How to use your Connected Casebook

Step 1: Go to **www.CasebookConnect.com** and redeem your access code to get started.

Access Code:

Step 2: Go to your **BOOKSHELF** and select your Connected Casebook to start reading, highlighting, and taking notes in the margins of your e-book.

Step 3: Select the **STUDY** tab in your toolbar to access a variety of practice materials designed to help you master the course material. These materials may include explanations, videos, multiple-choice questions, flashcards, short answer, essays, and issue spotting.

Step 4: Select the **OUTLINE** tab in your toolbar to access chapter outlines that automatically incorporate your highlights and annotations from the e-book. Use the My Notes area for copying, pasting, and editing your book notes or creating new notes.

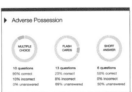

Step 5: If your professor has enrolled your class, you can select the **CLASS INSIGHTS** tab and compare your own study center results against the average of your classmates.

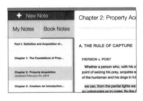

Is this a used casebook? Access code already scratched off?

You can purchase the Digital Version and still access all of the powerful tools listed above.
Please visit CasebookConnect.com and select Catalog to learn more.

CRIMINAL LAW

ASPEN CASEBOOK SERIES

CRIMINAL LAW
DOCTRINE, APPLICATION, AND PRACTICE

Second Edition

JENS DAVID OHLIN
Vice Dean and Professor of Law
Cornell Law School

Wolters Kluwer

Published by Wolters Kluwer in New York.

Wolters Kluwer Legal & Regulatory U.S. serves customers worldwide with CCH, Aspen Publishers, and Kluwer Law International products. (www.WKLegaledu.com)

To contact Customer Service, e-mail customer.service@wolters kluwer.com, call 1-800-234-1660, fax 1-800-901-9075, or mail correspondence to:

Wolters Kluwer
Attn: Order Department
PO Box 990
Frederick, MD 21705

Printed in the United States of America.

1 2 3 4 5 6 7 8 9 0

ISBN 978-1-4548-9491-9

Library of Congress Cataloging-in-Publication Data

Names: Ohlin, Jens David, author.
Title: Criminal law : doctrine, application, and practice / Jens David Ohlin,
    Vice Dean and Professor of Law, Cornell Law School.
Description: 2nd edition. | New York : Wolters Kluwer, [2018] |
Series: Aspen
    casebook series | Includes bibliographical references and index.
Identifiers: LCCN 2018005495 | ISBN 9781454894919
Subjects: LCSH: Criminal law—United States. | LCGFT: Casebooks.
Classification: LCC KF9219 .O35 2018 | DDC 345.73—dc23
LC record available at https://lccn.loc.gov/2018005495

Certified Chain of Custody
Promoting Sustainable Forestry
www.sfiprogram.org
SFI-01681

SFI label applies to the text stock

About Wolters Kluwer Legal & Regulatory U.S.

Wolters Kluwer Legal & Regulatory U.S. delivers expert content and solutions in the areas of law, corporate compliance, health compliance, reimbursement, and legal education. Its practical solutions help customers successfully navigate the demands of a changing environment to drive their daily activities, enhance decision quality and inspire confident outcomes.

Serving customers worldwide, its legal and regulatory portfolio includes products under the Aspen Publishers, CCH Incorporated, Kluwer Law International, ftwilliam.com and MediRegs names. They are regarded as exceptional and trusted resources for general legal and practice-specific knowledge, compliance and risk management, dynamic workflow solutions, and expert commentary.

For George Fletcher,
for rethinking criminal law

Summary of Contents

TABLE OF CONTENTS

PART V
JUSTIFICATIONS & EXCUSES

CHAPTER 23
SELF-DEFENSE

PREFACE

I wrote this casebook not just to use as teaching materials for my own class, but also to provide professors and students everywhere with a set of crisp and flexible materials for the study of criminal law. The book is divided into 28 chapters, followed by an appendix with selections from the Model Penal Code. I deliberately wrote a larger number of shorter chapters so that each chapter would correspond to a single topic. The goal of the book is to help students learn the criminal law and to stimulate a wider discussion of it among students and scholars alike.

Each chapter is divided into three major sections. The A Section focuses on a doctrinal overview of the subject, presented without using secondary materials such as law review excerpts. The goal of this section is to give the reader a bird's-eye view of the chapter's topic. I find this is helpful so that readers have a sense of the outer scope of the topic before they delve into more particular investigations of each doctrine. In short, students need some context before they learn the particulars. Then, the B Section (labeled "Application") focuses on applying the doctrine to new and complex fact patterns. Readers are presented with appellate opinions, followed by notes and questions, which will help develop and hone an essential skill: applying the law to novel facts. Consequently, cases are selected with an eye towards this pedagogical goal. Instead of reprinting cases that merely announce the law, the chapter focuses on cases that present complicated and contested applications of the law. Many of the cases are new—from the past 15 years—though I have also kept many of the older canonical cases that are rightly regarded as classics of criminal law teaching. Finally, each chapter concludes with a brief section labeled "Practice and Policy" that asks students to consider some of the deeper implications, both practical and theoretical, of the material they have learned in each chapter.

Please note that I have followed several conventions while selecting and editing the cases in the book. First, internal citations within the cases are omitted without indication, in order to make the cases more readable. Second, deletions within cases are marked by ellipses (. . .) rather than asterisks (* * *). Third, the ellipses at the beginning or end of a paragraph may indicate that sentences were deleted from the paragraph or that entire paragraphs were deleted. In other words, the reader should not assume that ellipses at the end of a paragraph indicate that the deleted material was solely contained within that original paragraph. Finally, parallel citations were removed without indication.

The second edition includes several notable additions. First, this edition includes a new chapter on "Other Offenses Against the Person" (Chapter 15), which covers physical battery, assault, and kidnapping. As these topics are tested on the bar exam, some professors may wish to add this chapter to their syllabuses.

Second, the new edition includes integrated prompts directing students to watch and analyze the fact patterns in a series of original courtroom videos at https://www.casebookconnect.com/ that were written and produced to accompany *Criminal Law: Doctrine, Application, and Practice*. There are four major vignettes, each one broken into four short segments of about three or four minutes in length. The idea behind the videos is to give students an extra opportunity to understand the implications of the legal rules that they are studying, and also another opportunity to *apply* the law to a hypothetical example—this time rendered in vivid detail on the screen. My assumption is that students will review the videos at home while they read the chapter. On occasion, though, professors may wish to replay the video during class to stimulate a discussion regarding the topic presented in the video. Learn more about the videos at https://www.wklegaledu.com/Ohlin-CriminalLaw2.

Third, I have added several new cases, especially in situations where jurisdictions adopt competing approaches to an issue; the goal, where possible, is to include one case for each approach.

Fourth, where appropriate, I have added more excerpts from statutes to give students practice analyzing and interpreting statutory language.

Please feel free to send comments and suggestions for the third edition; your feedback is both welcomed and essential for future revisions.

Jens David Ohlin
Cornell Law School
Ithaca, New York
March 2018

ACKNOWLEDGMENTS

Many people were instrumental in bringing this casebook to fruition.

I first discussed the idea of doing this casebook with Deborah Van Patten and Carol McGeehan. Nicole Pinard, John Devins, Kathy Langone, Troy Froebe, and Joe Stern were instrumental in helping me through the writing and editing process every step of the way, while Geoffrey Lokke assisted with permissions. Susanne Walker did a great job marketing the first edition. I also wish to thank Joe Terry.

Several colleagues at Cornell Law School, including Steve Shiffrin, offered advice about writing a casebook. In particular, Kevin Clermont spent countless hours with me discussing law school teaching pedagogy in general as well as the structure and content of my proposed casebook. He graciously provided a detailed editing of my first draft chapter.

I am indebted to several criminal law colleagues who read and provided feedback on early drafts of the entire manuscript, including Sherry Colb, Geoffrey Corn, Rob Sloane, Sasha Greenawalt, and Tom McDonnell. Also, several anonymous reviewers for Wolters Kluwer provided suggestions that made their way into the final version of this casebook. Rachel Lerman provided valuable research assistance.

The revisions for the second edition were, in many ways, a collaborative exercise. Several adopters sent back feedback that included rich ideas for new material or changes. However, two adopters in particular, Geoff Corn and Ken Simons, deserve special mention for sending me detailed suggestions for editorial changes both large and small. I am eternally grateful for their time and effort and for their commitment to this casebook.

Most importantly, Nancy Ohlin encouraged me to embark on this ambitious project in the first place. She suggested some of the news items that eventually became problem cases in the casebook. She also spent many hours listening to me, ultimately helping me to distinguish between my best and worst ideas. This book never would have become a reality without her hard work and dedication to my career.

I would also like to thank the following copyright holders for granting permission to reproduce these materials in the text:

Waseca Police Captain Kris Markeson and Superintendent Tom Lee, photograph. Copyright © 2014 by Glen Stubbe/Minneapolis Star Tribune/ZUMA Press. Reproduced by permission. All rights reserved.

Wolfgang Daschner, Frankfurt Police Department Vice President, and Magnus Gaefgen, photographs. Copyright © 2014 by Boris Roessler/EPA. Reproduced by permission. All rights reserved.

CRIMINAL LAW

PART I

—ຈຈຈ—

BASIC ELEMENTS
OF CRIMINALITY

CHAPTER 1

—⚬⚮⚬—

INTRODUCTION TO THE CRIMINAL PROCESS

A. DOCTRINE

Although this is a casebook in the substantive criminal law, not criminal *procedure*, it is nonetheless important to situate the substance of American criminal law within the system that it operates. Indeed, in debating about the criminal law, scholars and practitioners appeal to how the offense will be prosecuted and adjudicated in reality—surely a relevant consideration for anyone who cares about justice. Given this, the student of the criminal law needs at least a basic tour through the criminal justice system, and an introduction to the major stages of the process: the criminal complaint and its investigation, arrest, indictment or preliminary hearings, trial, sentencing, and appeal. Consequently, this introductory chapter, which provides such a tour, departs slightly from the structure used in the rest of the book. Section A examines the phases of the criminal justice system, with particular emphasis on the different evidentiary burdens that apply during each phase. Then, Section B considers the bedrock principle of the presumption of innocence and applies it in a concrete case. Section B then continues its examination of the fact-finding process with a concrete controversy: juries who refuse to convict even if they think a defendant is guilty. Section C provides an introduction in how to read, understand, and ultimately carve a penal statute into its component parts—an essential skill to acquire before proceeding to the rest of the material in this casebook.

1. Criminal Complaint and Investigation

The criminal process usually begins with a criminal complaint sworn by a victim in a case. There are exceptions to this general practice: If the police encounter evidence of law breaking they will investigate and pursue the case in anticipation that a victim will be found who will complain about the conduct. Also, if the police encounter evidence of criminal conduct directed at the public at large—or if they personally witness the crime—they will issue a citation on their own volition. But for major crimes, a case usually begins with a complaining victim for mostly pragmatic reasons: It is difficult to successfully prosecute an offender unless there is a witness to testify about the offending conduct.

The investigation will be conducted by the relevant police agency with jurisdiction over the crime. This is not limited to the municipal police and the FBI. There are a host of other agencies with criminal jurisdiction apart from your local city police and the federal government. This includes county sheriffs, state police, and numerous federal and state agencies with statutory grants of jurisdiction over particular crimes or territory: state agencies that patrol state parks; agencies that prosecute environmental or safety offenses; federal agencies like the Bureau of Alcohol, Tobacco, and Firearms; and hundreds of obscure agencies that rarely get public attention (e.g., the Library of Congress used to have its own police force until Congress merged it with the U.S. Capitol Police). Finally, universities and colleges in most states have their own public safety officers entitled to exercise the same duties as police officers. An "investigation" can be as swift or as protracted as the circumstances require.

2. Arrest

If the police believe that there is sufficient evidence that a particular individual committed a crime, they can either arrest the suspect or, if the crime is serious and the jurisdiction requires it, ask a judge to issue an arrest warrant. In every jurisdiction, if the police go to the suspect's home to arrest him or her, the Fourth Amendment requires an arrest warrant unless there are exigent circumstances. Outside the home, a police officer might perform an arrest on his or her own authority if he or she personally witnesses the crime or if the officer reasonably believes, based on an investigation, that the suspect committed the crime. As for the arresting officer's evidentiary burden, the standard is usually that there exists "probable cause" to believe that the suspect committed the crime—a standard that is much less demanding than the level of certainty required to convict someone at trial (proof beyond a reasonable doubt) or to find liability in a civil case (a preponderance of the evidence).

The police may question the suspect either before or after the arrest (or both). However, once the suspect is in police custody, the police must issue *Miranda* warnings and advise the suspect of his rights, including the right, during an interrogation, to counsel at public expense and the right to remain silent. See *Miranda v. Arizona*, 384 U.S. 436 (1966). Failure to advise a detained suspect of his rights could later trigger the exclusionary rule at trial. In some larger jurisdictions, such as New York City, professional investigators working directly for the district attorney will continue to work on the case pending the trial.

After being processed, arrested suspects will be brought before a judge for arraignment. Bail will either be granted or denied depending on various factors, including the severity of the offense and the risk that the defendant might flee the jurisdiction. If bail is granted, the suspect may either post cash (if he has enough) or apply for a bail bond. The defendant secures the bail bond by giving a percentage of the money and collateral to a bail bondsman. If the defendant flees the jurisdiction or otherwise refuses to appear for trial, the bail is forfeited. To recoup his loss, the bail bondsman will then attempt to locate the suspect and forcibly bring him to the court, or seize the collateral pledged by the defendant or his family. In many cases, the lightly regulated bail bondsman industry has provoked substantial concern because these private actors act as bounty hunters.

3. Indictment and Preliminary Hearings

After arrest, the local district attorney is usually not permitted to proceed directly to a trial. In the case of felonies, many jurisdictions require the successful completion of either a preliminary hearing or a grand jury indictment before a judge will schedule a trial. These two pre-trial mechanisms are radically different. Preliminary hearings are usually public, adversarial proceedings between a prosecutor and a defense attorney; the prosecutor has the burden to demonstrate to the judge that there is a sufficient factual basis to justify the charge and proceed to trial. In contrast, grand jury proceedings are non-adversarial and involve only a prosecutor presenting his or her side of the case to a grand jury in a closed-door and confidential proceeding. The prosecutor has the burden to present admissible evidence that provides reasonable cause to believe that the defendant committed the crime. A grand jury must indict the individual on a specific charge, which the prosecutor must then prove beyond a reasonable doubt at trial. In both mechanisms, if the prosecutor loses, the defendant is released. On the other hand, if the prosecutor wins and a trial is ordered, both sides then begin work to prepare for trial.

4. Trial

Before trial, prosecutors are required to meet the demands of discovery: turn over all relevant and probative evidence to defense counsel. This process eliminates the danger of unfair surprise and gives the defendant the opportunity to prepare for trial and select an appropriate defense strategy. Also, the defense attorney and prosecutor may make informal predictions about their chance of success at trial and then negotiate a plea bargain in order to reduce the risk of losing. Usually a plea bargain involves the defendant pleading guilty to a lesser charge and coming to some agreement about the length (or range) of the penalty. The deal is then presented to the judge for ratification and endorsement. Although judges are entitled to reject plea offers if they wish, in most cases they welcome them as a way to reduce their caseloads. In the absence of plea-bargaining, the criminal justice system in its current form would collapse.

After the judge dispenses with any pre-trial motions regarding inadmissible evidence or discovery disputes, the trial begins with *voir dire*, the selection of the jury. (Some jurisdictions dispense with juries but only in cases of minor infractions.) Each side may strike potential jurors with a limited number of peremptory challenges and an unlimited number of challenges for cause when there is evidence that a juror cannot be impartial.

The trial commences with the prosecutor's presentation of evidence and witnesses, who can be cross-examined by the defense attorney. The prosecutor bears the initial burden to establish a prima facie case, i.e., evidence that is legally sufficient to demonstrate that the defendant's behavior satisfied each element of the criminal offense, unless that evidence is disproved or rebutted by the defense. In theory then, a defendant could be acquitted without his lawyer presenting a shred of evidence, if the prosecutor fails to meet his prima facie burden. At the conclusion of the prosecution's case-in-chief, the judge can grant a dismissal if he or she determines that it would be unreasonable for any jury to convict (because of the paucity of evidence). Otherwise, the defense presents its case and argues for an acquittal, followed by closing arguments. If the defendant has selected a bench trial, the judge deliberates and then hands down a decision. In the case of a jury trial, the judge must "charge" the jury with a set of instructions that explain the law to lay individuals who do not have prior legal training. Jurors then retire to deliberate in secret. Not all jurisdictions require unanimous jury verdicts. Ultimately, the jury must decide whether the prosecution submitted enough admissible evidence to establish beyond a reasonable doubt that the defendant committed the crime. It is possible that the prosecution might submit enough evidence to meet its prima facie burden but not enough evidence to satisfy its ultimate burden of persuasion, especially in light of countervailing evidence presented by the defense. Those cases should result in acquittals by the jury.

5. Sentencing

If found guilty, a defendant will be subject to the criminal penalties defined by statute. In most cases the sentencing determination is bifurcated into a separate proceeding that allows the judge or jury to consider aggravating and mitigating circumstances that would not be relevant during the guilt phase of the trial. So, for example, defense counsel might call witnesses who could testify regarding the defendant's positive character or the factors beyond his control—such as early childhood abuse—that influenced his life trajectory. For some crimes, the statute will fix mandatory minimum and maximum penalties so as to constrain the discretion of the court in imposing its sentence. In some jurisdictions, a non-binding set of sentencing guidelines will provide a framework for the court to use in calculating an appropriate prison sentence or fine.

6. Appeal

After sentencing, defendants are permitted to appeal their conviction unless they have knowingly waived their right to appeal as part of a plea bargain. Generally speaking, the prosecutor cannot appeal an acquittal because the constitutional protection of double jeopardy attaches to the acquittal. The grounds of appeal by the defense are limited to questions of law, as opposed to the jury's assessment of the facts. That being said, matters of fact become reviewable as a question of law if an appellate court determines that no reasonable jury could find the defendant guilty under the evidence admitted in the case. Successful appeals also involve procedural irregularities at trial, mistakes regarding evidence that should have been excluded but was wrongfully submitted to the jury, or judges' mistakes in describing the law when charging the jury before its deliberations. An appellate court can uphold a conviction in spite of these mistakes if its judges believe they constituted "harmless error" that could not have affected the outcome of the case. If a defendant wins on appeal, the government usually has the option of retrying the case unless the appeals court orders a dismissal "with prejudice."

B. APPLICATION

1. The Presumption of Innocence

In the absence of proof of guilt, the defendant is presumed innocent. In many ways, this is an abstract principle. The rubber meets the road in the context of the prosecution's burden to establish the defendant's guilt beyond a reasonable doubt. What does it mean for this burden to fall on the prosecution side rather than on the defense side?

Owens v. State
Court of Special Appeals of Maryland
93 Md. App. 162 (1992)

MOYLAN, Judge.

This appeal presents us with a small gem of a problem from the borderland of legal sufficiency. It is one of those few occasions when some frequently invoked but rarely appropriate language is actually pertinent.

Ironically, in this case it was not invoked. The language is, "[A] conviction upon circumstantial evidence alone is not to be sustained unless the circumstances are inconsistent with any reasonable hypothesis of innocence."

We have here a conviction based upon circumstantial evidence alone. The circumstance is that a suspect was found behind the wheel of an automobile parked on a private driveway at night with the lights on and with the motor running. Although there are many far-fetched and speculative hypotheses that might be conjured up (but which require no affirmative elimination), there are only two unstrained and likely inferences that could reasonably arise. One is that the vehicle and its driver had arrived at the driveway from somewhere else. The other is that the driver had gotten into and started up the vehicle and was about to depart for somewhere else.

The first hypothesis, combined with the added factor that the likely driver was intoxicated, is consistent with guilt. The second hypothesis, because the law intervened before the forbidden deed could be done, is consistent with innocence. With either inference equally likely, a fact finder could not fairly draw the guilty inference and reject the innocent with the requisite certainty beyond a reasonable doubt. We are called upon, therefore, to examine the circumstantial predicate more closely and to ascertain whether there were any attendant and ancillary circumstances to render less likely, and therefore less reasonable, the hypothesis of innocence. Thereon hangs the decision.

The appellant, Christopher Columbus Owens, Jr., was convicted in the Circuit Court for Somerset County by Judge D. William Simpson, sitting without a jury, of driving while intoxicated. Upon this appeal, he raises the single contention that Judge Simpson was clearly erroneous in finding him guilty because the evidence was not legally sufficient to support such finding.

The evidence, to be sure, was meager. The State's only witness was Trooper Samuel Cottman, who testified that at approximately 11pm on March 17, 1991, he drove to the area of Sackertown Road in Crisfield in response to a complaint that had been called in about a suspicious vehicle. He spotted a truck matching the description of the "suspicious vehicle." It was parked in the driveway of a private residence.

The truck's engine was running and its lights were on. The appellant was asleep in the driver's seat, with an open can of Budweiser clasped between his legs. Two more empty beer cans were inside the vehicle. As Trooper Cottman awakened him, the appellant appeared confused and did not know where he was. He stumbled out of the vehicle. There was a strong odor of alcohol on his breath. His face was flushed and his eyes were red. When asked to recite the alphabet, the appellant "mumbled through the letters, didn't state any of the letters clearly and failed to say them in the correct order." His speech generally was "slurred and very unclear." When taken into custody, the appellant was "very argumentative . . . and uncooperative." A check with the Motor Vehicles Administration revealed, moreover, that the appellant had an alcohol restriction on his license. The appellant declined to submit to a blood test for alcohol.

After the brief direct examination of Trooper Cottman (consuming but 3½ pages of transcript), defense counsel asked only two questions, establishing that the driveway was private property and that the vehicle was sitting on that private driveway. The appellant did not take the stand and no defense witnesses were called. The appellant's argument as to legal insufficiency is clever. He chooses to fight not over the fact of drunkenness but over the place of drunkenness. He points out that his conviction was under the Transportation Article, which is limited in its coverage to the driving of vehicles on "highways" and does not extend to driving on a "private road or driveway."

We agree with the appellant that he could not properly have been convicted for driving, no matter how intoxicated, back and forth along the short span of a private driveway. The theory of the State's case, however, rests upon the almost Newtonian principle that present stasis on the driveway implies earlier motion on the highway. The appellant was not convicted of drunken driving on the private driveway, but of drunken driving on the public highway before coming to rest on the private driveway.

It is a classic case of circumstantial evidence. From his presence behind the wheel of a vehicle on a private driveway with the lights on and the motor running, it can reasonably be inferred that such individual either 1) had just arrived by way of the public highway or 2) was just about to set forth upon the public highway. The binary nature of the probabilities—that a vehicular odyssey had just concluded or was just about to begin—is strengthened by the lack of evidence of any third reasonable explanation, such as the presence beside him of an inamorata or of a baseball game blaring forth on the car radio. Either he was coming or he was going.

The first inference would render the appellant guilty; the second would not. Mere presence behind the wheel with the lights on and the motor running could give rise to either inference, the guilty one and the innocent one. For the State to prevail, there has to be some other factor to enhance the likelihood of the first inference and to diminish the likelihood of the second. We must look for a tiebreaker.

The State had several opportunities to break the game wide open but failed to capitalize on either of them. As Trooper Cottman woke the appellant, he asked him what he was doing there. The appellant responded that he had just driven the occupant of the residence home. Without explanation, the appellant's objection to the answer was sustained. For purposes of the present analysis, therefore, it is not in the case. We must look for a tiebreaker elsewhere.

In trying to resolve whether the appellant 1) had just been driving or 2) was just about to drive, it would have been helpful to know whether the driveway in which he was found was that of his own residence or that of some other residence. If he were parked in someone else's driveway with the motor still running, it would be more likely that he had just driven there a short time before. If parked in his own driveway at home, on the other hand, the relative strength of the inbound inference over the outbound inference would diminish.

The driveway where the arrest took place was on Sackertown Road. The charging document (which, of course, is not evidence) listed the appellant's address as 112 Cove Second Street. When the appellant was arrested, presumably his driver's license was taken from him. Since one of the charges against the appellant was that of driving in violation of an alcohol restriction on his license, it would have been routine procedure to have offered the license, showing the restriction, into evidence. In terms of our present legal sufficiency exercise, the license would fortuitously have shown the appellant's residence as well. Because of the summary nature of the trial, however, the license was never offered in evidence. For purposes of the present analysis, therefore, the appellant's home address is not in the case. We must continue to look for a tiebreaker elsewhere.

Three beer cans were in evidence. The presence of a partially consumed can of beer between the appellant's legs and two other empty cans in the back seat would give rise to a reasonable inference that the appellant's drinking spree was on the downslope rather than at an early stage. At least a partial venue of the spree, moreover, would reasonably appear to have been the automobile. One does not typically drink in the house and then carry the empties out to the car. Some significant drinking, it may be inferred, had taken place while the appellant was in the car. The appellant's state of unconsciousness, moreover, enforces that inference. One passes out on the steering wheel after one has been drinking for some time, not as one only begins to drink. It is not a reasonable hypothesis that one would leave the house, get in the car, turn on the lights, turn on the motor, and then, before putting the car in gear and driving off, consume enough alcohol to pass out on the steering wheel. Whatever had been going on (driving and drinking) would seem more likely to have been at a terminal stage than at an incipient one.

Yet another factor would have sufficed, we conclude, to break the tie between whether the appellant had not yet left home or was already abroad upon the town. Without anything further as to its contents being revealed, it was nonetheless in evidence that the thing that had brought Trooper Cottman to the scene was a complaint about a suspicious vehicle. The inference is reasonable that the vehicle had been observed driving in some sort of erratic fashion. Had the appellant simply been sitting, with his motor idling, on the driveway of his own residence, it is not likely that someone from the immediate vicinity would have found suspicious the presence of a familiar neighbor in a familiar car sitting in his own driveway. The call to the police, even without more being shown, inferentially augurs more than that. It does not prove guilt in and of itself. It simply makes one of two alternative inferences less reasonable and its alternative inference thereby more reasonable.

The totality of the circumstances are, in the last analysis, inconsistent with a reasonable hypothesis of innocence. They do not, of course, foreclose the hypothesis but such has never been required. They do make the hypothesis more strained and less likely. By an inverse proportion, the diminishing force of one inference enhances the force of its alternative. It makes the drawing of the inference of guilt more than a mere flip of a coin between guilt and innocence. It makes it rational and therefore within the proper purview of the factfinder. We affirm.

NOTES & QUESTIONS ON THE
PRESUMPTION OF INNOCENCE

1. *Burden of production vs. burden of persuasion.* The phrase "burden of proof" is often uttered, but it is an imprecise term. The burden of proof is composed of two more specific categories: "burden of production" and "burden of persuasion." In a criminal proceeding, the burden of production is one side's obligation to introduce sufficient evidence to make an issue a triable issue of fact for the fact finder (usually the jury) to resolve. The burden of persuasion is one side's obligation to introduce enough evidence to satisfy the fact finder according to the relevant standard of proof. In criminal cases, the standard of proof is proof beyond a reasonable doubt.

It is also important to distinguish how these burdens apply to the overall case versus a particular legal issue within a case. In criminal law cases, the prosecution retains the overall burden to persuade the fact finder of guilt beyond a reasonable doubt. For affirmative defenses, however, the defense bears an initial burden of production and must introduce sufficient facts regarding the defense to make it a triable issue of fact requiring resolution. Once the defense meets that initial burden of production, some states will shift the burden of persuasion to the prosecution to disprove the defense beyond a reasonable doubt to the jury. In some circumstances, however, a state might allocate the burden of persuasion on the affirmative defense to the defense side. In that case, the defense might need to demonstrate the affirmative defense by a preponderance of the evidence. For example, Ohio law allocates to the defendant the burden of proving self-defense by a preponderance of the evidence, a scheme that was upheld by the Supreme Court in *Moran v. Ohio*, 469 U.S.

948, 949 (1984). However, the Ohio scheme is rare; most states allocate to the prosecution the burden of disproving self-defense, since it is so closely connected to the state's overall burden of persuasion to demonstrate that the defendant committed the crime.

2. Jury Nullification

The following case involves two principles that come head-to-head when the jury goes into deliberations. On the one hand, the jury is supposed to follow and apply the law as described by the judge. On the other hand, the jury can do what it wants and can always refuse to return a guilty verdict, even in cases where evidence of guilt is sufficient to meet the legal standard of proof beyond a reasonable doubt. This is often referred to as jury nullification. Does the fact that the jury possesses this raw power entail that defense lawyers should be permitted to ask juries to nullify? In the following case, the New Jersey court grapples with this question.

State v. Ragland
Supreme Court of New Jersey
519 A.2d 1361, 105 N.J. 189 (1986)

WILENTZ, C.J.

. . . Defendant, Gregory Ragland, was convicted by a jury of conspiracy to commit armed robbery, unlawful possession of a weapon, and unlawful possession of a weapon without a permit. Another charge against him, possession of a weapon by a convicted felon, was severed on defense counsel's motion in order to avoid the inevitable prejudice in the trial of the other charges that would be caused by introducing defendant's prior felony conviction, an essential element in the severed charge. . . . Included in the trial court's instructions on the severed charge was the following:

> If you find that the defendant, Gregory Ragland, was previously convicted for the crime of robbery and that he was in possession of a sawed-off shotgun, as you have indicated . . . then you must find him guilty as charged by this Court. . . . If, on the other hand, you have any reasonable doubt concerning any essential element of this crime, then you will find him not guilty.

Defendant appealed. . . .

II

It is conceded that the "must" charge is widely used in New Jersey and has been as long as anyone can remember. Defendant refers to the instructions as "commonly used in this jurisdiction" and acknowledges that the "must" charge is found in our model jury charges—frequently, we might add. Defendant calls it "our current system of instructing jurors." We agree. While our review, for this purpose, of jury charges in criminal matters recently before us, as well as our recollection, indicates a great variety in the language used to instruct a jury concerning its responsibilities, the "must find him guilty" format is there in abundance. And so are many other formulations.

The defendant would require a charge that states, in effect, that if the jury does not find a, b and c beyond a reasonable doubt, it must find defendant not guilty, but that if it does find a, b and c beyond a reasonable doubt, then it may find defendant guilty. In support of this change in present practice, defendant contends that the jury's power of nullification—the unquestioned power of the jury to acquit with finality no matter how overwhelming the proof of guilt—is an essential attribute of a defendant's right to trial by jury; that use of the word "must" conflicts with that attribute, for it incorrectly advises the jury that if it finds the proof of guilt beyond a reasonable doubt it *must* convict, whereas the truth is that it need not do so, it may, in fact, acquit; that "must" convict, therefore, should never be used. While noting that the word "should" "is better than 'must,'" defendant would also prohibit the use of that word in connection with the guilty charge since when the court says it "should" convict, the jury will believe that the court means it "must."

While defendant's arguments suggest that the ultimate object is to assure that the jury is not impeded by this coercive language from performing its proper role, the effect of the change is somewhat different. Its only effect, its only tendency, is to make it more likely that juries will nullify the law, more likely, in other words, that no matter how overwhelming the proof of guilt, no matter how convinced the jury is beyond any reasonable doubt of defendant's guilt, despite the law, it will acquit. Even without an explicit charge on the power of nullification, the jury must understand from this contrasting language (*must* acquit but *may* convict) that it is quite properly free, and quite legally free (since it is the court who is telling it "may") to acquit even if it is convinced beyond a reasonable doubt of defendant's guilt. Whether the contrast is as clear as "must" and "may," or is expressed in some other way (e.g., "you are authorized to find the defendant guilty," "a guilty verdict would be considered valid or proper," "you have the responsibility to return a guilty verdict," "the State is entitled to the return of a guilty verdict"—all contrasting with "you must acquit"), the message, intended by the charge and so understood by the jury, is that you have the power to nullify and it is permissible for you to do so.

This change in our settled practice, this attempt to modify our present instructions to the jury in order to allow for the uninhibited, robust, exercise of its nullification power, is not commanded by the United States Constitution, the New Jersey Constitution, any statute, or by the common law. The implication of defendant's argument is that the use of the word "must" in this connection violates both his federal and state constitutional rights, since the protected right—nullification—is described in terms of an essential attribute of defendant's right to trial by jury. . . .

III

We conclude that the power of the jury to acquit despite not only overwhelming proof of guilt but despite the jury's belief, beyond a reasonable doubt, in guilt, is not one of the precious attributes of the right to trial by jury. It is nothing more than a power. By virtue of the finality of a verdict of acquittal, the jury simply has the *power* to nullify the law by acquitting those believed by the jury to be guilty. We believe that the exercise of that power, while unavoidable, is undesirable and that judicial attempts to strengthen the power of nullification are not only contrary to settled practice in this state, but unwise both as a matter of governmental policy and as a matter of sound administration of criminal justice.

It is only relatively recently that some scholars have characterized this power as part of defendant's right to trial by jury and have defended it as sound policy. Like defendant, they take the position that the exercise of the power is essential to preserve the jury's role as the "conscience of the community."

There are various elements in this view of the jury as the "conscience of the community." Some laws are said to be unfair. Only the jury, it is thought, is capable of correcting that unfairness—through its nullification power. Other laws, necessarily general, have the capacity of doing injustice in specific applications. Again, only the jury can evaluate these specific applications and thereby prevent injustice through its nullification power. Cast aside is our basic belief that only our elected representatives may determine what is a crime and what is not, and only they may revise that law if it is found to be unfair or imprecise; only they and not twelve people whose names are picked at random from the box.

Finally, there is an almost mystical element to this contention about the "conscience of the community": before anyone is imprisoned, that person is entitled to *more* than a fair trial even when such a trial is pursuant to a fair law. He is entitled to the benefit of the wisdom and compassion of his peers, entitled to the right to have them conclude that he is guilty beyond any doubt, but that he shall be acquitted and go free because of some irrational, inarticulable instinct, some belief, some observation, some value, or some other notion of that jury.

If the argument is that jury nullification has proven to serve society well, that proof has been kept a deep secret. It is no answer to point to the occasions when laws that are deemed unjust have, in effect, been nullified by the jury. That proves only that the power may have done justice in those limited instances, without reflecting on whether, even in those instances, the cost of that justice exceeded its benefit, or whether in other instances it has done more harm, on balance, than the good. We know so little about this power that it is impossible to evaluate it in terms of results. . . .

There is no mystery about the power of nullification. It is the power to act against the law, against the Legislature and the Governor who made the law. In its immediate application, it transforms the jury, the body thought to provide the ultimate assurance of fairness, into the only element of the system that is permissibly arbitrary. And in its immediate application, it would confuse any conscientious citizen serving on a jury by advising that person, after the meticulous definition of the elements of the crime, the careful description of the burden of proof, and the importance of the conscientious discharge of that person's duties, that, after all is said and done, he can do whatever he pleases. Spectators, formerly amazed at verdicts that clearly violated the law (namely, verdicts that suggested that the jury had nullified the law), will be comforted to know that there is nothing to be amazed about, that juries are not required to follow the law, that they are advised that one of their important functions is *not* to follow the law, and that this advice is given by the ultimate symbol of lawfulness, the judge. It is difficult to imagine a system more likely to lead to cynicism.

There is another point of view that accepts the existence of the power as a fact, regardless of its desirability, and concludes that if we cannot eliminate it, we should at least make its application equal by making sure every jury knows of it. There is a surface appeal to the equality advocated. If one believes, however, that the exercise of the power is essentially arbitrary, the position that every jury should be advised of this power is seen as leading not to more equality but to more arbitrary results. That is not the sole reason for opposing such a position, however. What may be more important than minimizing these arbitrary results is the question of society's determination to make the jury system work as rationally as possible. The cynicism and disbelief that are encouraged by such instructions to a jury, including, especially, the instruction that tells the jury it need not listen to instructions, are more to be avoided than even the arbitrariness likely to affect the jury's final determination.

The fundamental defect in jury nullification is obvious. It is a power that is absolutely inconsistent with the most important value of Western democracy, that we should live under a government of laws and not of men. There are many manifestations of the concept of a "government of laws," and one of the most important is its operation in the administration of criminal justice. It is there that the sovereign is visibly restrained, it is there that we can see most clearly the application of this hard-earned rule, the rule that no one, to the extent man is capable of achieving this goal, no one, shall be found to have violated society's commands unless that command is first announced and then only after a group of free people, hearing all of the evidence, determine that the accused has violated the command. With jury nullification, these free people are told, either explicitly or implicitly, that *they* are the law, that what the sovereign has pronounced ahead of time either may or may not be followed, and that if they want to, they may convict every poor man and acquit every rich man; convict the political opponent but free the crony; put the long-haired in jail but the crew-cut on the street; imprison the black and free the white; or, even more arbitrarily, just do what they please whenever they please.

One of the biggest problems in the administration of criminal justice is the inequality of its enforcement, an inequality that starts with the inability to find all of its violators (it is sometimes estimated that only one out of ten violators is apprehended) and then apply the law equally to those who are caught. The extent to which the inequality at that point varies depends upon prosecutorial discretion, the differences in the abilities of counsel, and the varying strength and wisdom of judges. But at every stage of the proceeding, from the work of the police and the prosecutor's office, to the actions of a grand jury and the work of the judiciary at trial, all elements strive, at least consciously, for one goal, and that is the equal application of the law to all accused, so that all who are guilty are found guilty and all who are innocent are acquitted. Absolutely nowhere in the system is there some notion that someone should have the power, arbitrarily, to pick and choose who shall live and who shall die. But that is precisely what jury nullification is: the power to undo everything that is precious in our system of criminal justice, the power to act arbitrarily to convict one and acquit another where there is absolutely no apparent difference between the two. It is a power, unfortunately, that is there, that this Court cannot terminate, but a power that should be restricted as much as possible. The defendant would enshrine that power, in effect pronounce it one of the precious rights of a defendant, and thereby weaken our system of criminal justice and our dedication to fairness in prosecuting criminals.

The underlying fault of nullification is its total arbitrariness. No one knows what causes it or whether what causes it in one instance causes it in another. No one knows what factors are at play. No one tells a jury what the standards are that should be considered in exercising jury nullification, and no jury advises what standards it applied, or that it applied any. The very nature of the power is that it is absolute, unguided, not to be explained. There is no quality that it lacks if the goal is arbitrariness; it is totally and perfectly arbitrary.

Its existence in our system of criminal justice is almost ludicrous. There is no system more carefully designed to assure not simply that the innocent go free, but that at every step of the way the proceedings are directed toward a rational result. The lengths to which we go to exclude irrelevant evidence, the expenditures made to protect defendants from juror prejudice, the energy, study, and work devoted to a particular prosecution, all of these are prodigious. Having gone through that process, admired by us both for its thoroughness and its goals, astonishing to others for its devotion to fairness and reason, it is incomprehensible that at the very end we should tell those who are to make the judgment that they may do so without regard to anything that went before and without guidance as to why they should disregard what went on before, and without the obligation of explaining why they so disregarded everything. Were anyone to suggest that the police had the right, for no reason whatsoever, to arrest one person but let another escape—intentionally—or that a prosecutor, for no reason whatsoever, and without the need to explain, could prosecute one person but intentionally not prosecute another, or that a grand jury could do the same, where there is no perceptible difference in the two cases, we would either demand the indictment of that policeman and that prosecutor or would immediately pronounce such a suggestion as so lacking in any understanding of the purposes of our criminal justice system as to be not worthy of response. But that is precisely the power that is proposed here to be given to a jury. And were the Legislature to pass a law making a particular course of conduct criminal, and, at the end of that statute, provide that regardless of the proof of criminality the jury shall have the power to acquit, that law would be stricken as unconstitutional.

Jury nullification is an unfortunate but unavoidable power. It should not be advertised, and, to the extent constitutionally permissible, it should be limited. Efforts to protect and expand it are inconsistent with the real values of our system of criminal justice. . . .

NOTES & QUESTIONS ON JURY NULLIFICATION

1. *Jury power or defendant right?*   Other courts generally agree with the New Jersey Supreme Court that jury nullification is an essential power of all juries implicit in their authority to issue an acquittal, but that this does not mean that *defendants* have an individual right to jury nullification. What is the proper role of the jury within our larger system of criminal justice? While the jury is the fact finder, the judge is arbiter of all matters of law. But if the jurors overstep this divide and refuse to convict a defendant simply because they disagree with the law, have they overstepped their role within the system? And if they do, what can judges do about it? Should judges go out of their way to tell juries that they *cannot* nullify? For some time, California courts used the following

anti-nullification instruction: "should . . . any juror refuse[ ] to deliberate or express . . . an intention to disregard the law or to decide the case based on penalty or punishment, or any other improper basis, it is the obligation of the other jurors to immediately advise the Court of the situation." The California Supreme Court concluded that the instruction did not infringe upon the defendant's constitutional right to a jury trial, though it still ruled, under its statutory power to supervise the lower courts, that the instruction should not be used because it may "intrude unnecessarily on the deliberative process." *People v. Engleman*, 28 Cal. 4th 436, 49 P.3d 209 (2002).

2. *"Must" versus "may."*   Some jurisdictions allow trial court judges to tell juries that they "may" convict a defendant if the prosecutor proves each material element beyond a reasonable doubt. Supposedly this implies, but does not say explicitly, that the jury has the raw power to nullify. Do you think most jurors will pick up on this linguistic subtlety? Is the permissive "may" sufficient to inform jurors of their power to nullify? What if the jury specifically asks the judge whether they can nullify? In *State v. Bonacorsi*, a trial judge instructed the jury that it "may" convict the defendant if the elements are proven beyond a reasonable doubt. During deliberations, the jury sent the following note to the judge: "During his summation [t]he defense attorney held up the copy of a law that supposedly allows the jury to come to a not guilty verdict even though they felt that the defendant is actually guilty—if they feel the consequences of this verdict would be harmful to all or anyone concerned. Is this in fact a law and could we be shown this." The trial judge refused to clarify his instructions and simply responded: "You are to follow the court's instructions." The defendant was convicted and appealed, arguing that the trial judge should have clarified that the word "may" implied jury nullification. The New Hampshire Supreme Court rejected the appeal and concluded that the judge was under no obligation to explain further. *Bonacorsi*, 139 N.H. 28, 648 A.2d 469 (1994). In other words, jurors are permitted to nullify but judges are under no obligation to hold their hands and walk them to an acquittal.

3. *Nullification strategy.*   Imagine you are a defense attorney. You want to coyly suggest to jurors that they should nullify even if they believe your client is guilty. The trial judge has given you strict instructions not to mention nullification to the jury. See *United States v. Sepulveda*, 15 F.3d 1161, 1190 (1st Cir. 1993) ("A trial judge . . . may block defense attorneys' attempts to serenade a jury with the siren song of nullification."). How can you plant the seed in the mind of the jury without referring to "nullification" by name? Should you tell them that they should be guided by deeper principles of justice? Another avenue might be to tell them to ask their hearts whether your client deserves to be punished. Can you think of another way to get the message across?

EXAMPLES   "Ladies and gentlemen, there are lots of things that you can use to look at in this matter—the records that have been entered here—and you can use your own sense of freedom, justice, and fair play in this. Ladies and gentlemen, I ask you: Is it fair for a person to be sentenced to serve a life sentence?" *Held*: The instruction was properly excluded because it argued impermissible nullification. *Craigmire v. State*, 1999 WL 508445 (Tenn. Ct. Crim. App.).

Defendant's counsel wanted to read a quote from *United States v. Spock*, 416 F.2d 165, 182 (1st Cir. 1969), which speaks of the historical role of the jury as "the conscience of the community." The trial judge disallowed it. *Held*: The instruction was properly excluded because it implied nullification. *United States v. Brown*, 548 F.2d 204 (7th Cir. 1977).

---

4. *Civil disobedience.*   Should jurors use nullification to send a message to the government? Various scholars have argued that juries should nullify in cases with African-American defendants—even when they know they are guilty—to

---

PROBLEM CASE

In 1994, former football player O.J. Simpson was put on trial for the murder of his ex-wife Nicole Brown Simpson and Ronald Goldman. The trial was exceptionally long: Opening statements started in January 1995 and the verdict was announced in October 1995. Although the trial took eight months, the jury deliberated for only a few hours. Despite DNA evidence linking Simpson to the crime scene, the jury acquitted Simpson on all counts. Many observers assumed that the jury had nullified, either because the jury considered the Los Angeles police racist or because the jury was upset that the trial took too long. Indeed, although Simpson's lawyers did not explicitly call for nullification, they did make race a primary issue in the trial. Afterward, one of his attorneys who disagreed with that strategy, Robert Shapiro, said: "[N]ot only did we play the race card, we dealt it from the bottom of the deck."

Some jurors insisted that the decision was motivated by their assessment of the evidence, not nullification. See Conan Nolan, *"Did He Do It? Maybe, Maybe Not": Simpson Juror Speaks Out*, NBC News, June 13, 2014. What do you think the jurors did? The case highlights that the

O.J. Simpson

jury room is a black hole—very little evidence about the nature of the deliberation escapes. One reason why the jury's power to nullify is unreviewable is because it is too difficult to figure out when a jury has nullified.

Consider the issue again: Should a defense lawyer be permitted to argue explicitly for jury nullification? How common do you think jury nullification is, even in cases where there is no nudging or prompting from defense counsel?

send a message regarding systemic racism in the judicial system. Paul Butler, *Racially Based Jury Nullification: Black Power in the Criminal Justice System*, 105 Yale L.J. 677 (1995). Another oft-heard rationale for jury nullification might be to protest the legislature's overly harsh penalties for, say, crack cocaine. Although Congress eventually eliminated the disparity in sentencing between crack and other forms of cocaine, the general point applies in other contexts. Criminal prohibitions and sanctions represent political and moral choices made by the legislature and some of those decisions might be suspect. No one would assert that the legislature *always* gets it right. The real question is whether nullification is an appropriate avenue for disputation when the legislature gets it wrong.

C. HOW TO READ A PENAL STATUTE

Before proceeding to our study of the substantive criminal law in the next chapters, a few words are in order about where criminal law comes from. In the criminal law, statutes are important. The content of the various criminal offenses is outlined specifically in penal statutes. Your goal should not be to memorize criminal law provisions but to learn how to *read* them.

Reading a criminal law provision sounds deceptively easy. In reality, the tightly packed words represent a complex web of interrelated ideas that must be carefully disentangled and carved up at the joints. What follows is a very brief *introduction* to the task that will only be complete once you have mastered the rest of the material in the casebook.

 ❧ **Material elements of the offense.** A criminal law provision is made up of *material elements*. These are the pieces of the crime, each of which must be proven beyond a reasonable doubt to the fact finder in the case. Defenses are not part of the material elements and are usually codified in separate provisions that can be asserted to negate criminal liability. The material elements can be grouped into the following categories:

1. Conduct (actus reus)
2. Mental state (mens rea)
3. Results
4. Causation (a link between the defendant's conduct and the results)
5. Attendant circumstances

We will learn about each of these material elements in due course in later chapters. But before learning about them, it is important to be able to look at a criminal law provision and identify the material elements even before you learn how to properly interpret and analyze their significance. In short, it is important to be able to carve up a criminal law provision at the joints, just as one learns to carve up an English sentence into a subject, verb, indirect object, and direct object. Just as there is a grammar to English sentences, you might think of the material elements as the "grammar" of criminal law.

As an example, let us consider a typical criminal law provision, selected almost at random. This is New York Penal Law § 120.10:

> A person is guilty of assault in the first degree when: 1. With intent to cause serious physical injury to another person, he causes such injury to such person or to a third person by means of a deadly weapon or a dangerous instrument. . . .

Although there are two other subsections that a prosecutor could use to convict someone of assault, we should concentrate for a moment on the first prong reproduced above. Take a first stab at identifying "chunks" of the provision that might count as material elements. As a frame of reference, use the categories described above: conduct, mental state, results, causation, and attendant circumstances. Again, without trying to analyze the content of the pieces, just pick out the separate elements:

1. With intent to cause serious physical injury to another person (mens rea);
2. Causing injury to another person (result and causation);
3. Using a weapon or instrument (conduct);
4. The status of the weapon or instrument as "deadly" or "dangerous" (attendant circumstance).

The first thing to notice is that the conduct element comes last in the statutory provision. It would be wrong to assume that there is no conduct requirement just because it is not listed at the beginning of the sentence. In fact, the defendant does need to engage in some conduct to be guilty of the offense. Also, the conduct element must be causally connected to a particular *result* (causing injury to another person). Then, "intent to cause serious physical injury" constitutes the mental element. What "intent" means is a complicated business and will be addressed in detail in Chapter 6. For the moment, do not worry about decoding all of the implications of this particular mental element. The important point is to recognize a mental element when you come across it. Finally, the statute specifies an attendant circumstance that must apply in order for the defendant to be guilty: The weapon or instrument must qualify as "deadly" or "dangerous."

In order to see the joints between the material elements more carefully, a visual diagram might be more helpful. A person is guilty of assault in the first degree when:

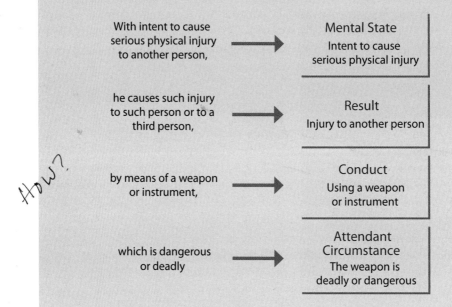

With intent to cause serious physical injury to another person, → **Mental State** Intent to cause serious physical injury

he causes such injury to such person or to a third person, → **Result** Injury to another person

by means of a weapon or instrument, → **Conduct** Using a weapon or instrument

which is dangerous or deadly → **Attendant Circumstance** The weapon is deadly or dangerous

How?

∾ **Canons of interpretation.** The process of extracting the material elements from a penal statute will not always be so simple and uncontroversial. In many cases reprinted in this casebook, the prosecution and the defense disagree over how the statute should be read or how it should be applied to the defendant's conduct. In many situations, the statute is ambiguous and the court must decide how to interpret and apply it. This process of statutory interpretation inevitably implicates the various theories of statutory interpretation that also apply in other contexts. Inevitably, judges differ substantially on their methodology for reading criminal law statutes, just as they differ on how to read civil statutes or the U.S. Constitution.

For example, one canon of interpretation calls on judges to determine the intent of the legislature when it passed the statute, in this case a penal statute penalizing certain conduct. This *classical intentionalism* often requires consultation of the legislative history: why the draft statute was first introduced, the nature and tenor of the legislative debate, the reasons for any amendments to the bill, and the reasons that various legislators had for their decision to vote in favor of the bill. This process requires the interpreter to extract the true legislative intent for the collective decision to enact the provision. In the criminal context, this analysis often places great weight on any differences between the criminal statute in question and other alternatives—such as prior versions of the statute or penal statutes in other jurisdictions—that were deliberately rejected. Another relevant point is whether the penal statute was designed to retain—or depart from—the way the crime was understood during the common law period when some crimes were prosecuted by judges without statutory definitions. All of this becomes relevant for determining legislative intent.

Some jurists adopt a purposive approach to criminal statutes. This interpretive methodology, often associated with Justice Stephen Breyer, looks to the overall purpose of the statute—i.e., what it is trying to accomplish. For example, looking at the statute holistically in relation to parallel provisions in the code might help illuminate the "purpose" of the statutory provision. In the context of penal statutes, a purposive method would attempt to determine overall which types of conduct are being prohibited and why—and then interpret individual words and sentences in the statute with that overall purpose in mind. While intentionalism is subjective (focusing on the subjective intent of the legislators who passed the law), most versions of purposivism are objective because they are based on the objective purpose of the statute and do not depend on an examination of the subject intent of specific lawmakers.

Finally, textualists often place greater priority on the "ordinary meaning" of the words used in a statute and prefer to ignore both legislative history and legislative intent. See John Manning, *Textualism and Legislative Intent*, 91 Va. L. Rev. 419 (2005). One argument for textualism is that the legislator voted on and adopted the text of the statute—not its legislative history. Under this approach, an interpreter should give preference to the words of the statute and their "ordinary meaning," to the extent possible. This would suggest ignoring deeper questions about why the state legislature decided to pass the penal statute and what problems it was trying to solve when it did so.

Correctly interpreting and applying penal statutes will occupy the rest of the semester. As you digest each area of the substantive law and grapple with its consequences, identify when each of these canons of interpretation is deployed by appellate judges. Finally, you should also: (i) develop a refined capacity to accurately *predict* how a future court will interpret these statutes, which is crucial for any counselor advising a client; (ii) learn how to *advocate* for the interpretation of the statute that advances the interests of your client, whether the "people" or a defendant; and (iii) come to your own assessment about the correct interpretation of the statute, all things considered. All three aspects are essential tasks for a practicing criminal attorney.

—ϭ/ϭ/ϭ—

PUNISHMENT

A. DOCTRINE

Why does punishment require special justification? One might find it obvious that the state is permitted to punish wrongdoers. However, punishment involves deprivations of liberty that in any other context would constitute kidnapping and be immoral. When the state takes someone away to prison, though, that deprivation of liberty is called "punishment" and is sanctioned both by law and morality. This is uncontroversial, but disagreements emerge as soon as one asks for the *reason* why punishment is permitted.

The standard accounts of punishment generally fall into two basic categories: utilitarian and deontological. Utilitarian theories are forward-looking and justify punishment because it has positive consequences to society, either through deterrence, incapacitation of the offender, or rehabilitation of the offender. The most prominent deontological theory is retributivism, which is backward-looking and holds that defendants should be punished because they should receive their just deserts. A final theory, expressivism, does not fall neatly into either of the two categories. All of the theories require that the punishment should be proportional, though what counts as proportional depends on the aim of the punishment.

1. Deterrence, Incapacitation, and Rehabilitation

For some lawyers, the goal of the criminal law is to make society better, and on that score punishment works because it generates positive consequences for the community, i.e., it improves overall social utility. The most important benefit for society is the prevention or reduction of crime. For example, the philosopher John Stuart Mill famously said that the "only purpose for which power can be rightfully exercised over any member of a civilized community, against his will, is to prevent harm to others." J.S. Mill, *On Liberty and Other Essays* 14

(Oxford University Press 1991) (1859). Punishment is consistent with this "Harm Principle" because it prevents others from being victimized by crime. The *mechanism* for this prevention changes depending on the particular theory.

In the case of deterrence, society benefits because would-be criminals will be dissuaded from their misbehavior because they fear punishment. In other words, a defendant's punishment is an example to the rest of the world: Break the law and you too will go to jail. The hope is that this possibility will influence people's behavior and promote compliance with the law. If it does, putting people in prison is morally justified. As will be explored in more detail below, there are two forms of deterrence: general and specific. When a criminal is incarcerated, that *specific* criminal might be deterred from reoffending when they get out of prison. In addition, though, society *generally* might be deterred from committing that crime when they see what happened to the defendant when he broke the law.

There are other ways that society might benefit from punishing offenders. If the criminal is incapacitated while in prison, he cannot harm others. Other punishments, such as chemical castration for serial rapists, might follow a similar logic. Although the former sex offender is no longer incarcerated, he is functionally "incapacitated" by the procedure. Rehabilitation also produces positive benefits for society because the offender is returned as a functioning member of society and unlikely to repeat his or her criminal mistakes. Decreasing the rate of recidivism will lower the community's crime rate.

2. Retributivism or "Just Deserts"

The philosopher Immanuel Kant believed that punishment was justified because offenders should receive their just deserts for their wrongdoing. He objected to utilitarian theories of punishment because they treat criminals as mere means to a particular end. For example, deterrence punishes a defendant in order to send a message to future miscreants who might be tempted to misbehave. For Kant, turning a criminal into an instrument of social policy violates the inherent moral dignity of each person. Why would improving society overall justify imposing harm to some subcategory of its members? Under this view, punishment is based on the notion that the defendant's wrongful action is a proper basis for blaming him and for the state giving the defendant what he justly deserves. For retributivists, punishment is not an occasion to hold up the perpetrator as an example for the world to see in the hopes that this message will deter others from breaking the law.

Kant supported a retributive theory of punishment, although many other philosophers have made retributive arguments over the years. Retributivists argue that punishment is permitted simply because wrongdoers deserve to suffer for their wrongdoing. For some, this smacks of impermissible vengeance, a form of rough eye-for-an-eye justice. But for Kant and other modern-day retributivists, what would otherwise constitute private vengeance is transformed into legitimate punishment when state officials mete it out under the rule of law.

3. Expressivism

For others, the handing down of a punishment allows society to express its disapproval of the defendant's criminal conduct. One normally thinks of the court's *conviction* of the defendant as expressing this disproval, but for expressivists the process of punishment—the imposition of harm—expresses society's moral condemnation of the offender's behavior. Expressivism can be combined with deterrence or retributivism to produce hybrid theories of punishment. For example, one might say that society's expression of condemnation will deter future lawbreakers, or that punishment allows society to express its retributive feelings.

Does this account of punishment require any particular type or severity of punishment, or might a token slap on the wrist be sufficient to express social approval? Or think of a shaming penalty, like publishing the convict's picture in the local newspaper, that brings him social humiliation. While these creative sentences might work in some situations, expressivism generates its own demand for proportional punishment. Only by imposing severe penalties for severe crimes does society adequately express its outrage regarding the worst offenses such as murder.

B. APPLICATION

1. Deterrence

In the following case, the sentencing judge must assess and weigh the competing rationales for punishment and apply all of them to the defendant's criminal conduct. As you read the following case, pay particular attention to the judge's assessment of the possibility that incarceration will deter future offenders. Why is he so skeptical of deterrence in this case?

Petitioner

United States v. Brewer

U.S. District Court for the Western District of Texas
978 F. Supp. 2d 710 (2013)

FRED BIERY, CHIEF JUDGE.

THE INDICTMENT

Defendant

Donald Dean Brewer and Sherri Lynn Brewer were indicted by a grand jury of citizens on seventeen counts of conspiracy to defraud, wire fraud and major fraud against the United States, alleging creation of a sham contracting operation which led to $6,445,370 in ill gotten gains, half of which went to the Brewers, and all of which were stolen from the taxpayers.

THE PUNISHMENT

The advisory sentencing guidelines called for incarceration of Mr. Brewer for 108 to 135 months and Mrs. Brewer for 70 to 87 months. For the reasons stated in the Court's judgment and those that follow, the Court severely punished the Brewers without imposing a prison sentence, in addition to the punishment inflicted by the Brewers upon themselves and their family.

The Brewers have been ordered to disgorge all of their assets except for one vehicle and their personal belongings. After many years of a legitimate $150,000 to $200,000 annual income, they now exist on $2,800 per month from Social Security and disability.

The assets to be forfeited include a $930,000 note receivable, the loss of $7,000 per month in so-called "retirement" income, a vehicle, a home and Mrs. Brewer's ownership interest in a grocery store valued at several hundred thousand dollars.

Non-monetary punishment includes being shamed in their lifelong home-town of Clovis, New Mexico, population 39,197, and being ostracized by their professional friends, some of whom testified against defendant Donald Brewer. And for their crime, they will live out their lives as convicted federal felons.

LEGAL STANDARD

18 U.S.C. § 3553 provides in part that punishment should be decided taking into account:

(1) the nature and circumstances of the offense and the history and characteristics of the defendant;

(2) the need for the sentence imposed—

(A) to reflect the seriousness of the offense, to promote respect for the law, and to provide just punishment for the offense;

(B) to afford adequate deterrence to criminal conduct;

(C) to protect the public from further crimes of the defendant; and

(D) to provide the defendant with needed educational or vocational training, medical care, or other correctional treatment in the most effective manner. . . .

Section 3553(a)(2) calls upon the Court to consider the goals of sentencing. "[R]etribution, deterrence, incapacitation, and rehabilitation—are the four purposes of sentencing generally, and a court must fashion a sentence 'to achieve the[se] purposes . . . to the extent that they are applicable' in a given case."

APPLICATION OF LEGAL STANDARD

A. History and Characteristics of the Defendants

Section 3553(a)(1) requires the Court to consider "the nature and circumstances of the offense[s] and the history and characteristics of the defendant[s]." Here, the history and characteristics of the defendants weigh heavily on the Court.

Mr. and Mrs. Brewer are both 64 years of age. They wed in January of 1966, have remained married for forty-seven years, and have raised three children together. In August of 2004, Mr. Brewer was involved in an airplane crash. As a consequence of the crash and the related surgeries and procedures, Mr. Brewer has complete paralysis and constant nerve pain in his right leg, partial paralysis in his left leg, severe osteoporosis in his lower extremities, poor circulation, and poor temperature regulation. He has undergone several procedures to remove cysts from his tailbone, repair a broken hip, remove scar tissue near his spinal cord and treat various leg problems. Mr. Brewer is confined to a wheelchair 99% of the time. His injuries also require him to use a four-inch padded seat to avoid pressure sores, a shower chair and bar for the toilet, leg braces, a walker, a Medtronic Neurostimulation System which is implanted in his waist, and a regimen of half a dozen medications. Mr. Brewer also suffers from depression.

While a guidelines sentence of 108 to 135 months imprisonment for Mr. Brewer may be appropriate for a young or middle aged healthy individual found guilty of these crimes, such a term for a severely infirm 64-year-old man like Mr. Brewer is, as a practical matter, a life sentence. Mr. Brewer deserves to be punished. He does not deserve to die in prison.

Mrs. Brewer's history and characteristics also weigh on the Court. At the sentencing hearing, it was revealed that Mrs. Brewer's resistance to imprisonment stemmed, not from a fear for her own health, happiness and safety, but for the health, happiness and safety of her husband. Her defense counsel explained that Mrs. Brewer "lives to take care of Don Brewer." Indeed, while the Bureau of Prisons is equipped to care for prisoners of all levels of need, it would not likely meet the level of care that Mrs. Brewer has faithfully provided to Mr. Brewer in the years since the airplane crash. Consideration of these issues weigh in favor of a non-custodial sentence.

B. Retribution

While imprisonment is often necessary for retributive purposes, it is not always the most effective or the most fiscally sound option. The Bureau of Prisons calculated that the "fee to cover the average cost of incarceration for Federal inmates in Fiscal Year 2011 was $28,893.40." In this case, given Mr. Brewer's severe physical limitations and continuing medical issues, his incarceration would cost the government far more than the average federal inmate.

Recognizing these costs, in the age of sequestration, prison time should not be imposed where it is not necessary. The Attorney General of the United States recently recognized this fact in relation to certain drug cases. In his August 12, 2013 memorandum, Attorney General Holder instructed United States Attorneys to decline to charge quantities necessary to trigger mandatory minimum sentences for certain non-violent drug offenders without significant criminal histories. In establishing this policy, Attorney General Holder noted that "[r]ising prison costs have resulted in reduced spending on criminal justice initiatives, including spending on law enforcement agents, prosecutors, and prevention and intervention programs." The new policy has garnered support from some unlikely allies.

In the spirit of sparing dwindling resources by keeping non-violent offenders out of prison, the Court finds that non-custody retribution is appropriate for Mr. and Mrs. Brewer, who have and continue to suffer in other ways.

C. DETERRENCE

Section 3553(a)(2)(B) requires the Court to impose a sentence "to afford adequate deterrence to criminal conduct." At the sentencing hearing, the Government stated that its "big concern" with regard to sentencing was deterrence, explaining that there are many opportunities to take advantage when dealing with military contracts and citing "a tremendous amount of fraud in the procurement system." While the Court recognizes the importance of deterrence, it is also realistic about its limits, especially in the realm of white-collar crime, where the powers of greed and ambition are often stronger than any deterrent effect. The Brewers did not learn from the example of Bernie Madoff, who did not learn from the example of John Rigas, who did not learn from the example of Ivan Boesky. And these criminals did not learn from the horse thieves who came before them, hung in the American West in the name of deterrence. As journalist H.L. Mencken put it: "Hanging one scoundrel, it appears, does not deter the next." Indeed, despite the use of the cane in Singapore and the blade and stone in Saudi Arabia, Sudan and Nigeria, crimes continue to be committed around the world. The Court finds that incarceration of the Brewers would not significantly deter future offenders.

D. INCAPACITATION

Section 3553(a)(2)(C) concerns incapacitation, instructing the Court to impose a sentence "to protect the public from further crimes of the defendant." The Court finds the goal of incapacitation is sufficiently achieved by the conditions of probation in this case. In addition to the applicable mandatory and standard conditions, the Court also prohibited the defendants from becoming employed in any fiduciary position or becoming employed in a position requiring the handling of money or the disbursing of funds without the prior approval of the Probation Officer. Imprisonment is not necessary to keep the Brewers from committing financial crimes again.

E. Rehabilitation

Section 3553(a)(2)(D) concerns the rehabilitative goals of sentencing. It requires the Court to impose a sentence "to provide the defendant with needed educational or vocational training, medical care, or other correctional treatment in the most effective manner." The most relevant aspect of rehabilitation in this case is the defendant's need for medical care. As outlined above, Mr. Brewer requires extensive care for the injuries he sustained as a result of the crash. The Court finds these needs are best met outside of the prison system. . . .

NOTES & QUESTIONS ON DETERRENCE

1. *The relevance of age.* Did the Brewers receive an adequate sentence for their crimes? The judge seemed influenced by the personal circumstances of Mr. and Mrs. Brewer, including age and his medical condition. Are these relevant considerations? Should a younger defendant in good health have received a longer sentence, even if his crime was exactly the same as the Brewers?

2. *General versus specific deterrence.* Deterrence operates differently depending on whether it is aimed at the offender himself or other hypothetical criminals. Under the notion of general deterrence, the goal of punishment is to deter others from committing crime. With specific deterrence, the goal is to deter the offender from engaging in wrongdoing in the future. In *Brewer,* Judge Biery seemed particularly influenced by the concept of specific deterrence and the fact that the Brewers were unlikely to repeat their fraud. But might general deterrence—sending a message to other con men in society—have supported a prison sentence for the Brewers? The judge went so far as to claim that general deterrence *never* works, in part because society has never succeeded in stamping out crime. Is that true? In the absence of punishment, maybe the crime rate would have been even higher.

3. *Moral limits to deterrence.* Is it possible that deterrence justifies *too much* punishment? If the government were to punish a large number of citizens, people might be too scared to commit crimes because they are certain to be punished. What if the government started punishing innocent people as well?

As long as the community is *unaware* of that innocence, general deterrence would seem to support the punishment. (If the community was aware that innocent people were being punished, it might have the perverse effect of increasing crime because punishment would appear essentially random and unrelated to one's law breaking.) Consider a less extreme example. Suppose a city decides to impose a strict penalty for the regulatory offense of failing to register as a felon with the local police department. Some felons might be unaware of the regulatory requirement, but punishing them despite this fact might send a stern message to future offenders that crime does not pay. Is this appropriate? In answering this question, the U.S. Supreme Court concluded that it was unconstitutional. See *Lambert v. California*, 355 U.S. 255 (1957) (overturning conviction under felon registration ordinance when defendant had no actual knowledge of registration requirement). Should the holding from *Lambert* apply to sex offender registration statutes? As it happens, courts have generally upheld sex offender registration statutes. See, e.g., *Hatton v. Bonner*, 356 F.3d 955 (9th Cir. 2003) (holding that defendant knew he had to register as a sex offender). Why is that? Perhaps the legislature should be given greater flexibility when the crime sought to be controlled is so heinous? But see *Wallace v. Indiana*, 905 N.E.2d 371 (Ind. 2009) (refusing to apply registration statute that was enacted after defendant's original conviction because it would violate state ex post facto provision).

4. *Constitutional limits to deterrence.* The Eighth Amendment prohibits cruel and unusual punishment. Even if the government could prove that a particularly vile form of punishment had a deterrent effect, the Constitution might still not permit it. For example, in *Hope v. Pelzer*, 536 U.S. 730 (2002), the Supreme Court ruled that the Eighth Amendment prohibited prison officials from handcuffing an inmate to a hitching post for seven hours in the hot sun with only one or two water breaks and no bathroom breaks. See also *State v. Gardner*, 947 P.2d 630 (Utah 1997) ("[I]f fines are a good way to deter people from littering the streets or public parks, deterrence theory would conclude that stiffer fines or prison sentences would be even more effective. Pushing this principle to its ultimate conclusion, the deterrent effect of the law would be even stronger if the State enforced litter laws with the death penalty—deterrence might even be perfect. But such a punishment is obviously and unconstitutionally cruel—the evil it inflicts is far greater than the evil it seeks to prevent.").

5. *Proportionality.* It is a basic principle of criminal justice that offenders should receive punishment that is proportional to their wrongdoing. See *Weems v. United States*, 217 U.S. 349 (1910) (12 years of hard labor for falsifying records was excessive). But recently the U.S. Supreme Court has shown remarkably little interest in enforcing the proportionality principle outside of the death penalty context. For example, some state statutes impose truly draconian penalties for petty offenses committed by habitual offenders.

Consider the case of Gary Ewing who was prosecuted in California for shoplifting three golf clubs valued at $399. Ewing had prior convictions on his record for burglary, robbery, and battery, and his conviction for the new theft triggered California's "Three Strikes and You're Out" law and a penalty of 25 years to life imprisonment. The law was passed by the state legislature to incapacitate habitual recidivists and deter repeat offenders. In *Ewing v. California*, 538 U.S. 11 (2003), the Supreme Court concluded that the law was not disproportionate and did not constitute a cruel and unusual punishment: "When the California Legislature enacted the three strikes law, it made a judgment that protecting the public safety requires incapacitating criminals who have already been convicted of at least one serious or violent crime. Nothing in the Eighth Amendment prohibits California from making that choice." For a discussion of proportionality in capital punishment, see Chapter 3.

In her majority opinion in *Ewing v. California*, 538 U.S. at 29, Justice O'Connor wrote:

> In weighing the gravity of Ewing's offense, we must place on the scales not only his current felony, but also his long history of felony recidivism. Any other approach would fail to accord proper deference to the policy judgments that find expression in the legislature's choice of sanctions. In imposing a three strikes sentence, the State's interest is not merely punishing the offense of conviction, or the "triggering" offense: "[I]t is in addition the interest . . . in dealing in a harsher manner with those who by repeated criminal acts have shown that they are simply incapable of conforming to the norms of society as established by its criminal law." To give full effect to the State's choice of this legitimate penological goal, our proportionality review of Ewing's sentence must take that goal into account.

In contrast, Justice Breyer's dissent (for himself, Souter, Stevens, and Ginsburg), argued that:

> [W]e know that California has reserved, and still reserves, Ewing-type prison time, i.e., at least 25 real years in prison, for criminals convicted of crimes far worse than was Ewing's. Statistics for the years 1945 to 1981, for example, indicate that typical (nonrecidivist) male first-degree murderers served between 10 and 15 real years in prison, with 90 percent of all such murderers serving less than 20 real years. Moreover, California, which has moved toward a real-time sentencing system (where the statutory punishment approximates the time served), still punishes far less harshly those who have engaged in far more serious conduct. It imposes, for example, upon non-recidivists guilty of arson causing great bodily injury a maximum sentence of nine years in prison; it imposes upon those guilty of voluntary manslaughter a maximum sentence of 11 years. It reserves the sentence that it here imposes upon (former-burglar-now-golf-club-thief) Ewing for nonrecidivist, first-degree murderers.

Which side do you agree with? Was Ewing's sentence constitutionally proportionate or unconstitutionally disproportionate?

6. *Overlapping justifications.* Up until now, we have assumed that punishments should be supported by *one* of the major justifications for punishment. In reality, judges consider all of the standard theories and usually pool together a patchwork of arguments to justify the sentences that they hand down. The result is a set of overlapping justifications for the outcome in a particular case. In *Brewer,* the judge cycles through all of the theories of punishment in order to come to a final conclusion about an appropriate punishment. As a matter of strategy, why might a judge appeal to multiple theories of punishment during the sentencing phase? If the sentence is supported by multiple and independent grounds, might the sentence be less likely to be overturned on appeal as an abuse of discretion? For more discussion, see Michael H. Tonry, *Why Punish? How Much?: A Reader on Punishment* 159 (2011) (theories of punishment are not necessarily mutually exclusive).

PROBLEM CASE

In January 2015, a federal judge sentenced Shannon Maureen Conley to four years in prison after she pled guilty to conspiracy to provide material support to a designated foreign terrorist organization. Conley, a 19-year-old girl living in Colorado, was planning to travel to Turkey and then Syria to marry a member of ISIS (the Islamic State) and support its jihad. She was arrested at the Denver airport.

Judge Raymond P. Moore concluded that Conley needed some psychiatric help and was "a bit of a mess," though she was not legally insane. Federal prosecutors argued that a prison sentence was necessary to deter others and stem the flow of homegrown sympathizers traveling to fight for ISIS or other similar extremist organizations. Will a four-year sentence deter others who might be tempted, through the Internet, by the lure of radicalization?

In contrast, a federal judge in Minnesota authorized the pre-trial release of an 18-year-old Somali-American teenager, Abdullahi Yusuf, who was accused of trying to join ISIS. The judge seemed more animated by rehabilitation and asked court officials to come up with a plan to reintegrate the defendant into the community and reduce his feeling of alienation—a potential source of his desire to join ISIS. Is this a better plan? Which approach represents better social policy?

Shannon Maureen Conley

7. *Hard-to-detect crimes.* If the crime in question is hard to detect, then only a small proportion of offenders will ever be discovered and punished. Imagine that a wrongdoer estimates that he has a 5 percent chance of being discovered of committing a crime that carries a one-year sentence; he factors the likelihood of discovery when he considers whether the potential punishment outweighs the possible benefits of the crime. So he might commit the crime anyway. Some economists argue that deterrence requires us to increase penalties for hard-to-detect crimes, so that the wrongdoer will multiply 5 percent (the chance of discovery) against 10 years in prison (penalty if he is caught). For example, assume that a one-year sentence will yield an adequate deterrent effect for a crime that the offender estimates is 100 percent likely to be imposed. However, if the crime is only 5 percent likely to be detected and punished, then the state should increase the sentence to 20 years to compensate for the low detection rate. Do you agree? Should this economic approach be extended to all crimes? See Richard A. Posner, *An Economic Theory of Criminal Law*, 85 Colum. L. Rev. 1193, 1212 (1985) ("[H]anging of horse thieves in the nineteenth century American West is another example of a penalty whose great severity reflects the low probability of punishment more than the high social cost of the crime.").

2. Retributivism

Deterrence is not the only consideration when determining an appropriate sentence for a convicted criminal. In some cases, judges determine the quantum of punishment by evaluating how much punishment the defendant "deserves." Most judges determine that convicted murderers deserve to go to prison for a long time. However, the following case does not involve a crime of violence. The defendant was convicted of a financial crime—a multi-billion-dollar pyramid scheme lasting for decades—that devastated a huge number of victims. How much punishment does he deserve?

United States v. Madoff
Southern District of New York
Sentencing Hearing of June 29, 2009

DENNY CHIN, DISTRICT JUDGE:

I take into account what I have read in the presentence report, the parties' sentencing submissions, and the emails and letters from victims. I take into account what I have heard today. I also consider the statutory factors as well as all the facts and circumstances in the case.

In his initial letter on behalf of Mr. Madoff, Mr. Sorkin argues that the unified tone of the victims' letters suggests a desire for mob vengeance. He also writes that Mr. Madoff seeks neither mercy nor sympathy, but justice and objectivity. Despite all the emotion in the air, I do not agree with the suggestion that victims and others are seeking mob vengeance. The fact that many have sounded similar themes does not mean that they are acting together as a mob. I do agree that a just and proportionate sentence must be determined, objectively, and without hysteria or undue emotion.

Objectively speaking, the fraud here is staggering. It spanned more than 20 years. Mr. Madoff argues in his reply letter than the fraud did not begin until the 1990s. I guess it's more that the commingling did not begin until the 1990s, but it is clear that the fraud began earlier. And even if it is true that it only started in the 1990s, the fraud exceeded 10 years, still an extraordinarily long period of time. The fraud reached thousands of victims.

As for the amount of the monetary loss, there appears to be some disagreement. Mr. Madoff disputes that the loss amount is $65 billion or even $13 billion. But Mr. Madoff has now acknowledged, however, that some $170 billion flowed into his business as a result of his fraudulent scheme. The presentence report uses a loss amount of $13 billion, but as I understand it, that number does not include the losses from moneys invested through the feeder funds. That's what the PSR states. Mr. Madoff argues that the $13 billion amount should be reduced by the amounts that the SIPC trustee may be able to claw back, but that argument fails. Those clawbacks, if they happened, will result in others who suffered losses. Moreover, Mr. Madoff told his sons that there were $50 billion in losses. In any event, by any of these monetary measures, the fraud here is unprecedented.

Moreover, the offense level of 52 is calculated by using a chart for loss amount that only goes up to $400 million. By any of these measures, the loss figure here is many times that amount. It's off the chart by many fold.

Moreover, as many of the victims have pointed out, this is not just a matter of money. The breach of trust was massive. Investors—individuals, charities, pension funds, institutional clients—were repeatedly lied to, as they were told their moneys would be invested in stocks when they were not. Clients were sent these millions of pages of account statements that the government just alluded to confirming trades that were never made, attesting to balances that did not exist. As the victims' letters and emails demonstrate, as the statements today demonstrate, investors made important life decisions based on these fictitious account statements—when to retire, how to care for elderly parents, whether to buy a car or sell a house, how to save for their children's college tuition. Charitable organizations and pension funds made important decisions based on false information about fictitious accounts. Mr. Madoff also repeatedly lied to the SEC and the regulators, in writing and in sworn testimony, by withholding material information, by creating false documents to cover up his scheme.

It is true that Mr. Madoff used much of the money to pay back investors who asked along the way to withdraw their accounts. But large sums were also taken by him, for his personal use and the use of his family, friends, and colleagues. The PSR [pre-sentence report] shows, for example, that Mr. Madoff reported adjusted gross income of more than $250 million on his tax returns for the ten year period from 1998 through 2007. On numerous occasions, Mr. Madoff used his firm's bank accounts which contained customer funds to pay for his personal expenses and those of his family, including, for example, the purchase of a Manhattan apartment for a relative, the acquisition of two yachts, and the acquisition of four country club memberships at a cost of $950,000. Billions of dollars more were paid to individuals who generated investments for Mr. Madoff through these feeder funds.

Mr. Madoff argues a number of mitigating factors but they are less than compelling. It is true that he essentially turned himself in and confessed to the FBI. But the fact is that with the turn in the economy, he was not able to keep up with the requests of customers to withdraw their funds, and it is apparent that he knew that he was going to be caught soon. It is true that he consented to the entry of a $170 billion forfeiture order and has cooperated in transferring assets to the government for liquidation for the benefit of victims. But all of this was done only after he was arrested, and there is little that he could have done to fight the forfeiture of these assets. Moreover, the SIPC trustee has advised the Court Mr. Madoff has not been helpful, and I simply do not get the sense that Mr. Madoff has done all that he could or told all that he knows.

Mr. Madoff has stipulated to the transfer of some $80 million in assets to the government for the benefit of victims, but the record also shows that as it became clear that Mr. Madoff's scheme was unraveling, he made substantial loans to family members, he transferred some $15 million of firm funds into his wife's personal accounts, and he wrote out the checks that the government has just described.

I have taken into account the sentences imposed in other financial fraud cases in this district. But frankly, none of these other cases is comparable to this case in terms of the scope, duration and enormity of the fraud, and the degree of the betrayal.

In terms of mitigating factors in a white-collar fraud case such as this, I would expect to see letters from family and friends and colleagues. But not a single letter has been submitted attesting to Mr. Madoff's good deeds or good character or civic or charitable activities. The absence of such support is telling.

We have heard much about a life expectancy analysis. Based on this analysis, Mr. Madoff has a life expectancy of 13 years, and he therefore asks for a sentence of 12 years or alternatively 15 to 20 years. If

Mr. Sorkin's life expectancy analysis is correct, any sentence above 20 or 25 years would be largely, if not entirely, symbolic.

But the symbolism is important, for at least three reasons. First, retribution. One of the traditional notions of punishment is that an offender should be punished in proportion to his blameworthiness. Here, the message must be sent that Mr. Madoff's crimes were extraordinarily evil, and that this kind of irresponsible manipulation of the system is not merely a bloodless financial crime that takes place just on paper, but that it is instead, as we have heard, one that takes a staggering human toll. The symbolism is important because the message must be sent that in a society governed by the rule of law, Mr. Madoff will get what he deserves, and that he will be punished according to his moral culpability.

Second, deterrence. Another important goal of punishment is deterrence, and the symbolism is important here because the strongest possible message must be sent to those who would engage in similar conduct that they will be caught and that they will be punished to the fullest extent of the law.

Finally, the symbolism is also important for the victims. The victims include individuals from all walks of life. The victims include charities, both large and small, as well as academic institutions, pension funds, and other entities. Mr. Madoff's very personal betrayal struck at the rich and not-so-rich, the elderly living on retirement funds and social security, middle class folks trying to put their kids through college, and ordinary people who worked hard to save their money and who thought they were investing it safely, for themselves and their families.

I received letters, and we have heard from, for example, a retired forest worker, a corrections officer, an auto mechanic, a physical therapist, a retired New York City school secretary, who is now 86 years old and widowed, who must deal with the loss of her retirement funds. Their money is gone, leaving only a sense of betrayal.

I was particularly struck by one story that I read in the letters. A man invested his family's life savings with Mr. Madoff. Tragically, he died of a heart attack just two weeks later. The widow eventually went in to see Mr. Madoff. He put his arm around her, as she describes it, and in a kindly manner told her not to worry, the money is safe with me. And so not only did the widow leave the money with him, she eventually deposited more funds with him, her 401(k), her pension funds. Now, all the money is gone. She will have to sell her home, and she will not be able to keep her promise to help her granddaughter pay for college.

A substantial sentence will not give the victims back their retirement funds or the moneys they saved to send their children or grandchildren to college. It will not give them back their financial security or the freedom from financial worry. But more is at stake than money, as we have heard.

The victims put their trust in Mr. Madoff. That trust was broken in a way that has left many—victims as well as others—doubting our financial institutions, our financial system, our government's ability to regulate and protect, and sadly, even themselves.

I do not agree that the victims are succumbing to the temptation of mob vengeance. Rather, they are doing what they are supposed to be doing—placing their trust in our system of justice. A substantial sentence, the knowledge that Mr. Madoff has been punished to the fullest extent of the law, may, in some small measure, help these victims in their healing process.

Mr. Madoff please stand.

It is the judgment of this Court that the defendant, Bernard L. Madoff, shall be and hereby is sentenced to a term of 150 years. . . .

AFTERWORD   The Madoff scandal had a wide-ranging impact, not just on the victims of the Ponzi scheme, but also on Madoff's children. Bernie Madoff's two grown children, Mark and Andrew, both worked at the family firm, though neither apparently knew about the Ponzi scheme. In fact, the brothers were the ones who reported the fraud to the police, after their father confessed to them that the investment firm was really a multi-billion-dollar Ponzi scheme. The next day, their father was arrested. Andrew and Mark never spoke to their father again.

Bernie Madoff

Although Mark was never charged with a crime, he was embroiled in a series of civil lawsuits relating to assets and money that he, his wife, and his young children had received from his family.

Exactly two years to the day after Bernie Madoff was arrested, Mark hung himself in his apartment while his two-year-old son slept in an adjacent room. See Diana B. Henriques & Al Baker, *A Madoff Son Hangs Himself on Father's Arrest Anniversary*, N.Y. Times, Dec. 11, 2010.

NOTES & QUESTIONS ON RETRIBUTIVISM

1. *The quantum of punishment.*   Did the judge impose the correct sentence on Bernie Madoff? Although the crime was only financial in nature, its scope and the number of victims were massive. Is it right that Madoff gets a longer sentence than some individuals convicted of rape or murder? Compare the sentence in *Madoff* with the sentence in *Brewer*. What explains the radical

difference in the two sentences: 150 years for Madoff and no prison term at all for the Brewers? Do you think the widespread publicity of the *Madoff* case influenced the judge's decision?

2. *Mercy.*   Should the judge have shown Madoff some mercy? Under a retributive framework, mercy might be disfavored because it interrupts the defendant's receipt of his just deserts. Does mercy simply make the dispenser feel better or does it serve some legitimate penological purpose? Or perhaps mercy offends our retributive intuitions because the wrong type of actor—say the parole board or governor—exercises it. See Dan Markel, *Against Mercy*, 88 Minn. L. Rev. 1421, 1478 (2004) ("from the perspective of equal liberty under law, grants of mercy based on compassion are as problematic as grants of mercy based on caprice, sovereign grace, corruption, or bias"). This suggests that excessive mercy might offend the legitimate policy decisions made by the legislature that certain categories of crimes deserve certain punishments. Another argument is that excessive mercy violates the rights of victims. In *Gäfgen v. Germany*, Application 22978/05 (2010), the European Court of Human Rights ruled that Germany's mild punishment—small monetary fines—of police officers convicted of torture was grossly disproportionate and violated Germany's obligation to prohibit torture. This suggests that, in theory, mercy is not always a virtue—especially if it promotes impunity for wrongdoing. Others argue that mercy is good for the person exercising forgiveness because it is better for their character or soul. Would the same argument apply to society in general? Does it say something good about society when a community forgives an offender? See Martha Nussbaum, *Compassion: The Basic Social Emotion*, 13 Social Phil. & Pol'y 27 (1996). For one controversial example, consider the family members who explicitly told Dylann Roof—charged with murdering nine innocent victims in a 2015 church shooting rampage—during his initial court appearance that they forgave him. Said one family member: "You took something very precious away from me. I will never talk to her ever again. I will never be able to hold her again. But I forgive you. And have mercy on your soul." See also Meir Dan-Cohen, *Revising the Past: On the Metaphysics of Repentance, Forgiveness, and Pardon*, in *Forgiveness, Mercy, and Clemency* 117 (A. Sarat & N. Hussain eds., 2007).

3. *The utility of desert.*   It might be possible to combine utilitarianism with a just deserts theory. Most people have strong intuitions about moral desert, which actions should be criminalized by the state, and which actions are most culpable. Psychologists have studied these intuitions and at least some have argued that they are surprisingly uniform across individuals and even across cultures. Some scholars think that a good system of criminal justice should be designed to implement these common intuitions because it will make the system most effective. In other words, people start taking the system less seriously when it strays from deeply held community norms. The result is less

compliance with the law. See Paul H. Robinson & John M. Darley, *The Utility of Desert*, 91 Nw. U. L. Rev. 453 (1997).

4. *Private punishment.*   Does punishment have to be handed down by the state, or can private individuals engage in a more personal form of retribution? Obviously, a state system of justice is well equipped to make sensitive decisions about who needs to be punished and how much. Furthermore, only a just government has the political legitimacy to make fundamental decisions to violate a person's liberty (by putting them in prison). If this is true, then individuals cannot take the law into their own hands without degrading it back into vengeance. The state decides whom to punish so the state must be the one to punish them; the concept of private punishment is a non sequitur. See Alon Harel, *Why Only the State May Inflict Criminal Sanctions: The Argument from Moral Burdens*, 28 Cardozo L. Rev. 2629 (2007). Do you agree?

3. Shaming Penalties

Not every penalty involves monetary fines or incarceration. Some creative judges have tried more esoteric methods of punishing the guilty, including publicizing the defendant's conduct in order to cast shame upon him or her. In these cases, judges hope the mechanism of shame might deter both the defendant and the public and satisfy retributive aims as well. Are these penalties consistent with the U.S. Constitution and deeper principles of retributive justice?

United States v. Gementera

U.S. Court of Appeals for the Ninth Circuit
379 F.3d 596 (2004)

O'Scannlain, Circuit Judge:

We must decide the legality of a supervised release condition that requires a convicted mail thief to spend a day standing outside a post office wearing a signboard stating, "I stole mail. This is my punishment."

I

Shawn Gementera pilfered letters from several mailboxes along San Francisco's Fulton Street on May 21, 2001. A police officer who observed the episode immediately detained Gementera and his partner in crime, Andrew Choi, who had been stuffing the stolen letters into his jacket as Gementera anxiously kept watch. After indictment, Gementera entered a plea agreement pursuant to which he pled guilty to mail theft. . . .

On February 25, 2003, Judge Vaughn Walker of the United States District Court for the Northern District of California sentenced Gementera. The U.S. Sentencing Guidelines range was two to eight months incarceration; Judge Walker sentenced Gementera to the lower bound of the range, imposing two months incarceration and three years supervised release. He also imposed conditions of supervised release.

One such condition required Gementera to "perform 100 hours of community service," to consist of "standing in front of a postal facility in the city and county of San Francisco with a sandwich board which in large letters declares: 'I stole mail. This is my punishment.'" Gementera later filed a motion to correct the sentence by removing the sandwich board condition.

Judge Walker modified the sentence after inviting both parties to present "an alternative form or forms of public service that would better comport with the aims of the court." In lieu of the 100-hour signboard requirement, the district court imposed a four-part special condition in its stead. Three new terms, proposed jointly by counsel, mandated that the defendant observe postal patrons visiting the "lost or missing mail" window, write letters of apology to any identifiable victims of his crime, and deliver several lectures at a local school. It also included a scaled-down version of the signboard requirement:

> The defendant shall perform 1 day of 8 total hours of community service during which time he shall either (i) wear a two-sided sandwich board-style sign or (ii) carry a large two-sided sign stating, "I stole mail; this is my punishment," in front of a San Francisco postal facility identified by the probation officer. For the safety of defendant and general public, the postal facility designated shall be one that employs one or more security guards. Upon showing by defendant that this condition would likely impose upon defendant psychological harm or effect or result in unwarranted risk of harm to defendant, the public or postal employees, the probation officer may withdraw or modify this condition or apply to the court to withdraw or modify this condition.

II

We first address Gementera's argument that the eight-hour sandwich board condition violates the Sentencing Reform Act.

The Sentencing Reform Act affords district courts broad discretion in fashioning appropriate conditions of supervised release, while mandating that such conditions serve legitimate objectives. . . . Thus, to comply with this requirement, any condition must be "reasonably related" to "the nature and circumstances of the offense and the history and characteristics of the defendant." Moreover, it must be both "reasonably related" to and "involve no greater deprivation of liberty than is reasonably necessary" to "afford adequate deterrence to criminal conduct," "protect the public from further crimes of the defendant," and "provide the defendant with needed educational or vocational training, medical care, or other correctional treatment in the most effective manner." Accordingly, the three legitimate statutory

[handwritten margin note: Issue: Do the conditions of supervised release violate the Sentencing Reform Act?]

purposes of deterrence, protection of the public, and rehabilitation frame our analysis. [8]

Within these bounds, we have recognized the flexibility and considerable discretion the district courts exercise to impose conditions of supervised release, up to and including limits upon the exercise of fundamental rights. This reflects, in part, their greater knowledge of and experience with the particular offenders before them. We have, for example, upheld conditions barring possession of sexually stimulating material, contact with minors, association or membership in "motorcycle clubs," and access to the internet. . . .

A

Gementera first urges that the condition was imposed for an impermissible purpose of humiliation. He points to certain remarks of the district court at the first sentencing hearing:

> [H]e needs to understand the disapproval that society has for this kind of conduct, and that's the idea behind the humiliation. And it should be humiliation of having to stand and be labeled in front of people coming and going from a post office as somebody who has stolen the mail.

According to Gementera, these remarks, among others, indicate that the district court viewed humiliation as an end in itself and the condition's purpose.

Reading the record in context, however, we cannot but conclude that the district court's stated rationale aligned with permissible statutory objectives. At the second sentencing hearing, when the sentence was amended to what is now before us, the court explained: "[U]ltimately, the objective here is, one, to deter criminal conduct, and, number two, to rehabilitate the offender so that after he has paid his punishment, he does not reoffend, and a public expiation of having offended is, or at least it should be, rehabilitating in its effect." Although, in general, criminal punishment "is or at least should be humiliating," the court emphasized that "[h]umiliation is not the point." The court's written order similarly stresses that the court's goal was not "to subject defendant to humiliation for humiliation's sake, but rather to create a situation in which the public exposure of defendant's crime and the public exposure of defendant to the victims of his crime" will serve the purposes of "the rehabilitation of the defendant and the protection of the public."

The court expressed particular concern that the defendant did not fully understand the gravity of his offense. Mail theft is an anonymous crime and, by "bring[ing] home to defendant that his conduct has palpable significance to real people within his community," the court aimed to break the defendant of the illusion that his theft was victimless or not serious. In short, it explained:

> While humiliation may well be—indeed likely will be—a feature of defendant's experience in standing before a post office with such a sign, the humiliation or shame he experiences should serve the salutary purpose of bringing defendant in close touch with the real significance of the crime he has acknowledged committing. Such an experience should have a specific rehabilitative effect on defendant that could not be accomplished by other means, certainly not by a more extended term of imprisonment.

Moreover, "[i]t will also have a deterrent effect on both this defendant and others who might not otherwise have been made aware of the real legal consequences of engaging in mail theft."

Read in its entirety, the record unambiguously establishes that the district court imposed the condition for the stated and legitimate statutory purpose of rehabilitation and, to a lesser extent, for general deterrence and for the protection of the public.

B

Assuming the court articulated a legitimate purpose, Gementera asserts, under the second prong of our test, that humiliation or so-called "shaming" conditions are not "reasonably related" to rehabilitation. In support, he cites our general statements that conditions must be reasonably related to the statutory objectives, several state court decisions, and several law review articles that were not presented to the district court.

In evaluating probation and supervised release conditions, we have emphasized that the "reasonable relation" test is necessarily a "very flexible standard," and that such flexibility is necessary because of "our uncertainty about how rehabilitation is accomplished." While our knowledge of rehabilitation is limited, we have nonetheless explicitly held that "a public apology may serve a rehabilitative purpose." Of course, for Gementera to prevail, introducing mere uncertainty about whether the condition aids rehabilitation does not suffice; rather, he must persuade us that the condition's supposed relationship to rehabilitation is unreasonable.

We considered a similar question in *Clark*, a case involving two police officers convicted of perjury in a civil rights lawsuit they brought against their department. In a deposition, the officers lied about a past episode in which they had falsely phoned in sick while actually en route to a vacation. As a probation condition, the court required them to publish a detailed apology in the local newspaper and in the police department newsletter. Though they challenged the condition based upon the First Amendment, we applied the same test applicable here, concluding that "[b]ecause the probation condition was reasonably related to the permissible end of rehabilitation, requiring it was not an abuse of discretion."

Both *Clark* and *Gementera* involve defendants who seemingly failed to confront their wrongdoing, and the defendants in each case faced public expiation and apology. In *Clark*, the defendants had neither admitted guilt nor taken responsibility for their actions. Here, by contrast, the defendant pled guilty. His plea decision is unremarkable, though, given that he had been apprehended red-handed. Reflecting upon the defendant's criminal history, the court expressed concern that he did not fully understand the consequences of his continued criminality, and had not truly accepted responsibility. The court explained:

> [T]his is a young man who needs to be brought face-to-face with the consequences of his conduct. He's going down the wrong path in life. At age 24, committing this kind of an offense, he's already in a criminal history category 4, two-thirds of the way up the criminal history scale. He needs a wake-up call.

The court also determined that Gementera needed to be educated about the seriousness of mail crimes in particular, given that they might appear to be victimless:

> One of the features of Mr. Gementera's offense is that he, unlike some offenders did not, by the very nature of this offense, come face-to-face with his victims. . . . He needs to be shown that stealing mail has victims; that there are people who depend upon the integrity and security of the mail in very important ways and that a crime of the kind that he committed abuses that trust which people place in the mail. He needs to see that there are people who count on the mails and integrity of the mails. How else can he be made to realize that than by coming face-to-face with people who use the postal service? That's the idea.

As with *Clark*, the district court concluded that public acknowledgment of one's offense—beyond the formal yet sterile plea in a cloistered courtroom—was necessary to his rehabilitation.

It is true, of course, that much uncertainty exists as to how rehabilitation is best accomplished. Were that picture clearer, our criminal justice system would be vastly different, and substantially improved. By one estimate, two-thirds of the 640,000 state and federal inmates who will be released in 2004 will return to prison within a few years. The cost to humanity of our ignorance in these matters is staggering.

Gementera and amicus contend that shaming conditions cannot be rehabilitative because such conditions necessarily cause the offender to withdraw from society or otherwise inflict psychological damage, and they would erect a per se bar against such conditions. Though the district court had no scientific evidence before it, as Gementera complains, we do not insist upon such evidence in our deferential review. Moreover, the fact is that a vigorous, multifaceted, scholarly debate on shaming sanctions' efficacy, desirability, and underlying rationales continues within the academy. . . .

Criminal offenses, and the penalties that accompany them, nearly always cause shame and embarrassment. Indeed, the mere fact of conviction, without which state-sponsored rehabilitation efforts do not commence, is stigmatic. The fact that a condition causes shame or embarrassment does not automatically render a condition objectionable; rather, such feelings generally signal the defendant's acknowledgment of his wrongdoing. See *Webster's Ninth New Collegiate Dictionary* 1081 (1986) (defining shame as "a painful emotion caused by consciousness of guilt, shortcoming, or impropriety"). We have recognized that "the societal consequences that flow from a criminal conviction are virtually unlimited," and the tendency to cause shame is insufficient to extinguish a condition's rehabilitative promise, at least insofar as required for our flexible reasonable relation test.

While the district court's sandwich board condition was somewhat crude, and by itself could entail risk of social withdrawal and stigmatization, it was coupled with more socially useful provisions, including lecturing at a high school and writing apologies, that might loosely be understood to promote the offender's social reintegration. See Note, *Shame, Stigma, and Crime: Evaluating the Efficacy of Shaming Sanctions in Criminal Law*, 116 Harv. L. Rev. 2186 (2003) (proposing how shaming sanctions may be structured to promote social reintegration most effectively); John Braithwaite, *Crime, Shame and Reintegration* 55 (1989) ("The crucial distinction is between shaming that is reintegrative and shaming that is disintegrative (stigmatization). Reintegrative shaming means that expressions of community disapproval, which may range from mild rebuke to degradation ceremonies, are followed by gestures of reacceptance into the community of law-abiding citizens."). We see this factor as highly significant. In short, here we consider not a stand-alone condition intended solely to humiliate, but rather a comprehensive set of provisions that expose the defendant to social disapprobation, but that also then provide an opportunity for Gementera to repair his relationship with society—first by seeking its forgiveness and then by making, as a member of the community, an independent contribution to the moral formation of its youth. These provisions, tailored to the specific needs of the offender, counsel in favor of concluding that the condition passes the threshold of being reasonably related to rehabilitation.

Finally, we are aware that lengthier imprisonment was an alternative available to the court. The court, however, reasoned that rehabilitation would be better achieved by a shorter sentence, coupled with the additional conditions: "It would seem to me that he's better off with a taste of prison, rather than a longer prison sentence, and some form of condition of release that brings him face-to-face with the consequences of his crime." The judge's reasoning that rehabilitation would better be served by means other than extended incarceration and punishment is plainly reasonable, particularly in light of the significant economic disadvantages that attach to prolonged imprisonment.

Accordingly, we hold that the condition imposed upon Gementera reasonably related to the legitimate statutory objective of rehabilitation. In so holding, we are careful not to articulate a principle broader than that presented by the facts of this case. With care and specificity, the district court outlined a sensible logic underlying its conclusion that a set of conditions, including the signboard provision, but also including reintegrative provisions, would better promote this defendant's rehabilitation and amendment of life than would a lengthier term of incarceration. By contrast, a per se rule that the mandatory public airing of one's offense can *never* assist an offender to reassume his duty of obedience to the law would impose a narrow penological orthodoxy not contemplated by the Guidelines' express approval of "any other condition [the district court] considers to be appropriate." . . .

HAWKINS, CIRCUIT JUDGE, dissenting:

Conditions of supervised release must be reasonably related to and "involve no greater deprivation of liberty than is reasonably necessary" to deter criminal conduct, protect the public, and rehabilitate the offender. Clearly, the shaming punishment at issue in this case was intended to humiliate Gementera. And that is all it will do. Any attempt to classify the goal of the punishment as anything other than humiliation would be disingenuous. Because humiliation is not one of the three proper goals under the Sentencing Reform Act, I would hold that the district court abused its discretion in imposing the condition.

There is precious little federal authority on sentences that include shaming components, perhaps indicative of a recognition that whatever legal justification may be marshaled in support of sentences involving public humiliation, they simply have no place in the majesty of an Article III courtroom. Some state courts have reviewed such sentences and the results have been mixed.

People v. Hackler, 13 Cal. App. 4th 1049 (1993), involved a condition that required a shoplifting offender to wear a court-provided t-shirt whenever he left the house that read: "My record plus two six-packs equals four years" on the front and "I am on felony probation for theft" on the back. Applying a state sentencing regime similar to the federal guidelines—authorizing the imposition of reasonable conditions of probation to foster rehabilitation and to protect public safety—the court struck down the condition. The court held that the relationship between the required conduct (wearing the t-shirt) and the defendant's crime (stealing beer) was so incidental that it was not reasonable and that the true intent behind the condition was to expose Hackler to "public ridicule and humiliation" and not "to foster rehabilitation."

 As in Hackler's case, the purpose behind the sandwich board condition was not to rehabilitate Gementera, but rather to turn him into a modern day Hester Prynne. This sort of condition is simply improper under the Sentencing Reform Act. See also *Springer v. United States*, 148 F.2d 411, 415-16 (9th Cir. 1945) (invalidating a condition that a convicted draft dodger donate a pint of blood to the Red Cross).

Ballenger v. State, 210 Ga. App. 627 (1993), approved a condition that a convicted drunk driver wear a fluorescent pink identification bracelet identifying him as such. By my lights, the dissent in *Ballenger* is far more persuasive. Concluding that the purpose of the condition was clearly to humiliate, Judge Blackburn argued that "a rationale of rehabilitation may not be used to vest . . . authority [to prescribe this type of punishment] in the judiciary."

Just as in *Hackler* and *Ballenger*, the true intention in this case was to humiliate Gementera, not to rehabilitate him or to deter him from future wrongdoing. When the district court initially imposed the sandwich board condition, the judge explained that Gementera should have to suffer the "humiliation of having to stand and be labeled in front of people coming and going from a post office as somebody who has stolen the mail." Subsequently, Gementera filed a motion to correct the sentence by having the sandwich board condition removed. He urged that humiliation was not a legitimate objective of punishment or release conditions. Only at the hearing on Gementera's motion did the district court change its characterization of the shaming punishment, remarking that the punishment was one of deterrence and rehabilitation and not merely humiliation. . . .

Although I believe that the sandwich board condition violates the Sentencing Reform Act and we should reverse the district court for that reason, I also believe that this is simply bad policy. A fair measure of a civilized society is how its institutions behave in the space between what it may have the power to do and what it should do. The shaming component of the sentence in this case fails that test. "When one shames another person, the goal is to degrade the object of shame, to place him lower in the chain of being, to dehumanize him."

To affirm the imposition of such punishments recalls a time in our history when pillories and stocks were the order of the day. To sanction such use of power runs the very great risk that by doing so we instill "a sense of disrespect for the criminal justice system" itself. . . .

NOTES & QUESTIONS ON SHAMING PENALTIES

1. *Reintegrative versus disintegrative shaming.*   What was the judge's goal in shaming Mr. Gementera? Was he trying to rehabilitate him, deter him from future crime, or encourage the community to express its outrage over his conduct? Do you agree with the court's discussion—and application—of the various theories of punishment? The Ninth Circuit upheld the shaming penalty in *Gementera* because they found it reintegrative in nature, i.e., it would still allow him to rejoin society as a productive member after the shaming was complete. Compare the penalty to the letter of apology that the Brewers were ordered to publish in the local newspaper. How does reintegration work? On one level it might require that the community forgive the defendant and accept him back into the fold. But perhaps this is too idealistic, and maybe reintegration only happens when the community forgets the event and the offender is permitted some degree of anonymity.

2. *Social media shaming.*   The *Gementera* case was decided in 2004. If the sentence were handed down today, what would have happened when he stood on the sidewalk in front of the post office? Presumably, someone witnessing the strange scene would take a picture and post it to Twitter or Facebook, thus ensuring that the event would become a permanent scarlet letter. Would this change the outcome of the court's analysis, or yours? Is it important to the result in *Gementera* that the shame is temporary rather than permanent?

3. *Sex offender registration statutes.*   Many states have passed regulations requiring sex offenders to register with local police when they move to a new municipality. State officials maintain databases with photographs of each offender and information about their criminal convictions and the underlying facts of their offense. In many cases the databases are publicly searchable on the Internet and school districts mail out notifications to parents when a new offender moves into the community. Some municipalities place strict zoning requirements on where sex offenders can live, sometimes forcing them into homelessness or motels. Are these provisions integrative or disintegrative? If they have a disintegrative component, is it sufficiently outweighed by the demands of public policy (i.e., notification)?

Most courts reviewing these statutes have found them constitutional, but there are exceptions. In *In re J.B.*, 2014 WL 7369785 (Dec. 29, 2014), the Supreme Court of Pennsylvania struck down the portions of the state's Sex Offender Registration and Notification Act that required lifetime registration for juvenile sex offenders. The court concluded that "studies suggest that many of those who commit sexual offenses as juveniles do so as a result of impulsivity and sexual curiosity, which diminish with rehabilitation and general maturation." Several states have ruled that their notification requirements cannot be imposed retroactively on defendants sentenced before the Act was passed. See also *State v. Briggs*, 199 P.3d 935 (Utah 2008) (publishing information regarding the type of victims the offender might victimize implied that he was currently dangerous and violated due process because offender had no opportunity to prove he was not currently dangerous).

C. PRACTICE & POLICY

In the following section, we consider the ways in which strategic and policy questions implicate the theory and practice of punishment. In particular, we address: (i) the role of emotion in sentencing decisions; (ii) the strategic decision of when to admit guilt in order to argue for reduced punishment; (iii) the appropriate role of victim impact statements in the sentencing process; (iv) the tension between sentencing guidelines and individual discretion for judges; (v) the lack of consistent sentences across different jurisdictions, including those of international tribunals; and (vi) consecutive versus concurrent prison terms.

> ∾ **Appealing to emotion.**   How should a prosecutor convince a judge to give the defendant the maximum sentence in any case? One possibility is to research the judge's prior decisions to determine whether he leans toward deterrence, retributivism, incapacitation, or rehabilitation in making sentencing decisions. For a defense attorney, the same logic applies. However, many judges appeal to *all* of the theories in making their decisions, requiring lawyers to find reasons under each theory for the outcome that best serves their client. Even within a single theory of punishment, however, emotion may play a greater or lesser role in the decision. Prosecutors and defense attorneys will inevitably play to a jury's emotions—on the one hand their fear of the defendant and, on the other hand, their compassion for the defendant as a human being. Are judges any less immune from these considerations? See generally Samuel H. Pillsbury, *Emotional Justice: Moralizing the Passions of Criminal Punishment*, 74 Cornell L. Rev. 655 (1988); Stephen P. Garvey, *The Emotional Economy of Capital Sentencing*, 75 N.Y.U. L. Rev. 26 (2000).
>
> ∾ **The guilt paradox.**   Most defendants facing conviction are caught in an intractable paradox. They want to deny that they committed the crime, but if they are convicted they want to express remorse and argue that they will not do it again. These two statements are logically incompatible. For this reason, American criminal courts generally split the guilt phase from the sentencing phase. At least one reason for "bifurcating" the criminal

proceeding into two phases is to free defendants from this Hobson's choice. Defendants can proclaim their innocence at the beginning of trial but, if they are convicted, they can change strategy for the sentencing phase and admit guilt (and seek mercy). Not all jurisdictions in the world bifurcate their criminal proceedings in this way. For example, the International Criminal Tribunal for the Former Yugoslavia (ICTY), a war crimes tribunal located in The Hague, generally followed a unitary model, which required defendants to stick to a single strategy. Some observers considered this unfair. However, the new International Criminal Court (ICC), also in The Hague, allows either the defense or prosecutor to request a separate sentencing hearing.

∿ **Victim impact statements.** Should judges consider the opinions of victims before deciding sentences? The issue is hotly debated. On the one hand, judges should learn about the consequences of the criminal act they are passing judgment on, including the full range of consequences—some obvious, some less so—that have torn apart victims and their families. In many cases, the impacts are substantially downstream. For instance, Judge Chin in *Madoff* was particularly moved by the fact that one victim of the scam, a grandmother, would be unable to fulfill her promise to help pay for her grandchild's college education. Victim impact statements in capital cases were originally declared unconstitutional on Eighth Amendment grounds by the Supreme Court in *South Carolina v. Gathers*, 490 U.S. 805 (1989), but just two years later the Supreme Court reversed course and decided that the practice was permissible. See *Payne v. Tennessee*, 501 U.S. 808 (1991):

> Payne echoes the concern . . . that the admission of victim impact evidence permits a jury to find that defendants whose victims were assets to their community are more deserving of punishment than those whose victims are perceived to be less worthy. As a general matter, however, victim impact evidence is not offered to encourage comparative judgments of this kind—for instance, that the killer of a hardworking, devoted parent deserves the death penalty, but that the murderer of a reprobate does not. It is designed to show instead *each* victim's "uniqueness as an individual human being," whatever the jury might think the loss to the community resulting from his death might be. The facts of *Gathers* are an excellent illustration of this: The evidence showed that the victim was an out of work, mentally handicapped individual, perhaps not, in the eyes of most, a significant contributor to society, but nonetheless a murdered human being . . .

> We are now of the view that a State may properly conclude that for the jury to assess meaningfully the defendant's moral culpability and blameworthiness, it should have before it at the sentencing phase evidence of the specific harm caused by the defendant. "[T]he State has a legitimate interest in counteracting the mitigating evidence which the defendant is entitled to put in, by reminding the sentencer that just as the murderer should be considered as an individual, so too the victim is an individual whose death represents a unique loss to society and in particular to his family." . . .

In fact, federal law now explicitly protects the right of victims to be heard prior to sentencing in a *federal* criminal case. In 2004, Congress passed the Crime Victims' Rights Act, 18 U.S.C. § 3771, which codifies a victim's right to be heard at any district court proceeding resulting in the defendant's release, parole, plea, or sentencing. The Act also imposes affirmative obligations on the U.S. attorney prosecuting the case to confer with the victims and keep them apprised of developments in the case.

∞ Sentencing guidelines. In most cases, judges have sentencing ranges that limit their discretion regarding how much, or how little, to punish a particular offender. State penal codes often fix upper or lower limits (or both) for prison terms for each criminal charge. Within that range, the judge can take into account the individual facts of the case and the specific circumstances of the defendant in deciding an appropriate sentence. Or the sentence might be negotiated in a plea deal. Some jurisdictions try to guide the judge's discretion by promulgating sentencing guidelines that list the aggravating and mitigating factors that should impact the decision. In the case of the federal sentencing guidelines, which are applied in federal courts, the aggravating and mitigating factors are then quantified in a complex calculation that helps the judge determine how many months a defendant should spend in jail or how many dollars the defendant should pay as a fine (or both).

In *Blakely v. Washington*, 542 U.S. 296 (2004), the Supreme Court struck down Washington's state sentencing guidelines because the aggravating factors that would increase a defendant's sentence could be determined by the judge instead of the jury. The following year, in *United States v. Booker*, 543 U.S. 220 (2005), the Supreme Court concluded that the federal sentencing guidelines were unconstitutional for the same reason. Five years earlier, the Supreme Court had ruled in *Apprendi v. New Jersey*, 530 U.S. 466 (2000), that a state hate crimes statute violated the Sixth Amendment's right to a jury trial because it allowed a judge—not a jury—to find that a crime was committed with the purpose of intimidating a protected group, thus triggering an enhanced penalty. Many court watchers saw the writing on the wall after *Apprendi* and predicted that the court would attack state and federal sentencing guidelines because they too allowed a judge to make factual findings that impacted sentencing. The prediction came true. However, sentencing guidelines did not completely disappear after *Blakely* and *Booker*. In most cases, the guidelines persist as discretionary only, providing a framework that judges are free to accept or reject as they choose. Based on this remedy (recasting mandatory guidelines as discretionary guidelines), the *Blakely* and *Booker* decisions have not had the earth-shattering impact than some expected, though they probably increased inter-judge discrepancies. See Ryan W. Scott, *Inter-Judge Sentencing Disparity After Booker: A First Look*, 63 Stan. L. Rev. 1 (2010).

൸ **Consistency in punishment.** Sentencing guidelines promote consistency *within* a jurisdiction. Our federal system, though, leaves criminal law largely to the individual states, so that Oregon might have different penological policies—and different sentencing guidelines—from, say, Vermont or New Hampshire. This means that someone arrested for drug possession in the State of New York might receive a different sentence from someone convicted in New Mexico. Is this result fair to the individual defendants? Is justice universal or does it vary from state to state? The American system is unique compared to Canada or most European nations that have a single federal criminal code for the entire country. Perhaps the American system should be considered a virtue and a feature of community-oriented justice that allows each defendant to be tried and sentenced by a community of peers considered sensitive to local context. Or is the federal system a hindrance to developing a coherent criminological policy?

൸ **International crimes.** Domestic crimes range all the way from simple marijuana possession to first-degree murder. Some crimes, however, are magnified on an exponential scale. War crimes tribunals, operating in foreign jurisdictions or as international courts, adjudicate atrocities where thousands or even tens of thousands of innocent victims were killed, often under horrific circumstances. *Biljana Plavšić*

Defendants convicted of war crimes, crimes against humanity, or genocide sometimes receive life in prison, but often the sentences range from 10 to 30 years. (The death penalty is not currently available in any international tribunal.) How can this be squared with results typically handed down in an American courtroom? For example, Biljana Plavšić, the former Bosnian Serb president, pled guilty in 2002 to crimes against humanity, expressed remorse, and was sentenced by the ICTY to 11 years in prison. She served her sentence in a Swedish prison and was released after serving only seven years. She later admitted in an interview that her guilty plea was a lie—she was not sorry about anything she did. Compare Plavšić's sentence with the 150 years that Madoff received for his financial fraud. What accounts for the difference?

৵ **Consecutive versus concurrent sentences.** In a case with multiple charges, it makes a big difference whether the sentences are to run concurrently with each other or consecutively. In many cases the judge has discretion to select between the two options. Consider the case of Anders Breivik, who killed eight people in a bomb attack in Oslo, Norway, before taking a boat to an island and massacring 69 people, many of them teenagers, at a youth political rally. Breivik was convicted of the murders and sentenced to 21 years in prison because Norwegian law does not permit consecutive prison terms. As such, each of his prison terms runs concurrently. Doing the math, Breivik received less than four months in prison for each victim of his rampage. However, Norway also has a scheme of preventive detention that might permit incarceration on the basis of dangerousness even after the sentence is completed. In 2014, Breivik threatened a hunger strike over conditions at the prison and included a list of demands such as replacing his PlayStation 2 videogame console with a newer PlayStation 3 model. See Henry Chu, *Mass Killer Breivik Threatens Hunger Strike for Better Games and Gym*, L.A. Times, Feb. 18, 2014.

CHAPTER 3

—⟨⟩⟨⟩⟨⟩—

THE DEATH PENALTY

A. DOCTRINE

Capital punishment has a long history in American jurisprudence. At common law, capital punishment was once mandatory for certain felonies. Over time, the criminal law has narrowed the class of individuals subject to the death penalty and in many ways that process is still continuing today. In *Furman v. Georgia*, 408 U.S. 238 (1972), the Supreme Court ruled that the death penalty was too arbitrary to be constitutional, but just four years later it held in *Gregg v. Georgia*, 428 U.S. 153 (1976), that it was constitutional if a jury's discretion was appropriately guided by consideration of aggravating and mitigating circumstances. Under this standard of "guided discretion," capital punishment must be neither mandatory nor arbitrary. Since that time, the Supreme Court has consistently reaffirmed the constitutionality of the death penalty, though over time it has progressively narrowed both the categories of offenders and the offenses that are death-eligible. Also, some state courts have struck down the death penalty on independent state constitutional grounds.

1. Who Can Be Executed

The Eighth Amendment prohibition on cruel and unusual punishment prohibits the execution of juveniles and the mentally disabled. In 1988, the Court struck down capital punishment for offenders aged 16 or younger when they committed the crime, but in 1989 the Court refused to extend the prohibition to adolescents between 16 and 18. The Court reversed course in *Roper v. Simmons*, 543 U.S. 551 (2005), holding categorically that juveniles under 18 at the time of the crime's commission could not be put to death by the state, since juveniles lacked the same intellectual maturity and impulse control that adults enjoy. The

Court also ruled in *Atkins v. Virginia*, 536 U.S. 304 (2002), that the state could not execute mentally disabled offenders because it would not serve the death penalty's penological goals (retribution and deterrence).

2. Which Crimes Apply

There are substantial constitutional limits on which crimes may be punished with death. In 1977, the Supreme Court barred the death penalty for the rape of an adult in *Coker v. Georgia*, 433 U.S. 584 (1977), and followed suit by banning it for child rape in *Kennedy v. Louisiana*, 554 U.S. 407 (2008). Consequently, capital punishment is generally not available in non-homicide cases, though the Court has been careful to exclude from its reasoning public offenses against the state—such as treason. In these cases, as well as the cases mentioned above involving juvenile and mentally disabled defendants, the Court relied on the development of a trend against applying the death penalty under those circumstances.

3. Racial Disparities

Statistically, African-American defendants are disproportionately sentenced to death when compared to their white counterparts. Furthermore, a conviction for murdering a white victim is more likely to get an African American sentenced to death than if the victim had been African-American. So both the race of the defendant and the race of the victim correlate with outcomes regarding capital punishment. For many opponents of the death penalty, this suggests that the system is discriminatory. The Supreme Court rejected this argument in *McCleskey v. Kemp*, 481 U.S. 279 (1987), because the Justices saw only correlation where others saw causation. Without proof of overt discrimination on the part of a jury or the state legislature, the death penalty is constitutional.

4. Methods of Execution

Recent litigation in the circuit courts has focused extensively on methods of execution, in particular the drug "cocktail" used for lethal injection. In the past, most states used a three-drug sequence comprising of a barbiturate to sedate the prisoner into unconsciousness, a second drug to produce paralysis, followed by a third drug to stop the heart. After manufacturers stopped providing the barbiturates for the first step, some states shifted either to a single-drug protocol (at a high dose) while others developed new three-step sequences using midazolam instead of the barbiturates for the first step. Some executions have gone poorly, while others have produced a swift death. In *Glossip v. Gross*, 135 S. Ct. 2726 (2015), the Supreme Court upheld the constitutionality of the three-drug sequence in Oklahoma.

B. APPLICATION

1. Mental Disability

There is a class of individuals with mental disabilities who nonetheless are held criminally responsible for their actions. For many years, advocates have argued that defendants with mental disabilities are not appropriate subjects for the death penalty. In the following case, the Supreme Court evaluates this claim. As you read the following opinion, pick out the particular reasons why mental disability is inconsistent with the application of capital punishment. Does the Court's opinion rely on any particular theory of punishment?

Atkins v. Virginia
Supreme Court of the United States
536 U.S. 304 (2002)

STEVENS, J.

Those mentally retarded persons who meet the law's requirements for criminal responsibility should be tried and punished when they commit crimes. Because of their disabilities in areas of reasoning, judgment, and control of their impulses, however, they do not act with the level of moral culpability that characterizes the most serious adult criminal conduct. More-over, their impairments can jeopardize the reliability and fairness of capital proceedings against mentally retarded defendants. Presumably for these reasons, in the 13 years since we decided *Penry v. Lynaugh,* 492 U.S. 302 (1989), the American public, legislators, scholars, and judges have deliberated over the question whether the death penalty should ever be imposed on a mentally retarded criminal. The consensus reflected in those deliberations informs our answer to the question presented by this case: whether such executions are "cruel and unusual punishments" prohibited by the Eighth Amendment to the Federal Constitution.

I

Petitioner, Daryl Renard Atkins, was convicted of abduction, armed robbery, and capital murder, and sentenced to death. At approximately midnight on August 16, 1996, Atkins and William Jones, armed with a semiautomatic handgun, abducted Eric Nesbitt, robbed him of the money on his person, drove him to an automated teller machine in his pickup truck where cameras recorded their withdrawal of additional cash, then took him to an isolated location where he was shot eight times and killed. . . .

In the penalty phase, the defense relied on one witness, Dr. Evan Nelson, a forensic psychologist who had evaluated Atkins before trial and concluded that he was "mildly mentally retarded." His conclusion was based on interviews with people who knew Atkins, a review of school and court records, and the administration of a standard intelligence test which indicated that Atkins had a full scale IQ of 59.

The jury sentenced Atkins to death, but the Virginia Supreme Court ordered a second sentencing hearing because the trial court had used a misleading verdict form. At the resentencing, Dr. Nelson again testified. The State presented an expert rebuttal witness, Dr. Stanton Samenow, who expressed the opinion that Atkins was not mentally retarded, but rather was of "average intelligence, at least," and diagnosable as having antisocial personality disorder. The jury again sentenced Atkins to death. . . .

II

The Eighth Amendment succinctly prohibits "[e]xcessive" sanctions. It provides: "Excessive bail shall not be required, nor excessive fines imposed, nor cruel and unusual punishments inflicted." . . .

A claim that punishment is excessive is judged not by the standards that prevailed in 1685 when Lord Jeffreys presided over the "Bloody Assizes" or when the Bill of Rights was adopted, but rather by those that currently prevail. As Chief Justice Warren explained in his opinion in *Trop v. Dulles,* 356 U.S. 86 (1958): "The basic concept underlying the Eighth Amendment is nothing less than the dignity of man. . . . The Amendment must draw its meaning from the evolving standards of decency that mark the progress of a maturing society."

Proportionality review under those evolving standards should be informed by "objective factors to the maximum possible extent." We have pinpointed that the "clearest and most reliable objective evidence of contemporary values is the legislation enacted by the country's legislatures." Relying in part on such legislative evidence, we have held that death is an impermissibly excessive punishment for the rape of an adult woman, *Coker v. Georgia,* 433 U.S. 584, 593-596 (1977) or for a defendant who neither took life, attempted to take life, nor intended to take life, *Enmund v. Florida,* 458 U.S. 782, 789-793 (1982). . . .

III

The parties have not called our attention to any state legislative consideration of the suitability of imposing the death penalty on mentally retarded offenders prior to 1986. In that year, the public reaction to the execution of a mentally retarded murderer in Georgia apparently led to the enactment of the first state statute prohibiting such executions. In 1988, when Congress enacted legislation reinstating the federal death penalty, it expressly provided that a "sentence of death shall not be carried out upon a person who is mentally retarded." In 1989, Maryland enacted a similar prohibition. It was in that year that we decided *Penry*, and concluded that those two state enactments, "even when added to the 14 States that have rejected capital punishment completely, do not provide sufficient evidence at present of a national consensus."

Much has changed since then. Responding to the national attention received by the Bowden execution and our decision in *Penry*, state legislatures across the country began to address the issue. In 1990, Kentucky and Tennessee enacted statutes similar to those in Georgia and Maryland, as did New Mexico in 1991, and Arkansas, Colorado, Washington, Indiana, and Kansas in 1993 and 1994. In 1995, when New York reinstated its death penalty, it emulated the Federal Government by expressly exempting the mentally retarded. Nebraska followed suit in 1998. There appear to have been no similar enactments during the next two years, but in 2000 and 2001 six more States—South Dakota, Arizona, Connecticut, Florida, Missouri, and North Carolina—joined the procession. The Texas Legislature unanimously adopted a similar bill, and bills have passed at least one house in other States, including Virginia and Nevada.

It is not so much the number of these States that is significant, but the consistency of the direction of change. Given the well-known fact that anti-crime legislation is far more popular than legislation providing protections for persons guilty of violent crime, the large number of States prohibiting the execution of mentally retarded persons (and the complete absence of States passing legislation reinstating the power to conduct such executions) provides powerful evidence that today our society views mentally retarded offenders as categorically less culpable than the average criminal. The evidence carries even greater force when it is noted that the legislatures that have addressed the issue have voted overwhelmingly in favor of the prohibition. Moreover, even in those States that allow the execution of mentally retarded offenders, the practice is uncommon. Some States, for example New Hampshire and New Jersey, continue to authorize executions, but none have been carried out in decades. Thus there is little need to pursue legislation barring the execution of the mentally retarded in those States. And it appears that even among those States that regularly execute offenders and that have no prohibition with regard to the mentally retarded, only five have executed offenders possessing a known IQ less than 70 since we decided *Penry*. The practice, therefore, has become truly unusual, and it is fair to say that a national consensus has developed against it. . . .

IV

This consensus unquestionably reflects widespread judgment about the relative culpability of mentally retarded offenders, and the relationship between mental retardation and the penological purposes served by the death penalty. Additionally, it suggests that some characteristics of mental retardation undermine the strength of the procedural protections that our capital jurisprudence steadfastly guards.

As discussed above, clinical definitions of mental retardation require not only subaverage intellectual functioning, but also significant limitations in adaptive skills such as communication, self-care, and self-direction that became manifest before age 18. Mentally retarded persons frequently know the difference between right and wrong and are competent to stand trial. Because of their impairments, however, by definition they have diminished capacities to understand and process information, to communicate, to abstract from mistakes and learn from experience, to engage in logical reasoning, to control impulses, and to understand the reactions of others. There is no evidence that they are more likely to engage in criminal conduct than others, but there is abundant evidence that they often act on impulse rather than pursuant to a premeditated plan, and that in group settings they are followers rather than leaders. Their deficiencies do not warrant an exemption from criminal sanctions, but they do diminish their personal culpability.

In light of these deficiencies, our death penalty jurisprudence provides two reasons consistent with the legislative consensus that the mentally retarded should be categorically excluded from execution. First, there is a serious question as to whether either justification that we have recognized as a basis for the death penalty applies to mentally retarded offenders. *Gregg v. Georgia,* 428 U.S. 153, 183 (1976), identified "retribution and deterrence of capital crimes by prospective offenders" as the social purposes served by the death penalty. Unless the imposition of the death penalty on a mentally retarded person "measurably contributes to one or both of these goals, it 'is nothing more than the purposeless and needless imposition of pain and suffering,' and hence an unconstitutional punishment."

With respect to retribution—the interest in seeing that the offender gets his "just deserts"—the severity of the appropriate punishment necessarily depends on the culpability of the offender. Since *Gregg,* our jurisprudence has consistently confined the imposition of the death penalty to a narrow category of the most serious crimes. For example, in *Godfrey v. Georgia,* 446 U.S. 420 (1980), we set aside a death sentence because the petitioner's crimes did not reflect "a consciousness materially more 'depraved' than that of any person guilty of murder." If the culpability of the average murderer is insufficient to justify the most extreme sanction available to the State, the lesser culpability of the mentally retarded offender surely does not merit that form of retribution. Thus, pursuant to our narrowing jurisprudence, which seeks to ensure that only the most deserving of execution are put to death, an exclusion for the mentally retarded is appropriate.

With respect to deterrence—the interest in preventing capital crimes by prospective offenders—"it seems likely that 'capital punishment can serve as a deterrent only when murder is the result of premeditation and deliberation.'" Exempting the mentally retarded from that punishment will not affect the "cold calculus that precedes the decision" of other potential murderers. Indeed, that sort of calculus is at the opposite end of the spectrum from behavior of mentally retarded offenders. The theory of deterrence in capital sentencing is predicated upon the notion that the increased severity of the punishment will inhibit criminal actors from carrying out murderous conduct. Yet it is the same cognitive and behavioral impairments that make these defendants less morally culpable—for example, the diminished ability to understand and process information, to learn from experience, to engage in logical reasoning, or to control impulses—that also make it less likely that they can process the information of the possibility of execution as a penalty and, as a result, control their conduct based upon that information. Nor will exempting the mentally retarded from execution lessen the deterrent effect of the death penalty with respect to offenders who are not mentally retarded. Such individuals are unprotected by the exemption and will continue to face the threat of execution. Thus, executing the mentally retarded will not measurably further the goal of deterrence.

The reduced capacity of mentally retarded offenders provides a second justification for a categorical rule making such offenders ineligible for the death penalty. The risk "that the death penalty will be imposed in spite of factors which may call for a less severe penalty," is enhanced, not only by the possibility of false confessions, but also by the lesser ability of mentally retarded defendants to make a persuasive showing of mitigation in the face of prosecutorial evidence of one or more aggravating factors. Mentally retarded defendants may be less able to give meaningful assistance to their counsel and are typically poor witnesses, and their demeanor may create an unwarranted impression of lack of remorse for their crimes. . . .

2. The Juvenile Death Penalty

The following case asks many of the same questions for juvenile defendants. Why does the Supreme Court view juveniles as responsible enough to be prosecuted for their criminal behavior but not responsible enough to face execution?

Roper v. Simmons
Supreme Court of the United States
543 U.S. 551 (2005)

KENNEDY, J.

This case requires us to address, for the second time in a decade and a half, whether it is permissible under the Eighth and Fourteenth Amendments to the Constitution of the United States to execute a juvenile offender who was older than 15 but younger than 18 when he committed a capital crime. . . .

I

At the age of 17, when he was still a junior in high school, Christopher Simmons, the respondent here, committed murder. About nine months later, after he had turned 18, he was tried and sentenced to death. There is little doubt that Simmons was the instigator of the crime. Before its commission Simmons said he wanted to murder someone. In chilling, callous terms he talked about his plan, discussing it for the most part with two friends, Charles Benjamin and John Tessmer, then aged 15 and 16 respectively. Simmons proposed to commit burglary and murder by breaking and entering, tying up a victim, and throwing the victim off a bridge. Simmons assured his friends they could "get away with it" because they were minors.

The three met at about 2 A.M. on the night of the murder, but Tessmer left before the other two set out. (The State later charged Tessmer with conspiracy, but dropped the charge in exchange for his testimony against Simmons.) Simmons and Benjamin entered the home of the victim, Shirley Crook, after reaching through an open window and unlocking the back door. Simmons turned on a hallway light. Awakened, Mrs. Crook called out, "Who's there?" In response Simmons entered Mrs. Crook's bedroom, where he recognized her from a previous car accident involving them both. Simmons later admitted this confirmed his resolve to murder her.

Using duct tape to cover her eyes and mouth and bind her hands, the two perpetrators put Mrs. Crook in her minivan and drove to a state park. They reinforced the bindings, covered her head with a towel, and walked her to a railroad trestle spanning the Meramec River. There they tied her hands and feet together with electrical wire, wrapped her whole face in duct tape and threw her from the bridge, drowning her in the waters below.

By the afternoon of September 9, Steven Crook had returned home from an overnight trip, found his bedroom in disarray, and reported his wife missing. On the same afternoon fishermen recovered the victim's body from the river. Simmons, meanwhile, was bragging about the killing, telling friends he had killed a woman "because the bitch seen my face." . . .

III

The evidence of national consensus against the death penalty for juveniles is similar, and in some respects parallel, to the evidence *Atkins* held sufficient to demonstrate a national consensus against the death penalty for the mentally retarded. When *Atkins* was decided, 30 States prohibited the death penalty for the mentally retarded. This number comprised 12 that had abandoned the death penalty altogether, and 18 that maintained it but excluded the mentally retarded from its reach. By a similar calculation in this case, 30 States prohibit the juvenile death penalty, comprising 12 that have rejected the death penalty altogether and 18 that maintain it but, by express provision or judicial interpretation, exclude juveniles from its reach. *Atkins* emphasized that even in the 20 States without formal prohibition, the practice of executing the mentally retarded was infrequent. . . .

As in *Atkins,* the objective indicia of consensus in this case—the rejection of the juvenile death penalty in the majority of States; the infrequency of its use even where it remains on the books; and the consistency in the trend toward abolition of the practice—provide sufficient evidence that today our society views juveniles, in the words *Atkins* used respecting the mentally retarded, as "categorically less culpable than the average criminal."

A majority of States have rejected the imposition of the death penalty on juvenile offenders under 18, and we now hold this is required by the Eighth Amendment.

Because the death penalty is the most severe punishment, the Eighth Amendment applies to it with special force. Capital punishment must be limited to those offenders who commit "a narrow category of the most serious crimes" and whose extreme culpability makes them "the most deserving of execution." This principle is implemented throughout the capital sentencing process. States must give narrow and precise definition to the aggravating factors that can result in a capital sentence. In any capital case a defendant has wide latitude to raise as a mitigating factor "any aspect of [his or her] character or record and any of the circumstances of the offense that the defendant proffers as a basis for a sentence less than death." There are a number of crimes that beyond question are severe in absolute terms, yet the death penalty may not be imposed for their commission. The death penalty may not be imposed on certain classes of offenders, such as juveniles under 16, the insane, and the mentally retarded, no matter how heinous the crime. These rules vindicate the underlying principle that the death penalty is reserved for a narrow category of crimes and offenders.

Three general differences between juveniles under 18 and adults demonstrate that juvenile offenders cannot with reliability be classified among the worst offenders. First, as any parent knows and as the scientific and sociological studies respondent and his *amici* cite tend to confirm, "[a] lack of maturity and an underdeveloped sense of responsibility are found in youth more often than in adults and are more understandable among the young. These qualities often result in impetuous and ill-considered actions and decisions." It has been noted that "adolescents are overrepresented statistically in virtually every category of reckless behavior." In recognition of the comparative immaturity and irresponsibility of juveniles, almost every State prohibits those under 18 years of age from voting, serving on juries, or marrying without parental consent.

The second area of difference is that juveniles are more vulnerable or susceptible to negative influences and outside pressures, including peer pressure. This is explained in part by the prevailing circumstance that juveniles have less control, or less experience with control, over their own environment.

The third broad difference is that the character of a juvenile is not as well formed as that of an adult. The personality traits of juveniles are more transitory, less fixed.

These differences render suspect any conclusion that a juvenile falls among the worst offenders. The susceptibility of juveniles to immature and irresponsible behavior means "their irresponsible conduct is not as morally reprehensible as that of an adult." Their own vulnerability and comparative lack of control over their immediate surroundings mean juveniles have a greater claim than adults to be forgiven for failing to escape negative influences in their whole environment. The reality that juveniles still struggle to define their identity means it is less supportable to conclude that even a heinous crime committed by a juvenile is evidence of irretrievably depraved character. From a moral standpoint it would be misguided to equate the failings of a minor with those of an adult, for a greater possibility exists that a minor's character deficiencies will be reformed. Indeed, "[t]he relevance of youth as a mitigating factor derives from the fact that the signature qualities of youth are transient; as individuals mature, the impetuousness and recklessness that may dominate in younger years can subside." . . .

Once the diminished culpability of juveniles is recognized, it is evident that the penological justifications for the death penalty apply to them with lesser force than to adults. We have held there are two distinct social purposes served by the death penalty: "retribution and deterrence of capital crimes by prospective offenders.'" As for retribution, we remarked in *Atkins* that "[i]f the culpability of the average murderer is insufficient to justify the most extreme sanction available to the State, the lesser culpability of the mentally retarded offender surely does not merit that form of retribution." The same conclusions follow from the lesser culpability of the juvenile offender. Whether viewed as an attempt to express the community's moral outrage or as an attempt to right the balance for the wrong to the victim, the case for retribution is not as strong with a minor as with an adult. Retribution is not proportional if the law's most severe penalty is imposed on one whose culpability or blameworthiness is diminished, to a substantial degree, by reason of youth and immaturity.

As for deterrence, it is unclear whether the death penalty has a significant or even measurable deterrent effect on juveniles, as counsel for petitioner acknowledged at oral argument. In general we leave to legislatures the assessment of the efficacy of various criminal penalty schemes. Here, however, the absence of evidence of deterrent effect is of special concern because the same characteristics that render juveniles less culpable than adults suggest as well that juveniles will be less susceptible to deterrence. . . .

IV

Our determination that the death penalty is disproportionate punishment for offenders under 18 finds confirmation in the stark reality that the United States is the only country in the world that continues to give official sanction to the juvenile death penalty. This reality does not become controlling, for the task of interpreting the Eighth Amendment remains our responsibility. Yet at least from the time of the Court's decision in *Trop*, the Court has referred to the laws of other countries and to international authorities as instructive for its interpretation of the Eighth Amendment's prohibition of "cruel and unusual punishments."

As respondent and a number of *amici* emphasize, Article 37 of the United Nations Convention on the Rights of the Child, which every country in the world has ratified save for the United States and Somalia, contains an express prohibition on capital punishment for crimes committed by juveniles under 18. No ratifying country has entered a reservation to the provision prohibiting the execution of juvenile offenders. Parallel prohibitions are contained in other significant international covenants.

Respondent and his *amici* have submitted, and petitioner does not contest, that only seven countries other than the United States have executed juvenile offenders since 1990: Iran, Pakistan, Saudi Arabia, Yemen, Nigeria, the Democratic Republic of Congo, and China. Since then each of these countries has either abolished capital punishment for juveniles or made public disavowal of the practice. In sum, it is fair to say that the United States now stands alone in a world that has turned its face against the juvenile death penalty. . . .

It is proper that we acknowledge the overwhelming weight of international opinion against the juvenile death penalty, resting in large part on the understanding that the instability and emotional imbalance of young people may often be a factor in the crime. The opinion of the world community, while not controlling our outcome, does provide respected and significant confirmation for our own conclusions.

Over time, from one generation to the next, the Constitution has come to earn the high respect and even, as Madison dared to hope, the veneration of the American people. The document sets forth, and rests upon, innovative principles original to the American experience, such as federalism; a proven balance in political mechanisms through separation of powers; specific guarantees for the accused in criminal cases; and broad provisions to secure individual freedom and preserve human dignity. These doctrines and guarantees are central to the American experience and remain essential to our present-day self-definition and national identity. Not the least of the reasons we honor the Constitution, then, is because we know it to be our own. It does not lessen our fidelity to the Constitution or our pride in its origins to acknowledge that the express affirmation of certain fundamental rights by other nations and peoples simply underscores the centrality of those same rights within our own heritage of freedom. . . .

NOTES & QUESTIONS ON ATKINS AND ROPER

1. *Foreign law and the U.S. Constitution.*   Should the Supreme Court look to foreign jurisdictions to help determine whether the U.S. death penalty constitutes cruel and unusual punishment? Kennedy's opinion in *Roper* drew heavily on the global consensus against executing juveniles, with the exception of Iran, Pakistan, Saudi Arabia, Yemen, Nigeria, the Democratic Republic of Congo, and China. This methodology drew the ire of Justice Scalia, who argued in dissent that "the basic premise of the Court's argument—that American law should conform to the laws of the rest of the world—ought to be rejected out of hand." *Roper* at 624. He continued: "What these foreign sources 'affirm,' rather than repudiate, is the Justices' own notion of how the world ought to be, and their diktat that it shall be so henceforth in America." As a question of methodology, should the Court look to international human rights standards in order to fix the content of constitutional protections in the United States? Scalia complained that the reliance on foreign standards was one-way only. For example, plenty of foreign jurisdictions allow illegally obtained evidence in criminal trials. Should the United States follow suit and abandon the exclusionary rule? In past cases, the Court's majority has said no and has ignored the counter-trends in foreign jurisdictions. In a recent book, Justice Breyer argued that the world is so interconnected that foreign considerations are now inevitable in most questions pertaining to U.S. law that come before the Court. See Stephen Breyer, *The Court and the World: American Law and the New Global Realities* (2015). Do you agree?

2. *What is the correct remedy?* If one accepts Kennedy's conclusion that juvenile offenders are often immature when it comes to their moral agency, what is the correct remedy? One solution might be to establish a broad standard that the death penalty should only be used on a 17-year old when a court is satisfied that the defendant demonstrated the same level of emotional maturity as an adult. The lower appellate courts could then police this standard and overturn particular sentences that run afoul of it. But the Supreme Court refused to grant this discretion to lower courts and instead crafted a categorical bar in all cases, even as it recognized that some juveniles are very mature and some adults are immature. Why require a categorical rule barring the death penalty in all cases of juvenile offenders? Presumably the answer lies in the *risk* that an immature person might be condemned under the standard. But if we cannot trust the lower appellate courts to make this determination, can we trust them to do anything? Does the Court's unwillingness to tolerate this risk mean "death is different"?

3. Capital Punishment for Rape

Aside from the individuals that are exempt from capital punishment, some crimes are constitutionally exempt from the application of the death penalty. At the time *Kennedy* was decided, the Supreme Court had already ruled capital punishment for the rape of an adult was constitutionally impermissible. In the following case, the Court asks whether it should expand that holding to cases of child rape.

Kennedy v. Louisiana

Supreme Court of the United States
554 U.S. 407 (2008)

KENNEDY, J.

I

Petitioner's crime was one that cannot be recounted in these pages in a way sufficient to capture in full the hurt and horror inflicted on his victim or to convey the revulsion society, and the jury that represents it, sought to express by sentencing petitioner to death. At 9:18 A.M. on March 2, 1998, petitioner called 911 to report that his stepdaughter, referred to here as L.H., had been raped. He told the 911 operator that L.H. had been in the garage while he readied his son for school. Upon hearing loud screaming, petitioner said, he ran outside and found L.H. in the side yard. Two neighborhood boys, petitioner told the operator, had dragged L.H. from the garage to the yard, pushed her down, and raped her. Petitioner claimed he saw one of the boys riding away on a blue 10-speed bicycle.

When police arrived at petitioner's home between 9:20 and 9:30 A.M., they found L.H. on her bed, wearing a T-shirt and wrapped in a bloody blanket. She was bleeding profusely from the vaginal area. Petitioner told police he had carried her from the yard to the bathtub and then to the bed. Consistent with this explanation, police found a thin line of blood drops in the garage on the way to the house and then up the stairs. Once in the bedroom, petitioner had used a basin of water and a cloth to wipe blood from the victim. This later prevented medical personnel from collecting a reliable DNA sample.

L.H. was transported to the Children's Hospital. An expert in pediatric forensic medicine testified that L.H.'s injuries were the most severe he had seen from a sexual assault in his four years of practice. A laceration to the left wall of the vagina had separated her cervix from the back of her vagina, causing her rectum to protrude into the vaginal structure. Her entire perineum was torn from the posterior fourchette to the anus. The injuries required emergency surgery. . . .

Eight days after the crime, and despite L.H.'s insistence that petitioner was not the offender, petitioner was arrested for the rape. The State's investigation had drawn the accuracy of petitioner and L.H.'s story into question. Though the defense at trial proffered alternative explanations, the case for the prosecution, credited by the jury, was based upon the following evidence: An inspection of the side yard immediately after the assault was inconsistent with a rape having occurred there, the grass having been found mostly undisturbed but for a small patch of coagulated blood. Petitioner said that one of the perpetrators fled the crime scene on a blue 10-speed bicycle but gave inconsistent descriptions of the bicycle's features, such as its handlebars. Investigators found a bicycle matching petitioner and L.H.'s description in tall grass behind a nearby apartment, and petitioner identified it as the bicycle one of the perpetrators was riding. Yet its tires were flat, it did not have gears, and it was covered in spider webs. In addition police found blood on the underside of L.H.'s mattress. This convinced them the rape took place in her bedroom, not outside the house.

Police also found that petitioner made four telephone calls on the morning of the rape. Sometime before 6:15 A.M., petitioner called his employer and left a message that he was unavailable to work that day. Petitioner called back between 6:30 and 7:30 A.M. to ask a colleague how to get blood out of a white carpet because his daughter had "just become a young lady." At 7:37 A.M., petitioner called B&B Carpet Cleaning and requested urgent assistance in removing bloodstains from a carpet. Petitioner did not call 911 until about an hour and a half later.

About a month after petitioner's arrest L.H. was removed from the custody of her mother, who had maintained until that point that petitioner was not involved in the rape. On June 22, 1998, L.H. was returned home and told her mother for the first time that petitioner had raped her. And on December 16, 1999, about 21 months after the rape, L.H. recorded her accusation in a videotaped interview with the Child Advocacy Center. . . .

II

The Eighth Amendment, applicable to the States through the Fourteenth Amendment, provides that "[e]xcessive bail shall not be required, nor excessive fines imposed, nor cruel and unusual punishments inflicted." The Amendment proscribes "all excessive punishments, as well as cruel and unusual punishments that may or may not be excessive." The Court explained in *Atkins* and *Roper* that the Eighth Amendment's protection against excessive or cruel and unusual punishments flows from the basic "precept of justice that punishment for [a] crime should be graduated and proportioned to [the] offense." Whether this requirement has been fulfilled is determined not by the standards that prevailed when the Eighth Amendment was adopted in 1791 but by the norms that "currently prevail." The Amendment "draw[s] its meaning from the evolving standards of decency that mark the progress of a maturing society." This is because "[t]he standard of extreme cruelty is not merely descriptive, but necessarily embodies a moral judgment. The standard itself remains the same, but its applicability must change as the basic mores of society change."

Evolving standards of decency must embrace and express respect for the dignity of the person, and the punishment of criminals must conform to that rule. As we shall discuss, punishment is justified under one or more of three principal rationales: rehabilitation, deterrence, and retribution. It is the last of these, retribution, that most often can contradict the law's own ends. This is of particular concern when the Court interprets the meaning of the Eighth Amendment in capital cases. When the law punishes by death, it risks its own sudden descent into brutality, transgressing the constitutional commitment to decency and restraint.

For these reasons we have explained that capital punishment must "be limited to those offenders who commit 'a narrow category of the most serious crimes' and whose extreme culpability makes them 'the most deserving of execution.'" Though the death penalty is not invariably unconstitutional, the Court insists upon confining the instances in which the punishment can be imposed. . . .

Based both on consensus and our own independent judgment, our holding is that a death sentence for one who raped but did not kill a child, and who did not intend to assist another in killing the child, is unconstitutional under the Eighth and Fourteenth Amendments.

III

The existence of objective indicia of consensus against making a crime punishable by death was a relevant concern in *Roper, Atkins, Coker,* and *Enmund,* and we follow the approach of those cases here. The history of the death penalty for the crime of rape is an instructive beginning point.

In 1925, 18 States, the District of Columbia, and the Federal Government had statutes that authorized the death penalty for the rape of a child or an adult. Between 1930 and 1964, 455 people were executed for those crimes. To our knowledge the last individual executed for the rape of a child was Ronald Wolfe in 1964.

In 1972, *Furman* invalidated most of the state statutes authorizing the death penalty for the crime of rape; and in *Furman*'s aftermath only six States reenacted their capital rape provisions. Three States—Georgia, North Carolina, and Louisiana—did so with respect to all rape offenses. Three States—Florida, Mississippi, and Tennessee—did so with respect only to child rape. All six statutes were later invalidated under state or federal law.

Louisiana reintroduced the death penalty for rape of a child in 1995. Under the current statute, any anal, vaginal, or oral intercourse with a child under the age of 13 constitutes aggravated rape and is punishable by death. Mistake of age is not a defense, so the statute imposes strict liability in this regard. Five States have since followed Louisiana's lead: Georgia, Montana, Oklahoma, South Carolina, and Texas. Four of these States' statutes are more narrow than Louisiana's in that only offenders with a previous rape conviction are death eligible. Georgia's statute makes child rape a capital offense only when aggravating circumstances are present, including but not limited to a prior conviction.

By contrast, 44 States have not made child rape a capital offense. As for federal law, Congress in the Federal Death Penalty Act of 1994 expanded the number of federal crimes for which the death penalty is a permissible sentence, including certain nonhomicide offenses; but it did not do the same for child rape or abuse. Under 18 U.S.C. § 2245, an offender is death eligible only when the sexual abuse or exploitation results in the victim's death. . . .

The evidence of a national consensus with respect to the death penalty for child rapists, as with respect to juveniles, mentally retarded offenders, and vicarious felony murderers, shows divided opinion but, on balance, an opinion against it. Thirty-seven jurisdictions—36 States plus the Federal Government—have the death penalty. As mentioned above, only six of those jurisdictions authorize the death penalty for rape of a child. Though our review of national consensus is not confined to tallying the number of States with applicable death penalty legislation, it is of significance that, in 45 jurisdictions, petitioner could not be executed for child rape of any kind. . . .

IV

As we have said in other Eighth Amendment cases, objective evidence of contemporary values as it relates to punishment for child rape is entitled to great weight, but it does not end our inquiry. . . .

It must be acknowledged that there are moral grounds to question a rule barring capital punishment for a crime against an individual that did not result in death. These facts illustrate the point. Here the victim's fright, the sense of betrayal, and the nature of her injuries caused more prolonged physical and mental suffering than, say, a sudden killing by an unseen assassin. The attack was not just on her but on her childhood. For this reason, we should be most reluctant to rely upon the language of the plurality in *Coker,* which posited that, for the victim of rape, "life may not be nearly so happy as it was," but it is not beyond repair. Rape has a permanent psychological, emotional, and sometimes physical impact on the child. We cannot dismiss the years of long anguish that must be endured by the victim of child rape.

It does not follow, though, that capital punishment is a proportionate penalty for the crime. The constitutional prohibition against excessive or cruel and unusual punishments mandates that the State's power to punish "be exercised within the limits of civilized standards." Evolving standards of decency that mark the progress of a maturing society counsel us to be most hesitant before interpreting the Eighth Amendment to allow the extension of the death penalty, a hesitation that has special force where no life was taken in the commission of the crime. It is an established principle that decency, in its essence, presumes respect for the individual and thus moderation or restraint in the application of capital punishment.

To date the Court has sought to define and implement this principle, for the most part, in cases involving capital murder. One approach has been to insist upon general rules that ensure consistency in determining who receives a death sentence. At the same time the Court has insisted, to ensure restraint and moderation in use of capital punishment, on judging the "character and record of the individual offender and the circumstances of the particular offense as a constitutionally indispensable part of the process of inflicting the penalty of death." . . .

Our concern here is limited to crimes against individual persons. We do not address, for example, crimes defining and punishing treason, espionage, terrorism, and drug kingpin activity, which are offenses against the State. As it relates to crimes against individuals, though, the death penalty should not be expanded to instances where the victim's life was not taken. . . .

Consistent with evolving standards of decency and the teachings of our precedents we conclude that, in determining whether the death penalty is excessive, there is a distinction between intentional first-degree murder on the one hand and nonhomicide crimes against individual persons, even including child rape, on the other. The latter crimes may be devastating in their harm, as here, but "in terms of moral depravity and of the injury to the person and to the public," they cannot be compared to murder in their "severity and irrevocability." . . .

The goal of retribution, which reflects society's and the victim's interests in seeing that the offender is repaid for the hurt he caused, does not justify the harshness of the death penalty here. In measuring retribution, as well as other objectives of criminal law, it is appropriate to distinguish between a particularly depraved murder that merits death as a form of retribution and the crime of child rape.

There is an additional reason for our conclusion that imposing the death penalty for child rape would not further retributive purposes. In considering whether retribution is served, among other factors we have looked to whether capital punishment "has the potential . . . to allow the community as a whole, including the surviving family and friends of the victim, to affirm its own judgment that the culpability of the prisoner is so serious that the ultimate penalty must be sought and imposed." In considering the death penalty for nonhomicide offenses this inquiry necessarily also must include the question whether the death penalty balances the wrong to the victim.

It is not at all evident that the child rape victim's hurt is lessened when the law permits the death of the perpetrator. . . . Society's desire to inflict the death penalty for child rape by enlisting the child victim to assist it over the course of years in asking for capital punishment forces a moral choice on the child, who is not of mature age to make that choice. The way the death penalty here involves the child victim in its enforcement can compromise a decent legal system; and this is but a subset of fundamental difficulties capital punishment can cause in the administration and enforcement of laws proscribing child rape. . . .

In addition, by in effect making the punishment for child rape and murder equivalent, a State that punishes child rape by death may remove a strong incentive for the rapist not to kill the victim. Assuming the offender behaves in a rational way, as one must to justify the penalty on grounds of deterrence, the penalty in some respects gives less protection, not more, to the victim, who is often the sole witness to the crime. It might be argued that, even if the death penalty results in a marginal increase in the incentive to kill, this is counterbalanced by a marginally increased deterrent to commit the crime at all. Whatever balance the legislature strikes, however, uncertainty on the point makes the argument for the penalty less compelling than for homicide crimes. . . .

NOTES & QUESTIONS ON OFFENSE RESTRICTIONS

1. *Special risk of wrongful execution.* Among other things, the Court was concerned that child rape cases are prone to wrongful convictions due to the unreliability of child witnesses. Does this argument apply to other capital offenses or is it limited to offenses against children? Could the same argument be extended to all cases based solely on eyewitness testimony, which is sometimes unreliable? See Elizabeth F. Loftus, *Eyewitness Testimony* (1979). See also Kelly J. Minor, *Prohibiting the Death Penalty for the Rape of a Child While Overlooking Wrongful Execution:* Kennedy v. Louisiana, 54 S.D. L. Rev. 300, 325 (2009) ("Many child sexual abuse convictions, including the one in *Kennedy*, rely almost exclusively on the testimony of the child victim. The Salem witch trials of the early seventeenth century are the first recorded occurrences of child testimony. The trials drastically changed the positive perception of children as innocent and truthful."). Compare with Thomas D. Lyon, *The New Wave in Children's Suggestibility Research: A Critique*, 84 Cornell L. Rev. 1004, 1013-14 (1999) (suggesting that the law must balance two problems: the risk of wrongful convictions from false testimony and the risk that childhood abuse will go undetected because children are ignored). If the rules of evidence regarding admissibility of childhood testimony were tightened up, would that change the Court's calculation in *Kennedy*?

2. *The death penalty for treason.* The Court held in *Kennedy* that the death penalty is not available for non-homicide offenses like child rape, though the Court was careful to exclude from its holding "treason, espionage, terrorism, and drug kingpin activity." The Court distinguished these offenses because they are public offenses against the state itself. Why is this relevant? As for treason and terrorism, the Court was probably interested in preserving the government's authority to execute a terrorist for a large or complex terrorist plot that is foiled before it is brought to fruition. In that case, the terrorist would be guilty of an attempt but would not, strictly speaking, have caused the death of any victims. Similarly, a spy guilty of treason might have sold government secrets and betrayed his country without the government being able to prove that an individual was killed as a result of the security breach. In cases of treason, say by selling nuclear secrets, the country is *at risk* in the future, but no one has died in the present. Does drug "kingpin activity" fit this mold? Why was it included in the list? Are there other public offenses against the state that would be exempted from the Court's holding in *Kennedy*? For an argument that applying the death penalty in non-fatal treason cases might be inconsistent with the underlying rationale of *Kennedy*, see Kristen E. Eichensehr, *Treason in the Age of Terrorism: An Explanation and Evaluation of Treason's Return in Democratic States*, 42 Vand. J. Transnat'l L. 1443, 1506 (2009) ("Charging the death penalty in a non-death-causing treason case would raise serious constitutional questions, but the prosecutor can tilt this factor entirely in favor of charging

PROBLEM CASE

In May 2013, a passerby heard a woman screaming from inside the door of a house in Cleveland, Ohio, and helped her escape. When police arrived, they discovered a house of horror. Three women had been held captive inside for a decade, enduring years of beatings, rapes, and other degrading treatment. One of the victims had even borne a child fathered by her captor.

After the three women and the child were rescued, police charged the owner of the house, Ariel Castro. In an agreement with prosecutors, Castro pled guilty to 937 counts of rape and kidnapping, and agreed to a sentence of life plus 1,000 years to cover all of the charges. At his sentencing, Castro said: "I'm not a monster, I'm just sick." In September 2013, Castro committed suicide in prison by hanging himself with a bed sheet. See Timothy Williams & Michael Schwirtz, *Death in Prison of Man Who Held Ohio Women Captive Prompts Investigations*, N.Y. Times, Sept. 4, 2013.

What was the appropriate sentence for Castro? The sentence of life *plus* 1,000 years represented a symbolic attempt to express the full horror of his criminal behavior. More importantly, was Justice Kennedy correct when he concluded in *Kennedy v. Louisiana* that non-homicide cases are less blameworthy than

Ariel Castro

homicide cases? Is the distinction between killing and not killing a reliable barometer of which crimes are the most serious?

treason by declining to seek the death penalty in cases where the accused traitor has not caused death.").

4. Racial Disparities

Although the Supreme Court has narrowed the class of individuals and crimes subject to the death penalty, it has refused to declare capital punishment per se unconstitutional. In the following case, the Court considers substantial empirical evidence that racial considerations affect the application of the death penalty in this country. As you read the case, identify the exact reasons why the court rejects this constitutional argument.

McCleskey v. Kemp

Supreme Court of the United States
481 U.S. 279 (1987)

POWELL, J.

This case presents the question whether a complex statistical study that indicates a risk that racial considerations enter into capital sentencing determinations proves that petitioner McCleskey's capital sentence is unconstitutional under the Eighth or Fourteenth Amendment.

I

. . . In support of his claim, McCleskey proffered a statistical study performed by Professors David C. Baldus, Charles Pulaski, and George Woodworth, and (the Baldus study) that purports to show a disparity in the imposition of the death sentence in Georgia based on the race of the murder victim and, to a lesser extent, the race of the defendant. The Baldus study is actually two sophisticated statistical studies that examine over 2,000 murder cases that occurred in Georgia during the 1970's. The raw numbers collected by Professor Baldus indicate that defendants charged with killing white persons received the death penalty in 11% of the cases, but defendants charged with killing blacks received the death penalty in only 1% of the cases. The raw numbers also indicate a reverse racial disparity according to the race of the defendant: 4% of the black defendants received the death penalty, as opposed to 7% of the white defendants.

Baldus also divided the cases according to the combination of the race of the defendant and the race of the victim. He found that the death penalty was assessed in 22% of the cases involving black defendants and white victims; 8% of the cases involving white defendants and white victims; 1% of the cases involving black defendants and black victims; and 3% of the cases involving white defendants and black victims. Similarly, Baldus found that prosecutors sought the death penalty in 70% of the cases involving black defendants and white victims; 32% of the cases involving white defendants and white victims; 15% of the cases involving black defendants and black victims; and 19% of the cases involving white defendants and black victims.

Baldus subjected his data to an extensive analysis, taking account of 230 variables that could have explained the disparities on nonracial grounds. One of his models concludes that, even after taking account of 39 nonracial variables, defendants charged with killing white victims were 4.3 times as likely to receive a death sentence as defendants charged with killing blacks. According to this model, black defendants were 1.1 times as likely to receive a death sentence as other defendants. Thus, the Baldus study indicates that black defendants, such as McCleskey, who kill white victims have the greatest likelihood of receiving the death penalty. . . .

II

McCleskey's first claim is that the Georgia capital punishment statute violates the Equal Protection Clause of the Fourteenth Amendment. He argues that race has infected the administration of Georgia's statute in two ways: persons who murder whites are more likely to be sentenced to death than persons who murder blacks, and black murderers are more likely to be sentenced to death than white murderers. As a black defendant who killed a white victim, McCleskey claims that the Baldus study demonstrates that he was discriminated against because of his race and because of the race of his victim. In its broadest form, McCleskey's claim of discrimination extends to every actor in the Georgia capital sentencing process, from the prosecutor who sought the death penalty and the jury that imposed the sentence, to the State itself that enacted the capital punishment statute and allows it to remain in effect despite its allegedly discriminatory application. We agree with the Court of Appeals, and every other court that has considered such a challenge, that this claim must fail.

Our analysis begins with the basic principle that a defendant who alleges an equal protection violation has the burden of proving "the existence of purposeful discrimination." A corollary to this principle is that a criminal defendant must prove that the purposeful discrimination "had a discriminatory effect" on him. Thus, to prevail under the Equal Protection Clause, McCleskey must prove that the decisionmakers in *his* case acted with discriminatory purpose. He offers no evidence specific to his own case that would support an inference that racial considerations played a part in his sentence. Instead, he relies solely on the Baldus study. McCleskey argues that the Baldus study compels an inference that his sentence rests on purposeful discrimination. McCleskey's claim that these statistics are sufficient proof of discrimination, without regard to the facts of a particular case, would extend to all capital cases in Georgia, at least where the victim was white and the defendant is black.

The Court has accepted statistics as proof of intent to discriminate in certain limited contexts. First, this Court has accepted statistical disparities as proof of an equal protection violation in the selection of the jury venire in a particular district. Although statistical proof normally must present a "stark" pattern to be accepted as the sole proof of discriminatory intent under the Constitution, "[b]ecause of the nature of the jury-selection task, . . . we have permitted a finding of constitutional violation even when the statistical pattern does not approach [such] extremes." Second, this Court has accepted statistics in the form of multiple-regression analysis to prove statutory violations under Title VII of the Civil Rights Act of 1964.

But the nature of the capital sentencing decision, and the relationship of the statistics to that decision, are fundamentally different from the corresponding elements in the venire-selection or Title VII cases. Most importantly, each particular decision to impose the death penalty is made by a petit jury selected from a properly constituted venire. Each jury is unique in its composition, and the Constitution requires that its decision rest on consideration of innumerable factors that vary according to the characteristics of the individual defendant and the facts of the particular capital offense. Thus, the application of an inference drawn from the general statistics to a specific decision in a trial and sentencing simply is not comparable to the application of an inference drawn from general statistics to a specific venire-selection or Title VII case. In those cases, the statistics relate to fewer entities, and fewer variables are relevant to the challenged decisions. . . .

McCleskey also suggests that the Baldus study proves that the State as a whole has acted with a discriminatory purpose. He appears to argue that the State has violated the Equal Protection Clause by adopting the capital punishment statute and allowing it to remain in force despite its allegedly discriminatory application. . . . For this claim to prevail, McCleskey would have to prove that the Georgia Legislature enacted or maintained the death penalty statute *because of* an anticipated racially discriminatory effect. In *Gregg v. Georgia,* this Court found that the Georgia capital sentencing system could operate in a fair and neutral manner. There was no evidence then, and there is none now, that the Georgia Legislature enacted the capital punishment statute to further a racially discriminatory purpose.

Nor has McCleskey demonstrated that the legislature maintains the capital punishment statute because of the racially disproportionate impact suggested by the Baldus study. As legislatures necessarily have wide discretion in the choice of criminal laws and penalties, and as there were legitimate reasons for the Georgia Legislature to adopt and maintain capital punishment, we will not infer a discriminatory purpose on the part of the State of Georgia. Accordingly, we reject McCleskey's equal protection claims.

IV

In light of our precedents under the Eighth Amendment, McCleskey cannot argue successfully that his sentence is "disproportionate to the crime in the traditional sense." He does not deny that he committed a murder in the course of a planned robbery, a crime for which this Court has determined that the death penalty constitutionally may be imposed. His disproportionality claim "is of a different sort." McCleskey argues that the sentence in his case is disproportionate to the sentences in other murder cases.

On the one hand, he cannot base a constitutional claim on an argument that his case differs from other cases in which defendants *did* receive the death penalty. On automatic appeal, the Georgia Supreme Court found that McCleskey's death sentence was not disproportionate to other death sentences imposed in the State. The court supported this conclusion with an appendix containing citations to 13 cases involving generally similar murders. Moreover, where the statutory procedures adequately channel the sentencer's discretion, such proportionality review is not constitutionally required.

On the other hand, absent a showing that the Georgia capital punishment system operates in an arbitrary and capricious manner, McCleskey cannot prove a constitutional violation by demonstrating that other defendants who may be similarly situated did *not* receive the death penalty. . . .

Although our decision in *Gregg* as to the facial validity of the Georgia capital punishment statute appears to foreclose McCleskey's disproportionality argument, he further contends that the Georgia capital punishment system is arbitrary and capricious in *application,* and therefore his sentence is excessive, because racial considerations may influence capital sentencing decisions in Georgia. We now address this claim.

To evaluate McCleskey's challenge, we must examine exactly what the Baldus study may show. Even Professor Baldus does not contend that his statistics *prove* that race enters into any capital sentencing decisions or that race was a factor in McCleskey's particular case. Statistics at most may show only a likelihood that a particular factor entered into some decisions. There is, of course, some risk of racial prejudice influencing a jury's decision in a criminal case. There are similar risks that other kinds of prejudice will influence other criminal trials. The question "is at what point that risk becomes constitutionally unacceptable." McCleskey asks us to accept the likelihood allegedly shown by the Baldus study as the constitutional measure of an unacceptable risk of racial prejudice influencing capital sentencing decisions. This we decline to do. . . .

At most, the Baldus study indicates a discrepancy that appears to correlate with race. Apparent disparities in sentencing are an inevitable part of our criminal justice system. The discrepancy indicated by the Baldus study is "a far cry from the major systemic defects identified in *Furman*." As this Court has recognized, any mode for determining guilt or punishment "has its weaknesses and the potential for misuse." Specifically, "there can be no perfect procedure for deciding in which cases governmental authority should be used to impose death." Despite these imperfections, our consistent rule has been that constitutional guarantees are met when "the mode [for determining guilt or punishment] itself has been surrounded with safeguards to make it as fair as possible." Where the discretion that is fundamental to our criminal process is involved, we decline to assume that what is unexplained is invidious. In light of the safeguards designed to minimize racial bias in the process, the fundamental value of jury trial in our criminal justice system, and the benefits that discretion provides to criminal defendants, we hold that the Baldus study does not demonstrate a constitutionally significant risk of racial bias affecting the Georgia capital sentencing process. . . .

AFTERWORD   Warren McCleskey was executed in Georgia's electric chair on September 25, 1991. He declined his last meal. After he lost his Supreme Court case, his lawyers litigated several issues on his behalf in state and federal courts. Various last-minute appeals were also filed but rejected in the final hours before his execution. Justice Marshall dissented from the Court's refusal to issue a stay: "In refusing to grant a stay to review fully McCleskey's claims, the Court values expediency over human life. Repeatedly denying Warren McCleskey his constitutional rights is unacceptable. Executing him is inexcusable."

In an editorial after the execution, the *New York Times* wrote: "Some supporters of the death penalty are outraged that Mr. McCleskey lived so long, surviving through the ingenuity of writ-writing lawyers. But many other Americans are more interested in sure justice than in certain death. They are left to feel outrage for a different reason, and what makes it worse is that they cannot look for relief to the Supreme Court of the United States." *Warren McCleskey Is Dead*, N.Y. Times, Sept. 29, 1991.

---

5. Methods of Execution

Although capital punishment produces death, the Constitution's Cruel and Unusual Punishment Clause prohibits the infliction of unnecessary pain and suffering. Death penalty opponents have argued that condemned inmates subjected to lethal injection sometimes suffer impermissible pain during the execution process. In the following case, the Supreme Court determines whether this possibility makes lethal injection unconstitutional.

Glossip v. Gross
Supreme Court of the United States
135 S. Ct. 2726 (2015)

ALITO, J.

Prisoners sentenced to death in the State of Oklahoma filed an action in federal court . . . contending that the method of execution now used by the State violates the Eighth Amendment because it creates an unacceptable risk of severe pain. They argue that midazolam, the first drug employed in the State's current three-drug protocol, fails to render a person insensate to pain. After holding an evidentiary hearing, the District Court denied four prisoners' application for a preliminary injunction, finding that they had failed to prove that midazolam is ineffective. The Court of Appeals for the Tenth Circuit affirmed. . . .

For two independent reasons, we also affirm. First, the prisoners failed to identify a known and available alternative method of execution that entails a lesser risk of pain, a requirement of all Eighth Amendment method-of-execution claims. Second, the District Court did not commit clear error when it found that the prisoners failed to establish that Oklahoma's use of a massive dose of midazolam in its execution protocol entails a substantial risk of severe pain. . . .

IV

Our first ground for affirmance is based on petitioners' failure to satisfy their burden of establishing that any risk of harm was substantial when compared to a known and available alternative method of execution. In their amended complaint, petitioners proffered that the State could use sodium thiopental as part of a single-drug protocol. They have since suggested that it might also be constitutional for Oklahoma to use pentobarbital. But the District Court found that both sodium thiopental and pentobarbital are now unavailable to Oklahoma's Department of Corrections. The Court of Appeals affirmed that finding, and it is not clearly erroneous. On the contrary, the record shows that Oklahoma has been unable to procure those drugs despite a good-faith effort to do so.

Petitioners do not seriously contest this factual finding, and they have not identified any available drug or drugs that could be used in place of those that Oklahoma is now unable to obtain. Nor have they shown a risk of pain so great that other acceptable, available methods must be used. Instead, they argue that they need not identify a known and available method of execution that presents less risk. But this argument is inconsistent with the controlling opinion in *Baze*, 553 U.S., at 61, which imposed a requirement that the Court now follows. . . .

Readers can judge for themselves how much distance there is between the principal dissent's argument against requiring prisoners to identify an alternative and the view, now announced by Justices Breyer and Ginsburg, that the death penalty is categorically unconstitutional. The principal dissent goes out of its way to suggest that a State would violate the Eighth Amendment if it used one of the methods of execution employed before the advent of lethal injection. And the principal dissent makes this suggestion even though the Court held in *Wilkerson* that this method (the firing squad) is constitutional and even though, in the words of the principal dissent, "there is some reason to think that it is relatively quick and painless." Tellingly silent about the methods of execution most commonly used before States switched to lethal injection (the electric chair and gas chamber), the principal dissent implies that it would be unconstitutional to use a method that "could be seen as a devolution to a more primitive era." If States cannot return to any of the "more primitive" methods used in the past and if no drug that meets with the principal dissent's approval is available for use in carrying out a death sentence, the logical conclusion is clear. But we have time and again reaffirmed that capital punishment is not per se unconstitutional. We decline to effectively overrule these decisions.

V

We also affirm for a second reason: The District Court did not commit clear error when it found that midazolam is highly likely to render a person unable to feel pain during an execution. We emphasize four points at the outset of our analysis.

First, we review the District Court's factual findings under the deferential "clear error" standard. . . . Second, petitioners bear the burden of persuasion on this issue. . . . Third, numerous courts have concluded that the use of midazolam as the first drug in a three-drug protocol is likely to render an inmate insensate to pain that might result from administration of the paralytic agent and potassium chloride. . . . Fourth, challenges to lethal injection protocols test the boundaries of the authority and competency of federal courts. Although we must invalidate a lethal injection protocol if it violates the Eighth Amendment, federal courts should not "embroil [themselves] in ongoing scientific controversies beyond their expertise." Accordingly, an inmate challenging a protocol bears the burden to show, based on evidence presented to the court, that there is a substantial risk of severe pain.

Petitioners attack the District Court's findings of fact on two main grounds. First, they argue that even if midazolam is powerful enough to induce unconsciousness, it is too weak to maintain unconsciousness and insensitivity to pain once the second and third drugs are administered. Second, while conceding that the 500-milligram dose of midazolam is much higher than the normal therapeutic dose, they contend that this fact is irrelevant because midazolam has a "ceiling effect"—that is, at a certain point, an increase in the dose administered will not have any greater effect on the inmate. Neither argument succeeds.

The District Court found that midazolam is capable of placing a person "at a sufficient level of unconsciousness to resist the noxious stimuli which could occur from the application of the second and third drugs." This conclusion was not clearly erroneous. Respondents' expert, Dr. Evans, testified that the proper administration of a 500-milligram dose of midazolam would make it "a virtual certainty" that any individual would be "at a sufficient level of unconsciousness to resist the noxious stimuli which could occur from application of the 2nd and 3rd drugs" used in the Oklahoma protocol. And petitioners' experts acknowledged that they had no contrary scientific proof. . . .

Based on the evidence that the parties presented to the District Court, we must affirm. Testimony from both sides supports the District Court's conclusion that midazolam can render a person insensate to pain. Dr. Evans testified that although midazolam is not an analgesic, it can nonetheless "render the person unconscious and 'insensate' during the remainder of the procedure." In his discussion about the ceiling effect, Dr. Sasich agreed that as the dose of midazolam increases, it is "expected to produce sedation, amnesia, and finally lack of response to stimuli such as pain (unconsciousness)." Petitioners argue that midazolam is not powerful enough to keep a person insensate to pain after the administration of the second and third drugs, but Dr. Evans presented creditable testimony to the contrary. Indeed, low doses of midazolam are sufficient to induce unconsciousness and are even sometimes used as the sole relevant drug in certain medical procedures. Dr. Sasich conceded, for example, that midazolam might be used for medical procedures like colonoscopies and gastroscopies.

Petitioners emphasize that midazolam is not recommended or approved for use as the sole anesthetic during painful surgery, but there are two reasons why this is not dispositive. First, as the District Court found, the 500-milligram dose at issue here "is many times higher than a normal therapeutic dose of midazolam." The effect of a small dose of midazolam has minimal probative value about the effect of a 500-milligram dose. Second, the fact that a low dose of midazolam is not the best drug for maintaining unconsciousness during surgery says little about whether a 500-milligram dose of midazolam is constitutionally adequate for purposes of conducting an execution. We recognized this point in *Baze*, where we concluded that although the medical standard of care might require the use of a blood pressure cuff and an electrocardiogram during surgeries, this does not mean those procedures are required for an execution to pass Eighth Amendment scrutiny.

Oklahoma has also adopted important safeguards to ensure that midazolam is properly administered. The District Court emphasized three requirements in particular: The execution team must secure both a primary and backup IV access site, it must confirm the viability of the IV sites, and it must continuously monitor the offender's level of consciousness. The District Court did not commit clear error in concluding that these safeguards help to minimize any risk that might occur in the event that midazolam does not operate as intended. . . .

Petitioners assert that midazolam's "ceiling effect" undermines the District Court's finding about the effectiveness of the huge dose administered in the Oklahoma protocol. Petitioners argue that midazolam has a "ceiling" above which any increase in dosage produces no effect. As a result, they maintain, it is wrong to assume that a 500-milligram dose has a much greater effect than a therapeutic dose of about 5 milligrams. But the mere fact that midazolam has such a ceiling cannot be dispositive. Dr. Sasich testified that "all drugs essentially have a ceiling effect." The relevant question here is whether midazolam's ceiling effect occurs below the level of a 500-milligram dose and at a point at which the drug does not have the effect of rendering a person insensate to pain caused by the second and third drugs.

Petitioners provided little probative evidence on this point, and the speculative evidence that they did present to the District Court does not come close to establishing that its factual findings were clearly erroneous. . . . The principal dissent discusses the ceiling effect at length, but it studiously avoids suggesting that petitioners presented probative evidence about the dose at which the ceiling effect occurs or about whether the effect occurs before a person becomes insensate to pain. . . .

Petitioners' remaining arguments about midazolam all lack merit. . . . [P]etitioners argue that there is no consensus among the States regarding midazolam's efficacy because only four States (Oklahoma, Arizona, Florida, and Ohio) have used midazolam as part of an execution. Petitioners rely on the plurality's statement in *Baze* that "it is difficult to regard a practice as 'objectively intolerable' when it is in fact widely tolerated," and the plurality's emphasis on the fact that 36 States had adopted lethal injection and 30 States used the particular three-drug protocol at issue in that case. But while the near-universal use of the particular protocol at issue in *Baze* supported our conclusion that this protocol did not violate the Eighth Amendment, we did not say that the converse was true, i.e., that other protocols or methods of execution are of doubtful constitutionality. That argument, if accepted, would hamper the adoption of new and potentially more humane methods of execution. . . .

Fourth, petitioners argue that difficulties with Oklahoma's execution of Lockett and Arizona's July 2014 execution of Joseph Wood establish that midazolam is sure or very likely to cause serious pain. We are not persuaded. Aside from the Lockett execution, 12 other executions have been conducted using the three-drug protocol at issue here, and those appear to have been conducted without any significant problems. Moreover, Lockett was administered only 100 milligrams of midazolam, and Oklahoma's investigation into that execution concluded that the difficulties were due primarily to the execution team's inability to obtain an IV access site. And the Wood execution did not involve the protocol at issue here.

Wood did not receive a single dose of 500 milligrams of midazolam; instead, he received fifteen 50-milligram doses over the span of two hours. And Arizona used a different two-drug protocol that paired midazolam with hydromorphone, a drug that is not at issue in this case. When all of the circumstances are considered, the Lockett and Wood executions have little probative value for present purposes.

Finally, we find it appropriate to respond to the principal dissent's groundless suggestion that our decision is tantamount to allowing prisoners to be "drawn and quartered, slowly tortured to death, or actually burned at the stake." That is simply not true, and the principal dissent's resort to this outlandish rhetoric reveals the weakness of its legal arguments.

NOTES & QUESTIONS ON EXECUTION METHODS

1. *Historical evolution.* It was once common for the death penalty to be carried out by hanging, firing squad, or the electric chair. See *In re Kemmler*, 136 U.S. 436 (1890) (upholding New York state law allowing electrocution as more humane than hanging); *Wilkerson v. Utah*, 99 U.S. (9 Otto) 130 (1879) (upholding death by shooting). Now lethal injection is by far the most common method. However, the firing squad is now back in a few jurisdictions that have designated it as a "backup" method in case the preferred methods are unavailable. For example, Oklahoma designated death by firing squad as a third option after lethal injection and the electric chair. In a more extreme example, Utah passed a statute in March 2015 making the firing squad the state's preferred execution method if lethal injection was not available. Lawmakers rushed to pass the statute after Utah suffered from increasing difficulties in obtaining the necessary chemicals for its lethal injections. Utah had the firing squad until it was abolished in 2004, and defendants convicted for murder during the pre-2004 period were eligible for the firing squad if they selected it. In fact, the execution of Ronnie Lee Gardner in 2010 was carried out by firing squad. The March 2015 statute reinstating the firing squad was passed just weeks before the Supreme Court decided *Glossip*—a period when the constitutionality of lethal injection was somewhat in question. Now that the Supreme Court has spoken and upheld lethal injection, it is unclear whether Utah will need to use the firing squad again. Nonetheless, Utah regulations have codified the procedure. See Utah Admin. Code R251-107 ("If the judgment of death is to be carried out by firing squad . . . the executive director or his designee shall select a five-person firing squad of peace officers."). Recently, three Ohio inmates selected firing squad as their preferred method of execution. Michael Muskal, *Three of Utah's 8 Death Row Inmates Have Chosen Firing Squads*, L.A. Times, Mar. 24, 2015.

2. *Finding the vein.* Is the concern in *Glossip* regarding the drugs being used somewhat misplaced? In some instances of botched executions, the proximate cause for the prisoner's pain was the inability of the prison staff to successfully place an intravenous line into the prisoner's vein. If the drugs are not being directly injected into the condemned prisoner's system, it is not much of a surprise that they will not work as planned. Should the Supreme Court mandate a particular protocol for the actual delivery of the drugs, rather than concentrate its attention on the drugs themselves? At least part of the problem is the unwillingness of some medical professionals to participate in the execution process, thus leaving the job to prison staff with less medical training. In *Morales v. Hickman*, 438 F.3d 926 (9th Cir. 2006), a federal appeals court upheld a district judge's order that the state have a licensed anesthesiologist present during the execution to ensure the inmate was unconscious during the execution. According to the American Medical Association, "A physician, as a member of a profession dedicated to preserving life when there is hope of doing so, should not be a participant in a legally authorized execution." See AMA Opinion 2.06. What do you think of this policy? On the one hand it makes it more difficult for states to ensure that executions are painless, and in that sense might encourage more states to abolish capital punishment. On the other hand, if states do *not* abolish capital punishment, the result of the policy is not fewer executions but simply more *botched* executions. From the perspective of a capital punishment abolitionist, which is better?

PROBLEM CASE

On April 28, 2014, Oklahoma officials executed Clayton D. Lockett, who had been convicted in 2000 of murder, rape, forcible sodomy, kidnapping, and assault and battery. The first drug, a sedative, was administered at 6:23 P.M., and after he was declared unconscious, the execution team moved on to the second and third drugs. However, Lockett was not fully unconscious and he started to mumble "oh man." The doctor diagnosed that the IV line was compromised and not working properly. Prison officials closed a curtain so that witnesses could no longer see the prisoner. Mr. Lockett finally died of a heart attack at 7:06 P.M. See Erik Eckholm, *One Execution Botched, Oklahoma Delays the Next,* N.Y. Times, Apr. 29, 2014.

Was Mr. Lockett's death cruel and unusual punishment? Did he suffer unnecessary harm? More importantly, which standard should be used to answer this question? By historical standards, executed prisoners in the past have suffered pain before dying. However, contemporary practices allow prison officials to reduce or eliminate the pain by first sedating the prisoner. Perhaps the Eighth Amendment requires prison officials to do everything in their power to eliminate pain. But if the appropriate drugs are not available (because drug companies refuse to sell them), should the state be barred from implementing the death penalty entirely?

C. PRACTICE & POLICY

Capital sentencing has no shortage of strategic questions for practitioners, judges, and lawmakers. The following materials discuss: (i) using the threat of capital punishment to coerce defendants into pleading guilty; (ii) how much discretion to give jurors to impose the death penalty; (iii) strategic considerations in bifurcated trials where the same jury, though in different phases, determines both the guilt of the defendant and the appropriate punishment; and (iv) applying the death penalty for fetal homicide.

∾ **Bargaining in the shadow of death.** As a strategic matter, is it permissible for a prosecutor to threaten the death penalty in order to pressure a defendant into pleading guilty and accepting a life sentence? If this is impermissible, how would a state legislator eliminate the practice? Certainly it would not advance the interests of defendants to prevent them from plea-bargaining. For discussions of this, see John H. Blume & Rebecca K. Helm, *The Unexonerated: Factually Innocent Defendants Who Plead Guilty*, 100 Cornell L. Rev. 157, 180 (2014); James S. Liebman, *The Overproduction of Death*, 100 Colum. L. Rev. 2030, 2097 & n.165 (2000) (concluding that innocent defendants sometimes plead guilty in a plea arrangement to avoid a death sentence). Blume notes that two individuals, Phillip Bivens and Bobby Ray Dixon, pled guilty in 1979 in exchange for a life sentence, though a subsequent DNA test in 2010 exonerated them. Is there any legal mechanism that could be used to avoid this coercion? Certainly, it would not be advisable to *disallow* a plea bargain for life imprisonment after the death penalty is charged, because that would only encourage prosecutors to stick with their decision to pursue the death penalty. One might argue that the threat of the death penalty (and its inherent coerciveness) vitiates the *voluntariness* of the guilty plea in a plea bargain. For example, the Supreme Court concluded in 1968 that the death penalty clause in the Federal Kidnapping Act was unconstitutional for similar reasons. *United States v. Jackson*, 390 U.S. 570, 577-78 (1968). However, in *Boykin v. Alabama*, 395 U.S. 238 (1969), the Supreme Court declared that a guilty plea was constitutionally acceptable if there was an "affirmative showing that it was intelligent and voluntary." Rule 11 of the Federal Rules of Criminal Procedure requires that "[b]efore accepting a plea of guilty or nolo contendere, the court must address the defendant personally in open court and determine that the plea is voluntary and did not result from force, threats, or promises (other than promises in a plea agreement)." For criticism of this practice, see Robert Schehr, *The Emperor's New Clothes: Intellectual Dishonesty and the Unconstitutionality of*

Plea-Bargaining, 2 Tex. A&M L. Rev. 385, 401 (2015) (arguing that the federal rule is "without social, scientific, or constitutional merit").

ℛ **Return to guided discretion.** In *Gregg v. Georgia,* 428 U.S. 153 (1976), the Supreme Court imposed a system of guided discretion to make the death penalty fair. This system stands in between two opposite poles, both of which are constitutionally unacceptable. On the one hand, legislatures could make the death penalty mandatory in some cases, which would promote consistency but would prevent the jury from taking into account the particular circumstances of the case, in particular mitigating circumstances regarding the defendant's background. That is unconstitutional. On the other hand, giving juries *unlimited* discretion regarding when to hand down the death penalty would essentially make it random and arbitrary—like being struck by lightning. This too is unconstitutional. The solution, according to the Supreme Court, is to build a system in between these two extremes: *guide* the discretion of juries by giving them a list of aggravating and mitigating circumstances to consider. This makes the process less random but still permits the jury to exercise mercy and consider the particularities of the defendant's situation. Is the process of guided discretion a viable middle ground? Or is it a contradiction in terms? The more discretion you give to the jury, the more random it becomes. The less discretion you give the jury, the more the particularities of the defendant's circumstances get ignored. This paradox led Justice Blackmun to write this famous paragraph in his dissent from a denial of certiorari in *Callins v. Collins,* 510 U.S. 1141 (1994):

> From this day forward, I no longer shall tinker with the machinery of death. For more than 20 years I have endeavored—indeed, I have struggled—along with a majority of this Court, to develop procedural and substantive rules that would lend more than the mere appearance of fairness to the death penalty endeavor. Rather than continue to coddle the Court's delusion that the desired level of fairness has been achieved and the need for regulation eviscerated, I feel morally and intellectually obligated simply to concede that the death penalty experiment has failed. It is virtually self-evident to me now that no combination of procedural rules or substantive regulations ever can save the death penalty from its inherent constitutional deficiencies. The basic question— does the system accurately and consistently determine which defendants "deserve" to die?—cannot be answered in the affirmative. It is not simply that this Court has allowed vague aggravating circumstances to be employed, relevant mitigating evidence to be disregarded, and vital judicial review to be blocked. The problem is that the inevitability of factual, legal, and moral error gives us a system that we know must wrongly kill some defendants, a system that fails to deliver the fair, consistent, and reliable sentences of death required by the Constitution.

  ❧ **Strategy in bifurcated trials.** During the guilt phase, a murder defendant's first intuition will be to argue that he did not do it. However, if the defendant is found guilty, the strategy shifts. The defendant may now wish to plead for mercy and explain the circumstances of the crime, and his background, to convince the jury to spare his life. At this point, maintaining innocence might be a counterproductive strategy. In theory, bifurcating the trial into two proceedings—the first dealing solely with guilt and the second dealing with sentencing—allows the defendant to shift strategies. Indeed, in *Gregg v. Georgia*, the Supreme Court found that the death penalty was constitutional when states bifurcate trials in this way. Also, prosecutors like bifurcation because it allows them to introduce, during the sentencing phase, evidence regarding aggravating factors that would be inadmissible during the guilt phase. However, bifurcation will not completely solve the strategy dilemma. The jury in the sentencing phase is the same jury that decided guilt, so the shift in strategy might be viewed with suspicion. If the defendant lied about committing the crime, the jury might not believe what he says at the sentencing hearing. Can you come up with a strategy to solve this problem? For example, a lawyer might keep the client from taking the stand in the guilt phase and rely on the lawyer to make the argument about innocence. Then, if the jury convicts him, the defendant can take the stand during the sentencing phase for the first time, making the argument in the guilt phase seem more like a lawyering strategy that does not harm the defendant's credibility with the jury. Can you think of other strategies?

  ❧ **Ariel Castro case redux.** Reconsider the case of Ariel Castro, the Cleveland man accused of keeping three women captive in his house. What type of arguments might a prosecutor have used to apply the death penalty in this case, even with the restriction announced in *Kennedy v. Louisiana*? After Castro was arrested, the local prosecutor in Cuyahoga County announced that he was considering seeking the death penalty in the case. The prosecutor noted that Castro had beaten the women to force them to miscarry their fetuses, which could be the basis for a murder charge—or even several murder charges depending on how many times this occurred. Under this theory, Castro might have been convicted and executed for the murder of the unborn children that he fathered with his victims. See Trip Gabriel & Steven Yaccino, *Officials, Citing Miscarriages, Weigh Death Penalty in Ohio Case*, N.Y. Times, May 9, 2013. Do you agree with this legal theory? For more discussion, see Bicka A. Barlow, *Severe Penalties for the Destruction of "Potential Life"—Cruel and Unusual Punishment?*, 29 U.S.F. L. Rev. 463 (1995) (arguing that the death penalty for fetal homicide is disproportionate and therefore unconstitutional under the Eighth Amendment).

CHAPTER 4

—◦◦◦—

FUNDAMENTAL PRINCIPLES OF CRIMINAL LAW

A. DOCTRINE

In order for the criminal law to be fair, individuals need "fair notice," i.e., an opportunity to conform their behavior to the requirements of the law. Before punishment is imposed, then, the law must satisfy certain procedural and substantive requirements that are often described collectively as the "principle of legality." They include a written statute prohibiting the conduct, announced publicly, and enacted prior to the defendant's conduct (not applied retroactively). In that sense, a secret law or a retroactive law is not real "law" at all. Furthermore, the content of the statute must be sufficiently precise (as opposed to vague) that ordinary people understand what is—and is not—prohibited by the statute. If the law is ambiguous, courts should interpret it in favor of the defendant. These elements of the principle of legality are unified by a central vision of the criminal law: that defendants should only be condemned if they had fair warning about the law's requirements but disobeyed it anyway. In this vein, consider Justice Holmes's famous statement in *McBoyle v. United States*, 283 U.S. 25, 27 (1931): "[A]lthough it is not likely that a criminal will carefully consider the text of the law before he murders or steals, it is reasonable that a fair warning should be given to the world in language that the common world will understand, of what the law intends to do if a certain line is passed. To make the warning fair, so far as possible the line should be clear."

1. The Written Statute Requirement

The first requirement is that the criminal conduct be proscribed in a written statute. Broadly speaking this is a relatively new requirement of the criminal law. Historically, judges punished defendants for "common law crimes" that were defined in the case law as opposed to a written penal statute enacted by the state legislature. For example, assault, battery, burglary, larceny, rape, and murder were all common law crimes, though there were others as well. The elements of these offenses were articulated in prior judicial decisions rather than in penal statutes. What was the judge's authority for punishing common law crimes? That authority resided in the common law itself: Judges had always punished individuals for certain conduct. Citizens found the definitions of these crimes by consulting the case law or a book that described it. Or, more controversially, perhaps defendants were expected to consult their own conscience or their community's moral norms, under the broad assumption that common law crimes tracked these vague intuitions. This era of common law crimes has largely passed. Every state in the United States now has a written penal statute, and appellate courts in many states enforce a prohibition against prosecuting an old common law crime that was not carried over and codified in statute. See, e.g., *Valeriano v. Bronson*, 209 Conn. 75, 92 (1988) ("the adoption of the comprehensive penal code in 1969 abrogated the common law and set out substantive crimes and defenses in great detail").

2. Retroactivity

Just as important as the written nature of the legal prohibition is its temporal location: It must come *before* the defendant has committed the act in question. Anything else is retroactive punishment in violation of the Ex Post Facto Clause of Article I of the Constitution. The key point here is the reason why the Constitution prohibits ex post facto laws. Enacting the prohibition after the defendant has committed the crime robs the citizen of any chance to conform his or her behavior to the requirements of the law—to make the right choice. Moreover, knowing that the action is immoral or frowned upon by the community's social norms is insufficient to meet the demands of *legality*, which requires that an actual law prohibit the conduct in advance. That being said, retroactivity can creep into the law in unusual ways even if the statutes are passed well in advance. When a court issues a new interpretation of a statute, is it changing the law or simply discovering the correct interpretation that was there all along? Courts are much more rigorous in striking down ex post legislative enactments than ex post interpretations, which are allowed if the defendant had "fair warning" of the change.

3. Interpreting Statutes and the Common Law

Interpreting statutes is extremely difficult, especially since legislators do not always specify, with complete precision, every element of the offense.

Consequently, courts often interpret a statute with reference to its common law precursor, i.e., the unwritten version of the crime that was used by judges before it was codified into a statute. In many cases, the first step in this process is to determine whether the crime in question actually has a common law antecedent, or whether the crime was invented from whole cloth by the legislature. If the crime is not new, and bears some relationship to an older common law crime, courts will look to the case law—often ancient—to help determine what the legislature meant when they passed the law. The assumption here is that the legislature was certainly aware of the older common law background when it passed the law.

4. Vagueness

Retroactive or unwritten laws are just two ways that the government can deprive citizens of advance knowledge of the law's requirements. Another is to write a law that is so vague that no one knows how it will be applied in future cases. In those cases, courts can strike down the law on due process grounds under either the Fourteenth or Fifth Amendments. See *Connally v. Gen. Constr. Co.*, 269 U.S. 385, 391 (1926) ("a statute which either forbids or requires the doing of an act in terms so vague that men of common intelligence must necessarily guess at its meaning and differ as to its application violates the first essential of due process of law"). If a law is so open-ended that a defendant has no idea what it means for concrete cases, then the defendant had no chance to conform his conduct to the law. Distinguishing between precise and impermissibly vague laws is not so easy. One thing is certain: A law's use of a standard that must be applied by the jury (as opposed to a much more specific rule) does not necessarily constitute impermissible vagueness, since the criminal law is replete with doctrines that require application of existing standards to novel facts. In distinguishing an acceptable standard from an impermissibly vague standard, courts will ask whether the standard is so vague that its application by a court is unpredictable and fails to give the potential defendant some sense of its true meaning.

5. The Rule of Lenity

Criminal statutes are often ambiguous such that courts are called upon to resolve disputes over how to interpret them. When the text can be read in different ways, the court looks to plain meaning, legislative history, the common law, the purpose behind the statute, and social policy—all in the hopes of deriving the best interpretation of the provision. After consulting these factors, if a court believes that a genuine ambiguity still persists and the statute has multiple meanings, a court will sometimes invoke the rule of lenity and conclude that it should be read in favor of the defendant. To use a baseball analogy, a tie goes to the defendant. At least one rationale for the rule is that the defendant may have conformed his behavior to one interpretation rather than the other, and one should not condemn him unless the interpretation is definitely wrong. That being said, some jurisdictions have abolished the rule. And in jurisdictions that retain it, the rule of lenity is infrequently invoked because courts invariably find good reason to prefer one interpretation over another—so the ambiguity disappears.

B. APPLICATION

1. The Written Statute Requirement

Although most states have abolished common law crimes by statute, a few states are still willing to prosecute defendants for the older common law crimes. Prosecuting someone for a common law crime without a written statute poses many thorny questions. Among the most pressing is how severely the defendant should be punished if convicted. Some states have passed statutes that restrict the length of prison terms for common law prosecutions. But in the following case, there is no such statute. Are there any limits to the trial court's punishment of a defendant for a common law crime?

Street v. State

Court of Appeals of Maryland
307 Md. 262 (1986)

COLE, JUDGE.

The question presented in this case is whether a fine may be imposed as part of a sentence upon conviction of the common-law crime of false imprisonment.

We set forth the salient facts as follows. At 8:30 A.M. on August 8, 1983, Valerie McNeal, the prosecutrix, got into a cab driven by appellant, George Street. When the cab reached McNeal's destination, the meter read $2.50. McNeal had $2.46 in change, plus one ten-dollar bill and one twenty-dollar bill. When she discovered that she was four cents short in change, McNeal offered appellant the ten-dollar bill. Appellant refused the bill, citing a city ordinance which provides that cab drivers need not carry more than $5.00 in change. Appellant also rejected McNeal's suggestion that one or both of them obtain change for the ten-dollar bill at a nearby establishment. When McNeal attempted to get out of the cab, she found that the rear doors were locked. Despite McNeal's repeated requests, appellant refused to disengage the locks, which he controlled. The parties argued for approximately twenty-five minutes, with the meter running all the while. After being ignored by numerous pedestrians, McNeal finally managed to obtain the assistance of a passerby, Cora Williams. Williams, acting as mediator, persuaded appellant to accept the ten-dollar bill in payment of the fare, which now amounted to $5.20. Appellant gave Williams a five-dollar bill, which she promptly turned over to McNeal. Shortly thereafter, a police officer arrived on the scene and appellant finally released McNeal from the cab.

Appellant was charged with false imprisonment. He was tried and convicted in the Circuit Court for Baltimore City. The trial judge sentenced appellant to one-year imprisonment and a $500 fine with the prison term suspended in favor of three years probation . . .

At the outset, we note a few points concerning the history and development of fines as criminal sanctions at common law. The use of fines in criminal cases predates the Magna Carta, which prohibited the imposition of excessive fines and assessments. Compared with other forms of punishment used at common law, the imposition of a fine was a mild penalty indeed. Criminal sentences embodied a litany of abhorrent practices, including cutting off the hand or ears, slitting the nostrils, branding the hand or face, whipping, the pillory, and the ducking-stool. Moreover, Blackstone writes that "[d]isgusting as this catalogue (of punishments) may seem, it will afford pleasure to an English reader, and do honour to the English law, to compare it with that shocking apparatus of death and torment, to be met with in the criminal codes of almost every other nation in Europe." Thus, the development and use of pecuniary penalties, in the form of fines, contrasted sharply with the various methods of corporal punishment that had been employed as criminal sanctions at common law.

The earliest fines were agreements between the judge and the prisoner to avoid imprisonment, at a time when the judge had no power to impose pecuniary punishments. These fines constituted a major source of the royal power and revenue . . . At common law, a fine, either with or without imprisonment, was punishment for a misdemeanor. As to felonies, conviction entailed the automatic forfeiture of the felon's property. Thus, the power to impose a fine for a felony was not necessary. In exercising its discretion as to the amount of the fine, the court considered the egregiousness of the particular offense and the financial condition of the offender, as well as other factors.

In this case, appellant was charged with false imprisonment. This Court has defined false imprisonment as the "unlawful detention of a person against his will." It is a common-law offense in Maryland, the penalty for which is not statutorily prescribed. At common law, false imprisonment was classified as a misdemeanor. As set forth above, misdemeanors at common law were punishable by fine, imprisonment, or both.

We have noted on several occasions that the only restrictions on sentencing for a common-law crime are (absent a penalty prescribed by statute) that the sentence be within the reasonable discretion of the trial judge and that it not be cruel and unusual punishment. In *Burley v. State*, 226 Md. 94 (1961), the appellant asserted that a sentence of five years for common-law assault was excessive and thus violated the prohibition against cruel and unusual punishment set forth in Article 25 of the Maryland Declaration of Rights. We held that under the circumstances of that case, including appellant's conviction on prior occasions of crimes against the person, the sentence imposed did not constitute cruel and unusual punishment. In *Heath v. State*, 198 Md. 455 (1951), this Court rejected a similar contention as to appellant's five-year sentence for common-law assault. The Court declared:

> Still, from early times, when misdemeanors were punished by whatever fine or imprisonment the judge might deem it right to impose, it has been the judicial habit to look upon assaults as more or less aggravated by such attendant facts as appealed to the discretion for a heavy penalty. . . . An assault is deemed to be more or less enormous according to the facts of the particular case.

In light of the "attendant facts" involved, the Court concluded that the sentence imposed was within the discretion of the trial court and did not violate the constitutional provision against cruel and unusual punishment. In *Messina v. State*, 212 Md. 602 (1957), the appellant contended that a four-month sentence for the common-law offense of indecent exposure constituted cruel and unusual punishment. The court held that in light of the "corrupting effect" of appellant's act, the sentence "could scarcely be held to have been beyond a reasonable discretion, and certainly could not under the limitations of the decisions of this Court be declared either cruel or unusual."

In a separate line of Maryland cases, this Court has refused to limit sentences for common-law offenses where the legislature has not expressly so provided. In *Gleaton v. State*, 235 Md. 271 (1963), the appellant was charged with assault with intent to murder in the first count, simple assault in the second count, and assault and beating with intent to maim in the third count. The appellant pleaded guilty to the second count, and the prosecuting attorney nol prossed the first and third counts. The appellant received a sentence of ten years on the second count.

On appeal, he argued that the ten-year sentence for common-law assault was excessive and unreasonable when compared to the maximum sentences for the two charges that were nol prossed. The greater statutory offense of assault with intent to murder carried a maximum fifteen year sentence, while the statutory offense of assault and beating with intent to maim carried a maximum ten-year sentence. Initially, the Court noted that no limitation on the penalty for common-law assault existed at common law. The Court refused to interpret the penal limits applicable to the statutory assaults as imposing any restriction on the maximum sentence for the lesser common law offense. The Court concluded that the matter of imposing sentences for common law offenses is left to the sound discretion of the trial court, subject only to the constitutional prohibition against cruel and unusual punishment . . . All of these cases demonstrate the reluctance of this Court to place strict limitations on the trial judge's discretion in sentencing an individual convicted of a common-law crime . . .

Here, the trial judge examined the conduct of appellant giving rise to his conviction. He also considered appellant's financial condition with regard to his ability to pay the fine. Under these circumstances, the imposition of a $500 fine constituted a reasonable exercise of the judge's discretion. No extended discussion is necessary in these circumstances to conclude that a fine of $500 does not constitute cruel and unusual punishment . . . Accordingly, we shall affirm the judgment of the Court of Special Appeals.

NOTES & QUESTIONS ON WRITTEN STATUTES

1. *Common law saving clause.* A few state legislatures have enacted common law "saving" clauses that specifically authorize courts to continue punishing defendants for common law crimes. For example, Michigan's statute says: "Any person who shall commit any indictable offense at the common law, for the punishment of which no provision is expressly made by any statute of this state, shall be guilty of a felony, punishable by imprisonment in the state prison not more than 5 years or by a fine of not more than $10,000.00, or both in the discretion of the court." Mich. Comp. Laws § 750.505. Rhode Island has a similar statute:

> Every act and omission which is an offense at common law, and for which no punishment is prescribed by the general laws, may be prosecuted and punished as an offense at common law. Every person who shall be convicted of any offense which is a misdemeanor at common law shall be imprisoned for a term not exceeding one year or be fined not exceeding five hundred dollars ($500). Every person who shall be convicted of any offense which is a felony at common law shall be imprisoned for a term not exceeding five (5) years or be fined not exceeding five thousand dollars ($5,000).

11 R.I. Gen. Laws § 11-1-1. Are these statutes sufficient to resolve legality concerns? Does it matter that the crimes referred to in the saving clauses are defined by judicial decision rather than by legislative enactment? For a criticism of Michigan's common law saving clause, see Marvin Zalman et al., *Michigan's Assisted Suicide Three Ring Circus—An Intersection of Law and Politics*, 23 Ohio N.U. L. Rev. 863, 901 (1997) ("Certain rule of law concepts are so basic that they are assumed in a normally functioning legal system. Chief among these is the core notion that the government is not above the law,

and that law must be as certain as is possible when dealing with words. One way to insure that law be as certain as possible is to require that it be written.").

2. *Contempt of court.* Offenses against the administration of justice, including contempt of court (ignoring a judicial order) have a long history as common law crimes. Most states now have statutes penalizing contempt of court. See, e.g., N.Y. Penal Law § 215.50. But even in jurisdictions without a statute, prosecutions for contempt of court are common. Is this legitimate? One argument in favor of prosecuting contempt of court as a common law crime is that the contempt power is "inherent" in the judicial function. If the state had no authority to prosecute willful defiance of a judicial order, the judicial power would be meaningless. See, e.g., *State v. Price*, 672 A.2d 893, 896 (R.I. 1996); *People v. Barron*, 677 P.2d 1370, 1372 (Colo. 1984) ("The power to punish for criminal contempt is an inherent and indispensable power of the court and exists independently of legislative authorization."). When Colorado abolished common law crimes in 1971, it specifically excluded contempt of court: "Common-law crimes are abolished and no conduct shall constitute an offense unless it is described as an offense in this code or in another statute of this state, but this provision does not affect *the power of a court to punish for contempt*, or to employ any sanction authorized by law for the enforcement of an order lawfully entered, or a civil judgment or decree; nor does it affect the use of case law as an interpretive aid in the construction of the provisions of this code." Colo. Rev. Stat. § 18-1-104. Are there any limits to the contempt power?

2. Retroactivity

Everyone agrees that a criminal law statute cannot be passed by the legislature and then applied retroactively to a defendant who committed the action before the law was passed. But what if an appellate court in a state changes a particular *doctrine* and then applies it retroactively to the appellant who is appealing his conviction (which by definition occurred before the appeals court judgment)? Should the Constitution's ban on ex post facto laws apply in such a situation?

Rogers v. Tennessee
Supreme Court of the United States
532 U.S. 451 (2000)

O'CONNOR, J.

This case concerns the constitutionality of the retroactive application of a judicial decision abolishing the common law "year and a day rule." At common law, the year and a day rule provided that no defendant could be convicted of murder unless his victim had died by the defendant's act within a year and a day of the act. The Supreme Court of Tennessee abolished the rule as it had existed at common law in Tennessee and applied its decision to petitioner to uphold his conviction. The question before us is whether, in doing so, the court denied petitioner due process of law in violation of the Fourteenth Amendment.

I

Petitioner Wilbert K. Rogers was convicted in Tennessee state court of second degree murder. According to the undisputed facts, petitioner stabbed his victim, James Bowdery, with a butcher knife on May 6, 1994. One of the stab wounds penetrated Bowdery's heart. During surgery to repair the wound to his heart, Bowdery went into cardiac arrest, but was resuscitated and survived the procedure. As a result, however, he had developed a condition known as "cerebral hypoxia," which results from a loss of oxygen to the brain. Bowdery's higher brain functions had ceased, and he slipped into and remained in a coma until August 7, 1995, when he died from a kidney infection (a common complication experienced by comatose patients). Approximately 15 months had passed between the stabbing and Bowdery's death which, according to the undisputed testimony of the county medical examiner, was caused by cerebral hypoxia "secondary to a stab wound to the heart." . . .

II

Although petitioner's claim is one of due process, the Constitution's *Ex Post Facto* Clause figures prominently in his argument. The Clause provides simply that "[n]o State shall . . . pass any . . . ex post facto Law." . . .

We have observed, however, that limitations on *ex post facto* judicial decisionmaking are inherent in the notion of due process. In *Bouie v. City of Columbia*, 378 U.S. 347 (1964), we considered the South Carolina Supreme Court's retroactive application of its construction of the State's criminal trespass statute to the petitioners in that case. The statute prohibited "entry upon the lands of another . . . after notice from the owner or tenant prohibiting such entry. . . ." The South Carolina court construed the statute to extend to patrons of a drug store who had received no notice prohibiting their entry into the store, but had refused to leave the store when asked. Prior to the court's decision, South Carolina cases construing the statute had uniformly held that conviction under the statute required proof of notice before entry. None of those cases, moreover, had given the "slightest indication that that requirement could be satisfied by proof of the different act of remaining on the land after being told to leave."

We held that the South Carolina court's retroactive application of its construction to the store patrons violated due process. Reviewing decisions in which we had held criminal statutes "void for vagueness" under the Due Process Clause, we noted that this Court has often recognized the "basic principle that a criminal statute must give fair warning of the conduct that it makes a crime." Deprivation of the right to fair warning, we continued, can result both from vague statutory language and from an unforeseeable and retroactive judicial expansion of statutory language that appears narrow and precise on its face. For that reason, we concluded that "[i]f a judicial construction of a criminal statute is 'unexpected and indefensible by reference to the law which had been expressed prior to the conduct in issue,' [the construction] must not be given retroactive effect." We found that the South Carolina court's construction of the statute violated this principle because it was so clearly at odds with the statute's plain language and had no support in prior South Carolina decisions. . . .

III

Turning to the particular facts of the instant case, the Tennessee court's abolition of the year and a day rule was not unexpected and indefensible. The year and a day rule is widely viewed as an outdated relic of the common law. Petitioner does not even so much as hint that good reasons exist for retaining the rule, and so we need not delve too deeply into the rule and its history here. Suffice it to say that the rule is generally believed to date back to the 13th century, when it served as a statute of limitations governing the time in which an individual might initiate a private action for murder known as an "appeal of death"; that by the 18th century the rule had been extended to the law governing public prosecutions for murder; that the primary and most frequently cited justification for the rule is that 13th century medical science was incapable of establishing causation beyond a reasonable doubt when a great deal of time had elapsed between the injury to the victim and his death; and that, as practically every court recently to have considered the rule has noted, advances in medical and related science have so undermined the usefulness of the rule as to render it without question obsolete.

For this reason, the year and a day rule has been legislatively or judicially abolished in the vast majority of jurisdictions recently to have addressed the issue. Citing *Bouie,* petitioner contends that the judicial abolition of the rule in other jurisdictions is irrelevant to whether he had fair warning that the rule in Tennessee might similarly be abolished and, hence, to whether the Tennessee court's decision was unexpected and indefensible as applied to him. In discussing the apparent meaning of the South Carolina statute in *Bouie,* we noted that "[i]t would be a rare situation in which the meaning of a statute of another State sufficed to afford a person 'fair warning' that his own State's statute meant something quite different from what its words said." This case, however, involves not the precise meaning of the words of a particular statute, but rather the continuing viability of a common law rule. Common law courts frequently look to the decisions of other jurisdictions in determining whether to alter or modify a common law rule in light of changed circumstances, increased knowledge, and general logic and experience. Due process, of course, does not require a person to apprise himself of the common law of all 50 States in order to guarantee that his actions will not subject him to punishment in light of a developing trend in the law that has not yet made its way to his State. At the same time, however, the fact that a vast number of jurisdictions have abolished a rule that has so clearly outlived its purpose is surely relevant to whether the abolition of the rule in a particular case can be said to be unexpected and indefensible by reference to the law as it then existed.

Finally, and perhaps most importantly, at the time of petitioner's crime the year and a day rule had only the most tenuous foothold as part of the criminal law of the State of Tennessee. The rule did not exist as part of Tennessee's statutory criminal code. And while the Supreme Court of Tennessee concluded that the rule persisted at common law, it also pointedly observed that the rule had never once served as a ground of decision in any prosecution for murder in the State. Indeed, in all the reported Tennessee cases, the rule has been mentioned only three times, and each time in dicta. . . .

These cases hardly suggest that the Tennessee court's decision was "unexpected and indefensible" such that it offended the due process principle of fair warning articulated in *Bouie* and its progeny. This is so despite the fact that, as Justice Scalia correctly points out, the court viewed the year and a day rule as a "substantive principle" of the common law of Tennessee. As such, however, it was a principle in name only, having never once been enforced in the State. The Supreme Court of Tennessee also emphasized this fact in its opinion, and rightly so, for it is surely relevant to whether the court's abolition of the rule in petitioner's case violated due process limitations on retroactive judicial decisionmaking . . .

There is, in short, nothing to indicate that the Tennessee court's abolition of the rule in petitioner's case represented an exercise of the sort of unfair and arbitrary judicial action against which the Due Process Clause aims to protect. Far from a marked and unpredictable departure from prior precedent, the court's decision was a routine exercise of common law decisionmaking in which the court brought the law into conformity with reason and common sense. It did so by laying to rest an archaic and outdated rule that had never been relied upon as a ground of decision in any reported Tennessee case.

Scalia, J., dissenting.

The Court today approves the conviction of a man for a murder that was not murder (but only manslaughter) when the offense was committed. It thus violates a principle—encapsulated in the maxim *nulla poena sine lege*—which "dates from the ancient Greeks" and has been described as one of the most "widely held value-judgment[s] in the entire history of human thought." J. Hall, General Principles of Criminal Law 59 (2d ed. 1960). Today's opinion produces, moreover, a curious constitution that only a judge could love. One in which (by virtue of the *Ex Post Facto* Clause) the elected representatives of all the people cannot retroactively make murder what was not murder when the act was committed; but in which unelected judges can do precisely that. One in which the predictability of parliamentary lawmaking cannot validate the retroactive creation of crimes, but the predictability of judicial lawmaking can do so. I do not believe this is the system that the Framers envisioned—or, for that matter, that any reasonable person would imagine. . . .

Even if I agreed with the Court that the Due Process Clause is violated only when there is lack of "fair warning" of the impending retroactive change, I would not find such fair warning here. It is not clear to me, in fact, what the Court believes the fair warning consisted of. Was it the mere fact that "[t]he year and a day rule is widely viewed as an outdated relic of the common law"? So are many of the elements of common-law crimes, such as "breaking the close" as an element of burglary, or "asportation" as an element of larceny. Are all of these "outdated relics" subject to retroactive judicial rescission? Or perhaps the fair warning consisted of the fact that "the year and a day rule has been legislatively or judicially abolished in the vast majority of jurisdictions recently to have addressed the issue." But why not count in petitioner's favor (as giving him no reason to expect a change in law) those even more numerous jurisdictions that have chosen *not* "recently to have addressed the issue"? And why not also count in petitioner's favor (rather than *against* him) those jurisdictions that have abolished the rule *legislatively,* and those jurisdictions that have abolished it through *prospective* rather than *retroactive* judicial rulings (together, a large majority of the abolitions)? That is to say, even if it was predictable that the rule would be changed, it was *not* predictable that it would be changed *retroactively,* rather than in the *prospective* manner to which legislatures are restricted by the *Ex Post Facto* Clause, or in the *prospective* manner that most other courts have employed. . . .

I reiterate that the only "fair warning" discussed in our precedents, and the only "fair warning" relevant to the issue before us here, is fair warning *of what the law is.* That warning, unlike the new one that today's opinion invents, goes well beyond merely "safeguarding defendants against *unjustified* and *unpredictable* breaks with prior law." It safeguards them against *changes in the law after the fact.* But even accepting the Court's novel substitute, the opinion's conclusion that this watered-down standard has been met seems to me to proceed on the principle that a large number of almost-valid arguments makes a solid case. As far as I can tell, petitioner had nothing that could fairly be called a "warning" that the Supreme Court of Tennessee would retroactively eliminate one of the elements of the crime of murder. . . .

NOTES & QUESTIONS ON RETROACTIVITY

1. *Retroactivity and unforeseeable changes to the law.* In *Rogers*, the Court relies heavily on *Bouie v. City of Columbia*, 378 U.S. 347 (1964), a pivotal case in the Court's ex post facto jurisprudence. As described above, the case involved two African Americans arrested for trespassing in the restaurant area of a drugstore even though it lacked a sign declaring it whites-only. They were arrested after refusing an order to vacate the premises. The state court interpreted the statute as prohibiting not just entering another's property but also refusing to leave after being told to vacate. The U.S. Supreme Court decided the case on retroactivity grounds and concluded that the state Supreme Court interpretation of the statute constituted a retroactive change to the law since it was "unforeseeable" to the defendants. Thus, *Bouie* firmly established that the prohibition against retroactivity applies just as much to judicial interpretations as it does to legislative enactments. Is it odd that the Court used the *Bouie* case to make a statement about retroactivity? The Court had decided *Brown v. Board of Education* in 1954 and declared segregation unconstitutional a full decade before *Bouie*. Should the Court have simply stated that arresting the defendants violated their right to equal protection of the law? Normally, constitutional claims require some state action; is the involvement of the police sufficient state involvement to trigger constitutional scrutiny? As it happens, the Court decided to resolve the case on due process grounds and declined to resolve any questions presented on equal protection.

2. *Judicial enlargement of murder statutes.* In *Keeler v. Superior Court*, 470 P.2d 617 (1970), the Supreme Court of California ruled that a defendant could not be prosecuted for murder for assaulting a woman and causing the death of her fetus. The defendant intended to kill the fetus and shouted, "I'm going to stomp it out of you" as he assaulted the woman. After the assault, the woman sought medical treatment and the fetus was delivered stillborn. The legal question in the case is whether the statutory definition of murder as the "unlawful killing of a human being with malice aforethought" applies to the killing of a fetus. Keeler, the defendant, argued that the common law rule required the fetus to be born alive in order for its death to be classified as a murder. Applying *Bouie*, the California Supreme Court agreed, arguing that judicial enlargement of the state's homicide statute was not foreseeable to Mr. Keeler and that he had no advance notice that fetuses were covered by the California homicide statute. Incidentally, the state legislature subsequently amended its homicide statutes to cover unborn fetuses, so that future defendants could not succeed with the same argument that Keeler had raised. But in solving the retroactivity problem, the legislature created another: The draft language for the new statute appeared to criminalize abortions too. To rectify this, the legislature specifically excluded from the provision all lawful abortions as defined by the Therapeutic Abortion Act.

HYPOTHETICAL

Consider the following case. Mr. A is arrested for a felony charge of burglary and does not have enough money to make bail. While in the county jail waiting for his trial date, Mr. A murders a corrections officer and is charged with first-degree murder. Under the state's homicide statute, first-degree murder includes the intentional killing of a police officer and mandates a sentence of either 25 years to life or the death penalty. The local prosecutor decides to seek the death penalty. Mr. A argues that the term "police officer" in the homicide statute does not include correction officers serving in local jails, and cites prior intermediate appellate decisions in the state that have agreed with him. But the state's highest court disagrees with Mr. A and the lower courts and concludes that the first-degree murder statute covers local corrections officers. The death penalty charge is reinstated against Mr. A.

Is this result acceptable? Should the Ex Post Facto Clause prohibit this retroactive change in the interpretation of the law? Does your answer change depending on whether Mr. A had actual knowledge of the lower court decisions when he committed the murder?

3. Statutory Construction and the Common Law

When courts interpret criminal law statutes, they often consider the prior common law crime that was replaced by the statute. The rationale for doing so is that it helps the court get a handle on what the legislature was trying to accomplish by crafting the statute. As you read the following case, ask yourself whether regular citizens have adequate access to the old common law definitions and can interpret statutes in the same way.

Lewis v. Superior Court
Court of Appeal, Third District
California 217 Cal. App. 3d 379 (1990)

BLEASE, ASSOCIATE JUSTICE.

This petition for a writ of prohibition challenges the indictment of petitioner (defendant) for forgery. We are asked to determine whether the definition of forgery in Penal Code section 470 extends to the fabrication of a signature on a letter of endorsement of a candidate for public office. We answer "no" and will grant the relief sought.

Section 470 is derived from the common law and its reach is thereby limited. Under the controlling case law a letter bearing a false signature urging people to vote for a candidate for public office is not an instrument which could "prejudice, damage, or defraud" any person, as those terms are used in section 470. Unless the consequential harm of the fabrication is a loss, damage, or prejudice of a legal right, generally a pecuniary or property right, there is no harm of the kind to which the statute is directed and hence no forgery. The attempted persuasion of another to vote does not implicate such a right.

This conclusion does not imply condonation of the alleged conduct. Rather, as the Supreme Court once noted, in overturning a different forgery conviction: "whatever [a defendant's] misdeeds, he must not suffer for a crime which he has not committed."

FACTS AND PROCEDURAL BACKGROUND

Defendant John Lewis is charged by indictment with one count of forgery in violation of section 470. The indictment alleges that defendant "with the intent to defraud cause[d] to be counterfeited and forged the handwriting of another, to wit, PRESIDENT RONALD REAGAN and, further [caused to be passed], as true and genuine letters on behalf of certain candidates for the state Assembly which letters bore the counterfeit and forged signature and purported to be from PRESIDENT RONALD REAGAN, with the intent to prejudice, damage or defraud the voters in the various districts from which the candidates were seeking election." Though but one offense is alleged, two acts relating to the letters are made the predicate of criminal liability. The first is the "forging" of a signature to the letters. The second is their passing. . . .

Defendant is a member of the California Assembly. He directed members of his own staff, and other political consultants working for the Republican Party under his supervision, to draft six letters supporting fellow Republican candidates for state legislative office. The letters were mailed to registered voters in the "target" districts. They were printed on stationary bearing the letterhead "Ronald Reagan—The White House," and appeared to be signed by the former President. In fact, President Reagan did not sign the letters, nor did he authorize the use of his signature by facsimile or otherwise. Rather, the false signature was affixed to the letters, and the letters mailed, upon defendant's orders, even after he was advised that permission to use the President's name and signature on those communications had been sought and denied. . . .

DISCUSSION

Section 470 in pertinent part reads: "Every person who, [1] with intent to defraud, signs the name of another person, or a fictitious person, knowing that he or she has no authority so to do, to, or falsely makes, alters, forges, or counterfeits, any [of a list of more than 40 kinds of named documents concerning interests in tangible and intangible property]; [2] or counterfeits or forges the seal or handwriting of another; [3] or utters, publishes, passes, or attempts to pass, as true and genuine, any of the above-named false, altered, forged, or counterfeited matters, as above specified and described, knowing the same to be false, altered, forged, or counterfeited, with intent to prejudice, damage, or defraud any person; [4] or who, with intent to defraud, alters, corrupts, or falsifies any record of any will, codicil, conveyance, or other instrument, the record of which is by law evidence, or any record of any judgment of a court or the return of any officer to any process of any court, is guilty of forgery."

As indicated by its semicolons and our parenthetical numbering of the text, section 470 has four branches. The first branch pertains to acts regarding a list of named instruments. Here, there is no claim that the campaign letters are any of the named instruments. The fourth branch of the statute also is not pertinent since there is no claim that the campaign letters are an "instrument, the record of which is by law evidence. . . ." Hence, the conduct charged as forgery, to come within the statute, must constitute either [2] the "counterfeit[ing] or forg[ing] of . . . handwriting of another; or [3] . . . [passing] as true and genuine, any of the above-named false, altered, forged, or counterfeited matters, as above specified and described, knowing the same to be false, altered, forged, or counterfeited, with intent to prejudice, damage, or defraud any person. . . ."

This language, almost all of which was taken from section 73 of the Crimes and Punishments Act of 1850, was incorporated in section 470 of the Penal Code in 1872 and has remained essentially unaltered since that time. This section, like many of the early codes, was viewed as deriving from the common law and has been read by the controlling cases as incorporating significant provisions of the common law. . . .

The words of section 470 bear a "peculiar and appropriate meaning" taken from the common law. As was said in 1896, "[A]s to what constitutes forgery of instruments which are subjects of forgery, the definitions at common law and by our code are the same. 'Forgery, at common law, is the false making or material altering, with intent to defraud, of any writing which, if genuine, might apparently be of legal efficacy, or the foundation of a legal liability.'" That is evident in section 470 by the detailed attention which is shown in the listing of instruments which may be made the subjects of forgery.

The common law rule of forgery began as a species of treason, including such acts as falsifying the king's seal and counterfeiting money. Over time, case law broadened the offense to extend to fabrication and use of false documents as the means of accomplishing theft by false pretenses. The comment to Model Penal Code section 224.1 suggests that forgery developed as an offense independent of theft by false pretenses most importantly because of the narrowness of the law of attempt. The offense is maintained as a distinct, felony offense from theft by false pretenses because forgery threatens the system of written instruments upon which modern commerce critically depends.

The broadening of the offense is explained in the comment to section 224.1 of the Model Penal Code. "It is easy to understand how the original legislative concern for royal seals, money, and official documents was transferred to negotiable instruments and muniments of title as society became increasingly commercial. The pragmatic need in both classes of cases is a guarantee of authenticity of instruments and records upon which the community can rely in important transactions. This is the case with deeds and wills, which constitute links in the chain of devolution of title and which are usually entered of public record as notice to all. This is also true with instruments that pass from hand to hand in the manner of money—e.g., checks, notes, bills of lading, stocks, bonds, and other securities. It is a natural extension of this notion to include contracts, releases, authorizations, and other documents that purport to have legal effect."

In this context the common law rule concerning the apparent legal efficacy of the instrument is tailored to the harm that the common law offense addresses. The rule identifies the kinds of writings that are suited to occasion such harm. Making virtually any kind of false document affords an inference that the maker intends to deceive someone. However, only a document with apparent legal efficacy is naturally suited to perpetrate the kind of deception that is strictly speaking a defrauding. Fabricating such a document by that very act affords an inference of an intention to "defraud", namely by such deceit to detrimentally accomplish something akin to a theft by false pretenses.

Without some reference to the common law, the generalized provisions of the second branch of section 470, upon which the indictment is in part founded, would be perilously broad. The terse declaration that forgery is the counterfeiting or forging of the handwriting of another could extend to any imitation of another's handwriting for purposes of deception, whatever the harmlessness or triviality of the end in view, i.e., regardless of an intention to defraud. However, "The common law meaning of a statutory term is . . . a proper basis for defeating a claim of fatal uncertainty." No doubt for this reason, among others, it is has long been settled that, notwithstanding the absence of an explicit scienter provision, an intent to defraud is to be implied from and must be pled and proved under this branch of section 470. . . .

Our research has turned up only one forgery case, *Barnes v. Crawford* (1894) 115 N.C. 76, 20 S.E. 386, which approaches the kind of misrepresentation of political sentiments at issue here. The question was whether the forging of a declaration of support for supposed legislation purporting to be signed by a candidate for Congress was a criminal forgery. The case holds that the writing is not one of which forgery could be predicated. "[I]t is not alone sufficient that there be a writing, and that the writing be false: it must also be such as, if true, would be of some legal efficacy, real or apparent, since otherwise it has *no legal tendency to defraud*." . . .

In any event, it is too late in the day to urge a novel construction of section 470. As we have shown, the California Supreme Court has consistently stated that the statutory offense, whether it be of making or sending of a fabricated instrument, requires an intention to defraud. More importantly, the controlling case law plainly indicates that only schemes to prejudice, damage or defraud persons as to their legal rights, generally money or property, are within the ambit of section 470. If a broader scienter is to become the measure of the crime then notice of that shift must be afforded by the enactment of an appropriate statute. . . .

As this court explained in another context, the categorization of offenses by their allocation to different statutory structures may reveal how certain types of conduct should be treated and controlled. An examination of the laws of California regulating political activities and the campaign and election process shows an extensive body of enactments focused exclusively on these matters. The existence of this regulatory system suggests that political activities should be subjected to restrictions peculiar to that sphere. Numerous specific statutes prescribe criminal or civil sanctions for a variety of acts that interfere with the electoral process, including, in at least two instances, the forging of signatures. The conduct which defendant is alleged to have engaged in may be properly placed in this "political offense" category, which the Legislature has placed outside the ambit of the Penal Code, as with Election Code section 29300. This statutory pattern reinforces our view that the forging of President Reagan's signature to these political campaign tools is not punishable under section 470. . . .

NOTES & QUESTIONS ON STATUTORY CONSTRUCTION

1. *The seal of the King.* The court notes that the common law crime of forgery was originally based on forging the seal of the King on official documents and money. Indeed, forgery of the King's seal was a species of treason. See Jerome Hall, *Criminal Attempt—A Study of Foundations of Criminal Liability,* 49 Yale L.J. 789, 795 (1940). If that is the case, does it seem strange that signing President Ronald Reagan's name on a letter does not qualify as forgery? The court argued that long ago the common law crime evolved into the intent to defraud using an official legal document. Was Lewis trying to defraud someone? For money? The key to the case's resolution is that Lewis was not engaged in a fraud for financial gain, but rather was apparently motivated by political concerns.

2. *The common law and legality.* Does the process of *consulting* the common law violate the principle of legality? In Lewis's case, consideration of the common law ultimately narrowed the statute and generated his acquittal. But what if the situation were the reverse? Say the common law supported the broader interpretation and resulted in his conviction being upheld? Would that be consistent with the principle of legality? The whole point of codification of

the criminal law was to replace unwritten common law crimes with written statutes that were available to all—even laypersons—for consultation. But if judges use common law crimes to interpret the written statutes, are they smuggling the common law back in through the back door (as a methodology)? Are regular citizens aware of the common law antecedents of today's crimes and do they interpret the law the same way that judges do?

AFTERWORD   What happened to John R. Lewis after his indictment was nullified? After serving for a decade in the California State Assembly, Lewis went on to serve in the California State Senate between 1991 and 2000. (He is not related to Rep. John R. Lewis, the civil rights leader who represents Georgia in Congress.)

---

4. Vagueness

What if a statute is so vague that a potential defendant has no idea if his conduct will violate the law or not? In the following case, the Supreme Court evaluates a local ordinance that the defendant claimed was too vague to satisfy constitutional muster. As you read the case, ask yourself why vague statutes violate foundational principles of the criminal law. Ultimately, how much vagueness is permissible in a statute?

City of Chicago v. Morales
Supreme Court of the United States
527 U.S. 41 (1999)

Justice Stevens announced the judgment of the Court and delivered the opinion of the Court with respect to Parts I, II, and V, and an opinion with respect to Parts III, IV, and VI, in which Justice Souter and Justice Ginsburg join.

In 1992, the Chicago City Council enacted the Gang Congregation Ordinance, which prohibits "criminal street gang members" from "loitering" with one another or with other persons in any public place. The question presented is whether the Supreme Court of Illinois correctly held that the ordinance violates the Due Process Clause of the Fourteenth Amendment to the Federal Constitution.

I

Before the ordinance was adopted, the city council's Committee on Police and Fire conducted hearings to explore the problems created by the city's street gangs, and more particularly, the consequences of public loitering by gang members. Witnesses included residents of the neighborhoods where gang members are most active, as well as some of the aldermen who represent those areas. Based on that evidence, the council made a series of findings that are included in the text of the ordinance and explain the reasons for its enactment.

The council found that a continuing increase in criminal street gang activity was largely responsible for the city's rising murder rate, as well as an escalation of violent and drug related crimes. It noted that in many neighborhoods throughout the city, "the burgeoning presence of street gang members in public places has intimidated many law abiding citizens." Furthermore, the council stated that gang members "establish control over identifiable areas . . . by loitering in those areas and intimidating others from entering those areas; and . . . [m]embers of criminal street gangs avoid arrest by committing no offense punishable under existing laws when they know the police are present. . . ." It further found that "loitering in public places by criminal street gang members creates a justifiable fear for the safety of persons and property in the area" and that "[a]ggressive action is necessary to preserve the city's streets and other public places so that the public may use such places without fear." Moreover, the council concluded that the city "has an interest in discouraging all persons from loitering in public places with criminal gang members."

The ordinance creates a criminal offense punishable by a fine of up to $500, imprisonment for not more than six months, and a requirement to perform up to 120 hours of community service. Commission of the offense involves four predicates. First, the police officer must reasonably believe that at least one of the two or more persons present in a "public place" is a "criminal street gang membe[r]." Second, the persons must be "loitering," which the ordinance defines as "remain[ing] in any one place with no apparent purpose." Third, the officer must then order "all" of the persons to disperse and remove themselves "from the area." Fourth, a person must disobey the officer's order. If any person, whether a gang member or not, disobeys the officer's order, that person is guilty of violating the ordinance. . . .

III

The basic factual predicate for the city's ordinance is not in dispute. As the city argues in its brief, "the very presence of a large collection of obviously brazen, insistent, and lawless gang members and hangers-on on the public ways intimidates residents, who become afraid even to leave their homes and go about their business. That, in turn, imperils community residents' sense of safety and security, detracts from property values, and can ultimately destabilize entire neighborhoods." The findings in the ordinance explain that it was motivated by these concerns. We have no doubt that a law that directly prohibited such intimidating conduct would be constitutional, but this ordinance broadly covers a significant amount of additional activity. Uncertainty about the scope of that additional coverage provides the basis for respondents' claim that the ordinance is too vague. . . .

Vagueness may invalidate a criminal law for either of two independent reasons. First, it may fail to provide the kind of notice that will enable ordinary people to understand what conduct it prohibits; second, it may authorize and even encourage arbitrary and discriminatory enforcement. Accordingly, we first consider whether the ordinance provides fair notice to the citizen and then discuss its potential for arbitrary enforcement.

IV

"It is established that a law fails to meet the requirements of the Due Process Clause if it is so vague and standardless that it leaves the public uncertain as to the conduct it prohibits. . . ." The Illinois Supreme Court recognized that the term "loiter" may have a common and accepted meaning, but the definition of that term in this ordinance—"to remain in any one place with no apparent purpose"—does not. It is difficult to imagine how any citizen of the city of Chicago standing in a public place with a group of people would know if he or she had an "apparent purpose." If she were talking to another person, would she have an apparent purpose? If she were frequently checking her watch and looking expectantly down the street, would she have an apparent purpose?

Since the city cannot conceivably have meant to criminalize each instance a citizen stands in public with a gang member, the vagueness that dooms this ordinance is not the product of uncertainty about the normal meaning of "loitering," but rather about what loitering is covered by the ordinance and what is not. The Illinois Supreme Court emphasized the law's failure to distinguish between innocent conduct and conduct threatening harm. Its decision followed the precedent set by a number of state courts that have upheld ordinances that criminalize loitering combined with some other overt act or evidence of criminal intent. However, state courts have uniformly invalidated laws that do not join the term "loitering" with a second specific element of the crime.

The city's principal response to this concern about adequate notice is that loiterers are not subject to sanction until after they have failed to comply with an officer's order to disperse. "[W]hatever problem is created by a law that criminalizes conduct people normally believe to be innocent is solved when persons receive actual notice from a police order of what they are expected to do." We find this response unpersuasive for at least two reasons.

First, the purpose of the fair notice requirement is to enable the ordinary citizen to conform his or her conduct to the law. "No one may be required at peril of life, liberty or property to speculate as to the meaning of penal statutes." Although it is true that a loiterer is not subject to criminal sanctions unless he or she disobeys a dispersal order, the loitering is the conduct that the ordinance is designed to prohibit. If the loitering is in fact harmless and innocent, the dispersal order itself is an unjustified impairment of liberty. If the police are able to decide arbitrarily which members of the public they will order to disperse, then the Chicago ordinance becomes indistinguishable from the law we held invalid in *Shuttlesworth v. Birmingham*, 382 U.S. 87, 90 (1965). Because an officer may issue an order only after prohibited conduct has already occurred, it cannot provide the kind of advance notice that will protect the putative loiterer from being ordered to disperse. Such an order cannot retroactively give adequate warning of the boundary between the permissible and the impermissible applications of the law.

Second, the terms of the dispersal order compound the inadequacy of the notice afforded by the ordinance. It provides that the officer "shall order all such persons to disperse and remove themselves from the area." This vague phrasing raises a host of questions. After such an order issues, how long must the loiterers remain apart? How far must they move? If each loiterer walks around the block and they meet again at the same location, are they subject to arrest or merely to being ordered to disperse again? . . .

Lack of clarity in the description of the loiterer's duty to obey a dispersal order might not render the ordinance unconstitutionally vague if the definition of the forbidden conduct were clear, but it does buttress our conclusion that the entire ordinance fails to give the ordinary citizen adequate notice of what is forbidden and what is permitted. The Constitution does not permit a legislature to "set a net large enough to catch all possible offenders, and leave it to the courts to step inside and say who could be rightfully detained, and who should be set at large." This ordinance is therefore vague "not in the sense that it requires a person to conform his conduct to an imprecise but comprehensible normative standard, but rather in the sense that no standard of conduct is specified at all."

V

The broad sweep of the ordinance also violates "the requirement that a legislature establish minimal guidelines to govern law enforcement." There are no such guidelines in the ordinance. In any public place in the city of Chicago, persons who stand or sit in the company of a gang member may be ordered to disperse unless their purpose is apparent. The mandatory language in the enactment directs the police to issue an order without first making any inquiry about their possible purposes. It matters not whether the reason that a gang member and his father, for example, might loiter near Wrigley Field is to rob an unsuspecting fan or just to get a glimpse of Sammy Sosa leaving the ballpark; in either event, if their purpose is not apparent to a nearby police officer, she may—indeed, she "shall"—order them to disperse. . . .

Recognizing that the ordinance does reach a substantial amount of innocent conduct, we turn, then, to its language to determine if it "necessarily entrusts lawmaking to the moment-to-moment judgment of the policeman on his beat." As we discussed in the context of fair notice, the principal source of the vast discretion conferred on the police in this case is the definition of loitering as "to remain in any one place with no apparent purpose."

As the Illinois Supreme Court interprets that definition, it "provides absolute discretion to police officers to decide what activities constitute loitering." We have no authority to construe the language of a state statute more narrowly than the construction given by that State's highest court. "The power to determine the meaning of a statute carries with it the power to prescribe its extent and limitations as well as the method by which they shall be determined."

Nevertheless, the city disputes the Illinois Supreme Court's interpretation, arguing that the text of the ordinance limits the officer's discretion in three ways. First, it does not permit the officer to issue a dispersal order to anyone who is moving along or who has an apparent purpose. Second, it does not permit an arrest if individuals obey a dispersal order. Third, no order can issue unless the officer reasonably believes that one of the loiterers is a member of a criminal street gang.

Even putting to one side our duty to defer to a state court's construction of the scope of a local enactment, we find each of these limitations insufficient. That the ordinance does not apply to people who are moving—that is, to activity that would not constitute loitering under any possible definition of the term—does not even address the question of how much discretion the police enjoy in deciding which stationary persons to disperse under the ordinance. Similarly, that the ordinance does not permit an arrest until after a dispersal order has been disobeyed does not provide any guidance to the officer deciding whether such an order should issue. The "no apparent purpose" standard for making that decision is inherently subjective because its application depends on whether some purpose is "apparent" to the officer on the scene.

Presumably an officer would have discretion to treat some purposes—perhaps a purpose to engage in idle conversation or simply to enjoy a cool breeze on a warm evening—as too frivolous to be apparent if he suspected a different ulterior motive. Moreover, an officer conscious of the city council's reasons for enacting the ordinance might well ignore its text and issue a dispersal order, even though an illicit purpose is actually apparent.

It is true, as the city argues, that the requirement that the officer reasonably believe that a group of loiterers contains a gang member does place a limit on the authority to order dispersal. That limitation would no doubt be sufficient if the ordinance only applied to loitering that had an apparently harmful purpose or effect, or possibly if it only applied to loitering by persons reasonably believed to be criminal gang members. But this ordinance, for reasons that are not explained in the findings of the city council, requires no harmful purpose and applies to nongang members as well as suspected gang members. It applies to everyone in the city who may remain in one place with one suspected gang member as long as their purpose is not apparent to an officer observing them. Friends, relatives, teachers, counselors, or even total strangers might unwittingly engage in forbidden loitering if they happen to engage in idle conversation with a gang member. . . .

NOTES & QUESTIONS ON VAGUENESS

1. *Anti-gang legislation.*   As a state legislator responding to the *Morales* decision, how would you craft a legislation to target gang activity? Any statute that gives police officers complete discretion to determine who is a "gang member" will suffer from vagueness problems. Also, everyone has the right to appear on public property—indeed that is the definition of public property. The other possibility would be to use a range of prohibitions that could be equitably applied to all individuals, such as curfews, with the underlying policy goal of reducing gang activity. In response to the *Morales* decision, the City of Chicago passed a revised anti-loitering ordinance in 2000. See Chi. Ill. Mun. Code § 8-4-015(d)(1) (2000). In addition to specifying with greater clarity the locations to which the law applied, the law also included a new definition of loitering: "Gang loitering means remaining in any one place under circumstances that would warrant a reasonable person to believe that the purpose or effect of that behavior is to enable a criminal street gang to establish control over identifiable areas, to intimidate others from entering those areas, or to conceal illegal activities." The revision seemed inspired in part by Justice O'Connor, who stated in her concurring opinion in *Morales*:

In my view, the gang loitering ordinance could have been construed more narrowly. The term "loiter" might possibly be construed in a more limited fashion to mean "to remain in any one place with no apparent purpose other than to establish control over identifiable areas, to intimidate others from entering those areas, or to conceal illegal activities." Such a definition would be consistent with the Chicago City Council's findings and would avoid the vagueness problems of the ordinance as construed by the Illinois Supreme Court. As noted above, so would limitations that restricted the ordinance's criminal penalties to gang members or that more carefully delineated the circumstances in which those penalties would apply to nongang members.

City of Chicago v. Morales, 527 U.S. 41, 68 (1999).

2. *Anti-vagrancy statutes.* In *Papachristou v. City of Jacksonville,* 405 U.S. 156 (1972), the Supreme Court evaluated the following anti-vagrancy ordinance enacted by the City of Jacksonville, Florida:

> Rogues and vagabonds, or dissolute persons who go about begging, common gamblers, persons who use juggling or unlawful games or plays, common drunkards, common night walkers, thieves, pilferers or pickpockets, traders in stolen property, lewd, wanton and lascivious persons, keepers of gambling places, common railers and brawlers, persons wandering or strolling around from place to place without any lawful purpose or object, habitual loafers, disorderly persons, persons neglecting all lawful business and habitually spending their time by frequenting houses of ill fame, gaming houses, or places where alcoholic beverages are sold or served, persons able to work but habitually living upon the earnings of their wives or minor children shall be deemed vagrants and, upon conviction in the Municipal Court shall be punished as provided for Class D offenses.

The Supreme Court concluded that the statute was unconstitutionally vague because it "makes criminal activities which by modern standards are normally innocent" and "[i]t would certainly be dangerous if the legislature could set a net large enough to catch all possible offenders, and leave it to the courts to step inside and say who could be rightfully detained, and who should be set at large," quoting *United States v. Reese,* 92 U.S. 214, 221 (1875). As an exercise, try rewriting the above ordinance, with a narrower focus, in a manner that might pass constitutional muster.

5. The Rule of Lenity

In baseball, a tie at the base goes to the base runner. Similarly, under the rule of lenity, an ambiguous statute should be read in the defendant's favor, all other things being equal. Although courts rarely invoke the rule of lenity, it can sometimes provide a crucial factor that tips the scales in favor of the defendant. In the following case, identify the reasons why the Court applies the rule of lenity.

Bell v. United States

Supreme Court of the United States
349 U.S. 81 (1955)

FRANKFURTER, J.

Once more it becomes necessary to determine "What Congress has made the allowable unit of prosecution," under a statute which does not explicitly give the answer. This recurring problem now arises under what is familiarly known as the Mann Act. The relevant provisions of the Act in its present form are: "Whoever knowingly transports in interstate or foreign commerce . . . any woman or girl for the purpose of prostitution or debauchery, or for any other immoral purpose. . . . Shall be fined not more than $5,000 or imprisoned not more than five years, or both." 18 U.S.C. § 2421.

The facts need not detain us long. Petitioner pleaded guilty to violations laid in two counts, each referring to a different woman. Concededly, the petitioner transported the two women on the same trip and in the same vehicle. This was the basis of his claim that he committed only a single offense and could not be subjected to cumulative punishment under the two counts. The District Court rejected this conception of the statute and sentenced the petitioner to consecutive terms of two years and six months on each of the two counts. On appeal from denial of a motion to correct the sentence, the Court of Appeals affirmed the District Court. "While the act of transportation was a single one," it ruled, "the unlawful purpose must of necessity have been selective and personal as to each of the women involved. . . . We therefore believe that two separate offenses were committed in this case." This decision was in accord with decisions of other lower federal courts, but a contrary holding by the Court of Appeals for the Tenth Circuit raised a square conflict for settlement by this Court. This led us to bring the case here.

The punishment appropriate for the diverse federal offenses is a matter for the discretion of Congress, subject only to constitutional limitations, more particularly the Eighth Amendment. Congress could no doubt make the simultaneous transportation of more than one woman in violation of the Mann Act liable to cumulative punishment for each woman so transported. The question is: did it do so? It has not done so in words in the provisions defining the crime and fixing its punishment. Nor is guiding light afforded by the statute in its entirety or by any controlling gloss. The constitutional basis of the statute is the withdrawal of "the facility of interstate transportation," though, to be sure, the power was exercised in aid of social morality. Again, it will not promote guiding analysis to indulge in what might be called the color-matching of prior decisions concerned with "the unit of prosecution" in order to determine how near to, or how far from, the problem under this statute the answers are that have been given under other statutes.

It is not to be denied that argumentative skill, as was shown at the Bar, could persuasively and not unreasonably reach either of the conflicting constructions. About only one aspect of the problem can one be dogmatic. When Congress has the will it has no difficulty in expressing it—when it has the will, that is, of defining what it desires to make the unit of prosecution and, more particularly, to make each stick in a faggot[1] a single criminal unit. When Congress leaves to the Judiciary the task of imputing to Congress an undeclared will, the ambiguity should be resolved in favor of lenity. And this not out of any sentimental consideration, or for want of sympathy with the purpose of Congress in proscribing evil or anti-social conduct. It may fairly be said to be a presupposition of our law to resolve doubts in the enforcement of a penal code against the imposition of a harsher punishment. This in no wise implies that language used in criminal statutes should not be read with the saving grace of common sense with which other enactments, not cast in technical language, are to be read. Nor does it assume that offenders against the law carefully read the penal code before they embark on crime. It merely means that if Congress does not fix the punishment for a federal offense clearly and without ambiguity, doubt will be resolved against turning a single transaction into multiple offenses, when we have no more to go on than the present case furnishes.

Reversed.

NOTES & QUESTIONS ON LENITY

1. *The origins of lenity.* There is much dispute over the origins of the rule of lenity. At least some scholars trace it back to the historical roots of the common law when justice was often harsh and disproportionate. In particular, all felonies were subject to the death penalty; judges created legal doctrines to mitigate the harshness of capital sentencing. The rule of lenity was just one among many judicial doctrines used to narrow the range of cases that might end in conviction (and by extension, execution). See Philip M. Spector, *The Sentencing Rule of Lenity*, 33 U. Tol. L. Rev. 511 (2001). Instead of

---

1. Editor's note: Justice Frankfurter is using this word in accordance with its non-pejorative meaning as "a bundle of sticks, twigs, or small branches of trees bound together." See 5 *Oxford English Dictionary* 663 (2d ed. 2000).

striking down vague statutes as unconstitutional (the contemporary approach), courts applied a rule of construction that interpreted overboard statutes in favor of the defendant. See *Johnson v. United States,* 135 S. Ct. 2551, 2567 (2015) (Thomas, J., concurring). Does the rule of lenity still make sense now that the criminal law has abandoned the common law's harshness and unfairness? Or is the deprivation of liberty implicit in criminal punishment sufficiently important to ground the rule of lenity?

2. *The Model Penal Code.*   The Model Penal Code makes no mention of lenity by name and says that the "provisions of the Code shall be construed according to the fair import of their terms but when the language is susceptible of differing constructions it shall be interpreted to further the general purposes stated in this Section and the special purposes of the particular provision involved." MPC § 1.02(3). However, one purpose of the MPC is "to give fair warning of the nature of the conduct declared to constitute an offense." MPC § 1.02(1)(d).

3. *Lenity's demise?*   Following the Model Penal Code, many jurisdictions have explicitly repealed the doctrine of lenity. See, e.g., N.Y. Penal Law § 5.00 ("The general rule that a penal statute is to be strictly construed does not apply to this chapter, but the provisions herein must be construed according to the fair import of their terms to promote justice and effect the objects of the law."). Occasionally courts apply lenity even if the legislature has repealed it. For example, in *Keeler v. Superior Court,* the California Supreme Court said that "the defendant is entitled to the benefit of every reasonable doubt as to the true interpretation of words or the construction of language used in a statute," even though California abolished lenity in 1871. See Lawrence Solan, *The Language of Statutes* 191 (2010). On the other hand, enforcement of the rule of lenity in jurisdictions that still have it is "notoriously sporadic and unpredictable." Dan M. Kahan, *Lenity and Federal Common Law Crimes,* Sup. Ct. Rev. 345, 346 (1994).

C. PRACTICE & POLICY

The following section considers two examples of legal statutes that are mainstays of local criminal law practice, but that are somewhat vague and make it difficult to predict in advance which conduct will violate the ordinance in question. The examples include: (i) disorderly conduct; and (ii) endangering the welfare of the child. As you read the following materials, consider how a local prosecutor or defense attorney would approach these cases.

ॐ **Disorderly conduct.** Imagine that you are a local criminal law attorney representing an individual charged by city police with disorderly conduct—one of the most common violations charged in municipal courts. (In most jurisdictions, a "violation" is less severe than a misdemeanor.) Should you challenge the statute on some legality grounds, perhaps arguing that your client had no idea that his conduct violated the statute? Indeed, how does a regular person on the street know what a police officer will consider "disorderly"? Consider New York Penal Law § 240.20, which defines disorderly conduct in the following way:

A person is guilty of disorderly conduct when, with intent to cause public inconvenience, annoyance or alarm, or recklessly creating a risk thereof:

1. He engages in fighting or in violent, tumultuous or threatening behavior; or
2. He makes unreasonable noise; or
3. In a public place, he uses abusive or obscene language, or makes an obscene gesture; or
4. Without lawful authority, he disturbs any lawful assembly or meeting of persons; or
5. He obstructs vehicular or pedestrian traffic; or
6. He congregates with other persons in a public place and refuses to comply with a lawful order of the police to disperse; or
7. He creates a hazardous or physically offensive condition by any act which serves no legitimate purpose.

Is the statute sufficiently specific to put regular people on notice regarding which conduct will trigger an arrest? The required mens rea in the offense is the intent to cause, or recklessly creating a risk of, public inconvenience, annoyance, or alarm. But how does an individual know what conduct will annoy or alarm others? Doesn't that depend on factors beyond an individual's control? But see *People v. Tichenor*, 89 N.Y.2d 769 (1997) (New York disorderly conduct statute did not suffer from unconstitutional vagueness because it is limited to public conduct and the notion of "public offense" was an objective criterion).

ॐ **Endangering the welfare of a child.** Imagine that you are a state legislator considering amendments to your state's penal code. Most jurisdictions penalize conduct that endangers the welfare of a child. Examples include giving alcohol to a child or a parent failing to protect a child from physical abuse by someone else. Some jurisdictions also use the offense as an add-on in sexual abuse cases, so that defendants are charged both with sexual assault and endangering the welfare of the child. Should the statute specify which actions constitute endangering the welfare of a child or should that be left to the fact finder in individual cases? Say a parent lets a young child walk alone to the park at the end of the block. A concerned citizen sees the child alone and calls the police who charge the parents with endangering the welfare of the child. Is the parent under sufficient notice that this behavior was criminal? Community attitudes about leaving children alone have evolved quickly. In the 1950s some parents would let children walk alone, but in today's world most parents consider this too risky. For example, New York Penal Law § 260.10 defines the offense as:

1. He or she knowingly acts in a manner likely to be injurious to the physical, mental or moral welfare of a child less than seventeen years old or directs or authorizes such child to engage in an occupation involving a substantial risk of danger to his or her life or health; or

2. Being a parent, guardian or other person legally charged with the care or custody of a child less than eighteen years old, he or she fails or refuses to exercise reasonable diligence in the control of such child to prevent him or her from becoming an "abused child," a "neglected child," a "juvenile delinquent" or a "person in need of supervision". . . .

Would you revise the statute to be more specific? Should it explicitly list rules for when children can be left alone, or is it impossible to craft a statute with that level of specificity? See Donna St. George, *Parents Investigated For Neglect After Letting Kids Walk Home Alone*, Wash. Post, Jan. 14, 2015.

CHAPTER 5

ACT REQUIREMENT

A. DOCTRINE

Generally speaking, an individual should not be punished for evil thoughts alone. A culpable mental state must be accompanied by some prohibited act in order to sustain a conviction. The anticipated crime need not be completed; indeed, a whole chapter of this casebook (Chapter 17) will be devoted to prosecutions for *attempts*. But for now, we consider what *type* of act is required in order to sustain a conviction. Unfortunately, most criminal statutes are silent on what constitutes an act. It is generally considered implicit that a *voluntary* act is required. In some very limited and defined circumstances, the law penalizes an omission (the opposite of an act). Bystanders who let a crime occur are generally not subject to punishment in the United States, although basic tenets of morality and many foreign jurisdictions impose affirmative obligations on bystanders to intervene. Consequently, these three issues will be explored in this chapter: (i) the definition of a voluntary act; (ii) the scope of an actor's liability for an omission; and (iii) the law's general refusal to prosecute mere bystanders to criminal conduct.

1. Voluntary Acts

Voluntariness suggests a *willed* bodily movement. See Michael S. Moore, *Act and Crime* 79, 350 (1993). But what does that mean? In *Martin v. State*, 17 S.2d 427 (1944), the Alabama Supreme Court overturned the conviction of a man for public intoxication. Officers found him at his home and forcibly carried him outside where he was then drunk "in public." The court concluded that a "voluntary appearance is presupposed" by the statute. This case was easy to resolve because the involuntariness stemmed from the voluntary actions of the police officers. The more controversial cases involve actions that emanate from the accused's body but might be involuntary. The standard examples include sleepwalking (sometimes referred to as somnambulism or parasomnia), hypnosis, states of unconsciousness (automatism), and seizures. Jurisdictions differ on how to categorize these arguments. The most common approach is to consider them as a "failure of proof" defense that seeks to show that the prosecution cannot prove the required elements of the offense, one of which is the defendant's voluntary act. So, for example, if a defendant was sleepwalking, he might argue to a jury that it is impossible for the prosecution to establish that he committed the voluntary act necessary to be convicted for murder. In contrast, a few courts have entertained these arguments as an insanity plea that would lead to involuntary commitment if the defendant is found not guilty by reason of insanity. Finally, a few courts treat these as affirmative defenses with the burden of persuasion resting with the defense to convince the jury that the defendant was in a state of unconsciousness.

2. Omissions

Omissions are the opposite of acts—the failure to act or the absence of an act. In some situations, an omission can satisfy the act requirement—a somewhat paradoxical result since an omission is arguably no act at all. This has led some to argue that the act requirement is illusory. See Douglas Husak, *Rethinking the Act Requirement*, 28 Cardozo L. Rev. 2437 (2007). At the very least, it is probably more precise to say that the law requires either an act or a *culpable* omission. A conviction can be based on an omission only when the defendant had a legal *duty* to act. The situations where a duty to act is required are, like in tort law, very limited. A duty can be established by (i) statute; (ii) relationship between defendant and victim; (iii) contract; (iv) voluntary assumption of care; and (v) creation of risk. *Jones v. United States*, 308 F.2d 307 (D.C. Cir. 1962). For example, a statute might impose an affirmative obligation on all individuals to pay taxes, with criminal penalties for knowing noncompliance. In the absence of a statutory obligation to act, the law will look to one of the other categories, such as the relationship between the parties, to establish the legal obligation.

In order to give rise to a duty to act, the relationship between the defendant and the victim must be one that supports a legal duty to care for the individual, such as a parent-child relationship. For example, a parent's failure to rescue a child—though an omission instead of an act—could be the basis for a criminal prosecution, since all parents are legally required to care for their children. Similarly, a contract to care for an individual produces the same duty, though in that case it is an obligation that is voluntarily assumed in exchange for money. Other duties would include a doctor who has a professional duty to care for a patient, or a lifeguard who has a professional duty to safeguard the swimmers under his or her care. Similarly, fault in the creation of the peril can generate a duty to remediate. So someone who causes harm—such as a car accident—has a legal obligation to mitigate the harm and is therefore responsible for a failure to act. (In some cases, courts have imposed an obligation to act when the defendant's faultless behavior creates a harm.) On the other hand, a mere friend who fails to rescue someone could not be charged unless there was some other way to establish a duty to act, since friends are not legally obligated to care for each other. This state of affairs stands in stark contrast to some foreign jurisdictions—and some works of moral philosophy—that are more willing to impose robust obligations to act in many situations. However, this is a policy decision of American criminal law and certainly not a constitutional constraint. In other words, a state legislature could, at any time, pass a statute imposing obligations to act in additional circumstances, which would widen the scope of omission liability.

3. Bystanders

If a bystander witnesses a crime, she has no general legal obligation to intervene to stop the crime, unless she bears a legal duty to act under one of the categories described above. So, for example, a parent can be prosecuted for failing to protect a minor child from physical abuse, and a state statute might extend this duty to other officials (doctors, social workers, schoolteachers, etc.). But a pure bystander could not be convicted for failing to call the police. Despite this fact, bystanders can be prosecuted if they encouraged, incited, or assisted the crime in some way that transformed them from "mere" bystanders into actual accomplices or conspirators, though this is rare. The full criteria for becoming an accomplice through acts of encouragement will be explored in greater detail in Chapter 19 on Accomplices. For present purposes, it is sufficient to note that "pure" bystanders, who do not encourage the commission of the crime, cannot be prosecuted because they do not satisfy the law's act requirement, unless—as noted above—they are subject to a preexisting duty to act to stop the crime.

B. APPLICATION

1. Voluntary Acts

Physical acts produced by automatism—that is, during a state of unconsciousness—are not usually subject to criminal punishment. In the following case, the court heard testimony that the defendant's behavior was a "conditioned response" resulting from his prior military service. As you examine the evidence in the case, consider whether the defendant's behavior qualifies as a voluntary act.

State v. Utter

Court of Appeals of Washington
479 P.2d 946 (1971)

FARRIS, JUDGE.

Claude Gilbert Utter was charged by an information filed January 16, 1969, with the crime of murder in the second degree. He was convicted by a jury of the crime of manslaughter. He appeals from that conviction.

Appellant and the decedent, his son, were living together at the time of the latter's death. The son was seen to enter his father's apartment and shortly after was heard to say, "Dad, don't." Shortly thereafter he was seen stumbling in the hallway of the apartment building where he collapsed, having been stabbed in the chest. He stated, "Dad stabbed me" and died before he could be moved or questioned further.

Mr. Utter entered the armed services in December of 1942 and was honorably discharged in October of 1946. He was a combat infantryman. As a result of his service, he was awarded a 60 per cent disability pension.

Appellant testified that on the date of his son's death he began drinking during the morning hours. He was at the liquor store at 9 A.M. and purchased a quart of Thunderbird wine and a quart of port wine and drank the bottle of port wine with the exception of two drinks. Mr. Utter went for more liquor around noon. At that time he purchased 2 quarts of whiskey and 4 quarts of wine. Upon his return from the liquor store, he and another resident of the apartment "sat around drinking whiskey out of water glasses." Appellant remembers drinking with his friend and the next thing he remembers was being in jail subsequent to the death of his son. He has no recollection of any intervening events.

Appellant introduced evidence on "conditioned response" during the trial. Conditioned response was defined by Dr. Jarvis, a psychiatrist, as "an act or a pattern of activity occurring so rapidly, so uniformly as to be automatic in response to a certain stimulus." Mr. Utter testified that as a result of his jungle warfare training and experiences in World War II, he had on two occasions in the 1950's reacted violently towards people approaching him unexpectedly from the rear.

The trial court ruled that conditioned response was not a defense in Washington and instructed the jury to disregard all evidence introduced on this subject. Appellant contends that this evidence was not introduced as a defense. In this assertion, appellant is incorrect since if the evidence was received and believed by the jury, the result would be his exculpation. Therefore, it must be considered to be a defense to the crime.

The major issue presented on appeal is whether it was error for the trial court to instruct the jury to disregard the evidence on conditioned response. The trial court held that the defendant was attempting to present a defense of irresistible impulse—a theory of criminal insanity that has consistently been rejected in this state. In so holding, the trial court considered the defense to be one of mental incapacity. This was not so.

There are two components of every crime. One is objective—the actus reus; the other subjective—the mens rea. The actus reus is the culpable act itself, the mens rea is the criminal intent with which one performs the criminal act. However, the mens rea does not encompass the entire mental process of one accused of a crime. There is a certain minimal mental element required in order to establish the actus reus itself. This is the element of volition.

In the present case, the appellant was charged with second degree murder and found guilty of manslaughter. The actus reus of both is the same—homicide. Thus, in order to establish either, the fact of homicide must first be established.

Appellant contends that his evidence was presented for the purpose of determining whether in fact a homicide had been committed. He argues that his evidence, if believed, establishes that no "act" was committed within the definition of homicide (RCW 9.48.010):

> Homicide is the killing of a human being by the act, procurement or omission of another and is either (1) murder, (2) manslaughter, (3) excusable homicide or (4) justifiable homicide.

What is the meaning of the word "act" as used in this statute?

> It is sometimes said that no crime has been committed unless the harmful result was brought about by a "voluntary act." Analysis of such a statement will disclose, however, that as so used the phrase "voluntary act" means no more than the mere word "act." An act must be a willed movement or the omission of a possible and legally-required performance. This is essential to the Actus reus rather than to the mens rea. "A spasm is not an act."

R. Perkins, *Criminal Law* 660 (1957).

> (A)n "act" involves an exercise of the will. It signifies something done voluntarily. It necessarily implies intention. We find these statements abundantly sustained by the text-writers and decisions of our courts.

Heiman v. Pan American Life Ins. Co., 183 La. 1045, 1061 (1935).

Thus, to invert the statement of Perkins, the word "act" technically means a "voluntary act."

It is the appellant's contention that any of the alleged "acts" he committed were not those which involved mental processes, but rather were learned physical reactions to external stimuli which operated automatically on his autonomic nervous system. Although the theory sought to be presented by the appellant is similar to one of mental incapacity, it is nevertheless distinct from that concept. . . .

An "act" committed while one is unconscious is in reality no act at all. It is merely a physical event or occurrence for which there can be no criminal liability. However, unconsciousness does not, in all cases, provide a defense to a crime. When the state of unconsciousness is voluntarily induced through the use and consumption of alcohol or drugs, then that state of unconsciousness does not attain the stature of a complete defense. Thus, in a case such as the present one where there is evidence that the accused has consumed alcohol or drugs, the trial court should give a cautionary instruction with respect to voluntarily induced unconsciousness.

The issue of whether or not the appellant was in an unconscious or automatistic state at the time he allegedly committed the criminal acts charged is a question of fact. Appellant's theory of the case should have been presented to the jury if there was substantial evidence in the record to support it.

It is the function and province of the jury to weigh evidence and determine credibility of witnesses and decide disputed questions of fact. However, a court should not submit to the jury an issue of fact unless there is substantial evidence in the record to support it.

We find that the evidence presented was insufficient to present the issue of defendant's unconscious or automatistic state at the time of the act to the jury. There is no evidence, circumstantial or otherwise from which the jury could determine or reasonably infer what happened in the room at the time of the stabbing; the jury could only speculate on the existence of the triggering stimulus. . . .

NOTES & QUESTIONS ON VOLUNTARINESS

1. *Post-traumatic stress disorder.* Should returning combat veterans be permitted to argue that psychological afflictions made their actions involuntary? There are many elements of PTSD, but they include flashbacks "in which the individual feels or acts as if the traumatic event(s) were recurring" as well as behavior changes including "angry outbursts . . . reckless or self-destructive behavior, hypervigilance, and exaggerated startle response. . . ." *Diagnostic and Statistical Manual of Mental Disorders* (DSM) 309.81 (5th ed. 2013). In describing its diagnostic features, the DSM refers to "exposure to war as a combatant or civilian" as the very first example of a triggering event. Are actions produced or colored by PTSD "involuntary" or is it a mental condition that should be evaluated under the insanity plea? See Melissa Hamilton, *Reinvigorating Actus Reus: The Case for Involuntary Actions by Veterans with Post-Traumatic Stress Disorder*, 16 Berkeley J. Crim. L. 340, 387 (2011) ("Empirical

evidence substantially supports the perspective that the stress of war trauma has impaired the cognitive, physiological, and behavioral functioning of veterans with PTSD to the extent that some of their aggressive actions may be deprived of any internal component of voluntariness, will, or control."). Compare with Erin M. Gover, *Iraq as a Psychological Quagmire: The Implications of Using Post-Traumatic Stress Disorder as a Defense for Iraq War Veterans*, 28 Pace L. Rev. 561, 579 (2008) ("unconsciousness defense is only available to those who experience dissociative flashbacks as a symptom of PTSD"). Do you believe that the actions of a former soldier who "snapped" because of PTSD could be described as involuntary?

2. *Sleepwalking.* Consider the defendant who commits a crime while sleepwalking. Courts generally permit defendants to argue this to the jury if there is sufficient factual evidence presented at trial to support the claim. However, they are split on how to characterize the argument. First, it could be viewed as a denial of the voluntary act requirement implicit in almost any criminal offense and part of the prosecution's case-in-chief. This is the most common approach. In a few jurisdictions, it could be couched as a form of mental illness or insanity and judged under the regular standards for insanity as an excuse. See, e.g., *United States v. Harvey*, 66 M.J. 585, 588 (U.S.A.F. Ct. Crim. App. 2008). Third, in a few jurisdictions, it could be viewed as its own affirmative defense based on a state of unconsciousness. See, e.g., *Fulcher v. State*, 633 P.2d 142, 147 (Wyo. 1981); *Riley v. Commonwealth*, 277 Va. 467 (2009). In practice, it can be hard to determine after the fact whether someone was sleepwalking. The mere fact that someone does not remember the incident is not dispositive of their state of consciousness when they committed the act. They could, for example, be aware of their actions at the moment of commission but later forget what they did. See *People v. Rogers*, 39 Cal. 4th 826 (2007). In *Rogers*, the defendant was a sheriff's deputy who shot and killed a 20-year-old woman and a 15-year-old woman on two separate occasions. A psychiatrist testified that the defendant did not remember the shootings. The trial court refused to instruct the jury on the issue of unconsciousness, and the California Supreme Court upheld the decision because lack of memory did not entail that the defendant was not aware of his actions at the moment he performed them. *Rogers*, 39 Cal. 4th at 887.

3. *Hypnosis and seizures.* The Model Penal Code includes a specific provision declaring that "conduct during hypnosis or resulting from hypnotic suggestion" is not voluntary. See MPC § 2.01. As for seizures, courts generally permit defendants to argue that epilepsy or some other condition caused the prohibited bodily movement. See *Virgin Islands v. Smith*, 278 F.2d 169, 174 (3d Cir. 1960) (defendant argued that epileptic seizure caused fatal automobile accident). Also, a man's conviction for telephone harassment was overturned

because he suffered from Tourette's Syndrome. See *People v. Nelson*, 2 N.E.3d 613 (3d Dist. Ill. 2013). In *Nelson*, the court concluded that the defendant's utterances, which included repeated lewd comments, were involuntary because he "was not taking his medication at the time he made the phone calls and therefore he could not control his tics." Could the voluntary act requirement be satisfied in this case because the defendant failed to take his medication? According to the court: No, because "Nelson's failure to take his medication constitutes an omission, not an action. 'Not taking his pills' was not an affirmative act. Rather, Nelson engaged in nonaction—he simply did not take medication." *Id.* at 621. Nelson's omission could not be considered a voluntary act because omissions are only penalized by the law if the defendant was under a preexisting obligation or duty under the law to perform the action. According to the court, Nelson had no obligation to take his medication. Do you agree? Do patients have a duty to take medication to lower or eliminate the risk that their unconscious behavior will harm others?

4. *Possession*. Drug cases involve the possession of a particular type of contraband, usually a narcotic, and juries convict defendants every day for possessing drugs. For example, New York Penal Law § 220.21 states that "A person is guilty of criminal possession of a controlled substance in the first degree when he or she knowingly and unlawfully possesses: 1. one or more preparations, compounds, mixtures or substances containing a narcotic drug and said preparations, compounds, mixtures or substances are of an aggregate weight of eight ounces or more . . . ." Is the state of possession an act? If yes, it is an odd kind of act (as opposed to *receiving* stolen goods, for example). The Model Penal Code has a specific provision declaring that "possession is an act, within the meaning of this Section, if the possessor knowingly procured or received the thing possessed or was aware of his control thereof for a sufficient period to have been able to terminate his possession." MPC § 2.01(4). Does the MPC provision suggest that the voluntary act requirement is illusory (or at the very least exaggerated) and that the criminal law can be based on the defendant's "control" instead? See Andrew Ashworth, *The Unfairness of Risk-Based Possession Offences*, 5 Crim. L. & Phil. 237, 241 (2011). For more discussion, see Markus Dirk Dubber, *Policing Possession: The War on Crime and the End of Criminal Law*, 91 J. Crim. L. & Criminology 829, 859-60 (2001) ("Possession . . . does away with the traditional requirement that criminal liability must be predicated on an actus reus, an affirmative act or at least a failure to act (rather than a status, like being in possession of something)."). In some limited circumstances, courts have been willing to impose limitations on the theory of possession-as-an-act. See, e.g., *State v. Murphy*, 2010 WL 1254267 (Ct. App. Ohio 2010) (drug possession was involuntary when car driver threw drugs at his passenger as police approached).

PROBLEM CASES

Consider the following two cases:

Lindy Deer was a 52-year-old woman charged and convicted of third-degree rape for allegedly having sex with a 15-year-old boy named R.R. The relationship began when R.R. moved in with his aunt, for whom Deer was working as an administrative assistant. Deer started giving R.R. "kissing lessons," which eventually evolved into sex. R.R. revealed the relationship to an official at school and Deer was subsequently arrested. See *State v. Deer*, 175 Wash. 2d 725 (2012).

Deer argued that she was asleep during several of the sexual acts; since she did not act with volition, she could not be guilty of rape. The Washington statute governing rape of a child in the third degree reads: "A person is guilty of rape of a child in the third degree when the person has sexual intercourse with another who is at least fourteen years old but less than sixteen years old and not married to the perpetrator and the perpetrator is at least forty-eight months older than the victim." RCW 9A.44.079(1). This is commonly called "statutory rape" because the charge is based on the age of the victim and the consent or lack of consent of the victim is legally irrelevant.

Should Deer have been permitted to argue involuntariness to the jury? On appeal, the Washington Supreme Court concluded that Deer could argue a lack of conscious action, but also concluded that her claim of "sleep sex" should be treated as an affirmative defense, just like intoxication or insanity, with the burden of proof resting with the defense. Her conviction was upheld. Is this the correct result? Is voluntary action a logical prerequisite for the government's case? Does the result depend on the underlying statute in question, which in this case was a statutory rape provision based on strict liability?

In contrast, Kenneth Parks was acquitted by a jury in Canada after attacking his father-in-law and killing his mother-in-law. Although Parks drove a car 14 miles to get to the site of the murder, he claimed that he was sleepwalking during the entire encounter, including the drive, and he seemed unaware of his own injuries when he presented himself to the local police station in a dazed and confused state after the murders. A jury acquitted him of all charges. The prosecution appealed the acquittal (which is allowed in Canada) and argued that he should have been found not guilty by reason of insanity and committed to an asylum. The Supreme Court of Canada disagreed and held that this was a case of non-insane automatism. *R. v. Parks*, 2 S.C.R. 871 (1992).

Kenneth Parks

2. Omissions

As noted above, an omission can only be the basis for a criminal prosecution if the defendant owed a duty to act. As you read the following case, examine the *source* of the defendant's legal duty to act and ask yourself whether you agree with the court's analysis of the relationship between the defendants and the victim.

Commonwealth v. Pestinikas

Superior Court of Pennsylvania
617 A.2d 1339 (1992)

WIEAND, JUDGE:

The principal issue in this appeal is whether a person can be prosecuted criminally for murder when his or her failure to perform a contract to provide food and medical care for another has caused the death of such other person. The trial court answered this question in the affirmative and instructed the jury accordingly. The jury thereafter found Walter and Helen Pestinikas guilty of murder of the third degree in connection with the starvation and dehydration death of ninety-two (92) year old Joseph Kly. On direct appeal from the judgment of sentence, the defendants contend that the trial court misapplied the law and gave the jury incorrect instructions. . . .

Joseph Kly met Walter and Helen Pestinikas in the latter part of 1981 when Kly consulted them about pre-arranging his funeral. In March, 1982, Kly, who had been living with a stepson, was hospitalized and diagnosed as suffering from Zenker's diverticulum, a weakness in the walls of the esophagus, which caused him to have trouble swallowing food. In the hospital, Kly was given food which he was able to swallow and, as a result, regained some of the weight which he had lost. When he was about to be discharged, he expressed a desire not to return to his stepson's home and sent word to appellants that he wanted to speak with them. As a consequence, arrangements were made for appellants to care for Kly in their home on Main Street in Scranton, Lackawanna County.

Kly was discharged from the hospital on April 12, 1982. When appellants came for him on that day they were instructed by medical personnel regarding the care which was required for Kly and were given a prescription to have filled for him. Arrangements were also made for a visiting nurse to come to appellants' home to administer vitamin B-12 supplements to Kly. Appellants agreed orally to follow the medical instructions and to supply Kly with food, shelter, care and the medicine which he required.

According to the evidence, the prescription was never filled, and the visiting nurse was told by appellants that Kly did not want the vitamin supplement shots and that her services, therefore, were not required. Instead of giving Kly a room in their home, appellants removed him to a rural part of Lackawanna County, where they placed him in the enclosed porch of a building, which they owned, known as the Stage Coach Inn. This porch was approximately nine feet by thirty feet, with no insulation, no refrigeration, no bathroom, no sink and no telephone. The walls contained cracks which exposed the room to outside weather conditions. Kly's predicament was compounded by appellants' affirmative efforts to conceal his whereabouts. Thus, they gave misleading information in response to inquiries, telling members of Kly's family that they did not know where he had gone and others that he was living in their home.

After Kly was discharged from the hospital, appellants took Kly to the bank and had their names added to his savings account. Later, Kly's money was transferred into an account in the names of Kly or Helen Pestinikas, pursuant to which moneys could be withdrawn without Kly's signature. Bank records reveal that from May, 1982, to July, 1983, appellants withdrew amounts roughly consistent with the three hundred ($300) dollars per month which Kly had agreed to pay for his care. Beginning in August, 1983 and continuing until Kly's death in November, 1984, however, appellants withdrew much larger sums so that when Kly died, a balance of only fifty-five ($55) dollars remained. In the interim, appellants had withdrawn in excess of thirty thousand ($30,000) dollars.

On the afternoon of November 15, 1984, when police and an ambulance crew arrived in response to a call by appellants, Kly's dead body appeared emaciated, with his ribs and sternum greatly pronounced. Mrs. Pestinikas told police that she and her husband had taken care of Kly for three hundred ($300) dollars per month and that she had given him cookies and orange juice at 11:30 A.M. on the morning of his death. A subsequent autopsy, however, revealed that Kly had been dead at that time and may have been dead for as many as thirty-nine (39) hours before his body was found. The cause of death was determined to be starvation and dehydration. Expert testimony opined that Kly would have experienced pain and suffering over a long period of time before he died.

At trial, the Commonwealth contended that after contracting orally to provide food, shelter, care and necessary medicine for Kly, appellants engaged in a course of conduct calculated to deprive Kly of those things necessary to maintain life and thereby cause his death. The trial court instructed the jury that appellants could not be found guilty of a malicious killing for failing to provide food, shelter and necessary medicines to Kly unless a duty to do so had been imposed upon them by contract. . . . Appellants contend that this was error.

The applicable law appears at 18 Pa.C.S. § 301(a) and (b) as follows:

(a) General rule.—A person is not guilty of an offense unless his liability is based on conduct which includes a voluntary act or the omission to perform an act of which he is physically capable.

(b) Omission as basis of liability.—Liability for the commission of an offense may not be based on an omission unaccompanied by action unless:

(1) the omission is expressly made sufficient by the law defining the offense; or

(2) a duty to perform the omitted act is otherwise imposed by law.

With respect to subsection (b), Toll, in his invaluable work on the Pennsylvania Crimes Code, has commented:

> . . . [Subsection (b)] states the conventional position with respect to omissions unaccompanied by action as a basis of liability. Unless the omission is expressly made sufficient by the law defining the offense, a duty to perform the omitted act must have been otherwise imposed by law for the omission to have the same standing as a voluntary act for purposes of liability. *It should, of course, suffice, as the courts now hold, that the duty arises under some branch of the civil law. If it does, this minimal requirement is satisfied, though whether the omission constitutes an offense depends as well on many other factors.*

Toll, Pennsylvania Crimes Code Annotated, § 301, at p. 60, quoting Comment, Model Penal Code § 2.01 (emphasis added).

In *State v. Brown*, 129 Ariz. 347, 631 P.2d 129 (1981), the Court of Appeals for Arizona affirmed a manslaughter conviction of the operator of a boarding home in connection with the starvation death of a ninety-eight year old resident. . . . A similar rationale was employed by the Supreme Court of Virginia in *Davis v. Commonwealth*, 230 Va. 201, 335 S.E.2d 375 (1985), which upheld the conviction of a woman for involuntary manslaughter in the death by starvation and exposure of her elderly mother. The *Davis* Court held that the evidence had established the breach of an implied contract to care for her mother, in return for which the defendant had been permitted to live in her mother's home and share her mother's social security benefits. . . .

Consistently with this legal thinking we hold that when, in 18 Pa. C.S. § 301(b)(2), the statute provides that an omission to do an act can be the basis for criminal liability if a duty to perform the omitted act has been imposed by law, the legislature intended to distinguish between a legal duty to act and merely a moral duty to act. A duty to act imposed by contract is legally enforceable and, therefore, creates a legal duty. It follows that a failure to perform a duty imposed by contract may be the basis for a charge of criminal homicide if such failure causes the death of another person and all other elements of the offense are present. Because there was evidence in the instant case that Kly's death had been caused by appellants' failure to provide the food and medical care which they had agreed by oral contract to provide for him, their omission to act was sufficient to support a conviction for criminal homicide, and the trial court was correct when it instructed the jury accordingly.

Our holding is not that every breach of contract can become the basis for a finding of homicide resulting from an omission to act. A criminal act involves both a physical and mental aspect. An omission to act can satisfy the physical aspect of criminal conduct only if there is a duty to act imposed by law. A failure to provide food and medicine, in this case, could not have been made the basis for prosecuting a stranger who learned of Kly's condition and failed to act. Even where there is a duty imposed by contract, moreover, the omission to act will not support a prosecution for homicide in the absence of the necessary mens rea. For murder, there must be malice. Without a malicious intent, an omission to perform duties having their foundation in contract cannot support a conviction for murder. In the instant case, therefore, the jury was required to find that appellants, by virtue of contract, had undertaken responsibility for providing necessary care for Kly to the exclusion of the members of Kly's family. This would impose upon them a legal duty to act to preserve Kly's life. If they maliciously set upon a course of withholding food and medicine and thereby caused Kly's death, appellants could be found guilty of murder. . . .

NOTES & QUESTIONS ON OMISSIONS

1. *Contract.* How much does it matter that the court in *Pestinikas* construed the arrangement as a formal contract? What if the appellants were viewed as mere babysitters? Presumably a babysitter works for money and pursuant to an implicit contract for remuneration, but not always. Sometimes a "babysitter" is just someone who plays with a child. Would the result in *Pestinikas* have changed if the oral contract was invalid or unenforceable under that jurisdiction's law of contracts? In *Florio v. State*, Texas prosecutors charged a man with injury of a child by omission because it was unclear who had harmed the baby. He was convicted and sentenced to 60 years in prison. Florio was the mother's live-in boyfriend. Texas Penal Code § 6.01 provides that a person commits an offense if he "voluntarily engages in conduct, including an act, omission, or possession." A mid-level appeals court upheld the conviction because Florio had "assumed responsibility" for the child. 758 S.W.2d 351, 354 (1988). But the conviction was later reversed when a higher court concluded that

although Florio was a "babysitter, disciplinarian and caretaker of the deceased," he had no legal duty to care for the child because he was not a parent. See *Florio v. State*, 784 S.W.2d 415 (Tex. Ct. Crim. App. 1990). Does it seem odd that if Florio had accepted money in exchange for caring for the child, the result would have been different? Perhaps Florio should be responsible under a theory of "voluntary assumption of care" and his relationship to the mother was irrelevant.

2. *Families, de jure and de facto.*   Parents always have a legal duty toward their minor children. Other adults in a position of *in loco parentis*, including foster parents, have the same duties to their young charges, and can be prosecuted for failing to stop child abuse. But consider the case of Melissa Norris, a young mother who was suffering from mental illness and caring for a three-month-old child. A Good Samaritan named Joyce Lillian Pope provided Norris and her child shelter for the weekend. Norris was seriously disturbed (claiming she was God) and beat her child during the weekend, and Pope never intervened or called the police. When the child died, Pope was charged with child abuse. The Maryland Court of Appeals overturned the conviction against Pope because the mother was always present and the child was never officially left in Pope's care. "It would be most incongruous that acts of hospitality and kindness, made out of common decency and prompted by sincere concern for the well-being of a mother and her child, subjected the Good Samaritan to criminal prosecution for abusing the very child he sought to look after. . . ." *Pope v. State*, 396 A.2d 1054 (Maryland, 1979). Is this the correct result? If you were a creative prosecutor, what arguments could you make regarding the mother's presence? Was she really *present* in a deeper sense, given her obvious mental infirmity?

3. *Spouses.*   Are spouses responsible for providing assistance to each other? Normally the case law deals with children, who are by definition vulnerable. But sick or injured spouses can also be vulnerable. What is the source of the legal duty? Consider the oft-quoted wedding vow "in sickness and in health." See *State v. Mally*, 366 P.2d 868 (Mont. 1961) (husband guilty of involuntary manslaughter for not fetching medical assistance for wife with kidney disease who fell and broke her arms). What if the two individuals are not married? Compare *People v. Beardsley*, 113 N.W. 1128 (Mich. 1907) (married man did not owe a duty to care for another woman with whom he engaged in a non-family relationship), with *State ex rel. Kuntz v. Montana Thirteenth Judicial Dist. Court*, 995 P.2d 951 (Mont. 2000) (duty applied to unmarried couple living together for six years). Should the result depend on whether a state recognizes common law marriage?

4. *Terminating medical treatment.*   Patients in medical hospitals sometimes die from the *lack* of medical treatment. Courts generally treat these cases as omissions. In *Barber v. Superior Court*, 147 Cal. App. 3d

[handwritten margin note: Argue: The children were in her care — in her residence — especially b/c mother unstable]

HYPOTHETICAL

Some omission cases involve intoxicated individuals who eventually die of alcohol poisoning. Consider the following hypothetical. A college student who belongs to a fraternity goes out for an evening of drinking. He later returns to the fraternity house in an intoxicated state and passes out. His fraternity brothers put him on a couch and do not check on him again. He dies from alcohol poisoning in the middle of the night. Did his fraternity brothers have a duty to call an ambulance or take him the hospital? Does their "fraternity brother" relationship impose any special obligations on them toward each other?

1006 (1983), two doctors were charged with murder and conspiracy to commit murder for withdrawing life support from a patient. The patient, Clarence Herbert, had suffered cardiorespiratory arrest after recuperating from surgery, and was left in a persistent vegetative state. Were the doctors criminally liable for removing his IV feeding tube? The court analyzed the case as an *omission* of medical nutrition and hydration, which would only be criminal if there were an underlying duty. The court concluded that while doctors are usually under a legal duty to provide treatment to their patients, a "physician has no duty to continue treatment, once it has proven to be ineffective." Since there was no chance that Herbert could recover, the doctors had no legal duty to continue treatment.

5. *Acts and omissions.* Reconsider the *Barber* case. Why does the withdrawal of the breathing tube have to be an omission? Could it be re-described as an act (pulling out the tube)? Indeed, perhaps every omission could be re-described as some kind of act. At least one scholar thinks that we should make up a new word to describe them. See Luis E. Chiesa, *Actmissions*, 116 W. Va. L. Rev. 581 (2014) ("An actmission is conduct that is both active and omissive in morally relevant ways. Actmissions are active because they include a willed bodily movement that contributes significantly to causing harm, yet omissive because they entail a failure to do something that would prevent harm from materializing."). According to Chiesa, the act-omission dichotomy is reductive and ultimately unhelpful for facilitating legal analysis. In response, he suggests a three-tiered approach with acts, omissions, and actmissions as a hybrid category. Under this view, actmissions are more culpable than omissions, but less culpable than affirmative acts. Actmissions would include situations where a doctor turns off a life support machine for a patient, or a mountain climber lets go of a fellow climber in distress instead of pulling him to safety. Do you agree that the act-omission dichotomy is ultimately unhelpful and requires revision?

Review the casebook video, *People v. Robert Dale* (Part 1: Acts and Omissions). Was the defendant, Robert Dale, under a legal obligation to assist his neighbor? If yes, what was the source of that obligation? If not, is it appropriate for Robert Dale to escape criminal liability for his omission? If you were the prosecutor, what is the best argument you could make to establish a legal duty to act?

3. Bystanders

Bystanders usually fall under the rule for omissions—they are not liable for doing nothing unless they had a duty to act. Consequently, they are rarely charged. But in rare cases, a prosecutor might try to stretch the legal categories in order to establish criminal liability for the bystander. One way is to suggest that the bystander "encouraged" the crime and in so doing became an accomplice. Another way is to squeeze the facts of the case into one of the defined legal categories that establishes a relationship between the defendant and the victim (and thus a duty to act). As you read the following case, ask yourself whether you agree with the court's evaluation of these legal positions.

State v. Davis

Supreme Court of Appeals of West Virginia
388 S.E.2d 508 (1989)

Miller, Justice:

The principal issue in this appeal is whether there was sufficient evidence to sustain the conviction of the defendant, Dewey Davis, for the offense of second-degree sexual assault. The defendant was also convicted of abduction and first-degree sexual abuse. The State acknowledges that since the defendant aided and abetted Gerald Davis, his son, in these crimes, it is bound by our holding in *State v. Davis,* 180 W. Va. 357, 376 S.E.2d 563 (1988). In that decision, we held that the abduction and first-degree sexual abuse convictions were invalid.

The State's position is that while the abduction and sexual abuse convictions must be set aside, the conviction of second-degree sexual assault is valid. . . .

The salient facts are that on February 18, 1986, the victim, who was a close friend of the Davis family, went to the defendant's mobile home to pick up her laundry. While she was in the defendant's home, the defendant's son, Gerald Davis, followed her to the laundry room and asked her to go with him to his bedroom. She refused and Gerald tried to force her to come with him to the bedroom. In an attempt to get away from Gerald, she ran to the living room and pleaded with the defendant to help her. The defendant, who had been drinking, told her he could not help her. She tried to keep the defendant between Gerald and herself, but the defendant moved out of the way. Gerald then dragged her down the hall and into the bedroom. The defendant followed his son and the victim into the bedroom and lay next to them on the bed while Gerald raped her. Although she pleaded with the defendant to help her, the defendant merely patted her hand and told her not to worry.

We reject the defendant's contention that under the foregoing facts, he was not chargeable with the sexual assault committed by his son. We recently discussed, at some length, the sufficiency of the evidence to convict a person who is not the principal perpetrator in *State v. Fortner*, 387 S.E.2d 812 (1989). We outlined in *Fortner* the traditional roles of parties to a crime. We also indicated that, based on *State v. Petry*, 273 S.E.2d 346 (1980), and W. Va. Code, 61-11-6 (1923), a conviction could be obtained so long as the evidence showed that the defendant fit any one of these roles. We defined these categories in Syllabus Points 5 and 6 of *Fortner:*

> 5. A person who is the absolute perpetrator of a crime is a principal in the first degree, and a person who is present, aiding and abetting the fact to be done, is a principal in the second degree.
>
> 6. An accessory before the fact is a person who being absent at the time and place of the crime, procures, counsels, commands, incites, assists or abets another person to commit the crime, and absence at the time and place of the crime is an essential element of the status of an accessory before the fact.

Additionally, in *Fortner,* we dealt with the types of conduct that bear upon criminal culpability. These were summarized in Syllabus Points 9, 10, and 11:

> 9. Merely witnessing a crime, without intervention, does not make a person a party to its commission unless his interference was a duty, and his noninterference was one of the conditions of the commission of the crime; or unless his noninterference was designed by him and operated as an encouragement to or protection of the perpetrator.
>
> 10. Proof that the defendant was present at the time and place the crime was committed is a factor to be considered by the jury in determining guilt, along with other circumstances, such as the defendant's association with or relation to the perpetrator and his conduct before and after the commission of the crime.

Under the concerted action principle, a defendant who is present at the scene of a crime and, by acting with another, contributes to the criminal act, is criminally liable for such offense as if he were the sole perpetrator.

Syllabus Point 9 of *Fortner* holds that merely witnessing a crime without interference is not culpable. Here, however, the defendant was not merely an unconnected passive bystander. The assault occurred in his home, and his son was the perpetrator. Furthermore, the victim looked upon the defendant as a family member because of her long association with him and referred to him as "Uncle Dewey."

The victim initially tried to get the defendant to intervene by pleading with him to help her and positioning herself behind him and away from his son. Yet, the defendant responded that he could not help her and moved out of Gerald's way. When she was dragged into the bedroom by Gerald, the defendant followed. He lay on the bed next to them watching Gerald rape her and patted her hand while advising her not to worry. These actions were sufficient to make him culpable.

Other jurisdictions have come to the same conclusion on similar facts. In both *State v. Goodwin,* 118 N.H. 862 (1978), and *Commonwealth v. Henderson,* 249 Pa. Super. 472 (1977), neither of the defendants actually participated in the sexual assaults of the victims, but had sat by passively while their companions sexually assaulted the victims. The courts, in both cases, concluded that the evidence was sufficient to support the jury's findings that the defendant's presence facilitated and encouraged the perpetrator's actions. *See also Diaz v. State,* 444 N.E.2d 340 (Ind. App. 1983); *Sutton v. Commonwealth,* 228 Va. 654 (1985); *State v. McBee,* 644 S.W.2d 425 (Tenn. Crim. App. 1982). Thus, we find sufficient evidence before us to support the defendant's conviction as a principal in the second degree to second-degree sexual assault.

NOTES & QUESTIONS ON BYSTANDER LIABILITY

1. *Witnesses and encouragement.* Explain the different results in *Davis* and the Richmond High School case. Why did the police not charge the witnesses in the high school attack? Some media reports suggested that some witnesses at the school took videos on their cell phones. Could this be considered a form of tacit encouragement? What was the source of the defendant's duty to act in *Davis*? Did he have a duty to act because he witnessed the attack? Or because it took place in his home? Or because the victim thought of him as family? For an argument that states should impose criminal liability for witnessing a gang rape, see Allen, *supra,* at 840 ("states should adopt a new approach to gang rape that considers gang rapists' motivations and recognizes the nature of the crime as one that involves a group"). Allen notes that several jurisdictions have passed statutes penalizing the attendance and witnessing of an illegal drag race. Courts have upheld convictions under these statutes. See *Commonwealth v. Holstein,* 927

PROBLEM CASE

On the evening of October 24, 2009, police responded to a report of a disturbance in the courtyard of Richmond High School in California. What they found shocked them. A 15-year-old girl was naked, unconscious, and badly beaten. According to police, she had been gang-raped in a dimly lit area of the campus over the course of two and a half hours while a homecoming dance was held in the school gymnasium.

Richmond High School

According to news reports, as many as 20 people may have witnessed the assault but did nothing to stop it or report it to the police. One witness told a reporter: "They were kicking her in her head and they were beating her up, robbing her and ripping her clothes off; it's something you can't get out your mind . . . . I saw people, like, dehumanizing her; I saw some pretty crazy stuff." Another witness said: "She was pretty quiet; I thought she was like dead for a minute but then I saw her moving around, I was like, 'Oh,' . . . I really wanted to help her but I don't know, I just didn't . . . . I feel like I could have done something but I don't feel like I have any responsibility for anything that happened." See Cecilia Vegna, *Richmond Rape Witness Describes the Assault*, ABC7news.com, Nov. 12, 2009.

Several men were charged and went on trial for perpetrating the assault, though in keeping with the American bystander rule, none of the witnesses were charged. Should the law be changed to impose a statutory duty to rescue? See Kimberley K. Allen, *Guilt by (More Than) Association: The Case for Spectator Liability in Gang Rapes*, 99 Geo. L.J. 837 (2011).

A.2d 628, 2007 Pa. Super. 184 (2007). If a jurisdiction can penalize watching a drag race, why not pass a similar statute for watching a gang rape? See also *Arredondo v. State*, 270 S.W.3d 676, 680 (Tex. Ct. App. 2008) ("[A]fter C.B. passed out, Arredondo raped her while everyone watched, laughed, and cheered him on. . . . This may be sufficient evidence to establish that the people who encouraged Arredondo or Maldonado committed some criminal activity, but we disagree that it is evidence that Arrendodo and Maldonado acted in concert to sexually assault C.B."), cited in Allen, *supra*, at 854.

2. *New statutory duties.* Although bystander liability is generally disfavored in American law, some states are bucking the trend and imposing liability, usually for a separate, lesser offense with a minor punishment. For

example, Florida recently passed a statute, F.S.A. § 794.027, imposing a duty to assist victims of sexual assault:

> A person who observes the commission of the crime of sexual battery and who:
>
> (1) Has reasonable grounds to believe that he or she has observed the commission of a sexual battery;
> (2) Has the present ability to seek assistance for the victim or victims by immediately reporting such offense to a law enforcement officer;
> (3) Fails to seek such assistance;
> (4) Would not be exposed to any threat of physical violence for seeking such assistance;
> (5) Is not the husband, wife, parent, grandparent, child, grandchild, brother, or sister of the offender or victim, by consanguinity or affinity; and
> (6) Is not the victim of such sexual battery
>
> is guilty of a misdemeanor of the first degree, punishable as provided in § 775.082 or § 775.083.

Apply this statute to the Richmond High School assault. If this statute applied in California, could the witnesses be prosecuted? Despite the majority rule in American jurisprudence, a few states do impose on bystanders a *general* duty to render assistance, usually when aid "can be rendered without danger or peril to himself or without interference with important duties owed to others." 12 V.S.A. § 519. Other statutes involve automobile accidents. R.I. Gen. Laws § 11-56-1. But other than these exceptions, bystanders generally cannot be prosecuted because they have not performed a voluntary act and their omissions are not subject to punishment in the absence of an underlying duty to act.

C. PRACTICE & POLICY

In every case, the prosecution must establish a voluntary act or an omission in violation of a preexisting duty to act. The following materials explore the strategic choices that prosecutors face in making their prima face case with regard to a voluntary act. We first examine a unique strategy where a prosecutor argued to the court that a defendant committed either an act *or* a culpable omission—but the prosecutor did not know which one. The section concludes with a reconsideration of sleepwalking and asks whether the failure to seek appropriate medical care could itself satisfy the voluntary act requirement.

❧ **The omission strategy.** How can a prosecutor use the omission doctrine to his or her advantage? One obvious situation is when the prosecutor cannot prove *who* committed the blameworthy act in a particular case. Consider the case of Eugene and Mary Wong. The Wongs were a New York City couple hired to provide 24-hour care for a baby named Kwok-Wei Jiang, whose parents both worked long hours and could not care for the child. The baby lived in the home of the Wongs and the parents would visit the baby one day a week. One night after a lengthy crying fit at the Wong home, Kwok-Wei became unresponsive and was taken to the hospital and declared dead. After forensic investigation, the police concluded that the baby died from internal brain injuries caused "by shaken baby syndrome" and that the Wongs must have violently shaken the baby.

The New York prosecutors had a problem. They could not establish whether it was Eugene or Mary who shook the baby. So the prosecutors proceeded under a novel theory: *Both* caretakers were responsible for manslaughter because it did not matter which one had shaken the baby. The one who performed the shaking was guilty of manslaughter for having performed the act, while the one who did not perform the shaking—the "passive" caretaker—was guilty under an omission theory for failing to render assistance to Kwok-Wei and not calling 911. Since both theories (act and omission) were sufficient to ground a manslaughter charge, the jury need not decide who committed the shaking. The New York State Court of Appeals agreed with the general theory because both individuals, as hired caretakers, were under a legal duty to care for the child. See *People v. Wong*, 619 N.E.2d 377 (N.Y. 1993).

As a defense attorney, which arguments could be marshaled against this legal strategy? Was the "passive" caretaker—whoever it was—under sufficient notice that something was wrong and that Kwok-Wei needed urgent medical attention? Shaken Baby Syndrome can be hard to spot with the naked eye by someone without medical training. A baby suffering from the syndrome will stop crying and eventually lapse into a coma, though at a quick glance this state could be confused with sleep. So the "passive" caretaker might have assumed that the baby had simply stopped crying and fallen back asleep. The only clue to the baby's real neurological state would be a sustained observation of the child to see if it was subtly moving around as is typical during sleep. The Court of Appeals ultimately concluded that these doubts were fatal to the case:

> Accordingly, we conclude that the convictions of both defendants must be reversed even though that conclusion means that one clearly guilty party will go free. The result in this case is an especially difficult one because of the heinousness of the crime as well as the evident culpability of one of the two appealing parties. Nonetheless, we are duty bound to reverse these two defendants'

convictions because the alternative—incarcerating both individuals for a crime of which only one is demonstrably culpable—is an unacceptable option in a system that is based on personal accountability and presumes each accused to be innocent until proven otherwise.

Wong, 619 N.E.2d at 383. Do you agree with the court's decision? Did the prosecutor make a strategic error by relying on omission—or was there no other choice? Can you imagine a different case where the omission strategy might work better for a prosecutor? Incidentally, some doctors and experts who previously diagnosed shaken baby syndrome now question the validity of the medical diagnosis. See Debbie Cenziper, *Prosecutors Build Murder Cases on Disputed Shaken Baby Syndrome Diagnosis*, Wash. Post, Mar. 20, 2015 ("Testing has been unable to show whether violent shaking can produce the bleeding and swelling long attributed to the diagnosis, and doctors have found that accidents and diseases can trigger identical conditions in babies.").

∾ **Sleepwalking redux.**   In 2009, a British man named Brian Thomas stood trial for murdering his wife while they slept in a camper trailer. Thomas claimed that he had a dream that he was being attacked by intruders and killed his wife during this dream state. After medical experts validated his claim that he suffered from night terrors, the prosecution argued that he should be declared not guilty by reason of insanity and institutionalized. But the jury eventually declared him not guilty under a theory of sane automatism and he was released. See Steven Morris, *Devoted Husband Who Strangled Wife in His Sleep Walks Free from Court*, The Guardian, Nov. 20, 2009. Does it make a difference if there was a history of sleepwalking or night terrors? There was evidence that Thomas had suffered from sleep disturbances for 50 years. Could a prosecutor in a similar case argue that a defendant, put on notice of violent sleep behavior, had a duty to get medical treatment, and that failure to get medical treatment or take necessary precautions (such as sleeping in separate rooms) might be the basis for a criminal conviction? As a defense attorney, how would you rebut this argument?

CHAPTER 6

———⟨⟨∅∅⟩⟩———

MENTAL STATES

A. DOCTRINE

With very few exceptions, an act is only criminal if it is performed in accordance with a culpable mental state. This is an ancient requirement expressed in the Latin maxim *actus non facit reum nisi mens sit rea*, or "an act does not make a person guilty unless his mind (or intention) is guilty." *Black's Law Dictionary* 1617 (7th ed. 1999). A more modern expression of the same principle would be *nullem crimen sine culpa*, or "no crime without culpability," a maxim that is often described as the principle of culpability. These phrases link culpability with the inner blameworthiness necessary for punishment. In order to make punishment morally justified, the actor's mind must have displayed a culpable mental state while performing the prohibited action. This culpable mental state is often called mens rea.

It is important to distinguish mens rea from motive, because the terms are often confused in the popular imagination. Mens rea is the particular mental state that accompanied the defendant's action: Did the defendant commit the act intentionally or was it a reckless accident? Was the defendant aware of the risk that his behavior imposed on others? These are all mental attitudes that are the domain of mens rea. In contrast, motive is the *why*: The defendant committed murder to gain the life insurance money, or revenge for a prior misdeed, for example. As a practical matter, motive can be indirect evidence of mens rea. So if the prosecutor convinces a jury that the defendant killed the victim for insurance money, this entails that the defendant committed the killing intentionally.

Mental states also perform another essential function in the criminal law: They provide a scheme for distinguishing between levels of culpability. The offenses codified by criminal law include higher and lower offenses, and the goal of the criminal law is not simply to define which acts are criminal but also which acts are *more* blameworthy than others. This helps to reduce the guesswork in punishment. If crimes fall on some hierarchy from most to least blameworthy, it is at least plausible to suggest that (all other things being equal), the least blameworthy offenses receive lighter sentences, and the most blameworthy offenses received higher sentences. The underlying mental states of each offense begin that conversation (though other factors are no doubt relevant too). Of course, an offense's relatively severity (compared to other offenses) is based on far more than just its associated mental state. But that being said, a structured approach to mental states promotes coherence in the doctrine that might, in turn, promote sensible and just sentencing outcomes.

Historically, courts and statutes in different jurisdictions used different terms to explain the various mental states, or worse yet, similar words to express different concepts, leading to immense confusion over the difference between the various mental states. At common law, convicting a defendant for certain felonies required that the defendant acted with *malice*, a large and somewhat imprecise term encompassing various mental states and normative judgments about the defendant's state of mind.

In contrast, the drafting of the Model Penal Code in 1962 was a major attempt to harmonize the confusing landscape of mental states with a consistent terminology across different jurisdictions, and to get beyond the concept of malice in favor of more precise categories. Although not every jurisdiction has adopted the Model Penal Code provision on mental states, the new terminology is by far one of the most influential and successful reforms crafted by the model code. It quickly provides a common set of terms and definitions for scholars and practitioners alike. The basic categories of mens rea recognized by the Model Penal Code include:

1. Acting purposely;
2. Acting knowingly;
3. Acting recklessly; and
4. Acting negligently.

1. Malice

Although courts often defined malice differently, typical definitions for malice included acting with a "wicked" motive or with an "evil" intent. However, defining malice by referring to value-laden concepts like wickedness or evil was, of course, shockingly imprecise, and seemed to offer limited guidance to juries. Over time, courts tried to add greater precision to their definitions of malice. For example, in the classic case of *Regina v. Cunningham*, 2 Q.B. 396 (1957), the defendant was arrested for ripping a gas meter from the basement of a house and stealing it (and the coins inside of it). Cunningham's removal of the gas meter caused a gas leak that sickened and endangered a neighbor. In order for the defendant to be convicted for endangering the life of the neighbor through poisonous gas, the judge instructed the jury that the law required that the defendant acted maliciously. In defining malice, the trial judge stated: "'Malicious' for this purpose means wicked—something which he has no business to do and perfectly well knows it. 'Wicked' is as good a definition as any other which you would get." An appeals court overturned the conviction, concluding that this definition might confuse the jury into convicting the defendant simply because his decision to steal the gas meter was wicked. According to the appeals court, the defendant acted maliciously toward the victim only if he "foresaw that the removal of the gas meter might cause injury to someone but nevertheless removed it." The case is a good example of how some jurisdictions have sought to evolve the definition of malice from a wicked or evil state of mind to something more precise.

The concept of malice was especially important in murder prosecutions. For example, the classic common law definition of murder is a killing performed "with malice aforethought." Over time, courts added increasingly complex subdivisions to the category of malice, such as "express malice" versus "implied malice." As will be explored in greater depth in the chapter on murder, express malice involved the commission of a crime, such as murder, with the deliberate intention to bring about the victim's death. On the other hand, implied malice involved the defendant's indifference to a particular result brought about by a level of carelessness or inattention so severe that it demonstrated the defendant's malice. So, for example, shooting someone in the head was classified as express malice murder because the defendant intended the result. In contrast, causing someone's death by a horrific and avoidable accident might have been classified as implied malice murder.

Although the language of malice has waned and many jurisdictions no longer make reference to the concept, it still lingers in jurisdictions that cling to the older common law terminology. Consequently, lawyers and judges today still must grapple with the concept of malice and find a way to add clarity to an imprecise legal concept.

2. Acting Purposely

Historically, the bedrock principle for expressing culpability was the concept of *intent*, as in the distinction between intentional and unintentional killings. Unfortunately, the language of intent is fundamentally ambiguous because it is often unclear whether we are talking about intended actions or intended consequences. Consider the following situation. Say a perpetrator throws a grenade at victim A in an effort to kill him. This is clearly an intentional killing. But suppose a second, individual—call him victim B—is standing nearby and the perpetrator realizes that throwing the grenade at victim A will also kill victim B (perhaps because they are standing so close together). Is the killing of victim B also *intentional*? This question perplexed jurists for decades, in part because the language of intent is so ambiguous. In other words, the answer depends on what you mean by *intent*. That word has different meanings.

Enter now the Model Penal Code, which dissolved the ambiguity by de-emphasizing the language of "intent" in its description of mental states. In its place, the Model Penal Code offered two more specific categories, acting purposefully and acting knowingly. Usually, the mental states of purpose and knowledge explain the actor's attitude with regard to a particular result or circumstance element. In the example provided above, the two more specific categories would track the different attitudes regarding the killing of victim A and victim B. Specifically, the perpetrator would be acting with the purpose to bring about victim A's death (a result) because the purpose of his actions was to kill victim A. In contrast, the perpetrator would not be acting with the purpose to produce the death of B because although he is aware that his actions will inevitably kill B, he is indifferent to that result. Therefore, the perpetrator's mental state with regard to causing the death of B is one of knowledge.

The Model Penal Code provision on mental states, § 2.02, says that an individual acts purposely:

> (i) if the element involves the nature of his conduct or a result thereof, it is his conscious object to engage in conduct of that nature or to cause such a result; and
>
> (ii) if the element involves the attendant circumstances, he is aware of the existence of such circumstances or he believes or hopes that they exist.

The key phrase here is *conscious object*. The defendant desires to commit the act or produce the relevant result (depending on what the crime in question requires).

3. Acting Knowingly — *practically certain*

In the above hypothetical, the perpetrator acted *knowingly* in killing B, because he was aware that killing A would also involve the death of B (because the grenade would hit both of the victims given their proximity). The new Model Penal Code categories therefore sidestep the old common law conundrum of whether the act was performed intentionally—and replace that with two more precise questions: Was it performed with purpose and was it performed with knowledge? The Model Penal Code states that an individual acts knowingly:

> (i) if the element involves the nature of his conduct or the attendant circumstances, he is aware that his conduct is of that nature or that such circumstances exist; and
>
> (ii) if the element involves a result of his conduct, he is aware that it is practically certain that his conduct will cause such a result.

The key phrase here is *practically certain*. The perpetrator in the hypothetical above is aware that throwing the grenade is practically certain to strike and kill victim B, so the perpetrator's mens rea, as to the result, is knowledge. There is no mathematical formula for describing the level of probability embodied by the "practically certain" standard. It is a question of law application to fact for the fact finder to decide.

What of defendants who deliberately avoid acquiring incriminating information? The classic example is the drug courier who refuses to look in the trunk of his car so that he may profess ignorance of the contraband. The law declares such a person "willfully blind"—like an ostrich burying its head in the sand—and often provides that he can still be convicted for acting knowingly.

4. Recklessness and Negligence — *possibility*

In contrast to higher mental states such as purpose and knowledge, recklessness involves the defendant's awareness of the *possibility* that his or her behavior will cause a prohibited result. In other words, crimes of recklessness involve penalizing defendants for their risk-taking behavior. A classic example is involuntary manslaughter, which penalizes a defendant who engages in risky behavior that results in the death of another.

The difference between acting knowingly and recklessly is the likelihood that the prohibited result will occur. If the defendant is practically certain that the result will occur, he acts knowingly. If the defendant is aware of a strong possibility that the result might occur, he acts recklessly. Determining the exact level of risk required for crimes of recklessness is one of the most difficult areas of the criminal law.

So, the reckless defendant *consciously disregards* a *substantial and unjustifiable risk*. In the words of the Model Penal Code, the "risk must be of such a nature and degree that, considering the nature and purpose of the actor's conduct and the circumstances known to him, its disregard involves a gross deviation from the standard of conduct that a law-abiding person would observe in the actor's situation."

Negligence also involves the taking of a substantial and unjustified risk, but the defendant may be completely unaware of it. Instead, the law declares that he *should have been aware* of the risk and his "failure to perceive it, considering the nature and purpose of his conduct and the circumstances known to him, involves a gross deviation from the standard of care that a reasonable person would observe in the actor's situation." So, the distinction between recklessness and negligence is not the level of risk, but rather the defendant's *awareness* of the risk. In recklessness, the defendant is aware of the risk and somewhat callously decides to pursue the risky action nonetheless. In negligence, the defendant is not aware of the risk but should have been aware of it (because the defendant should have been more attentive).

5. Strict Liability Offenses

In rare circumstances, the law allows for the conviction of a perpetrator who acts without a culpable mental state. In that case, mens rea is largely irrelevant. Strict liability is most often found in regulatory offenses, with minor penalties, that have a public welfare rationale. Classic examples include medical and environmental regulations or the regulation of inherently dangerous materials (such as chemicals or some weapons). However, as will be explored below, strict liability offenses can be very controversial, since the defendant's fault or awareness of the situation is irrelevant to the criminal case. The argument in favor of strict liability offenses is that they place the onus on each individual to ensure that their behavior complies with the law and causes no harm to others. If the defendant does violate the law, he or she will be criminally responsible even if he or she was faultlessly unaware of the circumstances giving rise to the violation. Strict liability is harsh and is generally limited to minor offenses, though the Supreme Court has never articulated a constitutional limit on its use.

B. APPLICATION

1. Malice

What does malice mean? In the following case, Florida courts wrestled with the question of how to explain the concept to jurors. Does it simply mean that the defendant had a wicked or evil mind, or does it mean something more precise? Is the court's decision below consistent with the outcome in the *Cunningham* case described above? Is it appropriate for juries to convict defendants based on a requirement of "evil intent"?

Young v. State

District Court of Appeal of Florida
753 So. 2d 725 (2000)

WEBSTER, J.

In this direct criminal appeal, appellant challenges her conviction, following a jury trial, of aggravated child abuse. Because we conclude that the standard jury instruction on aggravated child abuse given by the trial court included a prejudicially erroneous definition of the word "maliciously" as used in section 827.03(2)(b), we reverse and remand for a new trial.

Appellant was charged by amended information with aggravated child abuse of her seven-year-old son. The information alleged that appellant "did maliciously punish the said child, by striking said child with a cord, in violation of Section 827.03(2)(b), Florida Statutes." To the extent pertinent, section 827.03(2)(b), Florida Statutes (Supp.1996), provides that "'[a]ggravated child abuse' occurs when a person . . . maliciously punishes . . . a child."

The evidence presented at trial was as follows. Appellant had called the sheriff's office to complain that a relative was teaching her two boys how to steal. Appellant was upset. Since the boys had not yet stolen anything, the deputy who responded to the call explained that there was nothing he could do. The next day, the same deputy responded to another call. Upon arriving, he observed several bruises and abrasions on the back, neck, arms and chest of appellant's seven-year-old son. The child told the deputy that appellant had questioned him about some missing money, and had then hit him with a telephone cord. Appellant told the deputy that she had "blacked out," and did not remember what had happened.

A nurse testified that she had counted 17 separate "marks" on the child, which appeared to have been inflicted within the previous two days. An investigator with the Department of Children and Families testified that the child had told her that his mother had hit him with an extension cord as punishment for stealing a dollar from her. Appellant told the investigator that the child had become upset because she had told him that he could not go on an outing, and had thrown the joy stick of a computer game at her. Appellant said that she responded by hitting the child with the computer cord. Appellant also told the investigator that her two sons were "out of control"; that the child had stolen money from her purse; that she had called the authorities seeking help in disciplining the boys; and that, after the incident, she had tried to drop the boys off at the Juvenile Justice Center but, finding it closed, had taken them to their father's home instead.

The child testified that appellant had punished him for something he had not done by spanking him with a folded extension cord. He denied any recollection of having spoken to either the deputy or the investigator from the Department of Children and Families about the incident.

After the state rested, appellant moved for a judgment of acquittal, arguing that the evidence failed to establish that the punishment inflicted had been maliciously motivated, as required by section 827.03(2)(b). The trial court denied the motion. The defense then rested, without offering any evidence.

During the charge conference, appellant requested that the following instruction be given, instead of the standard instruction:

Before you can find the defendant guilty of aggravated child abuse as charged in this case, the State must prove the following two elements beyond a reasonable doubt:

1. The Defendant:
a. Maliciously punished [the child].
b. [The child] was under the age of eighteen years.

A parent does not commit a crime by inflicting corporal punishment on a child if the parent remains within the legal limits of the exercise of that authority.

To prove that the Defendant . . . overstepped the legal limits in this case, the State must prove beyond a reasonable doubt that the punishment allegedly imposed upon the child by her was motivated by malice.

"Malice" means ill will, hatred, spite, an evil intent.

According to appellant, the standard jury instruction included a definition of malice that was at odds with the definition found in prior decisions of the supreme court and this court and was, therefore, erroneous. The prosecutor responded that the standard instruction was legally correct, and should be given. The trial court agreed to emphasize to the jury that malice was a prerequisite to a finding of guilt. However, it refused to give the definition of malice proposed by appellant, saying that it would give the definition contained in the standard instruction, because it believed that it was obliged to do so. The trial court subsequently acknowledged that appellant had sufficiently preserved for appellate purposes all of her objections to the instructions that would be given.

The trial court instructed the jury as follows regarding the elements of aggravated child abuse, as charged in the case:

[T]he defendant in this case[] has been accused of the crime of aggravated child abuse. And before you can find her guilty of aggravated child abuse, the State must prove the following two elements beyond a reasonable doubt: First of all, that she maliciously punished [the child].

Now, a parent does not commit a crime by inflicting corporal punishment on a child if a parent does so with an absence of malice.

. . . [A]nd the second element that must be proven beyond a reasonable doubt is that [the child] was under the age of 18 years when the alleged event occurred.

For purposes of the alleged offense, the word maliciously means wrongfully, intentionally, without legal justification or excuse.

The jury found appellant guilty as charged. Appellant moved for a new trial, arguing (among other things) that the trial court had incorrectly instructed the jury regarding the meaning of "maliciously" as used in section 827.03(2)(b). The motion was denied, and appellant was adjudicated guilty and sentenced to 67 months in prison. This appeal follows.

Initially, we conclude that the question of the correctness of the definition of malice provided to the jury was adequately preserved for appellate review. However, even if it had not been, as the state properly concedes, failure correctly to instruct a jury on a disputed element of a crime is fundamental error.

To establish that appellant had committed the crime with which she was charged, the state was required to prove that she "maliciously punishe[d]" the child. There was no dispute about the fact that the child had been punished. The only contested issue was whether that punishment had been "maliciously" inflicted. "Maliciously" is not defined in chapter 827.

In *State v. Gaylord,* 356 So. 2d 313 (Fla. 1978), the court held that section 827.03(3), Florida Statutes (1975), which treated "maliciously punish[ing] a child" as aggravated child abuse, was not unconstitutionally vague. In order to do so, the court was obliged to determine whether the word "maliciously" "provide[d] a definite standard of conduct understandable by a person of ordinary intelligence." The court concluded that it did, stating that "[m]alice means ill will, hatred, spite, an evil intent." That definition of malice has since been consistently employed in aggravated child abuse cases. Notwithstanding the definition adopted in *Gaylord,* however, without explanation, the standard jury instruction on aggravated child abuse includes a different definition—"'Maliciously' means wrongfully, intentionally, without legal justification or excuse."

The difference between the definition adopted in *Gaylord* and that included in the standard jury instruction is significant. The former is generally referred to as actual malice, or malice in fact; whereas the latter is generally referred to as legal, or technical, malice. Actual malice, or malice in fact, requires proof of evil intent or motive. In contrast, legal malice merely requires proof of an intentional act performed without legal justification or excuse. Legal malice may be inferred from one's acts, and does not require proof of evil intent or motive.

As best we have been able to determine, the standard instruction on aggravated child abuse was one of the standard instructions initially adopted by the court in 1981, and has never been subsequently amended. The trial court believed that, because of the inclusion of the instruction in the Florida Standard Jury Instructions in Criminal Cases, it was obliged to give the instruction as written, regardless of its views as to its correctness. This was a mistaken impression . . .

We hold that the trial court erred when it gave the jury the definition of "maliciously" included in the standard instruction, rather than that adopted by the court in *Gaylord,* and requested by appellant. The instruction given permitted the jury to return a guilty verdict based upon a finding of only legal, or technical, malice, rather than actual malice, or malice in fact. The effect of the error was to permit the jury to return a guilty verdict without finding that appellant actually harbored "ill will, hatred, spite, [or] an evil intent" when she punished her son, thereby reducing the state's burden of proof on an essential element of the offense charged. Because the jury might well have concluded from the evidence that appellant had not acted "maliciously" had it been properly charged, we hold, further, that the error was harmful. Accordingly, we reverse appellant's conviction, and remand the case for a new trial.

NOTES & QUESTIONS ON MALICE

1. *Other Definitions of Malice.* State penal codes offer a variety of other definitions of malice. For example, the California Penal Code defines malice in the following way: "The words 'malice' and 'maliciously' import a wish to vex, annoy, or injure another person, or an intent to do a wrongful act, established either by proof or presumption of law." Cal. Penal Code § 7. Is this a better definition than the one used in Florida? In Wyoming, the model jury instructions define malice in the following way:

> The term "malice" means that the act(s) constituting the offense charged was/ were done intentionally, without legal justification or excuse or that the act(s) was/were done in such a manner as to indicate hatred, ill will, or hostility towards another. "Maliciously" means acting in the state of mind in which an intentional act is done without legal justification or excuse. The term "maliciously" conveys the meaning of hatred, ill will, or hostility toward another.

In *State v. Wilkerson*, 2013 WL 8743241 (Wyo. Dist.), a murder defendant objected to the model instructions and urged the court to replace them with this: "The definition of 'malice' requires proof of either (a) actual intent to cause the particular harm which is produced or harm of the same or general nature; or (b) the wanton and willful doing of an act with awareness of a plain and strong likelihood that such harm may result." The court rejected the argument and held that the model jury instructions were more appropriate. Do you agree?

2. Acting Purposely

One of the great difficulties of the criminal law is distinguishing the concepts of purpose and knowledge. Purpose usually involves a desire to produce a particular outcome, while knowledge usually refers to an awareness that a result is practically certain to occur or awareness of a circumstance element. The following case deals with an escape from federal prison. As you read the case, identify why the outcome of the case is tied to the Court's analysis of whether the federal escape statute requires that the defendants acted with purpose or knowledge.

[handwritten margin note: purpose v. knowledge]

United States v. Bailey
Supreme Court of the United States
444 U.S. 394 (1980)

Mr. Justice Rehnquist delivered the opinion of the Court.

In the early morning hours of August 26, 1976, respondents Clifford Bailey, James T. Cogdell, Ronald C. Cooley, and Ralph Walker, federal prisoners at the District of Columbia jail, crawled through a window from which a bar had been removed, slid down a knotted bedsheet, and escaped from custody. Federal authorities recaptured them after they had remained at large for a period of time ranging from one month to three and one-half months. Upon their apprehension, they were charged with violating 18 U.S.C. § 751(a), which governs escape from federal custody. At their trials, each of the respondents adduced or offered to adduce evidence as to various conditions and events at the District of Columbia jail, but each was convicted by the jury . . .

I

. . . Respondents' defense of duress or necessity centered on the conditions in the jail during the months of June, July, and August 1976, and on various threats and beatings directed at them during that period. In describing the conditions at the jail, they introduced evidence of frequent fires in "Northeast One," the maximum-security cellblock occupied by respondents prior to their escape. Construed in the light most favorable to them, this evidence demonstrated that the inmates of Northeast One, and on occasion the guards in that unit, set fire to trash, bedding, and other objects thrown from the cells. According to the inmates, the guards simply allowed the fires to burn until they went out. Although the fires apparently were confined to small areas and posed no substantial threat of spreading through the complex, poor ventilation caused smoke to collect and linger in the cellblock.

Respondents Cooley and Bailey also introduced testimony that the guards at the jail had subjected them to beatings and to threats of death. Walker attempted to prove that he was an epileptic and had received inadequate medical attention for his seizures . . .

By a divided vote, the Court of Appeals reversed each respondent's conviction and remanded for new trials. The majority concluded that the District Court should have allowed the jury to consider the evidence of coercive conditions in determining whether the respondents had formulated the requisite intent to sustain a conviction under § 751(a). According to the majority, § 751(a) required the prosecution to prove that a particular defendant left federal custody voluntarily, without permission, and "with an intent to avoid confinement." The majority then defined the word "confinement" as encompassing only the "normal aspects" of punishment prescribed by our legal system. Thus, where a prisoner escapes in order to avoid "non-confinement" conditions such as beatings or homosexual attacks, he would not necessarily have the requisite intent to sustain a conviction under § 751(a) . . .

II

Criminal liability is normally based upon the concurrence of two factors, "an evil-meaning mind [and] an evil-doing hand. . . ." In the present case, we must examine both the mental element, or *mens rea*, required for conviction under § 751(a) and the circumstances under which the "evil-doing hand" can avoid liability under that section because coercive conditions or necessity negates a conclusion of guilt even though the necessary *mens rea* was present.

Few areas of criminal law pose more difficulty than the proper definition of the *mens rea* required for any particular crime. In 1970, the National Commission on Reform of Federal Criminal Laws decried the "confused and inconsistent ad hoc approach" of the federal courts to this issue and called for "a new departure." Although the central focus of this and other reform movements has been the codification of workable principles for determining criminal culpability, a byproduct has been a general rethinking of traditional *mens-rea* analysis.

At common law, crimes generally were classified as requiring either "general intent" or "specific intent." This venerable distinction, however, has been the source of a good deal of confusion . . . This ambiguity has led to a movement away from the traditional dichotomy of intent and toward an alternative analysis of *mens rea*. This new approach, exemplified in the American Law Institute's Model Penal Code, is based on two principles. First, the ambiguous and elastic term "intent" is replaced with a hierarchy of culpable states of mind. The different levels in this hierarchy are commonly identified, in descending order of culpability, as purpose, knowledge, recklessness, and negligence. Perhaps the most significant, and most esoteric, distinction drawn by this analysis is that between the mental states of "purpose" and "knowledge." As we pointed out in *United States v. United States Gypsum Co.*, 438 U.S. 422, 445 (1978), a person who causes a particular result is said to act purposefully if "he consciously desires that result, whatever the likelihood of that result happening from his conduct," while he is said to act knowingly if he is aware "that that result is practically certain to follow from his conduct, whatever his desire may be as to that result."

In the case of most crimes, "the limited distinction between knowledge and purpose has not been considered important since there is good reason for imposing liability whether the defendant desired or merely knew of the practical certainty of the result[s]." Thus in *Gypsum* we held that a person could be held criminally liable under § 1 of the Sherman Act if that person exchanged price information with a competitor either with the knowledge that the exchange would have unreasonable anticompetitive effects or with the purpose of producing those effects.

In certain narrow classes of crimes, however, heightened culpability has been thought to merit special attention. Thus, the statutory and common law of homicide often distinguishes, either in setting the "degree" of the crime or in imposing punishment, between a person who knows that another person will be killed as the result of his conduct and a person who acts with the specific purpose of taking another's life. Similarly, where a defendant is charged with treason, this Court has stated that the Government must demonstrate that the defendant acted with a purpose to aid the enemy. Another such example is the law of inchoate offenses such as attempt and conspiracy, where a heightened mental state separates criminality itself from otherwise innocuous behavior.

In a general sense, "purpose" corresponds loosely with the common-law concept of specific intent, while "knowledge" corresponds loosely with the concept of general intent. Were this substitution of terms the only innovation offered by the reformers, it would hardly be dramatic. But there is another ambiguity inherent in the traditional distinction between specific intent and general intent. Generally, even time-honored common-law crimes consist of several elements, and complex statutorily defined crimes exhibit this characteristic to an even greater degree. Is the same state of mind required of the actor for each element of the crime, or may some elements require one state of mind and some another? In *United States v. Feola*, 420 U.S. 671 (1975), for example, we were asked to decide whether the Government, to sustain a conviction for assaulting a federal officer under 18 U.S.C. § 111, had to prove that the defendant knew that his victim was a federal officer. After looking to the legislative history of § 111, we concluded that Congress intended to require only "an intent to assault, not an intent to assault a federal officer." What *Feola* implied, the American Law Institute stated: "[C]lear analysis requires that the question of the kind of culpability required to establish the commission of an offense be faced separately with respect to each material element of the crime[.]"

Before dissecting § 751(a) and assigning a level of culpability to each element, we believe that two observations are in order. First, in performing such analysis courts obviously must follow Congress' intent as to the required level of mental culpability for any particular offense. Principles derived from common law as well as precepts suggested by the American Law Institute must bow to legislative mandates. In the case of § 751(a), however, neither the language of the statute nor the legislative history mentions the *mens rea* required for conviction.

Second, while the suggested element-by-element analysis is a useful tool for making sense of an otherwise opaque concept, it is not the only principle to be considered. The administration of the federal system of criminal justice is confided to ordinary mortals, whether they be lawyers, judges, or jurors. This system could easily fall of its own weight if courts or scholars become obsessed with hair-splitting distinctions, either traditional or novel, that Congress neither stated nor implied when it made the conduct criminal.

As relevant to the charges against Bailey, Cooley, and Walker, § 751(a) required the prosecution to prove (1) that they had been in the custody of the Attorney General, (2) as the result of a conviction, and (3) that they had escaped from that custody. As for the charges against respondent Cogdell, § 751(a) required the same proof, with the exception that his confinement was based upon an arrest for a felony rather than a prior conviction. Although § 751(a) does not define the term "escape," courts and commentators are in general agreement that it means absenting oneself from custody without permission.

Respondents have not challenged the District Court's instructions on the first two elements of the crime defined by § 751(a). It is undisputed that, on August 26, 1976, respondents were in the custody of the Attorney General as the result of either arrest on charges of felony or conviction. As for the element of "escape," we need not decide whether a person could be convicted on evidence of recklessness or negligence with respect to the limits on his freedom. A court may someday confront a case where an escapee did not know, but should have known, that he was exceeding the bounds of his confinement or that he was leaving without permission. Here, the District Court clearly instructed the juries that the prosecution bore the burden of proving that respondents "knowingly committed an act which the law makes a crime" and that they acted "knowingly, intentionally, and deliberately. . . ." At a minimum, the juries had to find that respondents knew they were leaving the jail and that they knew they were doing so without authorization. The sufficiency of the evidence to support the juries' verdicts under this charge has never seriously been questioned, nor could it be.

The majority of the Court of Appeals, however, imposed the added burden on the prosecution to prove as a part of its case in chief that respondents acted "with an intent to avoid confinement." While, for the reasons noted above, the word "intent" is quite ambiguous, the majority left little doubt that it was requiring the Government to prove that the respondents acted with the purpose—that is, the conscious objective—of leaving the jail without authorization. In a footnote explaining their holding, for example, the majority specified that an escapee did not act with the requisite intent if he escaped in order to avoid "non-confinement conditions" as opposed to "normal aspects of confinement."

We find the majority's position quite unsupportable. Nothing in the language or legislative history of § 751(a) indicates that Congress intended to require either such a heightened standard of culpability or such a narrow definition of confinement. As we stated earlier, the cases have generally held that, except in narrow classes of offenses, proof that the defendant acted knowingly is sufficient to support a conviction. Accordingly, we hold that the prosecution fulfills its burden under § 751(a) if it demonstrates that an escapee knew his actions would result in his leaving physical confinement without permission . . .

NOTES & QUESTIONS ON PURPOSE AND INTENT

1. *Understanding specific and general intent.* In *Bailey*, the Court notes the prevalence of the terms "general intent" and "specific intent" before the Model Penal Code provisions on mens rea were adopted in an attempt to de-emphasize the language of intent in American criminal law. The terms general and specific intent are notoriously confusing, in part because they have different meanings and are used inconsistently by various judges, legislators, and lawyers. One common use of the terms "general intent" and "specific intent" involves whether the mens rea of the defendant applies to multiple elements of the offense. So, for example, common law burglary is often described as a specific intent crime because it requires the breaking and entering of another's dwelling with the intent to commit another crime inside. See, e.g., 13 V.S.A. § 1201 ("A person is guilty of burglary if he or she enters any building or structure knowing that he or she is not licensed or privileged to do so, with the intent to commit a felony, petit larceny, simple assault, or unlawful mischief."). Burglary is a specific intent crime because it requires *two levels* of mens rea. First, the defendant must have the intent to enter the building. Second, the defendant must have the further intent to commit a second crime, such as theft, rape, murder, or other crime. To denote the two levels of intent, scholars and jurists sometimes referred to this mens rea as specific intent. A crime with only one level of intent is general intent. Sometimes specific intent refers to the two levels of mens rea in a *result* offense. So, for example, a murder statute might require that the defendant commit an intentional act (say, firing a gun) and also that the defendant intend a particular result (the death of the victim). For this reason, intentional murder is sometimes referred to as a specific intent crime. The Model Penal Code replaces this notion of specific intent with the mental state of purposely causing a result, because the defendant's purpose in firing the gun was to produce the death of the victim.

2. *The doctrine of transferred intent.* Consider a variation of the hypothetical from the beginning of the chapter. A perpetrator fires a weapon at his target and accidentally hits an innocent bystander. Using the mental states described above, what is his attitude regarding the result? Arguably he is guilty of the attempted murder of his original target and the reckless killing of the actual victim (since the perpetrator did not intend to kill him). But most jurisdictions impose a harsher result and apply the doctrine of transferred intent.

They take the defendant's intent with regard to the intended target and apply it to the actual target, so that the defendant can be convicted of intentional murder for the killing of the bystander. The popular phrase "intent follows the bullet" captures the intuition. *State v. Batson*, 96 S.W. 2d 384, 389 (Mo. 1936). Of course, this is a legal fiction, since the defendant did not intend to kill the bystander.

What is the justification for the doctrine of transferred intent? One possibility is that the defendant intended to kill the original target, and that is all the intent that the law requires. But is it? Is it fair to transform a crime of recklessness into a crime of intent? Maybe the doctrine is based on deterrence or the idea that culpable criminals should not benefit from a "lucky" miss. Under either theory, though, attempts should be punished just as harshly as completed crimes, which they rarely are. Some scholars are convinced that the doctrine of transferred intent is incoherent—a form of casuistry or magical thinking—and should be abolished. Indeed, the Model Penal Code categories do not support the doctrine of transferred intent. Other scholars support the result but disagree about the underlying rationale for it. For a discussion of the various justifications, see Douglas N. Husak, *Transferred Intent*, 10 Notre Dame J.L. Ethics & Pub. Pol'y 65 (1996); William L. Prosser, *Transferred Intent*, 45 Tex. L. Rev. 650, 653 (1967).

ADVICE   The Model Penal Code was not entirely successful in excising specific intent from the criminal law, and the confusing phrase lingers in case law in many jurisdictions. When confronted with the phrase in a case or statute, a good lawyer should scrutinize which elements of the offense the "specific intent" attaches to and also ask how many layers of mens rea are included in the offense. Given the diverse meanings for the phrase, one cannot—and should not—mechanically assume a settled meaning when approaching it for the first time in a new context.

---

3. Knowledge and the Problem of "Willful Blindness"

Although "knowledge" sounds like a relatively simple mental state, in reality it is quite complex. As indicated above, knowledge, when attached to a result (as opposed to a circumstance element), requires the defendant's awareness that the result of a given state of affairs is practically certain to occur. What if the defendant deliberately and strategically *avoids* gaining affirmative evidence about the truth? The following case asks and answers that question.

United States v. Jewell
U.S. Court of Appeals for the 9th Circuit
532 F.2d 697 (1976)

BROWNING, CIRCUIT JUDGE.

Appellant defines "knowingly" in 21 U.S.C. § § 841[1] and 960[2] to require that positive knowledge that a controlled substance is involved be established as an element of each offense. On the basis of this interpretation, appellant argues that it was reversible error to instruct the jury that the defendant could be convicted upon proof beyond a reasonable doubt that if he did not have positive knowledge that a controlled substance was concealed in the automobile he drove over the border, it was solely and entirely because of the conscious purpose on his part to avoid learning the truth. The majority [of this court] concludes that this contention is wrong in principle, and has no support in authority or in the language or legislative history of the statute.

It is undisputed that appellant entered the United States driving an automobile in which 110 pounds of marihuana worth $6,250 had been concealed in a secret compartment between the trunk and rear seat. Appellant testified that he did not know the marijuana was present. There was circumstantial evidence from which the jury could infer that appellant had positive knowledge of the presence of the marihuana, and that his contrary testimony was false. On the other hand there was evidence from which the jury could conclude that appellant spoke the truth that although appellant knew of the presence of the secret compartment and had knowledge of facts indicating that it contained marijuana, he deliberately avoided positive knowledge of the presence of the contraband to avoid responsibility in the event of discovery. If the jury concluded the latter was indeed the situation, and if positive knowledge is required to convict, the jury would have no choice consistent with its oath but to find appellant not guilty even though he deliberately contrived his lack of positive knowledge. Appellant urges

---

1. Editor's Note: 21 U.S.C. § 841 provides: "(a) Unlawful acts. Except as authorized by this subchapter, it shall be unlawful for any person knowingly or intentionally—(1) to manufacture, distribute, or dispense, or possess with intent to manufacture, distribute, or dispense, a controlled substance; or (2) to create, distribute, or dispense, or possess with intent to distribute or dispense, a counterfeit substance."

2. Editor's Note: 21 U.S.C. § 960 provides: "(a) Unlawful acts. Any person who—(1) contrary to section 825, 952, 953, or 957 of this title, knowingly or intentionally imports or exports a controlled substance, (2) contrary to section 955 of this title, knowingly or intentionally brings or possesses on board a vessel, aircraft, or vehicle a controlled substance, or (3) contrary to section 959 of this title, manufactures, possesses with intent to distribute, or distributes a controlled substance, shall be punished as provided in subsection (b) of this section."

this view. The trial court rejected the premise that only positive knowledge would suffice, and properly so.

Appellant tendered an instruction that to return a guilty verdict the jury must find that the defendant knew he was in possession of marihuana. The trial judge rejected the instruction because it suggested that "absolutely, positively, he has to know that it's there." The court said, "I think, in this case, it's not too sound an instruction because we have evidence that if the jury believes it, they'd be justified in finding he actually didn't know what it was—he didn't because he didn't want to find it."

The court instructed the jury that "knowingly" meant voluntarily and intentionally and not by accident or mistake. The court told the jury that the government must prove beyond a reasonable doubt that the defendant "knowingly" brought the marihuana into the United States, and that he "knowingly" possessed the marihuana. The court continued:

> The Government can complete their burden of proof by proving, beyond a reasonable doubt, that if the defendant was not actually aware that there was marijuana in the vehicle he was driving when he entered the United States his ignorance in that regard was solely and entirely a result of his having made a conscious purpose to disregard the nature of that which was in the vehicle, with a conscious purpose to avoid learning the truth.

The legal premise of these instructions is firmly supported by leading commentators here and in England. Professor Rollin M. Perkins writes, "One with a deliberate antisocial purpose in mind . . . may deliberately 'shut his eyes' to avoid knowing what would otherwise be obvious to view. In such cases, so far as criminal law is concerned, the person acts at his peril in this regard, and is treated as having 'knowledge' of the facts as they are ultimately discovered to be." J. Ll. J. Edwards, writing in 1954, introduced a survey of English cases with the statement, "For well-nigh a hundred years, it has been clear from the authorities that a person who deliberately shuts his eyes to an obvious means of knowledge has sufficient mens rea for an offence based on such words as . . . 'knowingly.'" Professor Glanville Williams states, on the basis both English and American authorities, "To the requirement of actual knowledge there is one strictly limited exception. . . . (T)he rule is that if a party has his suspicion aroused but then deliberately omits to make further enquiries, because he wishes to remain in ignorance, he is deemed to have knowledge." Professor Williams concludes, "The rule that wilful blindness is equivalent to knowledge is essential, and is found throughout the criminal law."

The substantive justification for the rule is that deliberate ignorance and positive knowledge are equally culpable. The textual justification is that in common understanding one "knows" facts of which he is less than absolutely certain. To act "knowingly," therefore, is not necessarily to act only with positive knowledge, but also to act with an awareness of the high probability of the existence of the fact in question. When such awareness is present, "positive" knowledge is not required.

This is the analysis adopted in the Model Penal Code. Section 2.02(7) states: "When knowledge of the existence of a particular fact is an element of an offense, such knowledge is established if a person is aware of a high probability of its existence, unless he actually believes that it does not exist." As the Comment to this provision explains, "Paragraph (7) deals with the situation British commentators have denominated 'wilful blindness' or 'connivance,' the case of the actor who is aware of the probable existence of a material fact but does not satisfy himself that it does not in fact exist." . . .

Appellant's narrow interpretation of "knowingly" is inconsistent with the Drug Control Act's general purpose to deal more effectively "with the growing menace of drug abuse in the United States." Holding that this term introduces a requirement of positive knowledge would make deliberate ignorance a defense. It cannot be doubted that those who traffic in drugs would make the most of it. This is evident from the number of appellate decisions reflecting conscious avoidance of positive knowledge of the presence of contraband in the car driven by the defendant or in which he is a passenger, in the suitcase or package he carries, in the parcel concealed in his clothing.

It is no answer to say that in such cases the fact finder may infer positive knowledge. It is probable that many who performed the transportation function, essential to the drug traffic, can truthfully testify that they have no positive knowledge of the load they carry. Under appellant's interpretation of the statute, such persons will be convicted only if the fact finder errs in evaluating the credibility of the witness or deliberately disregards the law.

It begs the question to assert that a "deliberate ignorance" instruction permits the jury to convict without finding that the accused possessed the knowledge required by the statute. Such an assertion assumes that the statute requires positive knowledge. But the question is the meaning of the term "knowingly" in the statute. If it means positive knowledge, then, of course, nothing less will do. But if "knowingly" includes a mental state in which the defendant is aware that the fact in question is highly probable but consciously avoids enlightenment, the statute is satisfied by such proof.

It is worth emphasizing that the required state of mind differs from positive knowledge only so far as necessary to encompass a calculated effort to avoid the sanctions of the statute while violating its substance. "A court can properly find wilful blindness only where it can almost be said that the defendant actually knew." In the language of the instruction in this case, the government must prove, "beyond a reasonable doubt, that if the defendant was not actually aware . . . his ignorance in that regard was solely and entirely a result of . . . a conscious purpose to avoid learning the truth."

No legitimate interest of an accused is prejudiced by such a standard, and society's interest in a system of criminal law that is enforceable and that imposes sanctions upon all who are equally culpable requires it.

KENNEDY, CIRCUIT JUDGE, dissenting.

At the outset, it is arguable that the "conscious purpose to avoid learning the truth" instruction is inherently inconsistent with the additional mens rea required for count two intent to distribute. It is difficult to explain that a defendant can specifically intend to distribute a substance unless he knows that he possesses it. In any event, we would not approve the conscious purpose instruction in this case, because it falls short of the scienter independently required under both counts.

The majority opinion justifies the conscious purpose jury instruction as an application of the wilful blindness doctrine recognized primarily by English authorities. A classic illustration of this doctrine is the connivance of an innkeeper who deliberately arranges not to go into his back room and thus avoids visual confirmation of the gambling he believes is taking place. The doctrine is commonly said to apply in deciding whether one who acquires property under suspicious circumstances should be charged with knowledge that it was stolen.

One problem with the wilful blindness doctrine is its bias towards visual means of acquiring knowledge. We may know facts from direct impressions of the other senses or by deduction from circumstantial evidence, and such knowledge is nonetheless "actual." Moreover, visual sense impressions do not consistently provide complete certainty.

Another problem is that the English authorities seem to consider willful blindness a state of mind distinct from, but equally culpable as, "actual" knowledge. When a statute specifically requires knowledge as an element of a crime, however, the substitution of some other state of mind cannot be justified even if the court deems that both are equally blameworthy.

Finally, the wilful blindness doctrine is uncertain in scope. There is disagreement as to whether reckless disregard for the existence of a fact constitutes wilful blindness or some lesser degree of culpability. Some cases have held that a statute's scienter requirement is satisfied by the constructive knowledge imputed to one who simply fails to discharge a duty to inform himself. There is also the question of whether to use an "objective" test based on the reasonable man, or to consider the defendant's subjective belief as dispositive.

The approach adopted in section 2.02(7) of the Model Penal Code clarifies, and, in important ways restricts, the English doctrine: "When knowledge of the existence of a particular fact is an element of an offense, such knowledge is established if a person is aware of a high probability of its existence, unless he actually believes that it does not exist."

This provision requires an awareness of a high probability that a fact exists, not merely a reckless disregard, or a suspicion followed by a failure to make further inquiry. It also establishes knowledge as a matter of subjective belief, an important safeguard against diluting the guilty state of mind required for conviction. It is important to note that section 2.02(7) is a definition of knowledge, not a substitute for it; as such, it has been cited with approval by the Supreme Court.

In light of the Model Penal Code's definition, the "conscious purpose" jury instruction is defective in three respects. First, it fails to mention the requirement that Jewell have been aware of a high probability that a controlled substance was in the car. It is not culpable to form "a conscious purpose to avoid learning the truth" unless one is aware of facts indicating a high probability of that truth. To illustrate, a child given a gift-wrapped package by his mother while on vacation in Mexico may form a conscious purpose to take it home without learning what is inside; yet his state of mind is totally innocent unless he is aware of a high probability that the package contains a controlled substance. Thus, a conscious purpose instruction is only proper when coupled with a requirement that one be aware of a high probability of the truth.

The second defect in the instruction as given is that it did not alert the jury that Jewell could not be convicted if he "actually believed" there was no controlled substance in the car. The failure to emphasize, as does the Model Penal Code, that subjective belief is the determinative factor, may allow a jury to convict on an objective theory of knowledge that a reasonable man should have inspected the car and would have discovered what was hidden inside. One recent decision reversed a jury instruction for this very deficiency—failure to balance a conscious purpose instruction with a warning that the defendant could not be convicted if he actually believed to the contrary.

Third, the jury instruction clearly states that Jewell could have been convicted even if found ignorant or "not actually aware" that the car contained a controlled substance. This is unacceptable because true ignorance, no matter how unreasonable, cannot provide a basis for criminal liability when the statute requires knowledge. A proper jury instruction based on the Model Penal Code would be presented as a way of defining knowledge, and not as an alternative to it. . . .

NOTES & QUESTIONS ON WILLFUL BLINDNESS

1. *Moral foundations for the doctrine.*   What is the basis for punishing someone who is willfully blind? Is the *refusal* to acquire knowledge the same thing as *having* knowledge? Or is the refusal to acquire information a morally culpable decision in and of itself? See *United States v. Giovannetti,* 919 F.2d 1223 (7th Cir. 1990) ("A deliberate effort to avoid guilty knowledge is all the guilty knowledge the law requires."). Was Jewell really in a state of ignorance about the nature of the drugs he was delivering? What do you think really happened in this case? Is the rule regarding willful blindness really about mental states or does it simply lower the prosecutor's burden in situations where the defendant claims he never acquired the relevant information?

2. *Motive and willful blindness.*   In *United States v. Heredia,* 483 F.3d 913, 917 (9th Cir. 2007), the defendant was charged with possession of marijuana with intent to distribute after she was stopped by border control agents. Heredia testified at trial that she suspected that her car contained drugs because her mother, who was traveling with her in the car, was nervous and was carrying a large amount of cash, but she never actually searched the car to confirm her suspicions. At trial, the judge granted the prosecutor's request to charge the jury on willful blindness. On appeal, Heredia argued that the jury should have been charged that her *motive* for not inquiring further was relevant and that motive to avoid punishment should be a discrete prong required by the doctrine of willful blindness. In her case, Heredia stated that she did not look in the trunk after her suspicions were aroused because stopping the car to investigate further at that point was not practicable or safe. The Ninth Circuit disagreed and concluded that the "requirement that defendant have *deliberately* avoided learning the truth, provides sufficient protections for defendants in these situations. . . . A decision influenced by coercion, exigent circumstances or lack of meaningful choice is, perforce, not deliberate. A defendant who fails to investigate for these reasons has not deliberately chosen to avoid learning the truth." For a discussion, see *Criminal Law—Willful Blindness,* 121 Harv. L. Rev. 1245, 1248 (2008) ("The *Heredia* court, in failing to preserve the requirement that the willfully blind actor have a motive to avoid criminal punishment, removed an important protection for defendants.").

3. *The Supreme Court speaks.*   In 2011, the Supreme Court expressed its view on the contours of the willful blindness doctrine. In *Global-Tech Appliances v. SEB,* 563 U.S. 754 (2011), the defendant was sued for patent infringement. The Federal Circuit below had concluded that patent infringement under 35 U.S.C. § 271 requires that a plaintiff demonstrate that the patent infringer "knew or should have known that his actions would induce actual infringements." According to the Federal Circuit, although there was no evidence that the defendant knew of the patent, the defendant "deliberately disregarded a known risk" that the patent existed. The Federal Circuit

concluded that this disregard "is a form of actual knowledge." The Supreme Court reversed and concluded that the Federal Circuit had misapplied—and watered down—the concept of willful blindness. According to the Supreme Court, a finding of willful blindness requires that: "(1) the defendant must subjectively believe that there is a high probability that a fact exists and (2) the defendant must take deliberate actions to avoid learning of that fact." The Federal Circuit definition of deliberately disregarding a known risk did not "require active efforts by an inducer to avoid knowing about the infringing nature of the activities," which the doctrine of willful blindness requires. 563 U.S. at 770. Although the Supreme Court interpretation of willful blindness would not be binding on state courts applying the doctrine as a matter of state penal law, it is an authoritative statement of the doctrine as it applies in federal law.

4. *The Model Penal Code solution.* The Model Penal Code has a unique solution to the problem of willful blindness. In § 2.02(7) the Code states that knowledge of the existence of a fact is established if "a person is aware of a *high probability* of its existence, unless he actually believes that it does not exist." What if the defendant engineers the situation so that the likelihood of the attendant circumstance is *less than* 50 percent? Consider the following hypothetical: A drug dealer gives three couriers one suitcase each. The drugs are only in one of the suitcases. Each courier is aware that there is a 33.3 percent chance that he or she is smuggling the drugs. Does this satisfy the Model Penal Code "high probability" standard? See Douglas N. Husak & Craig A. Callender, *Wilful Ignorance, Knowledge, and the "Equal Culpability" Thesis: A Study of the Deeper Significance of the Principle of Legality*, 1994 Wis. L. Rev. 29 (1994).

4. Recklessness Versus Negligence

Articulating the dividing line between recklessness and negligence is fraught with conceptual and factual difficulties. In most jurisdictions, the distinction between the two concepts is not the level of risk but the nature of the defendant's *awareness* of the risk. In a criminal case, determining the defendant's level of awareness is a complex assessment for the jury to make. The following case involves the most frequent type of accident: a car crash resulting in death. As you read the facts and the legal analysis, evaluate whether the defendant was reckless or negligent.

State v. Olsen

Supreme Court of South Dakota
462 N.W.2d 474 (1990)

SABERS, JUSTICE.

The State appeals a magistrate court order dismissing a charge of manslaughter in the second degree against Michael K. Olsen.

About 5:00 P.M. on May 24, 1989, Olsen was driving a tractor west on Highway 46, approximately one mile east of the Beresford city limits. Visibility was good as it was a clear, sunny day. Olsen entered the highway from a field where he had been working and was travelling between five and fifteen miles per hour. After travelling approximately one-half mile on the highway, Olsen pulled over to the side of the road to allow a car that was following him to pass. A second vehicle, driven by Lloyd Saugstad, was a short distance farther back.

Shortly after pulling over to the side of the road, Olsen turned left toward a gravel road leading to his parents' home. As he was crossing the eastbound lane of the highway, the front of the tractor was struck by a car travelling east in that lane. The collision resulted in the immediate death of the driver of the eastbound vehicle. When Saugstad approached the accident scene, Olsen ran from the tractor saying "I didn't see it." After rescue personnel arrived, Olsen was taken to the Beresford clinic and treated for shock.

The State filed a complaint against Olsen on May 30, 1989, charging him with one count of manslaughter in the second degree. A preliminary hearing was held on July 27, 1989. At the hearing, Saugstad testified that he saw the eastbound vehicle coming and knew that a crash was imminent when Olsen turned his tractor. The South Dakota highway patrol trooper who investigated the accident testified that he interviewed Olsen the evening of the accident. Olsen told the trooper that before attempting to make his turn he looked both behind and forward, but did not see the approaching vehicle.

Following the presentation of the State's case at the preliminary hearing, Olsen moved to dismiss the complaint against him. The magistrate granted Olsen's motion and dismissed the manslaughter charge because "the factual situation fails to meet the burden to sustain a charge of felony manslaughter." The State petitioned this court for permission to appeal the intermediate order of the magistrate court. We granted the petition, but deny the relief sought. . . .

SDCL 22-16-20 treats "[a]ny reckless killing" as manslaughter in the second degree. The definition of "reckless" for the purpose of this statute is set forth in SDCL 22-1-2(1)(d). That definition states: "The words "reckless, recklessly" and all derivatives thereof, import a conscious and unjustifiable disregard of a substantial risk that the offender's conduct may cause a certain result or may be of a certain nature . . ."

In other words, for someone's conduct to be deemed reckless, they must consciously disregard a substantial risk. Consequently, someone cannot be reckless if they are unaware of the risk their behavior creates as they cannot disregard that risk if they are unaware of it. As the North Dakota

Supreme Court has stated: "In order that conduct be considered reckless it must create a high degree of risk of which the actor is *actually aware.*"

Recklessness requires more than ordinary negligent conduct. Evidence of carelessness, inadvertence or other similar behavior is insufficient to sustain a conviction where reckless conduct is required. The difference between reckless behavior and negligent behavior is primarily measured by the state of mind of the individual. As explained in 1 C. Torcia, *Wharton's Criminal Law* § 27 at 140 (1978):

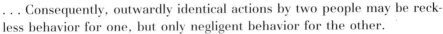

> The difference between the terms "recklessly" and "negligently", as usu-
> ally defined, is one of kind, rather than of degree. Each actor creates a
> *risk* of harm. The reckless actor is *aware* of the risk and disregards it; the
> negligent actor is *not aware* of the risk but should have been aware of it.

. . . Consequently, outwardly identical actions by two people may be reckless behavior for one, but only negligent behavior for the other.

Although it is not always possible for the State to directly establish that a defendant was aware of a risk, it can be done indirectly through the defendant's conduct. Awareness can be established if the defendant acts in a manner that indicates a reckless disregard for the safety of others. However, the operation of a motor vehicle in violation of the law is not in and of itself sufficient to constitute reckless conduct, even if a person is killed as a result thereof. As explained in *Commonwealth v. Kaulback,* 256 Pa. Super. 13 (1978), the evidence must show more than a mere violation of the law before criminal responsibility for a death will arise:

> [N]ot every violation of law or unlawful act in the operation of a motor
> vehicle will render the operator criminally responsible for deaths which
> may result. Such an operator, to be criminally responsible, must evidence
> a disregard of human life or an indifference to the consequences of his
> acts. This is based on the sound principle that there must be found from
> the evidence some degree of culpable behavior or reckless disregard for
> the safety of others before a conviction may be sustained. Criminal
> responsibility for death resulting from the operation of a motor vehicle
> in violation of the law will result only if the violation is done in such a
> manner as to evidence a reckless disregard for the safety of others. Mere
> carelessness or inadvertence or thoughtless omission is insufficient.

In the present case, the State has failed to introduce evidence of Olsen's conduct that would rise above the level of negligence. Nothing in the evidence of Olsen's behavior suggests that he was in any way aware of the risk he was creating when he turned his tractor towards the gravel road. Although it appears he did not properly yield the right-of-way, as the court explained in *Clowser:* "We are of the opinion that a mere failure to yield the right-of-way is not such evidence of culpable or criminal negligence as will support the charge of involuntary manslaughter." The State has failed to offer evidence indicating that Olsen's failure to yield the right-of-way was done in such a manner as to suggest a reckless disregard for the safety of others. While the State need not introduce evidence that Olsen could foresee a death resulting from his conduct, the State must introduce evidence that would allow a trier of fact to conclude that Olsen was aware of the dangerous nature of his conduct. . . .

NOTES & QUESTIONS ON
RECKLESSNESS AND NEGLIGENCE

1. *Awareness of risk.* The court concluded that Olsen could not be convicted of a crime of recklessness because he did not *consciously* disregard the risk of killing the other driver. He was only negligent in his behavior. How does the state prove that a defendant was consciously aware of a substantial and unjustified risk in any case? Why was Olsen not aware of the risk? Is it because he did not see the oncoming traffic? What evidence would have supported an inference that the defendant was aware of the risk? Remember, the prosecution must prove that the defendant was aware not just of a risk, but aware of a substantial and unjustified risk. The use of the term unjustified involves an objective assessment, by the judicial system, of the nature of the risk. However, the adjective "substantial" arguably involves a subjective component. A defendant might be aware of a *de minimis* risk—a trivial possibility that harm might result from the behavior—but not realize that the risk is substantial. This would not be sufficient to satisfy the requirement of conscious disregard.

In the past, some jurisdictions defined recklessness differently and concluded that a defendant could be reckless even if he or she was not consciously aware of the risk. Under this older definition, recklessness could be established if the *level* of the risk was sufficiently egregious, regardless of whether the defendant was consciously aware of it. In this vein, some jurisdictions distinguished between *advertent* and *inadvertent* recklessness. What is *inadvertent* recklessness? For example, in *Commonwealth v. Welansky*, 316 Mass. 383, 399, 55 N.E.2d 902, 910 (1944), a defendant was charged with 16 counts of manslaughter in connection with a nightclub fire that resulted in multiple fatalities. The court stated that the "essence of wanton or reckless conduct is intentional conduct, by way either of commission or of omission where there is a duty to act, which conduct involves a high degree of likelihood that substantial harm will result to another." The *Welansky* court did not require actual foresight of the risk. Under this old theory of inadvertent recklessness, what distinguishes recklessness from negligence is the degree of risk associated with the defendant's conduct. Is this a coherent definition? If you translate inadvertent recklessness into Model Penal Code language, which mental state would it be? The answer, of course, is that the concept of inadvertent recklessness is inconsistent—by definition—with the mental states used in the Model Penal Code. If the defendant is unaware of the risk, he or she is negligent, not reckless. For a discussion, see Andrew Ashworth, *Principles of Criminal Law* 183 (2d ed. 1995). Today, courts almost universally reject the concept of inadvertent recklessness.

2. *A theory of criminal negligence.*   Why is negligence considered a lower mental state than recklessness? After all, an individual might be so self-centered that they are clueless and impervious to the riskiness of their behavior and therefore will not satisfy the "conscious disregard" standard. Is this mental attitude of total cluelessness worse or better than recklessness? For this reason, some observers find the law's distinction between recklessness and negligence artificial. On the other hand, some observers have the opposite intuition: Negligence should not be criminalized *at all*. Indeed, negligent defendants are not *aware* that they did anything wrong. So, what is the foundation for their culpability if there is no conscious mental state to support it? For this reason, some think that negligence should be relegated to tort law and *never* generate criminal punishment. See, e.g., Larry Alexander & Kimberly Kessler Ferzan, *Crime & Culpability: A Theory of Criminal Law* (2009) (with Stephen J. Morse) ("A culpability-based criminal law will not include liability for negligence. Culpability entails control, and the negligent actor does not have this requisite control."). Under this view, negligence would be the exclusive purview of tort law and subject only to private remedies (i.e., monetary damages).

Do you agree? Although tort law does not impose "punishment" per se, its monetary damages do have the capacity to deter future behavior. Furthermore, the possibility of punitive damages includes an element of social opprobrium to the remedy imposed in the case. What more does criminal law add to the mix? Put simply, should negligent harm-doers go to jail? See also George P. Fletcher, *The Theory of Criminal Negligence: A Comparative Analysis*, 119 U. Penn. L. Rev. 401, 435 (1971) (concluding that criminal negligence "is a parallel rationale for criminal culpability, less culpable than intentional and reckless conduct, yet adequate to support the fair imposition of criminal sanctions"). Fletcher concludes that criminal negligence involves a *normative* conception of mens rea. In other words, instead of basing criminal liability on the mere fact that the defendant has a particular mental state (as is the case with purpose, knowledge, or recklessness), criminal law bases negligence liability on a society's normative assessment of the defendant's state of mind—a condemnation of the defendant for his or her lack of attention to the matter. Finally, some scholars advocate for an intermediate position and conclude that the minimum standard for criminal responsibility should be "culpable indifference." See, e.g., Kenneth W. Simons, *Culpability and Retributive Theory: The Problem of Criminal*

Negligence, 5 J. Contemp. Legal Issues 365, 381 (1994) ("Culpable indifference, by contrast, captures the idea that an inadvertent defendant who *would* have disregarded the risk if she had been aware is as blameworthy as an advertent defendant who did disregard the risk. For both defendants display callous insensitivity to the risk.").

5. Strict Liability

Strict liability offenses dispense with mental states entirely. The defendant is responsible simply for committing a particular action or causing a particular result—regardless of their state of mind. However, it can be difficult to determine whether a particular penal statute is strict liability or not. Unfortunately, statutes rarely include a label on top that says whether they are strict liability or not. The following case provides an example of the inherent difficulties of statutory interpretation.

Staples v. United States
Supreme Court of the United States
511 U.S. 600 (1994)

THOMAS, JUSTICE.

I

The National Firearms Act makes it unlawful for any person to possess a machinegun that is not properly registered with the Federal Government. Petitioner contends that, to convict him under the Act, the Government should have been required to prove beyond a reasonable doubt that he knew the weapon he possessed had the characteristics that brought it within the statutory definition of a machinegun. We agree and accordingly reverse the judgment of the Court of Appeals.

The National Firearms Act (Act), 26 U.S.C. § § 5801-5872, imposes strict registration requirements on statutorily defined "firearms." The Act includes within the term "firearm" a machinegun, § 5845(a)(6), and further defines a machinegun as "any weapon which shoots, . . . or can be readily restored to shoot, automatically more than one shot, without manual reloading, by a single function of the trigger," § 5845(b). Thus, any fully automatic weapon is a "firearm" within the meaning of the Act. Under the Act, all firearms must be registered in the National Firearms Registration and Transfer Record maintained by the Secretary of the Treasury. Section 5861(d) makes it a crime, punishable by up to 10 years in prison, for any person to possess a firearm that is not properly registered.

Upon executing a search warrant at petitioner's home, local police and agents of the Bureau of Alcohol, Tobacco and Firearms (BATF) recovered, among other things, an AR-15 rifle. The AR-15 is the civilian version of the military's M-16 rifle, and is, unless modified, a semiautomatic weapon. The M-16, in contrast, is a selective fire rifle that allows the operator, by rotating a selector switch, to choose semiautomatic or automatic fire. Many M-16 parts are interchangeable with those in the AR-15 and can be used to convert the AR-15 into an automatic weapon. No doubt to inhibit such conversions, the AR-15 is manufactured with a metal stop on its receiver that will prevent an M-16 selector switch, if installed, from rotating to the fully automatic position. The metal stop on petitioner's rifle, however, had been filed away, and the rifle had been assembled with an M-16 selector switch and several other M-16 internal parts, including a hammer, disconnector, and trigger. Suspecting that the AR-15 had been modified to be capable of fully automatic fire, BATF agents seized the weapon. Petitioner subsequently was indicted for unlawful possession of an unregistered machinegun in violation of § 5861(d).

At trial, BATF agents testified that when the AR-15 was tested, it fired more than one shot with a single pull of the trigger. It was undisputed that the weapon was not registered as required by § 5861(d). Petitioner testified that the rifle had never fired automatically when it was in his possession. He insisted that the AR-15 had operated only semiautomatically, and even then imperfectly, often requiring manual ejection of the spent casing and chambering of the next round. According to petitioner, his alleged ignorance of any automatic firing capability should have shielded him from criminal liability for his failure to register the weapon. He requested the District Court to instruct the jury that, to establish a violation of § 5861(d), the Government must prove beyond a reasonable doubt that the defendant "knew that the gun would fire fully automatically."

The District Court rejected petitioner's proposed instruction and instead charged the jury as follows: "The Government need not prove the defendant knows he's dealing with a weapon possessing every last characteristic [which subjects it] to the regulation. It would be enough to prove he knows that he is dealing with a dangerous device of a type as would alert one to the likelihood of regulation."

Petitioner was convicted and sentenced to five years' probation and a $5,000 fine. . . .

II

Whether or not § 5861(d) requires proof that a defendant knew of the characteristics of his weapon that made it a "firearm" under the Act is a question of statutory construction. As we observed in *Liparota v. United States,* 471 U.S. 419 (1985), "[t]he definition of the elements of a criminal offense is entrusted to the legislature, particularly in the case of federal crimes, which are solely creatures of statute." Thus, we have long recognized that determining the mental state required for commission of a federal crime requires "construction of the statute and . . . inference of the intent of Congress." *United States v. Balint,* 258 U.S. 250, 253.

The language of the statute, the starting place in our inquiry, provides little explicit guidance in this case. Section 5861(d) is silent concerning the *mens rea* required for a violation. It states simply that "[i]t shall be unlawful for any person . . . to receive or possess a firearm which is not registered to him in the National Firearms Registration and Transfer Record." Nevertheless, silence on this point by itself does not necessarily suggest that Congress intended to dispense with a conventional *mens rea* element, which would require that the defendant know the facts that make his conduct illegal. On the contrary, we must construe the statute in light of the background rules of the common law, in which the requirement of some *mens rea* for a crime is firmly embedded. As we have observed, "[t]he existence of a *mens rea* is the rule of, rather than the exception to, the principles of Anglo-American criminal jurisprudence." See also *Morissette v. United States,* 342 U.S. 246, 250 (1952) ("The contention that an injury can amount to a crime only when inflicted by intention is no provincial or transient notion. It is as universal and persistent in mature systems of law as belief in freedom of the human will and a consequent ability and duty of the normal individual to choose between good and evil.").

There can be no doubt that this established concept has influenced our interpretation of criminal statutes. Indeed, we have noted that the common-law rule requiring *mens rea* has been "followed in regard to statutory crimes even where the statutory definition did not in terms include it." Relying on the strength of the traditional rule, we have stated that offenses that require no *mens rea* generally are disfavored, and have suggested that some indication of congressional intent, express or implied, is required to dispense with *mens rea* as an element of a crime.

According to the Government, however, the nature and purpose of the Act suggest that the presumption favoring *mens rea* does not apply to this case. The Government argues that Congress intended the Act to regulate and restrict the circulation of dangerous weapons. Consequently, in the Government's view, this case fits in a line of precedent concerning what we have termed "public welfare" or "regulatory" offenses, in which we have understood Congress to impose a form of strict criminal liability through statutes that do not require the defendant to know the facts that make his conduct illegal. In construing such statutes, we have inferred from silence that Congress did not intend to require proof of *mens rea* to establish an offense.

For example, in *Balint,* we concluded that the Narcotic Act of 1914, which was intended in part to minimize the spread of addictive drugs by criminalizing undocumented sales of certain narcotics, required proof only that the defendant knew that he was selling drugs, not that he knew the specific items he had sold were "narcotics" within the ambit of the statute.

Such public welfare offenses have been created by Congress, and recognized by this Court, in "limited circumstances." Typically, our cases recognizing such offenses involve statutes that regulate potentially harmful or injurious items. In such situations, we have reasoned that as long as a defendant knows that he is dealing with a dangerous device of a character that places him "in responsible relation to a public danger," he should be alerted to the probability of strict regulation, and we have assumed that in such cases Congress intended to place the burden on the defendant to "ascertain at his peril whether [his conduct] comes within the inhibition of the statute." Thus, we essentially have relied on the nature of the statute and the particular character of the items regulated to determine whether congressional silence concerning the mental element of the offense should be interpreted as dispensing with conventional *mens rea* requirements.

The Government argues that § 5861(d) defines precisely the sort of regulatory offense described in *Balint.* In this view, all guns, whether or not they are statutory "firearms," are dangerous devices that put gun owners on notice that they must determine at their hazard whether their weapons come within the scope of the Act. On this understanding, the District Court's instruction in this case was correct, because a conviction can rest simply on proof that a defendant knew he possessed a "firearm" in the ordinary sense of the term.

The Government seeks support for its position from our decision in *United States v. Freed,* 401 U.S. 601 (1971) which involved a prosecution for possession of unregistered grenades under § 5861(d). The defendant knew that the items in his possession were grenades, and we concluded that § 5861(d) did not require the Government to prove the defendant also knew that the grenades were unregistered. To be sure, in deciding that *mens rea* was not required with respect to that element of the offense, we suggested that the Act "is a regulatory measure in the interest of the public safety, which may well be premised on the theory that one would hardly be surprised to learn that possession of hand grenades is not an innocent act." Grenades, we explained, "are highly dangerous offensive weapons, no less dangerous than the narcotics involved in *United States v. Balint.*" But that reasoning provides little support for dispensing with *mens rea* in this case.

As the Government concedes, *Freed* did not address the issue presented here. In *Freed,* we decided only that § 5861(d) does not require proof of knowledge that a firearm is *unregistered.* The question presented by a defendant who possesses a weapon that is a "firearm" for purposes of the Act, but who knows only that he has a "firearm" in the general sense of the term, was not raised or considered. And our determination that a defendant need not know that his weapon is unregistered suggests no conclusion concerning whether § 5861(d) requires the defendant to know of the features that make his weapon a statutory "firearm"; different elements of the same offense can require different mental states. Moreover, our analysis in *Freed* likening the Act to the public welfare statute in *Balint* rested entirely on the assumption that the defendant *knew* that he was dealing with hand grenades—that is, that he knew he possessed a particularly dangerous type of weapon (one within the statutory definition of a "firearm"), possession of which was not entirely "innocent" in and of itself. The predicate for that analysis is eliminated when, as in this case, the very question to be decided is *whether* the defendant must know of the particular characteristics that make his weapon a statutory firearm.

Notwithstanding these distinctions, the Government urges that *Freed's* logic applies because guns, no less than grenades, are highly dangerous devices that should alert their owners to the probability of regulation. But the gap between *Freed* and this case is too wide to bridge. In glossing over the distinction between grenades and guns, the Government ignores the particular care we have taken to avoid construing a statute to dispense with *mens rea* where doing so would "criminalize a broad range of apparently innocent conduct." *Liparota*, 471 U.S. at 426. In *Liparota*, we considered a statute that made unlawful the unauthorized acquisition or possession of food stamps. We determined that the statute required proof that the defendant knew his possession of food stamps was unauthorized, largely because dispensing with such a *mens rea* requirement would have resulted in reading the statute to outlaw a number of apparently innocent acts. Our conclusion that the statute should not be treated as defining a public welfare offense rested on the commonsense distinction that a "food stamp can hardly be compared to a hand grenade."

Neither, in our view, can all guns be compared to hand grenades. Although the contrast is certainly not as stark as that presented in *Liparota*, the fact remains that there is a long tradition of widespread lawful gun ownership by private individuals in this country. Such a tradition did not apply to the possession of hand grenades in *Freed* or to the selling of dangerous drugs that we considered in *Balint*. In fact, in *Freed* we construed § 5861(d) under the assumption that "one would hardly be surprised to learn that possession of hand grenades is not an innocent act." Here, the Government essentially suggests that we should interpret the section under the altogether different assumption that "one would hardly be surprised to learn that owning a gun is not an innocent act." That proposition is simply not supported by common experience. Guns in general are not "deleterious devices or products or obnoxious waste materials," that put their owners on notice that they stand "in responsible relation to a public danger."

The Government protests that guns, unlike food stamps, but like grenades and narcotics, are potentially harmful devices. Under this view, it seems that *Liparota*'s concern for criminalizing ostensibly innocuous conduct is inapplicable whenever an item is sufficiently dangerous—that is, dangerousness alone should alert an individual to probable regulation and justify treating a statute that regulates the dangerous device as dispensing with *mens rea*. But that an item is "dangerous," in some general sense, does not necessarily suggest, as the Government seems to assume, that it is not also entirely innocent. Even dangerous items can, in some cases, be so commonplace and generally available that we would not consider them to alert individuals to the likelihood of strict regulation. As suggested above, despite their potential for harm, guns generally can be owned in perfect innocence. Of course, we might surely classify certain categories of guns—no doubt including the machineguns, sawed-off shotguns, and artillery pieces that Congress has subjected to regulation—as items the ownership of which would have the same quasi-suspect character we attributed to owning hand grenades in *Freed*. But precisely because guns falling outside those categories traditionally have been widely accepted as lawful possessions, their destructive potential, while perhaps even greater than that of some items we would classify along with narcotics and hand grenades, cannot be said to put gun owners sufficiently on notice of the likelihood of regulation to justify interpreting § 5861(d) as not requiring proof of knowledge of a weapon's characteristics.

On a slightly different tack, the Government suggests that guns are subject to an array of regulations at the federal, state, and local levels that put gun owners on notice that they must determine the characteristics of their weapons and comply with all legal requirements. But regulation in itself is not sufficient to place gun ownership in the category of the sale of narcotics in *Balint*. The food stamps at issue in *Liparota* were subject to comprehensive regulations, yet we did not understand the statute there to dispense with a *mens rea* requirement. Moreover, despite the overlay of legal restrictions on gun ownership, we question whether regulations on guns are sufficiently intrusive that they impinge upon the common experience that owning a gun is usually licit and blameless conduct. Roughly 50 percent of American homes contain at least one firearm of some sort, and in the vast majority of States, buying a shotgun or rifle is a simple transaction that would not alert a person to regulation any more than would buying a car.

If we were to accept as a general rule the Government's suggestion that dangerous and regulated items place their owners under an obligation to inquire at their peril into compliance with regulations, we would undoubtedly reach some untoward results. Automobiles, for example, might also be termed "dangerous" devices and are highly regulated at both the state and federal levels. Congress might see fit to criminalize the violation of certain regulations concerning automobiles, and thus might make it a crime to operate a vehicle without a properly functioning emission control system. But we probably would hesitate to conclude on the basis of silence that Congress intended a prison term to apply to a car owner whose vehicle's emissions levels, wholly unbeknownst to him, began to exceed legal limits between regular inspection dates.

Here, there can be little doubt that, as in *Liparota,* the Government's construction of the statute potentially would impose criminal sanctions on a class of persons whose mental state—ignorance of the characteristics of weapons in their possession—makes their actions entirely innocent. The Government does not dispute the contention that virtually any semiautomatic weapon may be converted, either by internal modification or, in some cases, simply by wear and tear, into a machinegun within the meaning of the Act. Such a gun may give no externally visible indication that it is fully automatic. But in the Government's view, any person who has purchased what he believes to be a semiautomatic rifle or handgun, or who simply has inherited a gun from a relative and left it untouched in an attic or basement, can be subject to imprisonment, despite absolute ignorance of the gun's firing capabilities, if the gun turns out to be an automatic.

We concur in the Fifth Circuit's conclusion on this point: "It is unthinkable to us that Congress intended to subject such law-abiding, well-intentioned citizens to a possible ten-year term of imprisonment if . . . what they genuinely and reasonably believed was a conventional semi-automatic [weapon] turns out to have worn down into or been secretly modified to be a fully automatic weapon." . . .

The potentially harsh penalty attached to violation of § 5861(d)—up to 10 years' imprisonment—confirms our reading of the Act. Historically, the penalty imposed under a statute has been a significant consideration in determining whether the statute should be construed as dispensing with *mens rea.* Certainly, the cases that first defined the concept of the public welfare offense almost uniformly involved statutes that provided for only light penalties such as fines or short jail sentences, not imprisonment in the state penitentiary.

As commentators have pointed out, the small penalties attached to such offenses logically complemented the absence of a *mens rea* requirement: In a system that generally requires a "vicious will" to establish a crime, imposing severe punishments for offenses that require no *mens rea* would seem incongruous. Indeed, some courts justified the absence of *mens rea* in part on the basis that the offenses did not bear the same punishments as "infamous crimes," and questioned whether imprisonment was compatible with the reduced culpability required for such regulatory offenses. Similarly, commentators collecting the early cases have argued that offenses punishable by imprisonment cannot be understood to be public welfare offenses, but must require *mens rea.*

In rehearsing the characteristics of the public welfare offense, we, too, have included in our consideration the punishments imposed and have noted that "penalties commonly are relatively small, and conviction does no grave damage to an offender's reputation." We have even recognized that it was "[u]nder such considerations" that courts have construed statutes to dispense with *mens rea. . . .*

QUESTIONS ON STRICT LIABILITY

1. *Inherent dangerousness.* In 2012, Adam Lanza killed his mother and then used a Bushmaster XM15 assault rifle to massacre 20 children and 6 adults at the Sandy Hook Elementary School in Newtown, Connecticut. He then committed suicide. The Bushmaster XM15 is based on the AR-15 assault rifle platform. Do you agree with the majority in *Staples* that a grenade is inherently dangerous but an AR-15 is not?

Sandy Hook Elementary School

2. *Regulatory offenses.* In what circumstances is strict liability legitimate? Consider the case of *United States v. Apollo Energies*, 611 F.3d 679 (10th Cir. 2010). The defendants were convicted of a misdemeanor for violating the Migratory Bird Treaty Act when dead birds were found in oil drilling equipment. The equipment in question was heater-treaters that separate oil from water after the oil-rich liquid is pumped out of the ground. Birds had a habit of nesting in the equipment and then dying. The act makes it unlawful to "take [or] . . . attempt to take . . . any migratory bird. . . ." Implementing regulations defined "take" as "pursue, hunt, shoot, wound, kill, trap, capture, or collect." 50 C.F.R. § 10.12. The court concluded that the Act imposed strict liability and that it did not matter that the defendants did not intend to kill the birds. Is this result fair? Apply the criteria from *Staples*, i.e., whether the offense is regulatory and the applicable punishment. Does it matter whether the offense is a felony or a misdemeanor? See *United States v. Wulff*, 758 F.2d 1121, 1123, 1125 (6th Cir. 1985) (invalidating the felony provision of the Migratory Bird Treaty Act because its "severe penalty and grave damage to reputation" was only appropriate if "the defendant acted with some degree of scienter").

3. *Strict liability and affirmative defenses.*   Is strict liability morally justified? Some jurisdictions, such as Canada, place greater constraints on the government's power to criminalize strict liability offenses. In *Regina v. Sault Ste. Marie*, 2 S.C.R. 1299 (1978), the Supreme Court of Canada distinguished between "absolute liability" and "strict liability" offenses. The municipality of Sault Ste. Marie was convicted of violating the Water Resources Commission Act for the improper disposal of trash at a landfill that polluted a nearby creek. An independent contractor hired by the city conducted the improper trash disposal. The city was charged under the theory that the offense was strict liability and no mens rea was required. On appeal, the Supreme Court of Canada distinguished *three* categories: (i) traditional mens rea offenses; (ii) strict liability without mens rea but where a defendant can argue reasonable mistake of fact or reasonable care; and (iii) absolute liability offenses where conviction is automatic regardless of the defendant's fault and no defenses are permitted. The Supreme Court concluded that the first category embodied criminal law offenses, the second category involved public welfare offenses, and the third category was unconstitutional. The court explained its reasoning:

> There is no evidence that a higher standard of care results from absolute liability. If a person is already taking every reasonable precautionary measure, is he likely to take additional measures, knowing that however much care he takes, it will not serve as a defence in the event of breach? If he has exercised care and skill, will conviction have a deterrent effect upon him or others? Will the injustice of conviction lead to cynicism and disrespect for the law, on his part and on the part of others?

In contrast, the U.S. Supreme Court has never imposed a categorical exclusion on what the Canadians call "absolute liability" offenses.

Apply the standard announced in *Sault Ste. Marie*. Would you acquit the municipality of violating the regulatory statute because it hired an independent contractor to dispose of its trash and it assumed that the contractor would do it properly? What sort of "reasonable care" is required by a municipality to ensure that its contractors follow relevant regulations, or is it reasonable for them to simply assume that their contractors will always follow the law?

4. *Strict liability and political pressure on legislators.*   Should the legislature enact more strict liability offenses? In *Morissette,* the Supreme Court stated that the "purpose and obvious effect of doing away with the requirement of a guilty intent is to ease the prosecution's path to conviction." 342 U.S. at 263. If the goal of the criminal law is to deter future lawbreakers, strict liability might induce more compliance by increasing the number of convictions. On the other hand, if one of the goals of the criminal law is to give just deserts to those who act with a culpable state of mind, strict liability should be sharply curtailed. Put yourself in the shoes of a state legislator in New Jersey deciding whether to pass the following statute, 2C:35-9(a), Strict Liability for Drug-Induced Deaths:

Any person who manufactures, distributes or dispenses methamphetamine, lysergic acid diethylamide, phencyclidine or any other controlled dangerous substance classified in Schedules I or II, or any controlled substance analog thereof . . . is strictly liable for a death which results from the injection, inhalation or ingestion of that substance, and is guilty of a crime of the first degree.

Would you vote yes?

C. PRACTICE & POLICY

The following section explores the difficulties inherent in proving to a jury that a defendant had a particular state of mind. In this order, we consider: (i) the process of inferring mental states from a defendant's conduct; (ii) whether it is advisable for a prosecutor to undercharge a defendant in order to lower the prosecution's burden regarding the required mental element; (iii) the nature of mental states as sorting mechanisms for distinguishing between greater and lesser crimes; and (iv) how mental states are categorized in foreign jurisdictions.

∽ **Prosecutorial strategy.** How should a prosecutor go about proving a mental state? In some situations the defendant will have announced his intent, either by testifying at trial or providing pre-trial statements to investigators or grand juries. But in many situations the defendant will have consistently invoked his right to remain silent. Or, more commonly, the prosecutor will need to prove that the defendant's own words obscure rather than illuminate his intent. In other words, the prosecutor may need to prove that the defendant *lied*. How is this accomplished? A prosecutor catalogues the defendant's behavior and asks the jury to *infer* the defendant's mental state. In the absence of direct scientific or neurological evidence about what was going on in the defendant's brain, this is the *only* way of proving intent. The prosecutor tells the jury a particular story and argues that the defendant's behavior can only be explained if we assume that he or she had a particular mental state at the relevant moment. Defense attorneys contesting mens rea will do the exact same thing: argue that their client's behavior makes better sense if the jury assumes that he or she had a different state of mind. Although a criminal trial brings mental states to the forefront, it is important to understand that this process of *ascribing* mental states is everywhere in regular life. If you see someone drinking a glass of water, you ascribe to them a desire to drink water because that best explains why they picked up the glass. It is firmly established that juries are permitted to infer mens rea from the available facts. However, the court cannot use this presumption as a way of lowering or shifting its burden of persuasion. See *Sandstrom v. Montana*, 442 U.S. 510 (1979) (overturning jury instruction that the law "presumes that a person intends the ordinary consequences of his voluntary acts"). The law permits the jury to draw these inferences but never demands it.

∾ **Strategic charging.** When should a prosecutor proceed with a charge based on acting purposely? Charging decisions regarding mens rea are not made in a vacuum and are often carefully calibrated with desired results. If the prosecutor has a choice between two charges with similar penalties but different mens rea requirements, which one do you think he or she should select? Consider N.Y. Penal Law 125.25, which provides a lengthy penalty for second-degree murder, a category that includes intentional (purposeful) killings *or* causing someone's death with depraved indifference to human life. Could a prosecutor proceed with a "depraved indifference" charge simply to reduce his burden of persuasion with regard to mens rea, even if he or she believes the killing was committed intentionally? Does the prosecutor have an ethical duty to select a charge that accurately tracks his or her view of the facts? See Bennett L. Gershman, *The Prosecutor's Duty to Truth*, 14 Geo. J. Legal Ethics 309 (2001). In his article, Gershman focuses almost exclusively on prosecutorial tactics that are common but that may harm the interests of the defendant. For example, Gershman refers to the "moral courage to decline prosecution." *Id.* at 350. Should the same "duty to the truth" also apply to prosecutorial conduct—such as strategic undercharging—that *benefits* the defendant? In that case, the prosecutor would need moral courage to engage in the prosecution, even if expedience would suggest settling for a conviction for a lesser crime. Which approach is more correct?

∾ **Mental states as sorting mechanisms.** Mental states are often used as a sorting mechanism to distinguish between more and less blameworthy offenses. In general, legislatures provide for harsher penalties for crimes committed purposely and more lenient penalties for crimes of recklessness or negligence. Ask yourself whether this is always the case. The U.S. Sentencing Guidelines incorporate a complex set of mitigating and aggravating factors to determine the length of a sentence, but many states rely on more rudimentary sentencing ranges written into their state codes. Compare a defendant who commits one act of purposeful murder with another defendant responsible for a fire with multiple fatalities. Who should go to jail for longer? Daniel Biechele, the manager of the music group Great White, was sentenced to 15 years in prison after pleading guilty in connection to a fire at the Station nightclub in Rhode Island that killed 100 concertgoers. Biechele set off pyrotechnics that ignited nearby acoustic foam, causing the entire building to quickly go up in flames. The judge suspended 11 years of the sentence and Biechele was paroled and released from prison less than 2 years after he was sen-

Daniel Biechele

tenced. How should the gravity of an offense be calculated? All other things being equal, it seems legitimate to rank intentional crimes as more culpable than crimes of recklessness or negligence. For example, psychologist John Darley has concluded that laypeople have remarkably consistent intuitions about the severity of certain crimes, including that intentional crimes are more blameworthy than reckless or negligent ones. See John M. Darley, *Citizens' Assignments of Punishments for Moral Transgressions: A Case Study in the Psychology of Punishment*, 8 Ohio St. J. Crim. L. 101 (2010). For a description of more of this empirical research, see Paul H. Robinson & John M. Darley, *Justice, Liability, and Blame: Community Views and the Criminal Law* (1995). Of course, in most situations all other things are *not* equal, and in determining the correct sentence, courts usually take into account *both* the severity of the mental state and the magnitude of the harm caused by the defendant. But in the case of Biechele, it seems the court based the sentence almost entirely on the mental state and ignored the magnitude of harm—otherwise the sentence would have been much harsher in order to reflect the fact that 100 people died. Which approach would you follow?

∾ **Mental states in foreign jurisdictions.** The basic categories of mens rea are deeply intuitive but not strictly speaking universal in all jurisdictions across the world. For example, civil law jurisdictions in Europe often carve up the landscape of intent differently than American or British systems. Criminal lawyers in Europe often talk of *dolus eventualis*, a mental state that is most closely associated with American-style recklessness. Although there are multiple and competing definitions, one well-known formulation of *dolus eventualis* says that a defendant should be convicted if he or she is aware that his actions might fulfill the elements of the offense and he or she "reconciles himself [or herself]" to that result. See George P. Fletcher, *Rethinking Criminal Law* 445-46 (1978). This sounds close to common law recklessness, but in many European systems *dolus eventualis* is considered a subcategory of "intent." This stands in stark contrast to American criminal law where generally speaking the language of "intent" includes only acting purposely or knowingly. Definitions of mental states are often inconsistent—across national boundaries and even among competing local jurisdictions.

CHAPTER 7

181-194

MISTAKES

A. DOCTRINE

Mistakes are divided into two categories: mistakes of fact and mistakes of law. Historically, common law judges applied different standards for adjudicating the different categories, but over time most jurisdictions have evolved a unified standard that applies to all mistakes and can be stated quite simply: A mistake is relevant if it negates a required mental element of the offense. So it is impossible to figure out how to handle mistakes until you identify the precise contours of an offense's mens rea requirements. In this sense, a mistake is not really a defense at all, but just the negation of a required element of the prosecutor's case. For that reason, although it is the defense that will assert mistake of fact or mistake of law as a defense, the burden of persuasion falls to the prosecution to establish, beyond a reasonable doubt, that the defendant acted with the required mental state.

[handwritten margin note: burden on prosecution / that def. acted w/ required mens rea]

1. Mistakes of Fact

Historically, judges displayed mixed feelings about mistakes. On the one hand, judges looked for doctrines to acquit defendants whom they found sympathetic, especially since all felonies were subject to the death penalty. On the other hand, judges were wary of exonerating defendants who came up with flimsy excuses or made irrational mistakes. In order to mediate between these competing impulses, some jurisdictions imposed the "moral wrong" doctrine. Under the moral wrong doctrine, a defendant was not able to assert mistake of fact if what she subjectively believed that she was doing amounted to something immoral. Because this required engaging with moral philosophy, over time some jurisdictions switched to the "legal wrong" doctrine: Defendants were not permitted to argue mistake of fact if what they subjectively believed they were doing still amounted to committing some lesser *crime*.

Today, courts have looked to the required mental element of the offense to determine whether a mistake of fact is relevant or not. In the case of strict liability offenses, a mistake of fact is not relevant for the simple reason that the statute requires no mens rea. More specifically, if a crime includes some strict liability *aspect*, a mistake of fact is not relevant if it pertains to the element of the offense that is strict liability. So, for example, if a statutory rape statute is strict liability regarding the age of the victim, then a mistake regarding the victim's age would not be relevant. In the case of a "specific intent" offense, judges ask whether the mistake negates a required mental element of the offense, i.e., the part of the offense that requires a specific intent. Finally, in the case of "general intent" offenses, courts usually require that the mistake be *reasonable* before allowing the defense. Expressed in the negative, unreasonable mistakes are not a defense to general intent offenses.

The Model Penal Code, and any state statute modeled after it, has simplified this scheme and distilled it to its essence: A mistake of fact is a defense if and only if it negates the required mental element of the offense: "purpose, knowledge, belief, recklessness or negligence." MPC § 2.04(1). So, for example, if the defendant was reckless in the formation of her mistaken belief, she could still be convicted of a crime of recklessness. Similarly, if the defendant were charged with a crime of negligence, a negligent mistake would not negate the required mens rea. This recodification is not surprising since the MPC abandoned the language of specific and general intent as mental state categories, so those categories were not available to the drafters when they conceived the mistake provisions. The MPC dispensed entirely with the concept of reasonableness that characterized the prior jurisprudence.

2. Mistakes of Law

The old common law rule was that ignorance of the law was no excuse (*ignorantia legis neminem excusat*). Judges were particularly concerned that recognizing this excuse would open the floodgates for acquittals and give people perverse incentives. If ignorance of the law were an excuse, people would have no reason to learn about the law's requirements—doing so could only increase legal liability. The more modern approach, embodied in the Model Penal Code, takes a more sympathetic approach and recognizes that legal mistakes might be relevant if knowledge or awareness of the law is a material element of the offense. In reality, this is rare. In most cases, knowing that you are breaking the law is not a material element that the prosecutor is required to prove.

For example, murder involves killing another human being but nothing in the definition of the crime requires that the defendant know that murder is illegal.

But in some cases the definition of the crime stipulates that the defendant knows that she acts unlawfully, such as tax evasion. Consequently, the only way to figure out the relevancy of a mistake of law is to determine the precise contours of the mental requirement and determine whether it applies to any attendant circumstances that contain a legal element. If the mental state applies to the legal element referred to in the crime's definition, then a mistake of law could "negate" the required mens rea.

Finally, some jurisdictions (as well as the Model Penal Code), recognize mistake of law when it is the product of reasonable reliance on an official statement of the law that is later determined to be erroneous or invalid. See MPC § 2.04(3)(b). In order for the defense to apply, the statement must have appeared in a judicial order or decision, a formal administrative order, or an official interpretation of the law proffered by an officer "with responsibility for the interpretation, administration or enforcement of the law defining the offense." Also, in theory, a defendant could argue mistake of law based on the fact that the law or statute was secret or not published—a truly rare circumstance in today's world. MPC § 2.04(3)(a). In that situation, ignorance of the law would constitute an excuse because the defendant's ignorance was unavoidable.

B. APPLICATION

1. Mistakes of Fact

The first case below, *Navarro*, applies the rule that even unreasonable mistakes may be a defense to a specific intent crime if the mistake negates the required mens rea. The second case, *Sexton*, is more complicated and requires careful attention to the Model Penal Code rule that mistakes are a defense if they negate a required mental element of the offense. When the required mental element for an offense is recklessness, how should a court determine if the defendant's mistake negated that element? As you read *Sexton*, evaluate whether the defendant's mistake *negated* his recklessness or whether his mistake *constituted* his recklessness.

People v. Navarro

Appellate Department, Superior Court, Los Angeles County
160 Cal. Rptr. 692 (1979)

Dowds, Judge.

Defendant, charged with a violation of Penal Code section 487.1, grand theft, appeals his conviction after a jury trial of petty theft, a lesser but necessarily included offense. His contention on appeal is that the jury was improperly instructed. The only facts set forth in the record on appeal are that defendant was charged with stealing four wooden beams from a construction site and that the state of the evidence was such that the jury could have found that the defendant believed either (1) that the beams had been abandoned as worthless and the owner had no objection to his taking them or (2) that they had substantial value, had not been abandoned and he had no right to take them . . .

Accordingly, the question for determination on appeal is whether the defendant should be acquitted if there is a reasonable doubt that he had a good faith belief that the property had been abandoned or that he had the permission of the owner to take the property or whether that belief must be a reasonable one as well as being held in good faith.

A recent decision by the California Supreme Court throws light on this question. In *People v. Wetmore*, 149 Cal. Rptr. 265 (1978), defendant was charged with burglary, like theft a specific intent crime. The Supreme Court held that the trial court had erroneously refused to consider the guilt phase of the trial evidence that, because of mental illness, defendant was incapable of forming the specific intent required for conviction of the crime, instead receiving such evidence only in respect of his plea of not guilty by reason of insanity . . .

The instant case, does not, of course, involve evidence of mental illness. Evidence was presented, however, from which the jury could have concluded that defendant believed that the wooden beams had been abandoned and that the owner had no objection to his taking them, i.e., that he lacked the specific criminal intent required to commit the crime of theft (intent permanently to deprive an owner of his property). A similar situation existed in *People v. Photo*, 45 Cal. App. 2d 345 (1941), where defendant's conviction of grand theft for the taking of certain boxes of oranges which he thought he had purchased was reversed . . .

Earlier California cases are to the same effect. In *People v. Devine*, 95 Cal. 227 (1892), defendant's conviction of larceny was reversed. He had driven away in a wagon, without any attempt at secrecy, a number of hogs, his own and three bearing another's mark or brand. The Supreme Court pointed out: "There are cases in which all the knowledge which a person might have acquired by due diligence is to be imputed to him. But where a felonious intent must be proven it can be done only by proving what the accused knew. One cannot intend to steal property which he believes to be his own. He may be careless, and omit to make an effort to ascertain that the property which he thinks his own belongs to another; but so long as he believes it to be his own he cannot feloniously steal it." . . .

Cases in other jurisdictions also hold that where the law requires a specific criminal intent, it is not enough merely to prove that a reasonable man would have had that intent, without meeting the burden of proof that the defendant himself also entertained it . . .

Other cases from other jurisdictions setting forth the same rule could be cited and we appreciate that other cases can be found in which its application is not so clear. The proper rule, it seems to us, is set forth in *Perkins on Criminal Law* 940-41 (2d ed. 1969): "If no specific intent or other special mental element is required for guilt of the offense charged, a mistake of fact will not be recognized as an excuse unless it was based upon reasonable grounds . . . (On the other hand), because of the requirement of a specific intent to steal there is no such thing as larceny by negligence. One does not commit this offense by carrying away the chattel of another in the mistaken belief that it is his own, no matter how great may have been the fault leading to this belief, if the belief itself is genuine." . . .

{ analysis

In the instant case the trial court in effect instructed the jury that even though defendant in good faith believed he had the right to take the beams, and thus lacked the specific intent required for the crime of theft, he should be convicted unless such belief was reasonable. In doing so it erred. It is true that if the jury thought the defendant's belief to be unreasonable, it might infer that he did not in good faith hold such belief. If, however, it concluded that defendant in good faith believed that he had the right to take the beams, even though such belief was unreasonable as measured by the objective standard of a hypothetical reasonable man, defendant was entitled to an acquittal since the specific intent required to be proved as an element of the offense had not been established . . .

{ result: (trial court erred

State v. Sexton
Supreme Court of New Jersey
733 A.2d 1125 (1999)

O'HERN, J. . . .

On May 10, 1993, Shakirah Jones, a seventeen-year-old friend of defendant and decedent, overheard the two young men having what she described as a "typical argument." The two young men walked from a sidewalk into a vacant lot. Jones saw defendant with a gun in his hand, but she did not see defendant shoot Matthews.

Jones heard Matthews tell defendant, "there are no bullets in that gun," and then walk away. Defendant called Matthews back and said, "you think there are no bullets in this gun?" Matthews replied, "yeah." Jones heard the gun go off. A single bullet killed Matthews.

Acting on information received from Jones, police recovered a small caliber automatic pistol near the crime scene. The police did not trace the ownership of the gun, which may have been owned by Matthews's grandmother.

A ballistics expert testified that there was a spring missing from the gun's magazine, which prevented the other bullets from going into the chamber after the first bullet was discharged. In this condition, the gun would have to be loaded manually by feeding the live cartridge into the chamber prior to firing.

The expert later clarified that, if the magazine had been removed after one round had been inserted into the chamber, it would be impossible to see whether the gun was loaded without pulling the slide that covered the chamber to the rear. The expert agreed that, for someone unfamiliar with guns, once the magazine was removed, it was "probably a possible assumption" that the gun was unloaded.

Defendant's version was that when the two young men were in the lot, Matthews showed defendant a gun and "told me the gun was empty." Defendant "asked him was he sure," and "he said yes." When Matthews asked if defendant would like to see the gun, defendant said "yes." Defendant "took the gun and was looking at it, and 'it just went off.'" He never unloaded the gun or checked to see if there were any bullets in the gun. He had never before owned or shot a gun.

A grand jury indicted defendant for purposeful or knowing murder, possession of a handgun without a permit, and possession of a handgun for an unlawful purpose. At the close of the State's case, defendant moved to dismiss the murder charge because the victim had told him that the gun was not loaded. The court denied the motion.

The court charged murder and the lesser-included offenses of aggravated manslaughter and reckless manslaughter. Concerning defendant's version of the facts, the court said:

> Defense contends this was a tragic accident. That Alquadir [Matthews], says the defense, handed the gun to Ronald [defendant]. Alquadir told Ronald, you know, the gun was not loaded. Ronald believed the gun was not loaded. Ronald did not think the gun was pointed at Alquadir when it went off. But the gun went off accidentally and, says the defense, that is a very tragic and sad accident but it is not a crime.
>
> If, after considering all the evidence in this case, including the evidence presented by the defense as well as the evidence presented by the State, if you have a reasonable doubt in your mind as to whether the State has proven all the elements of any of these crimes: murder, aggravated manslaughter, or reckless manslaughter, you must find the defendant not guilty of those crimes.

The jury found defendant not guilty of murder, aggravated manslaughter, or possession of a handgun for an unlawful purpose, but guilty of reckless manslaughter and unlawful possession of a handgun without a permit. . . .

II

. . . The 1979 New Jersey Code of Criminal Justice followed the mental-state formulation of the MPC. The Code provides generally that no person should be guilty of an offense unless the person "acted purposely, knowingly, recklessly or negligently, as the law may require, with respect to each material element of the offense." The precise delineation of these four states of criminal culpability, each drawn from the MPC and each defined in N.J.S.A. 2C:2-2b, represented an effort, as a framer of the Code described it, "to achieve greater individual justice through a closer relation between guilt and culpability, requiring workable definitions of the various culpability factors. These factors must be related precisely to each element of an offense, defense, or mitigation, and all unnecessary limitations upon individual culpability should be eliminated." "[T]he material elements of an offense vary in that they may involve (1) conduct per se, (2) the attendant circumstances of conduct, or (3) the result of conduct. The MPC attempts to define culpability status for each."

The MPC also contains an express provision for mistake-of-fact defenses. "Its mistake of fact provision, while creating potential for conceptual confusion by continuing the common law characterization of the doctrine as a 'defense,' in fact sought to clarify the common law." The MPC expressly recognized that the doctrine did not sanction a true defense, but rather was an attack on the prosecution's ability to prove the requisite culpable mental state for at least one objective element of the crime. Hence, unlike enactments in many pre-MPC states, "the MPC expressly recognizes that the mistake of an accused need not be a reasonable mistake unless the Legislature has expressly decided that the requisite culpable mental state was minimal—'negligence' or perhaps, 'recklessness.'"

The MPC provides that, "Ignorance or mistake as to a matter of fact or law is a defense if: (a) the ignorance or mistake negatives the purpose, knowledge, belief, recklessness or negligence required to establish a material element of the offense; or (b) the law provides that the state of mind established by such ignorance or mistake constitutes a defense." MPC § 2.04 (1962).

Whether a mistake would negate a required element of the offense, depended, of course, on the nature of the mistake and the state of mind that the offense required. This led commentators to observe:

> Technically, such provisions [for a mistake of fact defense] are unnecessary. They simply confirm what is stated elsewhere: "No person may be convicted of an offense unless each element of such offense is proven beyond a reasonable doubt." If the defendant's ignorance or mistake makes proof of a required culpability element impossible, the prosecution will necessarily fail in its proof of the offense.

The Commentary to the Hawaii Criminal Code gives an easy example of how, under the MPC, a mistake of fact may negate culpability.

> [I]f a person is ignorant or mistaken as to a matter of fact . . . the person's ignorance or mistake will, in appropriate circumstances, prevent the person from having the requisite culpability with respect to the fact . . . as it actually exists. For example, a person who is mistaken (either reasonably, negligently, or recklessly) as to which one of a number of similar umbrellas on a rack is the person's and who takes another's umbrella should be afforded a defense to a charge of theft predicated on either intentionally or knowingly taking the property of another. . . . A reckless mistake would afford a defense to a charge requiring intent or knowledge—but not to an offense which required only recklessness or negligence. Similarly, a negligent mistake would afford a defense to a charge predicated on intent, knowledge, or recklessness—but not to an offense based on negligence.

State legislatures, however, "in emulating the Model Penal Code's three culpability provisions (its culpability definitions, its guidelines for resolving the requisite culpable mental state, and its mistake of fact doctrine), have not always understood their interrelationship. Hence, these states have failed to coordinate the enactment of these three types of culpability provisions." States have restricted the mistake-of-fact doctrine by imposing a reasonableness requirement. By thinking in terms of the reasonable person while failing to appreciate that the MPC's mistake-of-fact and culpability provisions are interrelated, these states have undermined the structure of the MPC.

To explain, we may consider again the case of the absent-minded umbrella thief. If only a reasonable mistake will provide a defense to the charge of theft, the absent-minded but careless restaurant patron will have no defense to a charge of theft. *People v. Navarro,* 160 Cal. Rptr. 692 (1979), explains how a mistake of fact, even though it is unreasonable, may constitute a defense to a crime requiring a culpable mental state higher than recklessness or negligence. In *Navarro,* defendant took some wooden beams from a construction site. He was charged with theft. He claimed that he thought the owner had abandoned the beams. The trial court instructed the jury that this would be a valid defense only if the scavenger's belief was reasonable. The reviewing court held that such an instruction was erroneous because if the jury "concluded that defendant in good faith believed that he had the right to take the beams, even though such belief was unreasonable . . . , defendant was entitled to an acquittal since the specific intent required to be proved as an element of the offense had not been established." Otherwise, one would end up imposing liability for theft on a lesser basis than knowledge or purpose to steal the property of another.

How then shall we resolve the problem created by the selective inclusion and exclusion of the culpability provisions of the MPC?

III

The issue posed by our grant of certification was whether a mistake of fact was a defense to the charge of reckless manslaughter. The short answer to that question is: "It depends." The longer answer requires that we relate the type of mistake involved to the essential elements of the offense, the conduct proscribed, and the state of mind required to establish liability for the offense. Defendant insists that the State is required to disprove, beyond a reasonable doubt, his mistake-of-fact defense. Most states would agree with that statement. In *State v. Savoie*, 67 N.J. 439, 463 n.8 (1975), the Court similarly said that once the defense of mistake of fact is raised, the burden of persuasion is on the State. Just what does that mean? Does it mean that the State must prove that the mistake was unreasonable? We must begin by examining the language of the statute.

N.J.S.A. 2C:2-4a allows a defense of ignorance or mistake "if the defendant reasonably arrived at the conclusion underlying the mistake and" the mistake either "negatives the culpable mental state required to establish the offense" or "[t]he law provides that the state of mind established by such ignorance or mistake constitutes a defense." The crime of manslaughter is a form of criminal homicide. "A person is guilty of criminal homicide if [the actor] purposely, knowingly [or] recklessly . . . causes the death of another human being." . . . Criminal homicide constitutes manslaughter, a second-degree crime, "when . . . [i]t is committed recklessly," that is, when the actor has recklessly caused death . . . The culpable mental state of the offense is recklessness. N.J.S.A. 2C:2-2b(3) states:

> A person acts recklessly with respect to a material element of an offense when [the actor] consciously disregards a substantial and unjustifiable risk that the material element exists or will result from [the actor's] conduct. The risk must be of such a nature and degree that, considering the nature and purpose of the actor's conduct and the circumstances known to [the actor], its disregard involves a gross deviation from the standard of conduct that a reasonable person would observe in the actor's situation. . . .

The State argues that "[i]t is obvious that the firing of a gun at another human being without checking to see if it is loaded disregards a substantial risk." The State argues that at a minimum there must be some proof establishing that defendant "reasonably arrived at the conclusion underlying the mistake." To return to the language of N.J.S.A. 2C:2-4a, does the mistake about whether the gun was loaded "negative [ ] the culpable mental state required to establish the offense," or does "the law provide[ ] that the state of mind established by such ignorance or mistake constitutes a defense"? Of itself, a belief that the gun is loaded or unloaded does not negate the culpable mental state for the crime of manslaughter. Thus, one who discharges a gun, believing it to be unloaded, is not necessarily innocent of manslaughter.

The State notes that under N.J.S.A. 2C:12-1b(4), a defendant is criminally liable for fourth-degree aggravated assault when the actor, "[k]nowingly under circumstances manifesting extreme indifference to the value of human life points a firearm . . . at or in the direction of another, whether or not the actor believes it to be loaded." The State contends that a defendant should not be able to assert a mistake-of-fact defense when charged with manslaughter, if such a defense would not be available against a charge of aggravated assault. In the case of certain offenses, state of mind is simply not an essential or material element.

On the other hand, the Sixth Amendment allows a defendant to assert any fact that will negate a material element of a crime. The material elements of manslaughter are the killing of another human being with a reckless state of mind. The culpable mental state is recklessness—the conscious disregard of a substantial and unjustified risk that death will result from the conduct. What mistaken belief will negate this state of mind?

> [T]he translation is uncertain at its most critical point: in determining the kind of mistake that provides a defense when recklessness, the most common culpability level, as to a circumstance is required. Recall that a negligent or faultless mistake negates . . . recklessness. While a "negligent mistake" may be said to be an "unreasonable mistake," all "unreasonable mistakes" are not "negligent mistakes." A mistake may also be unreasonable because it is reckless. Reckless mistakes, although unreasonable, will not negate recklessness. Thus, when offense definitions require recklessness as to circumstance elements, as they commonly do, the reasonable-unreasonable mistake language inadequately describes the mistakes that will provide a defense because of the imprecision of the term "unreasonable mistake." Reckless-negligent-faultless mistake language is necessary for a full and accurate description.

Thus, to disprove a reasonable mistake by proving that it is unreasonable, will turn out to be a mixed blessing for defendant. If the State may disprove a reasonable mistake by proving that the mistake was unreasonable, defendant may be convicted because he was negligent, as opposed to reckless, in forming the belief that the gun was unloaded. If recklessness is required as an element of the offense, "a merely negligent or faultless mistake as to that circumstance provides a defense."

Correctly understood, there is no difference between a positive and negative statement on the issue—what is required for liability versus what will provide a defense to liability. What is required in order to establish liability for manslaughter is recklessness (as defined by the Code) about whether death will result from the conduct. A faultless or merely careless mistake may negate that reckless state of mind and provide a defense.

How can we explain these concepts to a jury? We believe that the better way to explain the concepts is to explain what is required for liability to be established. The charge should be tailored to the factual circumstances of the case. The court should explain precisely how the offered defense plays into the element of recklessness. Something along the following lines will help to convey to the jury the concepts relevant to a reckless manslaughter charge:

> In this case, ladies and gentlemen of the jury, the defendant contends that he mistakenly believed that the gun was not loaded. If you find that the State has not proven beyond a reasonable doubt that the defendant was reckless in forming his belief that the gun was not loaded, defendant should be acquitted of the offense of manslaughter. On the other hand, if you find that the State has proven beyond a reasonable doubt that the defendant was reckless in forming the belief that the gun was not loaded, and consciously disregarded a substantial and unjustifiable risk that a killing would result from his conduct, then you should convict him of manslaughter.

. . . To sum up, evidence of an actor's mistaken belief relates to whether the State has failed to prove an essential element of the charged offense beyond a reasonable doubt. As a practical matter, lawyers and judges will undoubtedly continue to consider a mistake of fact as a defense. When we do so, we must carefully analyze the nature of the mistake in relationship to the culpable mental state required to establish liability for the offense charged. Despite the complexities perceived by scholars, the limited number of appeals on this subject suggests to us that juries have very little difficulty in applying the concepts involved. We may assume that juries relate the instructions to the context of the charge. For example, in the case of the carelessly purloined umbrella, we are certain that juries would have no difficulty in understanding that it would have been a reasonable mistake (although perhaps a negligent mistake) for the customer to believe that he or she was picking up the right umbrella.

To require the State to disprove beyond a reasonable doubt defendant's reasonable mistake of fact introduces an unnecessary and perhaps unhelpful degree of complexity into the fairly straightforward inquiry of whether defendant "consciously disregard[ed] a substantial and unjustifiable risk" that death would result from his conduct and that the risk was "of such a nature and degree that, considering the nature and purpose of the actor's conduct and the circumstances known to him, its disregard involve[d] a gross deviation from the standard of conduct that a reasonable person would observe in the actor's situation." . . .

NOTES & QUESTIONS ON MISTAKES OF FACT

1. *Reckless mistakes.*   Do you think Sexton was guilty of reckless man-slaughter? Given the description of the facts at the beginning of the case, do you have enough information in order to make a decision? What other facts would you, as a juror, need to have? Assuming that Sexton's statements are accurate, he did not know that the gun was loaded. So why isn't his ignorance—a bona fide mistake of fact—a complete defense? Essentially, Sexton is being prosecuted not in spite of his mistake but *because* of his mistake. In other words, his mistake did not negate his recklessness because his mistake *constituted* his recklessness. So the question for the jury is whether Sexton's jumping to an erroneous conclusion about the gun was reckless or not. Was it a reckless mistake? The bottom line is that reckless mistakes are no defense to a crime of recklessness—a formulation that sounds obvious.

2. *Is mistake of fact best classified as a defense?*   The previous note usefully highlights the fact that mistakes negate a required element of the offense, and in that sense are simply a failure of the prosecution to prove an essential element of its prima facie case. In that sense, perhaps we should stop calling mistake of fact a "defense." If not a defense, what other language could we use to describe it? Perhaps it should just be called a "negation" of a material element of the offense. That way of describing the doctrine helps clarify why the prosecutor retains the burden of disproving the mistake beyond a reasonable doubt. A defendant's argument about his mistake is often just the mirror image of the prosecutor's claim that the defendant acted with the required mens rea. For this reason, some scholars have concluded that mistake provisions are unnecessary in modern penal codes as long as the required mental elements are properly spelled out and understood. See Paul H. Robinson & Jane A. Grall, *Element Analysis in Defining Criminal Liability: The Model Penal Code and Beyond*, 35 Stan. L. Rev. 681, 732 (1983) ("[T]he mistake defense provisions and the accident provisions are both unnecessary. An offense's culpability requirements alone are adequate to determine precisely the mistakes or accidents that will provide a defense.").

3. *The moral wrong doctrine.*   In a previous era, courts would not allow defendants to claim mistake of fact if the defendant was aware that he was committing an immoral act. The analysis proceeded in the following way: Imagine the world as the defendant believed it to be. If the defendant believed that he was acting immorally, then he was not entitled to an acquittal based on a mistake of fact. A classic example is *Regina v. Prince*, L.R. 2 Crim. Cas. Res. 154 (1975). Prince was accused of taking a 14-year-old girl "out of the possession and against the will of her father or mother," which constituted a misdemeanor. Prince argued that he believed the girl was 18 years old at the time and therefore did not fall under the statute, which only applied to girls aged 16 or younger. Regardless, Prince was convicted because he knew that his actions

were immoral; he knew that taking an 18-year-old girl away from her parents was "immoral." What justifies a conviction in this case? Did Prince have the required mens rea for the offense? The court reasoned that knowledge of the immorality of his actions demonstrated enough culpability to justify punishing him. Many observers disagree with the moral wrong doctrine, going so far as to find it offensive. If you find it distasteful for a court to use morality so explicitly as a basis for a conviction, ask yourself *why*. What goes wrong when a court of law bases its decisions on morality? Is it because morality is not written down anywhere and therefore it violates the principle of legality? Or is it hopelessly vague because defendants cannot reliably predict what a court will consider immoral? Or perhaps some other reason?

4. *The legal wrong doctrine.*   Because of the well-known problems with the moral wrong doctrine described above, common law courts switched to the legal wrong doctrine, a close cousin to the moral wrong doctrine, which retains its basic structure but avoids its problematic appeal to morality. Under the legal wrong doctrine, the court asks whether the defendant believed that he was committing some *legal* wrong. If the answer is yes, then the defendant cannot claim a mistake of fact. For example, say a defendant transfers drug proceeds between two bank accounts and is charged with larceny for taking the money from a drug dealer. He argues mistake of fact because he genuinely thought that he was entitled to the money. However, he also was engaged in money laundering when he transferred the funds—a legal *wrong*. Under the doctrine he can still be prosecuted for larceny. In practice, the legal wrong doctrine allows a court to convict a defendant of a greater crime when the defendant believed he was committing a lesser crime. For this reason it is also sometimes referred to as the "lesser-offense doctrine." What is the rationale for the legal wrong doctrine? It seems to appeal to the equitable principle of clean hands. Since the defendant engaged in wrongdoing, he cannot complain about his treatment. Is this enough to justify the doctrine? As a judge, would you be comfortable applying the legal wrong doctrine now that it is based entirely on legal considerations as opposed to moral assessments? Nevertheless, the doctrine still allows defendants to be prosecuted for higher offenses when they thought they were committing a lesser offense. Is that appropriate?

The Model Penal Code includes a hybrid approach to this issue that in a formal sense follows the legal wrong doctrine but in a deeper sense rejects the legal wrong doctrine. First, the MPC says in § 2.04(2) that mistake is no defense "if the defendant would be guilty of another offense had the situation been as he supposed." This suggests that the MPC supports the legal wrong doctrine, because it denies the application of the defense in these cases and clarifies that these defendants will not be exonerated. But check out the next sentence. Section 2.04(2) goes on to say: "In such a case, however, the ignorance or mistake of the defendant shall reduce the grade and degree of the offense of which he may be convicted to those of the offense of which he would be guilty had the situation been as he supposed." This section rejects the *consequences* of the legal wrong doctrine (conviction for the greater offense) and attempts to correlate the defendant's criminal liability with the *level* of the lesser offense that he believed he was committing. In other words, the defendant who believes he was committing a lesser offense should be punished as if he had committed that lesser offense.

HYPOTHETICAL

A man sends money to an al-Qaeda operative and is charged with "knowingly" providing material support to a foreign terrorist organization. 18 U.S.C. § 2339B. The defendant knew that the man belonged to al-Qaeda but says he had no idea that al-Qaeda is a terrorist organization. The law requires that the defendant must know either that the organization is designated a "terrorist organization" by the federal government or, alternatively, that the organization has engaged in or engages in terrorist activity. If the defendant makes the incredible claim that he knew neither of these things, should he be allowed to make this argument to the jury? What would be the result under the older common law approach versus the modern Model Penal Code approach?

 Review the casebook video, *People v. David Savino* (Part 1: Mistakes). After watching the video, articulate the required mental element for the crime of robbery. Was the defendant's mistake of fact relevant to the case? Did the mistake negate a required element of the offense? Finally, is this a question of fact to be presented to a jury or a question of law that may be resolved by the judge?

2. Mistakes of Law

Mistake of law is relevant if the mistake negates a required mental element of the offense or (in some jurisdictions) if the defendant relied on an official interpretation of the law. Two cases are presented below. The first case, *Weiss*, demonstrates that penal statutes are not always explicit about whether the defendant must be aware of the legal assessment of his or her conduct. As you read *Weiss*, evaluate the crime of kidnapping and whether it requires that the defendant was aware of the illegal nature of his conduct. The second case, *Marrero*, deals with reliance on an official interpretation of the law. As you read *Marrero*, ask yourself whether the defendant's mistake was the product of his reliance on an official statement of the law or the product of his own *misinterpretation* of the law.

People v. Weiss

New York State Court of Appeals
276 N.Y. 384 (1938)

O'BRIEN, J.

These appellants [Schlossman and Weiss], without authority of law, seized and confined Paul H. Wendel, who was suspected or whom some pretended to suspect of the commission of a murder in New Jersey which had attracted attention throughout the country. They have been convicted of the crime of kidnapping as defined by section 1250 of the Penal Law, which provides; "A person who wilfully: 1. Seizes, confines, inveigles, or kidnaps another, *with intent* to cause him, *without authority of law,* to be confined or imprisoned within this state, or to be sent out of the state, or to be sold as a slave, or in any way held to service or kept or detained, against his will . . . is guilty of kidnapping. . . ."

The elements necessary to constitute the crime of kidnapping are different from those which are embraced within the torts of illegal arrest and false imprisonment. Where the detention is illegal, a civil action for damages will lie without regard to the innocence of the defendant in his *intentions.* In order to make out the crime of kidnapping, proof beyond a reasonable doubt must be produced that the defendant *willfully intended, without authority of law,* to confine or imprison another. To illustrate the difference: A reputable citizen is approached by a man, clothed in a police uniform and wearing a police shield, who requests him to assist in the arrest of one whom he describes as a murderer. The law-abiding citizen, in good faith and in the belief that he is performing his duty, assists the uniformed stranger and participates in the arrest of one who is entirely innocent. While the citizen may be answerable in damages in a civil action, he is not guilty of the crime of kidnapping, even though proof is later adduced that the uniformed stranger is an impostor and a kidnapper. In such a case, far from intending to seize or confine the prisoner *without authority of law,* he believed that his act was with such authority. In prosecutions for kidnapping, therefore, willful intent to seize a person without authority of law is the essential issue. Inferences of fact as to intent depend upon the degree of credibility accorded to witnesses by the jury and may be drawn from the defendant's disbelief or belief in the legality of his act. For the purpose of enabling the jury to draw its inference of fact, a defendant is entitled to the right of informing the jury in respect to his belief. His testimony may be of such a character as to fail to convince a jury, yet, nevertheless, he is entitled as a legal right to produce it for what it may be worth and to have it considered by the jury.

Appellant Schlossman testified that, prior to the seizure of Wendel, he had a conversation with appellant Weiss and with Ellis Parker, Jr., at a hotel in New York. His counsel attempted to introduce testimony in relation to statements by Parker, for the purpose of showing Schlossman's belief in his authority to act, but the offer was excluded and an exception taken. The following statement by Schlossman to Parker was, however, admitted: "I have got to have something to show that I am doing something within the law, helping you out this way, so he took out a badge, Secret Service of the State of New Jersey, and gave it to me and said he is hereby appointing me a special deputy to help him in the Lindbergh case." The questions, "Did you desire to help a detective solve any part of the Lindbergh mystery at that time?" and "Did you think at that time that you were taking part in some noble work?" were excluded and exceptions taken. The court stated: "That does not affect the question of his innocence or guilt, what he thought about those matters." Exception was taken to the exclusion of testimony by which appellant Weiss attempted to show that Parker had informed him of his official position and also to the exclusion of testimony by Weiss that he believed that the arrest of Wendel was made with authority of law. The following testimony in relation to a conversation between Weiss and Parker was stricken out and an exception noted: "I said, 'Now, listen. Suppose I arrest this man and we use these badges and he raises an outcry, and it proves to be an arrest illegally and there is police all over the street and the neighborhood and they should happen to come over. What happens then?' He [Parker] said: 'Well, that is what I am here for.' He says, 'You have the proper authority and if they question you I am there to prove who I am and whatever you done is the proper thing. Q. Did you believe that—what he told you? A. Yes.'" Exception was taken also to the ruling which sustained objection to this question directed to Weiss: "Did you believe that you were doing your Police work?"

Counsel for defendants requested: "That if the defendants, or either of them, acted in the honest belief that his act in seizing and confining Wendel was done with authority of law, even if they were mistaken in such belief, that they cannot be convicted of seizing, confining or kidnapping Wendel, *with intent, to cause him without authority of law* to be confined or imprisoned within the State, and the jury must acquit such defendants or defendant." To this request the court replied: "I not only decline to charge that but I repeat that the question of good faith is no defense." The jury was also instructed that "Even if they [defendants] did believe it, it is no defense in this case." If such interpretation is to prevail, then it must follow that in every instance where a defendant admits the fact that he *intended to make the arrest* and the courts later declare the arrest to have been made without authority of law, he must necessarily be convicted as a kidnapper, irrespective of his belief or his intentions to conform with the law. A peace officer, in the mistaken belief that he is acting with authority of law, makes an illegal arrest and later, in an effort to extort a confession, puts his prisoner through the third degree. He is guilty of the crime of assault or of official oppression, but he is certainly not a kidnapper. The question of assault is not in this case. So the trial judge charged.

The intent of defendants to seize and confine Wendel cannot be doubted, but their intent to perform these acts without authority of law depends upon the state of mind of the actors. If in good faith they believed that they were acting within the law, there could have been no intent to act "without authority of law." Their belief or disbelief indicates intent or lack of it and they were entitled to testify in respect to their intent based upon their belief.

No matter how doubtful the credibility of these defendants may be or how suspicious the circumstances may appear, we cannot say as matter of law, that, even in so strong a case as this for the prosecution, the jury was not entitled to consider the question whether defendants in good faith believed that they were acting with authority of law. We are, therefore, constrained to reverse the judgment of conviction and order a new trial for the purpose of submitting that question of fact to the jury.

The judgments should be reversed and a new trial ordered.

CRANE, CH. J. (dissenting).

I must dissent from the conclusions of Judge O'Brien in this case, upon three grounds:

First. I believe that the charge and rulings of the court were correct, and that the law has been well stated by Judge Johnston in the prevailing opinion. The fact that the defendants may have thought they had authority to confine Wendel is no excuse for the criminal act and no defense. The crime of kidnapping is committed when a person seizes and confines another with intent to cause him to be confined or imprisoned within the State, and the act is done without lawful authority. The fact that the person thought he had lawful authority has nothing to do with the matter. The intent applies to the seizing and to the confining. The defendants in this case intended to seize Wendel and to confine him within the State. In fact they confined him, bound, in Schlossman's home. Whether they thought they were acting according to law or not, or had legal authority, is no defense. They had no legal authority, and the judge so charged as matter of law. In this he was correct, for such is the law. In fact no one claims they had any legal authority. Where, therefore, one is seized, taken away and secretly confined, and it turns out that the person doing it had no legal authority to do it, the crime of kidnapping is committed. Of course if there be legal authority there is no crime, but the fact that the person mistakenly thought that they had authority does not lessen the crime. . . .

Second. The exceptions to the rulings of the judge excluding the evidence as to whether these defendants believed that they had authority to seize and imprison Wendel are harmless anyway, as both defendants testified as to the authority which young Parker told them they had, and the reasons given for not calling upon the New York police.

Third. Even if the law were different than I have stated it, we should not reverse for any of these rulings upon the plea that these men *believed* the law permitted them to seize Wendel, when both admit in their testimony before the grand jury that Wendel was taken to Schlossman's home, where Schlossman had prepared a stool or box posted in the cement upon which he and Weiss aided in fastening Wendel; that they saw him tied up with rope, and both participated in holding the straps while he was give the spread eagle, and kicked in the testicles; and both aided while he was pulled over backward by straps and tortured until he fainted. Such a case should not be reversed because these two men were not permitted to say that they believed they were aiding justice and obeying the law in committing such acts, all of which were part of the kidnapping. . . .

AFTERWORD   *People v. Weiss* is a bizarre case. It involves the crime of the century: the kidnapping of the baby of Charles Lindbergh, the famed aviator who gained prominence and social acclaim for flying solo and nonstop from Long Island to Paris. The kidnapping of his little boy transfixed the country. The defendants, Schlossman and Weiss, believed that Wendel—a lawyer—was involved in kidnapping the child, so they kidnapped and tortured Wendel until he confessed to the crime under duress. He later recanted. The Lindbergh baby was found dead; Richard Hauptmann was convicted and executed for the crime.

Lindbergh baby with nurse

People v. Marrero
New York Court of Appeals
69 N.Y.2d 382 (1987)

BELLACOSA, J.

. . . Defendant was a Federal corrections officer in Danbury, Connecticut, and asserted that status at the time of his arrest in 1977. He claimed at trial that there were various interpretations of fellow officers and teachers, as well as the peace officer statute itself, upon which he relied for his mistaken belief that he could carry a weapon with legal impunity.

The starting point for our analysis is the New York mistake statute as an outgrowth of the dogmatic common-law maxim that ignorance of the law is no excuse. The central issue is whether defendant's personal misreading or misunderstanding of a statute may excuse criminal conduct in the circumstances of this case.

The common-law rule on mistake of law was clearly articulated in *Gardner v. People* (62 NY 299). In *Gardner*, the defendants misread a statute and mistakenly believed that their conduct was legal. The court insisted, however, that the "mistake of law" did not relieve the defendants of criminal liability. The statute at issue, relating to the removal of election officers, required that prior to removal, written notice must be given to the officer sought to be removed. The statute provided one exception to the notice requirement: "removal . . . shall only be made after notice in writing . . . unless made while the inspector is actually on duty on a day of registration, revision of registration, or election, and for improper conduct." The defendants construed the statute to mean that an election officer could be removed without notice for improper conduct at any time. The court ruled that removal without notice could only occur for improper conduct on a day of registration, revision of registration or election.

In ruling that the defendant's misinterpretation of the statute was no defense, the court said:

> The defendants made a mistake of law. Such mistakes do not excuse the commission of prohibited acts. 'The rule on the subject appears to be, that in acts mala in se, the intent governs, but in those mala prohibita, the only inquiry is, has the law been violated?' The act prohibited must be intentionally done. A mistake as to the fact of doing the act will excuse the party, but if the act is intentionally done, the statute declares it a misdemeanor, irrespective of the motive or intent. . . . The evidence offered [showed] that the defendants were of [the] opinion that the statute did not require notice to be given before removal. This opinion, if entertained in good faith, mitigated the character of the act, but was not a defence [sic].

Gardner, 62 N.Y. 299, 304. This is to be contrasted with *People v. Weiss*, 276 N.Y. 384, where, in a kidnapping case, the trial court precluded testimony that the defendants acted with the honest belief that seizing and confining the child was done with "authority of law." We held it was error to exclude such testimony since a good-faith belief in the legality of the conduct would negate an express and necessary element of the crime of kidnapping, i.e., intent, without authority of law, to confine or imprison another. Subject to the mistake statute, the instant case, of course, falls within the *Gardner* rationale because the weapons possession statute violated by this defendant imposes liability irrespective of one's intent.

The desirability of the *Gardner*-type outcome, which was to encourage the societal benefit of individuals' knowledge of and respect for the law, is underscored by Justice Holmes' statement: "It is no doubt true that there are many cases in which the criminal could not have known that he was breaking the law, but to admit the excuse at all would be to encourage ignorance where the law-maker has determined to make men know and obey, and justice to the individual is rightly outweighed by the larger interests on the other side of the scales."

The revisors of New York's Penal Law intended no fundamental departure from this common-law rule in Penal Law § 15.20, which provides in pertinent part:

> 2. A person is not relieved of criminal liability for conduct because he engages in such conduct under a mistaken belief that it does not, as a matter of law, constitute an offense, unless such mistaken belief is founded upon an official statement of the law contained in (a) a statute or other enactment . . . (d) an interpretation of the statute or law relating to the offense, officially made or issued by a public servant, agency, or body legally charged or empowered with the responsibility or privilege of administering, enforcing or interpreting such statute or law.

This section was added to the Penal Law as part of the wholesale revision of the Penal Law in 1965. When this provision was first proposed, commentators viewed the new language as codifying "the established common law maxim on mistake of law, while at the same time recognizing a defense when the erroneous belief is founded upon an 'official statement of the law.'"

The defendant claims as a first prong of his defense that he is entitled to raise the defense of mistake of law under section 15.20(2)(a) because his mistaken belief that his conduct was legal was founded upon an official statement of the law contained in the statute itself. Defendant argues that his mistaken interpretation of the statute was reasonable in view of the alleged ambiguous wording of the peace officer exemption statute, and that his "reasonable" interpretation of an "official statement" is enough to satisfy the requirements of subdivision (2)(a). However, the whole thrust of this exceptional exculpatory concept, in derogation of the traditional and common-law principle, was intended to be a very narrow escape valve. Application in this case would invert that thrust and make mistake of law a generally applied or available defense instead of an unusual exception which the very opening words of the mistake statute make so clear, i.e., "A person is not relieved of criminal liability for conduct . . . unless" (Penal Law § 15.20). The momentarily enticing argument by defendant that his view of the statute would only allow a defendant to get the issue generally before a jury further supports the contrary view because that consequence is precisely what would give the defense the unintended broad practical application.

The prosecution further counters defendant's argument by asserting that one cannot claim the protection of mistake of law under section 15.20(2)(a) simply by misconstruing the meaning of a statute but must instead establish that the statute relied on actually permitted the conduct in question and was only later found to be erroneous. To buttress that argument, the People analogize New York's official statement defense to the approach taken by the Model Penal Code (MPC). Section 2.04(3) of the MPC provides: "A belief that conduct does not legally constitute an offense is a defense to a prosecution for that offense based upon such conduct when . . . (b) he acts in reasonable reliance upon an official statement of the law, *afterward determined to be invalid or erroneous*, contained in (i) a statute or other enactment" (emphasis added).

Although the drafters of the New York statute did not adopt the precise language of the Model Penal Code provision with the emphasized clause, it is evident and has long been believed that the Legislature intended the New York statute to be similarly construed. In fact, the legislative history of section 15.20 is replete with references to the influence of the Model Penal Code provision. The proposition that New York adopted the MPC general approach finds additional support in the comments to section 2. It is not without significance that no one for over 20 years of this statute's existence has made a point of arguing or noting or holding that the difference in wording has the broad and dramatically sweeping interpretation which is now proposed. Such a turnabout would surely not have been accidentally produced or allowed. New York's drafters may even have concluded that the extra clause in the MPC was mere surplusage in view of the clear exceptionability of the mistake authorization in the first instance. Moreover, adding specified conditions by judicial construction, as the dissenters would have to do to make the mistake exception applicable in circumstances such as these, would be the sheerest form of judicial legislation.

It was early recognized that the "official statement" mistake of law defense was a statutory protection against prosecution based on reliance of a statute that did in fact authorize certain conduct. "It seems obvious that society must rely on some statement of the law, and that conduct which is in fact 'authorized' . . . should not be subsequently condemned. The threat of punishment under these circumstances can have no deterrent effect unless the actor doubts the validity of the . . . official pronouncement—a questioning of authority that is itself undesirable." While providing a narrow escape hatch, the idea was simultaneously to encourage the public to read and rely on official statements of the law, not to have individuals conveniently and personally question the validity and interpretation of the law and act on that basis. If later the statute was invalidated, one who mistakenly acted in reliance on the authorizing statute would be relieved of criminal liability. That makes sense and is fair. To go further does not make sense and would create a legal chaos based on individual selectivity.

In the case before us, the underlying statute never in fact authorized the defendant's conduct; the defendant only thought that the statutory exemptions permitted his conduct when, in fact, the primary statute clearly forbade his conduct. Moreover, by adjudication of the final court to speak on the subject in this very case, it turned out that even the exemption statute did not permit this defendant to possess the weapon. It would be ironic at best and an odd perversion at worst for this court now to declare that the same defendant is nevertheless free of criminal responsibility.

The "official statement" component in the mistake of law defense in both paragraphs (a) and (d) adds yet another element of support for our interpretation and holding. Defendant tried to establish a defense under Penal Law § 15.20(2)(d) as a second prong. But the interpretation of the statute relied upon must be "officially made or issued by a public servant, agency or body legally charged or empowered with the responsibility or privilege of administering, enforcing or interpreting such statute or law." We agree with the People that the trial court also properly rejected the defense under Penal Law § 15.20(2)(d) since none of the interpretations which defendant proffered meets the requirements of the statute. The fact that there are various complementing exceptions to section 15.20, none of which defendant could bring himself under, further emphasizes the correctness of our view which decides this case under particular statutes with appropriate precedential awareness.

It must also be emphasized that, while our construction of Penal Law § 15.20 provides for narrow application of the mistake of law defense, it does not, as the dissenters contend, "rule out any defense based on mistake of law." To the contrary, mistake of law is a viable exemption in those instances where an individual demonstrates an effort to learn what the law is, relies on the validity of that law and, later, it is determined that there was a mistake in the law itself.

The modern availability of this defense is based on the theory that where the government has affirmatively, albeit unintentionally, misled an individual as to what may or may not be legally permissible conduct, the individual should not be punished as a result. This is salutary and enlightened and should be firmly supported in appropriate cases. However, it also follows that where, as here, the government is not responsible for the error (for there is none except in the defendant's own mind), mistake of law should not be available as an excuse . . .

Strong public policy reasons underlie the legislative mandate and intent which we perceive in rejecting defendant's construction of New York's mistake of law defense statute. If defendant's argument were accepted, the exception would swallow the rule. Mistakes about the law would be encouraged, rather than respect for and adherence to law. There would be an infinite number of mistake of law defenses which could be devised from a good-faith, perhaps reasonable but mistaken, interpretation of criminal statutes, many of which are concededly complex. Even more troublesome are the opportunities for wrongminded individuals to contrive in bad faith solely to get an exculpatory notion before the jury. These are not in terrorem arguments disrespectful of appropriate adjudicative procedures; rather, they are the realistic and practical consequences were the dissenters' views to prevail. Our holding comports with a statutory scheme which was not designed to allow false and diversionary stratagems to be provided for many more cases than the statutes contemplated. This would not serve the ends of justice but rather would serve game playing and evasion from properly imposed criminal responsibility . . .

Policy

NOTES & QUESTIONS ON MISTAKES OF LAW

1. *The mens rea of kidnapping.*   Were Weiss and Schlossman guilty of kidnapping? Put aside for a moment the allegations that they assaulted and tortured Wendel, and consider just the kidnapping charge. They argued that they believed that they were acting lawfully under state law as part of a police investigation into the Lindbergh crime. As it happens they were mistaken. Is their mistake of law relevant? The case highlights the need to determine the exact scope of the required mens rea. Both sides of the debate agree that the kidnapping requires an intentional confinement that is "without authority of law." But as written the statutory language is ambiguous. On one reading, "intentional" modifies the word "confinement" only. On the second reading, "intentional" modifies both "confinement" and "without authority of law." Whether the mistake of law is relevant depends entirely on how you read the mens rea of the offense. Which side gets the law of kidnapping correct? Does it penalize intentionally confining someone with the knowledge that the confinement is without legal authority, or does it penalize intentional confinements that just happen to be without legal authority (regardless of whether the defendant knows it)? That question must be answered first before proceeding to the issue of whether mistake of law is relevant in a kidnapping case.

2. *Tax evasion.*   Mistake of law is sometimes relevant in tax evasion cases. In *Cheek v. United States*, 498 U.S. 192 (1991), the Supreme Court analyzed 26 U.S.C. § 7203, which penalizes anyone who "willfully fails to" file an income tax return. The Court concluded that the word "willfully" implies that a defendant knew that he owed taxes but refused to file his return anyway. Consequently, defendants who honestly believe that they do not owe taxes cannot be convicted

of tax evasion, under some circumstances, though the IRS can assess them civil penalties. Cheek thought that he did not owe taxes because his wages were not income under the Internal Revenue Code. Although his legal interpretation was erroneous, perhaps even frivolous, the Supreme Court said that he could present his argument to a jury to determine if it negated the required mens rea. However, the court also rejected a similar mistake of law argument with respect to the constitutionality of the tax laws in general. In dissent, Justice Blackmun said that the decision would "encourage taxpayers to cling to frivolous views of the law in the hope of convincing a jury of their sincerity" and that "we have gone beyond the limits of common sense." Do you agree? Should Cheek get the benefit of his odd views of the Constitution? Ask yourself whether the phrase "ignorance of the law is no excuse" continues to be an accurate description of the doctrine today.

3. *Illegal structuring.* In *Ratzlaf v. United States*, 510 U.S. 135 (1994), the Supreme Court again had the opportunity to define the word "willfully" and again concluded that it required knowledge that the conduct was unlawful. Ratzlaf was charged with the federal crime of unlawful structuring, which involves configuring a financial transaction in such a way that a bank will not report the transaction to federal authorities. Most commonly this is accomplished by breaking up a large transaction into a number of smaller transactions, each of which are below $10,000. The Court concluded that the prosecution was required to demonstrate that Ratzlaf was willfully trying to evade the requirements of the law. Furthermore, the Court concluded that a prosecution for "willfully violating" the anti-structuring statute required that the defendant know that his conduct was criminal. A four-Justice minority strongly disagreed and accused the majority of confusing two different mental requirements. According to the dissenters, a defendant needs to know that his structuring of the transaction is designed to avoid the law's reporting requirements, but the defendant need not realize that this evasive behavior constitutes a *crime*. The dissent concluded that the law required the former state of awareness but not the latter. After all, why does it matter whether the defendant knows that structuring is a crime?

Although *Cheek* and *Ratzlaf* both interpreted the word "willfully" to require knowledge of law breaking, it would be wrong to assume that the term "willfully" can, or should, always be read in this way. In fact, the term is frequently used in penal statutes and does not always entail an intentional departure from the legal requirements of the law. In many instances it just means that the defendant committed an action deliberately without necessarily implying awareness of the illegal character of the behavior. Consequently, the only way to figure out what "willful" means in a particular statute is to analyze the context and purpose of the statute. There is no easy tip sheet for how to interpret the term.

4. *Reliance on official statements of the law.* In *Marrero*, the firearm possession statute exempted peace officers, who were defined as officials or guards "of any state correctional facility or of any penal correctional institution." Marrero worked as a guard at a federal prison and assumed (falsely, as it turned out) that he fell under the statutory exception. In your view, was his assumption reasonable? The Court of Appeals concluded that Marrero's mistake on this point was irrelevant. Marrero could assert mistake of law if he relied on a statute that was later deemed invalid or unconstitutional, or if he relied on a judicial interpretation by a court that is later found to be invalid. But the judges declined to extend the defense to situations, like Marrero's, where "a defendant misinterprets a potentially ambiguous statute not previously clarified by judicial decision and reasonably believes in good faith that the acts were legal." Is this fair to Marrero? If he was treated unfairly, was it because the court's interpretation of the statute was bad or because it should have granted him a mistake of law defense?

ADVICE   To assess the relevance of a mistake of law, you need to first examine the mental requirements for the offense. Structure your analysis in the following way:

1. Determine the elements of the offense, including conduct, mens rea, result, and any attendant circumstances.
2. Determine whether one of the attendant circumstances includes a legal status.
3. Determine the range of the mental requirement: Which elements of the offense does it apply to?
4. More specifically, determine whether the mens rea requires knowledge of the legal status referred to in the offense (which is rare).
5. If yes, ask yourself whether the defendant's mistake negates the required mens rea.

C. PRACTICE & POLICY

The following section considers some of the strategic concerns related to the use of mistake arguments in a criminal case. These include: (i) the dangers inherent in a defense counsel's decision to put a defendant on the stand to testify regarding a mistaken belief; and (ii) how to charge a jury on mistake of fact. Finally, this section concludes with a brief exegesis on the role that the concept of reasonableness has played in the evaluation of mistakes and why the MPC has moved away from the distinction between reasonable versus unreasonable mistakes.

∾ **The dangers of relying on mistake arguments.** How can a defense attorney establish the necessary facts for a strategy based on mistake of fact or mistake of law? Remember that although the prosecutor bears the burden of establishing that the defendant acted with the required mens rea for the offense, a defense attorney would be well advised to introduce evidence of the mistake to support this trial strategy. In other words, the defendant must offer at least *some* evidence that he labored under a relevant mistake if he hopes to convince the jury. In practice, the only way to present this evidence will be the defendant's own testimony about his state of mind when he committed the relevant act. As a defense attorney, would you counsel your client to take the stand? What risks are inherent in this strategy? In many cases, this will require the defendant to admit that he engaged in the relevant conduct, which could be risky for the defendant. If the jury rejects the mistake argument, the client has already admitted to the rest of the offense.

∾ **Charging a jury on mistakes.** If a judge determines that a defendant has established his initial burden of production regarding a mistake, he must then charge the jury on the issue. How should the judge describe the doctrine to them? In *People v. Gudz*, a man was charged with driving his car over a female bicyclist in an attempt to abduct her. Gudz argued at trial that he was laboring under a mistake of fact because he believed that the woman consented to the abduction. Specifically, he argued that he had corresponded with a woman named "Judith" on the Internet and planned a rendezvous that would begin with him kidnapping her while she rode a bicycle. He claimed that when he saw the real victim riding her bicycle, he mistakenly thought she was Judith. The trial judge delivered the following charge to the jury:

> In consideration of [defendant's mistake of fact defense], you must determine first what the defendant actually believed. That is, that he believed the victim had consented to such abduction. Next you must determine whether the defendant's mistake in identification of such individual was reasonable. That is, whether a reasonable person in defendant's position would, knowing what the defendant knew and being in the same circumstances, based on the known facts and availability of observations and investigation, have made the same mistake of fact. Thus, it is not sufficient that the defendant honestly believed in his own mind, that he was encountering the individual with which he had made this arrangement. An honest belief, no matter how genuine or sincere, may yet be unreasonable, and the mistake of fact must be such that a reasonable person in the defendant's position, knowing what the defendant knew, and being in the same circumstances, would have made the same mistake.

How would you evaluate the judge's description of the current state of the law of mistakes? Was it accurate? On appeal the conviction was reversed and a retrial was ordered. *People v. Gudz*, 793 N.Y.S.2d 556 (N.Y. App. Div. 2005). The appellate division concluded that the judge's reference to reasonableness was outmoded and not relevant. The sole issue for the jury to consider is whether the mistake negated the required mens rea of the offense, not whether it was objectively reasonable. But how should "negation" be explained to the jury? If you were a trial judge, what would you say to the jury?

∾ **Reasonableness redux.** Although it might seem crazy that the MPC approach does not technically require that a mistake of fact be reasonable, the Model Penal Code does not give defendants a free pass if they exhibit an unreasonable mistake. Remember, the Model Penal Code scheme requires that the mistake negate the required mens rea, and a reckless mistake will not negate the mens rea for a crime of recklessness. In the older common law doctrine, these mistakes might be called "unreasonable." What is the difference between the two approaches? Indeed there is a big difference. In the older common law approach, an unreasonable mistake would not be submitted to the jury and the defendant might be convicted of an *intentional* crime. In contrast, under the Model Penal Code, an unreasonable mistake might be labeled either negligent or reckless. A reckless mistake will negate the mens rea for an intentional crime but not a reckless crime, thus generating a conviction for a crime of recklessness. Similarly, a negligent mistake will negate the mens rea for a crime of recklessness (like manslaughter) but not for a crime of negligence (like negligent homicide). So in the older approach, the unreasonable defendant gets convicted of an intentional crime, while in the newer approach the defendant gets convicted of the lesser crime of recklessness or negligence (if a lesser crime exists).

CHAPTER 8

—⚬⚬⚬—

CAUSATION

A. DOCTRINE

The material elements of an offense will often require a particular *result*. So, for example, both murder and manslaughter require a resulting death caused by the defendant. Sometimes the material element is explicit about the causal relationship, but in other situations one can simply infer that talking about a prohibited result involves some causal connection. The criminal law generally follows the same two-step process used in tort law: First, establish whether there is any causal connection (sometimes also called a "but-for" cause, cause in fact, or actual cause), and then ask whether the causal connection is sufficiently close to hold the defendant responsible for the resulting harm (referred to as proximate cause or legal cause). In most cases, but-for causation will be relatively uncontroversial and the court will devote most of its energy to investigating proximate cause. The following sections outline the basic parameters for these two levels of the causation analysis.

1. Cause in Fact

The first step of the causal analysis is determining whether the defendant's behavior was a "cause in fact" of the prohibited result. This is usually determined by the "but-for" causation test: The court asks whether the result would have occurred "but for" the actions of the defendant. For this reason, lawyers often use the phrase "but-for causation" as a shorthand for "cause-in-fact causation" because the concept and its test are so deeply intertwined. If the defendant had refrained from acting, would the prohibited result have occurred anyway? If the answer is yes, then the defendant's action was not a cause in fact of the prohibited result.

There is one situation where cause-in-fact causation becomes contested and that is the problem of over-determination. Imagine that a firing squad shoots a condemned prisoner. If *one* of the guards had not fired his weapon, the prisoner would have died anyway (on account of the other bullets from the other guards). Or imagine that two people assault a victim and either punch was sufficient to cause the death. Taken literally, it seems that the "but-for" test is not satisfied in this case, because the result would have happened regardless of the defendant's action. Seemingly, the defendant made no difference to the result. The result is *over*-determined because any of the causes would have been sufficient to produce the harm.

But it would be absurd to conclude that there is insufficient causation in these cases—indeed, the problem is that there is *too much* causation, i.e., too many causes leading to the same result. Consequently, in these cases courts replace the but-for test and apply either a "substantial factor" test or an "acceleration" theory to determine cause-in-fact causation. Under the first test, courts ask whether the defendant's actions were a substantial factor in producing the result, regardless of whether the event might have occurred anyway. Under the second theory, courts ask whether the defendant's actions accelerated or hastened the result. The classic hypothetical is a victim pushed from the roof of a building. A second perpetrator, acting independently, shoots and kills the victim while he is already falling to his death. Is the second perpetrator a cause of the victim's death, given that he would have died anyway? Yes, because the second perpetrator *accelerated* the death (even if only by a second).

2. Proximate Cause

At common law, proximate cause was established with a rule of thumb: If the result occurred more than a year-and-a-day from the defendant's actions, the result could not be attributed to the defendant as a matter of law. Obviously, this doctrinal restriction was a crude proxy that liberated courts from getting their hands dirty in the messy business of determining causation. Although the doctrine still applies in many states, several jurisdictions have since abandoned the rule and recognize that some results come quickly and others take years to manifest themselves. For example, in one recent case, a man was indicted for murder because he violently shook a baby—who died as a teenager many years later. Victoria Cavaliere, *Washington State Teen Who Was Shaken as a Baby Dies; Father Likely to be Charged*, Reuters, Jan. 14, 2015. If the result was reasonably foreseeable, the defendant's actions are a proximate cause.

The most difficult cases involve intervening agents. Like in tort law, intervening agents who act negligently will not break the chain of causation, so a defendant can be prosecuted for putting someone in the hospital who later dies from negligent medical care (assuming this result is foreseeable). What if the intervening agents act intentionally? Unfortunately, this area of the law is deeply unsettled. Some courts ask whether the intervention was *normal* or *abnormal*; an abnormal intervention is unforeseeable and therefore breaks the chain of causation. The touchstone of this analysis is an objective analysis: Would a reasonable person foresee the intervention occurring? If yes, then the original actor is still responsible for the results that occur after the intervention.

In some cases, courts distinguish between *responding* and *coincidental* causes. If the second intervening agent is responding to the situation caused by the first actor, the causal chain is not broken and the first actor is still responsible. For example, suppose a defendant assaults and chases a boy into the street where he is struck and killed by a car. Does the intentional act of the boy (running into the street) break the causal chain? Arguably not, because the intervening act was a *response* to the situation caused by the defendant (the ongoing assault). *People v. Kern*, 545 N.Y.S.2d 4 (N.Y. App. Div. 1989) (upholding conviction). In contrast, a coincidental intervening cause will break the causal chain and the first actor will not be responsible. Suppose an assailant robs and assaults a victim and leaves him on the sidewalk. Then a second assailant, unconnected to the first crime, sees the victim lying on the ground and kills him. The intentional actions of the second assailant break the causal chain because they are a coincidence.

responding prox. cause ✓

coincidental prox. X cause

B. APPLICATION

1. Cause in Fact

The materials below present two cases where cause-in-fact causation was problematic. In the first case, *Oxendine*, the prosecution suggested that the defendant accelerated the death of the victim, but was there sufficient evidence to back up this claim? The second case, *Jennings*, involves over-determination: Experts testified that each cause was, by itself, sufficient to produce the victim's death. Notice how the court in *Jennings* applies the substantial factor test to solve the problem of over-determination. Would the substantial factor test change the outcome in *Oxendine* if that court applied it too?

Oxendine v. State
Supreme Court of Delaware
528 A.2d 870 (1987)

Reverse + Remand

HORSEY, JUSTICE:

Defendant, Jeffrey Oxendine, Sr., appeals his conviction in trial by jury in Superior Court of manslaughter in the beating death of his six-year-old son, Jeffrey Oxendine, Jr. Oxendine was sentenced to twelve years' imprisonment. On appeal, Oxendine's principal argument is that the Trial Court committed reversible error by denying his motion for a judgment of acquittal on the issue of causation. Specifically, he argues that the State's medical testimony, relating to which of the codefendants' admittedly repeated beatings of the child was the cause of death, was so vague and uncertain as to preclude his conviction of any criminal offense.

We conclude that the evidence upon causation was insufficient to sustain Oxendine's conviction of manslaughter, but that the evidence was sufficient to sustain his conviction of the lesser included offense of assault in the second degree. Therefore, we affirm the Trial Court's denial of Oxendine's motion for a judgment of acquittal, direct that he be convicted of assault in the second degree, and remand for entry of judgment of conviction and resentencing for that offense.

The facts may be summarized as follows: On the morning of January 18, 1984, Leotha Tyree, Oxendine's girlfriend, who lived with him, pushed Jeffrey into the bathtub causing microscopic tears in his intestines which led to peritonitis. During a break at work that evening, Oxendine telephoned home and talked to Jeffrey, who complained of stomach pains. When Oxendine returned home from work, he saw bruises on Jeffrey and knew that Tyree had beaten the child during the day. Although Jeffrey continued to complain of a stomachache, he apparently did not tell his father how or when he received the bruises.

The next morning at approximately 7:30 A.M., Oxendine went into Jeffrey's bedroom and began screaming at him to get up. A neighbor in the same apartment building testified to hearing sounds coming from the room of blows being struck, obscenities uttered by a male voice, and cries from a child saying, "Please stop, Daddy, it hurts." After hearing these sounds continue for what seemed like five to ten minutes, the witness heard a final noise consisting of a loud thump, as if someone had been kicked or punched "with a great blow."

Later that day, Jeffrey's abdomen became swollen. When Oxendine arrived home from work at about 5:00 P.M., Tyree told him of Jeffrey's condition and urged him to take Jeffrey to the hospital. Oxendine, apparently believing that Jeffrey was exaggerating his discomfort, went out, bought a newspaper, and returned home to read it. Upon his return, Tyree had prepared to take Jeffrey to the hospital. En route, Jeffrey stopped breathing; and was pronounced dead shortly after his arrival at the hospital.

I

In order to convict Oxendine of manslaughter, the State had to show that his conduct caused Jeffrey's death. 11 Del. C. § 261 defines causation as the "antecedent but for which the result in question would not have

Causation

Sts Theories of Causation

occurred." At trial, the State's original theories of causation were, alternatively, (1) a "combined direct effect," or (2) an "aggravation" theory.

During its case-in-chief, the State called medical examiners Dr. Inguito and Dr. Hameli, who both testified that Jeffrey's death was caused by intra-abdominal hemorrhage and acute peritonitis, occurring as a result of blunt force trauma to the front of the abdomen. Similarly, each pathologist identified two distinct injuries, one caused more than twenty-four hours before death, and one inflicted less than twenty-four hours before death.

Dr. Inguito could not separate the effects of the two injuries. In his view, it was possible that both the older and more recent hemorrhage could have contributed to the death of the child, but he was unable to tell which of the hemorrhages caused the death of the child. Dr. Inguito could not place any quantitative value on either of the hemorrhages nor could he state whether the fresh hemorrhage or the older hemorrhage caused the death. The prosecutor never asked, nor did Dr. Inguito give, an opinion on whether the second hemorrhage accelerated Jeffrey's death.

Both injuries possible cause

Dr. Hameli, on the other hand, was of the opinion that the earlier injury was the underlying cause of death. According to him, the later injury, i.e., the second hemorrhage, "was an aggravating, and probably some factors [sic] contributing," but it was the earlier injury that was the plain underlying cause of death.

1st underlying cause w/ 2nd aggravating

The prosecutor, however, did explicitly ask Dr. Hameli if the second injury accelerated Jeffrey's death. The relevant portion of the testimony is as follows:

> Prosecutor: Dr. Hameli, within a reasonable degree of medical certainty and in your expert opinion, did the second hemorrhage accelerate this child's death?
> Hameli: I do not know. If you are talking about timewise-I assume that's what you are talking about, exploration.
> Prosecutor: You cannot give an opinion of that area; is that correct?
> Hameli: No.

Oxendine moved for judgment of acquittal at the end of the State's case-in-chief. The Trial Court, however, denied his motion.

As part of her case, codefendant Tyree called Dr. Hofman, a medical examiner, who disagreed about the number of injuries. He perceived only one injury inflicted about twelve hours before death. Subsequently, the prosecutor asked Hofman the following hypothetical question that assumed two blows when Hofman only testified as to one blow:

(3) med. expert

> Prosecutor: In your expert medical opinion within a reasonable degree of medical certainty, if this child, given his weakened state as a result of the significant trauma to his abdominal cavity, suffered subsequently

another blunt force trauma to the same area, would it accelerate this child's death?

Hofman: My opinion, as in a general statement, not knowing this child, it certainly would have an impact on shortening this child's life.

Prosecutor: Is then, therefore, your answer yes?

Hofman: Yes.

At the end of trial, Oxendine again moved for judgment of acquittal. The Trial Court denied the motion and instructed the jury on the elements of recklessness, causation and on various lesser included offenses. The ultimate and only theory of causation on which the jury was charged was based on "acceleration." The Trial Court instructed the jury that "[a] defendant who causes the death of another . . . is not relieved of responsibility for causing the death if another later injury accelerates, that is, hastens the death of the other person. Contribution without acceleration is not sufficient." As previously noted, the jury returned verdicts of manslaughter against Oxendine and Tyree.

II

In this case, the evidence established that Oxendine inflicted a nonlethal injury upon Jeffrey after his son had, twenty-four hours earlier, sustained a lethal injury from a previous beating inflicted by Tyree. Thus, for Oxendine to be convicted of manslaughter in this factual context, the State was required to show for purposes of causation that Oxendine's conduct hastened or accelerated the child's death. The Superior Court correctly instructed the jury that "[c]ontribution [or aggravation] without acceleration is insufficient to establish causation." We do not equate aggravation with acceleration. It is possible to make the victim's pain more intense, i.e., aggravate the injury, without accelerating the time of the victim's death. Thus, in terms of section 261, and as applied to defendant, the relevant inquiry is: but for his infliction of the second injury, would the victim have died when he died? If the second injury caused his son to die any sooner, then defendant, who inflicted the second injury, would be deemed to have caused his son's death within the definition of section 261 . . .

The State's expert medical testimony, even when viewed in the light most favorable to the State, was (1) insufficient to sustain the State's original theories of causation (a "combined direct effect" or an "aggravation" theory); and (2) insufficient to sustain the State's ultimate theory of causation ("acceleration") on which the court instructed the jury. Both of the State's expert witnesses, Dr. Inguito and Dr. Hameli, were unable to state with any degree of medical certainty that the second injury contributed to the death of the child. Dr. Inguito could only testify that it was possible that both the older and more recent hemorrhage could have contributed to the death of the child. As for Dr. Hameli, he testified that the second injury independent of the first injury could have caused death but probably would not cause death. Furthermore, Dr. Hameli explicitly stated that he could not give an opinion as to whether the second injury accelerated Jeffrey's death. Similarly, Dr. Inguito was neither asked nor did he offer an opinion about acceleration . . .

The Trial Court, however, properly denied Oxendine's motion for judgment of acquittal at the close of the State's case because its medical testimony was sufficient for a rational trier of fact to conclude beyond a reasonable doubt that Oxendine was guilty of the lesser included offense of assault in the second degree, 11 Del. C. § 612(1). Therefore, we reverse Oxendine's conviction of manslaughter and remand the case to Superior Court for entry of a judgment of conviction and resentence of defendant for the lesser included offense of assault in the second degree.

[handwritten margin note: T.C. correct... D guilty of lesser offense]

ADVICE   The outcome of the *Oxendine* case offers an important lesson for practicing criminal lawyers. In a homicide case, if there is a failure of proof on causation, then in most cases the defendant will be guilty of a lesser-included offense such as aggravated battery, which does not require that the defendant caused the death of the victim. Consequently, a defense victory on the issue of causation is not necessarily a complete vindication; the defendant may still be sent to prison if convicted for the lesser-included offense. As a practicing attorney, would this change your defense strategy in some cases?

People v. Jennings

Supreme Court of California
114 Cal. Rptr. 3d 133, 237 P.3d 474 (2010)

GEORGE, C.J.

Defendant was tried together with his wife, Michelle Jennings. Defendant and Michelle had been together since Michelle ran away from home in 1989, when she was 14 years of age and defendant was 29. Arthur Jennings was born prematurely to defendant and Michelle on November 16, 1990. . . .

Approximately two weeks before Christmas in 1995, Phillip and Kevin Orand visited the Jenningses' home. Phillip saw Arthur with two black eyes and a mark on his mouth. Arthur was making an odd sound, rocking back and forth but staring straight ahead. When Phillip inquired what was wrong with Arthur, defendant said Michelle had "knocked him out." Michelle confirmed to Kevin that she had "socked the damn little brat between the eyes, knocked him out." . . .

Bernard Romaine saw Arthur in early January 1996 and recounted that he looked "pretty beat up." At the time, Arthur had two black eyes—one in particular that was "real bad" and appeared to require medical attention because it was swollen shut and seeping blood—and a bandaged hand that appeared to have been burned. Arthur also appeared very thin and undernourished. . . .

On February 4, 1996, while Michelle was away, Cora Grein, a neighbor, visited the Jenningses' home. Defendant and Arthur were watching a television program, and Grein joined them. Defendant instructed Arthur to go to his bedroom. Defendant then attempted to kiss Grein, but she resisted. During this attempt, Arthur reentered the room and subsequently was instructed by defendant to return to his bedroom. Grein testified that as Arthur began walking away, defendant grabbed him and struck him on the back of his head with a fireplace shovel. Defendant then picked up Arthur and threw him on the bed. He told Grein that if she said anything she would "see the bottom of a mine shaft." Grein told defendant she would remain quiet, and left.

Arthur died within an hour of being struck on the head with the shovel. The Jenningses initially buried Arthur's body in a shallow grave inside an old chicken coop. A few hours later, however, they unearthed Arthur's body and threw it down a nearby desert mine shaft. The Jenningses then attempted to scrub the blood off Arthur's bedroom walls. Defendant also burned Arthur's sheets and the gloves used to bury him, and placed Arthur's diaper, clothes, and glasses in the trash. . . .

Dr. Frank Sheridan, a forensic pathologist, performed the autopsy on Arthur's body. Dr. Sheridan testified that at the time of his death, Arthur was 3 feet 10 inches tall, and weighed only 35 pounds. His body as a whole was "severely emaciated and malnourished"; he had almost no body fat or fatty tissue, his muscles were wasted, and he had no food in his stomach when he died. Dr. Sheridan's examination of Arthur revealed no medical reason why Arthur would not have been eating or gaining weight. The severity of Arthur's condition indicated it was not something that had occurred over a short period of time.

Dr. Sheridan also testified concerning Arthur's numerous physical injuries, which he described as "generally painful to varying degrees" and as having required force to inflict. Visible injuries to Arthur's body included a bruise and an abrasion on the tip of Arthur's nose, bruising and a laceration in the area between the nose and the upper lip, bruises on the inside of his lips and gums, a lacerated oral frenulum (between the gum and the upper lip), and a slight bruise on the tip of his tongue. These injuries occurred shortly before death and were most consistent with smothering.

Arthur also had two injuries to the back of his head—one injury on the right side that was a few weeks old and had been sutured, and a second "fresh" injury on the left side that had occurred no more than six hours prior to his death, and possibly as recently as immediately preceding the time of death, but that was not itself life threatening. The remainder of Arthur's external injuries included a severe burn on his right hand, covering half of the palm and most of the fingers, that probably was several weeks old; abrasions on his left hand and arm, right elbow, and left buttock; "rug burn" abrasions and bruising on his left back; bruises on his chest, shoulders, right elbow and arm, left arm, and left buttock; a major hemorrhage to the right shoulder blade area; and a scar on the back of his lower right thigh.

An internal examination revealed extensive hemorrhaging to the deeper layers of Arthur's scalp that extended across the entire front of his forehead, indicating some kind of blow or impact to the area. This injury occurred shortly before Arthur's death but separately from his other recent head injury. Arthur also had a subdural hemorrhage on the left side of his head that was at least 10 days old, and hemorrhaging around the optic nerves of the back of the eyes from the same injuring event. Dr. Sheridan referred to this as an "acceleration/deceleration injury" consistent with a child who had been shaken violently, possibly causing permanent brain damage.

A microscopic examination of Arthur's lung tissue indicated he had acute pneumonia at the time of his death. Dr. Sheridan attributed this infection to the breakdown of Arthur's immune system and his overall failure to thrive.

Toxicology tests revealed that Arthur had three drugs in his blood system, all central nervous system depressants. The first drug was a significant amount of Unisom consistent with the administration of two sleeping pills. The dose was sufficient to cause seizures and cessation of breathing. The second drug was a small amount of Vicodin, a prescription painkiller, which would have added to the sedative or depressive effect of the Unisom. The third drug was a small amount of Valium, which would have played a minor contributing role in Arthur's condition.

When asked whether he had determined "a cause of death or causes of death," Dr. Sheridan replied, "Causes." On the death certificate, he listed the "main cause of death" as "combined drug toxicity," because although the level of Unisom alone was potentially fatal and the levels of Vicodin and Valium alone were not toxic, the three drugs together had a certain "additive effect" on sedation. Under the heading "Contributing Causes"— which Dr. Sheridan explained is "where you can list something else that contributed to death but is separate from the main one"—he listed "acute and chronic physical abuse and neglect." The term "acute" referred to Arthur's injuries inflicted shortly before death, and the term "chronic" referred to Arthur's older injuries as well as to the "very, very severe" emaciation and malnutrition. Also listed as a contributing cause was the acute pneumonia, which was a complication of Arthur's emaciated state.

Questioned further, Dr. Sheridan gave the cause of death as "the entire problem"—the drugs, the physical injuries, and the malnutrition and emaciation—"all working together," that brought about the resulting death. He described Arthur as in a "downhill slide" and "very near to the end of his life" because of malnutrition and "the whole body not functioning properly." Dr. Sheridan testified that even without the ingestion of drugs, Arthur likely would have died within a fairly short period of time if he were not given medical attention and food. Without the positive toxicology results, Dr. Sheridan would have concluded that acute abuse was the primary cause of death, most likely by smothering. . . .

Defendant . . . contends that even assuming he tortured Arthur, there is insufficient evidence that his torture was the "but for" cause of Arthur's death, which defendant attributes to the drugs. We disagree. There was sufficient evidence presented at trial from which a reasonable juror could have found that defendant's acts of physical violence and deliberate starvation of Arthur were concurrent causes of Arthur's death. . . .

If a defendant's acts of torture were a concurrent cause of the death, it is no defense that the conduct of some other person contributed to the death. "When the conduct of two or more persons *contributes concurrently as the proximate cause of the death,* the conduct of each is a proximate cause of the death if that conduct was also a substantial factor contributing to the result. A cause is concurrent if it was operative at the time of the death and acted with another cause to produce the death." "To be considered the proximate cause of the victim's death, the defendant's act must have been a substantial factor contributing to the result, rather than insignificant or merely theoretical." "[A]s long as the jury finds that without the criminal act the death would not have occurred when it did, it need not determine which of the concurrent causes was the principal or primary cause of death."

For this reason, defendant's focus upon "but for" causation, and whether the drugs were the "primary cause" of Arthur's death, is misplaced. "But for" or "sine qua non" causation provides that "[t]he defendant's conduct is a cause of the event if the event would not have occurred but for that conduct; conversely, the defendant's conduct is not a cause of the event, if the event would have occurred without it." By comparison, the "substantial factor" rule for concurrent causes "was developed primarily for cases in which application of the but-for rule would allow each defendant to escape responsibility because the conduct of one or more others would have been sufficient to produce the same result." As we have stated in the civil context, the tests for "but for" and "substantial factor" causation usually produce the same result, but the "substantial factor" standard states a clearer rule that subsumes and reaches beyond the "but for" test to more accurately address situations in which there are independent concurrent causes of an event.

In the present case, there was sufficient evidence from which a reasonable jury could have concluded that defendant's torture was at least a substantial factor in Arthur's death. Dr. Sheridan testified that the cause of Arthur's death was attributable to *the entire problem*—that it, the drugs, the physical injuries, and the malnutrition and emaciation—"*all working together*" to bring about the resulting death. Additionally, the expert toxicologist and Dr. Sheridan both concluded that the dosage of Unisom that was administered to Arthur was sufficient to account for Arthur's death *in light of his age and weight*. The jury reasonably could have inferred from this evidence that defendant's physical abuse and purposeful starvation of Arthur contributed to the lethal effect of the pills, and therefore was a substantial factor in his death. . . .

AFTERWORD   Martin Jennings was sentenced to death and currently sits on death row. His wife, Michelle Jennings, was sentenced to 25 years to life in prison.

Substantial
Factor

NOTES & QUESTIONS ON BUT-FOR CAUSATION

1. *Substantial factor test.* In *Jennings*, the court concluded that the defendant's actions were a substantial factor in the victim's death, even if other factors, such as the drugs in his system, were also prominent causes. What explains the use of the substantial factor test? Is it an ad hoc loosening of the requirement of but-for causation in difficult cases, or is there a deeper rationale for why the test should be used? Do you agree with the court's application of the doctrine in this case? Scholars are split over the coherence of the test. What is clear is that the best justification for the substantial factor test is that it simply avoids absurd results: letting a defendant go free just because the death of the victim was over-determined and would have happened anyway. That seems unjust, so the substantial factor test removes the loophole. See Michael Moore, *Causation in the Criminal Law*, in *The Oxford Handbook of Philosophy of Criminal Law* 168, 174 (J. Deigh & D. Dolinko eds., 2011) ("Notice that the substantial factor test 'solves' the overdetermination problem mostly because it does not say enough to get itself into trouble in the overdetermination cases. It thus allows our clear causal intuitions full play in these

cases."). For another case applying the substantial factor test, see *Commonwealth v. Nicotra*, 425 Pa. Super. 600, 625 A.2d 1259 (1993). Nicotra was charged with drunk driving and involuntary manslaughter (among other charges) in connection with a fatal car accident. The defendant argued that there was insufficient evidence that his intoxication or his speeding caused the accident; in other words, he argued that the accident would have occurred even if had been sober and had been driving slower. On appeal, the court sustained the conviction because a rational fact finder could conclude that the defendant's reckless conduct was a "substantial factor" in causing the death of the victim.

2. *The acceleration theory.* If a defendant accelerates the death of the victim, even if the victim's death was inevitable at a later point in time, courts will still convict the defendant. Why did the prosecution in *Oxendine* fail in its effort to prove acceleration? If you were the prosecutor in that case, would you have asked different questions? To better understand the acceleration theory, consider the following hypothetical. Ann poisons Bob with small doses of arsenic that take months to become fatal. In the interim, Charles shoots and kills Bob. Since Bob was dying anyway, Charles cannot be a "but-for" cause of Bob's death, unless you apply the acceleration theory. What is the justification for this doctrine? In a sense, everyone's death is inevitable at some point in time (we all die), so *any* killing prosecuted by the justice system is, in a sense, an acceleration of our inevitable demise. What is morally relevant is *when* we die and why. For more discussion, see Michael Moore, *Causation and Responsibility: An Essay in Law, Morals, and Metaphysics* 67 (2009).

3. *Likelihood of survival theory.* Sometimes the defendant's action does not accelerate death but merely makes survival less likely. Is that enough to establish causation? Imagine one perpetrator shoots the victim, who is injured but survives. A second perpetrator refuses to take the victim to the hospital and instead lets him die in the car. At trial, a surgeon testifies that he is unsure if he could have saved the victim with timely treatment, but concedes that the victim "would have had some chance" if promptly taken to the hospital. Did the second action—refusing to take the victim to the hospital—cause the resulting death? The "likelihood of survival" theory answers that question in the affirmative and makes the second actor (in addition to the shooter) responsible for the resulting death. Courts are split on this issue. Compare *State v. Montoya*, 61 P.3d 793 (N.M. 2002) (evidence sufficient to establish but-for causation because "[i]mmediate medical intervention possibly could have saved his life"), with *State v. Muro*, 695 N.W.2d 425 (Neb. 2005) (rejecting causation based on mere possibility that medical attention would save victim).

4. *Concurrence of the elements.* In addition to the causal requirements discussed in this section, there also must be a concurrence between the act and mental elements. In most cases, the concurrence comes naturally. But in

some rare situations, the act and mental elements peel apart, causing problems for the prosecution. For example, in *People v. Smith*, 78 Cal. App. 3d 698 (1978), the defendant was charged with the crime of burglary, which requires entering a dwelling (or similar structure) with the intent to commit a felony inside. The appeals court concluded, correctly, that burglary requires that the defendant have the intent to commit the felony when he *first* entered the dwelling. If the defendant entered the building for some other reason, and then decided to commit the larceny *after* he entered, this would not constitute burglary because there must be a concurrence of act and intent. Ultimately, in *Smith*, the defendant's appeal was dismissed, because the court concluded that "there was no room for a finding that the requisite specific intent to steal or to commit an assault by means of force likely to produce great bodily injury could have been formed after defendant's entry into [the] apartment." However, in a hypothetical case where a defendant enters a dwelling unlawfully but then forms the intent to commit the felony once inside, the proper result is acquittal on the burglary charge. In California, the concurrence requirement is codified by statute. See Cal. Penal Code § 20 ("In every crime or public offense there must exist a union, or joint operation of act and intent, or criminal negligence."). But this is rare. In most jurisdictions, the concurrence requirement is a creature of precedent based on logic and legal theory. Can you imagine other situations where concurrence is a problem?

2. Proximate Cause

Determining proximate cause is one of the most fraught areas of legal analysis in the criminal law. In the following case, the victim allegedly failed to follow medical advice after he was released from the hospital. The question is whether that decision should break the chain of causation that leads back to the defendant— who originally put the victim in the hospital in the first place. Pay attention to the role that the concept of foreseeability plays in the court's answer to this question.

State v. Smith
Court of Appeals of Ohio, Fourth District
2007 WL 1165822 (2007)

HARSHA, J.

John Smith appeals his convictions for felonious assault and involuntary manslaughter stemming from his assault of Bryan Biser, who died after being hit by a single punch to the head. Biser was diabetic and quit taking his medication after the incident. Prior to death, his blood sugar levels were extremely elevated and his bowels had become necrotic. Thus, Smith contends unforeseeable intervening events caused Biser's death. However, based on the testimony from the State's two expert witnesses, a reasonable juror could conclude that Smith's punch and Biser's resulting fall damaged the frontal lobes of Biser's brain. As a normal result of these injuries, Biser became apathetic and disinterested, which in turn, led to his failure to take required medication, and ultimately his death. Biser's lapse in attending to his own care was a response to Smith's assault. Because it was neither unforeseeable nor abnormal, it cannot be an intervening cause that broke the chain of legal causation stemming from the assault. . . .

FACTS

A grand jury indicted John Smith with one count of felonious assault and one count of involuntary manslaughter for allegedly causing the death of Bryan Biser by a closed-fist punch to the head. The case proceeded to a jury trial, which produced the following facts. . . .

On April 15, 2005, Bryan Biser spent the afternoon socializing with neighbors at the Hokolesqua Apartments just outside Frankfort, Ohio. Biser sat outside with his neighbor, Shanna Knapp, and split a six-pack of beer with her while watching the children playing in a playground just across the parking lot. As they watched the children, two of the kids around the age of five got into a fight. One of the children was a distant relative of Smith's.

When Smith learned that his nephew's child had been in a fight, he walked over to the playground and screamed obscenities at the children. Smith encouraged his five-year-old relative to beat up the other child. Ms. Knapp overheard Smith and approached him near the playground. Ms. Knapp told Smith to stop yelling obscenities and encouraging the children to fight. Ms. Knapp then got into an argument with Smith's nephew, John Rawlings.

Biser approached Ms. Knapp and Rawlings in the parking lot and attempted to stop the arguing by asking everyone to calm down. Smith then walked around a car towards Biser, yelled an obscenity at him, and hit him with a closed fist on the left side of his head while Biser stood with one hand to his side and one hand holding a beverage cup. Biser never raised his arms, squared to fight, or said a threatening word.

As Biser crumpled to the ground, the right side of his face hit a parked car, and then his head hit the pavement. Smith "danced" over Biser, as he lay unconscious, taunting him to get up and fight and challenging everyone else to fight him. Biser remained on the ground while a neighbor, Twila Jones, called 911. One of the children alerted Amy Preston, the apartment complex manager, who was also a nursing assistant, to attend to Biser.

Approximately fifteen minutes after receiving the call, emergency medical technicians (EMTs) Todd Smith and Sharon Flannery arrived on the

scene, along with EMT trainee Marilyn Chaffin. Biser regained consciousness, and the EMT's began treating his wounds and transported him to
Adena hospital. Biser stated to the EMT's that he was diabetic and had
taken his insulin that day. However, the EMT's were not able to take his
blood-glucose level because the Accu-check machine malfunctioned. Chaffin
testified that she noticed one of Biser's pupils was bigger than the other, but
she failed to note this in her report.

Dr. Kashubeck examined Biser at the emergency room of Adena Hospital. In his report, he noted that Biser's pupils were round and equal in
size, and that Biser denied any pain anywhere. The report also noted that
Biser complained of a laceration to his right eye and a bump to the back of
the head, and that he answered questions and followed commands appropriately. Biser refused emergency room treatment for his head injuries and
his diabetes, despite an elevated blood-glucose level of 465. Biser stated
that he had insulin to treat the diabetes at home and did not want to
purchase more at the hospital. He also refused a CAT Scan, which the
doctor had recommended. The doctor discharged Biser from the hospital,
but ordered him to return immediately if he experienced any vomiting,
confusion or vision problems.

Ms. Preston and Ms. Jones went to check on Biser following his return
from the hospital that same day, April 15, 2005. Ms. Preston testified that
Biser seemed confused and did not remember being involved in a fight, but,
instead, told her he had been singing karaoke that night. He acknowledged
being at the emergency room and gave Ms. Preston his paperwork from
that visit. The next day, April 16, 2005, Ms. Preston and Ms. Jones went
again to check on Biser. Ms. Jones testified that Biser did not invite them in,
but cracked the door and told them he felt sick to his stomach and asked
them to leave him alone.

Biser's cousin, Beth Spangler testified that she visited Biser on three
separate occasions on April 16, 2005. She first stopped by in the morning
and gave him Advil for his headache. She stopped by again at 1:00 PM, and
he continued to complain that his head hurt, and he wanted everyone to go
away. Finally, she returned at 5:00 PM and brought him food. She testified
that Biser told her he had taken his insulin that day. She also testified that
there were two bottles of insulin in the refrigerator.

Ms. Preston testified that on Tuesday, April 19, 2005, she received a
voicemail from one of Biser's family members, who had been unable to
contact him. Ms. Preston knocked on Biser's door, but received no
response. She opened his door with her master key and found Biser
lying on the floor, unconscious. She testified that Biser struggled to breathe,
and his feet and left arm had turned black. Ms. Preston instructed a
neighbor to call 911, and an ambulance arrived within seven to eight minutes to transport Biser to the hospital.

At the emergency room, Biser underwent a CAT scan of his head, which indicated that he had a possible skull fracture, a small subdural hematoma, and subarachnoid hemorrhage. Additionally, Biser's blood-glucose level was 1,169, and he was in severe diabetic ketoacidosis, a lethal condition resulting from a diabetic's failure to take prescribed insulin. Doctors transported Biser to Grant Medical Center in Columbus, Ohio, where he underwent exploratory surgery in his abdomen. The surgeons discovered that his right bowel and a portion of his right colon were necrotic, a condition from which no one could survive. Biser died several hours later. After performing an autopsy, Deputy Coroner Trent ruled the cause of death to be homicide due to blunt force craniocerebral injuries.

Dr. Glenn Roush, a radiologist, testified that he reviewed Biser's CAT Scan from Biser's emergency room visit on April 19, 2005. He testified that Biser's CAT Scan indicated he had a skull fracture and brain injury that had occurred recently. Dr. Roush also testified that he has "never seen anyone with this sort of injury be able to function."

Dr. William Cox, a forensic neuropathologist serving for the Franklin County Coroner, testified that he reviewed Biser's autopsy protocol, toxicology report, and medical records and determined that the cause of death listed by Dr. Trent on the death certificate was incorrect. Dr. Cox opined that Biser's death resulted from diabetic ketoacidosis. He testified that the punch Biser received and subsequent fall to the ground caused him to suffer contusions to his brain that damaged his frontal lobes. Dr. Cox testified that the damage to Biser's frontal lobes affected his cognitive ability and caused him to become apathetic, uninhibited and disinterested. He further testified that Biser's head injury substantially contributed to his death, and the damage to his frontal lobes "clearly would have adversely affected [Biser's] ability to look after himself."

A jury found Smith guilty on both counts of felonious assault and involuntary manslaughter. After merging the two counts, the trial court sentenced Smith to eight years in prison. . . .

SUFFICIENCY OF EVIDENCE

. . . Under the common law, a person could not be convicted of the offense of involuntary manslaughter unless the commission of the underlying offense was the "proximate cause" of the death of the victim. . . .

Here, Smith concedes that his felonious assault may have been the "but-for" cause of Biser's death. But he contends it did not proximately cause his death because multiple, unforeseeable events interfered with the natural and logical result of Smith's conduct. Smith argues that it was unforeseeable for Biser to refuse a recommended CAT scan and X-ray at the emergency room. Furthermore, it was unforeseeable for Smith to know that Biser was a diabetic and would refuse insulin at the emergency room. Smith claims that Biser's death resulted from his failure to take his insulin for several days, which caused his diabetic ketoacidosis. In light of these intervening circumstances, he contends the ultimate result is too remote from his conduct for the state to hold him accountable for Biser's death.

Courts generally treat the issue of legal causation in the criminal context similarly to that in tort cases because the situations are closely analogous. When dealing with claims of intervening causation, the proper analysis starts with a determination of whether the intervening act was a mere coincidence or alternatively, a response to the accused's prior conduct. An intervening cause is a coincidence when the defendant's act merely places the victim at a certain place at a certain time, thus subjecting the victim to the vagaries of the intervening cause. LaFave gives the example of "A" shoots at "B" but misses. "B" then varies from his intended route, is struck by lightening, and dies. Had "B" continued on his anticipated route, he would not have been injured. The lightening is a coincidence.

An intervening act is a response to the prior acts of the defendant where it involves reaction to the condition created by the defendant. Again from LaFave, "A" shoots "B" who is standing near the edge of a cliff. "B" impulsively jumps off the cliff rather than being the target of a second shot. This impulse may fairly be characterized as a normal response.

This distinction is important because the law will impose a less exacting standard of legal causation where the intervening cause is a response rather than a coincidence. A coincidence will break the chain of legal causation if it was unforeseeable. Thus, in the first example "A" is not criminally liable for "B's" death, notwithstanding he may be charged with an "attempt." However, for a response to break the chain, it must be both abnormal and unforeseeable. The distinction is premised upon a notion of fairness that finds less reason to hold a defendant liable for bad results where the defendant has merely caused the victim to "be at the wrong place at the wrong time." A defendant who has brought the intervening agency into play in response to the danger he has caused is subjected to a more stringent test if he is to break the chain of causation. Thus, in the second example, "A" will face potential criminal liability for "B's" death.

Here the primary intervening events that Smith relies upon to break the chain of causation are Biser's diabetes and failure to take his insulin. Initially, Smith contends it was unforeseeable that Biser would be a diabetic. But courts have routinely held both the tortfeasor and the accused take the victim as they find him. Thus, Biser's preexisting condition does not break the chain of causation.

We must now decide whether Biser's failure to medicate and take care of himself was a coincidence or a response. We conclude it can only be deemed a response. Biser's apathetic conduct occurred as a reaction to the head injuries that Smith caused. Biser's apathy did not happen because he was in the wrong place at the wrong time. This is not a case of "A" hits "B" in the head causing minor injuries; "B" goes to the hospital where he contracts a rare disease from his treating doctor. That sequence would present a coincidence.

Because we are dealing with a response, we must next decide whether Biser's failure to medicate and care for himself was both abnormal and unforeseeable. All the medical testimony in the record indicates the victim's conduct was neither. Dr. Roush testified a person suffering a skull fracture and brain injuries Biser received would not function normally. Dr. Cox testified Smith's punch and the resulting fall caused contusions to Biser's brain and damaged the frontal lobes. Dr. Cox indicated these injuries caused Biser's apathy and adversely affected his ability to care for himself. We believe that it is clearly foreseeable that someone with a fractured skull, a subdural hematoma and a subarachnoid hemorrhage might lose the ability to act rationally. In doing so, we rely on the proposition that an accused need not foresee the precise consequences of his conduct. To be actionable it is only necessary that the result is within the natural and logical scope of risk created by the conduct. Self-inflicted harm attributable to a victim's weakened conditions are quite normal and do not break the causal chain. Thus, we conclude Biser's failure to medicate and seek proper treatment is neither abnormal nor unforeseeable. In light of this conclusion, Biser's conduct is not an intervening cause that breaks the chain of legal causation set in motion by Smith. . . .

NOTES & QUESTIONS ON PROXIMATE CAUSE

1. *Responsive versus coincidental intervening agents.* Biser was an intervening agent. *He* decided not to seek appropriate medical treatment and not to take the required medicine—both decisions that compromised his health and led to his death. Did his intentional actions break the chain of causation leading back to Smith, who originally assaulted him? In a sense, why is it fair to hold Smith responsible for Biser's death when it was also caused by Biser's lackadaisical and cavalier attitude toward his health? The court's answer is that Biser's decisions were taken in *response* to Smith's actions and indeed his cavalier attitude was *caused* by Smith's assault (because it compromised his cognitive functions). What result if Smith had hit Biser in the gut (instead of the head), and Biser's cavalier attitude about his health were a long-term attitude that predated the assault? Would this count as a coincidental cause that breaks the causal chain? In that case, Biser's negligent attitude about his own healthcare would be attributable to him alone—and he would be responsible for his own death.

In general, courts are hesitant about declaring a second cause to be intervening and so rarely throw out convictions based on inadequate causation. For example, in *People v. Roberts*, the defendant was an inmate who fought and stabbed a fellow inmate named Charles Gardner, who was mortally wounded. Before dying, Gardner tried to retaliate against his attackers, but instead managed to stab and kill a prison guard named Albert Patch during the melee. Roberts, the original attacker, was charged with *both* murders, on the theory that Gardner would never have stabbed Patch if the first stabbing had never occurred. But wasn't the second stabbing by Gardner an intervening cause that broke the chain of causation leading back to Roberts? The court said no and apparently viewed Gardner's action as a responsive cause that could be attributed to the defendant. See *People v. Roberts*, 2 Cal. 4th 271, 317, 826 P.2d 274, 298 (1992) ("principles of proximate cause may sometimes assign homicide liability when, foreseeable or not, the consequences of a dangerous act directed at a second person cause an impulsive reaction that so naturally leads to a third person's death that the evil actor is deemed worthy of punishment"). See also Laura Schiesl Goodwin, *Causation in California Homicide*, 36 Loy. L.A. L. Rev. 1453, 1469 (2003) ("The dearth of case law on independent intervening acts reveals that courts are much more likely to see a positive finding of proximate cause. Many times, proximate cause is attributed to public policy concerns. As a result, courts do not take a definitive approach to the issue. It is fair to speculate that unless the intervening cause is overwhelmingly remote and unforeseeable it is unlikely that the intervening cause will overcome a proximate cause challenge.").

2. *The apparent safety doctrine.* It is not always easy to classify a particular intervening cause as responsive or coincidental. Consider *People v. Rideout*, 272 Mich. App. 602 (2006). The defendant was charged with drunk driving resulting in death. After the initial car crash caused by the defendant, Rideout, the victims in the other car went to the side of the road. However, the victim soon realized that his disabled car was in a precarious position in the middle of the road and he decided to reenter the roadway to put on his car's hazard lights. This turned out to be a dangerous and ultimately fatal decision: While tending to his vehicle, he was struck and killed by a passing car. Was Rideout responsible for the resulting death? In one sense the victim's decision to reenter the roadway was a responsive cause because his dilemma was caused by the first car crash. On the other hand, it was a mere coincidence that another car came barreling down the road at the moment the victim reentered the roadway. The court was more impressed with the "apparent safety doctrine" as a solution to the case. The victim was in a position of safety on the side of the road but decided on his own to reenter the roadway; by leaving his position of safety he broke the causal chain. Rideout's conviction was vacated. Do you agree that the distinction between coincidental and responsive is unhelpful for resolving

"likelihood of survival"?
neon

PROBLEM CASE

In 2015, Michelle Carter was charged with involuntary manslaughter in connection with the death of her boyfriend, Conrad Roy. Roy was 18 at the time of his death, Carter was 17, and both were students at the local high school. But this was no typical manslaughter case. Roy had killed himself by connecting the exhaust hose from a gas-powered water pump to the inside cabin of a pickup truck; he eventually succumbed to carbon monoxide poisoning and died.

Police charged Michelle Carter after they discovered that she had encouraged him to commit suicide over many months in a series of text messages. Some of the messages were comforting, while others expressed impatience and annoyance that he had not followed through on his talk of suicide. She allegedly wrote to him: "You always say you're gonna do it, but you never do. I just wanted to make sure tonight is the real thing." In another message, Carter wrote: "When are you gonna do it? Stop ignoring the question???" And in another: "You always seem to have an excuse." According to prosecutors, Roy also texted Carter during the actual suicide attempt as the truck was filling up with exhaust. He got out of the truck and texted with her; she allegedly told him to get back in to die. See Abby Phillip, *"It's Now or Never": Texts Reveal Teen's Efforts to Pressure Boyfriend into Suicide*, Wash. Post, Aug. 31, 2015.

Do you think that Carter is legally responsible for Roy's death? Her attorney said no, in part because causation is not established in this case: "What we have here is a young man who made a voluntary decision to end his own life. It was his voluntary decision. His death was not caused by Michelle Carter." See Stephanie Slifer, *Is it a Crime to "Encourage Suicide"? Teens' Texts Under Scrutiny*, CBS News, Mar. 3, 2015. If these facts are correct, it seems logical to conclude that Michelle Carter did play *some* causal role in Roy's death. However, the real question is whether Roy's voluntary decision to kill himself constituted an intervening cause that broke the chain of causation going back to Carter. Do you believe that proximate cause is established in this case or not?

Rideout's case? The court thought it was a coincidence that a car happened to be coming down the street at the exact moment that the victim went to his car. But that is only relevant if we are asking if the second car (coming down the highway) broke the causal chain. In fact, we are asking if the *victim's* act of reentering the roadway broke the causal chain. And *that* action was not coincidental—it was a direct response to the first accident. Would you have upheld Rideout's conviction?

3. *Abnormal and unforeseeable results.* Note that the court's analysis in *Smith* does not end with its classification of Biser as a responsive intervening agent. According to the court, for a response to break the chain of causation, the response must be both abnormal and unforeseeable. In this case, it is unlikely that Smith predicted this particular outcome. Does that matter? The court did not think so and concluded that "it is only necessary that the result is within the natural and logical scope of risk created by the conduct." Do you agree? Was Smith's reaction abnormal under the circumstances? On the one hand, it seems abnormal to refuse medical treatment. But on the other hand, it

is not abnormal for someone with a head injury to act irrationally. So maybe it was normal for him to act abnormally.

4. *Dangerous games.* Many cases with intervening agents involve drag races or Russian roulette. If two men go drag racing, and one of them gets into an accident (killing either himself or an innocent bystander), is the second drag racer responsible for the resulting death? Does the first driver's reckless driving break the causal chain, or should the second driver be held responsible for the death? Courts have upheld liability in these cases because participation in the game caused the deaths. However, in cases where the accident occurred *after* the drag race was over, courts have denied liability. *Velazquez v. State,* 561 So. 2d 347 (Dist. Ct. App. Fl. 1990). In Russian roulette cases, there is a similar dilemma regarding the scope of the game. If one man shoots himself in the head, is the other player in the game guilty as well, or does intentionally shooting yourself break the chain of causation? The answer depends in part on whether the two players are playing *together* or playing parallel games of

PROBLEM CASE

On March 30, 1981, John Hinckley, Jr. attempted to assassinate President Ronald Reagan as he emerged from the Washington Hilton Hotel in Washington, D.C. While Secret Service agents tackled Hinckley, other agents pushed Reagan into his limousine. At first they believed Reagan had escaped harm, but they soon realized that Reagan had been shot in the abdomen. In the melee, Press Secretary James Brady was shot in the head. One of the secret service agents also took a bullet. Although Brady survived, he was paralyzed and suffered substantial brain damage. Brady devoted the rest of his life to gun control. Hinckley was found not guilty by reason of insanity and was committed to a psychiatric facility. (Hinckley indicated that he wanted to assassinate Reagan to "impress" the actress Jodie Foster.)

    In 2014, Brady died at the age of 73. The local medical examiner ruled the death a homicide because his death was caused by his injuries in the 1981 assassination attempt. Nick Corasaniti, *Coroner Is Said to Rule James Brady's Death a Homicide, 33 Years After a Shooting,* N.Y. Times, Aug. 8, 2014.

The scene at the Washington Hilton Hotel after the assassination attempt

It is unclear whether the original insanity finding would preclude a second prosecution of Hinckley for Brady's death. But taking res judicata off the table, was Brady's death a proximate cause of Hinckley's assassination? Should prosecutors be permitted to file new murder charges against Hinckley, a full 33 years after the assassination attempt and long after the first trial ended?

solitaire. Is Russian roulette a two-person game like drag racing or is it a solitary game that can be played alone? *Commonwealth v. Attencio*, 345 Mass. 627 (1963) (upholding manslaughter indictment because Russian roulette involved "mutual encouragement in a joint enterprise").

5. *Taking the long view.*   Now that proximate cause is no longer limited by the old common law year-and-a-day rule, it is possible for courts to connect results back to conduct that occurred years—or decades—before the defendant died. Consider the case of Antonio Ciccarello, who was stabbed in New York City in 1958 or 1959, but recovered after going to the hospital. The perpetrator was not located. After a long life, Ciccarello died at the age of 97 in 2014, and the New York medical examiner ruled his death a homicide. Ciccarello died from a bowel obstruction that the medical examiner linked to the surgery he received in the 1950s. New York City police detectives dutifully investigated the homicide, though lack of evidence, and the fact that the perpetrators might long since have died, have prevented the police from solving the crime. J. David Goodman, *A Twist in the Murder of a 97-Year-Old Man: He Was Knifed 5 Decades Ago*, N.Y. Times, Jan. 24, 2015.

C. PRACTICE & POLICY

The following section considers three issues regarding the practice of causation analysis. The first part explores how causation is established at trial through expert testimony. The second part asks whether juries really make fine-grained decisions about causation or whether they rely more on gut intuition in deciding whether to find a defendant guilty. The last part examines the Model Penal Code's provision on causation, which simply asks whether liability is fair under the circumstances.

> ∾ **Establishing causation at trial.**   Causation is sometimes a matter of law that will be resolved by the judge before a jury even considers the issue. For example, if the prosecutor submits insufficient evidence to establish causation, the judge might dismiss the case as a matter of law. However, if there is sufficient evidence of causation for a reasonable jury to consider the issue, then causation will be decided by the jury. How should prosecutor elicit the necessary facts during witness examination to establish causation? Reconsider *State v. Montoya*, discussed above. During the trial, the prosecutor questioned a surgeon, Dr. Markey, about the nature of the victim's injuries. Here is how the witness examination proceeded:

Q: [A]ssuming that he bled for some period of time after this injury, if he promptly—and let's say maybe ten minutes to the hospital—promptly received medical treatment, would he have had a chance of [surviving]?
A: I think that he would have had some chance, yes.

. . .

Q: [I]n your opinion do you think it is more likely that he would have survived? Or more likely tha[t] he would have died anyway if he had been taken straight to the hospital?
A: I think it was still more likely that he would have died even if he would have been taken to the hospital.
Q: Okay, But, again, I gather you agree that being taken away from a hospital guaranteed his death?
A: Yes. Without medical treatment the wounds that were inflicted upon him would have resulted in his death.

Ultimately, this colloquy proved sufficient to convince the jury that causation was established; it also satisfied the appellate judges that there was sufficient evidence of causation on the record to justify the jury's decision. That being said, the doctor first appears to *reject* the likelihood of a success story when he testifies that "it was still more likely that he would have died even if he would have been taken to the hospital." This statement, somewhat mangled and confusing, suggests that he thought that death was inevitable and that going to the hospital was irrelevant to the outcome. But the prosecutor remains undeterred and comes back a second time to the witness to clarify the issue. Although generally lawyers cannot ask a witness the same question repeatedly in the hopes of getting a different answer, in this case the prosecutor alters the question and makes it more precise. In the end, he gets the doctor to admit that although death was probable anyway, the victim's death was *guaranteed* because he was not taken to the hospital. If the prosecutor had given up too easily, he could not have sustained a conviction in this case. As a side note, causation was the key legal and factual issue in this case. But do you think juries base their decisions on causation in such a fine-grained way, or do they end up making a more global judgment about the defendant's blameworthiness?

∾ **Arguing proximate cause to a jury.** How should a prosecutor or defense counsel make arguments to the jury about proximate cause? Consider again *State v. Smith*, above. The victim, Biser, died after being assaulted by the defendant, but it was clear that Smith never intended to kill Biser and his death was unexpected. Should his lawyer argue to the jury that holding him responsible for the resulting death is *unfair*? Or is this common-sense argument likely to fail since jurors might dislike Smith since he was the original aggressor? A lawyer can try to persuade the jury by focusing on each technical element of the legal doctrine, but at some point the jury is going to put the pieces together and just ask themselves what a just outcome would be.

ᴑ **The Model Penal Code approach.** The Model Penal Code takes a different approach to proximate cause and uses our common-sense notion of fairness to resolve these cases. Examine MPC § 2.03(3), which requires in cases of recklessness or negligence that "the result involves the same kind of injury or harm as the probable result and is not too remote or accidental in its occurrence to have a [just] bearing on the actor's liability or on the gravity of his offense." In short, causation is not established if the result is so remote that it makes punishing the defendant illegitimate. These moral and policy considerations are always in the background in debates about causation, but the Model Penal Code puts them front and center. Is this a smart approach? Could a jury be trusted to make decisions regarding causation based on such explicitly normative criteria? Or is causation always inevitably normative, so that the Code simply recognizes in explicit terms what is always lingering in the background?

PART II

OFFENSES

1st
2nd
voluntary man.
- involuntary man.
negligent Hom.

malice murder

Express / Implied

CHAPTER 9

⟞⟨⟩⟞

INTENTIONAL MURDER

A. DOCTRINE

Each jurisdiction classifies homicide offenses slightly differently, although a common progression is first-degree (or aggravated) murder, second-degree murder, voluntary manslaughter, involuntary manslaughter, and negligent homicide, each of which will be addressed in subsequent chapters. The following sections explain the different categories of intentional murder. Unfortunately, not every jurisdiction carves up homicide in the same way. For example, what constitutes first-degree murder in one jurisdiction might not be the same as another jurisdiction, and so on. Consequently, it is always essential to consult the definitions from the relevant statutes and case law in order to determine which scheme the state follows.

1. Express Malice Murder

At common law, murder required the killing of another human being with "malice aforethought." At the time, it was common for courts to define malice with reference to vague terms such as "wickedness," "evil disposition," or an "abandoned and malignant heart," which led to inconsistent decisions over how to establish the defendant's so-called wickedness, etc. Over time, some jurisdictions moved away from these definitions of malice in favor of more precise definitions tied to the mental states that were explored in Chapter 6.

Over time, courts eventually clarified that malice could be either express or implied. Express malice involved what would today be called intentional killing—an unlawful killing in which the actor desired the death of the victim. Implied malice involved reckless killings that demonstrated a depraved indifference to human life—a category of killings that will be addressed in Chapter 11 on reckless killings. In some jurisdictions, the terms "express malice murder" and "implied malice murder" remain in usage.

However, many jurisdictions have dropped the language of malice, in part because the Model Penal Code does not use the concept of malice. Instead, MPC § 210.12 simply defines intentional murder as a killing performed purposely or knowingly, and makes no attempt to distinguish between more or less blameworthy types of intentional murder. Across the United States, some jurisdictions cling to the older language of malice, while others follow the newer language and simply define murder as causing "the death of another human being with intent to kill that person," or with similar language. However, even those jurisdictions that have adopted the Model Penal Code definition of murder have insisted on adding degrees of murder to distinguish between the most severe forms of murder.

2. First-Degree or Aggravated Murder

As noted above, many jurisdictions reserve first-degree murder for cases of premeditation and deliberation, and then classify all other intentional murders as second-degree murder. Specifically, many states use the phrase "willful, deliberate, and premeditated" in their first-degree murder provisions. However, influenced in part by the difficulties associated with defining premeditation, some jurisdictions have abandoned premeditation as the hallmark of first-degree murder, and instead use other criteria, such as the killing of a police officer, the killing of a witness in a criminal proceeding, the use of torture or terrorism, a killing performed while incarcerated for a life term, or some other special circumstance. See, e.g., N.Y. Penal L. § 125.27. Some jurisdictions combine these approaches and define first-degree murder as involving *either* premeditation *or* one of the special circumstances. See, e.g., Iowa Code § 707.2. It is essential for students and practitioners alike to consult the latest code provisions in their jurisdictions to determine how aggravated murder is defined.

For example, consider the following two murder provisions. California defines murder as "the unlawful killing of a human being, or a fetus, with malice aforethought." See Cal. Penal L. § 187. California distinguishes between first-degree and second-degree murder in the following fashion:

> All murder which is perpetrated by means of a destructive device or explosive, a weapon of mass destruction, knowing use of ammunition designed primarily to penetrate metal or armor, poison, lying in wait, torture, or by any other kind of willful, deliberate, and premeditated killing, or which is committed in the perpetration of, or attempt to perpetrate, arson, rape, carjacking, robbery, burglary, mayhem, kidnapping, train

wrecking, or any act punishable under Section 206, 286, 288, 288a, or 289, or any murder which is perpetrated by means of discharging a firearm from a motor vehicle with the intent to inflict death, is murder of the first degree. All other kinds of murders are of the second degree.

In contrast, Pennsylvania distinguishes degrees of murder in the following way:

(a) Murder of the first degree.—A criminal homicide constitutes murder of the first degree when it is committed by an intentional killing. (b) Murder of the second degree.—A criminal homicide constitutes murder of the second degree when it is committed while defendant was engaged as a principal or an accomplice in the perpetration of a felony. (c) Murder of the third degree.—All other kinds of murder shall be murder of the third degree.

18 Penn. Con. Stat. § 2501. However, the Pennsylvania Code then defines "intentional killing" as "killing by means of poison, or by lying in wait, or by any other kind of willful, deliberate and premeditated killing." This language overlaps substantially with the California Penal Code.

3. Defining Premeditation and Deliberation

At first glance, it would seem that defining premeditation and deliberation would not be so difficult. The common-sense notion of premeditation suggests a murder planned in advance, perhaps with a careful or elaborate design. Many jurisdictions require that the defendant engaged in *both* premeditation and deliberation. That means both prior planning *and* consideration of whether to commit the crime—mental elements that are often closely intertwined in actual cases. Indeed, consideration of *how* to commit a crime often presupposes, by implication, that the defendant considered whether to commit the crime at all.

As a matter of legal interpretation, courts have generally focused on the *pre* in premeditation and have looked for some evidence that the defendant deliberated and then formed the intention to kill prior to the act of killing. The question is how long before the killing the defendant need form the intention in order for the killing to qualify as premeditated. As the following cases explore, some courts look for a time lag between the defendant's commitment to the plan and his execution of the act, but without defining exactly how long the lag needs to be—an issue that is reserved for the jury. In contrast, other jurisdictions think that deliberation and premeditation can occur virtually instantaneously in the moment before the act is carried out.

B. APPLICATION

1. Express Malice Murder

What does it mean for a defendant to commit a killing with malice? In the following case, the court must apply the concept of malice to a concrete crime. Do you think that express malice murder is the same thing as intentional murder, or does the malice label entail something especially heinous about the crime?

Taylor v. State
Supreme Court of Georgia
282 Ga. 44, 644 S.E.2d 850 (2007)

THOMPSON, JUSTICE.

Defendant Zachary Bouvier Taylor was convicted of malice murder and aggravated battery in connection with the death of Lamar Railey. . . .

Railey owned and operated a wrecker service in Hamilton, Georgia. After closing his business on the evening of February 13, 2004, Railey drove a wrecker to the J & A Tire Company where he stopped to purchase diesel fuel. When Railey finished fueling the wrecker, he headed for the business office to complete his purchase. Suddenly, Railey was struck by an accelerating motor vehicle. He was thrown into the air and landed on the pavement; he tried to get up, but was unable to do so. A passing motorist, who saw the vehicle strike Railey, called 911 and gave chase. As he followed the vehicle, described as a green sedan, the motorist was able to remain in contact with police and apprise them of the sedan's route. Soon, a police officer passed the motorist, fell in behind the sedan, and pulled it over. Other officers arrived on the scene. Defendant exited the vehicle and was placed under arrest.

Police noticed that marks on the front of defendant's vehicle were consistent with what one would expect after recently hitting a pedestrian. Officers conducted a search of the vehicle and found numerous items, including a manila envelope upon which the victim's name was written. Inside the envelope, police discovered various legal documents stemming from a year-long dispute between defendant and the victim.

In the meantime, the victim was taken to the hospital where he was admitted with multiple fractures and deep bruises to his right leg. After a short hospital stay, the victim was discharged and he was sent home to recuperate. On February 29, 2004, sixteen days after he was injured, the victim suddenly collapsed. Emergency personnel were summoned to the victim's home, but they were unable to revive him, and he died shortly thereafter. The medical examiner determined that pulmonary thromboemboli, which were the result of the injuries to the victim's right leg, caused the victim's death.

The evidence was sufficient to enable any rational trier of fact to find defendant guilty beyond a reasonable doubt of malice murder and aggravated battery. We reject defendant's assertion that, with regard to the murder conviction, the State failed to prove that defendant formed the intent to kill the victim, an essential element of malice murder.

> [T]he crime of malice murder is committed when the evidence shows either an express or, in the alternative, an implied intent to commit an unlawful homicide. This meaning of malice murder is consistent with the general rule that crimes which are defined so as to require that the defendant intentionally cause a forbidden bad result are usually interpreted to cover one who knows that his conduct is substantially certain to cause the result, whether or not he desires the result to occur. Thus, a malice murder can be shown not only by evidence that the defendant acted with the deliberate intention unlawfully to take the life of another human being which is manifested by external circumstances capable of proof, but also by evidence that the defendant acted where no considerable provocation appears and where all the circumstances of the killing show an abandoned and malignant heart. In other words, evidence that the defendant acted with implied malice is, for purposes of demonstrating his guilt of the crime of malice murder, no less probative than proof that he acted with a specific intent to kill.

We also find that, contrary to defendant's contention, the State introduced sufficient evidence to prove that the injuries to the victim's leg were the efficient, proximate cause of death. That is because the evidence shows that the injuries directly and materially contributed to the subsequently occurring pulmonary thromboemboli which immediately killed the victim.

In order to prove that defendant intended to kill the victim, the State introduced pleadings which defendant filed in a civil action he brought against the victim, as well as an affidavit supporting an arrest warrant through which defendant sought to have the victim arrested. . . .

NOTES & QUESTIONS ON MALICE

The concept of malice. Do you find the concept of malice confusing? The *Taylor* case makes clear that an intentional and unlawful killing will qualify for malice. If that is the case, what value does the "malice" label provide? The answer is historical continuity. At common law, murder was defined as killing with malice aforethought. Consequently, some jurisdictions, in order to preserve continuity with precedent, maintain the formal requirement that a murder conviction requires that the jury find that the defendant acted with "malice." But the problem is that the word "malice" lacks precision. Judges inevitably explain the concept to jurors using phrases like "intention" or "deliberate." Should every jurisdiction abandon the labels express and implied murder and confine them to the dustbin of history? For example, the Model Penal Code makes no reference to malice and instead talks of murder committed with purpose or knowledge. But even in jurisdictions that do not follow the Model Penal Code definitions of homicide, perhaps malice is more confusing than helpful. See, e.g., *People v. Woods*, 416 Mich. 581, 331 N.W.2d 707 (1982) (concluding that judges should charge juries using precise mental elements rather than referring to malice); *State v. Johnson*, 158 Vt. 508, 519, 615 A.3d 132, 137 (1992) ("continued use of the archaic and arcane language associated with the word 'malice' could only be a source of confusion to jurors").

2. Premeditation

How should the law distinguish between a spontaneous killing and a premeditated murder? The following case tackles this question by focusing on the moments prior to the defendant's final action and the nature of the defendant's deliberations. What guidelines does the appeals court give to trial judges in order to explain the difference to juries? Why is it important that the defendant had time to carefully consider his or her decision to kill?

State v. Guthrie
Supreme Court of Appeals of West Virginia
194 W.Va. 657, 461 S.E.2d 163 (1995)

CLECKLEY, JUSTICE:
. . . It is undisputed that on the evening of February 12, 1993, the defendant removed a knife from his pocket and stabbed his co-worker, Steven Todd Farley, in the neck and killed him. The two men worked together as dishwashers at Danny's Rib House in Nitro and got along well together before this incident. On the night of the killing, the victim, his brother, Tracy Farley, and James Gibson were joking around while working in the kitchen of the restaurant. The victim was poking fun at the defendant who appeared to be in a bad mood. He told the defendant to "lighten up" and snapped him with a dishtowel several times. Apparently, the victim had no idea he was upsetting the defendant very much. The dishtowel flipped the defendant on the nose and he became enraged.

The defendant removed his gloves and started toward the victim. Mr. Farley, still teasing, said: "Ooo, he's taking his gloves off." The defendant then pulled a knife from his pocket and stabbed the victim in the neck. He also stabbed Mr. Farley in the arm as he fell to the floor. Mr. Farley looked up and cried: "Man, I was just kidding around." The defendant responded: "Well, man, you should have never hit me in my face." The police arrived at the restaurant and arrested the defendant. He was given his *Miranda* rights. The defendant made a statement at the police station and confessed to the killing. The police officers described him as calm and willing to cooperate.

It is also undisputed that the defendant suffers from a host of psychiatric problems. He experiences up to two panic attacks daily and had received treatment for them at the Veterans Administration Hospital in Huntington for more than a year preceding the killing. He suffers from chronic depression (dysthymic disorder), an obsession with his nose (body dysmorphic disorder), and borderline personality disorder. The defendant's father shed some light on his nose fixation. He stated that dozens of times a day the defendant stared in the mirror and turned his head back and forth to look at his nose. His father estimated that 50 percent of the time he observed his son he was looking at his nose. The defendant repeatedly asked for assurances that his nose was not too big. This obsession began when he was approximately seventeen years old. The defendant was twenty-nine years old at the time of trial.

The defendant testified he suffered a panic attack immediately preceding the stabbing. He described the attack as "intense"; he felt a lot of pressure and his heart beat rapidly. In contrast to the boisterous atmosphere in the kitchen that evening, the defendant was quiet and kept to himself. He stated that Mr. Farley kept irritating him that night. The defendant could not understand why Mr. Farley was picking on him because he had never done that before. Even at trial, the defendant did not comprehend his utter overreaction to the situation. In hindsight, the defendant believed the better decision would have been to punch out on his time card and quit over the incident. However, all the witnesses related that the defendant was in no way attacked, as he perceived it, but that Mr. Farley was playing around. The defendant could not bring himself to tell the other workers to leave him alone or inform them about his panic attacks.

In contrast to his written statement, the defendant testified he was unable to recall stabbing the victim. After he was struck in the nose, he stated that he "lost it" and, when he came to himself, he was holding the knife in his hand and Mr. Farley was sinking to the floor . . .

It was the State's position that the facts supported a first degree murder conviction. At the close of the State's case-in-chief, the defense moved for a directed verdict contending the State failed to present evidence of malice and premeditation. This motion was denied. The defense argued the facts of the case supported voluntary manslaughter or, at worse, second degree murder. The jury returned a verdict finding the defendant guilty of first degree murder with a recommendation of mercy. . . .

The principal question before us under this assignment of error is whether our instructions on murder when given together deprive a criminal defendant of due process or are otherwise wrong and confusing. . . .

The jury was instructed that in order to find the defendant guilty of murder it had to find five elements beyond a reasonable doubt: "The Court further instructs the jury that murder in the first degree is when one person kills another person unlawfully, willfully, maliciously, deliberately and premeditatedly[.]" In its effort to define these terms, the trial court gave three instructions. State's Instruction No. 8, commonly referred to as the *Clifford* instruction, stated:

> The Court instructs the jury that to constitute a willful, deliberate and premeditated killing, it is not necessary that the intention to kill should exist for any particular length of time prior to the actual killing; it is only necessary that such intention should have come into existence for the first time at the time of such killing, or at any time previously.

See State v. Clifford, 59 W. Va. 1 (1906). State's Instruction No. 10 stated: "The Court instructs the jury that in order to constitute a 'premeditated' murder an intent to kill need exist only for an instant." State's Instruction No. 12 stated: "The Court instructs the jury that what is meant by the language willful, deliberate and premeditated is that the killing be intentional." State's Instruction Nos. 10 and 12 are commonly referred to as *Schrader* instructions. *See State v. Schrader,* 172 W. Va. 1 (1982).

The linchpin of the problems that flow from these instructions is the failure adequately to inform the jury of the difference between first and second degree murder. Of particular concern is the lack of guidance to the jury as to what constitutes premeditation and the manner in which the instructions infuse premeditation with the intent to kill.

At common law, murder was defined as the unlawful killing of another human being with "malice aforethought." Because the common law definition of "malice aforethought" was extremely flexible, "it became over time an 'arbitrary symbol' used by trial judges to signify any of the number of mental states deemed sufficient to support liability for murder." Nevertheless, most American jurisdictions maintained a law of murder built around common law classifications. . . .

In *State v. Hatfield,* 169 W. Va. 191 (1982), we made an effort to distinguish the degrees of murder by indicating that the elements that separate first degree murder and second degree murder are deliberation and premeditation in addition to the formation of the specific intent to kill. Deliberation and premeditation mean to reflect upon the intent to kill and make a deliberate choice to carry it out. Although no particular amount of time is required, there must be at least a sufficient period to permit the accused to actually consider in his or her mind the plan to kill. In this sense, murder in the first degree is a calculated killing as opposed to a spontaneous event. . . .

To allow the State to prove premeditation and deliberation by only showing that the intention came "into existence for the first time at the time of such killing" completely eliminates the distinction between the two degrees of murder. Hence, we feel compelled in this case to attempt to make the dichotomy meaningful by making some modifications to our homicide common law.

Premeditation and deliberation should be defined in a more careful, but still general way to give juries both guidance and reasonable discretion. Although premeditation and deliberation are not measured by any particular period of time, there must be some period between the formation of the intent to kill and the actual killing, which indicates the killing is by prior calculation and design. . . . This means there must be an opportunity for some reflection on the intention to kill after it is formed. The accused must kill purposely after contemplating the intent to kill. Although an elaborate plan or scheme to take life is not required, [the] notion of instantaneous premeditation and momentary deliberation is not satisfactory for proof of first degree murder. . . .

Thus, there must be some evidence that the defendant considered and weighed his decision to kill in order for the State to establish premeditation and deliberation under our first degree murder statute. This is what is meant by a ruthless, cold-blooded, calculating killing. Any other intentional killing, by its spontaneous and nonreflective nature, is second degree murder. . . .

Finally, we feel obligated to discuss what instruction defining premeditation is now acceptable. What came about as a mere suggestion in *Hatfield,* we now approve as a proper instruction under today's decision. . . .

> The jury is instructed that murder in the first degree consists of an intentional, deliberate and premeditated killing which means that the killing is done after a period of time for prior consideration. The duration of that period cannot be arbitrarily fixed. The time in which to form a deliberate and premeditated design varies as the minds and temperaments of people differ, and according to the circumstances in which they may be placed. Any interval of time between the forming of the intent to kill and the execution of that intent, which is of sufficient duration for the accused to be fully conscious of what he intended, is sufficient to support a conviction for first degree murder.

NOTES & QUESTIONS ON
PREMEDITATION AND DELIBERATION

1. *Evidence of premeditation.*   Did Guthrie premeditate his killing? Or did he simply snap? The West Virginia court cannot offer a clear account of what constitutes premeditation but it seems confident that whatever it is, there was no evidence of it in Guthrie's case. Which facts demonstrate most conclusively that Guthrie did not premeditate the killing? Is it his testimony? Or the testimony of his psychiatrists? Or his history of mental disorders? What inference should we draw from Guthrie's inability to remember the stabbing? As a defense attorney, how would you draw the line from Guthrie's memory loss to the conclusion that the crime was not premeditated?

2. *Jury arguments.*   How should a judge explain the concept of premeditation? It is clear that states like West Virginia require some time lag, but how much is enough? Consider *State v. Morton*, 277 Kan. 575, 585 (2004). The defendant, Joseph Morton, was fired from his job at a grocery store. He returned to the store to commit a robbery, at which point he shot the store manager. During the closing argument, the prosecutor said: "We know he walked off the job on Friday. We don't know, though, if he started thinking about it Saturday or Sunday or Monday or Tuesday. But we do know that he started thinking about it before he got to the Save-A-Lot store. And remember one thing. Premeditation means to have thought over the matter beforehand for any length of time." To demonstrate the point dramatically, the prosecutor then pointed her fingers and squeezed like she was firing a gun and said: "That can be premeditation under the laws of the State of Kansas. One squeeze of the trigger is all it takes." The prosecutor's statement was certainly effective pantomime, but was it a correct statement of the law? Kansas is one of the states that requires some time to evidence deliberation and premeditation but refuses to define the length of time. The Kansas Supreme Court concluded that the statement was inaccurate, reversed the conviction, and ordered a new trial.

3. *Prior calculation and design.*   Some states have abandoned the "deliberation and premeditation" formula and replaced it with a different definition of first-degree murder as killings performed with "prior calculation and design." Notice that the *Guthrie* court used the phrase "prior calculation and design" as a way of defining the length of time required for premeditation—if the time period was enough for the defendant to engage in calculation and design, then the period was long enough for premeditation to have occurred. But some states have gone further and used "prior calculation and design" as a replacement for premeditation entirely. At least some courts have interpreted the "prior calculation and design" standard as more stringent than the older formula because it accords with the common-sense notion, expressed at the beginning of this chapter, of a killing performed according to a plan or scheme. *State v. Jenkins*, 48 Ohio App. 2d 99

(1976). Why was the prior calculation and design standard adopted? Perhaps it was because some courts had so watered down the premeditation requirement that it strayed so far from the common sense understanding of the term. In response, state legislatures dumped the premeditation standard in favor of a new standard that explicitly required planning or scheming. So, the "prior calculation and design" standard can be viewed as a legislative override of the theory of instantaneous premeditation.

4. *Voluntary intoxication and deliberation.* Although jurisdictions are generally reluctant to grant a complete defense to defendants who commit a crime while in a state of voluntary intoxication, the situation is slightly different for first-degree murder. Some jurisdictions recognize that a state of voluntary intoxication may negate the necessary deliberation for the defendant to be convicted of first-degree murder. See, e.g., Cal. Penal Code § 22. The jury would be permitted to conclude that the defendant's intoxication was so severe—and so compromised the defendant's mental faculties—that it was impossible to engage in the necessary deliberation associated with premeditated murder. In this situation, though, the defendant would still be convicted of second-degree murder. This result is in keeping with a larger rule, in many jurisdictions, to allow evidence of voluntary intoxication to negate the required mens rea for any specific intent crime, but to reject voluntary intoxication for all general intent crimes. For more discussion, see Susan Dimock, *What Are Intoxicated Offenders Responsible For? The "Intoxication Defense" Re-examined*, 5 Crim. L. & Phil. 1, 2 (2011).

HYPOTHETICAL

Defendant has a wife who is suffering from terminal lung cancer. The treating physician has advised them to discontinue medical treatment because death is inevitable. The wife is suffering from agonizing pain and asks her husband to put her out of her misery. The husband considers the issue and, upon extensive reflection, he accedes to his wife's request. In particular, he understands that she will die anyway in a few days and all she has to look forward to is a few more days of physical pain. He gets a gun and shoots her in the head; she dies immediately. The local prosecutor charges the husband with premeditated first-degree murder, simply because the description of the crime matches the statutory definition of the crime—he carefully considered his course of action and decided to kill her anyway. The law classifies premeditated killings as among the most culpable and therefore deserving of special condemnation. Is that always the case? Should the law classify this hypothetical murder as among the most culpable and deserving of the maximum social opprobrium? What is more important, the nature of the deliberative process or the motive for the killing?

3. Instantaneous Premeditation

Not every jurisdiction defines premeditation in the same way as the *Guthrie* court. Other jurisdictions are much more permissive about what counts as premeditation and have all but eliminated the requirement of a meaningful temporal delay prior to final action. As you read the following case, ask yourself whether "near-instantaneous" premeditation is a viable category or whether it just collapses into regular intentional murder.

Commonwealth v. Carroll

Supreme Court of Pennsylvania
412 Pa. 525, 194 A.2d 911 (1963)

BELL, CHIEF JUSTICE.

The defendant, Carroll, pleaded guilty generally to an indictment charging him with the murder of his wife, and was tried by a Judge without a jury in the Court of Oyer and Terminer of Allegheny County. That Court found him guilty of first degree murder and sentenced him to life imprisonment. . . .

The defendant married the deceased in 1955, when he was serving in the Army in California. Subsequently he was stationed in Alabama, and later in Greenland. During the latter tour of duty, defendant's wife and two children lived with his parents in New Jersey. Because this arrangement proved incompatible, defendant returned to the United States on emergency leave in order to move his family to their own quarters. On his wife's insistence, defendant was forced first to secure a "compassionate transfer" back to the States, and subsequently to resign from the Army in July of 1960, by which time he had attained the rank of Chief Warrant Officer. Defendant was a hard worker, earned a substantial salary and bore a very good reputation among his neighbors.

In 1958, decedent-wife suffered a fractured skull while attempting to leave defendant's car in the course of an argument. Allegedly this contributed to her mental disorder which was later diagnosed as a schizoid personality type. In 1959 she underwent psychiatric treatment at the Mental Hygiene Clinic in Aberdeen, Maryland. She complained of nervousness and told the examining doctor "I feel like hurting my children." This sentiment sometimes took the form of sadistic "discipline" toward their very young children. Nevertheless, upon her discharge from the Clinic, the doctors considered her much improved. With this background we come to the immediate events of the crime.

In January, 1962, defendant was selected to attend an electronics school in Winston-Salem, North Carolina, for nine days. His wife greeted this news with violent argument. Immediately prior to his departure for Winston-

Salem, at the suggestion and request of his wife, he put a *loaded* .22 calibre pistol on the windowsill at the head of their common bed, so that she would feel safe. On the evening of January 16, 1962, defendant returned home and told his wife that he had been temporarily assigned to teach at a school in Chambersburg, which would necessitate his absence from home four nights out of seven for a ten week period. A violent and protracted argument ensued at the dinner table and continued until four o'clock in the morning.

Defendant's own statement after his arrest details the final moments before the crime: "We went into the bedroom a little before 3 o'clock on Wednesday morning where we continued to argue in short bursts. Generally she laid with her back to me facing the wall in bed and would just talk over her shoulder to me. I became angry and more angry especially what she was saying about my kids and myself, and sometime between 3 and 4 o'clock in the morning I remembered the gun on the window sill over my head. I think she had dozed off. *I reached up and grabbed the pistol and brought it down and shot her twice in the back of the head.*"

Defendant's testimony at the trial elaborated this theme. He started to think about the children,

> seeing my older son's feet what happened to them. I could see the bruises on him and Michael's chin was split open, four stitches. I didn't know what to do. I wanted to help my boys. Sometime in there she said something in there, she called me some kind of name. I kept thinking of this. *During this time I either thought or felt—I thought of the gun, just thought of the gun.* I am not sure whether I felt my hand move toward the gun—I saw my hand move, the next thing—the only thing I can recollect after that is right after the shots or right during the shots I saw the gun in my hand just pointed at my wife's head. She was still lying on her back—I mean her side. I could smell the gunpowder and I could hear something—it sounded like running water. I didn't know what it was at first, didn't realize what I'd done at first. Then I smelled it. I smelled blood before. . . .

"Q. At the time you shot her, Donald, were you fully aware and intend to do what you did?

"A. I don't know positively. All I remember hearing was two shots and feeling myself go cold all of a sudden."

Shortly thereafter defendant wrapped his wife's body in a blanket, spread and sheets, tied them on with a piece of plastic clothesline and took her down to the cellar. He tried to clean up as well as he could. That night he took his wife's body, wrapped in a blanket with a rug over it to a desolate place near a trash dump. He then took the children to his parents' home in Magnolia, New Jersey. He was arrested the next Monday in Chambersburg where he had gone to his teaching assignment.

Although defendant's brief is voluminous, the narrow and only questions which he raises on this appeal are as hereinbefore quoted. Both are embodied in his contention that the crime amounted only to second degree murder and that his conviction should therefore be reduced to second degree or that a new trial should be granted. . . .

If we consider only the evidence which is favorable to the Commonwealth, it is without the slightest doubt sufficient in law to prove first degree. However, even if we believe all of defendant's statements and testimony, there is no doubt that this killing constituted murder in the first degree. Defendant first urges that there was insufficient time for premeditation in the light of his good reputation. This is based on an isolated and oft repeated statement in *Commonwealth v. Drum*, 58 Pa. 9, 16, that "no time is too short for a wicked man to frame in his mind the scheme of murder." Defendant argues that, conversely, a long time is necessary to find premeditation in a "good man." We find no merit in defendant's analogy or contention. As Chief Justice Maxey appropriately and correctly said in *Commonwealth v. Earnest*, 342 Pa. 544, 549-550:

> Whether the intention to kill and the killing, that is, the premeditation and the fatal act, were within a brief space of time or a long space of time is immaterial if the killing was in fact intentional, wilful, deliberate and premeditated. . . . As Justice Agnew said in *Com. v. Drum*: "The law fixes upon no length of time as necessary to form the intention to kill, but leaves the existence of a fully formed intent as a fact to be determined by the jury, from all the facts and circumstances in the evidence."

Defendant further contends that the time and place of the crime, the enormous difficulty of removing and concealing the body, and the obvious lack of an escape plan, militate against and make a finding of premeditation legally impossible. This is a "jury argument"; it is clear as crystal that such circumstances do not negate premeditation. This contention of defendant is likewise clearly devoid of merit.

Defendant's most earnestly pressed contention is that the *psychiatrist's opinion of* what *defendant's state of mind must have been and was at the time of the crime*, clearly establishes not only the lack but also the legal impossibility of premeditation. Dr. Davis, a psychiatrist of the Allegheny County Behavior Clinic, testified that defendant was "for a number of years . . . passively going along with a situation which he . . . [was] not controlling and he . . . [was] not making any decisions, and finally a decision . . . [was] forced on him. . . . He had left the military to take this assignment, and he was averaging about nine thousand a year; he had a good job. He knew that if he didn't accept this teaching assignment in all probability he would be dismissed from the Government service, and at his age and his special training he didn't know whether he would be able to find employment. More critical to that was the fact that at this point, as we understand it, his wife issued an ultimatum that if he went and gave this training course she would leave him. . . . He was so dependent upon her he didn't want her to leave. He couldn't make up his mind what to do. He was trapped. . . ."

The doctor then gave *his opinion* that "rage," "desperation," and "panic" produced "an impulsive automatic reflex type of homicide, . . . as opposed to an intentional premeditated type of homicide. . . . Our feeling was that if this gun had fallen to the floor he wouldn't have been able to pick it up and consummate that homicide. And I think if he had to load the gun he wouldn't have done it. This is a matter of opinion, but this is our opinion about it."

There are three answers to this contention. First, as we have hereinbefore stated, neither a Judge nor a jury has to believe all or any part of the testimony of the defendant or of any witness. Secondly, the opinion of the psychiatrists was based to a large extent upon statements made to them by the defendant, which need not be believed and which are in some instances opposed by the facts themselves. Thirdly, a psychiatrist's opinion of a defendant's impulse or lack of intent or state of mind is, in this class of case, entitled to very little weight, and this is especially so when defendant's own actions, or his testimony or confession, or the facts themselves, belie the opinion. . . . Judgment and sentence affirmed.

NOTES & QUESTIONS ON INSTANTANEOUS PREMEDITATION

1. *The end of the temporal requirement.* Carroll said that he reached up for the gun, picked it up, and shot his wife. Is that enough to qualify for premeditation? There certainly was no evidence of prior calculation or a prearranged scheme that required days to consider. Indeed, the whole deliberative process, from start to finish, seemed to last a few seconds. Is instantaneous premeditation a contradiction in terms? One legal scholar, writing in 1882, called the doctrine just as coherent as a white blackbird or upward rain. J. Dos Passos, *Hints for Legislative Reform*, Papers Read Before the Medico-Legal Society of New York From Its Organization 506, 509 (1882). Or as a more recent scholar noted: "If premeditation is synonymous with intent to kill, why did the legislature choose to use the word premeditated instead of intentional? Why would the legislators not have said simply that all intentional murders are first degree murder?" See Matthew A. Pauley, *Murder by Premeditation*, 36 Am. Crim. L. Rev. 145, 154 (1999). Do you think the court in *Carroll* adequately responded to this argument regarding statutory interpretation?

2. *Lack of a plan.*   Carroll argued that his obvious lack of a plan implied that he did *not* act with premeditation. Do you accept this argument? Is it possible to premeditate a crime but not work out the details in advance? Or perhaps the operative distinction in this case is not premeditation versus no premeditation but rather premeditation done well versus premeditation done poorly. Some scholars believe that the existence of a prior plan is central to the deterrence rationale for punishing premeditated crimes more severely. See, e.g., Michael J. Zydney Mannheimer, *Not the Crime but the Cover-Up: A Deterrence-Based Rationale for the Premeditation-Deliberation Formula*, 86 Ind. L.J. 879, 921 (2011) ("Thus, the concept of murder, at its very origin, dealt specifically and explicitly with killings committed in secret so that either the perpetrator or the very act itself was concealed. The understanding that the premeditation-deliberation formula expresses a special concern for killings that take place after a period of planning sufficient to allow the killer to avoid or delay detection, apprehension, and punishment, therefore, accords well with the ancient roots of the law of murder."). Do you think that Carroll's crime fits this historical paradigm? Indeed, it would be strange for Carroll to receive a lighter penalty simply because his premeditated design was faulty or ill conceived.

C. PRACTICE & POLICY

The following section considers two practical and policy questions raised by the doctrine of premeditation. The first deals with the difficulties inherent in proving premeditation in a criminal court and the various *inferences* regarding premeditation that a jury can draw from the defendant's behavior. The second deals with the underlying policy assumption that premeditated killings are worse than non-premeditated killings.

    ॐ **Proving premeditation.**   How should a prosecutor prove that the defendant premeditated the killing? In many murder cases the defendant never takes the stand because his lawyer does not want to risk an unpredictable cross-examination by the prosecutor. If the defendant does not testify, he will not be cross-examined, and the prosecutor cannot independently call the defendant to the stand. This means that the prosecutor may not have the opportunity to *ask* the defendant about his state of mind during the killing. How then should the prosecutor prove premeditation? Like any issue of mens rea, the prosecutor can and should submit facts to the jury and ask them to infer the defendant's mental state. This process requires painting a picture of the defendant's behavior and then positing a particular mental attitude that best explains why the defendant acted the way he did. Indeed, premeditation is almost *always* established through this process of inference.

Consider, for example, *Thomas v. State*, 114 Nev. 1127 (1998). Thomas was fired from his job as a dishwasher at the Lone Star Steakhouse in Las Vegas. One morning Thomas and several members of his family drove to the restaurant to get his job back, but the restaurant was not open yet. Thomas and another family member (his brother-in-law) entered through an employee entrance and went to the manager's office. An argument ensued and the confrontation escalated when Thomas pulled out a gun, possibly to rob the restaurant (although the defendant denied this). Thomas then went to the bathroom where he confronted two employees, one of whom had a carving knife. He prevented the two of them from leaving and eventually stabbed one of them to death with the carving knife. Evidence suggested that he chased the second victim down and stabbed him too. The jury heard some evidence that Thomas had enticed the employees into the bathroom; the prosecutor's theory of the case was that Thomas had lured them into a confined space where he could then waylay them.

Was the killing in *Thomas* premeditated? At trial, the medical examiner testified that one of the victims was stabbed 19 times. The Nevada Supreme Court concluded that this was sufficient evidence from which to infer premeditation, especially when combined with the fact that Thomas had chased down the second employee to stab him too. The court concluded: "Taken together, the jury could reasonably conclude that Thomas premeditated the murders within moments of killing [the victims] even if he did not previously plan to kill them."

If you were on the jury, would you convict Thomas of premeditated murder based on these facts alone? Do you agree that multiple stab wounds suggest premeditation? Perhaps the jury should draw the opposite inference: A single wound, inflicted methodically, suggests premeditation, while a messy and savage killing might suggest a *lack* of planning. Nevada permits instantaneous premeditation, which makes the evidentiary burden that much easier. *Scott v. State*, 92 Nev. 552, 555 (1976). What result in a jurisdiction that *rejects* instantaneous premeditation? What arguments could a prosecutor make? Should the prosecutor try to convince the jury that Thomas went to the restaurant intent on revenge from the very beginning?

∾ **Hierarchy of blameworthiness.** Should the criminal law continue its struggle to define premeditation? The opposite strategy is to jettison premeditation and use other criteria to define first-degree murder. An even more radical strategy is to collapse the distinction between first-degree and second-degree murder entirely. Why is the distinction important at all? One reason is that the law can impose different sentencing schemes for first-degree and second-degree murder. (For example, first-degree murder might make the defendant eligible for the death penalty, if the jurisdiction has it, or life in prison without the possibility of parole.) If this is the real point of the distinction, then its true function is to impose legislative constraints on sentencing that reduce (but do not eliminate) the discretion that the trial court has to determine the appropriate sentence. But is that the only point of it? Consider whether the labels "first-degree" or "aggravated" murder have a special stigmatizing effect, separate from the greater punishment attached to them. What role do the labels play? Some legal scholars refer to this as "fair labeling" and conclude that defendants have a moral right that the criminal law appropriately label their offending conduct in such a way that it neither inflates nor diminishes their degree of blameworthiness. Andrew Ashworth, *Principles of Criminal Law* 87 (2d ed. 1995) ("Fairness demands that offenders be labelled and punished in proportion to their wrongdoing; the label is important both in public terms and in the criminal justice system, for deciding on appropriate maximum penalties, for evaluating previous convictions, prison classification, and so on.").

CHAPTER 10

VOLUNTARY MANSLAUGHTER

A. DOCTRINE

A murder charge can be downgraded to voluntary manslaughter in limited circumstances. At common law, this mitigation applied when the killing was performed with provocation (also known as sudden "heat of passion"), which only applied to a closed list of situations. Many jurisdictions still apply the provocation doctrine, although a few have replaced it with a broader standard that downgrades a killing to manslaughter when the killing is performed with "extreme emotional disturbance." The punishment associated with voluntary manslaughter is usually far less severe than the punishment for murder, so there is a lot at stake for the average defendant.

1. Provocation

Provocation functions as a partial defense in the sense that it mitigates the blameworthiness associated with murder to a lesser offense frequently called voluntary manslaughter (though some jurisdictions use different terminology). In a jurisdiction that defines murder as an intentional killing, provocation is a *partial* defense because although the killing is intentional, its severity is downgraded to manslaughter. In jurisdictions that still define murder as killing with malice aforethought, the provocation could be considered a "failure of proof theory" because it establishes that the defendant did not act with the required malice and therefore cannot be convicted of murder, but instead must be prosecuted for manslaughter.

In order to qualify as provocation, courts often require that the killing meet the following general requirements:

1. adequate provocation;
2. killing in the heat of passion;

3. performed suddenly before reasonable opportunity for passions to cool;
4. causal connection between provocation, passion, and killing.

What constitutes adequate provocation? The action must be committed in the heat of passion, which courts have long defined as situations "calculated to inflame the passion of a reasonable man and tend to cause him to act for the moment from passion rather than reason." *Girouard v. State*, 321 Md. 532 (1991). Courts applying this heat-of-passion standard have generally required that the provocation must fall into one of the recognized categories:

1. extreme assault on the defendant;
2. mutual combat;
3. illegal arrest of the defendant;
4. injury or serious abuse of close relative (or friend);
5. sudden discovery of spousal adultery.

While some courts interpret the categories liberally, other jurisdictions zealously guard them—in some cases refusing to expand the category of spousal adultery to girlfriends and boyfriends or romantic infidelity falling short of actual adultery. *State v. Turner*, 708 So. 2d 232 (Ala. Crim. App. 1997) (no provocation defense for unmarried couple cohabitating). For example, some courts have said that "mere words" never constitute provocation and that the defendant must *witness* the adultery or injury. In contrast, other jurisdictions concede that words can be enough if they *inform* the defendant of the underlying incident.

2. Extreme Emotional Disturbance

Jurisdictions looking for a more flexible approach have jettisoned the provocation doctrine in favor of a broader standard. For example, MPC § 210.3 downgrades a killing to manslaughter when "committed under the influence of extreme mental or emotional disturbance for which there is reasonable explanation or excuse." New York Penal Law § 125.25 uses similar language to establish mitigation that transforms second-degree murder into first-degree manslaughter. The effect of the move to the "extreme emotional disturbance" standard is to discard the relatively inflexible categories of provocation in favor of a functional standard designed to catch *any* circumstance that produces the mental disruption. It codifies a much broader approach to provocation while also downgrading other killings to the category of voluntary manslaughter that are not, strictly speaking, cases of "provocation" at all. In other words, there are many situations other than the actor being "provoked" that could trigger an extreme emotional disturbance for which there is a reasonable explanation or excuse.

Furthermore, it should be noted that some jurisdictions, such as California, reach the result of permitting a flexible reasonable person test for provocation without using the Model Penal Code formula. This result is achieved simply by dropping the strict provocation categories described in the prior section, but without using the concept of "extreme emotional disturbance."

B. APPLICATION

1. Provocation

The following materials present two cases on provocation with opposite outcomes. The first case, *Girouard*, involves a verbal dispute that turned violent. As you read the case, ask yourself why words are not enough to establish provocation. The second case, *Castagna*, involves mob behavior that demonstrates humanity at its worst. How does the court apply the doctrine of provocation to the facts of the murder? Which category of provocation does *Castagna* fall under? For both cases, after you understand the nature of the alleged provocation, assess whether it is sufficient to mitigate the defendant's liability for a brutal murder.

Girouard v. State

Court of Appeals of Maryland

321 Md. 532 (1991)

[handwritten margin note: Words not enough]

Cole, Judge.

In this case we are asked to reconsider whether the types of provocation sufficient to mitigate the crime of murder to manslaughter should be limited to the categories we have heretofore recognized, or whether the sufficiency of the provocation should be decided by the factfinder on a case-by-case basis. Specifically, we must determine whether words alone are provocation adequate to justify a conviction of manslaughter rather than one of second degree murder.

The Petitioner, Steven S. Girouard, and the deceased, Joyce M. Girouard, had been married for about two months on October 28, 1987, the night of Joyce's death. Both parties, who met while working in the same building, were in the army. They married after having known each other for approximately three months. The evidence at trial indicated that the marriage was often tense and strained, and there was some evidence that after marrying Steven, Joyce had resumed a relationship with her old boyfriend, Wayne.

On the night of Joyce's death, Steven overheard her talking on the telephone to her friend, whereupon she told the friend that she had asked her first sergeant for a hardship discharge because her husband did not love her anymore. Steven went into the living room where Joyce was on the phone and asked her what she meant by her comments; she responded, "nothing." Angered by her lack of response, Steven kicked away the plate of food Joyce had in front of her. He then went to lie down in the bedroom.

Joyce followed him into the bedroom, stepped up onto the bed and onto Steven's back, pulled his hair and said, "What are you going to do, hit me?" She continued to taunt him by saying, "I never did want to marry you and you are a lousy fuck and you remind me of my dad." The barrage of insults continued with her telling Steven that she wanted a divorce, that the marriage had been a mistake and that she had never wanted to marry him. She also told him she had seen his commanding officer and filed charges against him for abuse. She then asked Steven, "What are you going to do?" Receiving no response, she continued her verbal attack. She added that she had filed charges against him in the Judge Advocate General's Office (JAG) and that he would probably be court martialed.

When she was through, Steven asked her if she had really done all those things, and she responded in the affirmative. He left the bedroom with his pillow in his arms and proceeded to the kitchen where he procured a long handled kitchen knife. He returned to Joyce in the bedroom with the knife behind the pillow. He testified that he was enraged and that he kept waiting for Joyce to say she was kidding, but Joyce continued talking. She said she had learned a lot from the marriage and that it had been a mistake. She also told him she would remain in their apartment after he moved out. When he questioned how she would afford it, she told him she would claim her brain-damaged sister as a dependent and have the sister move in. Joyce reiterated that the marriage was a big mistake, that she did not love him and that the divorce would be better for her.

After pausing for a moment, Joyce asked what Steven was going to do. What he did was lunge at her with the kitchen knife he had hidden behind the pillow and stab her 19 times. Realizing what he had done, he dropped the knife and went to the bathroom to shower off Joyce's blood. Feeling like he wanted to die, Steven went back to the kitchen and found two steak knives with which he slit his own wrists. He lay down on the bed waiting to die, but when he realized that he would not die from his self-inflicted wounds, he got up and called the police, telling the dispatcher that he had just murdered his wife.

When the police arrived they found Steven wandering around outside his apartment building. Steven was despondent and tearful and seemed detached, according to police officers who had been at the scene. He was unconcerned about his own wounds, talking only about how much he loved his wife and how he could not believe what he had done. Joyce Girouard was pronounced dead at the scene.

At trial, defense witness, psychologist, Dr. William Stejskal, testified that Steven was out of touch with his own capacity to experience anger or express hostility. He stated that the events of October 28, 1987, were entirely consistent with Steven's personality, that Steven had "basically reach[ed] the limit of his ability to swallow his anger, to rationalize his wife's behavior, to tolerate, or actually to remain in a passive mode with that. He essentially went over the limit of his ability to bottle up those strong emotions. What ensued was a very extreme explosion of rage that was intermingled with a great deal of panic." Another defense witness, psychiatrist, Thomas Goldman, testified that Joyce had a "compulsive need to provoke jealousy so that she's always asking for love and at the same time destroying and undermining any chance that she really might have to establish any kind of mature love with anybody."

Steven Girouard was convicted, at a court trial in the Circuit Court for Montgomery County, of second degree murder and was sentenced to 22 years incarceration, 10 of which were suspended . . .

Petitioner relies primarily on out of state cases to provide support for his argument that the provocation to mitigate murder to manslaughter should not be limited only to the traditional circumstances of: extreme assault or battery upon the defendant; mutual combat; defendant's illegal arrest; injury or serious abuse of a close relative of the defendant's; or the sudden discovery of a spouse's adultery. Petitioner argues that manslaughter is a catchall for homicides which are criminal but that lack the malice essential for a conviction of murder. Steven argues that the trial judge did find provocation (although he held it inadequate to mitigate murder) and that the categories of provocation adequate to mitigate should be broadened to include factual situations such as this one.

The State counters by stating that although there is no finite list of legally adequate provocations, the common law has developed to a point at which it may be said there are some concededly provocative acts that society is not prepared to recognize as reasonable. Words spoken by the victim, no matter how abusive or taunting, fall into a category society should not accept as adequate provocation. According to the State, if abusive words alone could mitigate murder to manslaughter, nearly every domestic argument ending in the death of one party could be mitigated to manslaughter. This, the State avers, is not an acceptable outcome. Thus, the State argues that the courts below were correct in holding that the taunting words by Joyce Girouard were not provocation adequate to reduce Steven's second degree murder charge to voluntary manslaughter.

Initially, we note that the difference between murder and manslaughter is the presence or absence of malice. Voluntary manslaughter has been defined as "an intentional homicide, done in a sudden heat of passion, caused by adequate provocation, before there has been a reasonable opportunity for the passion to cool."

There are certain facts that may mitigate what would normally be murder to manslaughter. For example, we have recognized as falling into that group: (1) discovering one's spouse in the act of sexual intercourse with another; (2) mutual combat; (3) assault and battery. There is also authority recognizing injury to one of the defendant's relatives or to a third party, and death resulting from resistance of an illegal arrest as adequate provocation for mitigation to manslaughter. Those acts mitigate homicide to manslaughter because they create passion in the defendant and are not considered the product of free will.

In order to determine whether murder should be mitigated to manslaughter we look to the circumstances surrounding the homicide and try to discover if it was provoked by the victim. Over the facts of the case we lay the template of the so-called "Rule of Provocation." The courts of this State have repeatedly set forth the requirements of the Rule of Provocation:

1. There must have been adequate provocation;
2. The killing must have been in the heat of passion;
3. It must have been a sudden heat of passion—that is, the killing must have followed the provocation before there had been a reasonable opportunity for the passion to cool;
4. There must have been a causal connection between the provocation, the passion, and the fatal act.

We shall assume without deciding that the second, third, and fourth of the criteria listed above were met in this case. We focus our attention on an examination of the ultimate issue in this case, that is, whether the provocation of Steven by Joyce was enough in the eyes of the law so that the murder charge against Steven should have been mitigated to voluntary manslaughter. For provocation to be "adequate," it must be "calculated to inflame the passion of a reasonable man and tend to cause him to act for the moment from passion rather than reason." The issue we must resolve, then, is whether the taunting words uttered by Joyce were enough to inflame the passion of a reasonable man so that that man would be sufficiently infuriated so as to strike out in hot-blooded blind passion to kill her. Although we agree with the trial judge that there was needless provocation by Joyce, we also agree with him that the provocation was not adequate to mitigate second degree murder to voluntary manslaughter.

Although there are few Maryland cases discussing the issue at bar, those that do hold that words alone are not adequate provocation. Most recently, in *Sims v. State*, 319 Md. 540, we held that "[i]nsulting words or gestures, no matter how opprobrious, do not amount to an affray, and standing alone, do not constitute adequate provocation." That case involved the fling-ing of racial slurs and derogatory comments by the victim at the defendant. That conduct did not constitute adequate provocation.

In *Lang v. State*, 6 Md. App. 128 (1969), the Court of Special Appeals stated that it is "generally held that mere words, threats, menaces or ges-tures, however offensive and insulting, do not constitute adequate provo-cation." Before the shooting, the victim had called the appellant "a chump" and "a chicken," dared the appellant to fight, shouted obscenities at him and shook his fist at him. The provocation, again, was not enough to mit-igate murder.

The court in *Lang* did note, however, that words can constitute ade-quate provocation if they are accompanied by conduct indicating a present intention and ability to cause the defendant bodily harm. Clearly, no such conduct was exhibited by Joyce in this case. While Joyce did step on Ste-ven's back and pull his hair, he could not reasonably have feared bodily harm at her hands. This, to us, is certain based on Steven's testimony at trial that Joyce was about 5'1" tall and weighed 115 pounds, while he was 6'2" tall, weighing over 200 pounds. Joyce simply did not have the size or strength to cause Steven to fear for his bodily safety. Thus, since there was no ability on the part of Joyce to cause Steven harm, the words she hurled at him could not, under the analysis in Lang, constitute legally sufficient provocation.

Other jurisdictions overwhelmingly agree with our cases and hold that words alone are not adequate provocation. One jurisdiction that does allow provocation brought about by prolonged stress, anger and hostility caused by marital problems to provide grounds for a verdict of voluntary man-slaughter rather than murder is Pennsylvania. The Pennsylvania court left the determination of the weight and credibility of the testimony regard-ing the marital stress and arguments to the trier of fact . . .

Thus, with no reservation, we hold that the provocation in this case was not enough to cause a reasonable man to stab his provoker 19 times. Although a psychologist testified to Steven's mental problems and his need for acceptance and love, we agree with the Court of Special Appeals speaking through Judge Moylan that "there must be not simply provocation in psychological fact, but one of certain fairly well-defined classes of prov-ocation recognized as being adequate as a matter of law." The standard is one of reasonableness; it does not and should not focus on the peculiar frailties of mind of the Petitioner. That standard of reasonableness has not been met here. We cannot in good conscience countenance holding that a verbal domestic argument ending in the death of one spouse can result in a conviction of manslaughter. We agree with the trial judge that social necessity dictates our holding. Domestic arguments easily escalate into furious fights. We perceive no reason for a holding in favor of those who find the easiest way to end a domestic dispute is by killing the offending spouse.

We will leave to another day the possibility of expansion of the categories of adequate provocation to mitigate murder to manslaughter. The facts of this case do not warrant the broadening of the categories recognized thus far.

———

Mob
No Time to
"cool off"

State v. Castagna

Superior Court of New Jersey, Appellate Division
376 N.J. Super. 323, 870 A.2d 653 (2005)

FUENTES, J.

The legal issues raised by these three appeals arise from one violent incident that brutally took the life of a man named Bennett Grant. The details of this crime reveal the darkest aspects of the human character and provide a limited insight into the dynamics of mob behavior and how it can, at times, overtake the individuals composing the group. Notwithstanding our unmitigated condemnation of the indisputably barbaric acts that brought about the destruction of this human life, we are compelled to reverse the convictions. . . .

Defendants, Jean Morales, Josephine Castagna, and Thomas D'Amico, were tried together as individual assailants and as part of the mob that chased down and killed Grant. Morales was convicted of murder . . . The State argued to the jury that Morales dropped the stone on Grant's head, while he lay on the ground, battered, bruised and defenseless. On the murder conviction, Morales was sentenced to a term of fifty years . . . D'Amico, who was a full-time police officer for the City of Elizabeth at the time this incident took place, was convicted of first-degree aggravated manslaughter . . . Castagna was convicted of the lesser-included offense of second-degree aggravated assault, attempting to cause serious bodily injury, and acquitted of murder, aggravated manslaughter, and two weapons offenses.

In addition to these three defendants, the State also indicted Violet Arias, Carmine Perrotti, Alvin Baez, and Edward Gentile. All of these defendants pled guilty, pursuant to negotiated plea agreements, to second-degree reckless manslaughter . . . As an express condition of their agreements with the State, all of the individuals who pled guilty also agreed to testify as witnesses for the prosecution against the three defendants who elected to stand trial.

. . . With respect to Morales, we . . . hold that the trial court committed reversible error when it failed to sua sponte instruct the jury on the elements of passion/provocation manslaughter, as a lesser included offense of the crime of murder. . . .

FACTS

On the night of October 23, 1999, Arthur McKeown and his friend Bennett Grant went to Sinners Go-Go Bar (Sinners), which was located at the corner of Bayway Avenue and South First Street in the City of Elizabeth. The relocated Bayway Avenue Bridge was located about 300 to 400 yards down the street from Sinners. Grant was a thirty-seven-year-old African American man who stood over six feet tall and weighed 220 pounds. . . .

At about 11:00 P.M., Carmine Perrotti, Lewis Rodriguez, Christopher Longo and defendant D'Amico arrived at Sinners in Perrotti's maroon Jeep Cherokee. That night, D'Amico was off duty as a full-time police officer for the Elizabeth Police Department. He had held this position since July 1996. The four men went to the main bar to drink and watch the boxing match. They were seated across the bar from McKeown and Grant. Longo went home after the boxing match.

About 11:30 P.M., Violet Arias, Ann Truzzolino, Alvin Baez and defendant Castagna entered the back door of Sinners and went into the sports bar. Arias was five foot two, thinly built, and was wearing a white t-shirt and a red vest. All of these individuals, including the three co-defendants involved in this appeal, knew each other either from high school or from the neighborhood.

Witnesses' accounts of what transpired at this point varied widely. There is a general consensus, however, that: (1) Arias had some sort of confrontation with Grant and McKeown outside Sinners around 2:00 A.M.; (2) Grant went back inside Sinners and another conflict developed with Arias in the bar, which eventually spilled out onto the street; (3) as a result, a crowd gathered outside Sinners and surrounded Grant; (4) Grant broke free and ran down Bayway Avenue towards the relocated bridge with the crowd chasing him; (5) all of the people named in the indictment pursued Grant; and (6) all of the pursuers and, indeed, most of the other patrons in Sinners that night, had consumed alcohol, some to the point of inebriation. . . .

Morales arrived at Sinners just as the confrontation outside the bar was taking place. By this time, the crowd that had been chasing Grant had degenerated into a raging mob. . . .

Elizabeth Mojica resides in the area where the bridge is located. She saw Grant running from the rear side of her house to the front and then onto the bridge. She also saw the mob continue to chase Grant and heard female voices yelling, "Get him. Kill him. Fuck'em up. Get his black ass. . . . He had no business doing this to me." . . .

Elizabeth's husband, Jose Mojica, testified that he saw the Jeep stop and pick up two people. The Jeep then went the wrong way on the relocated bridge, heading straight toward Grant. Mr. Mojica then saw the front passenger side door of the Jeep swing open and hit Grant. In an attempt to keep his balance, Grant grabbed the front of the vehicle. The Jeep then suddenly stopped and jerked forward, knocking Grant to the ground with the right front bumper. Arias and Baez corroborated the Mojicas' testimony.

The mob reached Grant, as he lay directly in front of the Jeep. Testimony from those who were on the bridge and from the residents in the area provide a chilling description of the chaotic and violent scene that transpired next. Punctuated by the screams of the participants, exhorting each other to the point of convulsive frenzy, the mob kicked, stomped and beat Grant as he lay in front of the Jeep. . . .

According to Morales's statement to police, he hit or kicked Grant two or three times "in the back and punched him in the shoulder and punched him in the chest and then [Morales] got bumped out of the way by someone." Morales also stated that, while Grant was being kicked and beaten, a woman was also "beating the shit out of" him with what looked like a bat or a stick or a pipe.

Fragoso identified Arias as that assailant. He described the object used by Arias to beat Grant as some type of car or truck molding, about two feet in length and three to four inches in width, flat on one side, and black with a chrome strip running through it on the other side. According to Fragoso, Arias was enraged, and repeatedly called Grant a racial epithet while she swung the piece of chrome.

Arias denied that she struck Grant and accused Castagna of beating Grant with a "pipe, kicking him and saying, 'Why the fuck did you hit me, you stupid nigger.'" Gentile and Baez corroborated Arias's testimony in this respect. Gentile described the object that Castagna allegedly used against Grant as a "broomstick." Baez simply stated that it was "a long object."

As Grant lay on the ground, helplessly enduring the mob's barrage of blows and kicks, the most egregious assault upon his person was about to take place. According to Fragoso, he saw a "Hispanic [man], five-nine, five-ten, heavy build, short black hair, [wearing a] gray fleece, blue jeans with reflective letter on his pants" holding a rock. This object was subsequently identified as a Belgian block weighing approximately twenty-five pounds. Using both his hands, the assailant raised the block above his head and "immediately dropped it on the victim's head." . . .

There was total silence after the block was dropped on Grant's head. Fragoso testified that it looked as if part of the victim's forehead had fallen off, blood was "gushing out," and his breathing became erratic. Fragoso dropped to his knees to check on Grant and pushed the crowd away. . . .

PASSION/PROVOCATION CHARGE AS TO MORALES

For the first time on appeal, Morales contends that the trial court committed reversible error by not *sua sponte* charging the jury on passion/provocation manslaughter, in light of testimony that the victim had violently attacked Castagna and Arias, both friends of Morales. We agree.

While discussing charging the jury on the offenses of murder, aggravated manslaughter and reckless manslaughter, the trial judge remarked that "in this case there is only reckless manslaughter or manslaughter as a lesser included offense," and that "passion/provocation is not in this case." . . .

Criminal homicide constitutes manslaughter when: "A homicide which would otherwise be murder under [N.J.S.A.] 2C:11-3 is committed in the heat of passion resulting from a reasonable provocation." N.J.S.A. 2C: 11-4(b)(2). This mitigating element is only available, however, when the killing occurs before sufficient time has passed for an ordinary person in similar circumstances to have cooled off.

Passion/provocation manslaughter has four specific elements: (1) reasonable and adequate provocation; (2) insufficient cooling-off time; (3) actual passion caused by the provocation; and (4) no actual cooling off. The first two criteria are objective. That is, both the adequacy of the provocation and the lack of time to cool off must be judged against the standard of a reasonable person in the defendant's position. The last two elements are subjective. That is, if a reasonable person would have been provoked but the defendant was not, the passion/provocation defense will not be available. Thus, because of the objective nature of the first two elements, if they are supported by the evidence, a court must instruct the jury on the lesser-included offense.

With respect to the first element, "the judge must determine whether a reasonable fact-finder could conclude that the loss of self control was a reasonable reaction." Moreover, a trial judge "should view the situation in the light most favorable to the defendant" when deciding whether to instruct a jury on passion/provocation manslaughter. "If no jury could rationally conclude that the State had not proven beyond a reasonable doubt that the asserted provocation was insufficient to inflame the passions of a reasonable person, the trial court should withhold the charge."

It is clear that words alone, no matter how offensive or insulting, never constitute sufficient provocation. Nor would a "bump" and "insulting language," in the absence of a severe battery, constitute sufficient provocation. However, mutual combat, under certain circumstances, could constitute adequate provocation to reduce murder to manslaughter.

It is also well settled that a person can be provoked by conduct that causes injury to a relative or close friend. This type of provocation need not be witnessed by the accused, provided that he or she is informed of the actual event.

Here, Morales argues that the trial court should have charged passion/provocation manslaughter because, viewing the evidence in the light most favorable to the defense, this case involved a group of people, including Morales, who had responded to Grant's "violent attack" upon Arias, who fell against the cigarette machine in the bar when Grant hit her, and upon Castagna, who fell like "a sack of potatoes" in the street in front of the bar when Grant struck her.

The record supports Morales's position. There was evidence presented from which a jury could find that Morales was told about Grant assaulting these two women. From this there is a rational basis to conclude that there was no opportunity for a reasonable person in Morales's position to have cooled off.

As Grant ran for his life, the evidence shows that the mob reached a state of frenzy. Once it reached the victim, the mob mercilessly beat and kicked the helpless Grant, as he attempted to shield himself from the blows. Under these circumstances, a rational jury could have found that Morales, as one of those caught up in these events, did not have an opportunity to cool off. It is also the jury's function to determine whether Morales's attack against Grant was a response proportionate to the force allegedly used against Arias and Castagna. . . .

NOTES & QUESTIONS ON PROVOCATION

1. *Mob violence.* Do you agree that there was enough evidence in the record to put the issue of Morales's provocation to the jury? The court seemed highly influenced by the collective nature of the violence—the "frenzy" of the mob. But at the end of the day, the source of the provocation had nothing to do with the mob. Grant had allegedly assaulted one of Morales's friends in the bar (Arias), which falls under the "injury to close family or friend" prong of the standard. The existence of the mob is relevant under a different prong of the standard: insufficient cooling off time. According to Morales's lawyer, the incitement of the mob prevented Morales from cooling off and regaining control over his senses. Is there anything worrisome about that argument? Each member of the mob whips the others into a state of frenzy, with the result that they *all* end up meeting the standard for provocation. Should the law treat individuals so charitably when they engage in mob violence?

2. *The nature of the relationship.* Morales gets to argue provocation to the jury because Grant allegedly assaulted his friend Arias in the bar. Although there is no family relationship between the two, New Jersey permits the provocation doctrine when a close friend is assaulted or injured. However, other

jurisdictions require a *family* relationship between the defendant and the original target of the assault—a rule that would have barred the provocation doctrine for Morales. Moreover, the defense usually applies when the killing is triggered by a sufficiently heinous or severe assault; a minor assault is not likely to make a reasonable person lose control. Compare *Paz v. State*, 777 So. 2d 983 (Dist. Ct. App. Fla. 2000) (permitting defense for defendant who stabbed the man who had just raped his wife), with *High v. United States*, 972 A.2d 829 (D.C. Ct. App. 2009) (no provocation defense because defendant "was not suddenly reacting to a heinous assault upon a close family member or in response to discovering that a young relative was abused by a trusted friend"). In *High*, the defendant suspected that the victim had just slept with his 29-year-old stepsister with whom the defendant was not particularly close. Was there evidence that Grant committed an especially heinous assault? What result if the defendants lost control not because of the severity of the original assault but because of their racial animus? In fact, the court in *Castagna* heard ample evidence that race was a factor in Grant's killing. Indeed, witnesses testified that Grant was subjected to horrible racial epithets during the attack. However, the judge instructed the jury to disregard some of the statements because the state did not charge the murder as a hate crime. Can and should the jury ignore this distasteful aspect of the crime?

3. *Witnessing versus learning.*   In *Castagna*, the court said that Morales should be entitled to argue the provocation defense even though he never witnessed the alleged assault committed by the victim. Indeed, Morales arrived on the scene much later, after Arias had already been allegedly assaulted in the bar. But the court concluded that his *learning* of the assault could be sufficient to constitute provocation as a matter of law, and constitutes an exception to the old adage that "words are never enough." Several jurisdictions permit the defense when the defendant suddenly learns of sexual abuse that happened in the past. *State v. Munoz*, 113 N.M. 489, 827 P.2d 1303 (1992). In *Munoz*, the defendant learned from his wife that she had been repeatedly molested as a child by her stepfather and uncle. The defendant got his rifle, went to the stepfather's house, confronted him, and then killed him. The court concluded that the jury could consider the provocation caused by the original abuse, even though the defendant only learned of it years later. What mattered was that the defendant lost control *immediately* upon learning of the mistreatment.

4. *The rekindling doctrine.*   Does the crime always have to occur immediately upon learning of the original act? In a few instances, courts have suggested that a new incident can rekindle the passion elicited from a prior encounter, or a long-standing course of provocation. Under this theory, the original provocation ignites the passions of the defendant, but over a period of time the defendant cools off. Then, a new incident (or new conversation) rekindles the original provocation, leading the defendant to commit the murder.

For example, imagine that an individual is physically abused as a teenager. Although the abuse would have been sufficient to ground a claim of provocation at the time, the abuse victim does nothing violent in response. Then, many years later, the abuse victim is confronted unexpectedly with the presence of the abuser, thus triggering the abuse victim to commit the killing under a heat of passion. See also *People v. Berry*, 18 Cal. 3d 509, 516, 556 P.2d 777, 781 (1976) (long course of provocatory conduct negated cooling off period); *United States v. Jack*, 483 F. App'x 427, 429 (10th Cir. 2012) (discussing rekindling). However, many courts refuse to apply the doctrine. *State v. Gounagias*, 88 Wash. 304, 153 P. 9 (1915).

5. *Attempted voluntary manslaughter.*   Consider a defendant who is provoked but the killing is unsuccessful and the victim survives. What is the correct outcome in that case? May the defendant be convicted of attempted voluntary manslaughter? Some jurisdictions have answered yes. The rationale for this conclusion is that provocation negates the malice associated with either murder or attempted murder, thus downgrading responsibility to either voluntary manslaughter or attempted voluntary manslaughter. See, e.g., *State v. Jernigan*, 139 N.M. 1 (2013); *People v. Van Ronk*, 171 Cal. App. 3d 818 (1985) ("There is nothing illogical or absurd in a finding that a person who unsuccessfully attempted to kill another did so with the intent to kill which was formed in the heat of passion . . ."). Several jurisdictions have rejected the category of attempted manslaughter and declared it illogical, but these cases typically involve involuntary manslaughter convictions. See, e.g., *State v. Howard*, 405 A.2d 206 (Me. 1979). Why is attempted voluntary manslaughter logical but attempted involuntary manslaughter illogical? To understand the difference, pay particular attention to the required mens rea for the different forms of manslaughter.

ADVICE   Do not forget that the provocation doctrine is not the only "partial defense" that may downgrade murder to voluntary manslaughter. There are other avenues to a conviction for voluntary manslaughter. For example, in some jurisdictions, a defendant who acts with "imperfect self-defense" will be convicted of voluntary manslaughter. Imperfect self-defense involves an actor who commits a killing with a sincere but *unreasonable* belief in imminent harm. Since self-defense requires acting with a *reasonable* belief in imminent harm, these actors are not entitled to complete exoneration, but their liability is downgraded to voluntary manslaughter. Second, an actor who commits a killing while suffering from a "diminished mental capacity" might also be convicted of voluntary manslaughter. A diminished mental capacity involves a mental disruption that fails to meet the criteria for the full excuse of legal insanity, but nonetheless is sufficiently grave that it negates the required mens rea for murder. These two doctrines are explored in more detail in the chapters on self-defense and insanity respectively.

2. Extreme Emotional Disturbance

The doctrine of extreme emotional disturbance, or EED for short, is designed to broaden the number of situations that can be classified as voluntary manslaughter. Instead of a defined list of categories, extreme emotional disturbance offers a functional standard regarding the defendant's state of mind. This adds flexibility to the doctrine but it also increases the jury's discretion. As you read the facts of this case, ask yourself whether the defendant should qualify for mitigation under EED.

State v. White
Supreme Court of Utah
251 P.3d 820 (2011)

JUSTICE NEHRING, opinion of the Court:

Brenda White was charged with the attempted murder of her ex-husband, Jon White, after she chased and hit him with her car at Mr. White's workplace. Shortly after she was charged, Ms. White filed a pretrial motion asking the trial judge to instruct the jury on the extreme emotional distress defense. In her motion, Ms. White argued that the defense was warranted because, on the date of the incident, stress she felt from her divorce, along with financial difficulties and other emotional problems, overwhelmed her ability to act rationally and caused her to lose all self-control. The trial judge denied Ms. White's motion. The court of appeals affirmed. Because we conclude that the court of appeals applied the wrong standard when it evaluated the availability of the extreme emotional distress defense, we reverse the decision of the court of appeals with instructions to remand to the trial court to reevaluate evidence in support of the defense in a manner consistent with this opinion.

BACKGROUND

Brenda and Jon White were married for eleven years. Both parties admit the marriage was difficult and that talk of divorce was common. According to Ms. White, Jon was addicted to pornography and suggested that Ms. White participate in "sexual threesomes" with him and his co-worker. Ms. White further alleges that during the marriage Jon was having an affair with another woman. These behaviors caused Ms. White to experience feelings of great anxiety, anger, and agitation, and they eventually led to the couple's divorce.

Following the divorce, Ms. White's stress increased. She struggled financially to support her two daughters and, as a result of having to work more hours, saw less of her children. Throughout this period of time, Ms. White claims that Jon began to withdraw from the children and failed to pay child

under commonlaw not going to be enough for EED claim

support. Jon canceled Ms. White's medical insurance, which left her unable to pay for medication she needed to treat her anxiety and depression.

As part of the divorce settlement, Ms. White was awarded the couple's house. Because of her financial troubles, Ms. White attempted to refinance the home, but learned that she would not be able to complete the refinancing process without Jon's assistance and signatures.

On April 26, 2006, Brenda went to Jon's office to speak to him about refinancing the house. Jon spoke to the mortgage broker by phone, but told Brenda the issue would ultimately need to be resolved at a later time. Following the call, Jon walked out to the parking lot with Brenda. Brenda asked Jon to sign a quit-claim deed to the marital home, but Jon refused to do so until Brenda took his name off the two mortgages encumbering the property. The conversation escalated in intensity and Brenda became extremely upset. She climbed into her vehicle and turned on music with the lyrics, "I want to kill you; I want to blow you away." During the song, she joined her hands together to mimic a gun and pointed her fingers at Jon. She then told Jon he was a "parasite" and that she was going to wipe him off the earth. Jon went back into the office, and Brenda drove away.

That same afternoon, around 4:30 P.M., Ms. White returned to Jon's workplace to again discuss refinancing the home. When she arrived, Jon was leaving the office building. Brenda observed him talking on a cell phone—a cell phone that she claims Jon had repeatedly denied owning. Ms. White testified that at that moment she was overcome with all the anger, agitation, loss, grief, and disappointment she had experienced throughout her relationship and the divorce. Ms. White claims at that point, her emotions took over and she lost all self-control.

As she watched Jon talk on his cell phone, Ms. White drove her vehicle toward him, accelerating quickly. When Jon heard tires screeching, he jumped between two parked cars, over a small cement wall, and back into his office building. Ms. White continued to follow Jon, driving her car through the building's double glass doors. After entering the lobby with her car, Ms. White struck Jon twice with her vehicle. Jon flew over the hood of the car and landed on the ground, injuring his left leg.

Brenda was arrested and charged with attempted murder and criminal mischief. In preparation for trial, she filed a motion in limine requesting the court to instruct the jury on the defense of extreme emotional distress found in Utah Code section 76-5-203. In her motion, Ms. White argued that under this section she was entitled to let a jury consider whether during the relevant events Ms. White was acting "under the influence of extreme emotional distress" for which there was a "reasonable explanation or excuse."

The State opposed her motion. It proffered evidence from Mr. White's sister, who testified that Brenda called her shortly after the events and told her that she thought she had just killed Jon. Mr. White's sister testified that Brenda's tone was "matter-of-fact" and "unemotional." The State also introduced the statement of the officer who responded to the scene just after the events occurred. The officer testified that when he approached Ms. White, she was still in her car. He observed that she was not crying and did not appear upset.

After the trial court heard argument on the issue, it denied Ms. White's pretrial motion and declined to give the affirmative defense jury instruction. In its order, the trial court stated that "[t]he extreme emotional distress defense is available only to defendants who have been subjected to stress that would cause the average reasonable person to have an extreme emotional reaction and experience a loss of self control." The trial court concluded that while Ms. White may have been angry and under stress, the stressors she claimed caused her to attack her ex-husband were "common occurrences" for divorced couples and happened "several weeks to years" before the day of her violent attack. The trial court also found that Ms. White's return to Jon's workplace four hours after their argument, along with her negotiation of a "complicated driving pattern" indicated she "was aware of what she was doing and was in control of her faculties at the time in question."

Ms. White filed a petition for an interlocutory appeal to challenge the trial court's decision to deny her motion.

The court of appeals affirmed the trial court's decision. The court of appeals reasoned that to be eligible for an extreme emotional distress defense instruction, a defendant must show that the "defendant's loss of self-control be in reaction to a *highly provocative triggering event*" that is "*contemporaneous* with the defendant's loss of self-control." In its application of this rule to Ms. White's case, the court stated:

> Ultimately, the only contemporaneous, provocative event that preceded [Ms. White's] loss of self-control was [Jon's] use of a cell phone that he had previously denied possessing. This event is not sufficiently provocative, even when viewed in its unique context, to entitle [Ms. White] to a jury instruction on the affirmative defense of extreme emotional distress.

The court of appeals reasoned that Ms. White "had the opportunity to proffer as much evidence as she deemed necessary to show that she qualified" for the defense, but the only information she actually proffered—"marital difficulties, financial stress, parenting issues, other difficulties with divorce, and the death of a therapist—lack[ed] the requisite contemporaneous relationship to her loss of self-control." Finally, the court of appeals held that the availability of the extreme emotional distress defense must be evaluated using an objective standard and based on the expected conduct of a reasonable person under the then-existing circumstances, not the subjective point of view of Ms. White . . .

ANALYSIS

We granted certiorari to determine whether the court of appeals erred in holding that Ms. White was required to demonstrate a *highly provocative and contemporaneous triggering event* as a prerequisite to an affirmative defense of extreme emotional distress.

Ms. White contends the court of appeals erred when it required her to show a "highly provocative and contemporaneous triggering event" because this language does not appear in the statute and this standard is more demanding than the language of the statute and our case law requires. Ms. White urges us to reverse the decision of the court of appeals and hold that she is entitled to let the jury consider this defense at trial.

The State asks us to affirm the decision of the court of appeals. The State concedes, as it must, that the extreme emotional distress defense statute does not contain the "highly provocative and contemporaneous triggering event" language, but it nevertheless argues that case law interpreting the extreme emotional distress defense statute clearly requires application of this rigorous standard.

We do not decide whether Ms. White is entitled to an extreme emotional distress defense jury instruction at trial because this is not the question presented to us. But we do conclude that the court of appeals' decision imposes a standard more exacting than the statute mandates. We therefore reverse the decision of the court of appeals and remand with instructions to remand this matter to the trial court for reevaluation of the evidence supporting Ms. White's request for an extreme emotional distress defense instruction under the standard we announce in this opinion . . .

We begin our discussion by turning to the language of the extreme emotional distress defense statute. Utah Code section 76-5-203(4)(a)(i) provides that "[i]t is an affirmative defense to a charge of . . . attempted murder" if the defendant was [1] acting "under the influence of extreme emotional distress [2] for which there was a reasonable explanation or excuse." Although the statute does not define these terms, the extreme emotional distress defense has a long history in our case law in which we have conferred meaning for each of the elements. We find it useful to briefly discuss this history here.

Utah's extreme emotional distress defense was codified in 1973 and was largely patterned after the defense contained in the Model Penal Code. The extreme emotional distress defense was generally enacted by states in response to the unworkable nature of the heat of passion defense. The defense was meant to "substantially *enlarge*[ ] the class of cases that might be reduced to manslaughter" and "to do away with categories of adequate provocation which had developed in the cases."

Although we briefly touched on the extreme emotional distress defense in two earlier cases, we did not have an opportunity to squarely consider the contours of the defense until we decided *State v. Bishop* in 1988. In *Bishop*, we singled out a New York case, *People v. Shelton*, as a "well-reasoned" decision that helped define what "extreme emotional disturbance" would mean under our statute. Relying on *Shelton*, we adopted a similar definition for extreme emotional distress under Utah law. We stated that a person acts under the influence of extreme emotional distress when "he is exposed to extremely unusual and overwhelming stress" that would cause the average reasonable person under the same circumstances to "experience a loss of self-control," and "be overborne by intense feelings, such as passion, anger, distress, grief, excessive agitation, or other similar emotions."

Although the court of appeals' decision correctly identifies the definition of extreme emotional distress, the court of appeals erred in applying it to Ms. White's case because it linked this definition to an additional requirement not present in the statute or our case law. Specifically, the court of appeals stated:

> Although [Ms. White] had the opportunity to proffer as much evidence as she deemed necessary to show that she qualified for [the extreme emotional distress defense], the only other factors actually proffered— marital difficulties, financial stress, parenting issues, other difficulties with divorce, and the death of a therapist—*lack the requisite contemporaneous relationship to her loss of self-control.*

As we discuss in more detail below, this "contemporaneous" requirement is not a prerequisite to asserting the defense and the court of appeals' imposition of this standard was an improper retreat into our heat of passion jurisprudence.

We first conclude that the court of appeals improperly relied on *State v. Clayton*. *Clayton* was decided in 1983, before we developed the requirements of the extreme emotional distress defense in *Bishop*. In *Bishop*, we announced our intent to distance ourselves from the heat of passion analysis and to "substantially enlarge[ ] the class of cases" where the defense would be available to defendants. Since our decision in *Bishop*, we have employed a more generous approach to this defense and the court of appeals erred in narrowing its scope.

Second, we conclude that the court of appeals erred by requiring Ms. White to show a "highly provocative triggering event" that was "contemporaneous" with her loss of self-control. The word "contemporaneous" does not appear anywhere in the statute or our extreme emotional distress defense case law. And unlike the former "heat of passion" defense, "[a]n action influenced by an extreme emotional [distress]" need not be an immediate trigger for criminal conduct. "Rather, it may be that a significant mental trauma has affected a defendant's mind for a substantial period of time, simmering in the unknowing subconscious and then inexplicably coming to the fore." Our recent decision in *State v. Shumway* illustrates this principle. In *Shumway*, two teenage boys, Christopher and Brookes, were playing video games at a sleepover. According to Brookes, Christopher was irritated with Brookes for beating him at the games, went into the kitchen, and began playing with a knife. Christopher began throwing the knife in the air and catching it, and then lunged at Brookes and began poking him with the knife. The boys wrestled over control of the knife and in his anger, Brookes stabbed Christopher, killing him. We held that Brookes was entitled to an extreme emotional distress defense instruction. In our decision, we noted that Brookes had "been bullied and pushed around by his peers since he was in the third grade, and that all of this 'came out on Chris' when the boys fought over the knife."

This case demonstrates that when a person reacts to a situation, that reaction cannot be viewed in isolation. Rather, a reaction to an event must be evaluated in its broader context. This context is relevant, maybe essential, to acquiring an accurate picture of the past experiences and emotions that give meaning to that reaction. Those past experiences must be taken into account to determine whether an individual is acting "under the influence of extreme emotional distress."

Although a building emotional reaction to a series of events may *contribute* to extreme emotional distress, an external triggering event is also required. An external trigger is a necessary predicate to access the defense because other preeminent causes of emotional distress—organic causes relating to mental illness and self-inflicted causes—are expressly rejected as a form of distress under the statute. Thus, "some external initiating circumstance must bring about" the defendant's distress and resulting conduct. In many cases this triggering event will naturally occur just before the criminal act; however, we find no language in our precedent that *requires* the triggering event be *contemporaneous* with the defendant's loss of self-control. A close temporal tie between provocation and the criminal act was necessary under the "heat of passion" formulation because manslaughter was not available if there was time for the defendant to "cool off." No such requirement exists to assert the extreme emotional distress defense.

In summary, the court of appeals' "contemporaneous" requirement represents, in our view, an improper retreat into the realm of "heat of passion" manslaughter. As we discussed above, the extreme emotional distress defense was meant to "reformulate[ ] and *enlarge*[ ] the heat of passion standard" to make it more accessible to criminal defendants and to move away from a case-by-case examination of whether the "type" of provocation rendered the defendant's reaction reasonable. Thus, we conclude that the court of appeals erred by improperly limiting the extreme emotional distress defense to defendants who can point to a "highly provocative" and "contemporaneous" triggering event. This is not what the law requires. We therefore reverse and remand this case to the court of appeals with instructions to remand the case to the trial court. On remand, we instruct the trial court to use this opinion as a guide to reevaluate whether Ms. White has demonstrated "any reasonable basis" upon which the jury should be allowed to consider the extreme emotional distress defense at trial.

We now take the opportunity to briefly comment on the "reasonable explanation or excuse" element of the extreme emotional distress defense statute. While technically outside the scope of the narrow certiorari question presented to us, we nevertheless address this issue in order to provide guidance to the trial court on remand.

On appeal, Ms. White argues that the court of appeals erred when it failed to evaluate the reasonableness of the explanation for her distress from her subjective point of view. We disagree.

The extreme emotional distress statute provides that "[t]he reasonableness of an explanation or excuse . . . shall be determined from the viewpoint of a *reasonable person under the then existing circumstances.*" As the court of appeals noted:

> Although a trial court is statutorily required to consider the circumstances surrounding a defendant's extreme emotional distress, those circumstances must be viewed from the viewpoint of a reasonable person. Thus, the legal standard is whether the circumstances were "such that the average reasonable person would react by experiencing a loss of self-control."

This standard requires a trier of fact to put herself in the shoes of a reasonable person in the defendant's situation to determine whether the defendant's reaction to a series of events was reasonable. The standard is not whether the defendant thought her reaction was reasonable, but whether a reasonable person facing the same situation would have reacted in a similar way. We conclude that the court of appeals correctly identified this legal standard. This same standard should be applied when the trial court evaluates Ms. White's extreme emotional distress defense on remand . . .

Brenda White

AFTERWORD   After extensive legal wrangling and a mistrial, Brenda White pled guilty to aggravated assault and criminal mischief in a plea deal. She was sentenced to a year in jail; in exchange, prosecutors dropped the attempted murder charge. During sentencing, the victim stated: "I have a life-long leg injury. It's never going to go away, but I'll just move on every day with it. The thing is we can now finally say that, for the actions that happened on that day, she's being held accountable for it. And that's been the big question mark the whole time is, why is she not being held accountable for it? And everybody in my family can finally just breathe a sigh of relief that she's going to be held accountable." Meredith Forrest Kulwicki & David Wells, *Man Hit by Wife's SUV Speaks at Sentencing*, Fox 13, Jan. 8, 2013.

NOTES & QUESTIONS ON EXTREME EMOTIONAL DISTURBANCE

1. *Temporality.*   The Supreme Court of Utah concluded that the Court of Appeals was wrong to require White to point to an immediate triggering event. It is clear that jurisdictions with a traditional provocation doctrine want to see an immediate reaction based on a triggering stimulus, rather than a chronic pattern of low-level conduct. However, should the same apply when the jurisdiction applies "extreme emotional disturbance"? The Model Penal Code provision on which Utah based its provision was meant to broaden the old provocation standard and get away from its rigid doctrinal requirements. The editors' notes to Model Penal Code § 210.3 state that "[t]he traditional requirement of a sudden heat of passion based on adequate provocation is broadened by the Model Code, though the new version still retains both objective and subjective components." Do you agree with the Supreme Court of Utah that the Utah legislature was similarly motivated by a desire to broaden the doctrine of provocation?

2. *The reasonable person standard.*   MPC § 210.3 states that the "extreme emotional disturbance" standard will apply when there is no "reasonable explanation or excuse." The reasonableness of the explanation or excuse will be "determined from the viewpoint of a person in the actor's situation under the circumstances as he believes them to be." Jurisdictions that adopted this MPC language have interpreted the standard subjectively. For example, in *People v. Casassa*, 49 N.Y.2d 668 (1980), the New York Court of Appeals stated that the determination "should be made by viewing the subjective, internal situation in which the defendant found himself and the external circumstances as he perceived them at the time, however inaccurate that perception may have been, and assessing from that standpoint whether the explanation or excuse for his

emotional disturbance was reasonable. . . ." Think for a second about why New York courts would use a subjective approach. Is it because "extreme emotional disturbance" is a partial *excuse* based on the mental infirmity of the defendant? In *White*, however, the Utah Court of Appeals rejected the subjective approach, distinguished *Casassa*, and concluded that the Utah provision required a more objective assessment of the reasonableness of the explanation or excuse. The New York statute at issue in *Casassa* required that the analysis be "determined from the viewpoint of a person in the defendant's situation under the circumstances as the defendant believed them to be." In contrast, Utah Code § 76-5-203(4) dictates that "[t]he reasonableness of an explanation or excuse . . . be determined from the viewpoint of a reasonable person under the then existing circumstances." Pay attention to the language from the New York Statute that is conspicuously missing from the Utah provision. With this difference in mind, did the Utah judges read the Utah statute correctly?

3. *A mini insanity defense.* The Model Penal Code doctrine of "extreme emotional disturbance" does double duty. In addition to replacing the provocation defense with a broader standard, it was also designed to allow jurisdictions to consider mental problems that fall short of qualifying for the full insanity defense. Some jurisdictions call this "diminished capacity," and it will be considered in greater depth in Chapter 28. The result of the doctrine is that a fully insane defendant should be acquitted and sent to a mental hospital, while a defendant with lesser mental problems should still be entitled to introduce psychiatric evidence that will downgrade a murder charge to manslaughter. The rationale for this approach is that the law should recognize any emotional disturbance that mitigates the defendant's responsibility for the killing, regardless

---

HYPOTHETICAL

Ann and Bob have a troubled marriage and frequently engage in verbal fights that turn physical, requiring the police to show up. Both have been arrested for domestic violence, though in both cases the charges were dropped when each refused to testify. The latest fight happened in March and again the police were called. When they arrived, both individuals had scratches on their faces.

In April, during one particularly bad verbal argument, Bob screams at Ann: "I'm going to sleep with your sister tomorrow!" Although there is no hitting during the argument, the comment enrages Ann, who takes a knife and stabs Bob to death.

At trial, Ann's lawyer argues that she is only guilty of manslaughter. During the trial, Ann's sister testifies that she had been engaged in a lengthy affair with Bob, although they had both kept the affair secret, and Ann was not aware of it. Ann's lawyer argues that she was more likely than a typical reasonable person to snap because of her long history of domestic disturbances.

What result under the provocation doctrine? What result under the standard of extreme emotional disturbance?

of whether the source of the disturbance is a mental illness or a specific provoking event. Either way, the defendant's mental condition was compromised by something for which there is a "reasonable explanation or excuse," thus mitigating the defendant's blameworthiness.

C. PRACTICE & POLICY

This section begins with a dialogue over the status of provocation and EED: Are they partial excuses, partial justifications, or neither? We also ask whether the provocation defense is applied in a discriminatory fashion because most of the defendants who qualify for the defense are abusive men who kill women. This raises a deeper question: Should the doctrine be eliminated entirely?

> ◌ **Provocation as partial justification.**   Provocation is clearly a *partial* defense because it does not result in an acquittal. But is it a justification or an excuse? Justifications usually mean that the defendant's actions are, in a sense, rightful. So the victim is partially responsible for the resulting situation because he provoked the incident. This makes a provoked killing less wrongful than an unprovoked killing. (Think of the doctrine of comparative negligence in tort law, which in some situations reduces the amount of a plaintiff's recovery because of his own contribution to the injury.) This view of the provocation defense has fallen out of favor, particularly because it blames the victim. If the provoking act is adultery, the theory seems particularly inapt because adultery is no longer a crime. If the provoking act is injury or assault, the theory implies that killing the original provoker is partially justified even if the killing does not meet the doctrinal requirements for self-defense.
>
> ◌ **Provocation as partial excuse.**   Maybe provocation is a partial excuse because the defendant loses control and has difficulty conforming his behavior to the requirements of the law. See Joshua Dressler, *Provocation: Partial Justification or Partial Excuse?*, 51 Modern L. Rev. 467, 480 (1988) (provocation doctrine is a "concession to human weakness"). This view is by far the most common approach to the doctrine. It is also consistent with the approach taken by the extreme emotional disturbance standard, which places provocation cases on a spectrum of emotional problems that might also be caused by mental illness. In this way, provocation is clearly a partial excuse because it mirrors the excuse-like nature of the insanity defense, which is based on the inability of the defendant to follow

the law because of mental infirmity. A final possibility is that the provocation doctrine has *both* elements of justification and excuse mixed together. See, e.g., Mitchell N. Berman & Ian P. Farrell, *Provocation as Partial Justification and Partial Excuse*, 52 Wm. & Mary L. Rev. 1027 (2011). In Berman's and Farrell's view, the defense should only apply when the defendant loses mental control (the excuse) because the victim engaged in some wrongdoing (the justification). Under this approach, both aspects are essential and necessary elements of the doctrine.

∽ Arguing provocation to the jury. Which standard do you think would be most beneficial for a defense attorney: provocation based on heat of passion, or extreme emotional disturbance? Would a defense attorney prefer to argue for manslaughter under the provocation formula or EED? On the one hand, the extreme emotional disturbance formula is *broader* and more forgiving than a provocation standard based on a closed list of situations—and the perpetrator might have acted under a situation not covered by the list. In that case, the extreme emotional disturbance formula will give the defendant the doctrinal space to argue for mitigation. (Also, a few jurisdictions such as California dispense with the closed list and allow defendants to argue provocation based on a reasonable person approach.) On the other hand, the "closed-list" version of the provocation doctrine concentrates on the episodic and exceptional nature of the defendant's behavior (because it was based on a triggering event). Juries might be more forgiving of the defendant because they see the crime as unlikely of being repeated, and by extension, the defendant as less dangerous to the public. So, the jury might be more willing to convict on the lesser charge. In contrast, an argument based on extreme emotional disturbance could, in theory, involve a chronic emotional deficiency that might make the jury very anxious about the defendant's potential to commit more crimes in the future, thus suggesting a need for longer incarceration.

∽ Domestic violence and adultery. In cases dealing with adultery, the husband usually kills the wife. It is rare for a wife to kill her husband and successfully argue provocation. Is it problematic that provocation provides a partial defense for men who kill wives who stray from the marriage? Is it based on an antiquated and offensive notion that wives were property under the dominion of their husbands? Lawrence Friedman, *Crime and Punishment in American History* 221 (1993). The law is now facially neutral, but the empirical facts show that in practice the defense more often mitigates the criminal responsibility of men engaged in domestic violence rather than women. Compare Emily L. Miller, Comment, *(Wo)manslaughter: Voluntary Manslaughter, Gender, and the Model Penal Code,*

50 Emory L.J. 665, 667 (2001) (criticizing the discriminatory nature of the doctrine in practice), with Aya Gruber, *A Provocative Defense*, 103 Calif. L. Rev. 273, 332 (2015) ("The defense does not necessarily burden women unfairly nor does it particularly privilege sexist men."). Historically, the defense may have been premised—in part—on the idea that adultery was illegal. In American law today, adultery is no longer illegal in most states, though several states still have adultery laws on the books (that are almost never used). See Gabrielle Viator, *The Validity of Criminal Adultery Prohibitions After Lawrence v. Texas*, 39 Suffolk U.L. Rev. 837 (2006) (suggesting that adultery laws are unconstitutional). This would imply that adultery should remain a provocation in jurisdictions, like the U.S. military and its Uniform Code of Military Justice, that still criminalize adultery. Do you agree? Some scholars question whether adultery should qualify as a provocation at all. Others find the entire analysis too focused on the "justification" aspect of provocation at the expense of the "excuse" aspect.

∾ Abolishing provocation.   Some scholars would jettison the defense entirely. See, e.g., Stephen J. Morse, *Undiminished Confusion in Diminished Capacity*, 75 J. Crim. L. & Criminology 1, 28-36 (1984). Morse argues that we "cheapen both life and our conception of responsibility by maintaining the provocation/passion mitigation." For Morse and some other scholars, the provocation doctrine provides an overly charitable outcome for killers who become enraged by events that most other individuals would suffer through without resorting to lethal violence. As he says, "most intentional killers deserve little sympathy." If the provocation defense is *defensible*, on their view it has to be because the defendant has lost partial control of their behavior through no fault of their own. Is this an accurate description of perpetrators who kill in the heat of passion? Or is "partial loss of control" a meaningless concept? Compare with Victoria Nourse, *Passion's Progress: Modern Law Reform and the Provocation Defense*, 106 Yale L.J. 1331, 1337 (1997) ("The passion defense should be retained as a partial excuse but only in the limited set of cases in which the defendant and the victim stand on an equal emotional and normative plane.").

CHAPTER 11

—◁∘⁄∘▷—

RECKLESS KILLINGS

A. DOCTRINE

A reckless killing can fall into two categories: murder or involuntary manslaughter. Involuntary manslaughter applies when the defendant engages in conduct that constitutes a substantial and unjustified risk that results in someone's death. So, for example, imagine three young men are on a highway overpass and drop a bunch of heavy (ten-pound) rocks on cars passing below, as a "prank." One of the rocks falls through a car windshield and kills a passenger. Throwing a rock in this manner creates a substantial and unjustified risk of death—unjustified because the rock was thrown for no reason other than the teenagers' amusement and substantial because of the degree of risk of death from the behavior. If the teenagers were aware of the degree of risk and consciously disregarded it (by engaging in the action anyway), this qualifies as a reckless killing. In some jurisdictions, unintentional killings can also qualify as murder if the defendant's actions are so reckless that they demonstrate either implied malice or a depraved indifference to human life (depending on the jurisdiction). The following sections explain the difference between these forms of reckless killing; the chapter concludes with a discussion of the misdemeanor manslaughter rule.

1. Involuntary Manslaughter   *Mens Rea = Recklessness*

Involuntary manslaughter is an unintentional killing based on the defendant's *unjustified* risk-taking behavior. In almost all jurisdictions, the required mental state is recklessness, though a few jurisdictions only require negligence for manslaughter. As discussed in Chapter 6, recklessness requires that the perpetrator "consciously disregard[ ] a substantial and unjustified risk." In the words of

subjective risk

Model Penal Code § 2.02(2), disregarding the risk "involves a gross deviation from the standard of conduct that a law-abiding person would observe in the actor's situation." Consequently, it is not enough for the prosecutor to establish that the defendant engaged in risk-taking behavior. In addition, the prosecution must demonstrate that a reasonable person—viewed objectively—would not have taken the risk. In theory, many accidents resulting in death could meet this standard if they stemmed from an unjustified and substantial risk and were accompanied by the appropriate mental state (conscious awareness). For example, imagine an artist builds a large ice sculpture and is aware that there is a substantial risk that the ice sculpture might topple over and cause a potentially lethal injury to a child. The risk in this situation also might be unjustified if there was a sensible precaution, such as a small safety perimeter for viewing the sculpture, that might have prevented the deadly accident. If the artist consciously disregarded the risk, he could be convicted of involuntary manslaughter. More controversially, one writer has suggested that executives at some car companies should be prosecuted for ignoring safety problems that result in fatal collisions. Rena I. Steinzor, *(Still) "Unsafe at Any Speed": Why Not Jail for Auto Executives?*, 9 Harvard L. & Pol'y Rev. 901 (2015). So, if a food company executive knows that his peanut butter is tainted with a potentially lethal strain of salmonella but tells his subordinates to "ship it anyway," a jury could conclude that the risk was so substantial and unjustified that the executive should be convicted of involuntary manslaughter.

2. Implied Malice and Extreme Indifference Murder

A reckless killing can rise to the level of murder, though the labels change slightly depending on the jurisdiction. Some penal codes refer to reckless murder as "implied malice murder." The phrase originates in the common law definition of murder, which is the killing of another human being with "malice aforethought." At common law, that malice was demonstrated expressly when the defendant committed the killing intentionally. However, judges eventually broadened their understanding of malice so that defendants who committed non-intentional killings could also, in extreme cases, be convicted of murder. Those cases were defined as "implied malice murder" if the depravity evinced by the defendant was especially severe or evidence of an "abandoned and malignant heart." Although the "implied malice murder" label is in decline and has been abandoned by many courts, it still endures in some jurisdictions.

In contrast, other jurisdictions classify reckless killings as murder if they were committed while manifesting an "extreme indifference to the value of human life." MPC § 210.2(b). For example, N.Y. Penal Law § 125.25 defines second-degree murder as reckless "conduct which creates a grave risk of death to another person" that evinces a "depraved indifference to human life." In this context, the terms "depraved indifference" and "extreme indifference" are functional synonyms. Determining whether a particular case of reckless conduct involves a depraved or extreme indifference to human life will inevitably be a fact-dependent inquiry of law application to fact, and one that will fall under the jury's discretion. Although in exceptional circumstances an appellate court could overturn as unreasonable a jury finding of depraved or extreme indifference, in reality it is rare for a court to disturb the jury's discretion in this area.

3. Misdemeanor Manslaughter Rule

Some jurisdictions apply the "misdemeanor manslaughter rule" (also known as the "unlawful act doctrine"), which permits a conviction for involuntary manslaughter if the defendant commits an underlying misdemeanor that results in death. The required mental state is the mens rea for the underlying misdemeanor, and the doctrine does not require that the prosecutor independently demonstrate that the defendant acted with recklessness with respect to the resulting death. Instead, the defendant's recklessness is *presumed* by statute, on account of the defendant's commission of the underlying misdemeanor. Prosecutors love the doctrine because it allows them to prosecute a manslaughter case in situations where the defendant committed a regulatory misdemeanor, without having to independently prove the required recklessness. Of course, the prosecution must still demonstrate a sufficient causal link (proximate cause) between the underlying misdemeanor and the resulting death.

B. APPLICATION

1. Involuntary Manslaughter

The following case involves the death of a young child who was forgotten in a car—a truly horrific death. The defendant was charged with involuntary manslaughter. As such, the court was tasked with determining whether the defendant acted with recklessness or whether the defendant simply committed an innocent mistake. As you read the details of the case, form your own conclusion about the defendant's mental state.

People v. Kolzow
Appellate Court of Illinois
301 Ill. App. 3d 1, 703 N.E.2d 424 (1998)

FROSSARD, J.

Following a bench trial, defendant Donna Kolzow was convicted of involuntary manslaughter for the death of her three-month-old son, who died of heat stroke after she left him unattended in a car for four hours. She was sentenced to three years' probation, with the conditions of counseling and six months in custody in the Cook County Department of Corrections. . . .

FACTS

Defendant related the following in her statements to police: On the night of August 11, 1996, defendant was out with her three-month-old baby, Jeffrey. From 11 P.M. until 2 A.M., she and the child were driving around in a car with a friend of defendant, Eileen Hoover. While driving around, defendant called Officer Jeffrey Simpson, an on-duty Riverside police officer, whom she and Hoover later met at a parking lot around 1 A.M. After feeding the child with a bottle at approximately 2 A.M., she drove Hoover home. In her initial statement to police, defendant said that she and the baby spent the night at Hoover's home until she drove home at 6:30 A.M. However, in a subsequent statement, defendant said that after she dropped Hoover off at home, she ran into Officer Simpson again, who asked her to meet him at the Riverside Swim Club. She met him, got out of the car to talk and drove home around 4:30 A.M. She and the baby arrived home around 5 A.M., but instead of going inside, defendant parked her car in a nearby parking lot and read a book. She stated that she did not go inside because she did not want to wake her sleeping stepmother. At 6:30 A.M., defendant said she noticed her stepmother's car was gone and parked her car in front of the house. She turned off the engine, closed the driver's window, and locked the car. Leaving the baby in the car, defendant then went in the house. She stated she immediately went to the bathroom as she had diarrhea. Defendant said she then set the alarm for 9:30 A.M., lay on the couch and fell asleep. She said she forgot about the baby, who was locked outside in the car.

Defendant stated the alarm never went off and that she awoke at 10:30 A.M. on her own. She said she remembered the baby was still in the car when she noticed he was not in the playpen. She went out to the car and saw the child's face was completely purple. After bringing him into the house, she said she felt his hands and knew he was dead. She then called her father and her workplace. When her sister called the house, defendant told her the baby was dead.

Officer James Glosniak of the Hillside police department arrived at the scene shortly after 11 A.M. on August 12, 1996, in response to a call from one of defendant's relatives. He testified that, when he arrived, the rear windows of the car were down about four inches and the front windows were closed. He said the car was facing west. The child was inside the house, and the officer found no pulse. The child's body was still warm, and his cheeks and hands were a dark, reddish purple color. Defendant told the officer that she had left the baby in the car from 7 A.M. until 10:30 A.M. that morning with the windows rolled up. However, when later asked whether she had rolled the windows down, she stated she had not touched anything in the car since she removed the baby. Realizing that the child could not be resuscitated, Officer Glosniak called his supervisor to the scene.

An autopsy conducted the next day revealed the baby died of heat stroke, and Dr. Edmond Donoghue of the Cook County medical examiner's office concluded that "parental neglect [was] a significant factor" in the child's death. Donoghue noted that the baby's nutrition, hydration and cleanliness were good and stated on cross-examination that it appeared the child had been well cared for.

After obtaining a search warrant, detectives retrieved an alarm clock from defendant's apartment. Detective Heldt said the clock was displaying the correct time before it was removed from the apartment, and the alarm was set for 6 A.M. On cross-examination, the detective acknowledged he did not test the alarm to see if it functioned properly . . .

George Gourley, who lived across the street from one of defendant's friends, was also called as a State witness. He testified that a few days prior to baby Jeffrey's death, he was sitting on his front porch when he saw defendant park her car on the street and go inside the friend's house. He testified that it was a very hot evening, and the windows of the car were rolled up. About 20 minutes later, defendant came out of the house and retrieved the baby, who had been in the car. Gourley further testified that "at least half a dozen times" he witnessed defendant leave the child unattended in a parked car while she went inside her friend's house. . . .

ANALYSIS

Defendant . . challenges the sufficiency of the evidence supporting her conviction. Specifically, she asserts that the evidence fails to prove she acted recklessly by leaving her three-month-old son unattended in a car for four hours, resulting in his death. . . .

Under the Illinois Criminal Code of 1961, a person commits involuntary manslaughter when he or she "unintentionally kills an individual without lawful justification . . . [and] his [or her] acts whether lawful or unlawful which cause the death are such as are likely to cause death or great bodily harm to some individual, and he [or she] performs them recklessly." Recklessness is defined as follows:

> A person is reckless or acts recklessly, when he consciously disregards a substantial and unjustifiable risk that circumstances exist or that a result will follow . . . and such disregard constitutes a gross deviation from the standard of care which a reasonable person would exercise in the situation.

Defendant asserts that in the present case, there was no evidence she knew the car would become so overheated that it was a danger to her baby and thus there was no evidence she consciously disregarded any risk. Therefore, she argues, there was insufficient proof of recklessness. We disagree, and find the record contains sufficient evidence to support a conviction for involuntary manslaughter; specifically, that defendant left her three-month-old son in the vehicle, consciously disregarding a substantial and unjustifiable risk of death or great bodily harm to her son.

We find that a rational trier of fact could certainly interpret the evidence presented, including the statement of defendant herself, as supporting the conclusion that defendant acted recklessly in leaving her baby unattended in the car. The evidence in the record supports the State's theory, and the trial court's conclusion, that defendant left the child unattended in an effort to get some uninterrupted sleep. First, defendant claimed to have set her alarm before she lay down to go to sleep, supporting the inference she purposely intended to nap rather than just fall asleep. In addition, she waited outside her stepmother's home from 5 A.M. to 6:30 A.M. even though she had been up all night, thereby avoiding any possibility that her decision to leave the child unattended would be questioned by the stepmother. Also, before defendant went into the house, leaving the baby in the car, she locked the car and closed the windows, further supporting the conclusion that she did not plan to come immediately back out to retrieve the child after going to the bathroom. Finally, the car was found with each back window opened about four inches, which indicates defendant was planning to leave the child in the car and knew it could become hot.

The trial court simply did not find defendant's claim that she "forgot" the child to be credible. A trial court's determination as to the witnesses' credibility and the weight given to their testimony is entitled to great deference. Defendant also asserts that, because she was a new mother, she was unaware of the danger of leaving the child unattended in the car, and she argues there was no indication she knew how high the temperature in the car could get. However, defendant was not charged with murder for intentionally killing her child; she was charged with involuntary manslaughter, which requires a mental state of recklessness. In general, a defendant acts recklessly when he or she is aware that his conduct might result in death or great bodily harm, although that result is not substantially certain to occur. We believe a reasonable person would be aware of the risks in leaving a three-month-old infant unattended in a parked car for four hours on a summer day, and find the evidence supports the trial court's finding that defendant acted recklessly by consciously disregarding that clear and obvious risk. . . .

NOTES & QUESTIONS ON INVOLUNTARY MANSLAUGHTER

1. *Honest mistake or recklessness?*   Should Kolzow have been convicted if she was only guilty of a simple mistake? Or was there a deeper theory of the case here? The Illinois court seemed particularly influenced by testimony that Kolzow had a habit of leaving her child in the car unattended. What role did this piece of evidence play in helping the prosecution to satisfy its burden of showing that she had consciously disregarded a substantial and unjustified risk? Presumably the argument was that Kolzow knew that there was a risk that something bad might happen to the child while he was left unattended in the car, but she continued this type of behavior anyway. What result if this had been a one-off situation, and Kolzow had never left the child in the car before? Could she still be convicted of involuntary manslaughter in that situation?

What result if a parent mistakenly forgets a child in a car because of absent-mindedness? Although this sounds like an unlikely event, some have argued that it is easier than one might think. Babies are often strapped in rear-facing child seats that make it difficult to see if they are occupied when a parent is in the driver's seat. Also, a sleeping baby might be quiet and therefore go unnoticed. As one mother wrote in an essay about her own experience: "Walking into the garden center, my husband turned to me and said: 'My God. We left Paloma in the car.' I screamed, dropped my purse, ran to the car and opened the door. The car was already warm. Her face already flushed. But she was fine and still sleeping. I was ashamed, embarrassed and horrified at what I had done. It dawned on me immediately—I could have killed my girl." Sunny Hostin, *I, Too, Left My Child in a Hot Car*, CNN, June 26, 2014. Hostin's child was fine. But if a forgotten child dies, should the parent be convicted of involuntary manslaughter? Is one parent more blameworthy than the other?

2. *Mitigated punishment for manslaughter.*   Kolzow received a relatively minor punishment: six months in jail, three years' probation, and counseling. Involuntary manslaughter is punished less harshly than murder, so it really matters whether a reckless defendant is charged and convicted of depraved indifference murder or involuntary manslaughter. Even so, Kolzow argued in her appeal that her sentence was too harsh, an argument that drew a sharp rebuke from one of the concurring justices:

> I would like to comment on defendant's complaint that the sentence was excessive. The range of a sentence for an involuntary manslaughter conviction is two to five years. In this case, the sentence was three years' probation, with the conditions of counseling and six months in custody. I believe the trial judge imposed a more than fair sentence considering that a three-month-old child died of heat stroke, and Dr. Donoghue concluded that "parental neglect [was] a significant factor" in the child's death.
>
> Jeffrey's life was every bit as precious as any other human being's. However, defendant's actions showed that her social life and sleep took precedence over Jeffrey's well-being. Defendant kept Jeffrey in the car all night

while she was out socializing, had a habit of leaving Jeffrey in the car alone, and, in a final act of selfishness, left Jeffrey in a severely hot car so she could get uninterrupted sleep. As a result, Jeffrey was left alone to cry in a car with temperatures exceeding 115 degrees. Unfortunately, Jeffrey's cries for his mother were to no avail. The exposure of Jeffrey's three-month-old body to the extreme heat caused sunburn, hemorrhages throughout his heart, and blood to fill his lungs. The cost of defendant's feeble attempt at motherhood is the untimely loss of an innocent young life. Defendant's mild sentence is in no way disproportionate to the heinous crime at issue here.

Do you agree with the judge's statement?

PROBLEM CASE

On the morning of June 18, 2014, Justin Ross Harris left his house for work, with his 22-month-old son strapped in the back of the car. On his way to work, Harris stopped at a fast-food restaurant for breakfast, which he ate inside the restaurant with his son at his side. After finishing breakfast, he strapped his son back into the car seat and drove to work. Police allege that instead of dropping his son off at daycare, Harris left him inside the hot car for the workday. When Harris left work at the end of the day, he pulled into a nearby shopping center parking lot and got out of the car screaming about his baby. Paramedics could not revive the child; he was dead.

Harris was charged with murder; police suggested that he left the child in the car deliberately because he wanted to live a child-free existence. But Harris's attorney argued that the charge was inappropriate because he was simply guilty of making a mistake. Harris was convicted of intentional murder in 2016 and his lawyers filed an appeal in 2017, asking for a new trial. Harris's supporters, including his ex-wife, still maintain that the death was an accident.

If you were prosecuting a similar case, what strategy would you adopt if you were convinced of the defendant's intent to kill the child? You could seek an indictment for murder if he intentionally killed the child, or you could proceed on a more modest charge of involuntary manslaughter based on the mental state of recklessness.

Justin Ross Harris

Review the casebook video, *People v. Robert Dale* (Part 5: Punishment for Manslaughter). What factors should the court consider in assessing the appropriate penalty for a conviction of manslaughter? In this case, Dale was not convicted of an intentional killing. On the other hand, manslaughter is a significant criminal offense. In the end, what length of imprisonment is appropriate for Dale's sentence?

2. Implied Malice and Extreme Indifference Murder

The first case deals with implied malice and the second case applies the extreme indifference to human life standard. As you read the following two cases, compare their standards. Do you think the standards made a difference or would both cases come out the same regardless of the standard used?

People v. Knoller

Supreme Court of California
41 Cal. 4th 139, 158 P.3d 731 (2007)

KENNARD, J.

On January 26, 2001, two dogs owned by defendant Marjorie Knoller and her husband, codefendant Robert Noel, attacked and killed Diane Whipple in the hallway of an apartment building in San Francisco. Defendant Knoller was charged with second degree murder and involuntary manslaughter; codefendant Noel, who was not present at the time of the attack on Whipple, was charged with involuntary manslaughter but not murder. . . . After a change of venue to Los Angeles County, a jury convicted defendants on all counts. Both moved for a new trial. . . .

not premeditated

FACTS AND PROCEEDINGS

. . . Defendant Knoller . . . contacted Dr. Donald Martin, a veterinarian for 49 years, and on March 26, 2000, he examined and vaccinated the dogs. With his bill to Knoller, Dr. Martin included a letter, which said in part: "I would be professionally amiss [*sic*] if I did not mention the following, so that you can be prepared. These dogs are huge, approximately weighing in the neighborhood of 100 pounds each. They have had no training or discipline of any sort. They were a problem to even get to, let alone to vaccinate. You mentioned having a professional hauler gather them up and taking them. . . . Usually this would be done in crates, but I doubt one could get them into anything short of a livestock trailer, and if let loose they would have a battle. [¶] To add to this, these animals would be a liability in any household, reminding me of the recent attack in Tehama

County to a boy by large dogs. He lost his arm and disfigured his face. The historic romance of the warrior dog, the personal guard dog, the gaming dog, etc. may sound good but hardly fits into life today." Knoller thanked Dr. Martin for the information and said she would pass it on to her client. . . .

Between the time defendants Noel and Knoller brought the dogs to their sixth-floor apartment in San Francisco and the date of the fatal mauling of Diane Whipple on January 26, 2001, there were about 30 incidents of the two dogs being out of control or threatening humans and other dogs. Neighbors mentioned seeing the two dogs unattended on the sixth floor and running down the hall. . . .

There were also instances when defendants' two dogs attacked or threatened people. David Moser, a fellow resident in the apartment building, slipped by defendants Knoller and Noel in the hallway only to have their dog Hera bite him on the "rear end." When he exclaimed, "Your dog just bit me," Noel replied, "Um, interesting." Neither defendant apologized to Moser or reprimanded the dog. Another resident, Jill Cowen Davis, was eight months pregnant when one of the dogs, in the presence of both Knoller and Noel, suddenly growled and lunged toward her stomach with its mouth open and teeth bared. Noel jerked the dog by the leash, but he did not apologize to Davis. Postal carrier John Watanabe testified that both dogs, unleashed, had charged him. He said the dogs were in a "snarling frenzy" and he was "terrified for [his] life." When he stepped behind his mail cart, the dogs went back to Knoller and Noel. On still another occasion, the two dogs lunged at a six-year-old boy walking to school; they were stopped less than a foot from him. . . .

On January 26, 2001, Whipple telephoned Smith to say she was going home early. At 4:00 P.M., Esther Birkmaier, a neighbor who lived across the hall from Whipple, heard dogs barking and a woman's "panic-stricken" voice calling, "Help me, help me." Looking through the peephole in her front door, Birkmaier saw Whipple lying facedown on the floor just over the threshold of her apartment with what appeared to be a dog on top of her. Birkmaier saw no one else in the hallway. Afraid to open the door, Birkmaier called 911, the emergency telephone number, and at the same time heard a voice yelling, "No, no, no" and "Get off." When Birkmaier again approached her door, she could hear barking and growling directly outside and a banging against a door. She heard a voice yell, "Get off, get off, no, no, stop, stop." She chained her door and again looked through the peephole. Whipple's body was gone and groceries were strewn about the hallway. Birkmaier called 911 a second time. . . .

An autopsy revealed over 77 discrete injuries covering Whipple's body "from head to toe." The most significant were lacerations damaging her jugular vein and her carotid artery and crushing her larynx, injuries typically inflicted by predatory animals to kill their prey. . . .

On February 8, 2001, both defendants appeared on the television show *Good Morning America* and basically blamed mauling victim Whipple for her own death. Defendant Knoller claimed that Whipple had already opened her apartment door when something about her interested Bane. He broke away, pulled Knoller across the lobby, and jumped up on Whipple, putting his paws on either side of her. Knoller said she pushed Whipple into Whipple's apartment, fell on top of Whipple, and then tried to shield Whipple with her own body. But Whipple's struggles must have been misinterpreted by the dog, and when Whipple struck Knoller with her fist, the dog began to bite Whipple. Knoller claimed that Whipple had ample opportunity to just slam the door of her apartment or stay still on the floor.

Codefendant Noel did not testify, but he presented evidence of positive encounters between the two dogs and veterinarians, friends, and neighbors . . . Asked whether she denied responsibility for the attack on Whipple, Knoller gave this reply: "I said in an interview that I wasn't responsible but it wasn't for the—it wasn't in regard to what Bane had done, it was in regard to knowing whether he would do that or not. And I had no idea that he would ever do anything like that to anybody. How can you anticipate something like that? It's a totally bizarre event. I mean how could you anticipate that a dog that you know that is gentle and loving and affectionate would do something so horrible and brutal and disgusting and gruesome to anybody? How could you imagine that happening?"

In rebuttal, the prosecution presented evidence that the minor character of defendant Knoller's injuries—principally bruising to the hands—indicated that she had not been as involved in trying to protect mauling victim Whipple as she had claimed. Dr. Randall Lockwood, the prosecution's expert on dog behavior, testified that good behavior by a dog on some occasions does not preclude aggressive and violent behavior on other occasions, and he mentioned the importance of training dogs such as Bane and Hera *not* to fight. . . .

THE ELEMENTS OF IMPLIED MALICE

Murder is the unlawful killing of a human being, or a fetus, with malice aforethought. Malice may be express or implied. At issue here is the definition of "implied malice."

Defendant Knoller was convicted of second degree murder as a result of the killing of Diane Whipple by defendant's dog, Bane. Second degree murder is the unlawful killing of a human being with malice aforethought but without the additional elements, such as willfulness, premeditation, and deliberation, that would support a conviction of first degree murder. Section 188 provides: "[M]alice may be either express or implied. It is

Abandoned + malignant → heart problematic

express when there is manifested a deliberate intention to take away the life of a fellow creature. It is implied, when no considerable provocation appears, or when the circumstances attending the killing show an abandoned and malignant heart."

Implied malice →

The statutory definition of implied malice, a killing by one with an "abandoned and malignant heart," is far from clear in its meaning. Indeed, an instruction in the statutory language could be misleading, for it "could lead the jury to equate the malignant heart with an evil disposition or a despicable character" instead of focusing on a defendant's awareness of the risk created by his or her behavior. "Two lines of decisions developed, reflecting judicial attempts 'to translate this amorphous anatomical characterization of implied malice into a tangible standard a jury can apply.'" Under both lines of decisions, implied malice requires a defendant's awareness of the risk of death to another.

The earlier of these two lines of decisions . . . originated in Justice Traynor's concurring opinion in *People v. Thomas*, 41 Cal. 2d 470, 480 (1953), which stated that malice is implied when "the defendant for a base, antisocial motive and with wanton disregard for human life, does an act that involves a high degree of probability that it will result in death." The later line dates from this court's 1966 decision in *People v. Phillips*, 51 Cal. Rptr. 225: Malice is implied when the killing is proximately caused by "an act, the natural consequences of which are dangerous to life, which act was deliberately performed by a person who knows that his conduct endangers the life of another and who acts with conscious disregard for life."

THE COURT OF APPEAL'S TEST FOR IMPLIED MALICE

Implied malice well-settled

As discussed in the preceding part, the great majority of this court's decisions establish that a killer acts with implied malice only when acting with an awareness of *endangering human life*. This principle has been well settled for many years, and it is embodied in the standard jury instruction given in murder cases, including this one. The Court of Appeal here, however, held that a second degree murder conviction, based on a theory of implied malice, can be based simply on a defendant's awareness of the risk of causing *serious bodily injury* to another.

Ct of Appeals

In cases decided shortly before and after *Conley*, we reiterated the established definition of implied malice as requiring an awareness of the risk that the defendant's conduct will result in the *death* of another. One year before *Conley* was filed, we stated in *People v. Washington*, 44 Cal. Rptr. 442, 402 P.2d 130 (1965), that implied malice required a "conscious disregard for life." *Conley* did not at all suggest that it intended to depart from the view expressed in *Washington*. And two months after *Conley*, this court in *People v. Phillips*, endorsed its earlier statement in Washington that implied malice requires a "conscious disregard for *life*." . . .

We conclude that a conviction for second degree murder, based on a theory of implied malice, requires proof that a defendant acted with conscious disregard of the danger to human life. In holding that a defendant's conscious disregard of the risk of serious bodily injury suffices to sustain such a conviction, the Court of Appeal erred. . . .

(handwritten marginalia: "H", "not risk of serious bodily injury")

AFTERWORD   On remand, Knoller's conviction for implied malice murder—and her sentence of 15 years to life—was upheld by a California appeals court in 2010. Her husband, Robert Noel, served his sentence for involuntary manslaughter and was released from prison. Whipple's partner, Sharon Smith, sued Knoller and Noel in a civil case for wrongful death. The case was heralded as a victory for gay rights, since at the time the lawsuit was filed in 2001, gay marriage was not legally recognized in California.

People v. Snyder

Supreme Court of New York, Appellate Division
937 N.Y.S.2d 429, 91 A.D.3d 1206 (2012)

GARRY, J.

. . . After the January 1996 death of her daughter (born in 1993), defendant was arrested and charged with, among other things, three counts of murder in the second degree, including intentional murder, depraved indifference murder, and depraved indifference murder of a person under 11 years old. She was also charged with attempted intentional murder of her son (born in 1992), and multiple counts of both assault in the first degree and reckless endangerment. In 2001, defendant was convicted by jury verdict of depraved indifference murder, assault in the first degree (four counts) and reckless endangerment in the first degree (eight counts), and was thereafter sentenced to an aggregate prison term of 50 years to life. . . .

A person is guilty of depraved indifference murder when, "[u]nder circumstances evincing a depraved indifference to human life, he [or she] recklessly engages in conduct which creates a grave risk of death to another person, and thereby causes the death of another person." N.Y. Penal L. § 125.25(2). Defendant's convictions of assault in the first degree required proof that, "[u]nder circumstances evincing a depraved indifference to human life, [she] recklessly engage[d] in conduct which create[d] a grave risk of death to another person, and thereby cause[d] serious physical injury to another person." N.Y. Penal L. § 120.10(3). Likewise, to support defendant's conviction of reckless endangerment in the first degree, the People were required to prove that "under circumstances evincing a depraved indifference to human life, [she] recklessly engage[d] in conduct which create[d] a grave risk of death to another person." N.Y. Penal L. § 120.25.

Although defendant advances a variety of challenges to her convictions, her primary challenge on appeal relates to the legal sufficiency and weight of the evidence. She argues that the evidence does not support a finding that she committed any of the acts alleged, that she possessed the necessary mens rea or that she caused injury to either of her children. We reject these contentions.

The People's case was based entirely on the theory that defendant attempted to cause breathing problems in both of her children by suffocating them for the purpose of collecting government benefits. To that end, the People presented extensive testimony from the numerous pediatricians, specialists, nurses, emergency personnel and social workers who cared for the children or otherwise interacted with defendant and her children from the birth of defendant's son in 1992 until the death of defendant's daughter in 1996. The mostly circumstantial evidence established that both children were admitted to the hospital—after experiencing difficulty breathing and being rushed to the emergency room—on numerous occasions following their births for what appeared to be apnea episodes. Each episode occurred during daytime hours, defendant was the only person present when the symptoms began and she was the sole source of information as to what occurred. Although numerous tests were performed, the results were routinely normal and medical personnel were unable to determine any organic cause for the children's identical breathing problems. One such test performed on defendant's daughter revealed that her apnea originated in the lung area, rather than in the brain, indicating that it was caused by something blocking her airway. According to various medical witnesses, there were other indicators that the children's problems were caused by suffocation, including reports of blood in their noses or mouths and certain recorded information on heart and respiratory rate monitors, which signified that their lungs were healthy but that the oxygen flow had been interrupted for a period of time.

Medical personnel who came in contact with defendant and her children at the hospital observed more than one incident that caused them to suspect that defendant was suffocating them. After one such incident, Donald Swartz, the pediatric pulmonologist for defendant's son, directed that defendant not be left alone with the child while he was in the hospital, and he experienced no further apnea episodes during the remainder of his hospital stay. Swartz thereafter discharged the son with orders that he not be left alone at home with defendant and made arrangements for nurses to regularly visit the home. When the son was later readmitted to the hospital, defendant and the child's father requested that Swartz not be involved in caring for him.

Subsequently, defendant's daughter was referred to Daniel Shannon, a pediatrician at Massachusetts General Hospital, who diagnosed her with a sinus node dysfunction with a possible seizure disorder and recommended surgery to implant a pacemaker. Despite such surgery, the daughter's apnea episodes continued and she was admitted to the emergency room several times thereafter with reported seizures. No seizures were ever documented during her hospital stays and none were actually witnessed by medical personnel.

Ultimately, in January 1996, defendant's daughter was rushed to the local hospital emergency room in respiratory and cardiac arrest. She was transferred to another hospital, where she died a few days later. Her death was determined to have resulted from a lack of oxygen and inadequate blood flow to the brain. The chief medical examiner who performed the autopsy on defendant's daughter testified that he was unable to rule out suffocation as the cause of death, and that he believed that the manner of death was "consistent with a homicide." The People's expert witness similarly testified that, in her opinion, both children's frequent hospitalizations resulted from suffocation, which carried a significant risk of death, and that the death of defendant's daughter was, in fact, caused by suffocation.

Pamela Marshall, an inmate at the Franklin County Jail when defendant was incarcerated there after her arrest, also testified for the People. According to Marshall, defendant spoke with her about the case on one occasion and told Marshall that she and her husband had been having financial difficulties and decided to try to get disability benefits for her children after learning that a friend had received such benefits for a child who was having breathing problems. During that conversation, defendant described several incidents—which were consistent with the testimony of other witnesses—in which she had attempted to induce such breathing problems in her children. Defendant also told Marshall that, on the day her daughter was taken to the hospital just prior to her death, she had attempted several times to put a pillow over her face in order to cause breathing problems in anticipation of the arrival of a home health nurse that day. Defendant stated that she "didn't mean for it to go as far as it did," but that the nurse who was scheduled to come to the house had arrived late.

In addition, a claims representative for the Supplemental Security Income (hereinafter SSI) program testified regarding defendant's applications for disability benefits on behalf of her children based upon alleged lung problems/obstructive apnea, which applications were ultimately successful. The People attempted to demonstrate a correlation between the timing of various aspects of the application process—including reviews of entitlement to benefits and payments made—and the occurrence or "remission" of the children's apnea events in order to prove that defendant induced their problems at particular times in her effort to obtain or maintain eligibility for such benefits.

Dapheny Wright, a salesperson for a mobile home company, testified that she first encountered defendant and her boyfriend in 1995 when they purchased a mobile home. Wright was concerned about their ability to secure financing for the purchase, as their income consisted of public assistance and SSI benefits. When Wright asked defendant whether the SSI benefits were permanent, defendant responded that the benefits were for her daughter, who was disabled due to "respiratory problems and weak blood," that she anticipated the condition to be a long-term disability and that the benefits would continue for the rest of the child's life. Wright further testified that defendant and her boyfriend presented themselves at her office on January 19, 1996—within days of the death of defendant's daughter—and informed her that they had lost their daughter, who was their main source of income, and indicated that they were in danger of losing their home.

. . . We readily conclude that the record contains legally sufficient evidence that defendant repeatedly suffocated her children knowing that she was subjecting them to a grave risk of death and caused them serious physical injury, and that, in doing so, she recklessly caused the death of her daughter. . . .

Mens rea may be demonstrated by circumstantial evidence. In the event of an unintentional killing of a single individual, depraved indifference may be established, as relevant here, where the "defendant—acting with a conscious objective not to kill but to harm—engages in torture or a brutal, prolonged and ultimately fatal course of conduct against a particularly vulnerable victim." The defendant's actions must "reflect wanton cruelty, brutality or callousness [and be] combined with utter indifference to the life or safety" of the victim. The Court of Appeals has stated that "depraved indifference is best understood as an utter disregard for the value of human life—a willingness to act not because one intends harm, but because one simply doesn't care whether grievous harm results or not." As set forth above, the proof here revealed that defendant repeatedly suffocated her two helpless children and forced them to undergo unnecessary medical procedures, callously causing repeated injury to each of them without regard to the risk of grievous harm posed by her actions, which ultimately resulted in her daughter's death. Defendant's indifference to the lives and safety of her children was further demonstrated in the testimony describing her behavior on the day that she last suffocated her daughter; the person whom defendant later described as a "home health nurse" arrived at defendant's home to find that the child was not breathing, had no pulse, was limp, colorless and "ice cold," and that defendant had not called for help. This individual, a parent monitor, testified at trial that although she repeatedly instructed defendant to perform rescue breathing, defendant did not do so. Instead, defendant "just [sat] there," tearless and doing nothing, while the monitor summoned rescue personnel and tended to the child. Defendant's state of apparent unconcern continued at the hospital; while medical personnel attempted to resuscitate her daughter, defendant remained outside the treatment room, calmly eating snacks.

The evidence revealed that defendant's sole reason for wishing that her children would not die as a result of her repeated, brutal acts was so that she might continue to torture them, and thereby continue to receive disability benefits. This wish—to be able to indefinitely continue brutalizing her children for financial gain—does not and cannot constitute anything but the most "utter disregard for the value of human life" and for her children's lives. Indeed, defendant's wish to continue to profit from her children's pain and suffering was cruelly depraved. Her desire for her children to continue living only to serve her cruel purpose cannot legally be deemed to constitute even the smallest shred of concern for their lives or safety. Thus, we find that the evidence of depraved indifference is legally sufficient to support defendant's convictions. . . .

NOTES ON IMPLIED MALICE AND DEPRAVED INDIFFERENCE

1. *What constitutes depravity?* According to the prosecutors, why did Snyder act with depraved indifference to human life? The prosecution's view was that Snyder never intended to kill her children. Instead, Snyder wanted to suffocate them in order to get state benefits—a plan that not only did not require that they die, it in fact depended on the children surviving. Nonetheless, the prosecution argued that Snyder consciously disregarded the risk that the suffocations might produce death. Furthermore, that conscious disregard constituted a depraved indifference to human life. Which aspect of it makes it depraved indifference? Is it because the victim was her own child? Or because she had a financial motive? The court in *Snyder* interpreted "depraved indifference" as an additional mens rea requirement over and above traditional recklessness. In the past, some New York courts had interpreted depraved indifference as an "objective" assessment of the defendant's *conduct*. Courts have since abandoned that view and clarified that the standard pertains to mens rea, so that the relevant inquiry is whether the defendant's risk-taking behavior was so extreme and unjustified that it evidenced a particularly depraved state of mind.

2. *Implied malice and risk.* In *Knoller*, the California Supreme Court clarified that implied malice murder requires that the defendant consciously disregard a risk of death—as opposed to a risk of serious bodily injury. Apply this standard to the facts of *Knoller*. Did the defendant realize that the dogs might *kill* someone (as opposed to merely injure someone)? In theory, almost

any case of serious bodily injury has the capacity to escalate into a death. Applying the "risk of death" standard articulated by the California Supreme Court, how would you vote if you were a juror hearing this case?

3. *Emotional disturbance.* The DSM-V recognizes "Factitious Disorder Imposed on Another" as a significant mental disorder. It was more commonly known in the past as "Münchausen syndrome by proxy" and involves "falsification of physical or psychological signs or symptoms, or *induction of injury* or disease, in another . . . " The manual specifically states that whereas "some aspects of factitious disorders might represent criminal behavior (e.g., factitious disorder imposes on another, in which the parent's actions represent abuse and maltreatment of a child), such criminal behavior and mental illness are not mutually exclusive." *Diagnostic and Statistical Manual of Mental Disorders* 325-26 (5th ed. 2013). If you were Snyder, would you have tried to introduce psychiatric evidence, either for a full insanity defense or as an "extreme emotional disturbance" qualifying her for manslaughter? Or would the strategy fail because of Snyder's financial motive for the crime?

PROBLEM CASE

In 1995, Dr. David Benjamin was convicted of second-degree murder for performing a botched abortion in Queens, NY. Local prosecutors argued that Benjamin did not have the requisite training to perform the late-term abortion on the patient, and that when the operation went awry, he misled paramedics who arrived at his clinic to take the patient to the hospital.

In his own defense, Benjamin testified that the problems started when he erroneously calculated the age of the fetus. He thought the fetus was younger, which would have resulted in an easier procedure. During the abortion, however, he realized that the fetus was older, but he pressed ahead with the procedure anyway, resulting in severe danger to the patient. Prosecutors contended that after the procedure he left the woman to bleed to death in the recovery room while he went to operate on another patient. Furthermore, prosecutors argued that Benjamin was fully aware of the level of risk to his patient associated with his conduct.

The jury deliberated for two hours before finding Benjamin guilty of second-degree murder under a theory of depraved indifference to human life. Lynette Holloway, *Abortion Doctor Guilty of Murder*, N.Y. Times, Aug. 9, 1995. Do you think the doctor was guilty of murder or just medical malpractice? Why?

 Review the casebook video, *People v. Robert Dale* (Part 3: Depraved Indifference). Assume that the defendant, Robert Dale, was under a legal obligation to feed his neighbor. Was his recklessness regarding his neighbor sufficiently depraved to support a conviction for second-degree murder? What facts would support such a finding? Is there enough evidence to present this issue to a jury or should it be dismissed by the judge?

3. Misdemeanor Manslaughter Rule

The misdemeanor manslaughter rule gives the prosecutor a "shortcut" to a manslaughter charge if the defendant committed a misdemeanor resulting in death. As you read the following case, ask yourself whether the misdemeanor manslaughter rule is a form of strict liability, and if so, whether it is appropriate. What limitations or restrictions does the court impose on the doctrine's application?

State v. Biechele
Superior Court of Rhode Island
2005 WL 3338331 (2005)

DARIGAN, J.

Before this Court is Defendant Daniel Biechele's ("Defendant") motion to dismiss one hundred counts of a grand jury indictment. . . . Defendant faces two hundred manslaughter counts. . . . The first one hundred counts charge Defendant with involuntary manslaughter resulting from criminal negligence; the second one hundred counts charge Defendant with involuntary manslaughter resulting from the commission of an unlawful act ("misdemeanor manslaughter"). Defendant moves to dismiss the misdemeanor manslaughter counts for failure to state an offense under Rhode Island law and for failure to provide fair warning. . . .

Defendant was the "tour manager" of "Great White," a band that performed at The Station, a nightclub located in Warwick, Rhode Island. On February 20, 2003, the Defendant allegedly ignited pyrotechnic devices inside the Station as part of the band's performance. The ignition of the pyrotechnics would constitute a misdemeanor if the Defendant was not licensed to possess, control, or use the pyrotechnics under § 11-13-1. The State alleges that the pyrotechnics started a fire inside The Station that proximately caused the deaths of one hundred people. . . .

Section 11-23-3 requires that "[e]very person who shall commit manslaughter shall be imprisoned not exceeding thirty (30) years." It is settled law in Rhode Island that because manslaughter is not defined within the statute, it takes the same meaning as defined in common law. . . .

Involuntary manslaughter in Rhode Island is defined as "an unintentional homicide without malice aforethought committed either in performance of an unlawful act not amounting to a felony or in the performance of a lawful act with criminal negligence." This definition clearly creates two distinct theories of involuntary manslaughter: one based on criminal negligence theory and one based on unlawful act theory ("misdemeanor manslaughter"). . . .

Defendant first claims that the State failed to allege the Defendant engaged in conduct that constitutes a misdemeanor under Rhode Island law. Defendant also argues § 11-13-1 does not apply to pyrotechnics. Further, Defendant contends § 11-13-1 failed to give adequate warning of the offense, in violation of due process protection. Defendant asserts that the firework misdemeanor's thirty-day statute of limitation precludes the State from bringing a manslaughter charge after thirty days.

Defendant contends that even if the ignition of the pyrotechnics constituted a misdemeanor under § 11-13-1, manslaughter could not be appropriately charged because the Defendant lacked the criminal scienter necessary for such a serious conviction. Defendant avers Rhode Island case law requires the misdemeanor underlying a misdemeanor manslaughter charge to be *malum in se,* and contends the firework statute is *malum prohibitum.* Additionally, Defendant argues that the indictment requires no criminal *mens rea* in violation of fundamental due process guarantees and State case law. . . .

The State asserts the clear language of the statute indicates the pyrotechnic devices used by the Defendant required a permit or prior approval under § 11-13-1 ("firework statute"). Further, the State argues that a reasonable person would know that the Defendant's conduct was within the ambit of the firework statute. The State avers the thirty-day statute of limitation for the firework misdemeanor is irrelevant, as the State does not seek to bring charges under the firework statute. Finally, the State contends that there is an element of criminal *mens rea* imbedded both in the misdemeanor and in the proximate cause required between the misdemeanor and the deaths. Thus, the State asserts that the level of criminal culpability embedded in the misdemeanor manslaughter counts is sufficient to satisfy due process guaranties and is also consistent with Rhode Island case law. . . .

CULPABILITY OF FIREWORK MISDEMEANOR

The State must first prove some criminal *mens rea* on the part of the Defendant in the possession, control, and ignition of the pyrotechnic devises. Although the statute on its face does not require any mental culpability, a criminal statute prohibiting possession of a specified object has repeatedly been held to require both intentional control of the object and knowledge of the object's nature. This holding has applied to many different criminal statutes. Such knowledge can be inferred from the acts, declarations, or conduct of the accused.

As the State recognized in oral argument, the rule to strictly construe verbs relating to possession in criminal statutes extends to the misdemeanor underlying the Defendant's indictment. Essentially, in order to prove the underlying misdemeanor, the State will not only have to prove the Defendant's possession and use of the pyrotechnics without a permit, but also must prove the Defendant intentionally controlled the pyrotechnics and knew of the characteristics of the devices. This is not to say the State will have to prove that the Defendant knew his conduct was illegal, but rather that the Defendant knew he was dealing with devices which had a combustible or explosive composition or that contained a substance prepared for the purpose of producing a visible or audible effect by combustion, explosion, deflagration, or detonation.

STATE ADEQUATELY ALLEGED DEFENDANT COMMITTED MISDEMEANOR MANSLAUGHTER

Whether the unlawful possession, control, and ignition of pyrotechnic gerbs could potentially serve as the requisite misdemeanor for a manslaughter conviction is a novel question in Rhode Island. The Court agrees with the Defendant's suggestion that without some element of *mens rea*, conviction of the Defendant would be inconsistent with both Rhode Island law and State and Federal Constitutional guarantees. However, the Court does not agree that the indictment as it stands does not require any underlying criminal *mens rea*; further, the Court holds that the criminal culpability required to convict the Defendant is consistent with state law and constitutional protections.

The allegation of manslaughter based on the firework misdemeanor is consistent with state law and constitutional protections. "To inflict substantial punishment upon one who is morally entirely innocent, who caused injury through reasonable mistake or pure accident, would so outrage the feelings of the community as to nullify its own enforcement." Sayre, *Public Welfare Offenses,* 33 Col. L. Rev. 55, 56 as in *Morissette v. United States,* 342 U.S. 246, 256 (1952). As manslaughter carries substantial punishment of up to thirty years, it would be unjust to convict the Defendant unless the Defendant had some guilty mental state. However, in addition to the knowledge implied in the misdemeanor, there is also criminal culpability embedded in the misdemeanor manslaughter theory of involuntary manslaughter.

In *State v. McLaughlin,* the Rhode Island Supreme Court articulated that proximate cause is an element of the crime of misdemeanor manslaughter. 621 A.2d 170 (R.I. 1993). In *McLaughlin,* the Court stated "[i]n order to find defendant guilty of involuntary manslaughter under the misdemeanor manslaughter theory, the state must prove two elements beyond a reasonable doubt. It must show first that a misdemeanor occurred and then that such misdemeanor was the *proximate cause* of the victim's death." . . .

Proximate Cause Requirement of Misdemeanor Manslaughter Heightens Culpability Required to Convict the Defendant

The requirement that the illegal conduct proximately cause the manslaughter eliminates concerns that the culpability required to convict the Defendant is too insignificant to uphold a manslaughter conviction. Logically, the Defendant's conduct must be of the type that could proximately cause death. LaFave's *Substantive Criminal Law* identifies how states have limited the use of misdemeanor manslaughter through proximate cause. States which adhere to the *malum in se/malum prohibitum* distinction generally do not require proof of proximate cause if the misdemeanor is *malum in se*. Those states would apply the three variations of limiting the underlying misdemeanor to *malum prohibitum* crimes; other states would use the variations as to all crimes. The three variations are 1) the unlawful act must proximately cause the death, 2) the unlawful excess must proximately cause the death, or 3) the unlawful act must amount to criminal negligence. The Court in *McLaughlin* adopted the first position, as it states the criminal conduct must proximately cause the death. . . .

The proximate cause limitation is perfectly consistent with the Rhode Island Supreme Court's reasoning in other criminal cases. In *State v. Benoit,* the defendant, while intoxicated beyond twice the legal limit, was driving in the high-speed lane. 650 A.2d 1230, 1231 (R.I. 1995). A car carrying one passenger, driving in the opposite direction of the defendant, crossed the dividing line and hit the defendant. The passenger in the other car was killed, and the driver of the other car was injured. The defendant was charged by way of information with § 31-27-2.2 and § 31-27-2.6. These statutes appeared to create a strict liability standard if an intoxicated defendant was operating a vehicle and death or injury resulted from such operation. Plainly, the operation of the vehicle was a "but for" cause of the accident; without the defendant's presence on the highway, no accident would have occurred. However, the Court held proof that the *manner* of operation proximately caused the death was necessary. In terms of proximate cause, the simple fact that the defendant was intoxicated while driving did not make it foreseeable that a car traveling at a high rate of speed would cross the center divider and strike the defendant's car. Because the State admitted that it could not prove the defendant's truck was anywhere but in its lane and only alleged the mere presence of the car on the highway, the Court dismissed the counts. The Court rejected the State's theory of strict liability and embraced the limitation that proximate cause must be shown between the *manner* of operation and not just the operation itself. Court also clarified that no showing of negligence or recklessness was necessary to convict the defendant under the two statutes. Sensibly, a harmless misdemeanor could not serve as the proximate cause of a death because death is not the natural consequence of harmless action.

PROXIMATE CAUSE INQUIRY IS FACT-INTENSIVE

With respect to the proximate cause inquiry, *State v. Benoit* is also significant because of the Court's focus on the facts of the case, not the general category of the crime. Drunk driving is a crime that the court blatantly considered to be conduct that proximately causes death. However, the Court did not consider whether the category in which the conduct was classified could proximately cause the crime, but rather looked to see if defendant's specific actions proximately caused the crime. . . .

The Defendant's contention that *malum prohibitum* crimes should be categorically excluded without inquiry into the specific facts would be contradictory to previous reasoning of the Rhode Island Supreme Court. The inquiry of this Court should not be whether a firework misdemeanor can underlie a misdemeanor manslaughter conviction, but whether the Defendant's alleged unlawful possession, control, and ignition of the pyrotechnics, in light of the specific circumstances and facts, could create a foreseeable risk of death. Although the Defendant had a duty under the statute to refrain from possession, control, and ignition of pyrotechnics without a permit, failing to do so does not automatically mean his conduct made death foreseeable. The alleged facts indicate that conditions in The Station nightclub might have been unusually dangerous, possibly constituting an intervening cause of death. Depending on the facts and circumstances, the effect of the pyrotechnics may not have been foreseeable. However, proximate cause and knowledge are facts for the jury to decide and are not appropriate for this Court to address in a motion to dismiss counts in an indictment. . . .

NO ADDITIONAL ELEMENTS APPLICABLE

This Court believes that the indictment sufficiently meets the modern day requirements of misdemeanor manslaughter articulated in *McLaughlin*. Because *McLaughlin* and other recent Rhode Island criminal law cases fail to adhere to the *malum in se/malum prohibitum* distinction, this Court does not believe it is necessary or appropriate to add any additional requirements to the crime of misdemeanor manslaughter. Proximate cause implicates a culpable mental state; a separate element for criminal culpability is not required. . . .

Classification of the alleged firework misdemeanor as *malum in se or malum prohibitum* is unnecessary. If the State can prove the Defendant disregarded the statutory requirements for possession and use of the pyrotechnic devices, and that disregard caused a foreseeable risk of death to hundreds of people, the Defendant's conduct would not be blameless. However, if the facts show that such disregard did not exist or did not create a foreseeable risk of death, then the Defendant could not be convicted of manslaughter.

This Court declines to dismiss the misdemeanor manslaughter counts on their face by promulgating a new judicial rule creating categorical limitations on the type of misdemeanor the State could use as the basis of a manslaughter charge. As this issue has not been presented to the Supreme Court of Rhode Island, it would be their prerogative to use these facts to further limit misdemeanor manslaughter if the court was so inclined. This Court notes that misdemeanor manslaughter has fallen into disfavor on a national level, and has been criticized as being harsh and archaic. However, it remains a viable cause of action in this jurisdiction. . . .

AFTERWORD   The fire at The Station was one of the deadliest nightclub fires in U.S. history. Biechele ended up pleading guilty to 100 counts of involuntary manslaughter. The prosecutor asked for a 10-year prison sentence; the judge imposed a 15-year sentence, but suspended 11 years from the sentence, thus requiring that Biechele only spend 4 years in prison. He was paroled from prison after serving less than 2 years in prison.

Jay McLaughlin, brother-in-law of The Station nightclub fire victims, Sandy and Michael Hoogasian

At his sentencing hearing, Biechele said: "Since the fire, I have wanted to tell the victims and their families how truly sorry I am for what happened that night and the part that I had in it. I never wanted anyone to be hurt in any way. I never imagined that anyone ever would be. . . . I know how this tragedy has devastated me, but I can only begin to understand what the people who lost loved ones have endured. I don't know that I'll never forgive myself for what happened that night, so I can't expect anybody else to."

The owners of the nightclub, two brothers named Michael and Jeffrey Derderian, received a similar fate. Michael was sentenced to 15 years in prison with 11 years suspended and eventually received early parole. Jeffrey served no prison time.

NOTES & QUESTIONS ON MISDEMEANOR MANSLAUGHTER

1. *Limitations on strict liability.*   How would you describe the culpability of Biechele, the tour manager? He improperly handled the fireworks and as a result 100 people lost their lives. As a strategic matter, was the misdemeanor

manslaughter rule even necessary? Could the prosecutor have succeeded under a theory of involuntary manslaughter without relying on the misdemeanor manslaughter rule? If the answer to that question is yes, then one way of understanding the misdemeanor manslaughter rule is that it lowers the prosecutorial burden with regard to mens rea in manslaughter cases (as long as the defendant committed an underlying misdemeanor). Is the prosecutorial burden lowered too far? The court in *Biechele* concedes that the misdemeanor manslaughter rule is disfavored and often criticized for its harshness. Nonetheless the doctrine stubbornly remains in many jurisdictions. See *People v. Datema*, 448 Mich. 585 (1995) (upholding misdemeanor manslaughter rule). Is the misdemeanor manslaughter rule a type of strict liability? The basic contour of the doctrine is that a misdemeanor resulting in death should be prosecuted as manslaughter. This would seem to alleviate the need for the prosecutor to demonstrate the defendant's recklessness, i.e., his conscious disregard of a substantial and unjustified risk. However, in Rhode Island, the prosecutor must still demonstrate proximate cause by showing that the result was reasonably foreseeable. Does this doctrinal limitation mitigate the harshness of the original rule? The Rhode Island court views the proximate cause limitation as imposing a heightened mens rea requirement. How would you describe it? If the resulting deaths must be reasonably foreseeable, does this imply something close to recklessness, or does it only imply negligence?

2. *Inherently dangerous misdemeanors.* Some jurisdictions impose additional limitations on the doctrine, such as limiting it to "inherently dangerous misdemeanors." Would that have changed the result in The Station nightclub case? Is the illegal possession or use of fireworks inherently dangerous? Moreover, should the question be evaluated in the abstract or with regard to the facts of the case? In this case the fireworks clearly *were* inherently dangerous, otherwise the result would not have been so catastrophic. Can the same be said of all fireworks in general? To answer the question, consider the public policy rationale for creating the regulations regarding fireworks in the first place. Did the legislature in Rhode Island create the misdemeanor because it recognized that fireworks were inherently dangerous?

C. PRACTICE & POLICY

The following materials discuss the strategic and legal implications of using "depraved indifference" and "implied malice" in cases that are best described as intentional—not reckless—murders. In terms of legislative grading, depraved indifference is a form of murder that in many jurisdictions is labeled second-degree murder. But depraved indifference is also a distinct—and in some sense mutually exclusive—description of how a killing occurred. Either the defendant desired the victim's death, or not. Do the labels matter or should we only be concerned with the resulting punishment?

    ∾ **Murder and mens rea.**   Prosecutors are increasingly making use of "depraved indifference to human life" as a basis for securing murder convictions. Consider the strategy behind this. Under normal circumstances, a prosecutor who charges a defendant with garden-variety second-degree murder must establish that the defendant acted with the intent to kill the victim. In many cases, intent can be difficult to prove and requires the jury to make an inference regarding the defendant's mental state on the basis of the available evidence. While there is nothing inherently impossible about that process, it does introduce a wild card into the calculation; the jury might decide that there is insufficient evidence of intent in the case and acquit the defendant of the murder charge. Consequently, prosecutors may wish to take a risk-averse approach and charge the defendant with depraved indifference to human life. In that case, the prosecutor can dispense with the need to prove intent entirely—all she needs to do is prove recklessness plus depraved indifference.

    ∾ **Murder and sentencing.**   The striking thing about the strategy is that it is increasingly being used in cases that, to the casual observer, certainly sound like intentional murder. In that case, the prosecutor really is lowering his or her evidentiary burden with regard to the mens rea. Why would the prosecutor do this? To understand the strategy, you need to look at the available penalties. For example, in New York State, second-degree murder potentially carries a sentence of 25 years to life in prison, regardless of whether the murder charge is based on intentional murder or recklessly causing death with depraved indifference to human life. Without a substantial statutory distinction in the applicable penalties, prosecutors have an incentive to charge a defendant with depraved indifference murder even if the prosecutor believes that the defendant intended to kill the victim.

    ∾ **Compromise verdicts.**   Why do juries convict intentional killers of "depraved indifference" murder? One possibility is that some juries might be confused into thinking that "depraved indifference" murder is actually a *higher* form of intentional murder, like aggravated murder (which it is not). When that happens, the jury might see the murder as especially heinous and jump to the erroneous conclusion that "depraved indifference" is the right legal category for it. But a more likely explanation is that the jury is reaching a compromise verdict. Indeed, a prosecutor might want to include "depraved indifference" murder in the indictment to *encourage* the jury to reach a compromise verdict. Unable to decide on guilt on the top count or a full acquittal, the jury might split the difference and find the defendant guilty of an intermediate charge like second-degree depraved indifference murder. Prosecutors often try to avoid compromise verdicts because the associated sentence might be too light (from their perspective). But in the case of second-degree depraved indifference murder, the prison term is likely to be almost as severe (or even equally severe) as for intentional murder, thus eliminating any qualms the prosecutor might have about encouraging the compromise verdict.

∾ New York courts respond. Recently, a few courts have started to clamp down on this prosecutorial strategy, though judicial pushback is still rare. But in a trio of decisions, New York's highest court has emphatically rejected the strategy. In *People v. Gonzalez*, 1 N.Y.3d 464, 775 N.Y.S.2d 224 (2004), the defendant was charged with murder after shooting the victim 10 times at close range. The New York Court of Appeals rejected the depraved indifference charge, concluding that the defendant was either guilty of intentional murder or nothing at all—the intermediate charge based on recklessness was completely inconsistent with the available evidence in the case. The effect of the decision was to prevent prosecutors from shoehorning intentional murder cases into the "depraved indifference" category simply to lower their burden on mens rea. As the court put the point: "Depraved indifference murder does not mean an extremely, even heinously, intentional killing. Rather, it involves a killing in which the defendant does not have a conscious objective to cause death but instead is recklessly indifferent, depravedly so, to whether death occurs. When defendant shot his victim at close range, he was not recklessly creating a grave risk of death, but was creating a virtual certainty of death born of an intent to kill."

Similarly, in *People v. Payne*, 3 N.Y.3d 266, 786 N.Y.S.2d 116 (2004), the defendant fatally shot the victim with a shotgun at point-blank range; the bullet hit the victim right below the heart. Once again, the New York Court of Appeals concluded that the evidence in the case was inconsistent with a theory of depraved indifference. In *Payne*, the jury convicted the defendant of depraved indifference after acquitting him of intentional murder, perhaps as a compromise verdict or perhaps for a different reason. The court noted that, "if a defendant fatally shoots the intended victim once, it could be murder, manslaughter in the first or second degree or criminal negligence (or self-defense), but not depraved indifference murder. Moreover, it should be obvious that the more the defendant shoots (or stabs or bludgeons) the victim, the more clearly intentional is the homicide. Firing more rounds or inflicting more wounds does not make the act more depravedly *indifferent*, but more intentional."

Finally, in *People v. Suarez*, 6 N.Y.3d 202, 811 N.Y.S.2d 267 (2005), the defendant stabbed his girlfriend in the throat, chest, and abdomen, and then fled the scene. Without medical assistance, the victim died. The New York State Court of Appeals reversed the depraved indifference conviction, again holding that the crime was intentional murder or not murder at all, but clearly not a crime of recklessness. "The proliferation of the use of depraved indifference murder as a fallback theory under which to charge intentional killers reflects a fundamental misunderstanding of the depraved indifference murder statute," the court concluded, before providing a re-education on the difference between intentional and reckless killings "to provide the guidance that will enable prosecutors, juries, trial courts and reviewing courts to function without risk of reversal." This line of cases suggests that court actors should take care that their legal theories adequately and truthfully describe the underlying facts of their cases.

CHAPTER 12

—⚬⁄⚬⁄⚬—

FELONY MURDER

A. DOCTRINE

The felony murder rule allows a court to convict a defendant who commits a felony that results in someone's death. The paradigmatic example is an armed robbery gone wrong where someone ends up dead. Normally the defendant would be guilty of armed robbery and maybe manslaughter if the defendant was reckless as to the resulting death. Under the felony murder rule, the defendant is guilty of murder, simply because he committed a triggering felony that resulted in death. While the list of felonies that can trigger the felony murder rule is different in each jurisdiction, a typical list includes arson, burglary, rape, and robbery. Some state statutes have a much longer list of triggering felonies; other statutes allow any felony of a particular category (e.g., forcible felonies or felonies of a particular degree); and some jurisdictions have no statutory limits on which felonies trigger the rule. It is essential for students and practitioners to consult the relevant statute since the enumerated list changes from jurisdiction to jurisdiction.

In recognition of the harshness of the felony murder rule, many jurisdictions now impose a series of doctrinal limitations that must be satisfied in order for a defendant to be convicted of felony murder. These limitations include: (i) the independent felony or merger limitation; (ii) the inherently dangerous felony limitation; and (iii) the "in furtherance of the felony" limitation. Each will be explained in depth.

The distinction between first-degree and second-degree felony murder differs across jurisdictions. In some jurisdictions, first-degree felony murder is reserved for *intentional* killings performed by the defendant during the commission of the underlying felony, and might be a capital offense. In contrast, *unintentional* deaths resulting from the felony (whether the fatal act is performed by a defendant or someone else) would be classified as second-degree felony murder. In other jurisdictions, though, the distinction between first-degree and second-degree felony murder hinges on whether the underlying felony was listed in the statute (first-degree felony murder) or not listed in the statute (second-degree). For this reason, lawyers sometimes distinguish between an "enumerated" felony murder provision or an "unenumerated" felony murder provision. For example, consider the following provision from the California Penal Code:

> All murder which is . . . committed in the perpetration of, or attempt to perpetrate, arson, rape, carjacking, robbery, burglary, mayhem, kidnapping, train wrecking, or any act punishable under Section 206, 286, 288, 288a, or 289, or any murder which is perpetrated by means of discharging a firearm from a motor vehicle, intentionally at another person outside of the vehicle with the intent to inflict death, is murder of the first degree. All other kinds of murders are of the second degree.

Cal. Penal Code § 189. Since California "enumerated" arson, rape, carjacking, robbery, burglary, mayhem, kidnapping, and train wrecking as triggering felonies, the legislature has already decided, by statute, that these felonies are "independent" and "inherently dangerous," thus eliminating the need for a trial court to apply these doctrinal limitations. If, however, the prosecution is for an unenumerated felony, then the trial court must assess whether the triggering felony charged by the prosecution does, or does not, run afoul of these doctrinal limitations.

1. Independent Felony or "Merger" Limitation

The triggering felony must also have a life of its own apart from the resulting death or killing. In other words, the felony cannot "merge" into the resulting killing. Consider a classic example. The defendant commits assault with a deadly weapon and the victim dies as a result. In that case, the felony is not independent of the resulting death. One way of determining whether the underlying felony is independent is by asking whether the felony would merge into the more serious offense of murder. In this case it would, because a perpetrator who shoots and kills someone cannot be convicted of both assault with a deadly weapon *and* murder. If the perpetrator is convicted of murder, the assault charge drops away because it merges into the more serious offense of murder. In this way, one can see the rationale for the merger limitation in felony murder cases. The equation for felony murder is: a triggering felony + resulting killing = felony murder. If the triggering felony disappears into the killing, then the two requirements for the doctrine no longer persist. In contrast, consider the commission of a rape that results in the death of the victim. Rape never merges into murder and rape is certainly not a lesser-included offense of murder. It is perfectly permissible for a jury to convict a defendant of both rape and murder for one criminal transaction. Again, this limitation is most important in jurisdictions without a statutory list of triggering felonies.

To understand the rationale for the merger limitation, imagine if manslaughter were applied as the triggering felony in a felony murder case. If that were allowed, every case of manslaughter would potentially trigger the application of the felony murder rule. Such an interpretation would undermine the legislative homicide scheme, which clearly contemplates that manslaughter is less serious than murder. The merger limitation solves this potential problem.

2. Inherently Dangerous Felony Limitation

In order to qualify for felony murder, the triggering felony must be "inherently dangerous" to human life. This limitation is particularly important in jurisdictions without a closed list of triggering felonies in their penal code. The requirement is designed to limit the application of the felony murder rule to situations where the defendant's underlying criminal behavior was sufficiently reckless or negligent. A non-dangerous felony resulting in an unintentional death might be a freakish occurrence, and one that courts would be uncomfortable classifying as felony murder. In assessing whether the felony is inherently dangerous, courts adopt one of two approaches. Either they look to the definition of the crime in the abstract and ask whether it always—by definition—involves dangerousness. Or, in contrast, the court looks to the facts of the case (and the defendant's behavior) to decide if the felony was sufficiently dangerous.

3. In Furtherance of the Felony Limitation

On the other hand, the killing cannot be too remote from the triggering felony. The killing must be performed "in furtherance of" or "in the perpetration of" the felony. What if the defendant is escaping from police *after* he robs a bank and runs over an innocent bystander? In most jurisdictions, escape and evasion of law enforcement after the felony is considered *part* of its commission, so the resulting death would be in furtherance of the felony. Also, many felony murder statutes now explicitly include the defendant's "immediate flight" from the commission of the felony. Tex. Penal Code § 19.02(b). In some jurisdictions, the "in furtherance of the felony" limitation is referred to as the *res gestae* limitation—a Latin phrase that refers to the temporal and geographical scope of the felony, i.e., its beginning and end points.

For example, consider what happens when the police respond to a felony in progress and kill the defendant's co-felon, his partner in crime. Can the defendant be charged with felony murder under the theory that he committed an underlying felony that resulted in someone's death? Should it matter that someone else—a police officer—committed the actual killing? Under the "prox-imate cause approach," all that matters is that the victim's death was set in motion by the defendant's behavior. In that sense, even the police officer's defensive killing is performed "in the perpetration" of the felony. Consequently, the proximate cause approach allows prosecutors to charge defendants for fel-ony murder for killings performed by police officers, first responders, and even victims who resist the underlying felony and fight back. In contrast, the "agency approach" says that it matters who performs the physical act of killing the vic-tim, and police killings do not count. Under this approach, the defendant is only deemed the cause of the death if he is the actual agent of the killing. Conse-quently, a defensive killing by a police officer, or a shop owner trying to stop a robbery, would not qualify as felony murder.

> Review the casebook video, *People v. David Savino* (Part 2: Felony Murder). What mental state best describes the defendant's attitude with regard to the resulting death? Was it an intentional killing or a reckless killing? Is it fair to hold Savino responsible for murder under these circumstances? Should the law describe this as a case of manslaughter or as a case of murder, as the felony murder rule requires?

B. APPLICATION

1. Independent Felony or "Merger" Limitation

If a felony "merges" away into the resulting death, then there is no underlying felony to trigger the felony murder rule. But which felonies merge? In the following case, the California Supreme Court tries to come up with a coherent scheme to divide the felonies that merge from those felonies that do not merge. What is the rule? Does the doctrine make sense?

People v. Sarun Chun
Supreme Court of California
45 Cal. 4th 1172, 203 P.3d 425 (2009)

CHIN, J.

In this murder case, the trial court instructed the jury on second degree felony murder with shooting at an occupied vehicle under Penal Code section 246 the underlying felony. We granted review to consider various issues concerning the validity and scope of the second degree felony-murder rule.

We first discuss the rule's constitutional basis. Although the rule has long been part of our law, some members of this court have questioned its constitutional validity. We conclude that the rule is based on statute, specifically section 188's definition of implied malice, and hence is constitutionally valid.

Next we reconsider the contours of the so-called merger doctrine this court adopted in *People v. Ireland*. After reviewing recent developments, primarily some of our own decisions, we conclude the current state of the law in this regard is untenable. We will overrule some of our decisions and hold that all assaultive-type crimes, such as a violation of section 246, merge with the charged homicide and cannot be the basis for a second degree felony-murder instruction. . . .

FACTS AND PROCEDURAL HISTORY

. . . Judy Onesavanh and Sophal Ouch were planning a party for their son's birthday. Around 9:00 P.M. on September 13, 2003, they and a friend, Bounthavy Onethavong, were driving to the store in Stockton in a blue Mitsubishi that Onesavanh's father owned. Onesavanh's brother, George, also drives the car. The police consider George to be highly ranked in the Asian Boys street gang (Asian Boys).

That evening Ouch was driving, with Onesavanh in the front passenger seat and Onethavong behind Ouch. While they were stopped in the left turn lane at a traffic light, a blue Honda with tinted windows pulled up beside them. When the light changed, gunfire erupted from the Honda, hitting all three occupants of the Mitsubishi. Onethavong was killed, having received two bullet wounds in the head. Onesavanh was hit in the back and seriously wounded. Ouch was shot in the cheek and suffered a fractured jaw.

Ouch and Onesavanh identified the Honda's driver as "T-Bird," known to the police to be Rathana Chan, a member of the Tiny Rascals Gangsters (Tiny Rascals), a criminal street gang. The Tiny Rascals do not get along with the Asian Boys. Chan was never found. The forensic evidence showed that three different guns were used in the shooting, a .22, a .38, and a .44, and at least six bullets were fired. Both the .38 and the .44 struck Onethavong; both shots were lethal. Only the .44 was recovered. It was found at the residence of Sokha and Mao Bun, brothers believed to be members of a gang.

Two months after the shooting, the police stopped a van while investigating another suspected gang shooting. Defendant was a passenger in the van. He was arrested and subsequently made two statements regarding the shooting in this case. He admitted he was in the backseat of the Honda at the time; T-Bird was the driver and there were two other passengers. Later, he also admitted he fired a .38-caliber firearm. He said he did not point the gun at anyone; he just wanted to scare them.

Defendant, who was 16 years old at the time of the shooting, was tried as an adult for his role in the shooting. He was charged with murder, with driveby and gang special circumstances, and with two counts of attempted murder, discharging a firearm from a vehicle, and shooting into an occupied vehicle, all with gang and firearm-use allegations, and with street terrorism. At trial, the prosecution presented evidence that defendant was a member of the Tiny Rascals, and that the shooting was for the benefit of a gang. Defendant testified, denying being a member of the Tiny Rascals or being involved in the shooting.

The prosecution sought a first degree murder conviction. The court also instructed the jury on second degree felony murder based on shooting at an occupied motor vehicle (§ 246) either directly or as an aider and abettor. The jury found defendant guilty of second degree murder. It found the personal-firearm-use allegation not true, but found that a principal intentionally used a firearm and the shooting was committed for the benefit of a criminal street gang. The jury acquitted defendant of both counts of attempted murder, shooting from a motor vehicle, and shooting at an occupied motor vehicle. It convicted defendant of being an active participant in a criminal street gang. . . .

THE MERGER RULE AND SECOND DEGREE FELONY MURDER

Although today we reaffirm the constitutional validity of the long-standing second degree felony-murder rule, we also recognize that the rule has often been criticized and, indeed, described as disfavored. We have repeatedly stated, as recently as 2005, that the rule "deserves no extension beyond its required application." For these reasons, although the second degree felony-murder rule originally applied to all felonies, this court has subsequently restricted its scope. . . .

The merger doctrine developed due to the understanding that the underlying felony must be an independent crime and not merely the killing itself. Thus, certain underlying felonies "merge" with the homicide and cannot be used for purposes of felony murder. The specific question before us is how to apply the merger doctrine. . . .

[W]e conclude we need to reconsider our merger doctrine jurisprudence. . . . In considering this question, we must also keep in mind the purposes of the second degree felony-murder rule. We have identified two. The purpose we have most often identified "is to deter felons from killing negligently or accidentally by holding them strictly responsible for killings they commit." Another purpose is to deter commission of the inherently dangerous felony itself. . . .

On reflection, we do not believe that a person who claims he merely wanted to frighten the victim should be subject to the felony-murder rule (*Robertson*), but a person who says he intended to shoot at the victim is not subject to that rule (*Randle*). Additionally, *Robertson* said that the intent to frighten is a collateral *purpose*, but *Randle* said the intent to rescue another person is not an independent purpose but merely a *motive*. It is not clear how a future court should decide whether a given intent is a purpose or merely a motive.

. . . In the past, we have treated the merger doctrine as a legal question with little or no factual content. Generally, we have held that an underlying felony either never or always merges, not that the question turns on the specific facts. Viewed as a legal question, the trial court properly decides whether to instruct the jury on the felony-murder rule, but if it does so instruct, it does not also instruct the jury on the merger doctrine. The *Robertson* and *Randle* test, however, turns on potentially disputed facts specific to the case. In *Robertson*, the defendant claimed he merely intended to frighten the victim, which caused this court to conclude the underlying felony did not merge. But the jury would not necessarily have to believe the defendant. Whether a defendant shot *at* someone intending to injure, or merely tried to frighten that someone, may often be a disputed factual question.

Defendant argues that the factual question whether the defendant had a collateral felonious purpose—and thus whether the felony-murder rule applies—involves an element of the crime and, accordingly, that the *jury* must decide that factual question. When the merger issue turns on potentially disputed factual questions, there is no obvious answer to this argument. Justice Kennard alluded to the problem in her dissent in *Robertson* when she observed that "the jury never decided whether he had that intent [to frighten]." Because this factual question determines whether the felony-murder rule applies under *Robertson* and *Randle*, and thus whether the prosecution would have to prove some other form of malice, it is not clear why the jury should not have to decide the factual question.

To avoid the anomaly of putting a person who merely intends to frighten the victim in a worse legal position than the person who actually intended to shoot at the victim, and the difficult question of whether and how the jury should decide questions of merger, we need to reconsider our holdings in *Robertson* and *Randle*. When the underlying felony is assaultive in nature, such as a violation of section 246 or 246.3, we now conclude that the felony merges with the homicide and cannot be the basis of a felony-murder instruction. An "assaultive" felony is one that involves a threat of immediate violent injury. In determining whether a crime merges, the court looks to its elements and not the facts of the case. Accordingly, if the elements of the crime have an assaultive aspect, the crime merges with the underlying homicide even if the elements also include conduct that is not assaultive. For example, in *People v. Smith*, the court noted that child abuse under section 273a "includes both active and passive conduct, i.e., child abuse by direct assault and child endangering by extreme neglect." Looking to the facts before it, the court decided the offense was "of the assaultive variety," and therefore merged. It reserved the question whether the nonassaultive variety would merge. Under the approach we now adopt, both varieties would merge. This approach both avoids the necessity of consulting facts that might be disputed and extends the protection of the merger doctrine to the potentially less culpable defendant whose conduct is not assaultive.

This conclusion is also consistent with our repeatedly stated view that the felony-murder rule should not be extended beyond its required application. We do not have to decide at this point exactly what felonies are assaultive in nature, and hence may not form the basis of a felony-murder instruction, and which are inherently collateral to the resulting homicide and do not merge. But shooting at an occupied vehicle under section 246 is assaultive in nature and hence cannot serve as the underlying felony for purposes of the felony-murder rule. . . .

NOTES & QUESTIONS ON THE MERGER LIMITATION

1. *California's felony murder rule.* What is left of California's second-degree felony murder rule after its decision in *Sarun Chun*? As one commentator put it, the California Supreme Court seems intent on "merging away" its felony murder doctrine by holding that no "assaultive felonies" can trigger second degree felony murder because they all merge with the resulting homicide. See David Mishook, *People v. Sarun Chun—In Its Latest Battle with Merger Doctrine, Has the California Supreme Court Effectively Merged Second-Degree Felony Murder out of Existence?*, 15 Berkeley J. Crim. L. 127, 157 (2010) ("By applying the assaultive-element test, the Court has limited felony murder to homicides that occur during the commission of inherently dangerous felonies in which, by their definition, death is least likely to be a foreseeable result."). Do you agree?

2. *Assaultive felonies.* What does the California court mean when it says that all "assaultive felonies" merge? The court defined an assaultive felony as "one that involves a threat of immediate violent injury." Does that accord with a standard definition of assault? The court noted that passive conduct that results in injury, such as child neglect, would constitute an "assaultive felony" and would merge. Why? What was the court's rationale? Was the court seeking to avoid a perverse system where active conduct merged and was unavailable for the felony murder rule, but less culpable passive conduct did not merge and therefore still triggered felony murder? For the court, that result would have been absurd. Consequently, child neglect, which does not sound inherently assaultive to a lay person, nevertheless was defined as an assaultive felony that merges.

2. Inherently Dangerous Felony Limitation

Some courts refuse to apply the felony murder rule if the underlying felony was not inherently dangerous. The question is: What does "inherently" mean? As you read the following case, pay careful attention to how the court understands "inherently" and the methodology the court uses to determine whether the underlying felony in this case—a motor-vehicle violation—is inherently dangerous. Do you agree with the analysis?

People v. Howard
Supreme Court of California
34 Cal. 4th 1129, 104 P.3d 107 (2005)

KENNARD, J.

Murder is the unlawful killing of a human being, with malice aforethought. But under the second degree felony-murder rule, the prosecution can obtain a conviction without showing malice if the killing occurred during the commission of an inherently dangerous felony. Is the crime of driving with a willful or wanton disregard for the safety of persons or property while fleeing from a pursuing police officer (Veh. Code, § 2800.2) an inherently dangerous felony for purposes of the second degree felony-murder rule? We conclude it is not.

I

At 12:40 A.M. on May 23, 2002, California Highway Patrol Officer Gary Stephany saw defendant driving a Chevrolet Tahoe (a sport utility vehicle) without a rear license plate, and signaled him to pull over. Defendant stopped on the side of the road. But when Officer Stephany and his partner, Officer Wayne Bernard, got out of their patrol car, defendant restarted the engine and sped to a nearby freeway. The officers gave chase at speeds of up to 90 miles per hour and radioed for assistance. Defendant left the freeway and drove onto a surface street, turning off his car's headlights. He ran two stop signs and a red light, and he drove on the wrong side of the road. His speed was 15 to 20 miles over the posted speed limit of 50 miles per hour. At some point, he made a sharp turn onto a small dirt road and escaped.

Minutes later, Officer Anthony Arcelus and his partner, Officer Bret Boss, who had been monitoring the pursuit on their car radio, saw the Tahoe with its headlights on again and took up the chase. Officer Arcelus, who was driving, estimated the Tahoe's speed at more than 80 miles per hour, and he saw it run a stop sign and a traffic light. By then, the car's headlights were again turned off. Up to that point, the chase had taken place in rural parts of Fresno County. When the Tahoe started heading toward downtown Fresno, Officer Arcelus gave up the pursuit, fearing that the high-speed chase might cause an accident.

About a minute after Officer Arcelus stopped chasing the Tahoe, he saw it run a red light half a mile ahead of him and collide with a car driven by Jeanette Rodriguez. Rodriguez was killed and her husband, a passenger in the car, was seriously injured. It turned out that the Tahoe that defendant was driving had been stolen earlier that day. Defendant, who was also injured in the crash, was arrested and charged with murder, with causing serious bodily injury while evading a police officer (§ 2800.3), and with evading a police officer in willful or wanton disregard for the safety of persons or property.

At trial, the prosecution called as a witness Laurie Bennett, defendant's passenger during the chase. She was evasive about the events leading up to the accident. Ultimately, she admitted that she had told the truth when she explained to a police officer that five or six times during the chase she had begged defendant to let her get out of the car, and that defendant had run a red light at the intersection where the fatal accident occurred. An accident reconstruction expert testified that at the time of the accident the Tahoe was traveling over 80 miles per hour, and Rodriguez's car was traveling close to the posted speed limit of 35 miles per hour. John Mikkelson, a pipeline inspector working near the intersection where the accident occurred, said he looked at the signal immediately after hearing the crash of the two colliding cars and saw that it was green for cars traveling in Rodriguez's direction (and thus presumably red for defendant).

Forensic toxicologist Roger Peterson, a witness for the defense, testified that defendant had a "high amount" of methamphetamine in his bloodstream at the time of the accident. A person under the influence of methamphetamine, Peterson said, might drive at excessive speeds, might have trouble staying in a single lane, and might not notice traffic lights and signs. Defendant also had marijuana in his bloodstream, but not enough to be under the influence. Victim Rodriguez's bloodstream contained morphine (a metabolite of heroin) and benzoyleconine (a metabolite of cocaine). Based on this evidence, toxicologist Peterson expressed his opinion that Rodriguez was under the influence of heroin and possibly cocaine when the accident occurred.

Defendant testified on his own behalf. He admitted stealing the Tahoe and fleeing from the Highway Patrol officers. He did so because his probation officer had told him he would go to prison if he was again caught in a stolen car. He could only remember bits and pieces of the chase. He described himself as a skilled driver; his cousin, a race car driver, had taught him to drive "sprint cars" at a race track. He saw the victims' car before the accident but could not recall hitting it. He could not remember what color the signal light was when he entered the intersection but admitted it was "most likely" red when the car he was driving crashed into the Rodriguez car. . . .

II

Because the second degree felony-murder rule is a court-made rule, it has no statutory definition. This court has described it thusly: "A homicide that is a direct causal result of the commission of a felony *inherently dangerous to human life* (other than the . . . felonies enumerated in Pen. Code, § 189) constitutes at least second degree murder." The rule "eliminates the need for proof of malice in connection with a charge of murder." It is not an evidentiary presumption but a substantive rule of law, which is based on the theory that "when society has declared certain inherently dangerous conduct to be felonious, a defendant should not be allowed to excuse himself by saying he was unaware of the danger to life because, by declaring the conduct to be felonious, society has warned him of the risk involved."

Because the second degree felony-murder rule is "a judge-made doctrine without any express basis in the Penal Code," its constitutionality has been questioned. And, as we have noted in the past, legal scholars have criticized the rule for incorporating "an artificial concept of strict criminal liability that 'erodes the relationship between criminal liability and moral culpability.'" Therefore, we have repeatedly stressed that the rule "'deserves no extension beyond its required application.'"

"In determining whether a felony is inherently dangerous [under the second degree felony-murder rule], the court looks to the elements of the felony *in the abstract,* 'not the "particular" facts of the case,' i.e., not to the defendant's specific conduct." That is, we determine whether the felony "by its very nature . . . cannot be committed without creating a substantial risk that someone will be killed. . . ."

Felonies that have been held inherently dangerous to life include shooting at an inhabited dwelling, poisoning with intent to injure, arson of a motor vehicle, grossly negligent discharge of a firearm, manufacturing methamphetamine, kidnapping, and reckless or malicious possession of a destructive device.

Felonies that have been held *not* inherently dangerous to life include practicing medicine without a license under conditions creating a risk of great bodily harm, serious physical or mental illness, or death; false imprisonment by violence, menace, fraud, or deceit; possession of a concealable firearm by a convicted felon; possession of a sawed-off shotgun; escape; grand theft; conspiracy to possess methedrine; extortion; furnishing phencyclidine; and child endangerment or abuse.

III

In determining whether section 2800.2 is an offense inherently dangerous to life, we begin by reviewing the statutory scheme . . . Section 2800.2, which was the basis for defendant's conviction under the second degree felony-murder rule, provides:

(a) If a person flees or attempts to elude a pursuing peace officer in violation of Section 2800.1 and the pursued vehicle is driven in a willful or wanton disregard for the safety of persons or property, the person driving the vehicle, upon conviction, shall be punished by imprisonment in the state prison, or by confinement in the county jail. . . . The court may also impose a fine . . . or may impose both that imprisonment or confinement and fine.

(b) For purposes of this section, a willful or wanton disregard for the safety of persons or property includes, but is not limited to, driving while fleeing or attempting to elude a pursuing peace officer during which time either three or more violations that are assigned a traffic violation point count under Section 12810 occur, or damage to property occurs.

In concluding that section 2800.2 is an inherently dangerous felony, the Court of Appeal relied heavily on *People v. Johnson*, 15 Cal. App. 4th 169 (1993). There the Court of Appeal, construing an earlier version of section 2800.2 that was essentially the same as what is now subdivision (a) of that section, held that driving with "willful or wanton disregard for the safety of persons or property" was inherently dangerous to life. We need not decide, however, whether *Johnson* was correct, because in 1996, three years after *Johnson* was decided, the Legislature amended section 2800.2 to add subdivision (b). Subdivision (b) very broadly defines the term "willful or wanton disregard for the safety of persons or property," as used in subdivision (a), to include *any* flight from an officer during which the motorist commits three traffic violations that are assigned a "point count" under section 12810, or which results in "damage to property."

Violations that are assigned points under section 12810 and can be committed without endangering human life include driving an unregistered vehicle owned by the driver, driving on a highway at slightly more than 55 miles per hour when a higher speed limit has not been posted, failing to come to a complete stop at a stop sign, and making a right turn without signaling for 100 feet before turning. . . .

The Attorney General contends that when the Legislature amended section 2800.2 to add subdivision (b), it did not intend to make the second degree felony-murder rule inapplicable to violations of that section. The legislative history of the amendment makes no mention, however, of the second degree felony-murder rule; nor does the legislative history pertaining to the original enactment in 1988 of section 2800.2. In all likelihood, the Legislature did not consider the effect that *either* the statute's original enactment *or* its amendment would have on murder prosecutions. In the absence of any evidence of legislative intent, we assume that the Legislature contemplated that we would determine the application of the second degree felony-murder rule to violations of section 2800.2 based on our long-established decisions holding that the rule applies only to felonies that are inherently dangerous in the *abstract*. As we have explained in this opinion, a violation of section 2800.2 is not, in the abstract, inherently dangerous to human life. Therefore, the second degree felony-murder rule does not apply when a killing occurs during a violation of section 2800.2. . . .

State v. Stewart

Supreme Court of Rhode Island
663 A.2d 912 (1995)

. . . On August 31, 1988, twenty-year-old Tracy Stewart (the defendant) gave birth to a son, Travis Young. Travis's father was Edward Young. Stewart and Young, who had two other children together, were not married at the time of Travis's birth. Travis lived for only fifty-two days, dying on October 21, 1988, from dehydration.

During the week prior to Travis's death, Stewart, Young, and a friend, Patricia McMasters, continually and repeatedly ingested cocaine over a two- to three-consecutive-day period at the apartment shared by Stewart and Young. The baby, Travis, was also present at the apartment while Stewart, Young, and McMasters engaged in this cocaine marathon . . . The cocaine binge continued uninterrupted for two to three days . . . During this entire time, McMasters saw defendant feed Travis only once. Travis was in a walker, and defendant propped a bottle of formula up on the walker, using a blanket, for the baby to feed himself. McMasters testified that she did not see defendant hold the baby to feed him nor did she see defendant change Travis's diaper or clothes during this period.

Ten months after Travis's death defendant was indicted on charges of second-degree murder, wrongfully causing or permitting a child under the age of eighteen to be a habitual sufferer for want of food and proper care, and manslaughter. The second-degree-murder charge was based on a theory of felony murder. The prosecution did not allege that defendant intentionally killed her son but rather that he had been killed during the commission of an inherently dangerous felony, specifically, wrongfully permitting a child to be a habitual sufferer. Moreover, the prosecution did not allege that defendant intentionally withheld food or care from her son. Rather the state alleged that because of defendant's chronic state of cocaine intoxication, she may have realized what her responsibilities were but simply could not remember whether she had fed her son, when in fact she had not . . .

Rhode Island's murder statute, § 11-23-1, enumerates certain crimes that may serve as predicate felonies to a charge of first-degree murder. A felony that is not enumerated in § 11-23-1 can, however, serve as a predicate felony to a charge of second-degree murder. Thus the fact that the crime of wrongfully permitting a child to be a habitual sufferer is not specified in § 11-23-1 as a predicate felony to support a charge of first-degree murder does not preclude such crime from serving as a predicate to support a charge of second-degree murder.

In Rhode Island second-degree murder has been equated with common-law murder. At common law, where the rule is unchanged by statute, "[h]omicide is murder if the death results from the perpetration or attempted perpetration of an inherently dangerous felony." To serve as a predicate felony to a charge of second-degree murder, a felony that is not specifically enumerated in § 11-23-1 must therefore be an inherently dangerous felony.

The defendant contends that wrongfully permitting a child to be a habitual sufferer is not an inherently dangerous felony and cannot therefore serve as the predicate felony to a charge of second-degree murder. In advancing her argument, defendant urges this court to adopt the approach used by California courts to determine if a felony is inherently dangerous. This approach requires that the court consider the elements of the felony "in the abstract" rather than look at the particular facts of the case under consideration. With such an approach, if a statute can be violated in a manner that does not endanger human life, then the felony is not inherently dangerous to human life . . .

In *Caffero*, 207 Cal. App. 3d at 683, a two-and-one-half-week-old baby died of a massive bacterial infection caused by lack of proper hygiene that was due to parental neglect. The parents were charged with second-degree felony murder and felony-child abuse, with the felony-child-abuse charge serving as the predicate felony to the second-degree-murder charge. Examining California's felony-child-abuse statute in the abstract, instead of looking at the particular facts of the case, the court held that because the statute could be violated in ways that did not endanger human life, felony-child abuse was not inherently dangerous to human life. By way of example, the court noted that a fractured limb, which comes within the ambit of the felony-child-abuse statute, is unlikely to endanger the life of an infant, much less of a seventeen-year-old. Because felony-child abuse was not inherently dangerous to human life, it could not properly serve as a predicate felony to a charge of second-degree felony murder . . .

We decline defendant's invitation to adopt the California approach in determining whether a felony is inherently dangerous to life and thus capable of serving as a predicate to a charge of second-degree felony murder. We believe that the better approach is for the trier of fact to consider the facts and circumstances of the particular case to determine if such felony was inherently dangerous in the manner and the circumstances in which it was committed, rather than have a court make the determination by viewing the elements of a felony in the abstract. We now join a number of states that have adopted this approach.

A number of felonies at first glance would not appear to present an inherent danger to human life but may in fact be committed in such a manner as to be inherently dangerous to life. The crime of escape from a penal facility is an example of such a crime. On its face, the crime of escape is not inherently dangerous to human life. But escape may be committed or attempted to be committed in a manner wherein human life is put in danger. Indeed in *State v. Miller,* this court upheld the defendant's conviction of second-degree murder on the basis of the underlying felony of escape when a prison guard was killed by an accomplice of the defendant during an attempted escape from the Rhode Island State prison. By way of contrast, the California Supreme Court has held that the crime of escape, viewed in the abstract, is an offense that is not inherently dangerous to human life and thus cannot support a second-degree felony-murder conviction.

The amendment of our murder statute to include any unlawful killing "committed during the course of the perpetration, or attempted perpetration, of felony manufacture, sale, delivery, or other distribution of a controlled substance otherwise prohibited by the provisions of chapter 28 of title 21" lends further support for not following California's approach to determining the inherent dangerousness of a felony. According to the statute a person who delivers phencyclidine (PCP) . . . to another person who then dies either as a result of an overdose or as a result of behavior precipitated by the drug use (such as jumping off a building because of the loss of spacial perception) could be charged with first-degree murder under § 11-23-1. Conversely, the California Court of Appeal has held that when viewed in the abstract, the standard used by California courts to determine whether a felony is inherently dangerous, the furnishing or selling of PCP is not a felony that carries a high probability that death will result. Consequently, the California Court of Appeal held that the felony of furnishing PCP could not serve as a predicate to a charge of second-degree felony murder. It is clear that there is a profound ideological difference in the approach of the Rhode Island Legislature from the holdings of the courts of the State of California concerning appropriate criminal charges to be preferred against one who furnishes PCP (and presumably a host of other controlled substances) to another person with death resulting therefrom. The lawmakers of the State of Rhode Island have deemed it appropriate to charge such a person with the most serious felony in our criminal statutes—first-degree murder. It appears that the appellate court of California, however, would hold that the most serious charge against one who furnishes PCP to another person with death resulting therefrom would be involuntary manslaughter.

The Legislature's recent amendment to our murder statute as well as this court's prior jurisprudence concerning second-degree felony murder reinforces our belief that we should not adopt the California approach to determine whether a felony is inherently dangerous. The proper procedure for making such a determination is to present the facts and circumstances of the particular case to the trier of fact and for the trier of fact to determine if a felony is inherently dangerous in the manner and the circumstances in which it was committed. This is exactly what happened in the case at bar. The trial justice instructed the jury that before it could find defendant guilty of second-degree murder, it must first find that wrongfully causing or permitting a child to be a habitual sufferer for want of food or proper care was inherently dangerous to human life "in its manner of commission." This was a proper charge. By its guilty verdict on the charge of second-degree murder, the jury obviously found that wrongfully permitting a child to be a habitual sufferer for want of food or proper care was indeed a felony inherently dangerous to human life in the circumstances of this particular case . . .

NOTES & QUESTIONS ON INHERENT DANGEROUSNESS

1. *Dangerousness in the abstract.*   Should Howard have been convicted of murder? Indeed, there was *ample* evidence in the record that Howard was driving dangerously. While evading the police, his car was traveling at speeds of more than 80 miles per hour, and ran both a stop sign and a red light. He had drugs in his system. Even his *passenger* was begging to be let out of the car because she worried about the dangerous driving. Why then did the court conclude that this was not a case of inherently dangerous driving? The court's analysis is a study in formalism. The court asked whether the felony was inherently dangerous when viewed in the abstract. Because *one* sub-section of the evasion statute permitted a conviction in the situations that were not dangerous, the court concluded that the underlying felony was not inherently dangerous, even though the defendant's conduct in this case was clearly dangerous. Why is this relevant? If the legislature had moved the non-dangerous sub-section into a separate section, with a new name as a distinct felony, then Howard's felony would have been inherently dangerous under the abstract approach and he would have been convicted. Does it make sense to tie the outcome of the analysis to such a contingent detail?

2. *Facts of the case.* While a few jurisdictions follow California's "in the abstract" methodology for determining inherent dangerousness, most jurisdictions instruct the jury to look at the facts of the case to determine whether the defendant's behavior in committing the underlying felony was greatly or inherently dangerous. If it was not, then felony murder is not permitted. But the standard for the inquiry is the facts of that case, not an abstract analysis of the felony as the legislature defined it. What rationale did the Supreme Court of Rhode Island articulate in *Stewart* for its "facts of the case" approach? If the inherent dangerousness limitation is designed to limit the felony murder rule to defendants with a sufficiently culpable mens rea, then it would seem to matter most whether that *particular* defendant was engaged in a dangerous activity. With that rationale in mind, why does California cling to the abstract approach? While there are many explanations, consider that courts in different jurisdictions might have radically different attitudes toward the felony murder rule. While some judges might like it, others might be hostile to it but feel constrained by statute or *stare decisis* to respect it. Unable to eliminate the felony murder rule, some judges might want to cabin it as much as possible. Adopting the abstract approach to inherent dangerousness is one way of knocking some felony murder cases out of court.

3. *Felony murder and jury discretion.* Just because the felony murder rule is unavailable because the underlying felony is not inherently dangerous does not automatically mean that the defendant cannot be prosecuted for murder. In the absence of the felony murder rule, the prosecutor could still argue to the jury that the defendant's behavior was sufficiently depraved to qualify for second-degree murder under an implied malice theory of murder. If you were on the *Howard* jury, would you have convicted the defendant of murder under a regular implied malice theory? Were there facts to support a legal conclusion that the defendant acted with an "abandoned and malignant heart" as required by the California Penal Code? Why then do prosecutors use the felony murder statute so readily? The issue is one of jury discretion. Under regular murder provisions, the jury must make a factual determination that the defendant's recklessness was sufficiently severe that it implied malice. In *Howard,* that would require the jury to find that the defendant acted with an abandoned and malignant heart by evading the police in such a dangerous manner. In a New York case, it would require the jury to find that the defendant acted with depraved indifference to human life. But if the prosecutor uses the felony murder rule, that issue is taken away from the jury. If the jury decides that the defendant committed the underlying felony, and it resulted in death, the issue of his depravity or malignant heart becomes totally irrelevant for the case. The doctrine allows the prosecutor to go straight to the conviction without demonstrating a particular mens rea with regard to the resulting death.

3. In Furtherance of the Felony Limitation

The name of this doctrine can be a bit confusing. In essence, the "in furtherance of the felony" limitation is a requirement of a connection between the felony and the resulting killing. As you read the following cases, analyze the connection between the defendant's commission of the felony and the victim's death, and ask yourself whether the two events are closely connected in the right way. The first case applies the proximate cause approach, while the second case applies the agency approach.

People v. Hernandez
Court of Appeals of New York
82 N.Y.2d 309, 604 N.Y.S.2d 524 (1993)

SIMONS, J.

This appeal raises the question whether a conviction of felony murder under Penal Law § 125.25(3) should be sustained where the homicide victim, a police officer, was shot not by one of the defendants but by a fellow officer during a gun battle following defendants' attempted robbery. Under the circumstances presented, we conclude that it should, and we therefore affirm.

I

Defendants Santana and Hernandez conspired to ambush and rob a man who was coming to a New York City apartment building to buy drugs. The plan was to have Santana lure him into the building stairwell where Hernandez waited with a gun. In fact, the man was an undercover State Trooper, wearing a transmitter, and backed up by fellow officers.

Once the Trooper was inside the building, Hernandez accosted him and pointed a gun at his head. A fight ensued during which the officer announced that he was a policeman, pulled out his service revolver and began firing. In the confusion, Hernandez, still armed, ran from the building into a courtyard where he encountered members of the police back-up unit. They ordered him to halt. Instead, he aimed his gun at one of the officers and moved toward him. The officers began firing, and one, Trooper Joseph Aversa, was fatally shot in the head. His body was found near the area where Hernandez was apprehended after being wounded. Santana was arrested inside the building.

The evidence at trial did not establish who killed Aversa, but the People concede that it effectively eliminated the possibility that either defendant was the shooter. Separate juries were empaneled for the two cases, and both defendants were convicted of felony murder and other charges.

On appeal, defendants contend that the felony murder charges should have been dismissed because neither one of them fired the fatal shot. The Appellate Division rejected that argument. Even though a fellow officer shot Aversa, the Court concluded that defendants were properly held responsible for felony murder because their conduct "unquestionably 'forged' a critical link in the chain of events that led to Trooper Aversa's death."

II

Some 30 years ago, this Court affirmed the dismissal of a felony murder charge on the grounds that neither the defendant nor a cofelon had fired the weapon that caused the deaths (*People v. Wood,* 8 N.Y.2d 48, 201 N.Y.S.2d 328). In *Wood,* the defendant and his companions were escaping from a fight outside a tavern when the tavern owner, attempting to aid police, fatally shot a bystander and one of defendant's companions. Defendant was charged with assault and felony murder. At the time, the relevant provision of section 1044 of the former Penal Law defined murder in the first degree as "[t]he killing of a human being . . . without a design to effect death, by a person engaged in the commission of, or in an attempt to commit a felony." We concluded that by the plain terms of the statute defendant could not be liable for murder, for the killing of the two men was not committed by a person "engaged in the commission of" a felony or a felony attempt. Relying on the statute's "peculiar wording," we decided the case without addressing whether a similar result would be required as a matter of common law. The *Wood* case acknowledged that other jurisdictions differed on whether to apply a proximate cause theory under which felons could be held responsible for homicides committed by nonparticipants or an agency theory under which felons would be responsible only if they committed the final, fatal act.

In 1965, the Legislature revised the felony murder statute by removing the language that had been dispositive in *Wood* and replacing it with a provision holding a person culpable for felony murder when, during the commission of an enumerated felony or attempt, either the defendant or an accomplice "causes the death of a person other than one of the participants." Thus, this appeal raises the question of whether *Wood* remains good law despite the recasting of the Penal Law. The question is one of first impression for this Court, although some Appellate Division panels have continued to adhere to the *Wood* rule that the shooter must be a participant in the underlying felony.

The People believe those Appellate Division decisions to be in error. They premise their argument on the established construction of the term "causes the death," which is now the operative language in the Penal Law. That term is used consistently throughout article 125 and has been construed to mean that homicide is properly charged when the defendant's culpable act is "a sufficiently direct cause" of the death so that the fatal result was reasonably foreseeable. In the People's view the evidence here meets that standard. They contend that it was highly foreseeable that someone would be killed in a shootout when Hernandez refused to put down his gun and instead persisted in threatening the life of one of the back-up officers. Thus, under the People's theory, Hernandez "caused the death" of Aversa. Because his attempt to avoid arrest was in furtherance of a common criminal objective shared with Santana, the People contend that the murder was properly attributed to Santana as well as under principles of accomplice liability.

In response, defendants assert that *People v. Wood,* though decided on narrow statutory grounds, states a rule that was followed for centuries at common law and one that has been embraced by a significant number of jurisdictions. The rationale for requiring that one of the cofelons be the shooter (or, more broadly, the person who commits the final, fatal act) has been framed in several ways. Some courts have held that when the victim or a police officer or a bystander shoots and kills, it cannot be said that the killing was in furtherance of a common criminal objective. Others have concluded that under such circumstances the necessary malice or intent is missing. Under the traditional felony murder doctrine, the malice necessary to make the killing murder was constructively imputed from the *mens rea* incidental to perpetration of the underlying felony. Thus, in *Wooden,* 222 Va. 758, the Virginia Supreme Court concluded that where a nonparticipant in the felony is the shooter, there can be no imputation of the necessary malice to him, and no party in the causal chain has both the requisite *mens rea* and culpability for the *actus reus.* Still other courts have expressed policy concerns about extending felony murder liability. They have asserted that no deterrence value attaches when the felon is not the person immediately responsible for the death, or have contended that an expansive felony murder rule might unreasonably hold the felons responsible for the acts of others—for instance, when an unarmed felon is fleeing the scene and a bystander is hit by the bad aim of the armed victim.

III

Analysis begins with the statute. The causal language used in our felony murder provision and elsewhere in the homicide statutes has consistently been construed by this Court according to the rule in *People v. Kibbe,* 35 N.Y.2d 407, 362 N.Y.S.2d 848, where we held that the accused need not commit the final, fatal act to be culpable for causing death. To accept defendants' analysis would require that we hold that the phrase "causes the death" in subdivision (3), the felony murder paragraph of section 125.25, means something entirely different than it does in subdivisions (1) and (2) of the very same section. That is contrary to the normal rules of statutory construction.

That rule of construction must bend, of course, if in fact the Legislature intended the language to have a unique meaning within the context of the felony murder provision, but the legislative history of the 1965 revision reveals nothing about whether the Legislature intended to overturn *People v. Wood*. Defendants read that silence to mean that no such substantive change in the law was envisioned by the Legislature, and they urge us to reaffirm the common law as it applied to felony murder to limit liability when a nonparticipant is the killer.

Defendants' position is problematic for several reasons. First, it asks us to find in the ambiguous silence of the legislative record grounds for contradicting the unambiguous language of the statute. Second, it assumes that the Legislature intended an unusually narrow construction of the word "causes" even though New York homicide decisions had defined causality more expansively. It assumes also that in choosing the statutory language the Legislature and the Temporary State Commission on Revision of the Penal Law and Criminal Code, which drafted the amended provision, disregarded the well-defined debate over the difference between "causing" a homicide and "committing" a homicide. The Legislature could easily have written into subdivision (3) the limitation endorsed by defendants—as it did with the limitation applying to the death of a cofelon—but it chose not to do so . . .

In light of the statutory language and the case law prior to the revision, we conclude that the Legislature intended what appears obvious from the face of the statute: that "causes" in the felony murder provision should be accorded the same meaning it is given in subdivisions (1) and (2) of section 125.25 of the Penal Law.

Unlike defendants and those courts adopting the so-called agency theory, we believe New York's view of causality, based on a proximate cause theory, to be consistent with fundamental principles of criminal law. Advocates of the agency theory suggest that no culpable party has the requisite *mens rea* when a nonparticipant is the shooter. We disagree. The basic tenet of felony murder liability is that the *mens rea* of the underlying felony is imputed to the participant responsible for the killing. By operation of that legal fiction, the transferred intent allows the law to characterize a homicide, though unintended and not in the common design of the felons, as an intentional killing. Thus, the presence or absence of the requisite *mens rea* is an issue turning on whether the felon is acting in furtherance of the underlying crime at the time of the homicide, not on the proximity or attenuation of the death resulting from the felon's acts. Whether the death is an immediate result or an attenuated one, the necessary *mens rea* is present if the causal act is part of the felonious conduct.

No more persuasive is the argument that the proximate cause view will extend criminal liability unreasonably. First, New York law is clear that felony murder does not embrace any killing that is coincidental with the felony but instead is limited to those deaths caused by one of the felons in furtherance of their crime. More than civil tort liability must be established; criminal liability will adhere only when the felons' acts are a sufficiently direct cause of the death. When the intervening acts of another party are supervening or unforeseeable, the necessary causal chain is broken, and there is no liability for the felons. Where a victim, a police officer or other third party shoots and kills, the prosecution faces a significant obstacle in proving beyond a reasonable doubt to a jury that the felons should be held responsible for causing the death . . .

In short, our established common-law rules governing determinations of causality and the availability of the statutory defense provide adequate boundaries to felony murder liability. The language of Penal Law § 125.25(3) evinces the Legislature's desire to extend liability broadly to those who commit serious crimes in ways that endanger the lives of others. That other States choose more narrow approaches is of no moment to our statutory scheme. Our Legislature has chosen not to write those limitations into our law, and we are bound by that legislative determination.

IV

Finally, we conclude that there was no error in the court's instructions on defendant Santana's culpability. The jury was properly charged that more than "but for" causation was required; that it must find the fatal result was the sufficiently direct and foreseeable result of Hernandez's acts.

The evidence established that Hernandez, when confronted by the officers in the courtyard, refused to surrender and continued to move toward one officer with his gun drawn. Immediate flight and attempts to thwart apprehension are patently within the furtherance of the cofelons' criminal objective. Moreover, it was highly foreseeable that when Hernandez continued toward the officer with his gun drawn that shots would be fired and someone might be hit. Foreseeability does not mean that the result must be the most likely event. Undoubtedly, in planning the robbery, defendants did not anticipate that their victim would be a State Trooper or that a back-up unit would be on the scene. Yet, it was foreseeable that police would try to thwart crime, and Hernandez was aware that police were on the scene at the point he resisted arrest and remained armed. As the Appellate Division concluded, it is simply implausible for defendants to claim that defendants could not have foreseen a bullet going astray when Hernandez provoked a gun battle outside a residential building in an urban area. . . .

State v. Sophophone

Supreme Court of Kansas
270 Kan. 703 (2001)

LARSON, J.:

This is Sanexay Sophophone's direct appeal of his felony-murder conviction for the death of his co-felon during flight from an aggravated burglary in which both men participated.

The facts are not in dispute. Sophophone and three other individuals conspired to and broke into a house in Emporia. The resident reported the break-in to the police. Police officers responded to the call, saw four individuals leaving the back of the house, shined a light on the suspects, identified themselves as police officers, and ordered them to stop. The individuals, one being Sophophone, started to run away. One officer ran down Sophophone, hand-cuffed him, and placed him in a police car.

Other officers arrived to assist in apprehending the other individuals as they were running from the house. An officer chased one of the suspects later identified as Somphone Sysoumphone. Sysoumphone crossed railroad tracks, jumped a fence, and then stopped. The officer approached with his weapon drawn and ordered Sysoumphone to the ground and not to move. Sysoumphone was lying face down but raised up and fired at the officer, who returned fire and killed him. It is not disputed that Sysoumphone was one of the individuals observed by the officers leaving the house that had been burglarized . . .

Sophophone moved to dismiss the felony-murder charges, contending the complaint was defective because it alleged that he and not the police officer had killed Sysoumphone . . . We consider only the question of law, upon which our review is unlimited, of whether Sophophone can be convicted of felony murder for the killing of a co-felon not caused by his acts but by the lawful acts of a police officer acting in self-defense in the course and scope of his duties in apprehending the co-felon fleeing from an aggravated burglary . . .

The applicable provisions of K.S.A. 21-3401 read as follows: "Murder in the first degree is the killing of a human being committed:. . . . (b) in the commission of, attempt to commit, or flight from an inherently dangerous felony as defined in K.S.A. 21-3436 and amendments thereto." Aggravated burglary is one of the inherently dangerous felonies as enumerated by K.S.A. 21-3436(10) . . .

Our cases are legion in interpreting the felony-murder statute, but we have not previously decided a case where the killing was not by the direct acts of the felon but rather where a co-felon was killed during his flight from the scene of the felony by the lawful acts of a third party (in our case, a law enforcement officer) . . .

The minority of the states whose courts have adopted the proximate cause theory believe their legislatures intended that any person, co-felon, or accomplice who commits an inherently dangerous felony should be held responsible for any death which is a direct and foreseeable consequence of the actions of those committing the felony. These courts apply the civil law concept of proximate cause to felony-murder situations . . .

The overriding fact which exists in our case is that neither Sophophone nor any of his accomplices "killed" anyone. The law enforcement officer acted lawfully in committing the act which resulted in the death of the co-felon. This does not fall within the language of K.S.A. 21-3205 since the officer committed no crime . . .

Of . . . assistance to us is our long-time rule of statutory interpretation: "[C]riminal statutes must be strictly construed in favor of the accused. Any reasonable doubt about the meaning is decided in favor of anyone subjected to the criminal statute. The rule of strict construction, however, is subordinate to the rule that judicial interpretation must be reasonable and sensible to effect legislative design and intent."

It appears to the majority that to impute the act of killing to Sophophone when the act was the lawful and courageous one of a law enforcement officer acting in the line of his duties is contrary to the strict construction we are required to give criminal statutes. There is considerable doubt about the meaning of K.S.A. 21-3401(b) as applied to the facts of this case, and we believe that making one criminally responsible for the lawful acts of a law enforcement officer is not the intent of the felony-murder statute as it is currently written . . .

It does little good to suggest one construction over another would prevent the commission of dangerous felonies or that it would deter those who engage in dangerous felonies from killing purposely, negligently, or accidentally. Actually, innocent parties and victims of crimes appear to be those who are sought to be protected rather than co-felons.

We hold that under the facts of this case where the killing resulted from the lawful acts of a law enforcement officer in attempting to apprehend a co-felon, Sophophone is not criminally responsible for the resulting death of Somphone Sysoumphone, and his felony-murder conviction must be reversed . . .

ABBOTT, J., dissenting:

. . . When an issue requires statutory analysis and the statute is unambiguous, we are limited by the wording chosen by the legislature. We are not free to alter the statutory language, regardless of the result. In the present case, the felony-murder statute does not require us to adopt the "agency" theory favored by the majority. Indeed, there is nothing in the statute which establishes an agency approach. The statute does not address the issue at all. The requirements, according to the statute, are: (1) there must be a killing, and (2) the killing must be committed in the commission, attempt to commit, or flight from an inherently dangerous felony. The statute simply does not contain the limitations discussed by the majority. There is nothing in K.S.A. 21-3401 which requires us to adopt the agency approach or that requires Sophophone to be the shooter in this case. The facts in this case, in my opinion, satisfy all of the requirements set forth in K.S.A. 21-3401(b) . . .

In my opinion, our statute is unambiguous and simply does not require the defendant to be the direct cause of the victim's death, nor does it limit application of the felony-murder rule to the death of "innocents." . . .

Here, Sophophone set in motion acts which would have resulted in the death or serious injury of a law enforcement officer had it not been for the highly alert law enforcement officer. This set of events could have very easily resulted in the death of a law enforcement officer, and in my opinion this is exactly the type of case the legislature had in mind when it adopted the felony-murder rule.

The majority has opened a Pandora's box and left the law grossly unsettled. It does not take much imagination to see a number of situations where a death is going to result from an inherently dangerous felony and the majority's opinion is going to prevent the accused from being charged with felony murder.

If there is to be a change in the law, it should be by the legislature and not by this court adopting a statutory scheme set forth by the legislatures of other states. I would continue to follow the proximate cause theory of liability for felony murder which holds that criminal liability attaches for any death proximately resulting from the unlawful activity notwithstanding the fact that the killing was by one resisting the crime . . .

NOTES & QUESTIONS ON "IN FURTHERANCE"

1. *The proximate cause approach and foreseeability.* The court in *Hernandez* used the proximate cause approach to hold the defendant responsible for a killing that was physically perpetrated by the police. Was Hernandez sufficiently aware that he might be held responsible for someone that the *police* killed during his felony? This concern could be described in constitutional terms as a violation of substantive due process. Or one could simply describe it as a concern stemming from legality, a fundamental principle of criminal law. At some point, do principles of vicarious attribution become so expansive that they become unpredictable to the regular citizen? The other way of articulating a concern about prosecuting Hernandez for murder is it violates the principle of

culpability. The principle of course requires that only culpable individuals be convicted and punished. But it also requires something far subtler: that punishment be *proportional* to a defendant's culpability. Was this principle violated in Hernandez's case? Or did the punishment fit the crime? Was the court correct when it found it "implausible" that the defendant could not foresee that someone might die from a gun battle between the perpetrators and the police?

2. *The agency approach.*   There are multiple reasons to support the competing agency approach articulated in *Sophophone*. First, it can be viewed as an ad hoc limitation on the felony murder rule. To some jurists, the felony murder rule is an over-expansive doctrine and judges should entertain any opportunity to restrict its application. The agency approach is one such opportunity. Second, there are more specific issues of culpability. In *State v. Severs*, 284 S.E.2d 811 (Tenn. Ct. Crim. App. 1988), the defendant and a co-perpetrator planned to commit a larceny. But the victim of the larceny fought back and killed the defendant's co-perpetrator. Nonetheless, the defendant was charged with felony murder for the resulting death. The court vacated the conviction because the death "resulted from the effort to thwart rather than to perpetrate the felony." Do you agree with this reasoning? In *Wooden v. Commonwealth*, 222 Va. 758 (1981), the defendant was charged with *two* counts of felony murder. Wooden and two co-perpetrators hatched a plan to wait in Walter Randolph's apartment and rob him when he returned home from work. When he arrived, Randolph ended up fighting back and killing one of Wooden's co-perpetrators. At that point, Wooden's other co-perpetrator shot and killed Randolph. The prosecutor tried to pin *both* deaths on Wooden by virtue of her willing participation in the endeavor, even though she was in a different room during the killings. The court concluded that Wooden could not be held responsible for Randolph's shooting of the co-perpetrator, though Wooden *could* be charged with the co-perpetrator's killing of Randolph. According to the court, the former was performed without "malice" and therefore did not fall under the felony murder statute. Randolph's killing of the co-perpetrator was justified by self-defense and therefore not malicious, but the other co-perpetrator's killing of Randolph was unjustified and therefore malicious. Do you agree with this result?

3. *The agency approach and attribution.*   What is the normative rationale for the agency approach? Some courts find it strange to attribute to the defendant a justified act by a responding police officer or a resisting victim. Since the police or the victim is acting lawfully by repelling the act, the vicarious attribution of that justified act to the defendant cannot trigger liability for the defendant. *Commonwealth v. Redline*, 391 Pa. 486 (1958) ("How can anyone, no matter how much of an outlaw he may be, have a criminal charge lodged against him for the consequences of the lawful conduct of another person? The mere statement of the question carries with it its own answer."). Of course, this assumes that felony murder is a form of vicarious attribution. Vicarious attribution means that a doctrine allows you to attribute the act of a third party to the defendant in order to hold

PROBLEM CASE

On October 3, 2012, five teenagers in Elkhart, Indiana, hatched a plan to burglarize a nearby home that they assumed was unoccupied. But they were wrong. The occupant, Rodney Scott, was home, and he charged downstairs with a shotgun. Two of the intruders were shot, and one of them, Danzele Johnson, died from his wounds.

Police charged the four surviving teenagers with felony murder with burglary as the triggering felony. Although the killing of their co-felon was performed by the homeowner, that didn't matter. Under the proximate cause approach, the teenagers were guilty of felony murder because their burglary was the proximate cause of their co-felon's death. The teenagers were not armed with weapons. One of the teenagers pled guilty in exchange for a 55-year sentence, with 10 years suspended, in return for his testimony. The rest were convicted and sentenced to either 50 or 55 years in prison.

In a 2015 decision, the Indiana Supreme Court reaffirmed that the felony murder doctrine applied even in cases where a co-felon is killed by a police officer or a civilian resisting the underlying felony. Nonetheless, the court reversed the convictions because the teenagers were not engaged in any "dangerously violent and threatening conduct." According to the court, "There was simply nothing about the Appellants' conduct or the conduct of their cohorts that was 'clearly the mediate or immediate cause' of their friend's death." See *Layman v. State*, 2015 WL 5474389, at *6 (Ind. Sept. 18, 2015). Do you agree? Would the shooting have occurred without the burglary?

Opponents of the felony murder rule applauded the decision, in part because they believed that the murder convictions against the teenagers were unduly harsh. Do you agree? Furthermore, do you agree with the court's analysis? The court's opinion seemed to impose a limiting principle to the proximate approach discussed above. According to the court, only if the defendants were engaged in violent and threatening conduct could proximate cause be established. Is this a question of proximate cause or should the court have labeled it as an "inherently dangerous felony" limitation?

them responsible for the act in question. Is that the right way of understanding felony murder? Or is it best understood as a form of "constructive malice," where the necessary malice for a murder charge is simply assumed because of the defendant's intentional participation in the underlying felony?

Review the casebook video, *People v. David Savino* (Part 5: Felony Murder Punishment). Having been found guilty, what punishment should Savino receive? Should he receive the harshest form of punishment, equal to that for an intentional killing? Or should he receive a discount because the killing was an unfortunate consequence? As you review the video, ask yourself whether killings committed during a triggering felony require additional punishment to adequately deter would-be felons who might engage in dangerous crimes.

C. PRACTICE & POLICY

The following materials highlight the vast differences in how felony murder is understood across various jurisdictions. The discussions below highlight the following policy differences: (i) The Model Penal Code rejects the doctrine but codifies its own "presumption" doctrine that creates a similar effect; (ii) some foreign jurisdictions reject the doctrine and view it with suspicion as an example of American penal excess; and (iii) criminal law scholars are highly critical of the felony murder rule, though the doctrine still has its defenders and in any event enjoys widespread legislative support.

> ∾ **The Model Penal Code approach.** It is sometimes said that the Model Penal Code rejects the felony murder rule. See MPC commentaries ("The effect of the Model Code, therefore, is to abandon felony murder as a separate basis for establishing liability for homicide. . . . "). In one sense this is correct, because there is nothing with that label in the Code. However, the MPC does include a provision that covers substantially similar ground. Consider MPC 210.2(1)(b), which defines a criminal homicide as murder when:
>
> > it is committed recklessly under circumstances manifesting extreme indifference to the value of human life. Such recklessness and indifference are presumed if the actor is engaged or is an accomplice in the commission of, or an attempt to commit, or flight after committing or attempting to commit robbery, rape or deviate sexual intercourse by force or threat of force, arson, burglary, kidnapping or felonious escape.
>
> How does this provision compare to a more typical felony murder rule? The MPC version simply creates a statutory *presumption* that a killing performed during a felony constitutes murder under the category of "extreme indifference to the value of human life." But instead of requiring a jury finding that the defendant's behavior rose to this level of indifference, a court may simply presume that the required indifference is satisfied since the killing occurred during the course of the felony. Is this analogous to how the felony murder rule works?
>
> The key element of the MPC version of felony murder depends on understanding the word "presumption." Is it a rebuttable presumption or a conclusive presumption? If it is conclusive, then it basically tracks the outlines of a typical felony murder provision. On the other hand, if it is rebuttable, then it works like an evidentiary provision to establish a particular baseline that shifts the burden of persuasion to the defense (to show that the defendant did not act with the required indifference).

The official commentaries to the Model Penal Code articulate the presumption as rebuttable: "[T]he presumption may, of course, be rebutted by the defendant or may simply not be followed by the jury." However, the commentaries suggest that the presumption *does not* shift the burden of persuasion from the prosecution to the defense because the prosecution must still demonstrate "beyond a reasonable doubt that the defendant acted recklessly and with extreme indifference." How can this be squared with the language of the MPC, which says that recklessness and indifference "are presumed" during the commission of a felony? It would seem that the drafters of the MPC meant that the jury *may presume* the requisite indifference but is not required to do so. In terms of the burden of proof, the defense would have the initial burden of production to rebut the presumption with some evidentiary showing, but the ultimate burden of persuasion would remain with the prosecution. If that is the case, the provision simply means that the jury is entitled to look to the underlying felony to find the requisite indifference—a process that would seem to be obvious and not in need of explicit codification.

ᘓ **Felony murder in the United States.** Felony murder is often described as a common law inheritance, but ironically Britain repealed its felony murder rule in its 1957 Homicide Act. However, it continues to live on today in the United States in almost every state, despite the fact that it is so often criticized abroad. Indeed, other common law countries, such as Canada, have followed the British example and have repudiated the doctrine. Adam Liptak, *Serving Life for Providing Car to Killers*, N.Y. Times, Dec. 4, 2007. In *R v. Vaillancourt*, 2 SCR 636 (1987), the Canadian Supreme Court struck down the doctrine as unconstitutional and specifically rejected the deterrent rationale for felony murder: "It is not necessary to convict of murder persons who did not intend or foresee the death and who could not even have foreseen the death in order to deter others from using or carrying weapons. If Parliament wishes to deter the use or carrying of weapons, it should punish the use or carrying of weapons." Would the U.S. Supreme Court ever issue a similar holding? Arguably not, since the Court has generally avoided constitutionalizing substantive criminal law (while at the same time placing heavy constitutional constraints on criminal *procedure*).

ᘓ **Normative foundation.** The strategy for using the felony murder rule is obvious. A prosecutor might charge a defendant with intentional murder, but if there is any doubt that the prosecutor can demonstrate an intent to kill, it might make more sense to switch to a felony murder theory and drop the intentional murder count. Of course, that assumes that the underlying felony has survived that jurisdiction's application of the merger rule discussed above. If the underlying felony is not available because it merges with the killing, then the prosecutor has no choice but to rely on more basic principles of homicide. So it is clear that prosecutors prefer to use the felony murder doctrine if it is available. But just because a doctrine makes it easier to prosecute people does not make it morally justified. What is the *normative* basis for the felony murder doctrine? Perhaps it is an expansive example of the doctrine of transferred intent: The perpetrator *intentionally* or *recklessly* commits an underlying felony. Can the mens rea for the triggering felony simply be transferred to the murder, so that the defendant is deemed to have committed the murder with the requisite mens rea? That might be a good doctrinal description of how the felony murder rule works, but it does not articulate a *justification* for the doctrine.

Some scholars argue that the doctrine is unsupportable. See, e.g., Nelson E. Roth & Scott E. Sundby, *The Felony-Murder Rule: A Doctrine at Constitutional Crossroads*, 70 Cornell L. Rev. 446 (1984) (reviewing criticisms that the felony murder rule is "astonishing," "monstrous," a "legal fiction," and an "unsightly wart on the skin of the criminal law"); Rudolph J. Gerber, *The Felony Murder Rule: Conundrum Without Principle*, 31 Ariz. St. L.J. 763, 763 (1999) ("The rule is unfair, unprincipled and inconsistent with other criminal and civil standards."). As with most critics, Gerber views the doctrine as being fundamentally incompatible with defensible principles of mens rea and culpability. Although the defendants intentionally commit the underlying felony, their attitude regarding the resulting death is recklessness at best, yet the doctrine makes them as guilty as intentional killers. This is true, but does it also suggest that it is immoral to convict a defendant of murder based on implied malice or depraved indifference to human life? Of course, the difference between the two is that the felony murder doctrine often *presumes* that the defendant was reckless in this way, while in a regular murder case the prosecutor has to *prove* that the defendant acted with depraved indifference to human life.

That being said, some legal scholars support the rule, provided that it is properly constrained by doctrinal limitations—as outlined in this chapter. For example, one scholar concludes that "felony murder liability is deserved for those who negligently cause death by attempting felonies inherently involving (1) violence or destruction and (2) an additional malign purpose independent of injury to the victim killed." See Guyora Binder, *The Culpability of Felony Murder*, 83 Notre Dame L. Rev. 965, 967 (2008). Would this be enough to alleviate any concerns stemming from criminal law theory? When those limitations are faithfully applied, innocent offenders are excluded from the scope of the felony murder rule. In short, the limitations function to ensure that the defendant has a culpable mental state and a close connection to the resulting death. Binder concludes that scholars should stop calling the doctrine arbitrary and immoral, because that only encourages courts to apply it poorly in cases where it should not apply:

"Instructed by scholars that the felony murder doctrine imposes strict liability, courts will more likely instruct juries to impose strict liability. . . . The result is a self-fulfilling prophecy that encourages the arbitrariness and injustice it professes to condemn." See Guyora Binder, *Felony Murder* 20 (2012). See also David Crump & Susan Waite Crump, *In Defense of the Felony Murder Doctrine*, 8 Harv. J.L. & Pub. Pol'y 359 (1985); David Crump, *Reconsidering the Felony Murder Rule in Light of Modern Criticisms: Doesn't the Conclusion Depend Upon the Particular Rule at Issue?*, 32 Harv. J.L. & Pub. Pol'y 1155, 1162 (2009) ("the felony murder rule reflects a judgment that a robbery that causes a human death is not merely a robbery but something more serious; it is more akin to a murder than to a robbery").

CHAPTER 13

⟁

NEGLIGENT HOMICIDE

[handwritten: no Recklessness only negligence (Reasonably prudent person)]

A. DOCTRINE

Unlike involuntary manslaughter, which in most jurisdictions requires a reckless state of mind, negligent homicide requires only negligence. As we have learned, the key element of recklessness is the defendant's *awareness* of the risk and his conscious disregard of it. For negligence, no such state of awareness is required. Consequently, negligent homicide covers the vast array of cases where the defendant's risky behavior causes death, though the defendant did not consciously disregard the risk. In short, the defendant is punished for his carelessness. Most prosecutions for negligent homicide involve automobile accidents or some other form of transportation, so much so that many jurisdictions have now carved out a distinct offense—vehicular homicide—for cases of negligent homicide with an automobile.

Negligence requires a deviation from the standard of care that a reasonably prudent person would follow under the circumstances. But how far must someone deviate from the norm to be classified as criminally negligent? Some jurisdictions only require ordinary negligence—akin to the negligence standard in tort law. In contrast, other jurisdictions require *gross* negligence. The difference is one of degree, not kind.

1. Ordinary Negligence

It takes a fact finder (usually a jury) to assess whether a particular individual's deviation from the standard of care is sufficiently negligent to generate a conviction for negligent homicide. In most jurisdictions, the deviation must represent a "substantial and unjustifiable risk." Some jurisdictions also require that the defendant engage in actions that are "naturally and inherently dangerous to life" in order to be convicted of negligent homicide. Ordinary negligence is sometimes referred to as civil negligence because it tracks the level of negligence required in a tort action. However, the term civil negligence can be confusing because it erroneously suggests that ordinary negligence is never applied in criminal cases. In fact, some jurisdictions use the standard in negligent homicide or vehicular homicide cases. That being said, the use of ordinary negligence in criminal cases is often criticized by scholars and judges, and some jurisdictions have responded to the criticism by switching from ordinary negligence to gross negligence.

2. Gross Negligence

Under the heightened standard of gross negligence, the defendant's behavior must represent a gross deviation from the standard of care that a reasonably prudent person would observe under the circumstances. It is roughly equivalent to the gross negligence standard sometimes used in tort actions. In criminal cases, gross negligence is sometimes referred to as "criminal negligence" so as to emphasize that criminal cases require a heightened level of negligence over and above what usually suffices in a civil case. The key point to remember is that the elevated standard of *gross* negligence is satisfied by the heightened degree of the departure from the standard of care, i.e., the level of risk. It does not suggest or require that the defendant be aware of the nature of the risk and consciously disregard it—that element of awareness characterizes the higher mens rea of recklessness, not gross negligence.

The category of negligent homicide is of recent vintage. At common law, there was no such crime. Defendants who were grossly negligent were often found guilty of involuntary manslaughter and placed in the same category as defendants who acted recklessly. In fact, a few jurisdictions retain this scheme and use involuntary manslaughter as an omnibus category for both crimes of recklessness and gross negligence; in those jurisdictions, there is no crime of negligent homicide.

B. APPLICATION

1. Ordinary Negligence

Critics of ordinary negligence as a standard for negligent homicide complain that it is too loose to meet the stringent standards for the criminal law. While ordinary negligence might be fine for tort law and monetary remedies, the critics argue that criminal punishment requires a heightened standard, i.e., gross negligence. Read the following case to understand how ordinary negligence is applied in practice and decide for yourself whether it is an appropriate standard.

People v. Traughber

Supreme Court of Michigan
432 Mich. 208 (1989)

RILEY, C.J.

FACTS AND PROCEEDINGS

After waiving his right to a jury trial, defendant was convicted in the Wayne Circuit Court of negligent homicide. The judge sentenced defendant to three years probation, with the first three months to be served in the county jail.

The accident occurred at approximately 12:15 A.M. on December 22, 1984, on Denton Road, a dark, unlighted two-lane road with a 45 mph speed limit, in rural Canton Township, Wayne County.

Defendant was traveling south on Denton Road at approximately 35 mph, an uncontested fact, when he noticed the oncoming headlights of Linus Parr's automobile approximately three-quarters of a mile in front of him. Mr. Parr testified that he was traveling between 45 and 50 mph. As the two cars approached each other, each in its respective lane, defendant suddenly saw a large metal sign, later identified as a real estate sign, lying flat on the road. The defendant, now approximately thirty feet from the oncoming car, was faced with a split-second decision in an attempt to avoid the sign. Judging that he had enough space between himself and Mr. Parr's automobile, the defendant swerved to the left, into the northbound lane, to go around the sign. Upon seeing defendant's car enter his lane and assuming it either would continue in the left lane or go completely off the road, Mr. Parr swerved his car into defendant's lane, the southbound lane. Simultaneously, as Mr. Parr was turning into the southbound lane, the defendant, now around the sign, was returning into his own lane. The two cars collided head-on just inside defendant's lane, the southbound lane. Rochelle Richmond, who was sitting in Parr's passenger seat, was fatally injured. Mr. Parr and the defendant, as well as Jennifer Sellers, who was riding in the back seat of Mr. Parr's car, and Irene Baker, who was riding in the passenger seat of the defendant's car, received relatively minor injuries. . . .

II

The . . . issue before this Court is whether defendant was held to the correct standard of care.

There is no question that the applicable standard of care in negligent homicide cases is that of a reasonable person. CJI 16:5:02(1) states: "For negligent homicide the prosecution must prove beyond a reasonable doubt that the defendant was guilty of ordinary negligence." This instruction goes on to explain that "[o]rdinary negligence is defined as want of reasonable care; that is, failing to do what an ordinarily sensible person would have done under the conditions and circumstances then existing. . . ." CJI 16:5:02(4).

This instruction is merely a reiteration of the rule that has been long standing in Michigan. In *People v. McMurchy,* 249 Mich. 147, 167, 228 N.W. 723 (1930), this Court said: "Every person driving upon the public highway, or in other places frequented by others, is bound to exercise reasonable care and caution to prevent injury to others."

Defendant asserts that the trial judge held him to a degree of care greater than that of a reasonable, or ordinary, person. His argument is premised on the statement of the trial judge at the conclusion of the bench trial:

> I'm not saying as I indicated before that there was anything gross in the negligence of the defendant here and from his experience as a truck driver it would be even hard to say that he was an inexperienced man and that is what adds to the situation here. It appears quite obvious to the Court that with his experience as a truck driver, he could have and he should have been able to make a judgment factor at the time of going thirty five miles an hour, having seen the car coming from the other direction as he said he did.

Defendant would have us believe that by commenting on his experience as a truck driver the trial judge held him to a standard higher than that of an ordinary motorist. We disagree.

A thorough reading of the monologue delivered by the judge when handing down his verdict illustrates that the reasonable-person standard was applied. The judge specifically held:

> I'm impressed that a reading of the standard instruction, definition of ordinary negligence is a thing that is involved here. Whatever the Court must decide has to be done on whether or not in its view and its judgment ordinary negligence has been made out. . . .
>
> If there was anything to be concerned with, it would be whether or not the acts of the defendant in this case reached the plateau of ordinary negligence.
>
> *The standard instruction under degrees of negligence and the instructions 16:5:02 states in paragraph 4,* "Ordinary negligence is defined as want of reasonable care. That is failing to do what an ordinary sensible person would have done under the conditions and circumstances

then existing or doing what an ordinarily sensible person would not have done under the conditions and circumstances then existing in view of probable injury." (Emphasis added.)

The judge's recitation then continued to CJI 16:5:02(5):

Ordinary negligence occurs in the doing of acts which are naturally and inherently dangerous to life, which a reasonable person ought to perceive are likely to produce injury to another. Ordinary negligence is greater than or above slight negligence, but less than gross negligence. Ordinary negligence is characterized by thoughtlessness, heedlessness and inattention.

After his recitation of CJI 16:5:02(4) and (5), the judge held:

I invite your attention to this summation so to speak of what ordinary negligence is. It is characterized by thoughtlessness, heedlessness and inattention. *It seems to the Court that that's the problem we have here and that is what is made out here in terms of Mr. Traughber's conduct.* (Emphasis added.)

The above excerpts clearly illustrate that the judge did identify the proper standard of care for determining whether or not the defendant's conduct evidenced want of reasonable care given all the existing circumstances. Accordingly, we find no error with the standard of care applied by the trial court. However, we do find error with the court's failure to apply the standard to the facts supported by the record. We find error with the court concluding that the defendant created an emergency as opposed to having been confronted by an emergency.

The evidence at trial established that a sudden and unexpected event occurred when the defendant came upon the real estate sign lying in the middle of his lane of traffic. Moreover, it was this unexpected event, coupled with the fact that there was no time to adequately weigh the alternatives, that prompted the defendant to instinctively and impulsively swerve his car to the left in an attempt to avoid the obstacle. On cross-examination, the defendant was asked:

Q: And even traveling at that slow speed [35 mph] you didn't have time to negotiate that space on the right, is that correct?

A: I seen the sign [s]o fast that it was make up your mind what you're going to do. *It was a split second decision. I couldn't negotiate which wa[y] to go or what to do at that amount. I didn't have time.* (Emphasis added.)

The defendant testified that the reason he instinctively swerved to the left was because on the right side of the road there was a "three or four foot ditch there with . . . small trees in it. . . ."

Notwithstanding this testimony, corroborated by both drivers, the trial judge found that the defendant's "judgment" in reflexively swerving to the left, rather than to the right, was the determinative factor for the guilty verdict:

> It appears quite obvious to the Court that with his experience as a truck driver, *he could have and he should have been able to make a judgment factor at the time of going thirty five miles an hour,* having seen the car coming from the other direction as he said he did. That instead of going to the left to go around the sign, notwithstanding whatever risk about the ditch or the condition of the berm on the side of the road that he should have slacked his car and he could have gone easily around the sign on the right side of the sign and could have avoided the emergency that he created by trying to swerve to the left and then tried to swerve back to the right.
>
> For the reasons mentioned and discussed and the findings which the Court has made, it is the conclusion of the Court that as to count I of the information the defendant is guilty as charged. (Emphasis added.)

Thus, we disagree with the conclusion that the defendant created the emergency. Not only was the defendant not responsible for the real estate sign having been in the road, but he had no reason to know his lane of travel would be obstructed. He reacted to the sign immediately after his headlights revealed it to be in his way. Therefore, the defendant did not "create" an emergency, but rather he reacted to an emergency.

In emergency situations, the driver is not to be held accountable for misjudgment. This Court in *Craddock v. Torrence Oil Co.*, quoted the rule of *Loucks v. Fox*, 261 Mich. 338, 343 (1933):

> In case of an emergency, a driver is not responsible for the selection of the safer method of avoiding a collision. If a reasonably prudent man would turn onto the wrong side of the road under similar circumstances, defendant is free from liability despite the untoward results.

Later, in *Maddux v. Donaldson*, 362 Mich. 425, 428 (1961), this Court reiterated:

> But [plaintiff's] actions are not to be judged in the light of hindsight. He was suddenly imperiled by a serious emergency not of his own making. In this situation, as we have so often held, the law makes allowance for lack of calm judgment, for failure "to adopt what subsequently and upon reflection may appear to have been a better method."

Here, the defendant, traveling at 35 mph, first noticed the real estate sign when he was approximately thirty feet from the oncoming car. Therefore, the time within which the defendant had to formulate his judgment was imperceptible. While the defendant's judgment may very well have been incorrect, this Court will not judge the actions of an automobile driver in an emergency situation from a retrospective point of view.

CONCLUSION

We find that . . . the trial judge correctly used the reasonable-person standard but failed to apply the standard to the emergency faced by the defendant as evidenced by the record. This being so, the defendant's conduct cannot be said to have been contrary to that of an ordinarily prudent person under similar circumstances. Accordingly, we reverse the decision of the Court of Appeals.

NOTES & QUESTIONS ON ORDINARY NEGLIGENCE

1. *Ordinary negligence.* Several jurisdictions use the ordinary negligence standard. In *Butts v. United States*, 822 A.2d 407 (D.C. Ct. App. 2003), the defendant was driving in Washington, D.C., when she struck and killed a homeless man crossing the street with the aid of a cane. She was driving about 25 miles per hour. A police officer testified that although it was a dark and rainy night, the area was lit with an overhead street light. The defendant tested positive for a blood alcohol level of 0.17, well over the legal limit of 0.08. The trial judge gave the jury the following definition of negligence: "to operate the vehicle without the exercise of that degree of care that a person of ordinary prudence would exercise under the same or similar circumstances. . . . It is a failure to exercise ordinary care." After defendant was convicted, she appealed and argued that a gross negligence standard should have applied. The court upheld the conviction and reaffirmed the ordinary negligence standard. Moreover, the court held that the evidence was sufficient to support a jury finding of guilt under ordinary negligence, because she was drunk at the time of the accident and might have been using her cell phone.

2. *Negligent manslaughter?* As noted in the doctrine section, some jurisdictions do not have a statutory offense of negligent homicide. Instead, they define second-degree manslaughter as a killing performed with negligence. In a jurisdiction like this, second-degree manslaughter covers the same conceptual ground as negligent homicide in another jurisdiction. In such jurisdictions, what is the best definition of negligence: ordinary or gross negligence? One example is the State of Washington. In *State v. Williams*, 4 Wash. App. 908, 484 P.2d 1167 (1971), the Washington Court of Appeals upheld the manslaughter conviction of two parents for failing to provide medical care to their 17-month-old daughter. The father was a 24-year-old man with a sixth-grade education, who worked as a laborer. The mother was 20 years old and had attended school until

eleventh grade. The child developed an abscessed tooth, which became severely infected. Two weeks later, the child died. The expert pathologist testified that if the baby had received adequate medical care in the first week of the infection, the baby should have lived, though taking the baby to the doctor by the second week would have been too late. The defendants were convicted of manslaughter under an ordinary negligence standard, in part because the baby's cheek had turned bluish and she would not eat. The trial court heard evidence that the parents might have delayed going to the hospital because they feared that social services might take their baby away from them. The Court of Appeals held that there was sufficient evidence of negligence under a standard of ordinary caution. However, the State of Washington later repealed the ordinary negligence standard and replaced it with gross negligence. Wash. Crim. Code § 9A.32.070 ("A person is guilty of manslaughter in the second degree when, with *criminal* negligence, he or she causes the death of another person."). Applying the newer standard, do you think the Williams parents should still have been convicted? Or would the more demanding standard require an acquittal?

2. Gross Negligence

Gross negligence represents a heightened standard for negligent homicide. The difference between the two standards is often obscure and only gains precision when applied in particular cases. As you read the following case, apply the "gross deviation" standard and articulate reasons why the defendant violated—or did not violate—that legal standard.

State v. Small

Supreme Court of Louisiana
100 So. 3d 797 (2012)

Victory, J.

FACTS AND PROCEDURAL HISTORY

On January 20, 2008, around midnight, S.S., age six, was found unconscious from smoke and soot inhalation inside her burning home. The fire originated on the back right burner of the kitchen stove. S.S.'s mother, defendant Satonia Small, had left S.S. and her brother J.D., age seven, asleep unsupervised in the second-story apartment at about 10 P.M. to go drink at the home of her friend, Patrina Gay. When a neighbor called Gay to tell her about the fire, defendant returned home and learned that J.D. had escaped by jumping out of a window, but that S.S. was found inside by firefighters, could not be revived, and was taken to the hospital. Defendant was arrested for cruelty to juveniles. A few days later, S.S. died at the hospital, and on March 18, 2008, the grand jury indicted defendant for second degree murder.

On November 10, 2008, the state gave notice that it intended to present evidence at trial that defendant pleaded guilty on May 2, 2007, to criminal abandonment in violation of La. R.S. 14:79.1, committed on December 4, 2006. At a hearing held on May 27, 2009, the state indicated that it intended to introduce at trial a transcript of the colloquy in which defendant pleaded guilty to criminal abandonment. In this colloquy, defendant recognized the gravity of her misconduct and promised she would not leave her children unattended again. The state argued that defendant's assurance that she would never leave her children alone again was relevant to proving her guilty knowledge and the absence of mistake. The trial court then ruled that the prior guilty plea colloquy would be admissible.

Trial began on August 25, 2010 . . . Officer Marcus Hines of the Shreveport Police Department testified that he was off duty when he saw the fire, and when he arrived, the entire upstairs of the building was engulfed in flames. He saw J.D. outside and residents informed him that S.S. was still inside. Officer Hines watched as firefighters extracted S.S. from the building, performed CPR, and then placed her in an ambulance. Defendant, who smelled strongly of alcohol, arrived about 20–30 minutes later . . .

DISCUSSION

Defendant was found guilty of second degree murder in violation of La. R.S. 14:30.1(A)(2), which provides "[s]econd degree murder is the killing of a human being: . . . When the offender is engaged in the perpetration or attempted perpetration of aggravated rape, forcible rape, aggravated arson, aggravated burglary, aggravated kidnapping, second degree kidnapping, aggravated escape, assault by drive-by shooting, armed robbery, first degree robbery, second degree robbery, simple robbery, *cruelty to juveniles, second degree cruelty to juveniles,* or terrorism, even though he has no intent to kill or to inflict great bodily harm." (Emphasis added). This section of La. R.S. 14:30.1 contains the circumstances under which a defendant can be found guilty under the felony murder rule, which dispenses with the necessity of proving mens rea accompanying a homicide—the underlying felony supplies the culpable mental state. The underlying felony that defendant was found to have committed was cruelty to juveniles, which is defined in La. R.S. 14:93(A)(1) as the "intentional or criminally negligent mistreatment or neglect by anyone seventeen years of age or older of any child under the age of seventeen whereby unjustifiable pain or suffering is caused to said child." Essentially, the state argued that defendant was criminally negligent for leaving her young children unsupervised and that her absence caused her daughter to die in the fire. . . .

Before this Court, defendant argues that she is not guilty of second degree murder, the underlying felony of cruelty to juveniles, or even negligent homicide, because the evidence was insufficient to prove that her absence from the home caused her daughter's death. Defendant contends that the evidence failed to establish a sufficient causal nexus between her absence and the accidental fire that killed the victim, and emphasizes that the victim died because of the intervening circumstance of the accidental fire rather than directly from defendant's own action in leaving the children unsupervised.

Generally, this Court has interpreted the felony murder rule to require that a direct act of a defendant or his accomplice cause the death of the victim and has refused to hold persons criminally culpable for setting in motion chains of events that ultimately result in the deaths of others. In the context of felony murder, this issue arises most often when death results from the responses of third parties fleeing, resisting, or pursuing a defendant. In *Garner,* this Court adopted the "agency test," which is also utilized by at least 14 other states and restricts criminal culpability to deaths directly caused by the defendant and co-felons, and rejected the "proximate cause" test, which holds the defendant responsible for all deaths that foreseeably result from the acts of defendant and co-felons. . . .

Thus, the agency test adopted in Louisiana requires that a "direct act" of the defendant or his accomplice commit the act of killing. Where a second degree murder is based on the underlying crime of cruelty to juveniles or second degree cruelty to juveniles, and that conduct involves the criminal negligence of lack of supervision, there is no "direct act" of killing; instead the act is a negative act. This makes the lack of a direct act of killing by the defendant in this case troubling under the agency test. . . .

However, unlike second degree murder, negligent homicide does not require a "direct act" of killing by the defendant. Negligent homicide is "the killing of a human being by criminal negligence." La. R.S. 14:32. "Criminal negligence exists when although neither specific nor general criminal intent is present, there is such disregard of the interest of others that the offender's conduct amounts to a gross deviation below the standard of care expected to be maintained by a reasonably careful man under like circumstances." La. R.S. 14:12. Ordinary negligence does not equate to criminal negligence; the state is required to show more than a mere deviation from the standard of ordinary care. There can be no debate that defendant's conduct was criminally negligent, especially because she had previously pled guilty to child abandonment and knew leaving her young children alone unsupervised was against the law.

Regarding causation, this Court has addressed the type of causal connection the state must show between a defendant's conduct and the victim's death for a defendant to be criminally culpable where multiple causes led to the death. In *State v. Matthews,* 450 So. 2d 644 (La. 1984), we held that "[i]t is not essential that the act of the defendant should have been the sole cause of the death; if it hastened the termination of life, or contributed, mediately or immediately, to the death, in a degree sufficient to be a clearly contributing cause, that is sufficient." The *Matthews* court noted that a similar standard for determining causation-in-fact approved by LaFave and Scott in their treatise on substantive criminal law was adopted by the Court in *State v. Durio,* 371 So. 2d 1158 (La. 1979). In *Durio,* this Court found that the state could establish causation by showing that the "defendant's conduct was a substantial factor in bringing about the forbidden result." . . .

In the present case, there was little direct evidence relating to the fire. Presumably, the fire had not started at the time defendant left the home, at approximately 10:00 P.M. Sometime after 11:00, a neighbor noticed the fire and called Ms. Gay. When the fire department arrived at the apartment building, the upstairs was engulfed in flames, and after the roof caved in, the firefighters were able to find S.S. in her bedroom. The fire investigators determined that a pan had melted to the back right burner where the fire originated, and that the fire had progressed from the stove, up through the vent, into the attic, and set the roof on fire. Testimony established that this fire would have produced a lot of smoke. Evidence was presented that the child victim suffered carbon monoxide poisoning from what is typically a slowly developing kitchen fire, which type of fire typically has a very low fatality rate, and further that young children typically respond inappropriately to fire and are thus less likely than adults to escape without assistance.

The trial court rejected defendant's contention that the child's death was not causally connected to neglect:

> During trial, the State proved beyond a reasonable doubt that the fire was caused by a pot left on a burning stovetop. The pot became so hot that it melted and caused a kitchen fire, which spread throughout the entire home. It is unclear whether the defendant left the stove on before she left the home, or if during her absence one of the children was responsible for turning on the stove. Under either possibility, had the defendant been home or provided adult supervision, the children could have been removed from the home, the fire could have been stopped earlier, or the fire could have been avoided all together. This fire was not a purely coincidental occurrence on which the defendant's absence had no effect. This was not an electrical fire caused by faulty wiring or a fire caused by lightning striking the home. This fire was directly linked to the defendant's negligent conduct and the victim's death was a consequence of that underlying felony. . . .

. . . [W]e find that the evidence, viewed in the light most favorable to the state, was sufficient to convince a rational trier of fact that defendant's neglect was a legal cause of her daughter's death. A rational trial of fact could certainly have found that had defendant not left her children unsupervised, either the fire would not have occurred or she and the children would have been able to escape to safety before the apartment was engulfed in flames. Because the child died as a result of defendant's criminal negligence, she is guilty of negligent homicide. . . .

. . . Evidence that defendant previously pleaded guilty to criminal abandonment has probative value to show the improbability that defendant acted without the requisite intent or accidentally when she again left the children unsupervised. The state may fairly argue here that evidence defendant had been placed on notice by her prior conviction of the criminal consequences flowing from her neglect of her children bore on the jury's assessment of her moral culpability in neglecting them again. Further, it is relevant to show this was not mere ordinary negligence. . . .

NOTES & QUESTIONS ON GROSS NEGLIGENCE

1. *Small's culpability.*   How would you describe Small's level of culpability? She deliberately left her children alone in the house. When the fire started, there was no one there to help them escape; as a result, one of them died. The Louisiana Supreme Court had little doubt that this constituted the gross negligence required for negligent homicide, in part because leaving the children alone while going out for the night constituted a gross deviation from the ordinary standard of care. Indeed, at trial the prosecution convinced a jury to convict Small of murder under a felony murder theory. The underlying felony was cruelty to juveniles. However, Louisiana has a restrictive interpretation of the agency approach. As applied to this case, the Supreme Court said that Small was not the direct agent of the child's death. Although Small was a proximate cause of the child's death, the court found that fact insufficient to generate responsibility under felony murder.

2. *Prosecutorial strategy.*   Was it a strategic charging error on the part of the prosecutor to proceed with the felony murder theory (which was rejected by the court)? Would you have charged Small with implied malice murder (second-degree murder) or even involuntary manslaughter? That would have been a natural strategy. However, neither possibility was available in Louisiana, whose homicide statute is a bit of an outlier when compared with those of most other jurisdictions. First, Louisiana has no second-degree murder provision based on extreme or depraved indifference to human life. Second-degree murder in Louisiana is limited to intentional murder or felony murder based on one of 15 enumerated triggering felonies. Second, Louisiana's

manslaughter provision is limited to voluntary manslaughter based on provocation or heat of passion. Louisiana has no regular involuntary manslaughter provision, but rather a provision defining manslaughter as non-intentional homicide committed during the course of a felony or intentional misdemeanor. Consequently, regular acts of reckless killings must fall under the Louisiana provision for negligent homicide. In a sense, the Louisiana negligent homicide provision performs the work that involuntary manslaughter does in most other jurisdictions. Does this cause you to reevaluate the prosecutor's options in *Small*? Does it cause you to reevaluate Louisiana's decision to require gross negligence for negligent homicide?

3. *Gross negligence versus recklessness.* A few jurisdictions go even further and require something approaching recklessness for their negligent homicide statutes. *State v. Green*, 220 W. Va. 300, 647 S.E.2d 736 (W. Va. 2007). Although the crime is called negligent homicide, West Virginia courts interpret it as requiring recklessness because the negligent homicide statute provides that the defendant must drive in "reckless disregard" of the safety of others. In West Virginia, prosecutors can elect to prosecute a reckless driver either for involuntary manslaughter or negligent homicide—a result that did not bother the court because the statutes carried identical penalties.

4. *Gross negligence, a.k.a. "criminal" negligence.* Some jurisdictions use the term "criminal negligence" to refer to gross negligence. The Exxon Valdez oil spill of 1989 was, at the time, the largest environmental disaster in U.S. history. The Exxon Valdez oil tanker ran aground in Alaska, spilling 11 million gallons of crude oil into Prince William Sound, polluting the water and destroying the environment. The cleanup took years to finish. Prosecutors accused the tanker's captain, Joseph Hazelwood, of being drunk during the accident. Hazelwood was charged with reckless endangerment, operating a watercraft while intoxicated, and negligent discharge of oil, but he was only convicted of negligent discharge of oil. *State v. Hazelwood*, 946 P.2d 875 (Alaska 1997). While the case did not involve a prosecution for negligent homicide, it does provide an important case study regarding the definition of criminal negligence and the required deviation from the standard of care. The Alaskan Supreme Court described the difference between civil and criminal negligence in the following way:

> The difference between criminal and civil negligence although not major is distinct. Under both standards, a person acts "negligently" when he fails to perceive a substantial and unjustifiable risk that a particular result will occur. The two tests part ways in their descriptions of the relevant unobserved risk. Under ordinary negligence, "the risk must be of such a nature and degree that the failure to perceive it constitutes a deviation from the standard of care that a reasonable person would observe in the situation." Criminal negligence requires a greater risk. This standard is met only when the risk is of such a nature and degree that the failure to perceive it constitutes a *gross* deviation

from the standard of care that a reasonable person would observe in the situation. *Criminal negligence is something more than the slight degree of negligence necessary to support a civil action for damages and is negligence of a degree so gross as to be deserving of punishment.*

PROBLEM CASE

Skiing is a common recreational activity but it can also be dangerous. Collisions between skiers on the slopes can result in severe injuries or even death. If someone is skiing dangerously and crashes into an unsuspecting victim, should the defendant go to jail if the victim ends up dying?

That question was posed squarely in *People v. Hall*, 999 P.2d 207 (Col. 2000). Hall operated a ski lift at a resort in Vail, Colorado. When his shift was over, he decided to ski down the mountain, which by that point was not crowded. He gained excessive speed and was launched into the air on the moguls. While in the air he noticed that there were others in front of him, but at that point he could not stop. He landed on Allen Cobb, who died from brain injuries suffered in the collision. Cobb was skiing with his fiancée that day.

Hall was charged with reckless manslaughter and with a lesser-included offense of negligent homicide. Hall appealed to quash the indictment. Although the court conceded that skiing too fast "was not widely considered behavior that constitutes a high degree of risk," the court concluded that Hall's behavior was different. Hall, a ski racer, was skiing so fast that he could not stop or avoid a potential collision. The court ruled that the danger of a collision posed by Hall's skiing exceeded the inherent risks of skiing, which is characterized by "moments of high speeds and temporary losses of control."

The Colorado Supreme Court reinstated Hall's indictment and ruled that he should stand trial for reckless manslaughter. At trial, however, the jury refused to convict on the top count and instead convicted Hall of negligent homicide. Hall begged the trial judge for leniency and was sentenced to 90 days in jail. At his hearing, he said, "I know I'm guilty. . . . I stand before you guys knowing I've taken a human life, a life obviously very special and valued by a lot of people." *Skier Sentenced to 3 Months in Jail*, ABC, Feb. 1, 2001.

Do you agree with the result? Was Hall guilty of recklessness or negligence? Or neither? Hall is not the only skier or snowboarder to be convicted of negligent homicide. In 2006, snowboarder Greg Doda pled guilty to negligent homicide after he collided with a skier at Jackson Hole Mountain Resort and killed her. The judge sentenced Doda to a year in jail but stayed and suspended almost the entire sentence. The judge ordered Doda to spend the holiday season in jail, from Christmas to New Year's, in order to "impart upon you in some degree that emptiness that [the victim's] family feels every day." Noah Brenner, *Snowboarder Going to Jail*, Jackson Hole News & Guide, Dec. 22, 2006.

Greg Doda

In essence, then, the criminal negligence standard requires the jury to find negligence so gross as to merit not just damages but also punishment. It does not spill over into recklessness; there is still no requirement that the defendant actually be aware of the risk of harm. However, criminal negligence does require a more culpable mental state than simple, ordinary negligence.

Ultimately, the Alaskan Supreme Court ruled that Hazelwood could be convicted of the crime of negligent discharge of oil under an ordinary negligence standard. In other words, the court concluded that not all crimes require the use of the "criminal" negligence standard. This makes the use of the terminology "civil negligence" and "criminal negligence" somewhat misleading, since not all courts require the use of gross negligence in criminal cases.

Review the casebook video, *People v. Robert Dale* (Part 4: Negligent Homicide). How would you describe the defendant's mental state? Was he aware of, and consciously disregarded, a substantial and unjustifiable risk? Or was Dale genuinely unaware of the risk of death in this situation? In the absence of such awareness, should Dale be convicted for negligent homicide instead?

C. PRACTICE & POLICY

The following section explores several policy-related options associated with negligent homicide. These include: (i) the Model Penal Code's rationale for adopting the gross negligence standard; (ii) the possibility of an in-between or hybrid standard that combines ordinary and gross negligence; (iii) objective versus subjective interpretations of the negligence standard; and (iv) criminal prosecutions for medical malpractice. Each question implicates, in its own way, the essential controversy of negligent homicide: What is the dividing line between tort and criminal law?

~ **Model Penal Code approach.** As we saw in Chapter 6, MPC § 2.02 defines negligence in the following manner: "A person acts negligently with respect to a material element of an offense when he should be aware of a substantial and unjustifiable risk that the material element exists or will result from his conduct. The risk must be of such a nature and degree that the actor's failure to perceive it, considering the nature and purpose of his conduct and the circumstances known to him, involves a gross deviation from the standard of care that a reasonable person would observe in the actor's situation." In other words, the MPC requires gross negligence.

The official MPC commentaries offer only the barest of explanation for why the drafters sided with gross negligence. The editors noted that many typical statutory definitions of negligence, such as New York's definition prior to its 1965 revision, went like this: "[T]he terms 'negligent,' 'negligence,' 'neglect,' and 'negligently' import[] a want of such attention to the nature or probably consequences of the act or omission as a prudent man ordinarily bestows in acting in his own concerns." This language suggests ordinary negligence. Despite these statutory formulations, judges would often require something *extra* in order to punish a defendant for negligence. This something often went by different labels: wanton and willful negligence, gross negligence, or negligence more than required for tort liability. See Jerome Hall, *General Principles of Criminal Law* 124 (2d ed. 1960). Unfortunately, some of these labels confused negligence with recklessness. What was undeniable, however, was that common law judges often required something more than the statutory definition of ordinary negligence. When New York revised its penal law in 1965, it switched to gross negligence. For all of these reasons, the Model Penal Code sided with gross negligence.

ᔆ **The in-between standard.**   Not every jurisdiction uses the ordinary or gross negligence standards. Kansas once required something *in between* ordinary and gross negligence for a conviction under its negligent homicide statute. *State v. Randol*, 226 Kan. 347 (1979). This standard was codified in the Kansas vehicular homicide statute, K.S.A. § 21-5406 ("As used in this section, 'material deviation' means conduct amounting to more than simple or ordinary negligence but not amount[ing] to gross negligence."). Consequently, the alternatives for a jurisdiction deciding on the correct standard of negligent homicide actually involve *three* standards: ordinary negligence, material deviation (or intermediate negligence), and gross negligence. If you were a state legislator involved in codifying a new version of your state's penal code, which standard would you choose?

ᔆ **Subjective or objective.**   Should negligence be understood from the perspective of the defendant or from the perspective of the reasonable person? Or should it be assessed relative to a reasonable person with similar personal characteristics as the defendant (a hybrid standard)? Courts are very much divided on this question. To understand why this is a problem, consider the often used language that the deviation must be from a standard of care that a "reasonable person would observe in the actor's situation." What precisely is the "actor's situation"? Does it mean the objective circumstances of the moment, or does it include personal characteristics of the defendant? The commentaries to the Model Penal Code note that "if the actor were blind or if he had just suffered a blow or experienced a heart attack, these would certainly be facts to be considered in a judgment involving criminal liability, as they would be under traditional law." But the commentaries also continue with the following clarification: "[H]eredity, intelligence or temperament of the actor would not be held material in judging negligence, and could not be without depriving the criterion of all its objectivity." Commentaries at 242. Not all scholars agree with this conclusion. See George P. Fletcher, *The Theory of Criminal Negligence: A Comparative Analysis*, 119 U. Pa. L. Rev. 401 (1971). Even if you agree with the views expressed by the Model Penal Code, is it clear how this standard should be applied? What if the defendant is dyslexic? Or suffers from Attention Deficit Hyperactivity Disorder (ADHD)? Are these closer to blindness or instead to heredity and intelligence? Part of the problem is that these conditions have been increasingly medicalized since the Model Penal Code was drafted.

∾ **Criminal prosecutions for medical negligence.** In tort law, a large percentage of negligence cases involve medical malpractice. When a doctor or hospital deviates from the standard of care and the patient dies, it is clear that the patient's estate can sue for damages. But when should a doctor be held criminally responsible for causing a patient's death? Prosecutions for medical malpractice are rare, but not impossible. Usually prosecutors are inclined to let families seek justice privately through the tort system. In extreme cases, however, a prosecutor may feel that the case warrants public prosecution and criminal penalties. In these situations, should the prosecution be governed by ordinary or gross negligence? P.D.G. Skegg, *Criminal Prosecutions of Negligent Health Professionals: The New Zealand Experience*, 6 Med. L. Rev. 220 (1998) (noting that New Zealand shifted from ordinary to gross negligence).

In 2014, a New York plastic surgeon, Oleg Davie, pled guilty to negligent homicide after a patient died from a liposuction procedure that went horribly wrong. The patient, a 51-year-old model, died hours after the operation. The prosecutor argued that the doctor deviated from the standard of care by not consulting with the patient's cardiologist before performing the surgery. If he had done so, he would have learned that the patient had received a heart transplant years before and her arteries were severely clogged. On this basis, the prosecutor had originally charged the doctor with involuntary manslaughter under a theory of recklessness. In a plea agreement, the doctor pled guilty to negligent homicide and was sentenced to two months in jail. Oren Yaniv, *Brooklyn Plastic Surgeon Pleads Guilty to Criminally Negligent Homicide After Former Model Dies Following Botched Liposuction*, N.Y. Daily News, May 7, 2014. Do you agree with the prosecutor's decision, which was controversial in the medical community, or would you have left this case to the civil system for an appropriate remedy? (The family also filed a civil case against the doctor.)

Oleg Davie

CHAPTER 14

⟨◦⟩

RAPE

A. DOCTRINE

Rape law has undergone a tremendous evolution in a short period of time. Various jurisdictions have reformed their rape provisions to varying degrees and in some jurisdictions judicial interpretations have transformed rape law in lieu of explicit recodification by state legislatures. Much of the evolution of the law took place in response to vigorous questions about rape law's content. Some of that criticism came from well-known feminist scholars and activists, from within the legal academy and related academic disciplines, but much of the criticism also came from practicing lawyers and judges who identified areas of the law that required revision. In a famous law review article, Susan Estrich concluded: "Sexism in the law of rape is no matter of mere historical interest; it endures, even where some of the most blatant testaments to that sexism have disappeared. Corroboration requirements unique to rape may have been repealed, but they continue to be enforced as a matter of practice in many jurisdictions. The victim of rape may not be required to resist to the utmost as a matter of statutory law in any jurisdiction, but the definitions accorded to force and consent may render 'reasonable' resistance both a practical and a legal necessity. In the law of rape, supposedly dead horses continue to run." Susan Estrich, *Rape*, 95 Yale L.J. 1087, 1091 (1986).

Much of that law has changed since Estrich wrote her assessment in 1986, but some of these elements endure. Although the process of reform is incomplete, the following elements remain relevant for understanding the law and practice of rape prosecutions. Rape is usually defined by statute as non-consensual sexual intercourse completed by force or threat of force, although some jurisdictions have either eliminated the force requirement or substantially redefined it. The general category of sexual assault includes several related offenses, such as aggravated

357

rape, rape, and various forms of sexual assault that usually are punished less severely than rape. Aggravated rape, which triggers heightened penalties, applies when the rape is committed during another violent offense, such as assault with a deadly weapon or armed robbery. The labels for these terms differ widely across jurisdictions so it is imperative to consult the statutory scheme carefully.

The following sections outline the major elements of the crime of rape with an eye toward identifying the major points of departure among jurisdictions. Although almost every crime in American law is plagued by substantial divergence across state jurisdictions, this is especially pertinent in the context of rape. The material in this chapter, like much of the casebook, is disturbing; descriptions of sexual violence are inevitably upsetting. Great care has been taken to present materials that will spur a sophisticated, sensitive, and nuanced discussion of the topic.

1. Force

Most jurisdictions still require that the perpetrator accomplish the act of sexual intercourse with either physical force or the threat of physical force. However, both legislatures and courts have amended the force requirement over time, often in response to criticism that the force requirement, as applied, exonerated defendants who ought to have been convicted. In short, critics complained that the force requirement was unnecessary. At issue was the very definition of rape: Is it a crime of non-consensual sex (which does not require force) or is it a crime of violence (which entails force)? See, e.g., David P. Bryden, *Redefining Rape*, 3 Buff. Crim. L. Rev. 317 (2000); Robin D. Wiener, *Shifting the Communication Burden: A Meaningful Consent Standard in Rape*, 6 Harv. Women's L.J. 143 (1983); Robin L. West, *Legitimating the Illegitimate: A Comment on Beyond Rape*, 93 Colum. L. Rev. 1442, 1445 (1993) ("Many, if not most, rape law commentators from a range of perspectives have addressed the underenforcement of laws against sexual assault by arguing that rape should be defined simply as non-consensual sex—by dropping, in effect, the force requirement altogether.").

Under the force prong (as opposed to the threat of physical force), the prosecution is required to demonstrate that the act was completed through forcible compulsion, though jurisdictions disagree over what level of force is required. Some jurisdictions interpret "force" as just the physical act of sexual penetration. In contrast, other jurisdictions require some level of force beyond the force required for achieving sexual penetration. In these jurisdictions, the level of force required is sometimes defined as that force which is sufficient to overcome the resistance of the victim. However, resistance can be defined in two ways. Some courts require that the victim *physically* resist and that the defendant overpowered the victim's resistance. In contrast, other jurisdictions allow *verbal* resistance to meet the requirement. For example, if the victim says "no" but the defendant uses force to overcome the verbal objection, the force requirement would be met. The recognition of "verbal resistance" in some jurisdictions represented a substantial victory for reform advocates. See, e.g., Lani Anne Remick, *Read Her Lips: An Argument for a Verbal Consent Standard in Rape*, 141 U. Pa. L. Rev. 1103, 1105 (1993).

2. Threats of Force

Threats are best viewed as a distinct pathway toward a conviction, as an alternative to the force requirement. At common law, courts often struggled over how to deal with perpetrators who completed a rape by threatening physical force but never actually using force. The early doctrinal solution was to label threats as "constructive force," but now modern statutes explicitly refer to force or *threats* of force. Again, the question is what severity of threat is required. Most jurisdictions require that the threat prevent the victim from resisting due to a reasonable fear or apprehension regarding the victim's safety. What constitutes a *reasonable* apprehension or fear is a question of fact for a jury to decide. Non-physical threats (such as threatening financial harm or professional retaliation) do not constitute rape but might trigger the application of some other criminal or civil statute. One difficulty with applying the threat doctrine involves the interpretation of "reasonable" apprehension. Should reasonableness be determined objectively or subjectively? If subjectively, should it be from the subjective perspective of the victim or the subjective perspective of the defendant? Generally speaking, courts have interpreted the "reasonable apprehension" standard as requiring both a subjective component (a sincere fear) with an objective overlay (the fear was objectively reasonable).

3. Consent

The victim's lack of consent to the sexual act is key to a rape conviction. At common law, courts once established the victim's lack of consent by requiring that the victim "resisted to her utmost." That requirement has been abandoned as a relic of the common law past. Now, jurisdictions require simply that the victim did not consent to the sexual act. The difficulty stems from how to define consent. Is it a communicative act or a state of mind? Some courts view it as a communicative act, which could be established either by conduct or by the victim saying "yes" during the encounter. Other courts view it as a state of mind, which requires asking whether the victim wanted the encounter to occur or not. This opens up the possibility for defendants to argue mistake of fact regarding the victim's lack of consent. Some jurisdictions allow the mistake of fact defense on the theory that knowledge of the victim's lack of consent is an essential element of the crime's mental state. However, other jurisdictions disallow the defense under the theory that what matters is whether the victim consented, not whether the defendant was aware of the victim's state of mind. The best way of understanding this view is by recognizing that the victim's lack of consent is an attendant circumstance. Since the defendant is not required to have knowledge of this attendant circumstance, the defendant's mistake regarding this element of the offense is irrelevant.

4. Rape by Fraud

What if the defendant procures the victim's consent by lying or making some fraudulent representation? In this one instance the old common law rule has remained relatively stable and unchanged. Courts historically distinguished between "fraud in the factum" and "fraud in the inducement." Fraud in the factum involved a lie about the nature of the act itself, i.e., the defendant told the victim that they were not having sex when they actually *were* having sex. One example of fraud in the factum would be a sexual assault that occurs during a medical appointment. If the victim consented to a physical examination with a medical instrument, but the doctor engaged in sexual intercourse instead, this would be fraud in the factum. American courts classify this as rape, though such situations are very rare. The more common occurrence is fraud in the inducement, where the defendant lies about something in order to convince the victim to have sex. In that situation, the victim knows that he or she is having sex but only agrees to it because of the lie. For example, consider an individual who consents to sexual intercourse with someone who professes interest in a serious relationship leading to marriage. If, after the fact, the victim learns that these were not sincere proclamations of love but were, in fact, part of an elaborate ruse designed to secure consent for a one-time encounter, this would be fraud in the inducement. Fraud in the inducement is generally *not* punishable as rape in the United States. The result of this rule is that even egregious cases of inducement fraud—as long as the victim knows that he or she is engaging in sex—cannot be punished. This result has prompted a few state jurisdictions to broaden their rape statutes to include a wider range of fraudulent misrepresentations. Also, some jurisdictions will prosecute perpetrators who impersonate the victim's spouse in order to fraudulently achieve consent. (These cases often occur in the middle of the night in a darkened bedroom.)

5. Statutory Rape and Lack of Capacity

A defendant can also be convicted of rape if the victim is legally incapable of consenting to sex. The most common reason is the victim's young age, which is commonly referred to as statutory rape. However, most sexual assault statutes include several factual scenarios that make the victim incapable of consenting to the sexual act. These include the victim's incapacitation from drugs and alcohol or a mental defect associated with mental disease or illness. Many jurisdictions also list specific professional relationships (corrections officer, doctor, therapist, high school teacher) that make consent legally impossible. The underlying rationale for these statutes is that certain relationships are so inherently unequal—with complex power dynamics—as to prevent the formation of true consent between the partners. In the case of teachers and students, the power involves mentorship and educational opportunities. In the case of prison guards and their prisoners, the power is more physical and literal. The difficult cases for juries to resolve involve situations where the victim's judgment is partially impaired but not completely destroyed, either in a temporary way through alcohol use or in a permanent way from a cognitive disability. In such cases, the court cannot rely on the nature of the relationship between the parties. Instead, the jury must determine whether the victim's thought process was sufficiently unencumbered to allow for meaningful consent to occur.

B. APPLICATION

1. Force

Jurisdictions have struggled to define the type and quantum of force required to sustain a rape conviction. Should the force be "extrinsic" to the act of sexual intercourse (like an assault) or can the force be "intrinsic" to the sexual act itself (such as the act of penetration)? In reading the following case, examine how the court interprets the force requirement, as well as its relationship to the victim's resistance. Pay particular attention to how the court applies these concepts to the interaction between the defendant and the victim in this case.

State v. Jones

Court of Appeals of Idaho
2011 WL 4011738 (2011)

GUTIERREZ, J.

FACTS AND PROCEDURE

Jones, A.S., and Craig Carpenter had been friends for approximately fifteen years in the spring of 2008. A.S. and Carpenter were engaged and had children together. However, unbeknownst to Carpenter, Jones and A.S. had been having a sexual relationship for approximately four years. On May 22, 2008, after spending the night alone together in Jackpot, Nevada, Jones and A.S. returned to A.S.'s apartment—deciding on the drive back to Idaho they should end their affair. However, the next morning they engaged in consensual sex. Afterwards, A.S. went to the bathroom and when she returned to the bedroom Jones was on the computer looking at pornographic material. He sat down on the bed next to her and began to touch her. A.S. reacted by telling Jones, "[I] thought we had decided that the time before that was the last time and it wasn't going to happen anymore." Jones stopped touching her, got up, and walked around behind her. A.S. got up on her elbows and saw that Jones was unfastening his pants. She protested that she did not want to engage in intercourse, but he "leaned forward" and A.S. was "pushed down . . . to where [she] couldn't get up" and her arms were pinned beneath her body. Jones then moved A.S.'s underwear aside and had intercourse with her. Afterward, Jones apologized to A.S., asked her if she was alright, and told her that she could "press charges" if she wanted to because he was "out of line" and had "lost control." After Jones left the residence, A.S. called the Women's Center at Boise State University and spoke to a counselor. After telling the counselor that she had been raped, she was advised to call the police, which she did not do. She continued to be in contact with Jones, including going with him again to Jackpot.

Several days later on May 27, Jones came to watch movies at A.S.'s residence. Jones spent the night on A.S.'s couch and remained in the apartment after Carpenter left for work and A.S.'s children left for school. A.S. testified that during this time she was taking a prescribed anti-anxiety medication which caused her to experience marked drowsiness and had taken an over-the-counter antihistamine to treat a bee sting, which also caused her to feel drowsy. Due to her drowsiness, A.S. lay down on the couch in the living room, while Jones used the computer in her bedroom. Jones entered the living room, sat next to her, and began to stroke her hair. A.S. testified that Jones pulled her hair, but A.S. did not respond and pretended to be asleep. Jones then grabbed at A.S.'s breasts, forcefully touched her private area, and proceeded to engage in intercourse with her while she was lying on the couch and not moving. A.S. testified that she was "paralyzed by fear" and neither physically resisted Jones nor made any verbal protest. A.S. testified that she had hoped Jones would cease if she did not respond to him physically. . . .

Jones was charged with two counts of forcible rape, based on the May 22 incident in the bedroom (Count I) and the May 27 incident on the couch (Count II). . . . The jury convicted Jones of both. . . .

SUFFICIENCY OF THE EVIDENCE

Jones contends that there was insufficient evidence to support the jury's verdicts on both counts because the State failed to prove, beyond a reasonable doubt, both that A.S. physically resisted Jones and that her resistance was overcome by force or violence, elements that are required by the statute. . . . At the time of the charged offenses, the statute provided that: "Rape is defined as the penetration, however slight, of the oral, anal or vaginal opening with the perpetrator's penis accomplished with a female under any one of the following circumstances: . . . . (3) Where she resists but her resistance is overcome by force or violence." Idaho Code § 18-6101(3).

The term "resistance" is not defined in the statute, nor is there any attendant legislative history. We note that at common law a state had to prove beyond a reasonable doubt that the woman resisted her assailant to the utmost of her physical capacity to prove that an act of sexual intercourse was rape—known as the "utmost resistance" standard. Thus, legal decision-makers have historically ignored evidence of a woman's verbal resistance; under the law, verbal resistance was simply inadequate to prove anything.

When it became apparent that the "utmost" resistance standard made rape nearly impossible to prove, many states began to abandon the requirement. In its place, some states required that women exert only "earnest" resistance to establish that an act of sexual intercourse was without consent and by force—a standard which remains codified in two states. Rejecting the "utmost" and "earnest" resistance requirements, other jurisdictions have moved to require only "reasonable" resistance on the part of the rape victim. This standard, still codified by six states, requires that a woman offer resistance which is "reasonable under the circumstances," and she is not required to actively resist if she reasonably believes that resistance would be useless and would result in serious bodily injury.

Eventually, however, approximately thirty-two states, the Model Penal Code, the District of Columbia Code, and the Uniform Code of Military Justice eliminated the formal resistance requirement altogether by not mentioning resistance in the statutory language describing rape, allowing prosecutors to establish that a rape occurred even in the absence of any resistance by the woman. Six more states explicitly note in their criminal codes that physical resistance is not required to substantiate a rape charge. Thus, Idaho remains one of few states that still statutorily require resistance to prove forcible rape and one of even fewer whose statute does not specify the requisite amount of resistance that will suffice. . . .

Also helpful in elucidating the issue, we note that Washington's forcible rape statute, like Idaho's, references the "overcoming" of resistance, but does not specify the type and amount of resistance that a victim must employ. Specifically, the Washington statutory scheme defines "forcible compulsion," referenced in its first and second degree rape statutes, as "physical force which *overcomes resistance*. . . ." In interpreting this language, Washington courts have repeatedly held that to prove forcible compulsion, the state need not show that the victim physically resisted, but rather the question of whether resistance occurred is a fact-sensitive determination based on the totality of the circumstances, including the victim's words and conduct. *State v. McKnight*, 54 Wash. App. 521 (1989). . . .

The court then turned to the facts of the case—the victim, a fourteen-year-old girl, had invited a casual acquaintance, a seventeen-year-old boy, into her home because she was "bored and lonely." The two started kissing, but the victim testified that when she told the defendant to stop he started to slowly push her down on the couch and take off her clothes. She continued to tell him to stop and testified that at this point she was "scared." The defendant then lay on top of her and had sexual intercourse with her. It was undisputed that the victim had not physically resisted the defendant. However, the court concluded, looking at the totality of the facts, that there was sufficient evidence that she had resisted the defendant. Specifically, there was testimony that she was "physically weak" and therefore a reasonable trier of fact could conclude that she was incapable of physically resisting. There was also evidence that she had never dated a boy, it was her first sexual intercourse experience, and she was "unsophisticated and naïve." . . . Overall, the court concluded that the victim's resistance was *reasonable under the circumstances*. . . .

Given Idaho's statutory and case law history, we, like the Washington court, ascertain that "resist" as it is used in Idaho's forcible rape statute does not require that the victim have *physically* resisted. First and foremost, the plain language of the statute does not indicate that resistance must be physical. In addition, it has also been established that a victim need not resist to the utmost of her ability, and that the importance of resistance by the victim is simply to show two elements of the crime—the assailant's intent to use force in order to have sexual intercourse and the victim's non-consent. To interpret the statute rigidly as requiring physical resistance is contrary to the general tenor of these decisions. Accordingly, we hold that whether the evidence establishes the element of resistance is a fact-sensitive determination based on the totality of the circumstances, *including the victim's words* and conduct. . . .

Turning to the facts of the instant case, we conclude that there was substantial evidence that the jury could find that A.S. resisted Jones's advances. A.S. testified that she "kept yelling at [Jones] and pleading for him to stop and please quit" and was unable to physically resist because he was on top of her, pinning her arms beneath her body. Jones's statements to her afterwards indicate that he knew she did not want to engage in the act—including telling her that he had "lost control." This evidence unequivocally shows that A.S. explicitly communicated to Jones her non-consent to sexual intercourse. Accordingly, we conclude that there was substantial evidence for a reasonable trier of fact to conclude that A.S. "resisted" as required by the statute.

Jones also contends there was insufficient evidence to prove that he used force or violence to overcome A.S.'s resistance. Specifically, he notes that there was no evidence presented that he was violent towards A.S., nor that he applied any physical force beyond that required to accomplish the actual penetration. The State counters, contending evidence that

Jones pushed A.S. down, pinned her arms under her, adjusted her underwear, and proceeded to engage her sexually was sufficient evidence of force or violence.

While Idaho's forcible rape statute identifies the necessary *effect* of the force (that it overcome the victim's resistance), it does not otherwise indicate the *quantum* of force required. The amount of force required by the forcible rape statute—specifically, whether the force exerted must be more than is inherent in the sexual act—is an issue of first impression in Idaho.

A prominent commentator has noted that because the statutes defining the crime of rape typically do not establish an amount of physical coercion sufficient to demonstrate that sexual activity was accomplished "by force," the requisite degree of force mandated by the courts has been subject to considerable dispute and variation. For the most part, however, the treatment by the courts of this issue reflects one of two standards—which represent different approaches to the force element and to the degree and mechanisms of force that the prosecution must show in order to obtain a rape conviction—the intrinsic force standard and the extrinsic force standard. The latter approach reflects the more traditional view, which is that the force requirement ordinarily requires proof of use of force or threat of force *above and beyond* that inherent in the act of non-consensual intercourse, while the intrinsic force standard is the opposite, that force inherent in the act itself suffices.

An over one-hundred-year-old United States Supreme Court case, *Mills v. United States,* 164 U.S. 644 (1897), set the precedent that in certain instances, the defendant must have demonstrated force beyond the act of raping the victim in order for a rape conviction to be sustained. This extrinsic force standard is still the most commonly adopted. In *Commonwealth v. Berkowitz,* 537 Pa. 143 (1994), the Pennsylvania Supreme Court applied the standard, holding that the defendant had not committed rape because the victim failed to show that the defendant had used the requisite force or threat of force to compel her to have intercourse. The victim in the case had entered the defendant's dorm room in search of the defendant's roommate. After locking the door, the defendant sat beside the victim, lifted up her shirt, and fondled her breasts. The victim offered no physical resistance as he proceeded to engage in sexual intercourse with her, but testified that she had repeatedly stated "no" during the encounter. Noting that the issue of force is "relative and depends on the facts of the case," the court determined that the prosecution had not demonstrated the forcible compulsion element, focusing primarily on the actual degree of physical force exerted by the defendant—specifically the precise degree of the shove by which the defendant had put the victim on the bed and whether the untying of her sweatpants was the only physical contact made with the defendant. . . .

On the other hand, the adoption of the intrinsic force standard is indicative of a modern trend toward the eradication of the element of force and is most clearly observed in recent court opinions that narrowly construe sexual assault provisions in favor of the victim. In New Jersey, for example, forcible sexual assault is defined as "sexual penetration with another person" with the use of "physical force or coercion." Such statutes have traditionally been interpreted as requiring demonstrative force beyond the act of penetration, an interpretation that a lower state court adopted in *In re M.T.S.*, 247 N.J. Super. 254 (1991), *rev'd* 129 N.J. 422, 609 A.2d 1266 (1992), holding that the mere act of penetration itself could not satisfy the element of "physical force or coercion" since such an interpretation would render the statute "meaningless." The New Jersey Supreme Court disagreed, however, adopting the intrinsic force standard which effectively eliminates the need for the prosecution to demonstrate any extra force beyond the actual intercourse with the victim. In *M.T.S.*, the victim testified that she fell asleep on her bed and awoke to find that her shorts and underwear were removed and the defendant was lying on top of her in the act of penetration. . . .[1]

The court then concluded, for several reasons, including the fact that the elements of non-consent and resistance had been removed from the statute, that the legislature had intended to redefine rape consistent with the law of assault and battery—which require only offensive touching without reference to a degree of force. As such, the court reasoned that an interpretation of the statutory crime of sexual assault to require physical force in addition to that entailed in an act of involuntary or unwanted sexual penetration would be fundamentally inconsistent with the legislative purpose to eliminate any consideration of whether the victim resisted or expressed non-consent and would essentially reintroduce a resistance requirement into the sexual assault law. On this basis, the court held that the definition of "physical force" is satisfied under the rape statute if the defendant applies any amount of force against another person in the absence of what a reasonable person would believe to be affirmative and freely-given permission to the act of sexual penetration.

While generally considered progress in the area of rape law reform, the intrinsic force standard essentially renders the issue of force moot, instead shifting the analysis to the issue of consent. It removes rape from the special category of violent crimes where most courts have pigeonholed it, placing it in the group of assaultive crimes where contact is measured by its

---

1. [Editor's Note: In *M.T.S.*, the trial court discounted the testimony of both teenagers, ultimately concluding that the victim had not been asleep. Rather, the trial court concluded that the teenagers were initially engaged in consensual touching but that the victim did not consent to sexual intercourse. 129 N.J. 422, 428.]

unlawfulness and not by the degree of forcefulness. In this sense, it is incompatible with Idaho's statutory scheme, which places significant emphasis on the element of force—prescribing that it must be sufficient to "overcome" a victim's resistance. . . .

Most courts with similar language to that found in Idaho's rape statute, requiring that the force or violence "overcome" resistance, have interpreted their statutes to require extrinsic force. Quite simply, this terminology implies that force other than that inherent in the proscribed sexual act be used to overcome a victim's resistance—implying that the force must occur before penetration. The Idaho Legislature has not undertaken the rape law reform that characterizes those states which have departed from the traditional extrinsic force standard. Thus, we conclude that the extrinsic force standard is applicable in regard to Idaho's forcible rape statute.

In the conduct charged as Count I here, it is undisputed that the extent of Jones's physical contact with A.S. during the incident, aside from penetration, was coming up from behind her, laying on top of her, pushing her down from being propped up on her elbows, thus causing her arms to be pinned beneath her by his body weight, and moving her underwear aside. Accordingly, we must determine whether Jones exerted the requisite force beyond penetration to overcome A.S.'s resistance.

One criticism of the extrinsic force standard is that it is inherently more ambiguous than the intrinsic force standard because it requires more evidence and naturally gives rise to the question of just how much more will suffice. . . . As a result, the outcomes are generally all over the map. . . .

For example, on one end of the spectrum is the holding in *Berkowitz*, 641 A.2d at 1164, where the Pennsylvania Supreme Court held that the requisite force had not been shown where the defendant had not verbally threatened the victim, the defendant's hands were not restraining her in any manner during the actual penetration, and the weight of his body on top of her was the only force applied. On the other hand, numerous jurisdictions have found the requisite force under circumstances similar to those in *Berkowitz*. In *State v. Jacques*, 536 A.2d 535, 538 (1988), after adopting the extrinsic force standard as we discussed above, the Rhode Island Supreme Court applied the standard to the facts of the case. There, the defendant who was allegedly performing a photo shoot, instructed the victim to walk to a wing-back chair, which was against the wall opposite the desk. As she proceeded toward the chair, the defendant told her that he was getting excited by her body. The victim testified that at this point she became very frightened. As she arrived at the chair, she felt the pressure of the defendant's chest pushing against her back. This pressure caused her to fall into a kneeling position onto the chair facing the wall, after which he sexually assaulted her. On appeal, the defendant contended that he had not exerted the requisite force to be convicted of first degree sexual assault. The Supreme Court disagreed, noting that "the force of [the defendant's] chest pushing against her caused her to kneel in the chair" such that "[a]s a result of [the defendant's] approach from the rear, [the victim] was forced into a position of helplessness" and that "[o]nce [the victim] was in this position, [the defendant] moved to the attack." . . .

While we are not bound by the above-described cases, we find their holdings, excepting *Berkowitz,* to be persuasive. As a whole, we conclude that these jurisdictions have not interpreted the extrinsic force standard to require significant impositions of force above, for example, the pushing of a victim into a prone position or down on her knees, the removal of the victim's clothes and/or underwear, or the weight of a defendant's body on top of the victim, where they were taken over the victim's verbal and/or physical resistance and lead to subsequent sexual acts. This leads us to conclude that in this case, reasonable minds could have determined that Jones utilized more force in addition to that inherent in the sexual act and thus satisfied the force element. Jones's use of his body weight on top of A.S. to push her down from having been propped up on her arms and to pin her arms beneath her, rendered her unable to physically resist or escape his grasp and overcame her verbal resistance. Like in *Jacques,* A.S. was "forced into a position of helplessness" by Jones, after which he initiated the sexual act—to which A.S. had clearly communicated her resistance and non-consent. We conclude that there was sufficient evidence to satisfy the resistance and force elements of Count I.

NOTES & QUESTIONS ON FORCE

1. *Intrinsic versus extrinsic force.* Jurisdictions that maintain a force requirement are split over whether the force must be extrinsic to the sexual act or not. In *Berkowitz,* the Pennsylvania courts supported the extrinsic approach and vacated a rape conviction because they found insufficient evidence of physical force other than the act of sexual intercourse. On the other hand, the New Jersey courts in *M.T.S.* supported the intrinsic view and concluded that even the force "intrinsic" in the sexual act could constitute the force required for a rape conviction. Which approach did the Idaho court adopt in *Jones*? Why did it reject New Jersey's argument that the extrinsic approach risks bringing back the old common law resistance requirement through the back door? On appeal, the Supreme Court of Idaho affirmed *Jones.* 299 P.3d 219.

In the end, the Idaho court rejected the intrinsic approach and concluded that Pennsylvania's extrinsic approach was the better interpretation of the statute: A rape conviction under the statute requires some evidence of force that is extrinsic to the act of intercourse. Ultimately, though, the *Jones* court suggests that the Pennsylvania court got the *Berkowitz* case extremely wrong—not in the approach it adopted but rather in how the court *applied* it to the facts of its case. The Idaho court viewed its own case as factually similar to the *Berkowitz* case and concluded that even under the extrinsic approach, a conviction was appropriate in *Jones* because the defendant's body weight pinned the victim's arms beneath her during the act—which the Idaho court concluded was extrinsic because that was not strictly speaking necessary for intercourse. Do the Idaho justices think the *Berkowitz* case should have come out differently too?

2. *Verbal resistance.*   The *Jones* decision is a strong statement in favor of treating verbal resistance as sufficient for a rape conviction. In Idaho, the penal statute criminalizing rape requires that the defendant utilize force sufficient to overcome the victim's resistance. Not all jurisdictions define force relative to resistance, but in those that do, resistance is often understood in *physical* terms. The idea is that the perpetrator uses whatever force is required to overcome the physical resistance of the victim, such as attempting to push the perpetrator's body off during the assault. In contrast, the Idaho court noted that "resistance" can be either physical or verbal, and that simply saying "no" is evidence of resistance to the encounter. Then, if the perpetrator used some element of force to continue the act over the verbal objection of the victim, the act constituted rape. For more discussion of verbal resistance, see Michelle J. Anderson, *Reviving Resistance in Rape Law*, 1998 U. Ill. L. Rev. 953, 991 (1998) ("Verbal resistance should be the legal equivalent of physical resistance. From the victim's point of view, verbal resistance is meant to accomplish the same thing and is offered for the same reasons as physical resistance. Like those who physically resist, women verbally resist to stop the assailant from proceeding, to change his mind, and to express their will of opposition. Verbal resistance is an act to stop the sexual advance. From the victim's point of view, verbal resistance is not meaningfully different from physical resistance.").

2. Threats of Force

Force is not always required for a rape conviction. Every jurisdiction recognizes that threats of force are sufficient. Again, jurisdictions are faced with defining the type and level of threat required. If the perpetrator threatens the victim with death or serious bodily injury if the victim resists, this clearly satisfies the threat requirement, but what of more modest or diffuse threats? In reading the following case, look for the court's standard for evaluating these threats.

Rusk v. State

Court of Special Appeals of Maryland
43 Md. App. 476, 406 A.2d 624 (1979)

THOMPSON, JUDGE.

. . . Edward Salvatore Rusk, the appellant, was convicted in the Criminal Court of Baltimore of rape in the second degree and of assault. He was sentenced to concurrent terms of ten years for the rape and five years for the assault. The appellant does not challenge the conviction for assault but only for the rape. We will, therefore, affirm the assault conviction.

The prosecutrix was a twenty-one year old mother of a two-year old son. She was separated from her husband but not yet divorced. Leaving her son with her mother, she attended a high school reunion after which she and a female friend, Terry, went bar hopping in the Fells Point area of Baltimore. They drove in separate cars. At the third bar the prosecutrix met appellant. . . .

They had a five or ten minute conversation in the bar; at the end of which the prosecutrix said she was ready to leave. Appellant requested a ride home and she agreed. When they arrived at appellant's home, the prosecutrix parked at the curb on the side of the street opposite his rooming house but did not turn off the ignition. She put the car in park and appellant asked her to come up to his apartment. She refused. He continued to ask her to come up, and she testified she then became afraid. While trying to convince him that she didn't want to go to his apartment she mentioned that she was separated and if she did, it might cause her marital problems particularly if she were being followed by a detective. The appellant then took the keys out of the car and walked over to her side of the car, opened the door and said, "Now will you come up?" The prosecutrix then told him she would. She stated:

> At that point, because I was scared, because he had my car keys. I didn't know what to do. I was someplace I didn't even know where I was. It was in the city. I didn't know whether to run. I really didn't think, at that point, what to do. Now, I know that I should have blown the horn. I should have run. There were a million things I could have done. I was scared, at that point, and I didn't do any of them.

The prosecutrix followed appellant into the rowhouse, up the stairs, and into the apartment. When they got into appellant's room, he said that he had to go to the bathroom and left the room for a few minutes. The prosecutrix made no attempt to leave. When appellant came back, he sat on the bed while she sat on the chair next to the bed. He turned the light off and asked her to get on the bed with him. He started to pull her onto the bed and also began to remove her blouse. She stated she took off her slacks and removed his clothing because "he asked (her) to do it." After they both undressed, prosecutrix stated:

> I was still begging him to please let, you know, let me leave. I said, "you can get a lot of other girls down there, for what you want," and he just kept saying, "no," and then I was really scared, because I can't describe, you know, what was said. It was more the look in his eyes; and I said, at that point I didn't know what to say; and I said, "If I do what you want, will you let me go without killing me?" Because I didn't know, at that point, what he was going to do; and I started to cry; and when I did, he put his hands on my throat, and started lightly to choke me; and I said "If I do what you want, will you let me go?" And he said, yes, and at that time, I proceeded to do what he wanted me to.

She stated that she performed oral sex and they then had sexual intercourse.

The appellant testified as did two of his friends who were at the bar in which the parties met. Their testimony painted the episode in a manner more favorable to the accused, but there is no need for us to recite that testimony because, as we have stated earlier, we are obligated to view the evidence in the light most favorable to the prosecution.

The Court of Appeals of Maryland last spoke on the amount of force required to support a rape conviction in *Hazel v. State*, 221 Md. 464, 469 (1960), when the Court said: "Force is an essential element of the crime and to justify a conviction, the evidence must warrant a conclusion either that the victim resisted and her resistance was overcome by force or that she was prevented from resisting by threats to her safety."

In all of the victim's testimony we have been unable to see any resistance on her part to the sex acts and certainly can we see no fear as would overcome her attempt to resist or escape as required by *Hazel*. Possession of the keys by the accused may have deterred her vehicular escape but hardly a departure seeking help in the rooming house or in the street. We must say that "the way he looked" fails utterly to support the fear required by *Hazel*. . . .

Appellee argues first that the issue as to whether or not intercourse was accompanied by force or threats of force is one of credibility to be resolved by the triers of the fact. We cannot follow the argument. As we understand the law, the trial judge in ruling on a motion to acquit must first determine that there is legally sufficient evidence for the jury to find the victim was reasonably in fear. That is the rule set forth in *Hazel* and in each of our cases cited above. Contrary to the State's argument, there is no issue of credibility before us, because we accept the testimony that is most damaging to the accused before applying the rule. The State argues further that the evidence that the accused "started lightly to choke me" as well as the circumstances of being in a somewhat strange part of town late at night were sufficient to overcome the will of a normal twenty-one year old married woman. We are not impressed with the argument. When at oral argument it was pointed out to the State that the cases require that the fear must be reasonable, the appellee answered first that the cases so requiring were wrong and should be overruled and secondly, that a rapist took his victim as he found her. Thus, the argument goes, even though the victim was unreasonable in being afraid, that was the chance a man took in having intercourse with someone not his wife. In other words, in any situation where the victim testified that she consented because she was afraid, the verdict of the jury would be conclusive and all such cases should be submitted to the jury for consideration. Whatever appeal this argument might have in other cases, it has none here where there is nothing whatsoever to indicate that the victim was anything but a normal, intelligent, twenty-one year old, vigorous female.

Cases from other jurisdictions have followed the rule that the victim's fear which overcomes her will to resist must be a reasonable fear. . . .

Applying this reasoning to the record before us, we find the evidence legally insufficient to warrant a conclusion that appellant's words or actions created in the mind of the victim a reasonable fear that if she resisted, he would have harmed her, or that faced with such resistance, he would have used force to overcome it. The prosecutrix stated that she was afraid, and submitted because of "the look in his eyes." After both were undressed and in the bed, and she pleaded to him that she wanted to leave, he started to lightly choke her. At oral argument it was brought out that the "lightly choking" could have been a heavy caress. We do not believe that "lightly choking" along with all the facts and circumstances in the case, were sufficient to cause a reasonable fear which overcame her ability to resist. In the absence of any other evidence showing force used by appellant, we find that the evidence was insufficient to convict appellant of rape.

WILNER, J., dissenting.

With the deepest respect for the generally superior wisdom of my colleagues who authored or endorsed the majority Opinion, but with the equally profound conviction that, in this case, they have made a serious mistake, I record this dissent.

The majority's error, in my judgment, is not in their exposition of the underlying principles of law that must govern this case, but rather in the manner that they have applied those principles. The majority have trampled upon the first principle of appellate restraint. Under the guise of judging the sufficiency of the evidence presented against appellant, they have tacitly perhaps unwittingly, but nonetheless effectively substituted their own view of the evidence (and the inferences that may fairly be drawn from it) for that of the judge and jury. In so doing, they have not only improperly invaded the province allotted to those tribunals, but, at the same time, have perpetuated and given new life to myths about the crime of rape that have no place in our law today. . . .

Md. Annot. Code art. 27, § 463(a) considers three types of conduct as constituting second degree rape. We are concerned only with the first: a person is guilty of rape in the second degree if he (1) engages in vaginal intercourse with another person, (2) by force or threat of force, (3) against the will, and (4) without the consent of the other person. There is no real question here as to the first, third, or fourth elements of the crime. The evidence was certainly sufficient to show that appellant had vaginal intercourse with the victim, and that such act was against her will and without her consent. The point at issue is whether it was accomplished by force or threat of force; and I think that in viewing the evidence, that point should remain ever clear. Consent is not the issue here, only whether there was sufficient evidence of force or the threat of force.

Unfortunately, courts, including in the present case a majority of this one, often tend to confuse these two elements force and lack of consent and to think of them as one. They are not. They mean, and require, different things. What seems to cause the confusion—what, indeed, has become a common denominator of both elements—is the notion that the victim must actively resist the attack upon her. If she fails to offer sufficient resistance (sufficient to the satisfaction of the judge), a court is entitled, or at least presumes the entitlement, to find that there was no force or threat of force, or that the act was not against her will, or that she actually consented to it, or some unarticulated combination or synthesis of these elements that leads to the ultimate conclusion that the victim was not raped. Thus it is that the focus is almost entirely on the extent of resistance: The victim's acts, rather than those of her assailant. Attention is directed not to the wrongful stimulus, but to the victim's reactions to it. Right or wrong, that seems to be the current state of the Maryland law; and, notwithstanding its uniqueness in the criminal law, and its illogic, until changed by statute or the Court of Appeals, I accept it as binding.

But what is required of a woman being attacked or in danger of attack? How much resistance must she offer? Where is that line to be drawn between requiring that she either risk serious physical harm, perhaps death, on the one hand, or be termed a willing partner on the other? . . .

Pat was completely unfamiliar with appellant's neighborhood. She had no idea where she was. When she pulled up to where appellant said he lived, she put the car in park, but left the engine running. She said to appellant, "Well, here, you know, you are home." Appellant then asked Pat to come up with him and she refused. He persisted in his request, as did she in her refusal. She told him that even if she wanted to come up, she dared not do so. She was separated and it might cause marital problems for her. Finally, he reached over, turned off the ignition, took her keys, got out of the car, came around to her side, opened the door, and said to her, "Now, will you come up?"

It was at this point that Pat followed appellant to his apartment, and it is at this point that the majority of this Court begins to substitute its judgment for that of the trial court and jury. We know nothing about Pat and appellant. We don't know how big they are, what they look like, what their life experiences have been. We don't know if appellant is larger or smaller than she, stronger or weaker. We don't know what the inflection was in his voice as he dangled her car keys in front of her. We can't tell whether this was in a jocular vein or a truly threatening one. We have no idea what his mannerisms were. The trial judge and the jury could discern some of these things, of course, because they could observe the two people in court and could listen to what they said and how they said it. But all we know is that, between midnight and 1:00 A.M., in a neighborhood that was strange to Pat, appellant took her car keys, demanded that she accompany him, and most assuredly implied that unless she did so, at the very least, she might be stranded. . . .

———

Rusk v. State

Court of Appeals of Maryland
289 Md. 230, 424 A.2d 720 (1981)

Murphy, C.J.

. . . We think the reversal of Rusk's conviction by the Court of Special Appeals was in error for the fundamental reason so well expressed in the dissenting opinion by Judge Wilner when he observed that the majority had "trampled upon the first principle of appellate restraint . . . (because it had) substituted (its) own view of the evidence (and the inferences that may fairly be drawn from it) for that of the judge and jury . . . (and had thereby) improperly invaded the province allotted to those tribunals." In view of the evidence adduced at the trial, the reasonableness of Pat's apprehension of fear was plainly a question of fact for the jury to determine. . . . Of course, it was for the jury to observe the witnesses and their demeanor, and to judge their credibility and weigh their testimony. Quite obviously, the jury disbelieved Rusk and believed Pat's testimony. From her testimony, the jury could have reasonably concluded that the taking of her car keys was intended by Rusk to immobilize her alone, late at night, in a neighborhood with which she was not familiar; that after Pat had repeatedly refused to enter his apartment, Rusk commanded in firm tones that she do so; that Pat was badly frightened and feared that Rusk intended to rape her; that unable to think clearly and believing that she had no other choice in the circumstances, Pat entered Rusk's apartment; that once inside Pat asked permission to leave but Rusk told her to stay; that he then pulled Pat by the arms to the bed and undressed her; that Pat was afraid that Rusk would kill her unless she submitted; that she began to cry and Rusk then put his hands on her throat and began "lightly to choke" her; that Pat asked him if he would let her go without killing her if she complied with his demands; that Rusk gave an affirmative response, after which she finally submitted.

Just where persuasion ends and force begins in cases like the present is essentially a factual issue, to be resolved in light of the controlling legal precepts. That threats of force need not be made in any particular manner in order to put a person in fear of bodily harm is well established. Indeed, conduct, rather than words, may convey the threat. That a victim did not scream out for help or attempt to escape, while bearing on the question of consent, is unnecessary where she is restrained by fear of violence.

Considering all of the evidence in the case, with particular focus upon the actual force applied by Rusk to Pat's neck, we conclude that the jury could rationally find that the essential elements of second degree rape had been established and that Rusk was guilty of that offense beyond a reasonable doubt.

NOTES & QUESTIONS ON THREATS OF FORCE

1. *Threats of force.* Whether defined as constructive force or simply as a distinct prong in the statute, it is clear that threats of force are sufficient to generate a rape conviction, if the threats give the victim enough reason not to fight back. Whether the threat was sufficient to put the victim into a reasonable apprehension of violence is a question of fact for the jury to decide. Do you agree that Pat was laboring under a reasonable apprehension of violence? Even if a fact finder were to conclude that Rusk did not intend to produce this apprehension (which is debatable), do you think he was aware that Pat felt this way? What facts in the case support this inference? In *State v. Edwards*, 221 N.C. App. 434 (2012), the defendant's rape conviction was upheld because the defendant wielded a shotgun and verbally threatened the victim several times when she was in his house, told her that she could not leave, and eventually hit her. The court concluded that the sexual acts occurred during a period of captivity that constituted constructive force. Do you agree? Is it possible that a rape conviction could have been sustained under a theory of regular force as opposed to resorting to constructive force?

2. *Model Penal Code approach.*   In MPC § 213.1, the code drafters limited the crime of rape to threats of "imminent death, serious bodily injury, extreme pain or kidnapping." Is that standard too restrictive? What if the perpetrator threatens the victim with something less than extreme pain or seriously bodily injury? This would appear to be a grievous moral wrong deserving of punishment. Aware of this possibility, the drafters of the Model Penal Code crafted a separate offense of "gross sexual imposition," which is defined as sexual intercourse by a perpetrator who compels the victim to submit "by any threat that would prevent resistance by a woman of ordinary resolution." See MPC § 213.1(2). The drafters concluded that the provision "rests on the judgment that using one's ability to cause harm in order to override the will of a reluctant female is wrongful and should be punished. Although threat of economic injury may be deemed less serious than threat of physical attack, threat of either description may be sufficient to deny the freedom of choice that the law or rape and related offenses seeks to protect and to subject a woman to unwanted and degrading sexual intimacy." For example, imagine a high school teacher who coerces a student into a sexual relationship by threatening to fail the student or threatening to have the student expelled from school. Or, consider a government employee who threatens to terminate the victim's entitlement to a food stamp program unless she submits to a sexual relationship. If either threat is one that would prevent resistance by someone "of ordinary resolution," it would constitute gross sexual imposition.

3. Consent

Simply put, jurisdictions are split over how to understand lack of consent. Which part is more important, that the victim did not consent or that the perpetrator *knew* that the act was non-consensual? These are different phenomena. In reading the following case, ask yourself how rape's mental element should be defined and what that implies for the relevance of a mistake of fact argument.

Commonwealth v. Lopez
Supreme Judicial Court of Massachusetts
433 Mass. 722, 745 N.E.2d 961 (2001)

SPINA, J.

The defendant, Kenny Lopez, was convicted on two indictments charging rape and one indictment charging indecent assault and battery on a person over the age of fourteen years. We granted his application for direct appellate review. The defendant claims error in the judge's refusal to give a mistake of fact instruction to the jury. He asks us to recognize a defendant's honest and reasonable belief as to a complainant's consent as a defense to the crime of rape, and to reverse his convictions and grant him a new trial. Based on the record presented, we decline to do so, and affirm the convictions.

BACKGROUND

We summarize facts that the jury could have found. On May 8, 1998, the victim, a seventeen year old girl, was living in a foster home in Springfield. At approximately 3 P.M., she started walking to a restaurant where she had planned to meet her biological mother. On the way, she encountered the defendant. He introduced himself, asked where she was going, and offered to walk with her. The victim met her mother and introduced the defendant as her friend. The defendant said that he lived in the same foster home as the victim and that "they knew each other from school." Sometime later, the defendant left to make a telephone call. When the victim left the restaurant, the defendant was waiting outside and offered to walk her home. She agreed.

The two walked to a park across the street from the victim's foster home and talked for approximately twenty to thirty minutes. The victim's foster sisters were within earshot, and the victim feared that she would be caught violating her foster mother's rules against bringing "a guy near the house." The defendant suggested that they take a walk in the woods nearby. At one point, deep in the woods, the victim said that she wanted to go home. The defendant said, "trust me," and assured her that nothing would happen and that he would not hurt her. The defendant led the victim down a path to a secluded area.

The defendant asked the victim why she was so distant and said that he wanted to start a relationship with her. She said that she did not want to "get into any relationship." The defendant began making sexual innuendos to which the victim did not respond. He grabbed her by her wrist and began kissing her on the lips. She pulled away and said, "No, I don't want to do this." The defendant then told the victim that if she "had sex with him, [she] would love him more." She repeated, "No, I don't want to. I don't want to do this." He raised her shirt and touched her breasts. She immediately pulled her shirt down and pushed him away.

The defendant then pushed the victim against a slate slab, unbuttoned her pants, and pulled them down. Using his legs to pin down her legs, he produced a condom and asked her to put it on him. The victim said, "No." The defendant put the condom on and told the victim that he wanted her to put his penis inside her. She said, "No." He then raped her, and she began to cry. A few minutes later, the victim made a "jerking move" to her left. The defendant became angry, turned her around, pushed her face into the slate, and raped her again. The treating physician described the bruising to the victim's knees as "significant." The physician opined that there had been "excessive force and trauma to the [vaginal] area." . . .

The defendant told the victim that she "would get in a lot of trouble" if she said anything. He then grabbed her by the arm, kissed her, and said, "I'll see you later." The victim went home and showered. She told her foster mother, who immediately dialed 911. The victim cried hysterically as she spoke to the 911 operator.

The defendant's version of the encounter was diametrically opposed to that of the victim. He testified that the victim had been a willing and active partner in consensual sexual intercourse. Specifically, the defendant claimed that the victim initiated intimate activity, and never once told him to stop. Additionally, the defendant testified that the victim invited him to a party that evening so that he could meet her friends. The defendant further claimed that when he told her that he would be unable to attend, the victim appeared "mildly upset."

Before the jury retired, defense counsel requested a mistake of fact instruction as to consent. The judge declined to give the instruction, saying that, based "both on the law, as well as on the facts, that instruction is not warranted." Because the defendant's theory at trial was that the victim actually consented and not that the defendant was "confused, misled, or mistaken" as to the victim's willingness to engage in sexual intercourse, the judge concluded that the ultimate question for the jury was simply whether they believed the victim's or the defendant's version of the encounter. The decision not to give the instruction provides the basis for this appeal.

MISTAKE OF FACT INSTRUCTION

The defendant claims that the judge erred in failing to give his proposed mistake of fact instruction. The defendant, however, was not entitled to this instruction. In *Commonwealth v. Ascolillo,* 405 Mass. 456, 541 N.E.2d 570 (1989), we held that the defendant was not entitled to a mistake of fact instruction, and declined to adopt a rule that "in order to establish the crime of rape the Commonwealth must prove *in every case* not only that the defendant intended intercourse but also that he did not act pursuant to an honest and reasonable belief that the victim consented" (emphasis added). Neither the plain language of our rape statute nor this court's decisions prior to the *Ascolillo* decision warrant a different result.

A fundamental tenet of criminal law is that culpability requires a showing that the prohibited conduct (actus reus) was committed with the concomitant mental state (mens rea) prescribed for the offense. The mistake of fact "defense" is available where the mistake negates the existence of a mental state essential to a material element of the offense. . . . In determining whether the defendant's honest and reasonable belief as to the victim's consent would relieve him of culpability, it is necessary to review the required elements of the crime of rape.

At common law, rape was defined as "the carnal knowledge of a woman forcibly and against her will." 4 W. Blackstone, Commentaries 210. Since 1642, rape has been proscribed by statute in this Commonwealth. While there have been several revisions to this statute, the definition and the required elements of the crime have remained essentially unchanged since its original enactment. The current rape statute, G.L. c. 265, § 22(b), provides in pertinent part:

> Whoever has sexual intercourse or unnatural sexual intercourse with a person and compels such person to submit by force and against his will, or compels such person to submit by threat of bodily injury, shall be punished by imprisonment in the state prison for not more than twenty years.

This statute follows the common-law definition of rape, and requires the Commonwealth to prove beyond a reasonable doubt that the defendant committed (1) sexual intercourse (2) by force or threat of force and against the will of the victim. See *Commonwealth v. Sherry*, 386 Mass. 682, 687 (1982) ("The essence of the crime of rape, whether aggravated or unaggravated, is sexual intercourse with another compelled by force and against the victim's will or compelled by threat of bodily injury.").

As to the first element, there has been very little disagreement. Sexual intercourse is defined as penetration of the victim, regardless of degree. The second element has proven to be more complicated. We have construed the element, "by force and against his will," as truly encompassing two separate elements each of which must independently be satisfied. Therefore, the Commonwealth must demonstrate beyond a reasonable doubt that the defendant committed sexual intercourse (1) by means of physical force; nonphysical, constructive force; or threats of bodily harm, either explicit or implicit; and (2) at the time of penetration, there was no consent.

Although the Commonwealth must prove lack of consent, the "elements necessary for rape do not require that the defendant intend the intercourse be without consent." Historically, the relevant inquiry has been limited to consent in fact, and no mens rea or knowledge as to the lack of consent has ever been required.

A mistake of fact as to consent, therefore, has very little application to our rape statute. Because G.L. c. 265, § 22, does not require proof of a defendant's knowledge of the victim's lack of consent or intent to engage in nonconsensual intercourse as a material element of the offense, a mistake as to that consent cannot, therefore, negate a mental state required for commission of the prohibited conduct. Any perception (reasonable, honest, or otherwise) of the defendant as to the victim's consent is consequently not relevant to a rape prosecution.

This is not to say, contrary to the defendant's suggestion, that the absence of any mens rea as to the consent element transforms rape into a strict liability crime. It does not. Rape, at common law and pursuant to G.L. c. 265, § 22, is a general intent crime, and proof that a defendant intended sexual intercourse by force coupled with proof that the victim did not in fact consent is sufficient to maintain a conviction.

Other jurisdictions have held that a mistake of fact instruction is necessary to prevent injustice. New Jersey, for instance, does not require the force necessary for rape to be anything more than what is needed to accomplish penetration. See *In re M.T.S.*, 129 N.J. 422, 444 (1992) ("physical force in excess of that inherent in the act of sexual penetration is not required for such penetration to be unlawful"). Thus, an instruction as to a defendant's honest and reasonable belief as to consent is available in New Jersey to mitigate the undesirable and unforeseen consequences that may flow from this construction. By contrast, in this Commonwealth, unless the putative victim has been rendered incapable of consent, the prosecution must prove that the defendant compelled the victim's submission by use of physical force; nonphysical, constructive force; or threat of force. Proof of the element of force, therefore, should negate any possible mistake as to consent.

We also have concerns that the mistake of fact defense would tend to eviscerate the long-standing rule in this Commonwealth that victims need not use any force to resist an attack. A shift in focus from the victim's to the defendant's state of mind might require victims to use physical force in order to communicate an unqualified lack of consent to defeat any honest and reasonable belief as to consent. The mistake of fact defense is incompatible with the evolution of our jurisprudence with respect to the crime of rape.

We are cognizant that our interpretation is not shared by the majority of other jurisdictions. States that recognize a mistake of fact as to consent generally have done so by legislation. Some State statutes expressly require a showing of a defendant's intent as to nonconsent. Alaska, for example, requires proof of a culpable state of mind. "Lack of consent is a 'surrounding circumstance' which under the Revised Code, requires a complementary mental state as well as conduct to constitute a crime." Because no specific mental state is mentioned in Alaska's statute governing sexual assault in the first degree, the State "must prove that the defendant acted 'recklessly' regarding his putative victim's lack of consent." So understood, an honest and reasonable mistake as to consent would negate the culpability requirement attached to the element of consent.

The New Jersey statute defines sexual assault (rape) as "any act of sexual penetration engaged in by the defendant without the affirmative and freely-given permission of the victim to the specific act of penetration."

A defendant, by claiming that he had permission to engage in sexual intercourse, places his state of mind directly in issue. The jury must then determine "whether the defendant's belief that the alleged victim had freely given affirmative permission was reasonable."

The mistake of fact "defense" has been recognized by judicial decision in some States. In 1975, the Supreme Court of California became the first State court to recognize a mistake of fact defense in rape cases. See *People v. Mayberry*, 15 Cal. 3d 143 (1975) (en banc). Although the court did not make a specific determination that intent was required as to the element of consent, it did conclude that, "[i]f a defendant entertains a reasonable and bona fide belief that a prosecutrix [*sic*] voluntarily consented . . . to engage in sexual intercourse, it is apparent he does not possess the wrongful intent that is a prerequisite under Penal Code section 20 to a conviction of . . . rape by means of force or threat." Thus, the intent required is an intent to engage in nonconsensual sexual intercourse, and the State must prove that a defendant intentionally engaged in intercourse and was at least negligent regarding consent.

Other State courts have employed a variety of different constructions in adopting the mistake of fact defense. . . . However, the minority of States sharing our view is significant. . . .

This case does not persuade us that we should recognize a mistake of fact as to consent as a defense to rape in *all* cases. Whether such a defense might, in some circumstances, be appropriate is a difficult question that we may consider on a future case where a defendant's claim of reasonable mistake of fact is at least arguably supported by the evidence. This is not such a case.

People v. Newton
New York Court of Appeals
8 N.Y.3d 460 (2007)

READ, J.

On March 19, 2003, defendant James W. Newton, Jr. was indicted for the crimes of sodomy in the first degree, sexual abuse in the first degree, and sodomy in the third degree. The three-count indictment accused defendant of engaging in oral sex with a 19-year-old male by forcible compulsion and without consent (by virtue of something other than incapacity). In light of these allegations, a declaration of delinquency charged defendant with violating the conditions of the sentence of probation imposed upon him in 2000 after his conviction for second-degree assault. Defendant contended that the alleged victim did not resist or otherwise communicate a lack of consent, and that he perceived the sexual act to be consensual. It is undisputed that defendant had been consuming beer steadily in the hours before this incident.

At trial, defense counsel asked the court to instruct the jury on intoxication with respect to both sodomy counts. See Penal Law § 15.25 (while "(i)ntoxication is not, as such, a defense to a criminal charge," evidence of a defendant's intoxication may be offered whenever "relevant to negative an element of the crime charged"). Instead, the court charged the jury on intoxication with respect to first-degree sodomy only, reasoning that this crime called for the factfinder to conclude beyond a reasonable doubt that defendant intended to engage in forcible compulsion. See *People v. Williams*, 81 N.Y.2d 303, 316-317 (1993) ("intent is implicitly an element of" first-degree rape and first-degree sodomy, and "(t)he intent required is the intent to perform the prohibited act—i.e., the intent to forcibly compel another to engage in intercourse or sodomy").

Regarding third-degree sodomy, however, the court instructed the jury that "intoxication is not a defense under any circumstances" because there was no element of intent or other subjective mental state required for this crime. "Rather, . . . sodomy in the third degree involves an allegation that a reasonable person in the defendant's situation would have understood the . . . alleged victim's words and acts as an expression of a lack of consent." As a result, the court charged the jury that "if the defendant failed to so understand solely as a result of intoxication[,] such would not be a defense under the law" to third-degree sodomy. The jury ultimately acquitted defendant of sodomy in the first degree, and convicted him of sodomy in the third degree . . .

To be guilty of third-degree sodomy under Penal Law § 130.40(3), defendant was required to have engaged in the sexual act "with another person without such person's consent where such lack of consent [was] by reason of some factor other than incapacity to consent." The Sexual Assault Reform Act fleshed out this crime by specially defining "lack of consent" for purposes of third-degree sodomy as

> circumstances under which, at the time of the [sexual act], the victim clearly expressed that he or she did not consent to engage in such act, and a reasonable person in the actor's situation would have understood such person's words and acts as an expression of lack of consent to such act under all the circumstances.

Penal Law § 130.05(2)(d). This provision was

> designed to address the so-called date rape or acquaintance rape situations [where] there [might] be consent to various acts leading up to the sexual act, but at the time of the act, the victim clearly says no or

otherwise expresses a lack of consent, and a reasonable person in the actor's situation would understand that the victim was expressing a lack of consent.

Donnino, Main Volume Supp. Practice Commentary, McKinney's Cons. Laws of N.Y., Book 39, Penal Law art. 130, at 220. Further,

"[t]he use of the term 'reasonable person' in the 'actor's situation' imports an objective element into the determination of whether there was a clear expression of non-consent to the [sexual act]. Although the 'reasonable person' must stand in the shoes of the actor, if such a person would understand that the victim was expressing a lack of consent, *then it does not matter that the accused thought otherwise*."

In short, the proper inquiry for the factfinder is not whether a defendant actually perceives a lack of consent, but whether the victim, by words or actions, clearly expresses an unwillingness to engage in the sexual act in such a way that a neutral observer would have understood that the victim was not consenting. Otherwise, it would not be enough for a victim simply to say "No." Every prosecution would devolve into a dispute over whether the particular defendant might have misapprehended whether "No" really meant "No" for one reason or another. As the People point out, if the Legislature had, in fact, intended to take a defendant's subjective mental state into account, it could have drafted the statute to require the accused to know or have reason to know that the victim was not consenting; or the Legislature could have furnished an accused with an affirmative defense of lack of knowledge. See, e.g., N.Y. Penal Law § 130.10(1) (providing for an affirmative defense of lack of knowledge of incapacity where victim's lack of consent is based solely upon incapacity to consent because of mental disability, mental incapacity or physical helplessness).

Because a defendant's subjective mental state is not an element of the crime of third-degree sodomy, evidence of intoxication at the time of the sexual act is irrelevant. Thus, the trial judge in this case properly declined to instruct the jury on intoxication with respect to the charge of this crime . . .

NOTES & QUESTIONS ON CONSENT

1. *Mistake of fact and resistance.*   What is the relationship between mistakes of fact and the old resistance requirement? In Massachusetts, a defendant cannot claim mistake of fact regarding a victim's consent. The *Lopez* court argued that allowing the mistake of fact defense might force victims into an impossible choice. If they do not fight back, the defendant might later argue that he was laboring under a mistake of fact, because he took the victim's

lack of resistance as a false indication of consent. This would end with the defendant's acquittal. On the other hand, if the victim fights back vigorously to remove any doubt in the perpetrator's mind, the victim might get beaten up or even killed by the perpetrator. The court concluded that the law should not impose this inappropriate choice on the victim.

2. *The reasonable person standard.* In New York, lack of consent is understood according to a reasonable person standard. As the New York State Court of Appeals explained in *Newton*, what matters is not whether the defendant was subjectively aware that the victim was not consenting, but whether a reasonable person in the actor's situation would be aware that the victim was not consenting. Should the "actor's situation" include the actor's state of intoxication? In other words, in a case where the defendant was intoxicated, should the court ask whether a reasonable sober person would have perceived the lack of consent or whether a reasonable drunk person would have perceived the lack of consent? Based on the outcome of the *Newton* case, which rule was the court articulating?

3. *Mistake of fact and ambiguity.* In jurisdictions that allow mistakes of fact regarding consent, the defendant must usually establish that the situation was ambiguous in some way. Why impose this as a restriction on mistake of fact arguments? In order to understand the limitation, remember that the mistake doctrine only applies if the victim did not consent to the encounter and the defendant was mistaken regarding this fact. If the defendant testifies that the victim unambiguously and expressly consented to the encounter, how can the defendant also claim that he was mistaken about the victim's state of mind? In *Tyson v. State*, 619 N.E.2d 276 (Ind. App. 1993), the boxer Mike Tyson tried to argue mistake of fact. The court disallowed the defense because it concluded there was no factual basis for Tyson to argue that he was confused regarding the victim's consent. Tyson's testimony at trial was that the victim unambiguously consented. If that is the defendant's version of events, the defendant is not entitled to a jury instruction on mistake of fact. In other words, the defendant cannot have it both ways: Either the defendant argues that the victim consented or the defendant argues that the victim did not consent and the defendant was mistaken about this fact. But the defendant cannot make both arguments at once.

4. *Sleeping and consent.* Victims are incapable of consenting in certain situations, such as being asleep. Some state statutes conclude that legally valid consent is absent if the victim is either "physically helpless" or asleep. *State v. Stevens*, 311 Mont. 52 (2002) (massage therapist performed act on client who was sleeping and therefore incapable of expressing consent). But consider *State v. Smith*, 170 N.C. App. 461, 613 S.E.2d 304 (2005). In *Smith*, the trial court gave the following instruction to the jury: "Force and lack of consent are implied in law if at the time . . . the victim is sleeping or

similarly incapacitated." On appeal, the instruction was deemed deficient because the court never explained to the jury that the legal implication of non-consent could be rebutted by the defendant. In other words, the appeals court concluded that the trial judge confused a mandatory presumption with a permissive inference. The trial judge suggested to the jury that they were *required* to assume that sleeping negated consent, while he should have told them that they were *entitled* to infer non-consent from sleeping. What kind of evidence would be sufficient to rebut the presumption that a sleeping individual is not consenting to sexual relations? See note 4, immediately below.

5. *Pre-consent and retroactive consent.* What if the victim consents in advance to sexual intercourse during a state of unconsciousness? For example, what if a married individual tells her partner that he has permission to initiate sex during sleep—should the law protect this arrangement or discourage it? In 2011, the Canadian Supreme Court heard a case involving the consent of an unconscious partner. *Regina v. J.A.*, 2 S.C.R. 440 (2011). During sex, J.A. choked his partner, K.D., until she lost consciousness. They then engaged in various sexual practices. K.D. had consented to both the choking and the sexual relations, and she had anticipated that she might lose consciousness during the events. The Canadian Supreme Court concluded this was rape because the consent was not contemporaneous with the sex. Specifically, the court concluded that "Parliament defined consent in a way that requires the complainant to be conscious throughout the sexual activity in question." Consent procured prior to the sexual event is not valid if the defendant is not conscious during the act itself. In other words, it is never lawful to engage in sexual relations with an unconscious partner because the partner—by definition—is incapable to expressing consent at the moment when the act occurs.

Most situations like *Regina v. J.A.* will not reach a court because the consenting partner will not file a police complaint if she desired the event. However, in *J.A.*, the victim first told police that she did not consent to the sex. She later conceded that she had consented to the sex and had only lied to the police because she became embroiled in a child custody dispute with her partner. At this point, the Supreme Court ruled that the change in story was immaterial and that even if she had consented in advance, that consent was legally ineffective.

4. Rape by Fraud

What types of fraud vitiate the victim's consent? As the following case demonstrates, the fraud has to rise to a particularly high level (fraud in the factum) before it is deemed rape. In reading the following case, ask yourself why the law distinguishes between fraud in the factum and fraud in the inducement, and whether the rule is overbroad or under-broad.

Boro v. Superior Court

Court of Appeal, First District, California
163 Cal. App. 3d 1224, 210 Cal. Rptr. 122 (1985)

NEWSOM, J.

By timely petition filed with this court, petitioner Daniel Boro seeks a writ of prohibition to restrain further prosecution of count II of the information on file against him in San Mateo County Superior Court . . . charging him with a violation of Penal Code section 261(4), rape: "an act of sexual intercourse accomplished with a person not the spouse of the perpetrator, under any of the following circumstances: . . . (4) Where a person is at the time unconscious of the nature of the act, and this is known to the accused."

Petitioner contends that his motion to dismiss should have been granted with regard to count II because the evidence at the preliminary hearing proved that the prosecutrix, Ms. R., was aware of the "nature of the act" within the meaning of section 261(4). The Attorney General contends the opposite, arguing that the victim's agreement to intercourse was predicated on a belief—fraudulently induced by petitioner—that the sex act was necessary to save her life, and that she was hence unconscious of the *nature* of the act within the meaning of the statute.

In relevant part the factual background may be summarized as follows. Ms. R., the rape victim, was employed as a clerk at the Holiday Inn in South San Francisco when, on March 30, 1984, at about 8:45 A.M., she received a telephone call from a person who identified himself as "Dr. Stevens" and said that he worked at Peninsula Hospital.

"Dr. Stevens" told Ms. R. that he had the results of her blood test and that she had contracted a dangerous, highly infectious and perhaps fatal disease; that she could be sued as a result; that the disease came from using public toilets; and that she would have to tell him the identity of all her friends who would then have to be contacted in the interest of controlling the spread of the disease.

"Dr. Stevens" further explained that there were only two ways to treat the disease. The first was a painful surgical procedure—graphically described—costing $9,000, and requiring her uninsured hospitalization for six weeks. A second alternative, "Dr. Stevens" explained, was to have sexual intercourse with an anonymous donor who had been injected with a serum which would cure the disease. The latter, nonsurgical procedure would only cost $4,500. When the victim replied that she lacked sufficient funds the "doctor" suggested that $1,000 would suffice as a down payment. The victim thereupon agreed to the nonsurgical alternative and consented to intercourse with the mysterious donor, believing "it was the only choice I had."

After discussing her intentions with her work supervisor, the victim proceeded to the Hyatt Hotel in Burlingame as instructed, and contacted

"Dr. Stevens" by telephone. The latter became furious when he learned Ms. R. had informed her employer of the plan, and threatened to terminate his treatment, finally instructing her to inform her employer she had decided not to go through with the treatment. Ms. R. did so, then went to her bank, withdrew $1,000 and, as instructed, checked into another hotel and called "Dr. Stevens" to give him her room number.

About a half hour later the defendant "donor" arrived at her room. When Ms. R. had undressed, the "donor," petitioner, after urging her to relax, had sexual intercourse with her.

At the time of penetration, it was Ms. R.'s belief that she would die unless she consented to sexual intercourse with the defendant: as she testified, "My life felt threatened, and for that reason and that reason alone did I do it."

Petitioner was apprehended when the police arrived at the hotel room, having been called by Ms. R.'s supervisor. Petitioner was identified as "Dr. Stevens" at a police voice lineup by another potential victim of the same scheme. . . .

The People's position is stated concisely: "We contend, quite simply, that at the time of the intercourse Ms. R., the victim, was 'unconscious of the nature of the act': because of [petitioner's] misrepresentation she believed it was in the nature of a medical treatment and not a simple, ordinary act of sexual intercourse." Petitioner, on the other hand, stresses that the victim was plainly aware of the *nature* of the act in which she voluntarily engaged, so that her motivation in doing so (since it did not fall within the proscription of section 261(2)) is irrelevant.

Our research discloses sparse California authority on the subject. A victim need not be totally and physically unconscious in order that section 261(4) apply. In *People v. Minkowski*, 204 Cal. App. 2d 832, 23 Cal. Rptr. 92 (1962), the defendant was a physician who "treated" several victims for menstrual cramps. Each victim testified that she was treated in a position with her back to the doctor, bent over a table, with feet apart, in a dressing gown. And in each case the "treatment" consisted of the defendant first inserting a metal instrument, then substituting an instrument which "felt different"—the victims not realizing that the second instrument was in fact the doctor's penis. The precise issue before us was never tendered in *People v. Minkowski* because the petitioner there *conceded* the sufficiency of evidence to support the element of consciousness.

The decision is useful to this analysis, however, because it exactly illustrates certain traditional rules in the area of our inquiry. Thus, as a leading authority has written, "if deception causes a misunderstanding as to the fact itself (fraud in the *factum*) there is no legally-recognized consent because what happened is not that for which consent was given; whereas consent induced by fraud is as effective as any other consent, so far as direct and immediate legal consequences are concerned, if the deception relates not to the thing done but merely to some collateral matter (fraud in the inducement)." Perkins & Boyce, Criminal Law 1079 (3d ed. 1982).

The victims in *Minkowski* consented, not to sexual intercourse, but to an act of an altogether different nature, penetration by medical instrument. The consent was to a pathological, and not a carnal, act, and the mistake was, therefore, in the *factum* and not merely in the inducement. . . .

. . . [In the present case] her testimony was clear that she precisely understood the "nature of the act," but, motivated by a fear of disease, and death, succumbed to petitioner's fraudulent blandishments.

To so conclude is not to vitiate the heartless cruelty of petitioner's scheme, but to say that it comprised crimes of a different order. . . .

NOTES & QUESTIONS ON FRAUD

1. *Fraud in the factum versus fraud in the inducement.*   The settled rule in American jurisdictions produces unsatisfactory results. The victim in *Boro* was duped into consenting to sex—shouldn't that fact vitiate her consent since it was procured under false pretenses? One way of understanding the rule, for what it is worth, is that it produces a relatively clear categorization that is easy to apply. However, one cost of this categorization is that the rule is under-inclusive and fails to describe some situations as rape that truly deserve the label. What is the alternative? If courts allowed fraud in the inducement to vitiate consent, how would they distinguish between the serious fraud found in *Boro* with the more mundane fraud of a suitor who exaggerates his or her employment status or net worth? Can you think of a more satisfying way? For a discussion, see Joel Feinberg, *Victims' Excuses: The Case of Fraudulently Procured Consent*, 96 Ethics 330 (1986); Stuart P. Green, *Lies, Rape, and Statutory Rape*, in *Law and Lies: Deception and Truth-Telling in the American Legal System* (Austin Sarat ed., 2015).

2. *Legislative solution.*   After *Boro*, California amended § 261 to include within rape's ambit any situation where the victim "was not aware, knowing, perceiving, or cognizant of the essential characteristics of the act due to the perpetrator's fraudulent representation that the sexual penetration served a professional purpose when it served no professional purpose." Cal. Penal Code § 261(4)(D). However, some other jurisdictions have no such rule. Some statutes penalize sexual relations between doctors and patients as non-consensual based on the nature of the doctor-patient relationship, but what if the doctor is not a real doctor at all?

3. *Extortion.* Could Daniel Boro be prosecuted for extortion instead of rape? Why or why not? Consider Model Penal Code § 223.4 on "Theft by Extortion" or § 223.3 on "Theft by Deception." The first states that "a person is guilty of theft if he purposely obtains property of another by deception" and the second states that "a person is guilty of theft if he obtains property of another by threatening. . . ." Can sex ever constitute "property"? Arguably not, which explains why prosecutors do not punish fraud in the inducement rape cases as extortion or fraud. But see Donald A. Dripps, *Beyond Rape: An Essay on the Difference Between the Presence of Force and the Absence of Consent*, 92 Colum. L. Rev. 1780, 1786 (1992) (suggesting that rape involves the theft of a commodity—sex). As Dripps explains: "This is a quite unromantic notion of sex, a view I shall call the commodity theory. In the labor market at large, overwhelming considerations of dignity and efficiency support assigning the entitlement to a person's body to that person. According to the commodity theory, sexual cooperation is a service much like any other, which individuals have a right to offer for compensation, or not, as they choose." Do you agree with this interpretation of sex?

4. *Impersonation cases.* Although the distinction between fraud in the factum and fraud in the inducement is well settled in the United States, there is lingering confusion over how to deal with cases of mistaken identity. In the typical case, the victim wakes up and engages in sexual relations with a person that the victim assumes to be his partner. Some jurisdictions classify this as fraud in the inducement—and therefore not rape—since the victim is clearly aware that he is engaging in sex. Under this view, the identity of the partner is not an essential feature of the sexual act. See *Suliveres v. Commonwealth*, 865 N.E.2d 1086, 1088 (Mass. 2007) (man who impersonated his own brother to have sex with his brother's girlfriend could not be prosecuted for rape). However, other jurisdictions punish such cases as rape—as long as the victim is married—under the theory that the identity of the spouse is an essential feature of marital sex. Under this view, the impersonation constitutes fraud in the factum because the partner is consenting to *marital sex*—not adultery, an altogether different act. This view might have made sense in an older era when adultery was a crime, but should the theory remain viable today? What is the relevant factum, sex or the partner? A few jurisdictions now criminalize *any* impersonation during sex. Cal. Penal Code § 261(a)(4) ("a person submits under the belief that the person committing the act is someone known to the victim other than the accused, and this belief is induced by any artifice, pretense, or concealment practiced by the accused, with intent to induce the belief"). For a discussion, see Jacqueline Syrnick, *Challenging the Use of Fraud to Get into Bed After* Suliveres v. Commonwealth—*A Call for Legislative Reform*, 43 New Eng. L. Rev. 321, 337 (2009) (describing a Tennessee statute that defines fraud as including any "deceit, trickery, misrepresentation and subterfuge").

PROBLEM CASE

In 2010, a District Court in Jerusalem convicted Sabbar Kashur of rape. The conviction arose from a plea agreement and a stipulation of facts negotiated between the prosecution and the defense. According to that stipulation, Kashur procured the consent of a woman to engage in sex after representing to her that he was a Jewish man interested in a lasting relationship that could result in having children and raising a family. On the contrary, neither of these facts were correct. Kashur was neither Jewish nor looking to settle down and raise a family. Kashur was Arab and already married to someone else.

The District Court entered a conviction for rape under the theory that the fraudulent misrepresentations vitiated the consent of the victim. Israeli law, like many foreign jurisdictions, does not recognize the fraud in the factum and fraud in the inducement distinction that operates in American and other common law courts. The *Kashur* case received widespread publicity in Israel, in part for the ethnic nature of the misrepresentation and resulting rape conviction.

Under the Israeli approach to resolving rape by deception cases, the court asks whether the defendant's misrepresentations were critical to the victim's decision to consent and then secondly whether the victim's consideration of those elements was objectively reasonable or not. The last element of the standard is designed to preclude cases where the defendant's consent would have hinged on unreasonable or truly marginal factors. For more comparative analysis of fraudulent rape cases, see Amit Pundik, *Coercion and Deception in Sexual Relations*, 28 Can. J.L. Juris. 97 (2015).

Sabbar Kashur

5. Statutory Rape and Legal Barriers to Consent

As explained above, it is best to understand statutory rape as a crime that involves a legal barrier to effective consent to sexual relations. The typical cases involve partners who are too young to consent. But other sexual situations also involve relationships that, by statute, vitiate any putative consent between the partners. In most jurisdictions, that makes the defendant responsible for either rape or sometimes a lesser offense specifically drafted by the legislature to respond to particular instances of predatory conduct. Read the following case to understand the factual circumstances that can prevent the establishment of consent as a matter of law.

State v. Hirschfelder

Supreme Court of Washington
170 Wash. 2d 536 (2010)

Stephens, J.

This case requires us to interpret the statutory language prohibiting sexual relations between a student and a school employee. At issue is whether, under the statute, the term "minor" includes students between the ages of 18 and 21, or just those under 18. Also at issue is whether the statute is unconstitutionally vague or violates the defendant's right to equal protection. We reverse the Court of Appeals and hold that the statute at issue criminalizes sexual misconduct between school employees and full time registered students 16 or older. We further hold that the statute is neither unconstitutionally vague nor violative of the defendant's equal protection rights.

FACTS AND PROCEDURAL HISTORY

Matthew Hirschfelder was employed as a choir teacher at Hoquiam High School. He had sexual intercourse in his office with a member of the high school choir, A.N.T., several days prior to her graduation in 2006. At the time, Hirschfelder was 33 and A.N.T. was 18. Hirschfelder was charged with sexual misconduct with a minor in the first degree under former RCW 9A.44.093(1)(b). That statute provided in relevant part:

> A person is guilty of sexual misconduct with a minor in the first degree when: . . . the person is a school employee who has, or knowingly causes another person under the age of eighteen to have, sexual intercourse with a registered student of the school who is at least sixteen years old and not married to the employee, if the employee is at least sixty months older than the student.

Former RCW 9A.44.093(1)(b).

Hirschfelder filed a motion to dismiss the charge . . . arguing that because the statute criminalized sexual intercourse with "minors," he committed no crime when he had sexual intercourse with an 18-year-old adult. . . .

STATUTORY INTERPRETATION

. . . Hirschfelder argues that the former statute, entitled "[s]exual misconduct with a minor in the first degree," was not intended to criminalize sexual intercourse between school employees and registered students age 18 or older because of the statute's use of the term "minor." Alternatively, Hirschfelder argues that the term "minor" is ambiguous and that we should apply the rule of lenity to resolve the ambiguity in his favor. The Court of Appeals agreed with Hirschfelder, concluding "that for the purposes of

RCW 9A.44.093(1)(b), the common and legal definitions of 'students' conflict with those of 'minor' because the two words refer to groups who may be of differing age ranges (between 18 and 21 and under 18, respectively)." The Court of Appeals turned to the former statute's legislative history and concluded that the legislature intended that former RCW 9A.44.093(1)(b) criminalize only the behavior of school employees who have sexual intercourse with registered students who are 16 or 17 years old. . . .

Focusing as we must on the plain language of the statute, we conclude that former RCW 9A.44.093(1)(b) prohibits sexual relations between school employees and registered students. The word "minor" is self-defined by the specific descriptions of the victims in each of the alternative scenarios under the statute's sections. Under the subsection at issue, a minor is a registered student of the school who is at least 16 years old. Former RCW 9A.44.093(1)(b). At the time of the incident with A.N.T., a registered student included an individual up to 21 years of age. Thus, "minor" as used in former RCW 9A.44.093(1)(b) includes registered students between the ages of 16 and 21. Reading "minor" as Hirschfelder urges—to exclude those students 18 or older—renders the words "registered student" in the statute meaningless.

Hirschfelder argues that "minor" as it is used in the provision at issue must exclude students 18 or older because a separate statute, RCW 26.28.010, provides that a person has reached the age of majority, and is therefore no longer a minor according to dictionary definition, at age 18 *unless otherwise specified by law.* This argument is unpersuasive. A registered student is a minor for the purposes of former RCW 9A.44.093(1)(b), and a registered student is specified by law to include persons up to the age of 21. By its terms, RCW 26.28.010's definition of "minor" does not apply to former RCW 9A.44.093(1)(b). . . .

Hirschfelder, however, argues that former RCW 9A.44.093(1)(b) is ambiguous, and that the rule of lenity should resolve this case in his favor. We do not agree that the statute at issue is ambiguous, reasoning as we do that the word "minor" in the context of the statute plainly includes registered students age 16 to 21. Even if we were to agree that the statute is ambiguous, we would not be forced to turn to the rule of lenity. "If a statute is ambiguous, the rule of lenity requires us to interpret the statute in favor of the defendant *absent legislative intent to the contrary.*" Here, there is legislative intent to the contrary. When RCW 9A.44.093(1)(b) was first introduced as House Bill 1091, it prohibited sex between a school employee and a student 16 or 17 years old. A substitute bill removed the "under the age of 18" requirement. A legislative report explained that "[t]he substitute bill eliminates the requirement that the student be under the age of 18, thus covering registered students over the age of 18 who are completing independent education plans." The bill, as eventually passed by the legislature, contained no requirement that the student victim be under 18. Legislative history therefore suggests the legislature intended to criminalize sex with any registered student age 16 or older. . . .

In the end, a common sense reading of former RCW 9A.44.093(1)(b) must prevail. We hold that the former statute's plain language unambiguously defines minor as a registered student and thus includes students up to the age of 21. Because the statute is unambiguous, we need not resort to interpretive tools such as legislative history, but nevertheless note that the history supports our plain reading. We also stress that the result here is by no means novel. Several of our sexual misconduct laws focus on the special relationship between a perpetrator and a victim, even where the victim is over 18 or even 21. For example, we criminalize sex with vulnerable adults or adults over whom the perpetrator has supervisory authority, RCW 9A.44.050, and sex between employees of custodial institutions and those in custody. RCW 9A. 44.160. That the legislature saw fit to criminalize sex between school employees and high school students—even those who reach the age of majority while registered as students—is a policy choice that recognizes the special position of trust and authority teachers hold over their students. . . .

NOTES & QUESTIONS ON BARRIERS TO CONSENT

1. *Minors and consensual sex.*   Under the law, minors are not permitted to engage in sexual relations with adults. Statutory laws are designed to protect children from the predatory conduct of adults. But does the law deny adolescents their agency and freedom of choice, especially in situations that might involve meaningful consent with a partner who is only slightly older than the adolescent? Unlike the rules for fraudulent rape, which are arguably under-inclusive, maybe the rules for statutory rape are intentionally overbroad. The safety valve is prosecutorial discretion; most cases of adolescent sex are never prosecuted in a court of law. For a discussion, see Kathleen Fultz, *Griswold for Kids: Should the Privacy Right of Sexual Autonomy Extend to Minors?*, 21 J. Juv. L. 40, 54 (2000) (answering in the negative); Michelle Oberman, *Regulating Consensual Sex with Minors: Defining a Role for Statutory Rape*, 48 Buff. L. Rev. 703, 753 (2000) (noting that "existing mechanisms for selecting statutory rape cases for prosecution are flawed"). However, Oberman also concludes that statutory rape laws are designed to protect young teenagers from unwanted sexual encounters; in many situations, young girls are too timid to express lack of consent to an unwanted sexual experience. Is there a good mechanism for distinguishing these cases from more quotidian situations that should remain outside of the legal system? Or would you recommend universal enforcement of statutory rape laws?

2. *Romeo and Juliet laws.* Several states have codified provisions that exempt from statutory rape law relationships between teenagers of a similar age. For example, N.Y. Penal Law § 130.25 defines second-degree rape as sex by a person at least 18 years old with someone 15 years old or younger. Third-degree rape involves sex by a person at least 21 years old with someone less than 17 years old. Although the legislative inspiration for these statutes is teenagers involved in a relationship, the precise construction of the statute usually makes no reference to the relationship status of the individuals involved and is simply triggered by their relative ages, though other limitations might apply. See, e.g., Tex. Penal Code Ann. § 21.11(b)(1); Ariz. Rev. Stat. Ann. § 13-1407(F). For more discussion, see Carissa Byrne Hessick & Judith M. Stinson, *Juveniles, Sex Offenses, and the Scope of Substantive Law*, 46 Tex. Tech L. Rev. 5, 26 (2013).

However, several legal commentators have complained that some Romeo and Juliet statutes are written in gendered terms that only grant the exception in cases involving older males who have sex with younger females. By these terms, some gay teenagers would not be entitled to the exemption and would be treated discriminatorily under the statutory scheme. For example, an 18-year-old Kansas teenager named Matthew Limon was charged with statutory rape for engaging in relations with a victim who was just shy of 15 years of age. The Kansas Romeo and Juliet statute mitigates the severity of the statutory rape charge (but does not eliminate liability entirely) in cases where the age deferential is less than 4 years. However, Limon was not covered by the statute because his was a gay encounter with another male and the statute refers to "members of the opposite sex." After the Supreme Court handed down *Lawrence v. Texas*, 539 U.S. 558 (2003), the Supreme Court ordered Limon's conviction vacated and remanded the case to the Kansas courts for reconsideration. The Kansas Supreme Court concluded that "the United States Supreme Court's decision in *Lawrence* controls our analysis and, when considered in conjunction with several equal protection decisions of the United States Supreme Court, requires us to hold that the State does not have a rational basis for the statutory classification created in the Romeo and Juliet statute." *State v. Limon*, 280 Kan. 275, 277, 122 P.3d 22, 24 (2005). In new proceedings, Limon pled guilty in exchange for a lower sentence. This suggests that any state statute penalizing homosexual statutory rape more severely than heterosexual statutory rape would be unconstitutional. See *Kansas Supreme Court Invalidates Unequal Punishments for Homosexual and Heterosexual Teenage Sex Offenders*, 119 Harv. L. Rev. 2276 (2006).

3. *Alcohol and sex.* Severe intoxication can vitiate the victim's consent. Most courts do not require that the victim be incapacitated or unconscious

from intoxication; substantial impairment is enough if the victim is too intoxicated to engage in the judgment required for consensual sexual relations. *People v. Giardino*, 82 Cal. App. 4th 454 (2000). What if *both* individuals are intoxicated? Legally, the intoxication negates the victim's consent but the perpetrator's intoxication requires reference to the underlying rules regarding the defense of intoxication. Generally speaking, voluntary intoxication is only a defense if it negatives the required mens rea for the offense. So in a rape case, it matters whether the defendant must have knowledge of the victim's lack of consent. In a jurisdiction that requires this level of knowledge, intoxication might be relevant. But in jurisdictions that do not require the perpetrator to have knowledge of the victim's lack of consent, the intoxication is not relevant because it does not negate an element of the offense.

In 2015, two Vanderbilt University football players were convicted of raping a female student who was intoxicated to the point of unconsciousness. University officials investigating an unrelated crime saw security footage of the players carrying the unconscious woman into a room, where prosecutors said the assault occurred. The victim could not recall the incident but was shown video evidence of the assault. At trial, the defendants argued that they too were drunk during the assault and should be acquitted. The jury disagreed and convicted both of them. Alan Blinder & Richard Pérez-Peña, *Vanderbilt Rape Convictions Stir Dismay and Denial*, N.Y. Times, Jan. 28, 2015.

4. *Evaluating consent in disability cases.*   Consent can sometimes be difficult to evaluate when the victim is not available to testify. In 2013, the chair of the philosophy department at Rutgers University was charged with rape for having sexual relations with a 33-year-old man with cerebral palsy named "D.J." The philosophy professor, Anna Stubblefield, was using "facilitated communication" to help D.J. speak by guiding his use of a computer keyboard. D.J.'s family said that he had never communicated at all before working with Stubblefield. At some point in the process, Stubblefield (who is married) announced that she and D.J. had fallen in love and had engaged in consensual sexual relations. The family went to the police, who filed charges. The local prosecutor contended that Stubblefield's use of facilitated communication with D.J. was fraudulent and his "consent" was entirely illusory—a product of her own wishful thinking. The trial focused in part on the scientific validity of facilitated communication. Thomas Zambito, *Rutgers-Newark Philosophy Chairwoman Fights Criminal Sexual Assault Charges*, N.J. Advance Media, Apr. 20, 2014. Stubblefield was convicted by the jury and started sobbing uncontrollably after the verdict was read, but was granted a second trial when an appeals court ruled that the trial judge improperly excluded evidence related to facilitated communication.

PROBLEM CASE

What if the victim suffers from a mental disease or cognitive defect that makes meaningful consent impossible? Typical cases involve individuals with developmental disabilities and require scientific evaluation, possibly at trial, to determine whether the victim had the cognitive sophistication to consent to sex. These cases are especially difficult if the victim claims the capability to consent while the prosecution asserts the opposite.

Or consider the unique case of Henry Rayhons, who was charged with rape after allegedly having sex with his wife, Donna, in a nursing home. Rayhons's wife was suffering from Alzheimer's disease. Her adult children from a previous marriage and the nursing home doctor believed she was no longer capable of consenting to sexual relations. Her husband disagreed and was later put on trial for rape.

The issue of dementia and consent is fraught with difficulty because an Alzheimer's patient might seem relatively lucid in the morning but then grow increasingly disoriented as the day progresses. Under the law, what matters is the victim's capacity to consent at the moment the act occurs.

The jury ultimately acquitted Mr. Rayhons. Donna Rayhons died of Alzheimer's before the trial started. Pam Belluck, *Iowa Man Found Not Guilty of Sexually Abusing Wife with Alzheimer's*, N.Y. Times, Apr. 22, 2015.

Henry Rayhons

C. PRACTICE & POLICY

The rapid development of rape law, and its differing interpretation across jurisdictions, leads to many strategic challenges for practitioners. It also raises difficult questions about how society should respond to the growing problem of sexual violence. In this section, we consider three key developments of practice and policy: (i) "affirmative consent" proposals; (ii) adjudicating rape under university judicial codes; and (iii) strategic charging decisions in sex assault cases.

    ☙ Affirmative consent. In a rape prosecution (as in any prosecution), the burden is on the prosecution to establish, beyond a reasonable doubt to the satisfaction of the fact finder, the required elements of the offense. In the context of rape, courts once asked whether the victim resisted the attack, under the assumption that resistance communicated lack of consent.

Over time, the resistance requirement has waned and courts more often look to whether the sex was non-consensual. But as we saw above, some jurisdictions still require *verbal* resistance, i.e., they require that the victim said "no" to the defendant.

The "no means no" standard of verbal resistance assumes a baseline of consent. In the absence of "no," the assumption is that the sexual activity is desired and consensual. To put the point sharply, the assumption is that silence indicates consent. The onus is on the victim to affirmatively declare his or her lack of consent. But why should this be the baseline assumption? The alternate possibility is certainly coherent: The victim needs to say "yes," otherwise the law will presume that the action is non-consensual. The default rule would be that silence indicates *lack* of consent. This change in the default rule is precisely what "affirmative consent" proposals seek to accomplish. Do you agree with this change?

In 2014, the State of California passed legislation that mandated an "affirmative consent" policy across every California college and university—both public and private. The legislation would mandate the substantive rule to be applied in campus judicial proceedings: Sexual interactions without affirmative consent would constitute sexual assaults. The law includes the following definition:

> "Affirmative consent" means affirmative, conscious, and voluntary agreement to engage in sexual activity. It is the responsibility of each person involved in the sexual activity to ensure that he or she has the affirmative consent of the other or others to engage in the sexual activity. Lack of protest or resistance does not mean consent, nor does silence mean consent. Affirmative consent must be ongoing throughout a sexual activity and can be revoked at any time. The existence of a dating relationship between the persons involved, or the fact of past sexual relations between them, should never by itself be assumed to be an indicator of consent. Cal. Educ. Code § 67386.

In 2015, Governor Andrew Cuomo proposed and then signed into law similar legislation for New York state colleges and universities. The New York law defines affirmative consent in the following terms: "Affirmative consent is a knowing, voluntary, and mutual decision among all participants to engage in sexual activity. Consent can be given by words or actions, as long as those words or actions create clear permission regarding willingness to engage in the sexual activity. Silence or lack of resistance, in and of itself, does not demonstrate consent. The definition of consent does not vary based upon a participant's sex, sexual orientation, gender identity, or gender expression." N.Y. Educ. Law § 6441. Both laws are linked to the institution's eligibility to receive state funding—a substantial incentive for the colleges to comply with the new regulations.

∾ **Campus judicial codes.** Apart from the substantive law to be applied in rape cases, colleges and universities are struggling over the proper procedures for adjudicating rape allegations. In 2011, the U.S. Department of Education sent a "dear colleague" letter to every college and university regarding how campus judicial proceedings should handle rape complaints. The letter constituted the department's interpretation of federal law, Title IX of the Education Amendments of 1972 (Title IX), 20 U.S.C. § 1681, which prohibits discrimination on the basis of sex in educational institutions receiving federal funding. The department concluded that schools should use a "preponderance of the evidence" standard for resolving rape complaints, as opposed to "beyond a reasonable doubt"—the standard used in state and federal criminal proceedings. Civil lawsuits use the preponderance standard; it simply requires that the allegations are more likely true than false, i.e., about a 51 percent likelihood.

In response, some colleges and universities have reformed their campus judicial codes to implement the preponderance of the evidence standard. Other schools have gone further and eliminated the right to a disciplinary hearing; a campus judicial officer interviews both sides, collects the relevant evidence, and issues a determination without conducting an adversarial proceeding with both parties present. One argument for this process is that allowing an alleged perpetrator's lawyer to cross-examine the complainant is too traumatic for the victim. But this has led some students who have been expelled to sue their universities, arguing that the process that led to their expulsion denied them adequate due process.

Underneath this controversy is a more fundamental question: What is the nature of campus judicial proceedings? Are they criminal proceedings? Or educational events? Or administrative proceedings? This question is key for determining whether "due process" is even relevant at all. The issue is difficult to resolve because of the hybrid nature of the proceedings. On the one hand, the substantive norms being applied (rape, sexual assault, etc.) are borrowed from the criminal law. On the other hand, the relevant "punishment" is not imprisonment but disciplinary sanction including possible expulsion from the institution, which is not technically "punishment" in the sense in which criminal lawyers understand the term.

∾ **The Model Penal Code responds.** In light of the rapid development of sexual assault law over the last two decades, the American Law Institute undertook a comprehensive revision of the sexual assault and related provisions of the Model Penal Code. The Code was originally adopted in 1962; its sexual assault provisions were hopelessly out of date. A team of scholars and experts drafted a variety of proposals, including the addition of the principle of affirmative consent. MPC § 213.0(3) (Discussion Draft No. 2, 2015) ("'Consent' means a person's *positive* agreement, communicated by either words or actions, to engage in a specific act of sexual penetration or sexual contact.") (emphasis added). However, the membership of the ALI rejected this definition and the word "positive" was removed in Discussion Draft No. 3. Second, the discussion draft originally stated that sexual assault can include the touching of a *non-intimate body part* when performed for the purpose of sexual gratification, humiliation, degradation, or arousal. Again, however, the ALI membership rejected this element of the proposal, and the reference to the touching of non-intimate body parts was removed from the next draft. MPC § 213.0(6) (Discussion Draft No. 3, 2017). Third, the new provisions codify a rule that sex between a client and a mental-health professional (therapist) constitutes a felony called "sexual penetration by exploitation," though it excludes doctors treating physical (as opposed to mental or emotional) conditions. MPC § 213.4(2) (Discussion Draft No. 3, 2017). The new provisions also prohibit relationships between clients and lawyers—a violation that most states handle exclusively under rules of professional responsibility (leading to disbarment) rather than the criminal law. In the case of lawyers, the new proposed rule is limited to criminal defense attorneys and lawyers involved in a "domestic-relations" matter (e.g., divorce or custody), presumably under the assumption that their clients are especially vulnerable. Finally, the proposals will continue to be debated and revised before eventual adoption by the ALI.

   ◦ Prosecutorial strategy.   When dealing with a case of sexual assault, prosecutors have a menu of options at their disposal for charging the defendant. If force or threat of force is alleged, then the prosecutor can seek an indictment for rape. However, there are lesser forms of sexual assault in each jurisdiction with lower prosecutorial burdens. In particular, if there is any doubt whether the prosecution can successfully prove penetration, the prosecution may wish to proceed on a top count of sexual assault, even if the prosecutor believes that a much more serious crime occurred. Similarly, some convictions for statutory rape, for example based on the victim's age, may originally have involved allegations of forcible conduct. However, statutory rape laws obviate the need to establish either force or lack of consent, and drastically reduce the scope of the trial's fact-finding process. The whole proceeding focuses only on whether the individuals engaged in sex and the age of the victim (and possibly the defendant's knowledge of the victim's age if the jurisdiction requires it).

CHAPTER 15

≈≈≈≈≈≈

OTHER OFFENSES AGAINST THE PERSON

A. INTRODUCTION

Homicide and rape are not the only offenses classified as "offenses against the person." Assault and battery are important offenses against the person that make up a local prosecutor's bread-and-butter practice and fill up a court's docket. For assault and battery, our task is to separate verbal and physical disputes undeserving of criminal intervention from the more serious altercations that may give rise to a criminal conviction and punishment. For kidnapping, our task is to appreciate the technical elements of that offense and determine when a kidnapping charge may be combined with another charge without constituting an impermissible double counting.

At common law, there was a strict and important distinction between battery and assault. Battery required some physical contact, however slight, against the victim. The classic example of a physical battery was a punch to the face, but other less extreme contact would also suffice. Assault, on the other hand, was defined as an *attempted* battery—for example, a punch that missed its target and never made contact with the victim's body. Over time, however, most states have broadened the definition of assault to include situations where the defendant places the victim in reasonable apprehension of bodily injury—yet another situation where physical contact is not required. A classic example might be brandishing a knife, or cocking a fist, while screaming threatening words at the victim. Even if the threat is never consummated, the defendant's actions place the victim in a reasonable apprehension of bodily injury and thus support a conviction for assault.

To add a further layer of complication, many states have followed the lead of the Model Penal Code in eliminating the arcane historical distinction between battery and assault. The result in these jurisdictions is that one crime, called assault, covers all three of the above scenarios: physical contact, attempted physical contact, and causing reasonable apprehension of bodily injury. See, e.g., MPC § 211.1. However, the language of battery lingers in a few jurisdictions that have retained the older, common law classifications. In understanding and applying the law, the key is to look beyond the labels and master the three major approaches to criminal liability in these cases.

1. Physical Battery

There are three major elements to a physical battery—the act and mental state requirements combined with a result element. To be convicted, the defendant must (a) engage in an unlawful application of physical force; (b) resulting in either a physical (bodily) injury or an offensive touching; (c) acting with purpose, knowledge, or recklessness (or negligence under a few statutes) to cause the prohibited result. However, despite the agreement over this tripartite structure, the content of these elements varies considerably across jurisdictions.

The application of physical force could be conventionally direct, as with a punch, or it might involve a more complex chain of events set in motion by the defendant, that results in physical force being applied to the defendant by his falling down, or by an object falling on his head, for example. Regardless of whether the physical force is direct or indirect, it is presumed that the application of physical force must be unlawful/unjustified. So, for example, force used for purposes of self-defense or for any other lawful reason would not constitute a battery, nor would a physical touching that is appropriate under the circumstances, such as when a swim instructor grabs a novice swimmer to prevent them from drowning, or when a crossing guard restrains a wayward pedestrian from crossing into incoming traffic.

As for the result requirement, all jurisdictions conclude that a bodily injury satisfies the result requirement. (In some jurisdictions, if the bodily injury is severe, or if the injury is caused by a weapon, the defendant will be guilty of aggravated battery.) However, the bodily injury result requirement is arguably under-broad, since many cases of physical force will not cause injury. Consequently, some jurisdictions allow an "offensive" touching to qualify—if the physical force results in the victim being touched in some offensive way, the defendant is guilty. Depending on the jurisdiction, examples include slapping someone on the face, touching an intimate area of the body (such as an unwanted kiss), or throwing some disgusting liquid or object on the victim's body. However, jurisdictions are very much split on this issue, with many preferring to limit physical battery to situations causing a physical injury. In these jurisdictions, cases of unwanted touching that produces no injury might still be prosecuted as sex offenses, depending on what part of the body is touched.

2. Assault

As noted above, there are two avenues that can lead to an assault conviction. The first is an attempted battery. In that case, the act and mental state requirements remain the same as physical battery—with the only difference being the result requirement. There is no requirement of a physical injury for this type of assault because the assault is based on the mere *attempt* to commit a battery against the victim.

The second avenue for an assault conviction (available in most jurisdictions) involves placing the victim in a reasonable apprehension of bodily harm. One might think of this class of assault as pertaining to threats. For example, Model Penal Code § 211.1 describes this as the attempt "by physical menace to put another in fear of imminent serious bodily injury." Other jurisdictions might use phrases like "immediate harm" or other qualifiers meant to express a temporal restriction. Vague or distant harms, though threatening, usually do not qualify as an assault. So, for example, if the perpetrator threatens to harm the victim at some later point in time, that may not qualify as an assault. But if the perpetrator pulls out a gun and says he is going to shoot the victim, and by doing so places the victim in a reasonable apprehension of imminent bodily injury, the crime of assault has occurred even if the victim is never touched.

In most jurisdictions, the mental state for this form of the assault offense is the intent to cause the required apprehension in the victim. In these jurisdictions, if the perpetrator is genuinely unaware that his or her behavior is threatening to the victim, then the perpetrator has not committed an assault under the "apprehension" prong of the offense. The mental state and the result element are connected through the word "reasonable" in the phrase "reasonable apprehension." So, for example, an assault does not take place if the victim only comes to fear bodily injury because the victim is unreasonably sensitive and fearful in a way that is out of step with a typical person's reaction to the events. However, a few courts have held that the proper mental state for this type of assault is simply the purpose to commit the underlying conduct and that the defendant need not intend to cause apprehension in the victim. This judicial interpretation treats reasonable apprehension in the victim as a pure result element unconnected to the perpetrator's mental state.

3. Kidnapping

The crime of kidnapping is based on the confinement of the victim or the restriction of the victim's movement. Of course, this confinement or restriction must be unlawful, otherwise every arrest performed by a police officer or other law enforcement official (such as a prison guard) would constitute kidnapping, which would be absurd. The basic requirements for a kidnapping include:

(a) confining or carrying away the victim; (b) forcibly or by threat or fear or deception; (c) for a nefarious purpose.

The first requirement, the carrying away (also known as "asportation") is often the most controversial element. At common law, kidnapping was once based on asportation out of the jurisdiction (transporting the victim to another city or state). In modern times, courts in jurisdictions that require asportation will often look to the slightest movement of the victim by the perpetrator to satisfy the requirement, as long as the movement was not integral to the commission of another crime. So, for example, the forcible removal of an individual from the seat of a car to the sidewalk might not count as asportation because it is the integral element of carjacking. To prosecute the individual for both kidnapping and carjacking in that scenario would constitute impermissible double counting. However, jurisdictions that require asportation in all cases are in the distinct minority; the far more common scheme is to allow either asportation *or* confinement to satisfy the act requirement. In jurisdictions that require asportation for kidnapping, cases of mere confinement would be punishable as the less serious offense of unlawful confinement or false imprisonment.

As for the act requirement, all jurisdictions agree that accomplishing the confinement or asportation by *force* is sufficient, though some jurisdictions also allow other means to satisfy the requirement. For example, the Model Penal Code notes that the confinement or asportation may be accomplished by "force, threat or deception." See MPC § 212.1.

The mental state for kidnapping usually requires intent or purpose, though the question is what type of purpose. Kidnapping statutes often list a variety of improper purposes. For example, the MPC lists the following purposes: "(a) to hold for ransom or reward, or as a shield or hostage; or (b) to facilitate commission of any felony or flight thereafter; or (c) to inflict bodily injury on or to terrorize the victim or another . . ." Other state statutes include a longer list including a variety of purposes, such as the purpose to subject the victim to a sexual assault, to place the victim in servitude (i.e., slavery), or some form of custodial interference. In some jurisdictions, the existence of one of the statutorily defined purposes will trigger a higher-grade kidnapping offense; if the perpetrator kidnaps the victim for some other purpose, it is still kidnapping but a lesser grade. Application of the kidnapping statute requires careful attention to its technical requirements, which vary across jurisdictions.

B. APPLICATION

1. Physical Battery

As noted above, a physical battery requires some physical contact with the victim, regardless of whether it is a battery that causes physical injury or a battery that results in an offensive touching. However, the contact need not necessarily be *direct* contact. In the following case, the Illinois statute requires that the defendant "makes physical contact of an insulting or provoking nature with an individual." What type of conduct does this provision criminalize? As you read the following case, ask yourself whether the definition of "insulting or provoking" is sufficiently objective. Is it judged subjectively based on what the victim finds insulting/provoking or is it based on how a reasonable person in the circumstances might react?

People v. Peck
Appellate Court of Illinois, Fourth District
260 Ill. App. 3d 812 (1994)

JUSTICE STEIGMANN delivered the opinion of the court:

In October 1992, a jury found defendant, Sean A. Peck, guilty of aggravated battery to a police officer and resisting a peace officer. The trial court imposed concurrent sentences of six years in prison on the conviction of aggravated battery and 364 days in jail on the conviction of resisting a peace officer. Defendant appeals, arguing that (1) the State failed to prove him guilty beyond a reasonable doubt; and (2) the conviction of resisting a peace officer must be vacated because it was based upon the same physical act as the conviction of aggravated battery . . . We affirm.

The essential facts underlying defendant's convictions are as follows. In June 1992, the police were summoned to defendant's residence to quell a neighborhood disturbance. Several police officers responded and spoke with the local residents, including defendant. As the officers spoke with defendant, he was belligerent and spit on one officer's face, glasses, and cheek. The officers then attempted to arrest him, but he fought them by kicking and pulling away while they tried to restrain and place handcuffs on him. Ultimately, three police officers subdued defendant and placed him under arrest.

At trial, the State presented six witnesses, three of whom were the police officers at the scene, and three were neighbors. The defense introduced testimony from defendant's then-girlfriend and defendant himself, who claimed that any spitting that occurred was accidental. The jury found defendant guilty of one count of aggravated battery and one count of resisting a peace officer and acquitted him of another count of aggravated battery.

Defendant first argues that the State failed to prove him guilty of aggravated battery beyond a reasonable doubt. In essence, defendant contends that spitting alone cannot sustain an aggravated battery conviction. We disagree.

Section 12-4(b)(6) of the Criminal Code of 1961 provides as follows:

(b) A person who, in committing a battery, commits aggravated battery if he . . .

(6) Knows the individual harmed to be a peace officer . . . while such officer . . . is engaged in the execution of any of his official duties including arrest or attempted arrest, or to prevent the officer . . . from performing his official duties, or in retaliation for the officer . . . performing his duties. . . .

Section 12-3(a)(2) of the Code provides, in pertinent part, as follows: "A person commits battery if he intentionally or knowingly without legal justification and *by any means* . . . makes physical contact of an insulting or provoking nature with an individual."

In order to prove aggravated battery based upon this section of the Code, the State must establish that the defendant committed a battery to "a peace officer . . . engaged in the execution of any of his official duties." In this case, no dispute exists that the victim was a police officer engaged in his official duties. Thus, the only issue is whether defendant committed a battery by spitting on the officer.

Defendant bases his argument that "mere" spitting on another cannot amount to insulting or provoking contact on the contentions that spitting on another constitutes neither (1) physical contact, nor (2) sufficiently insulting or provoking behavior. We disagree with both contentions.

The language of the battery statute clearly provides that a battery can be committed if the accused has contact with the victim "by any means." Discussing this language, the committee comments to section 12-3 of the Code note that since the development of early common law, spitting has been recognized as an act sufficient to support a battery conviction.

Regarding the insulting or provoking nature of spitting on another, we note that "a particular physical contact may be deemed insulting or provoking based upon the factual context in which it occurs." *People v. d'Avis*, 250 Ill. App. 3d 649, 651 (1993) . . . Although we can envision contexts in which a defendant's spitting might not constitute insulting or provoking behavior, defendant's spitting in the face of a police officer in this case clearly amounts to insulting or provoking contact. We hold that defendant's conduct easily reached "physical contact of an insulting or provoking nature" within the meaning of section 12-3(a)(2) of the Code. . . .

NOTES & QUESTIONS ON PHYSICAL BATTERY

1. *Reasonably insulting.* Most other courts that have considered spitting have concluded that it is sufficiently insulting to sustain a conviction. For example, in *United States v. Lewellyn*, 481 F.3d 695, 697 (9th Cir. 2007), the defendant was convicted under a federal statute after he spit on patients

at a Veterans Administration hospital (a federal government facility). The federal court quoted Blackstone for the proposition that "[t]he least touching of another's person willfully, or in anger, is a battery; for the law cannot draw the line between different degrees of violence, and therefore totally prohibits the first and lowest stages of it: every man's person being sacred, and no other having a right to meddle with it, in any the slightest manner." As for whether spitting qualifies, the court concluded that "[a]s a matter of common sense, intentionally spitting in another person's face easily falls within the scope of an offensive touching."

2. *Verbal arguments.*   Courts have sometimes rejected battery convictions where prosecutors alleged that a touching was offensive or insulting, but otherwise *de minimis.* For example, in *State v. Cabana*, 315 N.J. Super. 84, 85 (1997), a local politician was engaged in a verbal dispute on a dance floor, at a Republican social event, with a rival candidate for local office when the knuckle of his finger made physical contact with the victim's chin. The contact occurred while the defendant was talking and gesticulating and waving a printed flyer in front of her face. The flyer was a campaign advertisement from the victim that was highly critical of the defendant. The court noted that "[e]ach were seasoned politicians, familiar with the rigors of political debate" and that the touching was "incidental to the sequence of events rather than the result of assaultive intent." The court concluded with the following observation regarding the dividing line between the criminal and non-criminal: "Not all inappropriate behavior leads to criminal liability. There are instances, such as this, where public opinion will be the better judge of conduct. The what, why and how of which may call for an apology, not criminal charges. The court is hopeful that the same courage shown by these parties to give of themselves and commit to public service will again be displayed by such a resolution." Is this statement consistent with Blackstone's edict that the "least touching of another's person willfully, or in anger, is a battery"?

HYPOTHETICAL

Consider the following case. A surgeon is told to amputate a patient's left leg due to a severe bacterial infection that cannot be controlled. The patient, named Bob, consents to the amputation. However, the surgeon confuses the patient with Carl, who is scheduled to have his right arm amputated later that day. Consequently, the surgeon amputates Bob's healthy arm by mistake, with the result that Bob now has both an infected leg and a missing right arm. Bob clearly has a viable tort case against the surgeon and the hospital for medical malpractice. However, Bob also asks the local prosecutor to charge the surgeon with battery. Bob's argument is that the physical contact was unlawful because Bob never consented to the amputation of his healthy arm. He only consented to the removal of his leg. Moreover, the contact caused a severe bodily injury (the removal of the healthy arm). Should the prosecutor charge the surgeon with battery or should the prosecutor let the case be resolved by the civil justice system? Is the correct remedy in this case civil or criminal or both?

2. Assault

As discussed above, the two major theories of assault are assault as reasonable apprehension of fear and assault as attempted battery. The following two cases offer classic examples of each theory. As you read the first case, *Birthmark*, ask yourself whether the defendant intended to put the victim in a reasonable apprehension of fear. Is that a subjective or objective standard? As you read the second case, *Boodoosingh*, ask yourself whether the jury was unanimous in concluding that the defendant committed an attempted battery. If the *Boodoosingh* jury was uncertain about which type of assault the defendant had committed, should the defendant be acquitted?

State v. Birthmark
Supreme Court of Montana
369 Mont. 413 (2013)

CHIEF JUSTICE MIKE MCGRATH delivered the Opinion of the Court.

Michael Todd Birthmark appeals from his conviction of the offense of Partner or Family Member Assault (PFMA), a felony, after a jury trial on June 21, 2011. We affirm the conviction and remand for correction of the written judgment . . .

In November 2010 Birthmark visited Glasgow, Montana, and stayed at the house shared by his mother, brother and sister. Late on the night of November 16 Birthmark and his sister went to a party at his aunt's nearby house. He got into an argument with someone at the party and at about 1:30 A.M. returned to his mother's house angry and intoxicated. When he arrived, his brother was awake and watching TV, while his mother was asleep. Birthmark was loud enough that he woke his mother and she came into the living room. Birthmark then began staring at his mother and brother, and called them "inbreds" and snitches. He grabbed a piece of lumber and said he was going to "bash [their] heads in;" that he was going to slice their necks and kill them; and that he would do the same to the people at the party. This conduct went on for some time.

When Birthmark left the living room for the kitchen, saying he was going to find a knife, his mother left the house and called 911. Glasgow Police Officer Weber responded and found Birthmark's mother outside the house. She was upset, crying and "scared to death." Weber saw Birthmark's brother coming out of the house with Birthmark close behind, but when Birthmark saw Weber he quickly went back inside. Birthmark's brother was concerned for his mother and warned Weber that Birthmark had a knife. Birthmark came out of the house at Weber's request without the piece of lumber or a knife. Weber observed that Birthmark was intoxicated and "worked up."

The State charged Birthmark with PFMA in violation of § 45-5-206(1)(c), MCA, for causing reasonable apprehension of bodily injury by his mother and brother. The charge was his third or subsequent such offense and was therefore a felony. At trial, Birthmark testified that he had been "jumped" by people at the party; that he was concerned for his sister who was at the party; and that his anger displayed at his mother's house was not directed at his mother and brother but was directed toward the people at the party. Birthmark testified that his mother and brother "inferred . . . or assumed" that his threats were directed at them.

At trial, Birthmark's attorney did not offer any proposed jury instructions, and stated that he had no objection to the instructions proposed by the State. The jury convicted Birthmark of PFMA and the District Court sentenced him to the Department of Corrections for four years with one year suspended and with credit for 273 days served. Birthmark appeals and requests that this Court undertake plain error review of the jury instruction issue . . .

Birthmark contends that his trial attorney provided ineffective assistance of counsel by not objecting to the instructions given by the District Court. To prevail on an IAC claim the defendant must establish that his attorney's performance was deficient and that the deficiency prejudiced the defense. A defendant must establish both of these factors in order to establish a claim of ineffective assistance of counsel.

Birthmark was charged with PFMA under § 45-5-206(1)(c), MCA, which provides that a person commits PFMA if he "purposely or knowingly causes reasonable apprehension of bodily injury in a partner or family member." . . . The District Court instructed the jury that "[a] person acts purposely when it is his conscious object to engage in conduct of that nature," and, in a separate instruction, that "[a] person acts knowingly when the person is aware of his or her conduct." The District Court also instructed the jury that

> Purpose and knowledge ordinarily may not be proved directly because there is no way of fathoming or scrutinizing the operations of the human mind. But you may infer the Defendant's state of mind, including his purpose and knowledge, from the Defendant's acts and all other facts and circumstances in evidence which indicate his state of mind.

Birthmark contends that the District Court's definitions of "purposely" and "knowingly" were improper because they were "conduct-based" definitions and not "result-based" definitions.

Birthmark did not materially contest his actions at his mother's house: staring at his brother and mother, using loud language, name-calling, picking up a large stick, talking about finding a knife, threatening to bash their heads in and to slit their throats. His defense was that he did not intend these actions to cause his brother and mother to have a reasonable apprehension of bodily injury. He contends that the jury should have been instructed that the State was required to prove that he intended his actions to cause his mother and brother to have reasonable apprehension of bodily injury.

Birthmark's subjective intent while he undertook his actions was not the issue in the PFMA charge. It is well established that under the "reasonable apprehension" portion of the PFMA statute, the standard for determining whether there has been an offense is whether a reasonable person under similar circumstances as the victim would have a reasonable apprehension of bodily injury. "The standard is objective, asking whether a reasonable person under similar circumstances would have reasonably apprehended bodily injury." The only mental state required to convict is that the defendant have a "conscious object to engage in [the] conduct" or that he be "aware of his . . . conduct" as defined in § 45-2-101(35) and (65), MCA. Those conduct definitions were in the instructions that the District Court gave to the jury here.

In *State v. Martin,* 305 Mont. 123 (2001), Martin was charged with a number of offenses following an attempt to cash a forged check at a bank. He was charged with felony assault under § 45-5-202(2)(b), MCA, for purposely or knowingly causing reasonable apprehension of seriously bodily injury after pointing a pistol at a pursuing officer. Martin testified that he did not intend to cause the officer to reasonably apprehend serious bodily injury, and argued on appeal that his mental state, and not the perception of the officer, determined the mental state required for conviction. This Court disagreed, holding that the only mental state required as to Martin was proof that he acted purposely or knowingly. The separate element of the offense—causing reasonable apprehension of serious bodily injury—is established by the perception of the victim.

The District Court properly instructed the jury in the applicable law on the mental state for the PFMA offense. Birthmark was not entitled to an instruction that the jury be required to find that he intended to cause his mother and brother to have reasonable apprehension of bodily injury. If such an instruction had been offered the District Court could have properly refused to give it. . . .

State v. Boodoosingh

Appeals Court of Massachusetts
85 Mass. App. Ct. 902 (2014)

On appeal from a conviction of assault by means of a dangerous weapon, the defendant argues that (1) the evidence of assault under an attempted battery theory was insufficient, and (2) the judge's instruction on that theory of assault gives rise to a substantial risk of a miscarriage of justice. We affirm.

Nancy Lizardo, the victim's mother, related that during the encounter between the defendant and her son, Luis, she jumped between the two young men and told them that if they were to fight at all, they should not fight with weapons. Despite her entreaty, the defendant refused to drop the baseball bat in his hand and yelled, "I'm going to fuck him up." The defendant lifted his hand to try to hit Luis with the bat, but Nancy pushed the defendant away from Luis, who stood only a foot behind her. Viewed in the light most favorable to the Commonwealth, this evidence suffices to establish assault under an attempted battery theory. See *Commonwealth v. Porro,* 458 Mass. 526, 530 (2010) (to prove attempt, Commonwealth must prove that defendant either committed last act necessary to complete crime, such as where combatant swings and misses, or committed overt acts that brought him very near in time and ability to commission of completed crime). We reject the defendant's contention that because the defendant did not "swing" the bat, his overt actions toward accomplishing the battery were insufficient. See *Commonwealth v. Purrier,* 54 Mass. App. Ct. 397, 402-403 (2002) (evidence of attempted battery sufficient where defendant stepped closer to male victim and female stepped in between them). The evidence that the defendant rushed toward Luis with a bat in his hands, rejected Nancy's entreaties, raised the bat as if to strike Luis, and came within a few feet of doing so before he was pushed aside by Nancy suffices to establish that he came "reasonably close" in time and ability to accomplishing the intended battery.

As requested by the parties, the judge instructed on assault . . . The defendant now contends that the requested instruction is error because, unlike its District Court counterpart, the Superior Court instruction on assault under an attempted battery theory fails to apprise that the Commonwealth must prove that the defendant came "reasonably close" to accomplishing the intended act. For its part, the Commonwealth maintains that the Superior Court instruction, which requires that the defendant "intended to physically harm" the victim, "did an act toward [that end]," and had "the actual ability or apparent ability to inflict bodily harm," conveys the necessary essentials of attempt—the defendant's overt acts brought him very near, in time and ability, to the actual commission of the completed crime.

While the District Court model instruction provides a clearer statement of assault by attempted battery, and is cited more frequently in appellate decisions, we need not resolve the adequacy of its Superior Court counterpart because even were we to assume that the challenged instruction is erroneous, the defendant's conviction must be affirmed. On the facts of this case, any error in the judge's instruction on assault under the attempted battery theory would not give rise to a substantial risk of a miscarriage of justice. As noted in *Commonwealth v. Porro*, 458 Mass. at 534, "Because attempted battery and threatened battery 'are closely related,' . . . we do not require that a jury be unanimous as to which theory of assault forms the basis for their verdict; a jury may find a defendant guilty of assault if some jurors find the defendant committed an attempted battery (because they are convinced the defendant intended to strike the victim and missed) and the remainder find that he committed a threatened battery (because they are convinced that the defendant intended to frighten the victim by threatening an assault)." We do not require the jury to signify by special verdict the theory of assault under which the verdict is returned.

The defense at trial, directed primarily to the more serious charge of armed assault with intent to murder, was that the defendant was only present at the scene and did nothing that rose to the level of criminal culpability. To find the defendant guilty under either theory of assault, the jury were necessarily required to reject the defendant's claim and credit the Commonwealth's proof that the defendant rushed at Luis with a raised baseball bat in his hands and threatened to harm him, only to have Luis's mother step in the way at the last moment and prevent a battery. . . .

NOTES & QUESTIONS ON ASSAULT

1. *Objective reasonableness.* Several courts have considered whether standards such as "reasonable apprehension" of bodily injury are unconstitutionally vague. Most courts have rejected these "void for vagueness" challenges, concluding that the use of an objective "reasonable person" standard regarding the resulting apprehension or fear makes the statute sufficiently clear and predictable. See, e.g., *Crandall v. State*, 125 Nev. 1029 (2009) (assault with a deadly weapon statute not void for vagueness because "an individual of ordinary intelligence recognizes that using a deadly weapon in a manner intended to unlawfully threaten bodily harm is a criminal offense"). What does it mean for someone to be placed in a state of reasonable apprehension of imminent bodily harm? Since the standard is objective, it is judged not just from the perspective of the victim, but from the perspective of what a reasonable person in the victim's situation would have felt. For example, in *United States v. Acosta-Sierra*, 690 F.3d 1111 (9th Cir. 2012), the defendant threw a "baseball-size piece of jagged concrete" at a customs agent at the border crossing. Although the rock did not strike the officer, it came within two feet of his head. The only problem with the prosecution's case was that the officer neither saw the defendant launch the projectile nor saw the projectile while it was flying through the air. The victim only became aware of it when he heard the projectile hit a metal gate behind him. Applying an objective standard of reasonable

apprehension, the Court of Appeals for the Ninth Circuit concluded that the officer "did not see Acosta-Sierra before he threw the rock and did not realize what had happened until after the threat of imminent bodily harm had passed. A reasonable person observing what [the officer] observed, therefore, would not have been aware of any threat." Under these facts, would you convict the defendant for assault under an attempted battery theory instead?

2. *Civil versus criminal assault.* There is substantial overlap between the definition of assault in tort law and the definition of assault in the criminal law. Indeed, over time, criminal assault has come to look more and more like civil assault (with the criminalization of threatened harm), resulting in an overarching harmonization of assault jurisprudence in the civil and criminal realms. But should the standard for criminal assault be higher? Does simple assault, as opposed to aggravated assault, transform everyday disputes into crimes? As one legal historian has written, "[a]ssault is a commonplace crime with uncommon potential for shedding light on the American criminal justice system. It lives on the periphery of American legal historiography, and yet, because of the ubiquity of small-scale violence, it has for centuries been a perennial and pesky nuisance threatening to overwhelm courts everywhere." See Joshua Stein, *Privatizing Violence: A Transformation in the Jurisprudence of Assault,* 30 Law & Hist. Rev. 423 (2012). Do you agree? Or do minor assaults portend more dangerous events and therefore justify early intervention from law enforcement before violence escalates?

HYPOTHETICAL

Consider the following hypothetical. Arnold and Charles are having an intense and increasingly belligerent verbal argument. Arnold is holding a knife but Charles is unarmed. Suddenly, Arnold holds the knife up and lunges in the direction of Charles's abdomen. Luckily for Charles, a bystander named David intervenes and tackles Arnold just as he is lunging forward. The knife narrowly misses Charles's body. What is the correct result in this case?

On the one hand, Arnold's action sounds like assault as an attempted battery. He lunged with the knife but simply failed to connect with its intended target because of the bystander's intervention. On the other hand, Arnold's action also sounds like assault as a reasonable apprehension of injury, since Charles no doubt feared a bodily injury during the interaction. In practical terms, the dividing line between the two theories is razor thin, since many (or perhaps most) cases of attempted battery will also produce a reasonable apprehension of injury. Did Arnold have the requisite mens rea to cause a reasonable apprehension of injury?

The local prosecutor charges Arnold with two counts of assault, each count based on a different theory of assault. The jury convicts Arnold on both counts. On appeal, Arnold argues that the jury may consider both theories but cannot convict him twice for the same criminal transaction. Arnold asks the appeals court to quash one of the convictions. If you are a judge on the appeals court, how would you rule? Should the jury be restricted to convicting Arnold once even if it finds both theories of assault applicable in this case?

3. Kidnapping

The following case is a good example of how courts will oversee the technical requirements of the kidnapping offense. The Georgia kidnapping statute requires asportation—a physical movement—of the victim. How does the court determine whether the defendant committed an asportation? In making this determination, what role is played by the other offenses committed by the defendant? In this case, the defendant committed sexual assaults and, according to the prosecution, kidnapping as well. As you read the case, ask yourself whether the movement of the victim was a necessary part of the sexual assault or whether the asportation was separate enough to ground a conviction for kidnapping.

Goolsby v. State
Court of Appeals of Georgia
311 Ga. App. 650 (2011)

McFADDEN, JUDGE

A jury convicted Terry Lee Goolsby of 13 felony counts in connection with the invasions of the homes and the rapes of S.P. and H.M.M. Six counts arise out of two separate invasions of S.P.'s home, including one count of kidnapping with bodily injury. Seven counts arise out of an invasion of H.M.M.'s home, also including one count of kidnapping with bodily injury. Goolsby appeals only from his convictions for kidnapping with bodily injury, focusing on the asportation element of the kidnapping with bodily injury charges. He challenges the sufficiency of the evidence and the trial court's instruction to the jury as to that element.

We hold that the evidence of asportation was insufficient to sustain Goolsby's convictions for the kidnapping with bodily injury of S.P. But as to H.M.M., we find the evidence of asportation not only sufficient to sustain Goolsby's conviction, but also sufficient to render harmless any error in the jury charge. Accordingly, we reverse Goolsby's conviction for kidnapping with bodily injury of S.P. and affirm his other convictions.

Reviewing a challenge to the sufficiency of the evidence to sustain a conviction, we view the evidence in the light most favorable to the jury verdict, and the defendant no longer has a presumption of innocence. We do not weigh the evidence or evaluate witness credibility; we only determine if the evidence was sufficient for a rational trier of fact to find the defendant guilty beyond a reasonable doubt of the charged offenses. Even though the evidence may be contradicted, if some evidence exists to support each necessary element of the State's case, we will uphold the jury's verdict.

So viewed, the evidence established that on September 8, 2002, while S.P., a 70-year-old woman who required constant use of an oxygen tank, was sleeping on her couch, Terry Lee Goolsby broke into her home and sexually assaulted her. Goolsby fled when something startled him.

Eleven days later, S.P., after hearing suspicious noises at around 4:00 A.M., got up from her couch where she was watching television and took a few steps toward her kitchen. Goolsby stepped out of the kitchen, grabbed both of her arms near the wrists, and forcefully walked her backward a couple of steps to the couch. He pushed her down on the couch, raped her, and subsequently fled.

At 4:00 A.M. on December 21, 2002, in the same mobile home community where S.P. lived, H.M.M. awoke to a loud noise. She got up to investigate and walked into her dining room where she saw Goolsby in the utility room inside her house. After seeing Goolsby, H.M.M. turned and ran for the front door, but Goolsby caught her from behind and pulled her away from the door. H.M.M. struggled to free herself. Goolsby attempted to tie H.M.M.'s hands together with a string as he was pulling her away from the door toward her bedroom. When H.M.M. clung to another door, Goolsby pulled out a knife, held it to her back, and beat her until she let go. Goolsby eventually tied H.M.M.'s hands in front of her and forced her into her bedroom. Once in the bedroom, he put her on the bed where he raped her. Following the attack, H.M.M. was able to convince Goolsby that she needed to go to the hospital, and he let her leave.

DNA evidence established that Goolsby had sexual contact with both victims. Furthermore, fingerprints lifted from a glass in H.M.M.'s home matched Goolsby's fingerprints, and H.M.M. picked him out of a live lineup as the person who raped her.

On April 2, 2003, Goolsby was indicted on charges of criminal attempt to commit rape, burglary, and sexual battery for his attack on S.P. on September 8, 2002. For his attack on S.P. on September 19, 2002, Goolsby was indicted on charges of burglary, rape, and kidnapping with bodily injury (Count 6). For the incident with H.M.M. in December 2002, Goolsby was indicted on charges of kidnapping with bodily injury (Count 7), rape, aggravated assault, burglary, aggravated sodomy, possession of a knife during the commission of a felony, and sexual battery. Goolsby was convicted on all counts. In October 2004, he received an aggregate sentence of life plus 45 years, including multiple concurrent and consecutive life sentences . . .

Goolsby contends that the evidence of asportation is insufficient to sustain his conviction of kidnapping S.P. He relies on *Garza v. State*, 284 Ga. 696 (2008), which changed the law as to that element of kidnapping, noting that his appeal was in the "pipeline" when Garza was handed down. We agree and reverse Goolsby's conviction on Count 6.

"A person commits the offense of kidnapping when such person abducts or steals away another person without lawful authority or warrant and holds such other person against his or her will." OCGA § 16-5-40(a). For a kidnapping conviction, the State must show that the defendant has "abducted" or "stolen away" the victim. In other words, the State must prove an unlawful movement, or asportation, of the victim has occurred against his or her will.

According to state law at the time of Goolsby's crimes in 2002 and his conviction and sentencing in 2004, the State could establish the element of asportation with proof of any movement of the victim, however slight. In 2008, however, our Supreme Court decided *Garza*, and established a four-part test to determine whether movement of the victim constitutes asportation:

> (1) the duration of the movement; (2) whether the movement occurred during the commission of a separate offense; (3) whether such movement was an inherent part of that separate offense; and (4) whether the movement itself presented a significant danger to the victim independent of the danger posed by the separate offense.

The purpose of the test is to determine "whether the movement in question is in the nature of the evil the kidnapping statute was originally intended to address—i.e., movement serving to substantially isolate the victim from protection or rescue—or merely a 'criminologically insignificant circumstance' attendant to some other crime."

Although the Georgia legislature has since amended the kidnapping statute to re-establish the rule that slight movement is sufficient proof of kidnapping as long as the movement was not incidental to another crime, that amendment applies to crimes committed on or after the revision's effective date of July 1, 2009. Because Goolsby's case was on direct review or not yet final when the Supreme Court of Georgia decided *Garza*, it was in the pipeline when *Garza* was handed down, and we apply the *Garza* test to determine whether the movement of the victim sufficiently establishes the element of asportation.

Applying the four-factor *Garza* test to Goolsby's attack on S.P., we find the evidence insufficient to establish asportation. The duration of the movement was minimal. When Goolsby grabbed S.P. in front of her kitchen, he forced her back "just a few steps" to her couch. Even though the movement occurred before the actual rape, it was movement incidental and in furtherance of the rape. In *Garza*, our Supreme Court expressly rejected a previous standard under which movement "designed to better carry out the criminal activity" was sufficient to sustain a kidnapping conviction. Here, the movement of the victim was not a necessary element of the crime of rape, but it allowed Goolsby to exercise control over S.P. during his conduct of the rape and was, therefore, an inherent part of the rape. See *Williams v. State*, 304 Ga. App. 787, 790 (2010) (asportation proven where movement of victims during a bank robbery did not isolate the victims, but rather allowed defendant to simultaneously confine and exercise control over the victims during the conduct of the armed robbery). Finally, the movement itself presented no significant danger to the victim independent of the danger posed by the rape itself because nothing changed in regard to S.P.'s isolation or potential rescue as a result of the movement to the couch. So, the movement in question was not in the "nature of the evil the kidnapping statute was originally intended to address." As the movement does not establish the element of asportation under the *Garza* test, Goolsby's conviction under Count 6 for kidnapping with bodily injury as it pertains to S.P. must be reversed. See *Escoffier v. State*, 303 Ga. App. 317, 318 (2010) (evidence of asportation insufficient where defendant used a knife to order the victim from the driver's seat to the passenger's seat in order to get in the car and steal it, movement of the victim occurred during the commission of the separate offense of hijacking a motor vehicle and did not significantly increase the danger to the victim independent of the underlying offense); *Moore v. State*, 301 Ga. App. 220 (2009) (where defendant forced the victim's car off a dark, rural road at 4:00 A.M., pulled her out of the car, dragged her into a ditch, and sexually assaulted her, movement of the victim did not significantly increase the danger to her); *Rayshad v. State*, 295 Ga. App. 29, 33-34 (2008) (reversing one of defendant's two kidnapping convictions because there was no evidence that the movements significantly enhanced the danger the victim already faced during the commission of the aggravated assault or armed robbery crimes).

Goolsby also contends that the evidence is insufficient to sustain his conviction on Count 7, kidnapping with bodily injury of H.M.M. We disagree. After assessing the evidence of the attack on H.M.M. under the *Garza* standard . . . we conclude that the evidence was sufficient to establish the asportation element of the crime of kidnapping with bodily injury. Therefore, we affirm Goolsby's conviction Count 7.

Applying the four factors to the evidence here, Goolsby's movement of H.M.M. from the front door, through the house, and into her bedroom establishes the element of asportation. Although the record does not establish the duration of the movement, in cases where the *Garza* standard applies, not all four factors must be met to establish the element of asportation. In fact, asportation has been established on the basis of only two of the *Garza* factors shown.

Considering the second and third factors, the movement of H.M.M. from the front door to the bedroom did not occur during the commission of the rape or the aggravated assault, and it was not an inherent part of either the rape or the aggravated assault. The movement happened before and was separate from the rape. Moreover, Goolsby did not continue to assault H.M.M. after he pulled her to the back bedroom; he assaulted her to subdue her, then forced her into the bedroom and onto the bed.

Finally, the movement created a significant danger to H.M.M. independent of the danger posed by the rape or the aggravated assault. The movement of H.M.M. enhanced Goolsby's control over her and isolated her from protection or potential rescue. Before Goolsby managed to pull H.M.M. into her bedroom, H.M.M. was at the front door where she could have made her escape or alerted her neighbors to provide help.

Accordingly, the evidence was sufficient to sustain Goolsby's conviction of kidnapping with bodily injury of H.M.M., and thus Goolsby's conviction is affirmed. . . .

NOTES & QUESTIONS ON KIDNAPPING

1. *Asportation.* Do courts take an unnecessarily broad view of asportation? In *Goolsby*, the court rejected kidnapping regarding one victim but upheld it for another, based on an intricate analysis of the exact movements of the perpetrator and the victim. Should courts return to the original understanding of asportation at common law, which involved carrying the victim out of the jurisdiction? For an argument that courts are far too willing to consider any slight movement an asportation, see Melanie A. Prince, *Two Crimes for the Price of One: The Problem with Kidnapping Statutes in Tennessee and Beyond*, 76 Tenn. L. Rev. 789, 790 (2009) ("To remedy this long-standing problem, Tennessee and other states should modify or dispense with their current kidnapping statutes and remove from prosecutors' ability [the power] to impose kidnapping charges for slight movements or detentions that are part of the underlying crime."). Do the *Garza* factors applied in the *Goolsby* case above resolve these concerns?

2. *Kidnapping and mistake of law.* Consider again the facts of *People v. Weiss*, 276 N.Y. 384 (1938), reprinted in Chapter 7 (Mistakes). In *Weiss*, the defendants were convicted of kidnapping though they were allegedly operating under the illusion that they were legally authorized the detain the victim. The New York Court of Appeals concluded that their conviction was only sustainable if they acted with the knowledge that they had no legal authority to detain the victim. Although some commentators refer to this as a mistake of law, it would be more accurate to describe it as a "mistake of legal element," because the element of the crime that refers to the unlawfulness of the victim's detention requires a legal determination. For a true mistake of law situation, consider *State v. Clark*, 346 N.W.2d 510 (Iowa 1984). In *Clark*, the defendants were

aware that forcibly placing the victim in a van and transporting him to another location would subject them to criminal responsibility for assault, but remained unaware that this conduct violated the kidnapping statute. The Iowa Supreme Court concluded that this mistake was irrelevant. The crime of kidnapping requires that the defendant know that the detention is without legal authority but is not required to know that the detention violates a particular criminal statute. The Iowa Supreme Court concluded: "As was the case in *Weiss,* defendants would have been entitled to an instruction on this defense if their alleged mistake went to whether or not they had authority to remove or confine the victim. Here, defendants did not claim to be mistaken as to their authority to seize and confine the victim. They merely testified they did not know their activities violated the kidnapping statute. Knowledge they were violating the statute is not an element of the offense." *Id.* at 513.

C. PRACTICE & POLICY

The following materials consider two new crimes that were enacted to respond to particular social problems. The first, stalking, is an extension of the crime of assault. The second, custodial interference, is an extension of the crime of kidnapping when it occurs during custody dispute situations. For both crimes, do the statutes adequately respond to the social problem? Are they overbroad or narrowly tailored to the unique harm that legislatures sought to resolve?

> ✍ Anti-stalking statutes. Responding to a wave of public concern about high-profile cases of stalking in the late 1980s, states responded in the 1990s by passing new statutes criminalizing stalking. One of the most public cases was the murder of actress Rebecca Schaeffer, who starred in the CBS sitcom *My Sister Sam*. In 1989, Schaeffer was killed at the doorstep of her Los Angeles home by an obsessed fan, Robert John Bardo, who had stalked her for months. State legislatures responded by defining the new crime of "stalking" and attaching heightened penalties to the conduct. A key element of the anti-stalking statutes is the result element—the creation of a feeling of fear or apprehension in the mind of the victim. In this sense, stalking is a legal extension of the assault jurisprudence that criminalizes creating a reasonable apprehension of bodily injury in the mind of the assault victim. Stalking statutes exhibit a similar structure. Although the content of these statutes varies considerably from jurisdiction to jurisdiction, especially regarding the type of fear created or the specific conduct or mental state of the perpetrator, many of the statutes are built from the same raw materials as the assault offenses discussed above. For example,

consider the following example of the Illinois stalking statute, 720 Ill. Comp. Stat. § 12-7.3:

> (a) A person commits stalking when he or she knowingly engages in a course of conduct directed at a specific person, and he or she knows or should know that this course of conduct would cause a reasonable person to:
>> (1) fear for his or her safety or the safety of a third person; or
>> (2) suffer other emotional distress.
>
> (a-3) A person commits stalking when he or she, knowingly and without lawful justification, on at least 2 separate occasions follows another person or places the person under surveillance or any combination thereof and:
>> (1) at any time transmits a threat of immediate or future bodily harm, sexual assault, confinement or restraint and the threat is directed towards that person or a family member of that person; or
>> (2) places that person in reasonable apprehension of immediate or future bodily harm, sexual assault, confinement or restraint to or of that person or a family member of that person.

In what ways is stalking similar to assault? Can you imagine a situation where a defendant would not be guilty of assault but would be guilty of stalking under the Illinois statute? What gaps does the stalking statute fill? For more discussion on stalking statutes, see B. Benjamin Haas, *The Formation and Viability of Anti-Stalking Laws*, 39 Vill. L. Rev. 1387, 1415 (1994) ("Traditional remedies proved ill-suited to deal effectively with the offense of stalking. Therefore, states drafted statutes that dealt specifically with stalking. However, in drafting such statutes, state legislatures encountered difficulty in balancing the need for an effective anti-stalking statute with the requirement that the statute not be unconstitutionally vague.").

∾ **Reasonable apprehension and vagueness.** Reconsider the materials above regarding "reasonable apprehension" as a standard for assault. As noted above, stalking statutes rely on similar standards, triggering some of the same void-for-vagueness arguments discussed above in assault cases. In the context of stalking statutes, consider *Monhollen v. Commonwealth*, 947 S.W.2d 61, 62 (Ky. Ct. App. 1997) and *Parker v. Commonwealth*, 24 Va. App. 681 (1997), both upholding stalking statutes from constitutional challenge. However, a few courts have struck down state stalking statutes, particularly when they were found not to include a reasonable person standard. See, e.g., *Long v. State*, 931 S.W.2d 285, 289 (Tex. Crim. App. 1996) (concluding that the phrase "reasonably likely to harass, annoy, alarm, abuse, torment, or embarrass that person" does not encompass a reasonable person standard because of the inclusion of the words "that person" in the provision). Some states revised their stalking statutes after courts refused to apply them on vagueness grounds. To understand why the reasonable person standard is so important in this context, consider the following explanation from the Supreme Court of Kansas in *State v. Bryan*, 259 Kan. 143, 154-55 (1996):

The danger in this situation is obvious. In the absence of an objective standard, the terms "annoys," "alarms" and "harasses" subject the defendant to the particular sensibilities of the individual victim. Different persons have different sensibilities, and conduct which annoys or alarms one person may not annoy or alarm another. The victim may be of such a state of mind that conduct which would never annoy, alarm, or harass a reasonable person would seriously annoy, alarm, or harass this victim. In such a case, the defendant would be guilty of stalking, a felony offense, under the 1994 statute, even though a reasonable person in the same situation would not be alarmed, annoyed, or harassed by the defendant's conduct.

Contrast this statutory language with language requiring that the following must be such that it would cause "a reasonable person to suffer substantial emotional distress" or place such person in reasonable fear for such person's safety. At the very least, under this language the finder of fact would not be left with the subjective state of mind of the victim as the determining factor but instead would have an objective reasonable person standard by which to determine whether the defendant committed the crime. Similarly, just as the finder of fact would be provided with an objective standard, so too would anyone subject to this law be provided with an objective standard to determine what conduct would constitute the crime of stalking. In the stalking statute's 1994 form, persons of common intelligence must necessarily guess at its meaning and differ as to its application.

∾ **Custodial interference.** Imagine that a father is involved in a dispute with his ex-wife over the custody of their children. The wife files a petition in family court requesting full custody, arguing that the father is unfit to care for the children. Sensing that he might lose custody of his kids, and firmly believing that his ex-wife is the one who is not fit to raise the children, the father absconds with the children and flees the state. In such a case, has the father committed a kidnapping? To respond to uniqueness of these cases, several jurisdictions enacted statutes criminalizing custodial interference. Consider the following example from Vermont, 13 Vt. Stat. § 245:

> (a) A person commits custodial interference by taking, enticing or keeping a child from the child's lawful custodian, knowingly, without a legal right to do so, when the person is a relative of the child and the child is less than 18 years old . . .
>
> (c) It shall be a defense to a charge of keeping a child from the child's lawful custodian that the person charged with the offense was acting in good faith to protect the child from real and imminent physical danger. Evidence of good faith shall include the filing of a nonfrivolous petition documenting that danger and seeking to modify the custodial decree in a Vermont court of competent jurisdiction. This petition must be filed within three business days of the termination of visitation rights. This defense shall not be available if the person charged with the offense has left the State with the child.

In the hypothetical above, would the father be guilty of custodial interference under this statute?

In some cases, parents who abscond with their children while a custody proceeding is pending may be found guilty of criminal contempt for ignoring a judge's court order. If that happens, can the parent also be convicted of custodial interference subsequently? Is it a violation of double jeopardy for the parent to be convicted twice? For an argument that this result does *not* constitute double jeopardy, see Valerie Brummel, *Parental Kidnapping, Criminal Contempt of Court, and the Double Jeopardy Clause: A Recommendation for State Courts*, 106 J. Crim. L. & Criminology 315, 353 (2016) ("Due to the material differences between the crimes of parental kidnapping and contempt of court, giving the state power to prosecute under its parental kidnapping statutes would not cause any person to 'be subject for the same offence to be twice put in jeopardy of life or limb.'").

CHAPTER 16

—◦◦◦—

THEFT

A. INTRODUCTION

At common law, theft offenses were segregated into separate offenses based on the manner in which the property was unlawfully obtained: larceny, theft by false pretenses, and embezzlement. What distinguishes the offenses is *how* the actor gets the property.

Larceny is defined as the trespassory taking and carrying away of another's property with the intent to permanently deprive the possessor of the property. In the context of larceny, "trespass" refers to the notion of a legal trespass, that is, a violation of a legal interest by taking the property without consent or justification. Over time, courts developed a subcategory of larceny called "larceny by trick," which involved the use of fraud to unlawfully gain possession over the item. In other words, larceny involved either a physical taking or a ruse to secure the item. In either case, the "intent to permanently deprive" the possessor of the property is the mental element, that is, in more colloquial terms, the intent to steal the item.

Theft by false pretenses is very similar to larceny by trick, except that theft by false pretenses requires that the actor receive actual *title* to the property (as opposed to mere possession) through the fraud. In many ways, this is a formalistic distinction that relies on the concept of title as it is understood in property law. So, for example, if the actor used fraud to convince the owner to convey a piece of jewelry, and by doing so the owner took title to the jewelry, the actor has committed theft by false pretenses. The offense of false pretenses differs from larceny because in false pretenses the owner intends to transfer title to the property (induced by the fraudulent representation), while in larceny the owner does not.

Embezzlement involves an actor's lawful possession of another's personal property, which is then converted or appropriated by the actor with the intent

423

to permanently deprive the owner of the property. In this respect, embezzlement focuses on an abuse of trust: The actor received possession of the item for one purpose (such as the money in a bank account) but converted it for personal use. So, if the treasurer of a local charity has possession of its funds to pay for the charity's activities, but converts those funds to pay for personal expenses, the treasurer has committed embezzlement. These situations cannot be covered by larceny because larceny requires that the defendant did *not* have lawful possession of the item. To close this gap, the common law offense of embezzlement was crafted by judicial invention.

To further understand the difference between larceny and embezzlement, consider a different hypothetical. Imagine that a shopper at a department store tries on a sweater, looks at herself in the mirror, and then leaves the store without paying for the merchandise. At first glance this might sound like an embezzlement, because the shopper had permission to try on the sweater but then converted the property. But this would be the wrong analysis. The shopper never had lawful possession of the sweater, which is required for embezzlement. The shopper had mere "custody" of the sweater when she tried it on, and that custody was transformed into possession—an *unlawful* possession—when she exited the store. She is guilty of larceny, not embezzlement.

Finally, there is a fourth property offense that is closely related to the three theft offenses described above. Extortion statutes prohibit obtaining possession of something by threat or fear, such as by threatening to expose a secret or by accusing the victim of a crime. Strictly speaking, extortion is legally distinct from larceny, false pretenses, and embezzlement, because the actor does not use trespass, fraud, or conversion to deprive the owner of the property. For example, an actor is guilty of extortion if he threatens to accuse someone of a crime to extract money from the victim. If the property was procured with a lie, the actor would be guilty of false pretenses, but in this case the threat makes it extortion.

Many jurisdictions continue to apply these common law categories for theft offenses or modern variations on them. However, the Model Penal Code consolidated the various offenses into a single omnibus theft offense with different subcategories for how the theft occurred. The Model Penal Code scheme was influential and several states consolidated their theft offenses along this line. In any event, whether a jurisdiction has a single theft provision with subcategories (as in the Model Penal Code) or multiple provisions for different types of theft (following the old common law scheme), these statutes require one or more of the following requirements. The defendant must (i) physically take and carry away or (ii) use deception, fraud, or extortion to take (iii) the victim's property (iv) with the intent to permanently deprive the victim of the property. Each element raises intense problems of application.

1. Unlawful Taking

Theft is often called larceny when it involves the physical taking and "carrying away" of the victim's property. The defendant must gain possession of the property for at least an instant. At common law, "carrying away" required some movement of the property but not necessarily the successful removal of the item from the building or location. For example, it would be enough for a thief to take control of an item from someone's apartment and place the item in her pocket; if the thief is arrested before leaving the apartment, the pocketing of the item constitutes sufficient "asportation" to generate a conviction for theft. However, in situations where the item is not moved, the defendant cannot be convicted of larceny and would have to be charged with attempted larceny instead.

2. Fraud, Extortion, Blackmail, and Embezzlement

If the taking is completed through less physical means, such as deception or coercion, the theft is classified as fraud or extortion. These offenses all involve situations where the victim gives the perpetrator access to the property, but some deceit or coercion vitiates the supposed "consent" that the victim has given the perpetrator to use the property. At common law, there were two types of fraud: larceny by trick and theft by false pretenses. For both crimes, the perpetrator convinces the owner to convey the property through deception. For example, if the perpetrator convinces the victim to give him $1,000 for a charity that supports leukemia patients, but instead uses the money to buy a car because the charity organization does not exist, then the transaction constitutes fraud. As mentioned above, theft by false pretenses covers situations where the perpetrator gains actual title, while larceny by trick only requires possession of the item. Model Penal Code § 223.3 consolidates this somewhat esoteric distinction in a provision called "theft by deception" that covers all situations where the actor "obtains property of another by deception," such as creating or reinforcing a false impression "as to law, value, intention, or other states of mind."

In the case of extortion, which the Model Penal Code classifies as a type of theft in § 223.4, the perpetrator convinces the owner to convey the property in exchange for the perpetrator promising not to engage in some unlawful act. For example, if the perpetrator coerces the victim into giving up $1,000 in exchange for a promise not to assault his son, then the transaction constitutes extortion. But what if the perpetrator coerces the victim into giving up the money by threatening to perform a *lawful* act, e.g., disclosing damaging information to the victim's wife or business partners? This is clearly illegal too—though the label of the crime changes depending on the jurisdiction. In states that follow the old common law scheme for defining their theft offenses, the crime of receiving property by threatening to perform a lawful act is called *blackmail*. However, the MPC does not have a separate offense for blackmail and instead rolls it into its provision on extortion, which includes threats to perform both lawful and unlawful actions.

Finally, if the victim has given the perpetrator access to the property for one purpose but the perpetrator converts it for his own use, then the transaction is embezzlement. So if the perpetrator is the trustee of a bank account to be used for a child's educational expenses, but instead uses the money to buy himself a sports car, the transaction constitutes embezzlement. The key element is that the victim *consents* to the transfer of the property to the actor for a particular use, but that condition is violated by the actor. The Model Penal Code has no separate embezzlement provision but instead includes it within the ambit of "theft by unlawful taking or disposition," which includes "exercising unlawful control" over movable property or unlawfully transferring "immovable property of another . . . to benefit himself or another not entitled thereto." MPC § 223.2.

3. Property

The material taken must constitute private property. At common law, the crime of theft generally involved tangible, moveable property, but over time our understanding of what constitutes property has expanded. Consequently, intellectual property, including patents and copyrighted material, are considered property as well. Jurisdictions have grappled over whether to define services as a type of property. Some courts refused to equate services with property, leading those jurisdictions to close that gap by expressly outlawing theft of services as a distinct crime. Finally, it is not required that the victim has an absolute right to the property that is stolen; some lesser possessory interest is sufficient. In other words, the victim must have "possession" of the property but not necessarily true "ownership" of the property. For example, imagine that a thief steals someone's property. Then, a second thief steals the property from the first thief. The second thief is still guilty of theft even though the first thief was not a legitimate owner of the property. There are some obvious public policy reasons for this result; if it were legally impossible to steal from a thief, instances of theft-like behavior might rise dramatically without any criminal punishment associated with the behavior.

4. Intent to Deprive

The perpetrator must act with the intent to permanently deprive the victim of his enjoyment of the property. If the perpetrator borrows the victim's car with the intent to return it tomorrow, he has not stolen the car. Many factual scenarios are difficult to classify. Courts have labeled as theft the taking of property with the intent to later return it for the purpose of claiming a reward, because the defendant's intent to return is contingent on securing the reward. Likewise, courts have labeled as theft the taking of property from a store with the intent to return it for a false refund, again because the intent to return is contingent upon receiving the illegitimate refund. Finally, some courts have interpreted "permanently" quite expansively, so that a perpetrator's intent to deprive the victim of the property during the entire time when the property would be useful to the victim would also be sufficient to constitute the crime of theft.

An important question regarding the mental element is the defendant's awareness of the victim's ownership status of the property. As noted above, theft requires that the victim have a possessory interest in the property but not an ownership interest, and the mens rea requirement tracks this attendant circumstance: The defendant need only be aware that the victim has possession over the property. However, there is an affirmative defense when the actor "was unaware that the property or service was that of another" or "acted under an honest claim of right to the property or service involved or that he had a right to acquire or dispose of it as he did." MPC § 223.1(3).

5. Robbery

Robbery involves the use of physical force to accomplish a theft. According to Model Penal Code § 222.1, a person is guilty of robbery if, in the course of committing a theft, he: "(a) inflicts serious bodily injury upon another; or (b) threatens another with or purposely puts him in fear of immediate serious bodily injury; or (c) commits or threatens immediately to commit any felony of the first or second degree." This means, by definition, that robbery involves the taking of property in the *presence* of the victim and that it be accomplished with force that is greater than the force required to achieve the taking. In other words, the force inherent in picking up an item and carrying it away is not sufficient to meet the requirements for robbery—that is simply the physical activity of taking implicit in any larceny. The classic example is pickpocketing. Although that involves some *de minimis* level of force (the reaching into the pocket), it does not include sufficient force to constitute robbery and is therefore an example of larceny. Since robbery legally requires an underlying theft as one of its elements, a legal defense to the theft will also serve as a defense to the robbery charge as well. In most jurisdictions, the use of a weapon during the theft turns the offense into the more serious crime of armed robbery.

B. APPLICATION

1. Unlawful Taking

If larceny requires a physical taking and carrying away, the question is how much of a taking is required. Taking the property home to your house certainly qualifies, but what if the perpetrator simply *moves* the property? Does that constitute theft?

State v. Carswell

Supreme Court of North Carolina
296 N.C. 101 (1978)

Upon a proper bill of indictment defendant was tried and convicted of felonious breaking and entering and felonious larceny. Respective consecutive sentences of ten and five years were imposed. He appealed both convictions to the Court of Appeals but they reversed as to the larceny conviction only and we allowed discretionary review thereon.

The State's evidence tended to show the following:

On the morning of 18 April 1976, Donald Ray Morgan was at the Day's Inn Motel where he was employed as a security guard. With him was Richard Strickland, a helper, and Mrs. Strickland, Richard's mother, who had brought her son some food. The motel was not in use at that time as it was still under construction. Upon inspection of the premises that morning, Mr. Morgan discovered that five or six rooms had been broken into during the night. In one of these, Room 158, the window air conditioner had been pried away from the base on which it rested in the bottom of the window, but it had not been removed.

Mr. Morgan asked Mrs. Strickland to stay at the motel while he called to report the incident to the Sheriff's Department. While he was gone, a pickup truck pulled into the motel with three people in it, one of them being the defendant. They wanted to get into the motel building and claimed that they were sent there by their boss. They left after Mrs. Strickland would not let them in.

Instead of relocking the doors that had been broken into, Mr. Morgan stayed at the motel and guarded the rooms from a point on the balcony of the second level some fifty to seventy-five feet away. Around 10:30 P.M. that night, the defendant and another man walked onto the premises of Day's Inn Motel from some nearby woods and entered Room 158. Through the window running across the entire front of the room, Mr. Morgan saw the two men take the air conditioner off its stand in the window and put it on the floor. The unit was moved approximately four to six inches toward the door.

After setting the air conditioner on the floor, the men left Room 158. Mr. Morgan stopped them as they appeared to be entering another room. The guard sent Mrs. Strickland, who again had come to the motel that night with food for her son, to the nearby Holiday Inn to call the Sheriff's Department.

Later that night, a pickup truck was seen driving up and down a road adjacent to the Day's Inn Motel. Mrs. Strickland testified that it was the same truck she had seen the defendant in that morning at the motel.

The defendant's evidence tended to show the following:

On 18 April 1976, the defendant and a friend had been drinking at a bar in Cleveland County and later at a club called The Shamrock in Burke

County. They walked up the road to the Day's Inn Motel. The two men decided to go into a room to lie down because they were tired and drunk and could not get a ride home.

They entered a room that had its door ajar; however, the two of them left because "it stunk so bad in there." As they started down the sidewalk outside the room, a man yelled and ordered them to stop. Thereafter they were arrested.

Defendant testified that he did not touch the air conditioner at any time. He also stated that he had not gone to the Day's Inn Motel earlier that day and had never seen Mrs. Strickland before.

COPELAND, J.

The Court of Appeals held that the movement of the air conditioner in this case was an insufficient taking and asportation to constitute a case of larceny against the defendant. Because we believe that there was enough evidence to send the larceny charge to the jury, we reverse the Court of Appeals on this point. . . .

Larceny has been defined as "a wrongful taking and carrying away of the personal property of another without his consent, . . . with intent to deprive the owner of his property and to appropriate it to the taker's use fraudulently." "A bare removal from the place in which he found the goods, though the thief does not quite make off with them, is a sufficient asportation, or carrying away." 4 W. Blackstone, Commentaries 231.

In *State v. Green*, 81 N.C. 560 (1879), the defendant unlocked his employer's safe and completely removed a drawer containing money. He was stopped before any of the money was taken from the drawer. This Court found these actions sufficient to constitute asportation of the money, and we upheld the larceny conviction.

The movement of the air conditioner in this case off its window base and four to six inches toward the door clearly is "a bare removal from the place in which the thief found (it)." The Court of Appeals apparently agreed; however, it correctly recognized that there is a taking element in larceny in addition to the asportation requirement. 4 W. Blackstone, supra at 231. The Court of Appeals stated that "here the problem with the State's case is that the evidence of asportation does not also constitute sufficient evidence of taking."

This Court has defined "taking" in this context as the "severance of the goods from the possession of the owner." Thus, the accused must not only move the goods, but he must also have them in his possession, or under his control, even if only for an instant. This defendant picked the air conditioner up from its stand and laid it on the floor. This act was sufficient to put the object briefly under the control of the defendant, severed from the owner's possession.

In rare and somewhat comical situations, it is possible to have an asportation of an object without taking it, or gaining possession of it.

"In a very famous case a rascal walking by a store lifted an overcoat from a dummy and endeavored to walk away with it. He soon discovered that the overcoat was secured by a chain and he did not succeed in breaking the chain. This was held not to be larceny because the rascal did not at any time have possession of the garment. He thought he did until he reached the end of the chain, but he was mistaken." R. Perkins, *Criminal Law* 222 (1957).

The air conditioner in question was not permanently connected to the premises of Day's Inn Motel at the time of the crime. It had previously been pried up from its base; therefore, when defendant and his companion moved it, they had possession of it for that moment. Thus, there was sufficient evidence to take the larceny charge to the jury.

The defendant's and the Court of Appeals' reliance on *State v. Jones*, 65 N.C. 395 (1871), is misplaced. In that case, the defendant merely turned a large barrel of turpentine, that was standing on its head, over on its side. This Court held that shifting the position of an object without moving it from where it was found is insufficient asportation to support a larceny conviction. The facts of this case show that there was an actual removal of the air conditioner from its base in the window to a point on the floor four to six inches toward the door. Thus, *Jones* is not controlling.

For the reasons stated above, the decision of the Court of Appeals is reversed, and the larceny judgment reinstated.

NOTES & QUESTIONS ON TAKINGS

1. *Asportation.* Other offenses require asportation. For example, the crime of kidnapping requires that the defendant carry away the victim, even if only slightly. Indeed, the element of asportation is what distinguishes kidnapping from false imprisonment where the defendant merely confines, but does not move, the victim. In the context of kidnapping, asportation can be relatively slight (e.g., forcibly moving victim from dining room to closet), so much so that the Supreme Court of Georgia noted that the "definition of asportation has evolved to the point where it seems that the only type of movement considered insufficient as evidence of asportation is movement immediately resulting from a physical struggle." *Garza v. State*, 284 Ga. 696, 670 S.E.2d 73 (2008). The Georgia Supreme Court pushed back against the modern trend toward expansive definitions of asportation and concluded that courts should look to the following factors: "(1) the duration of the movement; (2) whether the

movement occurred during the commission of a separate offense; (3) whether such movement was an inherent part of that separate offense; and (4) whether the movement itself presented a significant danger to the victim independent of the danger posed by the separate offense."

2. *Custody versus possession.*   In order to qualify as a taking, the victim must deprive the victim of possession of the property. But what if the victim voluntarily hands the property to an actor—such as a courier—with instructions to deliver the property to a particular location. If the actor takes the property for himself instead, has he committed larceny? The defendant could argue that he already had possession of the property and therefore did not take the property from the victim's possession. The answer to this riddle lies in the common law's distinction between custody and possession. Consider the case of *United States v. Mafnas*, 701 F.2d 83 (9th Cir. 1983). Mafnas worked for an armored car company that transported bags of money from the Bank of Hawaii and the Bank of America. On multiple occasions, Mafnas opened the bags and took some of the money. Mafnas argued in defense that he was innocent because he already had possession of the bags of money and did not take them from the banks. His conviction was upheld because he was given "custody" but not "possession" of the bags. According to the court, "Mafnas was given temporary custody only, to deliver the money bags to their various destinations. The later decision to take the money was larceny, because it was beyond the consent of the owner, who retained constructive possession until the custodian's task was completed."

HYPOTHETICAL

Suppose Bob is a college student who gets hold of his final exam before it will be administered. This is clearly cheating, but is it theft? Assume for the sake of argument that the student acted fraudulently in obtaining the exam, but that he never removed the physical paper from its proper location. In other words, instead of taking the exam paper with him, he simply *read* the information on the sheet and left it in its place. Can this constitute larceny?

In a case with similar facts, *Oxford v. Moss*, 68 Crim. App. Rep. 183 (1979), a British court refused to convict the student of theft, presumably because the student neither carried away the exam nor planned to keep it. As you read the following materials, try to determine if a court could convict a cheating student based on some other theory of this case. For more analysis, see Stuart P. Green, *Thirteen Ways to Steal a Bicycle* 237 (2012).

2. Fraud, Extortion, Blackmail, and Embezzlement

What distinguishes the different theft offenses is the level of *control* that the victim has over the property (custody, possession, or title) and the *manner* in which the perpetrator convinces the victim to give up the property. In the following case, pay particular attention to the *reason* the victim had for giving up the money. The key idea is that the victim consents to transfer of property to the defendant, but that consent is obtained through impermissible means. What precisely was impermissible about the defendant's actions in this case?

United States v. Villalobos

U.S. Court of Appeals for the Ninth Circuit
748 F.3d 953 (2014)

SMITH, CIRCUIT JUDGE.

Defendant-Appellant Alfred Nash Villalobos appeals from his conviction for attempted extortion, in violation of 18 U.S.C. § 1951(a), and endeavoring to obstruct justice, in violation of 18 U.S.C. § 1503(a). Villalobos claims that the district court erred in instructing the jury that all threats to testify or provide information are "wrongful" under the Hobbs Act if made with the intent to induce or take advantage of fear, and in precluding a claim of right defense to the attempted extortion charge. We hold that even though the district court's jury instruction was erroneous, that error was harmless. We also hold that the district court did not err in precluding Villalobos's claim of right defense. We affirm.

FACTUAL AND PROCEDURAL BACKGROUND

This appeal arises out of the government's investigation of Rabbi Amitai Yemeni (Rabbi Yemeni), the director of the Los Angeles Chabad Israel Center (Center), because of his efforts to help Israeli nationals obtain visas to come to the United States under the pretext that they were religious workers at the Center. Pursuant to Rabbi Yemeni's scheme, such individuals would not work at the Center, but would be paid as if they were. They would then return to Rabbi Yemeni the money paid to them by the Center.

Orit Anjel (Orit) came to the United States, allegedly as a religious worker at the Center. Orit was accompanied by her husband Avraham Anjel (Avi). Orit purportedly worked at the Center, and Avi received her paychecks. Avi regularly cashed the checks at a bank, and, in turn, gave the money to Rabbi Yemeni. In 2009, Orit received a letter from Rabbi Yemeni terminating her work at the Center.

When Orit was terminated, Avi engaged Villalobos, a lawyer, to help him recoup the money he had paid to Rabbi Yemeni. Through his discussions with Avi, Villalobos learned that the government wanted to interview Orit as part of its investigation into Rabbi Yemeni's scheme. Villalobos then approached Rabbi Yemeni, and later Rabbi Yemeni's lawyer, Benjamin Gluck (Gluck), and demanded payment. Villalobos contends that he was merely helping the Anjels recover back wages for Orit's work at the Center that Rabbi Yemeni had improperly required them to remit to him. The government, on the other hand, contends that Villalobos was attempting to extort Rabbi Yemeni, and that in return for payment, Villalobos promised that Orit would do "whatever it is we need her to do," including impeding the investigation, lying to investigating Assistant U.S. Attorney Keri Axel (Axel), and repeating those lies to the grand jury.

Gluck informed Axel about Villalobos's demands for payment, and agreed to record his subsequent communications with Villalobos. FBI Special Agent Gary Bennett was assigned to supervise Gluck's communications with Villalobos. Gluck recorded his conversations with Villalobos, both in person and over the phone, in which they discussed various aspects of the plan to pay Villalobos in return for Orit's favorable testimony during the investigation.

Villalobos was arrested after Gluck gave him a cash payment, shortly before Orit's scheduled meeting with Axel. Villalobos was charged with one count of attempted extortion, 18 U.S.C. § 1951(a), and one count of endeavoring to obstruct justice, 18 U.S.C. § 1503(a). After a five day trial, the jury returned a guilty verdict on both counts, and the district court entered judgment. Villalobos timely appealed.

DISCUSSION

Extortion is defined in the Hobbs Act as "the obtaining of property from another, with his consent, induced by *wrongful* use of actual or threatened force, violence, or fear, or under color of official right." 18 U.S.C. § 1951(b)(2) (emphasis added).

Villalobos contends that the district court erred when it instructed the jury that all threats to testify or provide information are "wrongful" under the Hobbs Act if made with the intent to induce or take advantage of fear. Closely related to his initial contention, Villalobos also argues that the district court erred when it precluded him from presenting a claim of right defense to the extortion charge. More specifically, Villalobos contends that he had a lawful claim to the property he demanded on behalf of Orit, and that as such his actions were not "wrongful" in the sense required by the Hobbs Act.

In *United States v. Enmons,* 410 U.S. 396 (1973), the Supreme Court concluded that the use of force to achieve legitimate labor ends was not extortion. The Court interpreted the word "wrongful" in the Hobbs Act to "limit[ ] the statute's coverage to those instances where the obtaining of the property would itself be 'wrongful' because the alleged extortionist has no lawful claim to that property." It reasoned that "[t]he term 'wrongful,' which on the face of the statute modifies the use of each of the enumerated means of obtaining property—actual or threatened force, violence, or fear—would be superfluous if it only served to describe the means used. For it would be redundant to speak of 'wrongful violence' or 'wrongful force' since . . . any violence or force to obtain property is 'wrongful.'" The Court thus held that violence in the labor context is not wrongful for purposes of extortion if the defendant has a lawful claim to the property, or a "claim of right."

In *United States v. Daane*, 475 F.3d 1114, 1119-20 (9th Cir. 2007), we held that the claim of right defense described in *Enmons* is unavailable in cases involving physical violence outside of the labor context, because such violence is inherently wrongful. We agreed with the reasoning of *United States v. Zappola*, 677 F.2d 264 (2d Cir. 1982), which concluded that "Congress meant to punish as extortion any effort to obtain property *by inherently wrongful means* . . . regardless of the defendant's claim of right to the property." In other words, we recognized in *Daane* that outside the labor context, there are some attempts to obtain property that are so inherently wrongful that whether the defendant had a lawful claim to the property demanded is not relevant in determining whether extortion or attempted extortion has been proven.

In the present case, we consider whether *nonviolent* threats outside the labor context can be "wrongful" under the Hobbs Act. The threats at issue in this case—threats to cooperate with an ongoing criminal investigation—are unlike the threats of force or violence outside the labor context discussed in *Daane,* because the threats at issue here are not inherently wrongful. Indeed, our law encourages individuals to cooperate with ongoing criminal investigations and proceedings.

We conclude that where a nonviolent threat to obtain property is not, by its nature, inherently wrongful, a court must first consider whether the threat, as actually used in the case at issue (the "means"), is wrongful, without regard to the property demanded by the defendant (the "ends"). If a nonviolent threat is wrongful under the circumstances, then it is sufficient to sustain a conviction for extortion or attempted extortion. In such situations, a court need not consider whether the defendant has a lawful claim to the property demanded. This approach is consistent with *Daane,* which recognized that certain "means" to obtain property are "wrongful" under the Hobbs Act without regard to the "ends" sought by the defendant. A similar means-ends framework was adopted by the First Circuit in *United States v. Sturm,* 870 F.2d 769 (1st Cir. 1989).

Here, Villalobos's "means" were his threats to have Orit cooperate with the investigation of Rabbi Yemeni, contingent upon payment, and his "ends" were the money, fraudulent tax receipts for donations, and a job or job recommendation for Orit that he demanded from Rabbi Yemeni. Unlike violent threats, threats to cooperate with an ongoing criminal investigation are clearly not wrongful per se under the Hobbs Act. However, if Villalobos's threats were wrongful under the circumstances, they are sufficient to sustain a conviction for attempted extortion, without regard to the "ends" Villalobos sought.

The district court instructed the jury that a threat of testifying or providing information was "wrongful" under the Hobbs Act "if it [wa]s made with the intent to induce or take advantage of fear. . . ." But by their nature, threats are intended to induce or take advantage of fear. Accordingly, an instruction that threats are wrongful if intended to induce or take advantage of fear would necessarily lead a jury to conclude that all threats are wrongful. The district court's instruction was thus erroneous because it essentially read the "wrongful" element out of the Hobbs Act.

Since the district court's instruction was erroneous, we must consider whether the district court's error was "harmless beyond a reasonable doubt."

To determine whether the district court's error was harmless, we first evaluate whether Villalobos's threats to cooperate with the ongoing investigation were wrongful. The evidence is clear beyond a reasonable doubt that any rational jury would have found Villalobos guilty absent the erroneous jury instruction because Villalobos's "means" to obtain the property—his threats to have his client Orit cooperate with, or alternatively, impede, the ongoing investigation, contingent upon payment—were unlawful, and therefore clearly wrongful under the circumstances. The evidence overwhelmingly shows that Villalobos threatened to have Orit change the story she would provide to the investigating authorities, depending on whether Rabbi Yemeni paid him. For example, Villalobos repeatedly promised to influence Orit to have her "shade[ ]" things as necessary and to "do whatever it is [they] need her to do" during her interview with Axel if Rabbi Yemeni paid him. Villalobos made clear through his conversations with Gluck that what Orit would tell government agents and the grand jury depended on whether Rabbi Yemeni acceded to his demands.

As evidence of the unlawfulness of Villalobos's conduct, the jury necessarily found that Villalobos's conduct was unlawful when it found him guilty of endeavoring to obstruct justice by instructing Orit to make false and misleading statements to the investigators in exchange for payment. The district court instructed the jury that in order to prove obstruction of justice, the government had to prove beyond a reasonable doubt that Villalobos sought payment and other compensation "from the target of a pending federal grand jury investigation in exchange for an agreement that [Villalobos] would cause his client, Orit . . . , to make false and misleading statements to [Axel] or the grand jury conducting that investigation. . . ." Because the record makes clear beyond a reasonable doubt that any rational jury would have found that Villalobos's threats were wrongful because they were unlawful, his threats were sufficient to sustain a conviction for attempted extortion.

In light of the above, although the district court's jury instruction on wrongfulness was erroneous, that error was harmless. Because Villalobos's threats were wrongful under the Hobbs Act, we need not reach the question whether a claim of right defense is available in this context. Even if available, such a claim would do nothing to shield Villalobos from conviction of attempted extortion. The district court did not err by not providing a claim of right instruction.

NOTES & QUESTIONS ON FRAUD AND EXTORTION

1. *Means versus ends.* Why should Villalobos be convicted for promising that his client would help with a police investigation? Isn't that what all law-abiding citizens should do (cooperate with the authorities)? Furthermore, if Villalobos's client was entitled to the money because the target of the extortion scheme had acted inappropriately in the first place, Villalobos's prosecution seems especially harsh. The key to understanding the Ninth Circuit's decision is that the court considered Villalobos's threat to be "wrongful" because he made the client's cooperation with the authorities *conditional* on the receipt of the payment from the target of the extortion scheme. That condition is what made the process wrongful because it made the target of the scheme fearful of a negative outcome if she did not provide the money. The Ninth Circuit also focused on the lawyer's promise that the client would "shade" things and do whatever was necessary to make the investigation come to a particular conclusion. This suggested lies, deceit, or obstruction of an official investigation. Without this element to the case—say if the lawyer had simply promised that the client would help the authorities in only appropriate ways—would it still have constituted extortion?

2. *Lawyers and extortion.* Lawyers pressure those on the other side of the table all the time. "Pay my client what you owe him or we will sue you." "Settle this case or we will take it to trial and you will lose big." "Close this deal on our terms otherwise we will walk." These types of strong-arm tactics are often part of hard-nose lawyering. When do they cross the line into extortion? Consider, for example, *State v. Harrington*, 260 A.2d 692 (Vt. 1969). In that case, a woman was embroiled in a contentious divorce. Her lawyer told the husband that he needed to agree to a favorable settlement of the divorce because otherwise the lawyer would divulge information regarding the husband's illegal

conduct to the authorities. This constituted the crime of extortion. *Harrington* was an easy extortion case because the lawyer allegedly used the threat to obtain a better settlement than what he would have obtained in the absence of the threat. But in *Villalobos*, the extorted property was simply the money that the lawyer's client was already due. The application of the crime of extortion to legal negotiations is unsettled and young lawyers are often advised to tread carefully in this area. Some jurisdictions have passed statutory exemptions to specifically clarify that extortion does not apply when "the property obtained by threat of accusation, exposure, lawsuit or other invocation of official action was honestly claimed as restitution or indemnification for harm done in the circumstances to which such accusation, exposure, lawsuit or other official action relates, or as compensation for property or lawful services." 18 Pa. Const. Stat. § 3923(b).

3. *The concept of consent.* There is something paradoxical about fraud, extortion, and embezzlement. In each of these cases, the defendant "consents" to giving the perpetrator the property, but something about the consent is problematic or invalid. So did the victim consent to the property being taken or not? The answer is yes and no—at the same time. For more discussion of this paradox, see Stuart P. Green, *Consent and the Grammar of Theft Law*, 28 Cardozo L. Rev. 2505 (2007). Green suggests that the seeming paradox stems from different senses of the phrase "consent." The first is expressive consent, where the victim *says* that the perpetrator can have the property. The second is prescriptive consent, where the victim voluntarily and meaningfully consents to the transfer. In extortion, the victim "consents" in the first sense but not in the second sense.

PROBLEM CASE

In 2012, Janet Miller was arrested and charged with grand larceny and fortune telling, which is a misdemeanor offense in the State of New York. The district attorney predicated the grand larceny charge on a fraud theory, alleging that Miller convinced one of her fortune-telling clients to give her $600,000 in fees in exchange for cleansing the woman of evil spirits. The fortuneteller claimed that she was able to procure images of the client's dead relatives and even suggested a positive resolution to the cancer that was devastating the client's father. Miller eventually pleaded guilty to the grand larceny charge. Russ Buettner, *Fortuneteller Pleads Guilty to Grand Larceny Charge*, N.Y. Times, May 10, 2013. Did the government's prosecution of the fortuneteller have to do with the falsity of her spiritual claims regarding evil spirits and images of the victim's dead relatives? If a spiritual advisor for an established church had convinced a worshipper to donate her money to a charity or the church itself, would larceny by fraud apply to that transaction as well?

3. Property

In order to engage in theft, one must steal *something*. But what does that something have to *be*? It has to be personal property. In this day and age, property can sometimes mean more than tangible physical objects and might also include less physical entities. In the following case, determine the outer scope of "property" as the concept is understood in theft law.

Penley v. Commonwealth
Court of Appeals of Virginia
51 Va. App. 166 (2008)

ANNUNZIATA, J.

Appellant was convicted in a jury trial of obtaining utility service by fraud in violation of Code § 18.2-187.1. He contends that the evidence was insufficient to prove that he obtained utility services valued at more than $200 and that the trial court erred when it failed to strike the Commonwealth's case. We agree and reverse appellant's conviction.

BACKGROUND

The facts are not in dispute. On April 29, 2005, a Dominion Virginia Power ("Dominion") employee, Carl Wohlleb, visited appellant's house to determine whether electricity continued to be used following an earlier meter removal. Wohlleb discovered that an illegal meter had been installed at appellant's house. Appellant asked Wohlleb to "look the other way and leave the meter in place." When Wohlleb refused, appellant told Wohlleb to get off his property.

Wohlleb went to his car and called a serviceman to disconnect the power at the pole that supplied power to the illegal meter. He also called the police.

Officer Matt Connelly arrested appellant for utility fraud. Subsequently, appellant admitted that his power had been turned off on April 5, 2005, that he owed Dominion $1,200, and that he had "incurred three hundred dollars since then."

Kevin Woolridge, a Dominion employee, testified that the power provided to appellant between April 5, 2005 and April 29, 2005 was valued at $82.29. Woolridge also testified the following costs were associated with appellant's service, and the court included them in its calculation of the value of the services appellant had wrongfully obtained:

a. Fee to turn off meter on April 5, 2005 $34.12
b. Fee for service investigator visit (Wohlleb) $34.48
c. Fee for service technician to turn off power at pole $75.00
d. Monthly flat fee for being a Dominion Power customer $7.00
e. Utility and taxes $4.67

Concluding that the value of the services appellant fraudulently obtained from the power company was greater than $200, the court denied appellant's motion to strike the Commonwealth's case.

ANALYSIS

Appellant argues the "value of service, credit or benefit procured" under Code § 18.2-187.1(D) only includes the value of the electrical current received. On that ground, he argues that the Commonwealth failed to prove the value of the services he fraudulently obtained was greater than $200. He reasons that Code § 18.2-187.1 makes a distinction between "value of services received" and "costs" and that the latter are only recoverable as restitution. We agree.

Code § 18.2-187.1 provides, in relevant part:

B. It shall be unlawful for any person to obtain or attempt to obtain oil, electric, gas, water, telephone, telegraph, cable television or electronic communication service by the use of any scheme, device, means or method, or by a false application for service with intent to avoid payment of lawful charges therefor.

. . .

D. Any person who violates any provisions of this section, if the value of service, credit or benefit procured is $200 or more, shall be guilty of a Class 6 felony; or if the value is less than $200, shall be guilty of a Class 1 misdemeanor. In addition, the court may order restitution for the value of the services unlawfully used and for all costs. Such costs shall be limited to actual expenses, including the base wages of employees acting as witnesses for the Commonwealth, and suit costs. However, the total amount of allowable costs granted hereunder shall not exceed $250, excluding the value of the service.

In *Lund v. Commonwealth,* 217 Va. 688, 232 S.E.2d 745 (1977), the Supreme Court of Virginia held that the common law offense of larceny did not include the theft of computer time or services. In response to *Lund,* the General Assembly enacted Code § 18.2-98.1 and several related statutes, including Code § 18.2-187.1, to include certain services as the subject of larceny.

We hold that the offense created under Code § 18.2-187.1 is a species of larceny. As such, the "value of service, credit or benefit procured" is to be measured at the time the services were taken. The Commonwealth's argument that the court properly considered the additional expenses charged to appellant's account because such expenses would be charged "to any customer . . . whose power was being disconnected[,]" and because they were "a direct result of the illegal actions of Penley," is not consistent with these well-established common law principles governing the prosecution of larceny offenses.

> Any additional "costs" incurred by the electric company as a result of the theft must be excluded from the court's calculation of value. Accordingly, the trial court erred in denying appellant's motion to strike the Commonwealth's case because the evidence failed to establish that the value of services obtained was $200 or more. . . .

NOTES & QUESTIONS ON PROPERTY

1. *Intellectual property.*   Academic researchers often produce inventions that receive patent protection. If the patent has some commercial application, the patent can be licensed to third parties for a huge amount of money—sometimes millions of dollars. For example, if the patent involves a process important for drug manufacturing, the licensing fees are very lucrative. Generally speaking, universities retain the right to the patents emerging from the work performed by their employees. Occasionally, disputes arise between former employees and universities over this intellectual property. In 2003, a federal district court ruled that Dr. John Fenn had engaged in civil theft by failing to disclose his chemical mass spectometry invention to his employer, Yale University. Under Yale's intellectual property policy, the university retained rights to the patent with licensing fees to be shared between the scientist and the institution. Since Fenn failed to disclose the patent to Yale, the university sued him for theft. Although the case involved civil, rather than criminal, theft, the basic property principles are the same. The court concluded that Fenn's actions could be described either as theft by false pretense (fraud) or theft by embezzlement because he converted Yale's intellectual property—which he had professional access to—for personal gain. *Fenn v. Yale University*, 2005 WL 327138 (D. Conn. 2005).

On the criminal law side, intellectual property theft is usually prosecuted by the federal government. According to the FBI, "intellectual property theft costs U.S. businesses billions of dollars a year and robs the nation of jobs and lost tax revenues. Preventing intellectual property theft is a priority of the FBI's criminal investigative program. We specifically focus on the theft of trade secrets and infringements on products that can impact consumers' health and safety, such as counterfeit aircraft, car, and electronic parts. Key to our success is linking the considerable resources and efforts of the private sector with law enforcement partners on local, state, federal, and international levels." For a discussion of intellectual property as property, see Stephen L. Carter, *Does It Matter Whether Intellectual Property Is Property?*, 68 Chi.-Kent L. Rev. 715 (1993).

4. Intent to Deprive Permanently

The mental element for theft offenses requires that the defendant intended to deprive the victim of the property "permanently." This requires consideration of an imagined future, since by definition the defendant is arrested and prosecuted before the end of time. The operative question becomes: Did the defendant intend to keep the property or was she going to return it? As you read the following case, look for how the court structures its inquiry into the defendant's future intentions with regard to the property.

Marsh v. Commonwealth
Court of Appeals of Virginia
57 Va. App. 645 (2011)

HUMPHREYS, J.

Bernard Chesley Marsh ("Marsh") was convicted in a bench trial of grand larceny, in violation of Code § 18.2-95, and was sentenced to four years incarceration with all but sixty days suspended. On appeal, Marsh argues that the trial court erred in finding the evidence sufficient to support his conviction of grand larceny. Specifically, he contends that he never intended to permanently deprive Rhonda Gazda ("Gazda") of her property. For the following reasons, we disagree and affirm the trial court's conviction.

BACKGROUND

. . . On October 17, 2008, Marsh went to Gazda's apartment to attend a birthday party with her. Gazda, Marsh's girlfriend of approximately two years, was getting ready when she noticed she was missing a ring from her jewelry box along with some other items. She asked Marsh if he had taken the missing items. Marsh replied he had needed some quick cash so he had pawned the items, but he would get the jewelry back when he got paid the next day. They then attended the birthday party together. Upon returning to her apartment after the party, Gazda told Marsh she did not want him staying with her. After Marsh left, Gazda called the police, and reported the missing items as stolen property. Gazda testified that she never allowed Marsh to take items or pawn items before even though he had done so in March 2008, with some of the same pieces and had subsequently returned them.

Detective Richard Buisch, with the Fairfax County Police Department, became involved with the case when he came in contact with Gazda on an unrelated matter. Gazda informed Detective Buisch that she had reported the stolen property, and asked what had happened with regards to the report. Detective Buisch contacted Marsh, and made arrangements with him for the return of the items. Marsh returned some of the items that he had pawned to Detective Buisch, and informed him that he was trying to save up money to purchase the other items back. After giving Marsh two to three weeks to come up with the money to retrieve the rest of the items, Detective Buisch placed a hold on them when Marsh did not obtain the rest of the items, retrieved them from Vienna Jewelry and Estate Buyers in Vienna, Virginia, and returned them to Gazda. . . .

Marsh took the stand at trial and testified that he had taken the items and pawned them to help carry him through a job he was working on. Marsh stated that he had initially needed approximately $500. When asked why he continued to pawn more items after he received that amount, he replied "[b]y then I was in a position where I was robbing Peter to pay Paul . . . [t]hat was Ms. Gazda to pay the shop." He also stated that he had informed Gazda he would get her items back when he was paid the next day. Marsh further testified that it was always his intent "to redeem [the jewelry] and give it back to her" as soon as he received his check.

At trial, Marsh made a motion to strike the charge against him, contending that the evidence was insufficient to prove he intended to permanently deprive Gazda of the jewelry. The trial court denied the motion, and found him guilty of grand larceny. . . .

ANALYSIS

. . . "In Virginia, larceny is a common law crime. We have defined larceny as 'the wrongful or fraudulent taking of personal goods of some intrinsic value, belonging to another, without his assent, and with the intention to deprive the owner thereof permanently.'" "Stated simply, larceny requires that there be a taking and asportation of the seized goods, coupled with an intent to steal those goods."

. . . However, "'[o]ne who takes another's property intending at the time he takes it to use it temporarily and then to return it unconditionally within a reasonable time—and having a substantial ability to do so—lacks the intent to steal required for larceny.'" "An intent to return, however, must be unconditional. Thus it is no defense to larceny that the taker intends to return the property only if he should receive a reward for its return, or only upon some other condition which he has no right to impose."

As noted above, it is not a defense to larceny merely to have an intent to return the property; in addition one must, at the time of taking, have a substantial ability to do so (even though, as events turn out, it may later become impossible to do so). . . . So too, an intent to pawn the property, accompanied by an intent later to redeem the property and return it to its owner, is a defense only if the taker's financial situation is such that he has an ability to redeem it.

Marsh acknowledges that there was a trespassory taking of Gazda's property, but argues that the evidence was insufficient to prove that he intended to *permanently* deprive her of that property rather than temporarily. While the fact finder could have reasonably inferred from Marsh's acknowledgment that he took the property that he intended to steal it, Marsh contends that the facts do not support this inference because they do not establish beyond a reasonable doubt that he intended to permanently deprive her of the jewelry—that there is "counterveiling evidence of intention otherwise." Specifically, he argues that the evidence negates any inference that he intended to permanently deprive her of the property because the transactions were written up as loans, he had made several payments on those loans, none of the loans had gone past their maturity except the ones the police placed a hold on, and he had redeemed some of the items.

In response, the Commonwealth asks this Court to broaden the conditions excluded under the "unconditional" return requirement of the intent to permanently deprive defense to include this type of situation where the return of the property was conditioned on Marsh's receipt of his paycheck and on the condition that he subsequently redeem the property from the pawnshop. However, we decline the Commonwealth's invitation to do so. In this case, Marsh was not placing a condition on Gazda that she has to pay off the loans in order to receive the property back, nor is he placing some other condition on her that he has no right to impose. As has been noted by our Supreme Court, "it is no defense to larceny that the taker intends to return the property only if he should receive a reward for its return, or only upon some other condition which he has no right to impose." The Supreme Court noted that "[t]o take property by trespass for the purpose of 'selling' it to the owner is larceny."

The cases in which courts have declined to find the lack of an intent to permanently deprive a defense to larceny due to a condition imposed have all involved the defendant placing a condition on the original owners of the property, and not a condition the defendant has imposed upon himself or that is imposed upon him by a third party. Because the condition in this case is not one placed on Gazda, we do not find that the return of the property was based on a condition Marsh had no right to impose, and we decline to apply the "unconditional" return requirement to the facts of this case.

Rather, in turning to the facts of this case, we hold the evidence was sufficient to support the fact finder's conclusion that Marsh did not have the substantial ability to return the property to Gazda at the time he took it because of his financial situation. Marsh testified that he took the items because he was having money troubles, and needed money in order to carry him through a job he was working on. In order to redeem the property, Marsh would need $3,272.50. However, the only job he had at that time was a contract for carpentry work in which he would receive a total of $2,000 in installments as the work was completed. In addition, he was behind on other bills, and the initial $800 installment that he received from the $2,000 went towards payment of those outstanding bills. The evidence shows that he did not have that amount at the time he pawned the items, nor was he able to get that amount when Detective Buisch gave him a few weeks to do so. Marsh had neither the present ability nor the prospective ability at the time he took the items because of his financial situation to return the property. Thus, he did not have the substantial ability required, and his stated intent to return the property is not a defense to larceny.

In addition, the trial judge, as the fact finder, was not required to believe Marsh's testimony that he intended to return the jewelry to Gazda the next day when he got paid and could retrieve the items from the pawnshop. . . .

For these reasons, we find the evidence supports the trial court's factual finding that Marsh intended to permanently deprive Gazda of her property. Accordingly, we hold that the trial court did not err in holding the evidence sufficient to find Marsh guilty of grand larceny in violation of Code § 18.2-95, and affirm.

NOTES & QUESTIONS ON INTENT TO DEPRIVE

1. *Ability to return.*   The court in *Marsh* agreed with the prosecutor's argument that the defendant did not intend to return the property. However, the court offered a completely different rationale for this conclusion than the one submitted by the prosecutor. The government position was that the intention to return was conditional on Marsh's receiving his next paycheck, as opposed to unconditional. The court was unwilling to sustain a conviction for larceny on that theory. Instead, the court concluded that Marsh had no ability to get the property back because even when he received his next paycheck he still would not have enough cash to repossess the jewelry from the pawn shop. Thus, even if he had a putative "intention" to return the property, he had no ability to do so, thus rendering his intention illusory in some sense. One way of putting the point is that he had the desire to return the property but no means to do so, thus making his intention no more than an abstract wish.

2. *Conditional returns.*   As the court conceded in *Marsh*, there is a long line of cases holding that a defendant's conditional intent to return the property is insufficient to generate a defense to a theft charge. So taking store merchandise with the intent to claim a false refund later constitutes theft because the return of the item is conditional on the defendant's receiving the false refund. But is this the correct way to analyze such cases? Perhaps the defendant should be charged with fraud for improperly claiming the refund—money that the shopper clearly intends to keep forever. If the shopper is caught before claiming the refund, should he be charged with attempted fraud for trying to get the refund or larceny for taking the store item?

Consider the case of *State v. Hauptma*
which arose from the kidnapping of fam
Hauptman was charged with multiple off
and murder of the Lindbergh boy. One of
the theft of the *clothes* the boy was wearing
idence. Hauptman had sent the clothes back t
he was the real kidnapper and that the ranso
Thus, Hauptman argued that he did not have th
the property because he returned it. However
return was not unconditional. Instead, the return
paying the ransom for the boy. Do you agree? T
certainly meant to *induce* payment of the ransom
thing as making the return of the clothing *condition*
The clothes were sent during the negotiations befoi   ..as paid.

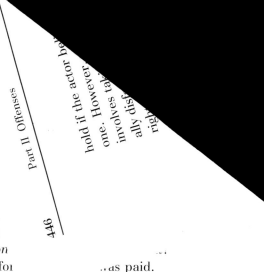

3. *Mistake of fact and larceny.* What if the actor believes that he has a valid claim of right to the property that he takes? Recall that a mistake of fact may be a defense if it negatives a required element of the offense. In the case of larceny, the mental element is that the actor intends to permanently deprive another of his or her property. In theory, the actor's belief that he is the rightful owner of the property will negate this mental state, even if the belief is unreasonable. In that situation, he cannot intend to deprive another of property if he does not believe that the property belongs to another. The same result would

---

HYPOTHETICAL

Imagine that the Hamburglar steals B's hamburger. The Hamburglar—ever hungry—immediately wolfs down the hamburger, which is now gone. Has he committed theft? The defendant must have the intent to permanently deprive the victim of the property, but in this case the hamburger is now destroyed and no one has it. What result?

Courts have not always defined the temporal concept literally. For example, in *People v. Avery*, 115 Cal. Rptr. 2d 403 (2002), the California Supreme Court clarified that "an intent to take the property for so extended a period as to deprive the owner of a major portion of its value or enjoyment satisfies the

common law, and therefore California, intent requirement." The court continued: "[T]here is an intent to steal when the *nature* of the property is such that even a temporary taking will deprive the owner of its primary economic value, e.g., when the property is dated material or perishable in nature or good for only seasonal use." Examples include taking cut flowers from a florist with the intent to return them a week later (once they had died), taking a lawn mower for the summer with the intent to return it in the fall, or taking property with the intent to abandon it later so the owner cannot recover it. Which category best describes the theft of the hamburger?

lieves that the property is abandoned and not owned by any-
the same result would not necessarily hold for robbery, which
ing property with physical force. Such self-help measures are gener-
avored, even if the actor honestly believes that he has a legitimate claim of
t to the property. See, e.g., *People v. Green*, 5 N.Y.3d 538, 544 (2005).

C. PRACTICE & POLICY

One of the biggest sources of theft—broadly construed—is financial fraud. Some of these cases are prosecuted by local authorities. In the following section, we consider two types of financial fraud: securities fraud by corporate managers and insider trading based on confidential information. In both cases, it is genuinely unclear what type of harm is being penalized by the government. Is it based on the property loss to the wronged investor, as in theft, or is it based on some deeper principle of honesty and fair dealing?

    ∾ Securities fraud.   The biggest frauds occur in the financial and securities context. Although these cases are usually prosecuted by the federal government under specific securities fraud statutes, the underlying principles all flow from basic principles of common law theft. A typical securities fraud case involves senior management who manipulate the reporting of their corporation's financial success to make the company appear more profitable than it actually is. Senior managers might be motivated to misrepresent the financial health of the company because doing so keeps the stock price high. This in turn increases the value of management's stock options. However, when the truth is then discovered and disclosed to the market, the stock price often plummets. The victims of this type of fraud include the shareholders who bought shares at the inflated prices and lost money when the value of their investments plummeted. These cases are often called "fraud on the market" cases because the fraudulent information corrupts the market's valuation of the stock and causes the stock purchaser to pay an inflated price. See, e.g., *Basic Inc. v. Levinson*, 485 U.S. 224 (1988). If the firm ends up closing as a result of the fraud, employees and retirees are often collateral victims of the fraud.

    In 2001, the energy giant Enron collapsed. It was once a corporate powerhouse but fell quickly into bankruptcy when its balance sheets were revealed to be fraudulent. Through a series of complex financial transactions that shifted liabilities off its balance sheet, the firm was able to maintain the illusion of profitability when in fact it was struggling financially.

When it went bankrupt, investors lost billions of dollars through the devaluation of their stock holdings. Founder Kenneth Lay, Chief Executive Officer Jeffrey Skilling, and Chief Financial Officer Andrew Fastow (pictured here) were all prosecuted for their role in the fraud.

The Justice Department also pursued Enron's financial auditors, the global accounting firm Arthur Andersen LLP, for its role in the scandal and for obstructing the securities fraud investigation into Enron. The criminal charges effectively led to the dissolution of the accounting firm, although the Supreme Court eventually overturned the conviction. But by that time the firm had already ceased operating as an accounting and auditing firm. Employees of Arthur Andersen, including those whose work had nothing to do with the Enron account, lost their jobs. Was prosecuting Arthur Andersen LLP the right prosecutorial decision?

Enron CFO Andrew Fastow

In order to reduce the likelihood of these frauds, Congress passed the Sarbanes-Oxley Act in 2002. The legislation requires senior managers and lawyers to personally certify that the corporation's financial balance sheets are accurate. Signing financial documents that are knowingly false can lead to civil and criminal penalties for these corporate officers. Is this the correct way of reducing securities fraud? Should the Justice Department pursue criminal charges against accountants and lawyers or should it rely on civil lawsuits (often called shareholder derivative suits) to deter wrongdoing?

∾ Insider trading. Both federal and local prosecutors struggle to combat insider trading—a type of fraud with a huge distortionary effect on market prices. The "victims" of insider trading fraud are often diffuse and difficult to identify. Insider trading usually involves the purchase and sale of stock based on insider information that remains unknown to the general market. Typically, the trader receives the information from someone with a duty of confidentiality, such as a corporate officer or a lawyer with access to confidential information about an upcoming deal. The result is that the trader makes a profit because he has privileged access to information that allows him to make the transaction before the information goes public. As a result, the trader can predict which way the stock's price will go and trade accordingly. Is insider trading a type of theft? Are the victims the traders who buy and sell the stocks at disadvantageous prices? Not everyone agrees. For example, one scholar has written that "[a]n investor who trades in a security contemporaneously with insiders having access to material nonpublic information likely will allege injury in that he sold at the wrong price. . . . The investor's claim, however, is fundamentally flawed. It is purely fortuitous that an insider was on the other side of the transaction. The gain corresponding to shareholder's 'loss' is reaped not just by inside traders, but by all contemporaneous purchasers whether they had access to the undisclosed information or not." Stephen Bainbridge, *Insider Trading: An Overview*, in *Encyclopedia of Law & Economics* (2000). Or maybe insider trading fraudulently induces third-party traders to make trades they would not ordinarily make.

Strangely, there is no statutory definition of insider trading. The concept is elucidated by case law, based on the statutory prohibition against using or employing "in connection with the purchase or sale of any security registered on a national securities exchange or any security not so registered, or any securities-based swap agreement any manipulative or deceptive device or contrivance in contravention of such rules and regulations as the Commission may prescribe as necessary or appropriate in the public interest or for the protection of investors." 15 U.S.C. § 78j(b) (2006). When a deceptive device is used in insider trading, should its use be a crime? Moreover, is it a *serious* crime? In 2011, trader Raj Rajaratnam was sentenced to 11 years in prison for insider trading—a sentence that some thought was too harsh for a non-violent offense.

PART III

⚯

INCHOATE OFFENSES

CHAPTER 17

⟨⟨ ⟩⟩

ATTEMPT

A. DOCTRINE

Attempt liability is a form of inchoate liability. A criminal need not complete a crime in order to be convicted. If he takes the last step he believes necessary to commit a crime but still fails in his effort, the law calls this a "complete attempt" and he can still be prosecuted and punished. If he starts the crime but is caught by the police before he can finish the effort, the law calls this an "incomplete attempt" and he is also subject to criminal liability. Indeed, society wants to give police officers the incentive to intervene in a burgeoning criminal endeavor and prevent the perpetrator from consummating the offense. If intervention and thwarting the crime were a bar to prosecution, the police would wait for the criminal to finish before catching him—hardly a desirable result for the victim. Generally speaking, the requirements for a punishable attempt are that (i) the defendant has the specific intent or purpose to bring about the crime and that (ii) he takes sufficient steps towards committing the crime to satisfy the jurisdiction's actus reus test (to be discussed below). Then, two defenses might apply if (iii) the crime is impossible to complete or (iv) the defendant abandoned the effort.

1. Specific Intent or Purpose

Some jurisdictions refer to attempt as a "specific intent" offense because the defendant must intend to engage in the conduct and also must intend to bring about the crime. This heightened mens rea requirement is often thought to "compensate" or "balance" the lower act requirement for attempts (which by definition does not require the defendant to complete the crime's actus reus). Another way of justifying the heightened mental requirement is that the *harm* associated with the crime never materializes because it is only an attempt and not a completed offense. To prevent over-criminalization, the law bumps up the required mental element. Model Penal Code § 5.01 requires that the defendant "purposely engages in conduct that would constitute the crime" and when causing a result is an element of the crime, also acts with the purpose to bring about the result. In this regard, the "purpose" mens rea can be regarded as roughly equivalent to the older "specific intent" language that still lingers in many jurisdictions. However, the MPC purpose requirement only applies to the *conduct*. As for other mental elements, including attendant circumstances, the defendant only needs to act "with the kind of culpability otherwise required for commission of the crime."

Since attempt liability requires a heightened mens rea (either specific intent or purpose) for both the conduct and the result, it is unclear whether it is possible to hold a defendant responsible for attempting to commit a crime of recklessness such as involuntary manslaughter. Courts are split on this issue, though most that have considered the issue have concluded that crimes of recklessness—by definition—involve defendants who do not intend the resulting harm, such as the death of the victim. Since attempt liability requires that the defendant intend to bring about the crime, most jurisdictions regard attempted manslaughter as a non sequitur. In jurisdictions that accept this argument, there also is no such thing as attempted felony murder or attempted implied malice murder. Both felony murder and implied malice murder are offenses where, like involuntary manslaughter, the actor need not intend the death of the victim, thus creating a similar incongruity with the heightened mens rea for attempt liability.

2. Distinguishing Attempts from Mere Preparation

The law has no shortage of standards for articulating the required act for attempts: How far must the defendant get with the completed crime in order to be punished for an attempt? The six tests include:

1. *The slight-acts test,* which allows liability if the design of a person to commit the crime is clearly shown and the actor commits even "slight acts" in furtherance of that design.
2. *The physical proximity test,* where the defendant must be close in time and space to the final act that completes the crime.
3. *The dangerous proximity test* is more conceptual and asks whether the defendant was dangerously close to consummating the offenses—proximity here being a causal concept, not a geographic one.
4. *The unequivocality test* asks whether the defendant's conduct unequivocally demonstrates the defendant's intent to commit the crime—an actus reus requirement that loops back and refers to the mental element.
5. *The probable desistance test* requires that the defendant's conduct would result in the completed crime "in the ordinary and natural course of events" if the actor had not been interrupted by a third party (such as the police).

6. *The MPC substantial step test* requires that the defendant engage in a "substantial step in a course of conduct planned to culminate in his commission of the crime."

3. Impossibility

Defendants frequently assert an impossibility defense to attempt prosecutions. These arguments rarely work. In the past, courts traditionally distinguished between "factual impossibility" and "legal impossibility"; legal impossibility was often considered a defense while factual impossibility was not.

Factual impossibility "occurs when the objective of the defendant is proscribed by the criminal law but a circumstance unknown to the actor prevents him from bringing about that objective." *United States v. Oviedo*, 525 F.2d 881, 883 (5th Cir. 1976). Factual impossibility is usually not a defense because it simply involves a factual element that prevented the defendant from completing the crime. So, if the perpetrator pulls the trigger but his gun jams, he is still guilty of attempted murder even though it was factually impossible to achieve the desired result (the death of the victim). The victim could not die because though the defendant pulled the trigger, the bullet was never going to leave the gun.

Legal impossibility is more complicated, because it is sometimes considered a defense and sometimes not. To keep these two outcomes clear, some scholars distinguish between two types of legal impossibility: "pure" legal impossibility and "hybrid" legal impossibility. The first category of pure legal impossibility covers the rather trivial circumstances where the defendant engages in conduct that he thinks is illegal but is not. In those situations, the defendant cannot be convicted of an attempt. For example, if the defendant walks in a public park at 10:00 P.M. after what he believes to be the curfew, he cannot be convicted of attempted trespassing if the curfew is really 11:00 P.M. This should not be surprising because the defendant has done nothing wrong; he falsely believes that the law is more restrictive than it is, which should not be the basis for criminal liability.

In contrast, hybrid legal impossibility "exists if [defendant's] goal was illegal, but commission of the offense was impossible due to a factual mistake by her regarding the legal status of some factor relevant to her conduct. This version of impossibility is a 'hybrid' because . . . [defendant's] impossibility claim includes both a legal and a factual aspect to it." *People v. Thousand*, 465 Mich. 149, 159 (2001) (quoting J. Dressler, Understanding Criminal Law). Unfortunately, this conceptual distinction has not helped matters, because almost every case of factual impossibility could be re-described as a case of hybrid legal impossibility, as many courts and commentators have noted. For this reason, courts have largely abandoned the distinction because it proved difficult to classify cases as one or the other.

The more modern approach is to disallow impossibility defenses unless they constitute pure legal impossibility. As the Model Penal Code states in § 5.01(1)(c), an actor is guilty of attempt if he "purposely engages in conduct which would constitute the crime if the attendant circumstances were as he believes them to be . . ." In other words, neither factual impossibility nor hybrid legal impossibility are defenses under the modern approach, thus eliminating the need to carefully distinguish the two categories.

4. Abandonment

If the criminal abandons the effort and reverses course, is he still guilty of an attempt? The abandonment defense applies if the perpetrator "voluntarily and completely" renounced his criminal purpose. However, the abandonment must be truly voluntary as opposed to a result of resistance from the victim or of fear of apprehension. For example, if a perpetrator abandons a robbery after the victim fights back or because the police are responding to the scene of the robbery, he cannot claim abandonment. Because the defendant desisted from the robbery because he was motivated by a fear of apprehension by law enforcement (or alternatively the victim's resistance), the abandonment will not be considered sufficiently *voluntary* to confer the defense. These limitations substantially limit the number of factual situations that will qualify as abandonment. Also, not all jurisdictions recognize the defense.

B. APPLICATION

1. Specific Intent or Purpose

What does it mean to say that the defendant must specifically intend—or have the purpose to commit—the crime? Indeed, the question is ill formed because a crime is composed of multiple elements and the defendant's mental attitude with regard to each element can be different. As you read the following case, ask yourself whether the specific intent (or purpose) requirement applies to each element of the offense or only some parts of it.

People v. Gentry

Appellate Court of Illinois, First District
157 Ill. App. 3d 899 (1987)

JUSTICE LINN delivered the opinion of the court:

Following a jury trial, defendant, Stanley Gentry, was convicted of attempted murder and aggravated battery. At the sentencing hearing, the trial court merged the aggravated battery conviction with the attempted murder conviction and on the charge of attempted murder sentenced Gentry to the Illinois Department of Corrections for a term of 45 years' imprisonment. On appeal, Gentry asserts that his conviction should be reversed because . . . the trial court's instruction regarding the intent necessary for attempted murder was prejudicially erroneous . . .

The record indicates that on December 13, 1983, Gentry and Ruby Hill, Gentry's girlfriend, were in the apartment they shared at 1756 North Talman in Chicago, Illinois. At approximately 9 P.M. the couple began to argue. During the argument, Gentry spilled gasoline on Hill, and the gasoline on Hill's body ignited. Gentry was able to smother the flames with a coat, but only after Hill had been severely burned. Gentry and Hill were the only eyewitnesses to the incident.

Police and paramedics were called to the scene. James Fahey was the first Chicago police officer to arrive. Fahey testified that when he entered Gentry and Hill's apartment, he found Hill's upper body (including her head, face, and arms) to be badly burned . . .

The victim, Ruby Hill . . . testified at trial. Hill stated that she and Gentry had been drinking all afternoon and that both of them were "pretty high." She further testified that Gentry had poured gasoline on her and that the gasoline ignited only after she had gone near the stove in the kitchen. Hill also related how Gentry tried to snuff the fire out by placing a coat over the flames.

Hill also testified as to her relationship with Gentry. She stated that she had lived with Gentry for three years prior to the accident, that she wanted to marry Gentry, and that she still loved Gentry notwithstanding the fire incident. Hill claimed that the entire episode was an accident and that she intended to again live with Gentry after the case was over.

In addition, over the objection of Gentry's counsel, the prosecution proffered certain impeachment evidence. The claimed purpose of this evidence was to impeach Hill as to her assertion that the fire incident was an accident. The prosecution first established the foundation for the impeachment by asking Hill if she had previously claimed that Gentry had threatened her with matches after he had poured gasoline on her. Hill denied it. The prosecution also asked her if she had previously claimed that she was terrified of Gentry. Hill again denied making such a statement. Hill also denied ever stating that she was afraid of Gentry and denied that Gentry had ever tried to choke her while she was taking a bath in the apartment's bathtub.

After Hill denied making positive answers to the aforementioned questions posed by the prosecution, the prosecution set out to "prove-up" the impeachment. First, the prosecution called Jeffrey Zitzka, a Chicago police officer who interviewed Hill while she was in the hospital after the incident.

Zitzka testified that Hill had nodded "no" when asked if the incident was an accident and had nodded "yes" as to whether she wanted to press charges.

Diane Meyer, a law clerk for the State's Attorney's office, then testified. Meyer stated that she had heard Hill tell prosecutors that Gentry had lit matches after pouring gasoline on her, that Hill had claimed that the incident was not an accident, and that Hill had also said that she was afraid of Gentry . . .

During the prosecution's closing argument, the record reveals that the prosecutors relied heavily on the impeachment testimony and invited the jury to consider the evidence for its substantive value as well as for what it revealed about Hill's credibility.

At the close of the case, the jury found Gentry guilty of attempted murder and aggravated battery. The lesser aggravated battery conviction was merged into the greater attempted murder conviction at sentencing, where Gentry was sentenced to the Illinois Department of Corrections for a term of 45 years. From his conviction for attempted murder and his sentence, Gentry now appeals . . .

At the close of the presentation of evidence in this case, the following instructions were given. First, the trial court defined "attempt" as it relates to the underlying felony of murder: "A person commits the offense of murder when he, with intent to commit the offense of murder does any act which constitutes a substantial step toward the commission of the offense of murder. The offense attempted need not have been completed."

Second, after giving this definition, the trial court set forth the necessary elements of attempted murder, to wit, an act and intent: "To sustain the charge of attempt, the State must prove the following propositions: First: That the defendant performed an act which constituted a substantial step towards the commission of the offense of murder; and Second: That the defendant did so with intent to commit the crime of murder."

Finally, the trial court defined the crime of murder, including all four culpable mental states: "A person commits the crime of murder where he kills an individual if, in performing the acts which cause the death, he intends to kill or do great bodily harm to that individual; or he knows that such acts will cause death to that individual; or he knows that such acts create a strong probability of death or great bodily harm to that individual."

Gentry contends that the inclusion of all the alternative states of mind in the definitional murder instruction was erroneous because the crime of attempted murder requires a showing of specific intent to kill. Gentry posits that inclusion of all four alternative states of mind permitted the jury to convict him of attempted murder upon a finding that he intended to harm Hill, or acted with the knowledge that his conduct created a strong probability of death or great bodily harm to Hill, even if the jury believed that Gentry did not act with specific intent to kill. We agree with Gentry's position that the jury was misinstructed in this case.

Our supreme court has repeatedly held that a finding of specific intent to kill is a necessary element of the crime of attempted murder. Indeed, a trial court instructing a jury on the crime of attempted murder must make it clear that specific intent to kill is the pivotal element of that offense, and that intent to do bodily harm, or knowledge that the consequences of defendant's act may result in death or great bodily harm, is not enough . . . Accordingly, the instructions given in this case were erroneous, since it is clear that the jury was permitted to convict Gentry without specifically finding that Gentry intended to kill Hill. Few errors are more highly prejudicial than the trial court's failure to give the proper instruction on the intent element of a crime.

The State attempts to minimize the significance of this error by arguing that the instructions as given actually did require the jury to find specific intent to kill. The State labels as illogical those cases which distinguish between the specific intent to kill and the three other alternative states of mind also found in the definitional murder instruction.

The State would read the attempted murder instruction as requiring a showing of any of the alternative mental states sufficient for a conviction of murder. In other words, the State makes no distinction between the mental state required to prove murder and the mental state required to prove attempted murder. We find the State's analysis and conclusion to be erroneous and lacking in legal substance since it fails to contain the judicial reasoning which recognizes the distinction between the intent elements of murder and attempted murder.

Specifically, we cite the *Kraft* case, where defendant's attempted murder conviction was reversed where the jury instructions would have permitted a conviction without a finding of specific intent to kill. *People v. Kraft*, 133 Ill. App. 3d 294 (1985). In reversing the defendant's attempted murder conviction in that case, the *Kraft* court analyzed the distinction between the culpable mental states required for murder and attempted murder, noting as follows:

> Our criminal code contains separate statutory definitions for the four culpable mental states of intent, knowledge, recklessness, and negligence, with knowledge encompassing a distinct and less purposeful state of mind than intent. . . . [O]ur State legislature manifested a desire to treat intent and knowledge as distinct mental states when imposing criminal liability for conduct. . . . Knowledge is not intent as defined by our statutes, and the jury instructions should reflect this distinction. Accordingly, we hold that in a prosecution for attempted murder, where alternative culpable mental states will satisfy the target crime of murder, but only one is

compatible with the mental state imposed by our attempt statute, the incompatible elements must be omitted from the jury instructions.

Consequently, it is sufficient only for us to say that we recognize the distinction between the alternative states of mind delineated in the definitional murder instruction, as well as the fact that only the specific intent to kill satisfies the intent element of the crime of attempted murder. Accordingly, the State's assertion that the instructions as given actually required the jury to find that Gentry had a specific intent to kill Hill is doomed . . .

In the instant case, it is clear that the essential task before the jury was the determination of whether Gentry sufficiently formed the specific intent to kill, in order to satisfy the elements of attempted murder. This is evidenced by the State's efforts to prove that Gentry knew that splashing gasoline on Hill would kill her, as well as by the State's attempts to impeach Hill's testimony that the incident was accidental. As such, we are faced with a situation where proving that Gentry formed the intent to kill was a necessary predicate to a finding of his guilt . . .

In conclusion, based upon the discussion of law and fact stated above, we reverse defendant's conviction and sentence and remand this cause for a new trial in front of a properly instructed jury.

NOTES & QUESTIONS ON SPECIFIC INTENT AND PURPOSE

1. *Attempted involuntary manslaughter.* Does the heightened mental element for attempt (specific intent or purpose) apply to just the defendant's conduct or to the result as well? One way of getting a handle on this seemingly abstract issue is to ask whether the crime of "attempted involuntary manslaughter" exists. Most jurisdictions that have considered the question have said no. See, e.g., *State v. Holbron*, 904 P.2d 912 (Haw. 1995); *State v. Almeda*, 189 Conn. 303, 455 A.2d 1326 (Conn. 1983) ("[T]he crime of attempted involuntary manslaughter requires a logical impossibility, namely, that the actor in his attempt intend that an unintended death result. Such an anomaly the legislature could scarcely have intended."); *Taylor v. State*, 444 So. 2d 931, 934 (Fla. 1983) (attempted manslaughter applicable in cases of voluntary manslaughter but *not* involuntary manslaughter); *Bailey v. State*, 100 Nev. 562, 564 (1984) ("Since the crime of 'attempted involuntary manslaughter' does not exist, appellant's conviction therefor must be reversed."); *State v. Louis*, 305 Kan. 453 (2016). In these jurisdictions, it is impossible for an actor to *attempt* to commit a crime of *recklessness*, since the mental elements associated with those concepts are incompatible. For attempt, the actor must have the purpose or specific intent to both engage in the conduct and to bring about the result, while crimes

of recklessness (such as involuntary manslaughter) assume that the defendant did not intend to bring about a particular result.

However, at least one court has reached the opposite result. In *People v. Thomas*, 729 P.2d 972 (Col. 1986), Thomas received a phone call from his ex-girlfriend reporting that she had just been raped in her apartment by a neighbor. Thomas went to the building, located the neighbor, and forced him at gunpoint to return to the woman's apartment, where she identified the neighbor as her assailant. The neighbor fled and Thomas gave chase, eventually firing his gun three times at the neighbor, hitting him twice but not killing him. Since the neighbor survived the shooting, Thomas was charged with, among other things, attempted murder, but the jury convicted him of attempted reckless (involuntary) manslaughter instead.

The result in *Thomas* can be explained by referring to the Colorado attempt statute, Colo. Rev. Stat. § 18-2-101, which distinguishes between the defendant's intent to commit the conduct in question and the defendant's intent with regard to other elements of the offense:

> A person commits criminal attempt if, acting with the kind of culpability otherwise required for commission of an offense, he engages in conduct constituting a substantial step toward the commission of the offense. A substantial step is any conduct, whether act, omission, or possession, which is strongly corroborative of the firmness of the actor's purpose to complete the commission of the offense. . . .

Recalling the chapters on homicide earlier in the casebook, manslaughter requires that the defendant intentionally engage in conduct that results in someone's death; the defendant's mental attitude with regard to the resulting death need only constitute recklessness (consciously disregarding a substantial and unjustified risk). Since Thomas specifically intended the conduct (firing the weapon), he could be guilty of attempted manslaughter as long as he was reckless. The court explained its argument:

> [I]n order to be guilty of criminal attempt, the actor must act with the kind of culpability otherwise required for commission of the underlying offense and must engage in the conduct which constitutes the substantial step with the further intent to perform acts which, if completed, would constitute the underlying offense . . .
>
> In order to complete the offense of reckless manslaughter, it is necessary that the actor cause the death of another person by acting in a manner that involves a substantial and unjustifiable risk of death of that other person and that the actor be conscious of that risk and of its nature when electing to act. Attempted reckless manslaughter requires that the accused have the intent to commit the underlying offense of reckless manslaughter. The "intent to commit the underlying offense" . . . is the intent to engage in and complete the risk-producing act or conduct. It does not include an intent that death occur

even though the underlying crime, reckless manslaughter, has death as an essential element.

Is this result consistent with the Model Penal Code? The Colorado attempt provision is based on the MPC, with one notable difference. Section 5.01(1)(b) of the Model Penal Code states that "when causing a particular result is an element of the crime, [the actor is guilty of attempt when he] does or omits to do anything with the purpose of causing or with the belief that it will cause such result without further conduct on his part. . . ." However, this subsection of the MPC was never incorporated into the Colorado attempt provision. Would the *Thomas* case come out differently if this MPC provision were included in the Colorado Penal Code?

2. *Attempted felony murder.* The Court of Appeals of Maryland considered in 1989 whether a defendant could be convicted of attempted felony murder. See *Bruce v. State*, 317 Md. 642, 566 A.2d 103 (1989). In that case, Leon Bruce and two other men entered a shoe store. Bruce was armed and aimed his gun at the victim and demanded money. The victim indicated the cash register was empty and during the confrontation he was shot by Bruce, though he survived. Since no one died, a charge of felony murder was impossible, but the prosecution proceeded under a theory of attempted felony murder. The court rejected the theory because attempt is a specific intent crime. See also *State v. Lyerla*, 424 N.W.2d 908 (S.D. 1988) (crime of attempted second-degree murder does not exist in South Dakota).

3. *Attempt and strict liability.* But what about strict liability offenses? Can a defendant be convicted of attempting to commit a strict liability offense? The answer is yes, assuming that the statute offense makes the defendant strictly liable for certain *conduct* (as opposed to a particular result). For example, in *People v. Aponte*, 24 Misc. 3d 118, 886 N.Y.S.2d 547 (N.Y. App. Div. 2009), the defendant was convicted of attempted stalking. On appeal, the court rejected his argument that attempted stalking was an impossibility:

> On the issue of whether attempted stalking in the third degree is a legally cognizable offense, we conclude that it is. "[W]here a penal statute imposes strict liability for creating an unintended *result,* an attempt to commit that crime is not a legally cognizable offense. . . . By contrast, where a penal statute imposes strict liability for committing certain *conduct,* an attempt is legally cognizable, since one can attempt to engage in conduct." The crime of third-degree stalking does not "impose[ ] strict liability for creating an unintended result"—it does not predicate liability upon the (possibly unintended) result of harm experienced by the victim. Rather, it imposes "strict liability for committing certain conduct"—it predicates liability upon the intentional engaging in a "course of conduct" that is "likely" to inflict harm on the victim. Thus, the crime of attempted stalking in the third degree is not a legal impossibility.

ADVICE In determining whether attempt can apply to a particular crime, the first thing you need to do is determine the mens rea for that crime. If the mens rea is recklessness as to a particular result, then attempt liability is precluded, since it requires purpose or specific intent. If the crime is strict liability, you must determine whether the statute imposes strict liability for an unintended result or strict liability for committing some conduct. If the former, the rule for recklessness applies and attempt liability is impossible. If the latter, and the strict liability is for certain conduct, then attempt liability could apply. For example, in *People v. Levy*, 801 N.Y.S.2d 240 (N.Y. Sup. Ct. 2005), a New York court upheld a conviction for attempting to endanger the welfare of a child, because the provision only requires that "he or she intends to knowingly act in a manner likely to be injurious to the welfare of a child without actually acting in such a manner."

2. Distinguishing Attempts from Mere Preparation

At some point the law needs to draw a sharp line between mere "preparation" (which is not a crime) and a criminal attempt. Although in real life that line might be gray and uncertain, the law needs something approaching a clear line to distinguish between a conviction for attempt and an acquittal. As you read the following case, ask yourself if the defendants were preparing for, or perpetrating, a crime.

People v. Rizzo
New York State Court of Appeals
246 N.Y. 334, 158 N.E. 888 (1927)

CRANE, J.

The police of the city of New York did excellent work in this case by preventing the commission of a serious crime. It is a great satisfaction to realize that we have such wide-awake guardians of our peace. Whether or not the steps which the defendant had taken up to the time of his arrest amounted to the commission of a crime, as defined by our law, is, however, another matter. He has been convicted of an attempt to commit the crime of robbery in the first degree, and sentenced to state's prison. There is no doubt that he had the intention to commit robbery, if he got the chance. An examination, however, of the facts is necessary to determine whether his acts were in preparation to commit the crime if the opportunity offered, or constituted a crime in itself, known to our law as an attempt to commit robbery in the first degree. Charles Rizzo, the defendant, appellant, with three others, Anthony J. Dorio, Thomas Milo, and John Thomasello, on January 14th planned to rob one Charles Rao of a pay roll valued at about $1,200 which he was to carry from the bank for the United Lathing Company. These defendants, two of whom had firearms, started out in an automobile, looking for Rao or the man who had the pay roll on that day. Rizzo claimed to be able to identify the man, and was to point him out to the others, who were to do the actual holding up. The four rode about in their car looking for Rao. They went to the bank from which he was supposed to get the money and to various buildings being constructed by the United Lathing Company. At last they came to One Hundred and Eightieth street and Morris Park avenue. By this time they were watched and followed by two police officers. As Rizzo jumped out of the car and ran into the building, all four were arrested. The defendant was taken out from the building in which he was hiding. Neither Rao nor a man named Previti, who was also supposed to carry a pay roll, were at the place at the time of the arrest. The defendants had not found or seen the man they intended to rob. No person with a pay roll was at any of the places where they had stopped, and no one had been pointed out or identified by Rizzo. The four men intended to rob the pay roll man, whoever he was. They were looking for him, but they had not seen or discovered him up to the time they were arrested.

Does this constitute the crime of an attempt to commit robbery in the first degree? . . .

In *Hyde v. U.S.,* 225 U.S. 347, it was stated that the act amounts to an attempt when it is so near to the result that the danger of success is very great. "There must be dangerous promixity to success." Halsbury in his *Laws of England,* vol. 9, p. 259, says: "An act in order to be a criminal attempt must be immediately and not remotely connected with and directly tending to the commission of an offense."

Commonwealth v. Peaslee, 177 Mass. 267, 59 N.E. 55, refers to the acts constituting an attempt as coming *very near* to the accomplishment of the crime. . . .

How shall we apply this rule of immediate nearness to this case? The defendants were looking for the pay roll man to rob him of his money. This is the charge in the indictment. Robbery is defined in section 2120 of the Penal Law as "the unlawful taking of personal property from the person or in the presence of another, against his will, by means of force, or violence, or fear of injury, immediate or future, to his person"; and it is made robbery in the first degree by section 2124 when committed by a person aided by accomplices actually present. To constitute the crime of robbery, the money must have been taken from Rao by means of force or violence, or through fear. The crime of attempt to commit robbery was committed, if these defendants did an act tending to the commission of this robbery. Did the acts above described come dangerously near to the taking of Rao's property? Did the acts come so near the commission of robbery that there was reasonable likelihood of its accomplishment but for the interference? Rao was not found; the defendants were still looking for him; no attempt to rob him could be made, at least until he came in sight; he was not in the building at One Hundred and Eightieth street and Morris Park avenue. There was no man there with the pay roll for the United Lathing Company whom these defendants could rob. Apparently no money had been drawn from the bank for the pay roll by anybody at the time of the arrest. In a word, these defendants had planned to commit a crime, and were looking around the city for an opportunity to commit it, but the opportunity fortunately never came. Men would not be guilty of an attempt at burglary if they had planned to break into a building and were arrested while they were hunting about the streets for the building not knowing where it was. Neither would a man be guilty of an attempt to commit murder if he armed himself and started out to find the person whom he had planned to kill but could not find him. So here these defendants were not guilty of an attempt to commit robbery in the first degree when they had not found or reached the presence of the person they intended to rob.

For these reasons, the judgment of conviction of this defendant appellant must be reversed and a new trial granted. . . .

NOTES & QUESTIONS ON DANGEROUS PROXIMITY

1. *Reading* Rizzo.   What is your assessment of the *Rizzo* decision? Were the defendants attempting to commit a crime (which would make them liable) or were they simply looking for an opportunity to commit a crime (which is not punishable)? Does the opinion cause a problem for the police, who might be placed in the awkward position of stopping a potential crime but then be barred from prosecuting the criminals? Indeed, one of the goals of attempt liability is to give police a doctrinal hook to intervene in burgeoning criminal endeavors.

2. *Dangerous proximity*.   The dangerous proximity standard focuses on how "close" the defendants were to succeeding. But closeness is defined not in geographic or temporal terms, but in *causal* terms. To illustrate the point that causal closeness and physical closeness are distinct, consider that an actor might be physically close to the scene of the completed crime but there might be important work remaining before the crime comes to fruition. Conversely, an actor might be far away from the scene of the crime, but the work is all but finished. In *Rizzo*, the defendants were missing an essential element: information about the victim's location. Without that crucial information, the court viewed their plan as far from succeeding. Do you agree? As for the standard itself, can you think of any deficits to the dangerous proximity test? As one legal scholar has put it, "The dangerous proximity test is somewhat pragmatic in that it does not ask complex questions about what can be inferred about the person and his intentions. It simply requires citizens to avoid bringing plans for criminal

activities to a point at which they could be successfully completed." See Paul H. Robinson, *Testing Lay Intuitions of Justice: How and Why?*, 28 Hofstra L. Rev. 611, 623 (2000). Robinson conducted extensive surveys of regular citizens (i.e., non-lawyers) and found near-universal agreement among his subjects that liability and punishment were warranted when defendants satisfied the dangerous proximity test. For this reason, Robinson recommends that all jurisdictions follow the dangerous proximity standard.

3. *Methodology.* Shortly after the *Rizzo* decision was handed down, one legal academic wrote: "The courts, while usually admitting that each case must be decided on its particular facts, continue to confuse their opinions by citing long lists of cases of quite different kinds of crimes. Here also, to discuss whether acts done in an attempted robbery are comparable to acts done in an attempted incestuous marriage, as they relate to the general principle of proximateness, is as valuable as discussing whether Milton is more poetical than a pig is fat. Yet this is constantly being done, again with occasional absurd results." See Thurman W. Arnold, *Criminal Attempts—The Rise and Fall of an Abstraction*, 40 Yale L.J. 53, 72 (1930). Do you agree that there is no value to citing—and considering—examples of attempts drawn from other crimes? In fact, as we will see below, that is precisely the methodology used by the Model Penal Code, which provides content and precision to a vague standard (the substantial step test) by including a large list of factual examples that are deemed punishable attempts.

State v. Reeves
Supreme Court of Tennessee
916 S.W.2d 909 (1996)

DROWOTA, J.

The defendant, Tracie Reeves, appeals from the Court of Appeals' affirmance of the trial court's order designating her a delinquent child. The trial court's delinquency order, which was entered following a jury trial, was based on the jury's finding that the defendant had attempted to commit second degree murder—a violation of Tenn. Code Ann. § 39-12-101. The specific issue for our determination is whether the defendant's actions constitute a "substantial step" toward the commission of that crime. For the following reasons, we hold that they do, and therefore affirm the judgment of the Court of Appeals.

FACTS AND PROCEDURAL HISTORY

On the evening of January 5, 1993, Tracie Reeves and Molly Coffman, both twelve years of age and students at West Carroll Middle School, spoke on the telephone and decided to kill their homeroom teacher, Janice Geiger. The girls agreed that Coffman would bring rat poison to school the following day so that it could be placed in Geiger's drink. The girls also agreed that they would thereafter steal Geiger's car and drive to the Smoky Mountains. Reeves then contacted Dean Foutch, a local high school student, informed him of the plan, and asked him to drive Geiger's car. Foutch refused this request.

On the morning of January 6, Coffman placed a packet of rat poison in her purse and boarded the school bus. During the bus ride Coffman told another student, Christy Hernandez, of the plan; Coffman also showed Hernandez the packet of rat poison. Upon their arrival at school Hernandez informed her homeroom teacher, Sherry Cockrill, of the plan. Cockrill then relayed this information to the principal of the school, Claudia Argo.

When Geiger entered her classroom that morning she observed Reeves and Coffman leaning over her desk; and when the girls noticed her, they giggled and ran back to their seats. At that time Geiger saw a purse lying next to her coffee cup on top of the desk. Shortly thereafter Argo called Coffman to the principal's office. Rat poison was found in Coffman's purse and it was turned over to a Sheriff's Department investigator. Both Reeves and Coffman gave written statements to the investigator concerning their plan to poison Geiger and steal her car.

Reeves and Coffman were found to be delinquent by the Carroll County Juvenile Court, and both appealed from that ruling to the Carroll County Circuit Court. After a jury found that the girls attempted to commit second degree murder in violation of Tenn. Code Ann. § 39-12-101, the "criminal attempt" statute, the trial court affirmed the juvenile court's order and sentenced the girls to the Department of Youth Development for an indefinite period. Reeves appealed from this judgment to the Court of Appeals, which affirmed the judgment of the trial court. Reeves then applied to this Court for permission to appeal pursuant to Tenn. R. App. P. 11. Because we have not addressed the law of criminal attempt since the comprehensive reform of our criminal law undertaken by the legislature in 1989, we granted that application.

PRIOR AND CURRENT LAW OF CRIMINAL ATTEMPT

Before the passage of the reform legislation in 1989, the law of criminal attempt, though sanctioned by various statutes, was judicially defined. In order to submit an issue of criminal attempt to the jury, the State was required to present legally sufficient evidence of: (1) an intent to commit a specific crime; (2) an overt act toward the commission of that crime; and (3) a failure to consummate the crime.

Of the elements of criminal attempt, the second, the "overt act" requirement, was by far the most problematic. By attempting to draw a sharp

distinction between "mere preparation" to commit a criminal act, which did
not constitute the required overt act, and a "direct movement toward the
commission after the preparations had been made," which did, Tennessee
courts construed the term "overt act" very narrowly. The best example of
this extremely narrow construction occurred in *Dupuy*. In that case, the
Memphis police sought to lay a trap for a pharmacist suspected of
performing illegal abortions by sending a young woman to request these
services from him. After the woman had made several attempts to secure
his services, he finally agreed to perform the abortion. The pharmacist
transported the young woman to a hotel room, laid out his instruments
in preparation for the procedure, and asked the woman to remove her
clothes. At that point the police came into the room and arrested the pharmacist, who then admitted that he had performed abortions in the past.
The defendant was convicted under a statute that made it illegal to procure
a miscarriage, and he appealed to this Court.

A majority of this Court reversed the conviction. After admitting that
the defendant's "reprehensible" course of conduct would doubtlessly have
resulted in the commission of the crime "had he not been thwarted in his
efforts by the arrival of the police," the majority concluded that:

> While the defendant had completed his plan to do this crime the element
> of attempt [overt act] does not appear in this record. The proof shows
> that he did not use any of the instruments and did not touch the body of
> the girl in question. Under such facts we do not think that the defendant is
> guilty under the statute.

To support its holding, the *Dupuy* court quoted a treatise passage
concerning actions that constituted "mere preparation," as opposed to
actions that would satisfy the overt act requirement:

> In a general way, however, it may be said that preparation consists in
> devising or arranging the means or measures necessary for the
> commission of the offense and that the attempt [overt act] is the direct
> movement toward the commission after the preparations are made. Even
> though a person actually intends to commit a crime, his procurement of
> the instrumentalities adapted to that end will not constitute an attempt to
> commit the crime in the absence of some overt act.

To further illustrate the foregoing principle the majority provided the
following example: "the procurement by a prisoner of tools adapted to
breaking jail does not render him guilty of an attempt to break jail."

As indicated above, the sharp differentiation in *Dupuy* between "mere
preparation" and "overt act," or the "act itself," was characteristic of the
pre-1989 attempt law. In 1989, however, the legislature enacted a general
criminal attempt statute, Tenn. Code Ann. § 39-12-101, as part of its comprehensive overhaul of Tennessee's criminal law. In that statute, the

legislature did not simply codify the judicially-created elements of the crime, but utilized language that had up to then been entirely foreign to Tennessee attempt law. Section 39-12-101 provides, in pertinent part, as follows:

(a) A person commits criminal attempt who, acting with the kind of culpability otherwise required for the offense:

(1) Intentionally engages in action or causes a result that would constitute an offense if the circumstances surrounding the conduct were as the person believes them to be;

(2) Acts with intent to cause a result that is an element of the offense, and believes the conduct will cause the result without further conduct on the person's part; or

(3) Acts with intent to complete a course of action or cause a result that would constitute the offense, under the circumstances surrounding the conduct as the person believe them to be, and the conduct constitutes a substantial step toward the commission of the offense.

(b) Conduct does not constitute a substantial step under subdivision (a)(3) unless the person's entire course of action is corroborative of the intent to commit the offense.

THE SUBSTANTIAL STEP ISSUE

As stated above, our task is to determine whether the defendant's actions in this case constitute a "substantial step" toward the commission of second degree murder under the new statute. The "substantial step" issue has not yet been addressed by a Tennessee court in a published opinion, and the question is made more difficult by the fact that the legislature declined to set forth any definition of the term, preferring instead to "leave the issue of what constitutes a substantial step [to the courts] for determination in each particular case."

In addressing this issue, we first note that the legislature, in enacting § 39-12-101, clearly looked to the criminal attempt section set forth in the Model Penal Code. That section provides, in pertinent part, as follows:

(1) Definition of attempt. A person is guilty of an attempt to commit a crime if, acting with the kind of culpability otherwise required for commission of the crime, he:

(a) purposely engages in conduct which would constitute the crime if the attendant circumstances were as he believes them to be; or

(b) when causing a particular result is an element of the crime, does or omits to do anything with the purpose of causing or with the belief that it will cause such result, without further conduct on his part; or

(c) purposely does or omits to do anything which, under the circumstances as he believes them to be, is a *substantial step in a course of conduct planned to culminate in his commission of the crime*

Model Penal Code, Section 5.01 (emphasis added).

The State argues that the striking similarity of Tenn. Code Ann. § 39-12-101 and the Model Penal Code evidences the legislature's intention to abandon the old law of criminal attempt and instead adopt the Model Penal Code approach. The State then avers that the model code contains examples of conduct which, if proven, would entitle, but not require, the jury to find that the defendant had taken a "substantial step"; and that two of these examples are applicable to this case. The section of the model code relied upon by the State, § 5.01(2), provides, in pertinent part, as follows:

> (2) Conduct which may be held substantial step under paragraph (1)(c). Conduct shall not be held to constitute a substantial step under paragraph (1)(c) of this Section unless it is strongly corroborative of the actor's criminal purpose. Without negativing the sufficiency of other conduct, the following, if strongly corroborative of the actor's criminal purpose, shall not be held insufficient as a matter of law:
>
>   . . .
>
>   (e) possession of materials to be employed in the commission of the crime, which are specially designed for such unlawful use or which can serve no lawful purpose of the actor under the circumstances;
>   (f) possession, collection or fabrication of materials to be employed in the commission of the crime, at or near the place contemplated for its commission, where such possession, collection or fabrication serves no lawful purpose of the actor under the circumstances;

The State concludes that because the issue of whether the defendant's conduct constitutes a substantial step may be a jury question under the model code, the jury was justified in finding her guilty of attempting to commit second degree murder.

The defendant counters by arguing that despite the similarity of Tenn. Code Ann. § 39-12-101 and the Model Penal Code's attempt provision, the legislature intended to retain the sharp distinction between "mere preparation" and the "act itself" characteristic of such decisions as *Dupuy*. She supports this assertion by pointing out that although the legislature could have easily included the examples set forth in § 5.01(2) of the model code, the Tennessee statute does not include the examples. The defendant concludes that the new statute did not substantially change Tennessee attempt law, and that her conviction must be reversed because her actions constitute "mere preparation" under *Dupuy*.

Initially, we cannot accept the argument that the legislature intended to explicitly adopt the Model Penal Code approach, including the examples set forth in § 5.01(2). Although § 39-12-101 is obviously based on the model code, we agree with the defendant that the legislature could have, if it had so desired, simply included the specific examples in the Tennessee statute.

That it did not do so prohibits us from concluding that the legislature explicitly intended to adopt the model code approach in all its particulars.

This conclusion does not mean, however, that the legislature intended to retain the distinction between "mere preparation" and the "act itself." Moreover, while we concede that a strong argument can be made that the conviction conflicts with *Dupuy* because the defendant did not place the poison in the cup, but simply brought it to the crime scene, we also are well aware that the *Dupuy* approach to attempt law has been consistently and effectively criticized. One persistent criticism of the endeavor to separate "mere preparation" from the "act itself" is that the question is ultimately not one of kind but of degree; the "act itself" is merely one of the termini on a continuum of criminal activity. Therefore, distinguishing between "mere preparation" and the "act itself" in a principled manner is a difficult, if not impossible, task. The other principal ground of criticism of the *Dupuy* approach bears directly on the primary objective of the law—that of preventing inchoate crimes from becoming full-blown ones. Many courts and commentators have argued that failing to attach criminal responsibility to the actor—and therefore prohibiting law enforcement officers from taking action—until the actor is on the brink of consummating the crime endangers the public and undermines the preventative goal of attempt law.

The shortcomings of the *Dupuy* rule with respect to the goal of prevention are particularly evident in this case. As stated above, it is likely that under *Dupuy* no criminal responsibility would have attached unless the poison had actually been placed in the teacher's cup. This rigid requirement, however, severely undercuts the objective of prevention because of the surreptitious nature of the act of poisoning. Once a person secretly places a toxic substance into a container from which another person is likely to eat or drink, the damage is done. Here, if it had not been for the intervention of the teacher, she could have been rendered powerless to protect herself from harm.

After carefully weighing considerations of stare decisis against the persuasive criticisms of the *Dupuy* rule, we conclude that this artificial and potentially harmful rule must be abandoned. We hold that when an actor possesses materials to be used in the commission of a crime, at or near the scene of the crime, and where the possession of those materials can serve no lawful purpose of the actor under the circumstances, the jury is entitled, but not required, to find that the actor has taken a "substantial step" toward the commission of the crime if such action is strongly corroborative of the actor's overall criminal purpose. For the foregoing reasons, the judgment of the Court of Appeals is affirmed.

NOTES & QUESTIONS ON SUBSTANTIAL STEP

1. *The concept of corroboration.* The Model Penal Code "substantial step" test simply asks whether the step was substantial enough to corroborate the defendant's criminal purpose. How should we understand this requirement? It seems to refer back to the mens rea required for attempts. Does this make it redundant? One way of thinking of the substantial step test is that it requires substantial action but the amount of action required depends on an evidentiary assessment of the relationship between the defendant's actions and her mental attitude—her commitment to the criminal endeavor. In this sense, the substantial step test is similar to the unequivocality test, which also requires that the fact finder assess what the defendant's actions say about her commitment to the criminal enterprise. The unequivocality test states that an actor has fulfilled the actus reus requirement for attempt liability when his or her conduct "unequivocally" demonstrates his or her intent to bring about the crime. For both tests, then, the actus reus and mens rea requirements are linked together in their definition. Do you agree that Tracie Reeves had firmly decided to poison her teacher? Why were the girls giggling? Perhaps the giggling was indicative that this was a mere prank. If yes, what kind of prank was it? Had they decided to go through with the plan or were they still deliberating about it?

2. *The laundry list.* The Model Penal Code's substantial step test includes a laundry list of factual scenarios that constitute a substantial step: lying in wait, enticing, reconnoitering, unlawful entry, possession of materials specially designed for unlawful use, possession or collection or fabrication of lawful materials near the place of commission, and soliciting. What is the purpose of drafting a long laundry list of examples? Does it provide a meaningful standard for how to assess a factual scenario that is *not* on the list? The key point in understanding the list is that a jury is entitled, but not required, to find that these situations constitute a substantial step. In other words, the Model Penal Code is telling appellate courts not to disturb jury convictions for attempt when the defendant's conduct falls into one of these categories. But the list is not exhaustive and other factual scenarios can qualify as substantial steps despite the fact that they are not enumerated on this list. Another key reason for the Model Penal Code's inclusion of the laundry list is to emphasize that the substantial step test focuses on how much the defendant has done (in a positive sense), rather than what remains to be done in order to complete the crime (in a negative sense). The physical and dangerous proximity to success tests both focus on the negative analysis, while the MPC test pegs attempt liability to the defendant's affirmative acts.

PROBLEM CASE

In April 2014, police received a 911 call about a young male with a backpack whom the caller believed was breaking into a storage unit. Police arrived and found a 17-year-old boy named J.D.L. in the storage locker with the following bomb-making materials: a scale, packing material for red iron oxide, boxes for ammunition, and a pressure cooker. J.D.L. told the police that he had planned an elaborate series of murders: first, shoot his family to death; second, set a wildfire to distract and lure away fire and police responders; third, set off multiple bombs in the cafeteria at the local junior and senior high schools to kill as many students as possible. Police found several guns and three bombs at his house. At the time he was arrested, he told police that his preparations were still incomplete

Students, parents, and community members listen as the police captain and school superintendent speak at a news conference about the arrest

because he needed to steal a shotgun and purchase a second pressure cooker. He said that if the police had not intervened, he would have executed the plan as soon as he acquired the last two items.

Prosecutors charged J.D.L. with multiple counts of attempted murder. Is he guilty? Minnesota law uses a simplified version of the substantial step test that creates attempt liability for any individual who: "with intent to commit a crime, does an act which is a substantial step toward, and more than preparation for, the commission of the crime." Minn. Stat. § 609.17(1). Applying this substantial step test, the Court of Appeals of Minnesota quashed the case, concluding: "When the officers found J.D.L. in the storage unit on April 29, he was still preparing for his plan. J.D.L. told the officers that he had two things to do before he was ready. While J.D.L. planned for at least nine months, he did not engage in anything more than preparation for the commission of the crimes. The law in Minnesota does not prohibit J.D.L.'s conduct. We cannot invite speculation as to whether the acts would be carried out. At present, our attempt laws reach no further." *In re Welfare of J.D.L.*, 2015 WL 1014079 (Minn. 2015). Do you agree? What result under the unequivocality test?

3. Impossibility

If there is no way that the defendant's crime could succeed, can he claim a defense of impossibility? Or is he guilty of attempt? The following materials present two examples of impossible attempts. The first defendant shot a dead body while the second defendant bit a prison guard to give him HIV. As you read each case, ask yourself whether the defendant should go to prison even though the intended harm could not materialize.

People v. Dlugash

Court of Appeals of New York
41 N.Y.2d 725 (1977)

JASEN, JUDGE.

The criminal law is of ancient origin, but criminal liability for attempt to commit a crime is comparatively recent. At the root of the concept of attempt liability are the very aims and purposes of penal law. The ultimate issue is whether an individual's intentions and actions, though failing to achieve a manifest and malevolent criminal purpose, constitute a danger to organized society of sufficient magnitude to warrant the imposition of criminal sanctions.

Difficulties in theoretical analysis and concomitant debate over very pragmatic questions of blameworthiness appear dramatically in reference to situations where the criminal attempt failed to achieve its purpose solely because the factual or legal context in which the individual acted was not as the actor supposed them to be. Phrased somewhat differently, the concern centers on whether an individual should be liable for an attempt to commit a crime when, unknown to him, it was impossible to successfully complete the crime attempted . . .

The 1967 revision of the Penal Law approached the impossibility defense to the inchoate crime of attempt in a novel fashion. The statute provides that, if a person engages in conduct which would otherwise constitute an attempt to commit a crime, "it is no defense to a prosecution for such attempt that the crime charged to have been attempted was, under the attendant circumstances, factually or legally impossible of commission, if such crime could have been committed had the attendant circumstances been as such person believed them to be." Penal Law § 110.10. This appeal presents to us, for the first time, a case involving the application of the modern statute. We hold that, under the proof presented by the People at trial, defendant Melvin Dlugash may be held for attempted murder, though the target of the attempt may have already been slain, by the hand of another, when Dlugash made his felonious attempt.

On December 22, 1973, Michael Geller, 25 years old, was found shot to death in the bedroom of his Brooklyn apartment. The body, which had literally been riddled by bullets, was found lying face up on the floor. An autopsy revealed that the victim had been shot in the face and head no less than seven times. Powder burns on the face indicated that the shots had been fired from within one foot of the victim. Four small caliber bullets were recovered from the victim's skull. The victim had also been critically wounded in the chest. One heavy caliber bullet passed through the left lung, penetrated the heart chamber, pierced the left ventricle of the heart upon entrance and again upon exit, and lodged in the victim's torso. A second bullet entered the left lung and passed through to the chest, but without reaching the heart area . . .

Defendant was indicted by the Grand Jury of Kings County on a single count of murder in that, acting in concert with another person actually present, he intentionally caused the death of Michael Geller . . . For proof of defendant's culpability, the prosecution relied upon defendant's own admissions as related by the detective and the prosecutor. From the physicians, the prosecution sought to establish that Geller was still alive at the time defendant shot at him. Both physicians testified that each of the two chest wounds, for which defendant alleged Bush to be responsible, would have caused death without prompt medical attention. Moreover, the victim would have remained alive until such time as his chest cavity became fully filled with blood. Depending on the circumstances, it might take 5 to 10 minutes for the chest cavity to fill. Neither prosecution witness could state, with medical certainty, that the victim was still alive when, perhaps five minutes after the initial chest wounds were inflicted, the defendant fired at the victim's head.

The defense produced but a single witness, the former Chief Medical Examiner of New York City. This expert stated that, in his view, Geller might have died of the chest wounds "very rapidly" since, in addition to the bleeding, a large bullet going through a lung and the heart would have other adverse medical effects. "Those wounds can be almost immediately or rapidly fatal or they may be delayed in there, in the time it would take for death to occur. But I would say that wounds like that which are described here as having gone through the lungs and the heart would be fatal wounds and in most cases they're rapidly fatal." . . .

Preliminarily, we state our agreement with the Appellate Division that the evidence did not establish, beyond a reasonable doubt, that Geller was alive at the time defendant fired into his body. To sustain a homicide conviction, it must be established, beyond a reasonable doubt, that the defendant caused the death of another person. The People were required to establish that the shots fired by defendant Dlugash were a sufficiently direct cause of Geller's death. While the defendant admitted firing five shots at the victim approximately two to five minutes after Bush had fired three times, all three medical expert witnesses testified that they could not, with any degree of medical certainty, state whether the victim had been alive at the time the latter shots were fired by the defendant. Thus, the People failed to prove beyond a reasonable doubt that the victim had been alive at the time he was shot by the defendant. Whatever else it may be, it is not murder to shoot a dead body. Man dies but once . . .

The most intriguing attempt cases are those where the attempt to commit a crime was unsuccessful due to mistakes of fact or law on the part of the would-be criminal. A general rule developed in most American jurisdictions that legal impossibility is a good defense but factual impossibility is not. Thus, for example, it was held that defendants who shot at a stuffed deer did not attempt to take a deer out of season, even though they believed the dummy to be a live animal. The court stated that there was no criminal attempt because it was no crime to "take" a stuffed deer, and it is no crime to attempt to do that which is legal. These cases are illustrative of legal impossibility . . .

On the other hand, factual impossibility was no defense. For example, a man was held liable for attempted murder when he shot into the room in which his target usually slept and, fortuitously, the target was sleeping elsewhere in the house that night. Although one bullet struck the target's customary pillow, attainment of the criminal objective was factually impossible . . .

The New York cases can be parsed out along similar lines. One of the leading cases on legal impossibility is *People v. Jaffe*, 185 N.Y. 497, in which we held that there was no liability for the attempted receipt of stolen property when the property received by the defendant in the belief that it was stolen was, in fact under the control of the true owner. Similarly, in *People v. Teal*, 196 N.Y. 372, a conviction for attempted subornation of perjury was overturned on the theory that the testimony attempted to be suborned was irrelevant to the merits of the case. Since it was not subornation of perjury to solicit false, but irrelevant, testimony, "the person through whose procuration the testimony is given cannot be guilty of subornation of perjury and, by the same rule, an unsuccessful attempt to that which is not a crime when effectuated, cannot be held to be an attempt to commit the crime specified." Factual impossibility, however, was no defense. Thus, a man could be held for attempted grand larceny when he picked an empty pocket.

As can be seen from even this abbreviated discussion, the distinction between "factual" and "legal" impossibility was a nice one indeed and the courts tended to place a greater value on legal form than on any substantive danger the defendant's actions posed for society. The approach of the draftsmen of the Model Penal Code was to eliminate the defense of impossibility in virtually all situations. Under the code provision, to constitute an attempt, it is still necessary that the result intended or desired by the actor constitute a crime. However, the code suggested a fundamental change to shift the locus of analysis to the actor's mental frame of reference and away from undue dependence upon external considerations. The basic premise of the code provision is that what was in the actor's own mind should be the standard for determining his dangerousness to society and, hence, his liability for attempted criminal conduct.

In the belief that neither of the two branches of the traditional impossibility arguments detracts from the offender's moral culpability, the

Legislature substantially carried the code's treatment of impossibility into the 1967 revision of the Penal Law. Thus, a person is guilty of an attempt when, with intent to commit a crime, he engages in conduct which tends to effect the commission of such crime. It is no defense that, under the attendant circumstances, the crime was factually or legally impossible of commission, "if such crime could have been committed had the attendant circumstances been as such person believed them to be." N.Y. Penal L. § 110.10. Thus, if defendant believed the victim to be alive at the time of the shooting, it is no defense to the charge of attempted murder that the victim may have been dead.

Turning to the facts of the case before us, we believe that there is sufficient evidence in the record from which the jury could conclude that the defendant believed Geller to be alive at the time defendant fired shots into Geller's head. Defendant admitted firing five shots at a most vital part of the victim's anatomy from virtually point blank range. Although defendant contended that the victim had already been grievously wounded by another, from the defendant's admitted actions, the jury could conclude that the defendant's purpose and intention was to administer the coup de grace . . .

—◦◦◦—

State v. Smith

Superior Court of New Jersey, Appellate Division
262 N.J. Super. 487, 621 A.2d 493 (1993)

KING, P.J.A.D.

Defendant was a county jail inmate at the time of this criminal episode on June 11, 1989. He had, and knew he had, the human immunodeficiency virus (HIV). On several occasions before June 11 he had threatened to kill corrections officers by biting or spitting at them. On that day he bit an officer's hand causing puncture wounds of the skin during a struggle which he had precipitated. The jury found him guilty of attempted murder, aggravated assault and terroristic threats. The judge imposed an aggregate 25-year term with a 12-year period of parole ineligibility.

On this appeal each of defendant's claims of error arises from his premises that (1) without dispute a bite cannot transmit HIV, and (2) defendant knew this when he bit the officers. From these premises defendant urges that he was wrongfully convicted of attempted murder because he knew that his bite could not kill the officer. He insists that he was convicted of such a serious charge because of society's discrimination against persons infected with this deadly virus. He claims that at worst he was guilty only of assaultive conduct and should have been sentenced, as a third-degree offender, to a relatively short custodial term.

From our review of this record, we conclude that neither of defendant's two premises has been established. First, if HIV cannot possibly be spread by a bite, the evidence at trial did not establish that proposition. Indeed, we doubt that the proposition is presently provable scientifically, given the current state of medical knowledge. The apparent medical consensus is that there has never been a controlled study of a sufficiently large number of cases to establish to any scientific certainty if transmission of HIV is possible by a bite, and if so, the percentage of likely infection. The proposition was surely disputed at this trial. Second, whether defendant actually believed that his bite could result in death was a question of his credibility, a question the jury obviously resolved against him.

We cannot and need not decide if a bite can transmit HIV. We have applied the elements of the attempted murder statute as we would in a case involving a more traditional criminal methodology. We conclude that the attempted murder verdict was supported by proof, which the jury reasonably could accept, that the defendant subjectively believed that his conduct could succeed in causing the officer's death, regardless of whether his belief was objectively valid. For this reason, we affirm the conviction. . . .

ADVICE   Performing research on impossibility in a particular jurisdiction can be maddening because courts uses the term "legal impossibility" in different ways—further fueling the confusion regarding the doctrine. When some judges say "legal impossibility" they mean pure legal impossibility, i.e., the situation where the defendant has an overly restrictive understanding of the law. Courts always recognize this as a defense. See, e.g., *United States v. Oviedo*, 525 F.2d 881, 883 (5th Cir. 1976). However, sometimes judges say "legal impossibility" when they mean to refer to hybrid legal impossibility, which is now generally disfavored by courts. Consequently, the first thing you should determine on seeing the term "legal impossibility" is to ascertain its definition based on the context.

NOTES & QUESTIONS ON IMPOSSIBILITY

1. *AIDS and impossibility.*   In *Smith*, the court concluded that it was uncertain whether a bite could transmit HIV. The decision was written in 1993 and the court noted the inability of scientists to generate a large number of subjects for a rigorous scientific study regarding HIV transmission and saliva. Assuming

the evidence conclusively demonstrated that HIV cannot be transmitted through saliva, what is the correct result? Does it remain a factual impossibility or a legal impossibility? Assuming the defendant believed erroneously that saliva can transmit HIV, would it remain a case of factual impossibility?

2. *Factual impossibility.*   Some jurisdictions have statutes that specifically preclude factual impossibility as a defense. See, e.g., 21 Kan. Stat. Ann. § 5301(b) ("It shall not be a defense to a charge of attempt that the circumstances under which the act was performed or the means employed or the act itself were such that the commission of the crime was not possible."). Other jurisdictions employ the rule through judicial invention. Either way, there is near-universal agreement that factual impossibility is no defense. The argument for rejecting the defense is that the defendant was trying to commit a crime and from a subjective standpoint this demonstrates the perpetrator's culpability and danger-ousness. Indeed, the Model Penal Code seems to highlight this fact by noting in its general attempt provision the requirement that the defendant "purposely engages in conduct that would constitute the crime if the attendant circumstances were *as he believes them to be.*" MPC § § 5.01(1)(a) and 5.01(1)(c).

3. *Hybrid legal impossibility.*   In the past, courts had granted a defense of impossibility in some cases of factual impossibility but not in others. Some com-mentators have tried to explain these rare decisions by using a third label. This third category—hybrid legal impossibility—would include mistakes regarding the legal status of a fact that is necessary to establish a required element of the offense, though it encompasses other situations as well. So if the defendant takes merchandise that he believes to be stolen but is not stolen, he should not be convicted of attempted possession of stolen goods, according to the doc-trine of hybrid legal impossibility. *People v. Jaffe*, 185 N.Y. 497 (1906). Some jurists also describe the situation in *Dlugash*—shooting a dead body believing that the person was alive—as a case of hybrid legal impossibility.

However, most jurisdictions now deny that cases of hybrid legal impossibility should be excused. In *People v. Thousand*, 465 Mich. 149 (2001), the defendant chatted over the Internet with an undercover police officer that he believed was an underage girl. The court upheld the conviction for distributing pornography to a minor even though it was legally impossible for him to complete the offense because there was, in fact, no minor on the other end of the chat. Courts have also consistently denied the impossibility defense when a would-be murderer hires an undercover police officer whom he believes to be a hitman. See, e.g., *People v. Superior Court (Decker)*, 157 P.3d 1017 (Cal. 2007). And in *Dlugash,* the New York Court of Appeals upheld the conviction because the attendant circumstances constituted a crime as the defendant believed them to be. N.Y. Penal Law § 110.10 ("If the conduct in which a person engages otherwise constitutes an attempt to commit a crime pursuant to section

110.00, it is no defense to a prosecution for such attempt that the crime charged to have been attempted was, under the attendant circumstances, factually or legally impossible of commission, if such crime could have been committed had the attendant circumstances been as such person believed them to be."). In general, courts today are inclined to reject impossibility defenses regardless of how they are classified. *United States v. Farner*, 251 F.3d 510 (5th Cir. 2001) ("distinction between factual and legal impossibility is elusive at best"); *Collins v. Commonwealth*, 283 Va. 263, 720 S.E.2d 530 (2012) (explicitly rejecting the notion of hybrid legal impossibility); *United States v. Darnell*, 545 F.2d 595, 597 (8th Cir. 1976) ("tidy dichotomy of the theoretician becomes obscure in the courtroom"). Because of this new uniformity and the categories' lack of conceptual clarity, it is wise not to get bogged down with trying to distinguish cases of factual impossibility from hybrid legal impossibility, especially since today neither situation constitutes a valid defense.

HYPOTHETICAL

A is angry at B and plots to kill him. A's plan is to put his vocational voodoo training to good use to accomplish the murder. A constructs the voodoo doll, crafted in B's image, and sticks pins all over it. To A's dismay, nothing happens to B. Although A remains a devotee of voodoo, A's attorney argues at trial that A cannot be guilty of attempted murder because the murder could never have been completed. What result? More importantly, is there some way of classifying the crime as legal impossibility, or does it remain a factual impossibility? If the latter, should A be convicted? See *United States v. Coffman*, 94 F.3d 330 (7th Cir. 1996) ("There may be attempts so feeble, such as sticking a pin into a voodoo doll of your enemy in an effort to kill him, that the attempter is entitled to be acquitted, as a harmless fool. The defendants' scheme, though harebrained, was not that harebrained.").

The Model Penal Code, § 5.05(2), includes a special provision for this problem, and permits judges to exercise their discretion to mitigate punishment or even dismiss the prosecution if the result "is so inherently unlikely to result or culminate in the commission of a crime that neither such conduct nor the actor presents a public danger. . . ." According to George Fletcher, the "supposition is that those who try to kill by incantations either know in their hearts that their activity is harmless, or are so out of touch that they could not competently execute a plan to kill by more rational means." *Rethinking Criminal Law* 177 (2d ed. 2000).

4. Abandonment

If a perpetrator reverses course, should he still be convicted of an attempt? How does a criminal unwind his participation in a prior criminal endeavor that is not yet complete? Courts have struggled with this question, in part because they want to give criminals the incentive to give up and comply with the law.

Ross v. Mississippi

Supreme Court of Mississippi
601 So. 2d 872 (1992)

PRATHER, J.

This attempted-rape case arose on the appeal of Sammy Joe Ross from the ten-year sentence imposed on July 7, 1988 by the Circuit Court of Union County. The appellant timely filed a notice of appeal and dispositively raises the issue: Whether the trial court erred in denying the defendant's motion for directed verdict on the charge of attempted rape. This Court reverses and renders the conviction for attempted rape.

On September 16, 1987, sometime around 2:15 in the afternoon, Deputy Sheriff Edwards of the Union County Sheriff's Department was driving on Highway 30 heading east. Before he turned south onto Highway 9, he saw an oncoming truck, a white, late-model Ford pickup, turn left onto the first gravel road. Because the truck had out-of-county tags and turned down a road on which several crimes had occurred, Edwards jotted down the tag number, which action he described as routine practice.

Dorothy Henley and her seven-year-old daughter lived in a trailer on the gravel road. Henley was alone at home and answered a knock at the door to find Sammy Joe Ross asking directions. Henley had never seen Ross before. She stepped out of the house and pointed out the house of a neighbor who might be able help him. When she turned back around, Ross pointed a handgun at her. He ordered her into the house, told her to undress, and shoved her onto the couch. Three or four times Ross ordered Henley to undress and once threatened to kill her. Henley described herself as frightened and crying. She attempted to escape from Ross and told him that her daughter would be home from school at any time. She testified: "I started crying and talking about my daughter, that I was all she had because her daddy was dead, and he said if I had a little girl he wouldn't do anything, for me just to go outside and turn my back." As instructed by Ross, Henley walked outside behind her trailer. Ross followed and told her to keep her back to the road until he had departed. She complied. . . .

On December 21, 1987, a Union County grand jury indicted Sammy Joe Ross for the attempted rape of Henley. . . . On June 23, 1988, the jury found Ross guilty. . . .

Although other issues . . . are raised, the primary issue here is . . . whether Ross abandoned his attack as a result of outside intervention. Ross claims that the case should have gone to the jury only on a simple assault determination. Ross asserts that "it was not . . . Henley's resistance that prevented her rape nor any independent intervening cause or third person, but the voluntary and independent decision by her assailant to abandon his attack." The state, on the other hand, claims that Ross "panicked" and "drove away hastily." . . .

The trial court instructed the jury that if it found that Ross did "any overt act with the intent to have unlawful sexual relations with [the complainant] without her consent and against her will" then the jury should find Ross guilty of attempted rape. The court further instructed the jury that:

> before you can return a verdict against the defendant for attempted rape, that you must be convinced from the evidence and beyond a reasonable doubt, that the defendant was prevented from completing the act of rape or failed to complete the act of rape by intervening, extraneous causes. If you find that the act of rape was not completed due to a voluntary stopping short of the act, then you must find the defendant not guilty.

The crime of attempt to commit an offense occurs when a person "shall design and endeavor to commit an offense, and shall do any overt act toward the commission thereof, but shall fail therein, or shall be prevented from committing the same. . . ." Miss. Code Ann. § 97-1-7 (1972). Put otherwise, attempt consists of "1) an intent to commit a particular crime; 2) a direct ineffectual act done toward its commission; and 3) failure to consummate its commission."

The Mississippi attempt statute requires that the third element, failure to consummate, result from extraneous causes. Thus, a defendant's voluntary abandonment may negate a crime of attempt. Where a defendant, with no other impetus but the victim's urging, voluntarily ceases his assault, he has not committed attempted rape. In *Pruitt*, 528 So. 2d at 830-831, where the assailant released his throathold on the unresisting victim and told her she could go, after which a third party happened on the scene, the Court held that the jury could not have reasonably ruled out abandonment.

In comparison, this Court has held that where the appellant's rape attempt failed because of the victim's resistance and ability to sound the alarm, the appellant cannot establish an abandonment defense. *Alexander v. State*, 520 So. 2d 127, 130 (Miss. 1988). In the *Alexander* case, the evidence sufficiently established a question of attempt for the jury. The defendant did not voluntarily abandon his attempt, but instead fled after the victim, a hospital patient, pressed the nurse's buzzer; a nurse responded and the victim spoke the word "help." The Court concluded, "[T]he appellant ceased his actions only after the victim managed to press the buzzer alerting the nurse." In another case, the court properly sent the issue of attempt to the jury where the attacker failed because the victim resisted and freed herself. *Harden v. State*, 465 So. 2d 321, 325 (Miss. 1985).

Thus, abandonment occurs where, through the verbal urging of the victim, but with no physical resistance or external intervention, the perpetrator changes his mind. At the other end of the scale, a perpetrator cannot claim that he abandoned his attempt when, in fact, he ceased his efforts because the victim or a third party intervened or prevented him from furthering the attempt. Somewhere in the middle lies a case such as *Alexander,* where the victim successfully sounded an alarm, presenting no immediate physical obstacle to the perpetrator's continuing the attack, but sufficiently intervening to cause the perpetrator to cease his attack.

In this case, Ross appeals the denial of his motion for directed verdict; thus, he challenges only the sufficiency of the evidence, that is, whether it raised a sufficient factual issue to warrant a jury determination. Even under this rigorous standard of review, Ross's appeal should succeed on this issue. The evidence does not sufficiently raise a fact question as to whether he attempted rape. The evidence uncontrovertibly shows that he did not, but instead abandoned the attempt.

The key inquiry is a subjective one: what made Ross leave? According to the undisputed evidence, he left because he responded sympathetically to the victim's statement that she had a little girl. He did not fail in his attack. No one prevented him from completing it. Henley did not sound an alarm. She successfully persuaded Ross, of his own free will, to abandon his attempt. No evidence shows that Ross panicked and hastily drove away, but rather, the record shows that he walked the complainant out to the back of her trailer before he left. Thus, the trial court's failure to grant a directed verdict on the attempted rape charge constituted reversible error. As this Court stated in *Pruitt,* 528 So. 2d 831, this is not to say that Ross committed no criminal act, but "our only inquiry is whether there was sufficient evidence to support a jury finding that [Ross] did not abandon his attempt to rape [Henley]." This Court holds that there was not.

Ross raises a legitimate issue of error in the sufficiency of the evidence supporting his conviction for attempted rape because he voluntarily abandoned the attempt. This Court reverses and renders.

NOTES & QUESTIONS ON ABANDONMENT

1. *Abandonment and resistance.*   Did the court in *Ross* get the abandonment issue correct? The court applied a common restriction on the abandonment defense, which is that the abandonment must be voluntary and not induced by the victim's resistance or outside intervention. The court's application of this standard in this case seemed guided by a distinction between verbal resistance and physical resistance. So if a victim verbally resists and convinces the defendant to abandon the crime, the perpetrator is not guilty of an attempt. But if the victim physically resists and the defendant cannot complete the crime because of it, he is guilty of attempted rape. Should the distinction between

physical and verbal resistance continue to be relevant given that verbal resistance—saying no—is now enough in some jurisdictions to make the perpetrator guilty of rape? Also, did it matter to the court how far the attempted assault had proceeded? In *State v. Mahoney*, 264 Mont. 89 (1994), the Supreme Court of Montana rejected an abandonment defense when an attempted rapist called police after he saw how much the victim was bleeding after he had stabbed her. The court rejected the abandonment defense because the victim was resisting the attack and preventing the rapist from accomplishing his criminal goal. Does it matter that the nature of the resistance in *Mahoney* and *Ross* was different?

ADVICE   As discussed above, the abandonment doctrine requires that the would-be perpetrator desist for the right reason—i.e., voluntarily—as opposed to being motivated by victim resistance or police detection. However, the reason for the desisting is irrelevant if the actor has not even crossed the threshold from preparation to sufficient actus reus for attempt. Prior to that crossing, the actor need not meet the formal requirements for the abandonment doctrine since by its terms the doctrine only applies when the threshold has been crossed and the actor is otherwise responsible for the attempt. Before the threshold has been crossed, the actor can desist for any reason at all and still escape attempt liability. Consequently, when analyzing a potential abandonment fact pattern, be sure to first determine whether the requirements for attempt liability are satisfied; if yes, then analyze the abandonment issue.

---

2. *Abandonment statutes.*   The defense of abandonment is often codified by statute. 35 Ind. Code § 41-3-10 ("With respect to a charge under IC 35-41-2-4, IC 35-41-5-1, or IC 35-41-5-2, it is a defense that the person who engaged in the prohibited conduct voluntarily abandoned his effort to commit the underlying crime and voluntarily prevented its commission."); 45 Mont. Code Ann. § 4-103(4) ("A person shall not be liable under this section if, under circumstances manifesting a voluntary and complete renunciation of his criminal purpose, he avoided the commission of the offense attempted by abandoning his criminal effort."). Jurisdictions that reject the defense often do so by case law. *State v. Robbins*, 253 Wis. 2d 298, 316 (2002) ("The crime of attempt is complete when the intent to commit the underlying crime is coupled with sufficient acts to demonstrate the improbability of free will desistance; the actual intervention of an extraneous factor is not a 'third element' of the crime of attempt, although it is often part of the proof. There is no statutory defense of voluntary abandonment once an attempt is completed, and this court has declined to create such a defense at common law."). However, the application of these provisions is difficult unless

one has a stable definition of voluntariness, i.e., what it means to *voluntarily* abandon an effort. The Model Penal Code provision on abandonment includes an explicit definition:

> Within the meaning of this Article, renunciation of criminal purpose is not voluntary if it is motivated, in whole or in part, by circumstances, not present or apparent at the inception of the actor's course of conduct, which increase the probability of detection or apprehension or which make more difficult the accomplishment of the criminal purpose. Renunciation is not complete if it is motivated by a decision to postpone the criminal conduct until a more advantageous time or to transfer the criminal effort to another but similar objective or victim.

MPC § 5.01(4). Some jurisdictions have defined voluntariness through case law when the statute does not include an explicit definition. For example, see *Smith v. State,* 636 N.E.2d 124, 127 (Ind. 1994) ("To be considered voluntary, the decision to abandon must originate with the accused and not be the product of extrinsic factors that increase the probability of detection or make more difficult the accomplishment of the criminal purpose.").

3. *Abandonment and incentives.* Should courts more freely grant the abandonment defense in order to give criminals an incentive to stop? For a discussion of this issue, see Murat C. Mungan, *Abandoned Criminal Attempts: An Economic Analysis*, Ala. L. Rev. (forthcoming). However, there are also non-utilitarian reasons to support an abandonment defense, based on the idea that the defendant's voluntary change of course represents an erasure or substantial mitigation of his or her moral culpability. A third possibility is that a perpetrator's renunciation of criminal purpose negates his dangerousness. Model Penal Code Commentaries to § 5.01, at 359. A fourth possibility is that abandonment should simply mitigate punishment but not operate as an affirmative defense. Under this scheme, judges would simply lower the penalty for criminals who abandon their crimes but not fully exonerate them. For an argument supporting this result, see Gideon Yaffe, *Criminal Attempts*, 124 Yale L.J. 92, 147 (2014) ("when the defendant has changed his mind, one reason to give a sanction of some particular size is nullified"). Do you agree?

C. PRACTICE & POLICY

Perhaps the biggest policy question regarding attempts is how they should be punished. Having mastered the basic building blocks of criminal attempts, we can now address the larger and deeper question about why and how much these attempts should be punished. The chapter concludes with a brief exegesis on the crime of assault—which was originally an attempt crime.

∾ **Punishing attempts: why and how much.** The first issue is why we should punish attempts at all. Gideon Yaffe has written that "the prohibition of an action is also an implicit prohibition of an attempt to engage in that action; a prohibition of causing a result is an implicit prohibition of an attempt to cause that result." *Criminal Attempts*, 124 Yale L.J. 92, 131 (2014). Implicitly, then, the criminalization of attempts is the criminalization of *trying* to commit a crime—an idea already embedded in the structure of the criminal law. Simply by trying to commit a crime, the criminal has thumbed his nose at society's rules and social order. Similarly, see Stephen P. Garvey, *Are Attempts Like Treason?*, 14 New Crim. L. Rev. 173 (2011) (arguing that all attempts involve a treasonous rejection of the duty to comply with the law). Even if unsuccessful, criminal attempts are an expression of defiance of established and legitimate rules of public conduct. Do you agree?

When it comes to how severely to punish attempts, there are two major—and competing—impulses. The first is that the attempts are less serious because the defendant never produced the resulting harm. Since the criminal law cares about harm and results, criminal attempts are much less serious crimes. In most cases, the victim was not harmed, or if the victim *was* harmed it is only because the perpetrator managed to complete some other, lesser crime in addition to the attempted crime. On the other hand, there are substantial reasons to think that attempts should be punished just as seriously as completed crimes. (These arguments are stronger in the context of complete attempts than for incomplete ones.) First, perpetrators who fail to complete the crime are usually fully committed to the crime's commission; otherwise, they should never have been convicted of the attempt in the first place. If the crime was thwarted, it was only because of the perpetrator's poor luck that the gun jammed, or he missed the target, or the police thwarted the crime and arrested him before he could complete the task. These barriers to completing the crime are all *extraneous* to the defendant's actions—they stem from outside the perpetrator's moral agency. Why should the criminal law give the perpetrator a discount on punishment just because the perpetrator had the misfortune (or fortune, depending on your point of view) to get caught or to have poor aim? In the end, the inner culpability of the attempted murderer is just as severe as the murderer, because both desire the result and engage in actions to bring it about. The successful murderer does not have a deeper and more profound level of blameworthiness just because he succeeded in his endeavor.

One could appeal to the concept of dangerousness to respond to the skepticism about mitigating punishment for attempted murders. Given that the attempted murderer fails to achieve the resulting death, perhaps attempted crimes are less serious because they are less dangerous to society. This is certainly true if the inherent dangerousness of an offense comes from its immediate result or lack thereof. But perhaps dangerousness also involves the risk that the defendant will reoffend and commit more crimes. See Steven Shavell, *Deterrence and the Punishment of Attempts*, 19 J. Leg. Stud. 435, 458 (1990). Under this incapacitation framework, it seems just as likely that an attempted murderer will commit another crime as it is that the successful murderer will commit another crime. Indeed, perhaps the attempted murderer has even *greater* incentive to reoffend, since his original crime was not successful. The only reason that a utilitarian should have for viewing an attempted murderer as less dangerous is if the attempted murderer is a hapless or truly incompetent criminal. But that presumably is a small subset of the universe of attempted murderers.

∾ Assault and battery. At common law, assault was defined as an attempt to commit a physical battery. For example, if the actor punched the victim and his fist made contact with the victim's body, this was battery. However, if the actor threw a punch that missed, it would be assault, i.e., an attempted battery. Many attempt cases were prosecuted under the rubric of assault because some jurisdictions defined assaults more broadly as the attempt to commit a "violent injury" of another person. Consequently, assault was one of the first inchoate crimes based on a theory of attempt. This ancient pedigree has fallen out of usage in some jurisdictions whose statutes define an assault as intentionally causing an injury—which basically combines assault and battery into a single provision, with the inchoate nature of assault removed. For example, New York law simply defines third-degree assault as "with intent to cause physical injury to another person, he causes such injury to such person or to a third person; or . . . [h]e recklessly causes physical injury to another person; or . . . [w]ith criminal negligence, he causes physical injury to another person by means of a deadly weapon or a dangerous instrument." N.Y. Penal Law § 120.00. Assault in tort law also includes situations where the actor threatens the victim and by his conduct places the victim in reasonable fear or apprehension of imminent and serious bodily harm. Many jurisdictions have taken this tort theory of "reasonable apprehension" and added it to their criminal law as well. For example, an actor who points a gun at someone and threatens to shoot that person would be guilty of assault even if the actor never pulls the trigger.

CHAPTER 18

⤙✧⤚

INCHOATE CONSPIRACY

A. DOCTRINE

The definition of a conspiracy is an agreement between two or more individuals to commit an unlawful act. Since the crime is inchoate in nature, the ultimate crime to which the conspiracy is directed need not be performed. Indeed, this is the whole point of inchoate conspiracy. It gives police and prosecutors an opportunity to intervene in criminal endeavors before the criminal transaction is completed. The elements of the offense include:

1. agreement to commit an unlawful act,
2. specific intent or purpose to achieve the goal or object of the conspiracy, and
3. overt act in furtherance of the conspiracy.

1. Agreement to Commit Unlawful Act

The unlawful agreement is in many ways the signature element of the crime of conspiracy—its *sine qua non*. Once the agreement is formed (and an overt act is performed), the inchoate crime of conspiracy has been committed. The agreement itself is the criminal act of the offense. That is precisely what makes conspiracy such a powerful prosecutorial tool.

Our folk conception of a conspiracy is a secret agreement pursued in a smoke-filled backroom. While this certainly constitutes a conspiracy, the criminal offense does not require an explicit agreement. An implicit agreement between two or more individuals, even if never rendered in more explicit terms, qualifies as a conspiracy. Consequently, the government may prove the existence of the unlawful agreement through circumstantial evidence and inferences. A criminal conspiracy is rarely memorialized in writing—though email and text messages may be changing that. It often takes a jury to make the subtle factual determination over whether multiple individuals had an implicit agreement (which constitutes a conspiracy) or were merely engaging in "conscious parallelism" (which does not constitute a conspiracy).

What if the defendant forms an agreement with someone who only *feigns* agreement? This often happens when informants or undercover police officers pretend to form an agreement with the target of an investigation. Does it constitute an agreement when only one party sincerely agrees to the plan? Jurisdictions differ on the answer. Some, including most federal courts, adopt a bilateral approach and require two sincere parties to the agreement on the theory that it takes two to tango. However, some jurisdictions have followed the unilateral definition of unlawful agreements, which means that a single individual can create an agreement even if there is no true agreement with the other party.

2. Specific Intent or Purpose

In jurisdictions that use the language of specific intent, the mens rea requirement for conspiracy as a substantive offense is the specific intent that the group commit the crime. In jurisdictions that use the Model Penal Code language of purpose, the mens rea for conspiracy is "the purpose of promoting or facilitating its commission." MPC § 5.03(1). The defendant's specific intent or purpose will often be inferred based on the relevant facts and his behavior. Only rarely will the government have direct evidence, say an audio recording, where the defendant announces his specific intent or purpose with regard to the object of the conspiracy. Rarer still is witness testimony on the stand whereby the defendant admits his intent. The more usual scenario is for the government to produce factual evidence legally sufficient to generate an inference that the defendant intended the goal of the conspiracy. The defendant need not intend to personally commit the crime. The whole point of conspiracy is that the defendant intends that the group commit the crime and that the defendant performs his assigned role, consistent with the plan's division of labor.

3. The Overt Act Requirement

Jurisdictions usually have both a general conspiracy statute, penalizing any conspiracy to commit a crime, as well as specific conspiracy provisions tailored for particular criminal offenses. Most of the general conspiracy statutes—34 at most recent count—require an overt act in furtherance of the conspiracy. The requirement is meant to restrain the government's use of the conspiracy doctrine. Mere "bad" thoughts, after all, are not penalized in the absence of a culpable act, as discussed in Chapter 5 on the act requirement. However, many of the context-specific conspiracy statutes dispense with the requirement. For example, the

Exceptions to overt act.

Supreme Court has concluded that although the general federal conspiracy statute (18 U.S.C. § 371) requires an overt act, there is no overt act requirement in federal drug conspiracy cases (21 U.S.C. § 846), money laundering conspiracy (18 U.S.C. § 1956), and price-fixing conspiracies (15 U.S.C. § 1). The Model Penal Code splits the difference and dispenses with the overt act requirement for conspiracy to commit first-degree and second-degree felonies, but it requires an overt act for conspiracy to commit all other crimes.

Furthermore, statutes *with* an overt act requirement are often interpreted broadly. The defendant need not commit the overt act in question. It is sufficient if one member of the conspiracy commits the overt act. This is consistent with the view that conspiracies involve a division of labor between participants according to some pre-arranged or implicit plan. The plan may call for the first act to be performed by one member, with the others providing their contribution at a later point in time.

The goal of the overt act requirement is simply to distinguish between criminal agreements that are purely mental—existing only in the minds of the conspirators—and criminal agreements that have been actualized, if only minimally, in the outside world. What counts as an overt act is a question of fact for the jury to decide but can often be a minor act. For example, the act may be calling a confederate to inquire about procuring weapons, or checking a schedule to determine when a store—the target of a burglary—closes for the day.

4. Renunciation

Liability for conspiracy as an inchoate offense is not extinguished when the defendant stops pursuing the conspiratorial objective. The defendant must fully renounce the conspiracy by *thwarting* the conspiracy "under circumstances manifesting a complete and voluntary renunciation of his criminal purpose." MPC § 5.03(6). In practical terms, this means either contacting the police or otherwise depriving the conspiracy of its effectiveness. However, not all jurisdictions adopted the MPC version of renunciation. On the one hand, some jurisdictions have watered down the defense and allow it when defendants make *reasonable* efforts to stop the conspiracy. Ala. Code § 13A-4-3(c). On the other hand, a few jurisdictions, including the federal courts, refuse to recognize the defense entirely, presumably on the old common law rationale that the crime is complete once the agreement is formed and an overt act is committed, regardless of what happens next. See, e.g., *United States v. Gonzalez*, 797 F.2d 915, 917 (10th Cir. 1986). In these jurisdictions, the defendant has committed "conspiracy" once he agrees to the plan and performs the overt act; no amount of backtracking at that point will unwind his criminal liability for the charge of conspiracy. The deed is done, as they say, and the "deed" in this case is not the goal of the conspiracy (such as the murder) but rather the formation of the agreement coupled with the overt act.

5. Merger

Unlike attempts, conspiracy does not merge with its completed offense. That means that liability for conspiracy does not disappear once the conspiracy is successfully completed. The practical import of conspiracy's non-merger is that prosecutors can charge a defendant with both murder and conspiracy to commit murder at the same time, thus permitting what defense attorneys view as a form of double dipping. The rationale for the non-merger rule is that conspiracy, a form of collective criminality, represents a "distinct evil." Perhaps conspiracies, because they always include multiple criminals acting in concert, are more dangerous than the same crime committed by a single individual.

B. APPLICATION

1. Agreement to Commit Unlawful Act

The agreement is often referred to as the gravamen of the offense of conspiracy—its most essential element. How should a court assess whether an agreement existed? Specifically, does the agreement need two sincere parties, or can one individual form an agreement even if the other party is only feigning agreement?

Bilateral vs unilateral

State v. Pacheco
Supreme Court of Washington
125 Wash. 2d 150 (1994)

JOHNSON, J.

The Defendant, Herbert Pacheco, appeals his convictions for conspiracy to commit first-degree murder and conspiracy to deliver a controlled substance. He contends he did not commit conspiracy within the meaning of RCW 9A.28.040 because no genuine agreement existed between him and his sole coconspirator, an undercover police agent. We hold RCW 9A.28.040 and RCW 69.50.407 require an actual agreement between two coconspirators, and, therefore, reverse his convictions for conspiracy to commit murder in the first degree and conspiracy to deliver a controlled substance.

FACTS

Herbert Pacheco met Thomas Dillon in 1985, when Pacheco worked about 2 months for Dillon's private investigation firm. Pacheco bragged to Dillon about his involvement in illegal activities, including enforcement, collecting debts, procuring weapons, providing protection, and performing "hits."

In 1989, Dillon learned that Pacheco was a Clark County deputy sheriff. Dillon contacted the FBI and volunteered to inform on Pacheco. The FBI began an investigation of Pacheco. The Clark County Sheriff's office joined, and later directed the investigation. . . .

On March 26, 1990, according to a plan designed by the sheriff's office and the FBI, Dillon called Pacheco and told him he would like to meet to discuss a possible deal. Dillon and Pacheco met at a restaurant. Dillon said he had ties to the "Mafia" and offered Pacheco $500 in exchange for protection during a cocaine deal. Dillon told Pacheco that a buyer (an undercover FBI agent) would arrive shortly, and Pacheco was to protect Dillon during the transaction. Pacheco agreed. The undercover agent arrived and the purported drug transaction took place. Afterward, Dillon paid Pacheco $500. . . .

ANALYSIS

The Defendant contends he did not commit conspiracy within the meaning of RCW 9A.28.040 because his sole coconspirator was an undercover police agent who never "agreed" to commit the crime of murder in the first degree.

The Defendant argues the statute retains the common law, bilateral approach to conspiracy, which requires an actual agreement to commit a crime between the defendant and at least one other. Therefore, a government agent feigning agreement with the defendant does not constitute a conspiracy under the common law approach because no genuine agreement is reached. The Defendant asserts Washington is among those states whose statutes are patterned after the Model Penal Code but have been interpreted as adopting only a limited form of the code's unilateral approach, and retaining the requirement of a bilateral underlying agreement. . . .

The State contends RCW 9A.28.040 follows the code's purely unilateral approach. Under the code, actual agreement is not required as long as the defendant believes another is agreeing to commit the criminal act. Therefore, a purported agreement between a government agent and a defendant would satisfy the code's unilateral conspiratorial agreement approach.

Adopted in 1975, as a part of the overhaul of the criminal code, RCW 9A.28.040 provides in part:

(1) A person is guilty of criminal conspiracy when, with intent that conduct constituting a crime be performed, he agrees with one or more persons to engage in or cause the performance of such conduct, and any one of them takes a substantial step in pursuance of such agreement.

(2) It shall not be a defense to criminal conspiracy that the person or persons with whom the accused is alleged to have conspired:

(a) Has not been prosecuted or convicted; or

(b) Has been convicted of a different offense; or

(c) Is not amenable to justice; or

(d) Has been acquitted; or

(e) Lacked the capacity to commit an offense. . . .

Subsection (1) of RCW 9A.28.040 expressly requires an *agreement*, but does not define the term. Black's Law Dictionary defines *agreement* as, "[a] meeting of two or more minds; a coming together in opinion or determination; the coming together in accord of two minds on a given proposition." Similarly, *agreement* is defined in *Webster's* as "1a: the act of agreeing or coming to a mutual agreement . . . b: oneness of opinion. . . ." The dictionary definitions thus support the Defendant's argument.

Likewise, the common law definition of the agreement required for a conspiracy is defined not in unilateral terms but rather as a confederation or combination of minds. . . . A conspiratorial agreement necessarily requires more than one to agree because it is impossible to conspire with oneself. *Morrison v. California*, 291 U.S. 82, 92 (1934). We conclude that by requiring an agreement, the Legislature intended to retain the requirement of a genuine or bilateral agreement.

Subsection (2) provides the conspiratorial agreement may still be found even though the co-conspirator cannot be convicted. In this sense, the statute incorporates a limited form of the code's unilateral conspiracy in that it is no longer necessary that agreement be proved against both conspirators. Thus, under subsection (2)'s unilateral approach, the failure to convict an accused's sole coconspirator will not prevent proof of the conspiratorial agreement against the accused. However, this does not indicate the Legislature intended to abandon the traditional requirement of two criminal participants reaching an underlying agreement. . . .

Additionally, the unilateral approach fails to carry out the primary purpose of the statute. The primary reason for making conspiracy a separate offense from the substantive crime is the increased danger to society posed by group criminal activity. . . . However, the increased danger is nonexistent when a person "conspires" with a government agent who pretends agreement. In the feigned conspiracy there is no increased chance the criminal enterprise will succeed, no continuing criminal enterprise, no educating in criminal practices, and no greater difficulty of detection. . . .

Indeed, it is questionable whether the unilateral conspiracy punishes criminal activity or merely criminal intentions. The "agreement" in a unilateral conspiracy is a legal fiction, a technical way of transforming nonconspiratorial conduct into a prohibited conspiracy. . . . When one party merely pretends to agree, the other party, whatever he or she may believe about the pretender, is in fact not conspiring with anyone. Although the deluded party has the requisite criminal intent, there has been no criminal act. . . .

Another concern with the unilateral approach is its potential for abuse. In a unilateral conspiracy, the State not only plays an active role in creating the offense, but also becomes the chief witness in proving the crime at trial. . . . We agree with the Ninth Circuit this has the potential to put the State in the improper position of manufacturing crime. At the same time, such reaching is unnecessary because the punishable conduct in a unilateral conspiracy will almost always satisfy the elements of either solicitation or attempt. The State will still be able to thwart the activity and punish the defendant who attempts agreement with an undercover police officer. . . .

DURHAM, JUSTICE (dissenting).

The jury found that Herbert Pacheco, an aspiring hit man, planned a murder for money. Moreover, he took a substantial step toward that objective. Yet the majority overturns his conviction for conspiracy to commit murder solely because he conspired with a government agent rather than with another hit man. The Washington conspiracy statute does not require a co-conspirator to be a nongovernment actor. In fact, the statute explicitly envisages so-called unilateral conspiracies, as the majority admits. Because neither our case law, the statute, nor the rationale of conspiracy crimes compel the result arrived at by the majority, I dissent.

We accepted review solely to determine whether Washington's conspiracy statute countenances unilateral conspiracies. Yet the majority fails to provide even a cursory analysis of the essential differences between the bilateral and unilateral approaches to conspiracy. The bilateral approach asks whether there is an agreement between two or more persons to commit a criminal act. Its focus is on the content of the agreement and whether there is a shared understanding between the conspirators. The unilateral approach is not concerned with the content of the agreement or whether there is a meeting of minds. Its sole concern is whether the agreement, shared or not, objectively manifests the criminal intent of at least one of the conspirators. The majority does not even mention this crucial difference, and instead merely assumes that all conspiracies must be bilateral. In other words, the majority assumes precisely what it is supposed to prove; it begs the question. . . .

Next, the majority portrays the unilateral approach to conspiracy as an outdated relic from a bygone era. The Model Penal Code endorses unilateral conspiracies, the majority admits, but "[e]very federal court, which has since considered the issue" has adopted the bilateral approach. The majority neglects to mention that all the federal courts adopting bilateral conspiracy are construing a different statute, one whose language requires bilateral conspiracies. See 18 U.S.C. § 371 ("If two or more persons conspire . . . to commit any offense against the United States").

In contrast, the Model Penal Code defines conspiracy "in terms of one person's agreeing with another, rather than in terms of an agreement among or between two or more people."

The code embodies a significant change in emphasis. In its view, the major basis of conspiratorial liability is not the group nature of the activity but the firm purpose of an individual to commit a crime which is objectively manifested in conspiring. The Washington conspiracy statute tracks the Model Penal Code's language rather than the "two or more persons" language of the general federal conspiracy statute. In any event, far from being antiquated or obsolete, the "movement toward a unilateral theory of the crime is the modern trend in conspiracy law."

A comparison of the revised Washington conspiracy statute with its predecessor is far more revealing of legislative intent than the majority's simplistic and premature resort to dictionary definitions. . . . The predecessor statute used the phrase "[w]henever two or more persons shall conspire," which parallels the federal conspiracy statute and clearly requires bilateral conspiracy. The revised statute, in contrast, tracks the definitional language of the Model Penal Code, which adopts unilateral conspiracy. . . .

Next, the majority constructs a straw man by claiming that the primary purpose of conspiracy is "the increased danger to society posed by group criminal activity." Preventing group criminal activity is the rationale behind bilateral conspiracy, but that rationale was decisively rejected by the Model Penal Code. At best, controlling group criminal activity is only one rationale for conspiracy statutes.

A bilateral theory of conspiracy and the rigid standard of mutuality that it demands . . . are inconsistent with the recognition of an independent rationale for conspiracy law based on a conspirator's firm expectation of committing a crime. The majority compounds its own confusion by contending that unilateral conspiracies are factually impossible and therefore presumptively invalid ("When one party merely pretends to agree, the other party, whatever he or she may believe about the pretender, is in fact not conspiring with anyone."). This argument amounts to the truism that it is factually impossible to have a "meeting of minds" on the commission of a future crime if one of the minds is a government agent who does not intend to commit the criminal act. However, a "meeting of minds" is not a prerequisite of unilateral conspiracy. In any event, factual impossibility is not a recognized defense. The majority does nothing more than restate the discredited assumption that all conspiracies must be bilateral because conspiracy statutes attempt to target only group criminal activity.

Finally, I share the majority's concern about the potential for abuse of unilateral conspiracy. However, the majority fails to take into consideration the effect of the entrapment defense. The potential for abuse is further restricted by the statute itself, which requires not only an agreement to engage in criminal conduct but also "a substantial step in pursuance of such agreement." In the end, the majority succeeds only in providing a superfluous protection to criminal defendants at the price of hamstringing government attempts to nip criminal acts in the bud.

NOTES & QUESTIONS ON CONSPIRATORIAL AGREEMENTS

1. *Unilateral versus bilateral conspiracies.* As noted by the dissent in *Pacheco*, the modern trend (including in the Model Penal Code) is to recognize the unilateral approach to conspiracies, though jurisdictions are still divided. The majority concludes that a conspiracy necessarily requires two sincere partners. Is this the correct definition of an agreement? Is there a difference between *agreeing* to something and *forming an agreement*? The dissent seems to think so, but maybe the difference is merely semantic. The issue can be viewed as a theoretical dispute about the nature of agreements. Is it a verbal act—the act of saying "I agree"—or is it a deeper relationship between two or more individuals who jointly commit themselves to a collective project? The dissent clearly thinks it is the former.

2. *Utilitarian arguments.* Another way of approaching the issue is to think of it as a policy question for legislatures and appellate courts: Should police have the authority to prosecute would-be criminals who form "agreements" with undercover officers and informants? Is this a necessary tool for law enforcement? Consider what other strategies police officers could use if they were forced to abandon this popular practice. The court in *Pacheco* is not terribly concerned about taking conspiracy off the table, since undercover police officers could still catch would-be conspirators and charge them with solicitation, if that crime is recognized in that jurisdiction. Indeed, one might think of solicitation as a unilateral conspiracy. For a discussion, see Ira P. Robbins, *Double Inchoate Crimes*, 26 Harv. J. on Legis. 1, 36 (1989).

3. *The entrapment defense.* The dissent in *Pacheco* claims that the entrapment defense will solve any abuses created by the unilateral approach to conspiracy. Is this correct? The entrapment defense is often asserted but rarely successful. Why? For an entrapment defense to be successful, the defendant must show that he was not predisposed to commit the crime. In that sense, the government has entrapped him into doing something that he was *not* predisposed to do in the first place. The problem with this argument is that it requires convincing a jury that the defendant was not predisposed to commit the crime. Since the defendant *did* agree to commit the crime with an undercover police officer, jurors are often skeptical of defendants' entrapment arguments and are reluctant to return a potentially dangerous individual to their community. For further discussion, see Michael A. DeFeo, *Entrapment as a Defense to Criminal*

Responsibility: Its History, Theory, and Application, 1 U.S.F. L. Rev. 243 (1967); Jonathan C. Carson, *The Act Requirement and the Foundations of the Entrapment Defense,* 73 Va. L. Rev. 1011 (1987).

Review the casebook video, *People v. Daniella Forcheimes* (Part 1: Conspiracy). Did the defendant form an agreement to commit an unlawful act? Or does the fact that Forcheimes was talking with an undercover police agent preclude a judicial finding of an agreement between them? At the moment of "agreement," what were Forcheimes and the undercover police officer each *thinking* about the target of the conspiracy?

2. Specific Intent or Purpose

The defendant must have the specific intent to achieve the goal of the conspiracy. As with any mental state, courts usually infer the mental state from the defendant's behavior. In a conspiracy, these inferences are sometimes drawn from the defendant's conversations with others. As you read the following case, think about the different ways such conversations can be interpreted.

United States v. Valle

Federal District Court for the Southern District of New York
301 F.R.D. 53 (2014)

PAUL G. GARDEPHE, DISTRICT JUDGE.

The highly unusual facts of this case reflect the Internet age in which we live. To prove the kidnapping conspiracy alleged in Count One, the Government relied on numerous Internet "chats" in which (Gilberto) Valle and three alleged co-conspirators discuss in graphic detail kidnapping, torturing, raping, murdering, and cannibalizing women. Valle and his three alleged co-conspirators "met" on Dark Fetish Network or darkfetishnet.com ("DFN"), which bills itself as a fantasy sexual fetish website. Valle's DFN profile page stated: "I like to press the envelope but no matter what I say, it is all fantasy." Many of Valle's Internet communications involved him transmitting Facebook photographs of women he knew—whether his wife, her colleagues from work, or his college friends—and then "chatting" with other DFN users about committing acts of sexual violence against these women.

With respect to the kidnapping conspiracy charge, the primary issue raised in Valle's motion for a judgment of acquittal is whether the evidence and the reasonable inferences that may be drawn from that evidence are such that a rational jury could find that "criminal intent ha[d] crystallized"—that is, that Valle and his alleged co-conspirators entered into a genuine agreement to kidnap certain women and had the specific intent to actually kidnap these women.

Valle contends that his Internet chats are fantasy role-play, and that the Government did not prove beyond a reasonable doubt that he and his alleged co-conspirators entered into a "real" agreement to kidnap one or more women. The Government argues that the evidence shows that Valle entered into an illegal agreement to kidnap women with (1) a New Jersey man named Michael Van Hise; (2) an individual located in India or Pakistan who uses the screen name "Aly Khan"; and (3) a man using the screen name "Moody Blues," who lives in England. The alleged kidnapping conspiracy thus spanned three continents.

Although the alleged conspiracy lasted nearly a year, all communications between Valle and his alleged co-conspirators in New Jersey, India or Pakistan, and England took place over the Internet. None of the conspirators ever met or took steps to meet, nor did they ever speak by telephone. This is a conspiracy that existed solely in cyberspace. There is no evidence that the alleged conspirators ever exchanged telephone contact information or accurate information about the area in which they lived, or that they ever knew or sought to learn each other's true identities. Communication between the alleged conspirators was episodic and generally infrequent; months often passed between chats, with the alleged conspirators forgetting what had previously been discussed.

After reviewing thousands of Valle's Internet communications, the Government determined that Valle had discussed kidnapping, torturing, raping, murdering, and/or cannibalizing women with twenty-four individuals. At trial, the Government conceded that—as to twenty-one of these individuals—Valle's communications about kidnapping, torturing, raping, murdering, and cannibalizing women are nothing more than fantasy role-play. The Government nonetheless contends that Valle's communications with the remaining three—Van Hise, Aly Khan, and Moody Blues—reflect a "real" kidnapping conspiracy. . . . As is discussed in detail below, however, Valle's "chats" with a number of the individuals who the Government concedes are fantasy role-play correspondents are substantively indistinguishable from his chats with Van Hise, Aly Khan, and Moody Blues. . . .

Moreover, the nearly year-long kidnapping conspiracy alleged by the Government is one in which no one was ever kidnapped, no attempted kidnapping ever took place, and no real-world, non-Internet-based steps were ever taken to kidnap anyone. While the alleged conspirators discussed dates for kidnappings, no reasonable juror could have found that Valle actually intended to kidnap a woman on those dates. For example, under the Government's theory, Valle separately "agreed" with two co-conspirators to kidnap three different women on or about the same day,

February 20, 2012. Valle was to kidnap one woman in Manhattan; lure another to India or Pakistan; and kidnap a third in Columbus, Ohio.

No one was kidnapped on February 20, 2012, however, and no one was kidnapped on any other date "agreed to" or discussed by Valle and his alleged co-conspirators. Moreover, neither Valle nor any of his alleged co-conspirators ever even raised the issue of whether a "planned" kidnapping had taken place, and if not, why not. Dates for "planned" kidnappings pass without comment, without discussion, without explanation, and with no follow-up. The only plausible explanation for the lack of comment or inquiry about allegedly agreed-upon and scheduled kidnappings is that Valle and the others engaged in these chats understood that no kidnapping would actually take place. No other reasonable inference is possible. Because the point of the chats was mutual fantasizing about committing acts of sexual violence on certain women, there was no reason for discussion, inquiry, or explanation when the agreed-upon date for kidnapping a woman came and went.

The kidnapping conspiracy alleged by the Government also featured a steady stream of lies from Valle to his alleged co-conspirators about himself and numerous critical aspects of the alleged conspiracy. Valle lied about his age; about his marital status; about the city and area in which he lived; about whom he lived with; and about his job and the hours he worked. He also lied about whether he owned a house "in the middle of nowhere . . . in Pennsylvania"; about whether he owned a van that could be used to transport victims; about whether he had a "pulley-apparatus" in his basement; about whether he was soundproofing his basement; about whether he had a human-size oven and rotisserie; about whether he possessed address and contact information for the purported targets of the kidnapping conspiracy; about whether he was conducting surveillance of targeted women; about how often he was in contact with these women; and about whether he had obtained, or would obtain, rope, duct tape, and a stun gun for purposes of committing a kidnapping.

Similarly, the details Valle provided to his alleged co-conspirators concerning the targets of the kidnapping conspiracy were as to identification information all false. Valle lied about where the purported kidnapping targets lived, their last names, their occupations, their dates and places of birth, where they had attended or were attending college, and the degrees they had obtained. Despite repeated requests, Valle never provided his alleged co-conspirators with the last names and addresses that would have permitted them to locate and identify these women.

The Government, of course, is not required to prove that conspirators planning a kidnapping met in person, spoke over the telephone, or shared accurate information about their names and where they live, the names and addresses of kidnapping targets, or the resources each conspirator will contribute to the enterprise. Those engaged in criminal activity frequently lie to each other about all manner of things, including, for example, the amount and purity of drugs they possess, the value of items to be stolen, and the likelihood of getting caught. There is likewise no legal requirement that a kidnapping actually take place in order for a kidnapping conspiracy conviction to be sustained. Moreover, the fact that Valle had fantasy chats with twenty-one individuals about kidnapping, raping, and murdering women does not establish that his conversations with Van Hise, Aly Khan, and Moody Blues are likewise fantasy.

But the kidnapping conspiracy here was formed and is alleged to have taken place almost exclusively in cyberspace, and in a context in which—according to the Government—the Defendant engaged in countless fantasy role-play conversations with at least twenty-one other individuals about the same topics: kidnapping, torturing, raping, murdering, and cannibalizing women. Under these unique circumstances, in determining whether the Government proved beyond a reasonable doubt Valle's criminal intent—his specific intent to actually kidnap a woman—the fact that no kidnappings took place and that no real-world, concrete steps toward committing a kidnapping were ever undertaken, is significant. And in determining whether Valle and his alleged co-conspirators ever intended to actually commit a kidnapping, the fact that dates for kidnappings are repeatedly set and then pass without incident, inquiry, or comment is powerful evidence that Valle and the three individuals engaged in these allegedly "real" chats understood that no actual kidnapping was going to take place. . . .

Once the lies and the fantastical elements are stripped away, what is left are deeply disturbing misogynistic chats and emails written by an individual obsessed with imagining women he knows suffering horrific sex-related pain, terror, and degradation. Despite the highly disturbing nature of Valle's deviant and depraved sexual interests, his chats and emails about these interests are not sufficient—standing alone—to make out the elements of conspiracy to commit kidnapping. There must be evidence that Valle actually intended to act on these interests with an alleged co-conspirator.

Under the unique circumstances of this extraordinary case, and for the reasons discussed in detail below, the Court concludes that the evidence offered by the Government at trial is not sufficient to demonstrate beyond a reasonable doubt that Valle entered into a genuine agreement to kidnap a woman, or that he specifically intended to commit a kidnapping. . . .

The Government does not attempt to explain the "vanishing plots" phenomenon repeatedly seen in the evidence at trial. It simply argues that a court may sustain a conspiracy conviction even where the substantive crime that is its object is never consummated. While this is a correct statement of the law, it misses the point. If there was a genuine agreement to kidnap someone, and a specific intent to do so, it is inconceivable that the dates for planned kidnappings would repeatedly pass without inquiry, comment, or explanation from Valle or any of his alleged co-conspirators. Moreover, while this aspect of the allegedly "real" chats is entirely inconsistent with the notion that Valle was involved in plotting real kidnappings, it is entirely consistent with Valle's defense that he was engaged in fantasy role-play.

AFTERWORD   Officer Valle was fired by the New York City Police Department after his conviction. After Judge Gardephe overturned his conviction for conspiracy, Valle remained in prison to serve the rest of his one-year sentence for illegally accessing a law enforcement database, which contained information about the intended victims of his fantasy/conspiracy (depending on whether you accept the prosecution or defense view of his behavior). Valle was released from federal prison on July 1, 2014. His marriage ended in divorce in July 2013.

Van Hise was also prosecuted and convicted. "Moody Blues" was a pseudonym for a 57-year-old male nurse in Britain named Dale Bolinger, who was arrested by British police after his online activities were brought to light because of Valle's case. On July 21, 2014, Bolinger was convicted in Canterbury Crown Court for attempting to use the Internet to lure an underage girl to his residence.

NOTES & QUESTIONS ON SPECIFIC INTENT AND PURPOSE

1. *The jury's decision.*   Why did the jury convict Officer Gilberto Valle in *United States v. Valle*? Was it because the jury was convinced by the government's characterization of his online activities as planning (as opposed to fantasy)? Perhaps the jury assumed that he *was* fantasizing but the jury ignored the law and made a strategic calculation that those who fantasize about such things are likely to graduate from online fantasy to real-world crimes. After all, conspiracy law is based on the premise that conspiracies are especially dangerous to society. So perhaps even fake conspiracies are dangerous too. Or was he just convicted for having evil thoughts?

2. *The judge's decision.*   In a criminal trial, the defense needs to communicate to two audiences: the jury and the judge. In theory, each plays a separate role. The jury decides questions of fact and the judge decides matters of law. In practice, however, the two domains intersect. When a judge believes that no

reasonable jury could convict the defendant, the issue of fact is transformed into an issue of law for the judge to decide. Gilberto Valle failed to adequately convince the jury, but he successfully communicated his "fantasy" argument to the judge. At the outset of a trial, defense attorneys need to carefully calibrate their message to these dual audiences.

3. *Conspiracy to commit crimes of recklessness?* Given the specific intent or purpose requirement for the substantive crime of conspiracy, there is controversy over whether a defendant can be convicted of conspiracy to commit manslaughter or a similar crime of recklessness. Recall that in the *Thomas* case (discussed in Chapter 17), the Supreme Court of Colorado concluded that another inchoate offense—attempt—*did* apply to manslaughter and crimes of recklessness. But in a subsequent case, the court refused to extend that ruling to the crime of conspiracy. Aaron Palmer was convicted by a jury of conspiracy to commit reckless manslaughter for firing his weapon into a crowd of people, though no one was killed (which explains why he could not be convicted of manslaughter). Palmer appealed his conviction, and this time the Supreme Court of Colorado concluded that conspiracy to commit reckless manslaughter was *not* a crime in Colorado. See *Palmer v. People*, 964 P.2d 524, 526 (Colo. 1998). Is this result inconsistent with its *Thomas* holding? The Colorado Supreme Court said no, and distinguished the *Thomas* holding on the grounds that attempt liability focuses on conduct rather than results—and is therefore consistent with the heightened mens rea associated with attempt. On the other hand, the court concluded that "the culpability requirement for conspiracy and that for the crime of reckless manslaughter conflict. Conspiracy is always a specific intent crime, and conspiracy liability focuses on specifically intended results rather than on conduct. Unlike attempted reckless manslaughter, conspiracy to commit reckless manslaughter would require the accused to possess the specific intent to achieve an unintentional death, which we conclude is a legal and logical impossibility." Do you think the same reasoning should have applied to attempt as well?

3. Overt Act in Furtherance of the Conspiracy

A conspiracy conviction is supposed to require more than evil thoughts. Some statutes, though not all, require an overt act by someone within the conspiracy to show proof that the conspiracy moved from talk to *action*. That being said, the action does not have to be particularly significant. As you read the first case, ask yourself why Congress has sometimes included an explicit overt act requirement and in other cases has not. As you read the second case, ask yourself how weighty the overt act must be when a statute requires an overt act.

United States v. Shabani

Supreme Court of the United States
513 U.S. 10 (1994)

JUSTICE O'CONNOR delivered the opinion of the Court.

This case asks us to consider whether 21 U.S.C. § 846, the drug conspiracy statute, requires the Government to prove that a conspirator committed an overt act in furtherance of the conspiracy. We conclude that it does not.

According to the grand jury indictment, Reshat Shabani participated in a narcotics distribution scheme in Anchorage, Alaska, with his girlfriend, her family, and other associates. Shabani was allegedly the supplier of drugs, which he arranged to be smuggled from California. In an undercover operation, federal agents purchased cocaine from distributors involved in the conspiracy . . .

Congress passed the drug conspiracy statute as § 406 of the Comprehensive Drug Abuse Prevention and Control Act of 1970 . . . As amended by the Anti–Drug Abuse Act of 1988, the statute currently provides: "Any person who attempts or conspires to commit any offense defined in this subchapter shall be subject to the same penalties as those prescribed for the offense, the commission of which was the object of the attempt or conspiracy." 21 U.S.C. § 846. The language of neither version requires that an overt act be committed to further the conspiracy, and we have not inferred such a requirement from congressional silence in other conspiracy statutes. In *Nash v. United States*, 229 U.S. 373 (1913), Justice Holmes wrote, "[W]e can see no reason for reading into the Sherman Act more than we find there," and the Court held that an overt act is not required for antitrust conspiracy liability. The same reasoning prompted our conclusion in *Singer v. United States*, 323 U.S. 338 (1945), that the Selective Service Act "does not require an overt act for the offense of conspiracy."

Nash and *Singer* follow the settled principle of statutory construction that, absent contrary indications, Congress intends to adopt the common law definition of statutory terms. We have consistently held that the common law understanding of conspiracy "does not make the doing of any act other than the act of conspiring a condition of liability." Respondent contends that these decisions were rendered in a period of unfettered expansion in the law of conspiracy, a period which allegedly ended when the Court declared that "we will view with disfavor attempts to broaden the already pervasive and wide-sweeping nets of conspiracy prosecutions." *Grunewald v. United States*, 353 U.S. 391, 404 (1957). *Grunewald*, however, was a statute of limitations case, and whatever exasperation with conspiracy prosecutions the opinion may have expressed in dictum says little about the views of Congress when it enacted § 846.

As to those views, we find it instructive that the general conspiracy statute, 18 U.S.C. § 371, contains an explicit requirement that a conspirator "do any act to effect the object of the conspiracy." In light of this additional element in the general conspiracy statute, Congress' silence in § 846 speaks volumes. After all, the general conspiracy statute preceded and presumably provided the framework for the more specific drug conspiracy statute. "*Nash* and *Singer* give Congress a formulary: by choosing a text modeled on § 371, it gets an overt-act requirement; by choosing a text modeled on the Sherman Act, 15 U.S.C. § 1, it dispenses with such a requirement." Congress appears to have made the choice quite deliberately with respect to § 846; the same Congress that passed this provision also enacted the Organized Crime Control Act of 1970, § 802(a) of which contains an explicit requirement that "one or more of [the conspirators] does any act to effect the object of such a conspiracy," codified at 18 U.S.C. § 1511(a) . . .

Shabani reminds us that the law does not punish criminal thoughts and contends that conspiracy without an overt act requirement violates this principle because the offense is predominantly mental in composition. The prohibition against criminal conspiracy, however, does not punish mere thought; the criminal agreement itself is the actus reus and has been so viewed since *Regina v. Bass*, 11 Mod. 55, 88 Eng. Rep. 881, 882 (K.B. 1705) ("[T]he very assembling together was an overt act"); see also *Iannelli v. United States*, 420 U.S. 770, 777 (1975) ("Conspiracy is an inchoate offense, the essence of which is an agreement to commit an unlawful act") . . .

As the District Court correctly noted in this case, the plain language of the statute and settled interpretive principles reveal that proof of an overt act is not required to establish a violation of 21 U.S.C. § 846. Accordingly, the judgment of the Court of Appeals is reversed.

United States v. Abu Ghayth

Federal District Court for the Southern District of New York
17 F. Supp. 3d 289 (2014)

Lewis A. Kaplan, District Judge.

Defendant Sulaiman Abu Ghayth, a spokesman for Usama bin Laden and al Qaeda in the wake of the September 11, 2001 attacks on the World Trade Center and the Pentagon, was arrested abroad by U.S. authorities in 2013 and brought to this district. He ultimately was convicted by a jury of conspiring to kill United States nationals, conspiring to provide material support or resources, knowing or intending that they would be used in preparation for, or in carrying out, a conspiracy to kill United States nationals, and providing such material support or resources. . . .

Abu Ghayth appears to have become involved with al Qaeda in the summer of 2001—that is, after the 1998 Embassy bombings and the 2000 attack on the U.S.S. Cole, during the run up to the September 11, 2001 attacks, and the early stages of the shoe-bomb plot, but before September 11, 2001 and before the shoe-bomb plot was put in motion. In June 2001, he traveled to Afghanistan from his home in Kuwait, where he was a religious leader and teacher. Abu Ghayth admitted at trial that he met with bin Laden six or seven times during the summer of 2001, knowing all the while that bin Laden was believed to be responsible for the Embassy bombings and the attack on the U.S.S. Cole. Although Abu Ghayth denied having pledged bayat (an oath of allegiance) to bin Laden, he admittedly agreed to help him as a religious scholar and orator. He gave speeches to groups of men at al Qaeda training camps and spoke to a small group at an al Qaeda guesthouse about the concept of giving bayat, explaining that pledging bayat to bin Laden would be the equivalent of pledging bayat also to Mullah Omar, the leader of the Afghani Taliban.

In the course of that summer, Abu Ghayth returned briefly to Kuwait to retrieve his pregnant wife and seven children. He resettled his family in Kandahar, but it did not long remain in Afghanistan. Abu Ghayth claimed that his wife was pregnant and needed medical treatment and that he therefore took her and his children to Pakistan. Allegedly unsatisfied with the care available there, he then sent them back to Kuwait on approximately September 5, 2001. Knowing that "something big was going to happen" with al Qaeda and believing that he "had something to offer in the time to come," Abu Ghayth returned to Afghanistan on September 7, 2001, and did not accompany his family to Kuwait.

Four days later, al Qaeda suicide bombers flew hijacked airplanes into the World Trade Center and the Pentagon. Abu Ghayth claims to have learned about the attacks after they occurred from the media while staying at a Kuwaiti acquaintance's house in Kabul. Later that night, a messenger dispatched by bin Laden arrived at the house to retrieve Abu Ghayth. Bin Laden's driver drove Abu Ghayth for several hours from Kabul into the mountains of Afghanistan. When he arrived at bin Laden's hideout, bin Laden beckoned Abu Ghayth to speak with him and spared no time in claiming responsibility for the attacks. The two men talked late into the night. The next morning, Abu Ghayth woke to find bin Laden flanked by two of his senior deputies—Ayman al Zawahiri and Abu Hafs al Masri. Bin Laden invited Abu Ghayth to join them and then asked him to help deliver al Qaeda's message to the world. Abu Ghayth admitted that he agreed, allegedly after some equivocation. He, bin Laden, Zawahiri, and Abu Hafs then proceeded to make a video later published around the globe in which Abu Ghayth offered justifications and praise for the September 11 attacks.

Following the September 12, 2001 video, Abu Ghayth appeared as an al Qaeda spokesperson in videos dated October 2001, October 9, 2001, and October 13, 2001, and made several audio recordings in 2001 and 2002. Two of the videos contain language threatening the United States with a "storm of airplanes."

In the wake of the September 11 attacks, the U.S. military entered Afghanistan to combat al Qaeda and the Taliban. In the course of those operations, the military recovered several so-called brevity cards that were introduced into evidence. Some of those cards contain the name "Salman Abu Ghayth," which the government argued was a reference to Sulaiman Abu Ghayth. Of particular importance here, the brevity cards contain numbers for persons and places affiliated with al Qaeda, such as "Sheik Usama" and "Al-Faruq Camp," and unaffiliated persons and places, such as "Amir Al-Mu'minyn" and "Al-Tayyib Agha." Sergeant Major Karnes further testified to the fact that the brevity cards contain some words with no apparent relationship to violence or al Qaeda. . . .

Abu Ghayth first was indicted in the thirteenth superseding indictment in this case ("S13"), filed on March 1, 2013. S13 contained a single count, which charged Abu Ghayth with conspiring to kill United States nationals. It alleged as an overt act that Abu Ghayth gave a speech in which he threatened that "'the storms shall not stop, especially the Airplanes storm,' and advised Muslims, children, and opponents of the United States 'not to board any aircraft and not to live in high rises.'" Thus, the government explicitly alleged from the outset of the case that Abu Ghayth threatened storms of airplanes and that the threats were in furtherance of the alleged conspiracy to kill U.S. nationals. It could have sought to prove Abu Ghayth's complicity in the charged conspiracy in any number of ways, including by proving that the above quoted threats betrayed his knowledge of the shoe-bomb plot. . . .

[The court then rejected defendant's motion to obtain testimony from a member of the al Qaeda terrorist organization who was being detained at the U.S. Naval Facility at Guantanamo Bay, Cuba.]

NOTES & QUESTIONS ON OVERT ACTS

1. *The genesis of the overt act requirement.* As the Supreme Court makes clear in *Shabani*, conspiracy at common law did not require an overt act. However, when Congress crafted the federal general conspiracy statute, 18 U.S.C. § 371, it added an overt act requirement. Why did Congress move

beyond the common law definition and tighten the requirements for a conspiracy conviction? Furthermore, given this change from the common law scheme, why did the Supreme Court refuse to apply an overt act requirement for the conspiracy provision at issue in *Shabani*?

2. *Speech as overt acts.* Abu Ghayth's overt act was a videotaped speech saying "the storms shall not stop." Are there problems with using speech to fulfill the overt act requirement? Indeed, we should remember that the law treats speech as a *verbal act*, so giving a speech qualifies as an overt act in furtherance of a conspiracy. For an argument that modern conspiracy law infringes on First Amendment rights, see Martin H. Redish & Michael J.T. Downey, *Criminal Conspiracy as Free Expression*, 76 Alb. L. Rev. 697 (2012-2013); Steven R. Morrison, *Conspiracy Law's Threat to Free Speech*, 15 U. Pa. J. Const. L. 865 (2013). In some terrorism cases, prosecutors have focused on the giving of *bayat*, or the pledging of allegiance to al-Qaeda

---

PROBLEM CASE

In 2014, two students at South Pasadena High School were charged by police with plotting a massive attack against their fellow students. The Los Angeles District Attorney's Office charged the two students with conspiracy to commit murder and conspiracy to commit assault with a deadly weapon. According to police, the two students, who were 16 and 17 years old, used Skype to communicate with each other while they were planning the attack, which allegedly targeted three staff members at the school. Police alleged that the students also planned to kill as many fellow students as possible during the attack. A lawyer for one of the students strongly objected to the charges and said the police could not establish that the defendants committed an overt act because "[i]n this case they only have Internet research and phone calls." Adolfo Flores, *South Pasadena Teens in Alleged School Shooting Plot Face New Charges*, L.A. Times, Sept. 8, 2014.

Do you agree with the lawyer? Do the Skype sessions constitute an overt act in furtherance of the conspiracy? See, e.g., *United States v. Rommy*, 506 F.3d 108, 120 (2d Cir.

Arthur Miller, South Pasadena Chief of Police, holds a press conference on August 19, 2014, after two students were arrested on suspicion of plotting a mass shooting at South Pasadena High School

2007) ("It is beyond question that telephone calls can constitute overt acts in furtherance of a conspiracy."). But if the calls were between the conspirators, perhaps they are evidence of the underlying agreement, not an overt act. How about their online research on weapons or explosives—is that an overt act? In 2015, both students pled guilty in juvenile court to a single felony of making criminal threats and were sentenced to one year of home probation.

or Osama bin Laden specifically. What are the strategic reasons why prosecutors rely on *bayat* or speeches as the core evidence to anchor conspiracy prosecutions? Perhaps it has something to do with the public nature of such pronouncements, which defendants are unlikely to repudiate for religious reasons. For more on the use of the conspiracy doctrine in terrorism cases, see generally Wadie E. Said, *Crimes of Terror: The Legal and Political Implications of Federal Terrorism Prosecutions* (2015).

3. *Inchoate conspiracy versus complicity.* Inchoate conspiracy does not require a completed offense; it is sufficient that the defendant entered into the unlawful agreement and a co-conspirator performed the overt act (if required by statute) in furtherance of the conspiracy. That being said, a defendant can still be charged with inchoate conspiracy *even if* the completed offense comes to fruition. Why did the government charge Abu Ghayth with inchoate conspiracy to kill U.S. nationals instead of charging him with complicity in the 9/11 attacks that actually occurred? Did that decision make the case against Abu Ghayth easier to prosecute? Does the answer have something to do with causation?

4. Renunciation

If a conspirator changes his mind, can he undo his conspiracy even if he has already formed the unlawful agreement and performed the overt act? Courts are reluctant to grant the defense, but on the other hand they want to incentivize conspirators to reverse course. In the following case, ask yourself what it means for a conspirator to thwart a conspiracy in such a way that it manifests a complete and voluntary renunciation.

Commonwealth v. Nee

Supreme Judicial Court of Massachusetts
458 Mass. 174, 935 N.E.2d 1276 (2010)

MARSHALL, C.F.

On September 16, 2004, the defendant, Daniel Farley, and Joseph Sullivan, then all students at Marshfield High School (school), attended a meeting with five Marshfield police officers at the Marshfield police station. The meeting had been arranged at the defendant's request by Officer Helen Gray, a Marshfield police officer assigned to duty as the school's "resource officer." Over the course of a few hours the defendant and his companions informed the police officers that since the previous winter another student, Tobin Kerns, had developed an elaborate plot to "blow up the school." The defendant, in particular, described the plot in detail. None of the three friends indicated that they were involved in the plot, or implicated one another in the plot.

Marshfield police officers subsequently arrested Kerns and obtained a warrant to search his home, where they discovered, among other things, a list of supplies and weaponry in a notebook, and evidence of computer searches pertaining to weapons, pipe bombs, and other explosives.

The defendant did not testify at trial. Farley and Sullivan testified pursuant to grants of immunity. They testified that during the winter of 2003 and spring of 2004, they would "hang out" with Kerns and the defendant "[a]lmost every day." In the winter of 2003, the defendant told Farley of a plan to "shoot up" the school and asked whether Farley was interested in joining him. On a subsequent occasion when Kerns was also present, the defendant asked Kerns whether Kerns would be interested in joining the defendant in "shooting up the school." Kerns and the defendant together discussed the plan with Sullivan and asked him whether he would be interested in participating. The plan that Kerns and the defendant proposed involved a multifaceted assault on the school to take place the following school year on or near the anniversary of the murders at Columbine High School. Kerns and the defendant, along with Farley, Sullivan, and perhaps one other student, were to shoot and kill targeted students, teachers, and other staff at the school using an assortment of automatic and semiautomatic weapons. They would set trip wire explosives, line the hallway with napalm, and place bicycle locks on the main and rear doors to the school to prevent escape. The defendant told Farley that "he wanted to be exactly like Eric Harris," one of the perpetrators of the Columbine mass murder.

Together, Kerns and the defendant developed a list of ingredients for explosives and other necessary supplies, and a list of names of specific students and staff at the school whom they planned to kill. They took a map of the school from Officer Gray's office at the school and drew another map by hand; at least one map was labeled with entry points and other information relevant to the planned attack. In the spring of 2004, the defendant and Kerns together attempted to make napalm by mixing gasoline and Styrofoam. The defendant acquired copper tubing and other materials necessary to build a pipe bomb; he also tried to build an explosive device using gunpowder, duct tape, a plastic breath mint container, and a candle fuse, which he unsuccessfully attempted to ignite in the woods. The remnants of the device were later discovered by the police.

In April 2004, Kerns and the defendant asked another student, Timothy Courchene, to join the planned attack. During the conversation, the defendant showed Courchene a list of names, said that the plan was to "take out" certain people on the list, and discussed various details of the scheme, including the use of bicycle locks and pipe bombs. At the end of the conversation, at which Farley and Sullivan were also present, the defendant displayed a large knife and threatened to cut out the tongue of anyone who spoke to the police about the plot.

The defendant spoke about Columbine frequently. He dressed like the perpetrators of the Columbine attack, and stated that he believed what they had perpetrated was "cool" and that they were "heroes." He had a "fascination for weaponry," bragged about his ability to acquire firearms, and "several times" asked a fellow student to take firearms from the student's father for the defendant's use. He asked another student in the spring of 2004 whether her brother could "get him a gun." The defendant, Kerns, Farley, and Sullivan engaged in target practice using BB guns in the Ferry Hill Thicket, a wooded area in Marshfield. The defendant suggested that targets on the tree represented parts of the human body.

The defendant lived in Kerns' house for approximately one month in the late spring or early summer of 2004. He left when Kerns was hospitalized after attempting suicide. On one occasion, after visiting Kerns in the hospital, the defendant punched the roof of a car, said that the people at the hospital were "brainwashing" Kerns and that he should not be there, and suggested "breaking [Kerns] out."

In September 2004, shortly after the commencement of the school year, the defendant approached Officer Gray and told her that "Kerns was scaring him." He asked to return later that day with Farley, and at the later meeting both students told Officer Gray that they were frightened of Kerns and that "they really needed to talk about something that was going on." Officer Gray arranged a meeting for the defendant and Farley with herself and police officers at the Marshfield police station. Sullivan joined in the meeting. Because the circumstances of the meeting are significant in our consideration of this appeal, we summarize it in detail.

Prior to the meeting, the defendant told Farley and Sullivan that he would do the talking so as not to "incriminate" them. The defendant said that they were going to the meeting in order to tell the police "what [Kerns] was going to do and to keep our mouths shut."

The defendant began by telling the officers that Kerns had threatened him and his family. He stated that he was frightened, that Kerns had recounted to him in great detail certain tortures he knew about, and that Kerns had told the defendant that he spied on people when they were sleeping. The defendant also declared that Kerns had weapons and had threatened him in August with a knife in a dispute over Kerns' girlfriend. He stated that Kerns had an "obsession" with Satanism.

When the police officers asked whether the students had anything more to say, the defendant told his companions, "I'll do the talking," and proceeded to detail how Kerns "had a plot to blow up the school." Specifically, the defendant told the police officers that Kerns planned to use "napalm, pipes, propane gas bombs" and "Tech-9's, assault rifles" in the attack. He stated that Kerns said he would need the help of two others to carry out the attack, and that the three would enter the school at certain entrances, corral the students into specified areas, and separate the students and faculty to be killed from those who would remain unharmed. The defendant told the police that Kerns planned to cause diversionary explosions at gasoline stations at opposite ends of town in order to tie up emergency response operations. He claimed that Kerns planned to be on the school roof when emergency personnel arrived "so he could pick [them] off," and then to escape from a tunnel beneath the school. The defendant informed the police officers about the existence and contents of a notebook listing materials to be used in the attack, and told the police where in Kerns' home they could find the notebook. The defendant also told the police that he was present when Kerns attempted to detonate a homemade bomb in a wooded area.

Over the course of the several hours they spoke with the police officers, neither the defendant nor his friends indicated that they had planned to participate with Kerns in the attack. Rather, the defendant led the officers to believe, as Officer Gray testified, that Kerns "developed this whole thing himself and [the defendant] was just a follower," who was not in concert with Kerns. . . .

The defendant claims that the judge erred in refusing to recognize and apply the renunciation defense. Putting to one side the issue of the availability of that defense in Massachusetts, we conclude that there was no error because the evidence in this case would not entitle the defendant to the benefits of the renunciation defense under any reasonable interpretation of the defense as set out in Model Penal Code § 5.03(6).

First, the renunciation defense applies in circumstances where the defendant manifests a "complete and voluntary renunciation of *his* criminal purpose." To "renounce" is to "give up" or "abandon." Fundamentally, then, renunciation "posits prior participation." *State v. Hughes,* 215 N.J. Super. 295, 298 (1986) (renunciation defense not available to defendant who denied involvement in conspiracy in testimony at trial). For the defendant

to be entitled to the affirmative defense of renunciation, he must first have acknowledged that he conspired to commit a crime. This the defendant did not do.

At the meeting at the Marshfield police station the defendant did not inform the police of his own participation in the conspiracy to "shoot up" the school. Nor is there evidence that he informed Kerns, Farley, Sullivan, or anyone else that he was abandoning the conspiracy. Rather, when the defendant spoke to the police about the plan, he placed exclusive blame on Kerns. He cannot be found to have "renounced" an enterprise in which he denied participation. See MPC and Commentaries § 5.03(7)(c) at 384 (renunciation accomplished "only if and when [the defendant] advises those with whom he conspired of his abandonment or he informs the law enforcement authorities of the existence of the conspiracy *and of his participation therein.*"

Second, providing the protection of the renunciation defense in the circumstances of this case would have defeated the purpose of the defense. The drafters of the Model Penal Code explained that the renunciation defense seeks to avoid punishing individuals whose actions suggest that they do not merit such punishment, and to provide an incentive for individuals who have entered into a conspiracy to "desist from pressing forward with their criminal designs." *Id.* at § 5.03 comment 6, at 457-458. Neither of these aims would be furthered by granting the benefits of the renunciation defense to one who failed to reveal and renounce his own crime. . . .

NOTES & QUESTIONS ON RENUNCIATION

1. *Thwarting.* Why was Nee denied the benefit of the renunciation defense? The key to understanding the court's decision is the distinction between thwarting and complete renunciation. The law requires that the defendant thwart the conspiracy, but that is not all. More is required. The defendant must also thwart the conspiracy in such a way that it manifests his complete and voluntary renunciation. The court in *Nee* believed that the renunciation was not complete because the defendant refused to admit to the police his participation in the scheme. Do you agree that this is an essential element of a complete and voluntary renunciation? Or was the court using the guise of interpretation to covertly add a new requirement for the renunciation defense (one not codified in the Model Penal Code)?

2. *Conspiracy and incentives.* Why should legislatures allow a defendant to undo her liability for conspiracy? If defendants have no incentive to abandon their criminal endeavor, they probably will not. The crafting of a renunciation provision by state legislators represents a strategic calculation that at least some conspirators can be induced by the law to change their minds. Can the law have this effect in reality? As noted above, renunciation is not recognized as a defense to inchoate conspiracy in federal courts. The theory is that the toothpaste cannot be returned to the tube after the agreement is formed and the inchoate conspiracy is set in motion. But in that situation, will conspirators have reason to change their minds? One answer might be that inchoate conspiracy is a lesser offense with a lighter penalty than the completed crime (such as murder), so the conspirator still has an incentive to back out and reduce his exposure to criminal liability. Do you find this argument persuasive? Or should federal courts start recognizing renunciation as an applicable defense under the federal conspiracy statute?

C. PRACTICE & POLICY

Conspiracy is a distinctively American crime, one that is deeply embedded in U.S. legal culture and traditions. The following section addresses: (i) conspiracy's common law origins; (ii) its contested role in international law given its lack of support from non–English-speaking countries and its suitability in terrorism-related cases; and (iii) a brief explanation of the distinction between two doctrines of inchoate crime: conspiracy and attempt.

ᕗ Common law origins. Inchoate conspiracy is a common law doctrine with an ancient pedigree. The doctrine dates back at least as far as *Poulterers' Case*, 77 Eng. Rep. 813, 813-16 (K.B. 1611). Several members of the Poulterer family conspired to falsely accuse an in-law (Mr. Stone) of burglary in Essex County. The ruse quickly failed when Stone had an alibi; he was in London. The Star Chamber concluded that the Poulterers were still liable for conspiracy even though the crime failed and they never had the opportunity to give the false testimony at trial. Why should the law penalize conspirators for a crime that never occurs? Coke surmised that "the common law is a law of mercy, for it prevents the malignant from doing mischief, and the innocent from suffering it." See 5 Reports of Sir Edward Coke 99-101 (1826). Does this rationale still apply today? Does—and should—the law save conspirators from themselves? The crime of conspiracy has, from its very origins, been linked to the inherent dangers of collective criminality and the need to protect society from that danger.

Plenty of foreign jurisdictions, especially in the civil law, eschew inchoate conspiracy. These legal systems rely on attempt or solicitation provisions to punish inchoate crimes. Generally speaking, attempt requires that the criminal endeavor be much more developed before liability attaches. Consequently, lawyers from foreign jurisdictions often view the American obsession with conspiracy with considerable bemusement. However, the skepticism about conspiracy is not just from foreign sources. Plenty of American scholars and jurists have expressed unease with inchoate conspiracy too. See Phillip Johnson, *The Unnecessary Crime of Conspiracy*, 61 Calif. L. Rev. 1137 (1973). Nonetheless, both legislators and prosecutors continue to rely on it, so much so that Learned Hand referred to it as the "darling of the modern prosecutor's nursery." *Harrison v. United States*, 7 F.2d 259, 263 (2d Cir. 1925). What strategic benefit does conspiracy provide for prosecutors? Does it have something to do with the merger doctrine?

ᕗ Conspiracy and international law. Because conspiracy is not recognized in all judicial systems, it is generally not considered part of international law. The dispute over conspiracy goes back at least as far as the Nuremberg trials after the defeat of Germany in World War II. Before the end of the war, lawyers for the U.S. War Department decided that the conspiracy doctrine best described the full scope of the Nazi regime's criminality. When the indictments at the tribunal were prepared, Nazi leaders were charged with participating in perhaps the largest conspiracy in world history: a conspiracy dating back decades (since the end of World War I) to take control of Germany, wage a war of aggression across Europe, and commit countless atrocities in the process. The conspiracy involved thousands of co-conspirators at all levels of the military and civilian hierarchy. Ultimately, though, French jurists at the Nuremberg trial—which was an international tribunal—pushed back against the conspiracy theory, which was viewed as an overly American legal concept that was far too collective. In the end, conspiracy was rejected as a legal concept that could be applied at the tribunal, with the exception of crimes against peace (waging a war of aggression), which was viewed as already a collective crime anyway. The one other example where conspiracy is generally recognized in international law is conspiracy to commit genocide—an especially dangerous crime for which conspiracy's expansive liability is considered necessary.

The fate of conspiracy as an international crime is of more than just academic or historical interest. The conspiracy doctrine proved controversial when after 9/11 the U.S. government used a military commission to prosecute Osama bin Laden's bodyguard, Salim Hamdan, for conspiracy to commit war crimes. At the time, it was generally understood that the jurisdiction of the military commission was limited to offenses that were already violations of international law. Four members of the Supreme Court concluded that international law's rejection of inchoate conspiracy prevented the government from using the doctrine in a military commission. *Hamdan v. Rumsfeld*, 548 U.S. 557 (2006). Is inchoate conspiracy a necessary tool for prosecuting terrorists before they launch an attack? As we saw earlier in this chapter, the federal government often uses conspiracy statutes to prosecute would-be terrorists in federal district courts. Should the same principles be allowed in military commissions, even if conspiracy is not considered to be an international war crime? This also raises a deeper point, which is why some offenses are considered so dangerous that conspiracy is appropriate for them. Why is genocide considered especially dangerous such that it justifies the use of inchoate conspiracy? Using this logic, can the same thing be said about stopping terrorism? Compare Raha Wala, *From Guantanamo to Nuremberg and Back: An Analysis of Conspiracy to Commit War Crimes Under International Humanitarian*

Law, 41 Geo. J. Int'l L. 683, 709 (2010) ("the conspiracy to commit war crimes offense being used in U.S. military commissions is not supported by IHL"), with Benjamin J. Priester, *Who Is a "Terrorist"? Drawing the Line Between Criminal Defendants and Military Enemies,* 2008 Utah L. Rev. 1255, 1262 ("Inchoate offense liability, under conspiracy law in particular, provides a powerful tool for prosecuting, convicting, and punishing individuals whose objective is the commission of terrorist acts but whose plans are foiled before they can succeed.").

∿ Distinguishing inchoate conspiracy from attempt. What is the difference between prosecuting a defendant for inchoate conspiracy or attempt? Since the factual scenarios often overlap considerably, it can be difficult to keep the two doctrines separate. A conviction for attempt requires a more substantial actus reus requirement—the substantial step or whatever act is required by a competing standard (i.e., dangerous proximity to success, etc.). In contrast, inchoate conspiracy requires a much smaller actus reus requirement: A single overt act performed in furtherance of the conspiracy is enough to generate a conspiracy conviction, even if that act is not substantial enough to meet the more demanding standard for attempts. However, there is also an extra requirement for a conspiracy conviction: the element of duality or plurality of persons involved. By definition, a conspiracy requires multiple conspirators, either real or imagined depending on whether the jurisdiction recognizes unilateral conspiracies or not. But regardless of that dispute, conspiracy clearly penalizes collective conduct, while attempt liability works for solitary endeavors.

How should prosecutors decide which doctrine to use? First of all, prosecutors can charge *both* if the facts warrant it. Also, it is important to remember that the potential punishment might be different under the two doctrines, depending on the applicable statute. Although there are many different conspiracy offenses under state and federal law, the prosecutor's charging decision might be impacted by the different sentencing ranges allowable in that jurisdiction for attempt and conspiracy, which could substantially diverge.

CHAPTER 19

SOLICITATION

A. DOCTRINE

Like conspiracy, solicitation is both an inchoate offense and a mode of liability. A defendant who solicits another individual to commit a crime is guilty of the inchoate crime of solicitation; if the solicited individual then carries out the crime, the solicitor is guilty of that offense as well. For example, a defendant who hires a hit man is guilty of the inchoate crime of solicitation, even if the hit man never carries out the murder. However, if the hit man *does* perform the murder, both the defendant and the hit man are then guilty of murder as well. At that point, however, the solicitation charge usually disappears because it merges with the completed offense. For the inchoate crime of solicitation, the elements of the offense include:

1. specific intent or purpose,
2. to solicit (hire, command, request, encourage, or invite),
3. a third party to perform a crime.

Each element, by itself, is insufficient to generate a conviction for solicitation. The defendant must intend that the solicited individual carry out the crime; halfhearted suggestions, jokes, or insincere requests are not sufficient because in those cases the defendant does not truly desire that the other individual commit the crime. As for the solicitation, courts agree that the communication (whether a command, hire, request, encouragement, or invitation) must be sent; but courts are split on whether the communication must be received. Some courts have allowed solicitation in this context, while others consider it attempted solicitation. Punishment for inchoate solicitation varies across jurisdictions. In some jurisdictions inchoate solicitation is a lesser offense, but in other jurisdictions solicitation to commit murder is punishable as seriously as murder.

1. Distinguishing Solicitation from Conspiracy

The biggest difficulty in the doctrine is determining the dividing line between a solicitation and a conspiracy. As a factual matter, most cases of solicitation will qualify as a conspiracy, for the simple reason that hiring a hit man for money (or any other form of compensation) constitutes an agreement to commit an unlawful act and hence a conspiracy. As a legal matter, however, the requirements are different and it is possible for a defendant to be guilty of soliciting someone to commit a crime without going the further step of forming an agreement with them to commit the crime. First, conspiracy statutes often require an overt act performed in furtherance of the conspiracy, while most solicitation statutes do not. Second, and more fundamentally, the focus of the two crimes is slightly different. Solicitation focuses on the acts and mens rea of the defendant *alone*: Does he ask someone to commit the crime for him? The crime of solicitation does not depend on the *response* that the defendant receives from this request. So, for example, the defendant could demand or request that someone commit the crime and that individual could refuse; the defendant would still be guilty of solicitation. However, conspiracy focuses on the relationship between the parties; it requires that the second individual "agree" to the proposal, thus creating the agreement that forms the gravamen of the conspiracy offense.

2. Distinguishing Solicitation from Attempts

Since both attempts and solicitation require the defendant's specific intent or purpose to commit the underlying crime, the key difference between these inchoate offenses is their different act requirements. Some commentators have assumed that attempt liability requires a greater level of development than solicitation, but that formulation is inexact. As described above, solicitation requires no overt act, whereas attempt liability requires that the defendant perform whatever actions constitute a substantial step or place them in dangerous proximity to success or whatever type of action would meet that jurisdiction's standard for attempt liability. However, many cases of inchoate solicitation involve defendants who solicit a hit man to commit a murder, pay them money, and make arrangements for how they will commit the crime. The inchoate offense of solicitation is completed the minute the defendant solicits the hit man. Once the payment of money is arranged and the defendant has made further arrangements with the hit man to complete the crime, the issue of whether the defendant has passed the threshold of attempt liability becomes a question of fact for the jury to decide. Some jurisdictions would convict a defendant under these facts (see the *Decker* case below), but other jurisdictions would not.

3. Merger and Renunciation

There are two situations where a solicitor might escape liability for the crime of solicitation: merger and renunciation. With regard to the merger doctrine, most jurisdictions refuse to convict a defendant of both solicitation and the completed crime. The solicitation *merges* into the completed offense, just like an attempt. In this regard, solicitation is closer to attempts and conceptually distinct from inchoate conspiracy, to which the merger doctrine usually does not apply.

On the question of whether inchoate solicitation merges into inchoate conspiracy, jurisdictions are divided. In some jurisdictions, a defendant can be punished for both solicitation *and* conspiracy if they meet the elements for both. See, e.g., *People v. Hood*, 878 P.2d 89 (Colo. Ct. App. 1994) (upholding defendant's convictions for both solicitation and conspiracy); *Monoker v. State*, 321 Md. 214 (1990) (holding that since it is possible to form an agreement in the absence of a solicitation, merger is inappropriate). The argument for this legal result is that solicitation and conspiracy have different elements: solicitation is based on the *asking* while conspiracy is based on the *agreement*. Other jurisdictions disagree and require the merger of solicitation with conspiracy, on the theory that a conspiracy necessarily begins with a solicitation, making it a lesser-included offense. See, e.g., *State v. Dodson*, 118 Or. App. 154 (1993); *State v. Vallejos*, 129 N.M. 424 (2000).

As for the second avenue for escaping liability, jurisdictions are split on whether to recognize a renunciation defense for solicitation. Model Penal Code § 5.02(3) allows the defense if the defendant persuades or prevents the solicitee from carrying out the crime, and plenty of jurisdictions have adopted that rule. See, e.g., Ark. Ann. Stat. § 5-3-302. Like the defense of renunciation in conspiracy cases, the renunciation must be "complete and voluntary." But some jurisdictions refuse to recognize the defense on the grounds that the solicitation is complete—and cannot be undone—once the request is made. See, e.g., *State v. Lynch*, 330 Mont. 74, 125 P.3d 1148 (2005).

B. APPLICATION

1. Distinguishing Solicitation from Conspiracy

We have already learned that jurisdictions are split on the unilateral and bilateral approaches to inchoate conspiracies. But what about solicitation? Can a defendant be convicted of inchoate solicitation even though the solicited party is merely feigning participation in the scheme? In that case, nothing has truly been solicited, though the defendant thinks it has. As you read the following case, ask yourself whether solicitation should be treated differently from conspiracy.

People v. Breton
Appellate Court of Illinois, Second District
237 Ill. App. 3d 355, 603 N.E.2d 1290 (1992)

UNVERZAGT, J.

Defendant, Keith Breton, was convicted of solicitation of murder for hire and sentenced to a term of 30 years' imprisonment. . . .

The defendant sold cocaine to Gary Wehrmeister at least 20 times between 1980 and 1989. . . . Wehrmeister agreed on June 5, 1989, to cooperate with authorities against the defendant and testify against him at his trial. . . . On June 12, 1989, John Bivins, a fellow inmate of defendant, advised the State's Attorney's office through his attorney that the defendant was looking for a hit man to kill Wehrmeister. . . .

The Du Page County State's Attorney's office implemented a plan to allow defendant to contact an undercover investigator posing as a hit man. . . . With State's Attorney approval, Bivins also gave defendant the names "Dan" and "Bob" as persons defendant could call at the undercover number to arrange a hit. State's Attorney investigators Dan Callahan and Bob Holguin would answer the phone and pose as hit men. . . .

Defendant first called Callahan at the undercover phone number on June 15, 1989. During the conversation Callahan asked defendant what he wanted. Defendant responded "I gotta have a job done." Defendant stated the job involved "a guy" whom he identified as Gary Wehrmeister. When Callahan asked defendant what he wanted done to Wehrmeister defendant replied "I want him out. I only got about five days. He goes to trial. . . . He's gotta go." Defendant indicated that Wehrmeister had set him up for a drug charge, that he was not guilty, but that he did not want to take a chance of Wehrmeister testifying against him.

Also during the first call, defendant agreed to pay Callahan $5,000 for Wehrmeister's murder with $2,500 up front. Defendant stated he would need a day to make arrangements for the delivery of the up-front money. Defendant told Callahan he would call him the next day to further discuss the delivery of the up-front money.

Defendant called Callahan at the undercover phone number for the second time on June 16, 1989. Defendant told Callahan the up-front money was coming from out of town and Callahan could pick it up from Ken Drost, an attorney, at his downtown Chicago office. Defendant instructed Callahan to tell Drost he was an investigator there to pick up an envelope. Defendant also supplied Callahan with information to facilitate the murder of Wehrmeister. This occurred after Callahan told defendant "when your [*sic*] payin' me to kill somebody I need to know everything I can." In response, defendant told Callahan where Wehrmeister lived, discussed Wehrmeister's habits, and described Wehrmeister's living arrangements.

Defendant made his third call to Callahan at the undercover number on June 19, 1989. Defendant told Callahan the up-front money was available and gave Callahan Drost's phone number. Defendant stated Drost would have the money in an envelope. Defendant also instructed Callahan he should tell Drost he was an investigator working on something for Keith (the defendant) if Drost asked what the money was for.

At defendant's request, defendant's wife had sent $2,500 in the form of a money order to Drost. On June 20, 1989, Callahan went to Drost's office and met Drost. At that time Drost endorsed the money order and delivered it to Callahan for the defendant.

Defendant made his fourth call to Callahan on June 21, 1989. Callahan told defendant he received the money order from Drost and expressed concern that a paper trail had been established. Defendant replied that he had told Drost to cash the money order and give Callahan cash. Callahan told defendant Wehrmeister's murder was "set for tonight." Defendant told Callahan he could pick up the rest of the money from Drost the next day. . . .

At his trial, defendant contended he did not really intend to have Wehrmeister murdered. . . . Defendant also testified that after he discovered the hit man was a phony he went along with the scheme knowing no one would really be hurt. . . .

Defendant first contends that his conviction must be reversed because the State failed to prove the "agreement" element of its solicitation of murder for hire charge. . . . Solicitation of murder for hire is an offense created by statute in 1988. Section 8-1.2(a) of the statute provides: "A person commits solicitation of murder for hire when, with the intent that the offense of first degree murder be committed, he procures another to commit that offense pursuant to any contract, agreement, understanding, command or request for money or anything of value." . . . Defendant contends his conviction cannot stand because Callahan's feigned agreement does not satisfy the "agreement" element of the solicitation of murder for hire charge.

Defendant argues that the issue is analogous to a similar issue in conspiracy law in Illinois. He contends that, like the conspiracy statute, at least two parties must reach an actual agreement (both parties must really intend to do what they agree to do) to satisfy the agreement element of the solicitation of murder for hire statute. Defendant argues that since Callahan only feigned agreement, there was no solicitation of murder for hire pursuant to an agreement as charged here.

Defendant correctly argues that a conspiracy conviction requires the actual agreement of at least two parties to the conspiracy. A conspiracy conviction in Illinois requires an agreement based on the bilateral theory of conspiracy rather than the unilateral theory of conspiracy. An agreement based on the bilateral theory is one between a defendant and at least one other person where both parties actually intend to agree (a bilateral agreement). Under the bilateral theory of conspiracy, a purported agreement between a defendant and a government agent only feigning agreement will not support a conspiracy conviction because there is no actual agreement and actual agreement is a necessary element of conspiracy.

An agreement between a defendant and a governmental agent only feigning agreement is an agreement based on the unilateral theory. In such a unilateral agreement only one person actually intends to agree.

If conspiracy law requiring a bilateral agreement applies to solicitation of murder for hire pursuant to an agreement as defendant contends, then defendant is correct that the facts of this case could not support a conviction because in this case there was only a unilateral agreement. The question is whether conspiracy law and the bilateral theory of conspiracy should apply to the solicitation of murder for hire statute to require a bilateral agreement when the solicitation is pursuant to an agreement. . . .

There are fundamental differences between solicitation and conspiracy. Solicitation can be thought of as an attempted conspiracy. Solicitation generally requires a command, encouragement, or request of another to commit a crime (in solicitation of murder for hire it is the procurement of another). Conspiracy requires an agreement to commit a crime and an overt act in furtherance of the agreement. Neither solicitation nor conspiracy is a lesser included offense of the other. Solicitation and conspiracy each have a different *actus reus*. The *actus reus* of conspiracy is an agreement to commit a crime while the *actus reus* of solicitation involves an attempt to persuade another to commit a crime.

In its decision holding that the bilateral theory applies to conspiracy, the Illinois Supreme Court recognized that solicitation and conspiracy are different. In addressing the issue of whether the bilateral theory should apply to the conspiracy statute, the court noted the different natures of solicitation and conspiracy when it said "Illinois does have a solicitation statute which embraces virtually every situation in which one could be convicted of conspiracy under the unilateral theory." The court also commented that there was little need to adopt a unilateral theory of conspiracy because of the solicitation statute.

Because solicitation statutes embrace situations in which one could be convicted of conspiracy under the unilateral theory, solicitation statutes do not require bilateral agreements. Although the charge of solicitation of murder for hire pursuant to an agreement uses the same term, "agreement," as the conspiracy statute, there is no reason to construe the terms the same in both statutes. Because of the nature of solicitation, the solicitation statute is based on the unilateral theory, which only requires actual agreement by one of the parties.

If actual agreement by both parties was required and the procurement element was satisfied the elements of a conspiracy would be satisfied (a bilateral agreement plus an overt act in furtherance of the agreement). Requiring a bilateral agreement in the solicitation of murder for hire statute when the solicitation was pursuant to an agreement would effectively require a conspiracy. We do not believe the legislature intended to require proof of the elements of a conspiracy in order to prove a solicitation of murder for hire charge. . . . Procurement of another to commit murder pursuant to an agreement where a defendant agrees with a government agent feigning agreement is sufficient to support a conviction of solicitation of murder for hire. . . . The judgment . . . is affirmed.

NOTES & QUESTIONS ON SOLICITATION VERSUS CONSPIRACY

1. *Unilateral versus bilateral.* In *Breton*, the court concluded that the defendant solicited the crime, even though the hit man was really an undercover police officer. Do you think Breton engaged in solicitation or in attempted solicitation? In the end, does the difference really matter? One way of putting the question is whether Breton was guilty of an inchoate crime or a double-inchoate crime. What label best describes his behavior when he told Callahan: "He's gotta go"? Most jurisdictions subscribe to a unilateral theory of solicitation, even if they adopt a bilateral theory of conspiracy. Indeed, some courts have suggested that the two issues are linked; one reason to adopt a bilateral view of conspiracies is that unilateral situations should be described as solicitations, not conspiracies. Do you agree?

2. *Failed communications.* Does the communication have to be received? Jurisdictions are split. In *State v. Cotton*, 109 N.M. 769, 790 P.2d 1054 (1990),

the defendant was in jail awaiting trial on charges alleging that he sexually abused his 14-year-old stepdaughter. While in jail, Cotton composed a letter to his wife asking her to give the stepdaughter some money to leave the state so that she would be unable to testify at the upcoming trial. Cotton gave the letter to another inmate with instructions to obtain a stamp for the envelope. However, the inmate removed the letter, gave it to authorities, replaced it with a blank sheet of paper, and then gave the sealed and stamped envelope back to the defendant for him to mail later. The effect of the inmate's deception was that Cotton's wife never received the letter. Nonetheless, Cotton was still convicted of solicitation for requesting that his wife engage in witness intimidation. On appeal, the New Mexico court reversed, noting that the "offense of solicitation requires some form of actual communication from the defendant to either an intermediary or the person intended to be solicited, indicating the subject matter of the solicitation." Do you agree with the *Cotton* decision? The New Mexico statute requires that the defendant "solicits, commands, requests, induces, employs or otherwise attempts to promote or facilitate another person to engage in conduct constituting a felony within or without the state." N.M. Stat. Ann. § 30-28-3. How do you interpret the word "attempts" in the New Mexico statute?

3. *The Model Penal Code approach.* The Model Penal Code takes a different view and explicitly permits solicitation convictions in cases of failed communication. See MPC § 5.02(1) ("*Uncommunicated Solicitation.* It is immaterial . . . that the actor fails to communicate with the person he solicits to commit a crime if his conduct was designed to effect such communication."). According to the drafters, the MPC provision was designed to penalize cases of attempted solicitation. The argument for penalizing these attempts stems from the dangerousness of the conduct irrespective of the results: "The crucial manifestation of dangerousness lies in the endeavor to communicate the incriminating message to another person, it being wholly fortuitous whether the message was actually received. Liability should attach, therefore, even though the message is not received by the contemplated recipient, and should also attach even though further conduct might be required on the solicitor's part before the party solicited could proceed to the crime." Commentaries to § 5.02 at 381-82. Only a few states adopted this provision. See, e.g., Haw. Rev. Stat. § 705-510(2). Several jurisdictions explicitly recognize "attempted solicitation" as the proper charge in cases of failed communications. See *People v. Boyce*, 27 N.E.3d 77 (Ill. 2015); *People v. Saephanh*, 94 Cal. Rptr. 2d 910, 915-17 (2000); *State v. Andujar*, 899 A.2d 1209, 1219 (R.I. 2006).

PROBLEM CASE

In 2011, Kathy Rowe of San Diego was "devastated" when she lost out on the opportunity to buy a house that she considered her "dream house." Another couple that also wanted to buy the house outbid Rowe. Authorities alleged that Rowe hatched a plan to get her revenge on the successful couple. She placed several advertisements on sex-related websites, pretending to be from the other woman. The advertisements professed her desire for rough sex and several men responded to the postings. During one exchange with one of the men, she wrote: "I love to be surprised and have a man just show up at the door and force his way in the door and on me, totally taking me while I say no." That man never arrived, but she corresponded with another man who showed up at the house but could not get in because of a locked gate; he returned a second time but left because the husband was home. *Woman Posted Ads for Rape as Revenge for Losing Dream House: Prosecutors*, Associated Press, Apr. 9, 2014.

Prosecutors charged Rowe with soliciting forcible rape. Rowe's lawyers argued that the charges should be dropped because she allegedly used the man as an "innocent instrumentality" to perpetrate the crime. According to Rowe, she never "solicited" the men because the men never knew they would be committing a crime (because they had been duped). The California Court of Appeal rejected this argument and concluded that the unilateral nature of solicitation implied that the man's response—and even his knowledge of the illegality of his would-be conduct—was irrelevant: "We reach this conclusion because the crime of solicitation focuses on the intention and action of the solicitor, not the solicitee. The crime 'is complete once the verbal request is made with the requisite criminal intent; the harm is in asking, and it is punishable irrespective of the reaction of the person solicited.'" *People v. Rowe*, 170 Cal. Rptr. 3d 180 (2014).

Kathy Rowe

The Model Penal Code has a special rule just for these cases. Although soliciting an innocent agent does not count as solicitation, it *does* qualify for attempt liability under MPC § 5.01(2)(g), which lists "soliciting an innocent agent to engage in conduct constituting an element of the crime," as an example of conduct that satisfies the substantial step requirement.

2. Distinguishing Solicitation from Attempts

The prior problem case raises a larger issue: What is the dividing line between solicitation and attempt? Does a solicitation automatically constitute a punishable attempt, or does the solicitor need to do something extra before becoming liable for attempting the crime too? Read the following case and ask yourself if asking someone to commit a crime is the same thing as attempting it. Should it matter that the solicitor is not planning to personally commit the actus reus of the crime?

People v. Superior Court (Decker)
Supreme Court of California
58 Cal. Rptr. 3d 421, 157 P.3d 1017 (2007)

BAXTER, J.

Defendant and real party in interest Ronald Decker has been charged with the attempted willful, deliberate, and premeditated murder of his sister, Donna Decker, and her friend, Hermine Riley Bafiera. According to the evidence offered at the preliminary hearing, Decker did not want to kill these women himself—as he explained, "he would be the prime suspect" and "would probably make a mistake somehow or another"—so he sought the services of a hired assassin.

Decker located such a person (or thought he did). He furnished the hired assassin with a description of his sister, her home, her car, and her workplace, as well as specific information concerning her daily habits. He also advised the assassin to kill Hermine if necessary to avoid leaving a witness behind. Decker and the hired assassin agreed on the means to commit the murder, the method of payment, and the price. The parties also agreed that Decker would pay $5,000 in cash as a downpayment. Before Decker handed over the money, the assassin asked whether Decker was "sure" he wanted to go through with the murders. Decker replied, "I am absolutely, positively, 100 percent sure, that I want to go through with it. I've never been so sure of anything in my entire life." All of these conversations were recorded and videotaped because, unknown to Decker, he was talking with an undercover police detective posing as a hired assassin.

Decker does not dispute that the foregoing evidence was sufficient to hold him to answer to the charge of solicitation of the murder of Donna and Hermine but argues that this evidence was insufficient to support a charge of their attempted murder. . . .

BACKGROUND

. . . Decker and Holston [the undercover police officer] met . . . on September 7. This meeting was also videotaped and recorded. Decker gave

Holston $5,000 in cash, wrapped in two plastic bundles. He reiterated that Holston, after Donna had been murdered, should use a pay phone to leave him a voicemail message—Holston was to say that "the paint job has been completed"—and that Holston would get the rest of the money about a month later. Decker also reiterated that "if Hermine is in the car, with her, you cannot, I understand if I were in your business, I would never leave a witness. You have to take her out too. Whoever's with her you gotta take the other person out too. But don't charge me double."

Holston told Decker that he had already performed some intelligence work, that he was "convinced" he would see the victim the next day, and that he could get this "job" done quickly—eliciting another "marvelous" from Decker—and explained that "once I leave here, it's done. So, you sure you want to go through with it?" Decker replied, "I am absolutely, positively, 100 percent sure, that I want to go through with it. I've never been so sure of anything in my entire life. . . . [¶] [D]o it very fast . . . as fast as you can." At the end of the conversation, Decker seemed "very pleased" and thanked Holston and Wafer. A short time after Holston and Wafer drove off, Decker was arrested.

DISCUSSION

. . . Attempted murder requires the specific intent to kill and the commission of a direct but ineffectual act toward accomplishing the intended killing. The uncontradicted evidence that Decker harbored the specific intent to kill his sister (and, if necessary, her friend Hermine) was overwhelming. Decker expressed to both Wafer and Holston his desire to have Donna killed. He researched how to find a hired assassin. He spent months accumulating cash in small denominations to provide the hired assassin with a downpayment and had also worked out a method by which to pay the balance. He knew the layout of his sister's condominium and how one might enter it surreptitiously. He had tested the level of surveillance in the vicinity of her home and determined it was "not really that sharp." He chronicled his sister's daily routine at both her home and her office. He offered Holston recommendations on how his sister should be killed and what materials would be necessary. And, at both meetings with Holston, he insisted that Hermine, if she were present, be killed as well, so as to prevent her from being a witness.

The controversy in this case, as the parties readily concede, is whether there was also a direct but ineffectual act toward accomplishing the intended killings. For an attempt, the overt act must go beyond mere preparation and show that the killer is putting his or her plan into action; it need not be the last proximate or ultimate step toward commission of the crime or crimes, nor need it satisfy any element of the crime. However, as we have explained, "[b]etween preparation for the attempt and the attempt itself, there is a wide difference. The preparation consists in devising or arranging the means or measures necessary for the commission of the offense; the attempt is the direct movement toward the commission after the preparations are made." . . .

As simple as it is to state the terminology for the law of attempt, it is not always clear in practice how to apply it. . . . Indeed, we have ourselves observed that "none of the various 'tests' used by the courts can possibly distinguish all preparations from all attempts."

Although a definitive test has proved elusive, we have long recognized that "[w]henever the design of a person to commit crime is clearly shown, slight acts in furtherance of the design will constitute an attempt." Viewing the entirety of Decker's conduct in light of his clearly expressed intent, we find sufficient evidence under the slight-acts rule to hold him to answer to the charges of attempted murder.

Decker's plan was to get rid of his sister so that he could recover money that she owed him. He was concerned, however, that he would be considered an obvious suspect in her murder, so he sought out someone else to carry out his plan. To that end, he conducted research into the underworld of professional killers, he budgeted to pay for those services, he evaluated how and where the murder should be done, he tested the level of security around his sister's condominium, and he considered the possibility that there might be a witness and what should be done in that event. Once he met Detective Holston, who he believed was a professional assassin, they agreed Holston would kill Donna and (if necessary) her friend Hermine, they agreed on a price, and they agreed it would be done within the week. Decker provided Holston with all of the necessary information concerning his sister, her home and office, and her habits and demeanor. He also gave Holston the agreed-on downpayment of $5,000 cash. Before he did, Holston warned him, "I want you to know, once I leave here, it's done. So, you sure you want to go through with it?" Decker replied, "I am absolutely, positively, 100 percent sure, that I want to go through with it. I've never been so sure of anything in my entire life."

Accordingly, at the time Decker handed Holston the downpayment on the murder, Decker's intention was clear. It was equally clear that he was "actually putting his plan into action." Decker had secured an agreement with Holston to murder Donna (and, if necessary, her friend Hermine); had provided Holston with all the information necessary to commit the crimes; had given Holston the $5,000 downpayment; and had understood that "it's done" once Holston left with the money. These facts would lead a reasonable person to "believe a crime is about to be consummated absent an intervening force"—and thus that "the attempt is underway." Indeed, as Justice Epstein noted for the Court of Appeal, "[t]here was nothing more for Decker to do to bring about the murder of his sister." Although Decker did not himself point a gun at his sister, he did aim at her an armed professional who had agreed to commit the murder.

As contrary authority, Decker relies on *Adami,* 36 Cal. App. 3d 452, 111 Cal. Rptr. 544 (1973), which affirmed the dismissal of an attempted murder charge on similar facts, and relies also on the small number of out-of-state majority and minority opinions that have followed *Adami.* In *Adami,* the defendant sought to have his wife killed because she had stolen money from him. He agreed on a price with an undercover police agent posing as an assassin and supplied the agent with a photograph of the victim, a description of the victim and her residence and vehicles, and other pertinent information. The defendant gave the police agent $500 as a down-payment and announced he was not going to change his mind. *Adami* declared that these acts "consisted solely of solicitation or mere preparation" and concluded, in accordance with the "weight of authority," that "solicitation alone is not an attempt."

We perceive several flaws in *Adami's* analysis.

First, the opinion makes no mention of the slight-acts rule, which has long been the rule for attempted crimes in California. Indeed, *Adami's* progeny make no pretense of reconciling their analysis with the slight-acts rule and instead explicitly reject it. These cases thus conflict with well-established California law and with the law concerning attempted crimes in most jurisdictions.

Decker argues that the slight-acts rule should not be applied to the crime of attempted murder, but his argument lacks legal or logical support. . . . The cases on which Decker relies thus conflict not only with California law, but also with the "fairly general agreement . . . that slight acts are enough when the intent to murder is clearly shown." Indeed, where (as here) the crime involves concerted action—and hence a greater likelihood that the criminal objective will be accomplished—there is a *greater* urgency for intervention by the state at an *earlier* stage in the course of that conduct. . . .

Second . . . Decker similarly expends considerable effort to convince us that "solicitation of another to commit a crime is an attempt to commit that crime if, but only if, it takes the form of urging the other to join with the solicitor in perpetrating that offense, not at some future time or distant place, but here and now, and the crime is such that it cannot be committed by one without the cooperation and submission of another," quoting Perkins, *Criminal Law* 519 (1957). But a solicitation requires only that a person invite another to commit or join in an enumerated crime (including murder) with the intent that the crime be committed. The solicitation is complete once the request is made and is punishable "irrespective of the reaction of the person solicited." In this case, the solicitation was complete early in Decker's first conversation with Holston, when he asked Holston to kill Donna. But the People do not contend that this request was sufficient to prosecute Decker for attempted murder. They argue instead that the solicitation, in combination with Decker's subsequent conduct, revealed his plan to have Holston murder Donna (and, if necessary, her friend Hermine) and that Decker put this plan into operation no later than the point at which he completed the agreement with Holston, finalized the details surrounding the murders, and paid Holston $5,000 in earnest money.

The issue, then, is not whether "solicitation alone" is sufficient to establish an attempt but whether a solicitation to commit murder, combined with a completed agreement to hire a professional killer and the making of a downpayment under that agreement, can establish probable cause to believe Decker attempted to murder these victims. A substantial number of our sister states have held that it can. Additional jurisdictions have held that a solicitation to murder, in combination with a completed agreement to hire a professional killer and further conduct implementing the agreement, can similarly constitute an attempted murder. . . .

Third, *Adami* mistakenly assumes that there can be no overlap between the evidence that would tend to prove solicitation to murder and that which would tend to prove attempted murder. Indeed, Decker asserts that these are "mutually exclusive crimes." But it could not be plainer, as Chief Justice Holmes put it, that while "preparation is not an attempt," nonetheless "*some* preparations may amount to an attempt." *Commonwealth v. Peaslee*, 177 Mass. 267 (1901). . . . There is thus no error in resting a finding of attempted murder in part on evidence that *also* tends to establish solicitation to commit murder and vice versa. . . .

In finding the record sufficient to hold Decker to answer to the charges of attempted murder here, we do not decide whether an agreement to kill followed by a downpayment is *always* sufficient to support a charge of attempted murder. Whether acts done in contemplation of the commission of a crime are merely preparatory or whether they are instead sufficiently close to the consummation of the crime is a question of degree and depends upon the facts and circumstances of a particular case. . . .

Dissenting Opinion by WERDEGAR, J.

My colleagues hold that defendant's conduct in soliciting the murder of his sister, reaching an agreement with a hired assassin to do the killing, and making a downpayment under the agreement establishes probable cause to believe defendant himself attempted the murder. I respectfully dissent. "An attempt to commit a crime consists of two elements: a specific intent to commit the crime, and a direct but ineffectual act done toward its commission." Defendant's conduct in this case does not include "a direct but ineffectual act" done toward the murder's commission. Accordingly, he cannot be guilty of attempted murder.

As we have long recognized, the required act for an attempt under California law must be "directed towards immediate consummation" of the crime attempted. As the majority details, defendant's conduct included numerous *indirect* acts toward accomplishing the murder of his sister: He sought the services of a hired assassin; he located a person (actually an undercover police detective) he thought would act as such; he furnished the supposed assassin with a description of his sister, her home, her car and her workplace, as well as specific information concerning her daily habits; he discussed how the murder would be done and how and when he would pay for the work, agreeing to furnish $5,000 in cash as a down-payment; and, finally, just before he was arrested, he stated he was "absolutely, positively, 100 percent sure, that I want to go through with it" and urged the supposed assassin to do it "as fast as you can."

I agree with the majority that as evidence defendant harbored the specific intent to kill his sister, these facts are overwhelming. None of them, however, constitutes a *direct* but ineffectual act done toward the murder's commission. As the majority states, defendant "did not himself point a gun at his sister"; neither did he otherwise directly menace her. Instead, he relied on the person he thought had agreed to commit the murder to do the actual deed. The direct object of defendant's preparatory acts was the person he sought to engage as his agent—not the ultimate, intended victim of the scheme.

We previously have stated that for attempt, it must be "clear from a suspect's acts what *he* intends to do. . . ." In this case, what defendant intended to do was have his sister killed *by someone else*. Defendant's own conduct did not include even "slight" acts toward actual commission of the murder. That he hired another, supplied him with information, and paid him a downpayment only highlights his intention not to perform the act himself.

The California cases the majority purports to rely on generally involve single actors, i.e., defendants who acted directly on their victims. These cases simply confirm that for attempt a defendant must have committed a direct act toward commission of the crime. Defendant here committed no direct act toward commission of the murder, since his scheme interposed a third party between himself and his intended victim, and the third party never acted. . . .

NOTES & QUESTIONS ON SOLICITATION VERSUS ATTEMPTS

1. *California's slight-acts rule.* In California, is there any difference left between solicitation and attempt? Or has the court effectively unified the two concepts? The court in *Decker* claimed that the defendant did *more*

than just solicit the crime—he also made a downpayment. Is the payment morally and legally significant enough to raise a solicitation to an attempt? Furthermore, the holding in *Decker* seems linked to the California's "slight-acts" rule for attempt liability, which allows liability if the design of a person to commit the crime is clearly shown and the actor commits even "slight acts" in furtherance of that design. Should the result come out differently in a jurisdiction that rejects the slight-acts test and uses a different standard for attempt liability? Here is the assessment from one expert on attempt liability: "But, of course, the question of whether an act is 'slight' or less than slight (whatever that might mean) is no easier to answer than the question of whether Decker tried to kill his sister. The justices' problem was that while they were convinced that Decker tried to kill his sister, they were powerless to explain why that was true, and so they used a bit of entirely uninformative legal terminology to hide their confusion." See Gideon Yaffe, *Criminal Attempts*, 124 Yale L.J. 92, 96-97 (2014).

2. *Direct versus indirect.*   The dissent objects to the majority's decision because Decker never attempted anything—he paid someone *else* to attempt something. The dissent's argument assumes that attempt liability requires personal action as opposed to indirect action. Is this assumption correct? Imagine a defendant who hires an agent to commit a crime on her behalf. If the agent finishes the crime, the defendant is clearly responsible for the finished crime (as an accomplice, conspirator, or solicitor), even though the defendant did not personally commit the actus reus of the crime. Why should the result be any different with regard to attempts?

3. *Verbal solicitation as attempt.*   Other jurisdictions have considered the issue and held that verbal solicitations may constitute attempts under limited circumstances. In *Ward v. State*, 528 N.E.2d 52 (Ind. 1988), the Indiana Supreme Court held that verbal solicitation may constitute the substantial step required for attempt liability when: "1) the solicitation takes the form of urging; 2) the solicitation urges the commission of the crime at some immediate time and not in the future; and 3) the cooperation or submission of the person being solicited is an essential feature of the substantive crime." In *Ashford v. Commonwealth*, 47 Va. App. 676, 626 S.E.2d 464 (Va. Ct. App. 2006), an attempt charge was upheld for a defendant who "requested two different people to kill his wife[,] . . . formulated diagrams of his wife's house and workplace, detailed when she would be at home and when the children would be away, and completed the payment of two thousand dollars to the hit man for the murder." But see *Johnson v. Sheriff*, 91 Nev. 161, 163 (1975) (rejecting attempt charge for defendant who solicited murder). In *Johnson*, the court concluded that "although intent to commit the crime was shown, the discussions testified to by the feigned 'hit man' were but preparation; they did not constitute the second element, performance of an overt act toward the commission of the crime."

Review the casebook video, *People v. Daniella Forcheimes* (Part 2: Solicitation & Attempted Murder). As you listen to the discussion between the attorneys and the judge, ask yourself whether the defendant committed attempted murder. Apply the classic standards for attempt liability and ask yourself whether the solicitation of a hitman, with no other action, meets those standards. Does your answer depend on which legal standard for attempt liability is applied?

C. PRACTICE & POLICY

In this last section, we consider two questions. The first involves the use of undercover police officers or informers in solicitation cases and how defense lawyers might argue such cases. The second involves the public policy rationale for penalizing inchoate solicitation.

    ↄ **Undercover agents and defense arguments.**   The crime of inchoate solicitation is a key tool in the prosecutorial toolbox. Police departments routinely capture recorded conversations between defendants seeking to hire someone to commit a crime. If you were a lawyer for a defendant caught in such a sting, what type of arguments would you make to a jury to convince them to acquit your client for solicitation? Remember the mental elements of the offense, which includes the defendant's specific intent (or purpose) that the solicitee carry out the intended crime. If the request is recorded, one solution is for the defense counsel to argue to the jury that the conversation is fundamentally ambiguous or that the defendant was merely joking or not serious. In that case, although the defendant committed the actus reus, it would be unaccompanied by the necessary specific intent. Would this strategy move a jury to acquit?

    ↄ **The inherent dangerousness of solicitations.**   The public policy rationale for penalizing solicitations so heavily is that they are especially dangerous. Why would that be? One argument might be that solicitations involve a process of automation. Once the defendant solicits a professional agent to commit the crime, the agent is then motivated to complete the crime because of some fiscal incentive (payment)—not the original motive that inspired the solicitor. Why should this matter? When a machine is set in motion, the gears turn in automatic fashion and there is little opportunity for second-guessing or changing course—what the law refers to as renunciation. This is in marked contrast to crimes performed solely by a single individual.

Many of the cases described in this chapter could be described as "double inchoate" offenses because they involve multiple layers of inchoateness. For example, cases of inchoate solicitation with undercover police officers involve one level of inchoateness because the solicited murder is never committed. In these cases, the solicitation takes place with a police officer who is feigning his participation in the endeavor. Consequently, the defendant is attempting to solicit a hit man, but never really succeeds in accomplishing even that, since the hit man is no hit man at all. Is this the right way of looking at these cases? Given that the solicitation is complete, under the unilateral view, the moment the request is received, it would seem that the solicitation is complete regardless of the police officer's attitude about the request. See Ira P. Robbins, *Double Inchoate Crimes,* 26 Harv. J. on Legis. 1, 113-14 (1989). However, cases of failed communications might legitimately be viewed as "double inchoate" crimes under even the unilateral view, because the communication is never received by *anyone.* The question here is whether the doubly inchoate nature of these crimes is dangerous enough to meet the public policy rationale for punishing inchoate solicitation. Under a utilitarian framework, at some point do inchoate crimes become so inchoate that the law should expend its policing resources elsewhere? Conversely, does a retributive framework suggest that even highly inchoate crimes are deserving of punishment because the perpetrator has the inner culpability associated with his specific intent?

PART IV

MODES OF LIABILITY

CHAPTER 20

—◦◦◦—

ACCOMPLICES

A. DOCTRINE

At common law, perpetrators were divided into two large categories: principals and accessories. These were then sub-divided into smaller categories based on somewhat archaic distinctions. First-degree principals physically performed the actus reus of the crime; second-degree principals were present at the scene of the crime and "aiding, and abetting the fact to be done." However, "presence" at the scene could be either literal or constructive—the latter in the case of lookouts who were distant from the scene of the crime but nonetheless "constructively present" due to their importance in the scheme. Accessories *before-the-fact* were distant from the scene of the crime but still somehow "concerned" in its commission prior to the act. In contrast, accessories *after-the-fact* provided assistance after the crime's commission, such as help disposing of the body or evading capture and detection. See W. Blackstone, *Commentaries on the Laws of England*, Book II, § 34 (Philadelphia: J.B. Lippincott Co., 1893). Over time, these old common law distinctions were distilled and simplified into a modern framework, which now distinguishes between principals and *accomplices*. The term "accomplice"—and its adjective form "complicit"—basically covers everything that Blackstone would have referred to as second-degree principal *and below*, i.e. everyone but the physical perpetrator of the crime.

Today, when an accomplice assists in the commission of an offense, the accomplice becomes derivatively responsible for that crime, even though someone else (the principal perpetrator) committed it. As such, accomplice liability is a mode of liability, not an inchoate offense such as attempt. By statute and long-standing common law tradition, accomplices can be punished just as harshly as the principal perpetrators they assist. See 18 U.S.C. § 2 ("Whoever commits an offense against the United States or aids, abets, counsels, commands, induces or procures its commission, is punishable as a principal."). Accomplice liability is often referred to as a form of "complicity" because the defendant is complicit in the criminality by virtue of his *association* with the criminal endeavor. What makes it appropriate to hold someone responsible for a crime based on his or her complicity in it? The law requires (i) assistance or support to the principal perpetrator (ii) performed with the purpose or knowledge (depending on the jurisdiction) to facilitate the crime.

1. Assistance or Support

The act requirement for accomplice liability is very broad: It includes not only the familiar category of aiding and abetting (also known under the more contemporary label of "assisting"), but also more obscure types of support such as counseling, encouraging, advising, commanding, ordering, inducing, or soliciting. Although the type of support is quite broad, it is not completely open-ended. Usually, an accomplice is criminally responsible because he performs an affirmative act to support the principal, though even words of encouragement might constitute the relevant act of support. However, being a mere bystander (e.g., witnessing the crime and saying nothing) will not usually constitute encouragement because courts evaluate these situations as omissions. In rare circumstances, an omission will satisfy the act requirement, but only if the defendant had a preexisting duty to act—a topic that was first broached in Chapter 5. Finally, it should be noted that the assistance requirement does not necessarily require a strong causal connection between the accomplice's assistance and the crime committed by the principal perpetrator. In other words, if the jury finds that the principal would have found a way to complete the crime even in the absence of the accomplice's assistance, the accomplice could still be convicted. See Joshua Dressler, *Reassessing the Theoretical Underpinnings of Accomplice Liability: New Solutions to an Old Problem*, 37 Hastings L.J. 91, 102 (1985).

2. Purpose Versus Knowledge

An accomplice must intend to aid or assist the principal's perpetration of the crime. As discussed in prior chapters, the language of intent is fundamentally ambiguous: It can mean either knowledge or purpose depending on the circumstance. The same ambiguity plagues the law of complicity. Does the law require that the defendant simply know that his actions will assist the principal's perpetration of the crime, or must he engage in the action with the purpose of facilitating the principal's endeavor? The federal courts apply the purpose standard, which predictably is also referred to as "specific intent" in some cases. (In the rest of this chapter, the term purpose will be used to avoid confusion.) In describing the purpose standard, Learned Hand famously defined an accomplice as someone who "in some sort associate[s] himself with the venture, that he participate in it as in something that he wishes to bring about, that he seek by his action to make it succeed." *United States v. Peoni*, 100 F.2d 401 (2d Cir. 1938).

In contrast to the federal courts, the state courts are split: Some follow the purpose standard but others use the much lower knowledge requirement for complicity. The Model Penal Code supports the purpose standard: "A person is an accomplice of another person in the commission of an offense if: (a) with the *purpose* of promoting or facilitating the commission of the offense. . . ." See MPC § 2.06(3) (emphasis added). While some states explicitly adopted the MPC formulation, others copied the provision but used the word "knowledge" instead. For example, consider the following provision in Washington State:

> A person is an accomplice of another person in the commission of a crime if:
>> (a) With knowledge that it will promote or facilitate the commission of the crime, he or she:
>>> (i) Solicits, commands, encourages, or requests such other person to commit it; or (ii) Aids or agrees to aid such other person in planning or committing it; or
>> (b) His or her conduct is expressly declared by law to establish his or her complicity.

See R.C.W. 9A.08.020.

3. Natural and Probable Consequences Doctrine

Jurisdictions are also split on another key element of accomplice liability. What if the accomplice provides assistance to the principal perpetrator with an eye toward the commission of one crime, but the principal accomplishes a *different* crime? Is the accomplice liable for the greater crime? The classic example is the getaway driver who assists the bank robber by driving him to the bank. The robber intentionally kills a bank employee in the course of the robbery, while the driver waits outside. The driver is clearly complicit in (and therefore guilty of) armed robbery, but is the driver a *murderer* as well? Some jurisdictions say yes, if the resulting crime was a "natural and probable consequence" of the target offense that the accomplice was assisting. In such cases, the accomplice has put his lot in with the principal and so bears the burden that the criminal transaction might turn out differently than originally anticipated. The natural and probable consequences rule is a creature of both case law and statute. See, e.g., Wis. Stat. Ann. § 939.05(2)(c). However, many jurisdictions, including the federal courts and the Model Penal Code, reject the doctrine as an overly expansive form of guilt by association.

4. Innocent Instrumentality Rule

The general rule is that the perpetrator who performs the actus reus of the crime (such as firing the gun in a murder case) is the principal, while the criminal who remains "behind the scenes" is a mere accomplice. There is one exception to this general rule. Imagine a perpetrator uses a child or an insane individual to carry out the crime. In these and other situations involving an "innocent instrumentality," the behind-the-scenes person is classified as a principal perpetrator—not an accomplice. The idea behind the doctrine is that the innocent individual is a mere instrument—analogous to a gun or other murder weapon—deployed by the true perpetrator behind the scenes. However, the instrumentality must remain non-culpable for the doctrine to apply. The idea here is that a culpable individual is a free agent and therefore not a true "instrument" like a gun, knife, or poison. Consequently, if the instrument is a free agent responsible for committing the crime, the behind-the-scenes perpetrator must be classified as an accomplice. Examples of innocent instruments include not only children and the mentally ill, but also sane adults who are deliberately duped into performing an action that they do not realize is criminal in nature. The innocent instrumentality rule is codified by statute in some jurisdictions. See, e.g., Del. Code Ann. 11 § 271(1) ("A person is guilty of an offense committed by another person when: (1) Acting with the state of mind that is sufficient for commission of the offense, he causes an innocent or irresponsible person to engage in conduct constituting the offense. . . .").

5. Defenses

Some accomplices have tried to argue that they cannot be convicted because the principal was acquitted. To evaluate this defense, it is crucial to remember that complicity is a doctrine of *derivative* liability. The accomplice "inherits" the guilt that attaches to the principal perpetrator. However, it is entirely possible that the principal might not be found by the police or, if found, might not even be charged. More surprising are cases where the principal is acquitted but the accomplice is convicted. Although this seems strange at first glance, the result is completely acceptable because there is no requirement that separate jury verdicts in separate trials must be consistent. One jury might conclude that the crime happened and convict the accomplice while another jury next door might conclude that the crime never happened and acquit the perpetrator. Could this happen *within* the same trial? It depends. If the jury concludes that the crime never occurred then logically it must acquit both. However, a jury could reasonably convict the accomplice but acquit the principal on the theory that he was arrested on a case of mistaken identity. In that case, the jury would be concluding that the accomplice assisted *someone*, just not the "principal" who was arrested by the police.

A more straightforward defense is withdrawal or renunciation of the crime. Most jurisdictions accept the defense but the requirements vary. Typically, the accomplice must either deprive his complicity of its effectiveness, contact the police, or prevent the crime. MPC § 2.06(6).

B. APPLICATION

1. Assisting the Principal Perpetrator

How much does the defendant have to do in order to count as an accomplice? Although each jurisdiction has a slightly different laundry list of acts that satisfy the requirement, many statutory codes include "encouragement" as one mode of accomplice liability. Is presence or association with the principal enough to infer encouragement or some other type of assistance? As you read the following case, ask yourself whether the defendant performed enough action to meet the requirements for complicity.

State v. V.T.

Court of Appeals of Utah
5 P.3d 1234 (2000)

ORME, J.

On June 12, 1998, V.T. and two friends, "Moose" and Joey, went to a relative's apartment to avoid being picked up by police for curfew violations. The boys ended up spending the entire night at the apartment.

The next morning, the relative briefly left to run an errand, while the boys remained in her apartment. She returned about fifteen minutes later to find the boys gone, the door to her apartment wide open, and two of her guns missing. She immediately went in search of the group and found them hanging out together near her apartment complex. She confronted the boys about the theft of her guns and demanded that they return them to her. When they failed to do so, she reported the theft to the police.

Two days after the theft of her guns, she discovered that her camcorder, which had been in the apartment when the boys visited, was also missing, and she immediately reported its theft to the police. The police found the camcorder at a local pawn shop, where it had been pawned on the same day the guns were stolen.

Still inside the camcorder was a videotape featuring footage of V.T., Moose, and Joey. The tape included a segment where Moose telephoned a friend, in V.T.'s presence, and discussed pawning the stolen camcorder. V.T. never spoke or gestured during any of this footage.

V.T. was eventually picked up by the police, while riding in a car with Moose. V.T. was charged with two counts of theft of a firearm; one count of theft, relating to the camcorder; and, for having initially given the police a phony name, one count of giving false information to a peace officer. . . .

. . . V.T. was tried under an accomplice theory on the three theft charges. The court found that V.T. had committed class A misdemeanor theft of the camcorder and had provided false information to a peace officer. The juvenile court summarized the basis for its adjudication concerning the camcorder theft as follows:

> I am going to find him guilty and I think the additional information that I have here that brings me peace of mind is that he was present a second time, he was shown on the camcorder when the camcorder was being handled at a time when he could've distanced himself from the activity. Not only do I have him there once with the group . . . on the second incident . . . there is no gap on him being there when [the camcorder] is being handled and talked about and used in the confines of a room with a group of friends and those who were involved in this illegal activity.

V.T. appeals his adjudication concerning the theft of the camcorder. . . .

Utah's accomplice liability statute, Utah Code Ann. § 76-2-202 (1999), provides:

> Every person, acting with the mental state required for the commission of an offense who directly commits the offense, who solicits, requests, commands, encourages, or intentionally aids another person to engage in conduct which constitutes an offense shall be criminally liable as a party for such conduct.

As with any other crime, the State must prove the elements of accomplice liability beyond a reasonable doubt.

The State argues that V.T.'s continued presence during the theft and subsequent phone conversation about selling the camcorder, coupled with his friendship with the other two boys, is enough evidence to support the inference that he had "encouraged" the other two in committing the theft and that he is therefore an accomplice to the crime. *Black's Law Dictionary* defines encourage as: "[t]o instigate; to incite to action; to embolden; to help." The plain meaning of the word confirms that to encourage others to take criminal action requires some form of active behavior, or at least verbalization, by a defendant. Passive behavior, such as mere presence—even continuous presence—absent evidence that the defendant affirmatively did something to instigate, incite, embolden, or help others in committing a crime is not enough to qualify as "encouragement" as that term is commonly used.

The case law in Utah is consistent with this definition: "Mere presence, or even prior knowledge, does not make one an accomplice" to a crime absent evidence showing—beyond a reasonable doubt—that defendant "advise[d], instigate[d], encourage[d], or assist[ed] in perpetuation of the crime." *State v. Labrum,* 959 P.2d 120, 123 (Utah Ct. App. 1998).

In *Labrum,* the defendant was convicted of attempted criminal homicide due to his participation in a drive-by shooting. The juvenile court gave defendant an enhanced sentence, based on its finding that defendant had acted in concert with two or more persons in committing the shooting and was therefore subject to the "group crime enhancement." . . . For purposes of that statute, "in concert" means that the other individuals who participated with defendant would be criminally liable for the offense as accomplices under Section 76-2-202.

On appeal, we held that there was insufficient evidence to find that Behunin, one of the passengers in the car who defendant was alleged to have acted "in concert" with, would be guilty if tried under an accomplice liability theory for the shooting. The juvenile court's findings supporting the group crime enhancement showed only that Behunin had been present before, during, and after the shooting and later was in defendant's presence when he boasted to a third party about the shooting. Although Behunin apparently endorsed the boasting, we held these findings were insufficient to show that he solicited, requested, commanded, encouraged, or intentionally aided Labrum in committing the shooting.

Two other Utah cases further illuminate the level of participation necessary to establish criminal liability as an accomplice. In *State v. Smith,* 706 P.2d 1052 (Utah 1985), our Supreme Court concluded there was sufficient evidence to convict Smith of aggravated robbery and theft based on a theory of accomplice liability. But in that case, there was testimony that Smith had recruited one of his co-defendants to aid in the robbery, that he selected the house to rob, and that he provided and drove the getaway car to and from the crime scene. This testimony was sufficient to show that Smith had solicited and intentionally aided his co-defendants in committing the robbery.

In *State v. Webb,* 790 P.2d 65 (Utah Ct. App. 1990), we upheld Webb's conviction for aggravated robbery of a jewelry store under an accomplice theory. Although the evidence was conflicting, there was testimony that Webb had solicited a co-defendant to steal the getaway car and give it to him, that Webb said he knew someone who would sell the stolen goods for them, and that he had sorted through the stolen jewelry with his partners-in-crime at a friend's house. This evidence was sufficient to find that Webb had "solicited, requested, commanded, encouraged, or intentionally aided" in the robbery.

These three cases make it clear that something more than a defendant's passive presence during the planning and commission of a crime is required to constitute "encouragement" so as to impose accomplice liability in Utah. There must be evidence showing that the defendant engaged in some active behavior, or at least speech or other expression, that served to assist or encourage the primary perpetrators in committing the crime.

The juvenile court's conclusion that V.T. was an accomplice to the camcorder theft was not supported by the evidence in this case. No evidence whatsoever was produced indicating V.T. had encouraged—much less that he solicited, requested, commanded or intentionally aided—the other two boys in the theft of the camcorder.

Instead, the evidence, read in the light most favorable to the juvenile court's decision, shows only that V.T. was present with the other two youths, albeit at multiple times: when the camcorder was stolen; when they were confronted about the theft of the guns; and when the plan to pawn the camcorder was being discussed by Moose. In sharp contrast to *Smith* and *Webb,* however, there is no indication in the record that V.T. had instigated, incited to action, emboldened, helped, or advised the other two boys in planning or committing the theft. The circumstantial evidence presented in this case, which only shows V.T.'s continuous presence during the events surrounding the theft, is sufficient for finding only that V.T. was a witness—not an accomplice—to the theft of the camcorder. And knowledge of a theft, without more, does not make one an accomplice.

The juvenile court's conclusion of accomplice liability was heavily influenced by the videotape footage of V.T., who at the time of the filming was necessarily in the presence of the camcorder, after it had been stolen. In fact, the court found that even though there was not enough evidence presented to find that V.T. was an accomplice in the theft of the guns, which were stolen at the same time and from the same apartment as the camcorder, the videotape footage was enough to find that V.T. was an accomplice to the camcorder theft. The juvenile court's heavy reliance on this footage shows that it made its conclusion of accomplice liability based not on any evidence that V.T. had encouraged the others to steal the camcorder . . . but instead on the sole fact that V.T. allowed himself to remain in the company of Joey, Moose, and the stolen camcorder before, during, and immediately after the theft. As explained above, this "guilt by association" theory is not a basis on which accomplice liability can be premised under Utah law. . . .

NOTES & QUESTIONS ON THE ACT REQUIREMENT

1. *Encouragement.* It can be difficult to distinguish between passive presence and encouragement. Certainly, if a defendant urges the principal to commit the crime, that encouragement makes the defendant complicit in the crime. But what if the defendant says nothing? Can silence indicate a type of

encouragement? In most cases courts would treat silence as an omission and apply the regular rules on omissions discussed in Chapter 5 on the act requirement. American and most commonwealth jurisdictions are hesitant to penalize omissions and usually only do so when the law imposes an affirmative duty to act, either based on statute or some other special relationship with the victim. Recall *State v. Davis*, 182 W. Va. 482, 388 S.E.2d 508 (1989), reprinted in Chapter 5. In *Davis*, the defendant followed his son into the bedroom, knowing that his son was about to rape the victim. The defendant then laid down next to the victim while his son raped her. The court upheld the father's conviction for accomplice liability because his presence encouraged the principal perpetrator, his son. Although the encouragement was based on an omission, the court established the father's duty because the victim was in his house and "the victim looked upon the defendant as a family member because of her long association with him. . . ." For similar cases, see *State v. Goodwin*, 118 N.H. 862, 395 A.2d 1234 (1978), and *Commonwealth v. Henderson*, 249 Pa. Super. 472, 378 A.2d 393 (1977).

2. *Accessories after the fact.* At common law, it was possible for an accomplice to be convicted for assisting a principal perpetrator *after* the commission of the crime by, for example, giving him money to get out of town or a room to hide in. This was called being an "accessory after the fact." These cases were conceptually problematic because the assistance did not causally contribute—by definition—to the principal's commission of the offense. Indeed, how *could it* given that the assistance occurred after the offense? One solution to this problem was to define the criminal offense quite broadly so as to include evasion from police detection. Although flight or evasion from police is not usually listed as a formal element of the offense, one could view it as an implicit element of any felonious transaction.

In any event, the modern solution is to drop accessory after the fact as a form of accomplice liability. However, accessory after the fact lives on as a separate and distinct offense in most jurisdictions but carries a much smaller penalty than true accomplice liability. See, e.g., Mass. Gen. Laws ch. 274, § 4 ("Whoever, after the commission of a felony, harbors, conceals, maintains or assists the principal felon or accessory before the fact, or gives such offender any other aid, knowing that he has committed a felony or has been accessory thereto before the fact, with intent that he shall avoid or escape detention, arrest, trial or punishment, shall be an accessory after the fact, and, except as otherwise provided, be punished by imprisonment in the state prison for not more than seven years or in jail for not more than two and one half years or by a fine of not more than one thousand dollars.").

3. *Ineffectual assistance.* What if the defendant attempts and *fails* to provide assistance? Consider the famous case of Judge Tally. Tally was indicted for being complicit in the murder of R.C. Ross by the Skelton brothers. Judge Tally

was related to the Skelton brothers, who were angry that Ross had been "criminally intimate" with one of their sisters. Ross skipped town and the Skelton brothers eventually pursued him on horseback and with weapons. Someone sent a telegram to Ross warning him that the Skelton brothers were close behind and out to get him. However, Judge Tally intervened to prevent Ross from receiving the message. Specifically, Tally sent his own telegram to the telegraph operator, directing him not to deliver the first telegram to Ross or otherwise warn Ross about the Skelton brothers. Subsequently, the Skelton brothers committed the murder. The problem is that the Skeltons probably would have killed Ross anyway and it was unclear that Tally's intervention made any difference to the outcome. However, the Alabama Supreme Court upheld the conviction because "Ross' predicament was rendered infinitely more desperate, his escape more difficult, and his death of much more easy and certain accomplishment by the withholding from him of the message. . . ." *State v. Tally*, 102 Ala. 25, 15 So. 722 (1894). Many jurisdictions follow the rule from *Tally* and do not require a causal connection. *State v. Gelb*, 515 A.2d 1246 (N.J. 1986). As Christopher Kutz explains in *Causeless Complicity*, 1 Crim. L. & Phil. 289, 290 (2007): "Causation may be present . . . and causal relations feature in the justification of accomplice liability overall, but causation is not necessary to complicity." The Model Penal Code also rejects causation because it includes "attempts to aid" as one version of complicity. MPC § 2.06(3)(a)(ii). Indeed, the MPC goes beyond *Tally* because it allows liability even when we know for certain that an actor's attempt to aid the principal was causally ineffective. Furthermore, under the MPC provision, if the principal only commits an attempt rather than a completed crime, the accomplice can be guilty of attempt too, assuming that the mens rea and actus reus standards for accomplice liability are otherwise satisfied.

4. *Complicity for mere presence.* Can mere presence be sufficient to establish complicity in a crime when presence implies the accomplice's encouragement of the crime? Consider the famous case of *Wilcox v. Jeffery*, 1 All England L. Rep. 464 (K.B. 1951). In that case, the defendant Wilcox was held responsible as an accomplice for attending a jazz concert in London. The principal crime was the musician's violation of immigration and employment regulations (because the musician was from the United States and presumably did not have authorization to work in England). The court upheld Wilcox's liability as an accomplice, which certainly sounds like liability for mere presence at a criminal transaction. However, the court made much of the fact that Wilcox had *paid* for the privilege to hear the concert, thus suggesting a form of encouragement. Did that make the *whole* audience guilty as accomplices? Perhaps, but the court also noted that Wilcox was the owner of a jazz magazine and was attending the concert to write an article about it, thus suggesting a financial interest in the criminal endeavor.

5. *Present and ready to assist.* It is well-established law that presence at the scene of the crime is sufficient to establish accomplice liability if the accomplice has previously agreed to provide assistance but at the moment of the criminal act that assistance turns out to be unnecessary. *State v. Collins,* 76 Wash. App. 496, 501-02, 886 P.2d 243 (1995) ("Aid can be accomplished by being present and ready to assist."). What is the justification for this well-entrenched rule? Perhaps the existence of the pre-arrangement suggests that the defendant's mere presence is not equivocal or ambiguous. Rather, the defendant's presence is firmly corroborative of his criminal intent. Furthermore, why should the putative accomplice escape criminal liability just because the principal turned out to be more successful in his criminal endeavor than anticipated, thus rendering the accomplice's promise of assistance unnecessary? Critics of this doctrine object that the accomplice's lack of assistance negates the required actus reus for the crime—since the assistance is never provided, the complicity liability should evaporate too. However, the doctrine is predicated on the idea that the principal receives comfort in knowing that the assistance will be provided if it is necessary, thus encouraging the principal to go through with the crime. In that sense, promises of assistance that are ultimately unnecessary constitute a form of encouragement that causally contribute to the ultimate crime.

2. Purpose Versus Knowledge

Jurisdictions are split on the required mens rea for complicity. Some require that the defendant purposefully assist the principal, while others simply require that the defendant know that his actions will facilitate the principal's commission of the crime. Federal courts have traditionally applied the purpose standard for accomplice liability. The canonical formation of this standard requires that the actor "in some sort associate himself with the venture, that he participate in it as in something that he wishes to bring about, that he seek by his action to make it succeed." *United States v. Peoni,* 100 F.2d 401, 402 (2d Cir. 1938). However, in 2014, the Supreme Court complicated the picture somewhat by articulating a knowledge standard for complicity in the federal crime of using or carrying a firearm during drug trafficking. As you read the following case, ask yourself whether this knowledge standard is consistent with, or a departure from, the traditional standard articulated in *Peoni.*

Rosemond v. United States
Supreme Court of the United States
134 S. Ct. 1240 (2014)

JUSTICE KAGAN delivered the opinion of the Court.

A federal criminal statute, § 924(c) of Title 18, prohibits "us[ing] or carr[ying]" a firearm "during and in relation to any crime of violence or drug trafficking crime." In this case, we consider what the Government must show when it accuses a defendant of aiding or abetting that offense. We hold that the Government makes its case by proving that the defendant actively participated in the underlying drug trafficking or violent crime with advance knowledge that a confederate would use or carry a gun during the crime's commission. We also conclude that the jury instructions given below were erroneous because they failed to require that the defendant knew in advance that one of his cohorts would be armed.

I

This case arises from a drug deal gone bad. Vashti Perez arranged to sell a pound of marijuana to Ricardo Gonzales and Coby Painter. She drove to a local park to make the exchange, accompanied by two confederates, Ronald Joseph and petitioner Justus Rosemond. One of those men apparently took the front passenger seat and the other sat in the back, but witnesses dispute who was where. At the designated meeting place, Gonzales climbed into the car's backseat while Painter waited outside. The backseat passenger allowed Gonzales to inspect the marijuana. But rather than handing over money, Gonzales punched that man in the face and fled with the drugs. As Gonzales and Painter ran away, one of the male passengers—but again, which one is contested—exited the car and fired several shots from a semiautomatic handgun. The shooter then re-entered the vehicle, and all three would-be drug dealers gave chase after the buyers-turned-robbers. But before the three could catch their quarry, a police officer, responding to a dispatcher's alert, pulled their car over. This federal prosecution of Rosemond followed.

The Government charged Rosemond with, inter alia, violating § 924(c) by using a gun in connection with a drug trafficking crime, or aiding and abetting that offense under § 2 of Title 18. Section 924(c) provides that "any person who, during and in relation to any crime of violence or drug trafficking crime[,] . . . uses or carries a firearm," shall receive a five-year mandatory-minimum sentence, with seven- and ten-year minimums applicable, respectively, if the firearm is also brandished or discharged. 18 U.S.C. § 924(c)(1)(A). Section 2, for its part, is the federal aiding and abetting statute: It provides that "[w]hoever commits an offense against the United States or aids, abets, counsels, commands, induces or procures its commission is punishable as a principal."

Consistent with the indictment, the Government prosecuted the § 924(c) charge on two alternative theories. The Government's primary contention was that Rosemond himself used the firearm during the aborted drug transaction. But recognizing that the identity of the shooter was disputed, the Government also offered a back-up argument: Even if it was Joseph who fired the gun as the drug deal fell apart, Rosemond aided and abetted the § 924(c) violation . . .

II

The federal aiding and abetting statute, 18 U.S.C. § 2, states that a person who furthers—more specifically, who "aids, abets, counsels, commands, induces or procures"—the commission of a federal offense "is punishable as a principal." That provision derives from (though simplifies) common-law standards for accomplice liability. And in so doing, § 2 reflects a centuries-old view of culpability: that a person may be responsible for a crime he has not personally carried out if he helps another to complete its commission.

We have previously held that under § 2 "those who provide knowing aid to persons committing federal crimes, with the intent to facilitate the crime, are themselves committing a crime." Both parties here embrace that formulation, and agree as well that it has two components. As at common law, a person is liable under § 2 for aiding and abetting a crime if (and only if) he (1) takes an affirmative act in furtherance of that offense, (2) with the intent of facilitating the offense's commission.

The questions that the parties dispute, and we here address, concern how those two requirements—affirmative act and intent—apply in a prosecution for aiding and abetting a § 924(c) offense. Those questions arise from the compound nature of that provision. Recall that § 924(c) forbids "us[ing] or carr [ying] a firearm" when engaged in a "crime of violence or drug trafficking crime." The prosecutor must show the use or carriage of a gun; so too he must prove the commission of a predicate (violent or drug trafficking) offense. For purposes of ascertaining aiding and abetting liability, we therefore must consider: When does a person act to further this double-barreled crime? And when does he intend to facilitate its commission? . . .

Begin with (or return to) some basics about aiding and abetting law's intent requirement, which no party here disputes. As previously explained, a person aids and abets a crime when (in addition to taking the requisite act) he intends to facilitate that offense's commission. An intent to advance some different or lesser offense is not, or at least not usually, sufficient: Instead, the intent must go to the specific and entire crime charged—so here, to the full scope (predicate crime plus gun use) of § 924(c). And the canonical formulation of that needed state of mind—later appropriated by this Court and oft-quoted in both parties' briefs—is Judge Learned Hand's: To aid and abet a crime, a defendant must not just "in some sort associate himself with the venture," but also "participate in it as in something that he wishes to bring about" and "seek by his action to make it succeed." *Nye & Nissen v. United States,* 336 U.S. 613, 619 (1949), quoting *Peoni,* 100 F.2d, at 402.

We have previously found that intent requirement satisfied when a person actively participates in a criminal venture with full knowledge of the circumstances constituting the charged offense. In *Pereira . . .* we found the requisite intent for aiding and abetting because the defendant took part in a fraud "know[ing]" that his confederate would take care of the mailing. Likewise, in *Bozza v. United States,* 330 U.S. 160, 165 (1947), we upheld a conviction for aiding and abetting the evasion of liquor taxes because the defendant helped operate a clandestine distillery "know[ing]" the business was set up "to violate Government revenue laws." And several Courts of Appeals have similarly held—addressing a fact pattern much like this one—that the unarmed driver of a getaway car had the requisite intent to aid and abet armed bank robbery if he "knew" that his confederates would use weapons in carrying out the crime. So for purposes of aiding and abetting law, a person who actively participates in a criminal scheme knowing its extent and character intends that scheme's commission.

The same principle holds here: An active participant in a drug transaction has the intent needed to aid and abet a § 924(c) violation when he knows that one of his confederates will carry a gun. In such a case, the accomplice has decided to join in the criminal venture, and share in its benefits, with full awareness of its scope—that the plan calls not just for a drug sale, but for an armed one. In so doing, he has chosen (like the abettors in *Pereira* and *Bozza* or the driver in an armed robbery) to align himself with the illegal scheme in its entirety—including its use of a firearm. And he has determined (again like those other abettors) to do what he can to "make [that scheme] succeed." *Nye & Nissen,* 336 U.S., at 619. He thus becomes responsible, in the typical way of aiders and abettors, for the conduct of others. He may not have brought the gun to the drug deal himself, but because he took part in that deal knowing a confederate would do so, he intended the commission of a § 924(c) offense—i.e., an armed drug sale.

For all that to be true, though, the § 924(c) defendant's knowledge of a firearm must be advance knowledge—or otherwise said, knowledge that enables him to make the relevant legal (and indeed, moral) choice. When an accomplice knows beforehand of a confederate's design to carry a gun, he can attempt to alter that plan or, if unsuccessful, withdraw from the enterprise; it is deciding instead to go ahead with his role in the venture that shows his intent to aid an *armed* offense. But when an accomplice knows nothing of a gun until it appears at the scene, he may already have completed his acts of assistance; or even if not, he may at that late point have no realistic opportunity to quit the crime. And when that is so, the defendant has not shown the requisite intent to assist a crime involving a gun. As even the Government concedes, an unarmed accomplice cannot aid and abet a § 924(c) violation unless he has "foreknowledge that his confederate will commit the offense with a firearm." For the reasons just given, we think that means knowledge at a time the accomplice can do something with it—most notably, opt to walk away.*

Both parties here find something to dislike in our view of this issue. Rosemond argues that a participant in a drug deal intends to assist a § 924(c) violation only if he affirmatively desires one of his confederates to use a gun. The jury, Rosemond concedes, could infer that state of mind from the defendant's advance knowledge that the plan included a firearm. But according to Rosemond, the instructions must also permit the jury to draw the opposite conclusion—that although the defendant participated in a drug deal knowing a gun would be involved, he did not specifically want its carriage or use. That higher standard, Rosemond claims, is necessary to avoid subjecting persons of different culpability to the same punishment. Rosemond offers as an example an unarmed driver assisting in the heist of a store: If that person spent the drive "trying to persuade [his confederate] to leave [the] gun behind," then he should be convicted of abetting shoplifting, but not armed robbery.

We think not. What matters for purposes of gauging intent, and so what jury instructions should convey, is that the defendant has chosen, with full knowledge, to participate in the illegal scheme—not that, if all had been left to him, he would have planned the identical crime. Consider a variant of Rosemond's example: The driver of a getaway car wants to help rob a convenience store (and argues passionately for that plan), but eventually accedes when his confederates decide instead to hold up a national bank. Whatever his original misgivings, he has the requisite intent to aid and abet *bank* robbery; after all, he put aside those doubts and knowingly took part in that more dangerous crime. The same is true of an accomplice who knowingly joins in an armed drug transaction—regardless whether he was formerly indifferent or even resistant to using firearms. The law does not, nor should it, care whether he participates with a happy heart or a sense of foreboding. Either way, he has the same culpability, because either way he has knowingly elected to aid in the commission of a peculiarly risky form of offense.

---

* Of course, if a defendant continues to participate in a crime after a gun was displayed or used by a confederate, the jury can permissibly infer from his failure to object or withdraw that he had such knowledge. In any criminal case, after all, the factfinder can draw inferences about a defendant's intent based on all the facts and circumstances of a crime's commission.

A final, metaphorical way of making the point: By virtue of § 924(c), using a firearm at a drug deal ups the ante. A would-be accomplice might decide to play at those perilous stakes. Or he might grasp that the better course is to fold his hand. What he should not expect is the capacity to hedge his bets, joining in a dangerous criminal scheme but evading its penalties by leaving use of the gun to someone else. Aiding and abetting law prevents that outcome, so long as the player knew the heightened stakes when he decided to stay in the game . . .

NOTES & QUESTIONS ON PURPOSE VERSUS KNOWLEDGE

1. *Inferring purpose from knowledge.* How is the knowledge standard in *Rosemond* consistent with *Peoni's* older purpose standard? One possibility is that juries are entitled to *infer* purpose from knowledge. In other words, in some circumstances, the fact that an actor *knew* their behavior would facilitate the principal perpetrator's commission of the crime is sufficient for the fact finder to infer that the accomplice acted with *purpose* as well. Indeed, the Supreme Court in *Rosemond* specifically referred to such inferences in a footnote. However, in that circumstance, it would be appropriate to explain to the jury that the required mental element is purpose but that the jury is permitted, but not required, to infer that the defendant acted with purpose if the prosecution proves beyond a reasonable doubt that the defendant acted with knowledge. But the Supreme Court in *Rosemond* appeared to be going much further than that; the Court suggested that the correct standard is knowledge, full stop. Indeed, the Court then qualified the standard and suggested that the defendant must have advance knowledge of the gun and decide to participate in the criminal venture anyway. This does not sound consistent with a purpose standard for accomplice liability. Is *Peoni* still good law? For more discussion of how to interpret the *Rosemond* holding, see Stephen P. Garvey, *Reading Rosemond*, 12 Ohio St. J. Crim. L. 233 (2014), and Kit Kinports, *Rosemond, Mens Rea, and the Elements of Complicity*, 52 San Diego L. Rev. 133, 153-56 (2015).

2. *Criminal facilitation.* Federal courts apply the purpose standard for accomplice liability, though the individual circuits use different and sometimes conflicting definitions for what counts as purpose. State courts are split. Some, like Washington above, allow knowledge to qualify for accomplice liability, while other state courts follow the federal courts and require purpose. Which is the better approach? Some jurisdictions split the difference by requiring purpose for accomplice liability but then craft a separate offense based on knowledge. This crime, which is a separate offense, is often called criminal facilitation. See, e.g., N.Y. Penal Law § 115 ("A person is guilty of criminal

facilitation in the fourth degree when, believing it probable that he is rendering aid: 1. to a person who intends to commit a crime, he engages in conduct which provides such person with means or opportunity for the commission thereof and which in fact aids such person to commit a felony. . . ."). Since it is a separate offense, the accomplice is not derivatively responsible for the principal's crime but is independently responsible for her knowing facilitation of criminal conduct, and therefore receives a lower penalty. California has a similar scheme but refers to these knowing facilitators as "accessories."

3. *Different standards for different offenses.* There is another way to split the difference in the purpose/knowledge debate for accomplice liability. One might use different mens rea standards depending on the severity of the crime. See *United States v. Fountain*, 768 F.2d 790, 798 (7th Cir. 1985) ("there is support for relaxing this requirement [the purpose requirement] when the crime is particularly grave"). Under this approach, a jurisdiction could adopt purpose as the standard for complicity in most felonies, but allow knowledge as the appropriate standard for murder cases. This is not typically done, but if it were, would it be a good idea? Some scholars have even suggested that the mens rea for accomplice liability for some crimes should be even *lower* than knowledge (e.g., recklessness), though so far no jurisdiction in the United States has accepted this invitation. Under this view, a defendant would be responsible for the principal's crime if he consciously disregards a substantial and unjustified risk that his actions might assist the principal's commission of the offense. See Sanford Kadish, *Reckless Complicity*, 87 J. Crim. L. & Criminology 369 (1997).

4. *Community of purpose requirement.* Jurisdictions with a purpose or intent requirement for complicity sometimes refer to the "community of purpose" between accomplices and principals in their criminal endeavor. But can a true community of purpose exist when the criminals are working at cross-purposes with each other? In *People v. Russell*, 91 N.Y.2d 280, 693 N.E.2d 193 (1998), three defendants engaged in a gun battle in the Red Hook section of Brooklyn. Two of the defendants were part of the same gang, while the third defendant was a member of a rival gang. An innocent bystander was struck in the crossfire and died, although police could not identify which defendant fired the fatal shot. Prosecutors charged all three with being accomplices to second-degree murder under a theory of depraved indifference to human life. Defendants objected that they could not possibly have had a "community of purpose" with each other because they were having a gun battle and firing at each other. The Court of Appeals disagreed and concluded that the defendants shared the tacit intent to engage in the gun battle, even if each desired a different outcome to it. See also *State v. Garza*, 259 Kan. 826, 916 P.2d 9 (1996) (defendant working at cross-purposes to principal could still be accomplice if results

were reasonably foreseeable). Courts have sometimes applied the same theory in drag racing races. See, e.g., *People v. Abbott*, 445 N.Y.S.2d 344 (1981).

5. *The mens rea for results.*   What is the mental element requirement for an accomplice who assists a principal perpetrator who commits a crime of recklessness or negligence? Again, answering this question requires separating the different levels of intent. Generally speaking, the defendant must perform his action with either the purpose or the knowledge that his action supports the principal (depending on the jurisdiction). However, if the principal commits a result-crime based on recklessness, the accomplice need not intend that result. It is enough that the accomplice also is reckless or negligent as to the result. For example, the Model Penal Code simply concludes that "[w]hen causing a particular result is an element of an offense, an accomplice in the conduct causing such result is an accomplice in the commission of that offense, if he acts with the kind of culpability, if any, with respect to that result that is sufficient for the commission of the offense." MPC § 2.06(4). For example, imagine that the operator of an amusement park ride recklessly operates the ride, resulting in a client's death. If the operator has an assistant who purposely aids the risky conduct, the assistant need not have any heightened mens rea as to the result element to be guilty as an accomplice. It is enough that the assistant's mental state with regard to the result, like the principal's, is one of recklessness. Similarly, in *People v. Turner*, 336 N.W.2d 217 (Mich. 1983), the defendant gave loaded guns to two women he was living with for a "trial by battle." One of the

PROBLEM CASE

The facts in *People v. Riley*, 60 P.3d 204 (Alaska 2002), are even more startling. Riley and Portalla opened fire on a group of revelers gathered around a bonfire, hitting and seriously injuring two of them. No one died. The prosecutors could not prove which man fired the shots that hit the victims, and so Riley was eventually convicted of being an accomplice to first-degree assault, a crime that requires "recklessly placing another person in fear of imminent serious physical injury by means of a dangerous instrument." Could Riley be an accomplice to a crime of recklessness?

The court upheld the conviction: "Thus, Riley could properly be convicted . . . either upon proof that he personally shot a firearm into the crowd or (alternatively) upon proof that, acting with intent to promote or facilitate Portalla's act of shooting into the crowd, Riley solicited, encouraged, or assisted Portalla to do so. These are alternative ways of proving that Riley was accountable for the conduct that inflicted the injuries. The government was also obliged to prove that Riley acted with the culpable mental state specified by the first-degree assault statute. But regardless of whether Riley acted as a principal or an accomplice, the applicable culpable mental state remained the same: recklessness as to the possibility that this conduct would cause serious physical injury." Do you agree with the court's conclusion?

women raised the gun and it fired accidentally. Defendant was convicted of complicity in involuntary manslaughter because there was a "common and shared purpose to participate in the act" and the defendant was reckless as to the result.

Review the casebook video, *People v. Daniella Forcheimes* (Part 4: Purpose or Knowledge). The testimony of the witness, Ms. Honoré, portrays an ambiguous situation. She lent money to Forcheimes with at least some suspicion that Forcheimes might use the money for an unlawful enterprise. Is that enough to make Honoré an accomplice to the hiring of the hitman? If the purpose standard for complicity is applied, could a jury *infer* purpose based on Honoré's knowledge that her assistance might facilitate the commission of a crime?

3. The Natural and Probable Consequences Doctrine

What happens when an accomplice offers assistance to a principal to commit one crime, but the principal ends up committing another? Is the accomplice responsible for the more serious of the two crimes, even if he did not intend to assist that crime? Some courts say no. Others say yes. The first case presents a jurisdiction that rejects the doctrine, which it calls an "in for a dime, in for a dollar" theory of accomplice liability. The second case provides an example of a jurisdiction that accepts the theory. As you read the second case, identify the doctrinal limitations that the jurisdiction imposes on this expansive doctrine.

Waddington v. Sarausad
Supreme Court of the United States
555 U.S. 179 (2009)

JUSTICE THOMAS delivered the opinion of the Court.

This case arose from a fatal driveby shooting into a group of students standing in front of a Seattle high school. Brian Ronquillo was ultimately identified as the gunman; at the time of the shooting, he was a passenger in a car driven by respondent Cesar Sarausad II. A jury convicted Sarausad as an accomplice to second-degree murder, attempted murder, and assault; he was sentenced to just over 27 years of imprisonment . . .

The driveby shooting was the culmination of a gang dispute between the 23d Street Diablos, of which Cesar Sarausad was a member, and the Bad Side Posse, which was headquartered at Ballard High School in Seattle, Washington. A member of the Diablos, Jerome Reyes, had been chased from Ballard by members of the Bad Side Posse, so the Diablos decided to go "to Ballard High School to show that the Diablos were not afraid" of the rival gang. The Diablos started a fight with the Bad Side Posse, but left quickly after someone indicated that police were nearby. They went to a gang member's house, still angry because the Bad Side Posse had "called [them] weak." Brian Ronquillo retrieved a handgun, and the gang decided to return to Ballard and "get [their] respect back."

Sarausad drove, with Ronquillo in the front passenger seat and Reyes and two other Diablos in the back seat. En route, someone in the car mentioned "capping" the Bad Side Posse, and Ronquillo tied a bandana over the lower part of his face and readied the handgun. Shortly before reaching the high school, a second car of Diablos pulled up next to Sarausad's car and the drivers of the two cars talked briefly. Sarausad asked the other driver, "Are you ready?" and then sped the rest of the way to the high school. Once in front of the school, Sarausad abruptly slowed to about five miles per hour while Ronquillo fired 6 to 10 shots at a group of students standing in front of it. Sarausad "saw everyone go down," and then sped away. The gunfire killed one student; another student was wounded when a bullet fragment struck his leg.

Sarausad, Ronquillo, and Reyes were tried for the first-degree murder of Melissa Fernandes, the attempted first-degree murders of Ryan Lam and Tam Nguyen, and the second-degree assault of Brent Mason. Sarausad and Reyes, who were tried as accomplices, argued at trial that they could not have been accomplices to murder because they "had no idea whatsoever that Ronquillo had armed himself for the return trip." They claimed that they expected, at most, another fistfight with the Bad Side Posse and were "totally and utterly dismayed when Ronquillo started shooting." . . .

In response, the prosecutor focused much of her closing argument on the evidence of Sarausad's knowledge of a shooting. He had "slowed down before the shots were fired, stayed slowed down until the shots were over and immediately sped up." "There was no hesitation, there was no stopping the car. There was no attempt for Mr. Sarausad to swerve his car out of the way so that innocent people wouldn't get shot." She also argued that Sarausad knew when he drove back to the school that his gang's "fists didn't work, the pushing didn't work, the flashing of the signs, the violent altercation didn't work" because the Bad Side Posse still "laughed at them, they called them weak, they called them nothing." So, "[w]hen they rode down to Ballard High School that last time, . . . [t]hey knew they were there to commit a crime, to disrespect the gang, to fight, to shoot, to get that respect back. A fist didn't work, pushing didn't work. Shouting insults at them didn't work. Shooting was going to work. In for a dime, you're in for a dollar."

At the close of trial, the jury received two instructions that directly quoted Washington's accomplice-liability statute. Instruction number 45 provided: "You are instructed that a person is guilty of a crime if it is committed by the conduct of another person for which he is legally accountable.

A person is legally accountable for the conduct of another person when he is an accomplice of such other person in the commission of the crime." Instruction number 46 provided, in relevant part: "A person is an accomplice in the commission of a crime if, with knowledge that it will promote or facilitate the commission of the crime, he or she either: (1) solicits, commands, encourages, or requests another person to commit the crime or (2) aids or agrees to aid another person in planning or committing the crime." . . .

Shortly thereafter, the Washington Supreme Court clarified in an unrelated criminal case that "in for a dime, in for a dollar" is not the best descriptor of accomplice liability under Washington law because an accomplice must have knowledge of "the crime" that occurs. *State v. Roberts*, 142 Wash. 2d 471, 509-510 (2000). Therefore, an accomplice who knows of one crime—the dime—is not guilty of a greater crime—the dollar—if he has no knowledge of that greater crime. It was error, then, to instruct a jury that an accomplice's knowledge of "a crime" was sufficient to establish accomplice liability for "the crime." The Washington Supreme Court limited this decision to instructions containing the phrase "a crime" and explicitly reaffirmed its precedent establishing that jury instructions linking an accomplice's knowledge to "the crime," such as the instruction used at Sarausad's trial, comport with Washington law. An instruction that references "the crime" "copie[s] exactly the language from the accomplice liability statute" and properly hinges criminal punishment on knowledge of "the crime" for which the defendant was charged as an accomplice . . .

. . . The Washington courts reasonably concluded that the trial court's instruction to the jury was not ambiguous. The instruction parroted the language of the statute, requiring that an accomplice "in the commission of the crime" take action "with knowledge that it will promote or facilitate the commission of the crime." Wash. Rev. Code § § 9A.08.020(2)(c), (3)(a). It is impossible to assign any meaning to this instruction different from the meaning given to it by the Washington courts. By its plain terms, it instructed the jury to find Sarausad guilty as an accomplice "in the commission of the [murder]" only if he acted "with knowledge that [his conduct] will promote or facilitate the commission of the [murder]." . . .

Put simply, there was no evidence of ultimate juror confusion as to the test for accomplice liability under Washington law. Rather, the jury simply reached a unanimous decision that the State had proved Sarausad's guilt beyond a reasonable doubt . . . Given the strength of the evidence supporting the conviction, along with the jury's failure to convict Reyes—who also had been charged as an accomplice to murder and also had admitted knowledge of a possible fight—it was not objectively unreasonable for the Washington courts to conclude that the jury convicted Sarausad only because it believed that he, unlike Reyes, had knowledge of more than just a fistfight . . .

JUSTICE SOUTER, with whom JUSTICE STEVENS and JUSTICE GINSBURG join, dissenting.

The issue in this habeas case is whether it was objectively reasonable for the state court to find that there was no reasonable likelihood that the jury convicted respondent Cesar Sarausad on a mistaken understanding of Washington law. The underlying question is whether the jury may have thought it could find Sarausad guilty as an accomplice to murder on the theory that he assisted in what he expected would be a fistfight, or whether the jury knew that to convict him Washington law required it to conclude Sarausad aided in what he understood was intended to be a killing . . .

The majority's position is simply unrealistic. Even a juror with a preter-natural grasp of the statutory subtlety would have lost his grip after listening to the prosecutor's closing argument, which first addressed the state law of accomplice liability with a statement that was flatout error, followed that with a confusing argument that could have reflected either the correct or the erroneous view, and concluded with an argument that could have fit either theory but ended with a phrase defined to express the erroneous one.

In her first pass at the subject, the prosecutor said unequivocally that assaultive, not murderous, intent on Sarausad's part would suffice for the intent required of an accomplice to murder:

> Let me give you a good example of accomplice liability. A friend comes up to you and says, 'Hold this person's arms while I hit him.' You say, 'Okay, I don't like that person, anyway.' You hold the arms. The person not only gets assaulted, he gets killed. You are an accomplice and you can't come back and say, 'Well, I only intended this much damage to happen.' Your presence, your readiness to assist caused the crime to occur and you are an accomplice. The law in the State of Washington says, if you're in for a dime, you're in for a dollar. If you're there or even if you're not there and you're helping in some fashion to bring about this crime, you are just as guilty.

Thus, in what the majority would launder into "one problematic hypo-thetical," the prosecutor introduced the "in for a dime, in for a dollar" locu-tion, which she defined to mean that readiness to aid in the commission of any crime thought to be intended by the principal is enough intent for accomplice liability for whatever crime the principal actually commits. This leadoff misstatement of the law, never corrected by the trial judge, infects every further statement bearing on accomplice law the prosecutor made, for into each effort she consistently introduced the viral catchphrase "in for a dime, in for a dollar." . . .

The point here is not to excoriate the prosecutor, who tried this case in the period between *Roberts* and *Davis* and could fairly assume that her expansive ("in for a dime . . .") view of accomplice liability was good law in her State. The point is just the obvious one that cannot be evaded without playing make-believe with the record: an uncertain instruction by the trial judge was combined with confounding prosecutorial argument incorporating what the state courts now acknowledge was a clearly erroneous statement of law, in contrast to the view of the law argued by defense counsel. In these circumstances jury confusion is all but inevitable and jury error the reasonable likelihood . . .

People v. Prettyman

Supreme Court of California
14 Cal. 4th 248, 58 Cal. Rptr. 2d 827, 926 P.2d 1013 (1996)

KENNARD, J.

. . . In this case, defendant Debra Jane Bray was charged with the crime of murder; the prosecution's theory at trial was that she was guilty as an accomplice. The trial court instructed the jury that it could find Bray guilty of murder if it determined either that she had aided and abetted the murder or that the murder was a "natural and probable consequence" of any uncharged offense(s) that Bray had aided and abetted. The court did not, however, identify or describe any such uncharged target offense. At issue here is whether, absent a request by counsel, the court should have so instructed the jury. We conclude that when the prosecutor relies on the "natural and probable consequences" doctrine, the trial court must identify and describe the target crimes that the defendant might have assisted or encouraged . . .

FACTS

Codefendant Richard D. Prettyman and defendant Debra Jane Bray were charged with the murder of Gaylord "Vance" Van Camp. . . . Defendant Bray and codefendant Prettyman held themselves out as husband and wife. They, as well as victim Van Camp, were among the homeless living in the Pacific Beach area of San Diego. Van Camp was beaten to death with a steel pipe on the morning of July 20, 1992, while asleep in the courtyard of the Pacific Beach Presbyterian Church. The prosecution contended that Prettyman beat Van Camp to death with the pipe, and that Bray, described by the prosecutor as an "argumentative drunk," encouraged Prettyman to kill Van Camp in order to obtain Bray's wallet, which Bray had given to Van Camp for safekeeping the previous evening.

On the evening preceding the murder, defendant Bray and Van Camp had dinner at the church. Codefendant Prettyman was not present during the dinner, but he attended the religious service that followed. After the service, Bray, who was intoxicated, argued with Prettyman. According to prosecution witness Dennis Charette, a homeless man who observed the argument, Bray demanded that Prettyman return to her certain identification papers that she needed to collect a benefit check. When the argument became heated, Van Camp asked the church's preschool director, Stephanie Hansen, to intervene. . . . After talking to Bray and Prettyman, Hansen asked Van Camp to take Prettyman away from the church until the latter had calmed down. The two men left. Before they went, Bray handed her wallet to Van Camp. According to Charette, Bray told Van Camp to hold the wallet for safekeeping, to prevent Prettyman from stealing it. . . .

At 3:00 or 4:00 A.M., Edward Eash, a homeless man sleeping in a car near the church courtyard, was awakened by the sound of loud voices. Looking out a car window, he saw Bray and codefendant Prettyman. Bray repeatedly said: "We are going to get that fucker Vance. He has no idea who he is messing with. He ain't getting away with this shit." Prettyman nodded his head and said, "Yep. Okay." . . .

THE "NATURAL AND PROBABLE CONSEQUENCES" DOCTRINE

At common law, a person encouraging or facilitating the commission of a crime could be held criminally liable not only for that crime, but for any other offense that was a "natural and probable consequence" of the crime aided and abetted. Although the "natural and probable consequences" doctrine has been "subjected to substantial criticism," it is an "established rule" of American jurisprudence. It is based on the recognition that "aiders and abettors should be responsible for the criminal harms they have naturally, probably and foreseeably put in motion." . . .

In *People v. Kauffman*, 152 Cal. 331 (1907), the defendant and six friends planned to break into a safe at a cemetery. Armed with guns, a bottle of nitroglycerin (to blow open the safe), and burglary tools, they went to the cemetery, where they found an armed guard by the safe. They turned back. On their way home, an encounter with a police officer led to a gunfight in which the officer was killed. The defendant, who had been carrying the nitroglycerin, was unarmed and did not participate in the shooting, but he was charged with and convicted of the officer's murder. On appeal, the defendant argued that the evidence was insufficient to support his conviction. In affirming the defendant's conviction in *Kauffman*, this court said:

The general rule is well settled that where several parties conspire or combine together to commit any unlawful act, each is criminally responsible for the acts of his associates or confederates committed in furtherance of any prosecution of the common design for which they combine. . . . *Each is responsible for everything done by his confederates, which follows incidentally in the execution of the common design as one of its probable and natural consequences, even though it was not intended as a part of the original design or common plan.* Nevertheless the act must be the ordinary and probable effect of the wrongful act specifically agreed on, so that the connection between them may be reasonably apparent, and not a fresh and independent product of the mind of one of the confederates outside of, or foreign to, the common design.

We then concluded in *Kauffman* that, based on the evidence presented, the jury could reasonably find that the plan in which the defendant had conspired included not only breaking into the safe at the cemetery, but also protecting all members of the group from arrest or detection while going to and returning from the scene of the proposed burglary, and that the policeman's death was a natural and probable consequence of this unlawful enterprise. . . .

[U]nder the general principles of aiding and abetting, "an aider and abettor [must] act with knowledge of the criminal purpose of the perpetrator *and* with an intent or purpose either of committing, or of encouraging or facilitating commission of, the offense." Therefore, when a particular aiding and abetting case triggers application of the "natural and probable consequences" doctrine . . . the trier of fact must find that the defendant, acting with (1) knowledge of the unlawful purpose of the perpetrator; and (2) the intent or purpose of committing, encouraging, or facilitating the commission of a predicate or target offense; (3) by act or advice aided, promoted, encouraged or instigated the commission of the target crime. But the trier of fact must also find that (4) the defendant's confederate committed an offense *other than* the target crime; and (5) the offense committed by the confederate was a natural and probable consequence of the target crime that the defendant aided and abetted.

Until quite recently, the decisions involving application of the "natural and probable consequences" doctrine in aiding and abetting situations were limited to a consideration of whether the evidence was sufficient under the doctrine to support the defendant's conviction. These decisions most commonly involved situations in which a defendant assisted or encouraged a confederate to commit an assault with a deadly weapon or with potentially deadly force, and the confederate not only assaulted but also murdered the victim. In those instances, the courts generally had no difficulty in upholding a murder conviction, reasoning that the jury could reasonably conclude that the killing of the victim death was a "natural and probable consequence" of the assault that the defendant aided and abetted. Other cases applied the "natural and probable consequences" doctrine in situations where a defendant assisted in the commission of an armed robbery, during which a confederate assaulted or tried to kill one of the robbery victims. In those cases, courts upheld jury verdicts convicting the defendant of assault and/or attempted murder, on the ground that the jury could reasonably conclude that the crime was a natural and probable consequence of the robbery aided by the defendant. . . .

. . . In this case, defendant Bray . . . contends that the trial court should, on its own initiative, have . . . [specified] for the jury the target or predicate crime(s) that, under the evidence, Bray might have aided and abetted and that could have led, as a natural and probable consequence, to the murder of Van Camp by codefendant Prettyman. . . . We agree with Bray. . . .

In an aiding and abetting case involving application of the "natural and probable consequences" doctrine, identification of the target crime will facilitate the jury's task of determining whether the charged crime allegedly committed by the aider and abettor's confederate was indeed a natural and probable consequence of any uncharged target crime that, the prosecution contends, the defendant knowingly and intentionally aided and abetted. The facts of this case illustrate this point. If, for example, the jury had concluded that defendant Bray had encouraged codefendant Prettyman to commit an assault on Van Camp but that Bray had no reason to believe that Prettyman would use a deadly weapon such as a steel pipe to commit the assault, then the jury could not properly find that the murder of Van Camp was a natural and probable consequence of the assault encouraged by Bray. If, on the other hand, the jury had concluded that Bray encouraged Prettyman to assault Van Camp with the steel pipe, or by means of force likely to produce great bodily injury, then it could appropriately find that Prettyman's murder of Van Camp was a natural and probable consequence of that assault. Therefore, instructions identifying and describing the crime of assault with a deadly weapon or by means of force likely to produce great bodily injury as the appropriate target crime would have assisted the jury in determining whether Bray was guilty of Van Camp's murder under the "natural and probable consequences" doctrine. . . .

. . . [T]o convict a defendant of a crime under this doctrine, the jury need not unanimously agree on the particular target crime the defendant aided and abetted. In many cases in which the doctrine is applicable, the defendant is not charged with the target crime, but with another crime that was allegedly committed by the defendant's confederate. Nevertheless, at trial each juror must be convinced, beyond a reasonable doubt, that the defendant aided and abetted the commission of a *criminal act,* and that the offense actually committed was a natural and probable consequence of that act. . . . [A] conviction may not be based on the jury's generalized belief that the defendant intended to assist and/or encourage unspecified "nefarious" conduct. To ensure that the jury will not rely on such generalized beliefs as a basis for conviction, the trial court should identify and describe the target or predicate crime that the defendant may have aided and abetted. . . .

NOTES & QUESTIONS ON NATURAL AND PROBABLE CONSEQUENCES

1. *What was Bray's intent?* Why was the natural and probable consequences doctrine even necessary in the *Prettyman* case? The prosecution contended that Bray *wanted* Prettyman to kill Van Camp in order to get the wallet back. If that is the case, then Bray is an accomplice to murder even in the absence of the natural and probable consequences doctrine. However, the problem emerges if the jury *rejects* the prosecution's assumption and has a different view of the facts. According to the court testimony, Bray said: "We are going to get that fucker Vance. He has no idea who he is messing with. He ain't getting away with this shit." What did Bray mean by this? The jury could reasonably conclude that Bray only wanted Prettyman to assault the victim to get the wallet back—not kill him. In that case, Bray could only be convicted of murder if the jury applied the natural and probable consequences doctrine.

2. *A natural and probable controversy.* The natural and probable consequences doctrine is highly controversial and frequently criticized by legal scholars. Many state jurisdictions reject it. However, it remains viable in many states, including California, Delaware, Illinois, Indiana, Iowa, Kansas, Maine, Minnesota, Tennessee, Wisconsin, and others. See, e.g., *People v. Robinson*, 475 Mich. 1, 715 N.W.2d 44 (2006). Is the doctrine consistent with the language of most accomplice statutes, which usually define an accomplice as someone who provides assistance with "intent to promote or facilitate the commission of an offense"? Ariz. Rev. Stat. Ann. §§ 13-301. As a matter of statutory interpretation, does this linguistic construction require that the offense that the accomplice intends to facilitate be the same as the offense that the accomplice is then convicted for?

Formally, the Model Penal Code rejects the natural and probable consequences doctrine. However, MPC § 210.2(b) defines a criminal homicide as murder when "it is committed recklessly under circumstances manifesting extreme indifference to the value of human life." This is the MPC version of depraved heart or "implied malice" murder. The provision goes on to clarify that the "recklessness and indifference are presumed if the actor is engaged or is an accomplice in the commission of, or an attempt to commit, or flight after committing or attempting to commit robbery, rape or deviate sexual intercourse by force or threat of force, arson, burglary, kidnapping or felonious escape." Apply this provision to the facts of *Prettyman*. Would Bray be guilty of murder under the Model Penal Code?

3. *Doctrinal justification.*   What justifies holding an accomplice guilty of one crime when he intended to support a lesser crime? In its simplest terms, the idea is that the accomplice is not fully in control of the criminal endeavor and runs the risk that his assistance might facilitate the perpetration of a greater crime; this risk is inherent in being an accomplice. But what is the accomplice's mental state regarding the facilitation of the greater crime? Arguably, the accomplice intends to facilitate the target crime but is *reckless* with regard to the greater crime. In other words, the accomplice is aware of the risk that his assistance might facilitate the commission of a greater crime but he consciously disregards that risk and offers the assistance anyway. In the end, though, the greater crime (like murder) might be an intentional crime. The result is that the accomplice is convicted of an intentional crime even though his mens rea is only recklessness or only negligence. This produces a culpability inflation that might conflict with the principle of culpability, or the idea that conviction and punishment should be proportional to culpability. One solution to this culpability problem is to think of this as a special case of transferred intent. The accomplice intends to facilitate the target crime, and that intent is transferred to the resulting crime even if the accomplice did not intend to facilitate it. Does that argument work? Or should the argument rest simply on the need for enhanced penalties to deter accomplices?

4. *Limits on the doctrine.*   Some jurisdictions have placed judicial limits on the doctrine to limit its application. In *People v. Chiu*, 59 Cal. 4th 155, 325 P.3d 972 (2014), the defendant was convicted of first-degree premeditated murder under the natural and probable consequences doctrine. The case involved an "after-school" brawl with as many as 25 people outside of a pizza parlor near a Los Angeles high school, which resulted in someone getting shot. The defendant was not the shooter, but the jury concluded that he was an accomplice to the target crime of either assault or disturbing the peace, and thus guilty of first-degree murder under the natural and probable consequences doctrine. The California Supreme Court overturned the conviction because "where the direct perpetrator is guilty of first degree premeditated murder, the legitimate public policy considerations of deterrence and culpability would not be served by allowing a defendant to be convicted of that greater offense under the natural and probable consequences doctrine." The State of Washington goes even further. In that jurisdiction, the prosecution can only convict an accomplice of murder under the doctrine if the accomplice already knew he was assisting some type of homicide offense. *Sarausad v. State*, 109 Wash. App. 824, 39 P.3d 308 (2001).

5. *Objective or subjective.* For the doctrine to apply, does the accomplice need to be consciously *aware* that the more serious crime is a natural and probable consequence? The natural and probable consequences doctrine can be understood subjectively or objectively. Under the subjective view, the accomplice must be aware of the possibility and provide the assistance anyway. Under the objective view, the accomplice is guilty if "a reasonable person in the defendant's position would have or should have known that the nontarget offense was a reasonably foreseeable consequence of the act aided and abetted by the defendant." See *People v. Nguyen*, 21 Cal. App. 4th 518, 531 (1993). Which view is better for the defense? Most courts that have explicitly considered the issue have sided with California in adopting an objective approach to reasonable foreseeability—indeed that is the whole point of attaching the word "reasonable" to the concept of foreseeability.

6. *Temporal duration of the complicity.* If the accomplice assists the principal perpetrator, he is derivatively responsible for any foreseeable greater acts performed by the principal perpetrator. But for how long? And what type of connection does there need to be between the target crime and the greater crime? If the accomplice assists the principal in his perpetration of the target crime, but the principal then commits a wholly unrelated crime years later, the accomplice is not responsible for that crime even under the natural and probable consequences doctrine. But if the principal kills a police officer while evading arrest, the accomplice is guilty of murder. See, e.g., *United States v. Taylor*, 322 F.3d 1209 (9th Cir. 2003) ("escape phase of a crime is still part of the commission of the crime").

HYPOTHETICAL

Imagine that the defendant is an accomplice who assists the principal in perpetrating a crime. The crime is successful and both individuals return home and go their separate ways. The criminals never speak again. Twenty years later, a police detective reviewing a cold case file gets a big break on the case and goes to arrest the principal perpetrator at his residence. When the principal sees the police detective at the door, he knows that his criminal past has finally caught up with him. But the principal does not want to go to prison, so he shoots and kills the police officer. The principal is clearly guilty of murder, but should the accomplice be convicted of murder on the natural and probable consequences doctrine as well? How should the question be analyzed?

4. Innocent Instrumentality Rule

In most cases, the person who performs the actus reus is the principal perpetrator, while the person "behind the scenes" is the accomplice. In some cases, that rule would produce absurd results because the person behind the scenes is more culpable than the person doing the act. In reading the following case, examine the type of factual scenarios that will allow a court to apply the innocent instrumentality rule and declare the behind-the-scenes actor as the principal perpetrator.

Bailey v. Commonwealth
Supreme Court of Virginia
229 Va. 258, 329 S.E.2d 37 (1985)

CARRICO, C.J.

Indicted for involuntary manslaughter, Joseph A. Bailey was convicted in a jury trial and sentenced in accordance with the jury's verdict to serve six months in jail and to pay a fine of $1,000. The question on appeal is whether it was proper to convict Bailey of involuntary manslaughter when, in his absence, the victim was killed by police officers responding to reports from Bailey concerning the victim's conduct.

The death of the victim, Gordon E. Murdock, occurred during the late evening of May 21, 1983, in the aftermath of an extended and vituperative conversation between Bailey and Murdock over their citizens' band radios. During the conversation, which was to be the last in a series of such violent incidents, Bailey and Murdock cursed and threatened each other repeatedly.

Bailey and Murdock lived about two miles apart in the Roanoke area. On the evening in question, each was intoxicated. Bailey had consumed a "twelve-pack" of beer and a "fifth of liquor" since mid-afternoon; a test of Murdock's blood made during an autopsy showed alcoholic content of ".271% . . . by weight." Murdock was also "legally blind," with vision of only 3/200 in the right eye and 2/200 in the left. Bailey knew that Murdock had "a problem with vision" and that he was intoxicated on the night in question.

Bailey also knew that Murdock owned a handgun and had boasted "about how he would use it and shoot it and scare people off with it." Bailey knew further that Murdock was easily agitated and that he became especially angry if anyone disparaged his war hero, General George S. Patton. During the conversation in question, Bailey implied that General Patton and Murdock himself were homosexuals.

Also during the conversation, Bailey persistently demanded that Murdock arm himself with his handgun and wait on his front porch for Bailey to come and injure or kill him. Murdock responded by saying he would be waiting on his front porch, and he told Bailey to "kiss [his] mother or [his] wife and children good-bye because [he would] never go back home."

Bailey then made two anonymous telephone calls to the Roanoke City Police Department. In the first, Bailey reported "a man . . . out on the porch [at Murdock's address] waving a gun around." A police car was dispatched to the address, but the officers reported they did not "see anything."

Bailey called Murdock back on the radio and chided him for not "going out on the porch." More epithets and threats were exchanged. Bailey told Murdock he was "going to come up there in a blue and white car" and demanded that Murdock "step out there on the . . . porch" with his gun "in [his] hands" because he, Bailey, would "be there in just a minute."

Bailey telephoned the police again. This time, Bailey identified Murdock by name and told the dispatcher that Murdock had "a gun on the porch," had "threatened to shoot up the neighborhood," and was "talking about shooting anything that moves." Bailey insisted that the police "come out here and straighten this man out." Bailey refused to identify himself, explaining that he was "right next to [Murdock] out here" and feared revealing his identity.

Three uniformed police officers, Chambers, Beavers, and Turner, were dispatched to Murdock's home. None of the officers knew that Murdock was intoxicated or that he was in an agitated state of mind. Only Officer Beavers knew that Murdock's eyesight was bad, and he did not know "exactly how bad it was." Beavers also knew that Murdock would get "a little 10-96 (mental subject) occasionally" and would "curse and carry on" when he was drinking.

When the officers arrived on the scene, they found that Murdock's "porch light was on" but observed no one on the porch. After several minutes had elapsed, the officers observed Murdock come out of his house with "something shiny in his hand." Murdock sat down on the top step of the porch and placed the shiny object beside him.

Officer Chambers approached Murdock from the side of the porch and told him to "[l]eave the gun alone and walk down the stairs away from it." Murdock "just sat there." When Chambers repeated his command, Murdock cursed him. Murdock then reached for the gun, stood up, advanced in Chambers' direction, and opened fire. Chambers retreated and was not struck.

All three officers returned fire, and Murdock was struck. Lying wounded on the porch, he said several times, "I didn't know you was the police." He died from "a gunshot wound of the left side of the chest." In the investigation which followed, Bailey stated that he was "the hoss that caused the loss."

In an instruction granted below and not questioned on appeal, the trial court told the jury it should convict Bailey if it found that his negligence or reckless conduct was so gross and culpable as to indicate a callous disregard for human life and that his actions were the proximate cause or a concurring cause of Murdock's death. Bailey concedes that the evidence at trial, viewed in the light most favorable to the Commonwealth, would support a finding that his actions constituted negligence so gross and culpable as to indicate a callous disregard for human life. He contends, however, that he "did not kill Murdock."

Bailey argues that his conviction can be sustained only if he was a principal in the first degree, a principal in the second degree, or an accessory before the fact to the killing of Murdock. The Attorney General concedes that Bailey was not a principal in the second degree or an accessory before the fact, but maintains that he was a principal in the first degree.

Countering, Bailey argues he was not a principal in the first degree because only the immediate perpetrators of crime occupy that status. Here, Bailey says, the immediate perpetrators of Murdock's killing were the police officers who returned Murdock's fire. He was in his own home two miles away, Bailey asserts, and did not control the actors in the confrontation at Murdock's home or otherwise participate in the events that occurred there. Hence, Bailey concludes, he could not have been a principal in the first degree.

We have adopted the rule in this Commonwealth, however, that one who effects a criminal act through an innocent or unwitting agent is a principal in the first degree. . . .

Knowing that Murdock was intoxicated, nearly blind, and in an agitated state of mind, Bailey orchestrated a scenario on the evening of May 21, 1983, whose finale was bound to include harmful consequences to Murdock, either in the form of his arrest or his injury or death. Bailey angered Murdock with accusations of homosexuality concerning Murdock himself as well as his war hero. Bailey then demanded repeatedly that Murdock arm himself with his handgun and wait on his front porch for Bailey to arrive. Bailey also threatened repeatedly that when he arrived at Murdock's home he would inflict serious injury upon Murdock and even kill him.

Having aroused Murdock's wrath and having led him to expect a violent confrontation, Bailey made two anonymous telephone calls to the police. In those calls, he falsely reported Murdock's conduct by saying the latter had threatened to "shoot up" the neighborhood and to shoot anything that moved, when Murdock had not made such threats. Bailey falsified his own ability to observe Murdock's conduct by telling the police that he, Bailey, was "right next to [Murdock] out here," when he was actually two miles away. And Bailey neglected to tell the police that Murdock was intoxicated and blind and in an agitated state of mind.

From a factual standpoint, it is clear from the sum total of Bailey's actions that his purpose in calling the police was to induce them to go to Murdock's home and unwittingly create the appearance that Bailey himself had arrived to carry out the threats he had made over the radio. And, from a legal standpoint, it is clear that, for Bailey's mischievous purpose, the police officers who went to Murdock's home and confronted him were acting as Bailey's innocent or unwitting agents.

But, Bailey argues, he cannot be held criminally liable in this case unless Murdock's death was the natural and probable result of Bailey's conduct. Bailey maintains that either Murdock's own reckless and criminal conduct in opening fire upon the police or the officers' return fire constituted an independent, intervening cause absolving Bailey of guilt.

We have held, however, that "[a]n intervening act which is reasonably foreseeable cannot be relied upon as breaking the chain of causal connection between an original act of negligence and subsequent injury." Here, under instructions not questioned on appeal, the jury determined that the fatal consequences of Bailey's reckless conduct could reasonably have been foreseen and, accordingly, that Murdock's death was not the result of an independent, intervening cause but of Bailey's misconduct. At the least, the evidence presented a jury question on these issues. . . .

NOTES & QUESTIONS ON INNOCENT INSTRUMENTALITIES

1. *Other cases of innocent instruments.* In practice, the use of the innocent instrumentality rule is not common. When it is invoked, the crime in question is often rape. In *Morrisey v. State*, 620 A.2d 207 (Del. 1993), the defendant was charged with robbing two individuals he found in the park. After brandishing what appeared to be a pistol, the defendant forcibly led the two individuals to a secluded area of the park where he forced them to have sex with each other. The Delaware Supreme Court upheld the convictions under the innocent instrumentality rule and also clarified that the defendant could be charged as a principal for *two* counts of rape for each sexual encounter, since each act "denigrated two innocent individuals." Essentially, Morrisey was guilty for raping both individuals at the same time, via two innocent instruments. Each victim was *simultaneously* a victim and an innocent instrument. See also *State v. Brown*, 147 Vt. 324 (1986). Why is the innocent instrumentality rule not invoked more often? The answer lies in the fact that U.S. law generally allows courts to penalize accomplices just as severely as principals—a doctrinal consequence that mutes the need to carefully distinguish between principals and accomplices.

2. *Culpable instruments and the Control Theory.* Another factor that limits the application of the innocent instrumentality rule is the requirement that

the instrument be truly innocent. Foreign jurisdictions also use the instrumentality doctrine but several of them have dropped the requirement that the instrument must be innocent. For example, after the reunification of East and West Germany, the newly unified Germany commenced an investigation into the murder of East Germans who were shot while trying to escape to the west over the Berlin Wall during communist rule. It was clear that the border guards who personally shot the victims were guilty of murder. In addition, the German Supreme Court convicted former East German dictator Erich Honecker as an indirect principal perpetrator of the killings. That result was only possible because Germany, like several other civil law countries, has dropped the requirement that the instrument used by the principal must be innocent. In this case, both Honecker and the border guards were culpable. This broader version of the instrumentality doctrine is called the "Control Theory" and stipulates that whoever controls the crime—and determines whether it will be carried out or not—is the principal perpetrator, even if he did not perform the criminal act. The Control Theory is also applied in atrocity cases prosecuted at the International Criminal Court in The Hague. For a discussion of the doctrine's application, see Neha Jain, *Perpetrators and Accessories in International Criminal Law* 119 (2014).

5. Defenses

As explained above, the liability of the accomplice is parasitic on the criminal liability of the principal perpetrator. But that generates no shortage of conceptual puzzles when juries acquit a principal perpetrator. As you read the following case, think about the derivative nature of complicity and how that concept should apply when there are multiple fact finders, and separate trials, for the actors of a criminal enterprise.

Standefer v. United States
Supreme Court of the United States
447 U.S. 10 (1980)

Burger, C.J.

We granted certiorari in this case to decide whether a defendant accused of aiding and abetting in the commission of a federal offense may be convicted after the named principal has been acquitted of that offense.

I

In June 1977, petitioner Standefer was indicted on four counts of making gifts to a public official . . . and on five counts of aiding and abetting a revenue official in accepting compensation in addition to that authorized by law. . . . The indictment charged that petitioner, as head of Gulf Oil Corp.'s tax department, had authorized payments for five vacation trips to Cyril Niederberger, who then was the Internal Revenue Service agent in charge of the audits of Gulf's federal income tax returns. . . .

Prior to the filing of this indictment, Niederberger was separately charged in a 10-count indictment. . . . In February 1977, Niederberger was tried on these charges. He was convicted on four counts . . . in connection with the vacations in Miami, Absecon, Pebble Beach, and Las Vegas and of two counts . . . for the Pebble Beach and Las Vegas trips. He was acquitted on the . . . count involving the Pompano Beach trip and on the three counts . . . charging him with accepting payments from Gulf for trips to Pompano Beach, Miami, and Absecon.

In July 1977, following Niederberger's trial and before the trial in his own case commenced, petitioner moved to dismiss the counts . . . which charged him with aiding and abetting Niederberger in connection with the Pompano Beach, Miami, and Absecon vacations. Petitioner argued that because Niederberger, the only named principal, had been acquitted of accepting unlawful compensation as to those vacations, he could not be convicted of aiding and abetting in the commission of those offenses. The District Court denied the motion. . . .

II

Petitioner makes two main arguments: first, that Congress in enacting 18 U.S.C. § 2 did not intend to authorize prosecution of an aider and abettor after the principal has been acquitted of the offense charged; second, that, even if § 2 permits such a prosecution, the Government should be barred from relitigating the issue of whether Niederberger accepted unlawful compensation in connection with the Pompano Beach, Miami, and Absecon vacations. The first contention relies largely on the common law as it prevailed before the enactment of 18 U.S.C. § 2. The second rests on the contemporary doctrine of nonmutual collateral estoppel.

At common law, the subject of principals and accessories was riddled with "intricate" distinctions. In felony cases, parties to a crime were divided into four distinct categories: (1) principals in the first degree who actually perpetrated the offense; (2) principals in the second degree who were actually or constructively present at the scene of the crime and aided or abetted its commission; (3) accessories before the fact who aided or abetted the crime, but were not present at its commission; and (4) accessories after the fact who rendered assistance after the crime was complete. By contrast, misdemeanor cases "d[id] not admit of accessories either before or after the fact"; instead, all parties to a misdemeanor, whatever their roles, were principals.

Because at early common law all parties to a felony received the death penalty, certain procedural rules developed tending to shield accessories from punishment. Among them was one of special relevance to this case: the rule that an accessory could not be convicted without the prior conviction of the principal offender. Under this rule, the principal's flight, death, or acquittal barred prosecution of the accessory. And if the principal were pardoned or his conviction reversed on appeal, the accessory's conviction could not stand. In every way "an accessory follow[ed], like a shadow, his principal."

This procedural bar applied only to the prosecution of accessories in felony cases. In misdemeanor cases, where all participants were deemed principals, a prior acquittal of the actual perpetrator did not prevent the subsequent conviction of a person who rendered assistance. And in felony cases a principal in the second degree could be convicted notwithstanding the prior acquittal of the first-degree principal. Not surprisingly, considerable effort was expended in defining the categories—in determining, for instance, when a person was "constructively present" so as to be a second-degree principal. In the process, justice all too frequently was defeated.

To overcome these judge-made rules, statutes were enacted in England and in the United States. In 1848 the Parliament enacted a statute providing that an accessory before the fact could be "indicted, tried, convicted, and punished in all respects *like the Principal*." As interpreted, the statute permitted an accessory to be convicted "although the principal be acquitted." Several state legislatures followed suit. In 1899, Congress joined this growing reform movement with the enactment of a general penal code for Alaska which abrogated the common-law distinctions and provided that "all persons concerned in the commission of a crime, whether it be felony or misdemeanor, and whether they directly commit the act constituting the crime or aid and abet in its commission, though not present, are principals, and to be tried and punished as such." . . .

The enactment of 18 U.S.C. § 2 in 1909 was part and parcel of this same reform movement. The language of the statute, as enacted, unmistakably demonstrates the point: "Whoever directly commits any act constituting an offense defined in any law of the United States, or aids, abets, counsels, commands, induces, or procures its commission, *is a principal*."

The statute "abolishe[d] the distinction between principals and accessories and [made] them all principals." Read against its common-law background, the provision evinces a clear intent to permit the conviction of accessories to federal criminal offenses despite the prior acquittal of the actual perpetrator of the offense. It gives general effect to what had always been the rule for second-decree principals and for all misdemeanants.

The legislative history of § 2 confirms this understanding. . . . This history plainly rebuts petitioner's contention that § 2 was not intended to authorize conviction of an aider and abettor after the principal had been acquitted of the offense charged. With the enactment of that section, all participants in conduct violating a federal criminal statute are "principals." As such, they are punishable for their criminal conduct; the fate of other participants is irrelevant.

The doctrine of nonmutual collateral estoppel was unknown to the common law and to the Congress when it enacted § 2 in 1909. . . . Here, petitioner urges us to apply nonmutual estoppel against the Government; specifically he argues that the Government should be barred from relitigating Niederberger's guilt. . . . That issue, he notes, was an element of his offense which was determined adversely to the Government at Niederberger's trial.

This, however, is a criminal case, presenting considerations different from those in *Blonder-Tongue* or *Parklane Hosiery*. First, in a criminal case, the Government is often without the kind of "full and fair opportunity to litigate" that is a prerequisite of estoppel. Several aspects of our criminal law make this so: the prosecution's discovery rights in criminal cases are limited, both by rules of court and constitutional privileges; it is prohibited from being granted a directed verdict or from obtaining a judgment notwithstanding the verdict no matter how clear the evidence in support of guilt; it cannot secure a new trial on the ground that an acquittal was plainly contrary to the weight of the evidence; and it cannot secure appellate review where a defendant has been acquitted.

The absence of these remedial procedures in criminal cases permits juries to acquit out of compassion or compromise or because of "their assumption of a power which they had no right to exercise, but to which they were disposed through lenity." It is of course true that verdicts induced by passion and prejudice are not unknown in civil suits. But in civil cases, post-trial motions and appellate review provide an aggrieved litigant a remedy; in a criminal case the Government has no similar avenue to correct errors. Under contemporary principles of collateral estoppel, this factor strongly militates against giving an acquittal preclusive effect.

The application of nonmutual estoppel in criminal cases is also complicated by the existence of rules of evidence and exclusion unique to our criminal law. It is frequently true in criminal cases that evidence inadmissible against one defendant is admissible against another. The exclusionary rule, for example, may bar the Government from introducing evidence against one defendant because that evidence was obtained in violation of his constitutional rights. And the suppression of that evidence may result in an acquittal. The same evidence, however, may be admissible against other parties to the crime "whose rights were [not] violated." In such circumstances, where evidentiary rules prevent the Government from presenting all its proof in the first case, application of nonmutual estoppel would be plainly unwarranted. . . .

III

In denying preclusive effect to Niederberger's acquittal, we do not deviate from the sound teaching that "justice must satisfy the appearance of justice." This case does no more than manifest the simple, if discomforting, reality that "different juries may reach different results under any criminal statute. That is one of the consequences we accept under our jury system." While symmetry of results may be intellectually satisfying, it is not required. . . .

NOTES & QUESTIONS ON DEFENSES

1. *Justifications and accomplices.*   Consider the case of *United States v. Lopez*, 662 F. Supp. 1083 (N.D. 1987). Ronald McIntosh wanted to break his girlfriend Samantha Lopez out of prison; he procured a helicopter and landed it right on the grounds of the federal prison where she was incarcerated. At trial, Lopez asserted that her escape was justified on grounds of necessity because her life had been threatened while she was in prison. McIntosh requested that the judge instruct the jury that if they acquitted Lopez then they had to acquit McIntosh too. The district court agreed with McIntosh because it concluded that necessity was a justification. In other words, Lopez had done nothing wrong by escaping because her act was justified by necessity. If she did nothing wrong, then by definition McIntosh did nothing wrong by assisting her. The fates of the principal and accomplice were tied together.

2. *Two juries versus one jury.*   How is the *Lopez* decision consistent with *Standefer*? The *Lopez* trial involved *one* jury struggling to come to a coherent resolution to the case and passing judgment on the guilt of both the principal and accomplice. In contrast, *Standefer* is about two juries and whether the decision of the first jury should preclude the second jury from reconsidering the underlying precepts of the first jury's decision (the guilt of the principal). The key point to remember about the *Standefer* decision is that the Supreme Court recognized that the guilt of the accomplice was logically tied to the guilt of the principal—it just preserved the right of the second jury to make an independent judgment about the guilt of the principal even if the principal was not a defendant in its courtroom (because it had been acquitted earlier). Incidentally, the rule expressed in *Standefer* is followed in state courts too. Some jurisdictions even have statutes codifying the rule that an accomplice can be convicted even when the

principal is not. See, e.g., 11 Del. Code § 272, which allows an accomplice conviction when:

(1) The other person is not guilty of the offense in question because of irresponsibility or other legal incapacity or exemption, or because of unawareness of the criminal nature of the conduct in question or of the accused's criminal purpose, or because of other factors precluding the mental state required for the commission of the offense; or

(2) The other person has not been prosecuted for or convicted of any offense based on the conduct in question, or has previously been acquitted thereof, or has been convicted of a different offense or in a different degree, or has legal immunity from prosecution for the conduct in question; or

(3) The offense in question, as defined, can be committed only by a particular class of persons, and the defendant, not belonging to that class, is for that reason legally incapable of committing the offense in an individual capacity, unless imposing liability on the defendant is inconsistent with the purpose of the provision establishing the defendant's incapacity.

The other key difference between *Lopez* and *Standefer* is their different procedural postures. *Standefer* involves a post-conviction request to an appellate court to overturn a jury verdict of guilt. In contrast, *Lopez* involves a request for a jury instruction at trial. The standards for each are different. Courts explain the law to the jury in a way that promotes consistency in their application of the law to the facts of the case. However, if the jury refuses to listen to those instructions, appellate reversal is not always appropriate. Think of the point this way: Imagine that the trial judge in *Lopez* issued the requested instruction, because its logic was undeniable, but the jury ignored it and convicted McIntosh anyway. What result? Applying *Standefer*, the court should uphold the verdict, even though the instruction was appropriate. As a final point, what result if the court in *Lopez* had *denied* the request for the instruction and the jury convicted McIntosh? An appellate court in that case should reverse the guilty verdict and order a new trial, this time with the appropriate instruction given to the jury.

3. *Withdrawal.* The accomplice's link to the principal perpetrator—and his inheritance of the guilt—might be severed if the accomplice abandons his participation in the endeavor. However, the standard for a successful withdrawal is extremely high. Since the accomplice's complicity is based on his assistance to the principal, many jurisdictions follow the Model Penal Code and require that the accomplice: (i) unwind his participation by "depriving" his assistance of its effectiveness; or (ii) give timely warning to the police; or (iii) make proper efforts to prevent the commission of the crime. In other words, the defendant must try to neutralize the previous participation. Is there a difference between

PROBLEM CASE

In 2007, high school students in New Hampshire were arrested in connection with a cheating scandal. Several students decided to steal a math exam from the third floor of the school building. The defendant, Paul Formella, stayed behind and agreed to serve as a lookout. He was supposed to yell something to the thieves from a distance if anyone approached. However, Formella changed his mind. Without saying anything to the thieves, he left and did not serve as a lookout. Was Formella an accomplice to the theft or did he successfully withdraw?

On appeal, the Supreme Court of New Hampshire concluded that Formella had not successfully withdrawn from the crime because he never informed the thieves that he was not acting as a lookout. Why was this relevant? The thieves were encouraged in their endeavor by the assurance that Formella was acting as their lookout. Since they never learned that he withdrew, they completed the crime based on the original encouragement. Formella's withdrawal "did nothing to counter his prior complicity." *State v. Formella*, 158 N.H. 114, 960 A.2d 722 (2008). Do you agree with the court's characterization of Formella's complicity as encouragement?

Formella's sentence included a fine, community service, and a letter of apology. The judge told Formella to look up the word "lemming" in the dictionary. Susan J. Boutwell, *Student Sentenced in Exam Scandal*, Concord Monitor, Nov. 15, 2007. After college, Formella attended University of Chicago Law School.

Paul Formella

these requirements? The first requires a particular effect, but the latter two options only require an effort. The standard will apply differently depending on the nature of the complicity. If the actus reus was encouragement, the accomplice could terminate his participation by repudiating the endeavor—which would seem to be the opposite of encouragement. However, in cases where the actus reus involved more concrete forms of assistance, depriving that assistance of its effectiveness might require alerting the police and stopping the crime. For example, if the defendant provides a gun to the principal to commit a murder, the accomplice would need to either get the gun back or get the police to intervene. Some jurisdictions have a more demanding standard and require that the accomplice make a "substantial effort" to prevent the crime. See, e.g., N.Y. Penal Law § 40.10.

C. PRACTICE & POLICY

This last section addresses three policy issues raised by the prosecution of accomplices. The first is whether there are any constitutional constraints on the severity of an accomplice's punishment. The second is whether an individual may simultaneously be a victim and an accomplice of a crime. The third is whether the purpose or knowledge standard should apply when a federal court hears a civil lawsuit against a corporation charged with being an accomplice to human rights abuses abroad.

     ∾ **Constitutional constraints on punishing accomplices.** As noted above, federal and state statutes typically allow accomplices to be punished just as harshly as principals. One reason for that rule is that U.S. courts are somewhat ambivalent about the principal-accomplice distinction and concede that sometimes the criminal labeled as the accomplice is actually more culpable than the principal perpetrator. There are two ways of solving this problem. One solution would be to revise the definitions of principals and accomplices. However, that flies in the face of common law tradition that defined the principal as the criminal who performed the actus reus. The other solution is to stipulate—by fiat—that accomplices can be punished just as severely as principals, which is the American solution. This stands in marked contrast to foreign jurisdictions, such as Germany, whose penal codes stipulate that accomplices should be punished *less* than principals.

     But how far can the American solution be taken? In *Enmund v. Florida*, 458 U.S. 782 (1982), the defendant Earl Enmund was convicted of being an accomplice in the first-degree murder and robbery of an elderly couple in a Florida farmhouse. Enmund was the getaway driver and stayed in the car while his co-felons committed the robbery and the murder in the farmhouse. Enmund's conviction was based on his participation as an accomplice in the underlying felony, the robbery. The trial court never concluded that Enmund intended the couple to die. Consequently, the Supreme Court overturned his death sentence and concluded that the Cruel and Unusual Punishments Clause of the Eighth Amendment barred the execution of a defendant who is a mere accomplice who did not personally commit murder and who did not intend the killing. According to the Court: "Enmund did not kill or intend to kill and thus his culpability is plainly different from that of the robbers who killed; yet the State treated them alike and attributed to Enmund the culpability of those who killed the Kerseys. This was impermissible under the Eighth Amendment."

However, in *Tison v. Arizona*, 481 U.S. 137 (1987), the Supreme Court declined to extend that reasoning to a case involving killings performed during a prison break. Gary Tison was in prison serving a life sentence for murder. His three sons came to the prison to break out their father; his cellmate Randy Greenawalt also joined in the escape. After leaving the prison, the group flagged down a car to steal. The occupants of the car included John Lyons and his wife Donnelda. Also in the car was 2-year-old Christopher, their son, and Theresa Tyson, their 15-year-old niece. Tison and Greenawalt ended up executing all of them. The Tison sons were convicted of four counts of murder under felony murder and accomplice liability. The Tisons argued that the rule from *Enmund* barred their execution because they were mere accomplices. The Supreme Court disagreed because it concluded that the Tisons' level of participation and underlying mens rea were more substantial than Enmund's. Specifically, the Court concluded that a "reckless disregard for human life implicit in knowingly engaging in criminal activities known to carry a grave risk of death represents a highly culpable mental state, a mental state that may be taken into account in making a capital sentencing judgment when that conduct causes its natural, though also not inevitable, lethal result." Do you agree with this conclusion?

ᖈᖇ Victims as accomplices.   What if the "victim" of a crime is also an accomplice? Sound like a strange idea, but it is ultimately quite possible in cases where the victim's putative consent is legally irrelevant. Statutory rape is the classic example. Say the younger individual agrees to engage in a sexual relationship with the older individual. Since the younger individual is legally incapable of consenting, the older individual is guilty of statutory rape. But since the younger individual agreed to the encounter, might this constitute "encouragement" sufficient to satisfy the requirements for accomplice liability? In that case, the younger individual would be both a victim and an accomplice to her own victimization at the very same time. Can a prosecutor charge the victim with being an accomplice to statutory rape? Take another example. A 16-year-old high school student asks a second student to take a nude picture of her. The second student—the photographer—is guilty of various child pornography violations. Can the prosecutor also charge the subject of the photos with being an accomplice to the crime?

In both cases, there is something intuitively odd about charging a victim with being an accomplice to her own victimization. For that reason, the Model Penal Code has a specific provision to bar such prosecutions. MPC § 2.06(6) provides that "a person is not an accomplice in an offense committed by another person if: (a) he is a victim of that offense. . . ." On policy grounds, several states have adopted this Model Penal Code provision. It is also recognized as a general principle of criminal law even in the absence of an explicit statutory provision. For example, in *Gebardi v. United States*, 287 U.S. 112 (1932), the Supreme Court interpreted the federal Mann Act, which made it a crime to transport a woman across state lines for so-called immoral purposes. Prosecutors charged one such woman with being a conspirator to the Mann Act violation. The Supreme Court reversed the conviction. See also *Queen v. Tyrrell*, 1 Q.B. 710 (1894); *In re Meagan R.*, 42 Cal. App. 4th 17, 49 Cal. Rptr. 2d 325 (Cal. Ct. App. 1996) (girl could not be accomplice to her own statutory rape); *Whitaker v. Commonwealth*, 95 Ky. 632 (1894) (daughter not an accomplice to her father's crime of incest).

The policy rationale for such decisions is that the criminal provision is designed to protect a vulnerable class of individuals from some predatory or inappropriate conduct. As such, it would be counter to public policy to penalize the protected class, even if they were participants in the endeavor. Of course, this policy rationale depends on a determination that the crime in question is designed to protect a vulnerable class of individuals. Are there some crimes where the rule should be rejected? For example, someone paying a bribe to a government official can—and should—be convicted of conspiring with (and aiding and abetting) the officer regarding the payment. *May v. United States*, 175 F.2d 994 (D.C. Cir. 1949). That rule holds even though bribery provisions are designed in part to protect vulnerable citizens from being preyed upon by government officials seeking to extract bribes from them.

ল **Purpose versus knowledge in human rights.** The proper contours of accomplice liability is an issue of international concern that stretches far beyond the borders of the United States. The Alien Tort Statute (ATS) allows foreign plaintiffs to sue in U.S. federal court for violations of international law. Typically, such cases are filed against U.S. corporations accusing them of being complicit in human rights abuses perpetrated by foreign governments against their own citizens. For example, several corporations were sued under the ATS for their dealings with the government of South Africa during the apartheid era. In another prominent case, Nigerian plaintiffs brought claims against the Royal Dutch Petroleum Company for its alleged complicity in extrajudicial killings and torture that occurred in Nigeria. In these cases, the proper interpretation of accomplice liability comes front and center—especially the mens rea debate between purpose and knowledge. That legal issue is key because the purpose standard for accomplice liability is far more defense friendly, while the knowledge standard is far more plaintiff-friendly. To understand the point, imagine why a U.S. corporation might do business with a foreign government engaged in human rights abuses. Typically, the U.S. corporation is indifferent to the human rights violations and is motivated by financial incentives to pursue the business relationship with the foreign government. In that situation, is the corporation providing assistance to the foreign government with the *purpose* of facilitating its human rights abuses? Arguably not, because the corporation's goal is simply to increase its business. So under the purpose standard the corporation is not complicit. However, does the corporation *know* that its actions will facilitate the government's human rights abuses? Certainly. So the corporation's liability hangs in the balance of the purpose-knowledge debate.

Unfortunately, federal courts are divided on which jurisdiction's rules on accomplice liability should apply in ATS cases. If courts should apply the complicity standards from U.S. federal courts, then as described at the beginning of this chapter, the correct standard is purpose because that is the standard used by U.S. district courts. However, other courts have concluded that the rules on complicity should come from international law, since ATS cases involve human rights abuses that violate international law. That requires an investigation into precedents from the Nuremberg tribunals after World War II and the more recent international tribunals in The Hague. Applying that methodology, some courts have held that international law uses the purpose standard for complicity, while other courts have endorsed the knowledge standard. Compare *Presbyterian Church of Sudan v. Talisman Energy*, 582 F.3d 244 (2d Cir. 2009) (purpose standard), with *Doe v. Exxon Mobil Corp.*, 654 F.3d 11 (D.C. Cir. 2011) (knowledge standard).

CHAPTER 21

⤞◦∕◦◦⤟

CONSPIRACY LIABILITY

A. DOCTRINE

As discussed in Chapter 18, a conspiracy is an agreement between two or more individuals to commit an unlawful act. The exact requirements for determining the existence of a conspiracy were outlined and discussed in that chapter. In this chapter, we now build on that analysis in order to understand how the existence of a conspiracy can yield additional liability for its participants. Remember that conspiracy can be both an inchoate offense and a mode of liability. Under the latter flavor of the doctrine, the conspiracy is used as a link to make the defendant responsible for the crimes committed by her co-conspirators. Just like inchoate conspiracy, the defendant must specifically intend for the group to commit the target offense. To understand the doctrine, there are three essential questions: (i) How extensive is this vicarious liability; (ii) how does one define the outer scope of the "conspiracy" that the defendant is responsible for; and (iii) how does one withdraw from the conspiracy and terminate one's vicarious responsibility for the acts of co-conspirators?

1. *Pinkerton* Liability

In 1949, the Supreme Court examined the contours of conspiracy liability in *United States v. Pinkerton*, 328 U.S. 640 (1946). The Pinkerton brothers Walter and Daniel were involved in a bootlegging conspiracy that also involved violations of the Internal Revenue Code. Walter personally committed the crimes and was of course liable for them, but Daniel was guilty as well, under the theory that the conspiracy between them made Daniel vicariously responsible for Walter's acts too. In fact, Daniel was in prison when Walter committed the crimes, but the court concluded that this was no bar to Daniel's conviction under the doctrine of conspiracy.

Are there any limits to *Pinkerton* liability? In dicta, the court said that liability would not attach if the co-conspirator committed a crime that was not reasonably foreseeable to the defendant. This language of "reasonable foreseeability" has become the standard for *Pinkerton* liability. Conspirators are liable for crimes committed by co-conspirators that either (i) form part of the conspiratorial agreement or (ii) stray beyond the conspiratorial agreement but were nonetheless a reasonably foreseeable consequence of that agreement. One should therefore distinguish between two aspects of *Pinkerton* liability—one narrow and the other broad. Under the narrow aspect, the defendant is responsible for crimes perpetrated by co-conspirators that fall within the scope of the prior agreement. Under the broader aspect, the defendant is also responsible for crimes *outside* the scope of the agreement as long as they are reasonably foreseeable consequences of the conspiracy.

2. Scope of the Conspiracy

If the defendant is responsible not just for his own acts but also for the acts of his co-conspirators, it becomes essential to identify the temporal and geometric scope of the conspiracy. The wider the conspiracy, the greater the liability that the defendant will face. This issue is of immense importance in drug distribution conspiracies, which could be viewed as a collection of smaller, overlapping conspiracies, or as one big mega-conspiracy. For a defendant involved in this type of criminality, the difference is hugely important. If the distribution consists of an overlapping collection of smaller conspiracies, the defendant is only vicariously responsible for the crimes committed by the co-conspirators of his "local" conspiracy. However, if a court defines the distribution ring as composed of a single large conspiracy, then the defendant is vicariously responsible *for all of it*. This increases the number of counts as well as the total punishment the defendant will face. Courts are generally willing to aggregate overlapping conspiracies to a single overarching conspiracy when the defendant must have been aware that the endeavor involved other persons and transactions who are part of the agreement, even if the defendant never corresponded with, or even met, the other participants.

3. Withdrawing from a Conspiracy

How does a conspirator terminate his liability for the acts of conspirators? Generally speaking, acts already performed by co-conspirators cannot be disowned but the link to *future* acts could be severed if the defendant successfully withdraws from the conspiracy. The standard for withdrawal differs from jurisdiction to jurisdiction, but most require that the defendant perform an affirmative act to disavow or defeat the conspiracy. This can be accomplished in several ways: (i) informing the authorities of the criminal endeavor; (ii) communicating withdrawal to the co-conspirators; or (iii) dissolving the underlying agreement that forms the basis of the conspiracy. The common element among these possibilities is that the defendant must take some affirmative step to withdraw from the conspiracy; simply *refraining* from actively pursuing the objectives of the conspiracy is insufficient to satisfy the requirements of withdrawal. If the defendant has not successfully terminated his participation in the conspiracy, he remains vicariously responsible for the acts of co-conspirators, even if he is no longer actively engaged in supporting the criminality.

B. APPLICATION

1. *Pinkerton* Liability

The law has no shortage of doctrines that allow courts to attribute the actions of one individual to another. In the following case, the court applies the conspiracy doctrine to hold the defendant responsible for the actions of his co-conspirators. At the same time, though, the court struggles to articulate some outer limit on this practice. As you read the case, try to formulate the general rule regarding this limitation and how it might be applied in future cases.

United States v. Alvarez
U.S. Court of Appeals for the Eleventh Circuit
755 F.2d 830 (1985)

KRAVITCH, CIRCUIT JUDGE.

On December 2, 1982, in a run-down motel in the Little Havana section of Miami, Florida, a cocaine deal turned into tragedy when a shoot-out erupted between the dealers and two undercover special agents from the Bureau of Alcohol, Tobacco, and Firearms (BATF). During the shoot-out, one of the BATF agents was killed and the other agent, along with two of the cocaine dealers, was seriously wounded. Appellants Augustin Alvarez, Mario Simon, Victoriano "Macho" Concepcion, Eduardo Portal, Oscar Hernandez, Ramon Raymond, and Rolando Rios were convicted after a trial by jury on various charges arising from the cocaine deal and shoot-out. All of the appellants were convicted of conspiracy to possess with intent to distribute cocaine, 21 U.S.C. § 846, and possession with intent to distribute cocaine, 21 U.S.C. § 841(a)(1). In addition, Alvarez and Simon were convicted of first degree murder of a federal agent, 18 U.S.C. §§ 1111(a) and 1114, assault on a federal agent by means of a deadly and dangerous weapon, and use of a firearm to commit a felony. Portal, Concepcion, and Hernandez were convicted of second degree murder of a federal agent, and assault on a federal agent by means of a deadly and dangerous weapon.

The appellants now appeal their respective convictions, raising numerous claims of error. Among the issues raised by this appeal are . . . whether the second degree murder and assault convictions of Portal, Concepcion, and Hernandez were based on an improper extension of *Pinkerton v. United States*, 328 U.S. 640 (1946). After careful consideration of these issues and the others raised by the appellants, we conclude that the district court did not commit reversible error and the appellants received a fair trial in every respect. We therefore affirm the appellants' convictions.

FACTS

On December 1, 1982, at about 6:00 P.M., BATF Special Agents Joseph Benitez, Joseph Tirado, Ariel Rios, and Alex D'Atri, each acting in an undercover capacity, met with appellants Rolando Rios and Ramon Raymond in the parking lot of a convenience store in Homestead, Florida. The purpose of the meeting was to continue previously initiated negotiations for the purchase of two kilograms of cocaine. . . . A short time later, appellant Eduardo Portal arrived at the parking lot and began speaking with appellants Rios and Raymond. Portal informed Agents Rios, Tirado, and Benitez that he could make immediate delivery of two kilograms of cocaine. Portal then made a telephone call to appellant Victoriano "Macho" Concepcion. After the call, Portal told the agents that delivery of the cocaine could be made by noon the next day. . . .

The next day, at about 12:00 noon, Agent Rios telephoned Concepcion and arranged to meet with Concepcion and Portal in the parking lot of a restaurant in the Little Havana section of Miami. . . . The four men left the restaurant parking lot and proceeded, in two separate cars, to the Hurricane Motel on West Flagler Street in Miami. . . .

Inside the motel office, Concepcion and the two agents met appellants Augustin Alvarez and Oscar Hernandez. Hernandez was the manager of the Hurricane Motel, and Alvarez and Hernandez shared an apartment that adjoined the motel office. Alvarez told the agents that he was not the cocaine source, but that he would make a telephone call and arrange the cocaine delivery. Alvarez made the call and informed the agents that the cocaine would be delivered shortly. The five men waited in the living room of the Alvarez-Hernandez apartment. While they waited, Alvarez and Agent Rios conversed in Spanish, with Agent Rios translating into English for Agent D'Atri's benefit. According to D'Atri's testimony at trial, Alvarez stated, "In this business, you have to be careful. It's a dangerous business. You have to watch out for rip-offs and Federal agents." Alvarez also stated that he would never go back to prison, and that he would rather be dead than go back to prison. D'Atri answered, "It's always better to be alive than in prison." Alvarez then spoke to Hernandez in Spanish, and D'Atri asked Hernandez what Alvarez had said. Hernandez replied that Alvarez had said that he could never go back. . . .

At about 4:25 P.M., the agents noticed Simon's car in the parking lot of the motel. The agents entered the motel and found Simon, Alvarez, and Concepcion in the living room where the earlier meeting had taken place. Agent D'Atri asked Simon whether he had the cocaine, and Simon replied, "Yes, it is in the car." Simon went out to his car, and returned with a plastic bag. Concepcion took the bag from Simon and removed a cardboard box from the bag. Concepcion handed the box to D'Atri, who opened the box and found another plastic bag containing what appeared to be about one kilogram of cocaine. D'Atri then asked Agent Rios to go out to their car and get the money. . . . At about this time, the surveillance and backup agents began to converge on the motel.

D'Atri heard the surveillance and backup agents arrive at the door of the motel office. Suddenly, Agent Rios shouted, "No," and D'Atri heard a gunshot. . . . During this time, the surveillance and backup agents were attempting to force their way into the motel. The agents finally shot the lock off the door of the motel office and entered the living room. The agents found Agent Rios on the couch with a gunshot wound in the face . . .

WERE THE MURDER CONVICTIONS OF PORTAL, CONCEPCION, AND HERNANDEZ PROPER UNDER *PINKERTON V. UNITED STATES*?

Appellants Portal, Concepcion, and Hernandez contend that their murder convictions under Count III were based on an unprecedented and improper extension of *Pinkerton v. United States,* 328 U.S. 640 (1946). Under *Pinkerton,* each member of a conspiracy is criminally liable for any crime committed by a coconspirator during the course and in furtherance of the conspiracy, unless the crime "did not fall within the scope of the unlawful project, or was merely a part of the ramifications of the plan which could not be reasonably foreseen as a necessary or natural consequence of the unlawful agreement." The three appellants argue that murder is not a reasonably foreseeable consequence of a drug conspiracy, and that their murder convictions therefore should be reversed. We conclude that, although the murder convictions of the three appellants may represent an unprecedented application of *Pinkerton,* such an application is not improper.

Upon reviewing the record, we find ample evidence to support the jury's conclusion that the murder was a reasonably foreseeable consequence of the drug conspiracy alleged in the indictment. In making this determination, we rely on two critical factors. First, the evidence clearly established that the drug conspiracy was designed to effectuate the sale of a large quantity of cocaine. The conspirators agreed to sell Agents Rios and D'Atri three kilograms of cocaine for a total price of $147,000. The transaction that led to the murder involved the sale of one kilogram of cocaine for $49,000. In short, the drug conspiracy was no nickel-and-dime operation; under any standards, the amount of drugs and money involved was quite substantial.

Second, based on the amount of drugs and money involved, the jury was entitled to infer that, at the time the cocaine sale was arranged, the conspirators must have been aware of the likelihood (1) that at least some of their number would be carrying weapons, and (2) that deadly force would be used, if necessary, to protect the conspirators' interests. We have previously acknowledged the "nexus" between weapons and drugs, and we have also recognized that weapons have become "tools of the trade" for those involved in the distribution of illicit drugs. As the former Fifth Circuit has stated, "Experience on the trial and appellate benches has taught that substantial dealers in narcotics keep firearms on their premises as tools of the trade almost to the same extent as they keep scales, glassine bags, cutting equipment, and other narcotic equipment." In light of these observations, and in view of the amount of drugs and money involved in the instant case, the jury's inference was both reasonable and proper.

In our opinion, these two critical factors provided ample support for the jury's conclusion that the murder was a reasonably foreseeable consequence of the drug conspiracy alleged in the indictment. In addition, we note the evidence at trial indicating that at least two of the conspirators were extremely nervous about the possibility of a rip-off or a drug bust. During a lull in the negotiations, Alvarez observed, "In this business, you have to be careful. It's a dangerous business. You have to watch out for rip-offs and Federal agents." Alvarez also stated that he would never go back to prison, and that he would rather be dead than go back to prison. Alvarez' statements clearly implied that he contemplated the use of deadly force, if necessary, to avoid a rip-off or apprehension by Federal agents. The evidence also indicated that, immediately prior to the shoot-out, Simon looked nervously out the window while fidgeting with a leather pouch that was suspected to contain a weapon. The jury properly could take this additional evidence into account in reaching its conclusion about the foreseeability of the murder.

Because we find that the evidence in this case was more than sufficient to allow a reasonable jury to conclude that the murder was a reasonably foreseeable consequence of the drug conspiracy alleged in the indictment, we hold that the court did not err by submitting the *Pinkerton* issue to the jury.

The three appellants also contend that, even if the murder was reasonably foreseeable, their murder convictions nevertheless should be reversed. The appellants argue that the murder was sufficiently distinct from the intended purposes of the drug conspiracy, and that their individual roles in the conspiracy were sufficiently minor, that they should not be held responsible for the murder. We are not persuaded.

It is well established that, under the *Pinkerton* doctrine, "[a] co-conspirator is vicariously liable for the acts of another co-conspirator even though he may not have directly participated in those acts, his role in the crime was minor, or the evidence against a co-defendant more damaging." Thus, in a typical *Pinkerton* case, the court need not inquire into the individual culpability of a particular conspirator, so long as the substantive crime was a reasonably foreseeable consequence of the conspiracy.

We acknowledge that the instant case is not a typical *Pinkerton* case. Here, the murder of Agent Rios was not within the originally intended scope of the conspiracy, but instead occurred as a result of an unintended turn of events. We have not found, nor has the government cited, any authority for the proposition that all conspirators, regardless of individual culpability, may be held responsible under *Pinkerton* for reasonably foreseeable but originally unintended substantive crimes. Furthermore, we are mindful of the potential due process limitations on the *Pinkerton* doctrine in cases involving attenuated relationships between the conspirator and the substantive crime.

Nevertheless, these considerations do not require us to reverse the murder convictions of Portal, Concepcion, and Hernandez, for we cannot accept the three appellants' assessment of their individual culpability. All three were more than "minor" participants in the drug conspiracy. Portal served as a look-out in front of the Hurricane Motel during part of the negotiations that led to the shoot-out, and the evidence indicated that he was armed. Concepcion introduced the agents to Alvarez, the apparent leader of the conspiracy, and was present when the shoot-out started. Finally, Hernandez, the manager of the motel, allowed the drug transactions to take place on the premises and acted as a translator during part of the negotiations that led to the shoot-out.

In addition, all three appellants had actual knowledge of at least some of the circumstances and events leading up to the murder. The evidence that Portal was carrying a weapon demonstrated that he anticipated the possible use of deadly force to protect the conspirators' interests. Moreover, both Concepcion and Hernandez were present when Alvarez stated that he would rather be dead than go back to prison, indicating that they, too, were aware that deadly force might be used to prevent apprehension by Federal agents.

We find the individual culpability of Portal, Concepcion, and Hernandez sufficient to support their murder convictions under *Pinkerton,* despite the fact that the murder was not within the originally intended scope of the conspiracy. In addition, based on the same evidence, we conclude that the relationship between the three appellants and the murder was not so attenuated as to run afoul of the potential due process limitations on the *Pinkerton* doctrine. We therefore hold that *Pinkerton* liability for the murder of Agent Rios properly was imposed on the three appellants, and we decline to reverse their murder convictions on this ground. . . .

NOTES & QUESTIONS ON PINKERTON *LIABILITY*

1. *Vicarious responsibility.* The *Alvarez* case is a classic example of the broad version of *Pinkerton* liability. The target of the conspiratorial agreement was narcotics distribution. However, the members of the conspiracy also were prosecuted for murdering a federal agent—because one member of the conspiracy shot the undercover agents. Is it morally fair to hold everyone responsible for the murder even if that was not the original plan? Answer this question with reference both to utilitarian theories of deterrence and retributive theories based on the defendant's culpability. How would you describe the mental state of Portal, Concepcion, and Hernandez with regard to the resulting death? Was it purpose, knowledge, recklessness, or negligence? Viewed in this way, is the mental state sufficient to provide the foundation for a murder conviction? For an argument that the *Pinkerton* doctrine is inherently problematic, see Bruce A. Antkowiak, *The* Pinkerton *Problem,* 115 Penn St. L. Rev. 607, 610-11 (2011) ("Through *Pinkerton,* courts dilute and radically alter the elements of a substantive offense (especially its mens rea) in violation of the legislative will and a cornucopia of constitutional rights the United States Supreme Court has championed during the last twenty years.").

HYPOTHETICAL

The classic example is the getaway driver who conspires with a bank robber. The bank robber is armed with a gun and the getaway driver knows that the robber is carrying a gun. Before they get to the bank, the driver says to the robber: "Nobody gets hurt, OK? I want this to be a clean robbery. In and out without any violence." The robber replies: "Got it. Agreed." The robber gets out of the car and runs into the bank. When he comes out carrying the money, he tells the driver that he also killed the teller. What result? Assume that the bank robber was a convicted felon who had previously served time for murder.

The driver is clearly guilty of robbery because robbery was the target offense of the conspiracy. However, in a jurisdiction that applies *Pinkerton,* would you also convict the getaway driver for murder? The result depends on whether it was reasonably foreseeable that the robber would stray from the plan and commit violence. Should it matter why the robber committed the murder? Imagine that he did it simply because he acted impulsively and without provocation. What result? Now imagine that he committed the murder because the teller was about to press a panic button that would alert the police to the robbery. Same or different result?

2. *Minor participants and constitutional constraints.* The court in *Alvarez* notes that the Due Process Clause imposes limitations on the application of the *Pinkerton* rule. Although this limitation is not universally recognized, it is recognized in several circuits. See, e.g., *United States v. Castaneda*, 9 F.3d 761 (9th Cir. 1993). If a defendant is a truly minor participant in a conspiracy, or resides on the very outer margins of the endeavor, some courts will refuse to apply the *Pinkerton* rule. Mark L. Noferi, *Towards Attenuation: A "New" Due Process Limit on* Pinkerton *Conspiracy Liability*, 33 Am. J. Crim. L. 91 (2006). In *Alvarez*, though, the court refused to apply this limitation and concluded that Portal, Concepcion, and Hernandez were all sufficiently involved to be held responsible for murder. Why? Was it because they were deeply involved in the drug deal? Or was it because they were sufficiently put on notice that Alvarez was armed and had announced his intention to do whatever it took to avoid going back to prison? If it is the second, why is this relevant? Is it because this knowledge would be sufficient to meet the "depraved indifference to life" standard that applies in implied malice murder cases?

3. *Objective or subjective foreseeability.* *Pinkerton*'s notion of "reasonable foreseeability" can be understood objectively or subjectively. Under the objective view, the fact finder should ask whether the outcome was objectively foreseeable from the perspective of a reasonable person in similar circumstances. Under the subjective view, the fact finder should ask whether the outcome was reasonably foreseeable to the defendant in this case, i.e., whether he was aware of the possibility that a co-conspirator might commit the further offense. What is the difference between the subjective and objective interpretations of *Pinkerton*? Quite a lot, actually. Under the subjective view, the defendant must have been aware of the risk yet consciously disregarded it and participated anyway—a mental state akin to recklessness. Under the objective view, however, the defendant need not have been aware of the risk—though he should have been because a reasonable person in similarly circumstances would have foreseen the results. This latter mental state is similar to negligence. See Alex Kreit, *Vicarious Criminal Liability and the Constitutional Dimensions of* Pinkerton, 57 Am. U. L. Rev. 585, 589 (2008). Should *Pinkerton* liability be based on recklessness or negligence as an underlying mental state? Most jurisdictions that have considered the issue have understood *Pinkerton* as applying objective foreseeability. *State v. Bridges*, 133 N.J. 447 (1993) (upholding *Pinkerton* liability under New Jersey law based on an objective standard of reasonable foreseeability). A similar rule exists for accomplice liability. *State v. Earl*, 702 N.W.2d 711 (Minn. 2005) (upholding objective theory for accomplice liability); *People v. Brigham*, 216 Cal. App. 3d 1039, 1057 (1989).

4. Pinkerton *controversy.* Jurisdictions are split on the *Pinkerton* rule. Although the rule still applies in the federal courts and some state courts, it is disfavored in many state jurisdictions and the Model Penal Code rejects it. *People v. McGee,* 49 N.Y.2d 48 (1979). The basic criticism is that the expansive version of the doctrine makes liability for intentional crimes, such as murder, possible based on a defendant's lower mental state, including mere negligence. Many scholars consider this an illegitimate inflation of a defendant's culpability and blameworthiness. See Jens David Ohlin, *The Law of Conspiracy and Collective Reason,* 98 J. Crim. L. & Criminology 147 (2007). A few jurisdictions recognize the validity of the criticism but are unwilling to entirely dispense with *Pinkerton* liability and instead limit the doctrine to general intent crimes. *Bolden v. State,* 124 P.3d 191 (Nev. 2005) (rejecting *Pinkerton* liability for specific intent crimes). Other jurisdictions refuse to apply *Pinkerton* liability in first-degree murder cases because that crime requires specific intent. *United States v. Cherry,* 217 F.3d 811 (10th Cir. 2000).

5. *Conspiracy and accomplice liability compared.* Conspiracy liability requires an underlying agreement. Accomplice liability *may* involve an underlying agreement but need not. It could, for instance, involve assistance or encouragement provided in the absence of an agreement to commit the crime. In terms of their similarities, both doctrines have limited versions and expansive versions. Under their limited varieties, the accomplice or co-conspirator is responsible when someone else commits the target crime. Under their expansive varieties, the accomplice or conspirator is responsible when others stray from the target crime and commit a *greater* offense. Furthermore, both have similar limitations on the expansive version of the doctrine. Although the terms are sometimes interchangeable, the most common usage of the phrase for conspiracy is that the charged offense was reasonably foreseeable, while for accomplice liability it is that the charged offense was a natural and probable consequence of the endeavor.

For a clear illustration of the difference between pre-arrangement (conspiracy) and spontaneous contribution (accomplice liability), consider the disturbing facts of *Commonwealth v. Cook,* 10 Mass. App. Ct. 668, 411 N.E.2d 1326 (1980). In that case, the Cook brothers, Maurice and Dennis, were socializing with a 17-year-old girl. The three went for a short walk in a wooded area in order to get to a nearby gas station. When the girl tripped and fell to the ground, Maurice decided to rape her. Dennis shouted words of encouragement and also held Maurice's belt during the assault. Maurice was convicted of rape, but the more controversial question was Dennis's liability for the assault. Dennis was an accomplice to the rape due to his spontaneous assistance to his brother. But was Dennis also a conspirator? The court said no because there was no prearranged plan or agreement between the Cook brothers. The court continued:

PROBLEM CASE

Ross Ulbricht launched a website called "Silk Road," which was designed to facilitate anonymous, untraceable transactions between users of the site. In theory, users could use Silk Road to buy and sell anything. In reality, thousands of users almost always used the site to buy and sell illegal drugs. The transactions were paid for using Bitcoins—a decentralized virtual currency that is used both for legitimate business and illicit purposes.

Law enforcement authorities shut down Silk Road in October 2013. Ulbricht was charged by

Supporters of Ross Ulbricht protest in front of a Manhattan federal courthouse on the first day of jury selection for his trial

the Justice Department with engaging in a continuing criminal enterprise and narcotics distribution through the Internet. Ulbricht had not personally sold or purchased drugs himself but provided the infrastructure for others to do so. Nonetheless, federal prosecutors linked Ulbricht to the drug distribution through the conspiracy doctrine; essentially Silk Road was one massive conspiracy. Moreover, prosecutors contended that Ulbricht had a stake in the illegal transactions because he earned $13 million in commissions from them. His defense attorney argued that he created Silk Road as an economics experiment but turned over its daily operation to an anonymous administrator named "Dread Pirate Roberts." The jury convicted him anyway.

On May 29, 2015, District Judge Katherine B. Forrest sentenced Ulbricht to life in prison. She told him that his operation was "terribly destructive to our social fabric." Do you agree that Ulbricht was responsible as a conspirator for the illegal drug trade on his site? And if the answer is yes, was a life sentence the appropriate punishment?

"The fact that Maurice's attack began immediately after the victim found herself in a compromising situation suggests spontaneity of action on his part rather than the purposeful execution of a predetermined plan. From that point on, the defendant's conduct fits the classic paradigm of an accomplice adding encouragement to a crime in progress." *Id.* at 672.

2. Scope of the Conspiracy

Vicarious liability depends on the scope of the conspiracy. The larger the conspiracy, the more liability the defendant inherits from the co-conspirators. The following two cases represent opposing findings to this question. In one, the court finds a single conspiracy, while in the other the court finds a series of independent conspiracies. What is the crucial difference?

People v. Bruno

U.S. Court of Appeals for the Second Circuit
105 F.2d 921 (1939)

PER CURIAM.

Bruno and Iacono were indicted along with 86 others for a conspiracy to import, sell and possess narcotics; some were acquitted; others, besides these two, were convicted but they alone appealed. They complain, (1), that if the evidence proved anything, it proved a series of separate conspiracies, and not a single one, as alleged in the indictment; (2) that unlawful telephone "taps" were allowed in evidence against them; (3) that the judge refused to charge the jury properly as to the effect of their failure to take the stand; and (4) that there was not enough evidence to support the verdict.

The first point was made at the conclusion of the prosecution's case: the defendants then moved to dismiss the indictment on the ground that several conspiracies had been proved, and not the one alleged. The evidence allowed the jury to find that there had existed over a substantial period of time a conspiracy embracing a great number of persons, whose object was to smuggle narcotics into the Port of New York and distribute them to addicts both in this city and in Texas and Louisiana. This required the cooperation of four groups of persons; the smugglers who imported the drugs; the middlemen who paid the smugglers and distributed to retailers; and two groups of retailers—one in New York and one in Texas and Louisiana—who supplied the addicts. The defendants assert that there were, therefore, at least three separate conspiracies; one between the smugglers and the middlemen, and one between the middlemen and each group of retailers. The evidence did not disclose any cooperation or communication between the smugglers and either group of retailers, or between the two groups of retailers themselves; however, the smugglers knew that the middlemen must sell to retailers, and the retailers knew that the middlemen must buy of importers of one sort or another. Thus the conspirators at one end of the chain knew that the unlawful business would not, and could not, stop with their buyers; and those at the other end knew that it had not begun with their sellers. That being true, a jury might have found that all the accused were embarked upon a venture, in all parts of which each was a participant, and an abettor in the sense that the success of that part with which he was immediately concerned, was dependent upon the success of the whole. That distinguishes the situation from that in *United States v. Peoni*, 100 F.2d 401 (2d Cir. 1938), where Peoni, the accused, did not know that Regno, his buyer, was to sell the counterfeit bills to Dorsey, since Regno might equally well have passed them to innocent persons himself. It might still be argued that there were two conspiracies; one including the smugglers, the middlemen and the New York group, and the other, the smugglers, the middlemen and the Texas & Louisiana group, for there was apparently no privity between the two groups of retailers. That too would be fallacious. Clearly, quoad the smugglers, there was but one conspiracy, for it was of no moment to them whether the middlemen sold to one or more groups of retailers, provided they had a market somewhere. So too of any retailer; he knew that he was a necessary link in a scheme of distribution, and the others, whom he knew to be convenient to its execution, were as much parts of a single undertaking or enterprise as two salesmen in the same shop. We think therefore that there was only one conspiracy. . . .

The last point is as to the sufficiency of the evidence. There is nothing to be said about this as to Bruno, who was plainly guilty. Iacono was probably guilty also, but the evidence to establish his guilt was tenuous. All that was shown was that he had received in New York seven money orders from members of the Louisiana retailers, some of them taken out in assumed names. There were for about $6,800 in the aggregate, but it did not appear that they covered the proceeds from the sales of narcotics. Even if these documents were enough to convict Iacono of complicity in some sort of illicit enterprise—itself a somewhat gratuitous assumption—the accused were shown to have been a disreputable lot and all sorts of ventures may have been afoot among them. The remittances should have been more closely interwoven with the sale of narcotics. The case is close, but we think that not enough was shown.

Kotteakos v. United States
Supreme Court of the United States
328 U.S. 750 (1946)

RUTLEDGE, J.

The only question is whether petitioners have suffered substantial prejudice from being convicted of a single general conspiracy by evidence which the Government admits proved not one conspiracy but some eight or more different ones of the same sort executed through a common key figure, Simon Brown. Petitioners were convicted under the general conspiracy section of the Criminal Code, 18 U.S.C. § 88, 18 U.S.C.A. § 88, of conspiring to violate the provisions of the National Housing Act. . . .

The indictment named thirty-two defendants, including the petitioners. The gist of the conspiracy, as alleged, was that the defendants had sought to induce various financial institutions to grant credit, with the intent that the loans or advances would then be offered to the Federal Housing Administration for insurance upon applications containing false and fraudulent information. . . .

Simon Brown, who pleaded guilty, was the common and key figure in all of the transactions proven. He was president of the Brownie Lumber Company. Having had experience in obtaining loans under the National Housing Act, he undertook to act as broker in placing for others loans for modernization and renovation, charging a five per cent commission for his services. Brown knew, when he obtained the loans, that the proceeds were not to be used for the purposes stated in the applications.

In May, 1939, petitioner Lekacos told Brown that he wished to secure a loan in order to finance opening a law office, to say the least a hardly auspicious professional launching. Brown made out the application, as directed by Lekacos, to state that the purpose of the loan was to modernize a house belonging to the estate of Lekacos' father. Lekacos obtained the money. Later in the same year Lekacos secured another loan through Brown, the application being in the names of his brother and sister-in-law. Lekacos also received part of the proceeds of a loan for which one Gerakeris, a defendant who pleaded guilty, had applied.

In June, 1939, Lekacos sent Brown an application for a loan signed by petitioner Kotteakos. It contained false statements. Brown placed the loan, and Kotteakos thereafter sent Brown applications on behalf of other persons. Two were made out in the names of fictitious persons. The proceeds were received by Kotteakos and petitioner Regenbogen, his partner in the cigarette and pinball machine business. Regenbogen, together with Kotteakos, had indorsed one of the applications. Kotteakos also sent to Brown an application for a loan in Regenbogen's name. This was for modernization of property not owned by Regenbogen. The latter, however, repaid the money in about three months after he received it.

The evidence against the other defendants whose cases were submitted to the jury was similar in character. They too had transacted business with Brown relating to National Housing Act loans. But no connection was shown between them and petitioners, other than that Brown had been the instrument in each instance for obtaining the loans. In many cases the other defendants did not have any relationship with one another, other than Brown's connection with each transaction. As the Circuit Court of Appeals said, there were "at least eight, and perhaps more, separate and independent groups, none of which had any connection with any other, though all dealt independently with Brown as their agent." As the Government puts it, the pattern was "that of separate spokes meeting at a common center," though we may add without the rim of the wheel to enclose the spokes.

The proof therefore admittedly made out a case, not of a single conspiracy, but of several, notwithstanding only one was charged in the indictment. The Court of Appeals aptly drew analogy in the comment, "Thieves who dispose of their loot to a single receiver—a single 'fence'—do not by that fact alone become confederates: they may, but it takes more than knowledge that he is a 'fence' to make them such." It stated that the trial judge "was plainly wrong in supposing that upon the evidence there could be a single conspiracy; and in the view he took of the law, he should have dismissed the indictment." Nevertheless the appellate court held the error not prejudicial, saying among other things that "especially since guilt was so manifest, it was 'proper' to join the conspiracies," and "to reverse the conviction would be a miscarriage of justice." This is indeed the Government's entire position. It does not now contend that there was no variance in proof from the single conspiracy charged in the indictment. Admitting that separate and distinct conspiracies were shown, it urges that the variance was not prejudicial to the petitioners.

In *Berger v. United States*, 295 U.S. 78, this Court held that in the circumstances presented the variance was not fatal where one conspiracy was charged and two were proved, relating to contemporaneous transactions involving counterfeit money. . . . The Court held the variance not fatal, resting its ruling on what has become known as "the harmless error statute," section 269 of the Judicial Code. . . .

Applying that section, the Court likened the situation to one where the four persons implicated in the two conspiracies had been charged as conspirators in separate counts, but with a failure in the proof to connect one of them (Berger) with one of the conspiracies, and a resulting conviction under one count and acquittal under the other. . . . The question we have to determine is whether the same ruling may be extended to a situation in which one conspiracy only is charged and at least eight having separate, though similar objects, are made out by the evidence, if believed; and in which the more numerous participants in the different schemes were, on the whole, except for one, different persons who did not know or have anything to do with one another. . . .

The Government's theory seems to be, in ultimate logical reach, that the error presented by the variance is insubstantial and harmless, if the evidence offered specifically and properly to convict each defendant would be sufficient to sustain his conviction, if submitted in a separate trial. For reasons we have stated and in view of the authorities cited, this is not and cannot be the test under section 269. But in apparent support of its view the Government argues that there was no prejudice here because the results show that the jury exercised discrimination as among the defendants whose cases were submitted to it. As it points out, the jury acquitted some, disagreed as to others, and found still others guilty. From this it concludes that the jury was not confused and, apparently, reached the same result as would have been reached or would be likely, if the convicted defendants had been or now should be tried separately.

One difficulty with this is that the trial court itself was confused in the charge which it gave to guide the jury in deliberation. The court instructed: "The indictment charges but one conspiracy, and to convict each of the defendants of a conspiracy, the Government would have to prove, and you would have to find, that each of the defendants was a member of that conspiracy. You cannot divide it up. It is one conspiracy, and the question is whether or not each of the defendants or which of the defendants, are members of that conspiracy."

On its face, as the Court of Appeals said, this portion of the charge was plainly wrong in application to the proof made; and the error pervaded the entire charge, not merely the portion quoted. The jury could not possibly have found, upon the evidence, that there was only one conspiracy. The trial court was of the view that one conspiracy was made out by showing that each defendant was linked to Brown in one or more transactions, and that it was possible on the evidence for the jury to conclude that all were in a common adventure because of this fact and the similarity of purpose presented in the various applications for loans.

This view, specifically embodied throughout the instructions, obviously confuses the common purpose of a single enterprise with the several, though similar, purposes of numerous separate adventures of like character. It may be that, notwithstanding the misdirection, the jury actually understood correctly the purport of the evidence, as the Government now concedes it to have been; and came to the conclusion that the petitioners were guilty only of the separate conspiracies in which the proof shows they respectively participated. But, in the face of the misdirection and in the circumstances of this case, we cannot assume that the lay triers of fact were so well informed upon the law or that they disregarded the permission expressly given to ignore that vital difference.

As we have said, the error permeated the entire charge, indeed the entire trial. Not only did it permit the jury to find each defendant guilty of conspiring with thirty-five other potential co-conspirators, or any less number as the proof might turn out for acquittal of some, when none of the evidence would support such a conviction, as the proof did turn out in fact. It had other effects. One was to prevent the court from giving a precautionary instruction such as would be appropriate, perhaps, required, in cases where related but separate conspiracies are tried together under section 557 of the Code, namely, that the jury should take care to consider the evidence relating to each conspiracy separately from that relating to each other conspiracy charged. The court here was careful to caution the jury to consider each defendant's case separately, in determining his participation in "the scheme" charged. But this obviously does not, and could not, go to keeping distinct conspiracies distinct, in view of the court's conception of the case.

Moreover, the effect of the court's misconception extended also to the proof of overt acts. Carrying forward his premise that the jury could find one conspiracy on the evidence, the trial judge further charged that, if the jury found a conspiracy, "then the acts or the statements of any of those whom you so find to be conspirators between the two dates that I have mentioned, may be considered by you in evidence as against all of the defendants whom you so find to be members of the conspiracy." (Emphasis added.) The instructions in this phase also declared: "It is not necessary, as a matter of law, that an overt act be charged against each defendant. It is sufficient if the conspiracy be established and the defendant be found to be a member of the conspiracy—it is sufficient to allege overt acts on the part of any others who may have been members of the conspiracy, if those acts were done in furtherance of, and for the purpose of accomplishing the conspiracy."

On those instructions it was competent not only for the jury to find that all of the defendants were parties to a single common plan, design and scheme, where none was shown by the proof, but also for them to impute to each defendant the acts and statements of the others without reference to whether they related to one of the schemes proven or another, and to find an overt act affecting all in conduct which admittedly could only have affected some. True, the Court of Appeals painstakingly examined the evidence directly relating to each petitioner and concluded he had not been prejudiced in this manner. That judgment was founded largely in the fact that each was clearly shown to have shared in the fraudulent phase of the conspiracy in which he participated. Even so, we do not understand how it can be concluded, in the face of the instruction, that the jury considered and was influenced by nothing else.

All this the Government seeks to justify as harmless error. Again the basis is that because the proof was sufficient to establish the participation of each petitioner in one or more of several smaller conspiracies, none of them could have been prejudiced because all were found guilty, upon such proof, of being members of a single larger conspiracy of the same general character. . . .

We do not agree. . . . Numbers are vitally important in trial, especially in criminal matters. Guilt with us remains individual and personal, even as respects conspiracies. It is not a matter of mass application. There are times when of necessity, because of the nature and scope of the particular federation, large numbers of persons taking part must be tried together or perhaps not at all, at any rate as respects some. When many conspire, they invite mass trial by their conduct. Even so, the proceedings are exceptional to our tradition and call for use of every safeguard to individualize each defendant in his relation to the mass. Wholly different is it with those who join together with only a few, though many others may be doing the same and though some of them may line up with more than one group.

Criminal they may be, but it is not the criminality of mass conspiracy. They do not invite mass trial by their conduct. Nor does our system tolerate it. That way lies the drift toward totalitarian institutions. True, this may be inconvenient for prosecution. But our Government is not one of mere convenience or efficiency. It too has a stake, with every citizen, in his being afforded our historic individual protections, including those surrounding criminal trials. About them we dare not become careless or complacent when that fashion has become rampant over the earth.

Here toleration went too far. We do not think that either Congress, when it enacted section 269 . . . intended to authorize the Government to string together, for common trial, eight or more separate and distinct crimes, conspiracies related in kind though they might be, when the only nexus among them lies in the fact that one man participated in all. . . . But if the practice here followed were to stand, we see nothing to prevent its extension to a dozen, a score, or more conspiracies and at the same time to scores of men involved, if at all, only separately in them. The dangers for transference of guilt from one to another across the line separating conspiracies, subconsciously or otherwise, are so great that no one really can say prejudice to substantial right has not taken place. Section 269 had no purpose to go so far. The line must be drawn somewhere. . . . Accordingly the judgments are reversed. . . .

NOTES & QUESTIONS ON CONSPIRATORIAL SCOPE

1. *Hubs and spokes.* Are *Bruno* and *Kotteakos* consistent judgments? In one, the court said there was a single conspiracy, but in the other the court said there were multiple conspiracies. What is the relevant difference? *Bruno* involved a large narcotics distribution ring with multiple smugglers and retailers. Each had to know that there were others involved in the operations, even if they had never met their supposed confederates. It was enough that the retailers were not selling *all* of the drugs; by this fact alone they had to know that other retailers were engaged in selling the remaining drugs. Expressed in the metaphor of the wheel, the separate spokes were connected because each retailer knew that the wheel had other spokes. In contrast, *Kotteakos* involved a series of conspiracies overlapping with a common criminal, Simon Brown. Should that have been enough to consider Brown a hub at the center of one

large conspiracy? No, because unlike in *Bruno*, there was no reason for each conspirator to believe that Brown *required* other confederates to complete his transactions. The fact is, he *did* have other confederates, but this was a contingent fact—not a necessary fact. It was contingent on the fact that he was repeating the conspiracy multiple times, as opposed to in *Bruno* where a large stash of narcotics necessarily had to be divided up between retailers through a division of labor.

2. *Association of the parties.* In order for a court to hold that a single conspiracy existed between its members (as was the case in *Bruno*), the court must conclude that there was an agreement or association among them, rather than a common purpose between them, which is legally insufficient. For example, consider *United States v. McDermott*, 245 F.3d 133, 137 (2d Cir. 2001). The case involved an insider-trading conspiracy overlapping with a love triangle between the president of an investment bank (James McDermott), his mistress (Kathryn Gannon, an adult film actress), and her other lover that she was seeing on the side (Anthony Pomponio). Prosecutors alleged that McDermott passed the information to Gannon who in turn provided the information to Pomponio. Both Gannon and Pomponio made substantial profits from trades based on the stock tips. Was this a single conspiracy? McDermott knew that he was passing inside information to Gannon, but had no idea that she was also providing it to Pomponio, her other boyfriend. According to the court: "[T]he government here asks us to redefine a conspiracy by its purpose, rather than by the agreement of its members to that purpose. The government argues that from the perspective of Gannon and Pomponio, albeit not from McDermott's perspective, there was a unitary purpose to commit insider trading based on information furnished by McDermott. According to the government, therefore, McDermott was part of the conspiracy even though he did not agree to pass information to both Gannon and Pomponio." This argument, the court held, was inconsistent with the requirement that the underlying agreement extend to all members of the conspiracy.

3. *Temporal scope of the conspiracy.* Both *Bruno* and *Kotteakos* are about the geometric scope of the conspiracy. Similar questions can be asked about the temporal scope of the conspiracy. The longer it lasts, the longer the defendant is on the hook for the acts of the co-conspirators. But when does the conspiracy expire? The default answer is that the conspiracy expires when the conspiratorial objective is achieved, i.e., the target offense is successfully completed. However, in some instances prosecutors have argued that the conspiracy endured even after the target crime was committed, with the new objective of avoiding police detection and concealing evidence of the crime. Courts are generally skeptical of such arguments and require direct evidence of an explicit agreement (as opposed to a mere inference) to cooperate to conceal their criminality. *Grunewald v. United States*, 353 U.S. 391 (1957). What if the police

intervene and defeat the conspiracy? Some jurisdictions assume that this terminates the conspiracy, though the Supreme Court has asserted that for purposes
of federal law it does not. *United States v. Jimenez Recio*, 537 U.S. 270 (2003)
("conspiracy does not automatically terminate simply because the Government,
unbeknownst to some of the conspirators" has defeated the conspiracy's
object). Another way of putting the point is that a conspiracy may continue
even after the target of the conspiracy becomes *impossible* to achieve. Also,
it is clearly the case that a conspiracy can endure even after one of its members
has been arrested. *United States v. Collazo-Aponte*, 216 F.3d 163 (1st Cir.
2000); *United States v. Mealy*, 851 F.2d 890, 901 (7th Cir. 1988).

   4. *Retroactive liability.*   Generally speaking, joining a conspiracy does not
make the new member guilty of the substantive crimes committed by co-conspirators prior to the defendant's arrival in the conspiracy. In other words,
Pinkerton liability is not retroactive. *United States v. Blackmon*, 839 F.2d
900, 908 (2d Cir. 1988). However, prior acts of co-conspirators can be used
to build a case for conspiracy as a substantive offense to be applied against
the new member. These two issues are frequently confused. For conspiracy
as a substantive offense, there is no requirement that the defendant was a member of the conspiracy at its inception.

HYPOTHETICAL

Say a group of conspirators agrees to commit a murder and they make preparations to bring the plan to fruition. This includes the performance of several overt acts in furtherance of the conspiracy, such as procuring weapons and ammunition. During that time, one member of the conspiracy commits a robbery to steal an assault rifle. Then, before the murder is carried out, a new member joins the conspiracy. What is the scope of the new member's liability? The new member could be convicted of conspiracy to commit murder even though *that* conspiracy predated the defendant's joining the endeavor. But because *Pinkerton* liability is not retroactive, conspiracy as a mode of liability cannot be used to prosecute the new member for the substantive offense of robbery.

---

3. Withdrawal

Starting a conspiracy is easy: You agree to commit a crime. How do you get out?
That is not so easy. Courts have struggled to define the exact standard for withdrawing from a conspiracy and terminating one's *Pinkerton* liability for future
acts. The following case explains the standard but refuses to grant the defense
to the defendant.

United States v. Schweihs

U.S. Court of Appeals for the Seventh Circuit
971 F.2d 1302 (1992)

FAIRCHILD, SENIOR CIRCUIT JUDGE.

The fifteen counts of the indictment of Schweihs and Daddino all involved the Hobbs Act, 18 U.S.C. § 1951. The Act punishes anyone who affects interstate commerce by extortion, or attempts or conspires so to do. . . .

BACKGROUND

For purposes of this opinion, we construe the evidence in the light most favorable to the verdict. William Wemette was the owner of an adult video store in Chicago. He had a business assistant and friend by the name of Leonard Cross who lived with him. From about 1974 to 1988, Wemette and Cross paid "street tax" to members of the Chicago "Outfit," an organized crime group, apparently willing and able to harm anyone who would not pay. Wemette and Cross paid the "street tax" to protect themselves and their business from harm. In 1984, Wemette's business was having financial difficulties, but Amato, the current "street tax" collector, informed Wemette that if he did not pay the tax, his business would be shut down possibly by an accident or a fire. Wemette complained to other organized crime figures and was told to contact Frank Schweihs. He met with Schweihs, whom he knew had a reputation as a violent person, and Schweihs arranged for a new person, Anthony Daddino, to begin collecting the "street tax" payments. Thereafter, Daddino collected $1,100 per month from Wemette and Cross.

In 1987, Wemette contacted the FBI about the "street tax" payments. Wemette agreed to work undercover for the FBI and record his conversations with Daddino and Schweihs. After several months, Wemette, at the direction of the FBI, refused to make any further payments to Daddino until his protests about his competitor's expansion were heard by someone higher up in the "Outfit." Daddino advised him against withholding the payments and warned him that he might not like the next guy that came to collect. Schweihs then began to collect the monthly payments from Wemette and Cross. When Schweihs came to their apartment to collect the tax, he often discussed the possibility of expanding or moving Wemette's business and making himself a partner in that business. On numerous occasions, Schweihs mentioned his connections with the "Outfit." They also discussed the competition from Steven Toushin's nearby video business, and Schweihs asked Wemette and Cross for information about Toushin and his business. Video recordings and transcripts of most of these conversations were introduced at the trial. . . .

Jury Instructions

Daddino challenges the district court's refusal to give two of his proposed jury instructions, one on withdrawal from the conspiracy and the other on the elements of extortion. The district court refused to give any instruction on withdrawal from the conspiracy because it found no evidence in the record to support a finding of withdrawal by Daddino. The district court gave an instruction on the elements of extortion but did not use the wording proposed by Daddino.

Generally, a defendant is entitled to an instruction on any defense recognized in the law and supported by sufficient evidence to allow a reasonable jury to find in the defendant's favor. The defendant bears the burden of coming forward with evidence of withdrawal, but once the defendant advances sufficient evidence, the prosecution must disprove the defense of withdrawal beyond a reasonable doubt.

Daddino argues that the evidence supported an instruction on his withdrawal from the conspiracy. A reasonable jury could have found that on October 1, 1987, Wemette, according to Schweihs' instructions, told Daddino not to come to his place anymore and that Daddino responded, "Okay, buddy," and was never seen by Wemette again. The issue is whether this evidence was sufficient to raise a withdrawal defense and place the burden upon the government to disprove that defense.

 Withdrawal requires more than a mere cessation of activity on the part of the defendant; it requires some affirmative action which disavows or defeats the purpose of the conspiracy. *United States v. Andrus,* 775 F.2d 825, 850 (7th Cir. 1985); *see also, United States v. Patel,* 879 F.2d 292, 294 (7th Cir. 1989). Daddino argues that because Schweihs "kicked him out" of the conspiracy Daddino's abandonment of the conspiracy had been communicated to his coconspirators, as required in *Patel*. This argument is not consistent with the language and underlying policies in the *Patel* decision.

In *Patel* we recognized, as did the Supreme Court in *United States v. United States Gypsum Co.,* 438 U.S. 422, 464 (1978), that there may be other ways of withdrawing from a conspiracy aside from making a clean breast to the authorities or communicating one's abandonment of the conspiracy to one's coconspirators. However, in *Patel* this court emphasized the policy considerations underlying the stringent requirements for asserting the withdrawal defense. Examination of these policy considerations indicates that withdrawal requires an affirmative action *by* the defendant.

> [H]aving set in motion a criminal scheme, a conspirator will not be permitted by the law to limit his responsibility for its consequences by ceasing, however definitively, to participate. . . . You do not absolve yourself of guilt of bombing by walking away from the ticking bomb. And similarly the law will not let you wash your hands of a dangerous scheme that you

have set in motion and that can continue to operate and cause great harm without your continued participation.

Daddino walked away from a ticking bomb. There was no evidence to show that Daddino was no longer associated with Schweihs or the "Outfit." Without evidence of some affirmative action by Daddino, Daddino could continue silently to endorse the extortion plan although he had been relieved of the duty to participate physically by collecting the "street tax" payments. We hold that withdrawal requires proof of an affirmative action by the defendant and that, since there was no such action in this case, the district court properly denied the withdrawal instruction.

Daddino also argues that statements made by Schweihs after Daddino's alleged withdrawal could not properly have been considered against him as coconspirator's statements under Rule 801(d)(2)(E), Fed. R. Evid. That rule provides that statements made by a party's coconspirator during the course and in furtherance of the conspiracy are not hearsay and are, therefore, admissible against the party. Daddino does not argue that the statements were not made during the course and in furtherance of the conspiracy. Instead, he argues that he had previously withdrawn from the conspiracy, ending Schweihs' status as a coconspirator. As we explained above, Daddino did not withdraw from the conspiracy, and Schweihs' statements during the course and in furtherance of the conspiracy were admissible as statements of a coconspirator. . . .

NOTES & QUESTIONS ON WITHDRAWAL

Passive versus active withdrawal. Daddino says he was kicked out of the conspiracy. Shouldn't that be enough to sever his link to the conspiracy? Apparently not, according to the court, because he was a mere passive recipient of this decision. In other words, if he had affirmatively quit the conspiracy, and informed his conspirators thusly, he would have severed the link to them. But because they were the ones who allegedly kicked him out, the link remains in force. Do you agree with this reasoning? Or was the outcome motivated more by the court's assessment of Daddino's departure? Daddino argued that he was kicked out of the conspiracy due to a falling out with his partners; whereas the court implied that his services were no longer required but he was still a member of the conspiracy—a "no-show" conspiracy job. Which assessment do you agree with?

C. PRACTICE & POLICY

We now turn to two issues of practice and policy. The first involves the dual use of the conspiracy doctrine in both substantive criminal law and the law of evidence, and the relative role of the judge and the jury in deciding matters pertaining to the existence of a conspiracy. The second issue involves the importation of *Pinkerton* liability into international criminal law as a mode of liability applicable in atrocity cases before international tribunals.

> ✍ Conspiracy as procedure and substance. Defense attorneys need to do whatever they can to deny the existence of a conspiracy between their clients and other indicted and unindicted co-conspirators. That's because in practice the conspiracy doctrine does *triple* duty. First, it is a substantive offense based on the existence of the underlying agreement. Second, it is a mode of liability to connect a defendant to the crimes committed by co-conspirators. Third, it provides an exception to the hearsay rule in evidence law that usually prevents witnesses from testifying about statements uttered by third parties for the purpose of establishing "the truth of the matter." The hearsay rule is subject to many exceptions and one of the most important in practice is that a co-conspirator made the statement in furtherance of the conspiracy. In that case, the person who heard the statement is permitted to testify about it notwithstanding the hearsay rule. Fed R. Evid. 801(d)(2)(E). This exception poses complications for the trial process. In order to determine whether this exception to the hearsay rule applies, the judge must first determine whether a conspiracy existed. However, the *jury* is the ultimate decider about whether a conspiracy existed for purposes of finding the defendant guilty of conspiracy or guilty of the target offense via conspiracy as a mode of liability. What if the judge finds that a conspiracy existed, applies the exception to the hearsay rule, but the jury concludes that no conspiracy existed? If the jury acquits the defendant of the conspiracy-related charges but convicts him of other offenses, should an appellate court reverse the other convictions on the ground that the hearsay evidence should have been excluded? The answer to this quandary is no, because the actors are applying different standards. The judge decides the evidence question regarding the existence of the conspiracy under a "preponderance of the evidence standard," while the jury asks whether the prosecution has proved the existence of the conspiracy "beyond a reasonable doubt." It is therefore possible for a judge, using a lower standard of proof, to commit no reversible error by making a finding contrary to the jury.
>
> It was once the case that juries were involved in deciding the admissibility of co-conspirator statements. See *United States v. Petrozziello*, 548 F.2d 20, 22 (1st Cir. 1977); *United States v. Honneus*, 508 F.2d 566, 577 (1st Cir. 1974). However, the Federal Rules of Evidence, adopted in 1975, explicitly provided that this determination was within the sole purview of

the trial judge. Now, federal judges must decide for purpose of applying the hearsay exception whether there is sufficient non-hearsay evidence of the existence of a conspiracy. For more discussion, see Ben Trachtenberg, *Coconspirators, "Coventurers," and the Exception Swallowing the Hearsay Rule*, 61 Hastings L.J. 581, 611 (2010).

∾ Joint Criminal Enterprise. *Pinkerton's* influence flows well beyond the borders of the American legal system. The International Criminal Tribunal for Yugoslavia (ICTY) applies a mode of liability known as "Joint Criminal Enterprise," often abbreviated as JCE. The ICTY was created by the United Nations Security Council to prosecute and punish perpetrators guilty of international crimes committed on the territory of the former Yugoslavia. The JCE doctrine allows prosecutors to charge defendants with perpetrating atrocities even if the crimes were personally committed by other individuals, as long as the defendant participated in a common plan or endeavor to carry out the crimes. As ICTY Judge Antonio Cassese explained in his treatise, "all participants in a common criminal action are equally responsible if they (i) participate in the action, *whatever their position and the extent of their contribution*, and in addition (ii) *intend to engage in the common criminal action*. Therefore they are all to be treated as *principals*, although of course the varying degree of culpability may be taken into account at the sentencing stage." Cassese, *International Criminal Law* 181-82 (1st ed. 2003).

The JCE doctrine has three variants. In JCE I, the defendant is prosecuted for crimes that fall within the scope of the original criminal purpose or plan and the defendant shared the intent that the group carry out the crime. In JCE II, the defendant is prosecuted for participating in a system of mistreatment that leads to the commission of international crimes, such as in a concentration camp. In JCE III, the defendant is prosecuted for crimes that fall *outside* the scope of the original criminal plan, as long as those crimes were a reasonably foreseeable consequence of the common plan or purpose. Sound familiar? It should. Commentators have noted that JCE III represents an expansive form of liability that replicates, on the international level, the type of liability that American criminal lawyers understand as *Pinkerton* liability. Indeed, the very first decision from the ICTY to apply the JCE theory cited the *Pinkerton* decision with approval. *Prosecutor v. Tadić*, ICTY Appeals Judgment, Case No. IT-94-1-A, ¶ 224 n. 289 (July 15, 1999).

JCE III has been subject to withering criticism from the scholarly academy, on many of the same grounds that *Pinkerton* is often criticized. The argument is that it subjects some defendants to prosecution based on negligence or recklessness for crimes that should require higher levels of intent, i.e., knowledge or even purpose. On this view, the doctrine allows courts to prosecute minor players in large conspiracies for the full weight of the criminality performed by the collective organization. Some international lawyers have joked that JCE amounts to a "Just Convict Everyone" doctrine. See M.E. Badar, *"Just Convict Everyone!"—Joint Perpetration: From Tadić to Stakić and Back Again*, 6 Int'l Crim. L. Rev. 293 (2006). Do you agree with this criticism? Or do you agree with Judge Cassese's contention that all differences in culpability among the participants can be sorted out in the sentencing phase by giving lower-level conspirators lighter prison terms? Does this suggest a viable solution for mitigating the harshness of the *Pinkerton* rule in American criminal law as well?

CHAPTER 22

—◁ΘϾΘ▷—

CORPORATE CRIME

A. DOCTRINE

Corporate behavior is generating increasing levels of public scrutiny. When corporations break the law, they are usually subject to criminal sanctions just as much as individual human beings. The phrase "corporate criminal liability" usually refers to the liability of the corporation itself for criminal violations performed by members of the corporation. However, equally important is the reverse: liability of high-level managers and officers for the crimes committed by their corporations. In this chapter we consider both. Both are forms of vicarious liability that come with their own sets of doctrinal standards and constraints.

1. Prosecuting Corporations

As legal persons, corporations are subject to the criminal law. The vast majority of these prosecutions are for regulatory offenses in the health, safety, and financial contexts, although occasionally corporations are prosecuted for violating "regular" criminal law offenses of the type already outlined in this casebook, such as murder or manslaughter. In evaluating whether corporate liability is appropriate, courts usually consider legislative intent, i.e., whether the statute proscribing the conduct anticipated that corporations, and not just individuals, could be convicted for violating the provision. A good example is the Sherman Act, which prohibits anti-trust violations such as price-fixing. Courts have concluded that Congress intended to impose criminal liability on corporations when it passed the statute. *United States v. Hilton Hotels Corp.*, 467 F.2d 1000 (9th Cir. 1972).

The mere existence of employee misconduct is insufficient to generate corporate liability; more is required. Under a strict respondeat superior approach, actions of individual agents can be imputed to the corporation itself if the individual performs the criminal act within the scope of her employment and with the intent to benefit the corporation. The basic idea is that if the corporate official performs the action for purely personal gain, the act should not be attributed to the corporation. Some courts impose additional restrictions, such as the involvement of high managerial agents acting within the scope of their employment, either by engaging in the conduct themselves or by tolerating it when performed by underlings. In the words of Model Penal Code § 2.07(1), the conduct must be "authorized, requested, commanded, performed or recklessly tolerated by the board of directors or by a high managerial agent acting on behalf of the corporation within the scope of his office or employment." Consequently, a corporation can be prosecuted even if a low-rung employee performed the criminal act.

The Model Penal Code codifies a due diligence defense that has been applied by some courts and precludes liability "if the defendant proves by a preponderance of evidence that the high managerial agent having supervisory responsibility over the subject matter of the offense employed due diligence to prevent its commission." MPC § 2.07(5). However, the mere existence of a corporate directive prohibiting the illegal behavior may be insufficient to satisfy the defense if a court concludes that the corporation should have done more to implement or enforce those policies. After all, due diligence requires more than just drafting another memo. Indeed, corporations almost *always* have explicit policies prohibiting illegal and unethical conduct; the question is what procedures the corporation put in place to implement them.

2. Punishing Corporations

If a corporation is convicted, how should it be punished? Most corporate convictions end in fines, since it is difficult to imprison a corporation. In extreme cases, should corporations receive a "death penalty" by a judicially enforced dissolution of the corporate enterprise? Although this drastic measure is theoretically possible, in practice corporate punishment is limited to substantial fines and probation with conditions attached. But consider *United States v. Allegheny Bottling Co.*, 695 F. Supp. 856 (E.D. Va. 1988), a curious case where a district judge "imprisoned" a corporation by issuing an order for the seizure of its assets by the U.S. Marshal. Criminal fines are blunt instruments and might have collateral consequences on innocent third parties such as employees, shareholders, and even consumers (who might be harmed by higher prices). Mindful of this problem, federal prosecutors factor in these consequences when deciding whether to seek an indictment. Prosecutors also have the option of settling with the corporation and entering into a deferred prosecution agreement in exchange for the corporation's promise to engage in structural reforms or remediation.

3. Prosecuting Corporate Officers

Corporate and individual liability are not mutually exclusive. It is possible for prosecutors to charge both the individual officers and the corporation at the same time. It is also possible for the jury to acquit one but convict the other. But not every employee is responsible for the criminality of the corporation. Under the "responsible corporate officer doctrine," the defendant must have been responsible for the behavior in some way. In *United States v. Dotterweich*, 320 U.S. 277 (1943), the Supreme Court upheld convictions against a president and general manager for violations of the Federal Food, Drug, and Cosmetic Act because he had a responsible share in, or responsible relation to, the violations. This can include oversight responsibilities for the behavior in question. It can also include liability for omissions if the corporation had a statutory to duty to act. One obvious consequence of prosecuting corporate officers is that they—unlike the corporation itself—can be sent to prison. If a prosecutor believes that the corporate wrongdoing is so severe that it calls out for imprisonment, this fact might motivate the prosecutor to find a doctrinal pathway to convict the officers as individuals.

B. APPLICATION

1. Prosecuting Corporations

The Supreme Court has long recognized that corporations can be prosecuted and punished under the criminal law when the statute contemplates that result. This result is frequently upheld when the statute involves criminal wrongdoing or health and safety violations. But what of regular criminal law provisions? Can a corporation be prosecuted for murder?

State v. Far West Water & Sewer Inc.
Court of Appeals of Arizona
224 Ariz. 173 (2010)

WEISBERG, J.

Far West Water & Sewer, Inc. appeals its convictions and sentences for negligent homicide, aggravated assault, two counts of endangerment and violating a safety standard or regulation which caused the death of an employee. . . . For reasons that follow, we affirm Far West's convictions and sentences.

PROCEDURAL HISTORY

The charges arose from an incident that occurred on October 24, 2001 at a sewage collection and treatment facility owned and operated by Far West, an Arizona corporation. At that time, Santec Corporation was a subcontractor of Far West. A Far West employee, James Gamble, and a Santec employee, Gary Lanser, died in an underground tank after they were overcome by hydrogen sulfide gas. Another Far West employee, Nathan Garrett, suffered severe injuries when he attempted to rescue Gamble from the tank. . . .

Far West was indicted for two counts of manslaughter for the deaths of Gamble and Lanser, one count of aggravated assault as to Garrett, four counts of endangerment as to Gamble, Garrett and two Santec employees, Shawn Hackbarth and Eric Andre, and one count of violating a safety standard or regulation that caused the death of Gamble. Far West's president, Brent Weidman, one of its forepersons, Connie Charles, and Santec were also indicted for the same or similar charges.

Santec pled guilty to one count of violating a safety standard or regulation that caused the death of its employee, Lanser. It was placed on probation for two years and fined $30,000. Charles pled guilty to two counts of endangerment as to Gamble and Garrett and was placed on concurrent one-year terms of probation.

On the State's motion, the trial court severed the trials of Far West and Weidman. The jury acquitted Far West of both counts of manslaughter as to Gamble and Lanser, but found it guilty of one count of the lesser-included offense of negligent homicide for the death of Gamble, one count of aggravated assault as to Garrett, two counts of endangerment as to Gamble and Garrett, and one count of violating a safety standard or regulation that caused the death of Gamble.

The court ordered the sentences suspended and placed Far West on four years' probation for negligent homicide, five years' probation for aggravated assault and three years' probation for each count of endangerment and for violating a safety standard or regulation that caused the death of an employee. . . . The court imposed fines and penalties totaling $1,770,000. . . .

PROSECUTION NOT BARRED BY FEDERAL OR STATE LAW

In 1970, Congress enacted the Occupational Safety and Health Act ("OSHA"). . . . Congress authorized the states to adopt standards that substantially complied with OSHA. Under this authority, the Arizona legislature enacted the Arizona Occupational Safety and Health Act. It created a division of occupational health and safety within the Arizona Industrial Commission to recommend and enforce safety standards. . . . Under

A.R.S. § 23-403(A), "[e]ach employer shall furnish to each of his employees employment and a place of employment which are free from recognized hazards that are causing or likely to cause death or serious physical harm to his employees" ("the statutory duty"). Employers who knowingly violate the requirements . . . may be subject to criminal penalties. . . .

In 1977, the Arizona legislature enacted A.R.S. § 13-305, which permits an enterprise to be held criminally liable. An enterprise includes a corporation. . . .

Far West filed a motion to dismiss the charges brought under the Arizona Criminal Code for manslaughter, aggravated assault and endangerment ("Title 13 offenses"). Assuming that its criminal liability was based solely on a "failure to discharge a specific duty imposed by law" under A.R.S. § 13-305(A)(1) and a failure to provide a safe workplace under A.R.S. § 23-403(A), Far West argued that the OSHA provision set forth in 29 U.S.C. § 653(b)(4) ("the savings clause") preempted the State's prosecution under Title 13. . . .

While no Arizona case has addressed this issue, jurisdictions considering it have uniformly held that the OSHA savings clause does not preempt prosecution under state criminal laws. For example, in *People v. Chicago Magnet Wire Corp.*, 534 N.E.2d 962, 965 (Ill. 1989), corporate officers were charged with several criminal offenses after numerous employees suffered physical injuries due to their exposure to toxic substances, inadequate ventilation and dangerously overheated working conditions. The indictments claimed the defendants knowingly and recklessly caused the injuries by failing to provide the employees with necessary safety precautions to avoid harmful exposure to the poisonous substances. The defendants argued that OSHA preempted the prosecutions on several grounds. The Supreme Court of Illinois disagreed and reversed the appellate court, which had affirmed an order dismissing the indictments. . . .

FAR WEST AS A "PERSON" FOR CRIMINAL LIABILITY

In a motion to dismiss made during trial, Far West argued, among other issues, that it was not a "person" for purposes of imposing criminal liability for manslaughter, aggravated assault or endangerment because only human beings can be held criminally liable for those crimes. Although denying the motion to dismiss on other grounds, the trial judge expressed his complete disagreement with Far West's position.

Arizona's criminal code defines "person" as "a human being and, as the context requires, an enterprise, a public or private corporation, an unincorporated association, a partnership, a firm, a society, a government, a governmental authority or an individual or entity capable of holding a legal or beneficial interest in property." There is nothing to indicate that by inclusion of the phrase "as the context requires," the legislature sought to exclude corporations from the definition of "person" for certain offenses. Further, not only did the legislature include corporations in the definition of person, the legislature described how corporations, as enterprises, can commit criminal offenses through the acts or omissions of their directors, high managerial agents and/or agents.

Our interpretation is also supported by the language of the statutes that prescribe penalties for commission of criminal offenses. Section 13-603 sets forth the authorized disposition of offenders and contains provisions specific to an "enterprise" that commits a criminal offense. Section 13-803 provides for the imposition of fines against "enterprises" convicted of criminal offenses. We therefore conclude that Far West was a person for purposes of imposing criminal liability for Title 13 offenses. . . .

ELEMENTS OF OFFENSES

Far West claims the evidence was insufficient to support the convictions against Far West because (1) Weidman and Noll were not high managerial agents acting within the scope of their employment; (2) Weidman and Noll did not engage in conduct or possess the requisite culpable mental states required for commission of each offense; and (3) Far West did not cause Gamble's death or Garrett's injuries. . . .

The State presented substantial evidence that Weidman and Noll were high managerial agents of Far West acting within the scope of their authority. Weidman was President and Chief Operating Officer of Far West and a member of the board of directors. Noll was the supervisor for the sewage division of Far West, answered to Weidman and had considerable authority over Far West's employees. He was in charge of Far West's safety program. He and Weidman together formulated and developed policies and practices of Far West regarding entry into underground sewage tanks. They made decisions and took actions regarding training, safety and equipment necessary for entry into such tanks. A jury could reasonably conclude that Weidman and Noll were high managerial agents of Far West and were acting within the scope of their authority.

The State presented substantial evidence that Weidman and Noll engaged in acts and/or failed to act with the accompanying culpable mental states necessary to meet the statutory elements for each offense.

The State presented substantial evidence that Weidman and Noll were aware of the extreme risks to employees working at Far West. Both were industry professionals with extensive training and experience in sewage treatment plants. They knew the dangers associated with confined spaces and sewer environments. They knew about potentially lethal dangers posed by toxic gases found in underground tanks. Weidman posited that the death and injuries occurred due to the toxic gases. Noll admitted that working in underground tanks was unsafe. A jury could reasonably conclude that

Weidman and Noll were aware of the substantial and unjustifiable risk of death or physical injury involved in working in this environment.

The State presented substantial evidence that Weidman and Noll knew and understood the OSHA permit-required confined space regulations and knew Far West was required to follow OSHA regulations. Such regulations required that Far West, among other things, adopt a written permit space program, develop procedures and practices for safe entry into confined spaces, provide adequate training to employees, obtain necessary equipment for entry, testing and monitoring of permit spaces, establish a rescue plan, provide rescue equipment and emergency services and coordinate with third-party contractors.

Despite this knowledge, Weidman and Noll did not take steps to comply with OSHA. Instead, they devised a "clean-hole policy" in an apparent attempt to circumvent OSHA regulations. This policy, however, was never communicated to employees, never implemented and, in any event, could not have made the tanks safe for entry. Weidman and Noll knew Far West employees were entering permit-required confined spaces on a regular basis and knew they would enter the Tank on the day of the incident. A jury could reasonably conclude that Noll and Weidman consciously disregarded a substantial and unjustifiable risk of death or physical injury by knowingly violating OSHA regulations and permitting Far West employees to enter dangerous, life-threatening underground tanks without training, equipment, safety measures or rescue capability. . . .

The State presented substantial evidence that the conduct of Weidman and Noll constituted a gross deviation from the required standard of care and/or conduct. Several expert witnesses testified that the Tank was a permit-required confined space. Experts also testified that according to industry standards, once classified as a permit space, it is subject to mandatory OSHA regulations. They also testified that the "clean-hole policy" did not meet those requirements. Evidence supported the inference that Weidman and Noll simply ignored OSHA regulations. . . .

For the foregoing reasons, we affirm Far West's convictions and sentences.

NOTES & QUESTIONS ON CORPORATE LIABILITY

1. *Due diligence defense.*   As discussed above, the Model Penal Code and jurisdictions that adopted its corporate liability provisions recognize a due diligence defense. In *United States v. Hilton Hotels Corp.*, 467 F.2d 1000 (9th Cir. 1972), the Ninth Circuit upheld a corporate conviction for anti-trust violations, even though the corporation had an explicit policy against such behavior.

However, the due diligence defense might require more. With the knowledge that employees might stray from the requirements laid out in employee handbooks and the like, the due diligence defense would require corporations to take all required measures to prevent and remediate illegal behavior. Whether a corporation has gone far enough is a question of fact for a jury to decide. For other examples of the due diligence defense, see N.J. Stat. Ann. § 2C:2-7(c) (no liability if "the high managerial agent having supervisory responsibility over the subject matter of the offense employed due diligence to prevent its commission"). Even in jurisdictions that reject due diligence as a formal defense, it is usually taken into account during the sentence phase and is formally codified as a relevant criterion in the Federal Sentencing Guidelines. Applying this defense to *Far West*, do you think the company did all it could to prevent the accident? In short, were the deaths the result of a freak accident or the result of systemic safety problems at the company?

2. *Non-profit organizations.* Corporate criminality is not just limited to for-profit prosecutions, although this certainly represents the majority of prosecutions. In *State v. Zeta Chi Fraternity*, 142 N.H. 16 (1997), the New Hampshire State Attorney General prosecuted a fraternity at the University of New Hampshire for selling alcohol to a minor and prostitution, both violations of state law. The fraternity held a "rush" event at its house to recruit new members. According to state prosecutors, the event, which included several minors, included alcohol and a performance by a stripper. Lawyers for the fraternity argued that it could not be prosecuted as a corporation because the criminal acts were contrary to its stated policies. The fraternity had officially voted not to serve beer at the rush event and therefore the students who served the beer were not acting on behalf of the corporation or within the scope of their authority. However, citing *Hilton Hotels*, the court concluded that a corporation is criminally responsible for its agents' actions even when they are contrary to corporate directives, as long as the agents were acting within the scope of their actual or apparent authority. The court distinguished between express, implied, and apparent authority, and found that the students who provided the beer from a fraternity vending machine were acting under the apparent authority of the corporate entity. In making this finding, the court noted that "[i]t is the rare case in which the corporate leadership explicitly authorizes its agents to engage in criminal conduct."

3. *The academic controversy.* Corporate criminal liability has always been controversial, with many scholars arguing that corporate prosecutions are unnecessary, since everything they achieve can be better achieved by prosecuting corporate officials directly. One potential justification is expressivist. Punishing a corporation directly recognizes the reality of collective action and the undeniable fact that corporations have become market actors with significant influence

PROBLEM CASE

Pilot Andreas Lubitz allegedly told a friend that the world would one day know his name. That prediction came true on March 24, 2015, when Lubitz piloted a Germanwings Airbus 320 into the French Alps, killing all 150 individuals aboard. After investigators determined that the suicidal pilot deliberately crashed the airplane, prosecutors opened criminal investigations in both France and Germany. France had jurisdiction based on the location of the crash, and German jurisdiction was satisfied by the nationality of the pilot and many of the victims.

Since Lubitz is dead, the question is whether others are criminally responsible for the crash as well. Should Germanwings (or its corporate parent Lufthansa) be prosecuted for 150 counts of manslaughter? French law permits corporate criminal responsibility, while German law does not. According to investigators, Lubitz suffered from depression in 2009 that was so severe that it interrupted his instruction at a Lufthansa flight school. Clearly, Lufthansa was put on notice that there were potential problems with Lubitz's mental health. Did the company handle the situation appropriately? Should Lubitz have been barred from flying or placed under a more rigorous long-term monitoring protocol to assess whether the depression had returned? Did the Lufthansa and Germanwings officials employ the necessary due diligence to prevent Lubitz's crime?

Andreas Lubitz

on our daily lives—both economic and social. Indeed, a corporation is more than just an aggregation of individuals—it is a collective enterprise of like-minded individuals pursuing a collective objective through a specific decision procedure. See Christian List & Philip Pettit, *Group Agency* (2011); Sara Sun Beale, *A Response to the Critics of Corporate Criminal Liability*, 46 Am. Crim. L. Rev. 1481 (2009) (corporations "are very real and enormously powerful actors whose conduct often causes very significant harm both to individuals and society as a whole"). When corporate action goes wrong, society wants to express its disapproval of that deviance. The instrumental argument is that corporate liability deters malfeasance because it gives employees and corporate officers an incentive to monitor each other. Critics claim that both arguments are overbroad—like arguing that we should punish "all members of a group when one member eluded punishment for his crimes." Albert W. Alschuler, *Two Ways to Think About the Punishment of Corporations*, 46 Am. Crim. L. Rev. 1359 (2009).

2. Punishing Corporations

When the government decides whether to prosecute a corporation itself or its officers (or both), prosecutors are inevitably making a decision about whether they want the corporation itself punished. This assessment is complicated by the existence of collateral consequences for employees or shareholders who might be innocent of wrongdoing. The following document from the Justice Department lays out the government's current policy regarding when and how corporations should be punished.

Principles of Federal Prosecution of Business Organizations
U.S. Department of Justice
U.S. Attorney's Manual §§ 9-28.000-9-28.1300

GENERAL CONSIDERATIONS OF CORPORATE LIABILITY

A. General Principle: Corporations should not be treated leniently because of their artificial nature nor should they be subject to harsher treatment. Vigorous enforcement of the criminal laws against corporate wrongdoers, where appropriate, results in great benefits for law enforcement and the public, particularly in the area of white collar crime. Indicting corporations for wrongdoing enables the government to be a force for positive change of corporate culture, and a force to prevent, discover, and punish serious crimes.

B. Comment: In all cases involving corporate wrongdoing, prosecutors should consider the factors discussed further below. In doing so, prosecutors should be aware of the public benefits that can flow from indicting a corporation in appropriate cases. For instance, corporations are likely to take immediate remedial steps when one is indicted for criminal misconduct that is pervasive throughout a particular industry, and thus an indictment can provide a unique opportunity for deterrence on a broad scale. In addition, a corporate indictment may result in specific deterrence by changing the culture of the indicted corporation and the behavior of its employees. Finally, certain crimes that carry with them a substantial risk of great public harm—e.g., environmental crimes or sweeping financial frauds—may be committed by a business entity, and there may therefore be a substantial federal interest in indicting a corporation under such circumstances.

In certain instances, it may be appropriate, upon consideration of the factors set forth herein, to resolve a corporate criminal case by means other than indictment. Non-prosecution and deferred prosecution agreements, for example, occupy an important middle ground between declining prosecution and obtaining the conviction of a corporation. . . .

Where a decision is made to charge a corporation, it does not necessarily follow that individual directors, officers, employees, or shareholders should not also be charged. Prosecution of a corporation is not a substitute for the prosecution of criminally culpable individuals within or without the corporation. Because a corporation can act only through individuals, imposition of individual criminal liability may provide the strongest deterrent against future corporate wrongdoing. Only rarely should provable individual culpability not be pursued, particularly if it relates to high-level corporate officers, even in the face of an offer of a corporate guilty plea or some other disposition of the charges against the corporation.

Corporations are "legal persons," capable of suing and being sued, and capable of committing crimes. Under the doctrine of respondeat superior, a corporation may be held criminally liable for the illegal acts of its directors, officers, employees, and agents. To hold a corporation liable for these actions, the government must establish that the corporate agent's actions (i) were within the scope of his duties and (ii) were intended, at least in part, to benefit the corporation. In all cases involving wrongdoing by corporate agents, prosecutors should not limit their focus solely to individuals or the corporation, but should consider both as potential targets.

Agents may act for mixed reasons—both for self-aggrandizement (both direct and indirect) and for the benefit of the corporation, and a corporation may be held liable as long as one motivation of its agent is to benefit the corporation. See *United States v. Potter*, 463 F.3d 9, 25 (1st Cir. 2006) (stating that the test to determine whether an agent is acting within the scope of employment is "whether the agent is performing acts of the kind which he is authorized to perform, and those acts are motivated, at least in part, by an intent to benefit the corporation."). In *United States v. Automated Medical Laboratories, Inc.*, 770 F.2d 399 (4th Cir. 1985), for example, the Fourth Circuit affirmed a corporation's conviction for the actions of a subsidiary's employee despite the corporation's claim that the employee was acting for his own benefit, namely his "ambitious nature and his desire to ascend the corporate ladder." The court stated, "Partucci was clearly acting in part to benefit AML since his advancement within the corporation depended on AML's well-being and its lack of difficulties with the FDA." Moreover, the corporation need not even necessarily profit from its agent's actions for it to be held liable. . . .

FACTORS TO BE CONSIDERED

A. General Principle: Generally, prosecutors apply the same factors in determining whether to charge a corporation as they do with respect to individuals. Thus, the prosecutor must weigh all of the factors normally considered in the sound exercise of prosecutorial judgment: the sufficiency of the evidence; the likelihood of success at trial; the probable deterrent, rehabilitative, and other consequences of conviction; and the adequacy of noncriminal approaches. However, due to the nature of the corporate "person," some additional factors are present. In conducting an investigation, determining whether to bring charges, and negotiating plea or other agreements, prosecutors should consider the following factors in reaching a decision as to the proper treatment of a corporate target:

1. the nature and seriousness of the offense, including the risk of harm to the public, and applicable policies and priorities, if any, governing the prosecution of corporations for particular categories of crime;
2. the pervasiveness of wrongdoing within the corporation, including the complicity in, or the condoning of, the wrongdoing by corporate management;
3. the corporation's history of similar misconduct, including prior criminal, civil, and regulatory enforcement actions against it;
4. the corporation's timely and voluntary disclosure of wrongdoing and its willingness to cooperate in the investigation of its agents;
5. the existence and effectiveness of the corporation's pre-existing compliance program;
6. the corporation's remedial actions, including any efforts to implement an effective corporate compliance program or to improve an existing one, to replace responsible management, to discipline or terminate wrongdoers, to pay restitution, and to cooperate with the relevant government agencies;
7. collateral consequences, including whether there is disproportionate harm to shareholders, pension holders, employees, and others not proven personally culpable, as well as impact on the public arising from the prosecution;
8. the adequacy of the prosecution of individuals responsible for the corporation's malfeasance; and
9. the adequacy of remedies such as civil or regulatory enforcement actions.

B. Comment: The factors listed in this section are intended to be illustrative of those that should be evaluated and are not an exhaustive list of potentially relevant considerations. Some of these factors may not apply to specific cases, and in some cases one factor may override all others. For example, the nature and seriousness of the offense may be such as to warrant prosecution regardless of the other factors. In most cases, however, no single factor will be dispositive. In addition, national law enforcement policies in various enforcement areas may require that more or less weight be given to certain of these factors than to others. Of course, prosecutors must exercise their thoughtful and pragmatic judgment in applying and balancing these factors, so as to achieve a fair and just outcome and promote respect for the law.

In making a decision to charge a corporation, the prosecutor generally has substantial latitude in determining when, whom, how, and even whether to prosecute for violations of federal criminal law. In exercising that discretion, prosecutors should consider the following statements of principles that summarize the considerations they should weigh and the practices they should follow in discharging their prosecutorial responsibilities. In doing so, prosecutors should ensure that the general purposes of the criminal law—assurance of warranted punishment, deterrence of further criminal conduct, protection of the public from dangerous and fraudulent conduct, rehabilitation of offenders, and restitution for victims and affected communities—are adequately met, taking into account the special nature of the corporate "person."

SPECIAL POLICY CONCERNS

A. General Principle: The nature and seriousness of the crime, including the risk of harm to the public from the criminal misconduct, are obviously primary factors in determining whether to charge a corporation. In addition, corporate conduct, particularly that of national and multinational corporations, necessarily intersects with federal economic, tax, and criminal law enforcement policies. In applying these Principles, prosecutors must consider the practices and policies of the appropriate Division of the Department, and must comply with those policies to the extent required by the facts presented.

B. Comment: In determining whether to charge a corporation, prosecutors should take into account federal law enforcement priorities as discussed above. In addition, however, prosecutors must be aware of the specific policy goals and incentive programs established by the respective Divisions and regulatory agencies. Thus, whereas natural persons may be given incremental degrees of credit (ranging from immunity to lesser charges to sentencing considerations) for turning themselves in, making statements against their penal interest, and cooperating in the government's investigation of their own and others' wrongdoing, the same approach may not be appropriate in all circumstances with respect to corporations. As an example, it is entirely proper in many investigations for a prosecutor to consider the corporation's pre-indictment conduct, e.g., voluntary disclosure, cooperation, remediation or restitution, in determining whether to seek an indictment. However, this would not necessarily be appropriate in an antitrust investigation, in which antitrust violations, by definition, go to the heart of the corporation's business. With this in mind, the Antitrust Division has established a firm policy, understood in the business community, that credit should not be given at the charging stage for a compliance program and that amnesty is available only to the first corporation to make full disclosure to the government. . . .

PERVASIVENESS OF WRONGDOING WITHIN THE CORPORATION

A. General Principle: A corporation can only act through natural persons, and it is therefore held responsible for the acts of such persons fairly attributable to it. Charging a corporation for even minor misconduct may be appropriate where the wrongdoing was pervasive and was undertaken by a large number of employees, or by all the employees in a particular role within the corporation, or was condoned by upper management. On the other hand, it may not be appropriate to impose liability upon a corporation, particularly one with a robust compliance program in place, under a strict respondeat superior theory for the single isolated act of a rogue employee. There is, of course, a wide spectrum between these two extremes, and a prosecutor should exercise sound discretion in evaluating the pervasiveness of wrongdoing within a corporation.

B. Comment: Of these factors, the most important is the role and conduct of management. Although acts of even low-level employees may result in criminal liability, a corporation is directed by its management and management is responsible for a corporate culture in which criminal conduct is either discouraged or tacitly encouraged. As stated in commentary to the Sentencing Guidelines: "Pervasiveness [is] case specific and [will] depend on the number, and degree of responsibility, of individuals [with] substantial authority . . . who participated in, condoned, or were willfully ignorant of the offense. Fewer individuals need to be involved for a finding of pervasiveness if those individuals exercised a relatively high degree of authority. . . ."

THE CORPORATION'S PAST HISTORY

A. General Principle: Prosecutors may consider a corporation's history of similar conduct, including prior criminal, civil, and regulatory enforcement actions against it, in determining whether to bring criminal charges and how best to resolve cases.

B. Comment: A corporation, like a natural person, is expected to learn from its mistakes. A history of similar misconduct may be probative of a corporate culture that encouraged, or at least condoned, such misdeeds, regardless of any compliance programs. Criminal prosecution of a corporation may be particularly appropriate where the corporation previ-ously had been subject to non-criminal guidance, warnings, or sanctions, or previous criminal charges, and it either had not taken adequate action to prevent future unlawful conduct or had continued to engage in the miscon-duct in spite of the warnings or enforcement actions taken against it. The corporate structure itself (e.g., the creation or existence of subsidiaries or operating divisions) is not dispositive in this analysis, and enforcement actions taken against the corporation or any of its divisions, subsidiaries, and affiliates may be considered, if germane.

THE VALUE OF COOPERATION

Cooperation is a potential mitigating factor, by which a corporation—just like any other subject of a criminal investigation—can gain credit in a case that otherwise is appropriate for indictment and prosecution. Of course, the decision not to cooperate by a corporation (or individual) is not itself evidence of misconduct, at least where the lack of cooperation does not involve criminal misconduct or demonstrate consciousness of guilt (e.g., suborning perjury or false statements, or refusing to comply with lawful discovery requests). Thus, failure to cooperate, in and of itself, does not support or require the filing of charges with respect to a corporation any more than with respect to an individual.

A. General Principle: In determining whether to charge a corporation and how to resolve corporate criminal cases, the corporation's timely and voluntary disclosure of wrongdoing and its cooperation with the govern-ment's investigation may be relevant factors. In gauging the extent of the corporation's cooperation, the prosecutor may consider, among other things, whether the corporation made a voluntary and timely disclosure, and the corporation's willingness to provide relevant information and evidence and identify relevant actors within and outside the corporation, including senior executives.

B. Comment: In investigating wrongdoing by or within a corporation, a prosecutor is likely to encounter several obstacles resulting from the nature of the corporation itself. It will often be difficult to determine which individual took which action on behalf of the corporation. Lines of authority and responsibility may be shared among operating divisions or depart-ments, and records and personnel may be spread throughout the United States or even among several countries. Where the criminal conduct con-tinued over an extended period of time, the culpable or knowledgeable personnel may have been promoted, transferred, or fired, or they may have quit or retired. Accordingly, a corporation's cooperation may be cri-tical in identifying potentially relevant actors and locating relevant evidence, among other things, and in doing so expeditiously. . . .

ATTORNEY-CLIENT AND WORK PRODUCT PROTECTIONS

The attorney-client privilege and the attorney work product protection serve an extremely important function in the American legal system. The attorney-client privilege is one of the oldest and most sacrosanct privileges under the law. . . . The value of promoting a corporation's ability to seek frank and comprehensive legal advice is particularly important in the contemporary global business environment, where corporations often face complex and dynamic legal and regulatory obligations imposed by the federal government and also by states and foreign governments. The work product doctrine serves similarly important goals.

For these reasons, waiving the attorney-client and work product protections has never been a prerequisite under the Department's prosecution guidelines for a corporation to be viewed as cooperative. Nonetheless, a wide range of commentators and members of the American legal community and criminal justice system have asserted that the Department's policies have been used, either wittingly or unwittingly, to coerce business entities into waiving attorney-client privilege and work product protection. Everyone agrees that a corporation may freely waive its own privileges if it chooses to do so; indeed, such waivers occur routinely when corporations are victimized by their employees or others, conduct an internal investigation, and then disclose the details of the investigation to law enforcement officials in an effort to seek prosecution of the offenders. However, the contention, from a broad array of voices, is that the Department's position on attorney-client privilege and work product protection waivers has promoted an environment in which those protections are being unfairly eroded to the detriment of all.

The Department understands that the attorney-client privilege and attorney work product protection are essential and long-recognized components of the American legal system. What the government seeks and needs to advance its legitimate (indeed, essential) law enforcement mission is not waiver of those protections, but rather the facts known to the corporation about the putative criminal misconduct under review. In addition, while a corporation remains free to convey non-factual or "core" attorney-client communications or work product—if and only if the corporation voluntarily chooses to do so—prosecutors should not ask for such waivers and are directed not to do so. The critical factor is whether the corporation has provided the facts about the events, as explained further herein.

COOPERATION: DISCLOSING THE RELEVANT FACTS

Eligibility for cooperation credit is not predicated upon the waiver of attorney-client privilege or work product protection. Instead, the sort of cooperation that is most valuable to resolving allegations of misconduct by a corporation and its officers, directors, employees, or agents is disclosure of the relevant facts concerning such misconduct. In this regard, the analysis parallels that for a non-corporate defendant, where cooperation typically requires disclosure of relevant factual knowledge and not of discussions between an individual and his attorneys.

Thus, when the government investigates potential corporate wrong-doing, it seeks the relevant facts. For example, how and when did the alleged misconduct occur? Who promoted or approved it? Who was responsible for committing it? In this respect, the investigation of a corporation differs little from the investigation of an individual. In both cases, the government needs to know the facts to achieve a just and fair outcome. The party under investigation may choose to cooperate by disclosing the facts, and the government may give credit for the party's disclosures. If a corporation wishes to receive credit for such cooperation, which then can be considered with all other cooperative efforts and circumstances in evaluating how fairly to proceed, then the corporation, like any person, must disclose the relevant facts of which it has knowledge.

Individuals and corporations often obtain knowledge of facts in different ways. An individual knows the facts of his or others' misconduct through his own experience and perceptions. A corporation is an artificial construct that cannot, by definition, have personal knowledge of the facts. Some of those facts may be reflected in documentary or electronic media like emails, transaction or accounting documents, and other records. Often, the corporation gathers facts through an internal investigation. Exactly how and by whom the facts are gathered is for the corporation to decide. Many corporations choose to collect information about potential misconduct through lawyers, a process that may confer attorney-client privilege or attorney work product protection on at least some of the information collected. Other corporations may choose a method of fact-gathering that does not have that effect—for example, having employee or other witness statements collected after interviews by non-attorney personnel. Whichever process the corporation selects, the government's key measure of cooperation must remain the same as it does for an individual: has the party timely disclosed the relevant facts about the putative misconduct? That is the operative question in assigning cooperation credit for the disclosure of information—not whether the corporation discloses attorney-client or work product materials. Accordingly, a corporation should receive the same credit for disclosing facts contained in materials that are not protected by the attorney-client privilege or attorney work product as it would for disclosing identical facts contained in materials that are so protected. . . .

CORPORATE COMPLIANCE PROGRAMS

A. General Principle: Compliance programs are established by corporate management to prevent and detect misconduct and to ensure that corporate activities are conducted in accordance with applicable criminal and civil laws, regulations, and rules. The Department encourages such corporate self-policing, including voluntary disclosures to the government of any problems that a corporation discovers on its own. However, the existence of a compliance program is not sufficient, in and of itself, to justify not charging a corporation for criminal misconduct undertaken by its officers, directors, employees, or agents. In addition, the nature of some crimes, e.g., antitrust violations, may be such that national law enforcement policies mandate prosecutions of corporations notwithstanding the existence of a compliance program.

B. Comment: The existence of a corporate compliance program, even one that specifically prohibited the very conduct in question, does not absolve the corporation from criminal liability under the doctrine of respondeat superior. As explained in *United States v. Potter*, 463 F.3d 9 (1st Cir. 2006), a corporation cannot "avoid liability by adopting abstract rules" that forbid its agents from engaging in illegal acts, because "[e]ven a specific directive to an agent or employee or honest efforts to police such rules do not automatically free the company for the wrongful acts of agents." See also *United States v. Hilton Hotels Corp.*, 467 F.2d 1000, 1007 (9th Cir. 1972) (noting that a corporation "could not gain exculpation by issuing general instructions without undertaking to enforce those instructions by means commensurate with the obvious risks"); *United States v. Beusch*, 596 F.2d 871, 878 (9th Cir. 1979) ("[A] corporation may be liable for acts of its employees done contrary to express instructions and policies, but . . . the existence of such instructions and policies may be considered in determining whether the employee in fact acted to benefit the corporation.").

While the Department recognizes that no compliance program can ever prevent all criminal activity by a corporation's employees, the critical factors in evaluating any program are whether the program is adequately designed for maximum effectiveness in preventing and detecting wrongdoing by employees and whether corporate management is enforcing the program or is tacitly encouraging or pressuring employees to engage in misconduct to achieve business objectives. The Department has no formulaic requirements regarding corporate compliance programs. The fundamental questions any prosecutor should ask are: Is the corporation's compliance program well designed? Is the program being applied earnestly and in good faith? Does the corporation's compliance program work? In answering these questions, the prosecutor should consider the comprehensiveness of the compliance program; the extent and pervasiveness of the criminal misconduct; the number and level of the corporate employees involved; the seriousness, duration, and frequency of the misconduct; and any remedial actions taken by the corporation, including, for example, disciplinary action against past violators uncovered by the prior compliance program, and revisions to corporate compliance programs in light of lessons learned. Prosecutors should also consider the promptness of any disclosure of wrongdoing to the government. In evaluating compliance programs, prosecutors may consider whether the corporation has established corporate governance mechanisms that can effectively detect and prevent misconduct. For example, do the corporation's directors exercise independent review over proposed corporate actions rather than unquestioningly ratifying officers' recommendations; are internal audit functions conducted at a level sufficient to ensure their independence and accuracy; and have the directors established an information and reporting system in the organization reasonably designed to provide management and directors with timely and accurate information sufficient to allow them to reach an informed decision regarding the organization's compliance with the law.

Prosecutors should therefore attempt to determine whether a corporation's compliance program is merely a "paper program" or whether it was designed, implemented, reviewed, and revised, as appropriate, in an effective manner. In addition, prosecutors should determine whether the corporation has provided for a staff sufficient to audit, document, analyze, and utilize the results of the corporation's compliance efforts. Prosecutors also should determine whether the corporation's employees are adequately informed about the compliance program and are convinced of the corporation's commitment to it. This will enable the prosecutor to make an informed decision as to whether the corporation has adopted and implemented a truly effective compliance program that, when consistent with other federal law enforcement policies, may result in a decision to charge only the corporation's employees and agents or to mitigate charges or sanctions against the corporation. . . .

RESTITUTION AND REMEDIATION

A. General Principle: Although neither a corporation nor an individual target may avoid prosecution merely by paying a sum of money, a prosecutor may consider the corporation's willingness to make restitution and steps already taken to do so. A prosecutor may also consider other remedial actions, such as improving an existing compliance program or disciplining wrongdoers, in determining whether to charge the corporation and how to resolve corporate criminal cases.

B. Comment: In determining whether or not to prosecute a corporation, the government may consider whether the corporation has taken meaningful remedial measures. A corporation's response to misconduct says much about its willingness to ensure that such misconduct does not recur. Thus, corporations that fully recognize the seriousness of their misconduct and accept responsibility for it should be taking steps to implement the personnel, operational, and organizational changes necessary to establish an awareness among employees that criminal conduct will not be tolerated.

Among the factors prosecutors should consider and weigh are whether the corporation appropriately disciplined wrongdoers, once those employees are identified by the corporation as culpable for the misconduct. Employee discipline is a difficult task for many corporations because of the human element involved and sometimes because of the seniority of the employees concerned. Although corporations need to be fair to their employees, they must also be committed, at all levels of the corporation, to the highest standards of legal and ethical behavior. Effective internal discipline can be a powerful deterrent against improper behavior by a corporation's employees. Prosecutors should be satisfied that the corporation's focus is on the integrity and credibility of its remedial and disciplinary measures rather than on the protection of the wrongdoers.

In addition to employee discipline, two other factors used in evaluating a corporation's remedial efforts are restitution and reform. As with natural persons, the decision whether or not to prosecute should not depend upon the target's ability to pay restitution. A corporation's efforts to pay restitution even in advance of any court order is, however, evidence of its acceptance of responsibility and . . . may be considered in determining whether to bring criminal charges. Similarly, although the inadequacy of a corporate compliance program is a factor to consider when deciding whether to charge a corporation, that corporation's quick recognition of the flaws in the program and its efforts to improve the program are also factors to consider as to appropriate disposition of a case.

COLLATERAL CONSEQUENCES

A. General Principle: Prosecutors may consider the collateral consequences of a corporate criminal conviction or indictment in determining whether to charge the corporation with a criminal offense and how to resolve corporate criminal cases.

B. Comment: One of the factors in determining whether to charge a natural person or a corporation is whether the likely punishment is appropriate given the nature and seriousness of the crime. In the corporate context, prosecutors may take into account the possibly substantial consequences to a corporation's employees, investors, pensioners, and customers, many of whom may, depending on the size and nature of the corporation and their role in its operations, have played no role in the criminal conduct, have been unaware of it, or have been unable to prevent it. Prosecutors should also be aware of non-penal sanctions that may accompany a criminal charge, such as potential suspension or debarment from eligibility for government contracts or federally funded programs such as health care programs. Determining whether or not such non-penal sanctions are appropriate or required in a particular case is the responsibility of the relevant agency, and is a decision that will be made based on the applicable statutes, regulations, and policies.

Virtually every conviction of a corporation, like virtually every conviction of an individual, will have an impact on innocent third parties, and the mere existence of such an effect is not sufficient to preclude prosecution of the corporation. Therefore, in evaluating the relevance of collateral consequences, various factors already discussed, such as the pervasiveness of the criminal conduct and the adequacy of the corporation's compliance programs, should be considered in determining the weight to be given to this factor. For instance, the balance may tip in favor of prosecuting corporations in situations where the scope of the misconduct in a case is widespread and sustained within a corporate division (or spread throughout pockets of the corporate organization). In such cases, the possible unfairness of visiting punishment for the corporation's crimes upon shareholders may be of much less concern where those shareholders have substantially profited, even unknowingly, from widespread or pervasive criminal activity. Similarly, where the top layers of the corporation's management or the shareholders of a closely-held corporation were engaged in or aware of the wrongdoing, and the conduct at issue was accepted as a way of doing business for an extended period, debarment may be deemed not collateral, but a direct and entirely appropriate consequence of the corporation's wrongdoing.

On the other hand, where the collateral consequences of a corporate conviction for innocent third parties would be significant, it may be appropriate to consider a non-prosecution or deferred prosecution agreement with conditions designed, among other things, to promote compliance with applicable law and to prevent recidivism. Such agreements are a third option, besides a criminal indictment, on the one hand, and a declination, on the other. Declining prosecution may allow a corporate criminal to escape without consequences. Obtaining a conviction may produce a result that seriously harms innocent third parties who played no role in the criminal conduct. Under appropriate circumstances, a deferred prosecution or non-prosecution agreement can help restore the integrity of a company's operations and preserve the financial viability of a corporation that has engaged in criminal conduct, while preserving the government's ability to prosecute a recalcitrant corporation that materially breaches the agreement. Such agreements achieve other important objectives as well, like prompt restitution for victims. Ultimately, the appropriateness of a criminal charge against a corporation, or some lesser alternative, must be evaluated in a pragmatic and reasoned way that produces a fair outcome. . . .

OTHER CIVIL OR REGULATORY ALTERNATIVES

A. General Principle: Non-criminal alternatives to prosecution often exist and prosecutors may consider whether such sanctions would adequately deter, punish, and rehabilitate a corporation that has engaged in wrongful conduct. In evaluating the adequacy of non-criminal alternatives to prosecution—e.g., civil or regulatory enforcement actions—the prosecutor may consider all relevant factors, including:

1. the sanctions available under the alternative means of disposition;
2. the likelihood that an effective sanction will be imposed; and
3. the effect of non-criminal disposition on federal law enforcement interests.

B. Comment: The primary goals of criminal law are deterrence, punishment, and rehabilitation. Non-criminal sanctions may not be an appropriate response to a serious violation, a pattern of wrongdoing, or prior non-criminal sanctions without proper remediation. In other cases, however, these goals may be satisfied through civil or regulatory actions. In determining whether a federal criminal resolution is appropriate, the prosecutor should consider the same factors (modified appropriately for the regulatory context) considered when determining whether to leave prosecution of a natural person to another jurisdiction or to seek non-criminal alternatives to prosecution. . . .

SELECTING CHARGES

A. General Principle: Once a prosecutor has decided to charge a corporation, the prosecutor at least presumptively should charge, or should recommend that the grand jury charge, the most serious offense that is consistent with the nature of the defendant's misconduct and that is likely to result in a sustainable conviction.

B. Comment: Once the decision to charge is made, the same rules as govern charging natural persons apply. These rules require "a faithful and honest application of the Sentencing Guidelines" and an "individualized assessment of the extent to which particular charges fit the specific circumstances of the case, are consistent with the purposes of the Federal criminal code, and maximize the impact of Federal resources on crime." In making this determination, "it is appropriate that the attorney for the government consider, inter alia, such factors as the [advisory] sentencing guideline range yielded by the charge, whether the penalty yielded by such sentencing range . . . is proportional to the seriousness of the defendant's conduct, and whether the charge achieves such purposes of the criminal law as punishment, protection of the public, specific and general deterrence, and rehabilitation."

PLEA AGREEMENTS WITH CORPORATIONS

A. General Principle: In negotiating plea agreements with corporations, as with individuals, prosecutors should generally seek a plea to the most serious, readily provable offense charged. In addition, the terms of the plea agreement should contain appropriate provisions to ensure punishment, deterrence, rehabilitation, and compliance with the plea agreement in the corporate context. Although special circumstances may mandate a different conclusion, prosecutors generally should not agree to accept a corporate guilty plea in exchange for non-prosecution or dismissal of charges against individual officers and employees.

B. Comment: Prosecutors may enter into plea agreements with corporations for the same reasons and under the same constraints as apply to plea agreements with natural persons. This means, inter alia, that the corporation should generally be required to plead guilty to the most serious, readily provable offense charged. In addition, any negotiated departures or recommended variances from the advisory Sentencing Guidelines must be justifiable under the Guidelines or 18 U.S.C. § 3553 and must be disclosed to the sentencing court. A corporation should be made to realize that pleading guilty to criminal charges constitutes an admission of guilt and not merely a resolution of an inconvenient distraction from its business. As with natural persons, pleas should be structured so that the corporation may not later "proclaim lack of culpability or even complete innocence." Thus, for instance, there should be placed upon the record a sufficient factual basis for the plea to prevent later corporate assertions of innocence.

A corporate plea agreement should also contain provisions that recognize the nature of the corporate "person" and that ensure that the principles of punishment, deterrence, and rehabilitation are met. In the corporate context, punishment and deterrence are generally accomplished by substantial fines, mandatory restitution, and institution of appropriate compliance measures, including, if necessary, continued judicial oversight or the use of special masters or corporate monitors. In addition, where the corporation is a government contractor, permanent or temporary debarment may be appropriate. Where the corporation was engaged in fraud against the government (e.g., contracting fraud), a prosecutor may not negotiate away an agency's right to debar or delist the corporate defendant.

In negotiating a plea agreement, prosecutors should also consider the deterrent value of prosecutions of individuals within the corporation. Therefore, one factor that a prosecutor may consider in determining whether to enter into a plea agreement is whether the corporation is seeking immunity for its employees and officers or whether the corporation is willing to cooperate in the investigation of culpable individuals as outlined herein. Prosecutors should rarely negotiate away individual criminal liability in a corporate plea.

Rehabilitation, of course, requires that the corporation undertake to be law-abiding in the future. It is, therefore, appropriate to require the corporation, as a condition of probation, to implement a compliance program or to reform an existing one. As discussed above, prosecutors may consult with the appropriate state and federal agencies and components of the Justice Department to ensure that a proposed compliance program is adequate and meets industry standards and best practices. . . .

NOTES & QUESTIONS ON CORPORATE PUNISHMENT

1. *No soul to damn.*   It is extremely hard to punish a corporation, since it is a legal person as opposed to a natural person. One scholar summed up the problem succinctly: "[M]oderate fines do not deter, while severe penalties flow through the corporate shell to the relatively blameless." See John C. Coffee, Jr., *"No Soul to Damn: No Body to Kick": An Unscandalized Inquiry into the Problem of Corporate Punishment*, 79 Mich. L. Rev. 386 (1981). Coffee proposed an "equity fine" to help solve the problem: The convicted corporation would be required to issue shares to the state's victim compensation fund. The fund could then retain or sell the shares as it wishes. According to Coffee, "[l]ittle impact on employees, creditors or suppliers seems likely from the equity fine, since the capital of the corporation is not depleted." The only result is that the victims (or rather the state as their fiduciary) become part owners of the corporation. To date, the proposal has not been adopted. Do you think it would work?

2. *Collateral consequences.*   As the Federal Principles recognize, punishing a corporation can have devastating collateral consequences on innocent third parties. Three obvious examples include current employees who are innocent of wrongdoing, retirees who depend on the corporation for pension or healthcare benefits, and stockholders whose only connection to the company was their equity interest. As to the latter group, one might argue that some stockholders financially benefitted from the corporation's illegality, especially if it had a profit motive. But in this regard it is essential to distinguish between stockholders who sold at inflated prices (and benefited from the illegality) and stockholders who purchased at inflated prices and sold at depressed prices (and therefore were harmed by the criminal behavior). Employees and retirees are in a completely different situation and might be negatively impacted by a criminal prosecution.

PROBLEM CASE

On June 5, 2015, Chicago prosecutors announced that they had charged the Roman Catholic Archdiocese of St. Paul and Minneapolis with multiple counts of contributing to the delinquency of a minor and contributing to the "need for protection or services" in the case of a minor. Prosecutors had earlier charged and convicted a priest in the archdiocese, Curtis Wehmeyer, of multiple sex crimes. Prosecutors then went after the corporate entity, the local Archdiocese, and alleged in their criminal complaint that "a review of Archdiocesan priest files reveals a long history of an institutional failure to prevent and responsibly respond to child sexual abuse by clergy under the employ" of the Archdiocese. Priests received counseling and therapy and were sometimes reassigned to different parishes, but were rarely fired or turned over to police.

Do you agree with the court's decision to go after the church for its failure to adequately respond to the complaints about sex abuse? On the one hand, a criminal fine might harm other members of the church who are innocent third parties. On the other hand, perhaps a criminal case could be settled with a stipulation that the church implement appropriate monitoring and response mechanisms when it receives sex abuse allegations. Is the criminal process required to get these changes implemented or would a threat of civil action from victims be sufficient to generate change? Or is the criminal case justified on expressivist or retributive grounds, i.e., the public's need to condemn the church for its failure to act?

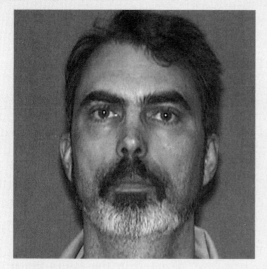

Curtis Wehmeyer

For this reason, federal prosecutors will often seek to punish the corporation without outright killing it (through dissolution). However, this thin line is not always easy to manage. Accounting firm Arthur Andersen was effectively put out of business after it was convicted of obstructing the government's investigation of Enron—a perilous result for employees who had no knowledge or involvement with the Enron account. Ironically, the Supreme Court ultimately vacated the conviction, though not in time for the firm to recover. *Arthur Andersen LLP v. United States*, 544 U.S. 696 (2005). As many as 28,000 employees were affected by the firm's dissolution. See Elizabeth K. Ainslie, *Indicting Corporations Revisited: Lessons of the Arthur Andersen Prosecution*, 43 Am. Crim. L. Rev. 107 (2006).

3. Prosecuting Corporate Officers

Corporate liability works in two directions. We first analyzed when the corporation can be held responsible for the acts of its officers or employees. Now we consider the reverse: When can corporate officers or managers be held responsible for the corporation's criminal behavior? As you read the following case, ask yourself whether the doctrine adequately identifies the culpable members of a corporation.

United States v. Park
Supreme Court of the United States
421 U.S. 658 (1975)

BURGER, C.J.

. . . Acme Markets, Inc., is a national retail food chain with approximately 36,000 employees, 874 retail outlets, 12 general warehouses, and four special warehouses. Its headquarters, including the office of the president, respondent Park, who is chief executive officer of the corporation, are located in Philadelphia, Pa. In a five-count information filed in the United States District Court for the District of Maryland, the Government charged Acme and respondent with violations of the Federal Food, Drug and Cosmetic Act. Each count of the information alleged that the defendants had received food that had been shipped in interstate commerce and that, while the food was being held for sale in Acme's Baltimore warehouse following shipment in interstate commerce, they caused it to be held in a building accessible to rodents and to be exposed to contamination by rodents. These acts were alleged to have resulted in the food's being adulterated. . . .

Acme pleaded guilty to each count of the information. Respondent pleaded not guilty. The evidence at trial demonstrated that in April 1970 the Food and Drug Administration (FDA) advised respondent by letter of insanitary conditions in Acme's Philadelphia warehouse. In 1971 the FDA found that similar conditions existed in the firm's Baltimore warehouse. An FDA consumer safety officer testified concerning evidence of rodent infestation and other insanitary conditions discovered during a 12-day inspection of the Baltimore warehouse in November and December 1971. He also related that a second inspection of the warehouse had been conducted in March 1972. . . .

The Government also presented testimony by the Chief of Compliance of the FDA's Baltimore office, who informed respondent by letter of the conditions at the Baltimore warehouse after the first inspection. There was testimony by Acme's Baltimore division vice president, who had responded to the letter on behalf of Acme and respondent and who described the steps taken to remedy the insanitary conditions discovered by both inspections. The Government's final witness, Acme's vice president for legal affairs and assistant secretary, identified respondent as the president and chief executive officer of the company and read a bylaw prescribing the duties of the chief executive officer. He testified that respondent functioned by delegating "normal operating duties," including sanitation, but that he retained "certain things, which are the big, broad, principles of the operation of the company," and had "the responsibility of seeing that they all work together." . . .

Respondent was the only defense witness. He testified that, although all of Acme's employees were in a sense under his general direction, the company had an "organizational structure for responsibilities for certain functions" according to which different phases of its operation were "assigned to individuals who, in turn, have staff and departments under them." He identified those individuals responsible for sanitation, and related that upon receipt of the January 1972 FDA letter, he had conferred with the vice president for legal affairs, who informed him that the Baltimore division vice president "was investigating the situation immediately and would be taking corrective action and would be preparing a summary of the corrective action to reply to the letter." Respondent stated that he did not "believe there was anything (he) could have done more constructively than what (he) found was being done."

On cross-examination, respondent conceded that providing sanitary conditions for food offered for sale to the public was something that he was "responsible for in the entire operation of the company," and he stated that it was one of many phases of the company that he assigned to "dependable subordinates." Respondent was asked about and, over the objections of his counsel, admitted receiving, the April 1970 letter addressed to him from the FDA regarding insanitary conditions at Acme's Philadelphia warehouse. He acknowledged that, with the exception of the division vice president, the same individuals had responsibility for sanitation in both Baltimore and Philadelphia. Finally, in response to questions concerning the Philadelphia and Baltimore incidents, respondent admitted that the Baltimore problem indicated the system for handling sanitation "wasn't working perfectly" and that as Acme's chief executive officer he was responsible for "any result which occurs in our company." . . .

I

The question presented by the Government's petition for certiorari in *United States v. Dotterweich*, 320 U.S. 277 (1943), and the focus of this Court's opinion, was whether "the manager of a corporation, as well as the corporation itself, may be prosecuted under the Federal Food, Drug, and Cosmetic Act of 1938 for the introduction of misbranded and adulterated articles into interstate commerce." In *Dotterweich*, a jury had disagreed as to the corporation, a jobber purchasing drugs from manufacturers and shipping them in interstate commerce under its own label, but had convicted Dotterweich, the corporation's president and general manager. The Court of Appeals reversed the conviction on the ground that only the drug dealer, whether corporation or individual, was subject to the criminal provisions of the Act, and that where the dealer was a corporation, an individual connected therewith might be held personally only if he was operating the corporation "as his 'alter ego.'"

In reversing the judgment of the Court of Appeals and reinstating Dotterweich's conviction, this Court looked to the purposes of the Act and noted that they "touch phases of the lives and health of the people which, in the circumstances of modern industrialism, are largely beyond self-protection." It observed that the Act is of "a now familiar type" which "dispenses with the conventional requirement for criminal conduct—awareness of some wrongdoing. In the interest of the larger good it puts the burden of acting at hazard upon a person otherwise innocent but standing in responsible relation to a public danger."

Central to the Court's conclusion that individuals other than proprietors are subject to the criminal provisions of the Act was the reality that "the only way in which a corporation can act is through the individuals who act on its behalf." The Court also noted that corporate officers had been subject to criminal liability under the Federal Food and Drugs Act of 1906, and it observed that a contrary result under the 1938 legislation would be incompatible with the expressed intent of Congress. . . .

At the same time, however, the Court was aware of the concern which was the motivating factor in the Court of Appeals' decision, that literal enforcement "might operate too harshly by sweeping within its condemnation any person however remotely entangled in the proscribed shipment." A limiting principle, in the form of "settled doctrines of criminal law" defining those who "are responsible for the commission of a misdemeanor," was available. In this context, the Court concluded, those doctrines dictated that the offense was committed "by all who . . . have . . . a responsible share in the furtherance of the transaction which the statute outlaws."

The Court recognized that, because the Act dispenses with the need to prove "consciousness of wrongdoing," it may result in hardship even as applied to those who share "responsibility in the business process resulting in" a violation. It regarded as "too treacherous" an attempt "to define or even to indicate by way of illustration the class of employees which stands in such a responsible relation." The question of responsibility, the Court said, depends "on the evidence produced at the trial and its submission—assuming the evidence warrants it—to the jury under appropriate guidance."...

II

The rule that corporate employees who have "a responsible share in the furtherance of the transaction which the statute outlaws" are subject to the criminal provisions of the Act was not formulated in a vacuum. Cases under the Federal Food and Drugs Act of 1906 reflected the view both that knowledge or intent were not required to be proved in prosecutions under its criminal provisions, and that responsible corporate agents could be subjected to the liability thereby imposed. Moreover, the principle had been recognized that a corporate agent, through whose act, default, or omission the corporation committed a crime, was himself guilty individually of that crime. The principle had been applied whether or not the crime required "consciousness of wrongdoing," and it had been applied not only to those corporate agents who themselves committed the criminal act, but also to those who by virtue of their managerial positions or other similar relation to the actor could be deemed responsible for its commission.

In the latter class of cases, the liability of managerial officers did not depend on their knowledge of, or personal participation in, the act made criminal by the statute. Rather, where the statute under which they were prosecuted dispensed with "consciousness of wrongdoing," an omission or failure to act was deemed a sufficient basis for a responsible corporate agent's liability. It was enough in such cases that, by virtue of the relationship he bore to the corporation, the agent had the power to prevent the act complained of....

III

We cannot agree with the Court of Appeals that it was incumbent upon the District Court to instruct the jury that the Government had the burden of establishing "wrongful action" in the sense in which the Court of Appeals used that phrase. The concept of a "responsible relationship" to, or a "responsible share" in, a violation of the Act indeed imports some measure of blameworthiness; but it is equally clear that the Government establishes a prima facie case when it introduces evidence sufficient to warrant a finding by the trier of the facts that the defendant had, by reason of his position in the corporation, responsibility and authority either to prevent in the first instance, or promptly to correct, the violation complained of, and that he failed to do so. The failure thus to fulfill the duty imposed by the interaction of the corporate agent's authority and the statute furnishes a sufficient causal link. The considerations which prompted the imposition of this duty, and the scope of the duty, provide the measure of culpability....

NOTES & QUESTIONS ON RESPONSIBLE OFFICERS

1. *The direction of legal responsibility.*   Was it fair to hold Park personally responsible for his company's FDA violations? *Park* is a classic case showing how corporate liability moves in both directions. Individual employees engaged in conduct that violated the FDA. The violations were attributable to the corporation, which was liable as a corporate entity. Then, responsibility flowed back *down* to all responsible corporate officers. Was Park responsible for the conduct? Did he have a responsible share in the violations? The Court said yes. Which facts in the record supported that conclusion? Was Park put on notice that there were problems at the plant and what corrective measures did he put in place to rectify the situation?

2. *The mens rea of corporate officers.*   Did Park have a sufficient mens rea to be convicted? Many cases of corporate officer liability rest on regulatory violations that are based on varying degrees of strict liability. It is one thing to hold a corporation responsible under that standard, but quite another to impute the behavior back to the corporate officer without establishing personal wrongdoing. How does the Court resolve this concern? The Court said that the existence of a responsible relationship to—or responsible share in—the violation demonstrates the necessary level of blameworthiness that makes individual liability appropriate. Do you agree? Courts continue to apply the responsible corporate officers doctrine and *Park*'s requirement that the defendant have a responsible relationship to, or a responsible share in, the violation. Indeed, some courts have applied this standard even when the defendant is not formally a corporate officer at all. For example, in *United States v. Hong*, 242 F.3d 528 (4th Cir. 2001), the defendant was involved in the operation of a wastewater treatment facility that violated the Clean Water Act by dumping untreated water into the sewage system on 12 occasions. The court concluded that although Hong was involved in the creation of the corporation and controlled its finances, he studiously avoided obtaining a corporate officer title at the company. Could the responsible corporate officers doctrine apply to non-officers? The court said yes because "the Government was not required to prove that Hong was a formally designated corporate officer. . . . The gravamen of liability as a responsible corporate officer is not one's corporate title or lack thereof; rather, the pertinent question is whether the defendant bore such a relationship to the corporation that it is appropriate to hold him criminally liable for failing to prevent the charged violations. . . ." *Id.* at 531. Applying this standard, the court noted that Hong was often on site and "substantially controlled corporate operations" even in the absence of a formal officer title. Hong was sentenced to three years in prison and fined $1.3 million.

C. PRACTICE & POLICY

Corporate criminal responsibility presents no shortage of practical issues for attorneys working on both sides of the aisle. In this section, we consider three issues of crucial importance for the criminal defense bar: (i) navigating both federal and state prosecutions; (ii) negotiating a deferred prosecution agreement; and (iii) deciding whether to waive the attorney-client and work product privileges.

    ∾ **State prosecutions.** Although most prosecutions of corporations are initiated by the federal government, this is not universally true. Some state jurisdictions are quite active in scrutinizing the conduct of corporations. We read about a regular manslaughter prosecution in Arizona in the *Far West* case, above. Some state jurisdictions are more active than others, depending on whether they prefer to conduct their own criminal enquiries against corporations or whether they rely on federal authorities. The State of New York is one obvious example. The New York State Attorney General has broad authority under state law to file civil cases against persons who engage in "repeated fraudulent or illegal acts or otherwise demonstrate persistent fraud or illegality in the carrying on, conducting or transaction of business." N.Y. Exec. Law § 63(12). Similarly, the New York State Attorney General has authority to prosecute corporations for anti-trust violations under the Donnelly Act. N.Y. Gen. Bus. Law § 340. See also *New York v. Haberstrumpf*, 404 N.Y.S.2d 245 (Sup. Ct. 1978) (civil and criminal remedies not mutually exclusive under state law). Indeed, the overlapping jurisdiction of federal and state authorities is of immense importance for attorneys working as corporate defense counsel. Successful negotiation and resolution of a federal enforcement matter does not preclude a piggyback prosecution by state authorities at a later point in time. Corporate defense counsel must therefore negotiate with both authorities to ensure appropriate resolution of all outstanding liability. Furthermore, admitting some allegations in exchange for preferential treatment in a federal investigation might result in unintended scrutiny during a subsequent state investigation. For example, in anti-trust investigations the Justice Department routinely promises favorable treatment to the first corporation to admit wrongdoing and cooperate with authorities. In making this decision, corporate counsel should factor in to their calculation the specter of a future state prosecution.

    ∾ **Deferred prosecution agreements.** When the Justice Department prosecutes a corporation, the charges are often resolved without a trial by the corporation agreeing to a "deferred prosecution agreement" or DPA. The basic contours of these agreements are that the federal government agrees to furlough the criminal case in exchange for promises from the corporation regarding reform and future behavior. The most common element of a deferred prosecution agreement is the implementation of a new or reformed compliance program to correct and prevent wrongdoing. Occasionally, DPAs might require the corporation to change how it conducts business. For example, a case against a pharmaceutical company for improper marketing of a drug for off-label uses might lead to a DPA where the corporation agrees to change its marketing practices. If the corporation fails to abide by the terms of the DPA, the government reserves the right to reinitiate the prosecution. The federal government encourages prosecutors to use DPA because it produces compliance and reform without the cost of a lengthy trial. Brandon L. Garrett, *Structural Reform Prosecution*, 93 Va. L. Rev. 853 (2007) (unlike legislative and administrative responses, "structural reform prosecutions raise questions about the reach of federal executive branch power"). The corporate defense bar often finds these agreements coercive because theoretically even innocent corporations are eager to avoid the disruption to their business interests that a trial would entail. See Wulf A. Kaal & Timothy A. Lacine, *The Effect of Deferred and Non-Prosecution Agreements on Corporate Governance: Evidence from 1993-2013*, 70 Bus. L. 61 (2015) (DPAs are "controversial because prosecutors, not judges or the legislature, are changing the governance of leading public corporations and entire industries"). Prosecutors retain unilateral authority to reinstate the prosecution if they believe that the corporation breached the non-prosecution agreement.

Similar issues arise when prosecutors and defense attorneys negotiate a consent judgment to settle an enforcement action that has already been filed. These cases frequently result in a negotiated "consent judgment" that requires formal approval by the judge in the case. In most cases, acceptance of the consent judgment is virtually pro forma. However, in *SEC v. Citigroup Global Markets*, 827 F. Supp. 2d 328 (S.D.N.Y. 2011), Judge Rakoff took the extraordinary step of rejecting the proposed consent judgment. Among other things, Rakoff complained that the negotiated judgment did not require Citigroup to admit wrongdoing. He continued:

> It is harder to discern from the limited information before the Court what the S.E.C. is getting from this settlement other than a quick headline. By the S.E.C.'s own account, Citigroup is a recidivist, and yet, in terms of deterrence, the $95 million civil penalty that the Consent Judgment proposes is pocket change to any entity as large as Citigroup. While the S.E.C. claims that it is devoted, not just to the protection of investors but also to helping them recover their losses, the proposed Consent Judgment, in the form

submitted to the Court, does not commit the S.E.C. to returning any of the total of $285 million obtained from Citigroup to the defrauded investors but only suggests that the S.E.C. "may" do so. In any event, this still leaves the defrauded investors substantially short-changed.

The Second Circuit overruled Rakoff and called his decision an abuse of discretion. 752 F.3d 285 (2d Cir. 2014).

∾ **Waiving attorney-client privilege.**   As the above "Principles of Federal Prosecution of Business Organizations" indicate, the government's decision to prosecute a corporation is based in part on an assessment of the corporation's level of cooperation. In the past, one component of the cooperation calculus was whether the corporation was willing to waive its attorney-client and work product privileges. Corporations often include multiple levels of legal review with corporate counsel throughout their daily operations and much of this activity is privileged and not discoverable if it took place within the context of a corporate attorney providing legal advice to the corporation or in anticipation of litigation. Frustrated by corporations using these privileges to shield information from the government, federal prosecutors sometimes asked corporations to "waive" these privileges and disclose relevant information to the government anyway. Why did corporations comply? They did so because the request often comes at the same time that the government is deciding whether to prosecute the corporation. Is it appropriate for the government to consider a corporation's unwillingness to waive the privilege when deciding whether to prosecute? Does this violate the spirit of the attorney-client privilege? See Oren M. Henry, *Privilege? What Privilege? Culture of Waiver in the Corporate World*, 20 Geo. J. Legal Ethics 679 (2007). In response to substantial public criticism, the Department of Justice announced in 2008 that it had revised its policy and would no longer consider a corporation's failure to waive attorney-client privilege when assessing cooperation credit, but rather would focus on whether the relevant facts were disclosed to the government.

PART V

JUSTIFICATIONS & EXCUSES

CHAPTER 23

⟞⟝⟞⟝⟞

SELF-DEFENSE

A. DOCTRINE

When faced with an imminent threat, the target of an attack need not simply
succumb to the intrusion. Certainly, non-deadly force is permitted in response
to a non-deadly threat. For example, a person faced with a physical battery
could use a battery of his own to stop the aggressor from connecting his
punch to the defender's face. In these and other situations, the law privileges
an act of defensive force that would otherwise constitute a crime. If taken in
response to an imminent threat of death or serious bodily injury, even deadly
force can be justified. For example, the use of deadly force is permitted to repel
a serious attack such as a rape, kidnapping, or—in some jurisdictions—a robbery. To satisfy the justification of self-defense in a homicide case, a defendant
must show that he acted according to a reasonable belief of an imminent threat
of death or serious bodily injury. Implicit in these requirements is that the
defensive force must be necessary (i.e., the defendant either could not escape
or was under no duty to escape) and that his response was proportionate to the
intrusion that he faced (i.e., the threatened injury was serious enough to
warrant deadly force). Each of these prongs will be explored in greater detail,
as well as the concept of imperfect self-defense that applies when the defendant's conduct does *not* meet one of the requirements.

1. Imminent Threat

A reasonable belief in a threat of death or severe bodily injury is not, by itself,
sufficient to ground a successful claim of self-defense. Indeed, the threat must
also be imminent. The rationale for the imminence requirement is that the
attack need not have already occurred before the target is entitled to a right

of response. For example, imagine an attacker points a gun at the victim and announces his intention to kill him. The law does not require that the attacker actually shoot the victim before the victim has a right to defend himself. That would be absurd. Indeed, it is sufficient that the threat is imminent, i.e., on the horizon, rather than fully manifest. However, the imminence requirement demands that the defensive force cannot be too far in advance. At that point, the defensive force becomes a pre-emptive strike designed to avert a potential or hypothetical threat that is not even imminent yet. The imminence requirement also outlaws defensive force that comes too late, after the threat has evaporated; at that point, force would be motivated by revenge or punishment, which is the exclusive purview of the state. The law only privileges defensive force that is prospective in nature and is designed to repel an imminent or ongoing attack. Imminence requires that self-defense be neither too soon nor too late. In determining how close in time the defensive force must be to the aggressive attack, juries exercise their discretion by engaging in a fact-intensive inquiry of the situation.

The imminence requirement was subjected to substantial criticism for being too strict. Some jurisdictions have flirted with loosening the requirement after hearing cases involving Battered Women's Syndrome—women who killed abusive partners even when they were not under direct assault at the moment they killed their partners. But the majority of state appellate courts (and legislatures) have not abandoned the imminence requirement. The issue remains highly controversial.

That being said, the Model Penal Code rejects the imminence requirement. In its place, the Model Penal Code simply requires that the defensive force be "immediately necessary" at the time of its deployment. MPC § 3.04(1). A handful of states have adopted this standard. Imagine that an attacker is about to administer a slow-acting poison that will kill the victim a year from now. Assume the poison has no known antidote. The victim's best and only chance to stop the attack is to repel it *now*, even though the threatened harm will only materialize a year from now. In that case, the defensive force is "immediately necessary" at the time the poison is administered. Or, imagine a prison inmate threatened with rape by his cellmate later that night. If the guards have done nothing to protect him, the inmate's only reasonable chance of success might be to use defensive force now rather than wait until the middle of the night when the sexual assault is in progress. Immediate necessity changes the temporal focus of the judicial inquiry from the time the harm materializes to the time that action is required to repel it, which in some situations might come at an earlier point in time.

2. Necessity and the Duty to Retreat

Defensive force must also be necessary in order to stop the attack. If the target of the aggressive force can repel the attack without resorting to deadly force, then she is required to avail herself of that opportunity. Specifically, if the target of the attack can safely retreat from the attack and avoid the necessity of using lethal force, the target is legally required to do so. Some jurisdictions refuse to apply the rule when the target of the aggressive attack is in her home. This "Castle Exception" to the duty to retreat has practical consequences for self-defense cases emerging from robberies and home invasions. If an intruder comes upon a homeowner inside the house, the homeowner need not run from the house or even retreat to a different room—say a bedroom upstairs. However, the Castle Doctrine does not automatically mean that the use of deadly force is justified whenever there is an intruder; it simply means that the homeowner is not required to retreat if the necessity standard is otherwise met. The elements of self-defense might not be satisfied for other reasons.

In recent years, some state legislatures have passed Stand Your Ground laws that abrogate the duty to retreat in a wide variety of situations—not just the home as the Castle Doctrine does. While the specifics of these laws vary, they usually repeal the duty to retreat as long as the actor who deploys defensive force was lawfully in that location. Some of these new statutes also include provisions that deal specifically with home invasions and create a legal presumption that the resident had a reasonable fear of death or serious bodily injury from an intruder who enters the home. In these jurisdictions, the combination of a statutory presumption of a reasonable fear, combined with a legal presumption that the killing was necessary, all but ensures that killings triggered by a home intruder will be deemed justified under the state statute. For this reason, the statutes are highly controversial.

3. Reasonable Belief

To qualify for self-defense, the defendant must sincerely *believe* that he faces a threat of death or severe bodily injury or sexual assault. In this sense, there is no requirement for an *actual* imminent threat. What is required is that the defendant believed that she faced an imminent threat and believed that lethal force was necessary to repel the threat. Consequently, self-defense requires the jury to view the situation through the eyes of the defendant. But there are limits to this subjectivity. The defendant's belief must also be *reasonable*. Courts have struggled with how to define reasonableness in this context, with some favoring a subjective approach and others favoring an objective approach. A subjective approach simply limits the analysis to whether the defendant's belief was reasonable *to him*. Under that analysis, reasonableness is not doing much work, since people are always inclined to think of their own beliefs as reasonable and well supported (otherwise they would not continue to entertain them or act upon them). So, the better and more popular view is the objective approach, where the analysis has two levels. First, the court asks whether the defendant sincerely and honestly believed that he faced a threat and that force was necessary to repel it. Second, the court asks whether that belief was objectively reasonable under the circumstances. In other words, would a reasonable person *in the same situation* have held the same belief? Materials in the application section will focus on the difficulties of applying the concept of reasonableness in concrete factual situations.

4. Imperfect Self-Defense

What if an actor believes that defensive force is necessary but he turns out to be wrong? Jurisdictions have two ways of handling these mistakes. In some jurisdictions, self-defense works like an ON-OFF switch: Either the defendant is justified or not. If the defendant is justified, he should be acquitted and go free. If the defendant is not justified, he should be convicted of murder, just as if he had never raised the self-defense argument in the first place. The result of this binary scheme is that actors who mistakenly use defensive force are placed in the same category as murderers who kill for more nefarious reasons (greed, avarice, sadism, etc.).

In response to dissatisfaction with the ON-OFF switch, some jurisdictions have created an interim category for actors who mistakenly use self-defense. These doctrines, known as imperfect self-defense or putative self-defense, recognize that cases of mistaken self-defense are less blameworthy than cases of cold-blooded murder. The result in these jurisdictions is that the defendant has his murder conviction downgraded from murder to voluntary manslaughter—a partial defense similar to provocation or extreme emotional disturbance. In an actual case, a defendant who pleads self-defense might begin his case by arguing to the jury that his actions were fully justified. If, however, the prosecution presents evidence that the defendant's actions were unjustified, the defendant might ask the judge to instruct the jury on the doctrine of imperfect self-defense. In the end, his lawyer might use this as a fallback argument: Even if the jury concludes that force was not justified, it should still conclude that the defendant mistakenly believed that defensive force was necessary and therefore convict him only of manslaughter.

B. APPLICATION

1. Imminence

A valid claim of self-defense requires a reasonable belief in an *imminent* threat. A threat far off in the future or an expired threat is insufficient. But what is the dividing line? As you read the following case, ask yourself whether the threat facing Norman was imminent and whether it was necessary for her to deploy lethal force when she did.

State v. Norman
Supreme Court of North Carolina
324 N.C. 253, 378 S.E.2d 8 (1989)

MITCHELL, J.

The defendant was tried at the 16 February 1987 Criminal Session of Superior Court for Rutherford County upon a proper indictment charging her with the first degree murder of her husband. The jury found the defendant guilty of voluntary manslaughter. The defendant appealed from the trial court's judgment sentencing her to six years imprisonment. The Court of Appeals granted a new trial, citing as error the trial court's refusal to submit a possible verdict of acquittal by reason of perfect self-defense. Notwithstanding the uncontroverted evidence that the defendant shot her husband three times in the back of the head as he lay sleeping in his bed, the Court of Appeals held that the defendant's evidence that she exhibited what has come to be called "the battered wife syndrome" entitled her to have the jury consider whether the homicide was an act of perfect self-defense and, thus, not a legal wrong.

We conclude that the evidence introduced in this case would not support a finding that the defendant killed her husband due to a reasonable fear of imminent death or great bodily harm, as is required before a defendant is entitled to jury instructions concerning either perfect or imperfect self-defense. Therefore, the trial court properly declined to instruct the jury on the law relating to self-defense. Accordingly, we reverse the Court of Appeals.

At trial, the State presented the testimony of Deputy Sheriff R.H. Epley of the Rutherford County Sheriff's Department, who was called to the Norman residence on the night of 12 June 1985. Inside the home, Epley found the defendant's husband, John Thomas Norman, lying on a bed in a rear bedroom with his face toward the wall and his back toward the middle of the room. He was dead, but blood was still coming from wounds to the back of his head. A later autopsy revealed three gunshot wounds to the head, two of which caused fatal brain injury. The autopsy also revealed a .12 percent blood alcohol level in the victim's body.

Later that night, the defendant related an account of the events leading to the killing, after Epley had advised her of her constitutional rights and she had waived her right to remain silent. The defendant told Epley that her husband had been beating her all day and had made her lie down on the floor while he slept on the bed. After her husband fell asleep, the defendant carried her grandchild to the defendant's mother's house. The defendant took a pistol from her mother's purse and walked the short distance back to her home. She pointed the pistol at the back of her sleeping husband's head, but it jammed the first time she tried to shoot him. She fixed the gun and then shot her husband in the back of the head as he lay sleeping.

After one shot, she felt her husband's chest and determined that he was still breathing and making sounds. She then shot him twice more in the back of the head. The defendant told Epley that she killed her husband because "she took all she was going to take from him so she shot him."

The defendant presented evidence tending to show a long history of physical and mental abuse by her husband due to his alcoholism. At the time of the killing, the thirty-nine-year-old defendant and her husband had been married almost twenty-five years and had several children. The defendant testified that her husband had started drinking and abusing her about five years after they were married. His physical abuse of her consisted of frequent assaults that included slapping, punching and kicking her, striking her with various objects, and throwing glasses, beer bottles and other objects at her. The defendant described other specific incidents of abuse, such as her husband putting her cigarettes out on her, throwing hot coffee on her, breaking glass against her face and crushing food on her face. Although the defendant did not present evidence of ever having received medical treatment for any physical injuries inflicted by her husband, she displayed several scars about her face which she attributed to her husband's assaults.

The defendant's evidence also tended to show other indignities inflicted upon her by her husband. Her evidence tended to show that her husband did not work and forced her to make money by prostitution, and that he made humor of that fact to family and friends. He would beat her if she resisted going out to prostitute herself or if he was unsatisfied with the amounts of money she made. He routinely called the defendant "dog," "bitch" and "whore," and on a few occasions made her eat pet food out of the pets' bowls and bark like a dog. He often made her sleep on the floor. At times, he deprived her of food and refused to let her get food for the family. During those years of abuse, the defendant's husband threatened numerous times to kill her and to maim her in various ways.

The defendant said her husband's abuse occurred only when he was intoxicated, but that he would not give up drinking. She said she and her husband "got along very well when he was sober," and that he was "a good guy" when he was not drunk. She had accompanied her husband to the local mental health center for sporadic counseling sessions for his problem, but he continued to drink.

In the early morning hours on the day before his death, the defendant's husband, who was intoxicated, went to a rest area off I-85 near Kings Mountain where the defendant was engaging in prostitution and assaulted her. While driving home, he was stopped by a patrolman and jailed on a charge of driving while impaired. After the defendant's mother got him out of jail at the defendant's request later that morning, he resumed his drinking and abuse of the defendant.

The defendant's evidence also tended to show that her husband seemed angrier than ever after he was released from jail and that his abuse of the defendant was more frequent. That evening, sheriff's deputies were called to the Norman residence, and the defendant complained that her husband had been beating her all day and she could not take it anymore. The defendant was advised to file a complaint, but she said she was afraid her husband would kill her if she had him arrested. The deputies told her they needed a warrant before they could arrest her husband, and they left the scene.

The deputies were called back less than an hour later after the defendant had taken a bottle of pills. The defendant's husband cursed her and called her names as she was attended by paramedics, and he told them to let her die. A sheriff's deputy finally chased him back into his house as the defendant was put into an ambulance. The defendant's stomach was pumped at the local hospital, and she was sent home with her mother.

While in the hospital, the defendant was visited by a therapist with whom she discussed filing charges against her husband and having him committed for treatment. Before the therapist left, the defendant agreed to go to the mental health center the next day to discuss those possibilities. The therapist testified at trial that the defendant seemed depressed in the hospital, and that she expressed considerable anger toward her husband. He testified that the defendant threatened a number of times that night to kill her husband and that she said she should kill him "because of the things he had done to her."

The next day, the day she shot her husband, the defendant went to the mental health center to talk about charges and possible commitment, and she confronted her husband with that possibility. She testified that she told her husband later that day: "J.T., straighten up. Quit drinking. I'm going to have you committed to help you." She said her husband then told her he would "see them coming" and would cut her throat before they got to him.

The defendant also went to the social services office that day to seek welfare benefits, but her husband followed her there, interrupted her interview and made her go home with him. He continued his abuse of her, threatening to kill and to maim her, slapping her, kicking her, and throwing objects at her. At one point, he took her cigarette and put it out on her, causing a small burn on her upper torso. He would not let her eat or bring food into the house for their children.

That evening, the defendant and her husband went into their bedroom to lie down, and he called her a "dog" and made her lie on the floor when he lay down on the bed. Their daughter brought in her baby to leave with the defendant, and the defendant's husband agreed to let her baby-sit. After the defendant's husband fell asleep, the baby started crying and the defendant took it to her mother's house so it would not wake up her husband. She returned shortly with the pistol and killed her husband.

The defendant testified at trial that she was too afraid of her husband to press charges against him or to leave him. She said that she had temporarily left their home on several previous occasions, but he had always found her, brought her home and beaten her. Asked why she killed her husband, the defendant replied: "Because I was scared of him and I knowed when he woke up, it was going to be the same thing, and I was scared when he took me to the truck stop that night it was going to be worse than he had ever been. I just couldn't take it no more. There ain't no way, even if it means going to prison. It's better than living in that. That's worse hell than anything."

The defendant and other witnesses testified that for years her husband had frequently threatened to kill her and to maim her. When asked if she believed those threats, the defendant replied: "Yes. I believed him; he would, he would kill me if he got a chance. If he thought he wouldn't a had to went to jail, he would a done it."

Two expert witnesses in forensic psychology and psychiatry who examined the defendant after the shooting, Dr. William Tyson and Dr. Robert Rollins, testified that the defendant fit the profile of battered wife syndrome. This condition, they testified, is characterized by such abuse and degradation that the battered wife comes to believe she is unable to help herself and cannot expect help from anyone else. She believes that she cannot escape the complete control of her husband and that he is invulnerable to law enforcement and other sources of help.

Dr. Tyson, a psychologist, was asked his opinion as to whether, on 12 June 1985, "it appeared reasonably necessary for Judy Norman to shoot J.T. Norman?" He replied: "I believe that . . . Mrs. Norman believed herself to be doomed . . . to a life of the worst kind of torture and abuse, degradation that she had experienced over the years in a progressive way; that it would only get worse, and that death was inevitable. . . ." Dr. Tyson later added: "I think Judy Norman felt that she had no choice, both in the protection of herself and her family, but to engage, exhibit deadly force against Mr. Norman, and that in so doing, she was sacrificing herself, both for herself and for her family."

Dr. Rollins, who was the defendant's attending physician at Dorothea Dix Hospital when she was sent there for evaluation, testified that in his opinion the defendant was a typical abused spouse and that "[s]he saw herself as powerless to deal with the situation, that there was no alternative, no way she could escape it." Dr. Rollins was asked his opinion as to whether "on June 12th, 1985, it appeared reasonably necessary that Judy Norman would take the life of J.T. Norman?" Dr. Rollins replied that in his opinion, "that course of action did appear necessary to Mrs. Norman."

Based on the evidence that the defendant exhibited battered wife syndrome, that she believed she could not escape her husband nor expect help from others, that her husband had threatened her, and that her husband's abuse of her had worsened in the two days preceding his death, the Court of Appeals concluded that a jury reasonably could have found that her killing of her husband was justified as an act of perfect self-defense. The Court of Appeals reasoned that the nature of battered wife syndrome is such that a jury could not be precluded from finding the defendant killed her husband lawfully in perfect self-defense, even though he was asleep when she killed him. We disagree.

The right to kill in self-defense is based on the necessity, real or reasonably apparent, of killing an unlawful aggressor to save oneself from *imminent* death or great bodily harm at his hands. Our law has recognized that self-preservation under such circumstances springs from a primal impulse and is an inherent right of natural law. . . .

The killing of another human being is the most extreme recourse to our inherent right of self-preservation and can be justified in law only by the utmost real or apparent necessity brought about by the decedent. For that reason, our law of self-defense has required that a defendant claiming that a homicide was justified and, as a result, inherently lawful by reason of perfect self-defense must establish that she reasonably believed at the time of the killing she otherwise would have immediately suffered death or great bodily harm. Only if defendants are required to show that they killed due to a reasonable belief that death or great bodily harm was imminent can the justification for homicide remain clearly and firmly rooted in necessity. The imminence requirement ensures that deadly force will be used only where it is necessary as a last resort in the exercise of the inherent right of self-preservation. It also ensures that before a homicide is justified and, as a result, not a legal wrong, it will be reliably determined that the defendant reasonably believed that absent the use of deadly force, not only would an unlawful attack have occurred, but also that the attack would have caused death or great bodily harm. The law does not sanction the use of deadly force to repel simple assaults.

The term "imminent," as used to describe such perceived threats of death or great bodily harm as will justify a homicide by reason of perfect self-defense, has been defined as "immediate danger, such as must be instantly met, such as cannot be guarded against by calling for the assistance of others or the protection of the law." Our cases have sometimes used the phrase "about to suffer" interchangeably with "imminent" to describe the immediacy of threat that is required to justify killing in self-defense.

The evidence in this case did not tend to show that the defendant reasonably believed that she was confronted by a threat of imminent death or great bodily harm. The evidence tended to show that no harm was "imminent" or about to happen to the defendant when she shot her husband. The uncontroverted evidence was that her husband had been asleep for some time when she walked to her mother's house, returned with the pistol, fixed the pistol after it jammed and then shot her husband three times in the back of the head. The defendant was not faced with an instantaneous choice between killing her husband or being killed or seriously injured. Instead, *all* of the evidence tended to show that the defendant had ample time and opportunity to resort to other means of preventing further abuse by her husband. There was no action underway by the decedent from which the jury could have found that the defendant had reasonable grounds to believe either that a felonious assault was imminent or that it might result in her death or great bodily injury. Additionally, no such action by the decedent had been underway immediately prior to his falling asleep. . . .

Additionally, the lack of any belief by the defendant—reasonable or otherwise—that she faced a threat of imminent death or great bodily harm from the drunk and sleeping victim in the present case was illustrated by the defendant and her own expert witnesses when testifying about her subjective assessment of her situation at the time of the killing. The psychologist and psychiatrist replied affirmatively when asked their opinions of whether killing her husband "appeared reasonably necessary" to the defendant at the time of the homicide. That testimony spoke of no *imminent* threat nor of any fear by the defendant of death or great bodily harm, imminent or otherwise. Testimony in the form of a conclusion that a killing "appeared reasonably necessary" to a defendant does not tend to show all that must be shown to establish self-defense. More specifically, for a killing to be in self-defense, the perceived necessity must arise from a reasonable fear of imminent death or great bodily harm.

Dr. Tyson additionally testified that the defendant "believed herself to be doomed . . . to a life of the worst kind of torture and abuse, degradation that she had experienced over the years in a progressive way; that it would only get worse, and that death was inevitable." Such evidence of the defendant's speculative beliefs concerning her remote and indefinite future, while indicating she had felt generally threatened, did not tend to show that she killed in the belief—reasonable or otherwise—that her husband presented a threat of *imminent* death or great bodily harm. Under our law of self-defense, a defendant's subjective belief of what might be "inevitable" at some indefinite point in the future does not equate to what she believes to be "imminent." Dr. Tyson's opinion that the defendant believed it was necessary to kill her husband for "the protection of herself and her family" was similarly indefinite and devoid of time frame and did not tend to show a threat or fear of *imminent* harm.

The defendant testified that, "I knowed when he woke up, it was going to be the same thing, and I was scared when he took me to the truck stop that night it was going to be worse than he had ever been." She also testified, when asked if she believed her husband's threats: "Yes. . . . [H]e would kill me if he got a chance. If he thought he wouldn't a had to went to jail, he would a done it." Testimony about such indefinite fears concerning what her sleeping husband might do at some time in the future did not tend to establish a fear—reasonable or otherwise—of *imminent death or great bodily harm* at the time of the killing.

We are not persuaded by the reasoning of our Court of Appeals in this case that when there is evidence of battered wife syndrome, neither an actual attack nor threat of attack by the husband at the moment the wife uses deadly force is required to justify the wife's killing of him in perfect self-defense. The Court of Appeals concluded that to impose such requirements would ignore the "learned helplessness," meekness and other realities of battered wife syndrome and would effectively preclude such women from exercising their right of self-defense. Other jurisdictions which have addressed this question under similar facts are divided in their views, and we can discern no clear majority position on facts closely similar to those of this case.

The reasoning of our Court of Appeals in this case proposes to change the established law of self-defense by giving the term "imminent" a meaning substantially more indefinite and all-encompassing than its present meaning. This would result in a substantial relaxation of the requirement of real or apparent necessity to justify homicide. Such reasoning proposes justifying the taking of human life not upon the reasonable belief it is necessary to prevent death or great bodily harm—which the imminence requirement ensures—but upon purely subjective speculation that the decedent probably would present a threat to life at a future time and that the defendant would not be able to avoid the predicted threat.

The Court of Appeals suggests that such speculation would have been particularly reliable in the present case because the jury, based on the evidence of the decedent's intensified abuse during the thirty-six hours preceding his death, could have found that the decedent's passive state at the time of his death was "but a momentary hiatus in a continuous reign of terror by the decedent [and] the defendant merely took advantage of her first opportunity to protect herself." Requiring jury instructions on perfect self-defense in such situations, however, would still tend to make opportune homicide lawful as a result of mere subjective predictions of indefinite future assaults and circumstances. Such predictions of future assaults to justify the defendant's use of deadly force in this case would be entirely speculative, because there was no evidence that her husband had ever inflicted any harm upon her that approached life-threatening injury, even during the "reign of terror." It is far from clear in the defendant's poignant evidence that any abuse by the decedent had ever involved the degree of physical threat required to justify the defendant in using deadly force, even when those threats were imminent. The use of deadly force in self-defense to prevent harm other than death or great bodily harm is excessive as a matter of law.

As we have stated, stretching the law of self-defense to fit the facts of this case would require changing the "imminent death or great bodily harm" requirement to something substantially more indefinite than previously required and would weaken our assurances that justification for the taking of human life remains firmly rooted in real or apparent necessity. That result in principle could not be limited to a few cases decided on evidence as poignant as this. The relaxed requirements for perfect self-defense proposed by our Court of Appeals would tend to categorically legalize the opportune killing of abusive husbands by their wives solely on the basis of the wives' testimony concerning their subjective speculation as to the probability of future felonious assaults by their husbands. Homicidal self-help would then become a lawful solution, and perhaps the easiest and most effective solution, to this problem. It has even been suggested that the relaxed requirements of self-defense found in what is often called the "battered woman's defense" could be extended in principle to *any type of case* in which a defendant testified that he or she subjectively believed that killing was necessary and proportionate to any perceived threat.

In conclusion, we decline to expand our law of self-defense beyond the limits of immediacy and necessity which have heretofore provided an appropriately narrow but firm basis upon which homicide may be justified and, thus, lawful by reason of perfect self-defense or upon which a defendant's culpability may be reduced by reason of imperfect self-defense. As we have shown, the evidence in this case did not entitle the defendant to jury instructions on either perfect or imperfect self-defense. . . .

MARTIN, J., dissenting.

. . . At the heart of the majority's reasoning is its unsubstantiated concern that to find that the evidence presented by defendant would support an instruction on self-defense would "expand our law of self-defense beyond the limits of immediacy and necessity." Defendant does not seek to expand or relax the requirements of self-defense and thereby "legalize the opportune killing of allegedly abusive husbands by their wives," as the majority overstates. Rather, defendant contends that the evidence as gauged by the existing laws of self-defense is sufficient to require the submission of a self-defense instruction to the jury. The proper issue for this Court is to determine whether the evidence, viewed in the light most favorable to the defendant, was sufficient to require the trial court to instruct on the law of self-defense. I conclude that it was. . . .

Evidence presented by defendant described a twenty-year history of beatings and other dehumanizing and degrading treatment by her husband. In his expert testimony a clinical psychologist concluded that defendant fit "and exceed[ed]" the profile of an abused or battered spouse, analogizing this treatment to the dehumanization process suffered by prisoners of war under the Nazis during the Second World War and the brainwashing techniques of the Korean War. The psychologist described the defendant as a woman incarcerated by abuse, by fear, and by her conviction that her husband was invincible and inescapable:

> Mrs. Norman didn't leave because she believed, fully believed that escape was totally impossible. There was no place to go. He, she had left before; he had come and gotten her. She had gone to the Department of Social Services. He had come and gotten her. The law, she believed the law could not protect her; no one could protect her, and I must admit, looking over the records, that there was nothing done that would contradict that belief. She fully believed that he was invulnerable to the law and to all social agencies that were available; that nobody could withstand his power. As a result, there was no such thing as escape. . . .

In addition to the testimony of the clinical psychologist, defendant presented the testimony of witnesses who had actually seen defendant's husband abuse her. These witnesses described circumstances that caused not only defendant to believe escape was impossible, but that also convinced *them* of its impossibility. Defendant's isolation and helplessness were evident in testimony that her family was intimidated by her husband into acquiescing in his torture of her. Witnesses also described defendant's experience with social service agencies and the law, which had contributed to her sense of futility and abandonment through the inefficacy of their protection and the strength of her husband's wrath when they failed. Where torture appears interminable and escape impossible, the belief that only the death of the oppressor can provide relief is reasonable in the mind of a person of ordinary firmness, let alone in the mind of the defendant, who, like a prisoner of war of some years, has been deprived of her humanity and is held hostage by fear.

In *State v. Mize,* 316 N.C. 48, 53, 340 S.E.2d 439, 442 (1986), this Court noted that if the defendant was in "no imminent danger" at the time of the killing, then his belief that it was necessary to kill the man who had pursued him eight hours before was unreasonable. The second element of self-defense was therefore not satisfied. In the context of the doctrine of self-defense, the definition of "imminent" must be informed by the defendant's perceptions. It is not bounded merely by measurable time, but by all of the facts and circumstances. Its meaning depends upon the assessment of the facts by one of "ordinary firmness" with regard to whether the defendant's perception of impending death or injury was so pressing as to render reasonable her belief that it was necessary to kill.

 Evidence presented in the case sub judice revealed no letup of tension or fear, no moment in which the defendant felt released from impending serious harm, even while the decedent slept. This, in fact, is a state of mind common to the battered spouse, and one that dramatically distinguishes Judy Norman's belief in the imminence of serious harm from that asserted by the defendant in *Mize*. Psychologists have observed and commentators have described a "constant state of fear" brought on by the cyclical nature of battering as well as the battered spouse's perception that her abuser is both "omnipotent and unstoppable." Constant fear means a perpetual anticipation of the next blow, a perpetual expectation that the next blow will kill. "[T]he battered wife is constantly in a heightened state of terror because she is certain that one day her husband will kill her during the course of a beating. . . . Thus from the perspective of the battered wife, the danger is constantly 'immediate.'" For the battered wife, if there is no escape, if there is no window of relief or momentary sense of safety, then the next attack, which could be the fatal one, is imminent. In the context of the doctrine of self-defense, "imminent" is a term the meaning of which must be grasped from the defendant's point of view. Properly stated, the second prong of the question is not whether the threat was *in fact* imminent, but whether defendant's belief in the impending nature of the threat, given the circumstances as she saw them, was reasonable in the mind of a person of ordinary firmness.

Defendant's intense fear, based on her belief that her husband intended not only to maim or deface her, as he had in the past, but to kill her, was evident in the testimony of witnesses who recounted events of the last three days of the decedent's life. This testimony could have led a juror to conclude that defendant reasonably perceived a threat to her life as "imminent," even while her husband slept. Over these three days, her husband's anger was exhibited in an unprecedented crescendo of violence. The evidence showed defendant's fear and sense of hopelessness similarly intensifying, leading to an unsuccessful attempt to escape through suicide and culminating in her belief that escape would be possible only through her husband's death.

Defendant testified that on 10 June, two days before her husband's death, he had again forced her to go to a rest stop near Kings Mountain to make money by prostitution. Her daughter Phyllis and Phyllis's boyfriend Mark Navarra accompanied her on this occasion because, defendant said, whenever her husband took her there, he would beat her. Phyllis corroborated this account. She testified that her father had arrived some time later and had begun beating her mother, asking how much money she had. Defendant said they all then drove off. Shortly afterwards an officer arrested defendant's husband for driving under the influence. He spent the night in jail and was released the next morning on bond paid by defendant's mother.

Defendant testified that her husband was argumentative and abusive all through the next day, 11 June. Mark Navarra testified that at one point defendant's husband threw a sandwich that defendant had made for him on the floor. She made another; he threw it on the floor, as well, then insisted she prepare one without touching it. Defendant's husband had then taken the third sandwich, which defendant had wrapped in paper towels, and smeared it on her face. Both Navarra and Phyllis testified that they had later watched defendant's husband seize defendant's cigarette and put it out on her neck, the scars from which defendant displayed to the jury.

A police officer testified that he arrived at defendant's home at 8:00 that evening in response to a call reporting a domestic quarrel. Defendant, whose face was bruised, was crying, and she told the officer that her husband had beaten her all day long and that she could not take it any longer. The officer told her that he could do nothing for her unless she took out a warrant on her husband. She responded that if she did, her husband would kill her. The officer left but was soon radioed to return because defendant had taken an overdose of pills. The officer testified that defendant's husband was interfering with ambulance attendants, saying "Let the bitch die." When he refused to respond to the officer's warning that if he continued to hinder the attendants, he would be arrested, the officer was compelled to chase him into the house.

Defendant's mother testified that her son-in-law had reacted to the discovery that her daughter had taken the pills with cursing and obscenities and threats such as, "Now, you're going to pay for taking those pills," and "I'll kill you, your mother and your grandmother." His rage was such that defendant's mother feared he might kill the whole family, and knowing defendant's sister had a gun in her purse, she took the gun and placed it in her own.

Defendant was taken to the hospital, treated, and released at 2:30 A.M. She spent the remainder of the night at her grandmother's house. Defendant testified that the next day, 12 June, she felt dazed all day long. She went in the morning to the county mental health center for guidance on domestic abuse. When she returned home, she tried to talk to her husband, telling him to "straighten up. Quit drinking. . . . I'm going to have you committed to help you." Her husband responded, "If you do, I'll see them coming and before they get here, I'll cut your throat."

Later, her husband made her drive him and his friend to Spartanburg to pick up the friend's paycheck. On the way, the friend testified, defendant's husband "started slapping on her" when she was following a truck too closely, and he periodically poured his beer into a glass, then reached over and poured it on defendant's head. At one point defendant's husband lay down on the front seat with his head on the arm rest, "like he was going to go to sleep," and kicked defendant, who was still driving, in the side of the head.

Mark Navarra testified that in the year and a half he had lived with the Normans, he had never seen defendant's husband madder than he was on 12 June, opining that it was the DUI arrest two days before that had ignited J.T.'s fury. Phyllis testified that her father had beaten her mother "all day long." She testified that this was the third day defendant's husband had forbidden her to eat any food. Phyllis said defendant's family tried to get her to eat, but defendant, fearing a beating, would not. Although Phyllis's grandmother had sent over a bag of groceries that day, defendant's husband had made defendant put them back in the bag and would not let anyone eat them.

Early in the evening of 12 June, defendant's husband told defendant, "Let's go to bed." Phyllis testified that although there were two beds in the room, her father had forbidden defendant from sleeping on either. Instead, he had made her lie down on the concrete floor between the two beds, saying, "Dogs don't lay in the bed. They lay in the floor." Shortly afterward, defendant testified, Phyllis came in and asked her father if defendant could take care of her baby while she went to the store. He assented and eventually went to sleep. Defendant was still on the floor, the baby on the small bed. The baby started to cry and defendant "snuck up and took him out there to [her] mother's [house]." She asked her mother to watch the baby, then asked if her mother had anything for headache, as her head was "busting." Her mother responded that she had some pain pills in her purse. Defendant went in to get the pills, "and the gun was in there, and I don't know, I just seen the gun, and I took it out, and I went back there and shot him."

From this evidence of the exacerbated nature of the last three days of twenty years of provocation, a juror could conclude that defendant believed that her husband's threats to her life were viable, that serious bodily harm was imminent, and that it was necessary to kill her husband to escape that harm. And from this evidence a juror could find defendant's belief in the necessity to kill her husband not merely reasonable but compelling. . . .

By his barbaric conduct over the course of twenty years, J.T. Norman reduced the quality of the defendant's life to such an abysmal state that, given the opportunity to do so, the jury might well have found that she was justified in acting in self-defense for the preservation of her tragic life. . . .

NOTES & QUESTIONS ON IMMINENCE

1. *Justification or excuse.* Evaluate the role that evidence of Battered Women's Syndrome plays in these cases. Does it tell us something about whether self-defense should be classified as a justification or an excuse? When a defendant misperceives a threat, self-defense sounds like an excuse based on a mistake of fact or a failure of rationality. On the other hand, some advocates think that defensive killings of this type should be legally justified because the woman had no other way out—an argument that speaks to self-defense as a justification. For a discussion, see George P. Fletcher, *Domination in the Theory of Justification and Excuse*, 57 U. Pitt. L. Rev. 553, 576 (1996) ("The prior relationship between the parties should bear on aspects of self-defense that sound in the theory of excuses, namely the recognition that the action is wrongful but nonetheless not a fit basis for blaming and punishing the person who resorts to violence."); Claire O. Finkelstein, *Self-Defense as a Rational Excuse*, 57 U. Pitt. L. Rev. 621 (1996).

2. *The Model Penal Code and immediate necessity.* Is the imminence standard morally justified? The Model Penal Code dispensed with imminence entirely and simply demands that the actor "believes that such force is immediately necessary for the purpose of protecting himself against the use of unlawful force. . . ." MPC § 3.04(1). What is the difference between imminent and immediate necessity? Imminence asks about the temporal relationship between the actor's defensive force and when the threatened harm will materialize. The two have to be close in time. In contrast, immediate necessity asks about the temporal relationship between the actor's defensive force and his last opportunity to avert the threat. In other words, what matters is whether it was necessary to use defensive force *at that moment* to stop the threat. In most cases, the two standards yield identical results but sometimes they diverge, especially in cases of slowly developing threats. The Model Penal Code standard of immediate necessity was not widely adopted but it is codified in a few states, including Texas. See Tex. Penal Code § 9.31; Neb. Rev. Stat. § 28-1409; Ariz. Rev. Stat. § 13-404. In New Jersey, which applies the immediate necessity standard, at least one defendant has tried to argue that he suffered from "Battered Child Syndrome" when he shot his father while he slept in his reclining chair. *State v. Mahoney*, 2012 N.J. Super. Unpub. LEXIS 2453 (upholding trial judge's decision to allow defense counsel to present Battered Child Syndrome defense to jury).

In Judy Norman's case, how would you evaluate her claim under the standard of immediate necessity? What would have happened if she had waited until her husband had woken up? Perhaps she could argue that shooting her husband while he slept was immediately necessary because once he woke up her ability to defend herself against the inevitable onslaught would be gone. Should advocates who support the Battered Women's Syndrome theory push for more states to switch from the imminence standard to immediate necessity?

2. Necessity and the Duty to Retreat

Defensive force is only justified if it is necessary to stop the attack and avert the harm. If the target can escape without injury, then in a sense the defensive force is not truly necessary. For this reason, the law has generally imposed a duty to retreat, if the actor can do so safely, instead of resorting to lethal force. The following case examines and applies the specific exceptions to this broad rule.

United States v. Peterson
U.S. Court of Appeals for the D.C. Circuit
483 F.2d 1222 (1973)

SPOTTSWOOD W. ROBINSON, III, CIRCUIT JUDGE:

Indicted for second-degree murder, and convicted by a jury of manslaughter as a lesser included offense, Bennie L. Peterson urges . . . reversal. . . . He contends . . . that the evidence was legally insufficient to establish his guilt of manslaughter, and that in consequence the judge erred in denying his motion for a judgment of acquittal. He complains . . . that the judge twice erred in the instructions given the jury in relation to his claim that the homicide was committed in self-defense. One error alleged was an instruction that the jury might consider whether Peterson was the aggressor in the altercation that immediately foreran the homicide. The other was an instruction that a failure by Peterson to retreat, if he could have done so without jeopardizing his safety, might be considered as a circumstance bearing on the question whether he was justified in using the amount of force which he did. After careful study of these arguments in light of the trial record, we affirm Peterson's conviction.

I

The events immediately preceding the homicide are not seriously in dispute. The version presented by the Government's evidence follows. Charles Keitt, the deceased, and two friends drove in Keitt's car to the alley in the rear of Peterson's house to remove the windshield wipers from the latter's wrecked car. While Keitt was doing so, Peterson came out of the house into the back yard to protest. After a verbal exchange, Peterson went back into the house, obtained a pistol, and returned to the yard. In the meantime, Keitt had reseated himself in his car, and he and his companions were about to leave.

Upon his reappearance in the yard, Peterson paused briefly to load the pistol. "If you move," he shouted to Keitt, "I will shoot." He walked to a point in the yard slightly inside a gate in the rear fence and, pistol in hand, said, "If you come in here I will kill you." Keitt alighted from his car, took a few steps toward Peterson and exclaimed, "What the hell do you think you are going to do with that?" Keitt then made an about-face, walked back to his car and got a lug wrench. With the wrench in a raised position, Keitt advanced toward Peterson, who stood with the pistol pointed toward him. Peterson warned Keitt not to "take another step" and, when Keitt continued onward shot him in the face from a distance of about ten feet. Death was apparently instantaneous. Shortly thereafter, Peterson left home and was apprehended 20-odd blocks away.

This description of the fatal episode was furnished at Peterson's trial by four witnesses for the Government. Peterson did not testify or offer any evidence, but the Government introduced a statement which he had given the police after his arrest, in which he related a somewhat different version. Keitt had removed objects from his car before, and on the day of the shooting he had told Keitt not to do so. After the initial verbal altercation, Keitt went to his car for the lug wrench, so he, Peterson, went into his house for his pistol. When Keitt was about ten feet away, he pointed the pistol "away of his right shoulder;" adding that Keitt was running toward him, Peterson said he "got scared and fired the gun. He ran right into the bullet." "I did not mean to shoot him," Peterson insisted, "I just wanted to scare him." . . .

IV

The trial judge's charge authorized the jury, as it might be persuaded, to convict Peterson of second-degree murder or manslaughter, or to acquit by reason of self-defense. On the latter phase of the case, the judge instructed that with evidence of self-defense present, the Government bore the burden of proving beyond a reasonable doubt that Peterson did not act in self-defense; and that if the jury had a reasonable doubt as to whether Peterson acted in self-defense, the verdict must be not guilty. The judge further instructed that the circumstances under which Peterson acted, however, must have been such as to produce a reasonable belief that Keitt was then about to kill him or do him serious bodily harm, and that deadly force was necessary to repel him. In determining whether Peterson used excessive force in defending himself, the judge said, the jury could consider all of the circumstances under which he acted.

These features of the charge met Peterson's approval, and we are not summoned to pass on them. There were, however, two other aspects of the charge to which Peterson objected, and which are now the subject of vigorous controversy. The first of Peterson's complaints centers upon an instruction that the right to use deadly force in self-defense is not ordinarily available to one who provokes a conflict or is the aggressor in it. Mere words, the judge explained, do not constitute provocation or aggression; and if Peterson precipitated the altercation but thereafter withdrew from it in good faith and so informed Keitt by words or acts, he was justified in using deadly force to save himself from imminent danger or death or grave bodily harm. And, the judge added, even if Keitt was the aggressor and Peterson was justified in defending himself, he was not entitled to use any greater force than he had reasonable ground to believe and actually believed to be necessary for that purpose. Peterson contends that there was no evidence that he either caused or contributed to the conflict, and that the instructions on that topic could only misled the jury.

It has long been accepted that one cannot support a claim of self-defense by a self-generated necessity to kill. The right of homicidal self-defense is granted only to those free from fault in the difficulty; it is denied to slayers who incite the fatal attack, encourage the fatal quarrel or otherwise promote the necessitous occasion for taking life. The fact that the deceased struck the first blow, fired the first shot or made the first menacing gesture does not legalize the self-defense claim if in fact the claimant was the actual provoker. In sum, one who is the aggressor in a conflict culminating in death cannot invoke the necessities of self-preservation. Only in the event that he communicates to his adversary his intent to withdraw and in good faith attempts to do so is he restored to his right of self-defense.

This body of doctrine traces its origin to the fundamental principle that a killing in self-defense is excusable only as a matter of genuine necessity. Quite obviously, a defensive killing is unnecessary if the occasion for it could have been averted, and the roots of that consideration run deep with us . . . In the case at bar, the trial judge's charge fully comported with these governing principles. The remaining question, then, is whether there was evidence to make them applicable to the case. A recapitulation of the proofs shows beyond peradventure that there was.

It was not until Peterson fetched his pistol and returned to his back yard that his confrontation with Keitt took on a deadly cast. Prior to his trip into the house for the gun, there was, by the Government's evidence, no threat, no display of weapons, no combat. There was an exchange of verbal aspersions and a misdemeanor against Peterson's property was in progress but, at this juncture, nothing more. Even if Peterson's post-arrest version of the initial encounter were accepted—his claim that Keitt went for the lug wrench before he armed himself—the events which followed bore heavily on the question as to who the real aggressor was.

The evidence is uncontradicted that when Peterson reappeared in the yard with his pistol, Keitt was about to depart the scene. Richard Hilliard testified that after the first argument, Keitt reentered his car and said "Let's go." This statement was verified by Ricky Gray, who testified that Keitt "got in the car and . . . they were getting ready to go;" he, too, heard Keitt give the direction to start the car. The uncontroverted fact that Keitt was leaving shows plainly that so far as he was concerned the confrontation was ended.

It demonstrates just as plainly that even if he had previously been the aggressor, he no longer was.

Not so with Peterson, however, as the undisputed evidence made clear. Emerging from the house with the pistol, he paused in the yard to load it, and to command Keitt not to move. He then walked through the yard to the rear gate and, displaying his pistol, dared Keitt to come in, and threatened to kill him if he did. While there appears to be no fixed rule on the subject, the cases hold, and we agree, that an affirmative unlawful act reasonably calculated to produce an affray foreboding injurious or fatal consequences is an aggression which, unless renounced, nullifies the right of homicidal self-defense. We cannot escape the abiding conviction that the jury could readily find Peterson's challenge to be a transgression of that character . . .

V

The second aspect of the trial judge's charge as to which Peterson asserts error concerned the undisputed fact that at no time did Peterson endeavor to retreat from Keitt's approach with the lug wrench. The judge instructed the jury that if Peterson had reasonable grounds to believe and did believe that he was in imminent danger of death or serious injury, and that deadly force was necessary to repel the danger, he was required neither to retreat nor to consider whether he could safely retreat. Rather, said the judge, Peterson was entitled to stand his ground and use such force as was reasonably necessary under the circumstances to save his life and his person from pernicious bodily harm. But, the judge continued, if Peterson could have safely retreated but did not do so, that failure was a circumstance which the jury might consider, together with all others, in determining whether he went further in repelling the danger, real or apparent, than he was justified in going.

Peterson contends that this imputation of an obligation to retreat was error, even if he could safely have done so. He points out that at the time of the shooting he was standing in his own yard, and argues he was under no duty to move. We are persuaded to the conclusion that in the circumstances presented here, the trial judge did not err in giving the instruction challenged.

Within the common law of self-defense there developed the rule of "retreat to the wall," which ordinarily forbade the use of deadly force by one to whom an avenue for safe retreat was open. This doctrine was but an application of the requirement of strict necessity to excuse the taking of human life, and was designed to insure the existence of that necessity. Even the innocent victim of a vicious assault had to elect a safe retreat if available, rather than resort to defensive force which might kill or seriously injure.

In a majority of American jurisdictions, contrarily to the common-law rule, one may stand his ground and use deadly force whenever it seems reasonably necessary to save himself. While the law of the District of Columbia on this point is not entirely clear, it seems allied with the strong minority adhering to the common law. In 1856, the District of Columbia Criminal Court ruled that a participant in an affray "must endeavor to retreat, . . . that is, he is obliged to retreat, if he can safely." The court added that "[a] man may, to be sure, decline a combat when there is no existing or apparent danger, but the retreat to which the law binds him is that which is the consequence." In a much later era this court, adverting to necessity as the soul of homicidal self-defense, declared that "no necessity for killing an assailant can exist, so long as there is a safe way open to escape the conflict." . . .

That is not to say that the retreat rule is without exceptions. Even at common law it was recognized that it was not completely suited to all situations. Today it is the more so that its precept must be adjusted to modern conditions nonexistent during the early development of the common law of self-defense. One restriction on its operation comes to the fore when the circumstances apparently foreclose a withdrawal with safety. The doctrine of retreat was never intended to enhance the risk to the innocent; its proper application has never required a faultless victim to increase his assailant's safety at the expense of his own. On the contrary, he could stand his ground and use deadly force otherwise appropriate if the alternative were perilous, or if to him it reasonably appeared to be. A slight variant of the same consideration is the principle that there is no duty to retreat from an assault producing an imminent danger of death or grievous bodily harm. "Detached reflection cannot be demanded in the presence of an uplifted knife," nor is it "a condition of immunity that one in that situation should pause to consider whether a reasonable man might not think it possible to fly with safety or to disable his assailant rather than to kill him."

The trial judge's charge to the jury incorporated each of these limitations on the retreat rule. Peterson, however, invokes another—the so-called "castle" doctrine. It is well settled that one who through no fault of his own is attacked in his home is under no duty to retreat therefrom. The oft-repeated expression that "a man's home is his castle" reflected the belief in olden days that there were few if any safer sanctuaries than the home. The "castle" exception, moreover, has been extended by some courts to encompass the occupant's presence within the curtilage outside his dwelling. Peterson reminds us that when he shot to halt Keitt's advance, he was standing in his yard and so, he argues, he had no duty to endeavor to retreat.

Despite the practically universal acceptance of the "castle" doctrine in American jurisdictions wherein the point has been raised, its status in the District of Columbia has never been squarely decided. But whatever the fate of the doctrine in the District law of the future, it is clear that in absolute form it was inapplicable here. The right of self-defense, we have said, cannot be claimed by the aggressor in an affray so long as he retains that unmitigated role. It logically follows that any rule of no-retreat which may protect an innocent victim of the affray would, like other incidents of a forfeited right of self-defense, be unavailable to the party who provokes or stimulates the conflict. Accordingly, the law is well settled that the "castle" doctrine can be invoked only by one who is without fault in bringing the conflict on. That, we think, is the critical consideration here.

We need not repeat our previous discussion of Peterson's contribution to the altercation which culminated in Keitt's death. It suffices to point out that by no interpretation of the evidence could it be said that Peterson was blameless in the affair. And while, of course, it was for the jury to assess the degree of fault, the evidence well nigh dictated the conclusion that it was substantial . . .

People v. Riddle

Supreme Court of Michigan
467 Mich. 116 (2002)

Young, J.

INTRODUCTION

The prosecution contends that Michigan law generally imposes a "duty to retreat" upon a person who would exercise deadly force in self-defense, and that the so-called "castle doctrine"—providing an exception to this duty to retreat when a person is attacked within his dwelling—does not extend to the area outside the dwelling. Defendant, on the other hand, contends that the castle doctrine should be extended to the curtilage and that he was not required to retreat when he was assaulted in his backyard.

Because Michigan's case law has become somewhat confused with respect to the concepts of retreat and the castle doctrine, we take this opportunity to clarify these principles as they apply to a claim of self-defense. We reaffirm today the following, according to the common-law principles that existed in Michigan when our murder statute was codified.

As a general rule, the killing of another person in self-defense by one who is free from fault is justifiable homicide if, under all the circumstances, he honestly and reasonably believes that he is in imminent danger of death or great bodily harm and that it is necessary for him to exercise deadly force. The necessity element of self-defense normally requires that the actor try to avoid the use of deadly force if he can safely and reasonably do so, for example by applying nondeadly force or by utilizing an obvious and safe avenue of retreat.

There are, however, three intertwined concepts that provide further guidance in applying this general rule in certain fact-specific situations. First, a person is *never* required to retreat from a sudden, fierce, and violent attack; nor is he required to retreat from an attacker who he reasonably believes is about to use a deadly weapon. In these circumstances, as long as he honestly and reasonably believes that it is necessary to exercise deadly force in self-defense, the actor's failure to retreat is never a consideration when determining if the necessity element of self-defense is satisfied; instead, he may stand his ground and meet force with force. That is, where it is uncontested that the defendant was the victim of a sudden and violent attack, the Court should not instruct the jury to consider whether retreat was safe, reasonable, or even possible, because, in such circumstances, the law does not require that the defendant engage in such considerations.

Second, Michigan law imposes an *affirmative obligation to retreat* upon a nonaggressor only in one narrow set of circumstances: A participant in voluntary mutual combat will not be justified in taking the life of another until he is deemed to have retreated as far as safely possible. One who is involved in a physical altercation in which he is a willing participant—referred to at common law as a "sudden affray" or a "chance medley"—is *required* to take advantage of any reasonable and safe avenue of retreat before using deadly force against his adversary, should the altercation escalate into a deadly encounter.

Third, regardless of the circumstances, one who is attacked in his dwelling is *never* required to retreat where it is otherwise necessary to exercise deadly force in self-defense. When a person is in his "castle," there is no safer place to retreat; the obligation to retreat that would otherwise exist in such circumstances is no longer present, and the homicide will be deemed justifiable. This is true even where one is a voluntary participant in mutual combat. Because there is no indication that this "castle doctrine" extended to outlying areas within the curtilage of the home at the time of the codification of our murder statute, however, we decline defendant's invitation to extend the doctrine in this manner; we hold instead that the doctrine is limited in application to the home and its attached appurtenances.

FACTUAL AND PROCEDURAL BACKGROUND

On the evening of August 15, 1997, defendant and two friends, Robin Carter and James Billingsley, convened at defendant's home. The three men were in the backyard just outside defendant's house, in the driveway near a detached garage, when defendant shot Carter in the legs eleven times with an automatic carbine rifle. After shooting Carter, defendant immediately drove to the Detroit River, where he disposed of the rifle. Carter, who did not have a weapon in his possession, was resuscitated at the scene but died as a result of the gunshot wounds three days later.

Although the facts in the preceding recitation are undisputed, at defendant's trial on charges of first-degree murder and felony-firearm the prosecution and the defense presented different versions of the events leading to the shooting. Billingsley testified for the prosecution that after Carter made a disparaging comment about ·defendant's fiancée, defendant went into the house, came back outside armed with a rifle, and began firing at Carter. Billingsley stated that Carter was not armed and did not approach defendant when he came out of the house with the weapon. Defendant, on the other hand, testified that he intervened in an argument between Carter and Billingsley and that he told Carter, whom he considered to be "the more aggressive one," to leave. Seeing a "dark object" in Carter's hand and believing it to be a gun, defendant immediately reached for his rifle, which he testified was in his detached garage. Defendant stated that he aimed the rifle at Carter's legs and pulled the trigger, intending only to scare him.

Defendant requested that the jury be instructed . . . that there is no duty to retreat in one's own home before exercising self-defense. The prosecution objected, contending that the instruction was not appropriate because the shooting took place outside the home, in the curtilage. Although defendant attempted to withdraw his request . . . the trial court proceeded to rule that the instruction was not appropriate under the circumstances of the case. The trial court instead instructed the jury . . . as follows:

> By law, a person must avoid using deadly force if he can safely do so. If the defendant could have safely retreated but did not do so, you can consider that fact along with all the other circumstances when you decide whether he went farther in protecting himself than he should have.
>
> However, if the defendant honestly and reasonably believed that it was immediately necessary to use deadly force to protect himself from an [imminent] threat of death or serious injury, the law does not require him to retreat. He may stand his ground and use the amount of force he believes necessary to protect himself.

The jury returned a verdict of guilty of the lesser offense of second-degree murder and guilty as charged of felony-firearm. . . .

SELF-DEFENSE AND RETREAT

At common law, a claim of self-defense, which "is founded upon necessity, real or apparent," may be raised by a nonaggressor as a legal justification for an otherwise intentional homicide. . . .

[T]he killing of another person in self-defense is justifiable homicide only if the defendant honestly and reasonably believes his life is in imminent danger or that there is a threat of serious bodily harm and that it is necessary to exercise deadly force to prevent such harm to himself.

We reaffirm today that the touchstone of *any* claim of self-defense, as a justification for homicide, is *necessity.* An accused's conduct in failing to retreat, or to otherwise avoid the intended harm, may in some circumstances—other than those in which the accused is the victim of a sudden, violent attack—indicate a lack of reasonableness or necessity in resorting to deadly force in self-defense. For example, where a defendant "invites trouble" or meets non-imminent force with deadly force, his failure to pursue an available, safe avenue of escape might properly be brought to the attention of the factfinder as a factor in determining whether the defendant acted in reasonable self-defense. . . .

The "Castle Doctrine"

It is universally accepted that retreat is not a factor in determining whether a defensive killing was necessary when it occurred in the accused's dwelling:

> Regardless of any general theory to retreat as far as practicable before one can justify turning upon his assailant and taking life in self-defense, the law imposes no duty to retreat upon one who, free from fault in bringing on a difficulty, is attacked at or in his or her own dwelling or home. Upon the theory that a man's house is his castle, *and that he has a right to protect it and those within it from intrusion or attack,* the rule is practically universal that when a person is attacked in his own dwelling he may stand at bay and turn on and kill his assailant if this is apparently necessary to save his own life or to protect himself from great bodily harm.

The rule has been defended as arising from "an instinctive feeling that a home is sacred, and that it is improper to require a man to submit to pursuit from room to room in his own house." Moreover, in a very real sense a person's dwelling is his primary place of refuge. Where a person is in his "castle," there is simply *no safer place* to retreat.

Defendant, who was outside his home in the driveway or yard between the home and a detached garage at the time of the homicide, contends that he was wholly excused from any obligation to retreat because he was in his "castle." We disagree and hold that the castle doctrine, as it applied in this state and as was codified in our murder statute in 1846, applies solely to the dwelling and its attached appurtenances. Although many courts have extended the castle exception to other areas, we conclude that there is simply no basis in the case law of this state, contemporaneous with the enactment of our initial murder statute, to justify extending the rule in this manner.

It is unknown whether the English common law applied the castle doctrine—which, as we have noted, was relevant only to the voluntary participant in a non-deadly encounter—to areas beyond the dwelling. . . . Because the only indication we have of the castle doctrine as it applied in Michigan at the time of the codification of our murder statute is that it applied *"in the dwelling,"* we lack the authority to now extend this rule to areas beyond "the dwelling" itself.

Defendant contends that this Court's statements in *Pond* indicate that Michigan's common law extended the castle doctrine to the curtilage surrounding the home. However, we agree with the prosecution's contention that *Pond* did not in any way purport to extend the self-defense castle exception to the curtilage area surrounding the dwelling. With respect to self-defense, this Court explained in *Pond* that

> [t]he danger resisted must be to life, or of serious bodily harm of a permanent character; and it *must be unavoidable by other means.* Of course, we refer to means within the power of the slayer, so far as he is able to judge from the circumstances as they appear to him at the time.
>
> *A man is not, however, obliged to retreat if assaulted in his dwelling,* but may use such means as are absolutely necessary *to repel the assailant from his house, or to prevent his forcible entry,* even to the taking of life. But here, as in the other cases, he must not take life if he can otherwise arrest or repel the assailant. [Emphasis supplied.]

This statement of the castle rule, taken from a case issued quite contemporaneously with the enactment of our murder statute, provides no basis from which to conclude that the rule applied anywhere but "in [the] dwelling," that is, an inhabited building and its attached appurtenances.

Pond, therefore, does not allow us to conclude that the castle doctrine, so far as it was a part of the common law of this state when our murder statute was enacted, extended to the curtilage surrounding the dwelling. Instead, by providing essentially the sole indication, contemporaneous with the enactment of the murder statute, concerning whether and to what extent any duty to retreat existed in our common law, *Pond* establishes that the castle doctrine applies in this State only to a residence. Thus, for example, while the castle doctrine applies to all areas of a dwelling—be it a room within the building, a basement or attic, or an attached appurtenance such as a garage, porch or deck—it does *not* apply to open areas in the curtilage that are not a part of a dwelling. . . .

CONCLUSION

We hold that the cardinal rule, applicable to *all* claims of self-defense, is that the killing of another person is justifiable homicide if, under all the circumstances, the defendant honestly and reasonably believes that he is in imminent danger of death or great bodily harm and that it is necessary for him to exercise deadly force. As part and parcel of the "necessity" requirement that inheres in every claim of lawful self-defense, evidence that a defendant could have safely avoided using deadly force is normally relevant in determining whether it was *reasonably necessary* for him to kill his assailant. However, (1) one who is without fault is *never* obligated to retreat from a sudden, violent attack or to retreat when to do so would be unsafe, and in such circumstances, the presence of an avenue of retreat cannot be a factor in determining necessity; (2) our law imposes an affirmative "duty to retreat" only upon one who is at fault in voluntarily participating in mutual nondeadly combat; and (3) the "castle doctrine" permits one who is within his dwelling to exercise deadly force even if an avenue of safe retreat is available, as long as it is otherwise reasonably necessary to exercise deadly force.

Defendant was not entitled to a "castle exception" instruction in this case because he was in his yard and not in his dwelling when he used deadly force. However, defendant was entitled to an instruction that adequately conveyed to the jury that, although he was required to avoid using deadly force if possible, he had no obligation to retreat if he honestly and reasonably believed that he was in imminent danger of great bodily harm or death and that it was necessary to use deadly force in self-defense. The standard jury instruction that was given adequately imparted these principles. Accordingly, we vacate the decision of the Court of Appeals in part and affirm defendant's convictions for the reasons expressed in this opinion.

NOTES & QUESTIONS ON DUTY TO RETREAT

1. *The Castle Doctrine and jury discretion.*   The Michigan Supreme Court took a narrow and formalistic approach to applying the Castle Doctrine to the facts of Riddle's case. What is the justification for limiting the Castle Doctrine to the physical building as opposed to its yard? On one interpretation, the Castle Doctrine is about the sanctity of private property and the homeowner's relationship to it; if that is the case, one would think it would apply to the yard as well. It would seem absurd to suggest that someone camping outdoors in a sleeping bag on a plot of land cannot appeal to the Castle Doctrine simply because his land does not include a physical "castle." On the other hand, perhaps the Castle Doctrine is based on the creation of a per se rule. It would seem too much to demand that a homeowner leave his own home, or retreat to a bedroom upstairs, before using deadly force to protect himself. Consequently, the law creates a per se rule that retreating from the home is *never* required. Should the law deploy per se rules? Why not simply push the question to the jury and ask whether retreat was reasonable under the circumstances and whether

PROBLEM CASE

On February 26, 2012, George Zimmerman and Trayvon Martin were locked in a deadly confrontation that ended with Zimmerman shooting Martin to death. The encounter began on the streets of a gated community in Sanford, Florida. Martin was 17 years old and was visiting his father's fiancée who lived nearby. While he was walking on the street, he was spotted by George Zimmerman, who was a volunteer with the local neighborhood watch group. Zimmerman thought he was suspicious and called 911 and told the dispatcher: "Hey we've had some break-ins in my neighborhood, and there's a real suspicious guy, uh, [near] Retreat View Circle, um, the best address I can give you is 111 Retreat View Circle. This guy looks like he's up to no good, or he's on drugs or something. It's raining and he's just walking around, looking about." Zimmerman stayed on the phone talking to the dispatcher and continued to monitor Martin, who eventually started to run away. Zimmerman gave chase even though the dispatcher said: "Ok, we don't need you to do that."

A confrontation and scuffle ensued between the two men that ended when Zimmerman shot Martin to death. The local police in Sanford declined to arrest Zimmerman, citing Florida's Stand Your Ground law and a general uncertainty about what transpired while the two men were wrestling on the ground. Although Zimmerman was not in his "castle," he had no duty to retreat as long as he had a right to be in that location. Eventually, the governor appointed a special prosecutor who charged Zimmerman with murder. The judge issued the following charge to the jury to guide its deliberations: "If George Zimmerman was not engaged in an unlawful activity and was attacked in any place where he had a right to be, he had no duty to retreat and had the right to stand his ground and meet force with force, including deadly force if he reasonably believed that it was necessary to do so to prevent death or great bodily harm to himself or another or to prevent the commission of a forcible felony."

As a juror, how would you have applied the Stand Your Ground law in this case? Does your answer depend on who was the aggressor? As a state legislator, would you vote to repeal or retain the Stand Your Ground law? Should Zimmerman have retreated if he had an opportunity to do so safely? Finally, was Zimmerman's assessment of Martin colored by race?

George Zimmerman

Trayvon Martin

defensive force was truly necessary? In essence, the Castle Doctrine functions to limit the discretion of jury and removes this issue from their consideration. By fiat, the law declares that retreat is unnecessary within the home. The Model Penal Code follows the Castle Doctrine and does not require retreat if the actor is in his own dwelling or workplace. However, the duty to retreat *does* apply if both individuals work in the same location. MPC § 3.04(2)(b)(ii). Can you explain why the Model Penal Code would have a specific rule for shared workspaces?

2. *Who is the aggressor?*   The law permits the *target* of an unlawful attack to respond with defensive force. However, the original aggressor is not then permitted to defend himself in response to that defensive force. Otherwise, the law would be saying that both parties have the right to respond against each other, which would be absurd. This scheme requires careful attention to who constitutes the aggressor. Say the target of an unlawful but non-deadly attack (Bob) decides to escalate the situation by trying to kill the original attacker (Charles). At that point, Bob's use of force is not justified because he has unnecessarily escalated the situation by resorting to lethal force when only non-lethal force is appropriate. At that point, Charles *is* entitled to defend himself, because although Charles was the original aggressor, Bob is the new aggressor by virtue of his unwarranted escalation of the encounter. See Alon Lagstein, *Beyond the George Zimmerman Trial: The Duty to Retreat and Those Who Contribute to Their Own Need to Use Deadly Self-Defense*, 30 Harv. J. Racial & Ethnic Just. 367 (2014).

3. Reasonable Belief

In order to qualify for the self-defense justification, the defendant must have a reasonable belief that she faces an imminent threat. But what does it mean for a belief to be *reasonable?* As you read the following case, ask yourself how the court understands reasonableness and what work the reasonable belief requirement does in the doctrine of self-defense.

People v. Goetz
New York State Court of Appeals
68 N.Y.2d 96, 497 N.E.2d 41 (1986)

WACHTLER, C.J.

A Grand Jury has indicted defendant on attempted murder, assault, and other charges for having shot and wounded four youths on a New York City subway train after one or two of the youths approached him and asked for $5. The lower courts, concluding that the prosecutor's charge to the Grand Jury on the defense of justification was erroneous, have dismissed the attempted murder, assault and weapons possession charges. We now reverse and reinstate all counts of the indictment.

I

The precise circumstances of the incident giving rise to the charges against defendant are disputed, and ultimately it will be for a trial jury to determine what occurred. We feel it necessary, however, to provide some factual background to properly frame the legal issues before us. Accordingly, we have summarized the facts as they appear from the evidence before the Grand Jury. We stress, however, that we do not purport to reach any conclusions or holding as to exactly what transpired or whether defendant is blameworthy. The credibility of witnesses and the reasonableness of defendant's conduct are to be resolved by the trial jury.

On Saturday afternoon, December 22, 1984, Troy Canty, Darryl Cabey, James Ramseur, and Barry Allen boarded an IRT express subway train in The Bronx and headed south toward lower Manhattan. The four youths rode together in the rear portion of the seventh car of the train. Two of the four, Ramseur and Cabey, had screwdrivers inside their coats, which they said were to be used to break into the coin boxes of video machines.

Defendant Bernhard Goetz boarded this subway train at 14th Street in Manhattan and sat down on a bench towards the rear section of the same car occupied by the four youths. Goetz was carrying an unlicensed .38 caliber pistol loaded with five rounds of ammunition in a waistband holster. The train left the 14th Street station and headed towards Chambers Street.

It appears from the evidence before the Grand Jury that Canty approached Goetz, possibly with Allen beside him, and stated "give me five dollars." Neither Canty nor any of the other youths displayed a weapon. Goetz responded by standing up, pulling out his handgun and firing four shots in rapid succession. The first shot hit Canty in the chest; the second struck Allen in the back; the third went through Ramseur's arm and into his left side; the fourth was fired at Cabey, who apparently was then standing in the corner of the car, but missed, deflecting instead off of a wall of the conductor's cab. After Goetz briefly surveyed the scene around him, he fired another shot at Cabey, who then was sitting on the end bench of the car. The bullet entered the rear of Cabey's side and severed his spinal cord.

All but two of the other passengers fled the car when, or immediately after, the shots were fired. The conductor, who had been in the next car, heard the shots and instructed the motorman to radio for emergency assistance. The conductor then went into the car where the shooting occurred and saw Goetz sitting on a bench, the injured youths lying on the floor or slumped against a seat, and two women who had apparently taken cover, also lying on the floor. Goetz told the conductor that the four youths had tried to rob him.

While the conductor was aiding the youths, Goetz headed towards the front of the car. The train had stopped just before the Chambers Street station and Goetz went between two of the cars, jumped onto the tracks and fled. Police and ambulance crews arrived at the scene shortly thereafter. Ramseur and Canty, initially listed in critical condition, have fully recovered. Cabey remains paralyzed, and has suffered some degree of brain damage.

On December 31, 1984, Goetz surrendered to police in Concord, New Hampshire, identifying himself as the gunman being sought for the subway shootings in New York nine days earlier. Later that day, after receiving *Miranda* warnings, he made two lengthy statements, both of which were tape recorded with his permission. In the statements, which are substantially similar, Goetz admitted that he had been illegally carrying a handgun in New York City for three years. He stated that he had first purchased a gun in 1981 after he had been injured in a mugging. Goetz also revealed that twice between 1981 and 1984 he had successfully warded off assailants simply by displaying the pistol.

According to Goetz's statement, the first contact he had with the four youths came when Canty, sitting or lying on the bench across from him, asked "how are you," to which he replied "fine." Shortly thereafter, Canty, followed by one of the other youths, walked over to the defendant and stood to his left, while the other two youths remained to his right, in the corner of the subway car. Canty then said "give me five dollars." Goetz stated that he knew from the smile on Canty's face that they wanted to "play with me." Although he was certain that none of the youths had a gun, he had a fear, based on prior experiences, of being "maimed."

Goetz then established "a pattern of fire," deciding specifically to fire from left to right. His stated intention at that point was to "murder [the four youths], to hurt them, to make them suffer as much as possible." When Canty again requested money, Goetz stood up, drew his weapon, and began firing, aiming for the center of the body of each of the four. Goetz recalled that the first two he shot "tried to run through the crowd [but] they had nowhere to run." Goetz then turned to his right to "go after the other two." One of these two "tried to run through the wall of the train, but . . . he had nowhere to go." The other youth (Cabey) "tried pretending that he wasn't with [the others]" by standing still, holding on to one of the subway hand straps, and not looking at Goetz. Goetz nonetheless fired his fourth shot at him. He then ran back to the first two youths to make sure they had been "taken care of." Seeing that they had both been shot, he spun back to check on the latter two. Goetz noticed that the youth who had been standing still was now sitting on a bench and seemed unhurt. As Goetz told the police, "I said '[y]ou seem to be all right, here's another,'" and he then fired the shot which severed Cabey's spinal cord. Goetz added that "if I was a little more under self-control . . . I would have put the barrel against his forehead and fired." He also admitted that "if I had had more [bullets], I would have shot them again, and again, and again."

II

. . . On October 14, 1985, Goetz moved to dismiss the charges contained in the second indictment alleging, among other things, that the evidence before the second Grand Jury was not legally sufficient to establish the offenses charged, and that the prosecutor's instructions to that Grand Jury on the defense of justification were erroneous and prejudicial to the defendant so as to render its proceedings defective.

On November 25, 1985, while the motion to dismiss was pending before Criminal Term, a column appeared in the *New York Daily News* containing an interview which the columnist had conducted with Darryl Cabey the previous day in Cabey's hospital room. The columnist claimed that Cabey had told him in this interview that the other three youths had all approached Goetz with the intention of robbing him. The day after the column was published, a New York City police officer informed the prosecutor that he had been one of the first police officers to enter the subway car after the shootings, and that Canty had said to him "we were going to rob [Goetz]." . . .

In an order dated January 21, 1986, Criminal Term granted Goetz's motion to the extent that it dismissed all counts of the second indictment, other than the reckless endangerment charge, with leave to resubmit these charges to a third Grand Jury. The court, after inspection of the Grand Jury minutes, first rejected Goetz's contention that there was not legally sufficient evidence to support the charges. It held, however, that the prosecutor, in a supplemental charge elaborating upon the justification defense, had erroneously introduced an objective element into this defense by instructing the grand jurors to consider whether Goetz's conduct was that of a "reasonable man in [Goetz's] situation." The court . . . concluded that the statutory test for whether the use of deadly force is justified to protect a person should be wholly subjective, focusing entirely on the defendant's state of mind when he used such force. It concluded that dismissal was required for this error because the justification issue was at the heart of the case. . . . On appeal by the People, a divided Appellate Division affirmed Criminal Term's dismissal of the charges. . . .

III

Penal Law article 35 recognizes the defense of justification, which "permits the use of force under certain circumstances." One such set of circumstances pertains to the use of force in defense of a person, encompassing both self-defense and defense of a third person. Penal Law § 35.15(1) sets forth the general principles governing all such uses of force: "[a] person may . . . use physical force upon another person when and to the extent he *reasonably believes* such to be necessary to defend himself or a third person from what he *reasonably believes* to be the use or imminent use of unlawful physical force by such other person" (emphasis added).

Section 35.15(2) sets forth further limitations on these general principles with respect to the use of "deadly physical force": "A person may not use deadly physical force upon another person under circumstances specified in subdivision one unless (a) He *reasonably believes* that such other person is using or about to use deadly physical force . . . or (b) He *reasonably believes* that such other person is committing or attempting to commit a kidnapping, forcible rape, forcible sodomy or robbery" (emphasis added).

Thus, consistent with most justification provisions, Penal Law § 35.15 permits the use of deadly physical force only where requirements as to triggering conditions and the necessity of a particular response are met. As to the triggering conditions, the statute requires that the actor "reasonably believes" that another person either is using or about to use deadly physical force or is committing or attempting to commit one of certain enumerated felonies, including robbery. As to the need for the use of deadly physical force as a response, the statute requires that the actor "reasonably believes" that such force is necessary to avert the perceived threat. . . .

When the prosecutor had completed his charge, one of the grand jurors asked for clarification of the term "reasonably believes." The prosecutor responded by instructing the grand jurors that they were to consider the circumstances of the incident and determine "whether the defendant's conduct was that of a reasonable man in the defendant's situation." It is this response by the prosecutor—and specifically his use of "a reasonable man"—which is the basis for the dismissal of the charges by the lower courts. As expressed repeatedly in the Appellate Division's plurality opinion, because section 35.15 uses the term "*he* reasonably believes," the appropriate test, according to that court, is whether a defendant's beliefs and reactions were "reasonable *to him*." Under that reading of the statute, a jury which believed a defendant's testimony that he felt that his own actions were warranted and were reasonable would have to acquit him, regardless of what anyone else in defendant's situation might have concluded. Such an interpretation defies the ordinary meaning and significance of the term "reasonably" in a statute, and misconstrues the clear intent of the Legislature, in enacting section 35.15, to retain an objective element as part of any provision authorizing the use of deadly physical force.

Penal statutes in New York have long codified the right recognized at common law to use deadly physical force, under appropriate circumstances, in self-defense. These provisions have never required that an actor's belief as to the intention of another person to inflict serious injury be correct in order for the use of deadly force to be justified, but they have uniformly required that the belief comport with an objective notion of reasonableness. . . .

[T]he Law Revision Commission, in a 1937 Report to the Legislature on the Law of Homicide in New York, summarized the self-defense statute as requiring a "reasonable belief in the imminence of danger," and stated that the standard to be followed by a jury in determining whether a belief was reasonable "is that of a man of ordinary courage in the circumstances surrounding the defendant at the time of the killing." The Report added that New York did not follow the view, adopted in a few States, that "the jury is required to adopt the subjective view and judge from the standpoint of the very defendant concerned."

In 1961 the Legislature established a Commission to undertake a complete revision of the Penal Law and the Criminal Code. . . . The drafting of the general provisions of the new Penal Law, including the article on justification, was particularly influenced by the Model Penal Code. While using the Model Penal Code provisions on justification as general guidelines, however, the drafters of the new Penal Law did not simply adopt them verbatim.

The provisions of the Model Penal Code with respect to the use of deadly force in self-defense reflect the position of its drafters that any culpability which arises from a mistaken belief in the need to use such force should be no greater than the culpability such a mistake would give rise to if it were made with respect to an element of a crime. Accordingly, under Model Penal Code § 3.04(2)(b), a defendant charged with murder (or attempted murder) need only show that he "*believe[d]* that [the use of deadly force] was necessary to protect himself against death, serious bodily injury, kidnapping or [forcible] sexual intercourse" to prevail on a self-defense claim (emphasis added). If the defendant's belief was wrong, and was recklessly, or negligently formed, however, he may be convicted of the type of homicide charge requiring only a reckless or negligent, as the case may be, criminal intent.

The drafters of the Model Penal Code recognized that the wholly subjective test set forth in section 3.04 differed from the existing law in most States by its omission of any requirement of reasonableness. The drafters were also keenly aware that requiring that the actor have a "reasonable belief" rather than just a "belief" would alter the wholly subjective test. . . .

New York did not follow the Model Penal Code's equation of a mistake as to the need to use deadly force with a mistake negating an element of a crime, choosing instead to use a single statutory section which would provide either a complete defense or no defense at all to a defendant charged with any crime involving the use of deadly force. The drafters of the new Penal Law adopted in large part the structure and content of Model Penal Code § 3.04, but, crucially, inserted the word "reasonably" before "believes."

The plurality below agreed with defendant's argument that the change in the statutory language from "reasonable ground," used prior to 1965, to "he reasonably believes" in Penal Law § 35.15 evinced a legislative intent to conform to the subjective standard contained in Model Penal Code § 3.04. This argument, however, ignores the plain significance of the insertion of "reasonably." Had the drafters of section 35.15 wanted to adopt a subjective standard, they could have simply used the language of section 3.04. "Believes" by itself requires an honest or genuine belief by a defendant as to the need to use deadly force. Interpreting the statute to require only that the defendant's belief was "reasonable to *him*," as done by the plurality below, would hardly be different from requiring only a genuine belief; in either case, the defendant's own perceptions could completely exonerate him from any criminal liability.

We cannot lightly impute to the Legislature an intent to fundamentally alter the principles of justification to allow the perpetrator of a serious crime to go free simply because that person believed his actions were reasonable and necessary to prevent some perceived harm. To completely exonerate such an individual, no matter how aberrational or bizarre his thought patterns, would allow citizens to set their own standards for the permissible use of force. It would also allow a legally competent defendant suffering from delusions to kill or perform acts of violence with impunity, contrary to fundamental principles of justice and criminal law.

We can only conclude that the Legislature retained a reasonableness requirement to avoid giving a license for such actions. The plurality's interpretation, as the dissenters below recognized, excises the impact of the word "reasonably." . . .

Goetz also argues that the introduction of an objective element will preclude a jury from considering factors such as the prior experiences of a given actor and thus, require it to make a determination of "reasonableness" without regard to the actual circumstances of a particular incident. This argument, however, falsely presupposes that an objective standard means that the background and other relevant characteristics of a particular actor must be ignored. To the contrary, we have frequently noted that a determination of reasonableness must be based on the "circumstances" facing a defendant or his "situation." As just discussed, these terms include any relevant knowledge the defendant had about that person. They also necessarily bring in the physical attributes of all persons involved, including the defendant. Furthermore, the defendant's circumstances encompass any prior experiences he had which could provide a reasonable basis for a belief that another person's intentions were to injure or rob him or that the use of deadly force was necessary under the circumstances.

Accordingly, a jury should be instructed to consider this type of evidence in weighing the defendant's actions. The jury must first determine whether the defendant had the requisite beliefs under section 35.15, that is, whether he believed deadly force was necessary to avert the imminent use of deadly force or the commission of one of the felonies enumerated therein. If the People do not prove beyond a reasonable doubt that he did not have such beliefs, then the jury must also consider whether these beliefs were reasonable. The jury would have to determine, in light of all the "circumstances," as explicated above, if a reasonable person could have had these beliefs. . . .

AFTERWORD   After the Court of Appeals reinstated the indictment, Bernhard Goetz went to trial. Although Goetz lost his legal case before the Court of Appeals, he won his case before the jury, which ultimately acquitted him. Cabey filed a civil suit against Goetz, which went to trial in 1996. Applying the lower civil standard of "preponderance of the evidence," the jury sided with Cabey and found Goetz responsible for the shooting. The damage award was $43 million and Goetz subsequently filed for bankruptcy. Though the

Bernhard Goetz

debt was not discharged in bankruptcy, it is unclear whether Goetz paid any money to Cabey. Goetz ran unsuccessfully for mayor of New York City in 2001 and public advocate in 2005.

NOTES & QUESTIONS ON REASONABLE BELIEFS

1. *Goetz's mental state.*   Why did the jury acquit Goetz? For his book on the trial, *A Crime of Self-Defense* (1988), George Fletcher interviewed several of the jurors, and their recollections of the deliberations revealed that they intermingled motive with intent, which pushed them closer to a "moral conception of intent." Since Goetz was trying to defend himself, they reasoned, he did not have the intent to commit murder. Fletcher reasoned that "[i]ndirectly and implicitly, they incorporated Goetz' purpose of defending himself into their

analysis of his intention under their various conceptions of intent. It would have been difficult to persuade [juror] Lesly, for example, that Goetz had a malicious motive to kill, for his apparent and presumptive motive was to ward off the attack." Fletcher concluded that "considerations of self-defense came into the jury's deliberations by the back door. . . ." Was the jury's view consistent with the law as explained by the Court of Appeals? Under the jury's view, *anyone* engaged in self-defense, so long as they honestly thought they were justified, could not be convicted of murder since they did not have the intent to kill. But the Court of Appeals held that objectively unreasonable beliefs were not eligible for self-defense and that those defendants should be found guilty of murder. The jury seemed to think that if you intend to defend yourself, you cannot intend to kill, but of course this is incorrect because you can intend the second as a means to the first. Does this result indicate a failure of advocacy on the part of the prosecutor, a failure of the judge to explain the relevant legal concepts, or neither? For more discussion, see Kenneth W. Simons, *Self-Defense, Mens Rea, and Bernard Goetz*, 89 Colum. L. Rev. 1179, 1193 (1989).

2. *Objective versus subjective.* At the heart of the dispute in the *Goetz* case is whether a defendant's belief in the existence of an imminent threat must be objectively or subjectively reasonable. Why did the Court of Appeals reject the subjective view? Arguably, the subjective view allows the defendant to set the conditions for his own defense, i.e., the defendant's *belief* that force is justified would automatically *make* that force justified. Did the court also have an argument for its objective standard based on statutory interpretation? Ultimately, the Court of Appeals concluded that the concept of reasonableness codifies, in the doctrine, an objective assessment of the defendant's perceptions. In a sense, it allows the community to say to the defendant: You sincerely believed that using force was necessary, but that belief was unreasonable and therefore your actions were indefensible.

3. *The hybrid standard.* In assessing reasonableness, courts have more than two options, objective or subjective. In *Goetz*, the court noted that the analysis should not be limited to what a "reasonable person"—in the abstract—would have done. A jury should be permitted to consider the physical attributes of the parties and the defendant's personal circumstances, including any relevant prior experiences. In that sense, perhaps it is best to describe the *Goetz* standard as neither objective nor subjective, but rather a highly contextualized hybrid standard. When using a hybrid standard, one needs to determine which contextualized factors should be included. What experiences of Goetz are relevant? The court offers some insights here but not a complete answer. If you were a trial judge overseeing a murder case in New York State, what would you consider to be the relevant experiences? Clearly, prior experiences that the defendant had had with the supposed attackers would be relevant. But what of prior experiences that Goetz had had with *others*, e.g., being mugged in the

past in the subway? Are Goetz's racial beliefs and understandings (particularly with regard to those prior muggings) relevant? These answers are crucial to the outcome because they determine how the reasonableness inquiry will play out. In asking whether it was objectively reasonable for Goetz to assess the situation as he did, we ask whether it was objectively reasonable for someone facing that situation on the subway. But if we add too many factors and prior experiences into the analysis, at some point the hybrid standard only picks out one person—Goetz—who is the only person who has had those experiences. And at that point the hybrid standard devolves into a subjective standard.

4. *Race.* The Goetz shooting and subsequent trial were both racially charged events, although the Court of Appeals opinion only gives a whiff of that context. Goetz was portrayed by some as a hero: the subway vigilante. To others, he was a racist who made a snap judgment to use violence because the young men were black and Goetz was white. Many legal scholars criticized the trial judge for not preventing the defense from covertly relying on the jurors' fears of inner-city violence: "If the jurors were inclined to empathize more with Goetz than his victims because of racial affinity, the jury instructions did nothing to discourage such racially selective empathy." Cynthia Kwei Yung Lee, *Race and Self-Defense: Toward a Normative Conception of Reasonableness*, 81 Minn. L. Rev. 367, 423 (1996). As a matter of legal doctrine, the question is how one crafts a hybrid standard that recognizes the defendant's prior experiences without indulging discriminatory attitudes. Are there other attitudes or beliefs that the law should consider per se unreasonable? In a provocative article, Stephen Garvey argued that a defendant should be excused if his mistaken assessment was the product of bias that he acquired involuntarily. In other words, if the defendant was racist because of his early upbringing or other factors beyond his control, then the mistakes should be excused. Stephen P. Garvey, *Self-Defense and the Mistaken Racist*, 11 New Crim. L. Rev. 119, 125-26 (2008) ("The choices we make at any moment in time, like the choice to kill, depend on the beliefs we possess at that moment. Our choices, moreover, are up to us. We can choose or not as we see fit. In contrast, the beliefs we possess at any moment are not up to us. We can choose to act or not act on our beliefs, but we cannot choose our beliefs."). Do you agree that some racist beliefs are involuntarily obtained by the racist?

> Review the casebook video, *People v. Derek Mann* (Part 1: Self-Defense). When Derek Mann exercised defensive force, was he acting pursuant to a reasonable belief? First, ask yourself what the victim meant when he said to Derek Mann, "I will hurt you." Second, reconstruct the defendant's perceptions of the encounter from his point of view. Third, assess whether those perceptions—and the conclusions he drew from them—were reasonable under the circumstances. Should the defendant be convicted of murder if his belief was unreasonable?

Now review the casebook video, *People v. Derek Mann* (Part 2: Stand Your Ground). Should Derek Mann have retreated rather than resorting to lethal force against the victim? How would you assess whether retreat is a reasonable option under the circumstances? Some jurisdictions have abolished the duty to retreat as long as the defendant was in a place where he was legally permitted to be. Does the statute apply in this case and should it exonerate Derek Mann?

4. Imperfect Self-Defense

In cases of *unreasonable* defensive force, states such as New York (in *Goetz*) require that the defendant be found guilty of murder because the self-defense justification failed. But some jurisdictions offer a middle ground that down-grades the conviction to manslaughter. The following case from California tests the limits of that doctrine and whether all cases of mistaken self-defense qualify for manslaughter.

People v. Elmore
Supreme Court of California
59 Cal. 4th 121, 172 Cal. Rptr. 3d 413, 325 P.3d 951 (2014)

CORRIGAN, J.

A killing committed because of an unreasonable belief in the need for self-defense is voluntary manslaughter, not murder. "Unreasonable self-defense, also called imperfect self-defense, obviates malice because that most culpable of mental states cannot coexist with an actual belief that the lethal act was necessary to avoid one's own death or serious injury at the victim's hand."

The question here is whether the doctrine of unreasonable self-defense is available when belief in the need to defend oneself is entirely delusional. We conclude it is not. No state, it appears, recognizes "delusional self-defense" as a theory of manslaughter. We have noted that unreasonable self-defense involves a mistake of *fact*. A purely delusional belief in the need to act in self-defense may be raised as a defense, but that defense is insanity. Under our statutory scheme, a claim of insanity is reserved for a separate phase of trial. At a trial on the question of guilt, the defendant may not claim unreasonable self-defense based on insane delusion.

BACKGROUND

The relevant facts are undisputed. Defendant was, by all accounts, mentally ill. He had repeatedly been institutionalized and diagnosed as psychotic. On the day of the killing, he was living in a rehabilitation center. While visiting his grandmother's house that morning, he became fidgety and anxious. At one point, he began to crawl under cars as his family and a friend tried to speak with him. He left his grandmother's home around 12:30 P.M.

Meanwhile, 53-year-old Ella Suggs was doing her weekend shopping. She wore a necklace with a charm in the shape of a turtle, which had a magnifying glass in place of the shell. She also wore reading glasses on a chain around her neck. About 1:00 P.M., Brandon Wilson looked out a restaurant window and noticed Suggs sitting at a bus stop across the street. He saw defendant walk past Suggs, stop, look in both directions, and return to confront her. Defendant did not seem to be talking to himself.

Defendant grabbed Suggs and appeared to pull on something around her neck. Suggs raised her hands defensively, stood, and tried to walk away. Defendant pushed her back to a seated position, brought his hands together over his head, and plunged them toward Suggs's chest. Then he fled, looking around as he ran. Suggs stood for a moment before falling. She had been stabbed with a paintbrush handle sharpened to a point. The weapon penetrated six or seven inches, through a lung and into her heart. Neither the turtle necklace nor the reading glasses were found at the scene or among Suggs's possessions.

Within half an hour, Wilson saw defendant return and approach the bus stop. He appeared to be puzzled, and fled. After Wilson alerted a security officer, police apprehended defendant. It took four officers to subdue him. His behavior was sufficiently bizarre that he was referred for psychiatric evaluation.

Charged with murder, defendant pleaded both not guilty and not guilty by reason of insanity. At the guilt phase, forensic psychiatrists were called by both prosecution and defense. They agreed that defendant suffered from schizophrenia, but disputed whether he was actively psychotic when he stabbed Suggs. . . .

The jury returned a first degree murder conviction. After the guilt phase, against the advice of counsel, defendant withdrew his plea of not guilty by reason of insanity and was sentenced to 25 years to life in prison. On appeal, he challenged the court's refusal to instruct on unreasonable self-defense and hallucination. . . .

THE LAW OF HOMICIDE AND UNREASONABLE SELF-DEFENSE

Homicide, the killing of one human being by another, is not always criminal. In certain circumstances, a killing may be excusable or justifiable. Murder and manslaughter are the forms of criminal homicide. . . .

Self-defense, when based on a *reasonable* belief that killing is necessary to avert an imminent threat of death or great bodily injury, is a complete justification, and such a killing is not a crime. A killing committed when that belief is *unreasonable* is not justifiable. Nevertheless, "one who holds an honest but unreasonable belief in the necessity to defend against imminent peril to life or great bodily injury does not harbor malice and commits no greater offense than manslaughter." We have also described this mental state as an "unreasonable but good faith belief" in the need for self-defense. However, it is most accurately characterized as an *actual* but unreasonable belief.

Here, defendant claims his request for an instruction on unreasonable self-defense should have been granted, even though his perception of a threat was entirely delusional. The claim fails, under both case law and statute. California cases reflect the understanding that unreasonable self-defense involves a misperception of objective circumstances, not a reaction produced by mental disturbance alone. And the statutory scheme, though it permits evidence of mental illness to show that the defendant did not harbor malice, reserves the issue of legal insanity for a separate phase of trial. As shall be seen, a belief in the need for self-defense that is purely delusional is a paradigmatic example of legal insanity. . . .

[U]nreasonable self-defense is not premised on considerations of mental disorder. From its earliest appearance in California law, unreasonable self-defense has been deemed to apply when the defendant's act was "*caused by the circumstances,*" rather than by cognitive defects alone. . . . [U]nreasonable self-defense "is based on a defendant's assertion that he lacked malice . . . because he acted under an unreasonable *mistake of fact*—that is, the need to defend himself against imminent peril of death or great bodily harm." . . .

We agree . . . that unreasonable self-defense, as a form of mistake of fact, has no application when the defendant's actions are entirely delusional. A defendant who makes a factual mistake misperceives the objective circumstances. A delusional defendant holds a belief that is divorced from the circumstances. The line between mere misperception and delusion is drawn at the absence of an objective correlate. A person who sees a stick and thinks it is a snake is mistaken, but that misinterpretation is not delusional. One who sees a snake where there is nothing snakelike, however, is deluded. Unreasonable self-defense was never intended to encompass reactions to threats that exist only in the defendant's mind. . . .

Defendant asserts a statutory basis for his claim in section 28(a). This provision states that evidence of mental disorders is admissible "on the issue of whether or not the accused actually formed a required specific intent, premeditated, deliberated, or harbored malice aforethought, when a specific intent crime is charged," a theory sometimes referred to as "diminished actuality." Section 28(a) bars evidence of the defendant's *capacity* to form a required mental state, consistent with the abolition of the diminished capacity defense.

Defendant contends the plain language of section 28(a) permits him to introduce evidence of the mental disorder that gave rise to his belief in the need for self-defense, and precluded him from actually harboring malice. If section 28(a) is viewed in isolation, this construction is logically defensible. However, it is unsustainable when the provision is considered in light of the statutory scheme governing evidence of mental illness, and the legislative history of section 28. . . .

Under California's statutory scheme, "[p]ersons who are mentally incapacitated" are deemed unable to commit a crime as a matter of law. Mental incapacity under section 26 is determined by the *M'Naghten* test for legal insanity. . . . Under *M'Naghten,* insanity is established if the defendant was unable either to understand the nature and quality of the criminal act, or to distinguish right from wrong when the act was committed.

A claim of unreasonable self-defense based solely on delusion is quintessentially a claim of insanity under the *M'Naghten* standard of inability to distinguish right from wrong. Its rationale is that mental illness caused the defendant to perceive an illusory threat, form an actual belief in the need to kill in self-defense, and act on that belief without wrongful intent. In *M'Naghten's Case* itself, the judges observed: "[I]f under the influence of [a] delusion [the defendant] supposes another man to be in the act of attempting to take away his life, and he kills that man, as he supposes, in self-defence, he would be exempt from punishment." . . .

Thus, what defendant attempted here was to assert a claim of legal insanity at the guilt phase of his trial. That is not allowed under our statutes. Section 1026 sets out the applicable procedure when, as in this case, the defendant pleads both not guilty and not guilty by reason of insanity. The trial is bifurcated, with the question of guilt tried first. The defendant is presumed innocent, of course, but in order to reserve the issue of sanity for the second phase of trial the defendant is also conclusively presumed to have been legally sane at the time of the offense. Evidence of the defendant's mental state may not be admitted at the guilt phase to prove insanity. If the defendant is found guilty, the trial proceeds to the sanity phase, where the defendant bears the burden of proof by a preponderance of the evidence. . . .

The bifurcated approach offers substantial benefits to the defense. At the guilt phase, the prosecution must prove beyond a reasonable doubt each element of the offense, including mens rea. The defendant has the opportunity to obtain an acquittal or a verdict on a lesser included offense, without having to claim insanity and risk the prospect of involuntary commitment for psychiatric treatment. The defense has available the panoply of strategies open to legally sane defendants, including unreasonable self-defense based on mistake of fact. It may choose to put on no evidence, or it may introduce any relevant and admissible evidence on the question of guilt. If the defendant is found not guilty, the trial is over. If there is a conviction, the trial moves to the second phase, devoted to the question of legal sanity. There the defendant bears the burden of proof by a preponderance of the evidence, and may be found not guilty by reason of insanity. This process affords the defense two chances at a favorable verdict.

However, the defense may not litigate the question of legal sanity at both phases. The defendant is presumed sane at the guilt phase, and cannot introduce evidence of insanity to counter the prosecution's showing of mens rea. A claim of self-defense based solely on delusion is more than a claim of unreasonable self-defense; as we have shown, it is a claim of legal insanity. If section 28(a) were applied to allow the defendant to make that claim at the guilt phase, the burden would shift to the prosecution to prove beyond a reasonable doubt that the defendant was not insane. The statutory scheme would be turned on its head. . . .

Accordingly, a claim of delusional belief in the need for self-defense is reserved for the sanity phase, where it may result in *complete exoneration* from criminal liability. It may not be employed to *reduce* a defendant's degree of guilt. When the Legislature enacted section 28, it certainly did not intend to allow defendants to . . . argue first that their mental condition made them guilty of a lesser crime, and then that the same condition made them not guilty at all by reason of insanity. . . .

NOTES & QUESTIONS ON IMPERFECT SELF-DEFENSE

1. *Imperfect self-defense as justification or excuse.*   In jurisdictions that recognize the doctrine, imperfect self-defense is clearly a *partial* defense because it does not generate complete exoneration; it simply mitigates the actor's responsibility and downgrades the liability to manslaughter. But is it best understood as a partial justification or excuse? Since self-defense is a justification and transforms a wrongful act into a rightful act, one might naturally conclude that imperfect self-defense is a partial justification. On the other hand, imperfect self-defense is also about a mistake of fact—the actor mistakenly believes that force is necessary and this belief was unreasonable. To help answer this question, consider *People v. McCoy*, 25 Cal. Rptr. 2d 188, 24 P.3d 1210 (2001). Dupree McCoy and Derrick Lakey were tried together for first-degree murder and both were convicted. McCoy was the shooter and Lakey was his accomplice. On appeal, McCoy's conviction was overturned because the trial judge improperly charged the jury on imperfect self-defense, which might have downgraded his conviction to voluntary manslaughter. Lakey's conviction was then thrown out as well on the assumption that the accomplice could not be

convicted of a greater crime than the principal perpetrator. But the Supreme Court of California disagreed and concluded that imperfect self-defense might apply to the shooter but not the accomplice. How is this possible? The defense is personal to the actor and does not automatically flow down to any accomplices, who might not be laboring under the same mistaken belief and might have a higher mens rea than the principal perpetrator. This implies that imperfect self-defense is a partial excuse. See George Fletcher, *The Law of Self-Defense* 27 (1988); Kenneth W. Simons, *Self-Defense: Reasonable Beliefs or Reasonable Self-Control?*, 11 New Crim. L. Rev. 51, 64-65 (2008).

2. *Imperfect self-defense for unintentional killings.*   Imagine that someone believes that he is being assaulted and therefore defends himself. Although he intends to thwart the attack, he does not intend to kill the aggressor—he simply wants to injure him enough to scare him away. Unfortunately, the aggressor ends up dying in the scuffle. Now assume that the defender's self-defense claim fails because his belief was unreasonable. He therefore argues that he should be eligible to argue imperfect self-defense and have his murder conviction downgraded. If the defense is accepted, what should the result be? Should he be convicted of voluntary manslaughter or involuntary manslaughter? Generally speaking, cases of imperfect self-defense result in voluntary manslaughter convictions, but this would be a case of an unintentional killing, which is usually classified as involuntary manslaughter. What result? In *People v. Blakeley*, 96 Cal. Rptr. 2d 451, 999 P.2d 675 (2000), the Supreme Court of California recognized this possibility and created the category of involuntary manslaughter resulting from imperfect self-defense in cases of unintentional killings.

3. *The Model Penal Code approach.*   Although the Model Penal Code does not use the phrase "imperfect self-defense," its provisions on self-defense replicate the same results. According to the MPC, a defendant need only *believe* that the use of force was immediately necessary to avert the threat. Accordingly, the MPC provisions are often described as codifying a subjective view of self-defense. While this is true, it comes with a major caveat. Consider this language in § 3.09(2):

> When the actor believes that the use of force upon or toward the person of another is necessary for any of the purposes for which such belief would establish a justification under Sections 3.03 to 3.08 but the actor is reckless or negligent in having such belief or in acquiring or failing to acquire any knowledge or belief which is material to the justifiability of his use of force, the justification afforded by those Sections is unavailable in a prosecution for an offense for which recklessness or negligence, as the case may be, suffices to establish culpability.

A defendant asserting this provision would therefore succeed in using it as a defense for intentional murder but could still be convicted of a homicide offense based on recklessness or negligence. This provision brings the MPC in line with its general approach toward mistakes generally, which are only relevant if they negate a required element of the offense. A reckless mistake about self-defense cannot negate the mens rea in a prosecution for a crime of recklessness, such as

PROBLEM CASE

On February 14, 2013, Oscar Pistorius fatally shot his girlfriend in their South African home. Pistorius is a world-class sprinter, affectionately nicknamed "Blade Runner" because he runs on two flexible carbon-fiber blades in lieu of feet, which were both amputated when he was an infant. He competed in the 2012 Summer Olympics after he successfully appealed a decision that his blades would give him an unfair advantage over other runners. Pistorius's girlfriend, Reeva Steenkamp, was a model and law school graduate.

Pistorius was arrested and charged with murder. Pistorius argued at trial that in the middle of night he heard noises that he attributed to an intruder in his home that he shared with Steenkamp. He testified that he rushed to get his gun and then shot into a locked bathroom, believing that Steenkamp was still in bed and that the intruder had gained access to the house through the bedroom window. (Gun ownership is widespread in South Africa, due in part to public fear of worsening street crime.) Instead, Steenkamp was the one in the bathroom and died from the gunshots. Pistorius

testified that he screamed in horror when he realized his tragic mistake. Prosecutors contended that the entire story was a fabrication designed to cover up Pistorius's premeditated killing of Steenkamp.

Pistorius was convicted of "culpable homicide" under South African law and sentenced to five years in prison. If you were the judge in his case, how would you decide his case? Assuming for the sake of argument that Pistorius's story is true, should the law grant partial excuses to defendants who make mistakes about the necessity of using defensive force? The trial judge concluded that Pistorius honestly believed that he faced an intruder but that he was negligent in forming this belief: "I am not persuaded that a reasonable person with the accused's disabilities would have fired four shots into that small toilet cubicle." *State v. Pistorius*, Case No. CC13/2013 (High Ct. Gauteng Div. 2014). Is it relevant to the analysis that Pistorius's disability caused him to feel vulnerable while he was sleeping without his prosthetics? In December 2015, an appeals court upgraded Pistorius's conviction to murder because he acted recklessly when he fired his weapon.

 Review the casebook video, *People v. Derek Mann* (Part 3: Imperfect Self-Defense). Assuming that Derek Mann was sincere in his belief that he faced an imminent threat, would it be fair to convict him of murder? Do you accept the defense counsel's argument that a manslaughter conviction would better capture his blameworthiness? Or should he go to jail for the rest of his life as a murderer?

manslaughter. Similarly, a negligent mistake about self-defense cannot negate the mens rea in a prosecution for a crime of negligence, such as a negligent homicide.

C. PRACTICE & POLICY

The law of self-defense is being extended in multiple domains. In this section, we examine: (i) so-called Stand Your Ground laws that widen a defender's latitude to use lethal force; (ii) the procedural immunities conferred by these statutes; (iii) how expansive notions of self-defense are being applied by analogy in international law; and (iv) what conception of imminence should apply when the government kills a suspected terrorist with a drone strike or conventional force.

  Stand Your Ground laws. Several jurisdictions have radically expanded the Castle Doctrine by crafting specific statutes that revoke the duty to retreat in many situations. For example, consider Florida's Stand Your Ground law, Fla. Stat. § 776.012, Use or Threatened Use of Force in Defense of Person:

(1) A person is justified in using or threatening to use force, except deadly force, against another when and to the extent that the person reasonably believes that such conduct is necessary to defend himself or herself or another against the other's imminent use of unlawful force. A person who uses or threatens to use force in accordance with this subsection does not have a duty to retreat before using or threatening to use such force.

(2) A person is justified in using or threatening to use deadly force if he or she reasonably believes that using or threatening to use such force is necessary to prevent imminent death or great bodily harm to himself or herself or another or to prevent the imminent commission of a forcible felony.

A person who uses or threatens to use deadly force in accordance with this subsection does not have a duty to retreat and has the right to stand his or her ground if the person using or threatening to use the deadly force is not engaged in a criminal activity and is in a place where he or she has a right to be.

The first paragraph basically replicates the background rules regarding self-defense. There is no requirement to retreat before using non-lethal force against a non-lethal threat. The second paragraph broadens the Castle Doctrine to any place where the individual has a right to be. So, for example, if the target of the aggression is on a public street, she has no duty to retreat and can shoot her attacker instead of running away. However, if the target of the aggression is trespassing, the law does not apply and the duty to retreat still applies.

The next section of the Florida statute, § 776.013, makes clear that deadly force is justified when someone breaks into a home, even if the intruder has no malicious intent once inside the dwelling and regardless of whether the defender believes the intruder is planning to attack the occupants:

> A person is presumed to have held a reasonable fear of imminent peril of death or great bodily harm to himself or herself or another when using or threatening to use defensive force that is intended or likely to cause death or great bodily harm to another if:
>
>> (a) The person against whom the defensive force was used or threatened was in the process of unlawfully and forcefully entering, or had unlawfully and forcibly entered, a dwelling, residence, or occupied vehicle, or if that person had removed or was attempting to remove another against that person's will from the dwelling, residence, or occupied vehicle; and
>>
>> (b) The person who uses or threatens to use defensive force knew or had reason to believe that an unlawful and forcible entry or unlawful and forcible act was occurring or had occurred.

So, if someone is breaking into a house, the law *presumes* that the homeowner had reasonable fear of peril that required deadly force. Do these provisions make the use of force too easy? What if the person breaking into the home was just a drunk neighbor who got confused about where he lived? Such situations are unfortunately all too common. See Dan Herbeck, *Haunted by a Fatal Decision: Homeowner Recalls Night of Fatal Shooting of Albany Teacher*, Buffalo News, Jan. 24, 2011. For a critical analysis, see Elizabeth Megale, *A Call for Change: A Contextual-Configurative Analysis of Florida's "Stand Your Ground" Laws*, 68 U. Miami L. Rev. 1051 (2014).

Some legal commentators have complained that Stand Your Ground laws are applied in a racially discriminatory fashion, in part because they exonerate defendants who commit questionable acts of "self-defense" against innocent black men who "look" dangerous. As one legal commentator put it, "[w]hen Zimmerman said of Trayvon Martin, 'these assholes always get away,' Trayvon as an individual disappeared. He was reduced to the dangerous essence that Trayvon's race and appearance represented in the mind of Zimmerman." D. Marvin Jones, *"He's a Black Male . . . Something Is Wrong with Him!" The Role of Race in the Stand Your Ground Debate*, 68 U. Miami L. Rev. 1025, 1031 (2014). Does this suggest that Stand Your Ground laws should be repealed? One way of framing the question is to ask what is the source of racially unjust outcomes in self-defense cases. Can the problem be traced to overly permissive rules regarding defensive force embodied in Stand Your Ground laws, or is the real problem police and lawyers who are insufficiently skeptical of white individuals who use deadly force? One professor argues that "[i]t is thus possible that repealing stand your ground will increase Florida murder convictions generally, but leave untouched, or possibly even exacerbate, racial disparities. In any case, the racial disparity question has been all but forgotten in the rush of arguments that stand your ground is too lenient on criminals and encourages violence." Aya Gruber, *Race to Incarcerate: Punitive Impulse and the Bid to Repeal Stand Your Ground*, 68 U. Miami L. Rev. 961, 965 (2014).

ᴪ **Procedural immunity.** The Florida "Stand Your Ground" statute also includes important procedural protections for actors who exercise their rights of self-defense. These provisions are of immense importance to the practical outcome of investigations and prosecutions into shootings where the actor claims self-defense. For example, Fla. Stat. § 776.032 provides defenders with "immunity" from arrest, prosecution, or civil suit. Immunity in this context means not only that the actor cannot be convicted of a crime but also should not be arrested. This provision is meant to deter police officers and prosecutors from arresting defenders and then letting a jury sort out the legitimacy of the self-defense claim. The law contemplates that the legal system will function as a screening system and not interfere with defenders who have a legitimate claim under the Stand Your Ground statute.

In practical terms for attorneys, the question is how the immunity should be enforced by courts. For civil suits, the law clearly provides that the "court shall award reasonable attorney's fees, court costs, compensation for loss of income, and all expenses incurred by the defendant in defense of any civil action brought by a plaintiff if the court finds that the defendant is immune from prosecution. . . ." However, the statute has no corresponding provision regarding enforcement of the immunity in criminal cases. What is the remedy if the prosecutor proceeds against a defendant who believes himself to be immune from prosecution? Normally, the protection against the prosecutor's decision is the requirement that the jury find the defendant guilty beyond a reasonable doubt. But that protection exists in *every* criminal case, so what additional protection is provided by the immunity provision in the Florida statute? In *Dennis v. State*, 51 So. 3d 456 (Fla. 2010), the Florida Supreme Court interpreted the statute as giving Florida defendants raising the immunity defense the right to a pretrial hearing before a judge, who must weigh the defendant's factual claims under the standard of "preponderance of the evidence"—a lower standard typically used in civil cases. Lawyers can use the procedural immunity to get a claim dismissed before it even gets to the jury. Is it wise to take away this decision from the jury using the lower civil standard?

ᴪ **Battered Nation Syndrome.** Strangely enough, the debate over imminence and Battered Women's Syndrome has had an impact on the debate about national self-defense under international law. Some scholars have suggested that a nation constantly under siege might misperceive the nature or severity of its threat, and should be excused as a "battered nation." Unfortunately, international lawyers generally avoid talk of excuses and simply judge international acts as justified or unjustified. For a discussion of this debate, see Michael Skopets, *Battered Nation Syndrome: Relaxing the Imminence Requirement of Self-Defense in International Law*, 55 Am. U. L. Rev. 753, 756 (2006). Even if one rejects the analogy from battered wives to nations under military threat, there is still an important debate in international law over the correct standard for self-defense. Although most scholars and state officials support the imminence standard, one could argue that international law could learn something from the Model Penal Code and should switch to the immediate necessity standard. See also Kimberly Kessler Ferzan, *Defending Imminence: From Battered Women to Iraq*, 46 Ariz. L. Rev. 213, 215 (2004); Jane Campbell Moriarty, *"While Dangers Gather": The Bush Preemption Doctrine, Battered Women, Imminence, and Anticipatory Self-Defense*, 30 N.Y.U. Rev. L. & Soc. Change 1 (2005).

∾ Imminence in targeted killing.   In recent years, the United States government has expanded the use of targeted killings, often using remotely piloted vehicles (or drones) to kill suspected terrorists located oversees. These killings are performed pursuant to the Law of Armed Conflict, the body of international law that governs hostilities between belligerents, in this case the United States and various terrorist organizations who constitute non-state actors. In one instance, the attacks targeted an American citizen, Anwar al-Awlaki, who was alleged to be a member of al-Qaeda. After mounting criticism of these attacks, the Obama Administration articulated in a policy speech by Attorney General Eric Holder the standards that it uses to determine when a strike against an American citizen is appropriate. One of these criteria is that the terrorist represents an imminent threat against the United States. However, Holder's definition of imminence was quite broad:

> The evaluation of whether an individual presents an "imminent threat" incorporates considerations of the relevant window of opportunity to act, the possible harm that missing the window would cause to civilians, and the likelihood of heading off future disastrous attacks against the United States. As we learned on 9/11, al Qaeda has demonstrated the ability to strike with little or no notice—and to cause devastating casualties. Its leaders are continually planning attacks against the United States, and they do not behave like a traditional military—wearing uniforms, carrying arms openly, or massing forces in preparation for an attack. Given these facts, the Constitution does not require the President to delay action until some theoretical

end-stage of planning—when the precise time, place, and manner of an attack become clear. Such a requirement would create an unacceptably high risk that our efforts would fail, and that Americans would be killed.

Does this standard equate with traditional interpretations of imminence or is it an attempt to stretch imminence like the defendant argued in *Norman*? Does Holder's standard sound more like the "immediate necessity" standard used by the Model Penal Code? Should Holder have simply come out and declared that the United States was rejecting the imminence standard in this context in favor of the immediate necessity standard? And one final question: Has the aggressive use of targeted killings made the United States safe? Conversely, would adherence to a stricter notion of imminence be more effective in upholding the moral authority of the United States? For a critical discussion, see Thomas M. McDonnell, *Sow What You Reap? Using Predator and Reaper Drones to Carry Out Assassinations or Targeted Killings of Suspected Islamic Terrorists*, 44 Geo. Wash. Int'l L.J. 443 (2012) (supporting imminence standard).

CHAPTER 24

⟨ᴥᴥᴥ⟩

DEFENSIVE FORCE BY POLICE OFFICERS

A. DOCTRINE

Police are subject to constitutional and statutory requirements that prohibit their use of excessive force. So they might be subject to: (i) a private lawsuit, filed under 42 U.S.C. § 1983, for exercising excessive force contrary to the Fourth Amendment; or (ii) federal criminal charges for violating the civil rights of the individual they assaulted or killed. However, since police officers are subject to the regular criminal law prohibition against unlawful killing, they might also be prosecuted for murder under state law. In that case, they can either appeal to the general justification of self-defense or defense of others (reasonable belief in an imminent threat of death or severe bodily injury), or to a specific statutory justification for police officers. For example, some states grant police officers a broader defense than the self-defense justification available to regular civilians.

1. Constitutional Limits

Historically, the old common law rule was that police officers could use deadly force to stop a fleeing felon but not a fleeing misdemeanant. Over time, this rule grew intolerable because the category of felonies grew from a short list of serious offenses (all of which were eligible for the death penalty) to a longer list of felonies that were codified by legislatures—some of which were serious and violent but others which were less so. Also, even before the list of felonies expanded, it was unclear whether all felons were necessarily dangerous to the public—and thus should be subject to deadly force in order to stop them from fleeing from an arrest. The felony classification was used as a proxy for dangerousness but it was an imperfect proxy at best.

693

The U.S. Supreme Court changed the rule when it decided *Tennessee v. Garner*, 471 U.S. 1 (1985). The new standard, still in effect today, is that a police officer may use deadly force against a fleeing suspect when the officer reasonably believes that the suspect poses an immediate danger to another person—either the police themselves or the public at large. Police who exceed this standard have violated the requirements of the Fourth Amendment, which prohibits the government from engaging in unreasonable search and seizures. In a sense, it might be odd to think of a police killing as a "seizure," since death is not the same as capture. However, the jurisprudence has viewed deadly force as one extreme of a continuum of government action that starts with arrest and detention and ends with killing.

Under the *Garner* framework, gone is the distinction between misdemeanors and felonies and indeed the suspect's prior crimes are no longer directly relevant. These crimes might be *indirectly* relevant only insofar as they might contribute to an officer's overall assessment that the suspect poses an immediate danger in his future conduct. But key to the analysis is the immediacy of the danger. In short, the common law standard was backward looking (what did the suspect do in the past?), while the new *Garner* standard is forward looking (what might the suspect do in the future if not immediately apprehended?). Deadly force is not appropriate to stop a fleeing suspect that poses no immediate danger. However, the Supreme Court in *Garner* conceded that police officers are entitled to infer dangerousness in some circumstances: "[I]f the suspect threatens the officer with a weapon or there is probable cause to believe that he has committed a crime involving the infliction or threatened infliction of serious physical harm, deadly force may be used if necessary to prevent escape, and if, where feasible, some warning has been given." *Garner*, 471 U.S. at 11-12. In that sense, the Supreme Court recognized that past conduct (in limited circumstances) can be dispositive regarding future dangerousness.

2. Civil Rights Violations

In addition to constitutional constraints, police officers are constrained in their use of force by statutory regulations. In particular, federal civil rights legislation prohibits the police from willfully subjecting any person to "the deprivation of any rights, privileges, or immunities secured or protected by the Constitution or laws of the United States." 18 U.S.C. § 242. In *Graham v. Connor*, 490 U.S. 386 (1989), the Supreme Court interpreted federal civil rights legislation as prohibiting the use of force that is "objectively unreasonable" when "judged from the perspective of a reasonable officer on the scene. . . ." The effect of § 242 is to *criminalize* these rights deprivations. Under the terms of the statute, *any* individual who violates these rights "under color of law" can be prosecuted and subject to fines and imprisonment. For incidents resulting in no injury, the maximum punishment is one year's imprisonment; for resulting injuries, ten years' imprisonment; for resulting deaths (or attempted killings), the maximum penalty is life imprisonment or even the death penalty.

The civil rights division of the Department of Justice prosecutes cases brought under this provision. A defendant may be subjected to prosecution by the federal government even if first acquitted by a jury in a local prosecution for murder or some other offense. These follow-on prosecutions by federal prosecutors do not violate the Constitution's Double Jeopardy Clause in the Fifth Amendment because the proceedings are launched by different "sovereigns"—the individual state and the federal government. See *Bartkus v. Illinois*, 359 U.S. 121 (1959); *Abbate v. United States*, 359 U.S. 187 (1959). For example, the police officers involved in the Rodney King beating in Los Angeles in 1991 were acquitted by a local jury in Ventura County. The beating had been videotaped and was widely circulated in the media; the acquittals sparked outrage and widespread rioting and violence across Los Angeles. The officers were subsequently prosecuted by the Justice Department; two were convicted and two acquitted. King sued the city of Los Angeles and received $3.8 million.

3. State Statutes Governing Police Use of Force

State statutes addressing police use of force vary in the amount of leeway that they grant to police officers. For example, Missouri law grants police officers a justification for killing in the following circumstances: in making an arrest or preventing escape from custody, the officer "reasonably believes that such use of deadly force is immediately necessary to effect the arrest and also reasonably believes that the person to be arrested: (a) has committed or attempted to commit a felony; or (b) is attempting to escape by use of a deadly weapon; or (c) may otherwise endanger life or inflict serious physical injury unless arrested without delay." Vernon's Ann. Mo. Stat. § 563.046. Because of the disjunction "or" in the sentence, the statutory justification is available if the officer believes that the individual has committed a felony, even if the individual is not endangering anyone's life or likely to inflict serious physical injury. In contrast, other jurisdictions have tighter justifications that require that the police officer believe that the arrestee committed a felony involving the use of deadly force *or* "the officer reasonably believes that the person will cause death or great bodily harm if the person's apprehension is delayed." Minn. Stat. Ann. § 609.066; Utah Code Ann. § 76-2-404. Still, these statutes sweep broader than the regular rules of self-defense because they permit deadly force based on the arrestee's prior behavior (not just future dangerousness). The key point to understand is that these statutes offer an additional affirmative defense that applies only to police officers; regular citizens must still rely on the more restricted standards for general self-defense. Also, some of these statutes might be inconsistent with the Supreme Court's jurisprudence on the Fourth Amendment described above. Consequently, a police officer might perform a killing that falls under one of these statutes but still violates the *Garner* standard. In that case, the police officer's actions would be unconstitutional—and consequently subject to a civil lawsuit from the victim's family—but the officer would have an affirmative defense in a prosecution for murder under the local state penal code.

B. APPLICATION

1. Constitutional Limits

How should a court evaluate a police officer's claim that use of force was justified under the *Tennessee v. Garner* framework? Inevitably, a court must determine whether the fleeing suspect posed an imminent danger by looking at the information available to the officer at the time. The following case involves a police chase that was recorded on video—thus giving the Court the opportunity to witness what the police officers saw as they were giving chase.

Scott v. Harris
Supreme Court of the United States
550 U.S. 372 (2007)

SCALIA, J.

We consider whether a law enforcement official can, consistent with the Fourth Amendment, attempt to stop a fleeing motorist from continuing his public-endangering flight by ramming the motorist's car from behind. Put another way: Can an officer take actions that place a fleeing motorist at risk of serious injury or death in order to stop the motorist's flight from endangering the lives of innocent bystanders?

I

In March 2001, a Georgia county deputy clocked respondent's vehicle traveling at 73 miles per hour on a road with a 55-mile-per-hour speed limit. The deputy activated his blue flashing lights indicating that respondent should pull over. Instead, respondent sped away, initiating a chase down what is in most portions a two-lane road, at speeds exceeding 85 miles per hour. The deputy radioed his dispatch to report that he was pursuing a fleeing vehicle, and broadcast its license plate number. Petitioner, Deputy Timothy Scott, heard the radio communication and joined the pursuit along with other officers. In the midst of the chase, respondent pulled into the parking lot of a shopping center and was nearly boxed in by the various police vehicles. Respondent evaded the trap by making a sharp turn, colliding with Scott's police car, exiting the parking lot, and speeding off once again down a two-lane highway.

Following respondent's shopping center maneuvering, which resulted in slight damage to Scott's police car, Scott took over as the lead pursuit vehicle. Six minutes and nearly 10 miles after the chase had begun, Scott decided to attempt to terminate the episode by employing a "Precision Intervention Technique ('PIT') maneuver, which causes the fleeing vehicle to spin to a stop." Having radioed his supervisor for permission, Scott was told to "[g]o ahead and take him out." Instead, Scott applied his push bumper to the rear of respondent's vehicle. As a result, respondent lost control of his vehicle, which left the roadway, ran down an embankment, overturned, and crashed. Respondent was badly injured and was rendered a quadriplegic.

Respondent filed suit against Deputy Scott and others under Rev. Stat. § 1979, 42 U.S.C. § 1983, alleging, inter alia, a violation of his federal constitutional rights, viz. use of excessive force resulting in an unreasonable seizure under the Fourth Amendment. . . .

III

The first step in assessing the constitutionality of Scott's actions is to determine the relevant facts. As this case was decided on summary judgment, there have not yet been factual findings by a judge or jury, and respondent's version of events (unsurprisingly) differs substantially from Scott's version. When things are in such a posture, courts are required to view the facts and draw reasonable inferences "in the light most favorable to the party opposing the [summary judgment] motion." In qualified immunity cases, this usually means adopting (as the Court of Appeals did here) the plaintiff's version of the facts.

There is, however, an added wrinkle in this case: existence in the record of a videotape capturing the events in question. There are no allegations or indications that this videotape was doctored or altered in any way, nor any contention that what it depicts differs from what actually happened. The videotape quite clearly contradicts the version of the story told by respondent and adopted by the Court of Appeals. For example, the Court of Appeals adopted respondent's assertions that, during the chase, "there was little, if any, actual threat to pedestrians or other motorists, as the roads were mostly empty and [respondent] remained in control of his vehicle." Indeed, reading the lower court's opinion, one gets the impression that respondent, rather than fleeing from police, was attempting to pass his driving test:

> [T]aking the facts from the non-movant's viewpoint, [respondent]
> remained in control of his vehicle, slowed for turns and intersections,

and typically used his indicators for turns. He did not run any motorists off the road. Nor was he a threat to pedestrians in the shopping center parking lot, which was free from pedestrian and vehicular traffic as the center was closed. Significantly, by the time the parties were back on the highway and Scott rammed [respondent], the motorway had been cleared of motorists and pedestrians allegedly because of police blockades of the nearby intersections.

The videotape tells quite a different story. There we see respondent's vehicle racing down narrow, two-lane roads in the dead of night at speeds that are shockingly fast. We see it swerve around more than a dozen other cars, cross the double-yellow line, and force cars traveling in both directions to their respective shoulders to avoid being hit. We see it run multiple red lights and travel for considerable periods of time in the occasional center left-turn-only lane, chased by numerous police cars forced to engage in the same hazardous maneuvers just to keep up. Far from being the cautious and controlled driver the lower court depicts, what we see on the video more closely resembles a Hollywood-style car chase of the most frightening sort, placing police officers and innocent bystanders alike at great risk of serious injury.

At the summary judgment stage, facts must be viewed in the light most favorable to the nonmoving party only if there is a "genuine" dispute as to those facts. As we have emphasized, "[w]hen the moving party has carried its burden under Rule 56(c), its opponent must do more than simply show that there is some metaphysical doubt as to the material facts. . . . Where the record taken as a whole could not lead a rational trier of fact to find for the nonmoving party, there is no 'genuine issue for trial.'" When opposing parties tell two different stories, one of which is blatantly contradicted by the record, so that no reasonable jury could believe it, a court should not adopt that version of the facts for purposes of ruling on a motion for summary judgment.

That was the case here with regard to the factual issue whether respondent was driving in such fashion as to endanger human life. Respondent's version of events is so utterly discredited by the record that no reasonable jury could have believed him. The Court of Appeals should not have relied on such visible fiction; it should have viewed the facts in the light depicted by the videotape.

Judging the matter on that basis, we think it is quite clear that Deputy Scott did not violate the Fourth Amendment. Scott does not contest that his decision to terminate the car chase by ramming his bumper into respondent's vehicle constituted a "seizure." "[A] Fourth Amendment seizure [occurs] . . . when there is a governmental termination of freedom of movement through means intentionally applied." It is also conceded, by both sides, that a claim of "excessive force in the course of making

[a] . . . 'seizure' of [the] person . . . [is] properly analyzed under the Fourth Amendment's 'objective reasonableness' standard." The question we need to answer is whether Scott's actions were objectively reasonable.

Respondent urges us to analyze this case as we analyzed *Garner*, 471 U.S. 1. We must first decide, he says, whether the actions Scott took constituted "deadly force." (He defines "deadly force" as "any use of force which creates a substantial likelihood of causing death or serious bodily injury.") If so, respondent claims that *Garner* prescribes certain preconditions that must be met before Scott's actions can survive Fourth Amendment scrutiny: (1) The suspect must have posed an immediate threat of serious physical harm to the officer or others; (2) deadly force must have been necessary to prevent escape; and (3) where feasible, the officer must have given the suspect some warning. Since these *Garner* preconditions for using deadly force were not met in this case, Scott's actions were per se unreasonable.

Respondent's argument falters at its first step; *Garner* did not establish a magical on/off switch that triggers rigid preconditions whenever an officer's actions constitute "deadly force." *Garner* was simply an application of the Fourth Amendment's "reasonableness" test to the use of a particular type of force in a particular situation. *Garner* held that it was unreasonable to kill a "young, slight, and unarmed" burglary suspect, by shooting him "in the back of the head" while he was running away on foot, and when the officer "could not reasonably have believed that [the suspect] . . . posed any threat," and "never attempted to justify his actions on any basis other than the need to prevent an escape." Whatever *Garner* said about the factors that might have justified shooting the suspect in that case, such "preconditions" have scant applicability to this case, which has vastly different facts. "*Garner* had nothing to do with one car striking another or even with car chases in general. . . . A police car's bumping a fleeing car is, in fact, not much like a policeman's shooting a gun so as to hit a person." Nor is the threat posed by the flight on foot of an unarmed suspect even remotely comparable to the extreme danger to human life posed by respondent in this case. Although respondent's attempt to craft an easy-to-apply legal test in the Fourth Amendment context is admirable, in the end we must still slosh our way through the factbound morass of "reasonableness." Whether or not Scott's actions constituted application of "deadly force," all that matters is whether Scott's actions were reasonable.

In determining the reasonableness of the manner in which a seizure is effected, "[w]e must balance the nature and quality of the intrusion on the individual's Fourth Amendment interests against the importance of the governmental interests alleged to justify the intrusion." Scott defends his actions by pointing to the paramount governmental interest in ensuring public safety, and respondent nowhere suggests this was not the purpose motivating Scott's behavior. Thus, in judging whether Scott's actions were reasonable, we must consider the risk of bodily harm that Scott's actions posed to respondent in light of the threat to the public that Scott was trying to eliminate. Although there is no obvious way to quantify the risks on either side, it is clear from the videotape that respondent posed an actual and imminent threat to the lives of any pedestrians who might have been present, to other civilian motorists, and to the officers involved in the chase. It is equally clear that Scott's actions posed a high likelihood of serious injury or death to respondent—though not the near certainty of death posed by, say, shooting a fleeing felon in the back of the head, or pulling alongside a fleeing motorist's car and shooting the motorist, cf. *Vaughan v. Cox*, 343 F.3d 1323, 1326-1327 (11th Cir. 2003). So how does a court go about weighing the perhaps lesser probability of injuring or killing numerous bystanders against the perhaps larger probability of injuring or killing a single person? We think it appropriate in this process to take into account not only the number of lives at risk, but also their relative culpability. It was respondent, after all, who intentionally placed himself and the public in danger by unlawfully engaging in the reckless, high-speed flight that ultimately produced the choice between two evils that Scott confronted. Multiple police cars, with blue lights flashing and sirens blaring, had been chasing respondent for nearly 10 miles, but he ignored their warning to stop. By contrast, those who might have been harmed had Scott not taken the action he did were entirely innocent. We have little difficulty in concluding it was reasonable for Scott to take the action that he did.

But wait, says respondent: Couldn't the innocent public equally have been protected, and the tragic accident entirely avoided, if the police had simply ceased their pursuit? We think the police need not have taken that chance and hoped for the best. Whereas Scott's action—ramming respondent off the road—was certain to eliminate the risk that respondent posed to the public, ceasing pursuit was not. First of all, there would have been no way to convey convincingly to respondent that the chase was off, and that he was free to go. Had respondent looked in his rear-view mirror and seen the police cars deactivate their flashing lights and turn around, he would have had no idea whether they were truly letting him get away, or simply devising a new strategy for capture. Perhaps the police knew a shortcut he didn't know, and would reappear down the road to intercept him; or perhaps they were setting up a roadblock in his path. Given such uncertainty, respondent might have been just as likely to respond by continuing to drive recklessly as by slowing down and wiping his brow.

Second, we are loath to lay down a rule requiring the police to allow fleeing suspects to get away whenever they drive so recklessly that they put other people's lives in danger. It is obvious the perverse incentives such a rule would create: Every fleeing motorist would know that escape is within his grasp, if only he accelerates to 90 miles per hour, crosses the double-yellow line a few times, and runs a few red lights. The Constitution assuredly does not impose this invitation to impunity-earned-by-recklessness. Instead, we lay down a more sensible rule: A police officer's attempt to terminate a dangerous high-speed car chase that threatens the lives of innocent bystanders does not violate the Fourth Amendment, even when it places the fleeing motorist at risk of serious injury or death.

The car chase that respondent initiated in this case posed a substantial and immediate risk of serious physical injury to others; no reasonable jury could conclude otherwise. Scott's attempt to terminate the chase by forcing respondent off the road was reasonable, and Scott is entitled to summary judgment. . . .

NOTES & QUESTIONS ON IMMEDIATE DANGER

1. *Videotape evidence.* In *Scott*, the Supreme Court had the luxury of videotape evidence. In fact, the majority opinion suggested that the correct conclusion was obvious once anyone viewed the videotape because the video would "speak for itself." The Court even went so far as to post the videotape on its website. The video is also posted on the companion website for this casebook. After you watch the video, ask yourself whether you agree with Scalia's assessment that Harris's driving constituted an immediate risk to the public on the road. The videotape evidence was apparently not obvious enough for Justice Stevens, who dissented from the judgment. He concluded that "[r]ather than supporting the conclusion that what we see on the video 'resembles a Hollywood-style car chase of the most frightening sort,' the tape actually confirms, rather than contradicts, the lower courts' appraisal of the factual questions at issue. More importantly, it surely does not provide a principled basis for depriving the respondent of his right to have a jury evaluate the question whether the police officers' decision to use deadly force to bring the chase to an end was reasonable." According to Stevens, the fact that other motorists rushed to pull over to the side of the road was not necessarily evidence that these motorists viewed the speeding car as inherently dangerous; this evidence was also consistent with the conclusion that they pulled over because that's what motorists are supposed to do when they hear sirens.

2. *Race and risk.* Scalia's opinion suggests that everyone will have the same reaction to the video. Is this true? In an empirical study, three law school professors studied the public's reaction to the video from *Scott v. Harris*. The video was shown to 1,350 Americans. The authors concluded that the majority agreed with Scalia's assessment that the actions of the police were objectively reasonable. However, the authors also concluded that viewers were less likely to consider the fleeing car as dangerous if they were African-Americans,

low-income workers, residents of the Northeast, or self-identified as liberals or Democrats. See Dan M. Kahan, David A. Hoffman & Donald Braman, *Whose Eyes Are You Going to Believe? Scott v. Harris and the Perils of Cognitive Illiberalism*, 122 Harv. L. Rev. 837 (2009). The authors suggested that members of different social sub-communities sometimes understand social reality differently. Consequently, they argued, *Scott v. Harris* should have been sent to a jury instead of resolved on summary judgment. Do you agree?

2. Civil Rights Violations

The Justice Department retains broad authority to criminally prosecute, under federal law, a police officer who violates the Fourth Amendment. The following

PROBLEM CASE

Two convicted murderers, Richard Matt and David Sweat, escaped from the maximum-security Clinton Correctional Facility in Dannemora, New York, in June 2015. They constructed dummies by stuffing sweatshirts and putting them in their beds to fool the guards into thinking that they were sleeping. In fact, they had drilled holes in the back of their prison cells, crawled through the bowels of the prison, and escaped into sewer pipes that led to a manhole on a nearby city street. By 5:30 A.M. when the guards discovered the ruse, they were long gone.

Matt and Sweat were supposed to meet a prison employee on the outside and drive to

Police stand over David Sweat after he was shot and captured near the Canadian border

Mexico, but when she got cold feet and did not show at the rendezvous point, they were forced to improvise a new plan. Over the course of the next three weeks, the escapees trekked through dense, upstate New York forest on their way to the Canadian border. Matt was confronted by a federal agent and shot in the head when he refused to drop his weapon—a shotgun stolen from a nearby hunting cabin. Sweat was spotted walking on a road by a New York state trooper who gave chase. Sweat refused orders to stop and when he reached the tree line of a nearby forest, the state trooper shot him twice in the back. Sweat was unarmed.

Was the shooting of Sweat consistent with the Fourth Amendment? In *Tennessee v. Garner*, 471 U.S. 1, 11-12 (1985), the Supreme Court said that "if the suspect threatens the officer with a weapon or there is probable cause to believe that he has committed a crime involving the infliction or threatened infliction of serious physical harm, deadly force may be used if necessary to prevent escape, and if, where feasible, some warning has been given." Since Sweat was a convicted murderer, he certainly had committed a crime involving the inflection of serious physical harm. Is this conclusion in tension with the broader *Tennessee v. Garner* standard that deadly force is only permitted when the fleeing suspect poses an immediate threat to someone?

excerpt of an official report on one such investigation shows the type of analysis that goes into the department's decision over whether a police shooting violated the civil rights of the victim. The shooting in this case sparked weeks of public demonstrations, a few riots, and a national conversation on race and the use of force by police.

Report Regarding the Criminal Investigation into the Shooting Death of Michael Brown by Ferguson, Missouri Police Officer Darren Wilson

U.S. Department of Justice
March 4, 2015

INTRODUCTION

At approximately noon on Saturday, August 9, 2014, Officer Darren Wilson of the Ferguson Police Department ("FPD") shot and killed Michael Brown, an unarmed 18-year-old. The Criminal Section of the Department of Justice Civil Rights Division, the United States Attorney's Office for the Eastern District of Missouri, and the Federal Bureau of Investigation ("FBI") (collectively, "The Department") subsequently opened a criminal investigation into whether the shooting violated federal law. The Department has determined that the evidence does not support charging a violation of federal law. This memorandum details the Department's investigation, findings, and conclusions. . . .

The Department conducted an extensive investigation into the shooting of Michael Brown. Federal authorities reviewed physical, ballistic, forensic, and crime scene evidence; medical reports and autopsy reports, including an independent autopsy performed by the United States Department of Defense Armed Forces Medical Examiner Service ("AFMES"); Wilson's personnel records; audio and video recordings; and internet postings. FBI agents, St. Louis County Police Department ("SLCPD") detectives, and federal prosecutors and prosecutors from the St. Louis County Prosecutor's Office ("county prosecutors") worked cooperatively to both independently and jointly interview more than 100 purported eyewitnesses and other individuals claiming to have relevant information. SLCPD detectives conducted an initial canvass of the area on the day of the shooting. FBI agents then independently canvassed more than 300 residences to locate and interview additional witnesses. Federal and local authorities collected cellular phone data, searched social media sites, and tracked down dozens of leads from community members and dedicated law enforcement email addresses and tip lines in an effort to investigate every possible source of information. . . .

In order to make the proper assessment . . . federal prosecutors evaluated physical, forensic, and potential testimonial evidence in the form of witness accounts. As detailed below, the physical and forensic evidence provided federal prosecutors with a benchmark against which to measure the credibility of each witness account, including that of Darren Wilson. We compared individual witness accounts to the physical and forensic evidence, to other credible witness accounts, and to each witness's own prior statements made throughout the investigations, including the proceedings before the St. Louis County grand jury ("county grand jury"). We worked with federal and local law enforcement officers to interview witnesses, to include re-interviewing certain witnesses in an effort to evaluate inconsistencies in their accounts and to obtain more detailed information. In so doing, we assessed the witnesses' demeanor, tone, bias, and ability to accurately perceive or recall the events of August 9, 2014.

We credited and determined that a jury would appropriately credit those witnesses whose accounts were consistent with the physical evidence and consistent with other credible witness accounts. In the case of witnesses who made multiple statements, we compared those statements to determine whether they were materially consistent with each other and considered the timing and circumstances under which the witnesses gave the statements. We did not credit and determined that a jury appropriately would not credit those witness accounts that were contrary to the physical and forensic evidence, significantly inconsistent with other credible witness accounts, or significantly inconsistent with that witness's own prior statements.

Based on this investigation, the Department has concluded that Darren Wilson's actions do not constitute prosecutable violations under the applicable federal criminal civil rights statute, 18 U.S.C. § 242, which prohibits uses of deadly force that are "objectively unreasonable," as defined by the United States Supreme Court. The evidence, when viewed as a whole, does not support the conclusion that Wilson's uses of deadly force were "objectively unreasonable" under the Supreme Court's definition. Accordingly, under the governing federal law and relevant standards set forth in the USAM, it is not appropriate to present this matter to a federal grand jury for indictment, and it should therefore be closed without prosecution.

SUMMARY OF THE EVIDENCE

Within two minutes of Wilson's initial encounter with Brown on August 9, 2014, FPD officers responded to the scene of the shooting, and subsequently turned the matter over to the SLCPD for investigation. SLCPD detectives immediately began securing and processing the scene and conducting initial witness interviews. The FBI opened a federal criminal civil rights investigation on August 11, 2014. Thereafter, federal and county authorities conducted cooperative, yet independent investigations into the shooting of Michael Brown.

The encounter between Wilson and Brown took place over an approximately two-minute period of time at about noon on August 9, 2014. Wilson was on duty and driving his department-issued Chevy Tahoe SUV westbound on Canfield Drive in Ferguson, Missouri when he saw Brown and his friend, Witness 101, walking eastbound in the middle of the street. Brown and Witness 101 had just come from Ferguson Market and Liquor ("Ferguson Market"), a nearby convenience store, where, at approximately 11:53 A.M., Brown stole several packages of cigarillos. As captured on the store's surveillance video, when the store clerk tried to stop Brown, Brown used his physical size to stand over him and forcefully shove him away. As a result, an FPD dispatch call went out over the police radio for a "stealing in progress." The dispatch recordings and Wilson's radio transmissions establish that Wilson was aware of the theft and had a description of the suspects as he encountered Brown and Witness 101.

As Wilson drove toward Brown and Witness 101, he told the two men to walk on the sidewalk. According to Wilson's statement to prosecutors and investigators, he suspected that Brown and Witness 101 were involved in the incident at Ferguson Market based on the descriptions he heard on the radio and the cigarillos in Brown's hands. Wilson then called for backup, stating, "Put me on Canfield with two and send me another car." Wilson backed up his SUV and parked at an angle, blocking most of both lanes of traffic, and stopping Brown and Witness 101 from walking any further. Wilson attempted to open the driver's door of the SUV to exit his vehicle, but as he swung it open, the door came into contact with Brown's body and either rebounded closed or Brown pushed it closed.

Wilson and other witnesses stated that Brown then reached into the SUV through the open driver's window and punched and grabbed Wilson. This is corroborated by bruising on Wilson's jaw and scratches on his neck, the presence of Brown's DNA on Wilson's collar, shirt, and pants, and Wilson's DNA on Brown's palm. While there are other individuals who stated that Wilson reached out of the SUV and grabbed Brown by the neck, prosecutors could not credit their accounts because they were inconsistent with physical and forensic evidence, as detailed throughout this report.

Wilson told prosecutors and investigators that he responded to Brown reaching into the SUV and punching him by withdrawing his gun because he could not access less lethal weapons while seated inside the SUV. Brown then grabbed the weapon and struggled with Wilson to gain control of it. Wilson fired, striking Brown in the hand. Autopsy results and bullet trajectory, skin from Brown's palm on the outside of the SUV door as well as Brown's DNA on the inside of the driver's door corroborate Wilson's account that during the struggle, Brown used his right hand to grab and attempt to control Wilson's gun. According to three autopsies, Brown sustained a close range gunshot wound to the fleshy portion of his right hand at the base of his right thumb. Soot from the muzzle of the gun found embedded in the tissue of this wound coupled with indicia of thermal change from the heat of the muzzle indicate that Brown's hand was within inches of the muzzle of Wilson's gun when it was fired. The location of the recovered bullet in the side panel of the driver's door, just above Wilson's lap, also corroborates Wilson's account of the struggle over the gun and when the gun was fired, as do witness accounts that Wilson fired at least one shot from inside the SUV.

Although no eyewitnesses directly corroborate Wilson's account of Brown's attempt to gain control of the gun, there is no credible evidence to disprove Wilson's account of what occurred inside the SUV. Some witnesses claim that Brown's arms were never inside the SUV. However, as discussed later in this report, those witness accounts could not be relied upon in a prosecution because credible witness accounts and physical and forensic evidence, i.e., Brown's DNA inside the SUV and on Wilson's shirt collar and the bullet trajectory and close-range gunshot wound to Brown's hand, establish that Brown's arms and/or torso were inside the SUV.

After the initial shooting inside the SUV, the evidence establishes that Brown ran eastbound on Canfield Drive and Wilson chased after him. The autopsy results confirm that Wilson did not shoot Brown in the back as he was running away because there were no entrance wounds to Brown's back. The autopsy results alone do not indicate the direction Brown was facing when he received two wounds to his right arm, given the mobility of the arm. However, as detailed later in this report, there are no witness accounts that could be relied upon in a prosecution to prove that Wilson shot at Brown as he was running away. Witnesses who say so cannot be relied upon in a prosecution because they have given accounts that are inconsistent with the physical and forensic evidence or are significantly inconsistent with their own prior statements made throughout the investigation.

Brown ran at least 180 feet away from the SUV, as verified by the location of bloodstains on the roadway, which DNA analysis confirms was Brown's blood. Brown then turned around and came back toward Wilson, falling to his death approximately 21.6 feet west of the blood in the roadway. Those witness accounts stating that Brown never moved back toward Wilson could not be relied upon in a prosecution because their accounts cannot be reconciled with the DNA bloodstain evidence and other credible witness accounts.

As detailed throughout this report, several witnesses stated that Brown appeared to pose a physical threat to Wilson as he moved toward Wilson. According to these witnesses, who are corroborated by blood evidence in the roadway, as Brown continued to move toward Wilson, Wilson fired at Brown in what appeared to be self-defense and stopped firing once Brown fell to the ground. Wilson stated that he feared Brown would again assault him because of Brown's conduct at the SUV and because as Brown moved toward him, Wilson saw Brown reach his right hand under his t-shirt into what appeared to be his waistband. There is no evidence upon which prosecutors can rely to disprove Wilson's stated subjective belief that he feared for his safety.

Ballistics analysis indicates that Wilson fired a total of 12 shots, two from the SUV and ten on the roadway. Witness accounts and an audio recording indicate that when Wilson and Brown were on the roadway, Wilson fired three gunshot volleys, pausing in between each one. According to the autopsy results, Wilson shot and hit Brown as few as six or as many as eight times, including the gunshot to Brown's hand. Brown fell to the ground dead as a result of a gunshot to the apex of his head. With the exception of the first shot to Brown's hand, all of the shots that struck Brown were fired from a distance of more than two feet. As documented by crime scene photographs, Brown fell to the ground with his left, uninjured hand balled up by his waistband, and his right, injured hand palm up by his side. Witness accounts and cellular phone video prove that Wilson did not touch Brown's body after he fired the final shot and Brown fell to the ground.

Although there are several individuals who have stated that Brown held his hands up in an unambiguous sign of surrender prior to Wilson shooting him dead, their accounts do not support a prosecution of Wilson. As detailed throughout this report, some of those accounts are inaccurate because they are inconsistent with the physical and forensic evidence; some of those accounts are materially inconsistent with that witness's own prior statements with no explanation, credible for otherwise, as to why those accounts changed over time. Certain other witnesses who originally stated Brown had his hands up in surrender recanted their original accounts, admitting that they did not witness the shooting or parts of it, despite what they initially reported either to federal or local law enforcement or to the media. Prosecutors did not rely on those accounts when making a prosecutive decision.

While credible witnesses gave varying accounts of exactly what Brown was doing with his hands as he moved toward Wilson—i.e., balling them, holding them out, or pulling up his pants up—and varying accounts of how he was moving—i.e., "charging," moving in "slow motion," or "running"—they all establish that Brown was moving toward Wilson when Wilson shot him. Although some witnesses state that Brown held his hands up at shoulder level with his palms facing outward for a brief moment, these same witnesses describe Brown then dropping his hands and "charging" at Wilson.

INITIAL LAW ENFORCEMENT INVESTIGATION

Wilson shot Brown at about 12:02 P.M. on August 9, 2014. Within minutes, FPD officers responded to the scene, as they were already en route from Wilson's initial radio call for assistance. Also within minutes, residents began pouring onto the street. At 12:08 P.M., FPD officers requested assistance from nearby SLCPD precincts. By 12:14 P.M., some members of the growing crowd became increasingly hostile in response to chants of "[We] need to kill these motherfuckers," referring to the police officers on scene. At around the same time, about 12:15 P.M., Witness 147, an FPD sergeant, informed the FPD Chief that there had been a fatal officer-involved shooting. At about 12:23 P.M., after speaking with one of his captains, the FPD Chief contacted the SLCPD Chief and turned over the homicide investigation to the SLCPD. Within twenty minutes of Brown's death, paramedics covered Brown's body with several white sheets.

The SLCPD Division of Criminal Investigation, Bureau of Crimes Against Persons ("CAP") was notified at 12:43 P.M. to report to the crime scene to begin a homicide investigation. When they received notification, SLCPD CAP detectives were investigating an armed, masked hostage situation in the hospice wing at St. Anthony's Medical Center in the south part of St. Louis County, nearly 37 minutes from Canfield Drive. They arrived at Canfield Drive at approximately 1:30 P.M. During that time frame, between about 12:45 P.M. and 1:17 P.M., SLCPD reported gunfire in the area, putting both civilians and officers in danger. As a result, canine officers and additional patrol officers responded to assist with crowd control. SLCPD expanded the perimeter of the crime scene to move the crowd away from Brown's body in an effort to preserve the crime scene for processing.

Upon their arrival, SLCPD detectives from the Bureau of Criminal Identification Crime Scene Unit erected orange privacy screens around Brown's body, and CAP detectives alerted the St. Louis County Medical Examiner ("SLCME") to respond to the scene. To further protect the integrity of the crime scene, and in accordance with common police practice, SLCPD personnel did not permit family members and concerned neighbors into the crime scene (with one brief exception). Also in accordance with common police practice, crime scene detectives processed the crime scene with Brown's body present. According to SLCPD CAP detectives, they have one opportunity to thoroughly investigate a crime scene before it is forever changed upon the removal of the decedent's body. Processing a homicide scene with the decedent's body present allows detectives, for example, to accurately measure distances, precisely document body position, and note injury and other markings relative to other aspects of the crime scene that photographs may not capture.

In this case, crime scene detectives had to stop processing the scene as a result of two more reports of what sounded like automatic weapons gunfire in the area at 1:55 P.M. and 2:11 P.M., as well as some individuals in the crowd encroaching on the crime scene and chanting, "Kill the Police," as documented by cell phone video. At each of those times, having exhausted their existing resources, SLCPD personnel called emergency codes for additional patrol officers from throughout St. Louis County in increments of twenty-five. Livery drivers sent to transport Brown's body upon completion of processing arrived at 2:20 P.M. Their customary practice is to wait on scene until the body is ready for transport. However, an SLCPD sergeant briefly stopped them from getting out of their vehicle until the gunfire abated and it was safe for them to do so. The SLCME medicolegal investigator arrived at 2:30 P.M. and began conducting his investigation when it was reasonably safe to do so. Detectives were at the crime scene for approximately five and a half hours, and throughout that time, SLCPD personnel continued to seek additional assistance, calling in the Highway Safety Unit at 2:38 P.M. and the Tactical Operations Unit at 2:44 P.M. Witnesses and detectives described the scene as volatile, causing concern for both their personal safety and the integrity of the crime scene. Crime scene detectives and the SLCME medicolegal investigator completed the processing of Brown's body at approximately 4:00 P.M., at which time Brown's body was transported to the Office of the SLCME.

THE LAW GOVERNING USES OF DEADLY FORCE BY A LAW ENFORCEMENT OFFICER

The federal criminal statute that enforces Constitutional limits on uses of force by law enforcement officers is 18 U.S.C. § 242, which provides in relevant part, as follows: "Whoever, under color of any law, . . . willfully subjects any person . . . to the deprivation of any rights, privileges, or immunities secured or protected by the Constitution or laws of the United States [shall be guilty of a crime]."

To prove a violation of Section 242, the government must prove the following elements beyond a reasonable doubt: (1) that the defendant was acting under color of law, (2) that he deprived a victim of a right protected by the Constitution or laws of the United States, (3) that he acted willfully, and (4) that the deprivation resulted in bodily injury and/or death. There is no dispute that Wilson, who was on duty and working as a patrol officer for the FPD, acted under color of law when he shot Brown, or that the shots resulted in Brown's death. The determination of whether criminal prosecution is appropriate rests on whether there is sufficient evidence to establish that any of the shots fired by Wilson were unreasonable, as defined under federal law, given the facts known to Wilson at the time, and if so, whether Wilson fired the shots with the requisite "willful" criminal intent.

In this case, the Constitutional right at issue is the Fourth Amendment's prohibition against unreasonable seizures, which encompasses the right of an arrestee to be free from "objectively unreasonable" force. *Graham v. Connor*, 490 U.S. 386, 396-97 (1989). "The 'reasonableness' of a particular use of force must be judged from the perspective of a reasonable officer on the scene, rather than with the 20/20 vision of hindsight." "Careful attention" must be paid "to the facts and circumstances of each particular case, including the severity of the crime at issue, whether the suspect poses an immediate threat to the safety of the officers or others, and whether he is actively resisting arrest or attempting to evade arrest by flight." Allowance must be made for the fact that law enforcement officials are often forced to make split-second judgments in circumstances that are tense, uncertain, and rapidly evolving.

The use of deadly force is justified when the officer has "probable cause to believe that the suspect pose[s] a threat of serious physical harm, either to the officer or to others." . . . As detailed throughout this report, the evidence does not establish that the shots fired by Wilson were objectively unreasonable under federal law. The physical evidence establishes that Wilson shot Brown once in the hand, at close range, while Wilson sat in his police SUV, struggling with Brown for control of Wilson's gun. Wilson then shot Brown several more times from a distance of at least two feet after Brown ran away from Wilson and then turned and faced him. There are no witness accounts that federal prosecutors, and likewise a jury, would credit to support the conclusion that Wilson fired at Brown from behind. With the exception of the two wounds to Brown's right arm, which indicate neither bullet trajectory nor the direction in which Brown was moving when he was struck, the medical examiners' reports are in agreement that the entry wounds from the latter gunshots were to the front of Brown's body, establishing that Brown was facing Wilson when these shots were fired. This includes the fatal shot to the top of Brown's head. The physical evidence also establishes that Brown moved forward toward Wilson after he turned around to face him. The physical evidence is corroborated by multiple eyewitnesses.

Applying the well-established controlling legal authority, including binding precedent from the United States Supreme Court and Eighth Circuit Court of Appeals, the evidence does not establish that it was unreasonable for Wilson to perceive Brown as a threat while Brown was punching and grabbing him in the SUV and attempting to take his gun. Thereafter, when Brown started to flee, Wilson was aware that Brown had attempted to take his gun and suspected that Brown might have been part of a theft a few minutes before. Under the law, it was not unreasonable for Wilson to perceive that Brown posed a threat of serious physical harm, either to him or to others. When Brown turned around and moved toward Wilson, the applicable law and evidence do not support finding that Wilson was unreasonable in his fear that Brown would once again attempt to harm him and gain control of his gun. There are no credible witness accounts that state that Brown was clearly attempting to surrender when Wilson shot him. As detailed throughout this report, those witnesses who say so have given accounts that could not be relied upon in a prosecution because they are irreconcilable with the physical evidence, inconsistent with the credible accounts of other eyewitnesses, inconsistent with the witness's own prior statements, or in some instances, because the witnesses have acknowledged that their initial accounts were untrue.

Federal law requires that the government must also prove that the officer acted willfully, that is, "for the specific purpose of violating the law." *Screws v. United States*, 325 U.S. 91, 101-107 (1945). The Supreme Court has held that an act is done willfully if it was "committed" either "in open defiance or in reckless disregard of a constitutional requirement which has been made specific or definite." The government need not show that the defendant knew a federal statute or law protected the right with which he intended to interfere. However, we must prove that the defendant intended to engage in the conduct that violated the Constitution and that he did so knowing that it was a wrongful act.

"[A]ll the attendant circumstances" should be considered in determining whether an act was done willfully. Evidence regarding the egregiousness of the conduct, its character and duration, the weapons employed and the provocation, if any, is therefore relevant to this inquiry. Willfulness may be inferred from blatantly wrongful conduct. Mistake, fear, misperception, or even poor judgment does not constitute willful conduct prosecutable under the statute.

As detailed below, Wilson has stated his intent in shooting Brown was in response to a perceived deadly threat. The only possible basis for prosecuting Wilson under 18 U.S.C. § 242 would therefore be if the government could prove that his account is not true—i.e., that Brown never punched and grabbed Wilson at the SUV, never attempted to gain control of Wilson's gun, and thereafter clearly surrendered in a way that no reasonable officer could have failed to perceive. There is no credible evidence to refute Wilson's stated subjective belief that he was acting in self-defense. As discussed throughout this report, Wilson's account is corroborated by physical evidence and his perception of a threat posed by Brown is corroborated by other credible eyewitness accounts. Even if Wilson was mistaken in his interpretation of Brown's conduct, the fact that others interpreted that conduct the same way as Wilson precludes a determination that he acted for the purpose of violating the law. . . .

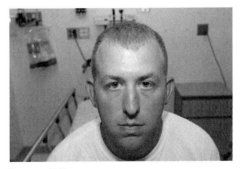

Darren Wilson

NOTES & QUESTIONS ON OBJECTIVE REASONABLENESS

1. *The killing of Michael Brown.*   Was it objectively reasonable for Officer Wilson to shoot Michael Brown? Do you believe it was reasonable for Officer Wilson to believe that Brown was trying to take his gun? Clearly, many people thought not and took to the streets to articulate that belief. The result was several days of peaceful demonstrations in Ferguson, Missouri, intermixed with episodes of rioting. The National Guard was deployed to quell the violence. Note that the Justice Department report makes a distinction between the correctness of Wilson's assessment and its reasonableness. In other words, the report concludes that even if Wilson was *wrong* about Brown's intentions, his belief was nonetheless objectively reasonable.

2. *The role of the prosecutor.*   Local prosecutor Robert P. McCulloch took the case to a grand jury, which refused to indict Darren Wilson. Several observers criticized the actions of the local prosecutor in presenting the evidence to the grand jurors. In most cases, the local prosecutor acts as an advocate for indictment of the defendant and presents evidence in order to make that case. In this case, however, the prosecutor vigorously questioned witnesses who said that they viewed Michael Brown surrendering. Later, McCulloch defended the tenor of his questioning because "[m]any witnesses to the shooting of Michael Brown made statements inconsistent with other statements they made and also conflicted with the physical evidence. Some were completely refuted by the physical evidence." What is the role of the prosecutor in the adversarial system? Is it to garner a conviction or is it to seek the truth? What role should prosecutorial discretion play in the system? For a critical evaluation of McCulloch's decisions in this case, see Ben Trachtenberg, *No, You "Stand Up": Why Prosecutors Should Stop Hiding Behind Grand Juries*, 80 Mo. L. Rev. (2016) ("it was his own failure to 'stand up' and take responsibility for the decisions of his office—instead of hiding behind the anonymous lay persons on the grand jury—that deprived Missouri of what the people pay for when they hire a prosecutor").

3. *Systemic racism.*   Although the Department of Justice found insufficient evidence to support the filing of federal civil rights charges against Officer Wilson, the Department issued a subsequent report addressing broader allegations that the Ferguson police department, and its local courts, had engaged in a pattern of conduct that was profoundly discriminatory. In a blistering report, the DOJ concluded:

> Ferguson's law enforcement practices are shaped by the City's focus on revenue rather than by public safety needs. This emphasis on revenue has compromised the institutional character of Ferguson's police department, contributing to a pattern of unconstitutional policing, and has also shaped its municipal court, leading to procedures that raise due process concerns and

PROBLEM CASE

The Ferguson case was just one of many police shootings that happen every month. In May 2015, Cleveland police officer Michael Brelo was acquitted of two counts of voluntary manslaughter for climbing the roof of a car and shooting its occupants. The incident stemmed from a 2012 chase of two individuals that police believed had fired a weapon. (In reality, the car had simply backfired and police mistook this sound for a gunshot.) The individuals in the car, Malissa Williams and Timothy Russell, were unarmed. The chase involved 60 police vehicles and ended when Williams and Russell were cornered in a parking lot. A total of 13 police officers fired 137 shots at Russell and Williams. The fatal shots were fired by Brelo, who climbed the hood of the car after the first volley of police gunfire, and fired the last gunshots into the victims. The prosecutor argued at trial that Williams and Russell were not moving and posed no danger to anyone when Brelo fired the last 15 shots while standing on the top of the car.

Brelo waived his right to a jury trial and selected a bench trial before a judge. This strategic decision proved prescient when the judge ruled that Brelo had violated police procedures

Michael Brelo

but had not broken the law. The judge concluded that the prosecutor had not established that Brelo did not have a reasonable belief that he faced an imminent danger when he fired the shots. The Department of Justice announced in 2015 that it was reviewing the case.

inflict unnecessary harm on members of the Ferguson community. Further, Ferguson's police and municipal court practices both reflect and exacerbate existing racial bias, including racial stereotypes. Ferguson's own data establish clear racial disparities that adversely impact African Americans. The evidence shows that discriminatory intent is part of the reason for these disparities. Over time, Ferguson's police and municipal court practices have sown deep mistrust between parts of the community and the police department, undermining law enforcement legitimacy among African Americans in particular.

Specifically, the report concluded that local courts issued over 9,000 warrants for minor traffic, parking, or code violations, resulting in jail time for local residents who failed to pay fines and court fees in a timely manner. This scheme ensured that Ferguson's poorest residents, who were disproportionately African-American, faced jail time for minor infractions simply because they did not have the same financial resources as their white counterparts.

C. PRACTICE & POLICY

In light of cases of alleged excessive force from police officers, policymakers might consider various reforms to reduce the likelihood that police officers will use deadly force against arrestees in situations when less extreme force might also accomplish the arrest. For example, the Doctrine section above outlined state statutes that grant wider affirmative defenses to police officers than to civilians. In light of the police killings described in this chapter, some politicians have argued that these statutes should be curtailed or repealed. In addition, two other proposals include: (i) encouraging police officers to abandon pursuits that might lead to deadly force; and (ii) the use of dashboard and body cameras.

> ∾ **Abandoning pursuit.** Some have suggested that Wilson escalated the confrontation by running after Brown. Instead of pursuing Brown, some say that Wilson should have simply let Brown escape. This would have avoided the necessity to use lethal force. While it is clear that Officer Wilson could have disengaged from the confrontation, the question is whether the law should require a police officer to do so. At the moment, Missouri law does not require that the police break off pursuit. Vernon's Ann. Mo. Stat. § 563.046 ("A law enforcement officer need not retreat or desist from efforts to effect the arrest, or from efforts to prevent the escape from custody, of a person he reasonably believes to have committed an offense because of resistance or threatened resistance of the arrestee."). What was the Justice Department report's conclusion on this point? Since multiple crimes had occurred at that point, Wilson was entitled to pursue Brown to effectuate an arrest. Should more police departments train officers to break off pursuit? Many departments already have written policies that officers should break off motorized pursuits when the risk of a crash would pose a substantial risk to innocent bystanders that outweighs the risk to the public posed by letting the arrestee escape. See *Oxford Handbook of Police and Policing* 316 (2014).
>
> Consider, as a representative example, the policies of the Cincinnati Police Department on foot pursuits. The policy requires that: "Police Officer should Terminate a Foot Pursuit: 1. If ordered by a supervisor. 2. If the

officer believes that the danger to the pursuing officers or the public outweighs the necessity for immediate apprehension of the suspect. 3. If the
suspect's identity is known and he is not an immediate threat to the safety of
the public or other officers, consider terminating the pursuit and apprehend
at a later date. 4. After termination of the foot pursuit, officers will notify
Police Communications Section (PCS) with the last known location of suspect or point of apprehension." See Cincinnati Police Department Procedure Manual § 12.536 (2015). Hypothetically, if this policy applied to
Officer Wilson in his pursuit of Michael Brown, do you believe the policy
would have required the police to retreat? Do you think this policy is
applied in practice by police officers working on the street? Should these
policies go further and take into account the potential harm against the
suspect?

ᐁ **Body cameras.** Many police departments, but not all, use dashboard cameras in their police cruisers or even require their officers to
wear body cameras. Should this relatively simple technology be standard
practice across the country? As a lawyer working for a city or county legal
department, what would you suggest to the local city council regarding these
police cameras? Do they increase or decrease the liability that the police
department and municipality might face? Or is that even the right question
for the lawyer to ask? As a lawyer representing the *municipality* (as
opposed to its officers), perhaps the lawyer should be more concerned
about what will be best for the residents of that municipality, rather than
focusing exclusively on the legal needs of its representatives.

For competing views about body cameras, see David A. Harris, *Picture
This: Body-Worn Video Devices (Head Cams) as Tools for Ensuring Fourth
Amendment Compliance by Police*, 43 Tex. Tech L. Rev. 357 (2010) ("if the
presence of the camera has an effect on the behavior of police officers,
making them more likely to hew to proper legal and constitutional standards, that is reason enough to move toward the use of these devices");
Developments in the Law: Policing, 128 Harv. L. Rev. 1794 (2015)
("This widespread galvanization over body cameras exemplifies the
human tendency, in times of tragedy, to latch on to the most readily available solution to a complex problem. But . . . even when high-quality, graphic
footage is available, officers may still not be indicted, let alone convicted.
Moreover, body cameras are a powerful—and indiscriminate—technology.
Their proliferation over the next decade will inevitably change the nature
of policing in unexpected ways, quite possibly to the detriment of the citizens the cameras are intended to protect.").

CHAPTER 25

⟨⟨⟨⟩⟩⟩

NECESSITY

A. DOCTRINE

Necessity is a powerful—and perhaps dangerous—doctrine. Under certain very limited circumstances, it allows a defendant to procure a get-out-of-jail-free card simply because committing the crime was "necessary." While this may sound outlandish, there is a deeper moral and legal principle behind the defense, which is broadly utilitarian: The defendant's criminal act was justified because violating the law produced better results. In other words, the benefits from violating the law outweighed the costs. Because this defense has the power to unwind almost any criminal prohibition (by granting exceptions when doing so promotes the lesser evil), the law imposes a substantial set of doctrinal constraints, which are outlined below.

1. Utilitarian Balancing and "Choice of Evils"

Jurisdictions differ in how they articulate the requirements for the necessity defense, although there exists a common core of doctrinal elements. The first and most essential aspect of the doctrine is that the defendant's violation of the law produces a lesser evil than had the defendant complied with the law. For this reason, the Model Penal Code and several jurisdictions refer to the doctrine as the "choice of evils" defense and require that "the harm, or evil sought to be avoided by such conduct is greater than that sought to be prevented by the law defining the offense charged. . . ." MPC § 3.02(1). So, for example, an individual without a driver's license might argue that his illegal use of the car outweighed the harm that would be caused if he did not drive a dying friend to the hospital.

717

Second, the danger sought to be avoided must represent a present, imminent, or immediate threat—the exact language changes depending on the jurisdiction. This requirement is arguably implicit in the notion of necessity—if the need to act is not acute at the moment the defendant commits the crime, then arguably the crime was not truly necessary. For this reason, the MPC dispenses with an explicit temporal requirement and simply requires that the actor believed that the action was "necessary to avoid a harm or evil to himself or to another." However, some jurisdictions have retained a temporal criterion. For example, Texas's necessity provision includes two temporal requirements and allows the justification only if "the actor reasonably believes the conduct is *immediately* necessary to avoid *imminent* harm." Texas Penal Code § 9.22.

Third, the defendant cannot be responsible for creating the very situation that produced the state of necessity. This means that even the defendant's recklessness or negligence is enough to limit his ability to appeal to that state of necessity as an affirmative defense. So, in the example above, if the defendant made the friend gravely ill by giving him tainted heroin, he cannot then claim necessity as a defense since he was responsible for the situation in the first place. This is consistent with an ancient principle in the criminal law that a defendant cannot voluntarily trigger the conditions of his own defense.

Fourth, the defendant must have no alternative but to violate the law. In the above example, if the defendant had access to a phone to call an ambulance, his use of the car was not truly necessary. Fifth, there must be a causal relationship between the criminal act and the harm to be avoided. In other words, the defendant must have a reasonable belief that committing the crime will contribute to averting the threatened harm. Sixth, the defendant must not have continued the illegal conduct after the harm was averted. If he does continue the conduct, at that point the *continuation* of the conduct is by definition unnecessary. If our hypothetical defendant drops the friend at the hospital but then uses the car to drive himself home, his necessity claim should fail because his drive home after the trip to the hospital was not sufficiently causally related to saving his friend.

Finally, most jurisdictions disallow the defense if the crime in question represents a legislative choice to disallow a claim of necessity. For example, imagine that a city with a heroin problem has a needle exchange program where addicts can turn in dirty needles and receive clean ones in order to reduce the transmission of AIDS or hepatitis. The state legislature dislikes the program and enacts a new law that defines the needles as prohibited drug paraphernalia under the state's penal code. In a prosecution for violating the law, the operators of the needle exchange cannot then claim that their actions were necessary to stop the transmission of AIDS or hepatitis, since the defense would effectively unwind the policy choice made by the legislature. See *Commonwealth v. Leno*, 616 N.E.2d 453 (Mass. 1993); MPC § 3.02(1)(c) (a condition of the lesser evils defense is that "a legislative purpose to exclude the justification claimed does not otherwise plainly appear").

2. Defense to Murder

In common law jurisdictions, necessity is generally unavailable in prosecutions for murder. A defendant cannot claim that killing an innocent individual was necessary to save a greater number of individuals—even if the killing represents a lesser evil under the circumstances. One might think of this constraint as being a deontological limit on what is otherwise a utilitarian doctrine. Although some crimes can be justified because they produce a lesser evil, there is an inherent moral limit to this argument and the law draws this line right at the crime of murder, which cannot be justified simply because the resulting death would help others. (Another way of putting the point is that every human life has an inherent moral worth that must be respected and cannot be "balanced" away in order to achieve social benefits.) Consequently, even though murdering an innocent individual might save a greater number of individuals, the criminal law will not recognize a necessity defense in that situation. This old common law rule was articulated in 1884 in *Dudley & Stephens* (reprinted below). However, support for the rule is not universal. The Model Penal Code has no such restriction and neither do some civil law countries in Europe, though the Model Penal Code has not been successful in getting states to abandon the old common law rule. The one situation where necessity would still be a defense to murder is in the felony murder context. Since necessity would be a successful defense to the triggering felony, there would be no triggering felony from which the prosecution could build a coherent felony murder theory.

3. Necessity and Prison Breaks

Necessity arguments are sometimes made by prisoners who argue that their escape was justified by the need to escape a threatened harm within the prison walls—such as the possibility of murder, rape, or beatings by other inmates. The standard requirements for necessity continue to apply, including that the threatened harm was imminent or immediate. In addition, most jurisdictions have developed additional doctrinal requirements for evaluating necessity claims in the prison context. In particular, the escapee must demonstrate that he exhausted all other avenues to resolve the threat, such as reporting the situation to the authorities, or that such actions were unfeasible or unavailable. Also, the escapee cannot continue the escape after the threat has been averted; instead, the escapee must report to authorities once he has obtained a position of safety. Both requirements stem from a strict reading of the underlying principle of absolute necessity. Once the defendant has escaped the prison, the threat has been averted and therefore a continued escape is no longer necessary. In reality, these requirements are often fatal to the defendant's legal position, since how many escapees report to their local precinct?

4. Necessity and Civil Disobedience

Another context in which courts have developed specific necessity doctrines is protest cases. Typically, the defendants are arrested for trespassing or some other act of vandalism during the course of a protest against a governmental or private policy that they consider unjust or unwise. The protestors then argue that their actions (such as trespassing) were necessary to avoid the greater evil caused by the policy. Courts that have considered the issue have distinguished between cases of direct and indirect civil disobedience; the necessity defense is more readily allowed for direct disobedience than indirect cases, though both categories might have difficulty meeting the other requirements for the necessity defense described above. Direct civil disobedience applies when the protestors break the very law that they are protesting—say a sit-in at a Woolworth's lunch counter in the segregated South. In that situation, the protestors are protesting segregation restrictions by refusing to comply with them. In contrast, an example of indirect civil disobedience would be protestors who commit vandalism of government property to protest its foreign policy (such as an unjust war). In that case, the violation of the law is a mere message and not directly connected to the harm associated with the policy. In these cases of indirect civil disobedience, courts are generally skeptical toward applying the necessity defense and protestors are generally not permitted to submit a necessity argument to the jury.

B. APPLICATION

1. Utilitarian Balancing and "Choice of Evils"

Courts are generally hesitant to allow necessity claims to go before a jury. The following case is no exception. The defendant clearly demonstrated he violated the law to avoid a greater evil. So as you read it, identify in general why the court is not more sympathetic to his claim. Specifically, identify the doctrinal requirements for the necessity defense that the defendant failed to satisfy.

United States v. Ridner

U.S. Court of Appeals for the Sixth Circuit
512 F.3d 846 (2008)

Merrit, Circuit Judge.

The defendant, Scotty Ridner, appeals the district court's *in limine* ruling that denied him the opportunity to present a necessity defense at trial to charges of being a felon-in-possession of ammunition. . . . The district court held that the defendant failed to establish a *prima facie* case of necessity pursuant to the five-factor test set forth in *United States v. Singleton,* 902 F.2d 471, 472 (6th Cir. 1990). Because we agree that the defendant has failed to present evidence to satisfy two of the *Singleton* factors, we affirm the district court's opinion.

On July 29, 2003, the McCreary County Sheriff's Office and the Kentucky State Police approached the home of Ella Mae Goodin in search of Scotty Ridner. Ella Mae Goodin is the ex-wife of Scotty's brother, Freddy Ridner. Prior to the officers' arrival, Freddy and Scotty were sitting on the front porch. Upon seeing the approaching officers, Scotty ran through the residence and exited the back door. Because the officers had an active arrest warrant for Scotty, they chased him and eventually apprehended him a short distance from the home. The officers proceeded to search Scotty and found him in possession of three rounds of shotgun ammunition. One of the officers escorted Scotty to a patrol car while the others returned to Ella Mae Goodin's residence to conduct a search of the premises. Within the home, they found a 12-gauge shotgun under the sofa.

. . . On April 21, 2004, a grand injury indicted Scotty Ridner for being a convicted felon in possession of a 12-gauge shotgun and three rounds of 12-gauge ammunition. . . . In anticipation of trial, the United States filed a motion *in limine* to prevent the defendant from producing any testimony or evidence that related to a necessity defense. Specifically, Ridner proposed to argue that he was only carrying ammunition to keep it away from his brother who was allegedly acting suicidal the morning of the arrest. . . . His version of events is as follows:

He spent the night prior to the arrest at his niece's trailer, which is proximately located to Ella Mae Goodin's home. Shortly after he awoke in the morning, Freddy Ridner and Ella Mae Goodin walked down to the niece's home and asked Scotty to walk to their home with them. During this walk, Ms. Goodin allegedly told Scotty that Freddy "was acting funny again, talking crazy" which traditionally meant, according to Scotty, that Freddy is "talking suicide" or "fixing to take a seizure." Upon reaching the home, Scotty and Freddy decided to sit on the front porch. Freddy went into the house and returned with a cup of coffee and three shotgun shells. While sitting on the porch, the two brothers allegedly discussed Freddy's desire to retrieve his gun from a pawnshop. Further, Scotty testified that Freddy "was talking that morning that he was going to kill hisself [sic]. He said he would be better off dead than having to live like he was." When Ms. Goodin brought Freddy another cup of coffee, he dropped the shells while switching hands. Scotty maintains that he picked up the shells and put them in his pocket "just a few minutes" before the officers arrived. To justify picking up the shells, Scotty testified that his brother Graylan shot and killed himself in 1992 in front of Scotty and that Freddy had attempted suicide, also with a gun, "a few years before." He further testified that

Freddy was in better spirits by the time the police arrived because Scotty had given him cigarettes. After the police arrived, Scotty ran through the front door and out the back with the shells in his pocket. Scotty admitted that he did not know of any gun located in the house on that particular day and that his primary concern was that his brother would attempt to retrieve the gun from the pawnshop, which he thought might be a 12-gauge shotgun. . . .

A defendant charged with being a felon-in-possession of a firearm may assert the necessity defense. *United States v. Singleton,* 902 F.2d 471, 472 (6th Cir. 1990) (explaining that even though the statute under which the defendant is charged does not provide an affirmative defense of justification, the defense still exists under common law). In essence, a "necessity defense, like other justification defenses, allows a defendant to escape responsibility despite proof that his actions encompassed all the elements of a criminal offense." This defense is limited to rare situations and should be "construed very narrowly." The Seventh Circuit, when analyzing this defense under similar facts, concluded "[t]he defense of necessity will rarely lie in a felon-in-possession case unless the ex-felon, not being engaged in criminal activity, does nothing more than grab a gun with which he or another is being threatened (the other might be the possessor of the gun, threatening suicide)." . . .

In *Singleton,* the Sixth Circuit adopted a five-factor test to determine when a defendant is entitled to a jury instruction presenting the necessity defense. The court emphasized that "the keystone of the analysis is that the defendant must have no alternative—either before or during the event—to avoid violating the law." Instructions on the defense are proper if the defendant produces evidence upon which a reasonable jury could conclude by a preponderance of the evidence that each of the following five requirements is met:

1. that defendant was under an unlawful and present, imminent, and impending threat of such a nature as to induce a well-grounded apprehension of death or serious bodily injury;
2. that defendant had not recklessly or negligently placed himself in a situation in which it was probable that he would be forced to choose the criminal conduct;
3. that defendant had no reasonable, legal alternative to violating the law, a chance both to refuse to do the criminal act and also to avoid the threatened harm;
4. that a direct causal relationship may be reasonably anticipated between the criminal action taken and the avoidance of the threatened harm; . . . and
5. [that the defendant] did not maintain the illegal conduct any longer than absolutely necessary.

The district court found that the defendant failed to produce sufficient evidence to satisfy the first and fifth *Singleton* requirements. Although the first criterion is phrased in terms of harm to the defendant himself, this Circuit also applies the necessity defense when "a defendant is acting out of a desire to prevent harm to a third party." Under the first element, the defendant must be under an "unlawful and present, *imminent,* and impending threat of such a nature as to induce a well-grounded apprehension of death or serious bodily injury." The district court held that the defendant failed to meet this requirement because it found that no reasonable jury could conclude that Scotty or his brother had a well-grounded fear of death or serious injury. The court reached this conclusion after focusing on the parts of Scotty's testimony wherein he indicated that he was unaware if any guns were present in Freddy's house and that he did not believe there was a gun located on the premises. Therefore, the closest gun that Scotty knew about at the time of the incident was at the nearby pawn shop. The court determined that the time it would take Freddy to retrieve a gun to use the ammunition vitiated the immediacy of the threat. Further, the court cited the Sixth Circuit case, *United States v. Hargrove,* 416 F.3d 486 (6th Cir. 2005), for the proposition that Scotty had to demonstrate that his brother was in immediate danger, not just that his brother might contemplate committing suicide in the future. In *Hargrove,* the defendant testified that he carried a firearm solely for his own protection after he was robbed. He further testified that on the morning of his arrest a man threatened him but did not follow him when he drove away in his vehicle. The court found that the circumstances fell short of constituting a "present, imminent, and impending [threat]" because the defendant could only support his defense with "speculation and conjecture" that did not reveal any immediate threat to his life. The logical connection between these two cases is clear: the legitimacy and nature of the threat cannot compensate for the lack of immediacy. Even assuming that Scotty Ridner genuinely believed that Freddy was contemplating suicide, Scotty was unaware of any gun located nearby that Freddy could use to carry out his threat. Consequently, we agree with the district court that the defendant has failed to meet his burden with respect to the first *Singleton* factor.

Scotty also fails to satisfy the fifth factor. It requires the defendant to show that "he did not maintain the illegal conduct any longer than absolutely necessary." The district court held that Scotty failed to present evidence to satisfy this requirement because he attempted to escape with the ammunition when the police arrived. Although he testified that he only possessed the ammunition for a few minutes before the police arrived, the police chased him for a quarter of a mile before arresting him. Further, Scotty testified that when the police arrived and the shells were in his pocket, Freddy's spirits had picked up and he was laughing. At this point, the court concluded the threat had subsided and Scotty could have handed the ammunition to the police and explained why he had taken possession of it. . . . Under our facts, Scotty Ridner does not contest that he ran from the police officers when they arrived. Further, he does not maintain . . . that he was running to escape harm; rather, it is clear that he was running to escape arrest. Scotty had the opportunity to dispose of the ammunition when the police arrived because they could have protected his brother from that moment forward. Consequently, no reasonable jury could find that Scotty did not possess the ammunition longer than absolutely necessary.

For the foregoing reasons, we affirm the judgment of the district court.

NOTES & QUESTIONS ON UTILITARIAN BALANCING

1. *Justified necessity.* For some time there was confusion over whether necessity represented a justification or an excuse. Part of the problem stemmed from the fact that the terms "justification" and "excuse" were once used rather loosely in the criminal law. Today, however, criminal lawyers work with common definitions: A justification negates the wrongfulness of the act while excuses simply negate the culpability of the actor. Since necessity is a largely utilitarian doctrine that requires a balancing of evils, most scholars agree that it constitutes a justification. When a defendant successfully argues necessity, the jury is concluding that the defendant did the right thing—or at least a permissible thing—by ignoring the law in exceptional circumstances. For more discussion, see Vera Bergelson, *Choice of Evils: In Search of a Viable Rationale*, 6 Crim. L. & Phil. 289, 290 (2012) ("necessity is widely regarded as the *paradigmatic justification*, 'the mother of all justifications'").

2. *Excused necessity.* But what if the defendant responds to an emergency by selecting a greater harm rather than a lesser harm? In that case, the defendant is not entitled to the necessity defense because he fails to satisfy the utilitarian "choice of evils" requirement that is so central to the necessity defense. But should the law view such an individual with charity? Imagine a parent who realizes that his child faces a substantial injury, and that saving him requires him to break the law. Now also assume that violating the law imposes a *greater* harm on others than the harm to the child that is averted. The parent would not be entitled to the necessity justification. Should some other doctrine apply? To take another example, consider a truck driver going down a hill towards a downtown intersection when his brakes fail. In order to save himself from being injured when his truck hits a building, the driver turns the truck towards two pedestrians, who are hurt when they are struck by the runaway truck. Justified necessity does not apply because the

motorist selected a course of action that imposed a greater—not lesser—evil (harming two to save one). The criminal law of Germany, as well as many other countries that draw their inspiration from German law, might apply "excused necessity"—a defense that applies in precisely these situations. StGB § 35. However, German law limits the defense to situations where the person being saved is a family member or has a special relationship to the defendant. "Excused necessity" as a category is not recognized in American law. For more information on the defense of excused necessity, see George P. Fletcher, *Rethinking Criminal Law* 818-29 (Oxford reprint ed. 2000); Michael Bohlander, *Principles of German Criminal Law* 123 (2009).

2. Defense to Murder

Despite the power of the necessity defense, its utilitarian logic does have its limits. At common law, there was a categorical bar to using the defense in murder cases. The question is why. In the following case, how sympathetic are the judges to the plight of Mr. Dudley and Mr. Stephens?

The Queen v. Dudley & Stephens
Queen's Bench Division
14 Q.B.D. 273 (1884)

INDICTMENT for the murder of Richard Parker on the high seas within the jurisdiction of the Admiralty.

At the trial before Huddleston, B., at the Devon and Cornwall Winter Assizes, November 7, 1884, the jury, at the suggestion of the learned judge, found the facts of the case in a special verdict which stated "that on July 5, 1884, the prisoners, Thomas Dudley and Edward Stephens, with one Brooks, all able-bodied English seamen, and the deceased also an English boy, between seventeen and eighteen years of age, the crew of an English yacht, a registered English vessel, were cast away in a storm on the high seas 1600 miles from the Cape of Good Hope, and were compelled to put into an open boat belonging to the said yacht. That in this boat they had no supply of water and no supply of food, except two 1 lb. tins of turnips, and for three days they had nothing else to subsist upon. That on the fourth day they caught a small turtle, upon which they subsisted for a few days, and this was the only food they had up to the twentieth day when the act now in question was committed. That on the twelfth day the remains of the turtle were entirely consumed, and for the next eight days they had nothing to eat. That they had no fresh water, except such rain as they from time to time caught in their oilskin capes. That the boat was drifting on the ocean, and was probably more than 1000 miles away from land. That on the eighteenth day, when they had been seven days without food and five without water, the prisoners spoke to Brooks as to what should be done if no succour came, and suggested that some one should be sacrificed to save the rest, but Brooks dissented, and the boy, to whom they were understood to refer, was not consulted. That on the 24th of July, the day before the act now in question, the prisoner Dudley proposed to Stephens and Brooks that lots should be cast who should be put to death to save the rest, but Brooks refused to consent, and it was not put to the boy, and in point of fact there was no drawing of lots. That on that day the prisoners spoke of their having families, and suggested it would be better to kill the boy that their lives should be saved, and Dudley proposed that if there was no vessel in sight by the morrow morning the boy should be killed. That next day, the 25th of July, no vessel appearing, Dudley told Brooks that he had better go and have a sleep, and made signs to Stephens and Brooks that the boy had better be killed. The prisoner Stephens agreed to the act, but Brooks dissented from it. That the boy was then lying at the bottom of the boat quite helpless, and extremely weakened by famine and by drinking sea water, and unable to make any resistance, nor did he ever assent to his being killed. The prisoner Dudley offered a prayer asking forgiveness for them all if either of them should be tempted to commit a rash act, and that their souls might be saved. That Dudley, with the assent of Stephens, went to the boy, and telling him that his time was come, put a knife into his throat and killed him then and there; that the three men fed upon the body and blood of the boy for four days; that on the fourth day after the act had been committed the boat was picked up by a passing vessel, and the prisoners were rescued, still alive, but in the lowest state of prostration. That they were carried to the port of Falmouth, and committed for trial at Exeter. That if the men had not fed upon the body of the boy they would probably not have survived to be so picked up and rescued, but would within the four days have died of famine. That the boy, being in a much weaker condition, was likely to have died before them. That at the time of the act in question there was no sail in sight, nor any reasonable prospect of relief. That under these circumstances there appeared to the prisoners every probability that unless they then fed or very soon fed upon the boy or one of themselves they would die of starvation. That there was no appreciable chance of saving life except by killing some one for the others to eat. That assuming any necessity to kill anybody, there was no greater necessity for killing the boy than any of the other three men." But whether upon the whole matter by the jurors found the killing of Richard Parker by Dudley and Stephens be felony and murder the jurors are ignorant, and pray the advice of the Court thereupon, and if upon the whole matter the Court shall be of opinion that the killing of Richard Parker be felony and murder, then the jurors say that Dudley and Stephens were each guilty of felony and murder as alleged in the indictment.

Lord Coleridge, C.J.

The two prisoners, Thomas Dudley and Edwin Stephens, were indicted for the murder of Richard Parker on the high seas on the 25th of July in the present year. . . .

From these facts, stated with the cold precision of a special verdict, it appears sufficiently that the prisoners were subject to terrible temptation, to sufferings which might break down the bodily power of the strongest man, and try the conscience of the best. Other details yet more harrowing, facts still more loathsome and appalling, were presented to the jury, and are to be found recorded in my learned Brother's notes. But nevertheless this is clear, that the prisoners put to death a weak and unoffending boy upon the chance of preserving their own lives by feeding upon his flesh and blood after he was killed, and with the certainty of depriving him, of any possible chance of survival. The verdict finds in terms that "if the men had not fed upon the body of the boy they would probably not have survived," and that "the boy being in a much weaker condition was likely to have died before them." They might possibly have been picked up next day by a passing ship; they might possibly not have been picked up at all; in either case it is obvious that the killing of the boy would have been an unnecessary and profitless act. It is found by the verdict that the boy was incapable of resistance, and, in fact, made none; and it is not even suggested that his death was due to any violence on his part attempted against, or even so much as feared by, those who killed him. Under these circumstances the jury say that they are ignorant whether those who killed him were guilty of murder, and have referred it to this Court to determine what is the legal consequence which follows from the facts which they have found. . . .

There remains to be considered the real question in the case whether killing under the circumstances set forth in the verdict be or be not murder. The contention that it could be anything else was, to the minds of us all, both new and strange, and we stopped the Attorney General in his negative argument in order that we might hear what could be said in support of a proposition which appeared to us to be at once dangerous, immoral, and opposed to all legal principle and analogy. . . .

It is, if possible, yet clearer that the doctrine contended for receives no support from the great authority of Lord Hale. . . . For in the chapter in which he deals with the exemption created by compulsion or necessity he thus expresses himself: "If a man be desperately assaulted and in peril of death, and cannot otherwise escape unless, to satisfy his assailant's fury, he will kill an innocent person then present, the fear and actual force will not acquit him of the crime and punishment of murder, if he commit the fact, for he ought rather to die himself than kill an innocent. . . ."

Is there, then, any authority for the proposition which has been presented to us? Decided cases there are none. . . . The American case cited by Brother Stephen in his Digest, from Wharton on Homicide, in which it was decided, correctly indeed, that sailors had no right to throw passengers overboard to save themselves, but on the somewhat strange ground that the proper mode of determining who was to be sacrificed was to vote upon the subject by ballot, can hardly, as my Brother Stephen says, be an authority satisfactory to a court in this country. . . .

Now, except for the purpose of testing how far the conservation of a man's own life is in all cases and under all circumstances, an absolute, unqualified, and paramount duty, we exclude from our consideration all the incidents of war. We are dealing with a case of private homicide, not one imposed upon men in the service of their Sovereign and in the defence of their country. Now it is admitted that the deliberate killing of this unoffending and unresisting boy was clearly murder, unless the killing can be justified by some well-recognised excuse admitted by the law. It is further admitted that there was in this case no such excuse, unless the killing was justified by what has been called "necessity." But the temptation to the act which existed here was not what the law has ever called necessity. Nor is this to be regretted. Though law and morality are not the same, and many things may be immoral which are not necessarily illegal, yet the absolute divorce of law from morality would be of fatal consequence; and such divorce would follow if the temptation to murder in this case were to be held by law an absolute defence of it. It is not so. To preserve one's life is generally speaking a duty, but it may be the plainest and the highest duty to sacrifice it. War is full of instances in which it is a man's duty not to live, but to die. The duty, in case of shipwreck, of a captain to his crew, of the crew to the passengers, of soldiers to women and children, as in the noble case of the Birkenhead;[1] these duties impose on men the moral necessity, not of the preservation, but of the sacrifice of their lives for others from which in no country, least of all, it is to be hoped, in England, will men ever shrink, as indeed, they have not shrunk. It is not correct, therefore, to say that there is any absolute or unqualified necessity to preserve one's life. . . . It would be a very easy and cheap display of commonplace learning to quote from Greek and Latin authors, from Horace, from Juvenal, from Cicero, from Euripides, passage after passage, in which the duty of dying for others

---

1. [Editor's Note: The HMS Birkenhead was shipwrecked in 1852. With insufficient lifeboats to save everyone, sailors and soldiers remained on board while passengers were evacuated to the boats. The chivalrous incident, in which many died, is said to be the origination of the popular concept "women and children first."]

has been laid down in glowing and emphatic language as resulting from the principles of heathen ethics; it is enough in a Christian country to remind ourselves of the Great Example whom we profess to follow. It is not needful to point out the awful danger of admitting the principle which has been contended for. Who is to be the judge of this sort of necessity? By what measure is the comparative value of lives to be measured? Is it to be strength, or intellect, or what? It is plain that the principle leaves to him who is to profit by it to determine the necessity which will justify him in deliberately taking another's life to save his own. In this case the weakest, the youngest, the most unresisting, was chosen. Was it more necessary to kill him than one of the grown men? The answer must be "No"—

> "So spake the Fiend, and with necessity
> The tyrant's plea, excused his devilish deeds."[2]

It is not suggested that in this particular case the deeds were "devilish," but it is quite plain that such a principle once admitted might be made the legal cloak for unbridled passion and atrocious crime. There is no safe path for judges to tread but to ascertain the law to the best of their ability and to declare it according to their judgment; and if in any case the law appears to be too severe on individuals, to leave it to the Sovereign to exercise that prerogative of mercy which the Constitution has intrusted to the hands fittest to dispense it.

It must not be supposed that in refusing to admit temptation to be an excuse for crime it is forgotten how terrible the temptation was; how awful the suffering; how hard in such trials to keep the judgment straight and the conduct pure. We are often compelled to set up standards we cannot reach ourselves, and to lay down rules which we could not ourselves satisfy. But a man has no right to declare temptation to be an excuse, though he might himself have yielded to it, nor allow compassion for the criminal to change or weaken in any manner the legal definition of the crime. It is therefore our duty to declare that the prisoners' act in this case was wilful murder, that the facts as stated in the verdict are no legal justification of the homicide; and to say that in our unanimous opinion the prisoners are upon this special verdict guilty of murder.

---

2. [Editor's Note: The quote is from John Milton's *Paradise Lost* (1667). The poem tells the biblical story of Adam and Eve and their descent into temptation and expulsion from the Garden of Eden. In the quote, Milton is lamenting that evil (or Satan) can almost always appeal to a state of necessity to "excuse" its wrongdoing, thus showing the danger of these arguments.]

NOTES & QUESTIONS ON NECESSITY AND MURDER

1. *Aftermath.*   Dudley and Stephens were convicted by the British courts and sentenced to death, but they fared far better before the court of public opinion. Many Brits were sympathetic to their plight and found their harsh treatment by the courts to be unconscionable. See Paul H. Robinson & Michael T. Cahil, *Law Without Justice: Why Criminal Law Doesn't Give People What They Deserve* 107 (2005). As a result, their death sentences were commuted to a prison term of six months. Do you think the court's decision was just? Did Dudley and Stephens deserve to die for their behavior? If you support the Crown's commutation of their death sentence, would you go even further and support a legislative rule that reinstates the necessity defense in cases of murder? Simply put, how sympathetic are you to the defendants in this case? For more discussion of this case, see A.W. Brian Simpson, *Cannibalism and the Common Law: The Story of the Tragic Last Voyage of the Mignonette and the Strange Legal Proceedings to Which It Gave Rise* (1984).

2. *Necessity and manslaughter.*   The rule from *Dudley & Stephens* is that necessity is no defense to the intentional killing of an innocent human being. Should the rule also apply to non-intentional killings in a prosecution for manslaughter or second-degree murder? Since *Dudley & Stephens* was clearly a case of an intentional killing, it is difficult to extrapolate how the rule should be applied in a different context. Few jurisdictions have explicitly ruled on this question. See, e.g., *Wood v. State*, 271 S.W.3d 329 (Ct. App. Tex. 2008) (suggesting that necessity is available as a defense to manslaughter). Some jurisdictions go in the opposite direction and have broadened the rule from *Dudley & Stephens* and apply it to a range of serious felonies. Mo. Ann. Stat. § 563.026 (necessity not applicable for murder or class A felonies). In Wisconsin, necessity is allowed as a *partial* defense to intentional murder and mitigates the defendant's responsibility from first-degree to second-degree intentional homicide. Wis. Stat. Ann. § 939.47. What result under the Model Penal Code? Recall that manslaughter and negligent homicide are based on the mental elements of recklessness and negligence respectively. MPC § § 210.3 and 210.4. Both mental states require a finding that the defendant's conduct constituted a substantial and *unjustifiable* risk. MPC § § 2.02(2)(c) and 2.02(2)(d). Could a defendant point to a necessity-type argument to show that his conduct was justifiable in some way? If yes, that might obviate the need to assert an independent necessity defense, since the analysis would be imported into the criterion for the mental element.

3. Necessity and Prison Breaks

When should a prisoner be entitled to argue necessity as a justification for breaking out of prison? In the following case, the Supreme Court articulated

PROBLEM CASE

Abortion opponents who have murdered abortion providers have sometimes tried to argue necessity as a justification for their actions. On May 31, 2009, Scott Roeder walked into a church service in Wichita, Kansas, and executed Dr. George Tiller, a local abortion provider. Roeder quickly confessed and argued that he acted to save unborn children.

In *State v. Roeder*, 300 Kan. 901, 336 P.3d 831 (2014), the Supreme Court of Kansas rejected Roeder's necessity argument. Although Kansas has no necessity defense codified in its penal code, courts in Kansas have applied necessity as a common law defense. However, the court rejected Roeder's argument for a number of reasons. First, since abortion is legal in Kansas, the abortions Roeder sought to prevent were not considered "evils" to be avoided. Although Roeder also argued that the clinic had engaged in procedural and administrative irregularities in performing the abortions, these could not be considered significant evils. Second, the harm was not imminent, since the victim was killed during a church service on a Sunday, not while he was at the clinic working. Third, the defendant had other alternatives at his disposal, such as convincing women not to have abortions through distributing literature or other protests. "Even for Roeder's professed purpose of stopping *all* abortions, not just illegal abortions, the Draconian measure of murder was not the only alternative," the court concluded.

Should the court have sidestepped this inquiry entirely and simply declared that it was following *Dudley & Stephens* in rejecting necessity in murder cases? Should the jury have been allowed to consider the necessity argument?

Scott Roeder

specific standards for evaluating these claims when the defendant escapes from federal custody. Several states have imposed similar constraints for prisoners who escape from state penitentiaries.

United States v. Bailey

Supreme Court of the United States
444 U.S. 394 (1980)

REHNQUIST, J.

In the early morning hours of August 26, 1976, respondents Clifford Bailey, James T. Cogdell, Ronald C. Cooley, and Ralph Walker, federal prisoners at the District of Columbia jail, crawled through a window from which a bar had been removed, slid down a knotted bedsheet, and escaped from custody. Federal authorities recaptured them after they had remained at large for a period of time ranging from one month to three and one-half months. Upon their apprehension, they were charged with violating 18 U.S.C. § 751(a), which governs escape from federal custody. At their trials, each of the respondents adduced or offered to adduce evidence as to various conditions and events at the District of Columbia jail, but each was convicted by the jury. The Court of Appeals for the District of Columbia Circuit reversed the convictions by a divided vote, holding that the District Court had improperly precluded consideration by the respective juries of respondents' tendered evidence. We granted certiorari and now reverse the judgments of the Court of Appeals. . . .

Respondents' defense of duress or necessity centered on the conditions in the jail during the months of June, July, and August 1976, and on various threats and beatings directed at them during that period. In describing the conditions at the jail, they introduced evidence of frequent fires in "Northeast One," the maximum-security cellblock occupied by respondents prior to their escape. Construed in the light most favorable to them, this evidence demonstrated that the inmates of Northeast One, and on occasion the guards in that unit, set fire to trash, bedding, and other objects thrown from the cells. According to the inmates, the guards simply allowed the fires to burn until they went out. Although the fires apparently were confined to small areas and posed no substantial threat of spreading through the complex, poor ventilation caused smoke to collect and linger in the cellblock.

Respondents Cooley and Bailey also introduced testimony that the guards at the jail had subjected them to beatings and to threats of death. Walker attempted to prove that he was an epileptic and had received inadequate medical attention for his seizures.

Consistently during the trial, the District Court stressed that, to sustain their defenses, respondents would have to introduce some evidence that they attempted to surrender or engaged in equivalent conduct once they had freed themselves from the conditions they described. But the court waited for such evidence in vain. Respondent Cooley, who had eluded the authorities for one month, testified that his "people" had tried to contact the authorities, but "never got in touch with anybody." He also suggested that someone had told his sister that the Federal Bureau of Investigation would kill him when he was apprehended.

Respondent Bailey, who was apprehended on November 19, 1976, told a similar story. He stated that he "had the jail officials called several times," but did not turn himself in because "I would still be under the threats of death." Like Cooley, Bailey testified that "the FBI was telling my people that they was going to shoot me."

Only respondent Walker suggested that he had attempted to negotiate a surrender. Like Cooley and Bailey, Walker testified that the FBI had told his "people" that they would kill him when they recaptured him. Nevertheless, according to Walker, he called the FBI three times and spoke with an agent whose name he could not remember. That agent allegedly assured him that the FBI would not harm him, but was unable to promise that Walker would not be returned to the D.C. jail. Walker testified that he last called the FBI in mid-October. He was finally apprehended on December 13, 1976.

At the close of all the evidence, the District Court rejected respondents' proffered instruction on duress as a defense to prison escape. The court ruled that respondents had failed as a matter of law to present evidence sufficient to support such a defense because they had not turned themselves in after they had escaped the allegedly coercive conditions. After receiving instructions to disregard the evidence of the conditions in the jail, the jury convicted Bailey, Cooley, and Walker of violating § 751(a).

Two months later, respondent Cogdell came to trial before the same District Judge who had presided over the trial of his co-respondents. When Cogdell attempted to offer testimony concerning the allegedly inhumane conditions at the D.C. jail, the District Judge inquired into Cogdell's conduct between his escape on August 26 and his apprehension on September 28. In response to Cogdell's assertion that he "may have written letters," the District Court specified that Cogdell could testify only as to "what he did . . . [n]ot what he may have done." Absent such testimony, however, the District Court ruled that Cogdell could not present evidence of conditions at the jail. Cogdell subsequently chose not to testify on his own behalf, and was convicted by the jury of violating § 751(a).

By a divided vote, the Court of Appeals reversed each respondent's conviction and remanded for new trials. The majority concluded that the District Court should have allowed the jury to consider the evidence of coercive conditions in determining whether the respondents had formulated the requisite intent to sustain a conviction under § 751(a). According to the majority, § 751(a) required the prosecution to prove that a particular defendant left federal custody voluntarily, without permission, and "with an intent to avoid confinement." The majority then defined the word "confinement" as encompassing only the "normal aspects" of punishment prescribed by our legal system. Thus, where a prisoner escapes in order to avoid "non-confinement" conditions such as beatings or homosexual attacks, he would not necessarily have the requisite intent to sustain a conviction under § 751(a). According to the majority:

> When a defendant introduces evidence that he was subject to such "non-confinement" conditions, the crucial factual determination on the intent issue is . . . whether the defendant left custody only to avoid these conditions or whether, in addition, the defendant *also* intended to avoid confinement. In making this determination the jury is to be guided by the trial

court's instructions pointing out those factors that are most indicative of the presence or absence of an intent to avoid confinement.

II

. . . Respondents also contend that they are entitled to a new trial because they presented (or, in Cogdell's case, could have presented) sufficient evidence of duress or necessity to submit such a defense to the jury. The majority below did not confront this claim squarely, holding instead that, to the extent that such a defense normally would be barred by a prisoner's failure to return to custody, neither the indictment nor the jury instructions adequately described such a requirement.

Common law historically distinguished between the defenses of duress and necessity. Duress was said to excuse criminal conduct where the actor was under an unlawful threat of imminent death or serious bodily injury, which threat caused the actor to engage in conduct violating the literal terms of the criminal law. While the defense of duress covered the situation where the coercion had its source in the actions of other human beings, the defense of necessity, or choice of evils, traditionally covered the situation where physical forces beyond the actor's control rendered illegal conduct the lesser of two evils. Thus, where A destroyed a dike because B threatened to kill him if he did not, A would argue that he acted under duress, whereas if A destroyed the dike in order to protect more valuable property from flooding, A could claim a defense of necessity.

Modern cases have tended to blur the distinction between duress and necessity. In the court below, the majority discarded the labels "duress" and "necessity," choosing instead to examine the policies underlying the traditional defenses. In particular, the majority felt that the defenses were designed to spare a person from punishment if he acted "under threats or conditions that a person of ordinary firmness would have been unable to resist," or if he reasonably believed that criminal action "was necessary to avoid a harm more serious than that sought to be prevented by the statute defining the offense." The Model Penal Code redefines the defenses along similar lines. See Model Penal Code § 2.09 (duress) and § 3.02 (choice of evils).

We need not speculate now, however, on the precise contours of whatever defenses of duress or necessity are available against charges brought under § 751(a). Under any definition of these defenses one principle remains constant: if there was a reasonable, legal alternative to violating the law, "a chance both to refuse to do the criminal act and also to avoid the threatened harm," the defenses will fail. Clearly, in the context of prison escape, the escapee is not entitled to claim a defense of duress or necessity unless and until he demonstrates that, given the imminence of the threat, violation of § 751(a) was his only reasonable alternative.

In the present case, the Government contends that respondents' showing was insufficient on two grounds. First, the Government asserts that the threats and conditions cited by respondents as justifying their escape were not sufficiently immediate or serious to justify their departure from lawful custody. Second, the Government contends that, once the respondents had escaped, the coercive conditions in the jail were no longer a threat and respondents were under a duty to terminate their status as fugitives by turning themselves over to the authorities.

Respondents, on the other hand, argue that the evidence of coercion and conditions in the jail was at least sufficient to go to the jury as an affirmative defense to the crime charged. As for their failure to return to custody after gaining their freedom, respondents assert that this failure should be but one factor in the overall determination whether their initial departure was justified. According to respondents, their failure to surrender "may reflect adversely on the bona fides of [their] motivation" in leaving the jail, but should not withdraw the question of their motivation from the jury's consideration.

We need not decide whether such evidence as that submitted by respondents was sufficient to raise a jury question as to their initial departures. This is because we decline to hold that respondents' failure to return is "just one factor" for the jury to weigh in deciding whether the initial escape could be affirmatively justified. On the contrary, several considerations lead us to conclude that, in order to be entitled to an instruction on duress or necessity as a defense to the crime charged, an escapee must first offer evidence justifying his continued absence from custody as well as his initial departure and that an indispensable element of such an offer is testimony of a bona fide effort to surrender or return to custody as soon as the claimed duress or necessity had lost its coercive force.

First, we think it clear beyond peradventure that escape from federal custody as defined in § 751(a) is a continuing offense and that an escapee can be held liable for failure to return to custody as well as for his initial departure. Given the continuing threat to society posed by an escaped prisoner, "the nature of the crime involved is such that Congress must assuredly have intended that it be treated as a continuing one." Moreover, every federal court that has considered this issue has held, either explicitly or implicitly, that § 751(a) defines a continuing offense. . . .

. . . [W]here a criminal defendant is charged with escape and claims that he is entitled to an instruction on the theory of duress or necessity, he must proffer evidence of a bona fide effort to surrender or return to custody as soon as the claimed duress or necessity had lost its coercive force. We have reviewed the evidence examined elaborately in the majority and dissenting opinions below, and find the case not even close, even under respondents' versions of the facts, as to whether they either surrendered or offered to surrender at their earliest possible opportunity. Since we have determined that this is an indispensable element of the defense of duress or necessity, respondents were not entitled to any instruction on such a theory. Vague and necessarily self-serving statements of defendants or witnesses as to future good intentions or ambiguous conduct simply do not support a finding of this element of the defense.

III

These cases present a good example of the potential for wasting valuable trial resources. In general, trials for violations of § 751(a) should be simple affairs. The key elements are capable of objective demonstration; the *mens rea*, as discussed above, will usually depend upon reasonable inferences from those objective facts. Here, however, the jury in the trial of Bailey, Cooley, and Walker heard five days of testimony. It was presented with evidence of every unpleasant aspect of prison life from the amount of garbage on the cellblock floor, to the meal schedule, to the number of times the inmates were allowed to shower. Unfortunately, all this evidence was presented in a case where the defense's reach hopelessly exceeded its grasp. Were we to hold, as respondents suggest, that the jury should be subjected to this potpourri even though a critical element of the proffered defenses was concededly absent, we undoubtedly would convert every trial under § 751(a) into a hearing on the current state of the federal penal system. . . .

NOTES & QUESTIONS ON PRISON BREAKS

Necessity and accomplices.   Since necessity is a justification and transforms what would otherwise be a wrongful act into a rightful act, it should also apply to any accomplices who assist the principal perpetrator. If indeed the defendant was justified, those who render assistance would not be guilty as accomplices—after all, they would have simply facilitated a rightful act. In *United States v. Lopez*, 662 F. Supp. 1083 (N.D. Cal. 1987), Ronald McIntosh landed a helicopter in a prison yard to break out his girlfriend Samantha Lopez from a state prison. At trial, Lopez claimed that her escape was justified by necessity because of an intolerable situation in the prison. McIntosh argued that the trial judge should instruct the jury that if it accepted Lopez's necessity defense, McIntosh should be acquitted as well. In a sense, the justification should roll down to the accomplices involved in the criminal transaction. The court agreed that McIntosh should be entitled to tie his fate to Lopez in this way since accomplice liability derives from the guilt of the principal. Ultimately, the jury convicted both of them.

4. Necessity and Civil Disobedience

Protestors often claim that it was "necessary" for them to break the law in order to achieve their larger objectives. As noted above, courts are generally skeptical of such claims. As you read the following case, ask yourself what a protestor would need to show in order to claim that an act of civil disobedience was justified by necessity.

United States v. Schoon
U.S. Court of Appeals for the Ninth Circuit
971 F.2d 193 (1991)

BOOCHEVER, CIRCUIT JUDGE.

Gregory Schoon, Raymond Kennon, Jr., and Patricia Manning appeal their convictions for obstructing activities of the Internal Revenue Service Office in Tucson, Arizona, and failing to comply with an order of a federal police officer. Both charges stem from their activities in protest of United States involvement in El Salvador. They claim the district court improperly denied them a necessity defense. Because we hold the necessity defense inapplicable in cases like this, we affirm.

I

On December 4, 1989, thirty people, including appellants, gained admittance to the IRS office in Tucson, where they chanted "keep America's tax dollars out of El Salvador," splashed simulated blood on the counters, walls, and carpeting, and generally obstructed the office's operation. After a federal police officer ordered the group, on several occasions, to disperse or face arrest, appellants were arrested.

At a bench trial, appellants proffered testimony about conditions in El Salvador as the motivation for their conduct. They attempted to assert a necessity defense, essentially contending that their acts in protest of American involvement in El Salvador were necessary to avoid further bloodshed in that country. While finding appellants motivated solely by humanitarian concerns, the court nonetheless precluded the defense as a matter of law, relying on Ninth Circuit precedent. The sole issue on appeal is the propriety of the court's exclusion of a necessity defense as a matter of law.

II

A district court may preclude a necessity defense where "the evidence, as described in the defendant's offer of proof, is insufficient as a matter of law to support the proffered defense." To invoke the necessity defense, therefore, the defendants colorably must have shown that: (1) they were faced with a choice of evils and chose the lesser evil; (2) they acted to prevent imminent harm; (3) they reasonably anticipated a direct causal relationship between their conduct and the harm to be averted; and (4) they had no legal alternatives to violating the law. We review *de novo* the district court's decision to bar a necessity defense.

The district court denied the necessity defense on the grounds that (1) the requisite immediacy was lacking; (2) the actions taken would not abate the evil; and (3) other legal alternatives existed. Because the threshold test for admissibility of a necessity defense is a conjunctive one, a court may preclude invocation of the defense if "proof is deficient with regard to any of the four elements."

While we could affirm substantially on those grounds relied upon by the district court, we find a deeper, systemic reason for the complete absence of federal case law recognizing a necessity defense in an indirect civil disobedience case. As used in this opinion, "civil disobedience" is the wilful violation of a law, undertaken for the purpose of social or political protest. Indirect civil disobedience involves violating a law or interfering with a government policy that is not, itself, the object of protest. Direct civil disobedience, on the other hand, involves protesting the existence of a law by breaking that law or by preventing the execution of that law in a specific instance in which a particularized harm would otherwise follow. This case involves indirect civil disobedience because these protestors were not challenging the laws under which they were charged. In contrast, the civil rights lunch counter sit-ins, for example, constituted direct civil disobedience because the protestors were challenging the rule that prevented them from sitting at lunch counters. Similarly, if a city council passed an ordinance requiring immediate infusion of a suspected carcinogen into the drinking water, physically blocking the delivery of the substance would constitute direct civil disobedience: protestors would be preventing the execution of a law in a specific instance in which a particularized harm—contamination of the water supply—would otherwise follow.

While our prior cases consistently have found the elements of the necessity defense lacking in cases involving indirect civil disobedience, we have never addressed specifically whether the defense is available in cases of indirect civil disobedience. Indeed, some other courts have appeared doubtful. Today, we conclude, for the reasons stated below, that the necessity defense is inapplicable to cases involving indirect civil disobedience.

III

Necessity is, essentially, a utilitarian defense. It therefore justifies criminal acts taken to avert a greater harm, maximizing social welfare by allowing a crime to be committed where the social benefits of the crime outweigh the social costs of failing to commit the crime. Pursuant to the defense, prisoners could escape a burning prison; a person lost in the woods could steal food from a cabin to survive; an embargo could be violated because adverse weather conditions necessitated sale of the cargo at a foreign port; a crew could mutiny where their ship was thought to be unseaworthy; and property could be destroyed to prevent the spread of fire.

What all the traditional necessity cases have in common is that the commission of the "crime" averted the occurrence of an even greater "harm." In some sense, the necessity defense allows us to act as individual legislatures, amending a particular criminal provision or crafting a one-time exception to it, subject to court review, when a real legislature would formally do the same under those circumstances. For example, by allowing prisoners who escape a burning jail to claim the justification of necessity, we assume the lawmaker, confronting this problem, would have allowed for an exception to the law proscribing prison escapes.

Because the necessity doctrine is utilitarian, however, strict requirements contain its exercise so as to prevent nonbeneficial criminal conduct. For example, "[i]f the criminal act cannot abate the threatened harm, society receives no benefit from the criminal conduct." Similarly, to forgive a crime taken to avert a lesser harm would fail to maximize social utility. The cost of the crime would outweigh the harm averted by its commission. Likewise, criminal acts cannot be condoned to thwart threats, yet to be imminent, or those for which there are legal alternatives to abate the harm.

Analysis of three of the necessity defense's four elements leads us to the conclusion that necessity can never be proved in a case of indirect civil disobedience. We do not rely upon the imminent harm prong of the defense because we believe there can be indirect civil disobedience cases in which the protested harm is imminent.

It is axiomatic that, if the thing to be averted is not a harm at all, the balance of harms necessarily would disfavor any criminal action. Indirect civil disobedience seeks first and foremost to bring about the repeal of a law or a change of governmental policy, attempting to mobilize public opinion through typically symbolic action. These protestors violate a law, not because it is unconstitutional or otherwise improper, but because doing so calls public attention to their objectives. Thus, the most immediate "harm" this form of protest targets is the *existence* of the law or policy. However, the mere existence of a constitutional law or governmental policy cannot constitute a legally cognizable harm.

There may be, of course, general harms that result from the targeted law or policy. Such generalized "harm," however, is too insubstantial an injury to be legally cognizable. We have in the past rejected the use of the necessity defense in indirect civil disobedience cases as a "'back door' attempt to attack government programs in a manner foreclosed by [federal] standing requirement[s]." The law could not function were people allowed to rely on their *subjective* beliefs and value judgments in determining which harms justified the taking of criminal action.

The protest in this case was in the form of indirect civil disobedience, aimed at reversal of the government's El Salvador policy. That policy does not violate the Constitution, and appellants have never suggested as much. There is no evidence that the procedure by which the policy was adopted was in any way improper; nor is there any evidence that appellants were prevented systematically from participating in the democratic processes through which the policy was chosen. The most immediate harm the appellants sought to avert was the existence of the government's El Salvador policy, which is not in itself a legally cognizable harm. Moreover, any harms resulting from the operation of this policy are insufficiently concrete to be legally cognizable as harms for purposes of the necessity defense.

Thus, as a matter of law, the mere existence of a policy or law validly enacted by Congress cannot constitute a cognizable harm. If there is no cognizable harm to prevent, the harm resulting from criminal action taken for the purpose of securing the repeal of the law or policy necessarily outweighs any benefit of the action.

This inquiry requires a court to judge the likelihood that an alleged harm will be abated by the taking of illegal action. In the sense that the likelihood of abatement is required in the traditional necessity cases, there will never be such likelihood in cases of indirect political protest. In the traditional cases, a prisoner flees a burning cell and averts death, or someone demolishes a home to create a firebreak and prevents the conflagration of an entire community. The nexus between the act undertaken and the result sought is a close one. Ordinarily it is the volitional illegal act alone which, once taken, abates the evil.

In political necessity cases involving indirect civil disobedience against congressional acts, however, the act alone is unlikely to abate the evil precisely because the action is indirect. Here, the IRS obstruction, or the refusal to comply with a federal officer's order, are unlikely to abate the killings in El Salvador, or immediately change Congress's policy; instead, it takes another *volitional* actor not controlled by the protestor to take a further step; Congress must change its mind.

A final reason the necessity defense does not apply to these indirect civil disobedience cases is that legal alternatives will never be deemed exhausted when the harm can be mitigated by congressional action. As noted above, the harm indirect civil disobedience aims to prevent is the continued existence of a law or policy. Because congressional action can *always* mitigate this "harm," lawful political activity to spur such action will always be a legal alternative. On the other hand, we cannot say that this legal alternative will always exist in cases of direct civil disobedience, where protestors act to avert a concrete harm flowing from the operation of the targeted law or policy.

The necessity defense requires the absence of any legal alternative to the contemplated illegal conduct which could reasonably be expected to abate an imminent evil. A prisoner fleeing a burning jail, for example, would not be asked to wait in his cell because someone might conceivably save him; such a legal alternative is ill-suited to avoiding death in a fire. In other words, the law implies a reasonableness requirement in judging whether legal alternatives exist.

Where the targeted harm is the existence of a law or policy, our precedents counsel that this reasonableness requirement is met simply by the possibility of congressional action. For example, in *Dorrell,* an indirect civil disobedience case involving a trespass on Vandenburg Air Force Base to protest the MX missile program, we rejected Dorrell's claims that legal alternatives, like lobbying Congress, were unavailable because they were futile. Dorrell, we said, "differ[ed] little from many whose passionate beliefs are rejected by the will of the majority legitimately expressed." We assumed there that the "possibility" that Congress will change its mind is sufficient in the context of the democratic process to make lawful political action a reasonable alternative to indirect civil disobedience. Without expressly saying so, *Dorrell* decided that petitioning Congress to change a policy is *always* a legal alternative in such cases, regardless of the likelihood of the plea's success. Thus, indirect civil disobedience can never meet the necessity defense requirement that there be a lack of legal alternatives.

As have courts before us, we could assume, as a threshold matter, that the necessity defense is conceivably available in these cases, but find the elements never satisfied. Such a decision, however, does not come without significant costs. First, the failure of the federal courts to hold explicitly that the necessity defense is unavailable in these cases results in district courts expending unnecessary time and energy trying to square defendants' claims with the strict requirements of the doctrine. Second, such an inquiry oftentimes requires the courts to tread into areas constitutionally committed to other branches of government. For example, in *May,* which involved trespass on a naval base to protest American nuclear weapons policy, we noted that, "[t]o consider defendants' argument [that trespassing was justified by the nefariousness of the Trident missile] would put us in the position of usurping the functions that the Constitution has given to the Congress and to the President." Third, holding out the possibility of the defense's applicability sets a trap for the unwary civil disobedient, rather than permitting the individual to undertake a more realistic cost-benefit analysis before deciding whether to break the law in political protest. Fourth, assuming the applicability of the defense in this context may risk its distortion in traditional cases. Finally, some commentators have suggested that the courts have sabotaged the usually low threshold for getting a defense theory before the jury as a means of keeping the necessity defense from the jury.

The real problem here is that litigants are trying to distort to their purposes an age-old common law doctrine meant for a very different set of circumstances. What these cases are really about is gaining notoriety for a cause—the defense allows protestors to get their political grievances discussed in a courtroom. It is precisely this political motive that has left some courts, like the district court in this case, uneasy. Because these attempts to invoke the necessity defense "force the courts to choose among causes they should make legitimate by extending the defense of necessity," and because the criminal acts, themselves, do not maximize social good, they should be subject to a *per se* rule of exclusion.

Thus, we see the failure of any federal court to recognize a defense of necessity in a case like ours not as coincidental, but rather as the natural consequence of the historic limitation of the doctrine. Indirect protests of congressional policies can never meet all the requirements of the necessity doctrine. Therefore, we hold that the necessity defense is not available in such cases. . . .

NOTES & QUESTIONS ON CIVIL DISOBEDIENCE

Other rationales.   Not every jurisdiction uses the distinction between direct and indirect civil disobedience to resolve necessity claims for protestors, but the result is usually the same: an unsympathetic courtroom for the political protestor. For example, in *Muller v. State*, 196 P.3d 815 (Alaska 2008), the defendant broke into the office of a U.S. Senator to protest the war in Iraq. At trial for criminal trespass, Muller tried to argue that his actions were justified by necessity. He fared no better than the defendants in *Schoon*, though for slightly different reasons. The Alaska Supreme Court concluded that there was insufficient causal connection between the crime and the harm sought to be avoided and that the protest would in no way solve the alleged problem: "Although Muller testified that he believed the only adequate alternative to halting the Iraq war was staying in Senator Stevens's office after closing—because he had already tried other types of protest and they had failed—he offered no evidence that coming back at 8:00 A.M. the following morning to finish reading the names of Iraq war casualties would have been any less effective. Moreover, Muller offered no evidence that, '[u]nder any possible set of hypotheses,' his actions had any realistic hope of ending the war in Iraq." See also *United States v. Santana*, 184 F. Supp. 2d 131 (D.P.R. 2001) (political protesters had legal alternatives to protest the Navy's use of Vieques island for training exercises); *State v. Marley*, 54 Haw. 450, 509 P.2d 1095 (1973) (trespassing at weapons manufacturer to protest alleged complicity in war crimes would not stop the Vietnam war). Do you agree that a mere protest cannot stop a war and change government policy?

C. PRACTICE & POLICY

Why do lawyers keep making necessity arguments if they so rarely work? The answer might have something to do with the fact that criminal defendants are sometimes using the trial to construct a larger narrative—one that extends far beyond the limited confines of guilt or innocence to a particular charge. They are also making moral arguments about the appropriateness of their conduct. The necessity defense speaks to a larger question about the limits of the criminal law. How far should we allow necessity arguments to go? The following materials consider three compelling examples of necessity arguments arising out of the 9/11 terrorism context: (i) Is it appropriate to torture someone to stop a terrorist attack; (ii) does torture violate human dignity; and (iii) should the government shoot down an airliner full of innocent passengers to stop terrorists from flying it into a skyscraper?

∾ **Torture and terrorism.** Would the prospect of a future terrorist attack justify torturing suspected terrorists who may have actionable intelligence that could help avert the threat? This question preoccupied the Administration of President George W. Bush, who unapologetically argued that torture was legally and morally justified under those circumstances. The argument was simple: A terrorist attack from al-Qaeda or another terrorist organization might kill thousands of innocent Americans; torture, though illegal, would be justified to avert that threat. Proponents of torture often use "ticking time bomb" hypotheticals; the bomb is about to go off, and the only way to stop it is to torture the terrorists already in custody. Although torture is wrong, it is outweighed by the need to save the many innocent victims who would be killed in the blast. Do you agree with this line of argument? Opponents of torture argue that the ticking time bomb hypotheticals have substantially distorted the moral and legal debate. In reality, it is almost never the case that there are no other viable alternatives to receive the information; indeed, conventional interrogation methods often produce better and more reliable information. See Henry Shue, *Torture in Dreamland: Disposing of the Ticking Bomb*, 37 Case W. Res. J. Int'l L. 231 (2005-2006); Ali Soufan, *The Black Banners: The Inside Story of 9/11 and the War Against al-Qaeda* (2011); Thomas M. McDonnell, *United States, International Law and the Struggle Against Terrorism* 91-96 (2011).

The terrorist attacks of 9/11 ushered in a lengthy national conversation about torture in the United States. In contrast, Israel had already been having this conversation for decades due to security threats from suicide bombers and other terrorist attacks. In 1999, the Israel Supreme Court concluded that even the need to avert a future terrorist attack was an insufficient reason for the government to authorize the torture of a detainee. *Public Committee Against Torture in Israel v. Israel*, HCJ 5100/94 (Supreme Court of Israel, 1999). However, the court also concluded that even though torture was not justified as an official *policy*, a security officer could still argue necessity as a defense to a criminal prosecution for torture. Can you understand why the court would draw this distinction? For a discussion, see Alon Harel & Assaf Sharon, *What Is Really Wrong with Torture?*, 6 J. Int'l Crim. Just. 241 (2008) ("[T]here is a compelling reason not to incorporate into the law exceptions to the prohibition on torture. Perhaps we can even say that the incorporation of an exception to the rule prohibiting torture, i.e., entrenching such an exception, is morally repugnant.").

Setting aside for the moment the issue of whether the government should ever codify a policy in favor of torture, consider simply the criminal law question. Assume that government security operatives receive credible information about an imminent terrorist attack. Also, assume that the operatives receive actionable intelligence that a detainee is connected to or involved in the plot and might have information that could help security officials foil the plot. If the interrogators cross the line and torture the detainee, can they argue necessity if they are prosecuted for the torture? Does the crime (the torture) constitute the lesser of two evils? Arguably yes, since many will die during the attack. Also, since the crime is not murder, the rule from *Dudley & Stephens* does not apply. Nonetheless, many people believe that torture would be immoral in this context and that a criminal law defense should not apply. Do you agree? In 2005, Congress passed a specific law designed to immunize interrogators from prosecution based on their reliance on official legal advice that torture was permissible. Detainee Treatment Act of 2005 § 1004(1), 42 U.S.C. § 2000dd-1 ("it shall be a defense that such officer, employee, member of the Armed Forces, or other agent did not know that the practices were unlawful and a person of ordinary sense and understanding would not know the practices were unlawful").

∾ **Torture and human dignity.** In Germany, recent court decisions have substantially restricted the availability of necessity as a defense to torture. In 2002, Wolfgang Daschner worked as a deputy police chief in Frankfurt, Germany. A detainee named Magnus Gäfgen was in custody, suspected of kidnapping an 11-year-old boy. Daschner and his lieutenants threatened to torture Gäfgen until he divulged the whereabouts of the boy. Gäfgen relented and police officers found the boy, who was already dead. (Gäfgen was eventually charged and convicted for kidnapping and murdering the boy.) Daschner was subsequently prosecuted for torture because

German law treats a threat to inflict severe pain as a form of mental torture even if the threat is never carried out. At trial, Daschner asserted a necessity defense. The Frankfurt Regional Court rejected both excused necessity and justified necessity in the case (German penal law has both). See Landgericht Frankfurt a.M. [LG] [Regional Court], Dec. 20, 2004, Neue Juristische Wochenschrift 692-96 (2005). As for excused necessity under the German Penal Code, the defense only applies if the defendant acts to save himself or a close family relation—and the kidnapped boy was neither. As for justified necessity, the German Penal Code requires that the defendant's action was an "appropriate means" to avert the danger. The court concluded that torturing the suspect violated his human dignity—and that violating someone's human dignity is *never* an appropriate means to averting a threat. Human dignity is protected in Article 1 of the German Constitution: "Human dignity shall be inviolable. To respect and protect it shall be the duty of all state authority." Despite convicting him, the court refused to throw Daschner in jail. The court imposed a monetary fine and suspended sentence. See Florian Jessberger, *Bad Torture—Good Torture? What International Criminal Lawyers May Learn from the Recent Trial of Police Officers in Germany*, 3 J. Int'l Crim. Just. 1059, 1073 (2005) ("Ultimately, police officers and other state agents may face a bitter choice if all legally available means of interrogation are exhausted: to make themselves guilty of a crime or to risk innocent lives. The 'choice of evils' is a price that must be paid for upholding the rule of law. This is something that should never be forgotten—even in times of a global 'war on terrorism.'").

Magnus Gäfgen and Wolfgang Daschner

∾ **Hijacked airliners and human dignity.**   Torture is not the only situation where the security needs of the state might conflict with an individual's human dignity. After 9/11, German security officials became concerned about the prospect that terrorists might try to repeat their 9/11 attacks by hijacking an airliner and crashing it into a skyscraper in a major German city. Consequently, the German legislature passed a law explicitly authorizing the chancellor to authorize military forces to shoot down a hijacked aircraft before it could be used to take down a building in the same manner as the hijacked airplanes in New York and Washington did on 9/11. Indeed, U.S. government officials indicated after 9/11 that had they had the opportunity to shoot down the aircraft, they would have done so. However, the German Constitutional Court struck down the law, concluding that it would violate the human dignity of the innocent passengers on the airplane. Although their deaths would be "outweighed" by the innocent lives that would be saved on the ground, the court concluded that they could not be deliberately killed in order to produce the "lesser evil" as contemplated by the necessity defense:

> This makes them objects not only of the perpetrators of the crime. Also the state which in such a situation resorts to the measure provided by § 14.3 of the Aviation Security Act treats them as mere objects of its rescue operation for the protection of others. The desperateness and inescapability which characterise the situation of the people on board the aircraft who are affected as victims also exist vis-à-vis those who order and execute the shooting down of the aircraft. Due to the circumstances, which cannot be controlled by them in any way, the crew and the passengers of the plane cannot escape this state action but are helpless and defenceless in the face of it with the consequence that they are shot down in a targeted manner together with the aircraft and as result of this will be killed with near certainty. Such a treatment ignores the status of the persons affected as subjects endowed with dignity and inalienable rights. By their killing being used as a means to save others, they are treated as objects and at the same time deprived of their rights; with their lives being disposed of unilaterally by the state, the persons on board the aircraft, who, as victims, are themselves in need of protection, are denied the value which is due to a human being for his or her own sake.

See *Aviation Security Case*, Constitutional Court (Germany), Judgment of the First Senate of 15 February 2006, 115 Entscheidungen des Bundesverfassungsgerichts [BVerfGE] 118 (F.R.G.). Do you agree that shooting down a hijacked airliner violates the human dignity of the innocent passengers? If you accept this argument, does it cast doubt on the entire logical structure of the necessity defense, which requires a balancing of evils? How does the supposedly "optimal result" justify, in any case in this chapter, the imposition of a criminal harm on an innocent victim? Perhaps the necessity defense should be outlawed in *all* cases, not just in cases of murder.

CHAPTER 26

—◦◦◦—

DURESS

A. DOCTRINE

The defense of duress traditionally differs from necessity in that the person who issues the threat is trying to coerce an otherwise innocent individual into committing a crime at his behest. If the innocent individual succumbs to the threat and commits the crime, her actions should be excused because the threat vitiated her autonomy. In order to satisfy the defense of duress, defendants must show that they committed the crime because: (i) They or a third party faced an imminent threat from another individual with no opportunity for reasonable escape; (ii) the threat was sufficiently severe in nature; (iii) the crime committed was not murder; and (iv) the defendant was not reckless or otherwise culpable in creating the circumstance that produced the duress. Each of these elements will now be explored in greater depth.

1. Threats That Vitiate Autonomy

In order to qualify for the duress defense, the defendant must show that she committed the crime in order to avoid a threat to herself or another individual. In the paradigmatic case, the coercer threatens someone by pointing a gun at her head and tells her that unless she commits a robbery, she will be shot. The individual succumbs to the threat and commits the robbery. At trial, she argues that the threat vitiated her autonomy and that she should be acquitted of the crime because the threat was immediate and she had no reasonable avenue of escape. In most jurisdictions, the defendant bears both the burden of production and the burden of persuasion, since it is an affirmative defense. In practical terms, this means that the defendant must make an initial showing of some factual evidence supporting the defense—for example, by testifying about the

747

threat and her decision to commit the crime in order to avoid the threatening result. Once this initial burden is satisfied, the judge should submit the issue to the jury and charge them that they should acquit the defendant if they believe she acted under duress. However, the Model Penal Code allocates the burden to the prosecution so as to remain consistent with other defenses, such as self-defense, which are typically the responsibility of the prosecution to disprove.

2. The Severity of the Threat

The threat facing the defendant must be sufficiently severe; a minor infringement certainly should not excuse serious criminal behavior. Some jurisdictions specify that the threat should be one of death or serious bodily injury, while other statutory formulations lean on the functional criteria of reasonable firmness. The difference between the two formulations comes down to a difference between a relatively bright-line rule (requiring death or serious bodily injury), or a hybrid standard that brings together subjective and objective criteria. For example, MPC § 2.09(1) requires that the threat involve an "unlawful force against his person or the person of another, which a person of reasonable firmness in his situation would have been unable to resist." In applying this "reasonable firmness" test, a court must first ask whether a person *in the defendant's situation* would have succumbed to the threat, which requires analyzing the threat from the subjective vantage point of the defendant. However, the court must then ask whether a person of *reasonable firmness* would have been unable to resist—a question of reasonableness that adds a clearly objective component to the analysis. In the end, the Model Penal Code test is best described as an objective-subjective hybrid test because it asks: Was it objectively reasonable for a person in similar circumstances as the defendant to succumb to the threat?

As to the object of the threat, some jurisdictions require that the threat be made against either the defendant or a close family relation, while others allow the defense when the threat is made against any third party, presumably on the assumption that an individual may feel compelled to succumb to a threat made against an innocent third party, even if the individuals bear no formal relation to each other. For example, imagine that a criminal takes a group of people hostage in a store. The criminal threatens to kill hostage A unless hostage B commits a particular crime. Hostage B commits the crime under duress because he wishes to avoid the death of the innocent hostage, even though they have no prior relationship.

Jurisdictions are split on whether the defendant needs to select the lesser of two evils (as generally required by the necessity defense). If the defendant saves someone's life by agreeing to commit a robbery, the lesser-evils requirement is satisfied. But what if the defendant agrees to torture someone in order to save a family member from a severe beating? In that case, the harm inflicted by the defendant is arguably *not* the lesser of the evils. The defendant is motivated to comply with the threat simply because he cares more about one individual than the other. This is a highly contested point, but the better view is that duress is an excuse, not a justification, so there is no requirement that the defendant select the "better" of the two options. Instead, the defense is an excuse based on the vitiation of the defendant's autonomy.

3. Defense to Murder

Like necessity, duress is usually unavailable as a defense to murder in the American criminal law system. Again, like necessity, both the Model Penal Code and some civil law systems in Europe take a different view and allow the defense. But at least in the United States and other commonwealth systems, the rule from *Dudley & Stephens* is interpreted as barring *both* necessity and duress as applicable defenses in homicide cases. The rationale for the rule is contested, but one might think of it as an ad hoc limitation designed to blunt the great power of the doctrine. The duress defense could, in theory, excuse all sorts of horrendous criminality performed by the individual who is coerced. Indeed, criminals could use the duress defense as a strategic ploy to escape liability. However, there is a limit to the law's tolerance in this area. For most crimes, the law will view with charity the individual who fails to live up to the demands of the law when coerced by someone who has threatened to impose a great harm. When the crime is murder, however, the charity comes to an end and the law expects—indeed demands—that the target of the coercion sacrifice herself rather than commit a murder. The one exception is felony murder, where duress might extinguish liability for the triggering felony and therefore make a conviction for felony murder impossible.

4. Recklessness in Creating the Threat

The duress defense is not available if the defendant is reckless or otherwise culpable in creating the very situation that gave rise to the duress. So if a defendant commits assault with a deadly weapon under a state of duress, but was reckless in contributing to the situation that gave rise to the duress, the defendant is guilty of the assault irrespective of the duress. For example, imagine that a defendant agrees to participate in a robbery with a co-felon. During the crime, the co-felon tells the defendant that he will kill him unless he commits a vicious assault. Although the defendant was coerced, he was culpable in the creation of the situation by participating in the original robbery, and thus the duress defense is unavailable to him. The rationale for the rule is that defendants should not be able to opportunistically create the conditions for their own defense—a principle that also limits other defenses such as voluntary intoxication. The Model Penal Code includes one such rule. Under MPC § 2.09(2), the defense is unavailable if the actor "recklessly placed himself in a situation in which it was probable that he would be subjected to duress." The end result of this provision is that if the defendant is charged with intentional murder and was reckless in creating the situation of duress, the defendant loses the duress defense entirely and is convicted of murder (and does not get a reduction to reckless manslaughter). The same section of the Model Penal Code states that the "defense is also unavailable if he was negligent in placing himself in such a situation, whenever negligence suffices to establish culpability for the offense charged." Consequently, if the defendant was negligent, the duress defense is unavailable for crimes of negligence, such as negligent homicide, but the duress defense would remain applicable as an excuse for a crime, such as murder, based on the mental states of purpose, knowledge, or recklessness. (Contrast this with the MPC provision on necessity, § 3.02(2), which is different: It allows the defendant who is reckless or negligent in creating the situation to still apply the defense of necessity for intentional crimes, and thus could achieve a reduction to reckless or negligent manslaughter.)

B. APPLICATION

1. Threats That Vitiate Autonomy

The following section presents two cases. The first deals with the burden of proof for duress. The prosecution always bears the burden of proving beyond a reasonable doubt that the defendant acted with the required mental state. Should the burden for disproving duress be similarly allocated? On the one hand, duress is closely related to mens rea (suggesting a prosecutorial burden), but on the other hand it is an affirmative defense. Most state jurisdictions allocate, to the defense, the burden of establishing duress by a preponderance of the evidence. In the first case, the Supreme Court must decide the question for federal crimes. The second case applies the general requirements for duress to a concrete case and analyzes whether the threat facing the defendant must be "inescapable."

Dixon v. United States

Supreme Court of the United States
548 U.S. 1 (2006)

Stevens, J.

In January 2003, petitioner Keshia Dixon purchased multiple firearms at two gun shows, during the course of which she provided an incorrect address and falsely stated that she was not under indictment for a felony. As a result of these illegal acts, petitioner was indicted and convicted on one count of receiving a firearm while under indictment in violation of 18 U.S.C. § 922(n) and eight counts of making false statements in connection with the acquisition of a firearm in violation of § 922(a)(6). At trial, petitioner admitted that she knew she was under indictment when she made the purchases and that she knew doing so was a crime; her defense was that she acted under duress because her boyfriend threatened to kill her or hurt her daughters if she did not buy the guns for him.

Petitioner contends that the trial judge's instructions to the jury erroneously required her to prove duress by a preponderance of the evidence instead of requiring the Government to prove beyond a reasonable doubt that she did not act under duress. The Court of Appeals rejected petitioner's contention; given contrary treatment of the issue by other federal courts, we granted certiorari.

At trial, in her request for jury instructions on her defense of duress, petitioner contended that she "should have the burden of production, and then that the Government should be required to disprove beyond a reasonable doubt the duress." . . .

The crimes for which petitioner was convicted require that she have acted "knowingly," § 922(a)(6), or "willfully," § 924(a)(1)(D). . . . Petitioner contends, however, that she cannot have formed the necessary *mens rea* for these crimes because she did not freely choose to commit the acts in question. But even if we assume that petitioner's will was overborne by the threats made against her and her daughters, she still *knew* that she was making false statements and *knew* that she was breaking the law by buying a firearm. The duress defense . . . may excuse conduct that would otherwise be punishable, but the existence of duress normally does not controvert any of the elements of the offense itself. As we explained in *United States v. Bailey,* "[c]riminal liability is normally based upon the concurrence of two factors, 'an evil-meaning mind [and] and evil-doing hand. . . . '" Like the defense of necessity, the defense of duress does not negate a defendant's criminal state of mind when the applicable offense requires a defendant to have acted knowingly or willfully; instead, it allows the defendant to "avoid liability . . . because coercive conditions or necessity negates a conclusion of guilt even though the necessary *mens rea* was present."

The fact that petitioner's crimes are statutory offenses that have no counterpart in the common law also supports our conclusion that her duress defense in no way disproves an element of those crimes. We have observed that "[t]he definition of the elements of a criminal offense is entrusted to the legislature, particularly in the case of federal crimes, which are solely creatures of statute." Here, consistent with the movement away from the traditional dichotomy of general versus specific intent and toward a more specifically defined hierarchy of culpable mental states, Congress defined the crimes at issue to punish defendants who act "knowingly," or "willfully." It is these specific mental states, rather than some vague "evil mind," or "'criminal' intent," that the Government is required to prove beyond a reasonable doubt. The jury instructions in this case were consistent with this requirement and, as such, did not run afoul of the Due Process Clause when they placed the burden on petitioner to establish the existence of duress by a preponderance of the evidence. . . .

As discussed above, the common law long required the defendant to bear the burden of proving the existence of duress. Similarly, even where Congress has enacted an affirmative defense in the proviso of a statute, the "settled rule in this jurisdiction [is] that an indictment or other pleading . . . need not negative the matter of an exception made by a proviso or other distinct clause . . . and that it is incumbent on one who relies on such an exception to set it up and establish it." Even though the Safe Streets Act does not mention the defense of duress, we can safely assume that the 1968 Congress was familiar with both the long-established common-law rule and the rule applied in *McKelvey* and that it would have expected federal courts to apply a similar approach to any affirmative defense that might be asserted as a justification or excuse for violating the new law. . . .

Indeed, for us to be able to accept petitioner's proposition, we would need to find an overwhelming consensus among federal courts that it is the Government's burden to disprove the existence of duress beyond a reasonable doubt. The existence today of disagreement among the Federal Courts of Appeals on this issue, however—the very disagreement that caused us to grant certiorari in this case—demonstrates that no such consensus has ever existed. Also undermining petitioner's argument is the fact that, in 1970, the National Commission on Reform of Federal Criminal Laws proposed that a defendant prove the existence of duress by a preponderance of the evidence. Moreover, while there seem to be few, if any, post-*Davis*, pre-1968 cases placing the burden on a defendant to prove the existence of duress, or even discussing the issue in any way, this lack of evidence does not help petitioner. The long-established common-law rule is that the burden of proving duress rests on the defendant. Petitioner hypothesizes that *Davis* fomented a revolution upsetting this rule. If this were true, one would expect to find cases discussing the matter. But no such cases exist.

It is for a similar reason that we give no weight to the publication of the Model Penal Code in 1962. As petitioner notes, the Code would place the burden on the government to disprove the existence of duress beyond a reasonable doubt. See Model Penal Code § 1.12 (stating that each element of an offense must be proved beyond a reasonable doubt); § 1.13(9)(c) (defining as an element anything that negatives an excuse for the conduct at issue); § 2.09 (establishing affirmative defense of duress). Petitioner argues that the Code reflects "well established" federal law as it existed at the time. But, as discussed above, no such consensus existed when Congress passed the Safe Streets Act in 1968. And even if we assume Congress' familiarity with the Code and the rule it would establish, there is no evidence that Congress endorsed the Code's views or incorporated them into the Safe Streets Act. . . .

Congress can, if it chooses, enact a duress defense that places the burden on the Government to disprove duress beyond a reasonable doubt. . . . In the context of the firearms offenses at issue—as will usually be the case, given the long-established common-law rule—we presume that Congress intended the petitioner to bear the burden of proving the defense of duress by a preponderance of the evidence. Accordingly, the judgment of the Court of Appeals is affirmed. . . .

—◦◦◦—

United States v. Contento-Pachon

U.S. Court of Appeals for the Ninth Circuit
723 F.2d 691 (1984)

BOOCHEVER, C.J.

This case presents an appeal from a conviction for unlawful possession with intent to distribute a narcotic controlled substance. . . . At trial, the defendant attempted to offer evidence of duress and necessity defenses. The district court excluded this evidence on the ground that it was insufficient to support the defenses. We reverse because there was sufficient evidence of duress to present a triable issue of fact.

FACTS

The defendant-appellant, Juan Manuel Contento-Pachon, is a native of Bogota, Colombia and was employed there as a taxicab driver. He asserts that one of his passengers, Jorge, offered him a job as the driver of a privately-owned car. Contento-Pachon expressed an interest in the job and agreed to meet Jorge and the owner of the car the next day.

Instead of a driving job, Jorge proposed that Contento-Pachon swallow cocaine-filled balloons and transport them to the United States. Contento-Pachon agreed to consider the proposition. He was told not to mention the proposition to anyone, otherwise he would "get into serious trouble." Contento-Pachon testified that he did not contact the police because he believes that the Bogota police are corrupt and that they are paid off by drug traffickers.

Approximately one week later, Contento-Pachon told Jorge that he would not carry the cocaine. In response, Jorge mentioned facts about Contento-Pachon's personal life, including private details which Contento-Pachon had never mentioned to Jorge. Jorge told Contento-Pachon that his failure to cooperate would result in the death of his wife and three year-old child.

The following day the pair met again. Contento-Pachon's life and the lives of his family were again threatened. At this point, Contento-Pachon agreed to take the cocaine into the United States.

The pair met two more times. At the last meeting, Contento-Pachon swallowed 129 balloons of cocaine. He was informed that he would be watched at all times during the trip, and that if he failed to follow Jorge's instruction he and his family would be killed.

After leaving Bogota, Contento-Pachon's plane landed in Panama. Contento-Pachon asserts that he did not notify the authorities there because he felt that the Panamanian police were as corrupt as those in Bogota. Also, he felt that any such action on his part would place his family in jeopardy.

When he arrived at the customs inspection point in Los Angeles, Contento-Pachon consented to have his stomach x-rayed. The x-rays revealed a foreign substance which was later determined to be cocaine.

At Contento-Pachon's trial, the government moved to exclude the defenses of duress and necessity. The motion was granted. We reverse.

DURESS

There are three elements of the duress defense: (1) an immediate threat of death or serious bodily injury, (2) a well-grounded fear that the threat will be carried out, and (3) no reasonable opportunity to escape the threatened harm. Sometimes a fourth element is required: the defendant must submit to proper authorities after attaining a position of safety.

Factfinding is usually a function of the jury, and the trial court rarely rules on a defense as a matter of law. If the evidence is insufficient as a matter of law to support a duress defense, however, the trial court should exclude that evidence.

The trial court found Contento-Pachon's offer of proof insufficient to support a duress defense because he failed to offer proof of two elements: immediacy and inescapability. We examine the elements of duress.

Immediacy: The element of immediacy requires that there be some evidence that the threat of injury was present, immediate, or impending. "[A] veiled threat of future unspecified harm" will not satisfy this requirement. The district court found that the initial threats were not immediate because "they were conditioned on defendant's failure to cooperate in the future and did not place defendant and his family in immediate danger."

Evidence presented on this issue indicated that the defendant was dealing with a man who was deeply involved in the exportation of illegal substances. Large sums of money were at stake and, consequently, Contento-Pachon had reason to believe that Jorge would carry out his threats. Jorge had gone to the trouble to discover that Contento-Pachon was married, that he had a child, the names of his wife and child, and the location of his residence. These were not vague threats of possible future harm. According to the defendant, if he had refused to cooperate, the consequences would have been immediate and harsh.

Contento-Pachon contends that he was being watched by one of Jorge's accomplices at all times during the airplane trip. As a consequence, the force of the threats continued to restrain him. Contento-Pachon's contention that he was operating under the threat of immediate harm was supported by sufficient evidence to present a triable issue of fact.

Escapability: The defendant must show that he had no reasonable opportunity to escape. The district court found that because Contento-Pachon was not physically restrained prior to the time he swallowed the balloons, he could have sought help from the police or fled. Contento-Pachon explained that he did not report the threats because he feared that the police were corrupt. The trier of fact should decide whether one in Contento-Pachon's position might believe that some of the Bogota police were paid informants for drug traffickers and that reporting the matter to the police did not represent a reasonable opportunity of escape.

If he chose not to go to the police, Contento-Pachon's alternative was to flee. We reiterate that the opportunity to escape must be reasonable. To flee, Contento-Pachon, along with his wife and three year-old child, would have been forced to pack his possessions, leave his job, and travel to a place beyond the reaches of the drug traffickers. A juror might find that this was not a reasonable avenue of escape. Thus, Contento-Pachon presented a triable issue on the element of escapability.

Surrender to Authorities: As noted above, the duress defense is composed of at least three elements. The government argues that the defense also requires that a defendant offer evidence that he intended to turn himself in to the authorities upon reaching a position of safety. Although it has not been expressly limited, this fourth element seems to be required only in prison escape cases. Under other circumstances, the defense has been defined to include only three elements. . . .

In cases not involving escape from prison there seems little difference between the third basic requirement that there be no reasonable opportunity to escape the threatened harm and the obligation to turn oneself in to authorities on reaching a point of safety. Once a defendant has reached a position where he can safely turn himself in to the authorities he will likewise have a reasonable opportunity to escape the threatened harm.

That is true in this case. Contento-Pachon claims that he was being watched at all times. According to him, at the first opportunity to cooperate with authorities without alerting the observer, he consented to the x-ray. We hold that a defendant who has acted under a well-grounded fear of immediate harm with no opportunity to escape may assert the duress defense, if there is a triable issue of fact whether he took the opportunity to escape the threatened harm by submitting to authorities at the first reasonable opportunity. . . .

NOTES & QUESTIONS ON DURESS AND AUTONOMY

1. *Duress as justification or excuse.*   Scholars and courts typically consider duress an excuse because the defendant's culpability is negated by a threat that compromises her ability to make a free choice. See Kyron Huigens, *Duress Is Not a Justification*, 2 Ohio St. J. Crim. L. 303 (2004). Although his choice is not completely eliminated, the nature of the threat is such that it places a thumb on the scale that makes compliance with the law seem difficult or unreasonable. However, at least some courts have interpreted the duress defense as a justification and have required that the defendant select the lesser evil (as with the necessity defense). See *State v. Heinemann*, 282 Conn. 281 (2007) ("in assessing the defense of duress, it is important to remember that, pursuant to the defense, the criminal act is justified because the defendant has avoided a harm of greater magnitude"); *State v. Rouleau*, 204 Conn. 240, 248-49 (1987) ("[t]he rationale of the defense is not that the defendant, faced with the unnerving threat of harm unless he does an act which violates the literal language of the criminal law, somehow loses his mental capacity to commit the crime in question . . . [but] rather . . . his conduct which violates the literal language of the criminal law is justified because he has thereby avoided a harm of greater magnitude"). For a scholarly defense of the lesser-evils requirement in duress cases, see Jerome Hall, *General Principles of Criminal Law* 448 (2d ed. 1960); Peter Westen & James Mangiafico, *The Criminal Defense of Duress: A Justification, Not an Excuse—and Why It Matters*, 6 Buff. Crim. L. Rev. 833 (2003). However, the weight of contemporary scholarly authority is behind duress as an excuse because it deals with threats that compromise the defendant's autonomy.

2. *Necessity and duress compared.*   In most jurisdictions, the crucial distinction between necessity and duress is not the source of the threat but the *reason* why the defendant commits the crime. In necessity, the defendant commits the crime in order to alleviate a threat coming from either the natural environment (such as the risk of drowning at sea) or a threat coming from another individual (such as a terrorist threatening to detonate a bomb). In the latter case, if the defendant tortures the terrorist to stop the terrorist attack, the crime is being committed to *thwart or frustrate* the will of the terrorist. In situations of duress, however, the defendant commits the crime in order to *implement or consummate* the will of the coercer. Consider the case of Contento-Pachon. Why did he break the law and transport the drugs? He did so to *implement* the will of the narco-traffickers because he was succumbing to their threat. If the defendant breaks the law to *defeat* the will of the third party, the legal claim should be classified as necessity.

3. *Duress compared with compulsion.*   Some jurisdictions codify a defense of "compulsion" rather than a defense of "duress." These statutory provisions are slightly broader than traditional duress provisions because they usually do

not require that the threat must come from another person (as opposed to a broader situation). For example, Illinois Criminal Code § 7-11 states that a "person is not guilty of an offense, other than an offense punishable with death, by reason of conduct that he or she performs under the compulsion of threat or menace of the imminent infliction of death or great bodily harm, if he or she reasonably believes death or great bodily harm will be inflicted upon him or her, or upon his or her spouse or child, if he or she does not perform that conduct." See also Kansas Stat. Ann. § 21-5206 ("A person is not guilty of a crime other than murder or voluntary manslaughter by reason of conduct which such person performs under the compulsion or threat of the imminent infliction of death or great bodily harm, if such person reasonably believes that death or great bodily harm will be inflicted upon such person or upon such person's spouse, parent, child, brother or sister if such person does not perform such conduct."). Do you think that Contento-Pachon's situation would be covered by these statutes as well as by more typical duress statutes? Could a police officer appeal to these provisions if he tortured or otherwise mistreated a detainee to obtain intelligence regarding an imminent terrorist attack? Notice that the provisions only apply if the individual facing the threat is the defendant or a close family relation.

2. The Severity of the Threat

Not just any threat can provide the foundation for a successful duress defense. Depending on the jurisdiction, the threat must involve either death or serious bodily injury, or it must be a threat that a person of reasonable firmness would be unable to resist. How should a court apply the "reasonable firmness" standard? In the following case, the Supreme Court of Pennsylvania articulates and applies the MPC standard in a way that combines objective and subjective elements together.

Commonwealth v. DeMarco

Supreme Court of Pennsylvania
570 Pa. 263, 809 A.2d 256 (2002)

NIGRO, J.

We granted allowance of appeal in the instant case to review whether the Court of Common Pleas of Monroe County committed reversible error during the trial of Appellant Richard DeMarco by refusing to charge the jury on the defense of duress. For the reasons that follow, we find that the trial court did err, and therefore, vacate Appellant's judgment of sentence and remand the case to the trial court for a new trial.

On February 16, 1998, Frank Larwa called the Pocono Mountain Regional Police Department to report that Salvatore Zarcone was at his home in Blakeslee, Pennsylvania, and had damaged his two cars. Shortly after Larwa's phone call, Officer Martin Reynolds arrived at Larwa's home and observed that two cars in the driveway next to the home were damaged. Officer Reynolds spoke with Larwa and Appellant, who were the only people present in the home. Larwa told Officer Reynolds that Zarcone had appeared at his home and when he refused to open the door to allow Zarcone inside, Zarcone threatened to injure him and vandalized his two cars. Appellant corroborated Larwa's statements. Officer Reynolds asked Larwa and Appellant to each make a written statement regarding their allegations and gave them forms on which to make those statements.

Officer Reynolds had to leave the home before Larwa and Appellant wrote their statements but he returned later that day to pick up the completed statements. Both Larwa's and Appellant's signed written statements substantiated what they had orally told Officer Reynolds earlier that day. Based on Larwa's and Appellant's allegations, Officer Reynolds filed a charge of terroristic threats against Zarcone. On April 9, 1998, a preliminary hearing was held concerning that charge. Appellant testified during the preliminary hearing in a manner consistent with his previous statements to Officer Reynolds. Based on the evidence presented at the preliminary hearing, the trial court determined that there was sufficient evidence to proceed to trial.

On November 10, 1998, a trial was held. . . . During the trial, Zarcone called Appellant to testify regarding the statements he made to Officer Reynolds and the testimony he gave during the preliminary hearing. Instead of confirming his prior statements and testimony, however, Appellant testified that his statements and testimony were not true accounts of what happened on February 16. According to Appellant's testimony at trial, Zarcone was not at Larwa's house on February 16 and, in fact, Larwa had vandalized his cars himself. Appellant also testified that Larwa had coerced him into telling the false story both to Officer Reynolds and at the preliminary hearing. The jury subsequently acquitted Zarcone of the terroristic threats charge.

Based on the inconsistencies between his earlier statements and his testimony at Zarcone's trial, Appellant was charged with two counts of perjury, two counts of false swearing, one count of unsworn falsification to authorities, and one count of false reports to law enforcement. Prior to trial, Appellant obtained a report from a medical expert in which the expert found that Appellant was coerced by Larwa into telling the false story to Officer Reynolds and at the preliminary hearing. Based on its receipt of the report, which Appellant planned to admit into evidence at his trial, on September 13, 1999, the day before Appellant's trial, the Commonwealth filed a motion in limine requesting that the trial court preclude Appellant from presenting any evidence regarding the duress defense provided for in 18 Pa. C.S. § 309. According to Section 309, the duress defense applies in the following circumstances:

> (a) General Rule.—It is a defense that the actor engaged in the conduct charged to constitute an offense because he was coerced to do so by the use of, or a threat to use, unlawful force against his person or the person of another, which a person of reasonable firmness in his situation would have been unable to resist.
>
> (b) Exception.—The defense provided by subsection (a) of this section is unavailable if the actor recklessly placed himself in a situation in which it was probable that he would be subjected to duress. The defense is also unavailable if he was negligent in placing himself in such a situation, whenever negligence suffices to establish culpability for the offense charged.

Alternatively, the Commonwealth argued that if the trial court allowed Appellant to present evidence of the duress defense, the trial court should exclude evidence from any medical experts regarding Appellant's mental condition.

On the morning of the first day of Appellant's trial, the trial court held a pretrial conference on the Commonwealth's motion in limine. The trial court ruled that Appellant could present evidence of the duress defense but that Appellant could not present any evidence from medical experts regarding his mental condition because, according to the trial court, such evidence would improperly bolster Appellant's credibility. Consequently, on the first day of his trial, Appellant argued that although he had made false statements to Officer Reynolds and at the preliminary hearing, Larwa had coerced him into making those statements. In support of his argument, Appellant presented evidence of his own testimony during Zarcone's trial in which he stated that Larwa had forced him to tell the false story by shooting him with a B.B. Gun and choking him, as well as Larwa's testimony at Zarcone's trial in which Larwa stated, "[Appellant's] brain doesn't work like yours and mine."

In addition, Appellant presented evidence from his mother, Charmaine Mesa. Mesa testified that Appellant's father hit Appellant in the head when he was just nine months old and, as a result, Appellant underwent several operations, and ultimately, had a metal plate placed in his head. According to Mesa, Appellant continues to suffer from severe headaches and seizures. Mesa also testified that Appellant's school informed her that Appellant is borderline mentally retarded and will not be able to intellectually develop above approximately a third-grade level. Furthermore, Mesa testified that both Appellant and his wife, Tracey Zook, notified her that Larwa was threatening Appellant. Mesa explained that she notified her local police in Philadelphia about the threats, but was told by the police that they could not help Appellant because he was outside of their jurisdiction.

Zook also testified at Appellant's trial. She confirmed that Appellant receives social security checks because he is mentally disabled. Zook further testified that she was living at Larwa's home with Appellant when Larwa coerced Appellant into falsely accusing Zarcone. According to Zook, she heard Larwa telling Appellant what he should say in court and threatening to either kill Appellant or take away his social security checks if he did not testify as rehearsed.

At the end of the first day of trial, the Commonwealth made a motion requesting that the trial court exclude any additional evidence regarding the duress defense and refrain from instructing the jury about that defense. The next morning, before the start of the second day of the trial, the trial court granted the Commonwealth's motion. In support of its ruling, the trial court initially noted that the duress defense is provided for in 18 Pa. C.S. § 309. Nevertheless, the trial court then determined that based on the Superior Court's decision in *Commonwealth v. Berger,* 417 Pa. Super. 473 (1992), in order to establish the duress defense, the evidence must show that: (1) the defendant was subject to a present and impending threat of death or serious bodily injury; (2) the defendant had a reasonable fear that the threatened harm would be made against him; and (3) the defendant had no reasonable opportunity to escape the threatened harm except by committing the criminal act.

Based upon its review of the evidence introduced on the first day of trial, the trial court found that the evidence was insufficient to support two of the three necessary elements set forth in *Berger,* namely, that Appellant was subject to a present and impending threat of death or serious bodily injury, and that he did not have a reasonable opportunity to escape the threatened harm except by committing the criminal offenses. Therefore, the trial court concluded that the duress defense was not a viable defense in the instant case. Moreover, the trial court determined that because the evidence indicated that by living with Larwa, Appellant recklessly placed himself in a situation where it was likely that he would be subject to duress, even if the evidence supported the duress defense, Appellant was not entitled to avail himself of the defense in light of the exception in 18 Pa. C.S. § 309(b).

Given its ruling on the Commonwealth's motion in limine, the trial court precluded Appellant from offering any additional evidence concerning the duress defense and refused, despite Appellant's requests, to instruct the jury regarding the defense. Indeed, in its charge to the jury, the trial court instructed, "as a matter of law, there is no legal application of duress that would apply in this particular case." Following deliberations, the jury convicted Appellant of one count each of perjury, false swearing, unsworn falsification to authorities, and false reports to law enforcement. The trial court subsequently sentenced Appellant to one to two years imprisonment for his perjury conviction, two concurrent terms of eleven and one-half to twenty-three months imprisonment for his false swearing and unsworn falsification to authorities convictions, and another concurrent term of six to twelve months imprisonment for his false reports to law enforcement conviction. . . .

In deciding whether a trial court erred in refusing to give a jury instruction, we must determine whether the court abused its discretion or committed an error of law. Where a defendant requests a jury instruction on a defense, the trial court may not refuse to instruct the jury regarding the defense if it is supported by evidence in the record. When there is evidence to support the defense, it is "for the trier of fact to pass upon that evidence and improper for the trial judge to exclude such consideration by refusing the charge."

As noted above, both lower courts in the instant case applied a stringent three-part test in determining whether the evidence was sufficient to support the duress defense. We conclude, however, that the three-part test applied by the lower courts is the wrong test for determining whether the evidence supports the duress defense. That test was the one followed at common law, which governed the law of duress prior to the enactment of 18 Pa. C.S. § 309 in 1972. When the General Assembly enacted Section 309, however, it abrogated the common law test, finding that it was too difficult for defendants to meet. Moreover, since the enactment of Section 309, this Court has repeatedly recognized that the test for determining whether the evidence supports the duress defense is the one set forth in the statute, rather than the common law test followed below. Accordingly, the trial court in the instant case committed an error of law by using the abrogated common law test to determine whether the evidence supported the duress defense here.

As set forth by the General Assembly in Section 309, in order to establish the duress defense in this Commonwealth, there must be evidence that: (1) there was a use of, or threat to use, unlawful force against the defendant or another person; and (2) the use of, or threat to use, unlawful force was of such a nature that a person of reasonable firmness in the defendant's situation would have been unable to resist it. Thus, to establish the duress defense under Section 309, unlike under the common law rule, the force or threatened force does not need to be of present and impending death or serious bodily injury. Instead, the relevant inquiry under Section 309 is whether the force or threatened force was a type of unlawful force that "a person of reasonable firmness in [*the defendant's*] *situation* would have been unable to resist." This test is a hybrid objective-subjective one. While the trier of fact must consider whether an objective person of reasonable firmness would have been able to resist the threat, it must ultimately base its decision on whether that person would have been able to resist the threat if he was subjectively placed in the defendant's situation. Therefore, in making its determination, the trier of fact must consider "stark, tangible factors, which differentiate the [defendant] from another, like his size or strength or age or health." Although the trier of fact is not to consider the defendant's particular characteristics of temperament, intelligence, courageousness, or moral fortitude, the fact that a defendant suffers from "a gross and verifiable" mental disability "that may establish irresponsibility" is a relevant consideration. Moreover, the trier of fact should consider any salient situational factors surrounding the defendant at the time of the alleged duress, such as the severity of the offense the defendant was asked to commit, the nature of the force used or threatened to be used, and the alternative ways in which the defendant may have averted the force or threatened force.

Even where the evidence is sufficient to establish the elements of the duress defense set forth in Section 309(a), however, the defendant still may not be entitled to avail himself of the defense under the exception in Section 309(b). According to that exception, the duress defense is not available if the evidence establishes that the defendant recklessly placed himself in a situation where it was probable that he would be subject to duress. 18 Pa. C.S. § 309(b). For purposes of Section 309, "recklessly" is defined as follows:

> A person acts recklessly with respect to a material element of an offense when he consciously disregards a substantial and unjustifiable risk that the material element exists or will result from his conduct. The risk must be of such a nature and degree that, *considering the nature and intent of the actor's conduct and the circumstances known to him,* its disregard involves a gross deviation from the standard of conduct that a reasonable person would observe *in the actor's situation.*

Therefore, like the test for determining whether the defendant was subject to duress, the test for determining whether a defendant acted recklessly under Section 309 is a hybrid objective-subjective one. The trier of fact must decide whether the defendant disregarded a risk that involves a gross deviation from what an objective "reasonable person" would observe if he was subjectively placed "in the [defendant's] situation." Thus, in making its determination, the trier of fact must again take into account the stark tangible factors that differentiate the defendant from another person and the salient situational factors surrounding the defendant.

Here, Appellant presented evidence at trial that Larwa shot him with a B.B. Gun, choked him, and threatened to deprive him of his social security checks or kill him if he did not corroborate Larwa's account of how his cars came to be damaged. Appellant also presented evidence of his situation when the threats occurred, including that he: (1) suffers from seizures, (2) is borderline mentally retarded with a third grade intellectual level, (3) receives social security because he is mentally disabled, and (4) was living with Larwa without transportation or sufficient money to move to alternative housing. We find that the above evidence was clearly sufficient to present a question for the jury as to whether Appellant was subject to duress pursuant to Section 309, *i.e.*, whether Appellant was subject to unlawful force and threats by Larwa that a person of reasonable firmness in Appellant's situation would not have been able to resist. . . .

Here, as noted by the trial court, there was evidence introduced at trial that Appellant had lived with Larwa in the past, had a bank account and an ATM card, had married several times, had worked, and was capable of contacting others via telephone. There was also evidence that Appellant had failed to seek the assistance of law enforcement officers in dealing with the alleged duress by Larwa when he was in the officers' presence. While these factors may call into question whether Appellant recklessly placed himself in a situation where it was probable that he would be subject to duress, we do not find that they made it completely obvious . . . that that was the case. This is particularly so in light of the evidence of Appellant's situation, including the fact that he suffers from borderline mental retardation and that he was living with Larwa without transportation or sufficient money to leave. Accordingly, we conclude that there was sufficient evidence to raise a question of fact as to whether or not Appellant had acted recklessly.

NOTES & QUESTIONS ON REASONABLE FIRMNESS

1. *The hybrid standard.* The Pennsylvania courts use a hybrid standard for understanding reasonable firmness. The Model Penal Code also uses a hybrid standard in § 2.09(1), which provides that the defense is only available if "a person of reasonable firmness *in his situation* would have been unable to resist." The MPC explanatory note refers to this as a "partially objective" standard in the sense that it requires reference to the actor's personal situation but with an objective overlay. However, neither the MPC nor the Pennsylvania Code explains which circumstances to take into account. Clearly, a jury should assess the defendant's personal situation and then ask whether it was objectively reasonable for a person in the defendant's situation to succumb to the threat. Should this include the fact that DeMarco has seizures and a mental disability? How about the fact that he was living with Larwa without independent transportation? In *DeMarco*, the court does not take a final position on whether the threat was significant enough to satisfy the duress defense, but does conclude

that there was enough evidence to justify submitting the issue to the jury. Given the above facts, if you were a juror, how would you vote?

2. *The objective standard.* The duress defense is only available if a person of reasonable firmness would have succumbed to the threat. But what if the defendant is not a person of reasonable firmness? In *Wood v. Quarterman*, 214 Fed. Appx. 473 (5th Cir. 2007), the petitioner was a death row inmate from Texas who filed a federal habeas corpus petition arguing that Texas's duress statute was unconstitutional because it denied him equal protection of the law. Wood was convicted of murder and his duress defense was unsuccessful. Under Tex. Penal Code § 8.05, duress applies if the defendant committed the crime because he was "compelled to do so by threat of imminent death or serious bodily injury," with compulsion defined as "the force or threat of force [that] would render a person of reasonable firmness incapable of resisting the pressure." Texas courts have interpreted the use of the word "reasonable" in this context as implementing an objective standard. Wood argued that "because he is not a person of reasonable firmness, the defense of duress is unavailable to him, and that this disparate treatment of the 'feeble minded' violates the Equal Protection Clause." The Fifth Circuit rejected the argument. Do you think the "feeble minded" are protected by the Equal Protection Clause in this way?

3. *Battered Women's Syndrome and duress.* Defendants have occasionally attempted to introduce evidence of Battered Women's Syndrome in an attempt to satisfy a duress defense. The basic idea is that the woman argues that she was coerced into violating the law by her abusive spouse or partner. The evidence of BWS would be particularly relevant when the court applies the "reasonable firmness" standard. If the court uses a subjective or hybrid standard, the jury might ask whether it was reasonable for a woman suffering from BWS to succumb to the threat and commit the crime, as opposed to reasonable for just any generic person. However, many states use a wholly objective standard in evaluating reasonable firmness.

In *State v. B.H.*, 183 N.J. 171 (2005), the New Jersey Supreme Court rejected a BWS argument, concluding that BWS is not relevant for determining whether a person of "reasonable firmness" would have succumbed or resisted the threat—which New Jersey courts have interpreted as an objective standard. The defendant, B.H., was convicted of first-degree aggravated sexual assault and third-degree endangering the welfare of a child for having sex with her seven-year-old stepson. At trial she argued that she was forced into the act by her husband, who had his hands on her throat at the time of the act, and that she suffered from Battered Women's Syndrome. Although the New Jersey court rejected the applicability of BWS in the reasonable firmness analysis, it did concede that BWS evidence could be presented to the jury to help it evaluate the defendant's "subjective perception of a threat from her abuser and, in that respect, can be relevant to her credibility."

PROBLEM CASE

In May 2015, Nicole F. Vaisey and Stephen Howells II pled guilty in separate charges relating to their kidnapping of two Amish girls in August 2014. Vaisey and federal prosecutors reached a plea agreement shortly after prosecutors filed a motion in limine in federal district court, seeking to prevent Vaisey from arguing at trial that she acted under duress.

Prosecutors laid out the following allegations in the motion. Vaisey and Howells participated in a relationship of dominance and submission, or what could also be described as a master-slave relationship. The parameters of the relationship were allegedly outlined in a so-called service agreement wherein Vaisey conveyed "full ownership and use of (her) body, spirit and mind" to Howells. See Brian Kelly,

Stephen Howells, Jr. and Nicole Vaisey

Prosecutors Claim Vaisey Was Not Forced into Alleged Sexual Exploitation of Children, Watertown Daily Times, May 13, 2015. Prosecutors contended that the evidence was insufficient to establish a duress defense because Vaisey was capable of leaving the relationship at any moment. Moreover, they noted that Vaisey's "service agreement" explicitly stated that she signed it of her own free will—as opposed to under threat of physical duress.

Under what conditions could a master-slave relationship give rise to a duress defense? If the relationship is accompanied by threat of physical force and a history of violence, then in theory the defense could work. In some circumstances, courts have entertained duress defenses when escape, though technically possible, was not a *reasonable* possibility. See *United States v. Contento-Pachon*, 723 F.2d 691 (9th Cir. 1984) ("To flee, Contento-Pachon, along with his wife and three year-old child, would have been forced to pack his possessions, leave his job, and travel to a place beyond the reaches of the drug traffickers. A juror might find that this was not a reasonable avenue of escape."). Should the duress defense exonerate defendants who voluntarily place themselves in relationships in which they are powerless?

For a discussion, see Laura K. Dore, *Downward Adjustment and the Slippery Slope: The Use of Duress in Defense of Battered Offenders*, 56 Ohio St. L.J. 665, 743-44 (1995) ("the behavioral and psychological characteristics that currently comprise the battered woman defense and that render battered offenders more susceptible to threats and less capable of resistance cannot be imported into the objective standard without gutting duress of its normative function"). Most jurisdictions that allow evidence of BWS in criminal cases have limited it to self-defense and have rejected it in duress cases. For a discussion of this divergent treatment, see Alafair S. Burke, *Rational Actors, Self-Defense, and Duress: Making Sense, Not Syndromes, Out of the Battered*

Woman, 81 N.C. L. Rev. 211 (2002). But see *Dando v. Yukins*, 461 F.3d 791 (6th Cir. 2006) (suggesting that BWS should be relevant in duress cases in Michigan because "those of us who are not so unfortunate to have to live with constant, imminent threats of violence might look at the actions of a defendant . . . from the relative comfort of a judge's chambers or a jury box and wonder what reasonable person would have facilitated [the boyfriend's] shocking crime spree[;] evidence of Battered Woman's Syndrome can explain why a reasonable person might resort to such actions given a history of violent abuse and the imminent violent threats"). The court in *Dando* noted that the defendant had suffered "a long history of violent sexual and physical abuse" and that her boyfriend "beat her and threatened to kill her immediately before she participated in the robberies."

3. Defense to Murder

Should duress apply in murder cases? The traditional common law answer was no, but the more modern Model Penal Code says yes. In the following case, the Supreme Court of California has to decide which rule to follow in its jurisdiction.

People v. Anderson
Supreme Court of California
28 Cal. 4th 767, 50 P.3d 368 (2002)

CHIN, J.

Over two centuries ago, William Blackstone, the great commentator on the common law, said that duress is no excuse for killing an innocent person: "And, therefore, though a man be violently assaulted, and hath no other possible means of escaping death, but by killing an innocent person, this fear and force shall not acquit him of murder; for he ought rather to die himself than escape by the murder of an innocent."

We granted review to decide whether these words apply in California. We conclude that, as in Blackstone's England, so today in California: fear for one's own life does not justify killing an innocent person. Duress is not a defense to murder. We also conclude that duress cannot reduce murder to manslaughter. Although one may debate whether a killing under duress should be manslaughter rather than murder, if a new form of manslaughter is to be created, the Legislature, not this court, should do it.

THE FACTS AND PROCEDURAL HISTORY

Defendant was charged with kidnapping and murdering Margaret Armstrong in a camp area near Eureka called the South Jetty. Defendant and others apparently suspected the victim of molesting two girls who resided in the camp. Ron Kiern, the father of one of the girls, pleaded guilty to Armstrong's second degree murder and testified at defendant's trial.

The prosecution evidence showed that a group of people, including defendant and Kiern, confronted Armstrong at the camp. Members of the group dragged Armstrong to a nearby field, beat her, put duct tape over her mouth, tied her naked to a bush, and abandoned her. Later, defendant and Kiern, in Kiern's car, saw Armstrong going naked down the street away from the jetty. The two grabbed Armstrong, forced her into the car, and drove away. They then put Armstrong into a sleeping bag, wrapped the bag with duct tape, and placed her, screaming, into the trunk of Kiern's car.

Witnesses testified that defendant picked up a large rock, brought it to the trunk, and handed it to Kiern. Kiern appeared to hit Armstrong with the rock, silencing her. Kiern testified that defendant said Armstrong had to die. After they put her into the trunk, defendant dropped a small boulder onto her head. Kiern also said that defendant picked up the rock again, handed it to Kiern, and told him to drop it on Armstrong or something would happen to his family. Kiern dropped the rock but believed it missed Armstrong. Kiern and defendant later commented to others that Armstrong was dead.

The evidence indicated that defendant and Kiern disposed of Armstrong's body by rolling it down a ravine. One witness testified that Kiern stated he had stepped on her neck until it crunched to ensure she was dead before putting her in the ravine. The body was never found.

Defendant testified on his own behalf. He said he had tried to convince Kiern to take Armstrong to the hospital after she had been beaten. When he and Kiern saw her going down the road beaten and naked, Kiern grabbed her and put her in the backseat of the car. Back at camp, Kiern put Armstrong in the sleeping bag and bound it with duct tape. At Kiern's instruction, defendant opened the trunk and Kiern put Armstrong inside. Kiern told defendant to retrieve a certain rock the size of a cantaloupe. Defendant said, "Man, you are out of your mind for something like that." Kiern responded, "Give me the rock or I'll beat the shit out of you." Defendant gave him the rock because Kiern was bigger than he and he was "not in shape" to fight. When asked what he thought Kiern would have done if he had said no, defendant replied: "Punch me out, break my back, break my neck. Who knows." Kiern hit Armstrong over the head with the rock two or three times. Kiern's wife was standing there yelling, "Kill the bitch."

Defendant testified that later they left in Kiern's car. They pulled over and Kiern opened the trunk. Armstrong was still moaning and moving around. Defendant tried to convince Kiern to take her to a hospital, but Kiern refused. Defendant got back into the car. A few minutes later, Kiern closed the trunk, got in the car, and said, "She's dead now. I stomped on her neck and broke it."

A jury convicted defendant of first degree murder and kidnapping. Based primarily on his testimony that Kiern threatened to "beat the shit out of" him, defendant contended on appeal that the trial court erred in refusing to instruct the jury on duress as a defense to the murder charge. The Court of Appeal concluded that duress is not a defense to first degree murder and affirmed the judgment. We granted defendant's petition for review to decide to what extent, if any, duress is a defense to a homicide-related crime, and, if it is a defense, whether the trial court prejudicially erred in refusing a duress instruction.

WHETHER DURESS IS A DEFENSE TO MURDER

At common law, the general rule was, and still is today, what Blackstone stated: duress is no defense to killing an innocent person. "Stemming from antiquity, the nearly 'unbroken tradition' of Anglo-American common law is that duress never excuses murder, that the person threatened with his own demise 'ought rather to die himself, than escape by the murder of an innocent.'"

The basic rationale behind allowing the defense of duress for other crimes "is that, for reasons of social policy, it is better that the defendant, faced with a choice of evils, choose to do the lesser evil (violate the criminal law) in order to avoid the greater evil threatened by the other person." This rationale, however, "is strained when a defendant is confronted with taking the life of an innocent third person in the face of a threat on his own life. . . . When the defendant commits murder under duress, the resulting harm—i.e., the death of an innocent person—is at least as great as the threatened harm—i.e., the death of the defendant." We might add that, when confronted with an apparent kill-an-innocent-person-or-be-killed situation, a person can always choose to resist. As a practical matter, death will rarely, if ever, inevitably result from a choice not to kill. The law should require people to choose to resist rather than kill an innocent person.

A state may, of course, modify the common law rule by statute. The Model Penal Code, for example, does not exclude murder from the duress defense. Defendant contends the California Legislature modified the rule in the 19th century and made duress a defense to some murders.

Since its adoption in 1872, Penal Code section 26 has provided: "All persons are capable of committing crimes except those belonging to the following classes: [¶] . . . [¶] . . . Persons (unless the crime be punishable with death) who committed the act or made the omission charged under threats of menaces sufficient to show that they had reasonable cause to and did believe their lives would be endangered if they refused." Defendant contends the reference to a "crime . . . punishable with death" means that the crimes to which duress is not a defense include only those forms of murder that are punishable with death, and that these forms change with changes in death penalty law. In 1872, when the current Penal Code was adopted, all first degree murder was punishable with death. Today only first degree murder with special circumstances is so punishable. Accordingly, defendant contends that today, duress is a defense to all murder except first degree murder with special circumstances. In effect, he argues that a killing under duress is either first degree murder with special circumstances or no crime at all. Because the prosecution did not allege special circumstances in this case, he continues, duress provides a full defense.

The sparse relevant California case law is inconclusive. In *People v. Martin*, 108 P. 1034 (1910), the court noted that "[i]t has ever been the rule that necessity is no excuse for killing an innocent person." It cited but did not construe section 26 and ultimately found duress was not available under the facts because the person was not in immediate danger. In both *People v. Son*, 79 Cal. App. 4th 224, 232-233 (2000), and *People v. Petro*, 56 P.2d 984 (1936), the court cited section 26 and stated that duress was not available as a defense, but in each case the defendant had been convicted of a form of murder then punishable with death. In *People v. Moran*, 114 Cal. Rptr. 413 (1974), the court stated in dicta, without analysis, that our decision in *People v. Anderson*, 493 P.2d 880 (1972), which had declared unconstitutional the death penalty law then in effect, "rendered meaningless the exception pertaining to capital crimes of Penal Code section 26," and therefore "the defense of compulsion was available to defendant at the time of trial." . . .

In this case, the Court of Appeal concluded that, because all first degree murders were punishable with death in 1872, when section 26 was enacted, duress is not a defense to any first degree murder. In effect, the court concluded that section 26's exception for a "crime . . . punishable with death" includes any crime punishable with death as of 1872 unaffected by later changes in death penalty law. As we explain, we agree, except that the Court of Appeal did not go back far enough in time. The exception for a crime punishable with death refers to a crime punishable with death as of *1850*, not 1872. Section 26 derives from section 10 of the original 1850 Act Concerning Crimes and Punishments, which similarly excepted a crime "punishable with death" from the duress defense. Section 5, enacted as part of the original Penal Code in 1872 and unchanged since, provides: "The provisions of this Code, so far as they are substantially the same as existing statutes, must be construed as continuations thereof, and not as new enactments." As relevant, section 26 was merely a continuation of the then existing 1850 statute. For this reason, we must "begin . . . by inquiring into the intent of the Legislature in 1850. . . ."

In 1850, all murder was punishable with death. Not until 1856 was murder divided into degrees, with death the punishment for first degree but not second degree murder. This means that in 1850, duress was no defense to any murder. Thus, like many of California's early penal statutes, section 26 effectively adopted the common law, although the Legislature used a problematic method in which to do so. The question before us is whether the exception for a crime punishable with death changes with every change in death penalty law, which would mean that by 1872, the exception included only first degree murder and today it includes only first degree murder with special circumstances. We think not, for several reasons.

We see no suggestion that the 1850, or any, Legislature intended the substantive law of duress to fluctuate with every change in death penalty law. That interpretation would create strange anomalies. For example, special circumstances were added to the murder laws in the 1970's to conform California's death penalty law to the requirements of the United States Constitution. Defendant's position would mean that constitutional death penalty jurisprudence would control the substantive law of duress, something we doubt the Legislature intended. Even more anomalously, defendant's position would mean that when the Legislature created special circumstances to give California a valid death penalty law, it simultaneously *expanded* the circumstances in which someone may kill an innocent person.

The presence or absence of special circumstances has no relationship to whether duress should be a defense to killing an innocent person. For example, because a prior murder conviction is a special circumstance, defendant's position would mean that a person with a prior murder conviction who intentionally kills an innocent person under duress without premeditating commits no crime, but if the person premeditates, the killing is a capital crime. A person without the prior conviction committing the same premeditated killing would commit no crime unless some other special circumstance happened to attach, in which case the killing would be a capital crime. The Legislature can hardly have intended such random results.

Defendant's interpretation would also force prosecutors to charge special circumstances to prevent duress from becoming a defense. As the Court of Appeal said in this case, "a rule making the availability of the duress defense turn on the manner in which prosecutorial discretion is exercised is potentially pernicious, and may do an unnecessary disservice to criminal defendants. The decision of whether to seek the death penalty . . . should not be encumbered by tactical considerations, such as blocking anticipated defenses. The charging decision must be governed by more sagacious considerations than whether the punishment charged will deprive a defendant of a defense to the crime." . . .

The original 1850 statute defining murder provided that the "punishment of any person convicted of the *crime of murder* shall be death." The 1856 statute that divided murder into degrees, with death the punishment only for first degree murder—and thus, under defendant's position, the statute that first abrogated the common law of duress—referred to determining "the degree of the crime." These statutes thus indicate that the "crime" was and remained "murder" even after it was divided into degrees. . . .

Other provisions of the Penal Code bolster this conclusion. Sections 195 and 197, both enacted in 1872, describe those situations in which homicide is excusable or justifiable. If the homicide is excusable or justifiable under these provisions, the person must be acquitted. The original 1850 law had provisions comparable to, although somewhat different from, sections 195 and 197. None of these provisions mentions duress as excusing or justifying homicide. It is unreasonable to suppose the Legislature carefully described the situations in which homicide is excusable or justifiable in those provisions, but also intended to create by oblique implication in section 26 (or any other statute) yet another form of excusable or justifiable homicide, especially when doing so would abrogate the settled common law rule that duress is no defense to killing an innocent person.

Moreover, no reason appears for the Legislature to have silently abrogated the common law rule. The reasons for the rule applied as well to 19th-century California as to Blackstone's England. They apply, if anything, with greater force in California today. A person can always choose to resist rather than kill an innocent person. The law must encourage, even require, everyone to seek an alternative to killing. Crimes are often committed by more than one person; the criminal law must also, perhaps especially, deter those crimes. California today is tormented by gang violence. If duress is recognized as a defense to the killing of innocents, then a street or prison gang need only create an internal reign of terror and murder can be justified, at least by the actual killer. Persons who know they can claim duress will be more likely to follow a gang order to kill instead of resisting than would those who know they must face the consequences of their acts. Accepting the duress defense for any form of murder would thus encourage killing. Absent a stronger indication than the language of section 26, we do not believe the Legislature intended to remove the sanctions of the criminal law from the killing of an innocent even under duress. . . .

Accordingly, we conclude that duress is not a defense to any form of murder.

WHETHER DURESS CAN REDUCE MURDER TO A LESSER CRIME

Defendant also argues that even if duress is not a complete defense to murder, at least it reduces the crime to manslaughter by negating malice.

"Manslaughter is 'the unlawful killing of a human being without malice.'" A defendant lacks malice and is guilty of voluntary manslaughter in limited, explicitly defined circumstances: either when the defendant acts in a "sudden quarrel or heat of passion," or when the defendant kills in "unreasonable self-defense"—the unreasonable but good faith belief in having to act in self-defense. Neither of these two circumstances describes the killing of an innocent person under duress. Nevertheless, defendant argues that we should make duress a third way in which a defendant lacks malice.

No California case has recognized the killing of an innocent person under duress as a form of manslaughter. Some states have provided by statute that a killing under duress is manslaughter. But California has not done so. The cases that have considered the question absent a statute have generally rejected the argument that duress can reduce murder to manslaughter. Relying heavily on *People v. Flannel,* 25 Cal. 3d 668, 160 Cal. Rptr. 84, 603 P.2d 1, and legal commentators, defendant argues that this court should do what the Legislature has not done: recognize a killing under duress as a form of manslaughter.

Some commentators do, indeed, argue that fear for one's own life, although not justifying the killing of an innocent, should at least mitigate murder to manslaughter. . . .

This court has never decided the question. The problem with making a killing under duress a form of manslaughter is that no statute so provides. The difference between murder and manslaughter "is that murder includes, but manslaughter lacks, the element of malice." Both forms of voluntary manslaughter currently recognized—provocation and imperfect self-defense—are grounded in statutory language. The provocation form of manslaughter is obviously based on statute. Section 192 "specif[ies] that an unlawful killing that lacks malice because committed 'upon a sudden quarrel or heat of passion' is voluntary manslaughter."

Although less obvious, the imperfect self-defense form of manslaughter is also based on statute. *People v. Flannel,* 25 Cal. 3d 668, 160 Cal. Rptr. 84, 603 P.2d 1, the leading case developing the doctrine, "had two *independent* premises: (1) the notion of mental capacity . . . and (2) a grounding in both well-developed common law and in the statutory requirement of malice." In 1981, the Legislature abolished diminished capacity, thus making the first premise no longer valid. But the second premise remains valid. Express malice exists "when there is manifested a deliberate intention *unlawfully* to take away the life of a fellow creature." A killing in self-defense is *lawful*. Hence, a person who actually, albeit unreasonably, believes it is necessary to kill in self-defense intends to kill lawfully, not unlawfully. "A person who actually believes in the need for self-defense necessarily believes he is acting lawfully." Because express malice requires an intent to kill unlawfully, a killing in the belief that one is acting lawfully is not malicious. The statutory definition of implied malice does not contain similar language, but we have extended the imperfect self-defense rationale to any killing that would otherwise have malice, whether express or implied. "[T]here is no valid reason to distinguish between those killings that, absent unreasonable self-defense, would be murder with express malice, and those killings that, absent unreasonable self-defense, would be murder with implied malice."

Defendant's reliance on *People v. Flannel*, and its recognition of unreasonable self-defense as a form of manslaughter, is thus misplaced. A killing in self-defense is lawful, but a killing of an innocent person under duress is unlawful. In contrast to a person killing in imperfect self-defense, a person who kills an innocent believing it necessary to save the killer's own life intends to kill unlawfully, not lawfully. Nothing in the statutes negates malice in that situation. Recognizing killing under duress as manslaughter would create a new form of manslaughter, which is for the Legislature, not courts, to do. . . .

We recognize that policy arguments can be made that a killing out of fear for one's own life, although not justified, should be a crime less than the same killing without such fear. On the other hand, because duress can often arise in a criminal gang context, the Legislature might be reluctant to do anything to reduce the current law's deterrent effect on gang violence. These policy questions are for the Legislature, not a court, to decide. Accordingly, we reject defendant's argument that we should create a new form of voluntary manslaughter. His arguments are better directed to the Legislature.

Defendant also argues that, at least, duress can negate premeditation and deliberation, thus resulting in second degree and not first degree murder. We agree that a killing under duress, like any killing, may or may not be premeditated, depending on the circumstances. If a person obeys an order to kill without reflection, the jury might find no premeditation and thus convict of second degree murder. As with implied malice murder, this circumstance is not due to a special doctrine of duress but to the legal requirements of first degree murder. The trial court instructed the jury on the requirements for first degree murder. It specifically instructed that a killing "upon a sudden heat of passion or *other condition precluding the idea of deliberation*" would not be premeditated first degree murder. Here, the jury found premeditation. In some other case, it might not. It is for the jury to decide. But, unless and until the Legislature decides otherwise, a malicious, premeditated killing, even under duress, is first degree murder.

On a final point, we note, contrary to the Attorney General's argument, that duress can, in effect, provide a defense to murder on a felony-murder theory by negating the underlying felony. If one is not guilty of the underlying felony due to duress, one cannot be guilty of felony murder based on that felony. Here, for example, the court instructed the jury that duress could be a defense to the kidnapping charge. It also instructed on felony murder with kidnapping as the underlying felony. If the jury had found defendant not guilty of kidnapping due to duress (it did not), it could not have found that he killed during the commission of that kidnapping. Defendant could not have killed during the perpetration of a crime of which he was innocent.

Our conclusion that duress is no defense to murder makes it unnecessary to decide whether the evidence would have warranted duress instructions in this case. . . .

NOTES & QUESTIONS ON DURESS AND MURDER

1. *The Model Penal Code approach.* The California Supreme Court decided to follow the common law rule on duress. This leaves the Model Penal Code as a distinct outlier in allowing the duress defense in homicide cases. Why did the drafters of the MPC take this position? They concluded that "[i]t is obvious that even homicide may sometimes be the product of coercion that is truly irresistible, that danger to a loved one may have greater impact on a person of reasonable firmness than a danger to himself, and, finally, that long and wasting pressure may break down resistance more effectively than a threat of immediate destruction." Do you think this is obvious? Even if it is, the more relevant question is whether the law should excuse or punish such behavior. If it punishes that behavior, it implicitly refuses to indulge defendants who prioritize their own lives (or the lives of a loved one) over the lives of an innocent third party. For an argument that coerced murder should be exonerated, see Rupert Cross, *Murder Under Duress*, 28 U. Toronto L.J. 369, 377 (1978) ("A punishment which is unjust because the majority of mankind would have done what the accused did does not cease to be unjust because the harm done by him was very great."). Compare *Wentworth v. State*, 29 Md. App. 110, 118 (1975) ("Whatever the psychological reality may be, the law, as a matter of social policy, has declared that the defense of duress may not extend to the taking of an innocent person's life."). On the basis of this argument, are you more or less sympathetic to Anderson's argument that Kiern threatened to "beat the shit out of" him?

2. *Duress and felony murder.* The court specifically concedes in *Anderson* that despite the general rule preventing duress claims in homicide cases, duress can still be a defense to felony murder. Why? Arguably, duress is a defense to felony murder because the coercion negates the defendant's responsibility for the triggering felony. If the triggering felony is excused, the felony murder rule cannot apply. See, e.g., *People v. Sims*, 374 Ill. App. 3d 231, 267 (2007);

McMillan v. State, 428 Md. 333 (2012) ("Disallowing the duress defense in the case of felony murder, absent a statutory imperative, would be unwarranted, in our view: a defendant could have a complete defense to the felony that forms the basis of a murder charge and be exonerated of that charge, yet, because unable to present it as a defense to the murder charge, still be convicted of felony murder."). Despite this logical argument, some jurisdictions have disallowed duress by statute in felony murder cases. See, e.g., Ariz. Rev. Stat. Ann. § 13-412(C) (duress unavailable for "offenses involving homicide or serious physical injury"); *People v. Doubleday*, 2012 WL 3746184 (Colo. Ct. App. 2012) (upholding felony murder conviction despite jury's acquittal of defendant of robbery based on duress). For a discussion of this split, see Steven J. Mulroy, *The Duress Defense's Uncharted Terrain: Applying It to Murder, Felony Murder, and the Mentally Retarded Defendant*, 43 San Diego L. Rev. 159, 186 (2006) (concluding that "allowing a duress defense to felony murder charges would not 'open the floodgates' to killers evading responsibility through flimsy claims of duress. If it is proven that a defendant participated in a felony leading to a death, jurors are not overly receptive to arguments for escaping responsibility for that death.").

3. *Imperfect duress.* The defendant in *Anderson* also argued that he should be entitled to an instruction of *imperfect duress*, even if his actions were unreasonable. To understand the rationale for this variation of the defense, consider self-defense. If the defendant acts reasonably in using defensive force, his actions are justified. If the defendant acts *unreasonably*, the defendant is either convicted of murder or his responsibility is downgraded to manslaughter under the doctrine of imperfect self-defense (depending on the jurisdiction). Should the same process apply in the duress cases? The court in *Anderson* answered this question in the negative. Can you think of relevant reasons for treating self-defense and duress differently in this regard? For cases dealing with imperfect duress, see *United States v. Pizzichiello*, 272 F.3d 1232, 1238 (9th Cir. 2001) (imperfect duress relevant for sentence reduction under federal sentencing guidelines); *People v. Son*, 79 Cal. App. 4th 224, 228, 93 Cal. Rptr. 2d 871, 873 (2000) (imperfect duress does not negate malice or specific intent and reduce murder charge to voluntary manslaughter).

4. *Duress and the innocent instrumentality rule.* As described in Chapter 20, a defendant can be considered a principal perpetrator (as opposed to a mere accomplice) if he uses an innocent instrumentality to carry out the crime. A key element of this doctrine is that the instrumentality—the actor who physically commits the criminal act—must be non-culpable. One way of demonstrating that the instrumentality is truly non-culpable is for the prosecution (as opposed to the defense) to argue that the physical perpetrator was acting under duress. In that case, the duress argument becomes a pathway for convicting the coercer as a principal in the crime that is committed by

the individual who was coerced. For an example, see *People v. Hack*, 219 Mich. App. 299, 302 (1996) (upholding abuse charges against 17-year-old defendant who coerced a young child into committing the acts against another child). Under this theory of the case, the defendant is directly guilty as a principal as opposed to indirectly or derivatively guilty as a mere accomplice.

ADVICE   Whenever you see a case involving duress, you should ask yourself whether the innocent instrumentality rule might apply to the individual who is the source of the coercion. Conversely, if you are confronted with a case involving the innocent instrumentality rule, you should inquire whether the duress defense might be relevant to the fact pattern. The two doctrines often accompany each other—though not always.

C. PRACTICE & POLICY

One of the most compelling and unsettled questions in international law is whether claims of duress should exonerate defendants accused of committing war crimes against innocent civilians. As demonstrated by the following material, the question has been controversial.

   ❧ **Duress and atrocity.** In 1995, a young man named Drazen Erdemović was living with a heavy conscience. Erdemović was a soldier assigned to the 10th Sabotage Detachment of the Bosnian Serb Army during the wars that followed from the disintegration of the former Yugoslavia. Bosnia, which was once a part of Yugoslavia, was engulfed in intense fighting between ethnic Serbs, Croats, and Muslims, whose populations were intermixed throughout Bosnia. Ethnic Serbs in Bosnia sought to carve out a breakaway republic within Bosnia in a region that was dominated by ethnic Serbs. Soon reports emerged that Bosnian Serb military forces were committing atrocities against Croats and Muslims and trying to forcefully expel them from the region in order to create an ethnically homogenous territory. When a television reporter came through the region to conduct interviews about the reports of atrocities, Erdemović did not shy away; he was eager to confess his sins. Here was his story:

On July 16, 1995, Erdemović's army detachment received busloads of Bosnian Muslim men who had been detained when Bosnian Serb forces captured Srebrenica. The buses were filled with men who the Bosnian Serb army considered to be of "fighting" age, which meant anyone from a teenager to about 60 years of age. The prisoners were taken in groups of ten and lined up against the wall of a building. Erdemović was told by his commander to execute them with his machine gun. At first, Erdemović refused, though very quickly the commander started to pressure Erdemović to complete the task. In later testimony, Erdemović described what happened next:

> Your Honour, I had to do this. If I had refused, I would have been killed together with the victims. When I refused, they told me: "If you are sorry for them, stand up, line up with them and we will kill you too." I am not sorry for myself but for my family, my wife and son who then had nine months, and I could not refuse because then they would have killed me.

Drazen Erdemović enters trial chamber

So Erdemović complied. Over the course of the afternoon, he murdered at point-blank range about 70 men with his gun.

When the United Nations Security Council created the International Criminal Tribunal for the Former Yugoslavia (ICTY), one of the first cases to be adjudicated was Erdemović's. He admitted his guilt but argued that he acted under duress. The judges of the ICTY Appeals Chamber were forced to reckon with a difficult question: Could a defense of duress exonerate a defendant accused of the war crime of murdering innocent civilians?

The legal question was complex for multiple reasons. First, the law on duress is different depending on which domestic legal system you look at. In American criminal law and most common law jurisdictions, duress (like necessity) is not available as a defense to murder. However, both the Model Penal Code and many civil law jurisdictions in Europe permit, in theory, duress to be applied in murder cases. Which rule should govern in international law when the crime involves a soldier's killing of innocent civilians?

The ICTY Appeals Chamber concluded in a sharply divided 3-2 opinion that duress should *not* be available in war crimes cases involving the deaths of innocent civilians. The majority concluded:

> . . . [W]e are of the view that soldiers or combatants are expected to exercise fortitude and a greater degree of resistance to a threat than civilians, at least

when it is their own lives which are being threatened. Soldiers, by the very nature of their occupation, must have envisaged the possibility of violent death in pursuance of the cause for which they fight. The relevant question must therefore be framed in terms of what may be expected from the ordinary soldier in the situation of the Appellant. What is to be expected of such an ordinary soldier is not, by our approach, analysed in terms of a utilitarian approach involving the weighing up of harms. Rather, it is based on the proposition that it is unacceptable to allow a trained fighter, whose job necessarily entails the occupational hazard of dying, to avail himself of a complete defence to a crime in which he killed one or more innocent persons.

Finally, we think, with respect, that it is inaccurate to say that by rejecting duress as a defence to the killing of innocent persons, the law "expects" a person who knows that the victims will die anyway to throw his life away in vain. If there were a mandatory life sentence which we would be bound to impose upon a person convicted of killing with only an executive pardon available to do justice to the accused, it may well be said that the law "expects" heroism from its subjects. Indeed, such a mandatory life-term was prescribed for murder in England at the time the relevant English cases were decided and featured prominently in the considerations of the judges. We are not bound to impose any such mandatory term. One cannot superficially gauge what the law "expects" by the existence of only two alternatives: conviction or acquittal. In reality, the law employs mitigation of punishment as a far more sophisticated and flexible tool for the purpose of doing justice in an individual case. The law, in our view, does not "expect" a person whose life is threatened to be hero and to sacrifice his life by refusing to commit the criminal act demanded of him. The law does not "expect" that person to be a hero because in recognition of human frailty and the threat under which he acted, it will mitigate his punishment. In appropriate cases, the offender may receive no punishment at all.

Do you agree that soldiers are required to make greater sacrifices than regular civilians? In short, if faced with a choice between dying or violating the law, the judges concluded that soldiers should die. Why should this duty be imposed on soldiers? Is it perhaps because they have a preexisting duty under the law of war to protect innocent civilians from the horrors of war? There is support for this view in a different context. In *United States v. Holmes*, 26 F. Cas. 360, 367 (C.C.E.D. Pa. 1842), a ship departed from Liverpool, bound for Philadelphia, but struck an iceberg off the coast of Newfoundland during the voyage. Holmes, the captain, directed his crew to throw overboard 14 male, and 2 female, passengers. The Pennsylvania court stated:

The passenger stands in a position different from that of the officers and seamen. It is the sailor who must encounter the hardships and perils of the voyage. Nor can this relation be changed when the ship is lost by tempest or other danger of the sea, and all on board have betaken themselves, for safety, to the small boats; for imminence of danger can not absolve from duty. The sailor is bound, as before, to undergo whatever hazard is necessary to preserve the boat and the passengers. Should the emergency become so extreme as to call for the sacrifice of life, there can be no reason why the law does not still remain the same. The passenger, not being bound either to labour or to incur the risk of life, cannot be bound to sacrifice his existence to preserve the sailor's.

Is the relationship between soldier and enemy civilian sufficiently analogous to that of sailor and passenger? Does the same duty of sacrifice apply in both contexts? The court's articulation of the sailor's duty to encounter the "hardships and peril" of the voyage could perhaps also describe the distinctive role of professional soldiers, who face the brutality of war so as to spare civilians from the same fate.

The majority in *Erdemović* conceded that although duress could not be a defense to war crimes, it could be considered as mitigation in punishment. Indeed, Erdemović was convicted and sentenced only to five years, after which he was relocated under witness protection and agreed to testify for the prosecution at future ICTY proceedings. Are you sympathetic to his plight or do you think he should have been punished more harshly?

In a sharply worded dissent, two judges concluded that duress, in theory, should be available as a defense to war crimes. Their argument was that since domestic legal systems are split on this issue, defendants at international tribunals should be entitled to the defense since it is not categorically rejected in all legal systems. One of the judges, Antonio Cassese, wrote:

> Thus the case law seems to make an exception for those instances where—on the facts—it is highly probable, if not certain, that if the person acting under duress had refused to commit the crime, the crime would in any event have been carried out by persons other than the accused. The commonest example of such a case is where an execution squad has been assembled to kill the victims, and the accused participates, in some form, in the execution squad, either as an active member—or as an organizer—, albeit only under the threat of death. In this case, if an individual member of the execution squad first refuses to obey but has then to comply with the order as a result of duress, he may be excused: indeed, whether or not he is killed or instead takes part in the execution, the civilians, prisoners of war, etc., would be shot anyway. Were he to comply with his legal duty not to shoot innocent persons, he would forfeit his life for no benefit to anyone and no effect whatsoever apart from setting a heroic example for mankind (which the law cannot demand him to set): his sacrifice of his own life would be to no avail. In this case the evil threatened (the menace to his life and his subsequent death) would be greater than the remedy (his refraining from committing the crime, i.e., from participating in the execution).

Do you think the massacre would have happened anyway even if Erdemović had refused to comply? Is this a good reason to exonerate him? For more discussion of this case, see Luis E. Chiesa, *Duress, Demanding Heroism and Proportionality: The Erdemović Case and Beyond*, 41 Vand. J. Trans. L. 741, 745 (2008) ("arguments in favor of permitting the defendant to claim duress weaken as the seriousness of the offense increases"); Rosa Ehrenreich Brooks, *Law in the Heart of Darkness: Atrocity and Duress*, 43 Va. J. Int'l L. 861 (2003); Sarah J. Heim, *The Applicability of the Duress Defense to the Killing of Innocent Persons by Civilians*, 46 Cornell Int'l L.J. 165 (2013) (concluding that the rule of heroic sacrifice required by the *Erdemović* decision should not apply with equal force to civilians who do not owe the same higher duty of care that soldiers owe to civilians).

Erdemović listens to his sentence in the trial chamber at the U.N. criminal tribunal

CHAPTER 27

INTOXICATION

A. DOCTRINE

There are generally two types of intoxication. Voluntary intoxication involves a defendant who willingly imbibes an intoxicating substance such as liquor or drugs, whether illegal or prescription. Involuntary intoxication involves a defendant who is drugged without her knowledge. At common law, judges were often unsympathetic to drunken defendants and feared that an intoxication defense would open the floodgates for acquittals. Consequently, neither voluntary nor involuntary intoxication were valid defenses. Over time, this harsh rule was replaced with a more sympathetic treatment of the phenomenon: Defendants could assert voluntary intoxication for specific intent crimes, but voluntary intoxication was no defense to a general intent crime. For reasons articulated below, this doctrinal solution is starting to break down; some states now allow intoxication as a defense if it negates a required mental element for the offense–a simpler doctrine that avoids the complicated business of determining which offenses are special intent crimes.

1. Negating Mens Rea

In order to mitigate the harshness of the old common law rule that intoxication was no defense, courts started to allow the defense for specific intent crimes but not for general intent crimes. The rationale for the rule is somewhat unclear, but at least in theory "specific intent" crimes require a higher or more sophisticated mental state; intoxication could interfere with the formation of these higher mental states. Long ago when the number of crimes punishable at common law was low, the category of "specific intent" crimes was relatively small and discrete, and included crimes such as intentional murder, assault, burglary, robbery, etc. But in a modern age of proliferating statutory crimes, the number of specific intent crimes has grown exponentially. Furthermore, the distinction is not as easy to apply as it once was; courts often struggle to determine whether a particular offense should be classified as "specific intent" or not—owing to the ambiguous definition of the concept. Also, it is unclear whether the distinction between specific intent and general intent crimes is a useful proxy for the distinction that the law wants to make between crimes subject to the intoxication defense and those that are not subject to it.

A few jurisdictions still use the distinction between general and specific intent for their intoxication defense. See, e.g., Iowa Code § 701.5 ("The fact that a person is under the influence of intoxicants or drugs neither excuses the person's act nor aggravates the person's guilt, but may be shown where it is relevant in proving the person's specific intent or recklessness at the time of the person's alleged criminal act or in proving any element of the public offense with which the person is charged."). However, a growing number of jurisdictions have expressed dissatisfaction with the scheme and have adopted the Model Penal Code approach. Section 2.08 of the Model Penal Code provides that intoxication is not a defense unless it "negatives an element of the offense." In most cases, this means that intoxication is a defense if it negates the mental element of the offense. For this reason, intoxication is sometimes referred to as a "failure of proof" defense, because at its core is evidence introduced by the defendant (the intoxication) that prevents the prosecution from proving the required mental element beyond a reasonable doubt. So, for example, if the statute requires acting with the purpose to do x but the defendant was too drunk to act purposefully, the defendant should be acquitted. Or, if the defendant was too drunk to know about x and the statute requires acting with a particular type of knowledge regarding x, the defendant would also be acquitted. In some cases, however, this does not generate a *complete* exoneration, because the jury could be asked to consider convicting the defendant of a lesser crime with a lower mental state that is not negated by the intoxication. One should always remember that exoneration under one criminal statute does not necessarily entail exoneration under *every* criminal statute.

However, in addition to this standard, the Model Penal Code adds an extra overlay provision pertaining solely to crimes of recklessness. MPC § 2.08(2) prevents voluntary intoxication from being a defense to crimes of recklessness: "When recklessness establishes an element of the offense, if the actor, due to self-induced intoxication, is unaware of a risk of which he would have been aware had he been sober, such unawareness is immaterial." Consider a defendant charged with reckless manslaughter. Although intoxication could, in theory, negate the conscious awareness of the risk that is the hallmark of recklessness as a mental state, § 2.08(2) specifically disallows that argument. In effect, the provision provides an ad hoc limitation to restrict the applicability of the general standard for intoxication outlined in the Model Penal Code.

2. Eliminating the Defense of Voluntary Intoxication

Some jurisdictions have sharply curtailed or even abandoned the defense of voluntary intoxication altogether—a partial return to the harshness of the old common law rule. For example, Florida abolished voluntary intoxication in 1999. See Fla. Stat. § 775.051 (voluntary intoxication not a defense "except when the consumption, injection, or use of a controlled substance . . . was pursuant to a lawful prescription issued to the defendant by a practitioner . . ."). This means that a defendant cannot introduce evidence of his intoxication to show that he did not have the required mental state for that particular offense. In these jurisdictions, evidence of intoxication will be inadmissible at trial and the jury will not be charged on the defense of voluntary intoxication prior to deliberations. Despite the misgivings of criminal law theorists, the Supreme Court has concluded that the Constitution permits eliminating the defense; nothing in the Due Process Clause prevents a state legislature from blocking a defendant from introducing evidence of voluntary intoxication as a way of escaping criminal liability. Courts in these jurisdictions have largely deferred to their state legislatures and have concluded that their state constitutions do not require the defense either.

State legislatures that eliminate the defense are often pursuing a law-and-order program to increase criminal liability, motivated either by deterrence or bare retributivism. Is there a deeper theoretical rationale for curtailing the defense? Criminal lawyers have long subscribed to the maxim that an act is free if it is free in its causes. In other words, an actor's drunken behavior is freely chosen because he voluntarily became intoxicated, even if, at the moment he committed the criminal act, his behavior seemed involuntary. A legal system that grants an intoxication defense allows an actor to set the conditions of his own defense by voluntarily creating the circumstance (intoxication) that will then exonerate him. This provides one argument for curtailing or eliminating the defense of voluntary intoxication.

3. Involuntary Intoxication

The general skepticism toward voluntary intoxication, as outlined above, does not carry over to cases of involuntary intoxication. When an actor is drugged against his will, almost everyone will agree that the actor is not responsible for his behavior if the intoxication causes the defendant to lack the required mental state for the offense. *People v. Scott*, 194 Cal. Rptr. 633 (1983) (punch at family reunion spiked with PCP). Consequently, involuntary intoxication is a legitimate defense. But there is a key constraint for the defense: There must be a causal connection between the actor's involuntary intoxication and the commission of the prohibited act. For example, one might have a situation where the defendant is drunk but still able to form the mental element required for the offense; in this situation, the defendant is still responsible.

The Model Penal Code resolves cases of involuntary intoxication with a "substantial capacity" formulation that treats involuntary intoxication as a form of temporary insanity. Model Penal Code § 2.08(4) stipulates that an actor is excused if he "lacks substantial capacity either to appreciate its criminality [wrongfulness] or to conform his conduct to the requirements of law." This provision replicates the MPC standard in insanity cases, suggesting that the MPC views involuntary intoxication as an infringement of the actor's agency—a form of temporary insanity that prevents the actor from acting lawfully. Similarly, in jurisdictions that do not apply the Model Penal Code, a defendant suffering from involuntary intoxication also might be able to plead not guilty by reason of temporary insanity if the defendant meets all of that jurisdiction's requirements for the insanity defense, which are detailed in Chapter 28, though such situations are rare.

The more complicated situations involve a defendant's voluntary decision to imbibe a substance that has an unpredictable effect on her system. If the defendant then commits a crime, should it be excused as the product of an involuntary intoxication? At least some courts have treated this situation under the rubric of involuntary intoxication, since the defendant did not *knowingly* consume a substance that she believed would cause a state of intoxication. Examples of common substances that defendants have argued produced their unpredictable intoxication include prescription medications, over-the-counter cough remedies, and insulin. Although rare, this defense can produce an acquittal if the defendant convinces a jury that the criminal act was caused by the intoxication and the defendant was not aware that the substance had intoxicating properties.

B. APPLICATION

1. Negating Mens Rea

When should intoxication negate the required mental element for an offense? Jurisdictions are split between the two major approaches: using general versus specific intent, or the broader Model Penal Code solution of allowing intoxication whenever it negates a required element of the offense except in cases of recklessness. In the following case, the Supreme Court of New Mexico debates which scheme to apply to depraved-mind murder.

State v. Brown

Supreme Court of New Mexico
122 N.M. 724 (1996)

Franchini, J.

Defendant Jimmy Brown ("Brown") appeals from a conviction of first-degree, depraved mind murder. Following a jury trial, Brown was sentenced to life imprisonment for the murder conviction. On appeal, we address a single issue: Whether the trial court erred in refusing to instruct the jury that Brown's intoxication could be considered in determining the mental state required for conviction of depraved mind murder. We hold that a fact finder may consider evidence of extreme intoxication when determining whether a defendant possessed the requisite mental state of "subjective knowledge" for first-degree depraved mind murder. Accordingly, we reverse and remand for new trial. . . .

On August 23, 1993, Oscar Zapata was shot and killed at the house of his girlfriend, Josephine Calanshe. The next morning, Brown was arrested and charged on an open count of murder. The evidence presented to the jury at Brown's trial, viewed in the light most favorable to sustain the verdict, established the following facts.

In early 1993, Brown met Josephine Calanshe ("Josephine"), and the two became friends. Though they dated briefly, by the summer of that same year, they were both dating other people. Nonetheless, Josephine and Brown remained friends; in fact, Brown and his friends would often "hang out" at her house drinking beer. Sometimes they would drink for a number of days in succession, which is what occurred prior to the murder in question.

On Monday, August 23, 1993, the day of the homicide, Brown, along with Toby and Richard Horton ("Toby" and "Richard"), began drinking beer around noon, and continued drinking throughout the afternoon. That evening they went to Josephine's house, where they continued to drink beer. Though all three men gave differing estimates of the amount of alcohol they consumed that day, by all estimates quite a large quantity of beer had been consumed throughout the day of the murder, approximately four and one-half cases (over 100 bottles of beer).

When Brown, Toby, and Richard arrived at Josephine's house, a number of people were already there, including Josephine, her boyfriend, Oscar Zapata (the victim), Brandy Matta ("Brandy"), Josephine's two children, and Brandy's younger brother and sister. Another person, Albert Padilla ("Albert"), arrived at Josephine's house shortly after Brown. Josephine introduced everyone to Oscar. Oscar and Brown shook hands and there was no apparent conflict or friction between the two. . . .

At the time of the homicide, Josephine and Oscar were kissing on the bed in Josephine's bedroom. Oscar was lying half-way on top of Josephine and half-way on the bed. Also in the bedroom were Josephine's two-year-old son, Arthur, who was standing by the bed, and Brandy. Brandy testified that while she was plugging a portable fan into the wall socket, she heard a loud sound. She then turned and saw Brown standing at the foot of the bed holding a shotgun. She saw Oscar lying on top of Josephine. He had been shot in the back of the head. Josephine yelled for Brandy to get Arthur out of the room. Brandy grabbed Arthur and began dragging him from the room. At that time, Brandy stated that Brown pointed the shotgun at her and Arthur, but he did not shoot. . . .

Defendant Brown took the stand and testified that he was so intoxicated on the night of the murder that he did not recall anything about the shooting. He testified that he had blackout episodes in the past due to excessive alcohol consumption and had been a heavy drinker since he was fifteen years old—he was nineteen at the time of the murder. He did, however, recall the earlier events of the day; he recalled going to Josephine's house, meeting Oscar, sitting in the living room, and showing the shotgun to Albert. He testified that he had just met Oscar that same night and that he had no reason to kill him. The last thing Brown remembered before the shooting was falling asleep on the couch. The next thing he remembered he was standing in the doorway of Josephine's room. At that point, he recalled hearing screaming but did not know the reason for the screams. He also recalled seeing Toby facing him holding a shotgun. When Toby told him to get out of there, Brown ran. Brown testified that, at that time, he did not know what had happened at Josephine's house or why Toby had told him to leave. . . .

We must first examine the elements of depraved mind murder to determine whether a jury may take into consideration evidence of intoxication when determining the existence of the mental state required for the offense. Because New Mexico is one of only a few states that divides unintentional murder based upon risk-creating conduct into two degrees of homicide, first-degree depraved mind murder and second degree murder, our inquiry must necessarily distinguish the elements of depraved mind murder from second-degree murder. We note that New Mexico is also one of only a few states to include depraved mind murder within the category of first degree murder, making it a capital felony. Because the consequences for committing first-degree murder are far more serious than those for second-degree murder, it follows that the legislature intended to sufficiently distinguish the offense of first-degree depraved mind murder from second-degree murder. . . .

Because depraved mind murder involves a higher degree of recklessness, one previously recognized distinction between the two degrees of homicide is the number of persons subjected to the risk of death. This factor alone, however, does not constitute the determinative factor in differentiating between first and second-degree murder. While "[t]he number of persons may be a factor in assessing the degree of the *risk* disregarded, . . . it should not be determinative of the degree of *murder* charged." Though the definitions of depraved mind murder and second-degree murder contain similar elements, a major distinction between the two degrees of murder is based upon the culpable mental states required by the two offenses.

First-degree murder is reserved for the most blameworthy or "the most heinous and reprehensible" class of homicides; thus, the difference in culpable mental states is crucial in justifying the more serious penal consequences of first-degree murder. Because the legislature has deemed that a killing performed with a depraved mind is an especially serious homicide, deserving of punishment equal to that imposed for other forms of first-degree murder, we conclude that the legislature intended the offense of depraved mind murder to encompass an intensified malice or evil intent.

Depraved mind murder "is the killing of one human being . . . by any act greatly dangerous to the lives of others, *indicating a depraved mind regardless of human life.*" Section 30-2-1(A)(3) (emphasis added). "Depraved mind" is defined as "[a] corrupt, perverted, or immoral state of mind" constituting "the highest grade of malice . . . equatable with malice in the commonly understood sense of ill will, hatred, spite or evil intent." The defendant's depraved-mind action must be performed with a "wicked and malignant heart." Accordingly, we have held that depraved mind murder requires proof that the defendant had "subjective knowledge" that his or her act was extremely dangerous to the lives of others. *State v. Ibn Omar–Muhammad,* 102 N.M. 274, 277 (1985); *State v. McCrary,* 100 N.M. 671, 673 (1984); *State v. Johnson,* 103 N.M. 364, 368 (1985).[1] The required *mens rea* element of "subjective knowledge" serves as proof that the defendant acted with a "depraved mind" or "wicked or malignant heart" and with utter disregard for human life. Second-degree murder, on the other hand, contains a component involving an "objective knowledge" of the risk, without the required showing that the risk-creating act was performed with a wicked and malignant heart. . . .

Therefore, to establish depraved mind murder requires that the state prove each of the elements beyond a reasonable doubt, including the "subjective knowledge" element. In this case, Brown must have had the *subjective or actual knowledge* of the high degree of risk involved in his conduct. As we will explain below, intoxication was relevant to determining the existence of the *mens rea* element of "subjective knowledge," and was therefore a valid consideration.

---

1. [Editor's Note: The "subjective knowledge" language is not contained in the penal statute but is, rather, a requirement that was articulated in the case law.]

In the instant case there was evidence that Brown was intoxicated, meaning that a "mental disturbance" resulted from his drinking which in turn caused his inability to recall the murder. This raises the question of whether Brown actually possessed the "subjective knowledge" or the requisite awareness that his acts were greatly dangerous to the lives of the others, indicating depraved-mind action performed with a wicked and malignant heart.

"'[I]ntoxication' means a disturbance of mental or physical capacities resulting from the introduction of substances into the body." "Like mistake and mental illness, a state of intoxication may also negate a required offense element, and when raised in this context, is a failure of proof defense." American jurisdictions early on expressed the policy that voluntary intoxication provided no defense to a criminal act. This area of law was greatly influenced by courts' moral disapproval of drunkenness. In addition, the courts' decisive rejection of the voluntary intoxication defense was based both on the belief that the defense could be easily fabricated and that such a personal vice should not be used as a shield to criminal liability. Recognizing the extreme harshness of this rule, gradually courts began to allow juries to consider evidence of the defendant's intoxication when relevant to the *mens rea* element. By the end of the nineteenth century, most American jurisdictions had adopted the common-law approach which permitted intoxication to be considered where it negates the required element of specific intent.

A "specific-intent crime" is defined as one for which a statute expressly requires proof of "intent to do a further act or achieve a further consequence." A general intent crime, however, requires only a "conscious wrongdoing," or "the purposeful doing of an act that the law declares to be a crime." New Mexico courts have long followed the same common law specific-general intent approach, allowing voluntary intoxication as a consideration only for specific-intent crimes, including premeditated first-degree murder. Under this approach, evidence of voluntary intoxication is not admissible for what are referred to as general-intent crimes.

We note, however, that this specific-general intent approach has been criticized because it is not always clear whether a particular offense is a specific-intent crime or a general-intent crime. Accordingly, some commentators have suggested rejecting this approach in favor of asking simply whether the defendant's intoxication was so severe as to negate whatever intent is required by the crime charged. In fact, a number of jurisdictions have rejected the common-law approach and instead follow the Model Penal Code § 2.08(1)-(2), which permits voluntary intoxication to negate purpose or knowledge, but not recklessness. This Court, however, recently affirmed New Mexico's approach by applying the general-specific intent analysis to exclude voluntary intoxication evidence for the crime of felony murder. Therefore, we do not, by this opinion, wholly abandon New Mexico's common law general-specific intent approach with respect to all offenses. In the instant case, however, we hold that the specific-general intent analysis does not apply to depraved mind murder.

The case before us presents a unique circumstance involving an express mental state, specifically that of "subjective knowledge." Until 1980 our homicide statutes contained no other express state of mind requirements besides specific intent and premeditation. We therefore must determine whether intoxication may also negate an express mental state besides the intent to achieve a further act or consequence.

Before 1980, murder was broadly defined as an unlawful killing with malice aforethought. In 1980, however, the legislature amended the murder statutes, eliminating the term "malice aforethought" and repealing the obsolete definitions of "express" and "implied" malice. In place of those expressions, the legislature introduced more descriptive terms for the required mental states. In *Ortega,* we concluded that the malice required for first and second-degree murder is "an intent to kill or an intent to do an act greatly dangerous to the lives of others or with the knowledge that the act creates a strong probability of death or great bodily harm." The malice required for depraved mind murder is an intent to commit an act imminently dangerous to others *or* with the subjective knowledge that the act creates a very high degree of risk to the lives of others, indicating a depraved mind regardless of human life.

As a consequence of these statutory changes, as interpreted by New Mexico courts, the legislature redefined and distinguished the mental states required for first-degree depraved mind murder and second-degree murder by introducing a new "subjective knowledge" element to first-degree depraved murder. Unlike second-degree murder, the new "subjective knowledge element" of depraved mind murder does not include the imputed knowledge that an ordinary person would be expected to have. Therefore, assuming as a result of Brown's intoxication, he did not subjectively know that his acts created a very high degree of risk to the lives of others, the only rationale for finding him guilty of depraved mind murder would be to exclude relevant evidence of voluntary intoxication. Such a specific exclusion would prevent intoxication evidence from being admitted to negate the mental state of "subjective knowledge." While the legislature could have easily written a specific exclusion rule into the change in the prior law, it did not.

In this case, the general-specific intent analysis is inapplicable to the definition of depraved mind murder because it requires proof of the specific *mens rea* element of "subjective knowledge" as a condition to criminal liability. The specific-general intent common-law approach does not take into consideration the existence of a "heightened" *mens rea* aside from specific intent. The capacity to possess "subjective knowledge" may be just as affected by intoxication as the capacity to intend to do a further act. Intoxication may affect mental processes and prevent a person from either coolly deliberating or subjectively realizing that his or her act creates a very high degree of risk to the lives of others. Intoxication, however, usually has no effect on whether a person is purposefully doing something declared to be a crime, that is, a general-intent crime. Even though depraved mind murder cannot be considered a "specific-intent" crime because it requires proof of "subjective knowledge," as we have explained, it does not fall squarely among the class of crimes referred to as the "general-intent" crimes. In fact, the depraved mind or extreme indifference aspect required for first-degree depraved mind murder brings it more in line with the "specific intent" or cool deliberation requirements of Section 30-2-1(A)(1) (first-degree premeditated or willful killing). For these reasons, absent express legislative guidance to the contrary, we consider evidence of intoxication relevant to the formation of the heightened *mens rea* element of depraved mind murder. . . .

Although we recognize concerns that a voluntary intoxication defense may be abused or fabricated, these concerns are no different from those arising with respect to any type of exculpatory evidence presented at trial. However, it is for the jury to weigh the credibility of the witnesses and the weight to be given that evidence. Moreover, such concerns should not lessen the state's burden to prove, beyond a reasonable doubt, all elements of the offense. . . .

According to Brown's theory of the case, he was so severely intoxicated that he was not subjectively aware of the seriousness of the risk entailed by his conduct, as required for depraved mind murder. At the time of the commission of the crime, Brown's lack of rancor and his apparent confusion in the aftermath of the murder appear to negate the "wicked and malignant heart" required for depraved mind murder. Brown had just been introduced to the victim that night, and they shook hands amicably a few hours before the shooting. In light of the undisputed evidence that there was no hostility between the victim and Brown prior to the murder, along with the evidence of Brown's excessive consumption of alcohol, the issue of whether Brown actually possessed a depraved mind, i.e., a subjective realization of the risk, is especially important.

Pursuant to Brown's theory of defense, he submitted a jury instruction that endeavored to instruct the jury to take into consideration the evidence of his intoxication and its effect on the requisite mental state of subjective knowledge. Despite the intoxication evidence, the trial court refused to give Brown's requested instruction on intoxication. When evidence at trial supports the giving of an instruction on a defendant's theory of the case, failure to so instruct is reversible error. . . .

NOTES & QUESTIONS ON NEGATING MENS REA

1. *The New Mexico approach.* In the end, the New Mexico Supreme Court concluded that Brown should be allowed to present the defense. Do you agree? Are you sympathetic to Brown's desire to take his argument to the jury? In essence, the court concluded that the Model Penal Code scheme worked best for depraved-mind murder. How does this square with the fact that New Mexico has historically used general intent versus specific intent as the dividing line? Did the court abandon the older approach? Strangely, the court said no—the intoxication defense remains unavailable for general intent crimes. The case of depraved-mind murder is just an exception to that general scheme. Does this ad hoc solution make sense to you? The New York Court of Appeals reached the opposite result in *People v. Register*, 60 N.Y.2d 270, 280, 457 N.E.2d 704, 709 (1983), holding that evidence of intoxication should be excluded in cases where recklessness is an element of the offense, such as depraved-mind (i.e., depraved indifference) murder. Essentially, the court concluded that "depraved indifference" related to objective circumstances, not state of mind. However, in *People v. Feingold*, 7 N.Y.3d 288, 294, 852 N.E.2d 1163, 1167 (2006), the New York Court of Appeals overruled *Register* and concluded that "depraved indifference" is a mental state. This suggests, in theory, that intoxication should be available as a defense to negate the mens rea. However, it is also true that both the Model Penal Code and the New York Penal Code exclude the intoxication defense for crimes of recklessness. The problem is that it is unclear whether the mental state of "depraved indifference" is the same as recklessness or something more. This led one New York judge to complain about the uncertainty: "I therefore write separately to point out that the Legislature, which is entrusted with determining social policy and degrees of culpability, should resolve this perplexing question of whether intoxication, to whatever extent, functions as a defense to depraved indifference crimes." *People v. Valencia*, 14 N.Y.3d 927, 931, 932 N.E.2d 871, 874 (2010) (Graffeo, J., concurring).

2. *Negating premeditation.* It is common for jurisdictions to permit defendants to use evidence of voluntary intoxication to negate the deliberation required for premeditated murder, which in theory could result in an acquittal for aggravated or first-degree murder. In these murder cases, it is sometimes said that voluntary intoxication produces "mitigation" rather than a complete defense, because the defendant could still be convicted of second-degree murder. See, e.g., *State v. Brooks*, 97 Wash. 2d 873 (1982) (finding that evidence of intoxication was sufficient for jury to conclude that it negated premeditation). The point here is that the "negation" performed by the intoxication defense need not be "all or nothing." In theory, it is possible for the jury to conclude that the defendant was just drunk enough to interfere with the process of deliberation inherent in premeditation, but not drunk enough to interfere

with the formation of the underlying mental state for murder. In such a case, the intoxication negates the extra mental element associated with the aggravating factors for first-degree murder. For example, in California, "[e]vidence of voluntary intoxication is admissible solely on the issue of whether or not the defendant actually formed a required specific intent, or, when charged with murder, whether the defendant premeditated, deliberated, or harbored express malice aforethought." Cal. Penal Code § 29.4. Noticeably absent in this provision is any reference to implied malice. Why? Remember that implied malice murder is based on the concept of a depraved heart which one might describe as a heightened form of recklessness, something akin to acting with depraved indifference to human life. Recall that the Model Penal Code § 2.08(2) renders voluntary intoxication irrelevant in recklessness cases, though it is unclear under the MPC whether intoxication is allowed, or disallowed, in cases of second-degree murder based on extreme indifference to human life.

3. *The time-shifting argument.*   An intoxicated individual may not be capable of forming the required mens rea if he was drunk during the commission of the criminal act. So if a prosecutor charges a drunk driver with murder, the intoxication defense might negate the required mental element. But what if the prosecutor changes her theory of the case? Consider the following hypothetical:

HYPOTHETICAL

John has a history of drinking problems and frequently drinks to the point of blacking out. He has been arrested four times for drunk driving and was convicted all four times. The third time, his license was suspended. On the fourth time, he hit a group of pedestrians on the sidewalk who were severely injured and spent two months in the hospital recuperating from injuries sustained when John's car ploughed into them.

One day, John starts drinking again. After ten drinks he gets so drunk that he loses control. Although his license is still suspended, he gets into his wife's car and speeds down the road. His driving is extremely erratic and he runs over a pedestrian on the sidewalk, killing him instantly. He flees from the scene and drives back home, where he passes out in his own driveway. The next day he has no memory of hitting the pedestrian or even driving the car. Should John be prosecuted? If so, for what? John's intoxication negated his mental state when he hit the pedestrian, because he was barely aware of his own actions at that point in time.

What if the prosecutor argues that John was reckless in his decision to *start* drinking that day? The decision to start drinking may have been reckless if John was aware of a substantial and unjustified risk and consciously disregarded it. Under this theory, the prosecutor would need to prove that John was aware of what happens when he drinks, including poor decisions regarding getting into a car. What evidence would the prosecutor need to marshal to make this case? John's prior convictions for drunk driving might help, as would the prior injuries to innocent bystanders. Both suggest that John was aware of the risk posed by his drinking. The key strategy in this argument is to shift the focus of the analysis back in time, to an early moment when John's actions were unclouded by alcohol intoxication. In that moment, was John a free agent in control of his behavior? For a discussion, see Susan Dimock, *Intoxication and the Act/ Control/Agency Requirement*, 6 Crim. L. & Phil. 341 (2012) (referring to these as "culpability in causing" cases).

Review the casebook video, *People v. Derek Mann* (Part 4: Intoxication). Is the defendant entitled to a jury instruction on intoxication? How should the court assess whether a defendant's intoxication negates the offense's mental element? In this case, the defendant was severely drunk when he left the bar in the moments before the crime. Is that enough to meet the requirements for the defense of voluntary intoxication in a murder case? Finally, does the end result depend on the jurisdiction or is the result the same regardless of jurisdiction?

Now review the casebook video, *People v. Derek Mann* (Part 5: Punishment). How severely should a court punish a defendant who commits a violent crime but who suffers from an obvious alcohol problem? Consider the relative merits of a lengthy prison sentence versus a referral to an alcohol rehabilitation center in lieu of traditional confinement.

2. Eliminating the Intoxication Defense

Several jurisdictions have cracked down on drunkenness by repealing the defense of voluntary intoxication. Some observers believe that this violates a defendant's right to due process. In the following case, the Supreme Court confronts this question in the case of a horrific murder committed after a drinking binge.

Montana v. Egelhoff
Supreme Court of the United States
518 U.S. 37 (1996)

SCALIA, J.

We consider in this case whether the Due Process Clause is violated by Montana Code Annotated § 45-2-203, which provides, in relevant part, that voluntary intoxication "may not be taken into consideration in determining the existence of a mental state which is an element of [a criminal] offense."

I

In July 1992, while camping out in the Yaak region of northwestern Montana to pick mushrooms, respondent made friends with Roberta Pavola and John Christenson, who were doing the same. On Sunday, July 12, the three sold the mushrooms they had collected and spent the rest of the day and evening drinking, in bars and at a private party in Troy, Montana. Some time after 9 P.M., they left the party in Christenson's 1974 Ford Galaxy station wagon. The drinking binge apparently continued, as respondent was seen buying beer at 9:20 P.M. and recalled "sitting on a hill or a bank passing a bottle of Black Velvet back and forth" with Christenson.

At about midnight that night, officers of the Lincoln County, Montana, sheriff's department, responding to reports of a possible drunk driver, discovered Christenson's station wagon stuck in a ditch along U.S. Highway 2. In the front seat were Pavola and Christenson, each dead from a single gunshot to the head. In the rear of the car lay respondent, alive and yelling obscenities. His blood-alcohol content measured .36 percent over one hour later. On the floor of the car, near the brake pedal, lay respondent's .38-caliber handgun, with four loaded rounds and two empty casings; respondent had gunshot residue on his hands.

Respondent was charged with two counts of deliberate homicide, a crime defined by Montana law as "purposely" or "knowingly" causing the death of another human being. Mont. Code Ann. § 45-5-102 (1995). A portion of the jury charge, uncontested here, instructed that "[a] person acts purposely when it is his conscious object to engage in conduct of that nature or to cause such a result," and that "[a] person acts knowingly when he is aware of his conduct or when he is aware under the circumstances his conduct constitutes a crime; or, when he is aware there exists the high probability that his conduct will cause a specific result." Respondent's defense at trial was that an unidentified fourth person must have committed the murders; his own extreme intoxication, he claimed, had rendered him physically incapable of committing the murders, and accounted for his inability to recall the events of the night of July 12. Although respondent was allowed to make this use of the evidence that he was intoxicated, the jury was instructed . . . that it could not consider respondent's "intoxicated condition . . . in determining the existence of a mental state which is an element of the offense." The jury found respondent guilty on both counts, and the court sentenced him to 84 years' imprisonment.

The Supreme Court of Montana reversed. . . .

II

The cornerstone of the Montana Supreme Court's judgment was the proposition that the Due Process Clause guarantees a defendant the right to present and have considered by the jury "*all relevant evidence to rebut the State's evidence on all elements of the offense charged.*" Respondent does not defend this categorical rule; he acknowledges that the right to present relevant evidence "has not been viewed as absolute." That is a wise concession, since the proposition that the Due Process Clause guarantees the right to introduce all relevant evidence is simply indefensible. As we have said: "The accused does not have an unfettered right to offer [evidence] that is incompetent, privileged, or otherwise inadmissible under standard rules of evidence." Relevant evidence may, for example, be excluded on account of a defendant's failure to comply with procedural requirements. And any number of familiar and unquestionably constitutional evidentiary rules also authorize the exclusion of relevant evidence. For example, Federal (and Montana) Rule of Evidence 403 provides: "*Although relevant,* evidence may be excluded if its probative value is substantially outweighed by the danger of unfair prejudice, confusion of the issues, or misleading the jury, or by considerations of undue delay, waste of time, or needless presentation of cumulative evidence." Hearsay rules, see Fed. Rule Evid. 802, similarly prohibit the introduction of testimony which, though unquestionably relevant, is deemed insufficiently reliable. Of course, to say that the right to introduce relevant evidence is not absolute is not to say that the Due Process Clause places *no* limits upon restriction of that right. But it is to say that the defendant asserting such a limit must sustain the usual heavy burden that a due process claim entails:

> [P]reventing and dealing with crime is much more the business of the States than it is of the Federal Government, and . . . we should not lightly construe the Constitution so as to intrude upon the administration of justice by the individual States. Among other things, it is normally "within the power of the State to regulate procedures under which its laws are carried out," . . . and its decision in this regard is not subject to proscription under the Due Process Clause unless "it offends some principle of justice so rooted in the traditions and conscience of our people as to be ranked as fundamental."

Our primary guide in determining whether the principle in question is fundamental is, of course, historical practice. Here that gives respondent little support. By the laws of England, wrote Hale, the intoxicated defendant "shall have no privilege by this voluntary contracted madness, but shall have the same judgment as if he were in his right senses." According to Blackstone and Coke, the law's condemnation of those suffering from *dementia affectata* was harsher still: Blackstone, citing Coke, explained that the law viewed intoxication "as an aggravation of the offence, rather than as an excuse for any criminal misbehaviour." This stern rejection of inebriation as a defense became a fixture of early American law as well. . . .

The historical record does not leave room for the view that the common law's rejection of intoxication as an "excuse" or "justification" for crime would nonetheless permit the defendant to show that intoxication prevented the requisite *mens rea.* Hale, Coke, and Blackstone were familiar, to say the least, with the concept of *mens rea,* and acknowledged that drunkenness "deprive[s] men of the use of reason." It is inconceivable that they did not realize that an offender's drunkenness might impair his ability to form the requisite intent; and inconceivable that their failure to note this massive exception from the general rule of disregard of intoxication was an oversight. Hale's statement that a drunken offender shall have the same judgment "as if he were in his right senses" must be understood as precluding a defendant from arguing that, because of his intoxication, he could not have possessed the *mens rea* required to commit the crime. . . .

Against this extensive evidence of a lengthy common-law tradition decidedly against him, the best argument available to respondent is the one made by his *amicus* and conceded by the State: Over the course of the 19th century, courts carved out an exception to the common law's traditional across-the-board condemnation of the drunken offender, allowing a jury to consider a defendant's intoxication when assessing whether he possessed the mental state needed to commit the crime charged, where the crime was one requiring a "specific intent." . . .

Eventually . . . the new view won out, and by the end of the 19th century, in most American jurisdictions, intoxication could be considered in determining whether a defendant was capable of forming the specific intent necessary to commit the crime charged.

. . . The burden remains upon respondent to show that the "new common-law" rule—that intoxication may be considered on the question of intent—was so deeply rooted at the time of the Fourteenth Amendment (or perhaps has become so deeply rooted since) as to be a fundamental principle which that Amendment enshrined.

That showing has not been made. Instead of the uniform and continuing acceptance we would expect for a rule that enjoys "fundamental principle" status, we find that fully one-fifth of the States either never adopted the "new common-law" rule at issue here or have recently abandoned it.

It is not surprising that many States have held fast to or resurrected the common-law rule prohibiting consideration of voluntary intoxication in the determination of *mens rea,* because that rule has considerable justification—which alone casts doubt upon the proposition that the opposite rule is a "fundamental principle." A large number of crimes, especially violent crimes, are committed by intoxicated offenders; modern studies put the numbers as high as half of all homicides, for example. Disallowing consideration of voluntary intoxication has the effect of increasing the punishment for all unlawful acts committed in that state, and thereby deters drunkenness or irresponsible behavior while drunk. The rule also serves as a specific deterrent, ensuring that those who prove incapable of controlling violent impulses while voluntarily intoxicated go to prison. And finally, the rule comports with and implements society's moral perception that one who has voluntarily impaired his own faculties should be responsible for the consequences.

There is, in modern times, even more justification for laws such as § 45-2-203 than there used to be. Some recent studies suggest that the connection between drunkenness and crime is as much cultural as pharmacological—that is, that drunks are violent not simply because alcohol makes them that way, but because they are behaving in accord with their learned belief that drunks are violent. This not only adds additional support to the traditional view that an intoxicated criminal is not deserving of exoneration, but it suggests that juries—who possess the same learned belief as the intoxicated offender—will be too quick to accept the claim that the defendant was biologically incapable of forming the requisite *mens rea*. Treating the matter as one of excluding misleading evidence therefore makes some sense.

In sum, not every widespread experiment with a procedural rule favorable to criminal defendants establishes a fundamental principle of justice. Although the rule allowing a jury to consider evidence of a defendant's voluntary intoxication where relevant to *mens rea* has gained considerable acceptance, it is of too recent vintage, and has not received sufficiently uniform and permanent allegiance, to qualify as fundamental, especially since it displaces a lengthy common-law tradition which remains supported by valid justifications today. . . .

"The doctrines of *actus reus, mens rea,* insanity, mistake, justification, and duress have historically provided the tools for a constantly shifting adjustment of the tension between the evolving aims of the criminal law and changing religious, moral, philosophical, and medical views of the nature of man. This process of adjustment has always been thought to be the province of the States." *Powell v. Texas,* 392 U.S. 514, 535-536 (1968). The people of Montana have decided to resurrect the rule of an earlier era, disallowing consideration of voluntary intoxication when a defendant's state of mind is at issue. Nothing in the Due Process Clause prevents them from doing so, and the judgment of the Supreme Court of Montana to the contrary must be reversed.

JUSTICE O'CONNOR, dissenting.

. . . This Court's cases establish that limitations placed on the accused's ability to present a fair and complete defense can, in some circumstances, be severe enough to violate due process. "The right of an accused in a criminal trial to due process is, in essence, the right to a fair opportunity to defend against the State's accusations." *Chambers v. Mississippi,* 410 U.S. 284, 294 (1973). Applying our precedent, the Montana Supreme Court held that keeping intoxication evidence away from the jury, where such evidence was relevant to establishment of the requisite mental state, violated the due process right to present a defense, and that the instruction pursuant to § 45-2-203 was not harmless error. In rejecting the Montana Supreme Court's conclusion, the plurality emphasizes that "any number of familiar and unquestionably constitutional evidentiary rules" permit exclusion of relevant evidence. It is true that a defendant does not enjoy an absolute right to present evidence relevant to his defense. But none of the "familiar" evidentiary rules operates as Montana's does. The Montana statute places a blanket exclusion on a category of evidence that would allow the accused to negate the offense's mental-state element. In so doing, it frees the prosecution, in the face of such evidence, from having to prove beyond a reasonable doubt that the defendant nevertheless possessed the required mental state. In my view, this combination of effects violates due process.

The proposition that due process requires a fair opportunity to present a defense in a criminal prosecution is not new. In *Chambers,* the defendant had been prevented from cross-examining a witness and from presenting witnesses on his own behalf by operation of Mississippi's "voucher" and hearsay rules. The Court held that the application of these evidentiary rules deprived the defendant of a fair trial. "[W]here constitutional rights directly affecting the ascertainment of guilt are implicated, the hearsay rule may not be applied mechanistically to defeat the ends of justice." The plurality's characterization of *Chambers* as "case-specific error correction," cannot diminish its force as a prohibition on enforcement of state evidentiary rules that lead, without sufficient justification, to the establishment of guilt by suppression of evidence supporting the defendant's case. . . .

NOTES & QUESTIONS ON ELIMINATING THE DEFENSE

1. *The aftermath of* Egelhoff.   The *Egelhoff* decision had a huge impact on the law of intoxication. Emboldened by the Supreme Court's holding that the Constitution did not require a defense of voluntary intoxication, several jurisdictions moved to sharply curtail or eliminate the defense entirely by statute. For an example of elimination, see Ind. Code Ann. § 35-41-2-5 ("Intoxication is not a defense in a prosecution for an offense and may not be taken into consideration in determining the existence of a mental state that is an element of the offense unless the defendant meets the requirements of" [involuntary intoxication]). State courts have upheld the statutes as constitutional. See *Sanchez v. State,* 749 N.E.2d 509 (Ind. 2001); *State v. Fanning,* 939 S.W.2d 941 (Mo. 1997); *State v. Birdsall,* 960 P.2d 729 (Haw. 1998).

2. *Intoxication defense as constitutional right.*   In *R. v. Daviault,* 3 S.C.R. 63 (1994), the Supreme Court of Canada concluded that the intoxication defense was protected by the Canadian Charter of Rights and Freedoms. The case involved a chronic alcoholic (Daviault) who had a blackout and was accused of sexually assaulting a friend of his wife. The trial judge determined that Daviault committed the assault but was so drunk that there was reasonable doubt that Daviault possessed the "general intent" required for a conviction of

sexual assault. The prosecution appealed to the Court of Appeals, which applied the common law rule that intoxication may be a defense to specific intent crimes but never for general intent crimes. Consequently, the Court of Appeals overturned the acquittal and entered a verdict of guilty for Daviault. On appeal, the Canadian Supreme Court held that the old common law rule—which prevents a defendant from introducing evidence of intoxication in a trial for a general intent offense—was unconstitutional in cases in which the defendant's intoxication approached a state of automatism. In other words, a defendant always has the constitutional right to present evidence that he did not meet the required mental state for the offense:

> The mental aspect of an offence has long been recognized as an integral part of crime, and to eliminate it would be to deprive an accused of fundamental justice. The mental element in general intent offences may be minimal; in this case it is simply an intention to commit the sexual assault or recklessness as to whether the actions will constitute an assault. The necessary mental element can ordinarily be inferred from the proof that the assault was committed by the accused, but the substituted *mens rea* of an intention to become drunk cannot establish the *mens rea* to commit the assault. Moreover, the presumption of innocence requires that the Crown bear the burden of establishing all elements of a crime, including the mental element of voluntariness. Assuming that voluntary intoxication is reprehensible, it does not follow that its consequences in any given situation are either voluntary or predictable. Further, self-induced intoxication cannot supply the necessary link between the minimal *mens rea* required for the offence and the *actus reus*. To deny that even a very minimal mental element is required for sexual assault offends the Charter in a manner that is so drastic and so contrary to the principles of fundamental justice that it cannot be justified under section 1 of the Charter.

Do you agree with the Canadian approach or the American approach? Is the right to argue voluntary intoxication a constitutionally protected right? Although the Canadian and U.S. Supreme Court decisions reflect mutually exclusive perspectives, they are each, in their own way, logically consistent with their prior jurisprudence. The Supreme Court of Canada has long overseen aspects of federal criminal law and has not hesitated to strike down criminal law provisions that impact substantive due process. In contrast, the United States Supreme Court rarely interferes with a state legislature's articulation of basic principles of criminal law, though the Court does vigorously oversee state criminal procedure for compliance with procedural due process. Incidentally, the *Daviault* decision did not sit well with Canadian legislators, who passed a new statute precluding intoxication as a defense when the defendant fails to exercise the appropriate "standard of reasonable care" toward others by voluntarily putting himself in an out-of-control state. R.S.C., c C-46, § 33.1(2).

3. Involuntary Intoxication

Most jurisdictions explicitly recognize a defense for involuntary intoxication. But how should the court *apply* the defense when the defendant claims he was unaware of the intoxicating nature of a substance he voluntarily consumed? These cases are especially hard to resolve when the defendant takes the substance for medical reasons pursuant to a prescription or the direction of a healthcare provider.

People v. Garcia
Supreme Court of Colorado
113 P.3d 775 (2005)

BENDER, J.

INTRODUCTION

We review the court of appeals' decision . . . which reversed Steve David Garcia, Jr.'s convictions for the attempted second degree murder and first degree assault of his wife.

Garcia, an insulin-dependent diabetic, asserted before trial that he had suffered from hypoglycemia, or low blood sugar level, at the time of the crimes and that he intended to raise involuntary intoxication as an affirmative defense. Hypoglycemia is a medical condition resulting from a diabetic's ingestion, or injection, of insulin coupled with a failure to eat appropriately. The trial court ruled, as a matter of law, that evidence of Garcia's hypoglycemic condition could not be presented under the affirmative defense of involuntary intoxication but, rather, could be presented only if Garcia entered a plea of not guilty by reason of insanity. As a result, Garcia entered a plea of not guilty by reason of insanity, abandoning his defense of involuntary intoxication. Pursuant to statute, the court then ordered a mental health examination on the issue of Garcia's sanity.

As a matter of law, we hold that the medical condition of insulin-induced hypoglycemia may, depending upon the particular facts and circumstances, constitute the affirmative defense of involuntary intoxication. We also hold that insanity and involuntary intoxication are legally separate and distinct defenses. Because the trial court ruled that insulin-induced hypoglycemia cannot constitute involuntary intoxication as a matter of law, it committed error. As a result of this improper ruling, the trial court deprived Garcia of the opportunity to meet his burden of going forward with evidence to raise his claimed affirmative defense of involuntary intoxication. Because Garcia was not given the opportunity to introduce evidence to raise this defense, we view the record before us as being limited on this issue. We therefore remand to the trial court to permit both parties to supplement, through offers of proof or evidence, the trial record on the issue of Garcia's claimed involuntary intoxication defense.

In view of all of the evidence and proffers, the trial court shall determine whether Garcia is entitled to raise the defense of involuntary intoxication for jury consideration. If he is so entitled, the trial court shall conduct a new trial. If the trial court concludes that Garcia has not met his burden of going forward with evidence to raise this defense, then Garcia's convictions shall be affirmed. Hence, we affirm in part, reverse in part, and remand this case to the court of appeals with directions to return it to the trial court to permit both parties the opportunity to supplement the record.

FACTS AND PROCEEDINGS BELOW

Garcia was charged with attempted first degree murder, first degree assault, domestic violence, and two counts of mandatory sentence for violent crimes for allegedly having hit his wife, Johnie Garcia, on the head with a hammer and then having run over her with a van.

Before trial, Garcia's counsel informed the court that Garcia would be asserting the affirmative defense of involuntary intoxication because he had suffered from hypoglycemia at the time of the alleged crimes. Hypoglycemia occurs when a diabetic injects, or ingests, insulin and then fails to eat properly. As part of this defense, Garcia's counsel proposed to call an endocrinologist, Dr. Daniel Bessesen, to testify that Garcia's injection of insulin on the morning of the alleged crimes, coupled with a lack of food, resulted in his hypoglycemic condition. Defense counsel stated that Dr. Bessesen would testify, based on Garcia's medical records, that Garcia suffers from diabetes, that he takes insulin for the condition, and that he has had prior occasions of hypoglycemia. According to counsel, Dr. Bessesen would not be able to testify as to whether Garcia was hypoglycemic at the time of the crimes. However, counsel stated that Dr. Bessesen would testify as to how hypoglycemia, in general, can affect a person, and coupled with evidence from other sources which would be presented at trial, counsel would be able to establish that Garcia was hypoglycemic at the time of the crimes: "Basically I will have to draw a link between the testimony of Dr. Bessesen and the testimony of the other evidence and other witnesses that I anticipate I will be bringing in about the events of that day." From defense counsel's description of Dr. Bessesen's proposed testimony, the trial court concluded that Dr. Bessesen would have testified that Garcia's hypoglycemia affected his "rational thought processes to a degree [so as to] . . . affect the mens rea of the Defendant or his ability to form a specific culpable mental state." The prosecution requested that the trial court exclude Dr. Bessesen's testimony, arguing the proposed testimony was tantamount to a "temporary insanity" defense and thus not permitted under Colorado law.

The trial court ruled that, as a matter of law, insulin-induced hypoglycemia could not constitute the affirmative defense of involuntary intoxication, under any circumstance, as that defense is defined. . . . The court also ruled that evidence pertaining to Garcia's hypoglycemia could be presented only if Garcia entered a plea of not guilty by reason of insanity. . . .

The court-appointed examiner, Dr. Robert Miller, concluded that Garcia had suffered an amnestic disorder due to insulin-induced hypoglycemia at the time of the crimes and that this disorder had caused him to be legally insane. At the request of the prosecution, the court ordered a second mental health evaluation by a second independent court-appointed examiner, Dr. Karen Fukutaki. Contrary to the findings of Dr. Miller, Dr. Fukutaki concluded that Garcia was legally sane at the time of the crimes.

Evidence at trial revealed that three days before the alleged crimes, Garcia's wife, Johnie Garcia, told him that she wanted a divorce, and Garcia moved out of their home. On the morning of July 11, 1999, in anticipation of eating cake and ice cream at his teenage daughter's afternoon birthday party, Garcia, who was a diagnosed diabetic and had been treated for diabetes for five years, injected himself with a large dosage of insulin. Garcia did not eat anything following this insulin injection. While he and Johnie were running errands in Johnie's van before the party, Johnie noticed that Garcia was "real quiet" with an "along-for-the-ride type attitude." She asked him at least three times during this timeframe: "Are you okay? Do you need something to eat?" He responded, "No, I'm fine, okay."

When they were exiting a store parking lot in the van at approximately 11:30 A.M., Garcia hit Johnie, who was driving the van at the time, on the right side of her head with what Johnie later learned was a hammer. Garcia did not say anything when he hit her. Johnie immediately got out of the van and began running. Garcia met her at the back of the van and tried to shove her into it through the back door. When an owner of a nearby shop came out and talked to Garcia, Johnie retrieved her purse from the van and ran away. As she was running through parking lots along the main road, Johnie saw Garcia drive past her and turn into a driveway in front of her. After she turned and ran in the opposite direction, Johnie looked to see where Garcia had driven to and discovered that he was directly behind her in the van. Before she could get away, Garcia ran over her with the van and then drove away. Johnie sustained a depressed skull fracture and abrasions and bruises to her entire body.

At trial, Garcia did not dispute that he committed these acts against Johnie. However, he argued that, as a result of his hypoglycemia at the time of the incident, he had no recollection of what had happened and was not legally responsible for his acts because he was insane at the time the acts were committed. Both the prosecution and the defense focused their cases on the issue of whether Garcia was hypoglycemic at the time of the crimes and, if so, whether his hypoglycemia made him insane.

Garcia did not testify at trial. However, a substantial amount of evidence was presented regarding his alleged hypoglycemic condition on the day of the incident and his previous episodes of hypoglycemia. Johnie described three previous episodes in which Garcia had suffered from hypoglycemia. She stated that doctors had instructed him on the importance of eating following an insulin injection. Dr. Bessesen testified about hypoglycemia in general, and both court-appointed psychiatric experts testified regarding the condition generally and in reference to Garcia specifically. Direct and cross-examination of the two court-appointed doctors focused on whether Garcia was hypoglycemic on the day of the crimes and, if so, whether his hypoglycemia made him insane. For example, defense counsel asked Dr. Fukutaki: "If Mr. Garcia was experiencing hypoglycemia on July 11th, 1999, and if that's why he became unpredictably violent, would he have been insane?" No testimony addressed whether Garcia was involuntarily intoxicated as a result of his hypoglycemic condition.

The trial court instructed the jury on the defense of insanity. No instruction was requested or given on involuntary intoxication as an affirmative defense. The jury convicted Garcia of attempted second degree murder and first degree assault.

On appeal, the court of appeals concluded that impairment as a result of intoxication is "not necessarily a mental defect or disease," as defined by the defense of insanity, and held that the trial court erred by not permitting Garcia to proceed under his claimed affirmative defense of involuntary intoxication. . . . We granted the People's petition for certiorari to review the judgment of the court of appeals on these issues and now affirm in part, reverse in part, and remand for further proceedings.

ANALYSIS

Although Garcia did not dispute that he committed the alleged acts against Johnie, he argued that he was not criminally responsible for his actions because he was suffering from hypoglycemia at the time of the crimes. While the central issue at trial concerned whether Garcia's alleged hypoglycemic condition excused his conduct, the jury was only permitted to consider such evidence in the context of Garcia's plea of not guilty by reason of insanity, and not in the context of the statutory affirmative defense of involuntary intoxication.

To determine whether Garcia's claimed defense of involuntary intoxication was properly rejected, we begin by deciding whether, as a matter of law, the medical condition of insulin-induced hypoglycemia could constitute the affirmative defense of involuntary intoxication as defined by section 18-1-804(3). . . .

Intoxication is defined as "a disturbance of mental or physical capacities resulting from the introduction of any substance into the body" and is either voluntary or involuntary. Voluntary, or self-induced, intoxication is caused by "substances which the defendant knows or ought to know have the tendency to cause intoxication and which he knowingly introduced or allowed to be introduced into his body, unless they were introduced pursuant to medical advice or under circumstances that would afford a defense to a charge of crime." Because involuntary intoxication, by definition, is intoxication which is "not self-induced," a person is involuntarily intoxicated when he or she takes a substance pursuant to medical advice, does not know that he or she is ingesting an intoxicant, or ingests a substance which is not known to be an intoxicating substance. Whether a defendant was intoxicated at the time of a particular incident, and whether such intoxication was voluntary or involuntary, are questions for the factfinder and thus depend upon the particular facts of each case.

The General Assembly has expressly provided that involuntary intoxication is an affirmative defense to a crime charged: "A person is *not criminally responsible* for his conduct if, by reason of intoxication that is *not self-induced* at the time he acts, he lacks capacity to conform his conduct to the requirements of the law." Because involuntary intoxication is statutorily defined as a complete defense to all crimes, an involuntarily intoxicated defendant is absolved of responsibility for all criminal acts. Involuntary intoxication is akin to "temporary insanity" because "there is no immoral or blameworthy stigma attached to the condition."

This Court has not previously addressed whether the medical condition of insulin-induced hypoglycemia may constitute involuntary intoxication as that affirmative defense is statutorily defined. However, we determined in *People v. Low* that the defendant could assert involuntary intoxication as a complete defense to the crimes charged where he was allegedly unable to conform his conduct to the requirements of law as a result of ingesting a large quantity of over-the-counter cough drops. Low claimed both that the manufacturer's warning did not advise him that intoxication was a potential side effect of consuming large quantities of the cough drops and that his own previous experience with taking the medicine did not forewarn him of that possibility either. Based on these claims and expert testimony that excessive quantities of the cough drops could have prevented Low from lawfully conforming his conduct, this Court determined that Low's ingestion of the medicine could have made him involuntarily intoxicated for purposes of raising the affirmative defense defined by section 18-1-804(3).

Similarly, in *People v. Turner,* 680 P.2d 1290, 1292 (Colo. App. 1983), the defendant claimed he had become involuntarily intoxicated as a result of overdosing on a prescription drug. Turner claimed that his resulting intoxication was involuntary because he had not been warned of the intoxicating side effect of an overdose of the drug and because his past experiences with the drug had led him to believe that an overdose would cause him to become fatigued, not intoxicated. The court of appeals concluded that based upon the defendant's evidence that he did not know of the potential intoxicating effect of an overdose of the drug, the defendant's overdose could constitute the affirmative defense of involuntary intoxication under section 18-1-804(3). The court ruled that the trial court erred by not permitting the defendant to present this affirmative defense for jury consideration.

Here, it is not disputed that Garcia took insulin—a substance—pursuant to prescription on the morning of the alleged crimes and that he failed to eat following this insulin injection. At Garcia's trial, three doctors testified as experts concerning the medical condition of hypoglycemia generally and Garcia's condition at the time of the crimes. According to their testimony, diabetes is a medical condition in which blood sugar, or glucose, is not regulated normally by the body. Normally, insulin is naturally produced by the body as a hormone which regulates a person's blood sugar level. A diabetic, however, must inject, or ingest, insulin to control his or her blood sugar level. A diabetic's treating physician will prescribe the dosage of insulin necessary for that particular person's condition. When a diabetic takes insulin and fails to eat, a low blood sugar level, or hypoglycemia, can result. Hypoglycemia, in turn, can affect one's physical capacities, causing a loss of motor skills, and can also create an "altered mental state," affecting "decision-making abilities" and "prevent[ing] rational thinking, planning, deliberation and even appreciation of what [one is] doing." Given that hypoglycemia is typically cured by the ingestion of sugar, these physical and mental effects are typically temporary in nature. Because a person with an inability to think rationally could necessarily lack the capacity to conform his or her conduct to the requirements of law, and given that insulin is a substance taken pursuant to prescription, *i.e.*, pursuant to medical advice, we conclude that the medical condition of insulin-induced hypoglycemia could constitute involuntary intoxication for the affirmative defense. . . .

Our research has disclosed that other jurisdictions have concluded that insulin-induced hypoglycemia can constitute the affirmative defense of involuntary intoxication. Similarly, while the New York appellate division did not reach the question of whether hypoglycemia could constitute involuntary intoxication, it did hold that insulin-induced hypoglycemia could constitute intoxication in general.

The People argue that insulin-induced hypoglycemia cannot constitute involuntary intoxication as a matter of law because Garcia's alleged hypoglycemic condition resulted not solely from the introduction of a substance into his body but, instead, from the combined injection of insulin with his failure to eat. We disagree. Applying Colorado's statutory language, intoxication is a substance-induced disturbance of mental or physical capacities. Insulin is a substance prescribed for diabetics by doctors, and insulin-induced hypoglycemia is thus a drug-induced disturbance of one's mental and/or physical capacities. Although the effect of insulin on one's mental and physical capacities may be impacted by a failure to eat, we agree with the conclusions reached by the other jurisdictions that insulin is a drug which can cause an intoxicated state.

We therefore conclude that, as a matter of law, the medical condition of insulin-induced hypoglycemia may, depending upon the particular facts and circumstances involved, constitute the affirmative defense of involuntary intoxication as that defense is defined by section 18-1-804(3). . . .

NOTES & QUESTIONS ON INVOLUNTARY INTOXICATION

1. Garcia *and recklessness.*   Are you sympathetic to Garcia's predicament? The Supreme Court of Colorado took no position on whether Garcia should be excused for the attempted murder but concluded that there was sufficient evidence of involuntary intoxication that the issue should be presented to a jury for resolution. On retrial, would you vote to acquit or convict? As a juror, how would you evaluate Garcia's decision not to eat after taking the insulin? The medical experts testified that Garcia's intoxication was caused by the combination of his ingestion of the insulin and his *failure* to eat afterward. Should he have predicted his own intoxication? Perhaps the prosecution's argument should be that he was reckless in not following his physician's advice for how to take the insulin, and that the attempted murder resulted from his conscious disregard of that substantial and unjustified risk.

2. *Pathological intoxication.*   One variation of involuntary intoxication involves defendants who argue that their intoxication was unpredictable because their body reacted in an abnormal or pathological manner to the ingestion of the substance. Consequently, the defendant's failure to anticipate the intoxication resulting from the voluntary ingestion of the substance is explained by the fact that most individuals have not become intoxicated by the substance. Some pathological aspect of the defendant's biology produced the intoxication when it was combined with the ingestion of the substance. For example, imagine an individual whose body chemistry makes him overly susceptible to alcohol—for reasons having to do with how his body processes alcohol; even a few sips of wine will produce an intense level of intoxication. Because this result is pathological, the defendant argues that his intoxication should be evaluated as involuntary rather than voluntary. Courts generally disallow this as an involuntary defense when the defendant voluntarily ingests an illegal intoxicant (like drugs) or legal intoxicants from which a person should "reasonably expect an adverse reaction." Compare *State v. Sette*, 259 N.J. Super. 156, 179 (App. Div. 1992) (denying defense for intoxication produced by combination of involuntary pesticide exposure and voluntary ingestion of cocaine, marijuana, and

Tylenol) with *City of Minneapolis v. Altimus*, 238 N.W.2d 851 (Minn. 1976) (allowing involuntary intoxication defense due to unpredictable reaction to prescription Valium). However, a few courts recognize involuntary "intoxication by mistake" when a defendant voluntarily takes one substance believing it to be another. *People v. Penman*, 271 Ill. 82, 110 N.E. 894 (1915) (defendant was told that cocaine tablets were breath mints).

PROBLEM CASE

On August 4, 1999, two young men set off on a hiking trip at the Carlsbad Caverns National Park in New Mexico. Carlsbad Caverns is a world marvel, drawing more than 380,000 visitors annually to admire its magical looking stalactites and stalagmites. Before visiting the caves, David Coughlin and Raffi Kodikian went for a hike on the nearby Rattlesnake Canyon trail. Coming from Boston, Coughlin and Kodikian were not prepared for the brutal heat conditions in the canyon and soon became lost. Within days, Coughlin was dead and Kodikian was charged with his murder.

Both men started suffering from dehydration when their inadequate water supply started to run out. Kodikian initially claimed that Coughlin was severely dehydrated and had begged to be put out of his misery—in essence a mercy killing. Police were skeptical of this claim, and wondered if Kodikian stabbed his friend to save himself when the water ran low, or perhaps for some other reason.

At trial, Kodikian conceded that he killed Coughlin but attempted to put on a defense of involuntary intoxication based on acute dehydration. In short, he argued that lack of water caused biochemical changes to his brain that constituted a form of intoxication. The trial judge denied the request to introduce the defense, in part because Kodikian never ingested a substance—his alleged intoxication was caused by his *failure* to ingest a substance. Kodikian pled guilty to second-degree murder and instead presented evidence of involuntary intoxication during the sentencing phase. He went to prison for two years.

Raffi Kodikian

Would you have acquitted Kodikian? Should the defense be available in cases of intoxication-by-omission? See Shawn Marie Boyne & Gary C. Mitchell, *Death in the Desert: A New Look at the Involuntary Intoxication Defense in New Mexico*, 32 N.M. L. Rev. 243, 267 (2002) ("[I]t is illogical to restrict the definition of intoxication to cases where a substance has been introduced into the body when the failure to introduce a substance may have an identical effect on the body. That restriction represents a pattern of logic crippled by the triumph of form over substance.").

C. PRACTICE & POLICY

How should the law deal with intoxicated criminals? In reading these materials, think outside the box and come up with new and innovative ways for handling these individuals. In particular, consider: (i) how to prosecute individuals who get drunk with the purpose of committing a crime; (ii) the possibility of creating a separate offense for drunken crimes; and (iii) the best strategy for a prosecutor faced with a defendant raising intoxication at trial.

✎ **Grand schemers.**   What if an actor deliberately gets drunk with the purpose of exonerating himself for crimes committed during his state of intoxication? This situation is more extreme than the case of the reckless drunk who decides to drink alcohol despite the *risk* that he might commit a crime during his state of intoxication. In the more extreme case, the defendant drinks the alcohol for the express purpose of establishing the conditions for his own defense. For example, imagine a soldier who gets drunk before committing a war crime in the hopes that his intoxication will serve as a defense. Or consider an abusive husband who knows that he tends to beat his wife when he blacks out during drinking binges. Suppose the husband decides to get drunk with the express purpose of murdering his wife during a state when he cannot be convicted of intentional murder. What is the appropriate resolution for this case? As a prosecutor, how would you construct a case to prosecute the husband?

The problem with the case is that the husband committed an intentional murder that ought to be prosecuted as first-degree or second-degree murder. But in a jurisdiction that allows intoxication in specific intent cases, the defendant could argue that his intoxication negated his specific intent because he had no idea what he was doing when he killed his victim. In a jurisdiction that follows the MPC scheme, the defendant could argue that his intoxication negated the required mental element for first-degree murder, and again he would be acquitted. Is this result justifiable?

One solution is to view the defendant's behavior as part of a single criminal transaction, a coherent plan from start to finish. Under this interpretation, the actor's culpability resides in intentionally setting in motion a sequence of events that leads to the commission of a crime. As to the defendant's mental state, the relevant question is not whether the defendant acted with purpose or knowledge when he committed the physical act of killing, but rather whether the defendant acted with purpose or knowledge when he set in motion the overall plan that would produce this result. See Dimock, *supra*, at 353 (using the phrase "grand schemers" to describe these cases). Although this argument is theoretically sound, it is unclear if it could be articulated at trial using a doctrine familiar to most criminal lawyers. Can you find a doctrine that would apply these insights? Query: Would the innocent instrumentality rule work? Is it possible for someone to be a principal perpetrator by using *himself*—at a later moment in time—as the innocent instrumentality? The later self would be innocent or non-culpable because he was unaware of his actions. Does this solution work or is it too clever by half?

〜 The "separate offense" solution. Taking a step back from the specific problems regarding intoxication, the entire subject suggests deep uncertainty over how to handle drunk defendants. At the heart of the problem is one simple tension: On the one hand, a drunk defendant might not exhibit the required mental elements for the offense, but on the other hand, intoxicated actors are often culpable for getting drunk and putting themselves into a position where they might lose control of their faculties and commit a crime. That result could be avoided by simply refraining from ingesting intoxicating substances, and actors who willingly take these substances run the risk that they might lose control while under their influence. Perhaps one solution is to make this a separate offense: the crime of being so drunk that you commit a crime. Is this a possible compromise solution to the problem of how to treat drunk criminals? As it happens, German criminal law includes precisely such a crime. Section 323(a) of the German Penal Code states: "Whosoever intentionally or negligently puts himself into a drunken state by consuming alcoholic beverages or other intoxicants shall be liable to imprisonment not exceeding five years or a fine if he commits an unlawful act while in this state and may not be punished because of it because he was insane due to the intoxication or if this cannot be excluded" (Michael Bohlander trans.). Would you support a legislative amendment in the United States that creates such a crime? Would it be a strict liability offense? At least in the German example, the law requires that the defendant was negligent in creating his own loss of control, i.e., he ought to have been aware that his conduct posed a substantial and unjustified risk. For more discussion, see George P. Fletcher, *Rethinking Criminal Law* 748 (Oxford reprint ed. 2000).

〜 Strategic charging and trial decisions. If you were a prosecutor, how would you respond to the possibility that a defendant in your case might raise a defense of voluntary intoxication? Assuming you are in a jurisdiction that still permits the defense of voluntary intoxication, the defendant's drunken state might prove a barrier to convicting him of intentional murder. He could argue at trial that his intoxication prevented him from forming that higher mental state. So the fallback strategy is to charge the defendant with either reckless murder or manslaughter. At least in some jurisdictions, his intoxication would be irrelevant to the state of awareness required for recklessness. Even in a jurisdiction with no such rule, one could charge the defendant with negligent homicide. As a prosecutor, one might be tempted to seek permission to present each of these charges to the jury, on the theory that the jury will convict on intentional murder if it rejects the defendant's intoxication defense, and will convict on a lesser count if it accepts the defendant's intoxication defense. Are there risks associated with this strategy? Once the jury gets a hold of the intoxication defense, they might acquit the defendant of *all charges*, notwithstanding the judge's explanation of the applicable law of intoxication. To avoid this poor outcome, would the prosecutor be advised to go into a court with a lesser charge as the top count and then convince the judge that evidence of intoxication is irrelevant and therefore per se inadmissible?

CHAPTER 28

—◁◦/◦/◦▷—

INSANITY

A. DOCTRINE

The insanity defense is ancient; over the years a number of competing standards have been used to determine whether a criminal was too insane to warrant criminal punishment. These include: (i) the cognitive test introduced in *M'Naghten*; (ii) the irresistible impulse or volitional test; and (iii) the Model Penal Code's "substantial capacity" test. With each of these standards, the defendant makes a formal plea of not guilty by reason of insanity; the fact finder then decides whether the defendant's insanity is sufficient to negate her culpability for committing the crime. If convicted the defendant can be punished, usually by prison; if acquitted the defendant is committed to psychiatric care. In acquitting someone by reason of insanity, the legal system determines that the defendant was not acting as a free moral agent whose behavior is worthy of social condemnation through the institution of punishment.

1. The Cognitive Test

The cognitive test was first articulated and summarized in *M'Naghten's Case*, 8 Eng. Rep. 718 (1843). Daniel M'Naghten attempted to assassinate the Prime Minister of England. He failed, but killed the prime minister's secretary. After the trial, the House of Lords issued an advisory opinion laying out the standard for finding a defendant not guilty by reason of insanity: "To establish a defense on the ground of insanity it must be clearly proved that, at the time of committing the act, the party accused was laboring under such a defect or reason, from disease of the mind, as not to know the nature and quality of the act he was doing, or if he did know it, that he did not know that what he was doing was wrong."

811

Distilled to its essence, the *M'Naghten* test concentrates on the impairment of a defendant's cognitive capacity. It always requires a finding that the defendant suffered from a mental disease or defect that caused a cognitive impairment. However, there are two prongs, either one of which would be sufficient to meet the standard. Under the first prong, the defendant believes she is committing one action but is actually committing another. For example, if the defendant squeezes the victim's neck but believes that she is squeezing a lemon, she remains unaware of the nature of the act. Under the second prong, the defendant correctly perceives the action but is unaware that it is wrongful. For example, if a delusional psychotic kills a man who he believes is about to assassinate the President, he does not understand the wrongfulness of his action. He knows full well that he is killing a human being, but he fails to appreciate the wrongfulness of his action due to his mental disease. Either situation is sufficient to meet the cognitive test.

2. The Irresistible Impulse Test

Over time, several jurisdictions have flirted with broadening the *M'Naghten* test. The most popular method of expanding the test is to include a volitional component as an additional prong to the preexisting cognitive test. Under this view, a defendant is legally insane if he meets the *M'Naghten* standard *or* if he suffers from a volitional defect that prevents him from complying with the demands of the law. This volitional component is often referred to as the "irresistible impulse" test because the actor is unable to control his behavior and comply with the law. The important point is that the irresistible impulse test supplements, rather than replaces, the cognitive test embodied in *M'Naghten*. Today, a few states retain the irresistible impulse test as a supplement, including Georgia, New Mexico, and Virginia.

3. The Model Penal Code Substantial Capacity Test

When the Model Penal Code was drafted, the American Law Institute sought to support both the *M'Naghten* test and the irresistible impulse test. Therefore both are included within the ambit of § 4.01, which states simply that "a person is not responsible for criminal conduct if at the time of such conduct as a result of mental disease or defect he lacks the substantial capacity either to appreciate the criminality [wrongfulness] of his conduct or to conform his conduct to the requirements of the law." The first prong ("appreciate") tracks the cognitive test, while the second prong ("conform") tracks the volitional test.

The great innovation of the Model Penal Code was its introduction of the notion of "substantial capacity." The phrase was meant to broaden the test for insanity and remove the all-or-nothing nature of the *M'Naghten* or irresistible impulse formulations. Under those tests, the defendant's capability to understand or control his criminal behavior had to be completely eviscerated in order to qualify for the insanity defense. In contrast, the new MPC test required only that the mental disease or defect negated a substantial capacity of the defendant to meet these requirements. That dovetails with the use of the term "appreciate" instead of "know," a shift designed to emphasize that the cognitive defect need not be total.

The MPC "substantial capacity" innovation was initially influential and ushered in a wave of mental illness reform in the criminal justice system in the 1960s and 1970s. However, many state governments eventually responded to public pressure to tighten up their standards for legal insanity, due in part to the public's (perhaps exaggerated) belief that too many defendants were being acquitted by reason of insanity. Many went back to a pure *M'Naghten* standard.

4. The Definition of Wrongfulness

The *M'Naghten* standard includes a fundamental ambiguity: It uses the term "wrong" or "wrongfulness" without defining the term. Does this use of the term "wrong" suggest "morally wrong" or "legally wrong"? Because of this ambiguity, the cognitive test can be understood in one of two ways: either the mental disease or defect prevented the actor from understanding that his actions were *morally* wrongful, or that his actions were *illegal*. These are quite different standards. At issue is whether the jury is supposed to ask whether the defendant's impairment was an obstacle to engaging in coherent moral reasoning or accurate legal analysis. Jurisdictions have taken competing positions on how to understand the wrongfulness element in the cognitive standard. Within jurisdictions that understand wrongfulness in moral terms, some use an objective standard and others a subjective standard. The objective standard asks whether the actor was able to understand that his actions violated society's view of morality; the subjective standard asks whether the actor was able understand that his actions violated his own personal moral code.

The drafters of the Model Penal Code took no position and left this issue unresolved; they included A and B options within § 4.01 so that state legislatures adopting the provision could use the term "criminality" or "wrongfulness" depending on which version of the cognitive test they preferred. In the MPC scheme, "wrongfulness" by itself refers to a moral concept, while "criminality" refers to legal wrongfulness. The drafters of the MPC apparently believed that both versions, while different from each other, represented a legitimate policy choice for lawmakers.

5. Diminished Capacity

The diminished capacity doctrine allows a defendant who does not plead insanity to still introduce evidence of mental illness to negate the mens rea that the prosecution must establish as part of its burden. If the mental illness negates the required mental element of the offense, the defendant's criminal liability is either downgraded to a lower crime or extinguished altogether, depending on the availability of other charges with a less significant mental element that is consistent with the defendant's psychic abnormality. Although diminished capacity is often referred to as a "doctrine," it is perhaps more properly classified as a rule of evidence. The rule simply allows the defense to present expert testimony regarding mental illness or abnormalities that might negate the prosecutor's case. Some jurisdictions have abrogated the rule by statute to *prevent* defendants from introducing psychiatric evidence unless they are pleading not guilty by reason of insanity. In these jurisdictions, in the absence of a full insanity plea, the psychiatric evidence is excluded from the trial. The stated rationale for disallowing psychiatric testimony is that it might confuse the jury. Also, defendants who successfully argue diminished capacity might be acquitted and never get mental treatment, while defendants who are found not guilty by reason of insanity are committed to a psychiatric facility until they are deemed no longer a threat to themselves or the community.

B. APPLICATION

1. The Cognitive Test

The following case applies the *M'Naghten* standard in the disturbing killing of two innocent grandparents. As you read the facts, try to make sense of the jury's decision to convict the defendant of one count and acquit him of the other. Does this make sense, given that the cognitive test evaluates whether the defendant suffered from a mental disease or defect that prevented him from understanding the nature or quality of his act or its wrongdoing?

Sanders v. State
Supreme Court of Mississippi
63 So. 3d 497 (2011)

Pierce, J.

More than twenty years after the murder of W.D. and Elma Crawford, their grandson Keir Sanders was arrested and indicted for their murders. He was tried by the Circuit Court of Tishomingo County, sitting, on a change of venue, in Lee County. Sanders was found not guilty of murder by reason of insanity on Count I, but the jury found that he remained insane and a danger to the community. On Count II, Sanders was found guilty of murder, and he was sentenced to life in prison as a habitual offender. . . .

FACTS AND PROCEDURAL HISTORY

On the morning of December 29, 1985, W.D. and Elma Crawford were attacked in their Tishomingo County home. While W.D. was cooking breakfast, someone shot him in the back with a shotgun and then killed him by bludgeoning him in the back of the head with a hammer. After killing W.D., the attacker proceeded to the bedroom and shot Elma with a shotgun while she was lying in bed. The attacker fled the scene in the couple's car.

Later that night, Officer Mike Kemp, chief deputy with the Tishomingo County Sheriff's Department in 1985, responded to a call concerning W.D. and Elma. Jannie Hadley, daughter of the couple, had called Tennessee authorities to say that she could not reach her parents. This was reported to Officer Kemp, who went to investigate with auxiliary deputy David Johnson.

Upon arriving, Officer Kemp discovered that the door was ajar, and he heard a voice coming from inside. Inside the house, he discovered Elma lying on the couch, covered in blood. According to Officer Kemp, Elma told him that her grandson, Sanders, had shot her and W.D. She did not know where Sanders was. Officer Kemp discovered that the phone had been pulled from the wall, so he returned to his squad car to call for backup.

Authorities searched the scene and discovered that Elma had been shot in the bedroom. After Sanders had shot her, she had crawled down a small flight of steps and had written "K D shotgun" on the floor using her own blood. W.D. was found face down on the floor of the kitchen. The hammer that Sanders had used to beat him was found in a trash can in the house. Neither the shotgun nor the couple's car was found at the scene.

Elma was taken to the hospital, where she spent several weeks in the intensive care unit. According to Sandra Puckett, who was the ICU supervisor and staff nurse at Iuka Hospital in 1985, Elma suffered a shotgun blast to her breast and right upper abdomen. Puckett said that Elma was afraid that she would never go home and that Sanders would finish her off. During Elma's stay in the hospital, she lost considerable amounts of blood, and she suffered multiple infections. She died on March 4, 1986. Sanders was twenty-one years old at the time of the shootings.

Authorities eventually located W.D.'s car parked in a motel parking lot in Memphis, Tennessee, on January 6, 1986. However, no more was heard from Sanders until 2005. In December 2005, Officer Guillermo Cantu, Jr., with the San Antonio Police Department, apprehended Sanders in San Antonio, Texas, after observing his suspicious behavior. Officer Guillermo found that Sanders was carrying his birth certificate, and he arrested Sanders after discovering the outstanding warrants for murder in Mississippi.

Mickey Baker, with the Mississippi Bureau of Investigation division of the Mississippi State Highway Patrol, traveled to San Antonio with a fingerprint card for Sanders. He discovered that Sanders had used six different aliases since 1990.

Sanders was transported back to Mississippi, and he was indicted by a grand jury in Tishomingo County for Count I, the murder of W.D., and Count II, the murder of Elma. Venue was changed from Tishomingo to Lafayette County. The trial resulted in a mistrial, and venue was changed to Lee County. In Sanders's defense during the trial in Lee County, he presented the testimony of his mother, Jannie, and stepfather, Gerald Hadley. He also called two experts to testify—Dr. John McCoy and Dr. Mark Webb.

Jannie testified concerning Sanders's childhood. She said that Sanders was diagnosed with schizophrenia at the age of eight or nine, and he changed when he was a teenager. Noticeable changes included Sanders quitting school, refusing to look in mirrors, screaming, hearing things, and sitting by himself for hours. Sanders was sent away for treatment at the Redemption Ranch in Pikeville, Tennessee; however, he ran away and was expelled. Jannie said that Sanders would spin around in his room and beat his head against the wall. When he came home, he was worse; he could not use utensils, he covered mirrors, and he stayed all alone. In 1982, after a confrontation, Sanders was sent away to Mid-South Hospital in Memphis. He later went to a halfway house, but he was asked to leave. Next, in 1984, Sanders was sent to the Mississippi State Hospital at Whitfield. However, he stayed for only a few weeks before he ran away from Whitfield and moved back in with his grandparents.

Sanders was treated at Mid-South from November 19, 1982, until he was discharged in August 1983. Dr. McCoy was a clinical psychologist at Mid-South during this time, and he treated Sanders. He described Sanders as follows: "He was really, very sick. He was the most mentally ill of all the patients in the hospital. He came in reporting bizarre symptoms. He was the sickest one that had been in that hospital in a long time." Dr. McCoy also described some of Sanders's symptoms: changing the pitch of his voice, burning Bibles, waking up cursing and fighting, talking to himself, covering or breaking mirrors, refusing to use toiletry articles except for toothpaste, sleeping on the top of the covers with his shoes on, slamming doors, jumping off the roof and out of windows at the behest of "voices," and attacking people. He also said Sanders was paranoid, disoriented as to the date and time, and had delusions of persecution.

Dr. McCoy diagnosed Sanders as suffering from a schizoaffective disorder. He described the disorder as a combination of schizophrenia and bipolar disorder. He said that such a person generally is socially incompetent, has no friends, and has delusions and auditory hallucinations. It was Dr. McCoy's opinion that Sanders never should have been discharged from Mid-South. Dr. McCoy also interviewed Sanders on May 10, 2008. It was Dr. McCoy's opinion that, at the time Sanders killed his grandparents, he was "laboring under a defect of reason from a disease of the mind." Dr. McCoy believed that Sanders understood the nature and quality of his actions, but that Sanders did not know that what he did was wrong.

Dr. Webb, a physician specializing in psychiatry with the Mississippi Neuropsychiatric Clinic in Jackson, evaluated Sanders on December 11, 2007, at the behest of the circuit court. Dr. Webb admitted that Sanders's situation was a close call; nevertheless, he agreed that, while Sanders understood the nature and quality of his actions, he did not know that his actions were wrong. Dr. Webb noted Sanders's possible history of aggressive and manipulative behavior, but he characterized Sanders as more paranoid than aggressive.

Dr. William Lott, a clinical psychologist, conducted a court-ordered forensic evaluation of Sanders on March 24, 2007. Dr. Lott noted the extended periods of time that Sanders was able to function successfully in society while not on any medications, and he also noted that Sanders had been off any medication for at least four years at the time of the examination. Dr. Lott testified that Sanders looked fine and that he did not appear to be psychotic. He also said that Sanders exhibited normal to above-average intelligence. In reviewing Sanders's history, Dr. Lott noted evidence of manipulative behavior and possible extensive drug use. Dr. Lott described Sanders as having a history of impulsive, aggressive behavior. He believed Sanders was spoiled as a result of being indulged. Dr. Lott also noted that the reports of Dr. Mona Carlyle, who had treated Sanders at and around the time he went to Mid-South and Whitfield, may have indicated that Sanders showed no signs of psychosis. However, Dr. Carlyle's final report on Sanders from October 15, 1984, diagnosed atypical psychosis.

Dr. Lott concluded that Sanders did understand the nature and quality of his actions. He noted that both Dr. McCoy and Dr. Webb initially had disagreed with this assessment. However, at trial, they had amended their opinions to agree with Dr. Lott. Contrary to the other doctors' assessments, Dr. Lott found that Sanders understood that what he did was wrong. According to Dr. Lott, Sanders's behavior during the murders was not random or psychotic; it was well-reasoned and well-intended. Supporting his conclusion was the fact that Sanders had unplugged the phone, wrapped the cord around it, and hid it under the sofa. Also, Sanders took his grandparents' car and immediately fled to Memphis, hiding the car in a busy parking lot. Sanders then made the trip to Texas and successfully avoided capture by adopting six different aliases over the next twenty years. Dr. Lott was suspicious that illegal drug use had played a part in Sanders's actions, even though there was little or no evidence that Sanders had used illegal drugs. Sanders did not testify in his own defense.

While deliberating, the jury sent out a note with questions for the circuit court. It read as follows: "What is the minimum sentence for someone that is found to be insane and a danger to the public? If the defendant is found 'not guilty' by reason of insanity BUT is a danger to the public . . . [w]ill the defendant be allowed to ever walk as a free man on the street?"

The circuit court did not answer the questions. The jury returned a verdict of not guilty on Count I, the murder of W.D., by reason of insanity, and found that Sanders had not been restored to his sanity and was dangerous to the community. On Count II, the murder of Elma, the jury found Sanders guilty. The circuit court sentenced Sanders to life in prison as a habitual offender on Count II. On Count I, the court ordered Sanders to be confined to the state psychiatric hospital until such time as he is restored to his sanity, with Sanders's confinement to be delayed until he had served his life sentence on Count II. . . .

DISCUSSION

. . . Sanders contends that his conviction on Count II, the murder of his grandmother, was against the overwhelming weight of the evidence. When this Court is asked to review the denial of a motion for a new trial based on the weight of the evidence, we review the evidence in the light most favorable to the verdict. Sitting as a thirteenth juror, we will disturb a verdict only when it is so contrary to the overwhelming weight of the evidence that to allow it to stand would sanction an unconscionable injustice. The motion, however, is addressed to the discretion of the court, which should be exercised with caution, and the power to grant a new trial should be invoked only in exceptional cases in which the evidence preponderates heavily against the verdict. Sanders does not dispute his role in killing his grandparents, but, rather, the finding that he was legally sane when he did so. In insanity defense cases, perhaps more than any other, a jury's verdict ought to be given great respect and deference. . . .

We are asked to determine whether the jury's determination that Sanders was legally sane was against the weight of the evidence. Mississippi follows the *M'Naghten* Rule for determining legal sanity. Under the *M'Naghten* Rule, a defendant may not be held criminally liable for his actions at the time of the alleged crime if he "was laboring under such a defect of reason from disease of the mind that either (a) he did not understand the nature and quality of his act, or (b) if he did understand the nature and quality of his act, he did not appreciate that the act was wrong." In applying this rule, the accused is presumed sane; and therefore, the burden is initially on the defendant to introduce evidence creating a reasonable doubt of his sanity. However, once the defendant has overcome this initial burden, it is the State's burden to present sufficient evidence to prove the defendant's sanity beyond a reasonable doubt. Though expert opinions frequently are used in cases in which the defendant claims insanity, expert opinions of psychiatrists are not conclusive upon the issue of insanity, which is, rather, a question to be resolved by the jury.

All three experts testified that they believed Sanders to have understood the nature and quality of his acts at the time. There is no indication in the record anywhere that Sanders did not understand that he was killing another human being. The only question is whether the evidence preponderates heavily against the jury's necessary determination that Sanders knew that the killing of his grandmother was wrong. On this point, there was conflicting evidence.

Dr. John McCoy, who treated Sanders at Mid-South, testified that Sanders was "the most mentally-ill patient" at the hospital and that he thought Sanders did not know right from wrong when he killed the Crawfords. Dr. Mark Webb testified that Sanders's paranoia had prevented him from understanding that his actions were wrong.

On the other hand, Dr. McCoy testified that Sanders had admitted that he was not hallucinating when he killed his grandmother. Dr. William Lott testified that, despite the fact that Sanders had not been medicated for schizophrenia for years, Sanders did not appear to be psychotic when Lott interviewed him in 2007. Dr. Lott further testified that symptoms of schizophrenia or schizoaffective disorder can "wax and wane," so diagnosed persons have periods of lucidity and know right from wrong. Further, the dying-declaration testimony of Elma was that her grandson had walked upstairs to her bedroom after killing her husband, had shot her, and then had hid the phone before leaving with the shotgun. Sanders then had eluded police for nearly twenty years. These facts and evidence suggest Sanders knew his conduct was wrong. . . .

Despite the expert testimony of Drs. McCoy and Webb and Sanders's history of mental illness, there is reasonable evidence to conclude that Elma was slain in an effort to avoid responsibility for the death of W.D. and not in a paranoid delusion. Only after arguing with and killing his grandfather did Sanders proceed upstairs and shoot his grandmother. Then he pulled the phone from the wall and hid it under a sofa before fleeing the scene. Just because a person is schizophrenic does not mean that person is M'Naghten insane. And, while no evidence of the circumstances surrounding this tragedy suggests that Sanders was in a paranoid delusional state of mind on the morning of these killings, his calculated flight and evasion of authorities immediately thereafter show deliberation and a guilty conscience.

In the past we have said that "the subjective aspects of sanity or insanity present difficult problems." This is especially true where, as here, the

PROBLEM CASE

On July 20, 2012, former University of Colorado student James Holmes walked into a late-night showing of a Batman film, *The Dark Knight Rises*, and started shooting. The dark theater was further clouded by teargas that Holmes deployed to sow confusion among the attendees. Armed with an assault rifle, Holmes murdered 12 people and injured more than 70, some with life-altering impairments.

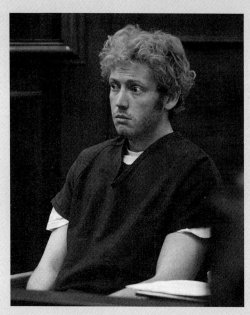

James Holmes

Holmes was captured by the police outside of the theater. He quickly confessed to the crime. Holmes had also booby-trapped his apartment with the apparent hope that responding police officers would be killed when they tried to enter his home.

Holmes had a history of psychiatric problems. He had seven sessions with a psychologist, Dr. Lynne Fenton, at the University of Colorado while he was enrolled in the school's graduate program in neuroscience, but that relationship soon soured. He threatened her; she reported to campus police that she considered him dangerous, though there is no evidence that municipal

police received this report. Right before the massacre, he mailed Dr. Fenton a notebook explaining his actions. Among other rambling statements explaining his desire to commit the killings, he also wrote: "The real me is fighting the biological me." Dr. Fenton later testified that Holmes was obsessed with homicidal thoughts, but she defended her decision not to seek an involuntary committal to a psychiatric facility because she said he never announced a specific plan to harm someone.

Holmes's notebook

At trial in June-July 2015, Holmes's lawyers argued that he was insane during the attack. Defense psychiatrists testified that he suffered from such severe schizophrenia that he could not tell the difference between right and wrong. Psychologists for the prosecution concluded that he was severely mentally ill but not legally insane, in part because his plan was well thought out and he listened to very loud music through headphones during the attack. For the state psychiatrists, this last detail was especially telling: It represented Holmes's desire to avoid sympathizing with his victims as real human beings during the attack, which presupposes that he knew that his actions were wrongful.

Jurors ultimately convicted Holmes of capital murder. As a juror, how would you have voted? Did Holmes know that his actions were wrong or did he simply not care?

defendant has a documented history of mental illness. However, the jury weighed the conflicting testimony of experts and Sanders's history of mental illness against his seemingly calculated flight. After being properly instructed regarding the burden of proving whether or not Sanders was legally sane, the jury found him guilty. To do so, the jury necessarily had to make a judgment concerning one of the most difficult questions of fact—legal sanity—with which a jury may be presented. We are in no position to make a better judgment than the jurors, so we cannot say that Sanders's conviction was against the overwhelming weight of the evidence. This issue is without merit. . . .

NOTES & QUESTIONS ON THE COGNITIVE TEST

The jury's verdict.   The court in *Sanders* goes to great lengths to find a coherent explanation for the jury's decision. The judges suggest that the jury might have concluded that the defendant was delusional for the first murder but then sane during the second crime, which was committed for more rational reasons (such as covering up the first crime). Do you buy this explanation? What other explanations might there be for the jury's decision? Is it possible that this was a compromise verdict meant to resolve an intractable dispute among the jurors over Sanders's insanity plea? In the end, do you believe that the jury's verdict was internally coherent? Did the decision reveal that the jurors misunderstood the nature of the *M'Naghten* test?

2. Irresistible Impulse Test

Over time, the cognitive test was criticized for being too narrow. What of criminals who know they are doing something wrong but cannot control their behavior? In the following case, the defendant was a police officer who understood the nature of his actions and their wrongfulness. But he was also severely disturbed. Should he be acquitted?

Pollard v. United States
U.S. Court of Appeals for the Sixth Circuit
282 F.2d 450 (1960)

McALLISTER, C.J.

Marmion Pollard, in April 1956, had been for several years a member of the Detroit Police Department. . . . In April 1956, while he was on police duty, his wife and small daughter were brutally murdered in their home by a drunken neighbor. After the murder, Pollard's three other children, all sons, continued to live with him and his mother-in-law, who cared for the children and the home. Gradually, Pollard became the victim of chronic depression or melancholia, appearing generally, to be overcome with fatigue, bursting into tears and crying and sobbing for considerable periods, and repeatedly threatening to commit suicide with his police gun. He continued his duties with the Police Department, but, to his fellow officers, he seemed always overcome by fatigue. Where he had appeared gay, smiling, and good humored, before the murder, he afterward was silent, morose, and expressionless, appearing for long periods not to hear questions addressed to him. His brother-in-law on one occasion prevented him from deliberately running onto a thruway, where he probably would have been killed by swiftmoving cars. On another occasion, his brother-in-law found him lying on the floor in his home, sobbing; his body was so limp he could hardly be lifted to the bed. After many of these incidents, Pollard seemed to recover and would become suddenly cheerful with no memory of what had happened.

A little more than two years after the murder of his wife and daughter, Pollard remarried, on May 22, 1958. On the day before this marriage, Pollard attempted to hold up a branch of the Detroit Bank & Trust Company about eleven o'clock in the morning. With a gun, he threatened the teller, ordering her to fill up a paper bag with money. The teller did so and handed the bag to Pollard, who ordered a bank official to accompany him to the exit. As they approached the door, the official suddenly threw his arms around Pollard, who then dropped the bag of money and ran out of the building.

On the afternoon of the same day, about 4:00 P.M., Pollard attempted to hold up a branch of the Bank of the Commonwealth. He walked to a railing behind which a bank employee was sitting and pointing his gun at him, told him to sit quietly. The employee, however, raised an alarm and Pollard ran out of the bank. After having held up two banks in one day and failed in the robberies, Pollard then planned on the same afternoon to rob a third bank, but finally decided not to do so when, as he said, he found it had too much window area, and felt that the chance of his being caught was too great. However, a few days later, on June 3, 1958, he entered another bank to attempt a hold-up. He went to an enclosure behind which two employees were sitting and with his gun, ordered one of them to come from behind the railing. As the employee arose, Pollard thought that she might have pushed an alarm button. He then ordered her to accompany him out of the bank, telling her to walk ahead of him. When they got outside, Pollard ran across an empty lot to his car and escaped. A week later, Pollard attempted to hold up a grocery market, but when the proprietor screamed, Pollard ran out of the building, leaving his car in the rear of the market. The car was placed under police surveillance, and later, when Pollard, who had changed to his police uniform, came to get the car, he was arrested by detectives of the Detroit Police Department. After his arrest, Pollard seemed greatly relieved, and confessed to eleven other attempted robberies, or robberies. . . .

Prior to being committed for examination and study to the United States Medical Center, appellant, as above stated, was examined by three psychiatrists: Dr. Milton R. Palmer, Dr. Alfred C. LaBine, and Dr. Herbert Alfred Raskin.

Dr. Milton R. Palmer, a psychiatrist, called on behalf of appellant, supported the defense that Pollard at the time of the conduct charged against him, was suffering from a disassociative reaction and that he acted under the compulsion of an irresistible impulse. In arriving at his conclusion, Dr. Palmer had been assisted by a psychiatric team, including Dr. Papano, a psychologist of the Veterans Administration, and Mr. Duncan, a psychiatric social worker of the Mental Hygiene Clinic of the Veterans Administration.

The government, then, voluntarily, and in a most commendable effort to submit to the District Court all evidence that it had obtained bearing upon appellant's claimed irresistible impulse—even contrary to its own theory and contentions—introduced the testimony of two experts in psychiatry, Dr. Alfred C. LaBine and Dr. Alfred Raskin. They agreed with appellant's witness, Dr. Palmer, and testified that, in their opinion, appellant had acted under an irresistible impulse when he attempted the robbery of the banks. . . .

In this case, therefore, it appears that six psychiatrists, a psychologist, a psychiatric social worker, and the Chief Medical Officer of the Medical Center for Federal Prisoners, including all of the expert witnesses, both for the government and appellant, were either of the opinion that appellant acted under an irresistible impulse when he attempted to rob the three banks, or that all the evidence available to them tended to show this fact. No expert, or non-expert testimony was submitted in opposition.

The District Court, after the filing of the Report of the United States Medical Center for Federal Prisoners with regard to Pollard's mental condition, filed its opinion in which it found, contrary to the opinions of the expert psychiatrists, that appellant did not act under an irresistible impulse and, accordingly, found him guilty of the crimes charged. The court based its conclusions on the testimony of lay witnesses, on certain statements taken from the testimony of the experts or official reports of the United States Medical Center, and on its own personal judgment of the matter. The court concluded that it had no reasonable doubt of appellant's guilt.

It is submitted by the government that whether appellant acted as a result of an irresistible impulse was a question of fact which was determinable by the trier of the facts—in this case, by the District Court, sitting without a jury, and that it properly found appellant guilty.

Appellant's counsel contends that the government did not prove appellant guilty beyond a reasonable doubt; and, further, that there was no evidence to sustain the trial court's finding that appellant was guilty beyond a reasonable doubt. . . .

In the instant case, the psychiatric witnesses had unanimously agreed that Pollard suffered from severe feelings of depression and guilt; that, in their opinion, he had an irresistible impulse to commit criminal acts; an unconscious desire to be apprehended and punished; and that he geared his behavior to the accomplishment of this end. The court, however, stated that his entire pattern of conduct during the period of his criminal activities militated against this conclusion, and that his conscious desire not to be apprehended and punished was demonstrably greater than his unconscious desire to the contrary. Without drawing any conclusions from the foregoing as to whether appellant's conscious or unconscious desires were the stronger, it is to be said that acts that appear rational are not to be taken by the factfinder as evidence of sanity, where all of the other evidence in the case is proof of a defendant's mental unsoundness.

It may here be mentioned, however, that in the Report of the Neuropsychiatric Staff Conference of the Medical Center for Federal Prisoners, it was pointed out that the attempted robberies by Pollard were bizarre and ineffectively planned and executed; that when he tried to leave one bank, he ordered a bank official to follow behind him instead of ahead of him, which resulted in his being caught from behind and barely escaping after a struggle, during which he dropped the paper bag of money he had collected; that on the various occasions of his attempted robberies, he would suddenly enter a bank that he had never seen before, without prior knowledge of the arrangement of the premises, or of the personnel. Taken in consideration with all of the other factors, such conduct, on the part of a highly intelligent police officer with a knowledge of how crimes are committed, has about it nothing of sanity.

It is true, as the government suggests, that the Report of the Neuropsychiatric Staff Conference of the Medical Center was an opinion that Pollard, during the period in question, may have been governed by unconscious drives which made it impossible for him to adhere to the right, and that the staff "acknowledges (its) inability either to marshall sufficient objective facts or formulate a completely satisfactory theory on which to base a solid opinion as to (Pollard's) responsibility during the period in question." However, the staff did conclude that "the weight of objective historical evidence available to us tends to support the conclusion of previous examiners" and that the current findings indicated that during the period of the attempted robberies "a disassociative state may have existed and that his actions may not have been consciously activated."

In its opinion, the trial court alluded to the testimony of lay witnesses, and stated that Pollard's conduct throughout the period following the murder of his wife and child by a drunken neighbor did not cause any concern among his colleagues, and that, in their opinion, he was sane; that his present wife married him a considerable time after the murders and that "It is a permissible inference that (his) conduct relative to his mental condition, as related by her, did not suggest to her that the defendant was insane."

As to Pollard's conduct, the record, stated in brief compass in this regard, discloses the following:

Before the murders of his wife and child, Pollard, as previously stated, was well adjusted, intelligent, of an active nature, pleasing personality, and happy disposition, with an excellent rating as a police officer, and a good husband and father, who had never been in any trouble. After the murders, Pollard became chronically depressed and continually seemed to be overcome by fatigue. He would repeatedly stare off into space and commence crying and would continue crying for as long as twenty minutes at a time. After such unusual conduct, including threats that he would commit suicide, he would wake up the next morning and remember nothing of such conduct.

His fellow officers in the Police Department noticed various changes about him after the death of his wife. They weren't abrupt changes. Sometimes a week would pass and he would seem all right; but then he would do something out of the ordinary. In the course of his duties as a policeman, on one day he would insist upon enforcing the law and issue loitering tickets for violation of ordinances, and the next day, he would express an opinion that he did not see anything wrong with such conduct. When he would be asked a question by his fellow policemen, while driving with them in a scout car, he would sometimes be silent for about ten minutes, and then answer the question as though he had just been asked. Sometimes when he came to work with a fellow officer, they might talk to each other normally. Other times he would sit for two hours at a time and say nothing. This was a change from his prior general demeanor, when he had always been very lively and talkative. Once when he drove the scout car, he constantly beat on the steering wheel with his fist for approximately half an hour. When, on this occasion, he was asked if anything was wrong, he acted as though he didn't know he was doing it, and would continue. His wife would call Pollard's fellow officers and ask if they couldn't possibly come over because Pollard was acting unusual and she was afraid; that he was very strange and "messing around" with a gun, and that she was afraid he would shoot her. When he responded to roll call at police headquarters, he was almost always late, contrary to his prior promptitude; he would come in and appear to be sleepy all of the time. He would act lifeless and the police officers, as one of them stated, all started worrying about him.

Shortly before he remarried, on occasion, he would attend a party and appear jovial, eating, dancing, and talking, and then would quickly change. He would suddenly sit down, stop dancing, refrain from eating with the others, and become very quiet. While, at all times, he regarded his present wife with affection, nevertheless, on one of the occasions mentioned, when he was at home with her, he kept holding his gun with the barrel pointed toward himself; and his wife became afraid of him, but kept talking to him, and trying to distract him by asking him to go to a party; but he started crying until tears streamed down his cheeks. Suddenly, in fear, his wife ran out of the house and called the police station, asking that his friends there come over. His fellow officers soon arrived and took his gun away from him, and had him go to the police station with them. He afterward called his wife from the station, but did not mention the incident and talked as though nothing had happened. At that time, he was in a jovial frame of mind, and, with his partner on the police force, returned home where they all conversed pleasantly for some time about things in general. His wife underwent several similar experiences. Often he appeared not to hear people talking to him. The officers all knew something was wrong; but one of them stated that they couldn't report every person that acts out of the ordinary.

From all of the evidence of the lay witnesses, which we have here summarized, it cannot be affirmatively concluded that Pollard was sane. Obviously, as a result of the murder of his wife and child while he was absent from his home, he was suffering from some grave disorder, and that disorder was, in the opinion of all the psychiatric and medical experts, a disassociative reaction resulting in Pollard's commission of the acts charged because of an irresistible impulse.

At the conclusion of the case and after the rendition of the court's opinion, but prior to certain slight amendments the court announced it would make therein, defense counsel submitted that the evidence of the three psychiatrists who testified in court was testimony offered by the best available scientific minds, and that, further, the official report of the psychiatrists of the United States Medical Center for Federal Prisoners, while not as conclusive as the testimony of the three psychiatric witnesses, would, in itself, raise a reasonable doubt as to appellant's responsibility for his acts. In reply, the trial judge stated that he had no reasonable doubt as to appellant's responsibility for his acts, and that, even if there were additional psychiatrists testifying for appellant, such evidence would not cause him to change his mind; that appellant knew what he was doing; that he knew right from wrong; that many wrongdoers, responsible for their conduct, commonly pleaded irresistible impulse; that simply because a man would not resist doing something he knew was wrong, was no excuse for his misdeeds; and that appellant was not suffering from that kind of diseased mind which excused and exculpated him from his criminal acts.

However, certain distinctions have been drawn by courts in applying the rule of irresistible impulse. While anger, greed, and passion are said, in ordinary parlance, to result in acts because of desires that have become irresistible, this is not, in law, the "irresistible impulse" that results from a mental defect or mental disease. Further, it is held that "emotional insanity," which is an unbridled passion lasting just long enough to enable the act complained of to be done, and then subsiding, does not relieve the accused of accountability, even in those jurisdictions where the doctrine of irresistible impulse, arising out of a mental defect, is recognized. . . .

The general rule is stated in 14 Am. Jur. 793: "Irresistible impulse as recognized by the courts is an impulse induced by, and growing out of, some mental disease affecting the volitive, as distinguished from the perceptive, powers, so that the person afflicted, while able to understand the nature and consequences of the act charged against him and to perceive that it is wrong, is unable, because of such mental disease, to resist the impulse to do it. It is to be distinguished from mere passion or overwhelming emotion not growing out of, and connected with, a disease of the mind. Frenzy arising solely from the passion of anger and jealousy, regardless of how furious, is not insanity." . . .

It is our conclusion from the record in this case that in the light of the unanimous testimony of the government's medical experts in psychiatry and appellant's expert witness, as well as the uncontradicted evidence of the lay witnesses, the presumption of sanity was overcome, and the government failed to sustain its burden of proving that appellant did not suffer from mental illness consequent upon the unprovoked murder of his wife and child while he was absent on police duty; and that it failed to prove that appellant did not act under irresistible impulse as a result of such mental illness. . . .

NOTES & QUESTIONS ON IRRESISTIBLE IMPULSES

1. *The foundation of the volitional test.*   Do you agree with the underlying principle of the volitional test? Even if you assume that Pollard could not control his behavior, does that mean he should be acquitted by reason of insanity? What if this argument is taken to its logical conclusion? Many individuals believe that some sex criminals are hopeless recidivists who cannot be reformed; some even believe that they are chemically driven to engage in their criminal sex acts. If this claim were supported by scientific evidence, would this entail that the worst sex offenders should all be acquitted by reason of insanity? Some observers find this outcome profoundly disturbing. But others would embrace it, as

long as it was combined with a system of prospective civil confinement for dangerous sex offenders. In other words, although the sex offender would be found not guilty by virtue of his irresistible impulses, he would still go into custody for continuous treatment of his disorder. For a discussion of these issues, see Katherine P. Blakely, *The Indefinite Civil Commitment of Dangerous Sex Offenders Is an Appropriate Legal Compromise Between Mad and Bad—A Study of Minnesota's Sexual Psychopathic Personality Statute*, 10 Notre Dame J.L. Ethics & Pub. Pol'y 227 (1996).

2. *The role of experts.* In *Pollard*, the trial judge substituted his own judgment for the judgment of the mental health professionals, whose opinions were all consistent with each other: Pollard could not control his behavior. The appeals court overturned the judge's decision because it was unsupported by any expert testimony. In essence, the appeals court criticized the trial judge for engaging in his own armchair psychiatry without any professional training. What lessons do you draw from this outcome? In practice, each side cannot rely on the judge simply rejecting the other side's psychiatric expert. To win, each side must find and present its own expert witness who will provide a scientific foundation for its legal arguments. In *Pollard*, the prosecution failed to do this, and one wonders why the federal prosecutors did not simply negotiate an insanity plea beforehand. For more on the role of psychiatric experts in criminal trials, see Winfred Overholser, *Psychiatric Expert Testimony in Criminal Cases Since* McNaghten—A Review, 42 J. Crim. L. Criminology & Police Sci. 283 (1951-1952); Christopher Slobogin, *Psychiatric Evidence in Criminal Trials: To Junk or Not to Junk?*, 40 Wm. & Mary L. Rev. 1 (1998). Do courts defer too much to psychiatric experts in making legal and moral assessments regarding culpability?

3. *The* Durham *product test.* In 1954, some courts decided to reform the legal standard for insanity by giving psychiatric testimony an even greater role in the legal determination. The test was first articulated by the U.S. Court of Appeals for the D.C. Circuit in *Durham v. United States*, 214 F.2d 862 (1954), which stated that "an accused is not criminally responsible if his unlawful act was the product of mental disease or mental defect." The goal of the product test (also known as the *Durham* test) was to avoid what some believed was the inevitable difficulty of the *M'Naghten* analysis: determining whether the defendant knew right from wrong. In contrast, the product test sidesteps that entire inquiry of wrongfulness and instead asks whether the defendant's behavior was caused by (i.e., the "product" of) the mental disease or defect. In theory, this would lead to a streamlined inquiry that would place psychiatric testimony at the heart of the trial without any confusing reference to moral norms. However, in practice the product test was criticized for being difficult to apply, in part because the concept of "productivity" was itself ambiguous. An individual human action has all sorts of complex psychological factors and

causes. But in applying the product test, one needs to know how much influence the mental disease needs to have on the resulting action to meet the standard. In *Carter v. United States*, 252 F.2d 608, 615-16 (D.C. Cir. 1957), the D.C. Circuit clarified that the product test requires "a reasonable inference that the act would not have been committed if the person had not been suffering from the disease." But in *Washington v. United States*, 390 F.2d 444 (D.C. Cir. 1967), the appeals court finally abandoned its experiment with the product test, in part because it relied too much on conclusory psychiatric labels from experts without reference to the deeper moral issue of the defendant's culpability. In other words, if psychiatry had a name for the mental defect, the defendant was acquitted; if psychiatry did not recognize the abnormality, the defendant was found guilty. In one case, the judges complained:

> The rule was devised to facilitate the giving of testimony by medical experts in the context of a legal rule, with the jury called upon to reach a composite conclusion that had medical, legal and moral components. However the pristine statement of the *Durham* rule opened the door to "trial by label." *Durham* did distinguish between "disease," as used "in the sense of a condition which is considered capable of either improving or deteriorating," and "defect," as referring to a condition not capable of such change "and which may be either congenital or the result of injury, or the residual effect of a physical or mental disease." But the court failed to explicate what abnormality of mind was an essential ingredient of these concepts. In the absence of a definition of "mental disease or defect," medical experts attached to them the meanings which would naturally occur to them—medical meanings—and gave testimony accordingly. The problem was dramatically highlighted by the weekend flip-flop case, *In re Rosenfield*, 157 F. Supp. 18 (D.D.C. 1957). The petitioner was described as a sociopath. A St. Elizabeths psychiatrist testified that a person with a sociopathic personality was not suffering from a mental disease. That was Friday afternoon. On Monday morning, through a policy change at St. Elizabeths Hospital, it was determined as an administrative matter that the state of a psychopathic or sociopathic personality did constitute a mental disease.

United States v. Brawner, 471 F.2d 969 (D.C. Cir. 1972). For a discussion, see Abe Krash, *The Durham Rule and Judicial Administration of the Insanity Defense in the District of Columbia*, 70 Yale L.J. 905, 906 (1961).

3. The Model Penal Code Substantial Capacity Test

The Model Penal Code represented a major effort to reform the insanity defense in the United States. The MPC "substantial capacity" test was designed to respond to the failures of the *M'Naghten*, irresistible impulse, and product tests. The following case explores the net positives of the MPC formulation in relation to prior standards.

United States v. Freeman
U.S. Court of Appeals for the Second Circuit
357 F.2d 606 (1966)

KAUFMAN, J.

IV

Efforts to supplement or replace the *M'Naghten* Rules with a more meaningful and workable test have persisted for generations, with varying degrees of success. Perhaps the first to receive judicial approval, however, was more an added fillip to *M'Naghten* than a true substitute: the doctrine which permits acquittal on grounds of lack of responsibility when a defendant is found to have been driven by an "irresistible impulse" to commit his offense. In one form or another, the "irresistible impulse" test has become encrusted on the law of several jurisdictions, including the District Courts of this Circuit, and is now a familiar part of the vocabulary of millions since it was successfully invoked by the defendant of Robert Travers' celebrated novel and motion picture, "Anatomy of a Murder."

As it has commonly been employed, however, we find the "irresistible impulse" test to be inherently inadequate and unsatisfactory. Psychiatrists have long questioned whether "irresistible impulses" actually exist; the more basic legal objection to the term "irresistible impulse" is that it is too narrow and carries the misleading implication that a crime impulsively committed must have been perpetrated in a sudden and explosive fit. Thus, the "irresistible impulse" test is unduly restrictive because it excludes the far more numerous instances of crimes committed after excessive brooding and melancholy by one who is unable to resist sustained psychic compulsion or to make any real attempt to control his conduct. In seeking one isolated and indefinite cause for every act, moreover, the test is unhappily evocative of the notions which underlay *M'Naghten*—unfortunate assumptions that the problem can be viewed in black and white absolutes and in crystal-clear causative terms.

In so many instances the criminal act may be the reverse of impulsive; it may be coolly and carefully prepared yet nevertheless the result of a diseased mind. The "irresistible impulse" test is therefore little more than a gloss on *M'Naghten*, rather than a fundamentally new approach to the problem of criminal responsibility. It is, as one professor explained, "a relatively unobnoxious attempt to improve upon *M'Naghten*."

With the exception of New Hampshire, American courts waited until 1954 and Judge Bazelon's opinion for the District of Columbia Circuit in *Durham v. United States*, for legal recognition that disease or defect of the mind may impair the whole mind and not a subdivided portion of it. The *Durham* court swept away the intellectual debris of a century and articulated a test which was as simple in its formulation as its sources were complex. A defendant is not criminally responsible, wrote Judge Bazelon, "if his unlawful act was the product of mental disease or mental defect."

The advantages of *Durham* were apparent and its arrival was widely hailed. The new test entirely eliminated the "right-wrong" dichotomy, and hence interred the overriding emphasis on the cognitive element of the personality which had for so long plagued *M'Naghten*. The fetters upon expert testimony were removed and psychiatrists were permitted and indeed encouraged to provide all relevant medical information for the common sense application of judge or jury.

Finally, *Durham* ended to a large degree the "professional perjury" decried by psychiatrists—the "juggling" of legal standards made inevitable by *M'Naghten* and rightly deplored by Justice Frankfurter. Too often, the unrealistic dogma of *M'Naghten* had compelled expert witnesses to "stretch" its requirements to "hard cases"; sympathetic to the plight of a defendant who was not, in fairness, responsible for his conduct, psychiatrists had found it necessary to testify that the accused did not know his act was "wrong" even when the defendant's words belied this conclusion. In its frank and express recognition that criminality resulting from mental disease or defect should not bring forth penal sanctions, *Durham* brought an end to this all too-frequent practice of "winking" at legal requirements, a practice which had contributed little to the self-respect and integrity of either medicine or the law.

In the aftermath of *Durham*, however, many students of the law recognized that the new rule, despite its many advantages, also possessed serious deficiencies. It has been suggested, for example, that *Durham*'s insistence that an offense be the "product" of a mental disease or defect raised near-impossible problems of causation, closely resembling those encountered by the *M'Naghten* and irresistible impulse tests.

The most significant criticism of *Durham*, however, is that it fails to give the fact-finder any standard by which to measure the competency of the accused. As a result, psychiatrists when testifying that a defendant suffered from a "mental disease or defect" in effect usurped the jury's function. This problem was strikingly illustrated in 1957, when a staff conference at Washington's St. Elizabeth's Hospital reversed its previous determination and reclassified "psychopathic personality" as a "mental disease." Because this single hospital provides most of the psychiatric witnesses in the District of Columbia courts, juries were abruptly informed that certain defendants who had previously been considered responsible were now to be acquitted. It seems clear that a test which permits all to stand or fall upon the labels or classifications employed by testifying psychiatrists hardly affords the court the opportunity to perform its function of rendering an independent legal and social judgment.

V

In 1953, a year before *Durham*, the American Law Institute commenced an exhaustive study of criminal conduct including the problem of criminal responsibility. In the ensuing months and years, under the scholarly direction of Professors Herbert Wechsler of Columbia University, its Chief Reporter, and Louis B. Schwartz of the University of Pennsylvania, Co-Reporter, the leading legal and medical minds of the country applied themselves to the task. Gradually and painstakingly a new definition of criminal responsibility began taking shape as Section 4.01 of the Model Penal Code was evolved. Before its penultimate articulation, drafts and redrafts of the section were submitted to and revised by an advisory committee comprised of distinguished judges, lawyers, psychiatrists, and penologists. After committee approval was obtained, successive drafts were debated and considered by the Council, and later by the full membership, of the Institute. Nine long years of research, exploration and consideration culminated in the definitive version of Section 4.01, which was finally adopted by the Institute in 1962.

Section 4.01 provides that "A person is not responsible for criminal conduct if at the time of such conduct as a result of mental disease or defect he lacks substantial capacity either to appreciate the wrongfulness of his conduct or to conform his conduct to the requirements of law." For reasons which will be more fully set forth, we believe this test to be the soundest yet formulated and we accordingly adopt it as the standard of criminal responsibility in the Courts of this Circuit.

The gravamen of the objections to the *M'Naghten* Rules is that they are not in harmony with modern medical science which, as we have said, is opposed to any concept which divides the mind into separate compartments—the intellect, the emotions and the will. The Model Penal Code formulation views the mind as a unified entity and recognizes that mental disease or defect may impair its functioning in numerous ways. The rule, moreover, reflects awareness that from the perspective of psychiatry absolutes are ephemeral and gradations are inevitable. By employing the telling word "substantial" to modify "incapacity," the rule emphasizes that "any" incapacity is not sufficient to justify avoidance of criminal responsibility but that "total" incapacity is also unnecessary. The choice of the word "appreciate," rather than "know" in the first branch of the test also is significant; mere intellectual awareness that conduct is wrongful, when divorced from appreciation or understanding of the moral or legal import of behavior, can have little significance.

While permitting the utilization of meaningful psychiatric testimony, the American Law Institute formulation, we believe, is free of many of the defects which accompanied *Durham*. Although it eschews rigid classification, the Section is couched in sufficiently precise terms to provide the jury with a workable standard when the judge charges in terms comprehensible to laymen. Expert testimony, in short, will be admissible whenever relevant but always as expert testimony—and not as moral or legal pronouncement. Relieved of their burden of divining precise causal relationships, the judge or jury can concentrate upon the ultimate decisions which are properly theirs, fully informed as to the facts.

Under the American Law Institute formulation, an inquiry based on meaningful psychological concepts can be pursued. The most modern psychiatric insights will be available, but, even more importantly, the legal focus will be sharper and clearer. The twin branches of the test, significantly phrased in the alternative, will remove from the pale of criminal sanctions precisely those who are in no meaningful sense responsible for their actions.

We do not delude ourselves in the belief that the American Law Institute test is perfect. Perfection is unattainable when we are dealing with a fluid and evolving science. Furthermore, we are aware that the Courts of Appeal for the District of Columbia, Third and Tenth Circuits have not adopted the American Law Institute test haec verba, but have employed their own language approaching the objectives of the Model Penal Code formulation. As an illustration, in the scholarly opinion of Chief Judge Biggs in *United States v. Currens*, the Third Circuit adopted the second branch of the Model Penal Code test—substantial capacity to conform one's conduct to the requirements of the law—but deleted the first, referring to "appreciation" of wrongfulness. While we can understand that Court's reluctance to stress the cognitive element of the personality in light of *M'Naghten*'s emphasis on that aspect, we cannot accept its formulation; the gravamen of psychiatric objections to the *M'Naghten* Rules, as we have seen, was not that they looked to the cognitive feature of the personality, undeniably a significant aspect of the total man, but that they looked to this element exclusively. . . .

We believe, in sum, that the American Law Institute test—which makes no pretension at being the ultimate in faultless definition—is an infinite improvement over the *M'Naghten* Rules, even when, as had been the practice in the courts of this Circuit, those Rules are supplemented by the "irresistible impulse" doctrine. All legal definitions involve elements of abstraction and approximation which are difficult to apply in marginal cases. The impossibility of guaranteeing that a new rule will always be infallible cannot justify continued adherence to an outmoded standard, sorely at variance with enlightened medical and legal scholarship. No one would suggest that a physician expert called to state an opinion with respect to a litigant's orthopedic or neurological condition should be restricted in his reply to a single isolated cause to the exclusion of other relevant and important findings and conclusions—much less to concepts developed at the outset of Victoria's reign. In a criminal trial, when life and liberty hang in the balance, such arbitrary limitations on expert and jury are all the less defensible.

The genius of the common law has been its responsiveness to changing times, its ability to reflect developing moral and social values. Drawing upon the past, the law must serve—and traditionally has served—the needs of the present. In the past century, psychiatry has evolved from tentative, hesitant gropings in the dark of human ignorance to a recognized and important branch of modern medicine. The outrage of a frightened Queen has for too long caused us to forego the expert guidance that modern psychiatry is able to provide. . . .

NOTES & QUESTIONS ON SUBSTANTIAL CAPACITY

1. *The rationale for the substantial capacity test.* The Model Penal Code's greatest innovation in reforming the insanity defense was adopting the substantial capacity standard. According to the MPC Commentaries, "the adoption of the standard of substantial capacity may well be the Code's most significant alteration of the prevailing tests. It was recognized, of course, that 'substantial' is an open-ended concept, but its quantitative connotation was believed to be sufficiently precise for purposes of practical administration. The law is full of instances in which courts and juries are explicitly authorized to confront an issue of degree. Such an approach was deemed to be no less essential and appropriate in dealing with this issue than in dealing with the questions of recklessness and negligence." In other words, ultimately it is up to the jury to decide *how much* psychological impairment the defendant was suffering from and what moral significance it had. Does this seem like an improvement over *M'Naghten*?

2. *The retreat from substantial capacity.* Many jurisdictions revised their insanity defense and adopted the MPC substantial capacity formulation. However, these reforms were short-lived in many jurisdictions. In 1981, President Ronald Reagan was shot by John Hinckley Jr., who claimed that he tried to assassinate Reagan to impress the actress Jodie Foster. Hinckley was found not guilty by reason of insanity and committed to a mental institution. The acquittal generated public dissatisfaction with the insanity defense and state legislatures soon rushed to make it more difficult for defendants to use the insanity defense. Some of the changes were procedural, such as shifting the burden of persuasion to the defendant to demonstrate by a preponderance of the evidence that he was insane, instead of the prior rule that required that the prosecution prove beyond a reasonable doubt that the defendant was sane. (The Supreme Court held in *Leland v. Oregon*, 343 U.S. 790 (1952), that burden-shifting statutes

were constitutional.) A few jurisdictions changed the substantive standard for legal insanity to ensure fewer acquittals. The practical effect of these reforms was to return to the old *M'Naghten* standard in some jurisdictions. For example, the federal Insanity Defense Reform Act of 1984 re-instituted the following standard for federal criminal cases: "It is an affirmative defense to a prosecution under any federal statute that, at the time of the commission of the acts constituting the offense, the defendant as a result of a severe mental disease or defect, was unable to appreciate the nature and quality or the wrongfulness of his acts. Mental disease or defect does not otherwise constitute a defense." 18 U.S.C. § 17. The federal provision also requires the defendant to prove insanity by "clear and convincing evidence."

John Hinckley Jr.

4. The Definition of Wrongfulness

The Model Penal Code represented a major effort to reform the insanity defense in the United States. In addition to introducing the "substantial capacity" test, the MPC also gave states the option of defining the cognitive test with reference to the defendant's understanding of moral wrongfulness or legal wrongfulness. The following case illustrates the difference between the legal and moral conceptions of wrongfulness and the difficulties inherent in defining them.

State v. Crenshaw

Supreme Court of Washington
98 Wash. 2d 789 (1983)

BRACHTENBACH, J.

Rodney Crenshaw was convicted by a jury of first degree murder. Finding that the trial court committed no reversible error, we affirm the conviction.

Petitioner Rodney Crenshaw pleaded not guilty and not guilty by reason of insanity to the charge of first degree murder of his wife, Karen Crenshaw. A jury found him guilty. . . .

Before turning to the legal issues, the facts of the case must be recounted. While defendant and his wife were on their honeymoon in Canada, petitioner was deported as a result of his participation in a brawl. He secured a motel room in Blaine, Washington and waited for his wife to join him. When she arrived 2 days later, he immediately thought she had been unfaithful—he sensed "it wasn't the same Karen . . . she'd been with someone else."

Petitioner did not mention his suspicions to his wife, instead he took her to the motel room and beat her unconscious. He then went to a nearby store, stole a knife, and returned to stab his wife 24 times, inflicting a fatal wound. He left again, drove to a nearby farm where he had been employed and borrowed an ax. Upon returning to the motel room, he decapitated his wife with such force that the ax marks cut into the concrete floor under the carpet and splattered blood throughout the room.

Petitioner then proceeded to conceal his actions. He placed the body in a blanket, the head in a pillowcase, and put both in his wife's car. Next, he went to a service station, borrowed a bucket and sponge, and cleaned the room of blood and fingerprints. Before leaving, petitioner also spoke with the motel manager about a phone bill, then chatted with him for awhile over a beer.

When Crenshaw left the motel he drove to a remote area 25 miles away where he hid the two parts of the body in thick brush. He then fled, driving to the Hoquiam area, about 200 miles from the scene of the crime. There he picked up two hitchhikers, told them of his crime, and enlisted their aid in disposing of his wife's car in a river. The hitchhikers contacted the police and Crenshaw was apprehended shortly thereafter. He voluntarily confessed to the crime.

The defense of not guilty by reason of insanity was a major issue at trial. Crenshaw testified that he followed the Moscovite religious faith, and that it would be improper for a Moscovite not to kill his wife if she committed adultery. Crenshaw also has a history of mental problems, for which he has been hospitalized in the past. The jury, however, rejected petitioner's insanity defense, and found him guilty of murder in the first degree.

Insanity is an affirmative defense the defendant must establish by a preponderance of the evidence. Sanity is presumed, even with a history of prior institutional commitments from which the individual was released upon sufficient recovery.

The insanity defense is not available to all who are mentally deficient or deranged; legal insanity has a different meaning and a different purpose than the concept of medical insanity. A verdict of not guilty by reason of insanity completely absolves a defendant of any criminal responsibility. Therefore, "the defense is available only to those persons who have lost contact with reality so completely that they are beyond any of the influences of the criminal law."

Petitioner assigned error to insanity defense instruction 10 which reads . . . "For a defendant to be found not guilty by reason of insanity you must find that, as a result of mental disease or defect, the defendant's mind was affected to such an extent that the defendant was unable to perceive the nature and quality of the acts with which the defendant is charged or was unable to tell right from wrong with reference to the particular acts with which defendant is charged. . . . What is meant by the terms 'right and wrong' refers to knowledge of a person at the time of committing an act that he was acting contrary to the law." Petitioner contends . . . that the trial court erred in defining "right and wrong" as legal right and wrong rather than in the moral sense. . . .

I

The definition of the term "wrong" in the *M'Naghten* test has been considered and disputed by many legal scholars. In Washington, we have not addressed this issue previously.

The confusion arises from apparent inconsistencies in the original *M'Naghten* case. In response to the House of Lords' first question, the justices replied that if an accused knew he was acting contrary to law but acted under a partial insane delusion that he was redressing or revenging some supposed grievance or injury, or producing some supposed public benefit, "he is nevertheless punishable . . . if he knew at the time of committing such crime that he was acting *contrary to law; . . . the law of the land.*" In this answer, the justices appear to approve the legal standard of wrong when there is evidence that the accused knew he was acting contrary to the law.

This has been characterized as inconsistent with the justices' response to the second and third questions, regarding how a jury should be instructed on the insanity defense:

> If the question were to be put [to a jury] as to the knowledge of the accused solely and exclusively with reference to the law of the land, it might tend to confound the jury, by inducing them to believe that an actual knowledge of the law of the land was essential in order to lead to a conviction; whereas the law is administered upon the principle that every one must be taken conclusively to know it, without proof that he does know it. If the accused was conscious that the act was one which he ought not to do, and if that act was at the same time contrary to the law of the land, he is punishable; and the usual course therefore has been to leave the question to the jury, whether the party accused had a sufficient degree of reason to know that he was doing an act that was wrong: and this course we think is correct, accompanied with such observations and explanations as the circumstances of each particular case may require.

This response appears to require both that the accused be "conscious that the act was one which he ought not to do" and that the act be "contrary to the law."

A close examination of these answers, however, shows they are reconcilable in the context of this case. First, the similarities between the hypothetical in the first question and Crenshaw's situation should afford that answer great weight. If, arguendo, Crenshaw was delusional, his delusion was only partial, for it related only to his perceptions of his wife's infidelity. His behavior towards others, i.e., the motel manager and the woman who loaned him the ax, at the time of the killing was normal. Crenshaw also "knew he was acting contrary to law," as evidenced by his sophisticated attempts to hide his crime and by the expert, psychiatric testimony. Furthermore, he acted with a view "of redressing or revenging [the] supposed grievance" of his wife's infidelity. Thus, the Crenshaw situation fits perfectly into the first hypothetical, and the trial court understandably relied on this passage in approving the challenged instruction.

Second, the answers to the second and third questions certainly do not forbid the additional comment found in instruction 10. The justices expressly provided that the instruction could be "accompanied with such observations and explanations as the circumstances of each particular case may require." In addition, the justices' hesitance to state the question exclusively with reference to the law stemmed from a fear that "it might tend to confound the jury, by inducing them to believe that an actual knowledge of the law of the land was essential in order to lead to a conviction." Therefore, in cases such as this where actual knowledge of the law is not an issue, an instruction in terms of legal wrong would not be improper.

In short, *M'Naghten* supports the propriety of the trial court's instruction in several ways: (1) the justices' answer to the first question was more analogous to Crenshaw's fact situation, and that answer referred only to legal wrong, (2) the *M'Naghten* justices provided that in some cases an additional statement by the court would be acceptable, and (3) in this case there was no danger that the jury would be induced to believe that actual knowledge of the law was essential, since Crenshaw demonstrated that he knew the illegality of his acts. Thus, the facts here permit resolution of the inconsistencies in *M'Naghten* in favor of the "legal" wrong standard.

Such an interpretation is consistent with Washington's strict application of *M'Naghten*. This court's view has been that "when *M'Naghten* is used, all who might possibly be deterred from the commission of criminal acts are included within the sanctions of the criminal law." . . . Given this perspective, the trial court could assume that one who knew the illegality of his act was not necessarily "beyond any of the influences of the criminal law," thus finding support for the statement in instruction 10.

II

Alternatively, the statement in instruction 10 may be approved because, in this case, legal wrong is synonymous with moral wrong. This conclusion is premised on two grounds.

First, in discussing the term "moral" wrong, it is important to note that it is society's morals, and not the individual's morals, that are the standard for judging moral wrong under *M'Naghten*. If wrong meant moral wrong judged by the individual's own conscience, this would seriously undermine the criminal law, for it would allow one who violated the law to be excused from criminal responsibility solely because, in his own conscience, his act was not morally wrong. This principle was emphasized by Justice Cardozo: "The anarchist is not at liberty to break the law because he reasons that all government is wrong. The devotee of a religious cult that enjoins polygamy or human sacrifice as a duty is not thereby relieved from responsibility before the law. . . ."

More recently the Arizona Supreme Court stated:

> We find no authority upholding the defendant's position that one suffering from a mental disease could be declared legally insane if he knew that the act was morally and legally wrong but he personally believed that act right. We believe that this would not be a sound rule, because it approaches the position of exonerating a defendant for his personal beliefs and does not take account of society's determination of defendant's capacity to conform his conduct to the law.

State v. Corley, supra at 243, 495 P.2d 470.

There is evidence on the record that Crenshaw knew his actions were wrong according to society's standards, as well as legally wrong. Dr. Belden testified: "I think Mr. Crenshaw is quite aware on one level that he is in conflict with the law *and with people*. However, this is not something that he personally invests his emotions in."

We conclude that Crenshaw knew his acts were morally wrong from society's viewpoint and also knew his acts were illegal. His personal belief that it was his duty to kill his wife for her alleged infidelity cannot serve to exculpate him from legal responsibility for his acts.

A narrow exception to the societal standard of moral wrong has been drawn for instances wherein a party performs a criminal act, knowing it is morally and legally wrong, but believing, because of a mental defect, that the act is ordained by God: such would be the situation with a mother who kills her infant child to whom she is devotedly attached, believing that God has spoken to her and decreed the act. Although the woman knows that the law and society condemn the act, it would be unrealistic to hold her responsible for the crime, since her free will has been subsumed by her belief in the deific decree.

This exception is not available to Crenshaw, however. Crenshaw argued only that he followed the Moscovite faith and that Moscovites believe it is their duty to kill an unfaithful wife. This is not the same as acting under a deific command. Instead, it is akin to "[t]he devotee of a religious cult that enjoins . . . human sacrifice as a duty [and] is *not* thereby relieved from responsibility before the law." Crenshaw's personal "Moscovite" beliefs are not equivalent to a deific decree and do not relieve him from responsibility for his acts.

Once moral wrong is equated with society's morals, the next step, equating moral and legal wrong, follows logically. The law is, for the most part, an expression of collective morality.

Most cases involving the insanity defense involve serious crimes for which society's moral judgment is identical with the legal standard.

Therefore, a number of scholars have concluded that, as a practical matter, the way in which a court interprets the word wrong will have little effect on the eventual outcome of a case.

As one scholar explained: "[S]ince by far the vast majority of cases in which insanity is pleaded as a defense to criminal prosecutions involves acts which are universally regarded as morally wicked as well as illegal, the hair-splitting distinction between legal and moral wrong need not be given much attention."

Society's morals and legal wrong are interchangeable concepts in the context of this case. Petitioner's crime, killing his wife by stabbing her 24 times then hacking off her head, is clearly contrary to society's morals as well as the law. Therefore by defining wrong in terms of legal wrong, the trial court did not alter the meaning of the *M'Naghten* test. . . .

NOTES & QUESTIONS ON WRONGFULNESS

1. *Moral versus legal wrongfulness.* The key move in *Crenshaw* is how the court defines moral wrongfulness. The defendant complained that the court defined wrongfulness in explicitly legal terms, instead of moral terms. On *that* question, the court basically agreed with Mr. Crenshaw and conceded that most courts have interpreted wrongfulness in explicitly moral terms. (That being said, the court concedes that the original *M'Naghten* case is ambiguous on this point.) However, the court still refuses to grant Crenshaw any relief, because it interprets moral wrongfulness in objective terms. In other words, it matters little whether the defendant subjectively believed that his actions were morally right. Rather, what matters is whether the defendant was aware that society would view his actions as morally wrong. And on that front, his mental illness had no effect on his judgments—he still knew that society would condemn his behavior as wrong. Do you agree with the court's objective interpretation of wrongfulness? As the court concedes, once you interpret moral wrongfulness in objective terms, the gap between moral wrongfulness and legal wrongfulness gets very thin. In most cases, societal morality will dovetail with the requirements of the law. Can you imagine a situation where the two notions might peel apart?

2. *The deific decree exception.* The court in *Crenshaw* notes that there is a widely held exception to the objective interpretation of moral wrongfulness. If a defendant argues that his actions were commanded by God, courts sometimes apply a subjective or individual standard of moral wrongfulness. These "deific decree" cases often involve individuals who say that God commanded them to kill someone. In these cases, the exception entails that a jury should still be entitled to consider the defense, even though the defendant was aware that society might condemn the killing. What is the basis for the deific decree defense? Why should hearing a message from God excuse a crime if the defendant was aware that both society and the law would condemn the action? From the defendant's perspective, what would happen if the defendant defied the deific command? What is the penalty for divine non-compliance? If the penalty is eternal damnation, perhaps the deific decree defense is based on the idea that it would be too much to expect the defendant to live up to the demands of the law—part insanity but also part "deific duress," in a sense. Also, the deific decree defense is a way of smuggling in a limited volitional component in jurisdictions that use a pure cognitive test under *M'Naghten*. For more debate on the defense, see Christopher Hawthorne, *"Deific Decree": The Short, Happy Life of a Pseudo-Doctrine*, 33 Loy. L.A. L. Rev. 1755, 1755-56 (2000) ("Such a narrow exception is rarely invoked, and when it is pleaded, it almost never meets with success.").

PROBLEM CASE

Consider the following facts from *State v. Applin*, 116 Wash. App. 818, 819 (2003): "Blaine Applin was a member of the Gatekeepers, a cult led by Christopher Turgeon. Turgeon was a self-proclaimed prophet who claimed to be in direct communication with God. In 1997, Turgeon learned Child Protective Services was seeking to remove children from some members' homes, so the Gatekeepers moved from Washington to southern California. To finance the move, Turgeon organized various schemes for thefts from local businesses, one of which

Chris Turgeon & Blaine Applin in handcuffs

involved issuing a forged check to Jaime's Transmission in Snohomish. Efforts by Jaime's Transmission to obtain payment eventually led the shop to contact Dan Jess.

"Jess had recently left the Gatekeepers. He was upset at being implicated in the scam, and had a combative phone conversation with Turgeon, during which he accused Turgeon of being a false prophet. That evening, Turgeon called a meeting of the male members of Gatekeepers. He told them he had heard the voice of God, and that God said Dan Jess must be killed.

"Believing he was God's 'chosen vessel' to kill Jess, Applin volunteered to help, telling Turgeon, 'God told me that I must be the one who does it.' He and Turgeon drove to Jess's home in Washington. Applin knocked on Jess's door. When Jess answered, Applin shot him numerous times. Turgeon and Applin returned to California and carried out several more robberies. They were eventually arrested and charged with first degree murder."

Applying the rule from the *Crenshaw* case, what is the correct result? Should Applin's fate be adjudicated under the objective or subjective interpretation of moral wrongfulness? Which standard is more friendly to the defense?

5. Diminished Capacity

Many jurisdictions allow defendants to assert the partial defense of diminished capacity—a doctrine that reduces, but does not eliminate, their responsibility for their behavior. The doctrine is of particular importance for defendants who are mentally ill but do not meet the strict standard for legal insanity. But Arizona's statutory scheme is all-or-nothing. Either the defendant is insane or not—evidence of diminished capacity is not admissible at trial. In the following case, the Supreme Court asks whether the doctrine of diminished capacity is constitutionally required. Based on the Court's prior pronouncements on substantive criminal law, can you guess the answer?

Clark v. Arizona

Supreme Court of the United States
548 U.S. 735 (2006)

SOUTER, J.

The case presents two questions: whether due process prohibits Arizona's use of an insanity test stated solely in terms of the capacity to tell whether an act charged as a crime was right or wrong; and whether Arizona violates due process in restricting consideration of defense evidence of mental illness and incapacity to its bearing on a claim of insanity, thus eliminating its significance directly on the issue of the mental element of the crime charged (known in legal shorthand as the *mens rea,* or guilty mind). We hold that there is no violation of due process in either instance.

I

In the early hours of June 21, 2000, Officer Jeffrey Moritz of the Flagstaff Police responded in uniform to complaints that a pickup truck with loud music blaring was circling a residential block. When he located the truck, the officer turned on the emergency lights and siren of his marked patrol car, which prompted petitioner Eric Clark, the truck's driver (then 17), to pull over. Officer Moritz got out of the patrol car and told Clark to stay where he was. Less than a minute later, Clark shot the officer, who died soon after but not before calling the police dispatcher for help. Clark ran away on foot but was arrested later that day with gunpowder residue on his hands; the gun that killed the officer was found nearby, stuffed into a knit cap.

Clark was charged with first-degree murder . . . for intentionally or knowingly killing a law enforcement officer in the line of duty. In March 2001, Clark was found incompetent to stand trial and was committed to a state hospital for treatment, but two years later the same trial court found his competence restored and ordered him to be tried. Clark waived his right to a jury, and the case was heard by the court.

At trial, Clark did not contest the shooting and death, but relied on his undisputed paranoid schizophrenia at the time of the incident in denying that he had the specific intent to shoot a law enforcement officer or knowledge that he was doing so, as required by the statute. Accordingly, the prosecutor offered circumstantial evidence that Clark knew Officer Moritz was a law enforcement officer. The evidence showed that the officer was in uniform at the time, that he caught up with Clark in a marked police car with emergency lights and siren going, and that Clark acknowledged the symbols of police authority and stopped. The testimony for the prosecution indicated that Clark had intentionally lured an officer to the scene to kill him, having told some people a few weeks before the incident that he wanted to shoot police officers. At the close of the State's evidence, the trial court denied Clark's motion for judgment of acquittal for failure to prove intent to kill a law enforcement officer or knowledge that Officer Moritz was a law enforcement officer.

In presenting the defense case, Clark claimed mental illness, which he sought to introduce for two purposes. First, he raised the affirmative defense of insanity, putting the burden on himself to prove by clear and convincing evidence, that "at the time of the commission of the criminal act [he] was afflicted with a mental disease or defect of such severity that [he] did not know the criminal act was wrong." Second, he aimed to rebut the prosecution's evidence of the requisite *mens rea,* that he had acted intentionally or knowingly to kill a law enforcement officer.

The trial court ruled that Clark could not rely on evidence bearing on insanity to dispute the *mens rea.* The court cited *State v. Mott,* 187 Ariz. 536, 931 P.2d 1046, which "refused to allow psychiatric testimony to negate specific intent," and held that "Arizona does not allow evidence of a defendant's mental disorder short of insanity . . . to negate the *mens rea* element of a crime."

As to his insanity, then, Clark presented testimony from classmates, school officials, and his family describing his increasingly bizarre behavior over the year before the shooting. Witnesses testified, for example, that paranoid delusions led Clark to rig a fishing line with beads and wind chimes at home to alert him to intrusion by invaders, and to keep a bird in his automobile to warn of airborne poison. There was lay and expert testimony that Clark thought Flagstaff was populated with "aliens" (some impersonating government agents), the "aliens" were trying to kill him, and bullets were the only way to stop them. A psychiatrist testified that Clark was suffering from paranoid schizophrenia with delusions about "aliens" when he killed Officer Moritz, and he concluded that Clark was incapable of luring the officer or understanding right from wrong and that he was thus insane at the time of the killing. In rebuttal, a psychiatrist for the State gave his opinion that Clark's paranoid schizophrenia did not keep him from appreciating the wrongfulness of his conduct, as shown by his actions before and after the shooting (such as circling the residential block with music blaring as if to lure the police to intervene, evading the police after the shooting, and hiding the gun).

At the close of the defense case consisting of this evidence bearing on mental illness, the trial court denied Clark's renewed motion for a directed verdict grounded on failure of the prosecution to show that Clark knew the victim was a police officer. The judge then issued a special verdict of first-degree murder, expressly finding that Clark shot and caused the death of Officer Moritz beyond a reasonable doubt and that Clark had not shown that he was insane at the time. The judge noted that though Clark was indisputably afflicted with paranoid schizophrenia at the time of the shooting, the mental illness "did not . . . distort his perception of reality so severely that he did not know his actions were wrong." For this conclusion, the judge expressly relied on "the facts of the crime, the evaluations of the experts, [Clark's] actions and behavior both before and after the shooting, and the observations of those that knew [Clark]." The sentence was life imprisonment without the possibility of release for 25 years. . . .

III

Clark's second claim of a due process violation challenges the rule adopted by the Supreme Court of Arizona in *State v. Mott*, 187 Ariz. 536 (1997). This case ruled on the admissibility of testimony from a psychologist offered to show that the defendant suffered from battered women's syndrome and therefore lacked the capacity to form the *mens rea* of the crime charged against her. . . . The state court held that testimony of a professional psychologist or psychiatrist about a defendant's mental incapacity owing to mental disease or defect was admissible, and could be considered, only for its bearing on an insanity defense; such evidence could not be considered on the element of *mens rea,* that is, what the State must show about a defendant's mental state (such as intent or understanding) when he performed the act charged against him.

Understanding Clark's claim requires attention to the categories of evidence with a potential bearing on *mens rea*. First, there is "observation evidence" in the everyday sense, testimony from those who observed what Clark did and heard what he said; this category would also include testimony that an expert witness might give about Clark's tendency to think in a certain way and his behavioral characteristics. This evidence may support a professional diagnosis of mental disease and in any event is the kind of evidence that can be relevant to show what in fact was on Clark's mind when he fired the gun. Observation evidence in the record covers Clark's behavior at home and with friends, his expressions of belief around the time of the killing that "aliens" were inhabiting the bodies of local people (including government agents), his driving around the neighborhood before the police arrived, and so on. . . .

Second, there is "mental-disease evidence" in the form of opinion testimony that Clark suffered from a mental disease with features described by the witness. As was true here, this evidence characteristically but not always comes from professional psychologists or psychiatrists who testify as expert witnesses and base their opinions in part on examination of a defendant, usually conducted after the events in question. The thrust of this evidence was that, based on factual reports, professional observations, and tests, Clark was psychotic at the time in question, with a condition that fell within the category of schizophrenia.

Third, there is evidence we will refer to as "capacity evidence" about a defendant's capacity for cognition and moral judgment (and ultimately also his capacity to form *mens rea*). This, too, is opinion evidence. Here, as it usually does, this testimony came from the same experts and concentrated on those specific details of the mental condition that make the difference between sanity and insanity under the Arizona definition. In their respective testimony on these details the experts disagreed: the defense expert gave his opinion that the symptoms or effects of the disease in Clark's case included inability to appreciate the nature of his action and to tell that it was wrong, whereas the State's psychiatrist was of the view that Clark was a schizophrenic who was still sufficiently able to appreciate the reality of shooting the officer and to know that it was wrong to do that.

A caveat about these categories is in order. They attempt to identify different kinds of testimony offered in this case in terms of explicit and implicit distinctions made in *Mott*. What we can say about these categories goes to their cores, however, not their margins. Exact limits have thus not been worked out in any Arizona law that has come to our attention, and in this case, neither the courts in their rulings nor counsel in objections invoked or required precision in applying the *Mott* rule's evidentiary treatment, as we explain below. Necessarily, then, our own decision can address only core issues, leaving for other cases any due process claims that may be raised about the treatment of evidence whose categorization is subject to dispute.

It is clear that *Mott* itself imposed no restriction on considering evidence of the first sort, the observation evidence. We read the *Mott* restriction to apply, rather, to evidence addressing the two issues in testimony that characteristically comes only from psychologists or psychiatrists qualified to give opinions as expert witnesses: mental-disease evidence (whether at the time of the crime a defendant suffered from a mental disease or defect, such as schizophrenia) and capacity evidence (whether the disease or defect left him incapable of performing or experiencing a mental process defined as necessary for sanity such as appreciating the nature and quality of his act and knowing that it was wrong).

Mott was careful to distinguish this kind of opinion evidence from observation evidence generally and even from observation evidence that an expert witness might offer, such as descriptions of a defendant's tendency to think in a certain way or his behavioral characteristics; the Arizona court made it clear that this sort of testimony was perfectly admissible to rebut the prosecution's evidence of *mens rea*. Thus, only opinion testimony going to mental defect or disease, and its effect on the cognitive or moral capacities on which sanity depends under the Arizona rule, is restricted.

In this case, the trial court seems to have applied the *Mott* restriction to all evidence offered by Clark for the purpose of showing what he called his inability to form the required *mens rea*. Thus, the trial court's restriction may have covered not only mental-disease and capacity evidence as just defined, but also observation evidence offered by lay (and expert) witnesses who described Clark's unusual behavior. Clark's objection to the application of the *Mott* rule does not, however, turn on the distinction between lay and expert witnesses or the kinds of testimony they were competent to present. . . .

Clark's argument that the *Mott* rule violates the Fourteenth Amendment guarantee of due process turns on the application of the presumption of innocence in criminal cases, the presumption of sanity, and the principle that a criminal defendant is entitled to present relevant and favorable evidence on an element of the offense charged against him.

The first presumption is that a defendant is innocent unless and until the government proves beyond a reasonable doubt each element of the offense charged, including the mental element or *mens rea*. Before the last century, the *mens rea* required to be proven for particular offenses was often described in general terms like "malice," but the modern tendency has been toward more specific descriptions, as shown in the Arizona statute defining the murder charged against Clark: the State had to prove that in acting to kill the victim, Clark intended to kill a law enforcement officer on duty or knew that the victim was such an officer on duty. As applied to *mens rea* (and every other element), the force of the presumption of innocence is measured by the force of the showing needed to overcome it, which is proof beyond a reasonable doubt that a defendant's state of mind was in fact what the charge states.

The presumption of sanity is equally universal in some variety or other, being (at least) a presumption that a defendant has the capacity to form the *mens rea* necessary for a verdict of guilt and the consequent criminal responsibility. This presumption dispenses with a requirement on the government's part to include as an element of every criminal charge an allegation that the defendant had such a capacity. The force of this presumption, like the presumption of innocence, is measured by the quantum of evidence necessary to overcome it; unlike the presumption of innocence, however, the force of the presumption of sanity varies across the many state and federal jurisdictions, and prior law has recognized considerable leeway on the part of the legislative branch in defining the presumption's strength through the kind of evidence and degree of persuasiveness necessary to overcome it.

There are two points where the sanity or capacity presumption may be placed in issue. First, a State may allow a defendant to introduce (and a factfinder to consider) evidence of mental disease or incapacity for the bearing it can have on the government's burden to show *mens rea*. In such States the evidence showing incapacity to form the guilty state of mind, for example, qualifies the probative force of other evidence, which considered alone indicates that the defendant actually formed the guilty state of mind. If it is shown that a defendant with mental disease thinks all blond people are robots, he could not have intended to kill a person when he shot a man with blond hair, even though he seemed to act like a man shooting another man. In jurisdictions that allow mental-disease and capacity evidence to be considered on par with any other relevant evidence when deciding whether the prosecution has proven *mens rea* beyond a reasonable doubt, the evidence of mental disease or incapacity need only support what the factfinder regards as a reasonable doubt about the capacity to form (or the actual formation of) the *mens rea,* in order to require acquittal of the charge. Thus, in these States the strength of the presumption of sanity is no greater than the strength of the evidence of abnormal mental state that the factfinder thinks is enough to raise a reasonable doubt.

The second point where the force of the presumption of sanity may be tested is in the consideration of a defense of insanity raised by a defendant. Insanity rules like *M'Naghten* . . . are attempts to define, or at least to indicate, the kinds of mental differences that overcome the presumption of sanity or capacity and therefore excuse a defendant from customary criminal responsibility, even if the prosecution has otherwise overcome the presumption of innocence by convincing the factfinder of all the elements charged beyond a reasonable doubt. The burden that must be carried by a defendant who raises the insanity issue, again, defines the strength of the sanity presumption. A State may provide, for example, that whenever the defendant raises a claim of insanity by some quantum of credible evidence, the presumption disappears and the government must prove sanity to a specified degree of certainty (whether beyond reasonable doubt or something less). Or a jurisdiction may place the burden of persuasion on a defendant to prove insanity as the applicable law defines it, whether by a preponderance of the evidence or to some more convincing degree. In any case, the defendant's burden defines the presumption of sanity, whether that burden be to burst a bubble or to show something more.

The third principle implicated by Clark's argument is a defendant's right as a matter of simple due process to present evidence favorable to himself on an element that must be proven to convict him. As already noted, evidence tending to show that a defendant suffers from mental disease and lacks capacity to form *mens rea* is relevant to rebut evidence that he did in fact form the required *mens rea* at the time in question; this is the reason that Clark claims a right to require the factfinder in this case to consider testimony about his mental illness and his incapacity directly, when weighing the persuasiveness of other evidence tending to show *mens rea,* which the prosecution has the burden to prove.

As Clark recognizes, however, the right to introduce relevant evidence can be curtailed if there is a good reason for doing that. "While the Constitution . . . prohibits the exclusion of defense evidence under rules that serve no legitimate purpose or that are disproportionate to the ends that they are asserted to promote, well-established rules of evidence permit trial judges to exclude evidence if its probative value is outweighed by certain other factors such as unfair prejudice, confusion of the issues, or potential to mislead the jury." *Holmes v. South Carolina*, 547 U.S. 319, 326 (2006). And if evidence may be kept out entirely, its consideration may be subject to limitation, which Arizona claims the power to impose here. State law says that evidence of mental disease and incapacity may be introduced and considered, and if sufficiently forceful to satisfy the defendant's burden of proof under the insanity rule it will displace the presumption of sanity and excuse from criminal responsibility. But mental-disease and capacity evidence may be considered only for its bearing on the insanity defense, and it will avail a defendant only if it is persuasive enough to satisfy the defendant's burden as defined by the terms of that defense. The mental-disease and capacity evidence is thus being channeled or restricted to one issue and given effect only if the defendant carries the burden to convince the factfinder of insanity; the evidence is not being excluded entirely, and the question is whether reasons for requiring it to be channeled and restricted are good enough to satisfy the standard of fundamental fairness that due process requires. We think they are.

The first reason supporting the *Mott* rule is Arizona's authority to define its presumption of sanity (or capacity or responsibility) by choosing an insanity definition . . . and by placing the burden of persuasion on defendants who claim incapacity as an excuse from customary criminal responsibility. No one, certainly not Clark here, denies that a State may place a burden of persuasion on a defendant claiming insanity. And Clark presses no objection to Arizona's decision to require persuasion to a clear and convincing degree before the presumption of sanity and normal responsibility is overcome.

But if a State is to have this authority in practice as well as in theory, it must be able to deny a defendant the opportunity to displace the presumption of sanity more easily when addressing a different issue in the course of the criminal trial. Yet, as we have explained, just such an opportunity would be available if expert testimony of mental disease and incapacity could be considered for whatever a factfinder might think it was worth on the issue of *mens rea*. As we mentioned, the presumption of sanity would then be only as strong as the evidence a factfinder would accept as enough to raise a reasonable doubt about *mens rea* for the crime charged; once reasonable doubt was found, acquittal would be required, and the standards established for the defense of insanity would go by the boards.

Now, a State is of course free to accept such a possibility in its law. After all, it is free to define the insanity defense by treating the presumption of sanity as a bursting bubble, whose disappearance shifts the burden to the prosecution to prove sanity whenever a defendant presents any credible evidence of mental disease or incapacity. In States with this kind of insanity rule, the legislature may well be willing to allow such evidence to be considered on the *mens rea* element for whatever the factfinder thinks it is worth. What counts for due process, however, is simply that a State that wishes to avoid a second avenue for exploring capacity, less stringent for a defendant, has a good reason for confining the consideration of evidence of mental disease and incapacity to the insanity defense.

It is obvious that Arizona's *Mott* rule reflects such a choice. The State Supreme Court pointed out that the State had declined to adopt a defense of diminished capacity (allowing a jury to decide when to excuse a defendant because of greater than normal difficulty in conforming to the law). The court reasoned that the State's choice would be undercut if evidence of incapacity could be considered for whatever a jury might think sufficient to raise a reasonable doubt about *mens rea,* even if it did not show insanity. In other words, if a jury were free to decide how much evidence of mental disease and incapacity was enough to counter evidence of *mens rea* to the point of creating a reasonable doubt, that would in functional terms be analogous to allowing jurors to decide upon some degree of diminished capacity to obey the law, a degree set by them, that would prevail as a stand-alone defense.

A State's insistence on preserving its chosen standard of legal insanity cannot be the sole reason for a rule like *Mott,* however, for it fails to answer an objection the dissent makes in this case. An insanity rule gives a defendant already found guilty the opportunity to excuse his conduct by showing he was insane when he acted, that is, that he did not have the mental capacity for conventional guilt and criminal responsibility. But, as the dissent argues, if the same evidence that affirmatively shows he was not guilty by reason of insanity (or "guilty except insane" under Arizona law, also shows it was at least doubtful that he could form *mens rea,* then he should not be found guilty in the first place; it thus violates due process when the State impedes him from using mental-disease and capacity evidence directly to rebut the prosecution's evidence that he did form *mens rea.*

Are there, then, characteristics of mental-disease and capacity evidence giving rise to risks that may reasonably be hedged by channeling the consideration of such evidence to the insanity issue on which, in States like Arizona, a defendant has the burden of persuasion? We think there are: in the controversial character of some categories of mental disease, in the potential of mental-disease evidence to mislead, and in the danger of according greater certainty to capacity evidence than experts claim for it.

To begin with, the diagnosis may mask vigorous debate within the profession about the very contours of the mental disease itself. And Members of this Court have previously recognized that the end of such debate is not imminent. Though we certainly do not "condem[n mental-disease evidence] wholesale," the consequence of this professional ferment is a general caution in treating psychological classifications as predicates for excusing otherwise criminal conduct.

Next, there is the potential of mental-disease evidence to mislead jurors (when they are the factfinders) through the power of this kind of evidence to suggest that a defendant suffering from a recognized mental disease lacks cognitive, moral, volitional, or other capacity, when that may not be a sound conclusion at all. Even when a category of mental disease is broadly accepted and the assignment of a defendant's behavior to that category is uncontroversial, the classification may suggest something very significant about a defendant's capacity, when in fact the classification tells us little or nothing about the ability of the defendant to form *mens rea* or to exercise the cognitive, moral, or volitional capacities that define legal sanity. The limits of the utility of a professional disease diagnosis are evident in the dispute between the two testifying experts in this case; they agree that Clark was schizophrenic, but they come to opposite conclusions on whether the mental disease in his particular case left him bereft of cognitive or moral capacity. Evidence of mental disease, then, can easily mislead; it is very easy to slide from evidence that an individual with a professionally recognized mental disease is very different, into doubting that he has the capacity to form *mens rea,* whereas that doubt may not be justified. And of course, in the cases mentioned before, in which the categorization is doubtful or the category of mental disease is itself subject to controversy, the risks are even greater that opinions about mental disease may confuse a jury into thinking the opinions show more than they do. Because allowing mental-disease evidence on *mens rea* can thus easily mislead, it is not unreasonable to address that tendency by confining consideration of this kind of evidence to insanity, on which a defendant may be assigned the burden of persuasion.

There are, finally, particular risks inherent in the opinions of the experts who supplement the mental-disease classifications with opinions on incapacity: on whether the mental disease rendered a particular defendant incapable of the cognition necessary for moral judgment or *mens rea* or otherwise incapable of understanding the wrongfulness of the conduct charged. Unlike observational evidence bearing on *mens rea,* capacity evidence consists of judgment, and judgment fraught with multiple perils: a defendant's state of mind at the crucial moment can be elusive no matter how conscientious the enquiry, and the law's categories that set the terms of the capacity judgment are not the categories of psychology that govern the expert's professional thinking. Although such capacity judgments may be given in the utmost good faith, their potentially tenuous character is indicated by the candor of the defense expert in this very case. Contrary to the State's expert, he testified that Clark lacked the capacity to appreciate the circumstances realistically and to understand the wrongfulness of what he was doing, but he said that "no one knows exactly what was on [his] mind" at the time of the shooting. And even when an expert is confident that his understanding of the mind is reliable, judgment addressing the basic categories of capacity requires a leap from the concepts of psychology, which are devised for thinking about treatment, to the concepts of legal sanity, which are devised for thinking about criminal responsibility. In sum, these empirical and conceptual problems add up to a real risk that an expert's judgment in giving capacity evidence will come with an apparent authority that psychologists and psychiatrists do not claim to have. We think that this risk, like the difficulty in assessing the significance of mental-disease evidence, supports the State's decision to channel such expert testimony to consideration on the insanity defense, on which the party seeking the benefit of this evidence has the burden of persuasion.

It bears repeating that not every State will find it worthwhile to make the judgment Arizona has made, and the choices the States do make about dealing with the risks posed by mental-disease and capacity evidence will reflect their varying assessments about the presumption of sanity as expressed in choices of insanity rules. The point here simply is that Arizona has sensible reasons to assign the risks as it has done by channeling the evidence. . . . The judgment of the Court of Appeals of Arizona is, accordingly, affirmed.

NOTES & QUESTIONS ON DIMINISHED CAPACITY

Abolishing the insanity defense. Some statutes have taken the extreme step of abolishing the insanity defense—essentially the *opposite* of the Arizona approach. For example, Montana abolished the insanity defense in 1979 and replaced it with a trifurcated system for considering evidence of mental illness. First, a court must satisfy itself that the defendant is mentally competent to stand trial. If the answer is yes, the defendant stands trial and can introduce evidence of mental illness to demonstrate that he did not act with the required mental state. If the jury acquits on that basis, the jury makes an explicit finding that their not guilty finding is based on "the reason that due to a mental disease or defect he could not have a particular state of mind that is an essential element of the offense charged. . . ." Mont. Code Ann. § 46-14-214. But if the jury convicts the defendant, the sentencing judge considers all psychiatric evidence presented at trial to determine whether "the defendant was able to appreciate the criminality of his acts or to conform his conduct to the law at the time he committed the offense"—essentially the MPC standard for insanity. On appeal, the Montana Supreme Court upheld the scheme. See *State v. Korell*, 213 Mont. 316 (1984) ("Our legislature has acted to assure that the attendant stigma of a criminal conviction is mitigated by the sentencing judge's personal consideration of the defendant's mental condition and provision for commitment to an appropriate institution for treatment, as an alternative to a sentence of imprisonment."). For other examples, see *State v. Searcy*, 798 P.2d 914 (Idaho 1990) (evidence of mental illness permitted only to negate mens rea); *State v. Herrera*, 993 P.2d 854 (Utah 1999).

As a defense attorney, which scheme would you prefer? Would you prefer the chance to convince a jury that your client's mental illness interfered with mens rea, or would you prefer that the judge explain the *M'Naghten* or MPC test to the jurors and have them apply the official insanity defense? One advantage of the Montana and Idaho scheme is that it relieves the jury from struggling with the complex standards for legal insanity embodied in the *M'Naghten* or MPC standards. As a matter of policy, there are two avenues of responding to a legal doctrine that is difficult to apply: You can revise the standard or you can abandon it entirely.

C. PRACTICE & POLICY

Jurisdictions are engaged in a constant process of revising both the procedure and substance of the insanity plea. The result is a set of fluid changes that alter how the criminal trial unfolds when a defendant argues that he was insane during the commission of the crime. The following materials canvass some of the most important procedural and substantive shifts. In each case, the strategy of the lawyers involved must adapt to the new procedural landscape.

ᖈ **Separate insanity phase.** Some jurisdictions have experimented with creating a separate insanity phase of the trial. In that situation, the "guilt" phase is separated from questions of mental illness that dominate the insanity phase. The trial starts with an inquiry into whether the defendant committed the crime; the jury must formally decide whether the defendant committed the crime and whether any justifications apply. If the jury finds that the defendant committed the crime, the defendant has the opportunity in the second phase to argue that he was legally insane during the commission of the crime. What is the value of bifurcating the trial in this manner? In California, for example, defendants have the option of arguing *both* not guilty and not guilty by reason of insanity—and need not chose one or the other. In the first phase, the defendant's lawyer tries to convince the jury that her client either did not commit the crime or was justified in doing so. Only if the defendant loses this phase does he need to argue that he was not guilty by reason of insanity in the second phase. For example, see Kathryn S. Berthot, *Bifurcation in Insanity Trials: A Change in Maryland's Criminal Procedure*, 48 Md. L. Rev. 1045 (1989). However, what seems like a due process—friendly procedure might have a shadow side. Some appellate courts have overturned on due process grounds state statutes mandating bifurcation when they prevent a defendant from raising evidence of mental illness to negate mens rea during the guilt phase. See, e.g., *State v. Shaw*, 106 Ariz. 103 (1970); *Sanchez v. State*, 567 P.2d 270, 274 (Wyo. 1977). Consequently, several states have since abandoned bifurcation and unified their trials again. See, e.g., Colo. Rev. Stat. § § 16-8-104.5 *et seq.* (requiring single trial but with a special verdict form so jury only needs to consider insanity issue if it finds that the defendant committed the crime). Which procedure do you think better protects the rights of defendants? If you were a defense attorney, which system would you prefer? The problem with bifurcation is that it is sometimes paired with an all-or-nothing scheme that blocks evidence of mental illness from negating mens rea. But if bifurcation is liberated from that constraint and mental illness evidence were permitted during the guilt phase as well, would that be more beneficial for defendants?

᠔ Guilty but mentally ill (GBMI) plea.   Some jurisdictions crave more options than the two extremes embodied by "guilty" and "not guilty by reason of insanity." What if the defendant is guilty but also mentally ill—just not crazy enough to be not responsible for the criminal conduct? In Delaware, as in a few other states, juries have the option of declaring the defendant responsible for his behavior but also mentally ill. See 11 Del. Code § 401(b). That provision provides:

> Where the trier of fact determines that, at the time of the conduct charged, a defendant suffered from a mental illness or serious mental disorder which substantially disturbed such person's thinking, feeling or behavior and/or that such mental illness or serious mental disorder left such person with insufficient willpower to choose whether the person would do the act or refrain from doing it, although physically capable, the trier of fact shall return a verdict of "guilty, but mentally ill."

The purpose of the provision is to give the criminal justice system the option of incarcerating the defendant and providing him with mandatory mental health treatment. Under the traditional scheme, the defendant gets one or the other—punishment or treatment, but not both. Although the provisions differ from jurisdiction to jurisdiction, the Delaware scheme would send the defendant to a mental hospital first and, once cured, to a prison to serve out the rest of his sentence. But not everyone applauded the new "third way" for handling mentally ill defendants. For example, one scholar wrote that the "possibility of improper convictions due to the guilty but mentally ill verdict is heightened by the difficulty of clearly instructing jurors about the difference between the definition of 'insanity' and the meaning of 'mental illness' in the context of the guilty but mentally ill verdict." Christopher Slobogin, *Guilty But Mentally Ill Verdict: An Idea Whose Time Should Not Have Come*, 53 Geo. Wash. L. Rev. 494 (1984-1985). Is there a risk that some defendants who are truly insane and not responsible for their behavior will be found "guilty but mentally ill" just because jurors do not want to run the risk that the defendant will someday be freed from mental health custody?

∾ **Too crazy to plead insanity.** Some defendants are too crazy to plead not guilty by reason of insanity. Consider the case of Colin Ferguson, who murdered six passengers and injured 19 more on board a Long Island Railroad train. The December 1993 massacre was horrendous and would have been worse had several passengers not intervened and wrestled him to the ground. Ferguson was initially represented by a legal team that included famed defense attorney William Kunstler. However, after a disagreement with them over defense strategy, Ferguson fired his attorneys and sought to represent himself at trial. The trial judge agreed with the request, which paved the way for a circus-like trial that included some bizarre ramblings during Ferguson's questioning of the victims of the shooting. During one speech to the judge he compared himself to John the Baptist. To many observers, Ferguson seemed mentally ill and perhaps legally insane—although the jury never got the chance to make that determination. Since Ferguson was declared competent to stand trial (i.e., capable of understanding the proceedings and assisting in his defense), the choice of pleading insanity was his to make. He declined to do so. He was convicted of six counts of murder and 19 counts of attempted murder. On appeal, the Second Department concluded that a "defendant who is competent to stand trial is necessarily competent to waive his right to counsel and proceed *pro se*." *People v. Ferguson*, 248 A.D.2d 725 (N.Y. App. Div. 1998). Do you agree that everyone who is deemed competent to stand trial should be permitted to represent himself? The problem with this rule is that some mentally ill individuals resent that label and will refuse it, even if it might exonerate them. If you were working as a defense attorney for such an individual, how would you define a good outcome for him: getting an acquittal or getting your client what he wants (which might not be the same thing)?

Colin Ferguson questioning witness at his trial

~ **The medical model to criminal insanity.** The law of insanity differs widely across foreign jurisdictions. For example, Norway has adopted a pure medical model for legal insanity. Under the Norwegian scheme, a defendant is not guilty by reason of insanity if the defendant was psychotic during the commission of the crime. Although this sounds unsurprising, notice the lack of any causal connection between the mental illness and the commission of the crime. For example, one obvious hallmark of the *M'Naghten* test is that the mental disease or defect caused the defendant to not understand the nature or quality of his act or its wrongfulness. Or, under the irresistible impulse test, there must be causal connection between the mental infirmity and the defendant's ability to control himself. In contrast, the Norwegian scheme requires none of these connections. The determination is purely medical. If the defendant is psychotic, the defense applies; if not, the defendant is guilty—full stop.

The Norwegian model gained international attention during the trial of Anders Behring Breivik, who was convicted of murdering 77 people during a bombing in Oslo followed by a shooting rampage on the island of Utøya at the site of a youth political camp. Many of the victims were teenagers. Breivik was first examined by two psychiatrists who declared him a paranoid schizophrenic—a finding that, if adopted by the court, would lead to an acquittal and psychiatric commitment. However, an evaluation with a second team of psychiatrists concluded that Breivik suffered from narcissistic personality disorder but was not psychotic per se. The court accepted the second evaluation and concluded that Breivik was responsible for his actions. Brevik was sentenced to 21 years in prison—the longest sentence available under Norwegian law.

The pure medical model seems bizarre when compared with the moral and legal assessments required by the *M'Naghten*, irresistible impulse, or substantial capacity tests. However, the model has its supporters in the United States as well. For example, Professor Michael Moore has written:

Anders Behring Breivik

> The familiar and persistent criticism of the medical model of insanity in America has long been that when we say (correctly) that insanity is a legal concept, not a medical one, the inference to be drawn is that some other, traditionally excusing notions (like compulsion or ignorance) are to be added to mental illness to construct a distinctively legal notion of insanity. . . . On this issue Norwegian law has it right, and the almost unanimous Anglo-American tradition has it wrong.

Michael S. Moore, *The Quest for a Responsibility Test: Norwegian Insanity Law After Breivik*, 9 Crim. L. & Phil. 645 (2014). As one of the judges in the Breivik case concluded, "[b]eing [mad] at the time of committing the act will unconditionally except the person from punishment, regardless of whether the offense is a result of the [madness]." See Oslo District Court Judgment, quoted in Moore, *supra*. Do you agree?

Consider the following hypothetical: Imagine a psychotic individual who hears voices telling him that the government is out to get him and that he should go shoot up a government building to stop the conspiracy against him. On the way to the government building, the individual passes a jewelry store with diamond rings in the window. The psychotic individual wants to propose marriage to his girlfriend but does not have enough money to buy the ring. He steals it, knowing full well that theft is wrong, and nothing in his mental illness prevented him from making this assessment. In other words, he knew that stealing the ring was wrong, and he just happened also to be insane at the same time. Should insanity excuse the theft as well as his attack against the government building?

APPENDIX

Model Penal Code
Published by the American Law Institute

PART I. GENERAL PROVISIONS
ARTICLE 1. PRELIMINARY

Section 1.02. Purposes; Principles of Construction.

(1) The general purposes of the provisions governing the definition of offenses are:

(a) to forbid and prevent conduct that unjustifiably and inexcusably inflicts or threatens substantial harm to individual or public interests;

(b) to subject to public control persons whose conduct indicates that they are disposed to commit crimes;

(c) to safeguard conduct that is without fault from condemnation as criminal;

(d) to give fair warning of the nature of the conduct declared to constitute an offense;

(e) to differentiate on reasonable grounds between serious and minor offenses.

(2) The general purposes of the provisions governing the sentencing and treatment of offenders are:

(a) to prevent the commission of offenses;

(b) to promote the correction and rehabilitation of offenders;

(c) to safeguard offenders against excessive, disproportionate or arbitrary punishment;

(d) to give fair warning of the nature of the sentences that may be imposed on conviction of an offense;

(e) to differentiate among offenders with a view to a just individualization in their treatment;

(f) to define, coordinate and harmonize the powers, duties and functions of the courts and of administrative officers and agencies responsible for dealing with offenders;

(g) to advance the use of generally accepted scientific methods and knowledge in the sentencing and treatment of offenders;

(h) to integrate responsibility for the administration of the correctional system in a State Department of Correction [or other single department or agency].

(3) The provisions of the Code shall be construed according to the fair import of their terms but when the language is susceptible of differing constructions it shall be

interpreted to further the general purposes stated in this Section and the special purposes of the particular provision involved. The discretionary powers conferred by the Code shall be exercised in accordance with the criteria stated in the Code and, insofar as such criteria are not decisive, to further the general purposes stated in this Section.

Section 1.03. Territorial Applicability.

(1) Except as otherwise provided in this Section, a person may be convicted under the law of this State of an offense committed by his own conduct or the conduct of another for which he is legally accountable if:

(a) either the conduct which is an element of the offense or the result which is such an element occurs within this State; or

(b) conduct occurring outside the State is sufficient under the law of this State to constitute an attempt to commit an offense within the State; or

(c) conduct occurring outside the State is sufficient under the law of this State to constitute a conspiracy to commit an offense within the State and an overt act in furtherance of such conspiracy occurs within the State; or

(d) conduct occurring within the State establishes complicity in the commission of, or an attempt, solicitation or conspiracy to commit, an offense in another jurisdiction which also is an offense under the law of this State; or

(e) the offense consists of the omission to perform a legal duty imposed by the law of the State with respect to domicile, residence or a relationship to a person, thing or transaction in the State; or

(f) the offense is based on a statute of this State which expressly prohibits conduct outside the State, when the conduct bears a reasonable relation to a legitimate interest of this State and the actor knows or should know that his conduct is likely to affect that interest.

(2) Subsection (1)(a) does not apply when either causing a specified result or a purpose to cause or danger of causing such a result is an element of an offense and the result occurs or is designed or likely to occur only in another jurisdiction where the conduct charged would not constitute an offense, unless a legislative purpose plainly appears to declare the conduct criminal regardless of the place of the result.

(3) Subsection (1)(a) does not apply when causing a particular result is an element of an offense and the result is caused by conduct occurring outside the State which would not constitute an offense if the result had occurred there, unless the actor purposely or knowingly caused the result within the State.

(4) When the offense is homicide, either the death of the victim or the bodily impact causing death constitutes a "result," within the meaning of Subsection (1)(a) and if the body of a homicide victim is found within the State, it is presumed that such result occurred within the State.

(5) This State includes the land and water and the air space above such land and water with respect to which the State has legislative jurisdiction.

Section 1.04. Classes of Crimes; Violations.

(1) An offense defined by this Code or by any other statute of this State, for which a sentence of [death or of] imprisonment is authorized, constitutes a crime. Crimes are classified as felonies, misdemeanors or petty misdemeanors.

(2) A crime is a felony if it is so designated in this Code or if persons convicted thereof may be sentenced [to death or] to imprisonment for a term which, apart from an extended term, is in excess of one year.

(3) A crime is a misdemeanor if it is so designated in this Code or in a statute other than this Code enacted subsequent thereto.

(4) A crime is a petty misdemeanor if it is so designated in this Code or in a statute other than this Code enacted subsequent thereto or if it is defined by a statute other than this Code which now provides that persons convicted thereof may be sentenced to imprisonment for a term of which the maximum is less than one year.

(5) An offense defined by this Code or by any other statute of this State constitutes a violation if it is so designated in this Code or in the law defining the offense or if no other sentence than a fine, or fine and forfeiture or other civil penalty is authorized upon conviction or if it is defined by a statute other than this Code which now provides that the offense shall not constitute a crime. A violation does not constitute a crime and conviction of a violation shall not give rise to any disability or legal disadvantage based on conviction of a criminal offense.

(6) Any offense declared by law to constitute a crime, without specification of the grade thereof or of the sentence authorized upon conviction, is a misdemeanor.

(7) An offense defined by any statute of this State other than this Code shall be classified as provided in this Section and the sentence that may be imposed upon conviction thereof shall hereafter be governed by this Code.

Section 1.05. All Offenses Defined by Statute; Application of General Provisions of the Code.

(1) No conduct constitutes an offense unless it is a crime or violation under this Code or another statute of this State.

(2) The provisions of Part I of the Code are applicable to offenses defined by other statutes, unless the Code otherwise provides.

(3) This Section does not affect the power of a court to punish for contempt or to employ any sanction authorized by law for the enforcement of an order or a civil judgment or decree.

Section 1.06. Omitted.

Section 1.07. Method of Prosecution When Conduct Constitutes More Than One Offense.

(1) *Prosecution for Multiple Offenses; Limitation on Convictions.* When the same conduct of a defendant may establish the commission of more than one offense, the defendant may be prosecuted for each such offense. He may not, however, be convicted of more than one offense if:

(a) one offense is included in the other, as defined in Subsection (4) of this Section; or

(b) one offense consists only of a conspiracy or other form of preparation to commit the other; or

(c) inconsistent findings of fact are required to establish the commission of the offenses; or

(d) the offenses differ only in that one is defined to prohibit a designated kind of conduct generally and the other to prohibit a specific instance of such conduct; or

(e) the offense is defined as a continuing course of conduct and the defendant's course of conduct was uninterrupted, unless the law provides that specific periods of such conduct constitute separate offenses.

(2) *Limitation on Separate Trials for Multiple Offenses.* Except as provided in Subsection (3) of this Section, a defendant shall not be subject to separate trials for multiple offenses based on the same conduct or arising from the same criminal episode, if such offenses are known to the appropriate prosecuting officer at the time of the commencement of the first trial and are within the jurisdiction of a single court.

(3) *Authority of Court to Order Separate Trials.* When a defendant is charged with two or more offenses based on the same conduct or arising from the same criminal episode, the Court, on application of the prosecuting attorney or of the defendant, may order any such charge to be tried separately, if it is satisfied that justice so requires.

(4) *Conviction of Included Offense Permitted.* A defendant may be convicted of an offense included in an offense charged in the indictment [or the information]. An offense is so included when:

(a) it is established by proof of the same or less than all the facts required to establish the commission of the offense charged; or

(b) it consists of an attempt or solicitation to commit the offense charged or to commit an offense otherwise included therein; or

(c) it differs from the offense charged only in the respect that a less serious injury or risk of injury to the same person, property or public interest or a lesser kind of culpability suffices to establish its commission.

(5) *Submission of Included Offense to Jury.* The Court shall not be obligated to charge the jury with respect to an included offense unless there is a rational basis for a verdict acquitting the defendant of the offense charged and convicting him of the included offense.

Section 1.08. When Prosecution Barred by Former Prosecution for the Same Offense.

When a prosecution is for a violation of the same provision of the statutes and is based upon the same facts as a former prosecution, it is barred by such former prosecution under the following circumstances:

(1) The former prosecution resulted in an acquittal. There is an acquittal if the prosecution resulted in a finding of not guilty by the trier of fact or in a determination that there was insufficient evidence to warrant a conviction. A finding of guilty of a lesser included offense is an acquittal of the greater inclusive offense, although the conviction is subsequently set aside.

(2) The former prosecution was terminated, after the information had been filed or the indictment found, by a final order or judgment for the defendant, which has not been set aside, reversed, or vacated and which necessarily required a determination inconsistent with a fact or a legal proposition that must be established for conviction of the offense.

(3) The former prosecution resulted in a conviction. There is a conviction if the prosecution resulted in a judgment of conviction which has not been reversed or vacated, a verdict of guilty which has not been set aside and which is capable of supporting a judgment, or a plea of guilty accepted by the Court. In the latter two cases failure to enter judgment must be for a reason other than a motion of the defendant.

(4) The former prosecution was improperly terminated. Except as provided in this Subsection, there is an improper termination of a prosecution if the termination is for reasons not amounting to an acquittal, and it takes place after the first witness is sworn but before verdict. Termination under any of the following circumstances is not improper:

   (a) The defendant consents to the termination or waives, by motion to dismiss or otherwise, his right to object to the termination.

   (b) The trial court finds that the termination is necessary because:

      (1) it is physically impossible to proceed with the trial in conformity with law; or

      (2) there is a legal defect in the proceedings which would make any judgment entered upon a verdict reversible as a matter of law; or

      (3) prejudicial conduct, in or outside the courtroom, makes it impossible to proceed with the trial without injustice to either the defendant or the State; or

      (4) the jury is unable to agree upon a verdict; or

      (5) false statements of a juror on voir dire prevent a fair trial.

Section 1.09. When Prosecution Barred by Former Prosecution for Different Offense. Although a prosecution is for a violation of a different provision of the statutes than a former prosecution or is based on different facts, it is barred by such former prosecution under the following circumstances:

(1) The former prosecution resulted in an acquittal or in a conviction as defined in Section 1.08 and the subsequent prosecution is for:

   (a) any offense of which the defendant could have been convicted on the first prosecution; or

   (b) any offense for which the defendant should have been tried on the first prosecution under Section 1.07, unless the Court ordered a separate trial of the charge of such offense; or

   (c) the same conduct, unless (i) the offense of which the defendant was formerly convicted or acquitted and the offense for which he is subsequently prosecuted each requires proof of a fact not required by the other and the law defining each of such offenses is intended to prevent a substantially different harm or evil, or (ii) the second offense was not consummated when the former trial began.

(2) The former prosecution was terminated, after the information was filed or the indictment found, by an acquittal or by a final order or judgment for the defendant which has not been set aside, reversed or vacated and which acquittal, final order or judgment necessarily required a determination inconsistent with a fact which must be established for conviction of the second offense.

(3) The former prosecution was improperly terminated, as improper termination is defined in Section 1.08, and the subsequent prosecution is for an offense of which the defendant could have been convicted had the former prosecution not been improperly terminated.

Section 1.10. Former Prosecution in Another Jurisdiction: When a Bar.

When conduct constitutes an offense within the concurrent jurisdiction of this State and of the United States or another State, a prosecution in any such other jurisdiction is a bar to a subsequent prosecution in this State under the following circumstances:

(1) The first prosecution resulted in an acquittal or in a conviction as defined in Section 1.08 and the subsequent prosecution is based on the same conduct, unless (a) the offense of which the defendant was formerly convicted or acquitted and the offense for which he is subsequently prosecuted each requires proof of a fact not required by the other and the law defining each of such offenses is intended to prevent a substantially different harm or evil or (b) the second offense was not consummated when the former trial began; or

(2) The former prosecution was terminated, after the information was filed or the indictment found, by an acquittal or by a final order or judgment for the defendant which has not been set aside, reversed or vacated and which acquittal, final order or judgment necessarily required a determination inconsistent with a fact which must be established for conviction of the offense of which the defendant is subsequently prosecuted.

Section 1.11. Former Prosecution Before Court Lacking Jurisdiction or When Fraudulently Procured by the Defendant.

A prosecution is not a bar within the meaning of Sections 1.08, 1.09 and 1.10 under any of the following circumstances:

(1) The former prosecution was before a court which lacked jurisdiction over the defendant or the offense; or

(2) The former prosecution was procured by the defendant without the knowledge of the appropriate prosecuting officer and with the purpose of avoiding the sentence which might otherwise be imposed; or

(3) The former prosecution resulted in a judgment of conviction which was held invalid in a subsequent proceeding on a writ of habeas corpus, coram nobis or similar process.

Section 1.12. Proof Beyond a Reasonable Doubt; Affirmative Defenses; Burden of Proving Fact When Not an Element of an Offense; Presumptions.

(1) No person may be convicted of an offense unless each element of such offense is proved beyond a reasonable doubt. In the absence of such proof, the innocence of the defendant is assumed.

(2) Subsection (1) of this Section does not:

(a) require the disproof of an affirmative defense unless and until there is evidence supporting such defense; or

(b) apply to any defense which the Code or another statute plainly requires the defendant to prove by a preponderance of evidence.

(3) A ground of defense is affirmative, within the meaning of Subsection (2)(a) of this Section, when:

(a) it arises under a section of the Code which so provides; or

(b) it relates to an offense defined by a statute other than the Code and such statute so provides; or

(c) it involves a matter of excuse or justification peculiarly within the knowledge of the defendant on which he can fairly be required to adduce supporting evidence.

(4) When the application of the Code depends upon the finding of a fact which is not an element of an offense, unless the Code otherwise provides:

(a) the burden of proving the fact is on the prosecution or defendant, depending on whose interest or contention will be furthered if the finding should be made; and

(b) the fact must be proved to the satisfaction of the Court or jury, as the case may be.

(5) When the Code establishes a presumption with respect to any fact which is an element of an offense, it has the following consequences:

(a) when there is evidence of the facts which give rise to the presumption, the issue of the existence of the presumed fact must be submitted to the jury, unless the Court is satisfied that the evidence as a whole clearly negatives the presumed fact; and

(b) when the issue of the existence of the presumed fact is submitted to the jury, the Court shall charge that while the presumed fact must, on all the evidence, be proved beyond a reasonable doubt, the law declares that the jury may regard the facts giving rise to the presumption as sufficient evidence of the presumed fact.

(6) A presumption not established by the Code or inconsistent with it has the consequences otherwise accorded it by law.

Section 1.13. General Definitions.

In this Code, unless a different meaning plainly is required:

(1) "statute" includes the Constitution and a local law or ordinance of a political subdivision of the State;

(2) "act" or "action" means a bodily movement whether voluntary or involuntary;

(3) "voluntary" has the meaning specified in Section 2.01;

(4) "omission" means a failure to act;

(5) "conduct" means an action or omission and its accompanying state of mind, or, where relevant, a series of acts and omissions;

(6) "actor" includes, where relevant, a person guilty of an omission;

(7) "acted" includes, where relevant, "omitted to act";

(8) "person," "he" and "actor" include any natural person and, where relevant, a corporation or an unincorporated association;

(9) "element of an offense" means (i) such conduct or (ii) such attendant circumstances or (iii) such a result of conduct as

(a) is included in the description of the forbidden conduct in the definition of the offense; or

(b) establishes the required kind of culpability; or

(c) negatives an excuse or justification for such conduct; or

(d) negatives a defense under the statute of limitations; or

(e) establishes jurisdiction or venue;

(10) "material element of an offense" means an element that does not relate exclusively to the statute of limitations, jurisdiction, venue or to any other matter similarly unconnected with (i) the harm or evil, incident to conduct, sought to be prevented by the law defining the offense, or (ii) the existence of a justification or excuse for such conduct;

(11) "purposely" has the meaning specified in Section 2.02 and equivalent terms such as "with purpose," "designed" or "with design" have the same meaning;

(2) "intentionally" or "with intent" means purposely;

(13) "knowingly" has the meaning specified in Section 2.02 and equivalent terms such as "knowing" or "with knowledge" have the same meaning;

(14) "recklessly" has the meaning specified in Section 2.02 and equivalent terms such as "recklessness" or "with recklessness" have the same meaning;

(15) "negligently" has the meaning specified in Section 2.02 and equivalent terms such as "negligence" or "with negligence" have the same meaning;

(16) "reasonably believes" or "reasonable belief" designates a belief which the actor is not reckless or negligent in holding.

ARTICLE 2. GENERAL PRINCIPLES OF LIABILITY

Section 2.01. Requirement of Voluntary Act; Omission as Basis of Liability; Possession as an Act.

(1) A person is not guilty of an offense unless his liability is based on conduct which includes a voluntary act or the omission to perform an act of which he is physically capable.

(2) The following are not voluntary acts within the meaning of this Section:

    (a) a reflex or convulsion;

    (b) a bodily movement during unconsciousness or sleep;

    (c) conduct during hypnosis or resulting from hypnotic suggestion;

    (d) a bodily movement that otherwise is not a product of the effort or determination of the actor, either conscious or habitual.

(3) Liability for the commission of an offense may not be based on an omission unaccompanied by action unless:

    (a) the omission is expressly made sufficient by the law defining the offense; or

    (b) a duty to perform the omitted act is otherwise imposed by law.

(4) Possession is an act, within the meaning of this Section, if the possessor knowingly procured or received the thing possessed or was aware of his control thereof for a sufficient period to have been able to terminate his possession.

Section 2.02. General Requirements of Culpability.

(1) *Minimum Requirements of Culpability.* Except as provided in Section 2.05, a person is not guilty of an offense unless he acted purposely, knowingly, recklessly or negligently, as the law may require, with respect to each material element of the offense.

(2) *Kinds of Culpability Defined.*

    (a) *Purposely.* A person acts purposely with respect to a material element of an offense when:

        (i) if the element involves the nature of his conduct or a result thereof, it is his conscious object to engage in conduct of that nature or to cause such a result; and

        (ii) if the element involves the attendant circumstances, he is aware of the existence of such circumstances or he believes or hopes that they exist.

    (b) *Knowingly.* A person acts knowingly with respect to a material element of an offense when:

(i) if the element involves the nature of his conduct or the attendant circumstances, he is aware that his conduct is of that nature or that such circumstances exist; and

(ii) if the element involves a result of his conduct, he is aware that it is practically certain that his conduct will cause such a result.

(c) *Recklessly*. A person acts recklessly with respect to a material element of an offense when he consciously disregards a substantial and unjustifiable risk that the material element exists or will result from his conduct. The risk must be of such a nature and degree that, considering the nature and purpose of the actor's conduct and the circumstances known to him, its disregard involves a gross deviation from the standard of conduct that a law-abiding person would observe in the actor's situation.

(d) *Negligently*. A person acts negligently with respect to a material element of an offense when he should be aware of a substantial and unjustifiable risk that the material element exists or will result from his conduct. The risk must be of such a nature and degree that the actor's failure to perceive it, considering the nature and purpose of his conduct and the circumstances known to him, involves a gross deviation from the standard of care that a reasonable person would observe in the actor's situation.

(3) *Culpability Required Unless Otherwise Provided.* When the culpability sufficient to establish a material element of an offense is not prescribed by law, such element is established if a person acts purposely, knowingly or recklessly with respect thereto.

(4) *Prescribed Culpability Requirement Applies to All Material Elements.* When the law defining an offense prescribes the kind of culpability that is sufficient for the commission of an offense, without distinguishing among the material elements thereof, such provision shall apply to all the material elements of the offense, unless a contrary purpose plainly appears.

(5) *Substitutes for Negligence, Recklessness and Knowledge.* When the law provides that negligence suffices to establish an element of an offense, such element also is established if a person acts purposely, knowingly or recklessly. When recklessness suffices to establish an element, such element also is established if a person acts purposely or knowingly. When acting knowingly suffices to establish an element, such element also is established if a person acts purposely.

(6) *Requirement of Purpose Satisfied if Purpose Is Conditional.* When a particular purpose is an element of an offense, the element is established although such purpose is conditional, unless the condition negatives the harm or evil sought to be prevented by the law defining the offense.

(7) *Requirement of Knowledge Satisfied by Knowledge of High Probability.* When knowledge of the existence of a particular fact is an element of an offense, such knowledge is established if a person is aware of a high probability of its existence, unless he actually believes that it does not exist.

(8) *Requirement of Wilfulness Satisfied by Acting Knowingly.* A requirement that an offense be committed wilfully is satisfied if a person acts knowingly with respect to the material elements of the offense, unless a purpose to impose further requirements appears.

(9) *Culpability as to Illegality of Conduct.* Neither knowledge nor recklessness or negligence as to whether conduct constitutes an offense or as to the existence, meaning or application of the law determining the elements of an offense is an element of such offense, unless the definition of the offense or the Code so provides.

(10) *Culpability as Determinant of Grade of Offense.* When the grade or degree of an offense depends on whether the offense is committed purposely, knowingly, recklessly or negligently, its grade or degree shall be the lowest for which the determinative kind of culpability is established with respect to any material element of the offense.

Section 2.03. Causal Relationship Between Conduct and Result; Divergence Between Result Designed or Contemplated and Actual Result or Between Probable and Actual Result.

(1) Conduct is the cause of a result when:

(a) it is an antecedent but for which the result in question would not have occurred; and

(b) the relationship between the conduct and result satisfies any additional causal requirements imposed by the Code or by the law defining the offense.

(2) When purposely or knowingly causing a particular result is an element of an offense, the element is not established if the actual result is not within the purpose or the contemplation of the actor unless:

(a) the actual result differs from that designed or contemplated, as the case may be, only in the respect that a different person or different property is injured or affected or that the injury or harm designed or contemplated would have been more serious or more extensive than that caused; or

(b) the actual result involves the same kind of injury or harm as that designed or contemplated and is not too remote or accidental in its occurrence to have a [just] bearing on the actor's liability or on the gravity of his offense.

(3) When recklessly or negligently causing a particular result is an element of an offense, the element is not established if the actual result is not within the risk of which the actor is aware or, in the case of negligence, of which he should be aware unless:

(a) the actual result differs from the probable result only in the respect that a different person or different property is injured or affected or that the probable injury or harm would have been more serious or more extensive than that caused; or

(b) the actual result involves the same kind of injury or harm as the probable result and is not too remote or accidental in its occurrence to have a [just] bearing on the actor's liability or on the gravity of his offense.

(4) When causing a particular result is a material element of an offense for which absolute liability is imposed by law, the element is not established unless the actual result is a probable consequence of the actor's conduct.

Section 2.04. Ignorance or Mistake.

(1) Ignorance or mistake as to a matter of fact or law is a defense if:

(a) the ignorance or mistake negatives the purpose, knowledge, belief, recklessness or negligence required to establish a material element of the offense; or

(b) the law provides that the state of mind established by such ignorance or mistake constitutes a defense.

(2) Although ignorance or mistake would otherwise afford a defense to the offense charged, the defense is not available if the defendant would be guilty of another offense had the situation been as he supposed. In such case, however, the ignorance or mistake of the defendant shall reduce the grade and degree of the offense of which he may be

convicted to those of the offense of which he would be guilty had the situation been as he supposed.

(3) A belief that conduct does not legally constitute an offense is a defense to a prosecution for that offense based upon such conduct when:

(a) the statute or other enactment defining the offense is not known to the actor and has not been published or otherwise reasonably made available prior to the conduct alleged; or

(b) he acts in reasonable reliance upon an official statement of the law, afterward determined to be invalid or erroneous, contained in (i) a statute or other enactment; (ii) a judicial decision, opinion or judgment; (iii) an administrative order or grant of permission; or (iv) an official interpretation of the public officer or body charged by law with responsibility for the interpretation, administration or enforcement of the law defining the offense.

(4) The defendant must prove a defense arising under Subsection (3) of this Section by a preponderance of evidence.

Section 2.05. When Culpability Requirements Are Inapplicable to Violations and to Offenses Defined by Other Statutes; Effect of Absolute Liability in Reducing Grade of Offense to Violation.

(1) The requirements of culpability prescribed by Sections 2.01 and 2.02 do not apply to:

(a) offenses which constitute violations, unless the requirement involved is included in the definition of the offense or the Court determines that its application is consistent with effective enforcement of the law defining the offense; or

(b) offenses defined by statutes other than the Code, insofar as a legislative purpose to impose absolute liability for such offenses or with respect to any material element thereof plainly appears.

(2) Notwithstanding any other provision of existing law and unless a subsequent statute otherwise provides:

(a) when absolute liability is imposed with respect to any material element of an offense defined by a statute other than the Code and a conviction is based upon such liability, the offense constitutes a violation; and

(b) although absolute liability is imposed by law with respect to one or more of the material elements of an offense defined by a statute other than the Code, the culpable commission of the offense may be charged and proved, in which event negligence with respect to such elements constitutes sufficient culpability and the classification of the offense and the sentence that may be imposed therefor upon conviction are determined by Section 1.04 and Article 6 of the Code.

Section 2.06. Liability for Conduct of Another; Complicity.

(1) A person is guilty of an offense if it is committed by his own conduct or by the conduct of another person for which he is legally accountable, or both.

(2) A person is legally accountable for the conduct of another person when:

(a) acting with the kind of culpability that is sufficient for the commission of the offense, he causes an innocent or irresponsible person to engage in such conduct; or

(b) he is made accountable for the conduct of such other person by the Code or by the law defining the offense; or

(c) he is an accomplice of such other person in the commission of the offense.

(3) A person is an accomplice of another person in the commission of an offense if:

(a) with the purpose of promoting or facilitating the commission of the offense, he

(i) solicits such other person to commit it; or

(ii) aids or agrees or attempts to aid such other person in planning or committing it; or

(iii) having a legal duty to prevent the commission of the offense, fails to make proper effort so to do; or

(b) his conduct is expressly declared by law to establish his complicity.

(4) When causing a particular result is an element of an offense, an accomplice in the conduct causing such result is an accomplice in the commission of that offense, if he acts with the kind of culpability, if any, with respect to that result that is sufficient for the commission of the offense.

(5) A person who is legally incapable of committing a particular offense himself may be guilty thereof if it is committed by the conduct of another person for which he is legally accountable, unless such liability is inconsistent with the purpose of the provision establishing his incapacity.

(6) Unless otherwise provided by the Code or by the law defining the offense, a person is not an accomplice in an offense committed by another person if:

(a) he is a victim of that offense; or

(b) the offense is so defined that his conduct is inevitably incident to its commission; or

(c) he terminates his complicity prior to the commission of the offense and

(i) wholly deprives it of effectiveness in the commission of the offense; or

(ii) gives timely warning to the law enforcement authorities or otherwise makes proper effort to prevent the commission of the offense.

(7) An accomplice may be convicted on proof of the commission of the offense and of his complicity therein, though the person claimed to have committed the offense has not been prosecuted or convicted or has been convicted of a different offense or degree of offense or has an immunity to prosecution or conviction or has been acquitted.

Section 2.07. Liability of Corporations, Unincorporated Associations and Persons Acting, or Under a Duty to Act, in Their Behalf.

(1) A corporation may be convicted of the commission of an offense if:

(a) the offense is a violation or the offense is defined by a statute other than the Code in which a legislative purpose to impose liability on corporations plainly appears and the conduct is performed by an agent of the corporation acting in behalf of the corporation within the scope of his office or employment, except that if the law defining the offense designates the agents for whose conduct the corporation is accountable or the circumstances under which it is accountable, such provisions shall apply; or

(b) the offense consists of an omission to discharge a specific duty of affirmative performance imposed on corporations by law; or

(c) the commission of the offense was authorized, requested, commanded, performed or recklessly tolerated by the board of directors or by a high managerial agent acting in behalf of the corporation within the scope of his office or employment.

(2) When absolute liability is imposed for the commission of an offense, a legislative purpose to impose liability on a corporation shall be assumed, unless the contrary plainly appears.

(3) An unincorporated association may be convicted of the commission of an offense if:

(a) the offense is defined by a statute other than the Code which expressly provides for the liability of such an association and the conduct is performed by an agent of the association acting in behalf of the association within the scope of his office or employment, except that if the law defining the offense designates the agents for whose conduct the association is accountable or the circumstances under which it is accountable, such provisions shall apply; or

(b) the offense consists of an omission to discharge a specific duty of affirmative performance imposed on associations by law.

(4) As used in this Section:

(a) "corporation" does not include an entity organized as or by a governmental agency for the execution of a governmental program;

(b) "agent" means any director, officer, servant, employee or other person authorized to act in behalf of the corporation or association and, in the case of an unincorporated association, a member of such association;

(c) "high managerial agent" means an officer of a corporation or an unincorporated association, or, in the case of a partnership, a partner, or any other agent of a corporation or association having duties of such responsibility that his conduct may fairly be assumed to represent the policy of the corporation or association.

(5) In any prosecution of a corporation or an unincorporated association for the commission of an offense included within the terms of Subsection (1)(a) or Subsection (3)(a) of this Section, other than an offense for which absolute liability has been imposed, it shall be a defense if the defendant proves by a preponderance of evidence that the high managerial agent having supervisory responsibility over the subject matter of the offense employed due diligence to prevent its commission. This paragraph shall not apply if it is plainly inconsistent with the legislative purpose in defining the particular offense.

(6)(a) A person is legally accountable for any conduct he performs or causes to be performed in the name of the corporation or an unincorporated association or in its behalf to the same extent as if it were performed in his own name or behalf.

(b) Whenever a duty to act is imposed by law upon a corporation or an unincorporated association, any agent of the corporation or association having primary responsibility for the discharge of the duty is legally accountable for a reckless omission to perform the required act to the same extent as if the duty were imposed by law directly upon himself.

(c) When a person is convicted of an offense by reason of his legal accountability for the conduct of a corporation or an unincorporated association, he is subject to the sentence authorized by law when a natural person is convicted of an offense of the grade and the degree involved.

Section 2.08. Intoxication.

(1) Except as provided in Subsection (4) of this Section, intoxication of the actor is not a defense unless it negatives an element of the offense.

(2) When recklessness establishes an element of the offense, if the actor, due to self-induced intoxication, is unaware of a risk of which he would have been aware had he been sober, such unawareness is immaterial.

(3) Intoxication does not, in itself, constitute mental disease within the meaning of Section 4.01.

(4) Intoxication which (a) is not self-induced or (b) is pathological is an affirmative defense if by reason of such intoxication the actor at the time of his conduct lacks substantial capacity either to appreciate its criminality [wrongfulness] or to conform his conduct to the requirements of law.

(5) *Definitions.* In this Section unless a different meaning plainly is required:

(a) "intoxication" means a disturbance of mental or physical capacities resulting from the introduction of substances into the body;

(b) "self-induced intoxication" means intoxication caused by substances which the actor knowingly introduces into his body, the tendency of which to cause intoxication he knows or ought to know, unless he introduces them pursuant to medical advice or under such circumstances as would afford a defense to a charge of crime;

(c) "pathological intoxication" means intoxication grossly excessive in degree, given the amount of the intoxicant, to which the actor does not know he is susceptible.

Section 2.09. Duress.

(1) It is an affirmative defense that the actor engaged in the conduct charged to constitute an offense because he was coerced to do so by the use of, or a threat to use, unlawful force against his person or the person of another, which a person of reasonable firmness in his situation would have been unable to resist

(2) The defense provided by this Section is unavailable if the actor recklessly placed himself in a situation in which it was probable that he would be subjected to duress. The defense is also unavailable if he was negligent in placing himself in such a situation, whenever negligence suffices to establish culpability for the offense charged.

(3) It is not a defense that a woman acted on the command of her husband, unless she acted under such coercion as would establish a defense under this Section. [The presumption that a woman, acting in the presence of her husband, is coerced is abolished.]

(4) When the conduct of the actor would otherwise be justifiable under Section 3.02, this Section does not preclude such defense.

Section 2.10. Military Orders.

It is an affirmative defense that the actor, in engaging in the conduct charged to constitute an offense, does no more than execute an order of his superior in the armed services which he does not know to be unlawful.

Section 2.11. Consent

(1) *In General.* The consent of the victim to conduct charged to constitute an offense or to the result thereof is a defense if such consent negatives an element of the offense or precludes the infliction of the harm or evil sought to be prevented by the law defining the offense.

(2) *Consent to Bodily Harm.* When conduct is charged to constitute an offense because it causes or threatens bodily harm, consent to such conduct or to the infliction of such harm is a defense if:

(a) the bodily harm consented to or threatened by the conduct consented to is not serious; or

(b) the conduct and the harm are reasonably foreseeable hazards of joint participation in a lawful athletic contest or competitive sport; or

(c) the consent establishes a justification for the conduct under Article 3 of the Code.

(3) *Ineffective Consent.* Unless otherwise provided by the Code or by the law defining the offense, assent does not constitute consent if:

(a) it is given by a person who is legally incompetent to authorize the conduct charged to constitute the offense; or

(b) it is given by a person who by reason of youth, mental disease or defect or intoxication is manifestly unable or known by the actor to be unable to make a reasonable judgment as to the nature or harmfulness of the conduct charged to constitute the offense; or

(c) it is given by a person whose improvident consent is sought to be prevented by the law defining the offense; or

(d) it is induced by force, duress or deception of a kind sought to be prevented by the law defining the offense.

Section 2.12. De Minimis Infractions.

The Court shall dismiss a prosecution if, having regard to the nature of the conduct charged to constitute an offense and the nature of the attendant circumstances, it finds that the defendant's conduct:

(1) was within a customary license or tolerance, neither expressly negatived by the person whose interest was infringed nor inconsistent with the purpose of the law defining the offense; or

(2) did not actually cause or threaten the harm or evil sought to be prevented by the law defining the offense or did so only to an extent too trivial to warrant the condemnation of conviction; or

(3) presents such other extenuations that it cannot reasonably be regarded as envisaged by the legislature in forbidding the offense.

The Court shall not dismiss a prosecution under Subsection (3) of this Section without filing a written statement of its reasons.

Section 2.13. Entrapment

(1) A public law enforcement official or a person acting in cooperation with such an official perpetrates an entrapment if for the purpose of obtaining evidence of the commission of an offense, he induces or encourages another person to engage in conduct constituting such offense by either:

(a) making knowingly false representations designed to induce the belief that such conduct is not prohibited; or

(b) employing methods of persuasion or inducement which create a substantial risk that such an offense will be committed by persons other than those who are ready to commit it.

(2) Except as provided in Subsection (3) of this Section, a person prosecuted for an offense shall be acquitted if he proves by a preponderance of evidence that his conduct occurred in response to an entrapment. The issue of entrapment shall be tried by the Court in the absence of the jury.

(3) The defense afforded by this Section is unavailable when causing or threatening bodily injury is an element of the offense charged and the prosecution is based on conduct causing or threatening such injury to a person other than the person perpetrating the entrapment.

ARTICLE 3. GENERAL PRINCIPLES OF JUSTIFICATION

Section 3.01. Justification an Affirmative Defense; Civil Remedies Unaffected.

(1) In any prosecution based on conduct which is justifiable under this Article, justification is an affirmative defense.

(2) The fact that conduct is justifiable under this Article does not abolish or impair any remedy for such conduct which is available in any civil action.

Section 3.02. Justification Generally: Choice of Evils

(1) Conduct which the actor believes to be necessary to avoid a harm or evil to himself or to another is justifiable, provided that:

    (a) the harm or evil sought to be avoided by such conduct is greater than that sought to be prevented by the law defining the offense charged; and

    (b) neither the Code nor other law defining the offense provides exceptions or defenses dealing with the specific situation involved; and

    (c) a legislative purpose to exclude the justification claimed does not otherwise plainly appear.

(2) When the actor was reckless or negligent in bringing about the situation requiring a choice of harms or evils or in appraising the necessity for his conduct, the justification afforded by this Section is unavailable in a prosecution for any offense for which recklessness or negligence, as the case may be, suffices to establish culpability.

Section 3.03. Execution of Public Duty.

(1) Except as provided in Subsection (2) of this Section, conduct is justifiable when it is required or authorized by:

    (a) the law defining the duties or functions of a public officer or the assistance to be rendered to such officer in the performance of his duties; or

    (b) the law governing the execution of legal process; or

    (c) the judgment or order of a competent court or tribunal; or

    (d) the law governing the armed services or the lawful conduct of war; or

    (e) any other provision of law imposing a public duty.

(2) The other sections of this Article apply to:

    (a) the use of force upon or toward the person of another for any of the purposes dealt with in such sections; and

    (b) the use of deadly force for any purpose, unless the use of such force is otherwise expressly authorized by law or occurs in the lawful conduct of war.

(3) The justification afforded by Subsection (1) of this Section applies:

(a) when the actor believes his conduct to be required or authorized by the judgment or direction of a competent court or tribunal or in the lawful execution of legal process, notwithstanding lack of jurisdiction of the court or defect in the legal process; and

(b) when the actor believes his conduct to be required or authorized to assist a public officer in the performance of his duties, notwithstanding that the officer exceeded his legal authority.

Section 3.04. Use of Force in Self-Protection.

(1) *Use of Force Justifiable for Protection of the Person.* Subject to the provisions of this Section and of Section 3.09, the use of force upon or toward another person is justifiable when the actor believes that such force is immediately necessary for the purpose of protecting himself against the use of unlawful force by such other person on the present occasion.

(2) *Limitations on Justifying Necessity for Use of Force.*

    (a) The use of force is not justifiable under this Section:

        (i) to resist an arrest which the actor knows is being made by a peace officer, although the arrest is unlawful; or

        (ii) to resist force used by the occupier or possessor of property or by another person on his behalf, where the actor knows that the person using the force is doing so under a claim of right to protect the property, except that this limitation shall not apply if:

            (1) the actor is a public officer acting in the performance of his duties or a person lawfully assisting him therein or a person making or assisting in a lawful arrest; or

            (2) the actor has been unlawfully dispossessed of the property and is making a re-entry or recaption justified by Section 3.06; or

            (3) the actor believes that such force is necessary to protect himself against death or serious bodily harm.

    (b) The use of deadly force is not justifiable under this Section unless the actor believes that such force is necessary to protect himself against death, serious bodily harm, kidnapping or sexual intercourse compelled by force or threat; nor is it justifiable if:

        (i) the actor, with the purpose of causing death or serious bodily harm, provoked the use of force against himself in the same encounter; or

        (ii) the actor knows that he can avoid the necessity of using such force with complete safety by retreating or by surrendering possession of a thing to a person asserting a claim of right thereto or by complying with a demand that he abstain from any action which he has no duty to take, except that:

            (1) the actor is not obliged to retreat from his dwelling or place of work, unless he was the initial aggressor or is assailed in his place of work by another person whose place of work the actor knows it to be; and

            (2) a public officer justified in using force in the performance of his duties or a person justified in using force in his assistance or a person justified in using force in making an arrest or preventing an escape is not obliged to desist from efforts to perform such duty, effect such arrest or prevent such escape

because of resistance or threatened resistance by or on behalf of the person against whom such action is directed.

(c) Except as required by paragraphs (a) and (b) of this Subsection, a person employing protective force may estimate the necessity thereof under the circumstances as he believes them to be when the force is used, without retreating, surrendering possession, doing any other act which he has no legal duty to do or abstaining from any lawful action.

(3) *Use of Confinement as Protective Force.* The justification afforded by this Section extends to the use of confinement as protective force only if the actor takes all reasonable measures to terminate the confinement as soon as he knows that he safely can, unless the person confined has been arrested on a charge of crime.

Section 3.05. Use of Force for the Protection of Other Persons.

(1) Subject to the provisions of this Section and of Section 3.09, the use of force upon or toward the person of another is justifiable to protect a third person when:

(a) the actor would be justified under Section 3.04 in using such force to protect himself against the injury he believes to be threatened to the person whom he seeks to protect; and

(b) under the circumstances as the actor believes them to be, the person whom he seeks to protect would be justified in using such protective force; and

(c) the actor believes that his intervention is necessary for the protection of such other person.

(2) Notwithstanding Subsection (1) of this Section:

(a) when the actor would be obliged under Section 3.04 to retreat, to surrender the possession of a thing or to comply with a demand before using force in self-protection, he is not obliged to do so before using force for the protection of another person, unless he knows that he can thereby secure the complete safety of such other person; and

(b) when the person whom the actor seeks to protect would be obliged under Section 3.04 to retreat, to surrender the possession of a thing or to comply with a demand if he knew that he could obtain complete safety by so doing, the actor is obliged to try to cause him to do so before using force in his protection if the actor knows that he can obtain complete safety in that way; and

(c) neither the actor nor the person whom he seeks to protect is obliged to retreat when in the other's dwelling or place of work to any greater extent than in his own.

Section 3.06. Use of Force for the Protection of Property.

(1) *Use of Force Justifiable for Protection of Property.* Subject to the provisions of this Section and of Section 3.09, the use of force upon or toward the person of another is justifiable when the actor believes that such force is immediately necessary:

(a) to prevent or terminate an unlawful entry or other trespass upon land or a trespass against or the unlawful carrying away of tangible, movable property, provided that such land or movable property is, or is believed by the actor to be, in his possession or in the possession of another person for whose protection he acts; or

(b) to effect an entry or re-entry upon land or to retake tangible movable property, provided that the actor believes that he or the person by whose authority he acts or a person from whom he or such other person derives title was unlawfully dispossessed of such land or movable property and is entitled to possession, and provided, further, that:

(i) the force is used immediately or on fresh pursuit after such dispossession; or

(ii) the actor believes that the person against whom he uses force has no claim of right to the possession of the property and, in the case of land, the circumstances, as the actor believes them to be, are of such urgency that it would be an exceptional hardship to postpone the entry or re-entry until a court order is obtained.

(2) *Meaning of Possession.* For the purposes of Subsection (1) of this Section:

(a) a person who has parted with the custody of property to another who refuses to restore it to him is no longer in possession, unless the property is movable and was and still is located on land in his possession;

(b) a person who has been dispossessed of land does not regain possession thereof merely by setting foot thereon;

(c) a person who has a license to use or occupy real property is deemed to be in possession thereof except against the licensor acting under claim of right.

(3) *Limitations on Justifiable Use of Force.*

(a) *Request to Desist.* The use of force is justifiable under this Section only if the actor first requests the person against whom such force is used to desist from his interference with the property, unless the actor believes that:

(i) such request would be useless; or

(ii) it would be dangerous to himself or another person to make the request; or

(iii) substantial harm will be done to the physical condition of the property which is sought to be protected before the request can effectively be made.

(b) *Exclusion of Trespasser.* The use of force to prevent or terminate a trespass is not justifiable under this Section if the actor knows that the exclusion of the trespasser will expose him to substantial danger of serious bodily harm.

(c) Resistance of Lawful Re-entry or Recaption. The use of force to prevent an entry or re-entry upon land or the recaption of movable property is not justifiable under this Section, although the actor believes that such re-entry or recaption is unlawful, if:

(i) the re-entry or recaption is made by or on behalf of a person who was actually dispossessed of the property; and

(ii) it is otherwise justifiable under paragraph (1)(b) of this Section.

(d) *Use of Deadly Force.* The use of deadly force is not justifiable under this Section unless the actor believes that:

(i) the person against whom the force is used is attempting to dispossess him of his dwelling otherwise than under a claim of right to its possession; or

(ii) the person against whom the force is used is attempting to commit or consummate arson, burglary, robbery or other felonious theft or property destruction and either:

(1) has employed or threatened deadly force against or in the presence of the actor; or

(2) the use of force other than deadly force to prevent the commission or the consummation of the crime would expose the actor or another in his presence to substantial danger of serious bodily harm.

(4) *Use of Confinement as Protective Force.* The justification afforded by this Section extends to the use of confinement as protective force only if the actor takes all reasonable measures to terminate the confinement as soon as he knows that he can do so with safety to the property, unless the person confined has been arrested on a charge of crime.

(5) *Use of Device to Protect Property.* The justification afforded by this Section extends to the use of a device for the purpose of protecting property only if:

(a) the device is not designed to cause or known to create a substantial risk of causing death or serious bodily harm; and

(b) the use of the particular device to protect the property from entry or trespass is reasonable under the circumstances, as the actor believes them to be; and

(c) the device is one customarily used for such a purpose or reasonable care is taken to make known to probable intruders the fact that it is used.

(6) *Use of Force to Pass Wrongful Obstructor.* The use of force to pass a person whom the actor believes to be purposely or knowingly and unjustifiably obstructing the actor from going to a place to which he may lawfully go is justifiable, provided that:

(a) the actor believes that the person against whom he uses force has no claim of right to obstruct the actor; and

(b) the actor is not being obstructed from entry or movement on land which he knows to be in the possession or custody of the person obstructing him, or in the possession or custody of another person by whose authority the obstructor acts, unless the circumstances, as the actor believes them to be, are of such urgency that it would not be reasonable to postpone the entry or movement on such land until a court order is obtained; and

(c) the force used is not greater than would be justifiable if the person obstructing the actor were using force against him to prevent his passage.

Section 3.07. Use of Force in Law Enforcement.

(1) *Use of Force Justifiable to Effect an Arrest.* Subject to the provisions of this Section and of Section 3.09, the use of force upon or toward the person of another is justifiable when the actor is making or assisting in making an arrest and the actor believes that such force is immediately necessary to effect a lawful arrest.

(2) Limitations on the Use of Force.

(a) The use of force is not justifiable under this Section unless:

(i) the actor makes known the purpose of the arrest or believes that it is otherwise known by or cannot reasonably be made known to the person to be arrested; and

(ii) when the arrest is made under a warrant, the warrant is valid or believed by the actor to be valid.

(b) The use of deadly force is not justifiable under this Section unless:

(i) the arrest is for a felony; and

(ii) the person effecting the arrest is authorized to act as a peace officer or is assisting a person whom he believes to be authorized to act as a peace officer; and

(iii) the actor believes that the force employed creates no substantial risk of injury to innocent persons; and

(iv) the actor believes that:

(1) the crime for which the arrest is made involved conduct including the use or threatened use of deadly force; or

(2) there is a substantial risk that the person to be arrested will cause death or serious bodily harm if his apprehension is delayed.

(3) *Use of Force to Prevent Escape from Custody.* The use of force to prevent the escape of an arrested person from custody is justifiable when the force could justifiably have been employed to effect the arrest under which the person is in custody, except that a guard or other person authorized to act as a peace officer is justified in using any force, including deadly force, which he believes to be immediately necessary to prevent the escape of a person from a jail, prison, or other institution for the detention of persons charged with or convicted of a crime.

(4) *Use of Force by Private Person Assisting an Unlawful Arrest.*

(a) A private person who is summoned by a peace officer to assist in effecting an unlawful arrest, is justified in using any force which he would be justified in using if the arrest were lawful, provided that he does not believe the arrest is unlawful.

(b) A private person who assists another private person in effecting an unlawful arrest, or who, not being summoned, assists a peace officer in effecting an unlawful arrest, is justified in using any force which he would be justified in using if the arrest were lawful, provided that (i) he believes the arrest is lawful, and (ii) the arrest would be lawful if the facts were as he believes them to be.

(5) *Use of Force to Prevent Suicide or the Commission of a Crime.*

(a) The use of force upon or toward the person of another is justifiable when the actor believes that such force is immediately necessary to prevent such other person from committing suicide, inflicting serious bodily harm upon himself, committing or consummating the commission of a crime involving or threatening bodily harm, damage to or loss of property or a breach of the peace, except that:

(i) any limitations imposed by the other provisions of this Article on the justifiable use of force in self-protection, for the protection of others, the protection of property, the effectuation of an arrest or the prevention of an escape from custody shall apply notwithstanding the criminality of the conduct against which such force is used; and

(ii) the use of deadly force is not in any event justifiable under this Subsection unless:

(1) the actor believes that there is a substantial risk that the person whom he seeks to prevent from committing a crime will cause death or serious bodily harm to another unless the commission or the consummation of the crime is prevented and that the use of such force presents no substantial risk of injury to innocent persons; or

(2) the actor believes that the use of such force is necessary to suppress a riot or mutiny after the rioters or mutineers have been ordered to disperse and warned, in any particular manner that the law may require, that such force will be used if they do not obey.

(b) The justification afforded by this Subsection extends to the use of confinement as preventive force only if the actor takes all reasonable measures to terminate the confinement as soon as he knows that he safely can, unless the person confined has been arrested on a charge of crime.

Section 3.08. Use of Force by Persons with Special Responsibility for Care, Discipline or Safety of Others.

The use of force upon or toward the person of another is justifiable if:

(1) the actor is the parent or guardian or other person similarly responsible for the general care and supervision of a minor or a person acting at the request of such parent, guardian or other responsible person and:

(a) the force is used for the purpose of safeguarding or promoting the welfare of the minor, including the prevention or punishment of his misconduct; and

(b) the force used is not designed to cause or known to create a substantial risk of causing death, serious bodily harm, disfigurement, extreme pain or mental distress or gross degradation; or

(2) the actor is a teacher or a person otherwise entrusted with the care or supervision for a special purpose of a minor and:

(a) the actor believes that the force used is necessary to further such special purpose, including the maintenance of reasonable discipline in a school, class or other group, and that the use of such force is consistent with the welfare of the minor; and

(b) the degree of force, if it had been used by the parent or guardian of the minor, would not be unjustifiable under Subsection (1)(b) of this Section; or

(3) the actor is the guardian or other person similarly responsible for the general care and supervision of an incompetent person; and:

(a) the force is used for the purpose of safeguarding or promoting the welfare of the incompetent person, including the prevention of his misconduct, or, when such incompetent person is in a hospital or other institution for his care and custody, for the maintenance of reasonable discipline in such institution; and

(b) the force used is not designed to cause or known to create a substantial risk of causing death, serious bodily harm, disfigurement, extreme or unnecessary pain, mental distress, or humiliation; or

(4) the actor is a doctor or other therapist or a person assisting him at his direction, and:

(a) the force is used for the purpose of administering a recognized form of treatment which the actor believes to be adapted to promoting the physical or mental health of the patient; and

(b) the treatment is administered with the consent of the patient or, if the patient is a minor or an incompetent person, with the consent of his parent or guardian or other person legally competent to consent in his behalf, or the treatment is administered in an emergency when the actor believes that no one competent to consent can be consulted and that a reasonable person, wishing to safeguard the welfare of the patient, would consent; or

(5) the actor is a warden or other authorized official of a correctional institution, and:

(a) he believes that the force used is necessary for the purpose of enforcing the lawful rules or procedures of the institution, unless his belief in the lawfulness of the rule or procedure sought to be enforced is erroneous and his error is due to ignorance or mistake as to the provisions of the Code, any other provision of the criminal law or the law governing the administration of the institution; and

(b) the nature or degree of force used is not forbidden by Article 303 or 304 of the Code; and

(c) if deadly force is used, its use is otherwise justifiable under this Article; or

(6) the actor is a person responsible for the safety of a vessel or an aircraft or a person acting at his direction, and

(a) he believes that the force used is necessary to prevent interference with the operation of the vessel or aircraft or obstruction of the execution of a lawful order, unless his belief in the lawfulness of the order is erroneous and his error is due to ignorance or mistake as to the law defining his authority; and

(b) if deadly force is used, its use is otherwise justifiable under this Article; or

(7) the actor is a person who is authorized or required by law to maintain order or decorum in a vehicle, train or other carrier or in a place where others are assembled, and:

(a) he believes that the force used is necessary for such purpose; and

(b) the force used is not designed to cause or known to create a substantial risk of causing death, bodily harm, or extreme mental distress.

Section 3.09. Mistake of Law as to Unlawfulness of Force or Legality of Arrest; Reckless or Negligent Use of Otherwise Justifiable Force; Reckless or Negligent Injury or Risk of Injury to Innocent Persons.

(1) The justification afforded by Sections 3.04 to 3.07, inclusive, is unavailable when:

(a) the actor's belief in the unlawfulness of the force or conduct against which he employs protective force or his belief in the lawfulness of an arrest which he endeavors to effect by force is erroneous; and

(b) his error is due to ignorance or mistake as to the provisions of the Code, any other provision of the criminal law or the law governing the legality of an arrest or search.

(2) When the actor believes that the use of force upon or toward the person of another is necessary for any of the purposes for which such belief would establish a justification under Sections 3.03 to 3.08 but the actor is reckless or negligent in having such belief or in acquiring or failing to acquire any knowledge or belief which is material to the justifiability of his use of force, the justification afforded by those Sections is unavailable in a prosecution for an offense for which recklessness or negligence, as the case may be, suffices to establish culpability.

(3) When the actor is justified under Sections 3.03 to 3.08 in using force upon or toward the person of another but he recklessly or negligently injures or creates a risk of injury to innocent persons, the justification afforded by those Sections is unavailable in a prosecution for such recklessness or negligence towards innocent persons.

Section 3.10. Justification in Property Crimes.

Conduct involving the appropriation, seizure or destruction of, damage to, intrusion on or interference with property is justifiable under circumstances which would establish a defense of privilege in a civil action based thereon, unless:

(1) the Code or the law defining the offense deals with the specific situation involved; or

(2) a legislative purpose to exclude the justification claimed otherwise plainly appears.

Section 3.11. Definitions.

In this Article, unless a different meaning plainly is required:

(1) "unlawful force" means force, including confinement, which is employed without the consent of the person against whom it is directed and the employment of which

constitutes an offense or actionable tort or would constitute such offense or tort except for a defense (such as the absence of intent, negligence, or mental capacity; duress; youth; or diplomatic status) not amounting to a privilege to use the force. Assent constitutes consent, within the meaning of this Section, whether or not it otherwise is legally effective, except assent to the infliction of death or serious bodily harm.

(2) "deadly force" means force which the actor uses with the purpose of causing or which he knows to create a substantial risk of causing death or serious bodily harm. Purposely firing a firearm in the direction of another person or at a vehicle in which another person is believed to be constitutes deadly force. A threat to cause death or serious bodily harm, by the production of a weapon or otherwise, so long as the actor's purpose is limited to creating an apprehension that he will use deadly force if necessary, does not constitute deadly force;

(3) "dwelling" means any building or structure, though movable or temporary, or a portion thereof, which is for the time being the actor's home or place of lodging.

ARTICLE 4. RESPONSIBILITY

Section 4.01. Mental Disease or Defect Excluding Responsibility.
(1) A person is not responsible for criminal conduct if at the time of such conduct as a result of mental disease or defect he lacks substantial capacity either to appreciate the criminality [wrongfulness] of his conduct or to conform his conduct to the requirements of law.

(2) As used in this Article, the terms "mental disease or defect" do not include an abnormality manifested only by repeated criminal or otherwise anti-social conduct.

Section 4.02. Evidence of Mental Disease or Defect Admissible When Relevant to Element of the Offense; [Mental Disease or Defect Impairing Capacity as Ground for Mitigation of Punishment in Capital Cases].
(1) Evidence that the defendant suffered from a mental disease or defect is admissible whenever it is relevant to prove that the defendant did or did not have a state of mind which is an element of the offense.

[(2) Whenever the jury or the Court is authorized to determine or to recommend whether or not the defendant shall be sentenced to death or imprisonment upon conviction, evidence that the capacity of the defendant to appreciate the criminality [wrongfulness] of his conduct or to conform his conduct to the requirements of law was impaired as a result of mental disease or defect is admissible in favor of sentence of imprisonment.]

Section 4.03. Mental Disease or Defect Excluding Responsibility Is Affirmative Defense; Requirement of Notice; Form of Verdict and Judgment When Finding of Irresponsibility Is Made.
(1) Mental disease or defect excluding responsibility is an affirmative defense.

(2) Evidence of mental disease or defect excluding responsibility is not admissible unless the defendant, at the time of entering his plea of not guilty or within ten days thereafter or at such later time as the Court may for good cause permit, files a written notice of his purpose to rely on such defense.

(3) When the defendant is acquitted on the ground of mental disease or defect excluding responsibility, the verdict and the judgment shall so state.

Section 4.04. Mental Disease or Defect Excluding Fitness to Proceed.

No person who as a result of mental disease or defect lacks capacity to understand the proceedings against him or to assist in his own defense shall be tried, convicted or sentenced for the commission of an offense so long as such incapacity endures.

Section 4.05. Psychiatric Examination of Defendant with Respect to Mental Disease or Defect.

(1) Whenever the defendant has filed a notice of intention to rely on the defense of mental disease or defect excluding responsibility, or there is reason to doubt his fitness to proceed, or reason to believe that mental disease or defect of the defendant will otherwise become an issue in the cause, the Court shall appoint at least one qualified psychiatrist or shall request the Superintendent of the _____ Hospital to designate at least one qualified psychiatrist, which designation may be or include himself, to examine and report upon the mental condition of the defendant. The Court may order the defendant to be committed to a hospital or other suitable facility for the purpose of the examination for a period of not exceeding sixty days or such longer period as the Court determines to be necessary for the purpose and may direct that a qualified psychiatrist retained by the defendant be permitted to witness and participate in the examination.

(2) In such examination any method may be employed which is accepted by the medical profession for the examination of those alleged to be suffering from mental disease or defect.

(3) The report of the examination shall include the following: (a) a description of the nature of the examination; (b) a diagnosis of the mental condition of the defendant; (c) if the defendant suffers from a mental disease or defect, an opinion as to his capacity to understand the proceedings against him and to assist in his own defense; (d) when a notice of intention to rely on the defense of irresponsibility has been filed, an opinion as to the extent, if any, to which the capacity of the defendant to appreciate the criminality [wrongfulness] of his conduct or to conform his conduct to the requirements of law was impaired at the time of the criminal conduct charged; and (e) when directed by the Court, an opinion as to the capacity of the defendant to have a particular state of mind which is an element of the offense charged.

If the examination can not be conducted by reason of the unwillingness of the defendant to participate therein, the report shall so state and shall include, if possible, an opinion as to whether such unwillingness of the defendant was the result of mental disease or defect.

The report of the examination shall be filed [in triplicate] with the clerk of the Court, who shall cause copies to be delivered to the district attorney and to counsel for the defendant.

Section 4.06. Determination of Fitness to Proceed; Effect of Finding of Unfitness; Proceedings if Fitness is Regained [; Post-Commitment Hearing].

(1) When the defendant's fitness to proceed is drawn in question, the issue shall be determined by the Court. If neither the prosecuting attorney nor counsel for the

defendant contests the finding of the report filed pursuant to Section 4.05, the Court may make the determination on the basis of such report. If the finding is contested, the Court shall hold a hearing on the issue. If the report is received in evidence upon such hearing, the party who contests the finding thereof shall have the right to summon and to cross-examine the psychiatrists who joined in the report and to offer evidence upon the issue.

(2) If the Court determines that the defendant lacks fitness to proceed, the proceeding against him shall be suspended, except as provided in Subsection (3) [Subsections (3) and (4)] of this Section, and the Court shall commit him to the custody of the Commissioner of Mental Hygiene [Public Health or Correction] to be placed in an appropriate institution of the Department of Mental Hygiene [Public Health or Correction] for so long as such unfitness shall endure. When the Court, on its own motion or upon the application of the Commissioner of Mental Hygiene [Public Health or Correction] or the prosecuting attorney, determines, after a hearing if a hearing is requested, that the defendant has regained fitness to proceed, the proceeding shall be resumed. If, however, the Court is of the view that so much time has elapsed since the commitment of the defendant that it would be unjust to resume the criminal proceeding, the Court may dismiss the charge and may order the defendant to be discharged or, subject to the law governing the civil commitment of persons suffering from mental disease or defect, order the defendant to be committed to an appropriate institution of the Department of Mental Hygiene [Public Health].

(3) The fact that the defendant is unfit to proceed does not preclude any legal objection to the prosecution which is susceptible of fair determination prior to trial and without the personal participation of the defendant.

[Alternative: (3) At any time within ninety days after commitment as provided in Subsection (2) of this Section, or at any later time with permission of the Court granted for good cause, the defendant or his counsel or the Commissioner of Mental Hygiene [Public Health or Correction] may apply for a special post-commitment hearing. If the application is made by or on behalf of a defendant not represented by counsel, he shall be afforded a reasonable opportunity to obtain counsel, and if he lacks funds to do so, counsel shall be assigned by the Court. The application shall be granted only if the counsel for the defendant satisfies the Court by affidavit or otherwise that as an attorney he has reasonable grounds for a good faith belief that his client has, on the facts and the law, a defense to the charge other than mental disease or defect excluding responsibility.]

[(4) If the motion for a special post-commitment hearing is granted, the hearing shall be by the Court without a jury. No evidence shall be offered at the hearing by either party on the issue of mental disease or defect as a defense to, or in mitigation of, the crime charged. After hearing, the Court may in an appropriate case quash the indictment or other charge, or find it to be defective or insufficient, or determine that it is not proved beyond a reasonable doubt by the evidence, or otherwise terminate the proceedings on the evidence or the law. In any such case, unless all defects in the proceedings are promptly cured, the Court shall terminate the commitment ordered under Subsection (2) of this Section and order the defendant to be discharged or, subject to the law governing the civil commitment of persons suffering from mental disease or defect, order the defendant to be committed to an appropriate institution of the Department of Mental Hygiene [Public Health].]

Section 4.07. Determination of Irresponsibility on Basis of Report; Access to Defendant by Psychiatrist of His Own Choice; Form of Expert Testimony When Issue of Responsibility Is Tried.

(1) If the report filed pursuant to Section 4.05 finds that the defendant at the time of the criminal conduct charged suffered from a mental disease or defect which substantially impaired his capacity to appreciate the criminality [wrongfulness] of his conduct or to conform his conduct to the requirements of law, and the Court, after a hearing if a hearing is requested by the prosecuting attorney or the defendant, is satisfied that such impairment was sufficient to exclude responsibility, the Court on motion of the defendant shall enter judgment of acquittal on the ground of mental disease or defect excluding responsibility.

(2) When, notwithstanding the report filed pursuant to Section 4.05, the defendant wishes to be examined by a qualified psychiatrist or other expert of his own choice, such examiner shall be permitted to have reasonable access to the defendant for the purposes of such examination.

(3) Upon the trial, the psychiatrists who reported pursuant to Section 4.05 may be called as witnesses by the prosecution, the defendant or the Court. If the issue is being tried before a jury, the jury may be informed that the psychiatrists were designated by the Court or by the Superintendent of the _____ Hospital at the request of the Court, as the case may be. If called by the Court, the witness shall be subject to cross-examination by the prosecution and by the defendant. Both the prosecution and the defendant may summon any other qualified psychiatrist or other expert to testify, but no one who has not examined the defendant shall be competent to testify to an expert opinion with respect to the mental condition or responsibility of the defendant, as distinguished from the validity of the procedure followed by, or the general scientific propositions stated by, another witness.

(4) When a psychiatrist or other expert who has examined the defendant testifies concerning his mental condition, he shall be permitted to make a statement as to the nature of his examination, his diagnosis of the mental condition of the defendant at the time of the commission of the offense charged and his opinion as to the extent, if any, to which the capacity of the defendant to appreciate the criminality [wrongfulness] of his conduct or to conform his conduct to the requirements of law or to have a particular state of mind which is an element of the offense charged was impaired as a result of mental disease or defect at that time. He shall be permitted to make any explanation reasonably serving to clarify his diagnosis and opinion and may be cross-examined as to any matter bearing on his competency or credibility or the validity of his diagnosis or opinion.

Section 4.08. Legal Effect of Acquittal on the Ground of Mental Disease or Defect Excluding Responsibility; Commitment; Release or Discharge.

(1) When a defendant is acquitted on the ground of mental disease or defect excluding responsibility, the Court shall order him to be committed to the custody of the Commissioner of Mental Hygiene [Public Health] to be placed in an appropriate institution for custody, care and treatment.

(2) If the Commissioner of Mental Hygiene [Public Health] is of the view that a person committed to his custody, pursuant to paragraph (1) of this Section, may be discharged or released on condition without danger to himself or to others, he shall make application for the discharge or release of such person in a report to the Court by which such person was committed and shall transmit a copy of such application and report to the prosecuting attorney of the county [parish] from which the defendant was committed. The Court shall thereupon appoint at least two qualified psychiatrists to examine such person and to report within sixty days, or such longer period as the Court determines to be necessary for the purpose, their opinion as to his mental condition. To facilitate such examination and the proceedings thereon, the Court may cause such person to be confined in any institution located near the place where the Court sits, which may hereafter be designated by the Commissioner of Mental Hygiene [Public Health] as suitable for the temporary detention of irresponsible persons.

(3) If the Court is satisfied by the report filed pursuant to paragraph (2) of this Section and such testimony of the reporting psychiatrists as the Court deems necessary that the committed person may be discharged or released on condition without danger to himself or others, the Court shall order his discharge or his release on such conditions as the Court determines to be necessary. If the Court is not so satisfied, it shall promptly order a hearing to determine whether such person may safely be discharged or released. Any such hearing shall be deemed a civil proceeding and the burden shall be upon the committed person to prove that he may safely be discharged or released. According to the determination of the Court upon the hearing, the committed person shall thereupon be discharged or released on such conditions as the Court determines to be necessary, or shall be recommitted to the custody of the Commissioner of Mental Hygiene [Public Health], subject to discharge or release only in accordance with the procedure prescribed above for a first hearing.

(4) If, within [five] years after the conditional release of a committed person, the Court shall determine, after hearing evidence, that the conditions of release have not been fulfilled and that for the safety of such person or for the safety of others his conditional release should be revoked, the Court shall forthwith order him to be recommitted to the Commissioner of Mental Hygiene [Public Health], subject to discharge or release only in accordance with the procedure prescribed above for a first hearing.

(5) A committed person may make application for his discharge or release to the Court by which he was committed, and the procedure to be followed upon such application shall be the same as that prescribed above in the case of an application by the Commissioner of Mental Hygiene [Public Health]. However, no such application by a committed person need be considered until he has been confined for a period of not less than [six months] from the date of the order of commitment, and if the determination of the Court be adverse to the application, such person shall not be permitted to file a further application until [one year] has elapsed from the date of any preceding hearing on an application for his release or discharge.

Section 4.09. Omitted

Section 4.10. Immaturity Excluding Criminal Convictions; Transfer of Proceedings to Juvenile Court.

(1) A person shall not be tried for or convicted of an offense if:

(a) at the time of the conduct charged to constitute the offense he was less than sixteen years of age [, in which case the Juvenile Court shall have exclusive jurisdiction*]; or

(b) at the time of the conduct charged to constitute the offense he was sixteen or seventeen years of age, unless:

(i) the Juvenile Court has no jurisdiction over him, or,

(ii) the Juvenile Court has entered an order waiving jurisdiction and consenting to the institution of criminal proceedings against him.

(2) No court shall have jurisdiction to try or convict a person of an offense if criminal proceedings against him are barred by Subsection (1) of this Section. When it appears that a person charged with the commission of an offense may be of such an age that criminal proceedings may be barred under Subsection (1) of this Section, the Court shall hold a hearing thereon, and the burden shall be on the prosecution to establish to the satisfaction of the Court that the criminal proceeding is not barred upon such grounds. If the Court determines that the proceeding is barred, custody of the person charged shall be surrendered to the Juvenile Court, and the case, including all papers and processes relating thereto, shall be transferred.

* The bracketed words are unnecessary if the Juvenile Court Act so provides or is amended accordingly.

ARTICLE 5. INCHOATE CRIMES

Section 5.01. Criminal Attempt.

(1) *Definition of Attempt.* A person is guilty of an attempt to commit a crime if, acting with the kind of culpability otherwise required for commission of the crime, he:

(a) purposely engages in conduct which would constitute the crime if the attendant circumstances were as he believes them to be; or

(b) when causing a particular result is an element of the crime, does or omits to do anything with the purpose of causing or with the belief that it will cause such result without further conduct on his part; or

(c) purposely does or omits to do anything which, under the circumstances as he believes them to be, is an act or omission constituting a substantial step in a course of conduct planned to culminate in his commission of the crime.

(2) *Conduct Which May Be Held Substantial Step Under Subsection (1)(c).* Conduct shall not be held to constitute a substantial step under Subsection (1)(c) of this Section unless it is strongly corroborative of the actor's criminal purpose. Without negating the sufficiency of other conduct, the following, if strongly corroborative of the actor's criminal purpose, shall not be held insufficient as a matter of law:

(a) lying in wait, searching for or following the contemplated victim of the crime;

(b) enticing or seeking to entice the contemplated victim of the crime to go to the place contemplated for its commission;

(c) reconnoitering the place contemplated for the commission of the crime;

(d) unlawful entry of a structure, vehicle or enclosure in which it is contemplated that the crime will be committed;

(e) possession of materials to be employed in the commission of the crime, which are specially designed for such unlawful use or which can serve no lawful purpose of the actor under the circumstances;

(f) possession, collection or fabrication of materials to be employed in the commission of the crime, at or near the place contemplated for its commission, where such possession, collection or fabrication serves no lawful purpose of the actor under the circumstances;

(g) soliciting an innocent agent to engage in conduct constituting an element of the crime.

(3) *Conduct Designed to Aid Another in Commission of a Crime.* A person who engages in conduct designed to aid another to commit a crime which would establish his complicity under Section 2.06 if the crime were committed by such other person, is guilty of an attempt to commit the crime, although the crime is not committed or attempted by such other person.

(4) *Renunciation of Criminal Purpose.* When the actor's conduct would otherwise constitute an attempt under Subsection (1)(b) or (1)(c) of this Section, it is an affirmative defense that he abandoned his effort to commit the crime or otherwise prevented its commission, under circumstances manifesting a complete and voluntary renunciation of his criminal purpose. The establishment of such defense does not, however, affect the liability of an accomplice who did not join in such abandonment or prevention.

Within the meaning of this Article, renunciation of criminal purpose is not voluntary if it is motivated, in whole or in part, by circumstances, not present or apparent at the inception of the actor's course of conduct, which increase the probability of detection or apprehension or which make more difficult the accomplishment of the criminal purpose. Renunciation is not complete if it is motivated by a decision to postpone the criminal conduct until a more advantageous time or to transfer the criminal effort to another but similar objective or victim.

Section 5.02. Criminal Solicitation.

(1) *Definition of Solicitation.* A person is guilty of solicitation to commit a crime if with the purpose of promoting or facilitating its commission he commands, encourages or requests another person to engage in specific conduct which would constitute such crime or an attempt to commit such crime or which would establish his complicity in its commission or attempted commission.

(2) *Uncommunicated Solicitation.* It is immaterial under Subsection (1) of this Section that the actor fails to communicate with the person he solicits to commit a crime if his conduct was designed to effect such communication.

(3) *Renunciation of Criminal Purpose.* It is an affirmative defense that the actor, after soliciting another person to commit a crime, persuaded him not to do so or otherwise prevented the commission of the crime, under circumstances manifesting a complete and voluntary renunciation of his criminal purpose.

Section 5.03. Criminal Conspiracy.

(1) *Definition of Conspiracy.* A person is guilty of conspiracy with another person or persons to commit a crime if with the purpose of promoting or facilitating its commission he:

(a) agrees with such other person or persons that they or one or more of them will engage in conduct which constitutes such crime or an attempt or solicitation to commit such crime; or

(b) agrees to aid such other person or persons in the planning or commission of such crime or of an attempt or solicitation to commit such crime.

(2) *Scope of Conspiratorial Relationship.* If a person guilty of conspiracy, as defined by Subsection (1) of this Section, knows that a person with whom he conspires to commit a crime has conspired with another person or persons to commit the same crime, he is guilty of conspiring with such other person or persons, whether or not he knows their identity, to commit such crime.

(3) *Conspiracy With Multiple Criminal Objectives.* If a person conspires to commit a number of crimes, he is guilty of only one conspiracy so long as such multiple crimes are the object of the same agreement or continuous conspiratorial relationship.

(4) *Joinder and Venue in Conspiracy Prosecutions.*

(a) Subject to the provisions of paragraph (b) of this Subsection, two or more persons charged with criminal conspiracy may be prosecuted jointly if:

(i) they are charged with conspiring with one another; or

(ii) the conspiracies alleged, whether they have the same or different parties, are so related that they constitute different aspects of a scheme of organized criminal conduct.

(b) In any joint prosecution under paragraph (a) of this Subsection:

(i) no defendant shall be charged with a conspiracy in any county [parish or district] other than one in which he entered into such conspiracy or in which an overt act pursuant to such conspiracy was done by him or by a person with whom he conspired; and

(ii) neither the liability of any defendant nor the admissibility against him of evidence of acts or declarations of another shall be enlarged by such joinder; and

(iii) the Court shall order a severance or take a special verdict as to any defendant who so requests, if it deems it necessary or appropriate to promote the fair determination of his guilt or innocence, and shall take any other proper measures to protect the fairness of the trial.

(5) *Overt Act.* No person may be convicted of conspiracy to commit a crime, other than a felony of the first or second degree, unless an overt act in pursuance of such conspiracy is alleged and proved to have been done by him or by a person with whom he conspired.

(6) *Renunciation of Criminal Purpose.* It is an affirmative defense that the actor, after conspiring to commit a crime, thwarted the success of the conspiracy, under circumstances manifesting a complete and voluntary renunciation of his criminal purpose.

(7) *Duration of Conspiracy.* For purposes of Section 1.06(4):

(a) conspiracy is a continuing course of conduct which terminates when the crime or crimes which are its object are committed or the agreement that they be committed is abandoned by the defendant and by those with whom he conspired; and

(b) such abandonment is presumed if neither the defendant nor anyone with whom he conspired does any overt act in pursuance of the conspiracy during the applicable period of limitation; and

(c) if an individual abandons the agreement, the conspiracy is terminated as to him only if and when he advises those with whom he conspired of his abandonment or he informs the law enforcement authorities of the existence of the conspiracy and of his participation therein.

Section 5.04. Incapacity, Irresponsibility or Immunity of Party to Solicitation or Conspiracy.

(1) Except as provided in Subsection (2) of this Section, it is immaterial to the liability of a person who solicits or conspires with another to commit a crime that:

(a) he or the person whom he solicits or with whom he conspires does not occupy a particular position or have a particular characteristic which is an element of such crime, if he believes that one of them does; or

(b) the person whom he solicits or with whom he conspires is irresponsible or has an immunity to prosecution or conviction for the commission of the crime.

(2) It is a defense to a charge of solicitation or conspiracy to commit a crime that if the criminal object were achieved, the actor would not be guilty of a crime under the law defining the offense or as an accomplice under Section 2.06(5) or 2.06(6)(a) or (b).

Section 5.05. Grading of Criminal Attempt, Solicitation and Conspiracy; Mitigation in Cases of Lesser Danger; Multiple Convictions Barred.

(1) *Grading.* Except as otherwise provided in this Section, attempt, solicitation and conspiracy are crimes of the same grade and degree as the most serious offense which is attempted or solicited or is an object of the conspiracy. An attempt, solicitation or conspiracy to commit a [capital crime or a] felony of the first degree is a felony of the second degree.

(2) *Mitigation.* If the particular conduct charged to constitute a criminal attempt, solicitation or conspiracy is so inherently unlikely to result or culminate in the commission of a crime that neither such conduct nor the actor presents a public danger warranting the grading of such offense under this Section, the Court shall exercise its power under Section 6.12 to enter judgment and impose sentence for a crime of lower grade or degree or, in extreme cases, may dismiss the prosecution.

(3) *Multiple Convictions.* A person may not be convicted of more than one offense defined by this Article for conduct designed to commit or to culminate in the commission of the same crime.

Section 5.06. Possessing Instruments of Crime; Weapons.

(1) *Criminal Instruments Generally.* A person commits a misdemeanor if he possesses any instrument of crime with purpose to employ it criminally. "Instrument of crime" means:

(a) anything specially made or specially adapted for criminal use; or

(b) anything commonly used for criminal purposes and possessed by the actor under circumstances which do not negative unlawful purpose.

(2) *Presumption of Criminal Purpose from Possession of Weapon.* If a person possesses a firearm or other weapon on or about his person, in a vehicle occupied by him, or otherwise readily available for use, it is presumed that he had the purpose to employ it criminally, unless:

(a) the weapon is possessed in the actor's home or place of business;

(b) the actor is licensed or otherwise authorized by law to possess such weapon; or

(c) the weapon is of a type commonly used in lawful sport.

"Weapon" means anything readily capable of lethal use and possessed under circumstances not manifestly appropriate for lawful uses which it may have; the term includes a firearm which is not loaded or lacks a clip or other component to render it immediately operable, and components which can readily be assembled into a weapon.

(3) *Presumptions as to Possession of Criminal Instruments in Automobiles.* Where a weapon or other instrument of crime is found in an automobile, it shall be presumed to be in the possession of the occupant if there is but one. If there is more than one occupant, it shall be presumed to be in the possession of all, except under the following circumstances:

(a) where it is found upon the person of one of the occupants;

(b) where the automobile is not a stolen one and the weapon or instrument is found out of view in a glove compartment, car trunk, or other enclosed customary depository, in which case it shall be presumed to be in the possession of the occupant or occupants who own or have authority to operate the automobile;

(c) in the case of a taxicab, a weapon or instrument found in the passengers' portion of the vehicle shall be presumed to be in the possession of all the passengers, if there are any, and, if not, in the possession of the driver.

Section 5.07. Omitted.

ARTICLE 6. AUTHORIZED DISPOSITION OF OFFENDERS

Section 6.01. Degrees of Felonies.

(1) Felonies defined by this Code are classified, for the purpose of sentence, into three degrees, as follows:

(a) felonies of the first degree;

(b) felonies of the second degree;

(c) felonies of the third degree.

A felony is of the first or second degree when it is so designated by the Code. A crime declared to be a felony, without specification of degree, is of the third degree.

(2) Notwithstanding any other provision of law, a felony defined by any statute of this State other than this Code shall constitute for the purpose of sentence a felony of the third degree.

Section 6.02.-6.03. Omitted.

Section 6.04. Penalties Against Corporations and Unincorporated Association; Forfeiture of Corporate Charter or Revocation of Certificate Authorizing Foreign Corporation to Do Business in the State.

(1) The Court may suspend the sentence of a corporation or an unincorporated association which has been convicted of an offense or may sentence it to pay a fine authorized by Section 6.03.

(2)(a) The [prosecuting attorney] is authorized to institute civil proceedings in the appropriate court of general jurisdiction to forfeit the charter of a corporation organized under the laws of this State or to revoke the certificate authorizing a foreign corporation to conduct business in this State. The Court may order the charter forfeited or the certificate revoked upon finding (i) that the board of directors or a high managerial agent acting in behalf of the corporation has, in conducting the corporation's affairs, purposely engaged in a persistent course of criminal conduct and (ii) that for the prevention of future criminal conduct of the same character, the public interest requires the charter of the corporation to be forfeited and the corporation to be dissolved or the certificate to be revoked.

(b) When a corporation is convicted of a crime or a high managerial agent of a corporation, as defined in Section 2.07, is convicted of a crime committed in the conduct of the affairs of the corporation, the Court, in sentencing the corporation or the agent, may direct the [prosecuting attorney] to institute proceedings authorized by paragraph (a) of this Subsection.

(c) The proceedings authorized by paragraph (a) of this Subsection shall be conducted in accordance with the procedures authorized by law for the involuntary dissolution of a corporation or the revocation of the certificate authorizing a foreign corporation to conduct business in this State. Such proceedings shall be deemed additional to any other proceedings authorized by law for the purpose of forfeiting the charter of a corporation or revoking the certificate of a foreign corporation.

Section 6.05. Young Adult Offenders.

(1) *Specialized Correctional Treatment.* A young adult offender is a person convicted of a crime who, at the time of sentencing, is sixteen but less than twenty-two years of age. A young adult offender who is sentenced to a term of imprisonment which may exceed thirty days [alternatives: (1) ninety days; (2) one year] shall be committed to the custody of the Division of Young Adult Correction of the Department of Correction, and shall receive, as far as practicable, such special and individualized correctional and rehabilitative treatment as may be appropriate to his needs.

(2) *Special Term.* A young adult offender convicted of a felony may, in lieu of any other sentence of imprisonment authorized by this Article, be sentenced to a special term of imprisonment without a minimum and with a maximum of four years, regardless of the degree of the felony involved, if the Court is of the opinion that such special term is adequate for his correction and rehabilitation and will not jeopardize the protection of the public.

[(3) *Removal of Disabilities; Vacation of Conviction.*

(a) In sentencing a young adult offender to the special term provided by this Section or to any sentence other than one of imprisonment, the Court may order that so long as he is not convicted of another felony, the judgment shall not constitute a conviction for the purposes of any disqualification or disability imposed by law upon conviction of a crime.

(b) When any young adult offender is unconditionally discharged from probation or parole before the expiration of the maximum term thereof, the Court may enter an order vacating the judgment of conviction.]

[(4) *Commitment for Observation.* If, after pre-sentence investigation, the Court desires additional information concerning a young adult offender before imposing sentence, it may order that he be committed, for a period not exceeding ninety days, to the custody of the Division of Young Adult Correction of the Department of Correction for observation and study at an appropriate reception or classification center. Such Division of the Department of Correction and the [Young Adult Division of the] Board of Parole shall advise the Court of their findings and recommendations on or before the expiration of such ninety-day period.]

Section 6.06. Sentence of Imprisonment for Felony; Ordinary Terms.

A person who has been convicted of a felony may be sentenced to imprisonment, as follows:

(1) in the case of a felony of the first degree, for a term the minimum of which shall be fixed by the Court at not less than one year nor more than ten years, and the maximum of which shall be life imprisonment;

(2) in the case of a felony of the second degree, for a term the minimum of which shall be fixed by the Court at not less than one year nor more than three years, and the maximum of which shall be ten years;

(3) in the case of a felony of the third degree, for a term the minimum of which shall be fixed by the Court at not less than one year nor more than two years, and the maximum of which shall be five years.

Alternate Section 6.06. Sentence of Imprisonment for Felony; Ordinary Terms.

A person who has been convicted of a felony may be sentenced to imprisonment, as follows:

(1) in the case of a felony of the first degree, for a term the minimum of which shall be fixed by the Court at not less than one year nor more than ten years, and the maximum at not more than twenty years or at life imprisonment;

(2) in the case of a felony of the second degree, for a term the minimum of which shall be fixed by the Court at not less than one year nor more than three years, and the maximum at not more than ten years;

(3) in the case of a felony of the third degree, for a term the minimum of which shall be fixed by the Court at not less than one year nor more than two years, and the maximum at not more than five years.

No sentence shall be imposed under this Section of which the minimum is longer than one-half the maximum, or, when the maximum is life imprisonment, longer than ten years.

Section 6.07. Omitted.

Section 6.08. Sentence of Imprisonment for Misdemeanors and Petty Misdemeanors; Ordinary Terms.

A person who has been convicted of a misdemeanor or a petty misdemeanor may be sentenced to imprisonment for a definite term which shall be fixed by the Court and shall not exceed one year in the case of a misdemeanor or thirty days in the case of a petty misdemeanor.

Section 6.09.-6.11. Omitted.

Section 6.12. Reduction of Conviction by Court to Lesser Degree of Felony or to Misdemeanor.

If, when a person has been convicted of a felony, the Court, having regard to the nature and circumstances of the crime and to the history and character of the defendant, is of the view that it would be unduly harsh to sentence the offender in accordance with the Code, the Court may enter judgment of conviction for a lesser degree of felony or for a misdemeanor and impose sentence accordingly.

Section 6.13. Civil Commitment in Lieu of Prosecution or of Sentence.

(1) When a person prosecuted for a [felony of the third degree,] misdemeanor or petty misdemeanor is a chronic alcoholic, narcotic addict [or prostitute] or person suffering from mental abnormality and the Court is authorized by law to order the civil commitment of such person to a hospital or other institution for medical, psychiatric or other rehabilitative treatment, the Court may order such commitment and dismiss the prosecution. The order of commitment may be made after conviction, in which event the Court may set aside the verdict or judgment of conviction and dismiss the prosecution.

(2) The Court shall not make an order under Subsection (1) of this Section unless it is of the view that it will substantially further the rehabilitation of the defendant and will not jeopardize the protection of the public.

ARTICLE 7. Omitted.

PART II. DEFINITION OF SPECIFIC CRIMES OFFENSES INVOLVING DANGER TO THE PERSON
ARTICLE 210. CRIMINAL HOMICIDE

Section 210.0. Definitions.

In Articles 210-213, unless a different meaning plainly is required:

(1) "human being" means a person who has been born and is alive;

(2) "bodily injury" means physical pain, illness or any impairment of physical condition;

(3) "serious bodily injury" means bodily injury which creates a substantial risk of death or which causes serious, permanent disfigurement, or protracted loss or impairment of the function of any bodily member or organ;

(4) "deadly weapon" means any firearm, or other weapon, device, instrument, material or substance, whether animate or inanimate, which in the manner it is used or is intended to be used is known to be capable of producing death or serious bodily injury.

Section 210.1. Criminal Homicide.

(1) A person is guilty of criminal homicide if he purposely, knowingly, recklessly or negligently causes the death of another human being.

(2) Criminal homicide is murder, manslaughter or negligent homicide.

Section 210.2. Murder

(1) Except as provided in Section 210.3(1)(b), criminal homicide constitutes murder when:

    (a) it is committed purposely or knowingly; or

(b) it is committed recklessly under circumstances manifesting extreme indifference to the value of human life. Such recklessness and indifference are presumed if the actor is engaged or is an accomplice in the commission of, or an attempt to commit, or flight after committing or attempting to commit robbery, rape or deviate sexual intercourse by force or threat of force, arson, burglary, kidnapping or felonious escape.

(2) Murder is a felony of the first degree [but a person convicted of murder may be sentenced to death, as provided in Section 210.6].

Section 210.3. Manslaughter.

(1) Criminal homicide constitutes manslaughter when:

(a) it is committed recklessly; or

(b) a homicide which would otherwise be murder is committed under the influence of extreme mental or emotional disturbance for which there is reasonable explanation or excuse. The reasonableness of such explanation or excuse shall be determined from the viewpoint of a person in the actor's situation under the circumstances as he believes them to be.

(2) Manslaughter is a felony of the second degree.

Section 210.4. Negligent Homicide.

(1) Criminal homicide constitutes negligent homicide when it is committed negligently.

(2) Negligent homicide is a felony of the third degree.

Section 210.5. Causing or Aiding Suicide.

(1) *Causing Suicide as Criminal Homicide.* A person may be convicted of criminal homicide for causing another to commit suicide only if he purposely causes such suicide by force, duress or deception.

(2) *Aiding or Soliciting Suicide as an Independent Offense.* A person who purposely aids or solicits another to commit suicide is guilty of a felony of the second degree if his conduct causes such suicide or an attempted suicide, and otherwise of a misdemeanor.

[Section 210.6. Sentence of Death for Murder; Further Proceedings to Determine Sentence].

(1) *Death Sentence Excluded.* When a defendant is found guilty of murder, the Court shall impose sentence for a felony of the first degree if it is satisfied that:

(a) none of the aggravating circumstances enumerated in Subsection (3) of this Section was established by the evidence at the trial or will be established if further proceedings are initiated under Subsection (2) of this Section; or

(b) substantial mitigating circumstances, established by the evidence at the trial, call for leniency; or

(c) the defendant, with the consent of the prosecuting attorney and the approval of the Court, pleaded guilty to murder as a felony of the first degree; or

(d) the defendant was under 18 years of age at the time of the commission of the crime; or

(e) the defendant's physical or mental condition calls for leniency; or

(f) although the evidence suffices to sustain the verdict, it does not foreclose all doubt respecting the defendant's guilt.

(2) *Determination by Court or by Court and Jury.* Unless the Court imposes sentence under Subsection (1) of this Section, it shall conduct a separate proceeding to determine whether the defendant should be sentenced for a felony of the first degree or sentenced to death. The proceeding shall be conducted before the Court alone if the defendant was convicted by a Court sitting without a jury or upon his plea of guilty or if the prosecuting attorney and the defendant waive a jury with respect to sentence. In other cases it shall be conducted before the Court sitting with the jury which determined the defendant's guilt or, if the Court for good cause shown discharges that jury, with a new jury empanelled for the purpose.

In the proceeding, evidence may be presented as to any matter that the Court deems relevant to sentence, including but not limited to the nature and circumstances of the crime, the defendant's character, background, history, mental and physical condition and any of the aggravating or mitigating circumstances enumerated in Subsections (3) and (4) of this Section. Any such evidence, not legally privileged, which the Court deems to have probative force, may be received, regardless of its admissibility under the exclusionary rules of evidence, provided that the defendant's counsel is accorded a fair opportunity to rebut such evidence. The prosecuting attorney and the defendant or his counsel shall be permitted to present argument for or against sentence of death.

The determination whether sentence of death shall be imposed shall be in the discretion of the Court, except that when the proceeding is conducted before the Court sitting with a jury, the Court shall not impose sentence of death unless it submits to the jury the issue whether the defendant should be sentenced to death or to imprisonment and the jury returns a verdict that the sentence should be death. If the jury is unable to reach a unanimous verdict, the Court shall dismiss the jury and impose sentence for a felony of the first degree.

The Court, in exercising its discretion as to sentence, and the jury, in determining upon its verdict, shall take into account the aggravating and mitigating circumstances enumerated in Subsections (3) and (4) and any other facts that it deems relevant, but it shall not impose or recommend sentence of death unless it finds one of the aggravating circumstances enumerated in Subsection (3) and further finds that there are no mitigating circumstances sufficiently substantial to call for leniency. When the issue is submitted to the jury, the Court shall so instruct and also shall inform the jury of the nature of the sentence of imprisonment that may be imposed, including its implication with respect to possible release upon parole, if the jury verdict is against sentence of death.

Alternative formulation of Subsection (2):

(2) *Determination by Court.* Unless the Court imposes sentence under Subsection (1) of this Section, it shall conduct a separate proceeding to determine whether the defendant should be sentenced for a felony of the first degree or sentenced to death. In the proceeding, the Court, in accordance with Section 7.07, shall consider the report of the presentence investigation and, if a psychiatric examination has been ordered, the report of such examination. In addition, evidence may be presented as to any matter that the Court deems relevant to sentence, including but not limited to the nature and circumstances of the crime, the defendant's character, background, history, mental and

physical condition and any of the aggravating or mitigating circumstances enumerated in Subsections (3) and (4) of this Section. Any such evidence, not legally privileged, which the Court deems to have probative force, may be received, regardless of its admissibility under the exclusionary rules of evidence, provided that the defendant's counsel is accorded a fair opportunity to rebut such evidence. The prosecuting attorney and the defendant or his counsel shall be permitted to present argument for or against sentence of death.

The determination whether sentence of death shall be imposed shall be in the discretion of the Court. In exercising such discretion, the Court shall take into account the aggravating and mitigating circumstances enumerated in Subsections (3) and (4) and any other facts that it deems relevant but shall not impose sentence of death unless it finds one of the aggravating circumstances enumerated in Subsection (3) and further finds that there are no mitigating circumstances sufficiently substantial to call for leniency.

(3) *Aggravating Circumstances.*

(a) The murder was committed by a convict under sentence of imprisonment.

(b) The defendant was previously convicted of another murder or of a felony involving the use or threat of violence to the person.

(c) At the time the murder was committed the defendant also committed another murder.

(d) The defendant knowingly created a great risk of death to many persons.

(e) The murder was committed while the defendant was engaged or was an accomplice in the commission of, or an attempt to commit, or flight after committing or attempting to commit robbery, rape or deviate sexual intercourse by force or threat of force, arson, burglary, or kidnapping.

(f) The murder was committed for the purpose of avoiding or preventing a lawful arrest or effecting an escape from lawful custody.

(g) The murder was committed for pecuniary gain.

(h) The murder was especially heinous, atrocious or cruel, manifesting exceptional depravity.

(4) *Mitigating Circumstances.*

(a) The defendant has no significant history of prior criminal activity.

(b) The murder was committed while the defendant was under the influence of extreme mental or emotional disturbance.

(c) The victim was a participant in the defendant's homicidal conduct or consented to the homicidal act.

(d) The murder was committed under circumstances which the defendant believed to provide a moral justification or extenuation for his conduct.

(e) The defendant was an accomplice in a murder committed by another person and his participation in the homicidal act was relatively minor.

(f) The defendant acted under duress or under the domination of another person.

(g) At the time of the murder, the capacity of the defendant to appreciate the criminality [wrongfulness] of his conduct or to conform his conduct to the requirements of law was impaired as a result of mental disease or defect or intoxication.

(h) The youth of the defendant at the time of the crime.]

ARTICLE 211. ASSAULT; RECKLESS ENDANGERING; THREATS

Section 211.0. Definitions.

In this Article, the definitions given in Section 210.0 apply unless a different meaning plainly is required.

Section 211.1. Assault.

(1) *Simple Assault.* A person is guilty of assault if he:

(a) attempts to cause or purposely, knowingly or recklessly causes bodily injury to another; or

(b) negligently causes bodily injury to another with a deadly weapon; or

(c) attempts by physical menace to put another in fear of imminent serious bodily injury.

Simple assault is a misdemeanor unless committed in a fight or scuffle entered into by mutual consent, in which case it is a petty misdemeanor.

(2) *Aggravated Assault.* A person is guilty of aggravated assault if he:

(a) attempts to cause serious bodily injury to another, or causes such injury purposely, knowingly or recklessly under circumstances manifesting extreme indifference to the value of human life; or

(b) attempts to cause or purposely or knowingly causes bodily injury to another with a deadly weapon.

Aggravated assault under paragraph (a) is a felony of the second degree; aggravated assault under paragraph (b) is a felony of the third degree.

Section 211.2. Recklessly Endangering Another Person.

A person commits a misdemeanor if he recklessly engages in conduct which places or may place another person in danger of death or serious bodily injury. Recklessness and danger shall be presumed where a person knowingly points a firearm at or in the direction of another, whether or not the actor believed the firearm to be loaded.

Section 211.3. Terroristic Threats.

A person is guilty of a felony of the third degree if he threatens to commit any crime of violence with purpose to terrorize another or to cause evacuation of a building, place of assembly, or facility of public transportation, or otherwise to cause serious public inconvenience, or in reckless disregard of the risk of causing such terror or inconvenience.

ARTICLE 212. KIDNAPPING AND RELATED OFFENSES; COERCION

Section 212.0. Definitions.

In this Article, the definitions given in Section 210.0 apply unless a different meaning plainly is required.

Section 212.1. Kidnapping.

A person is guilty of kidnapping if he unlawfully removes another from his place of residence or business, or a substantial distance from the vicinity where he is found, or if he unlawfully confines another for a substantial period in a place of isolation, with any of the following purposes:

    (a) to hold for ransom or reward, or as a shield or hostage; or

    (b) to facilitate commission of any felony or flight thereafter; or

    (c) to inflict bodily injury on or to terrorize the victim or another; or

    (d) to interfere with the performance of any governmental or political function.

Kidnapping is a felony of the first degree unless the actor voluntarily releases the victim alive and in a safe place prior to trial, in which case it is a felony of the second degree. A removal or confinement is unlawful within the meaning of this Section if it is accomplished by force, threat or deception, or, in the case of a person who is under the age of 14 or incompetent, if it is accomplished without the consent of a parent, guardian or other person responsible for general supervision of his welfare.

Section 212.2. Felonious Restraint.

A person commits a felony of the third degree if he knowingly:

    (a) restrains another unlawfully in circumstances exposing him to risk of serious bodily injury; or

    (b) holds another in a condition of involuntary servitude.

Section 212.3. False Imprisonment.

A person commits a misdemeanor if he knowingly restrains another unlawfully so as to interfere substantially with his liberty.

Section 212.4. Interference with Custody.

(1) *Custody of Children.* A person commits an offense if he knowingly or recklessly takes or entices any child under the age of 18 from the custody of its parent, guardian or other lawful custodian, when he has no privilege to do so. It is an affirmative defense that:

    (a) the actor believed that his action was necessary to preserve the child from danger to its welfare; or

    (b) the child, being at the time not less than 14 years old, was taken away at its own instigation without enticement and without purpose to commit a criminal offense with or against the child.

Proof that the child was below the critical age gives rise to a presumption that the actor knew the child's age or acted in reckless disregard thereof. The offense is a misdemeanor unless the actor, not being a parent or person in equivalent relation to the child, acted with knowledge that his conduct would cause serious alarm for the child's safety, or in reckless disregard of a likelihood of causing such alarm, in which case the offense is a felony of the third degree.

(2) *Custody of Committed Persons.* A person is guilty of a misdemeanor if he knowingly or recklessly takes or entices any committed person away from lawful custody when he is not privileged to do so. "Committed person" means, in addition to anyone committed under judicial warrant, any orphan, neglected or delinquent child, mentally defective or insane person, or other dependent or incompetent person entrusted to another's custody by or through a recognized social agency or otherwise by authority of law.

Section 212.5. Criminal Coercion.
(1) *Offense Defined.* A person is guilty of criminal coercion if, with purpose unlawfully to restrict another's freedom of action to his detriment, he threatens to:

(a) commit any criminal offense; or

(b) accuse anyone of a criminal offense; or

(c) expose any secret tending to subject any person to hatred, contempt or ridicule, or to impair his credit or business repute; or

(d) take or withhold action as an official, or cause an official to take or withhold action.

It is an affirmative defense to prosecution based on paragraphs (b), (c) or (d) that the actor believed the accusation or secret to be true or the proposed official action justified and that his purpose was limited to compelling the other to behave in a way reasonably related to the circumstances which were the subject of the accusation, exposure or proposed official action, as by desisting from further misbehavior, making good a wrong done, refraining from taking any action or responsibility for which the actor believes the other disqualified.

(2) *Grading.* Criminal coercion is a misdemeanor unless the threat is to commit a felony or the actor's purpose is felonious, in which cases the offense is a felony of the third degree.

ARTICLE 213. SEXUAL OFFENSES

Section 213.0. Definitions.
In this Article, unless a different meaning plainly is required:

(1) the definitions given in Section 210.0 apply;

(2) "Sexual intercourse" includes intercourse per os or per anus, with some penetration however slight; emission is not required;

(3) "Deviate sexual intercourse" means sexual intercourse per os or per anus between human beings who are not husband and wife, and any form of sexual intercourse with an animal.

Section 213.1. Rape and Related Offenses.
(1) *Rape.* A male who has sexual intercourse with a female not his wife is guilty of rape if:

(a) he compels her to submit by force or by threat of imminent death, serious bodily injury, extreme pain or kidnapping, to be inflicted on anyone; or

(b) he has substantially impaired her power to appraise or control her conduct by administering or employing without her knowledge drugs, intoxicants or other means for the purpose of preventing resistance; or

(c) the female is unconscious; or

(d) the female is less than 10 years old.

Rape is a felony of the second degree unless (i) in the course thereof the actor inflicts serious bodily injury upon anyone, or (ii) the victim was not a voluntary social companion of the actor upon the occasion of the crime and had not previously permitted him sexual liberties, in which cases the offense is a felony of the first degree.

(2) *Gross Sexual Imposition.* A male who has sexual intercourse with a female not his wife commits a felony of the third degree if:

(a) he compels her to submit by any threat that would prevent resistance by a woman of ordinary resolution; or

(b) he knows that she suffers from a mental disease or defect which renders her incapable of appraising the nature of her conduct; or

(c) he knows that she is unaware that a sexual act is being committed upon her or that she submits because she mistakenly supposes that he is her husband.

Section 213.2. Deviate Sexual Intercourse by Force or Imposition.

(1) *By Force or Its Equivalent.* A person who engages in deviate sexual intercourse with another person, or who causes another to engage in deviate sexual intercourse, commits a felony of the second degree if:

(a) he compels the other person to participate by force or by threat of imminent death, serious bodily injury, extreme pain or kidnapping, to be inflicted on anyone; or

(b) he has substantially impaired the other person's power to appraise or control his conduct, by administering or employing without the knowledge of the other person drugs, intoxicants or other means for the purpose of preventing resistance; or

(c) the other person is unconscious; or

(d) the other person is less than 10 years old.

(2) *By Other Imposition.* A person who engages in deviate sexual intercourse with another person, or who causes another to engage in deviate sexual intercourse, commits a felony of the third degree if:

(a) he compels the other person to participate by any threat that would prevent resistance by a person of ordinary resolution; or

(b) he knows that the other person suffers from a mental disease or defect which renders him incapable of appraising the nature of his conduct; or

(c) he knows that the other person submits because he is unaware that a sexual act is being committed upon him.

Section 213.3. Corruption of Minors and Seduction.

(1) *Offense Defined.* A male who has sexual intercourse with a female not his wife, or any person who engages in deviate sexual intercourse or causes another to engage in deviate sexual intercourse, is guilty of an offense if:

(a) the other person is less than [16] years old and the actor is at least [4] years older than the other person; or

(b) the other person is less than 21 years old and the actor is his guardian or otherwise responsible for general supervision of his welfare; or

(c) the other person is in custody of law or detained in a hospital or other institution and the actor has supervisory or disciplinary authority over him; or

(d) the other person is a female who is induced to participate by a promise of marriage which the actor does not mean to perform.

(2) *Grading.* An offense under paragraph (a) of Subsection (1) is a felony of the third degree. Otherwise an offense under this section is a misdemeanor.

Section 213.4. Sexual Assault.

A person who has sexual contact with another not his spouse, or causes such other to have sexual contact with him, is guilty of sexual assault, a misdemeanor, if:

(1) he knows that the contact is offensive to the other person; or

(2) he knows that the other person suffers from a mental disease or defect which renders him or her incapable of appraising the nature of his or her conduct; or

(3) he knows that the other person is unaware that a sexual act is being committed; or

(4) the other person is less than 10 years old; or

(5) he has substantially impaired the other person's power to appraise or control his or her conduct, by administering or employing without the other's knowledge drugs, intoxicants or other means for the purpose of preventing resistance; or

(6) the other person is less than [16] years old and the actor is at least [4] years older than the other person; or

(7) the other person is less than 21 years old and the actor is his guardian or otherwise responsible for general supervision of his welfare; or

(8) the other person is in custody of law or detained in a hospital or other institution and the actor has supervisory or disciplinary authority over him.

Sexual contact is any touching of the sexual or other intimate parts of the person for the purpose of arousing or gratifying sexual desire.

Section 213.5. Indecent Exposure.

A person commits a misdemeanor if, for the purpose of arousing or gratifying sexual desire of himself or of any person other than his spouse, he exposes his genitals under circumstances in which he knows his conduct is likely to cause affront or alarm.

Section 213.6. Provisions Generally Applicable to Article 213.

(1) *Mistake as to Age.* Whenever in this Article the criminality of conduct depends on a child's being below the age of 10, it is no defense that the actor did not know the child's age, or reasonably believed the child to be older than 10. When criminality depends on the child's being below a critical age other than 10, it is a defense for the actor to prove by a preponderance of the evidence that he reasonably believed the child to be above the critical age.

(2) *Spouse Relationships.* Whenever in this Article the definition of an offense excludes conduct with a spouse, the exclusion shall be deemed to extend to persons living as man and wife, regardless of the legal status of their relationship. The exclusion shall be inoperative as respects spouses living apart under a decree of judicial separation. Where the definition of an offense excludes conduct with a spouse or conduct by a woman, this shall not preclude conviction of a spouse or woman as accomplice in a sexual act which he or she causes another person, not within the exclusion, to perform.

(3) *Sexually Promiscuous Complainants.* It is a defense to prosecution under Section 213.3 and paragraphs (6), (7) and (8) of Section 213.4 for the actor to prove by a preponderance of the evidence that the alleged victim had, prior to the time of the offense charged, engaged promiscuously in sexual relations with others.

(4) *Prompt Complaint.* No prosecution may be instituted or maintained under this Article unless the alleged offense was brought to the notice of public authority within [3] months of its occurrence or, where the alleged victim was less than [16] years old or

otherwise incompetent to make complaint, within [3] months after a parent, guardian or other competent person specially interested in the victim learns of the offense.

(5) *Testimony of Complainants.* No person shall be convicted of any felony under this Article upon the uncorroborated testimony of the alleged victim. Corroboration may be circumstantial. In any prosecution before a jury for an offense under this Article, the jury shall be instructed to evaluate the testimony of a victim or complaining witness with special care in view of the emotional involvement of the witness and the difficulty of determining the truth with respect to alleged sexual activities carried out in private.

OFFENSES AGAINST PROPERTY
ARTICLE 220. ARSON, CRIMINAL MISCHIEF, AND OTHER PROPERTY DESTRUCTION

Section 220.1. Arson and Related Offenses.

(1) *Arson.* A person is guilty of arson, a felony of the second degree, if he starts a fire or causes an explosion with the purpose of:

    (a) destroying a building or occupied structure of another; or

    (b) destroying or damaging any property, whether his own or another's, to collect insurance for such loss. It shall be an affirmative defense to prosecution under this paragraph that the actor's conduct did not recklessly endanger any building or occupied structure of another or place any other person in danger of death or bodily injury.

(2) *Reckless Burning or Exploding.* A person commits a felony of the third degree if he purposely starts a fire or causes an explosion, whether on his own property or another's, and thereby recklessly:

    (a) places another person in danger of death or bodily injury; or

    (b) places a building or occupied structure of another in danger of damage or destruction.

(3) *Failure to Control or Report Dangerous Fire.* A person who knows that a fire is endangering life or a substantial amount of property of another and fails to take reasonable measures to put out or control the fire, when he can do so without substantial risk to himself, or to give a prompt fire alarm, commits a misdemeanor if:

    (a) he knows that he is under an official, contractual, or other legal duty to prevent or combat the fire; or

    (b) the fire was started, albeit lawfully, by him or with his assent, or on property in his custody or control.

(4) *Definitions.* "Occupied structure" means any structure, vehicle or place adapted for overnight accommodation of persons, or for carrying on business therein, whether or not a person is actually present. Property is that of another, for the purposes of this section, if anyone other than the actor has a possessory or proprietory interest therein. If a building or structure is divided into separately occupied units, any unit not occupied by the actor is an occupied structure of another.

Section 220.2. Causing or Risking Catastrophe.

(1) *Causing Catastrophe.* A person who causes a catastrophe by explosion, fire, flood, avalanche, collapse of building, release of poison gas, radioactive material or other

harmful or destructive force or substance, or by any other means of causing potentially widespread injury or damage, commits a felony of the second degree if he does so purposely or knowingly, or a felony of the third degree if he does so recklessly.

(2) *Risking Catastrophe.* A person is guilty of a misdemeanor if he recklessly creates a risk of catastrophe in the employment of fire, explosives or other dangerous means listed in Subsection (1).

(3) *Failure to Prevent Catastrophe.* A person who knowingly or recklessly fails to take reasonable measures to prevent or mitigate a catastrophe commits a misdemeanor if:

(a) he knows that he is under an official, contractual or other legal duty to take such measures; or

(b) he did or assented to the act causing or threatening the catastrophe.

Section 220.3. Criminal Mischief.

(1) *Offense Defined.* A person is guilty of criminal mischief if he:

(a) damages tangible property of another purposely, recklessly, or by negligence in the employment of fire, explosives, or other dangerous means listed in Section 220.2(1); or

(b) purposely or recklessly tampers with tangible property of another so as to endanger person or property; or

(c) purposely or recklessly causes another to suffer pecuniary loss by deception or threat.

(2) *Grading.* Criminal mischief is a felony of the third degree if the actor purposely causes pecuniary loss in excess of $5,000, or a substantial interruption or impairment of public communication, transportation, supply of water, gas or power, or other public service. It is a misdemeanor if the actor purposely causes pecuniary loss in excess of $100, or a petty misdemeanor if he purposely or recklessly causes pecuniary loss in excess of $25. Otherwise criminal mischief is a violation.

ARTICLE 221. BURGLARY AND OTHER CRIMINAL INTRUSION

Section 221.0. Definitions.

In this Article, unless a different meaning plainly is required:

(1) "occupied structure" means any structure, vehicle or place adapted for overnight accommodation of persons, or for carrying on business therein, whether or not a person is actually present.

(2) "night" means the period between thirty minutes past sunset and thirty minutes before sunrise.

Section 221.1. Burglary.

(1) *Burglary Defined.* A person is guilty of burglary if he enters a building or occupied structure, or separately secured or occupied portion thereof, with purpose to commit a crime therein, unless the premises are at the time open to the public or the actor is licensed or privileged to enter. It is an affirmative defense to prosecution for burglary that the building or structure was abandoned.

(2) *Grading.* Burglary is a felony of the second degree if it is perpetrated in the dwelling of another at night, or if, in the course of committing the offense, the actor:

(a) purposely, knowingly or recklessly inflicts or attempts to inflict bodily injury on anyone; or

(b) is armed with explosives or a deadly weapon.

Otherwise, burglary is a felony of the third degree. An act shall be deemed "in the course of committing" an offense if it occurs in an attempt to commit the offense or in flight after the attempt or commission.

(3) *Multiple Convictions.* A person may not be convicted both for burglary and for the offense which it was his purpose to commit after the burglarious entry or for an attempt to commit that offense, unless the additional offense constitutes a felony of the first or second degree.

Section 221.2. Criminal Trespass.

(1) *Buildings and Occupied Structures.* A person commits an offense if, knowing that he is not licensed or privileged to do so, he enters or surreptitiously remains in any building or occupied structure, or separately secured or occupied portion thereof. An offense under this Subsection is a misdemeanor if it is committed in a dwelling at night. Otherwise it is a petty misdemeanor.

(2) *Defiant Trespasser.* A person commits an offense if, knowing that he is not licensed or privileged to do so, he enters or remains in any place as to which notice against trespass is given by:

(a) actual communication to the actor; or

(b) posting in a manner prescribed by law or reasonably likely to come to the attention of intruders; or

(c) fencing or other enclosure manifestly designed to exclude intruders.

An offense under this Subsection constitutes a petty misdemeanor if the offender defies an order to leave personally communicated to him by the owner of the premises or other authorized person. Otherwise it is a violation.

(3) *Defenses.* It is an affirmative defense to prosecution under this Section that:

(a) a building or occupied structure involved in an offense under Subsection (1) was abandoned; or

(b) the premises were at the time open to members of the public and the actor complied with all lawful conditions imposed on access to or remaining in the premises; or

(c) the actor reasonably believed that the owner of the premises, or other person empowered to license access thereto, would have licensed him to enter or remain.

ARTICLE 222. ROBBERY

Section 222.1. Robbery.

(1) *Robbery Defined.* A person is guilty of robbery if, in the course of committing a theft, he:

(a) inflicts serious bodily injury upon another; or

(b) threatens another with or purposely puts him in fear of immediate serious bodily injury; or

(c) commits or threatens immediately to commit any felony of the first or second degree.

An act shall be deemed "in the course of committing a theft" if it occurs in an attempt to commit theft or in flight after the attempt or commission.

(2) *Grading*. Robbery is a felony of the second degree, except that it is a felony of the first degree if in the course of committing the theft the actor attempts to kill anyone, or purposely inflicts or attempts to inflict serious bodily injury.

ARTICLE 223. THEFT AND RELATED OFFENSES

Section 223.0. Definitions.

In this Article, unless a different meaning plainly is required:

(1) "deprive" means: (a) to withhold property of another permanently or for so extended a period as to appropriate a major portion of its economic value, or with intent to restore only upon payment of reward or other compensation; or (b) to dispose of the property so as to make it unlikely that the owner will recover it.

(2) "financial institution" means a bank, insurance company, credit union, building and loan association, investment trust or other organization held out to the public as a place of deposit of funds or medium of savings or collective investment.

(3) "government" means the United States, any State, county, municipality, or other political unit, or any department, agency or subdivision of any of the foregoing, or any corporation or other association carrying out the functions of government.

(4) "movable property" means property the location of which can be changed, including things growing on, affixed to, or found in land, and documents although the rights represented thereby have no physical location. "Immovable property" is all other property.

(5) "obtain" means: (a) in relation to property, to bring about a transfer or purported transfer of a legal interest in the property, whether to the obtainer or another; or (b) in relation to labor or service, to secure performance thereof.

(6) "property" means anything of value, including real estate, tangible and intangible personal property, contract rights, choses-in-action and other interests in or claims to wealth, admission or transportation tickets, captured or domestic animals, food and drink, electric or other power.

(7) "property of another" includes property in which any person other than the actor has an interest which the actor is not privileged to infringe, regardless of the fact that the actor also has an interest in the property and regardless of the fact that the other person might be precluded from civil recovery because the property was used in an unlawful transaction or was subject to forfeiture as contraband. Property in possession of the actor shall not be deemed property of another who has only a security interest therein, even if legal title is in the creditor pursuant to a conditional sales contract or other security agreement.

Section 223.1. Consolidation of Theft Offenses; Grading; Provisions Applicable to Theft Generally.

(1) *Consolidation of Theft Offenses*. Conduct denominated theft in this Article constitutes a single offense. An accusation of theft may be supported by evidence that it was committed in any manner that would be theft under this Article, notwithstanding the specification of a different manner in the indictment or information, subject only to the power of the Court to ensure fair trial by granting a continuance or other

appropriate relief where the conduct of the defense would be prejudiced by lack of fair notice or by surprise.

(2) *Grading of Theft Offenses.*

(a) Theft constitutes a felony of the third degree if the amount involved exceeds $500, or if the property stolen is a firearm, automobile, airplane, motorcycle, motor boat, or other motor-propelled vehicle, or in the case of theft by receiving stolen property, if the receiver is in the business of buying or selling stolen property.

(b) Theft not within the preceding paragraph constitutes a misdemeanor, except that if the property was not taken from the person or by threat, or in breach of a fiduciary obligation, and the actor proves by a preponderance of the evidence that the amount involved was less than $50, the offense constitutes a petty misdemeanor.

(c) The amount involved in a theft shall be deemed to be the highest value, by any reasonable standard, of the property or services which the actor stole or attempted to steal. Amounts involved in thefts committed pursuant to one scheme or course of conduct, whether from the same person or several persons, may be aggregated in determining the grade of the offense.

(3) *Claim of Right.* It is an affirmative defense to prosecution for theft that the actor:

(a) was unaware that the property or service was that of another; or

(b) acted under an honest claim of right to the property or service involved or that he had a right to acquire or dispose of it as he did; or

(c) took property exposed for sale, intending to purchase and pay for it promptly, or reasonably believing that the owner, if present, would have consented.

(4) *Theft from Spouse.* It is no defense that theft was from the actor's spouse, except that misappropriation of household and personal effects, or other property normally accessible to both spouses, is theft only if it occurs after the parties have ceased living together.

Section 223.2. Theft by Unlawful Taking or Disposition.

(1) *Movable Property.* A person is guilty of theft if he unlawfully takes, or exercises unlawful control over, movable property of another with purpose to deprive him thereof.

(2) *Immovable Property.* A person is guilty of theft if he unlawfully transfers immovable property of another or any interest therein with purpose to benefit himself or another not entitled thereto.

Section 223.3. Theft by Deception.

A person is guilty of theft if he purposely obtains property of another by deception. A person deceives if he purposely:

(1) creates or reinforces a false impression, including false impressions as to law, value, intention or other state of mind; but deception as to a person's intention to perform a promise shall not be inferred from the fact alone that he did not subsequently perform the promise; or

(2) prevents another from acquiring information which would affect his judgment of a transaction; or

(3) fails to correct a false impression which the deceiver previously created or reinforced, or which the deceiver knows to be influencing another to whom he stands in a fiduciary or confidential relationship; or

(4) fails to disclose a known lien, adverse claim or other legal impediment to the enjoyment of property which he transfers or encumbers in consideration for the property obtained, whether such impediment is or is not valid, or is or is not a matter of official record.

The term "deceive" does not, however, include falsity as to matters having no pecuniary significance, or puffing by statements unlikely to deceive ordinary persons in the group addressed.

Section 223.4. Theft by Extortion.

A person is guilty of theft if he purposely obtains property of another by threatening to:

(1) inflict bodily injury on anyone or commit any other criminal offense; or

(2) accuse anyone of a criminal offense; or

(3) expose any secret tending to subject any person to hatred, contempt or ridicule, or to impair his credit or business repute; or

(4) take or withhold action as an official, or cause an official to take or withhold action; or

(5) bring about or continue a strike, boycott or other collective unofficial action, if the property is not demanded or received for the benefit of the group in whose interest the actor purports to act; or

(6) testify or provide information or withhold testimony or information with respect to another's legal claim or defense; or

(7) inflict any other harm which would not benefit the actor.

It is an affirmative defense to prosecution based on paragraphs (2), (3) or (4) that the property obtained by threat of accusation, exposure, lawsuit or other invocation of official action was honestly claimed as restitution or indemnification for harm done in the circumstances to which such accusation, exposure, lawsuit or other official action relates, or as compensation for property or lawful services.

Section 223.5. Theft of Property Lost, Mislaid, or Delivered by Mistake.

A person who comes into control of property of another that he knows to have been lost, mislaid, or delivered under a mistake as to the nature or amount of the property or the identity of the recipient is guilty of theft if, with purpose to deprive the owner thereof, he fails to take reasonable measures to restore the property to a person entitled to have it.

Section 223.6. Receiving Stolen Property.

(1) *Receiving*. A person is guilty of theft if he purposely receives, retains, or disposes of movable property of another knowing that it has been stolen, or believing that it has probably been stolen, unless the property is received, retained, or disposed with purpose to restore it to the owner. "Receiving" means acquiring possession, control or title, or lending on the security of the property.

(2) *Presumption of Knowledge*. The requisite knowledge or belief is presumed in the case of a dealer who:

   (a) is found in possession or control of property stolen from two or more persons on separate occasions; or

(b) has received stolen property in another transaction within the year preceding the transaction charged; or

(c) being a dealer in property of the sort received, acquires it for a consideration which he knows is far below its reasonable value.

"Dealer" means a person in the business of buying or selling goods including a pawnbroker.

Section 223.7. Theft of Services.

(1) A person is guilty of theft is he purposely obtains services which he knows are available only for compensation, by deception or threat, or by false token or other means to avoid payment for the service. "Services" includes labor, professional service, transportation, telephone or other public service, accommodation in hotels, restaurants or elsewhere, admission to exhibitions, use of vehicles or other movable property. Where compensation for service is ordinarily paid immediately upon the rendering of such service, as in the case of hotels and restaurants, refusal to pay or absconding without payment or offer to pay gives rise to a presumption that the service was obtained by deception as to intention to pay.

(2) A person commits theft if, having control over the disposition of services of others, to which he is not entitled, he knowingly diverts such services to his own benefit or to the benefit of another not entitled thereto.

Section 223.8. Omitted.
Section 223.9. Unauthorized Use of Automobiles and Other Vehicles.

A person commits a misdemeanor if he operates another's automobile, airplane, motorcycle, motorboat, or other motor-propelled vehicle without consent of the owner. It is an affirmative defense to prosecution under this Section that the actor reasonably believed that the owner would have consented to the operation had he known of it.

ARTICLE 224. FORGERY AND FRAUDULENT PRACTICES

Section 224.0. Definitions.

In this Article, the definitions given in Section 223.0 apply unless a different meaning plainly is required.

Section 224.1. Forgery.

(1) *Definition*. A person is guilty of forgery if, with purpose to defraud or injure anyone, or with knowledge that he is facilitating a fraud or injury to be perpetrated by anyone, the actor:

(a) alters any writing of another without his authority; or

(b) makes, completes, executes, authenticates, issues or transfers any writing so that it purports to be the act of another who did not authorize that act, or to have been executed at a time or place or in a numbered sequence other than was in fact the case, or to be a copy of an original when no such original existed; or

(c) utters any writing which he knows to be forged in a manner specified in paragraphs (a) or (b).

"Writing" includes printing or any other method of recording information, money, coins, tokens, stamps, seals, credit cards, badges, trade-marks, and other symbols of value, right, privilege, or identification.

(2) *Grading*. Forgery is a felony of the second degree if the writing is or purports to be part of an issue of money, securities, postage or revenue stamps, or other instruments issued by the government, or part of an issue of stock, bonds or other instruments representing interests in or claims against any property or enterprise. Forgery is a felony of the third degree if the writing is or purports to be a will, deed, contract, release, commercial instrument, or other document evidencing, creating, transferring, altering, terminating, or otherwise affecting legal relations. Otherwise forgery is a misdemeanor.

Section 224.2.-224.14. Omitted.

OFFENSES AGAINST THE FAMILY
ARTICLE 230. OFFENSES AGAINST THE FAMILY

Section 230.1. Bigamy and Polygamy.

(1) *Bigamy*. A married person is guilty of bigamy, a misdemeanor, if he contracts or purports to contract another marriage, unless at the time of the subsequent marriage:

(a) the actor believes that the prior spouse is dead; or

(b) the actor and the prior spouse have been living apart for five consecutive years throughout which the prior spouse was not known by the actor to be alive; or

(c) a Court has entered a judgment purporting to terminate or annul any prior disqualifying marriage, and the actor does not know that judgment to be invalid; or

(d) the actor reasonably believes that he is legally eligible to remarry.

(2) *Polygamy*. A person is guilty of polygamy, a felony of the third degree, if he marries or cohabits with more than one spouse at a time in purported exercise of the right of plural marriage. The offense is a continuing one until all cohabitation and claim of marriage with more than one spouse terminates. This section does not apply to parties to a polygamous marriage, lawful in the country of which they are residents or nationals, while they are in transit through or temporarily visiting this State.

(3) *Other Party to Bigamous or Polygamous Marriage*. A person is guilty of bigamy or polygamy, as the case may be, if he contracts or purports to contract marriage with another knowing that the other is thereby committing bigamy or polygamy.

Section 230.2. Incest.

A person is guilty of incest, a felony of the third degree, if he knowingly marries or cohabits or has sexual intercourse with an ancestor or descendant, a brother or sister of the whole or half blood [or an uncle, aunt, nephew or niece of the whole blood]. "Cohabit" means to live together under the representation or appearance of being married. The relationships referred to herein include blood relationships without regard to legitimacy, and relationship of parent and child by adoption.

Section 230.3. Omitted.
Section 230.4. Endangering Welfare of Children.

A parent, guardian, or other person supervising the welfare of a child under 18 commits a misdemeanor if he knowingly endangers the child's welfare by violating a duty of care, protection or support.

Section 230.5. Persistent Non-Support.
A person commits a misdemeanor if he persistently fails to provide support which he can provide and which he knows he is legally obliged to provide to a spouse, child or other dependent.

OFFENSES AGAINST PUBLIC ADMINISTRATION
ARTICLE 240. BRIBERY AND CORRUPT INFLUENCE

Section 240.0. Definitions.
In Articles 240-243, unless a different meaning plainly is required:
(1) "benefit" means gain or advantage, or anything regarded by the beneficiary as gain or advantage, including benefit to any other person or entity in whose welfare he is interested, but not an advantage promised generally to a group or class of voters as a consequence of public measures which a candidate engages to support or oppose;
(2) "government" includes any branch, subdivision or agency of the government of the State or any locality within it;
(3) "harm" means loss, disadvantage or injury, or anything so regarded by the person affected, including loss, disadvantage or injury to any other person or entity in whose welfare he is interested;
(4) "official proceeding" means a proceeding heard or which may be heard before any legislative, judicial, administrative or other governmental agency or official authorized to take evidence under oath, including any referee, hearing examiner, commissioner, notary or other person taking testimony or deposition in connection with any such proceeding;
(5) "party official" means a person who holds an elective or appointive post in a political party in the United States by virtue of which he directs or conducts, or participates in directing or conducting party affairs at any level of responsibility;
(6) "pecuniary benefit" is benefit in the form of money, property, commercial interests or anything else the primary significance of which is economic gain;
(7) "public servant" means any officer or employee of government, including legislators and judges, and any person participating as juror, advisor, consultant or otherwise, in performing a governmental function; but the term does not include witnesses;
(8) "administrative proceeding" means any proceeding, other than a judicial proceeding, the outcome of which is required to be based on a record or documentation prescribed by law, or in which law or regulation is particularized in application to individuals.

Section 240.1. Bribery in Official and Political Matters.
A person is guilty of bribery, a felony of the third degree, if he offers, confers or agrees to confer upon another, or solicits, accepts or agrees to accept from another:
(1) any pecuniary benefit as consideration for the recipient's decision, opinion, recommendation, vote or other exercise of discretion as a public servant, party official or voter; or
(2) any benefit as consideration for the recipient's decision, vote, recommendation or other exercise of official discretion in a judicial or administrative proceeding; or
(3) any benefit as consideration for a violation of a known legal duty as public servant or party official.

It is no defense to prosecution under this section that a person whom the actor sought to influence was not qualified to act in the desired way whether because he had not yet assumed office, or lacked jurisdiction, or for any other reason.

Section 240.2. Threats and Other Improper Influence in Official and Political Matters.
(1) *Offenses Defined.* A person commits an offense if he:

(a) threatens unlawful harm to any person with purpose to influence his decision, opinion, recommendation, vote or other exercise of discretion as a public servant, party official or voter; or

(b) threatens harm to any public servant with purpose to influence his decision, opinion, recommendation, vote or other exercise of discretion in a judicial or administrative proceeding; or

(c) threatens harm to any public servant or party official with purpose to influence him to violate his known legal duty; or

(d) privately addresses to any public servant who has or will have an official discretion in a judicial or administrative proceeding any representation, entreaty, argument or other communication with purpose to influence the outcome on the basis of considerations other than those authorized by law.

It is no defense to prosecution under this Section that a person whom the actor sought to influence was not qualified to act in the desired way, whether because he had not yet assumed office, or lacked jurisdiction, or for any other reason.

(2) *Grading.* An offense under this Section is a misdemeanor unless the actor threatened to commit a crime or made a threat with purpose to influence a judicial or administrative proceeding, in which cases the offense is a felony of the third degree.

Section 240.3. Compensation for Past Official Action.
A person commits a misdemeanor if he solicits, accepts or agrees to accept any pecuniary benefit as compensation for having, as public servant, given a decision, opinion, recommendation or vote favorable to another, or for having otherwise exercised a discretion in his favor, or for having violated his duty. A person commits a misdemeanor if he offers, confers or agrees to confer compensation acceptance of which is prohibited by this Section.

Section 240.4. Retaliation for Past Official Action.
A person commits a misdemeanor if he harms another by any unlawful act in retaliation for anything lawfully done by the latter in the capacity of public servant.

Section 240.5.-240.7. Omitted.

ARTICLE 241. PERJURY AND OTHER FALSIFICATION IN OFFICIAL MATTERS

Section 241.0. Definitions.
In this Article, unless a different meaning plainly is required:

(1) the definitions given in Section 240.0 apply; and

(2) "statement" means any representation, but includes a representation of opinion, belief or other state of mind only if the representation clearly relates to state of mind apart from or in addition to any facts which are the subject of the representation.

Section 241.1. Perjury.

(1) *Offense Defined.* A person is guilty of perjury, a felony of the third degree, if in any official proceeding he makes a false statement under oath or equivalent affirmation, or swears or affirms the truth of a statement previously made, when the statement is material and he does not believe it to be true.

(2) *Materiality.* Falsification is material, regardless of the admissibility of the statement under rules of evidence, if it could have affected the course or outcome of the proceeding. It is no defense that the declarant mistakenly believed the falsification to be immaterial. Whether a falsification is material in a given factual situation is a question of law.

(3) *Irregularities No Defense.* It is not a defense to prosecution under this Section that the oath or affirmation was administered or taken in an irregular manner or that the declarant was not competent to make the statement. A document purporting to be made upon oath or affirmation at any time when the actor presents it as being so verified shall be deemed to have been duly sworn or affirmed.

(4) *Retraction.* No person shall be guilty of an offense under this Section if he retracted the falsification in the course of the proceeding in which it was made before it became manifest that the falsification was or would be exposed and before the falsification substantially affected the proceeding.

(5) *Inconsistent Statements.* Where the defendant made inconsistent statements under oath or equivalent affirmation, both having been made within the period of the statute of limitations, the prosecution may proceed by setting forth the inconsistent statements in a single count alleging in the alternative that one or the other was false and not believed by the defendant. In such case it shall not be necessary for the prosecution to prove which statement was false but only that one or the other was false and not believed by the defendant to be true.

(6) *Corroboration.* No person shall be convicted of an offense under this Section where proof of falsity rests solely upon contradiction by testimony of a single person other than the defendant.

Section 241.2.-241.9. Omitted.

ARTICLE 242. OBSTRUCTING GOVERNMENTAL OPERATIONS; ESCAPES

Section 242.0. Definitions.

In this Article, unless another meaning plainly is required, the definitions given in Section 240.0 apply.

Section 242.1. Obstructing Administration of Law or Other Governmental Function.

A person commits a misdemeanor if he purposely obstructs, impairs or perverts the administration of law or other governmental function by force, violence, physical interference or obstacle, breach of official duty, or any other unlawful act, except that this Section does not apply to flight by a person charged with crime, refusal to submit to arrest, failure to perform a legal duty other than an official duty, or any other means of avoiding compliance with law without affirmative interference with governmental functions.

Section 242.2. Resisting Arrest or Other Law Enforcement.

A person commits a misdemeanor if, for the purpose of preventing a public servant from effecting a lawful arrest or discharging any other duty, the person creates a substantial risk of bodily injury to the public servant or anyone else, or employs means justifying or requiring substantial force to overcome the resistance.

Section 242.3. Hindering Apprehension or Prosecution.

A person commits an offense if, with purpose to hinder the apprehension, prosecution, conviction or punishment of another for crime, he:

(1) harbors or conceals the other; or

(2) provides or aids in providing a weapon, transportation, disguise or other means of avoiding apprehension or effecting escape; or

(3) conceals or destroys evidence of the crime, or tampers with a witness, informant, document or other source of information, regardless of its admissibility in evidence; or

(4) warns the other of impending discovery or apprehension, except that this paragraph does not apply to a warning given in connection with an effort to bring another into compliance with law; or

(5) volunteers false information to a law enforcement officer.

The offense is a felony of the third degree if the conduct which the actor knows has been charged or is liable to be charged against the person aided would constitute a felony of the first or second degree. Otherwise it is a misdemeanor.

Section 242.4. Aiding Consummation of Crime.

A person commits an offense if he purposely aids another to accomplish an unlawful object of a crime, as by safeguarding the proceeds thereof or converting the proceeds into negotiable funds. The offense is a felony of the third degree if the principal offense was a felony of the first or second degree. Otherwise it is a misdemeanor.

Section 242.5. Compounding.

A person commits a misdemeanor if he accepts or agrees to accept any pecuniary benefit in consideration of refraining from reporting to law enforcement authorities the commission or suspected commission of any offense or information relating to an offense. It is an affirmative defense to prosecution under this Section that the pecuniary benefit did not exceed an amount which the actor believed to be due as restitution or indemnification for harm caused by the offense.

Section 242.6. Escape.

(1) *Escape.* A person commits an offense if he unlawfully removes himself from official detention or fails to return to official detention following temporary leave granted for a specific purpose or limited period. "Official detention" means arrest, detention in any facility for custody of persons under charge or conviction of crime or alleged or found to be delinquent, detention for extradition or deportation, or any other detention for law enforcement purposes; but "official detention" does not include supervision of probation or parole, or constraint incidental to release on bail.

(2) *Permitting or Facilitating Escape.* A public servant concerned in detention commits an offense if he knowingly or recklessly permits an escape. Any person who knowingly causes or facilitates an escape commits an offense.

(3) *Effect of Legal Irregularity in Detention.* Irregularity in bringing about or maintaining detention, or lack of jurisdiction of the committing or detaining authority, shall not be a defense to prosecution under this Section if the escape is from a prison or other custodial facility or from detention pursuant to commitment by official proceedings. In the case of other detentions, irregularity or lack of jurisdiction shall be a defense only if:

> (a) the escape involved no substantial risk of harm to the person or property of anyone other than the detainee; or
>
> (b) the detaining authority did not act in good faith under color of law.

(4) *Grading of Offenses.* An offense under this Section is a felony of the third degree where:

> (a) the actor was under arrest for or detained on a charge of felony or following conviction of crime; or
>
> (b) the actor employs force, threat, deadly weapon or other dangerous instrumentality to effect the escape; or
>
> (c) a public servant concerned in detention of persons convicted of crime purposely facilitates or permits an escape from a detention facility.

Otherwise an offense under this section is a misdemeanor.

Section 242.7.-242.8. Omitted.

ARTICLE 243. ABUSE OF OFFICE. Omitted.

OFFENSES AGAINST PUBLIC ORDER AND DECENCY
ARTICLE 250. RIOT, DISORDERLY CONDUCT, AND RELATED OFFENSES

Section 250.1. Riot; Failure to Disperse.

(1) *Riot.* A person is guilty of riot, a felony of the third degree, if he participates with [two] or more others in a course of disorderly conduct:

> (a) with purpose to commit or facilitate the commission of a felony or misdemeanor;
>
> (b) with purpose to prevent or coerce official action; or
>
> (c) when the actor or any other participant to the knowledge of the actor uses or plans to use a firearm or other deadly weapon.

(2) *Failure of Disorderly Persons to Disperse Upon Official Order.* Where [three] or more persons are participating in a course of disorderly conduct likely to cause substantial harm or serious inconvenience, annoyance or alarm, a peace officer or other public servant engaged in executing or enforcing the law may order the participants and others in the immediate vicinity to disperse. A person who refuses or knowingly fails to obey such an order commits a misdemeanor.

Section 250.2. Disorderly Conduct.

(1) *Offense Defined.* A person is guilty of disorderly conduct if, with purpose to cause public inconvenience, annoyance or alarm, or recklessly creating a risk thereof, he:

> (a) engages in fighting or threatening, or in violent or tumultuous behavior; or

(b) makes unreasonable noise or offensively coarse utterance, gesture or display, or addresses abusive language to any person present; or

(c) creates a hazardous or physically offensive condition by any act which serves no legitimate purpose of the actor.

"Public" means affecting or likely to affect persons in a place to which the public or a substantial group has access; among the places included are highways, transport facilities, schools, prisons, apartment houses, places of business or amusement, or any neighborhood.

(2) *Grading.* An offense under this section is a petty misdemeanor if the actor's purpose is to cause substantial harm or serious inconvenience, or if he persists in disorderly conduct after reasonable warning or request to desist. Otherwise disorderly conduct is a violation.

Section 250.3. Omitted.
Section 250.4. Harassment.

A person commits a petty misdemeanor if, with purpose to harass another, he:

(1) makes a telephone call without purpose of legitimate communication; or

(2) insults, taunts or challenges another in a manner likely to provoke violent or disorderly response; or

(3) makes repeated communications anonymously or at extremely inconvenient hours, or in offensively coarse language; or

(4) subjects another to an offensive touching; or

(5) engages in any other course of alarming conduct serving no legitimate purpose of the actor.

Section 250.5. Public Drunkenness; Drug Incapacitation.

A person is guilty of an offense if he appears in any public place manifestly under the influence of alcohol, narcotics or other drug, not therapeutically administered, to the degree that he may endanger himself or other persons or property, or annoy persons in his vicinity. An offense under this Section constitutes a petty misdemeanor if the actor has been convicted hereunder twice before within a period of one year. Otherwise the offense constitutes a violation.

Section 250.6. Loitering or Prowling.

A person commits a violation if he loiters or prowls in a place, at a time, or in a manner not usual for law-abiding individuals under circumstances that warrant alarm for the safety of persons or property in the vicinity. Among the circumstances which may be considered in determining whether such alarm is warranted is the fact that the actor takes flight upon appearance of a peace officer, refuses to identify himself, or manifestly endeavors to conceal himself or any object. Unless flight by the actor or other circumstance makes it impracticable, a peace officer shall prior to any arrest for an offense under this section afford the actor an opportunity to dispel any alarm which would otherwise be warranted, by requesting him to identify himself and explain his presence and conduct. No person shall be convicted of an offense under this Section if the peace officer did not comply with the preceding sentence, or if it appears at trial that the explanation given by the actor was true and, if believed by the peace officer at the time, would have dispelled the alarm.

Section 250.7.-250.10. Omitted.

Section 250.11. Cruelty to Animals.

A person commits a misdemeanor if he purposely or recklessly:

(1) subjects any animal to cruel mistreatment; or

(2) subjects any animal in his custody to cruel neglect; or

(3) kills or injures any animal belonging to another without legal privilege or consent of the owner.

Subsections (1) and (2) shall not be deemed applicable to accepted veterinary practices and activities carried on for scientific research.

Section 250.12. Omitted.

ARTICLE 251. PUBLIC INDECENCY

Section 251.1. Open Lewdness.

A person commits a petty misdemeanor if he does any lewd act which he knows is likely to be observed by others who would be affronted or alarmed.

Section 251.2. Prostitution and Related Offenses.

(1) *Prostitution.* A person is guilty of prostitution, a petty misdemeanor, if he or she:

(a) is an inmate of a house of prostitution or otherwise engages in sexual activity as a business; or

(b) loiters in or within view of any public place for the purpose of being hired to engage in sexual activity.

"Sexual activity" includes homosexual and other deviate sexual relations. A "house of prostitution" is any place where prostitution or promotion of prostitution is regularly carried on by one person under the control, management or supervision of another. An "inmate" is a person who engages in prostitution in or through the agency of a house of prostitution. "Public place" means any place to which the public or any substantial group thereof has access.

(2) *Promoting Prostitution.* A person who knowingly promotes prostitution of another commits a misdemeanor or felony as provided in Subsection (3). The following acts shall, without limitation of the foregoing, constitute promoting prostitution:

(a) owning, controlling, managing, supervising or otherwise keeping, alone or in association with others, a house of prostitution or a prostitution business; or

(b) procuring an inmate for a house of prostitution or a place in a house of prostitution for one who would be an inmate; or

(c) encouraging, inducing, or otherwise purposely causing another to become or remain a prostitute; or

(d) soliciting a person to patronize a prostitute; or

(e) procuring a prostitute for a patron; or

(f) transporting a person into or within this state with purpose to promote that person's engaging in prostitution, or procuring or paying for transportation with that purpose; or

(g) leasing or otherwise permitting a place controlled by the actor, alone or in association with others, to be regularly used for prostitution or the promotion of

prostitution, or failure to make reasonable effort to abate such use by ejecting the tenant, notifying law enforcement authorities, or other legally available means; or
(h) soliciting, receiving, or agreeing to receive any benefit for doing or agreeing to do anything forbidden by this Subsection.

(3) *Grading of Offenses Under Subsection (2).* An offense under Subsection (2) constitutes a felony of the third degree if:
(a) the offense falls within paragraph (a), (b) or (c) of Subsection (2); or
(b) the actor compels another to engage in or promote prostitution; or
(c) the actor promotes prostitution of a child under 16, whether or not he is aware of the child's age; or
(d) the actor promotes prostitution of his wife, child, ward or any person for whose care, protection or support he is responsible.
Otherwise the offense is a misdemeanor.

(4) *Presumption from Living off Prostitutes.* A person, other than the prostitute or the prostitute's minor child or other legal dependent incapable of self-support, who is supported in whole or substantial part by the proceeds of prostitution is presumed to be knowingly promoting prostitution in violation of Subsection (2).

(5) *Patronizing Prostitutes.* A person commits a violation if he hires a prostitute to engage in sexual activity with him, or if he enters or remains in a house of prostitution for the purpose of engaging in sexual activity.

(6) *Evidence.* On the issue whether a place is a house of prostitution the following shall be admissible evidence: its general repute; the repute of the persons who reside in or frequent the place; the frequency, timing and duration of visits by non-residents. Testimony of a person against his spouse shall be admissible to prove offenses under this Section.

Section 251.3. Loitering to Solicit Deviate Sexual Relations.

A person is guilty of a petty misdemeanor if he loiters in or near any public place for the purpose of soliciting or being solicited to engage in deviate sexual relations.

Section 251.4. Obscenity.

(1) *Obscene Defined.* Material is obscene if, considered as a whole, its predominant appeal is to prurient interest, that is, a shameful or morbid interest, in nudity, sex or excretion, and if in addition it goes substantially beyond customary limits of candor in describing or representing such matters. Predominant appeal shall be judged with reference to ordinary adults unless it appears from the character of the material or the circumstances of its dissemination to be designed for children or other specially susceptible audience. Undeveloped photographs, molds, printing plates, and the like, shall be deemed obscene notwithstanding that processing or other acts may be required to make the obscenity patent or to disseminate it.

(2) *Offenses.* Subject to the affirmative defense provided in Subsection (3), a person commits a misdemeanor if he knowingly or recklessly:
(a) sells, delivers or provides, or offers or agrees to sell, deliver or provide, any obscene writing, picture, record or other representation or embodiment of the obscene; or

(b) presents or directs an obscene play, dance or performance, or participates in that portion thereof which makes it obscene; or

(c) publishes, exhibits or otherwise makes available any obscene material; or

(d) possesses any obscene material for purposes of sale or other commercial dissemination; or

(e) sells, advertises or otherwise commercially disseminates material, whether or not obscene, by representing or suggesting that it is obscene.

A person who disseminates or possesses obscene material in the course of his business is presumed to do so knowingly or recklessly.

(3) *Justifiable and Non-Commercial Private Dissemination.* It is an affirmative defense to prosecution under this Section that dissemination was restricted to:

(a) institutions or persons having scientific, educational, governmental or other similar justification for possessing obscene material; or

(b) non-commercial dissemination to personal associates of the actor.

(4) *Evidence; Adjudication of Obscenity.* In any prosecution under this Section evidence shall be admissible to show:

(a) the character of the audience for which the material was designed or to which it was directed;

(b) what the predominant appeal of the material would be for ordinary adults or any special audience to which it was directed, and what effect, if any, it would probably have on conduct of such people;

(c) artistic, literary, scientific, educational or other merits of the material;

(d) the degree of public acceptance of the material in the United States;

(e) appeal to prurient interest, or absence thereof, in advertising or other promotion of the material; and

(f) the good repute of the author, creator, publisher or other person from whom the material originated.

Expert testimony and testimony of the author, creator, publisher or other person from whom the material originated, relating to factors entering into the determination of the issue of obscenity, shall be admissible. The Court shall dismiss a prosecution for obscenity if it is satisfied that the material is not obscene.

PART III. TREATMENT AND CORECTION (Omitted).

PART IV. ORGANIZATION AND CORRECTION (Omitted).

TABLE OF CASES

Principal cases are italicized.

INDEX